Lecture Notes in Computer Science   2840
Edited by G. Goos, J. Hartmanis, and J. van Leeuwen

Springer
*Berlin
Heidelberg
New York
Hong Kong
London
Milan
Paris
Tokyo*

Jack Dongarra   Domenico Laforenza
Salvatore Orlando (Eds.)

Recent Advances in Parallel Virtual Machine and Message Passing Interface

10th European PVM/MPI User's Group Meeting
Venice, Italy, September 29 - October 2, 2003
Proceedings

Springer

Series Editors

Gerhard Goos, Karlsruhe University, Germany
Juris Hartmanis, Cornell University, NY, USA
Jan van Leeuwen, Utrecht University, The Netherlands

Volume Editors

Jack Dongarra
University of Tennessee, Computer Science Department
1122 Volunteer Blvd, Knoxville, TN 37996-3450, USA
E-mail: dongarra@cs.utk.edu

Domenico Laforenza
Istituto di Scienza e Technologie dell'Informazione
Consiglio Nazionale delle Ricerche (ISTI-CNR)
Area della Ricerca CNR, Via G. Moruzzi, 1, 56126 Pisa, Italy
E-mail: domenico.laforenza@isti.cnr.it

Salvatore Orlando
Università Ca' Foscari di Venezia, Dipartimento di Informatica
Via Torino, 155, 30172 Venezia Mestre, Italy
E-mail: orlando@dsi.unive.it

Cataloging-in-Publication Data applied for

A catalog record for this book is available from the Library of Congress.

Bibliographic information published by Die Deutsche Bibliothek
Die Deutsche Bibliothek lists this publication in the Deutsche Nationalbibliografie;
detailed bibliographic data is available in the Internet at <http://dnb.ddb.de>.

CR Subject Classification (1998): D.1.3, D.3.2, F.1.2, G.1.0, B.2.1, C.1.2

ISSN 0302-9743
ISBN 3-540-20149-1 Springer-Verlag Berlin Heidelberg New York

This work is subject to copyright. All rights are reserved, whether the whole or part of the material is
concerned, specifically the rights of translation, reprinting, re-use of illustrations, recitation, broadcasting,
reproduction on microfilms or in any other way, and storage in data banks. Duplication of this publication
or parts thereof is permitted only under the provisions of the German Copyright Law of September 9, 1965,
in its current version, and permission for use must always be obtained from Springer-Verlag. Violations are
liable for prosecution under the German Copyright Law.

Springer-Verlag Berlin Heidelberg New York
a member of BertelsmannSpringer Science+Business Media GmbH

http://www.springer.de

© Springer-Verlag Berlin Heidelberg 2003
Printed in Germany

Typesetting: Camera-ready by author, data conversion by Olgun Computergrafik
Printed on acid-free paper   SPIN: 10961599   06/3142   5 4 3 2 1 0

Preface

The message passing paradigm is considered the most effective way to develop efficient parallel applications. PVM (Parallel Virtual Machine) and MPI (Message Passing Interface) are the most frequently used tools for programming message passing applications.

This volume includes the selected contributions presented at the 10th European PVM/MPI Users' Group Meeting (Euro PVM/MPI 2003), which was held in Venice, Italy, September 29–October 2, 2003. The conference was jointly organized by the Department of Computer Science of the Ca' Foscari University of Venice, Italy and the Information Science and Technologies Institute of the National Research Council (ISTI-CNR), Pisa, Italy.

The conference was previously held in Linz, Austria (2002), Santorini, Greece (2001), Balatonfüred, Hungary (2000), Barcelona, Spain (1999), Liverpool, UK (1998), and Krakow, Poland (1997). The first three conferences were devoted to PVM and were held in Munich, Germany (1996), Lyon, France (1995), and Rome, Italy (1994).

The conference has become a forum for users and developers of PVM, MPI, and other message passing environments. Interactions between these groups has proved to be very useful for developing new ideas in parallel computing, and for applying some of those already existent to new practical fields. The main topics of the meeting were evaluation and performance of PVM and MPI, extensions, implementations and improvements of PVM and MPI, parallel algorithms using the message passing paradigm, and parallel applications in science and engineering. In addition, the topics of the conference were extended to include Grid computing, in order to reflect the importance of this area for the high-performance computing community.

This year we received 115 submissions, and the Program Committee finally selected 64 regular papers, and 16 short papers. Besides the main track of contributed papers, the conference featured the second edition of the special session "ParSim 03 – Current Trends in Numerical Simulation for Parallel Engineering Environments." This volume also includes six short papers presented during the ParSim 03 session.

Two tutorials were presented during the meeting: "High-Level Programming in MPI" by William Gropp and Ewing Lusk, and "Programming Environments for Grids and Distributed Computing Systems" by Vaidy Sunderam. Finally, six invited talks were presented at the conference: the invited speakers were Geoffrey Fox, Al Geist, William Gropp, Ewing Lusk, Thierry Priol, and Marco Vanneschi. The contributions relating to the invited talks and tutorials are also included in this volume.

We would like to express our gratitude for the kind support of our sponsors (see below). We are also indebted to all the members of the Program Committee and the additional reviewers, who ensured the high quality of Euro PVM/MPI

2003 with their careful and timely work. Finally, we would like to express our gratitude to our colleagues in the ISTI-CNR and the University of Venice for their help and support during the conference organization. In particular, we would like to thank Tiziano Fagni, Paolo Palmerini, Raffaele Perego, Claudio Silvestri, Fabrizio Silvestri and Nicola Tonellotto.

September 2003

Jack Dongarra
Domenico Laforenza
Salvatore Orlando

Program Committee

General Chair

Jack Dongarra   University of Tennessee, Knoxville, USA

Program Chairs

Domenico Laforenza   ISTI CNR, Pisa, Italy
Salvatore Orlando   Ca' Foscari University of Venice, Italy

Program Committee Members

Vassil Alexandrov	University of Reading, UK
Ranieri Baraglia	ISTI CNR, Italy
Arndt Bode	Technical Univ. of Munich, Germany
Marian Bubak	AGH, Cracow, Poland
Jacques Chassin de Kergommeaux	LSR-IMAG, France
Yiannis Cotronis	Univ. of Athens, Greece
Jose C. Cunha	New University of Lisbon, Portugal
Erik D'Hollander	University of Ghent, Belgium
Marco Danelutto	Univ. of Pisa, Italy
Frederic Desprez	INRIA, France
Beniamino Di Martino	2nd Univ. of Naples, Italy
Graham Fagg	University of Tennessee, Knoxville, USA
Al Geist	Oak Ridge National Laboratory, USA
Michael Gerndt	Technical Univ. of Munich, Germany
Andrzej Goscinski	Deakin University, Australia
William Gropp	Argonne National Laboratory, USA
Rolf Hempel	DLR, Simulation Aerospace Center, Germany
Ladislav Hluchy	Slovak Academy of Sciences, Slovakia
Peter Kacsuk	MTA SZTAKI, Hungary
Dieter Kranzlmüller	Joh. Kepler University, Linz, Austria
Jan Kwiatkowski	Wroclaw University of Technology, Poland
Laurent Lefevre	INRIA/RESAM, France
Thomas Ludwig	University of Heidelberg, Germany
Emilio Luque	Universitat Autònoma de Barcelona, Spain
Ewing Lusk	Argonne National Laboratory, USA
Tomas Margalef	Universitat Autònoma de Barcelona, Spain
Shirley Moore	University of Tennessee, Knoxville, USA
Wolfgang Nagel	Dresden University of Technology, Germany
Benno J. Overeinder	Vrije Universiteit Amsterdam, The Netherlands
Raffaele Perego	ISTI CNR, Italy

Neil D. Pundit	Sandia National Labs, USA
Rolf Rabenseifner	University of Stuttgart, Germany
Andrew Rau-Chaplin	Dalhousie University, Canada
Ralf Reussner	DSTC, Monash University, Australia
Yves Robert	ENS Lyon, France
Casiano Rodriguez-Leon	Universidad de La Laguna, Spain
Miquel Senar	Universitat Autònoma de Barcelona, Spain
Joao Gabriel Silva	University of Coimbra, Portugal
Vaidy Sunderam	Emroy University, USA
Francisco Tirado	Universidad Complutense de Madrid, Spain
Bernard Tourancheau	SUN Labs Europe, France
Jesper Larsson Träff	NEC Europe Ltd., Germany
Pavel Tvrdik	Czech Technical University, Czech Republic
Umberto Villano	Università del Sannio, Italy
Jens Volkert	Joh. Kepler University, Linz, Austria
Jerzy Wasniewski	Danish Computing Centre, Denmark
Roland Wismüller	Technical Univ. of Munich, Germany

Additional Reviewers

Alba, Enrique
Almeida, Francisco
Angskun, Thara
Balis, Bartosz
Balogh, Zoltan
Baltzer, Oliver
Bautista, Alfredo
Beyls, Kristof
Bönisch, Homas
Bosilca, George
Brandes, Thomas
Caron, Eddy
Cortes, Ana
Cronk, David
De Sande, Francisco
Dobruchy, Miroslav
Eavis, Todd
Fagni, Tiziano
Ferrini, Renato
Franco, Daniel
Funika, Wlodzimierz
Fürlinger, Karl
Gabriel, Edgar
Garcia, Carlos
Gelas, Jean-Patrick
Giang, Nguyen T.
Guérin-Lassous, Isabelle
Habala, Ondrej
Halada, Ladislav
Haubold, Sven
Hermann, Gerd
Hernández, Porfidio
Hetze, Bernd
Heymann, Elisa
Iacono, Mauro
Keller, Ainer
Krämer-Fuhrmann, Ottmar
Legrand, Arnaud
León, Coromoto

L'Excellent, Jean-Yves
Luksch, Eter
Mairandres, Martin
Malawski, Maciej
Mancini, Emilio P.
Margalef, Tomas
Marques, Rui
Medeiros, Pedro
Mix, Hartmut
Moscato, Francesco
Müller-Pfefferkorn, Ralph
Nemeth, Zsolt
Palmerini, Paolo
Pedretti, Kevin
Pflüger, Stefan
Philippe, Laurent
Prieto-Matias, Manuel
Puppin, Diego
Rak, Massimiliano
Rastello, Fabrice
Rathmayer, Sabine
Renard, Hélène
Ripoll, Ana
Schaubschlaeger, Christian
Schmidt, Andreas
Senar, Miquel A.
Silvestri, Fabrizio
Simo, Branislav
Stamatakis, Alexandros
Suppi, Remo
Tonellotto, Nicola
Tran, Viet D.
Underwood, Keith
Venticinque, Salvatore
Vivien, Frédéric
Walter, Max
Weidendorfer, Osef
Worringen, Joachim
Zajac, Katarzyna

Sponsoring Institutions

(as of July 18th, 2002)

HP (Hewlett-Packard)
Sun Microsystems
Microsoft
ONRIFO (US Office of Naval Research – International Field Office)
Critical Software
DATAMAT SpA
Department of Computer Science, Ca' Foscari University of Venice
Information Science and Technologies Institute, National Research Council (ISTI-CNR), Pisa

Table of Contents

Invited Talks

Messaging Systems: Parallel Computing the Internet and the Grid 1
   G. Fox

Progress towards Petascale Virtual Machines 10
   A. Geist

Future Developments in MPI 15
   W.D. Gropp

Integrating Scalable Process Management
into Component-Based Systems Software.............................. 16
   E. Lusk

Programming High Performance Applications Using Components 23
   T. Priol

ASSIST High-Performance Programming Environment:
Application Experiences and Grid Evolution.......................... 24
   M. Vanneschi

Tutorials

High-Level Programming in MPI...................................... 27
   W. Gropp and E. Lusk

Programming Environments for Grids
and Distributed Computing Systems 28
   V. Sunderam

Evaluation and Performance Analysis

Performance Modeling and Evaluation
of Java Message-Passing Primitives on a Cluster 29
   G.L. Taboada, J. Touriño, and R. Doallo

Integrating New Capabilities into NetPIPE........................... 37
   D. Turner, A. Oline, X. Chen, and T. Benjegerdes

Off-Line Performance Prediction of Message-Passing Applications
on Cluster Systems... 45
   E. Mancini, M. Rak, R. Torella, and U. Villano

Complexity Driven Performance Analysis 55
  L. García, J.A. González, J.C. González, C. León, C. Rodríguez,
  and G. Rodríguez

Usefulness and Usage of SKaMPI-Bench 63
  W. Augustin and T. Worsch

The Performance of Parallel Disk Write Methods
for Linux Multiprocessor Nodes 71
  G.D. Benson, K. Long, and P.S. Pacheco

A Model for Performance Analysis of MPI Applications
on Terascale Systems 81
  S. Chakravarthi, C.R. Krishna Kumar, A. Skjellum, H.A. Prahalad,
  and B. Seshadri

Evaluating the Performance of MPI-2 Dynamic Communicators
and One-Sided Communication 88
  E. Gabriel, G.E. Fagg, and J.J. Dongarra

Ring Algorithms on Heterogeneous Clusters with PVM:
Performance Analysis and Modeling 98
  A. Corana

An MPI Tool to Measure Application Sensitivity to Variation
in Communication Parameters 108
  E.A. León, A.B. Maccabe, and R. Brightwell

Measuring MPI Latency Variance 112
  R. Riesen, R. Brightwell, and A.B. Maccabe

Parallel Algorithms Using Message Passing

CGM*graph*/CGM*lib*: Implementing and Testing CGM Graph Algorithms
on PC Clusters 117
  A. Chan and F. Dehne

Efficient Parallel Implementation of Transitive Closure of Digraphs 126
  C.E.R. Alves, E.N. Cáceres, A.A. Castro Jr, S.W. Song,
  and J.L. Szwarcfiter

A Scalable Crystallographic FFT 134
  J. Seguel and D. Burbano

Object-Oriented NeuroSys: Parallel Programs
for Simulating Large Networks of Biologically Accurate Neurons 142
  P.S. Pacheco, P. Miller, J. Kim, T. Leese, and Y. Zabiyaka

PageRank Computation Using PC Cluster 152
  A. Rungsawang and B. Manaskasemsak

An Online Parallel Algorithm for Remote Visualization of Isosurfaces 160
   A. Clematis, D. D'Agostino, and V. Gianuzzi

Parallel Algorithms for Computing the Smith Normal Form
of Large Matrices 170
   G. Jäger

Hierarchical MPI+OpenMP Implementation of Parallel PIC Applications
on Clusters of Symmetric MultiProcessors 180
   S. Briguglio, B. Di Martino, G. Fogaccia, and G. Vlad

Non-strict Evaluation of the FFT Algorithm
in Distributed Memory Systems 188
   A. Cristóbal-Salas, A. Tchernykh, and J.-L. Gaudiot

A Parallel Approach for the Solution of Non-Markovian Petri Nets 196
   M. Scarpa, S. Distefano, and A. Puliafito

Advanced Hybrid MPI/OpenMP Parallelization Paradigms
for Nested Loop Algorithms onto Clusters of SMPs 204
   N. Drosinos and N. Koziris

The AGEB Algorithm for Solving the Heat Equation in Two Space
Dimensions and Its Parallelization on a Distributed Memory Machine 214
   N. Alias, M.S. Sahimi, and A.R. Abdullah

A Parallel Scheme for Solving a Tridiagonal Matrix
with Pre-propagation 222
   A. Wakatani

Competitive Semantic Tree Theorem Prover with Resolutions 227
   C.K. Kim and M. Newborn

Explicit Group Iterative Solver on a Message Passing Environment 232
   M.A. Norhashidah Hj., A. Rosni, and J.L. Kok

Applying Load Balancing in Data Parallel Applications Using DASUD 237
   *A. Cortés, M. Planas, J.L. Millán, A. Ripoll, M.A. Senar,
   and E. Luque*

Performance Analysis of Approximate String Searching Implementations
for Heterogeneous Computing Platform 242
   P.D. Michailidis and K.G. Margaritis

Extensions, Improvements and Implementations of PVM/MPI

Using a Self-connected Gigabit Ethernet Adapter
as a `memcpy()` Low-Overhead Engine for MPI 247
   G. Ciaccio

Improving the Performance of Collective Operations in MPICH 257
  R. Thakur and W.D. Gropp

PVMWebCluster: Integration of PVM Clusters Using Web Services
and CORBA 268
  P. Czarnul

Lock-Free Collective Operations 276
  A. Supalov

Efficient Message-Passing within SMP Systems 286
  X. Chen and D. Turner

The Network Agnostic MPI – Scali MPI Connect 294
  L.P. Huse and O.W. Saastad

PC/MPI: Design and Implementation of a Portable MPI Checkpointer 302
  S. Ahn, J. Kim, and S. Han

Improving Generic Non-contiguous File Access for MPI-IO 309
  J. Worringen, J. Larsson Träff, and H. Ritzdorf

Remote Exception Handling for PVM Processes 319
  P.L. Kaczmarek and H. Krawczyk

Evaluation of an Eager Protocol Optimization for MPI 327
  R. Brightwell and K. Underwood

A Comparison of MPICH Allgather Algorithms on Switched Networks 335
  G.D. Benson, C.-W. Chu, Q. Huang, and S.G. Caglar

Network Fault Tolerance in LA-MPI 344
  R.T. Aulwes, D.J. Daniel, N.N. Desai, R.L. Graham, L.D. Risinger,
  M.W. Sukalski, and M.A. Taylor

MPI on BlueGene/L: Designing an Efficient General Purpose
Messaging Solution for a Large Cellular System 352
  G. Almási, C. Archer, J.G. Castaños, M. Gupta, X. Martorell,
  J.E. Moreira, W.D. Gropp, S. Rus, and B. Toonen

Porting P4 to Digital Signal Processing Platforms 362
  J.A. Rico, J.C. Díaz Martín, J.M. Rodríguez García,
  J.M. Álvarez Llorente, and J.L. García Zapata

Fast and Scalable Barrier Using RDMA and Multicast Mechanisms
for InfiniBand-Based Clusters 369
  S.P. Kini, J. Liu, J. Wu, P. Wyckoff, and D.K. Panda

A Component Architecture for LAM/MPI 379
  J.M. Squyres and A. Lumsdaine

ORNL-RSH Package and Windows '03 PVM 3.4 388
    P. Pfeiffer, S.L. Scott, and H. Shukla

MPI for the Clint Gb/s Interconnect 395
    N. Fugier, M. Herbert, E. Lemoine, and B. Tourancheau

Implementing Fast and Reusable Datatype Processing 404
    R. Ross, N. Miller, and W.D. Gropp

An MPI Implementation Supported by Process Migration
and Load Balancing 414
    A. Maloney, A. Goscinski, and M. Hobbs

PVM over the CLAN Network 424
    R. Sohan and S. Pope

Parallel Programming Tools

Distributed Configurable Application Monitoring on SMP Clusters 429
    K. Fürlinger and M. Gerndt

Integrating Multiple Implementations and Structure Exploitation
in the Component-Based Design of Parallel ODE Solvers 438
    J.M. Mantas, J. Ortega Lopera, and J.A. Carrillo

Architecture of Monitoring System for Distributed Java Applications 447
    M. Bubak, W. Funika, M. Smętek, Z. Kiliański, and R. Wismüller

A Communication API for Implementing Irregular Algorithms
on SMP Clusters 455
    J. Hippold and G. Rünger

TOM – Efficient Monitoring Infrastructure for Multithreaded Programs... 464
    B. Baliś, M. Bubak, W. Funika, R. Wismüller, and G. Kaplita

MPI Farm Programs on Non-dedicated Clusters 473
    N. Fonseca and J.G. Silva

Application Composition in Ensemble Using Intercommunicators
and Process Topologies 482
    Y. Cotronis

Improving Properties of a Parallel Program in ParJava Environment 491
    V. Ivannikov, S. Gaissaryan, A. Avetisyan, and V. Padaryan

Applications in Science and Engineering

Flow Pattern and Heat Transfer Rate
in Three-Dimensional Rayleigh-Benard Convection 495
    T. Watanabe

A Parallel Split Operator Method
for the Time Dependent Schrödinger Equation 503
    J.P. Hansen, T. Matthey, and T. Sørevik

A Parallel Software for the Reconstruction of Dynamic MRI Sequences . . . 511
    G. Landi, E. Loli Piccolomini, and F. Zama

Improving Wildland Fire Prediction on MPI Clusters 520
    B. Abdalhaq, G. Bianchini, A. Cortés, T. Margalef, and E. Luque

Building 3D State Spaces of Virtual Environments
with a TDS-Based Algorithm 529
    A. Křenek, I. Peterlík, and L. Matyska

Parallel Pencil-Beam Redefinition Algorithm 537
    P. Alderson, M. Wright, A. Jain, and R. Boyd

Dynamic Load Balancing for the Parallel Simulation
of Cavitating Flows 545
    F. Wrona, P.A. Adamidis, U. Iben, R. Rabenseifner, and C.-D. Munz

Message Passing Fluids: Molecules as Processes
in Parallel Computational Fluids 550
    G. Argentini

Parallel Implementation of Interval Analysis for Equations Solving 555
    Y. Papegay, D. Daney, and J.-P. Merlet

A Parallel System for Performing Colonic Tissue Classification
by Means of a Genetic Algorithm 560
    S.A. Amin, J. Filippas, R.N.G. Naguib, and M.K. Bennett

Eigenanalysis of Finite Element 3D Flow Models
by Parallel Jacobi–Davidson 565
    L. Bergamaschi, A. Martinez, G. Pini, and F. Sartoretto

Grid and Heterogeneous Computing

Executing and Monitoring PVM Programs
in Computational Grids with Jini 570
    G. Sipos and P. Kacsuk

Multiprogramming Level of PVM Jobs in a Non-dedicated Linux NOW . . . 577
    F. Giné, F. Solsona, J. Barrientos, P. Hernández, M. Hanzich,
    and E. Luque

Mapping and Load-Balancing Iterative Computations
on Heterogeneous Clusters 586
    A. Legrand, H. Renard, Y. Robert, and F. Vivien

Dynamic Topology Selection for High Performance MPI
in the Grid Environments 595
    K.-L. Park, H.-J. Lee, K.-W. Koh, O.-Y. Kwon, S.-Y. Park,
    H.-W. Park, and S.-D. Kim

Monitoring Message Passing Applications
in the Grid with GRM and R-GMA 603
    N. Podhorszki and P. Kacsuk

Component-Based System for Grid Application Workflow Composition ... 611
    M. Bubak, K. Górka, T. Gubała, M. Malawski, and K. Zając

Evaluating and Enhancing the Use of the GridFTP Protocol
for Efficient Data Transfer on the Grid 619
    M. Cannataro, C. Mastroianni, D. Talia, and P. Trunfio

Resource Monitoring and Management in Metacomputing Environments .. 629
    T. Wrzosek, D. Kurzyniec, D. Drzewiecki, and V. Sunderam

Generating an Efficient Dynamics Multicast Tree
under Grid Environment 636
    T. Vorakosit and P. Uthayopas

Topology-Aware Communication in Wide-Area Message-Passing 644
    C.A. Lee

Design and Implementation of Dynamic Process Management
for Grid-Enabled MPICH 653
    S. Kim, N. Woo, H.Y. Yeom, T. Park, and H.-W. Park

Scheduling Tasks Sharing Files on Heterogeneous Clusters 657
    A. Giersch, Y. Robert, and F. Vivien

Special Session: ParSim 03

Special Session of EuroPVM/MPI 2003: Current Trends in Numerical
Simulation for Parallel Engineering Environments – ParSim 2003 661
    C. Trinitis and M. Schulz

Efficient and Easy Parallel Implementation
of Large Numerical Simulations 663
    R. Revire, F. Zara, and T. Gautier

Toward a Scalable Algorithm for Distributed Computing
of Air-Quality Problems 667
    M. Garbey, R. Keller, and M. Resch

A Piloting SIMulator for Maritime and Fluvial Navigation: SimNav 672
    M. Vayssade and A. Pourplanche

Methods and Experiences of Parallelizing Flood Models 677
    L. Hluchy, V.D. Tran, D. Froehlich, and W. Castaings

padfem2 – An Efficient, Comfortable Framework
for Massively Parallel FEM-Applications 681
    S. Blazy, O. Kao, and O. Marquardt

AUTOBENCH/AUTO-OPT: Towards an Integrated Construction
Environment for Virtual Prototyping in the Automotive Industry 686
    A. Kuhlmann, C.-A. Thole, and U. Trottenberg

Author Index 691

Messaging Systems: Parallel Computing the Internet and the Grid

Geoffrey Fox

Indiana University
Computer Science, Informatics and Physics
Community Grids Computing Laboratory,
501 N Morton Suite 224, Bloomington IN 47404
gcf@indiana.edu

Abstract. We contrast the requirements and performance of messaging systems in parallel and distributed systems emphasizing the importance of the five orders of magnitude difference in network hardware latencies in the two cases. We note the importance of messaging in Grid and Web service applications in building the integrated system and the architectural advantages of a message based compared to a connection based approach. We illustrate these points using the NaradaBrokering system and its application to Audio-Video conferencing.

1 Message Passing in Parallel Computing

Parallel Computing has always understood the importance of message passing and PVM and MPI (the topics of this meeting) have dominated this field with other approaches readily mapped into these two systems. The appropriate programming model for parallel systems is of course a very active area with continued research on different architectures (openMP) and different high level approaches involving both domain specific systems and degrees of compiler generated parallelism. The issue has been further invigorated by the successes of the Japanese Earth Simulator system. However even when we use a high level model for parallel programming, message passing is typically essential as the low level primitive ("machine language") for parallelism between distributed memories. In understanding the requirements of message passing, it is useful to divide multi-processor (distributed memory) systems into three classes.

1. Classic massively parallel processor systems (MPP) with low latency high bandwidth specialized networks. One aims at message latencies of one to a few microseconds and scalable bisection bandwidth. Ignoring latency, the time to communicate a word between two nodes should be a modest multiple (perhaps 20) of time taken to calculate a floating point result. This communication performance should be independent of number of nodes in system.
2. Commodity clusters with high performance but non optimized communication networks. Latencies can be in the 100-1000 microsecond range typical of simple socket based communication interfaces.

3. Distributed or Grid systems with possibly very high internode bandwidth but the latency is typically 100 milliseconds or more as familiar from internet travel times.

Of course there is really a spectrum of systems with cost-performance increasing by a factor of 4 or so as one goes from 1) to 3). Here we will focus on the endpoints 1) and 3) – MPP's and the Grid and not worry about intermediate cases like 2). MPI especially is aimed at the class 1) with optimized "native" implementations exploiting particular features of the network hardware. Generic versions of PVM and MPI using socket based communication on a localized network illustrate 2) as do many other specialized programming environments (such as agent-based approaches). The latter typically cannot afford the development effort to optimize communication and as illustrated by our latter discussion of Grid messaging requires substantially more functionality than MPI and PVM. Grid systems are very diverse and there is little understanding at this stage as to critical performance and architecture (topology) characteristics. As we discuss in sections 2 and 3, they need a rich messaging environment very different from MPI and PVM. Note this doesn't mean that we shouldn't port systems like MPI to the Grid as in MPICH-G2 [1] and PACX-MPI [2]; there is clearly a need to run all messaging environments on all classes of machine.

The overriding "idea" of this paper is that messaging for an application with intrinsic (hardware) latency L, mustn't have software and routing overheads greater than this but certainly can afford extra software overheads of size around 0.1L without "noticing it". This implies that it should be expected that the application classes 1) 2) 3) have very different messaging semantics. MPI and PVM are not totally "barebones" but they are optimized for fast message processing and little communication overhead due to headers in the message packets.

Parallel computing can usually use very lean messaging as one is sending between different parts of the "same" computation; thus the messages can usually just contain data and assume that the recipient process understands the context in which the data should be interpreted.

2 Messaging in Grids and Peer-to-Peer Networks

Now let us consider messaging for the Grid and peer-to-peer (P2P) networks which we view as essentially identical concepts [3]. Here we are not given a single large scale simulation – the archetypical parallel computing application, Rather ab initio we start with a set of distributed entities – sensors, people, codes, computers, data archives – and the task is to integrate them together. For parallel computing one is decomposing applications into parts and messaging reflects that the parts are from the same whole. In distributed computing, the initial entities are often quite distinct and it is the messaging that links them together. Correspondingly the messaging for the Grid must carry the integration context and not just data; thus one has both the time (typically the 100 millisecond network latency) and the need for a much richer messaging system on the Grid than for parallel computing.

In parallel computing explicit message passing is a necessary evil as we haven't found a generally applicable high level expression of parallelism.. For Grids and P2P networks, messaging is the natural universal architecture which expresses the function of the system. In the next sections we compare the requirements for a messaging service in the two cases.

2.1 Objects and Messaging

Object-based programming models are powerful and should be very important in scientific computing even though up to now both C++ and Java have not achieved widespread use in the community [5]. The natural objects are items like the collection of physical quantities at a mesh point or at a larger grain size the arrays of such mesh points [6, 7]. There is some overhead attached with these abstractions but there are such natural objects for most parallel computing problems. However one can also consider the objects formed by the decomposed parts of a parallel application – it has *not* been very helpful to think of the decomposed parts of parallel applications as objects for these are not especially natural components in the system; they are what you get by dividing the problem by the number of processors. On the other hand, the linked parts in a distributed system (Web, Grid, P2P network) are usefully thought of objects as here the problem creates them; in contrast they are created for parallel computing by adapting the problem to the machine architecture. The Grid distributed objects are nowadays typically thought of as Web services and we will assume this below. We will also not distinguish between objects and services. Note that objects naturally communicate by messages linking the exposed interfaces (remote procedure calls or ports) of the distributed objects. So Grid messaging is the natural method to integrate or compose objects (services); parallel computing messaging is the natural representation of the hardware – not the application.

2.2 Requirements for a Grid Messaging Service

There are common features of messaging for distributed and parallel computing; for instance messages have in each case a source and destination. In P2P networks especially, the destination may be specified indirectly and determined dynamically while the message is en route using properties (published meta-data) of the message matched to subscription interest from potential recipients. Groups of potential recipients are defined in both JXTA [8] for P2P and MPI for parallel computing. Publish-subscribe is a particularly powerful way to dynamically define groups of message recipients. Collective communication – messages sent by hardware or software multicast – is important in all cases; much of the complexity of MPI is devoted to this. Again one needs to support in both cases, messages containing complex data structures with a mix of information of different types. One must also support various synchronization constraints between sender and receiver; messages must be acknowledged perhaps. These general characteristics are shared across messaging systems. There are also many differences where perhaps as discussed in section 1, performance is perhaps the most important issue.

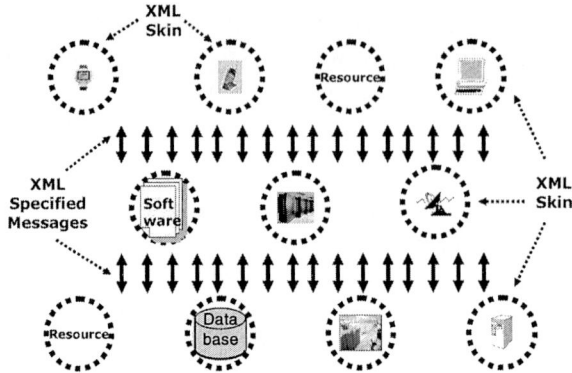

Fig. 1. XML Specified Resources linked by XML Specified Messages

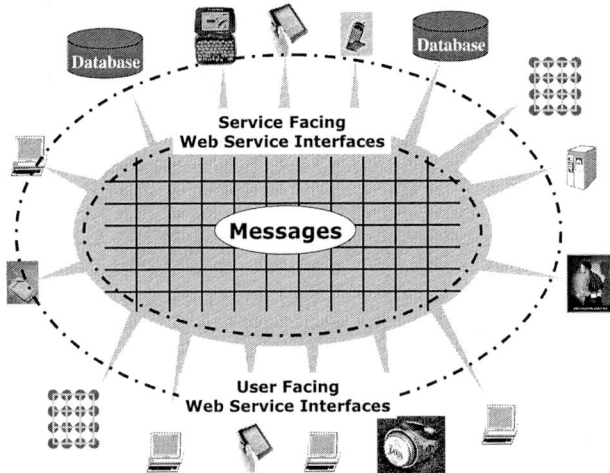

Fig. 2. A Peer-to-Peer Grid constructed from Web Services with both user-facing and service-facing ports to send and receive messages

Now consider message passing for a distributed system. Here we have elegant objects exchanging messages that are themselves objects. It is now becoming very popular to use XML for defining the objects and messages of distributed systems. Fig. 1 shows our simple view of a distributed system – a Grid or P2P Network – as a set of XML specified resources linked by a set of XML specified messages. A resource is any entity with an electronic signature; computer, database, program, user, sensor.

The web community has introduced SOAP [9] which is essentially the XML message format postulated above and "Web services" which are XML specified distributed objects. Web services are "just" computer programs running on one of the computers in our distributed set. Web services send and receive messages on so-called ports – each port is roughly equivalent to a subroutine or method call in the "old programming model". The messages define the name of the subroutine and its input and if necessary output parameters. This message interface is called WSDL (Web Service

Definition Language [10]) and this standard is an important W3C consortium activity. Using Web services for the Grid requires extensions to WSDL and the resultant OGSI [11] and OGSA (Open Grid Service Architecture [12]) standards are major efforts in the Grid forum [13] at the moment. OGSI is the component model and OGSA the interface standards that Grid services and messages must respect.

As seen in the peer-to-peer Grid of fig. 2, ports are either user-facing (messages go between user and Web Services) or service or resource-facing where messages are exchanged between different Web services. As discussed in [14] there is a special variant of WSDL for user-facing ports – WSRP (Web Services for Remote Portlets [15]) which defines a component model for user interfaces. This is one example of the context carried by Grid messages – WSRP indicates a user interface message that can be processed by aggregation portals like Apache Jetspeed [16].

One particularly clever idea in WSDL is the concept that one first defines not methods themselves but their abstract specification. Then there is part of WSDL that "binds" the abstract specification to a particular implementation. Here one can choose to bind the message transport not to the default HTTP protocol but to a different and perhaps higher performance protocol. For instance if one had ports linking Web services on the same computer, then these could in principle be bound to direct subroutine calls. This concept has interesting implications for building systems defined largely in XML at the level of both data structure and methods. Further one can imagine some nifty new branch of compilation which automatically converted XML calls on high performance ports and generated the best possible implementation.

2.3 Performance of Grid Messaging Systems

Now let us discuss the performance of the Grid messaging system. As discussed in section 1, the Grid messaging latency is very different from that for MPI as it can take several 100 milliseconds for data to travel between two geographically distributed Grid nodes; in fact the transit time becomes seconds if one must communicate between the nodes via a geosynchronous satellite. One deduction from this is that the Grid is often not a good environment for traditional parallel computing. Grids are not dealing with the fine grain synchronization needed in parallel computing that requires the few microsecond latency seen in MPI for MPP's. For us here, another more interesting deduction is that very different messaging strategies can be used in Grid compared to parallel computing. In particular we can perhaps afford to invoke an XML parser for the message and in general invoke high level processing of the message. Here we note that interspersing a filter in a message stream – a Web service or CORBA broker perhaps – increases the transit time of a message by about 0.5 millisecond; small compared to typical Internet transit times. This allows us to consider building Grid messaging systems which have substantially higher functionality than traditional parallel computing systems. The maximum acceptable latency is application dependent. Perhaps one is doing relatively tightly synchronized computations among multiple Grid nodes; the high latency is perhaps hidden by overlapping communication and computation. Here one needs tight control over the latency and reduce it as much as possible. On the other extreme, if the computations are largely independent or pipelined, one only needs to ensure that message latency is small compared to total execution time on each node. Another estimate comes from audio-video conferencing [17]. Here a typical timescale is 30 milliseconds – the time for a single frame of video conferencing or a high quality streaming movie. This 30 ms. scale is not really a limit on the latency but in its variation or jitter shown later in fig. 4. In most cases, a more or less constant offset (latency) can be tolerated.

Now consider, the bandwidth required for Grid messaging. Here the situation is rather different for there are cases where large amounts of information need to be transferred between Grid nodes and one needs the highest performance allowed by the Network. In particular numbers often need to be transferred in efficient binary form (say 64 bits each) and not in some XML syntax like <number>3.14159</number> with 24 characters requiring more bandwidth and substantial processing overhead. There is a simple but important strategy here and now we note that in fig. 1, we emphasized that the messages were specified in XML. This was to allow one to implement the messages in a different fashion which could be the very highest performance protocol. As explained above, this is termed binding the ports to a particular protocol in the Web service WSDL specification. So what do we have left if we throw away XML for the implementation? We certainly have a human readable interoperable interface specification but there is more which we can illustrate again by audio-video conferencing, which is straight-forward to implement as a Web service [18]. Here A/V sessions require some tricky set-up process where the clients interested in participating, join and negotiate the session details. This part of the process has no significant performance issues and can be implemented with XML-based messages. The actual audio and video traffic does have performance demands and here one can use existing fast protocols such as RTP. This is quite general; many applications need many control messages, which can be implemented in basic Web service fashion and just part of the messaging needs good performance. Thus one ends up with control ports running basic WSDL with possible high performance ports bound to a different protocol.

3 Narada Brokering Messaging Services

Shrideep Pallickara in the Community Grids Laboratory at Indiana has developed [19, 20] a message system for Web resources designed according to the principles sketched above. It is designed to be deployed as a hierarchical network of brokers that handle all aspects of Grid and Web distributed systems that can be considered as "only connected to the message". One critical design feature is that one considers the message and not the connection as the key abstraction. Destinations, formats and transport protocols are "virtualized" i.e. specified indirectly by the user at a high level. Messages are labeled by XML topics and used to bind source and destinations with a publish-subscribe mechanism. The transport protocol is chosen using a Network Weather Service [21] like evaluation of the network to satisfy quality of service constraints. A given message can be routed through a (logarithmic) network of Narada brokers using if needed a different protocol at each link. For example, an audio stream might have a TCP/IP link through a firewall followed by a UDP link across a high latency reliable satellite link. Currently there is support for TCP, UDP, Multicast, SSL, raw RTP and specialized PDA clients. Also NaradaBrokering (NB) provides the capability for communication through firewalls and proxies. It can operate either in a client-server mode like JMS (Java Message Service [22]) or in a completely distributed JXTA-like [8] peer-to-peer mode. Some capabilities of importance include.

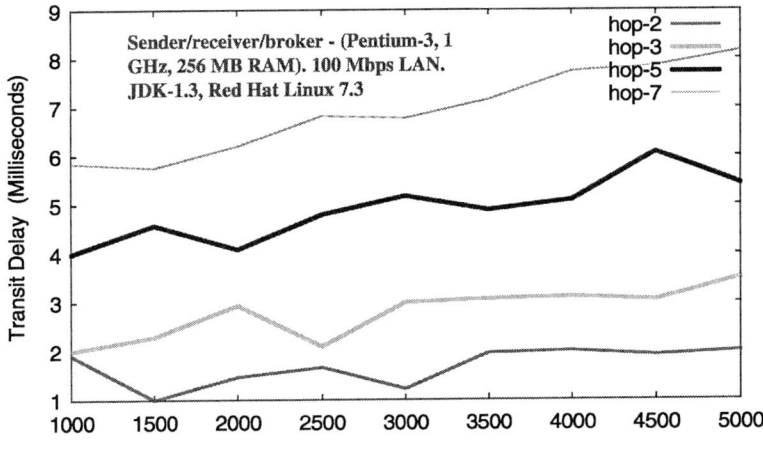

Fig. 3. Transit Delays for NaradaBrokering

(1) NB Supports heterogeneous network transportation and provides unified multipoint transportation

Software multicast – Since NB relies on software multicast, entities interested in linking collaboratively with each other need not set up a dedicated multicast group for communication. Each NB broker can handle hundreds of clients and can be arranged in general networks. Further as shown in fig. 3, the typical delay on a fast network is less than a millisecond per hop between brokers. Thus software multicast appears practical under general circumstances.

Communication over firewalls and proxy boundaries – NB incorporates strategies to tunnel through firewalls and authenticating proxies such as Microsoft's ISA and those from iPlanet and Checkpoint.

Communication using multiple transport protocols – We described above how this can be effectively used to provide quality of service.

(2) NB provides robust, scalable and high efficient multipoint transportation services

Availability and scalability – There is no single point of failure within the NB messaging system. Additional broker nodes may be added to support large heterogeneous distributed systems. NB's cluster based architecture allows the system to scale. The number of broker nodes may increase geometrically, but the communication *path lengths* between nodes increase logarithmically.

Efficient routing and bandwidth utilizations – NB efficiently computes destinations associated with an event. The resultant routing solution chooses links efficiently to reach the desired destinations. The routing solution conserves bandwidth by not overload links with data that should not be routed on them. Under conditions of high loads the benefits accrued from this strategy can be substantial.

Security – NB uses a message-based security mechanism that avoids difficulties with connection (SSL) based schemes and will track the emerging Web service standards in this area [23].

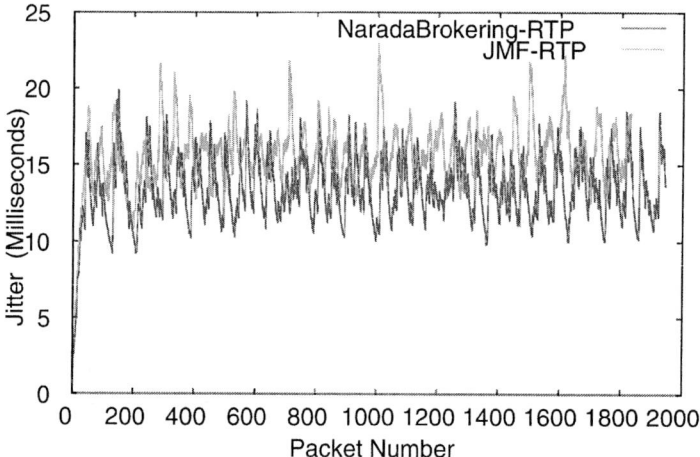

Fig. 4. Jitter (roughly standard deviation) in ms. for a single broker handling 400 video clients with a total bandwidth of 240 Mbps. The lower red lines are for NB using publish-subscribe and RTP transport; the upper green line is for a standard Java Media Framework video server. The mean interval between packets is 30 ms

Typical performance measurements for NB are given in figures 3 and 4. Further it compares well with the performance of commercial JMS and JXTA implementations. Future work will develop NB to support the emerging Web service messaging standards in areas of addressing [24], reliability [25] and security [23]. One can build Grid hosting environments on NaradaBrokering that allow efficient flexible federation of Grids with different architectures.

References

1. MPICH-G2 grid-enabled implementation of the MPI v1.1 standard based on the MPICH library http://www.nsf-middleware.org/NMIR3/components/mpichg2.asp
2. PACX-MPI described in M. Mueller , E. Gabriel and M. Resch, *A Software Development Environment for Grid Computing*, Concurrency and Computation: Practice and Experience Vol. 14, Grid Computing environments Special Issue 13-15, pages 1543-1552, 2002.

3. Geoffrey Fox, Dennis Gannon, Sung-Hoon Ko, Sangmi Lee, Shrideep Pallickara, Marlon Pierce, Xiaohong Qiu, Xi Rao, Ahmet Uyar, Minjun Wang, Wenjun Wu, *Peer-to-Peer Grids*, Chapter 18 of Reference [4].
4. *Grid Computing: Making the Global Infrastructure a Reality* edited by Fran Berman, Geoffrey Fox and Tony Hey, John Wiley & Sons, Chichester, England, ISBN 0-470-85319-0, March 2003. http://www.grid2002.org
5. High Performance Java http://www.hpjava.org.
6. Zoran Budimlic, Ken Kennedy, and Jeff Piper. *The cost of being object-oriented: A preliminary study*. Scientific Programming, 7(2):87-95, 1999.
7. S. Markidis, G. Lapenta and W.B. VanderHeyden, Parsek: *Object Oriented Particle in Cell Implementation and Performance Issues*. Java Grande Conference 2002 and Concurrency and Computation: Practice and Experience, to be published.
8. Project JXTA Peer-to-peer system http://www.jxta.org/
9. SOAP: Simple Object Access Protocol http://www.w3.org/TR/SOAP/
10. WSDL: Web Services Description Language http://www.w3.org/TR/wsdl.html.
11. OGSI Open Grid Service Infrastructure Working Group of Global Grid Forum http://www.gridforum.org/ogsi-wg/
12. Open Grid Services Architecture (OGSA) http://www.gridforum.org/ogsi-wg/drafts/ogsa_draft2.9_2002-06-22.pdf
13. Global Grid Forum http://www.gridforum.org
14. G. Fox, D. Gannon, M. Pierce, M. Thomas, *Overview of Grid Computing Environments*, Global Grid Forum Informational Document http://www.gridforum.org/documents/
15. OASIS Web Services for Remote Portlets (WSRP) http://www.oasis-open.org/committees/
16. Apache Jetspeed Portal http://jakarta.apache.org/jetspeed/site/index.html
17. Ahmet Uyar, Shrideep Pallickara and Geoffrey Fox *Audio Video Conferencing in Distributed Brokering Systems* in Proceedings of the 2003 International Conference on Communications in Computing, Las Vegas June 2003, http://grids.ucs.indiana.edu/ptliupages/publications/NB-AudioVideo.pdf.
18. Geoffrey Fox, Wenjun Wu, Ahmet Uyar, Hasan Bulut, Shrideep Pallickara, *A Web Services Framework for Collaboration and Videoconferencing*. WACE Conference Seattle June 2003. http://grids.ucs.indiana.edu/ptliupages/publications/finalwacepapermay03.doc.
19. NaradaBrokering from Indiana University http://www.naradabrokering.org
20. Shrideep Pallickara and Geoffrey Fox *NaradaBrokering: A Distributed Middleware Framework and Architecture for Enabling Durable Peer-to-Peer Grids* in Proceedings of ACM/IFIP/USENIX International Middleware Conference Middleware-2003, Rio Janeiro, Brazil June 2003. http://grids.ucs.indiana.edu/ptliupages/publications/NB-Framework.pdf
21. Network Weather Service NWS http://www.nsf-middleware.org/documentation/NMI-R3/0/NWS/index.htm.
22. JMS: Java Message Service http://java.sun.com/products/jms/.
23. Yan Yan, Yi Huang, Geoffrey Fox, Ali Kaplan, Shrideep Pallickara, Marlon Pierce and Ahmet Topcu, *Implementing a Prototype of the Security Framework for Distributed Brokering Systems* in Proceeedings of 2003 International Conference on Security and Management (SAM'03: June 23-26, 2003, Las Vegas, Nevada, USA, http://grids.ucs.indiana.edu/ptliupages/publications/SecurityPrototype.pdf.
24. Draft Web Service Addressing Standard from IBM and Microsoft http://msdn.microsoft.com/ws/2003/03/ws-addressing/
25. Draft Web Service Reliable Messaging Standard from BEA IBM Microsoft and TIBCO http://www-106.ibm.com/developerworks/library/ws-rm/.

Progress towards Petascale Virtual Machines

Al Geist

Oak Ridge National Laboratory,
PO Box 2008,
Oak Ridge, TN 37831-6367
gst@ornl.gov
http://www.csm.ornl.gov/~geist

Abstract. PVM continues to be a popular software package both for creating personal grids and for building adaptable, fault tolerant applications. We will illustrate this by describing a computational biology environment built on top of PVM that is used by researchers around the world. We will then describe or recent progress in building an even more adaptable distributed virtual machine package called Harness. The Harness project includes research on a scalable, self-adapting core called H2O, and research on fault tolerant MPI. The H2O core can be configured to support distributed web computing like SETI@home, parallel virtual machines like PVM, and OGSA compliant grid environments. The Harness software is being designed to scale to petascale virtual machines. We will describe work at Oak Ridge National Lab on developing algorithms for such petascale virtual machines and the development of a simulator to test these algorithms on simulated 100,000 processor systems.

1 Background

In 21st century scientific research programs, computation is becoming a third arm in scientific discovery along with theory and experiment. Computing was the key to unlocking the human genome and now is being used to decode the genomes of hundreds of other organisms. The next stage of genomics is encompassed by the U.S.A. Department of Energy's Genomes to Life project [1] where all the molecular machines in a microbe and their regulation will be determined. This 10 year effort will involve enormous data analysis and computational challenges.

Nanotechnology is another area where major advances are being made through advanced computer simulations. Over the last decade computational materials science has improved by three orders of magnitude through increased computing power and another eight orders of magnitude through advanced algorithms. With such improvements, computing has become a key method to push forward the nanotechnology frontier.

PVM and MPI are the key software packages used by scientific applications today and will continue to be the programming paradigm of choice for the foreseeable future. But as computers reach the 100 TF and upwards to a petaflop in the next 5 years, fault tolerance and adaptability may become as important as latency and bandwidth to both computational biology and nanotechnology applications. In anticipation of these needs, the developers of PVM started a new project, called Harness [2], that has all the features of PVM and MPI, but also has peer-to-peer distributed control, self adaptability, and the ability to survive multiple points of failure. These features are important to be able to scale to petascale virtual machines.

This paper describes the Genomes to Life project and uses it to illustrate PVM use today. Next we describe the Harness project and the features it has to help scale to petascale virtual machines. The paper discusses H2O, which is the self adapting core of Harness. Finally, we describe the latest developments in research going on at ORNL to develop multigrid and finite element algorithms that can self-adapt to failures on a petascale virtual machine.

2 Using PVM in Genomes to Life

The United States Department of Energy (DOE) initiated and ran the Human Genome project, which decoded all 3 billion bases in the human genome. That project finished this year and the DOE has embarked on an even more ambitious computational biology program called Genomes to Life. The plan for the 10-year program is to use DNA sequences from microbes and higher organisms, including humans, as starting points for systematically tackling questions about the essential processes of living systems. Advanced technological and computational resources will help to identify and understand the underlying mechanisms that enable organisms to develop, and survive under myriad environmental conditions. This approach ultimately will foster an integrated and predictive understanding of biological systems and offer insights into how both microbial and human cells respond to environmental changes. The applications of this level of knowledge will be extraordinary and will help DOE fulfill its broad missions in energy research, environmental remediation, and the protection of human health.

PVM plays a role in the Genomes to Life program through the Genome Integrated Supercomputer Toolkit (GIST). GIST is a middleware layer used to create the Genome Channel [3]. The Genome Channel is a computational biology workbench that allows biologists to transparently run a wide range of genome analysis and comparison studies on supercomputers at ORNL. When a request comes in to the Genome Channel, PVM is used to track the request, create a parallel virtual machine combining database servers, Linux clusters, and supercomputer nodes tailored to the nature of the request, and then spawning the appropriate analysis code on the virtual machine.

A key feature of PVM that is exploited in Genome Channel is fault tolerance. The creators of GIST require that their system be available 24/7 and that analyses that are running when a failure occurs are reconfigured around the problem and automatically restarted. PVM's dynamic programming model is ideal for this use. The Genome Channel has been cited in "Science" and used by thousands of researchers from around the world.

This is just one of many illustrations of PVM use today.

3 Harness – The Next Generation of PVM

Harness is the code name for the next generation heterogeneous distributed computing package being developed by the PVM team at Oak Ridge National Laboratory, the University of Tennessee, and Emory University. Harness is being designed to address the future needs of PVM and MPI application developers.

Harness version 1.9 was released last year and Harness 2 is scheduled to be released in November 2003.

The basic idea behind Harness is to allow users to dynamically customize, adapt, and extend a virtual machine's features to more closely match the needs of their application and to optimize the virtual machine for the underlying computer resources. For example, taking advantage of a high-speed communication channel. At the same time the software is being designed to be able to scale to petascale virtual machines through the use of distributed control and minimized global state.

As part of the Harness project, the University of Tennessee is developing a fault tolerant MPI called FT-MPI. This package which includes all the MPI 1.2 functions allows applications to be developed that can dynamically recover from task failures within an MPI job. FT-MPI supplies the means to notify the application that it has had a failure and needs to recover. In the simplest case recovery involves killing the application and restarting it from the last checkpoint. FT-MPI also allows an application to "run through" failure by recreating a new MPI_COMM_WORLD communicator on the fly and continue with the computation. MPI_COMM_SPAWN is included in FT-MPI to provide a means to replace failed tasks where appropriate. More fault tolerant MPI implementations and the use of them in super scalable algorithms is expected to increase significantly in the next decade.

Oak Ridge's part in the Harness project is to develop a distributed peer-to-peer control system that can survive and adapt to multiple points of failure. The development of such a control system is necessary to support petascale virtual machines. Fast updates of state and the ability to recreate state lost to failures are important attributes. Global state is minimized, replicated, and distributed across the virtual machine. The Harness peer-to-peer control system is felt to be much more scalable than the client-server system used in PVM. The control system is presently in the process of being incorporated into Harness 2.

Emory has taken the lead in the architectural design of Harness and development of the H2O core [4], which will be described in the next section. In developing Harness 1.9, it was realized that the distributed computing architecture could be generalized by creating a lower software level called H2O. A petascale virtual machine could then be built by adding distributed virtual machine plug-ins to the H2O plugable daemon.

4 H2O – The Harness Core

In Harness, the role now played by the PVM daemon is replaced with an H2O daemon. The H2O daemon starts out knowing little more than how to load and unload plug-ins from itself. It doesn't know anything about other daemons or the concept of a virtual machine. These are capabilities that the plug-ins provide. For example, a high-speed communication plug-in and a PVM plug-in can be loaded into the H2O daemon and it would have all the capabilities of a PVM daemon. In fact in the Harness 1.9 release, the PVM plug-in can run legacy PVM applications without recompiling. Load in an MPI plug-in and Harness is able to run MPI applications. With Harness a distributed virtual machine is no longer restricted to a give set of capabilities - new scalable features can be incorporated at any time.

But H2O is a general framework [4]. In the H2O model a dynamic collection of providers make their networked resources available to a defined set of clients. With this general model H2O is able to provide a framework for several different forms of distributed computing today.

To provide a PVM framework, the provider specifies only himself as a client, and he loads a PVM plug-in.

To provide a Grid framework, the provider specifies that any clients with a grid certificate can run on his resource. In addition he would most likely load a few OGSA plug-ins to provide a Grid interface for his grid clients.

To provide a web computing framework like SETI@HOME, the provider specifies one external client who can use his machine while it is idle. This client would then load and run a distributed application on thousands of such providers across the Internet.

Other frameworks can be supported by the H2O model. For example, a provider may sell use of his resource to one client. This client may in turn provide a popular software application (a game, or scientific program) that they then sell use of to other clients. Thus users of the resource may be a superset of the providers client list. Here is a hypothetical scenario. A client comes up with the next great "Google" software that instead of running on 6,000 node clusters, runs on idle Internet desktops. The client goes out and convinces many providers to supply their idle resources to him. This client in turn sets up his software and provides this service to many other people. These people, not the original client, are the ones who execute the software on the provider's resources.

While H2O is very flexible, our main focus in this paper is in using it to create Harness petascale virtual machines. To build such large systems distributed control and distributed state plug-ins are loaded into the daemon. These along with an MPI or PVM plug-in provide the basis for the next generation of distributed computing environment.

5 Algorithms for Petascale Virtual Machines

Exploiting Petascale Virtual Machines is going to take more than the Harness software. Fundamentally new approaches to application development will be required to allow programs to run across petascale systems with as many as 100,000 processors. With such large-scale systems the mean time to failure is less than the run time of most scientific jobs and at the same time checkpoint-restart is not a viable method to achieve fault tolerance due to IO requirements. Thus the algorithms in the next generation scientific applicationswill have to be both super scalable and fault tolerant.

ORNL has developed a meshless finite difference algorithm that is naturally fault tolerant. Parallel algorithms with "natural fault tolerance" have the property that they get the right answer even if one or more of the tasks involved in the calculations fail without warning or notification to the other tasks [5]. On a simulated 100,000 processor system the finite element algorithm gets the correct answer even if up to a hundred random parallel tasks are killed during the solution. Using a hiearchical implementation of the fault tolerant finite element algorithm, a "gridless multigrid" algorithm has now being developed and it's performance and fault tolerance results will be reported at the conference.

Global information is often needed in science applications to determine convergence, minimum energy, and other optimization values. ORNL has been able to create a naturally fault tolerant global maximum algorithm. Despite failures, all tasks (that are still alive) know the largest value when the algorithm finishes. The global max algorithm runs in logrithmic time, but unlike a typical binary tree, it is robust no matter which tasks die during the solution.

These examples are just the beginning of a new area of naturally fault tolerant algorithm development. Much research is still required to develop algorithms that can run effectively on petascale virtual machines.

6 Conclusion

Sciences such as genomics and nanotechnology are being driven by computation and PVM is helping to make that happen today. But tomorrow's discoveries are predicted to require computing capabilities 1,000 times greater than today's computers. Utilizing such Petascale Virtual Machines will require new approaches to developing application software that incorporate fault tolerance and adaptability. Our ongoing research in fault tolerant MPI and Harness are just beginning to address some of these needs. The new finite difference, global max, and multigrid algorithm results are encouraging but much research remains in order to understand the scalability and fault tolerance required for 100,000 processor systems.

References

1. G. Heffelfinger, et al, "Carbon Sequestration in Synechococcus Sp.: From Molecular Machines to Hierarchical Modeling", OMICS Journal of Integrative Biology. Nov. 2002 (www.genomes-to-life.org)
2. G. A. Geist, et al, "Harness", (www.csm.ornl.gov/harness)
3. M. Land, et al, "Genome Channel", (http://compbio.ornl.gov/channel)
4. D. Kurzyniec, et al, "Towards Self-Organizing Distributed Computing Frameworks: The H2O Approach", International Journal of High Performance Computing (2003).
5. G. A. Geist and C. Engelmann, "Development of Naturally Fault Tolerant Algorithms for Computing on 100,000 Processors", Parallel Computing (submitted) 2003. (PDF at www.csm.ornl.gov/ geist/Lyon2002-geist.pdf)

Future Developments in MPI*

William D. Gropp

Mathematics and Computer Science Division
Argonne National Laboratory
Argonne, IL
gropp@mcs.anl.gov
http://www.mcs.anl.gov/~gropp

Abstract. The Message Passing Interface (MPI) has been very successful at providing a programming model for computers from small PC clusters through the world's fastest computers. MPI has succeeded because it successfully addresses many of the requirements of an effective parallel programming model, including portability, performance, modularity, and completeness. But much remains to be done with MPI, both in terms of the performance of MPI and in the supporting the use of MPI in applications. This talk will look at three areas: programming models, implementations, and scalability.

The MPI programming model is often described as a supporting "only" basic message passing (point-to-point and collective) and (in MPI-2) simple one-sided communication. Such a description ignores the support in MPI for the creation of effective libraries built using MPI routines. This support has encouraged the development of powerful libraries that, working with MPI, provide a powerful high-level programming environment. This will be illustrated with two examples drawn from computational simulation.

MPI was designed to allow implementations to fully exploit the available hardware. It provides many features that support high performance, including a relaxed memory consistency model. While many MPI implementations take advantage of some of these opportunities, much remains to be done. This talk will describe some of the opportunities for improving the performance of MPI implementations, with particular emphasis on the relaxed memory model and both MPI's one-sided and parallel I/O operations.

Scalability is another goal of the MPI design and many applications have demonstrated scalability to thousands of processors. In the near future, computers with more than 64,000 processors will be built. Barriers to scalability in the definition and the implementation of MPI will be discussed, along with possible future directions for MPI developments. By avoiding a few very low usage routines and with the proper implementation, MPI should scale effectively to the next generation of massively parallel computers.

---

* This work was supported by the Mathematical, Information, and Computational Sciences Division subprogram of the Office of Advanced Scientific Computing Research, Office of Science, U.S. Department of Energy, under Contract W-31-109-ENG-38.

Integrating Scalable Process Management into Component-Based Systems Software*

Ewing Lusk

Mathematics and Computer Science Division
Argonne National Laboratory
Argonne, IL 60439, USA
lusk@mcs.anl.gov

Abstract. The Scalable Systems Software Project is exploring the design of a systems software architecture based on separate, replaceable components interacting through publicly defined interfaces. This talk will describe how a scalable process manager has provided the implementation of the process management component of that design. We describe a general, implementation-independent definition of process management and how a scalable process management system was used to provide its implementation.

1 Introduction

The work described here is motivated by the confluence of two research and development directions. The first has arisen from the MPICH project [5], which has had as its primary goal the development of a portable, open source, efficient implementation of the MPI standard. That work has led to the development of a standalone process management system called MPD [1, 2] for rapid and scalable startup of parallel jobs such as MPI implementations, in particular MPICH.

The second thrust has been in the area of scalable systems software in general. The Scalable Systems Software SciDAC project [6] is a collaboration among U. S. national laboratories, universities, and computer vendors to develop a standardized component-based architecture for open source software for managing and operating scalable parallel computers such as the large (greater than 1000 nodes) Linux clusters being installed at a number of institutions in the collaboration.

These two thrusts come together in the definition and implementation of a scalable process manager component. The definition consists concretely of the specification of an interface to other components being defined and developed as part of the Scalable Systems Software Project. Then multiple instantiations of this interface can evolve over time, along with multiple instantiations of other components, as long as the interfaces are adhered to. At the same time one

---

* This work was supported by the Mathematical, Information, and Computational Sciences Division subprogram of the Office of Advanced Scientific Computing Research, U.S. Department of Energy, under Contract W-31-109-Eng-38.

wants to present an implementation of the interface, both to test its suitability and to actually provide part of a usable suite of software for managing clusters. This talk outlines an interface that has been proposed to the Scalable Systems Software Project for adoption together with an implementation of it that is in actual use on some medium-sized clusters.

2 Defining Process Management

We define a process management component in an implementation-independent way, describing its functionality at an abstract level. A summary of how other components interact with this component are given in Section 2.4.

2.1 Goals and Assumptions

We assume that the process management component belongs to a family of system software components, with which it communicates using well-defined interfaces. Therefore the process management component need not concern itself with monitoring hardware or with assigning jobs to processors, since those tasks will be carried out by other components. We assume further that security concerns other than those internal to a specific instantiation of the process manager are handled by other components. Thus we take a minimalist position on what a process manager does. It should do a thorough and complete job of managing processes and leave other tasks to other components.

It is useful to introduce the concept of *rank* as a way of distinguishing and identifying the processes of a parallel job (at least the initial ones). We assume that an n-process job initially has processes with ranks $0,\ldots,n-1$. These need not necessarily coincide with MPI ranks, since there is nothing MPI-specific about job management, but the concept is the same. We will also need the concept of *pid*, which stands for process identifier, an integer assigned to a process that is unique on a particular host computer. Thus a single process in a parallel job may be identified by a (host, pid) pair, or more abstractly by a (job, rank) pair.

2.2 Not Included

The following functions are not included in the functionality of the process manager.

Scheduling. We assume that another component is responsible for making scheduling decisions. It will either specify which hosts various processes of the parallel job will run on, or specifically leave the choice up to the process manager, which is then free to make any decision it prefers.

Node monitoring. The state of a particular host is of interest to the scheduler, which should be responsible for deciding whether a node is available for starting a job. The scheduler can interact directory with a node monitor component to determine the information it needs.

Process monitoring. CPU usage, memory footprint, etc., are characteristics of the individual processes, and can be monitored by a separate component. The process manager can aid monitoring processes by either starting them (see *coprocesses* below) or by providing information on the process identifiers and hosts where particular processes of a job are running, in order to assist monitoring components.

Checkpointing. The process manager can help with checkpointing by delivering signals to the parallel job, but checkpointing itself is a separate function and should be carried out by a separate component.

2.3 Included

We are thus left with the following functions, which are the most appropriate for the process manager. We compensate for the limited number of functions described here by attempting to specify very flexible and complete versions of the functions that are included.

Starting a parallel job. The process manager is responsible for starting a parallel job, without restrictions. That is, the processes should be allowed to have separate executables, separate command-line arguments, and separate environments. Processes may even be run under different user names on different machines. Jobs will be started with appropriate user id's, group id's, and group memberships. It should be possible for the job submitter to assign a job identifier by which the job can be referred to later. A job-start request will be answered by a message confirming successful start or else a failure message with an error code. We allow multiple options for how standard I/O is handled.

Starting coprocesses for a parallel job. An advanced functionality we intend to explore is that of *coprocesses*, which we define to be separate processes started at the same time as the application process for scalability's sake, and passed the process identifiers of the application processes started on that host, together with other arguments. Our motivation is scalable startup of daemons for debugging or monitoring a particular parallel job.

Signaling a parallel job. It is possible to deliver a signal to all processes of a parallel job. Signals may be specified by either name ("STOP", "CONT", etc.) or by number ("43", "55", etc.) for signals that have no name on a particular operating system. The signals are delivered to all the processes of the job.

Killing a parallel job. Not only are all application processes killed, but also any "helper" processes that may have been started along with the job, such as the coprocesses. The idea is to clean the system of all processes associated with the job.

Reporting details of a parallel job. In response to a query, the process manager will report the hosts and process identifiers for each process rank. Queries can be forumalated in a variety of ways, specifying a host and asking for jobs on that host, for example, or specifying a user and retrieving hosts where that user has running jobs.

Reporting events. If there is an event manager, the process manager will report to it at least job start and job termination events.

Handling stdio. A number of different options for handling stdio are available. These include

- collecting stdout and stderr into a file with rank labels,
- writing stdout and stderr locally,
- ignoring stdout and stderr,
- delivering stdin to process 0 (a common default),
- delivering stdin to another specific process,
- delivering stdin to all processes.

Servicing the parallel job. The parallel job is likely to require certain services. We have begun exploring such services, especially in the MPI context, in [1]. Existing process managers tend to be part of resource management systems that use sophisticated schedulers to allocate nodes to a job, but then only execute a user script on one of the nodes, leaving to the user program the task of starting up the other processes and setting up communication among them. If they allow simultaneous startup of multiple processes, then all those processes must have the same executable file and command-line arguments. The process manager implementation we describe here provides services to a parallel job not normally provided by other process managers, which allow it to start much faster. In the long run, we expect to exploit this capability in writing parallel system utilities in MPI.

Registration with the service directory. If there is a service directory component, the process manager will register itself, and deregister before exiting.

2.4 Summary of Process Manager Interactions with Other Components

The Process Manager typically runs as root and interacts with other components bing defined and implemented as part of the Scalable Systems Software Project. These interactions are of two types: message exchanges initiated by the Process Manger and message exchanges initiated by other components and responded to by the Process Manager.

- Messages initiated by the Process Manager. These use the interfaces defined and published by other components.

  Registration/Deregistration. The Process Manager registers itself with the Service Directory so that other components in the system can connect to it. Essentially, it registers the host it is running on, the port where it is listening for connections, and the protocol that it uses for framing messages.

Events. The Process Manager communicates asynchronous events to other components by sending them to the Event Manager. Other components that have registered with the Event Manager for receipt of those events will be notified. by the Event Manager. Two such events that the Process Manager sends to the Event Manager are job start and job completion events.

- Messages responded to by the Process Manager. These can come from any authorized component. In the current suite of SSS components, the principal originators of such messages are the Queue Manager and a number of small utility components.

  Start job. This is the principal command that the Process Manager is responsible for. The command contains the complete specification of job as described in Section 2.3.

  Jobinfo. This request returns details of a running job. It uses the flexible XML query syntax that is used by a number of components in the project.

  Signal job. The Process Manager can deliver any signal to all the processes of a job.

  Kill job. The Process Manager can be asked to kill and clean up after a given job.

The XML that has been proposed to encode these messages is described in [3]. The appendix to that document presents the actual schemas.

3 Implementing a Process Manager Component

In order to provide a prototype implementation of the process manager component, we began by re-implementing the MPD system described in [2]. A new implementation was necessary because the original MPD system could not support the requirements imposed by the Scalable Systems Software Project, in particular the ability to provide separate specifications for each process. The relationship between the MPD system and the Scalable System Software process manager component is shown in Figure 1.

The process management component itself is written in Python, and uses Python's XML module for parsing. It invokes the `mpdrun` process startup command of the new MPD system. MPD is a ring of pre-existing and pre-connected daemons, running as root or as a user, which implements all the necessary requirements. The most notable one is that it provides an implementation of the process manager interface (PMI) used by MPICH to provide rapid startup of MPI programs and support for MPI-2 dynamic process functionality.

4 Experiments and Experiences

Our primary testbed has been the Chiba City testbed [4] at Argonne National Laboratory. We have carried out some preliminary experiments to test starting

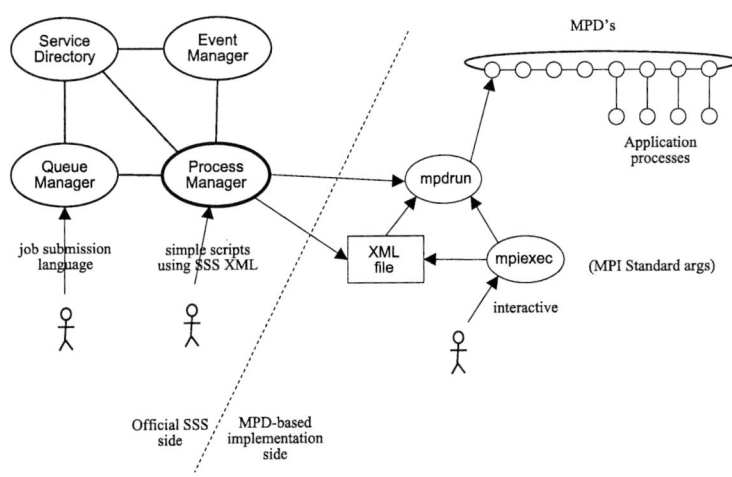

Fig. 1. Relationship of MPD to SSS components.

both MPI and non-MPI jobs, to illustrate the scalability of the MPD-based implementation of the Process Manager. Details are given in [3]; we summarize them here:

Command broadcast. The fact that the ring of MPD's is persistent and preconnected means that a message to execute a command (such as parallel job startup) can proceed quickly around the ring so that local process creation can occur in parallel. On a ring of 206 nodes, we could send a message ten times around the ring of MPD's in .89 seconds, simulating a ring of more than 2000 nodes. Thus just getting commands that come from other components out to the nodes is not a significant cost.

Starting non-MPI jobs. We ran hostname in parallel to test how fast non-communicating processes could be started. It took less than 4 seconds to start 200 instances and collect all of the stdout output. Times for varying numbers of processes were substantially sublinear, demonstrating that process startup is indeed occurring in parallel.

Starting MPI jobs. A feature of MPD not shared by most process managers is provision of services by which the processes of a parallel job can locate each other and create connections to support interprocess communication. Comparisons with the original process startup mechanism for MPICH shows improvements on the order of 100 times faster, nearly constant for up to 32 processes.

References

1. R. Butler, W. Gropp, and E. Lusk. A scalable process-management environment for parallel programs. In Jack Dongarra, Peter Kacsuk, and Norbert Podhorszki, editors, *Recent Advances in Parallel Virutal Machine and Message Passing Interface*, number 1908 in Springer Lecture Notes in Computer Science, pages 168–175, September 2000.

2. R. Butler, W. Gropp, and E. Lusk. Components and interfaces of a process management system for parallel programs. *Parallel Computing*, 27:1417–1429, 2001.
3. Ralph Butler, Narayan Desai, Andrew Lusk, and Ewing Lusk. The process management component of a scalable systems software environment. Technical Report ANL/MCS-P987-0802, Argonne National Laboratory, 2003.
4. Chiba City home page. http://www.mcs.anl.gov/chiba.
5. William Gropp, Ewing Lusk, Nathan Doss, and Anthony Skjellum. A highperformance, portable implementation of the MPI Message-Passing Interface standard. *Parallel Computing*, 22(6):789–828, 1996.
6. Scalable systems software center home page.
   http://www.scidac.org/scalablesystems.

Programming High Performance Applications Using Components

Thierry Priol

IRISA/INRIA
Campus de Beaulieu – 35042 Rennes Cedex, France
Thierry.Priol@irisa.fr
http://www.irisa.fr/paris/pages-perso/Thierry-Priol/welcome.htm

Abstract. Computational Grids promise to be the next generation of high-performance computing resources. However, programming suchcomputing infrastructures will be extremely challenging. Current programming practices tend to be based on existing and well understood models such as message-passing and SPMD (single program multiple data). On-going works based on Web services (OGSA) aims at programming Grids by specifying the coordination through the expression of interaction and dependencies between already deployed web services. This talk will focus on another alternative that aims at programming Grids with software components. With such an approach, it will be possible to install components on remote resources and to express interaction between components. This presentation will describe work in progress to develop a component-based software infrastructure, called Padico, for computational Grids based on the CORBA Component Model (CCM) from the Object Management Group (OMG). The objective of Padico is to offer a component model targeting multi-physics simulations or any applications that require the coupling of several codes (simulation or visualisation) within a high-performance environment. Two issues will be addressed during the talk: encapsulation of codes into components and runtime support for efficient communication between components within a Grid. This talk will look at the GridCCM component model, an extension to the CCM model to address the encapsulation of SPMD parallel codes into a component and a communication framework, called PadicoTM, able to efficiently support various communication runtime and middleware in an heterogeneous networking environment.

ASSIST High-Performance Programming Environment: Application Experiences and Grid Evolution*

Marco Vanneschi

Dipartimento di Informatica, University of Pisa, Italy

Extended Abstract. ASSIST (A Software development System based upon Integrated Skeleton Technology) is a new programming environment oriented to the development of parallel and distributed high-performance applications according to a unified approach. The main goals are: high-level programmability and software productivity for complex multidisciplinary applications, including data-intensive and interactive software; performance portability across different platforms, from homogenous parallel machines and possibly heterogeneous clusters to large-scale enabling platforms and computational Grids; effective reuse of parallel and distributed software; efficient evolution of applications through versions scalable according to the underlying technologies.

The programming model of ASSIST has been defined according to two main issues: i) evolution of structured parallel programming, starting from pros/cons of our past experience with the skeletons model, ii) joining the structured programming approach with the objects/components technology.

The design of applications is done by means of a coordination language, called ASSIST-CL, whose programming model has the following features:
a) parallel/distributed programs can be expressed by generic graphs;
b) the components can be parallel modules or sequential modules, with high flexibility of replacing components in order to modify the granularity and parallelism degree;
c) the parallel module, or *parmod*, construct, is introduced, which could be considered a sort of "generic" skeleton: it can be specialized to emulate the most common "classical" skeletons, and it is also able to easily express new forms of parallelism (e.g. optimized forms of task + data parallelism, nondeterminism, interactivity), as well as their variants and personalization. When necessary, the parallelism forms that are expressed could be at a lower abstraction level with respect to the "classical" skeletons;
d) the parallel and the sequential modules have an internal state. The parallel modules can have a nondeterministic behaviour;

---

* This work has been supported by the MIUR-CNR L449/97 Strategic Projects on Distributed Objects Complex Enabling ITC Platforms, "High-performance Distributed Platform" Project, and by the MIUR National Research Programme, FIRB Strategic Projects on Enabling Technologies for Information Society, Grid.it Project "Enabling Platforms for High-performance Computational Grid Oriented to Scalable Virtual Organizations".

e) composition of parallel and sequential modules is expressed, primarily, by means of the very general mechanisms of streams. In addition, modules can share objects implemented by forms of Distributed Shared Memory, invoked through their original APIs or methods;

f) the modules of a parallel application can refer to any kind of existing *external objects*, like CORBA and other commercial standards objects, as well to system objects, though their interfaces. In the same way, an ASSIST parallel application can be exported to other applications.

One of the basic features of structured parallel programming that we wish to preserve is related to the efficiency of implementation, and of the run-time support in particular. On the one hand, compared to "classical" skeletons, it is more difficult to define a simple cost model for a generic construct like parmod, and this can render optimizations at compile time more difficult. On the other hand, at least with the current knowledge of software development for large-scale platforms/Grids, we believe that run-time support optimizations are much more important than compile-time optimizations (which, anyway, remain a significant research issue).

This talk is organized in two parts. In the first part we discuss the utilization of ASSIST according to a set of application and benchmarking experiences performed during the last year. Such experiences have been done with the ASSIST 1.0 version of compiler and run-time system for Linux clusters; however, the run-time system is based upon ACE portable libraries, thus it is able to support ASSIST programs for heterogeneous clusters too. We show the expressive power and performance measures, and possible weaknesses to be overcame in the next versions of ASSIST. Among the classes of discussed applications:

1) problems that benefit from a flexible merging of task and data parallelism, possibly along with nondeterminism and flexible data distributions;

2) problems that benefit from a suitable mix of parallel/sequential modules and external objects, in particular data management, data repository and storage hierarchies in data intensive applications and interactive applications;

3) problems with a structure able to adapt itself to dynamic situations depending upon external data and/or nondeterministic events;

4) trade-offs in the utilization of ASSIST-CL *vs* the partial utilization of the lower level languages that are used in the design of ASSIST-CL run-time (namely, Assist-TaskCode and Assist-Lib), and that are available to the "expert" programmer.

In the second part we discuss the evolution of ASSIST for large-scale platforms and Grids. By now it is widely recognized that, at the programming model and environment level, the high-performance requirement for Grid platforms imposes new approaches able to take into account both the aspects related to the distribution of computations and resources, and the aspects related to parallelism. The development of Grid applications requires, in general, capabilities and properties beyond those needed in both sequential programming and in "classical" parallel/distributed programming, as it requires the management of computations and environments that are typically dynamic and heterogeneous in their nature and that include resource hierarchies with different features (e.g. memory and network). These issues are investigated in the Italian National Programme in Grid Computing (*Grid.it project*). Referring to such context, we discuss here some ideas and preliminary results:

1) description of Grid applications in terms of the features offered by ASSIST;
2) first results using a Grid- based version of ASSIST, called Assist-Conf, based upon the Globus toolkit;
3) evolution of the ASSIST programming model in terms of high-performance components that are consistent with emerging standards (CCA, CCM, and others);
4) re-thinking the ASSIST support in terms of high-performance components structuring;
5) evolution of the ASSIST implementation for Grid platforms.

High-Level Programming in MPI[*]

William D. Gropp and Ewing Lusk

Mathematics and Computer Science Division
Argonne National Laboratory
Argonne, IL 60439, USA
{gropp,lusk}@mcs.anl.gov

MPI is often thought of as a low-level approach, even as a sort of "assembly language," for parallel programming. This is both true and false. While MPI is designed to afford the programmer the ability to control the flow of data at a detailed level for maximum performance, MPI also provides highly expressive operations that support high-level programming. MPI's design has also encouraged the design of parallel libraries, which can provide performance while shielding the user from the details of MPI programming.

This tutorial will begin with the basics of MPI, so that attendees need not be familiar with MPI beforehand. We will focus, however, on using MPI as a high-level language by exploiting data type libraries, collective operations, and MPI-I/O. We will cover both MPI-1 and MPI-2 topics in this area, and will introduce some tools for analyzing performance of MPI programs. We will then familiarize attendees with libraries that have been built on MPI, such as ScaLAPACK, PETSc, and parallel NetCDF.

We will conclude with a hands-on, "class participation" project. Using whatever laptops attendees can bring to the tutorial together with a wireless network we will supply, we will set up a parallel computer and supply attendees with copies of MPICH-2, our all-new implementation of MPI-1 and MPI-2. If all goes well, we should thus be able to have a quite capable parallel computer available for some interesting demonstrations and experiments. Both Windows and Linux laptops will be accommodated.

---

[*] This work was supported by the Mathematical, Information, and Computational Sciences Division subprogram of the Office of Advanced Scientific Computing Research, U.S. Department of Energy, under Contract W-31-109-Eng-38.

Programming Environments for Grids and Distributed Computing Systems

Vaidy Sunderam

Dept. of Math & Computer Science
Emory University
Atlanta, GA 30322, USA
vss@mathcs.emory.edu

Abstract. Platforms for high-performance concurrent computing range from tightly-coupled multiprocessors to clusters, networks of workstations, and large-scale geographically distributed metacomputing systems. Effective application programming for each type of environment can be a challenge, given the wide variability and heterogeneity of the computational resources, communication interconnects, and level of dedicated access. In this tutorial, we will review and compare programming paradigms and associated runtime systems for high-performance concurrent computing in multiple types of distributed system environments. After a brief discussion of language-based approaches, we will analyze the underlying concurrent programming models embodied in MPI and PVM, with a particular focus on their suitability in loosely coupled distributed systems and grids. The emerging paradigm shift in computational grids to a standards-based service-oriented model will then be explored, and methodologies for developing and programming grid services will be discussed. Examples of writing and deploying grid services as well as clients will be included. The tutorial will conclude by summarizing the essential features and characteristics of programming different distributed computing environments and discussing approaches to application development using a combination of programming paradigms.

Performance Modeling and Evaluation of Java Message-Passing Primitives on a Cluster

Guillermo L. Taboada, Juan Touriño, and Ramón Doallo

Computer Architecture Group
Department of Electronics and Systems,
University of A Coruña, Spain
{taboada,juan,doallo}@udc.es

Abstract. The use of Java for parallel programming on clusters according to the message-passing paradigm is an attractive choice. In this case, the overall application performance will largely depend on the performance of the underlying Java message-passing library. This paper evaluates, models and compares the performance of MPI-like point-to-point and collective communication primitives from selected Java message-passing implementations on a cluster. We have developed our own microbenchmark suite to characterize the message-passing communication overhead and thus derive analytical latency models.

1 Introduction

Cluster computing architectures are an emerging option for organizations as they offer a reasonable price/performance ratio. The message-passing model provides programming flexibility and generally good performance on these architectures. Java message-passing libraries are an alternative to develop parallel and distributed applications due to appealing characteristics such as platform independence, portability and integrability into existing Java applications, although probably at a performance cost. In this work, Java message-passing libraries are analyzed in order to estimate overheads with simple expressions. Our goal is to identify design faults in the communication routines, as well as to provide performance results which can guide developers of Java parallel applications.

Related work about Java message-passing evaluation are the papers by Stankovic and Zhang [14], and by Getov et al. [6]. Both works do not derive performance analytical models. Moreover, the experimental results in [6] are restricted to point-to-point primitives using a JNI-wrapped version of LAM MPI on an IBM SP-2, and the scenarios of the experiments in [14] are not representative (eg, they carry out collective measures using up to 5 processors of different architectures connected via 10Mbps Ethernet). Finally, these works are based on currently out-of-date Java message-passing libraries and programming environments.

2 Java Message-Passing Libraries

Research efforts to provide MPI for Java are focused on two main types of implementations: Java wrapper and pure Java. On the one hand, the wrapper-based

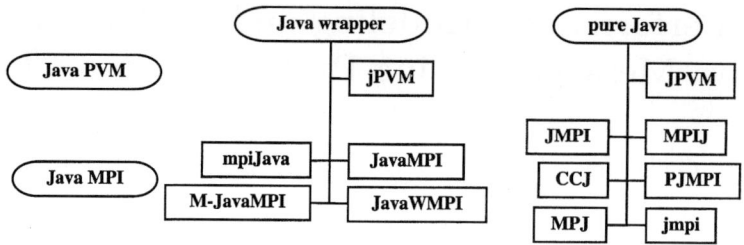

Fig. 1. Java-based message-passing libraries

approach provides efficient MPI communication through calling native methods (in C, C++ or Fortran) using the Java Native Interface (JNI). The major drawback is lack of portability: only a few combinations of platforms, message-passing libraries and JVMs are supported due to interoperability issues. The pure Java approach, on the other hand, provides a portable message-passing implementation since the whole library is developed in Java, although the communication could be relatively less efficient due to the use of the RMI protocol.

Figure 1 shows a taxonomy of Java message-passing libraries that use different approaches and APIs. Such variety is due to the lack of a standard MPI binding for Java, although the Message-Passing Working Group within the Java Grande Forum (www.javagrande.org) is working on a standard interface, named MPJ [2], in pure Java. One of the major issues that has arisen is how the Java mechanisms can be made useful in association with MPI: it is under study if and how Java's thread model can be used instead of the process-based approach of MPI.

In this work, we have focused on the following MPI-based libraries:

- mpiJava [1], a collection of wrapper classes that call the C++ binding of MPI through JNI. This is the most active Java wrapper project.
- JMPI [12], a pure Java implementation developed for academic purposes at the University of Massachusetts, following the MPJ specification.
- CCJ [13], a pure Java communication library with an MPI-like syntax not compliant with the MPJ specification. It makes use of Java capabilities such as a thread-based programming model or sending of objects.

Other Java message-passing libraries are:

- JavaMPI [11], an MPI Java wrapper created with the help of JCI, a tool for generating Java-to-C interfaces. The last version was released in January 2000.
- JavaWMPI [9] is a Java wrapper version built on WMPI, a Windows-based implementation of MPI.
- M-JavaMPI [8] is another wrapper approach with process migration support that runs on top of the standard JVM. Unlike mpiJava and JavaMPI, it does not use direct binding of Java programs and MPI. M-JavaMPI follows a client-server message redirection model that makes the system more portable, that is, MPI-implementation-independent. It is not publicly available yet.

- MPIJ is a pure Java MPI subset developed as part of the DOGMA project (Distributed Object Group Metacomputing Architecture) [7]. MPIJ has been removed from DOGMA since release 2.0.
- PJMPI [10] is a pure Java message-passing implementation strongly compatible with the MPI standard that is being developed at the University of Adelaide in conjunction with a non-MPI message-passing environment called JUMP (not publicly available yet).
- jmpi [4] is another pure Java implementation of MPI built on top of JPVM (see below). The project is dead.

Far less research has been devoted to PVM-based libraries. The most representative projects were JavaPVM (renamed as jPVM [15]), a Java wrapper to PVM (last released in April 1998), and JPVM [5], a pure Java implementation of PVM (last released in February 1999). Performance issues of both libraries were studied in [17].

3 Modeling Message-Passing Primitives

In order to characterize Java message-passing performance, we have followed the same approach as in [3] and [16], where the performance of MPI C routines was modeled on a PC cluster and on the Fujitsu AP3000 multicomputer, respectively.

Thus, in point-to-point communications, message latency (T) can be modeled as an affine function of the message length n: $T(n) = t_s + t_b n$, where t_s is the startup time, and t_b is the transfer time per data unit (one byte from now on). Communication bandwidth is easily derived as $Bw(n) = n/T(n)$. A generalization of the point-to-point model is used to characterize collective communications: $T(n,p) = t_s(p) + t_b(p)n$, where p is the number of processors involved in the communication.

The Low Level Operations section of the Java Grande Forum Benchmark Suite is not appropriate for our modeling purposes (eg, it only considers seven primitives and timing outliers are not discarded). We have thus developed our own microbenchmark suite which consists of a set of tests adapted to our specific needs. Regarding blocking point-to-point primitives, a ping-pong test takes 150 measurements of the execution time varying the message size in powers of four from 0 bytes to 1 MB. We have chosen as test time the 25th value of the increasingly ordered measurements to avoid distortions due to timing outliers. Moreover, we have checked that the use of this value is statistically better than the mean or the median to derive our models. As the millisecond timing precision in Java is not enough for measuring short message latencies, in these cases we have gathered several executions to achieve higher precision. The parameters t_s and t_b were derived from a linear regression of T vs n. Similar tests were applied to collective primitives, but also varying the number of processors (up to 16 in our cluster), so that the parameters of the model were obtained from the regression of T vs n and p. Double precision addition was the operation used in the experiments with reduction primitives. We have observed performance degradation due to network contention in some collective primitives for $n >$256KB

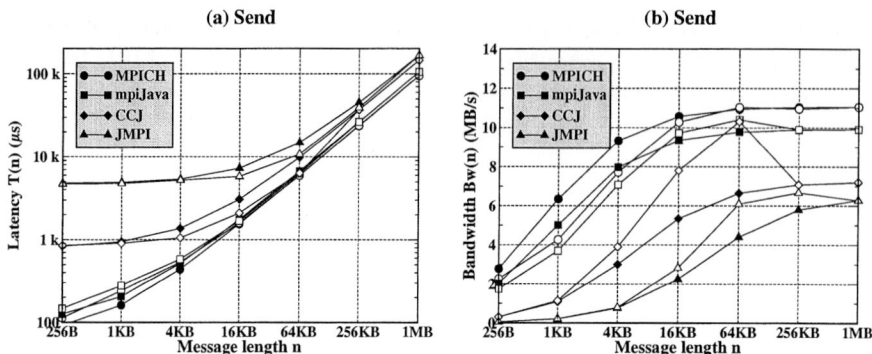

Fig. 2. Measured and estimated latencies and bandwidths of Send

(see, for instance, Allgather and Alltoall primitives in Figures 3(d) and 3(g), respectively). In these cases, the values were discarded in the modeling process.

4 Experimental Results

The tests were performed in a cluster with 16 single-processor nodes (PIII at 1 GHz with 512MB of memory) interconnected via Fast Ethernet. The OS is Linux Red Hat 7.1, kernel 2.4.7-10. We have used the following libraries: MPICH 1.2.4 (underlying MPI C library needed by mpiJava), mpiJava 1.2.5, CCJ 0.1 and JMPI. The C compiler is gcc 2.96 and the Java Runtime Environment is Sun 1.4.1 HotSpot. We have used the same benchmark codes for mpiJava and JMPI, whereas CCJ codes are quite different as this library does not follow the MPJ standard.

Table 1 presents the estimated parameters of the models (t_s and t_b) obtained for the standard Send (we have checked that it is the best choice in blocking point-to-point communications) and for collective communications. Some experimentally measured metrics ($T(n,p)$ for n=16 bytes and p=16, and $Bw(n,p)$ for n=1MB and p=16) are also provided in order to show short and long message-passing performance, respectively, as well as to compare the different libraries for each primitive. Reduction primitives are not implemented in the JMPI library and some advanced primitives (Alltoall, Reducescatter, Scan) are not available in the current version of CCJ. As we can see, transfer times ($t_b(p)$) in collective communications present $O(\log_2 p)$ complexities. This fact reveals a binomial tree-structured implementation of the primitives. Design faults were found in the JMPI implementation of the broadcast (it is $O(p)$), and in the CCJ Allreduce, where surprisingly the transfer time of this primitive is larger than the CCJ time of the equivalent Reduce+Broadcast.

Figure 2 shows experimental (empty symbols) and estimated (filled symbols) latencies and bandwidths of the Send primitive using various message sizes. In Figure 2(b) we can observe that the MPICH and mpiJava point-to-point bandwidths are very close to the theoretical bandwidth of Fast Ethernet (12.5 MB/s). MPICH achieves 88% of available bandwidth for a 1 MB send and mpiJava 79%,

Table 1. Message-passing analytical models and experimental metrics ($lp = \log_2 p$)

Primitive	Library	$t_s(p)$ $\{\mu s\}$	$t_b(p)$ $\{\mu s/byte\}$	$T(16_B, 16)$ $\{\mu s\}$	$Bw(1_{MB}, 16)$ $\{MB/s\}$
Send	MPICH	69	0.0903	72	11.061
	mpiJava	101	0.1007	105	9.923
	CCJ	800	0.1382	800	7.217
	JMPI	4750	0.1544	4750	6.281
Broadcast	MPICH	$7 + 117\lceil lp \rceil$	$-0.0003 + 0.0904\lceil lp \rceil$	483	2.764
	mpiJava	$19 + 124\lceil lp \rceil$	$0.0101 + 0.0905\lceil lp \rceil$	532	2.683
	CCJ	$-430 + 1430\lceil lp \rceil$	$0.0064 + 0.1304\lceil lp \rceil$	5200	1.878
	JMPI	$-9302 + 7151p$	$-0.1232 + 0.1757p$	97800	0.359
Scatter	MPICH	$92 + 18p$	$0.0397 + 0.0111\lceil lp \rceil$	370	12.364
	mpiJava	$95 + 19p$	$0.0526 + 0.0100\lceil lp \rceil$	391	11.203
	CCJ	$534 + 333p$	$0.0516 + 0.0202\lceil lp \rceil$	6400	7.028
	JMPI	$-5276 + 6938p$	$0.1021 + 0.0015\lceil lp \rceil$	101000	4.504
Gather	MPICH	$31 + 46p$	$0.0377 + 0.0133(lp)$	728	11.350
	mpiJava	$45 + 45p$	$0.0386 + 0.0141(lp)$	755	10.692
	CCJ	$780 + 210p$	$0.0471 + 0.0096(lp)$	4800	11.155
	JMPI	$2000 + 2000p$	$0.0708 + 0.0009(lp)$	34600	9.612
Allgather	MPICH	$-78 + 84p$	$0.0522 + 0.0112\lceil lp \rceil$	1319	1.678
	mpiJava	$-65 + 89p$	$0.0479 + 0.0152\lceil lp \rceil$	1369	1.608
	CCJ	$442 + 679p$	$0.0506 + 0.0766\lceil lp \rceil$	13000	1.337
	JMPI	$-5259 + 7929p$	$0.1086 + 0.0631\lceil lp \rceil$	118400	2.170
Reduce	MPICH	$103 + 25p$	$0.0027 + 0.0996\lceil lp \rceil$	518	2.489
	mpiJava	$113 + 25p$	$0.0119 + 0.0997\lceil lp \rceil$	532	2.330
	CCJ	$454 + 273p$	$0.0119 + 0.0927\lceil lp \rceil$	3800	2.683
Allreduce	MPICH	$90 + 32p$	$0.0030 + 0.1897\lceil lp \rceil$	608	1.312
	mpiJava	$102 + 32p$	$0.0166 + 0.1945\lceil lp \rceil$	632	1.261
	CCJ	$18 + 591p$	$-0.1108 + 0.3585\lceil lp \rceil$	8200	0.719
Alltoall	MPICH	$32 + 34p$	$0.0316 + 0.0371(lp)$	594	5.687
	mpiJava	$38 + 35p$	$0.0542 + 0.0373(lp)$	608	5.380
	JMPI	$-6836 + 8318p$	$0.1039 + 0.0656\lceil lp \rceil$	115800	2.124
Reducescatter	MPICH	$78 + 41p$	$0.0440 + 0.1100\lfloor lp \rfloor$	771	2.081
	mpiJava	$90 + 42p$	$0.0654 + 0.1127\lfloor lp \rfloor$	794	1.951
Scan	MPICH	$83 + 25p$	$-0.0902 + 0.0976\lfloor 2lp \rfloor$	627	1.464
	mpiJava	$91 + 27p$	$-0.0691 + 0.0993\lfloor 2lp \rfloor$	654	1.394
Barrier	MPICH	$26 + 33p$	N/A	N/A	N/A
	mpiJava	$44 + 33p$	N/A	N/A	N/A
	CCJ	$382 + 209p$	N/A	N/A	N/A
	JMPI	$1858 + 521p$	N/A	N/A	N/A

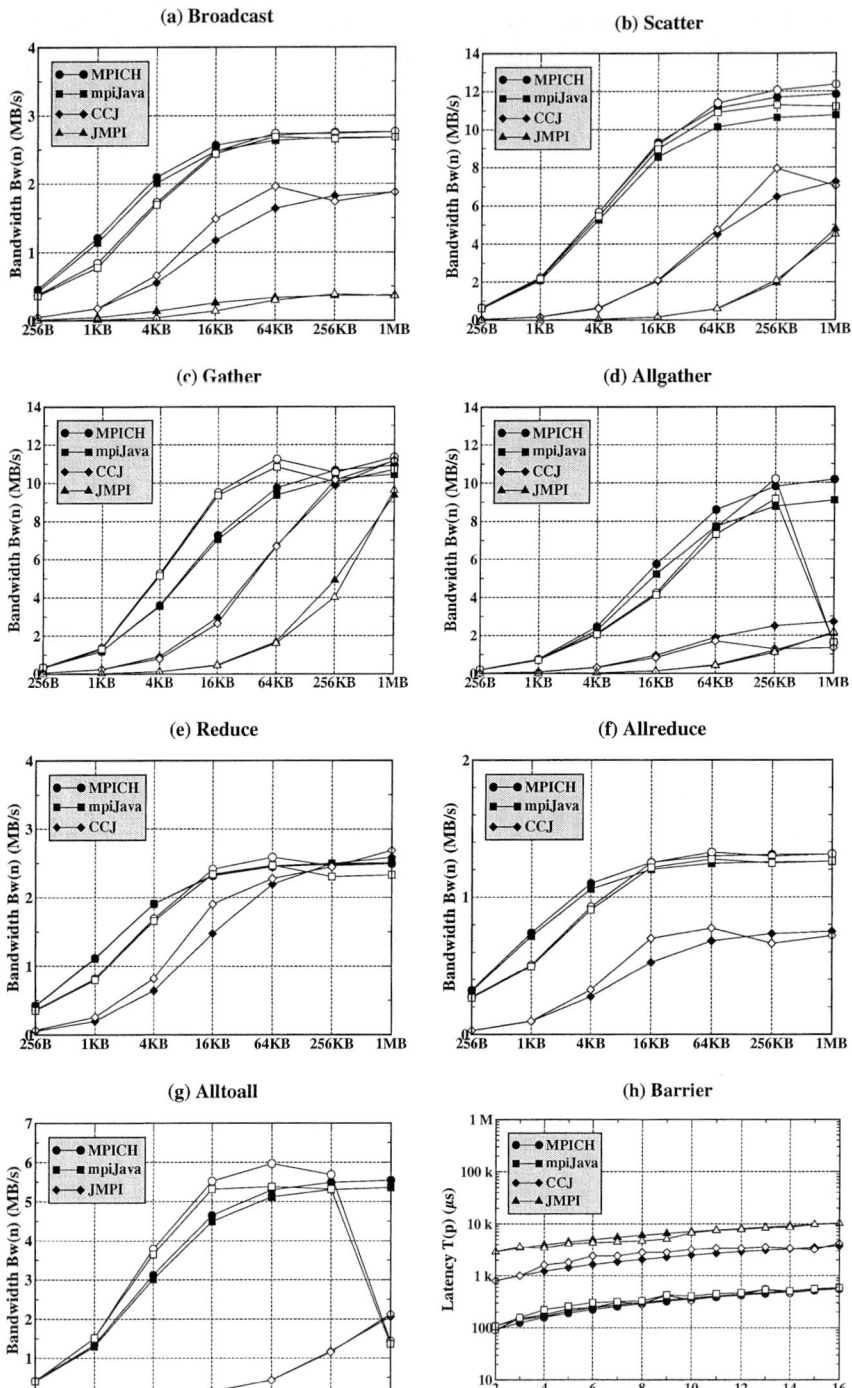

Fig. 3. Measured and estimated bandwidths for various message sizes on 16 nodes

whereas CCJ and JMPI only achieve 58% and 50%, respectively. Experimental and estimated bandwidths for collective primitives on 16 processors are depicted in Figure 3 (except the last graph that shows barrier latencies for different cluster configurations). In many cases, the estimated values are hidden by the measured values, which means a good modeling. The MPICH C primitives, which are used as a reference to compare the performance of the Java-based libraries, have the lowest communication overhead; mpiJava, as a wrapper implementation over MPICH, has slightly larger latencies due to the overhead of calling the native MPICH routines through JNI. Regarding pure Java implementations, both the transfer time and, mainly, the startup time increase significantly because of the use of RMI for interprocess communication, which adds a substantial overhead to each message passed. In fact, RMI was primarily designed for communication across the Internet, not for low latency networks. CCJ shows better performance than JMPI due to the use of asynchronous messages.

5 Conclusions

The characterization of message-passing communication overhead is an important issue in not well-established environments. As Java message-passing is an emerging option in cluster computing, this kind of studies serve as objective and quantitative guidelines for cluster parallel programming. We have selected the most outstanding Java-based libraries: mpiJava, CCJ and JMPI. The design of our own message-passing microbenchmark suite allowed us to obtain more accurate models. From the evaluation of the experimental results, we can conclude that mpiJava presents a good performance (mpiJava calls to native MPI have low overhead), although it is not a truly portable library. Pure Java implementations show poorer performance (particularly JMPI), mainly for short messages due to the RMI overhead. Research efforts should concentrate on this drawback to consolidate and enhance the use of pure Java message-passing codes. This is the topic of our future work, together with the evaluation of Java message-passing performance on Myrinet and SCI clusters.

Acknowledgments

This work was supported by Xunta de Galicia (Projects PGIDT01-PXI10501PR and PGIDIT02-PXI10502IF). We gratefully thank CESGA (Galician Supercomputing Center, Santiago de Compostela, Spain) for providing access to the cluster.

References

1. Baker, M., Carpenter, B., Fox, G., Ko, S., Lim, S.: mpiJava: an Object-Oriented Java Interface to MPI. In Proc. of 1st Int. Workshop on Java for Parallel and Distributed Computing (IPPS/SPDP'99 Workshop), San Juan, Puerto Rico, LNCS Vol. 1586, Springer (1999) 748–762
(http://www.npac.syr.edu/projects/pcrc/mpiJava/mpiJava.html)

2. Baker, M., Carpenter, B.: MPJ: a Proposed Java Message Passing API and Environment for High Performance Computing. In Proc. of 2nd Int. Workshop on Java for Parallel and Distributed Computing (IPDPS 2000 Workshop), Cancun, Mexico, LNCS Vol. 1800, Springer (2000) 552–559
3. Barro, J., Touriño, J., Doallo, R., Gulías, V.: Performance Modeling and Evaluation of MPI-I/O on a Cluster. Journal of Information Science and Engineering **18(5)** (2002) 825–836
4. Dincer, K.: Ubiquitous Message Passing Interface Implementation in Java: jmpi. In Proc. of 13th Int. Parallel Processing Symposium and 10th Symposium on Parallel and Distributed Processing, IPPS/SPDP'99, San Juan, Puerto Rico (1999) 203–207
5. Ferrari, A.: JPVM: Network Parallel Computing in Java. Concurrency: Practice & Experience **10(11-13)** (1998) 985–992
6. Getov, V., Gray, P., Sunderam, V.: MPI and Java-MPI: Contrasts and Comparisons of Low-Level Communication Performance. In Proc. of Supercomputing Conference, SC'99, Portland, OR (1999)
7. Judd, G., Clement, M., Snell, Q.: DOGMA: Distributed Object Group Metacomputing Architecture. Concurrency: Practice & Experience **10(11-13)** (1998) 977–983
8. Ma, R.K.K., Wang, C.-L., Lau, F.C.M.: M-JavaMPI: a Java-MPI Binding with Process Migration Support. In Proc. of 2nd IEEE/ACM Int. Symposium on Cluster Computing and the Grid, CCGrid'02, Berlin, Germany (2002) 255-262
9. Martin, P., Silva, L.M., Silva, J.G.: A Java Interface to WMPI. In Proc. of 5th European PVM/MPI Users' Group Meeting, EuroPVM/MPI'98, Liverpool, UK, LNCS Vol. 1497, Springer (1998) 121–128
10. Mathew, J.A., James, H.A., Hawick, K.A.: Development Routes for Message Passing Parallelism in Java. In Proc. of the ACM 2000 Java Grande Conference, San Francisco, CA (2000) 54–61
11. Mintchev, S., Getov, V.: Towards Portable Message Passing in Java: Binding MPI. In Proc. of 4th European PVM/MPI Users' Group Meeting, EuroPVM/MPI'97, Crakow, Poland, LNCS Vol. 1332, Springer (1997) 135–142
12. Morin, S., Koren, I., Krishna, C.M.: JMPI: Implementing the Message Passing Standard in Java. In Proc. of 4th Int. Workshop on Java for Parallel and Distributed Computing (IPDPS 2002 Workshop), Fort Lauderdale, FL (2002) 118–123 (http://euler.ecs.umass.edu/jmpi)
13. Nelisse, A., Maassen, J., Kielmann, T., Bal, H.E.: CCJ: Object-Based Message Passing and Collective Communication in Java. Concurrency and Computation: Practice & Experience **15(3-5)** (2003) 341–369 (http://www.cs.vu.nl/manta)
14. Stankovic, N., Zhang, K.: An Evaluation of Java Implementations of Message-Passing. Software - Practice and Experience **30(7)** (2000) 741–763
15. Thurman, D.: jPVM – A Native Methods Interface to PVM for the Java Platform (1998) (http://www.chmsr.gatech.edu/jPVM)
16. Touriño, J., Doallo, R.: Characterization of Message-Passing Overhead on the AP3000 Multicomputer. In Proc. of 30th Int. Conference on Parallel Processing, ICPP'01, Valencia, Spain (2001) 321–328
17. Yalamanchilli, N., Cohen, W.: Communication Performance of Java-Based Parallel Virtual Machines. Concurrency: Practice & Experience **10(11-13)**(1998) 1189–1196

Integrating New Capabilities into NetPIPE

Dave Turner, Adam Oline, Xuehua Chen, and Troy Benjegerdes

Ames Laboratory – Iowa State University
327 Wilhelm Hall, Ames, Iowa, 50011
turner@ameslab.gov

Abstract. The performance of the communication network can greatly affect the ability of scientific applications to make efficient use of the computational power available in high-performance computing systems. Many tools exist for analyzing network performance, but most concentrate on a single layer in the communication subsystem or on one type of network hardware. NetPIPE was developed to provide a complete and consistent set of analytical tools in a flexible framework that can be applied to analyze the message-passing libraries and the native software layers that they run on. Examples are given on how NetPIPE is being enhanced to enable research in channel bonding multiple Gigabit Ethernet interfaces, to analyze InfiniBand hardware and the MPI libraries being developed for it, and to optimize memory copy routines to make SMP message-passing more efficient.

1 Introduction

Performance losses can come from many sources in the communication network of clusters, Shared-memory Multi-Processor (SMP) and Massively Parallel Processing (MPP) systems. Internal limitations of the PCI and memory buses can restrict the rate that data can be transferred into and out of a node. The network hardware itself can impose limitations, as can improper tuning of the driver and OS parameters. The message-passing layer often requires tuning to achieve optimal performance, and the choice of a particular message-passing implementation can make a large difference.

Designing, building, and using high-performance computing systems requires careful measurement and tuning of the communication system to ensure that the processing power is being efficiently used. Many tools such as Netperf [1], Iperf [2], and the variants of ttcp are commonly used to analyze TCP performance between systems. Vendors often provide their own tools that allow users to measure the performance of the native software layer. Myricom provides a simple tool for analyzing the performance of Myrinet hardware at the GM layer, and Mellanox provides a tool for measuring the InfiniBand performance at the Verbs API (VAPI) layer.

While these tools are very good, they are somewhat limited in their scope. Most test only a single message size at a time, making it difficult to fully evaluate any communication system. All are aimed at testing only one layer, making it more difficult to directly compare performance at the native and message-passing layers.

The goal of the NetPIPE project is to provide a wide variety of features within a common framework that can be used to evaluate both message-passing libraries and the native software layers that they run on. Many new modules and features of Net-

PIPE will be introduced, with examples given of how they are being used to analyze cutting edge networking technology.

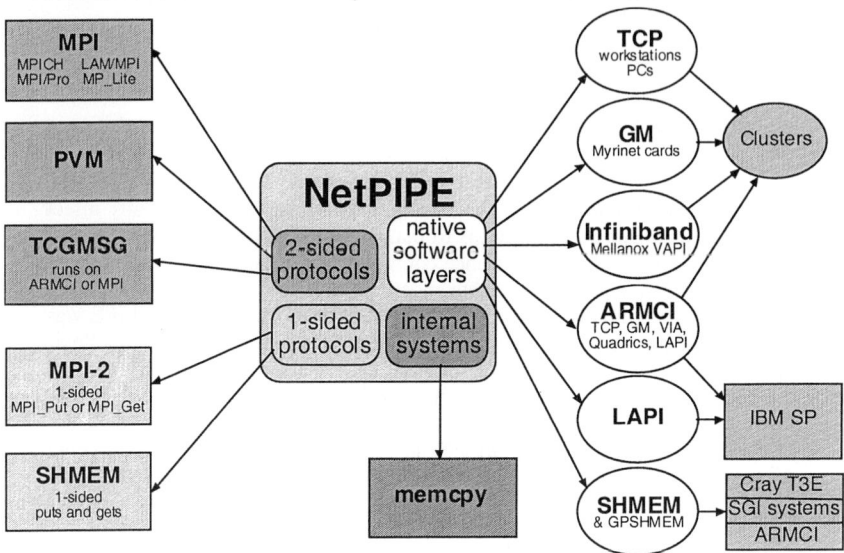

Fig. 1. A diagram showing the structure of NetPIPE and the modules developed for it.

2 NetPIPE

NetPIPE is the **Net**work **P**rotocol **I**ndependent **P**erformance **E**valuator [3-5], a tool originally developed to provide a more complete measurement of the communication performance at both the TCP and MPI layers. A message is repeatedly bounced between nodes to provide an accurate measurement of the transmission time for each message size. Message sizes are chosen at regular intervals and at slight perturbations to more fully evaluate the communication hardware and software layers. This produces an accurate measurement of the small message latency, taken to be half the round trip time for an 8-byte message, and a graph of the throughput across a broad range of message sizes.

The authors have taken this framework, and greatly expanded the modules supported to allow measurements on more message-passing libraries and native software layers. Additional testing options have been built into the code to provide more insight into the performance bottlenecks. New modules are allowing NetPIPE to look at internal properties such as memory copy rates that affect SMP message-passing performance greatly. Current research is extending NetPIPE beyond point-to-point measurements, allowing it to address more global network performance issues.

The diagram in fig. 1 shows the current structure of NetPIPE. The code consists of one central program that provides the same testing framework for all environments. Modules have been developed to test the 2-sided communications of MPI [6-7] implementations, the PVM library [8-9], and the TCGMSG library [10]. The 1-sided *get* and *put* operations of the MPI-2 and SHMEM standards can be tested with or without the synchronization imposed by intervening *fence* calls. The native software layers that message-passing implementations are built upon can be tested using the TCP, GM, InfiniBand, ARMCI [11], LAPI, and SHMEM modules.

Having all these modules in the same framework allows for direct comparison between the various message-passing libraries. The efficiency of each message-passing library can also be measured by directly comparing its performance to that of the native software layer it runs on.

A ping-pong measurement across the full range of message sizes is ideal for identifying many deficiencies in the communication system. Latencies are typically limited by the network hardware, but may be hurt by poorly written or optimized drivers, or by the message-passing layer. Instabilities and dropouts in the performance curves may be affected by OS and network parameters such as the socket buffer sizes or the MTU size, or by problems in the message-passing layer. Limitations to the maximum throughput may be due to poor optimization at any level. The type of problem demonstrated by the performance measurement can help direct the user toward the proper solution.

NetPIPE also has a streaming mode where messages are sent in only one direction. The source node simply pushes messages over the network to the destination node in rapid succession. While the ping-pong tests apply more closely to scientific applications, the streaming mode can be useful since it puts more stress on the network. The OS can coalesce many small messages together into packets, so the transmission time for small messages should not be taken as the latency time. Streaming messages at high rates can cause the OS to adjust the window size down, which restricts any subsequent performance. The sockets must therefore be reset for each data point to prevent interference with subsequent measurements.

SMP message-passing performance depends greatly on whether the data starts in cache or main memory. Some networking hardware is also fast enough now that it may be affected by the starting location of the data. A complete understanding of the performance of these systems therefore requires testing with and without cache effects. The default configuration is to test using cache effects, where each node sends and receives the message from the same memory buffer each time. Testing without cache effects involves sending the message from a different location in main memory each time.

NetPIPE can now do an integrity check instead of measuring performance. In this mode, each message is fully tested to ensure it has not been corrupted during transmission. A bi-directional mode has been added to test the performance when messages flow in both directions at the same time. Real applications often produce message traffic in multiple directions through a network, so this provides another useful probe for the communication system. Future work will add the capability to perform multiple, synchronized, pair-wise measurements within NetPIPE. This should prove ideal for investigating global properties of networks such as the maximum throughput of the back plane in a switch.

3 Gigabit Ethernet Performance

Even though Gigabit Ethernet technology is fairly mature, care must still be taken in choosing the hardware, optimizing the driver and OS parameters, and evaluating the message-passing software. Instabilities caused by poor drivers can sometimes be overcome by optimizing the drivers themselves, choosing a better driver for that card, or simply adjusting the TCP socket buffer sizes. Limitations to the maximum throughput, typical of graphs where the performance flattens out for large messages, can often be optimized away by increasing the TCP socket buffer sizes or increasing the MTU size if supported.

The NetPIPE TCP module provides an easy way to measure the performance of a system while varying the socket buffer sizes using the –b flag. The maximum socket buffer size is often limited by the OS, but this may be a tunable parameter in itself. If the socket buffer size is found to be a limiting factor, you may be able to change the default socket buffer size in the OS and you may also need to tune the message-passing library (set P4_SOCKBUFSIZE for MPICH [12-13], for example).

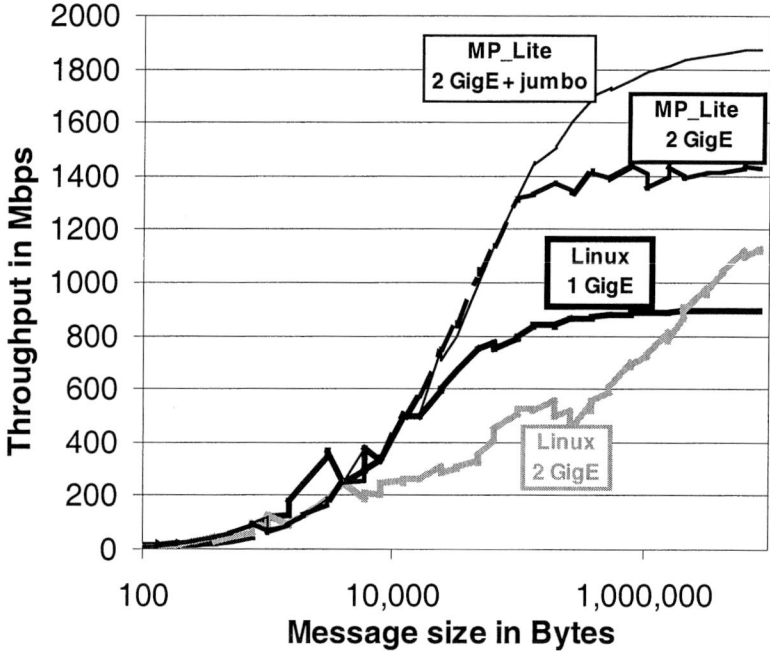

Fig. 2. The channel bonding performance using the built in Intel Pro/1000 ports on two SuperMicro X5DP8-G2 motherboards having 2.4 GHz Xeon processors running RedHat 7.3 Linux with the 2.4.18-10smp kernel.

The thick black line in fig. 2 shows the performance of the built in Intel Pro/1000 Gigabit Ethernet port between two SuperMicro X5DP8-G2 motherboards. This is good networking hardware, with a 62 μs latency and 900 Mbps throughput, but this lack of a nice smooth curve can sometimes indicate stability problems. Netgear GA302T Gigabit Ethernet cards have a lower latency at 24 μs and provide a much smoother performance curve. Both work well with the default socket buffer size, but can raise the throughput to 950 Mbps by setting the MTU size to 9000 Bytes.

Linux kernel level channel bonding across the two built in Gigabit Ethernet ports currently produces poorer performance than using just one of the ports. Using the MP_Lite message-passing library [14-16], channel bonding across the same two built in ports can be done with much greater efficiency by striping the data at the socket level. The benefit of using jumbo frames in this case is clear from the improvement from performance that flattens out at 1400 Mbps to a smoother curve that gets to nearly an ideal doubling of the single channel performance.

4 InfiniBand Research

InfiniBand [17] adapters are based on either the IBM or Mellanox chipsets. The current 4X technology is capable of operating at a maximum throughput of 10 Gbps. Many vendors such as Mellanox, DivergeNet, and JNI offer adaptors based on the Mellanox chipset, and programmed with the Mellanox VAPI or close variants.

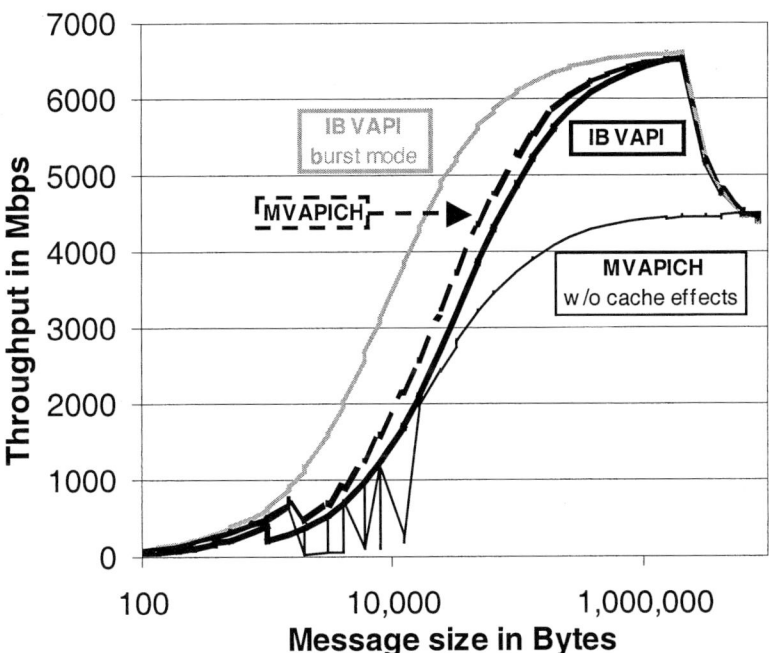

Fig. 3. The performance across Mellanox InfiniBand adapters between two 2.2 GHz Xeon systems running RedHat 7.3 Linux with the 2.4.18-10 kernel.

An InfiniBand module for NetPIPE was developed to assist in analyzing the characteristics of the hardware and Mellanox VAPI software. This also allows direct comparison with research versions of message-passing libraries such as MVAPICH 0.8 [18], an MPICH implementation for the Mellanox VAPI that grew out of an MPICH VIA module developed by the same group.

There are several unique features of InfiniBand that place new demands upon Net-PIPE. The most obvious is that the transfer rates are much greater than previous technologies have delivered. Fig. 3 shows the communication performance reaching 6500 Mbps for message sizes that fit in cache, after which the performance tails off to 4400 Mbps. Running the NetPIPE tests without cache effects limits the performance to the same 4400 Mbps. This is approximately the memcpy rate for these systems. It is therefore not certain whether this is a fundamental limit of the DMA speed of the adapters in transferring data into and out of main memory, or whether the adapters are just tuned better for transfers from cache rather than main memory.

The performance tool that Mellanox distributes runs in a burst mode, where all receives are pre-posted before a trial starts, and are therefore excluded from the total communication time. While this is not representative of the performance applications would see, it is useful in determining the amount of time spent in posting a receive. The burst mode (-B) was added to NetPIPE to allow it to duplicate the measurements seen with the Mellanox tool. Fig. 3 shows that a significant amount of the communication time is spent in posting the receive, making it an attractive target for optimization. Future efforts to optimize message-passing libraries can use this information to concentrate efforts on reducing the need to pin memory buffers that have been previously used.

MVAPICH uses an RDMA mechanism to provide impressive small message latencies of around 8 μs. Pre-allocated buffers are used that avoid the need to perform memory pinning for each incoming message. However, the MVAPICH performance measured without cache effects shows severe problems between 1500 Bytes and 16 kB that will need to be addressed.

5 Memory Copy Rates

NetPIPE can also be used to probe the internal performance of a node. The memcpy module simply copies data between two memory locations within the same process rather than transferring data between 2 processes or 2 nodes. Cache effects obviously play a large role in these evaluations, as does the choice of a compiler.

The thin lines in fig. 4 show the performance of the GNU memcpy function from the 686 version of glibc using cache effects. The top of the spikes represents the good performance for transfers of data where the size is divisible by 4 Bytes. Memory transfers for sizes not divisible by 4 Bytes are handled with a byte-by-byte transfer that reduces the performance by as much as an order of magnitude. The Intel 7.1 compiler achieves better performance by simply transferring the body of data 4 bytes at a time, and handling any bytes at the end and any preceding bytes due to misalignment separately. The 386 version of glibc also uses this approach, so it is not clear why the 686 version does not.

An optimized memory copy routine is vital in SMP message-passing systems. These same spikes have been observed in performance tests on most MPI implementations. While most messages will be 4-Byte aligned, with sizes divisible by 4 Bytes, it is easy to write an optimized memory copy routine that produces optimal results for even the odd cases. The MP_memcpy curve in fig. 4 also shows that the copy rate from main memory can be improved by up to 50% by using the non-temporal copy techniques available on Pentium 4 chips.

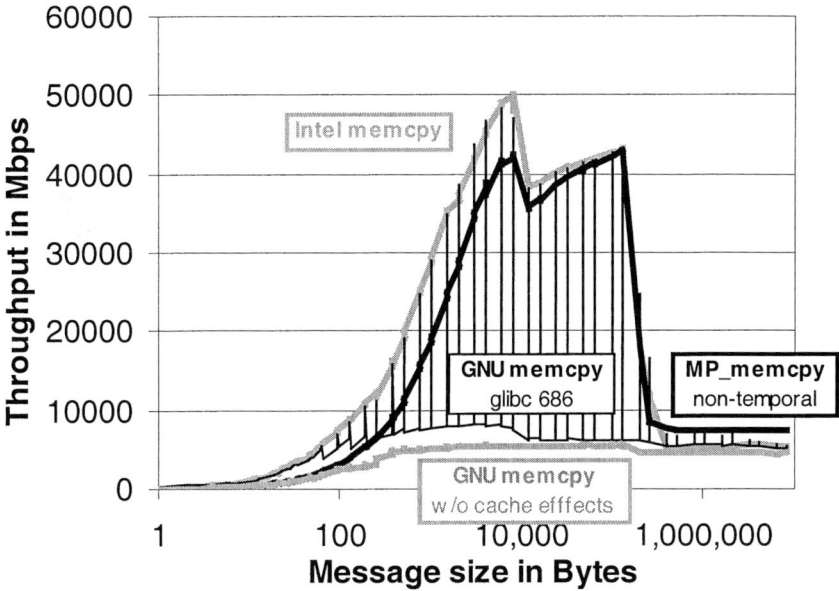

Fig. 4. The memory copy rates of the Intel compiler, the GNU compiler using the 386 and 686 versions of glibc, and an optimized routine using non-temporal memory copies.

6 Conclusions

The goal of the NetPIPE project is to provide a complete and consistent set of analytical tools within the same flexible framework to allow performance evaluations of both the message-passing libraries and the native software layers they run on. New modules have been developed to test 1-sided *get* and *put* operations of the MPI-2 and SHMEM interfaces, as well as native software layers such as GM, the Mellanox VAPI, ARMCI, and LAPI.

New capabilities have been built into the NetPIPE framework. Cache effects can now be fully investigated, and have been shown to play an important role in understanding InfiniBand and SMP message-passing performance. The streaming mode can now accurately handle the faster rates of cutting edge network hardware. Integrity tests can be used to determine if messages are being corrupted at some level in the communication system. A bi-directional mode allows testing of communications going in both directions at the same time, which more closely matches the message traffic in many applications. Adding the ability to do multiple pair-wise tests synchronized within NetPIPE will allow for a more global analysis of the capabilities of networks.

Acknowledgements

This project is funded by the DOE MICS department through the Applied Mathematical Sciences Program at Ames Laboratory. Ames Laboratory is operated for the U.S. Department of Energy by Iowa State University under Contract No. W-7405-Eng-82.

References

1. Netperf webpage: http://www.netperf.org/
2. Iperf webpage: http://dast.nlanr.net/Projects/Iperf/
3. NetPIPE webpage: http://www.scl.ameslab.gov/Projects/NetPIPE/
4. Snell, Q., Mikler, A., and Gustafson, J.: NetPIPE: A Network Protocol Independent Performance Evaluator. IASTED International Conference on Intelligent Management and Systems. (June 1996)
5. Turner, D., and Chen, X.: Protocol-Dependent Message-Passing Performance on Linux Clusters. Proceedings of the IEEE International Conference on Cluster Computing. (September 2002) 187-194
6. The MPI Standard: http://www.mcs.anl.gov/mpi/
7. MPI Forum. MPI: A Message-Passing Interface Standard. International Journal of Supercomputer Applications 8 (3/4). (1994) 165-416
8. PVM webpage: http://www.epm.ornl.gov/pvm/
9. Geist, A., Beguelin, A., Dongarra, J., Jiang, W., Manchek, R., and Sunderam, V.: PVM: Parallel Virtual Machine. The MIT Press (1994)
10. TCGMSG webpage: http://www.emsl.pnl.gov:2080/docs/parasoft/tcgmsg/tcgmsg.html
11. ARMCI webpage: http://www.emsl.pnl.gov:2080/docs/parasoft/armci/
12. MPICH webpage: http://www.mcs.anl.gov/mpi/mpich/
13. Gropp, W., Lusk, E., Doss, N., and Skjellum, A.: High-Performance, Portable Implementation of the MPI Message Passing Interface Standard. Parallel Computing 22(6). (September 1996) 789-828
14. MP_Lite webpage: http://www.scl.ameslab.gov/Projects/MP_Lite/
15. Turner, D., Chen, W., and Kendall, R.: Performance of the MP_Lite Message-Passing Library on Linux Clusters. Linux Clusters: The HPC Revolution. University of Illinois, Urbana-Champaign. (June 25-27, 2001)
16. Turner, D., Selvarajan, S., Chen, X., and Chen, W.: The MP_Lite Message-Passing Library. Fourteenth IASTED International Conference on Parallel and Distributed Computing and Systems. Cambridge Massachusetts. (November 4-6, 2002) 434-439
17. InfiniBand webpage: http://www.infinibandta.org/
18. MVAPICH webpage: http://nowlab.cis.ohio-state.edu/projects/mpi-iba/

Off-Line Performance Prediction of Message-Passing Applications on Cluster Systems[*]

E. Mancini[1], M. Rak[2], R. Torella[2], and U. Villano[3]

[1] RCOST, Università del Sannio, Via Traiano, 82100 Benevento, Italy
epmancini@unisannio.it
[2] DII, Seconda Università di Napoli, via Roma 29, 81031 Aversa (CE), Italy
massimiliano.rak@unina2.it, ganglio@kaiba.cc
[3] Dip. di Ingegneria, Università del Sannio, C.so Garibaldi 107, 82100 Benevento, Italy
villano@unisannio.it

Abstract. This paper describes a simulation-based technique for the performance prediction of message-passing applications on cluster systems. Given data measuring the performance of a target cluster in the form of standard benchmark results, along with the details of the chosen computing configuration (e.g., the number of nodes), it is possible to build and to validate automatically a detailed simulation model. This makes it possible to predict the performance of fully-developed or skeletal code off-line, i.e., without resorting to the real hardware. The reasonable accuracy obtained makes this approach particularly useful for preliminary performance testing of parallel code on non-available hardware. After a description of the approach and of the construction and validation of the simulation model, the paper presents a case study.

1 Introduction

The use of cluster architectures for solving computing-intensive problems is currently customary both in the industrial research and academic communities. The impressive computing power of even small-sized and self-made clusters has changed the way most people regards these architectures. As a matter of fact, clusters are no longer considered as the poor man's supercomputer, and currently more than 90 clusters are present in the list of the top 500 supercomputer sites [1].

The awareness of the high computing power and of the wide range of application software available for such systems has made the use of cluster architectures attractive, widening the number of possible users. The result is that now clusters are precious (and expensive) resources, potentially useful for a very high number of users. On the bad side, the often-conflicting computing needs of these users have to be suitably managed, thus calling for the adoption of effective job management systems. State-of-the-art job management systems (e.g., the Portable Batch System [2]) make it possible to enforce site-specific scheduling policies for running user jobs in both time-shared and space-shared modes. Many sites, besides a batching system, also

---

[*] This work was partially supported by Regione Campania, project l. 41/2000 "Utilizzo di predizioni del comportamento di sistemi distribuiti per migliorare le prestazioni di applicazioni client/server basate su web".

adopt an advanced scheduler (e.g., Maui [3]) providing mechanisms to optimize the use of computing resources, to monitor system performance, and, more generally, to manage effectively the system.

As a matter of fact, current cluster job management systems are not able to satisfy completely cluster user management needs, and the development of advanced schedulers and batching system will be a strategic research field in the near future. However, it is clear that a more efficient use of existing systems could be attained if:

- as many users as possible are diverted from the main system, encouraging them to use off-line facilities for software development and performance testing;
- for each submitted job, reasonable predictions of its impact on system workload (number of computing nodes used, running time, use of system resources, ...) are available. This would allow more effective scheduling decisions to be made.

In light of all the above, the adoption of simulation-based performance prediction techniques appears a particularly promising approach. A most obvious objective is to obtain off-line (i.e., without accessing the "real" cluster hardware) reasonably accurate predictions of software performance and resource usage to be used to guide scheduling choices. Less obvious, but probably of much greater importance, is the possibility to compare several different hardware configurations, in order to find one compatible with the expected performance. For example, preliminary simulation-based performance analysis could suggest the use of larger or of a differently configured system [4]. But the use of simulation-based performance analysis environments has also great potential for performance-driven parallel software development. This process uses quantitative methods to identify among the possible development choices the designs that are more likely to be satisfactory in terms of performance [5]. The final result is not only a reduction of the time and effort invested in design (and coding), but also less cluster workload, due to reduced testing and benchmarking times.

This paper proposes a complete development and performance analysis process for the performance prediction of message-passing applications on cluster systems. The method relies on the use of an existing and fairly mature simulation environment (HeSSE, [6,7,8]). Given data measuring the performance of a target cluster in the form of standard benchmark results, along with trivial details of the chosen computing configuration (e.g., the number of nodes), it is possible to build a detailed simulation model by means of a user-friendly graphical interface. A recently-developed software makes then possible to tune and to validate automatically the model. After that, the user can predict the performance of fully-developed or even skeletal code and to obtain information on program behavior (performance summaries, animations, activity traces,...) in a simulated environment, without resorting to the real hardware.

The reasonable accuracy obtained (errors are typically below 10%) makes this *off-line* approach particularly useful for preliminary performance testing of parallel code, during software development steps, or simply when access to the real cluster hardware is not possible or is uneconomical. A most important point to be stressed here is that the cluster performance is measured simply by running a customary benchmark suite. In other words, the benchmark outputs are not used to get qualitative information on cluster performance (as is done customarily), but to build a simulation model that can produce quantitative information on the hardware/software behavior. This approach has never been followed in our previous work, and, to the best of our knowledge, is not even present in the literature.

This paper is structured as follows. The next section will introduce the HeSSE simulation environment and its modeling methodology. Section 3 describes the proposed modeling process, describing the automatic validation system. Section 4 shows a case study, where the proposed process is applied to the modeling of a simple application on two different cluster systems. After an examination of related work, the paper closes with our conclusions and the directions of future research.

2 HeSSE (Heterogeneous System Simulation Environment)

HeSSE (*He*terogeneous *S*ystem *S*imulation *E*nvironment) is a simulation tool that can reproduce or predict the performance behavior of a (possibly heterogeneous) distributed system for a given application, under different computing and network load conditions [6-10]. The distinctive feature of HeSSE is the adoption of a compositional modeling approach. Distributed heterogeneous systems (DHS) are modeled as a set of interconnected components; each simulation component reproduces the performance behavior of a section of the complete system at a given level of detail. Support components are also provided, to manage simulation-support features such as statistical validation and simulation restart. System modeling is thus performed primarily at the logical architecture level.

HeSSE is capable of obtaining simulation models for DHS systems that can be even very complex, thanks to the use of component composition. A HeSSE simulation component is basically a hard-coded object that reproduces the performance behavior of a specific section of a real system. More detailed, each component has to reproduce both the *functional* and the *temporal behavior* of the subsystem it represents. In HeSSE, the functional behavior of a component is the collection of the services that it exports to other components. In fact, components can be connected, in such a way that they can ask other components for services. On the other hand, the temporal behavior of a component describes the time spent servicing.

Applications are described in HeSSE through traces. A trace is a file that records all the relevant actions of the program. For example, a typical HeSSE trace file for parallel PVM applications is a timed sequence of CPU bursts and of requests to the run-time environment. Each trace represents a single execution of a parallel program. Traces can be obtained by application instrumentation and execution on a host system [9,10], or through prototype-oriented software description languages [6,11,12].

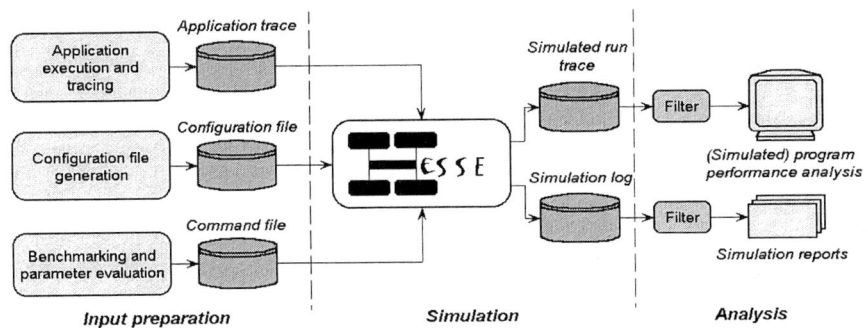

Fig. 1. HeSSE Performance Analysis Process

Parallel application behavioral analysis takes place as shown in Figure 1. The issue is further described in companion papers [4,6-12]. Previously published results show that the simulation environment is simple and effective to analyze real-world scientific applications with reasonable accuracy [4].

The stress in all the above-mentioned papers on the HeSSE simulation environment is on behavioral modeling of applications; the system modeling process is simply left to the performance analyzer expertise. In practice, a skilled analyzer can model system and application altogether, with relatively modest effort, and validate them as a whole. The procedure canonically followed requires getting the hardware parameters needed by the simulation environment through tests on the real system. These make it possible to reproduce correctly the application execution behavior. Successively, the tentative model is validated, by comparing its results with those obtained on the real system. It can be easily recognized that this simple approach fails whenever the target system is not readily available, thus precluding both the measurement of system parameters, needed for model construction, and its final validation. Off-line model construction and performance prediction is a challenging problem, and requires the use of new approaches.

The observation at the basis of the work described in this paper is that, even if the system is not available, it is almost always possible to obtain from cluster administrators the results of standard benchmarks, customarily used to evaluate the performance of their hardware. Benchmarks are commonly used to compare parallel and distributed systems, and they can be often considered as representative of the system "standard" use. As far as performance prediction and analysis is concerned, an obvious issue is to ascertain whether benchmarks can be used to tune and to validate a cluster simulation environment, or not. This is the problem tackled in the following section, where a modeling process based on benchmark results is proposed. The validity of the approach is considered in Section 4, which shows the accuracy results obtained for a simple problem on two different clusters.

3 The Proposed Modeling Process

Given a cluster system, the modeling and analysis process can be carried out in the HeSSE simulation environment in three macro steps ("macro" steps, since each step includes many different operations), which are briefly outlined in the following.

3.1 System High-Level Description

A very simple model of the system is obtained using natural language descriptions. This "base" model includes just information on the number of the computing nodes, the middleware adopted, and the network architecture.

High-level models can be built through the simple graphical interface provided by *HeSSEgraphs*. This is a visual tool that makes it possible to create interactively a visual model of a given DHS system. The HeSSEgraphs tool makes it also possible to obtain from the graphical description of the system the command and configuration files needed to simulate the system in the HeSSE environment. In HeSSEgraphs, a system is modeled as a plain graph, using predefined components collected in libraries. HeSSEgraphs shows all these components, grouped by library, in a left frame. The user can choose a component, and place it in a working drawing area by a drag-and-drop operation. The first step is the creation of nodes. Then he/she can add connections between them, and edit the properties of each node or connection using the mouse.

Figure 2 shows a screenshot of the visual tool HeSSEgraphs. The graph in the Figure is representative of a 4-node SMP system with Ethernet connectivity running a PVM application. Specialized off-the-shelf nodes model the computing node, the PVM daemons, every instance of the application, the NICs and a connecting Ethernet switch. It is of paramount importance to point out that the information managed at this level of abstraction can be easily retrieved from simple textual and rather informal descriptions of the cluster hardware. In practice, it is sufficient to know the number of nodes and their type (mono or multi-processor), and the network technology adopted to build the DHS graph using the nodes in the predefined libraries.

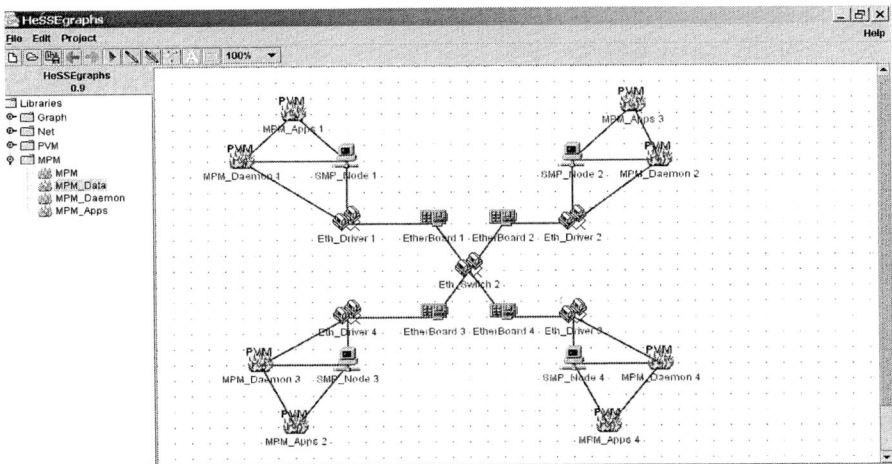

Fig. 2. HeSSEgraphs screenshot

3.2 Model Tuning and Benchmark Simulation

High-level descriptions can be built easily, thanks to the use of predefined components, but they cannot capture the behavior of real system, since they do not contain any type of temporal information. In fact, a high-level model does not describe a given cluster, but only a cluster class, to which the given target system belongs. The objective of the next modeling step, *Model Tuning*, is to define all the parameters that specialize the cluster class and allow to obtain a close description of the given computer system.

While high-level description was built by means of simple components, which can be gathered from a natural language description, parameters needed in the model tuning are not equally simple to be defined and understood. Furthermore, they should be gathered from the target cluster through dedicated experiments. As mentioned in the previous section, the canonical way to carry out this procedure is to rely on the analyzer experience and to perform intensive testing on the real hardware. The procedure followed here is based instead on the use of new HeSSE components that make it possible to perform the tuning in an automated way. The procedure is based on the use of previously collected cluster performance parameters. Instead of dedicated and proprietary tests, our choice was to adopt standard benchmarks for both parameters evaluation and simulation model validation.

The process takes place in the following steps:
- standard benchmark results are collected on the target system;
- a special HeSSE configuration file is built, adding tuning components to the high-level model previously defined;
- an automated learning process takes place;
- the simulation error is evaluated, validating the model.

3.2.1 Cluster Benchmarking

The Benchmark suite adopted for all the experiments described below is the Parkbench suite [13]. This is a well-known set of benchmark tests, freely available and largely used in the parallel computing community. With all the caveats linked to the use of standard benchmarks for cluster performance evaluation, the proposed tests are commonly considered very expressive of the overall system performance. In our experiments, we did not actually run the whole suite of benchmarks but only the MPBench group, aiming to tune the cluster configuration for MPI applications.

3.2.2 Tuner Configuration and Learning Process

The automation of the parameter fitting process relies on dedicated HeSSE components, able to manage a learning algorithm and benchmark reproduction. Usually benchmark programs contain loops whose body includes the tested operation sequence (along with timestamping instructions). A *Benchmark* component is able to reproduce the majority of available benchmarks, reading a benchmark description from a simple configuration file. A simple language was developed to describe this kind of benchmark tests, i.e., to provide information such as type and number of primitives to be tested (e.g. MPISend, MPIBroadcast, ...), and the number of test runs.

A *Trainer* component, instead, starts the simulation, asks the benchmark component to perform all the available tests, checks the time, compares the results with the reference ones (i.e., with the results of actual benchmark execution) and restarts the simulation with new parameters. The learning process stops when the accuracy is over a desired threshold. The learning procedure currently is based on simulated annealing fitting. The description of the learning algorithm details (e.g., convergence properties and execution time) can be found in [6].

3.2.3 Accuracy Evaluation and Model Validation

The trainer component reproduces only one half of the benchmark results available. For example, if the benchmarks are parameterized on message packet dimension, e.g. from 16 bytes to 1 MB in steps of 16 bytes, the simulation model reproduces the same tests in steps of 32 bytes. The remainder of the values (i.e., the other half of the benchmark results) is used to evaluate the model accuracy. This makes it possible to avoid obtaining a model that fits well the supplied benchmark values, but does not capture the overall performance behavior.

3.2.4 Application Analysis

Following up the evaluation of the model accuracy, the application performance analysis takes place, following the typical HeSSE steps: application tracing on a host system, simulation execution, and analysis of the performance results. The reader is referred to previous papers for details [4,6-12].

4 An Example: Cygnus and Cossyra Case Studies

The proposed approach was applied on two cluster systems of the PARSEC laboratory at the 2nd University of Naples, Cygnus and Cossyra. Though these systems are different as far as processors and node hardware are concerned, it will be shown that the accuracies obtained for their performance predictions are very similar.

Cygnus is a four SMP-node cluster. Each node is an SMP Compaq ProLiant 330 system, equipped with two Pentium IV, 512MB RAM memory. The network architecture is a Switched Fast Ethernet. The System is managed through Rocks [14], which currently includes Red Hat Linux 7.3 and well known administration tools, like PBS, MAUI and Ganglia. A Pentium III, 256 MB RAM, was adopted as frontend.

Cossyra is a 3 Alpha Workstation cluster. Each node is an AlphaStation 250, with Alpha RISC processor, 233 Mhz, 64MB RAM memory. Network is a standard 10 Mbs Ethernet. The operating system is Alpha Red Hat Linux 7.1.

4.1 Benchmark Results and Model Tuning

The benchmark-based model tuning was started by executing MPbench on both clusters. Then the automated tuning system was fed with the description of the benchmark set adopted and the benchmark results, thus starting the training phase. At the end of the learning step, all the simulation parameters found are collected in a report file. The resulting parameter values typically are a good fit to the training (benchmark) results. An example of the errors between the actual benchmark results and the tuned simulation model is proposed in Fig. 3. In this figure, the completion times of a simple *Roundtrip* benchmark are illustrated, as measured on the real cluster and obtained by simulation on the automatically-tuned system. Relative errors between measured data and simulation results, along with completion times, are reported in the same diagram in logarithmic scale and are always under 10%.

4.2 Target Application Performance Prediction

The application chosen to show the validity of the approach is a simple row-column square matrix multiplication. The algorithm adopted for parallel decomposition of the multiplication $C = A \times B$ works as follows: the master process splits the matrix A by rows in *numtask*-1 slices and sends one of them to each slave process. Then sends the matrix B to each slave. Slaves compute the row-column product between the slice of A and B, thus obtaining a slice of C that is sent back to the master. This simple algorithm [15] was chosen as a simple case study as the focus here is on the prediction methodology, rather than on parallel program development.

The application was instrumented and executed on a host system (the cluster frontend). The model was fed with the trace files thus obtained, and the application execution time was predicted for matrix sizes going from 10×10 to 500×500 in steps of 10. For each size, the tests on the real clusters were executed ten times. Each test, even for the largest matrices, required a few seconds of simulation. The actual and predicted performance results are shown in Figure 4. The proposed diagram shows (in logarithmic scale) both the real measurements on the cluster system and the simulation results, along with the resulting relative error. The target application simulation error has the same behavior shown in the benchmark execution. For both architectures, the resulting error is typically about 5%, and in any case under 10%. It is important to point out that the simulation results were obtained completely off-line, i.e., without resorting to the application execution on the clusters.

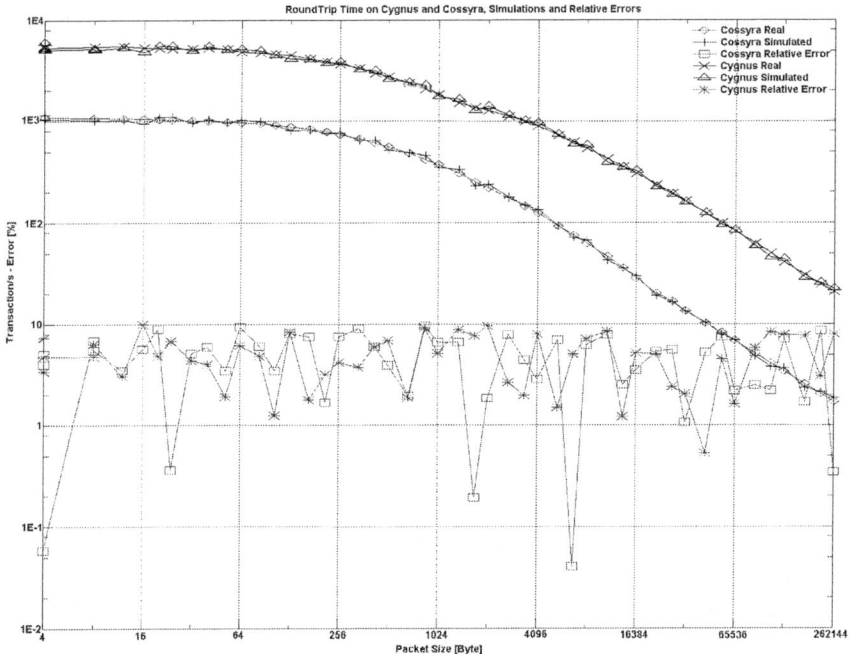

Fig. 3. Benchmark and simulation results after the learning phase, relative errors

5 Related Work

The problem of off-line cluster prediction has never been explicitly treated in existing literature. However, a wide number of papers deals with parallel and distributed system modeling and performance analysis [17-18], and it is likely that many existing simulation environments and tools could be applied to carry out performance analyses similar to those that are the object of this paper. Other authors focus their interest in tools for performance-driven software development, mainly in the context of Performance Engineering (see per example [19-20]).

Similarly, a wide body of literature deals with benchmarking and performance evaluation [21]. But benchmarking has never been used to characterize a system for performance simulation and to predict off-line the behavior of parallel applications.

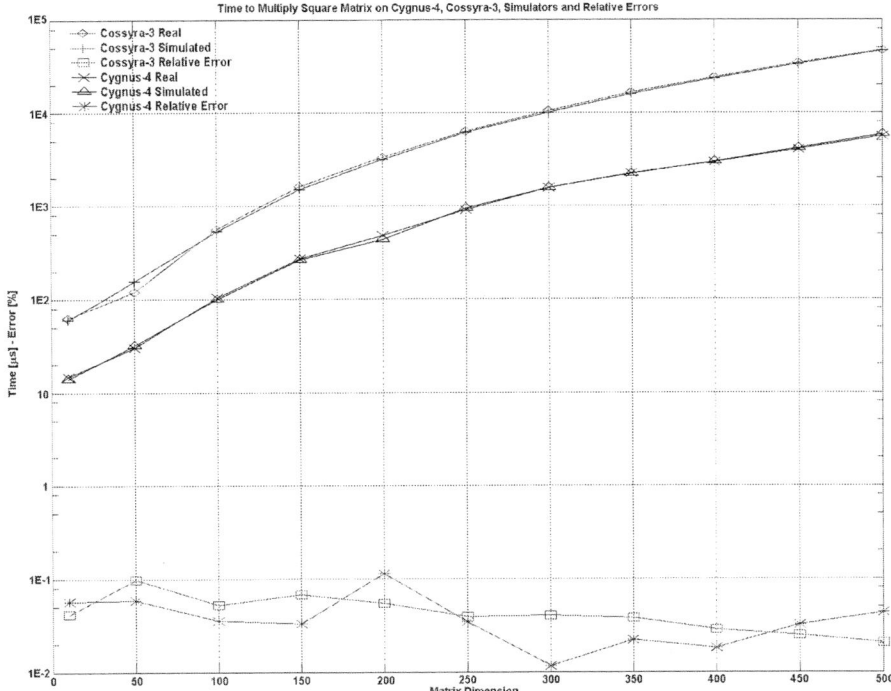

Fig. 4. Matrix multiplication actual and predicted performance results, relative errors

6 Conclusions and Future Work

This paper describes a modeling and performance prediction process that can be adopted even when the target system is not available. Standard benchmarks are used to tune and to validate the system simulation models, whose definition stems from simple natural language descriptions, and are obtained through a graphical interface. The accuracy results obtained (relative errors under 10%) make this approach attractive for off-line software development and analysis.

One of the main results of the work described here is the use of common benchmarks for tuning and validating the simulation models. The results obtained in our tests, some of which have been reported here, show that the execution of a benchmark is sufficient to fully characterize the target system for simulation.

A research field to be explored in the future is the possibility to compare the performance of proprietary applications on possibly unavailable target systems, using information gathered running standard benchmarks. This comparison can also be very useful when the clusters are components of large GRID systems. In this case, the objective can be to enable the user to choose the best system for his/her application execution, without expensive (in time and cost) test executions on the real hardware. A further evolution of the work documented in this paper is the prediction of benchmark results for non-existing clusters. We intend to study the possibility to predict the performance of applications by means only of artificial benchmark results.

References

1. TOP500 Supercomputer Sites, http://www.top500.org/
2. Portable Batch System, http://www.openpbs.org/main.html
3. Maui Scheduler, http://supercluster.org/maui/
4. Fahringer, T., Mazzocca, N., Rak, M., Villano, U., Pllana S., Madsen G.: Performance Modeling of Scientific Applications: Scalability Analysis of LAPW0. In Proc. PDP03 Conference, 3-7 February 2003, IEEE Press, Genova, Italy
5. Smith, C. U., Williams, L. G.: Performance Engineering Models of CORBA based Distributed-Object Systems. In: Computer Measurement Group Conf. Proceedings (1998)
6. Rak, M.: "A Performance Evaluation Environment for Distributed Heterogeneous Computer Systems Based on a Simulation Approach", Ph.D. Thesis, Facoltà di Ingegneria, Seconda Università di Napoli, Italy, 2002.
7. Mazzocca, N., Rak, M., Villano, U.: The Transition from a PVM Program Simulator to a Heterogeneous System Simulator: The HeSSE Project. In: Dongarra, J. et al. (eds.): Recent Advances in Parallel Virtual Machine and Message Passing Interface. LNCS, Vol. 1908. Springer-Verlag, Berlin (2000) 266-273
8. Mazzocca, N., Rak, M., Villano, U.: Predictive Performance Analysis of Distributed Heterogeneous Systems with HeSSE. In Proc. 2001 Conference Italian Society for Computer Simulation (ISCSI01), CUEN, Naples, Italy (2002) 55-60
9. Aversa, R., Mazzeo, A., Mazzocca, N., Villano, U.: Heterogeneous System Performance Prediction and Analysis using PS. IEEE Concurrency, Vol. 6 (1998) 20-29
10. Aversa, R., Mazzeo, A., Mazzocca, N., Villano, U.: Developing Applications for Heterogeneous Computing Environments using Simulation: a Case Study. Parallel Computing, Vol. 24 (1998) 741-761
11. Mazzocca, N., Rak, M., Villano, U.: MetaPL: a Notation System for Parallel Program Description and Performance Analysis. In: Malyshkin, V. (ed.): Parallel Computing Technologies. LNCS, Vol. 2127. Springer-Verlag, Berlin (2001) 80-93
12. Mazzocca, N., Rak, M., Villano, U.: The MetaPL approach to the performance analysis of distributed software systems. In: Proc. 3rd International Workshop on Software and Performance (WOSP02), IEEE Press (2002) 142-149
13. PARKBENCH Report: Public International Benchmarks for Parallel Computers. Scientific Programming, Vol. 3 (1994) 101-146 (http://www.netlib.org/parkbench/)
14. Papadopoulos, P. M., Katz, M. J., Bruno, G.: NPACI Rocks: Tools and Techniques for Easily Deploying Manageable Linux Clusters, In: Proc. IEEE Cluster 2001 (2001)
15. Center for Parallel Computer Training Courses, Matrix Multiplication Example http://www.pdc.kth.se/training/Tutor/MPI/Templates/mm/
16. Kerbyson, D. J., Papaefstatuiou, E., Harper, J. S., Perry, S. C., Nudd, G. R.: Is Predictive Tracing too late for HPC Users? In: Allan, M. F. Guest, D. S. Henty, D. Nicole and A. D. Simpson (eds.): Proc. HPCI'98 Conference: High Performance Computing. Plenum/Kluwer Publishing (1999) 57-67
17. Labarta, J., Girona, S., Pillet, V., Cortes T., Gregoris, L.: DiP: a Parallel Program Development Environment. Proc. Euro-Par '96, Lyon, France (Aug. 1996) Vol. II 665-674
18. Buck, J. T., et al.: A Framework for Simulating and Prototyping Heterogeneous Systems. Int. Journal of Comp. Simulation 4 (1994) 155-182
19. Smith C.U., Williams L.G.: Performance Engineering Evaluation of Object-Oriented Systems with SPEED. In: Marie, R. et. al. (eds.): Computer Perfomance Evaluation Modeling Techniques and Tools. LNCS, Vol. 1245, Springer-Verlag, Berlin (1997)
20. Menascé, D. A., Gomaa, H.: A Method for Design and Performance Modeling of Client/Server Systems. IEEE Trans. on Softw. Eng., Vol. 26 (2000) 1066-1085
21. Messina, P. et al.: Benchmarking advanced architecture computers, Concurrency: Practice and Experience, Vol. 2 (1990) 195-255

Complexity Driven Performance Analysis

L. García, J.A. González, J.C. González, C. León, C. Rodríguez, and G. Rodríguez

Dpto. Estadística, I.O. y Computación,
Universidad de La Laguna,
La Laguna, 38271, Spain
casiano@ull.es
http://nereida.deioc.ull.es/~call/

Abstract. This work presents a new approach to the relation between theoretical complexity and performance analysis of MPI programs. The performance analysis is driven by the information produced during the complexity analysis stage and supported at the top level by a complexity analysis oriented language and at the bottom level by a special purpose statistical package.

1 Introduction

Researchers have successfully developed simple analytical models like BSP [1], LogP [2] or the Collective Model [3] to obtain qualitative insights and bounds on the scalability of parallel programs as a function of input and system size. In contrast, tools for more detailed analysis performance have been primarily based on measurement and simulation rather than on analytical modeling. This paper introduces a general framework where different performance models can be instantiated, develops an approach that combines analytical modeling with measurement and simulation techniques and discuss a set of software tools giving support to the methodology.

The next section presents the idea of complexity-analysis driven measurement, establishes definitions and concepts and introduces a classification of the performance models according to the nature of the function that links the machine description with the algorithm description. Section 3 illustrates the concepts proving that the BSP and Collective Models belong to the class of linear models. In section 4 we propose a prediction method that can be used with any arbitrary linear model. Section 5 deals with non linear models. A general strategy to extend any linear model to a non-linear model is sketched. This way the model reflects the characteristics of the memory hierarchy. Finally, section 6 extends complexity-analysis driven measurement to the observation of alternative software performance indicators.

2 The Meta-model

Assuming that a processor has an instruction set $\{I_1, \ldots, I_t\}$ of size t, where the i-th instruction I_i takes time p_i, an approximation to the execution time $T^{\mathcal{P}}(\Psi)$ of an algorithm $\mathcal{P}$ with sizes of the input data $\Psi = (\Psi_1 \ldots \Psi_d) \in \Omega \subset \mathbb{N}^d$ is given by the formula:

$$T^{\mathcal{P}}(\Psi) \simeq \sum_{i=1}^{t} w_i(\Psi) \times p_i \tag{1}$$

where $w_i(\Psi)$ is the number of instructions of type I_i executed by the algorithm $\mathcal{P}$ with input data of size Ψ. On the other side, the "algorithm designer" counts the high level operations in $\mathcal{P}$ and provides a complexity formula

$$f^{\mathcal{P}}(\Psi) = \sum_{i=0}^{n} A_i \times f_i(\Psi) \tag{2}$$

that is an approximation to the execution time of the program expressed in terms of the input data. The f_i function depends only on the input Ψ and summarizes the repetitions of the different segments of code, while the constants A_i stand for the distribution of machine instructions corresponding to the "component" function f_i.

Our idea is that the C source code implementing the algorithm is annotated with the complexity Eq. (2). For example, for the classical matrix product algorithm it would be something like:

```
1  #pragma cll M M[0]+M[1]*N+M[2]*N*N+M[3]*N*N*N
2     for(i = 0; i < N; i++) {
3        for(j = 0; j < N; j++) {
4           sum = 0;
5           for(k = 0; k < N; k++)
6              sum += A(i, k) * B(k, j);
7           C(i,j) = sum;
8        }
9     }
10 #pragma cll end M
```

In this case, we have $n = 3$, $\Psi = N$, $f_0(N) = 1$, $f_1(N) = N$, $f_2(N) = N^2$ and $f_3(N) = N^3$, A_i=M[i] and $\mathcal{P}$ = code in lines 2...9. Using the information provided by the algorithm designer in line 1, a software system like the one presented here (named *CALL*), can provide the value of the algorithmic constants A_i.

The constant coefficients A_i introduced in Eq. (2) for an analytical model, are platform dependent and can be computed through multidimensional regression analysis on the gathered execution times.

The complexity analysis can be considered as the task of classifying the sequence of instructions executed by the algorithm in sets, so that all the elements in a set are executed approximately the same number of times. That number is given by the associated component function $f_i(\Psi)$. Thus, the complexity formula of the matrix product $A_0 + A_1 N + A_2 N^2 + A_3 N^3$ divides the instructions executed in four sets: those that were executed a constant number of times, those that were executed N times, and so on. Denoting by ξ_i the proportion of instructions I_i that were executed in the matrix product most inner loop (lines 5 and 6), we have:

$$\sum_{i=1}^{t} \xi_i \times p_i \simeq N^3 \times A_3 \qquad (3)$$

An therefore $A_3 \simeq \frac{\sum_{i=1}^{t} \xi_i \times p_i}{N^3}$. In general, the coefficient A_i represents the average time spent by the machine instructions that were executed approximately $f_i(\Psi)$ times.

Unfortunately, is not uncommon to observe a variation of the values A_i with the input size, that is, the A_i are not actually real fixed numbers but functions

$$A_i : \Omega \subset \mathbb{N}^d \to \mathbb{R}$$

Usually the assumption is that A_i a step-wise function of the input size $\Psi \in \Omega$.

The use of regression allow us to deduce the values of the coefficients A_i when we have access to the platform. When the platform is not available, we can use a "machine data base" that for each platform $\mathcal{M}$ contains the numeric vector $(\gamma_i^{\mathcal{M}})$ describing the machine. This data base is generated by an "architecture analyzer" program (these sort of programs are collectively named `probes`). The `bsp_probe` program included with the BSPlib library [4] is an example.

Let us denote by $\Gamma = \{\gamma_{i=0,m}\}$ the set of parameters which describe an architecture. We call each index or class evaluated by a `probe` program a "Universal Instruction Class" or UIC. The set of UICs constitutes the "machine profile". A particular example of a possible definition of UICs is given by the BSP model: $\Gamma = (s, g, L)$. they correspond to the universal instruction classes "computing", "communication" and "synchronization". The last one also stands for startup latency.

We assume that each coefficient A_i can be expressed as a function of the architecture parameters Γ,

$$A_i = X_i(\gamma_1 \ldots \gamma_m) \qquad i = 0 \ldots n \qquad (4)$$

A computational model determines the definition and construction of the triples (Γ, X, A) i.e. not only defines the nature of the parameters Γ and application coefficients A but the set of procedures to determine them and the methodology to build the functions X_i that permit to characterize the performance of a given algorithm.

Though the *convolution* functions X_i are not always linear, in not few cases they can be approached by a linear function. Some models assume such a linear behavior. Eq. (4) then becomes:

$$A_i = \sum_{j=0}^{m} x_{i,j} \times \gamma_j \qquad i = 0 \ldots n \qquad (5)$$

where $x_{i,j}$ denotes the contribution of the j-th UIC class to the i-th "component" function f_i.

Computational models can be classified as *linear* models, when they follow Eq. (5) and they assume the A_i to be constants in the whole range of the input size Ω. Otherwise we will call them non-linear (i.e. they provide a non linear function X_i or they assume a functional nature of the coefficients.

3 Examples of Linear Models

3.1 BSP

According to the former classification, BSP is a linear model. Let us illustrate this fact using a significant example: the Parallel Sorting by Regular Sampling (PSRS) algorithm proposed by Li et al. [5]. This is a synchronous algorithm that matches BSP style, even when using a library that is not oriented to that model. The algorithm uses a wide variety of MPI collective functions. As is usual in BSP, s is normalized (i.e. $s = 1$ and g and L are expressed in terms of s units) and the number of processors p is considered constant (i.e. a change in the number of processors implies a change of Γ: In fact the values of $g = g_P$ and $L = L_P$ depend on p). The BSP complexity of PSRS to sort an array of size n is given by a linear function of $\Gamma = (s, g, L)$. For this case the components of Eq. (2) are $\Psi = n$, $f_0(n) = n\log(n)$, $f_1(n) = n$ and $f_2(n) = 1$.

Theorem 1. *The coefficients (A_i) of the BSP complexity formula of any BSP algorithm are a linear function of (s, g, L).*

Proof. It derives from the model definition. Assume (s, g, L) are expressed in seconds. The three parameters only appear as factors in the complexity formula associated with each superstep:

$$s \times W_i(\Psi) + g \times h_i(\Psi) + L \qquad (6)$$

Where W_i denotes the computation time, h_i is the superstep h-relation and L is the synchronization time. The total complexity is the sum of the costs of the $N(\Psi)$ supersteps:

$$s \times \sum_{i=1}^{N(\Psi)} W_i(\Psi) + g \times \sum_{i=1}^{N(\Psi)} h_i(\Psi) + N(\Psi) \times L \qquad (7)$$

that is linear in s, g and L. Notice however that the dependence on the number of processors is non linear.

3.2 The Collective Model

Another example of linear model is the Collective Model introduced in [3]. That model is an adaptation of BSP to the analysis of MPI programs. The main difference with BSP is that it uses different bandwidths g_C and latencies L_C per collective operation C, where C belongs to the set of collective operations $MPI = \{MPI\_Scatter \ldots\}$ of the message passing library. Therefore, the different MPI functions define different UICs. The PSRS equation for such model is similar to the BSP complexity formula only that it involves a larger number of terms. Figure 1 illustrates some *CALL* pragmas annotating the code. Line 1 announces that is an MPI program: *CALL* will collect the measures in the different processors, synchronize them, etc. As a consequence of the declaration at line 3 all the Collective MPI operations will be measured and the times compared with the values predicted by the Collective model. Though in this case we know the complexity formula, line 5 is there to show that you can introduce partial knowledge: we declare that the time depends on the `size` of the vector but that we don't know the complexity formula. Using an evolutive algorithm that analyses the trace files *LLAC* will propose an analytical global formula.

```
1  #pragma cll parallel MPI
2  ....
3  #pragma cll model Collective
4  ....
5  #pragma cll sync sort sort[0]*unknown(size)
6    psrs(vector, size);
7  #pragma cll end sort
```

Fig. 1. Parallel Sort by Regular Sampling annotated with *CALL* pragmas

4 A Universal Prediction Method for Linear Models

Eq. (5) establishes a relationship where the response, output or dependent variables are the algorithmic constants A_i, the predictor or explanatory variables are the UIC classes γ_j and the unknown parameters are $x_{i,j}$. We can essay to use regression techniques to obtain $x_{i,j}$. We run the program for a sample of available platforms $(\Psi^r)_{r=0...q}$ and measure the running times $(T^\mathcal{P}(\Psi^r))_{r=0...q}$. We also run the probe program q times under the same conditions, obtaining different values of the UICs for the platforms we have available. From there, we use linear regression to evaluate $x_{i,j}$. Since the values A_i can be obtained using linear regression and the coefficients γ_j^r are provided by the probe program, we can have the values of $(x_{i,j})$, and therefore, predict the behavior of the algorithm $\mathcal{P}$ on a external (non available) machine $\mathcal{M}$, provided we know its UIC vector γ_i.

Rewriting Eq. (5) for different available platforms and repeating the executions of the probe program a number of times q lead us to the following linear equation system:

$$A_i^r = \sum_{j=0}^{m} x_{i,j} \times \gamma_j^r \qquad i = 0\ldots n \text{ and } r = 0\ldots q \qquad (8)$$

Taking $q = m+1$ we have a linear system with the same number of equations than the number of unknown variables $x_{i,j}$. Observe that, if only one machine under exactly the same performance conditions is used for the experience, then $\gamma_j^r \simeq \gamma_j^s$ for any r and s, and the matrix (γ_j^r) becomes singular.

An alternative path is to measure the amount of use $\gamma_j^\mathcal{P}(\Psi)$ of the UICs γ_j in algorihtm $\mathcal{P}$ for input Ψ. From these values we can derive the coefficients $x_{i,j}$ and consequently, the A_i.

Figure 2 a) presents the actual time (dots) and predicted time (continuous line) for the matrix product code presented in the former section, on a machine different from the ones used to get $(x_{i,j})$. The algorithmic constants for such machine were derived using Eq. (5). The figure on the right presents the same results for one of the machines that took part in solving 8. The accuracy in both cases is excellent. This is partly due to the fact that the target machine was built on the same technology than the polled machines (Intel and Linux). In general, if available, it seems sensible to include in the group of machines to poll any machine you have access whose technology (operating system, compiler, etc.) resembles the targeted platform.

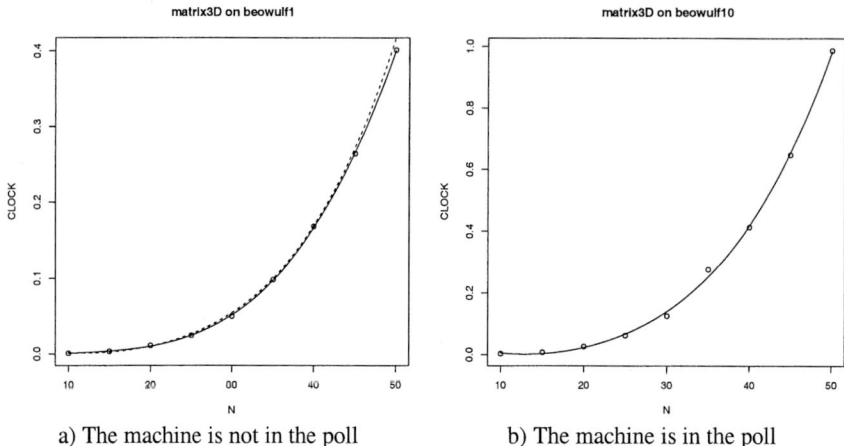

Fig. 2. Portability of the Performance Model

5 Piece-Wise Linear Models

For most scientific codes the main source of nonlinearity of the behavior of $T^\mathcal{P}(\Psi)$ is due to the influence of the memory hierarchy.

Let us assume the designer of the algorithm provide us with a complexity formula $\mathcal{M}^\mathcal{P}(\Psi)$ for the variation of the observable "memory" in the CALL experiment $\mathcal{P}$. Observe that, in general the input size $\Psi \in \mathbb{N}^d$ is a vector. For instance, for the matrix product algorithm, assuming the matrices have different dimensions $N \times R$ and $R \times M$ is $d = 3$, $\Psi = (N, R, M)$ and $\mathcal{M}^\mathcal{P}(N, R, M) = A_0 \times R \times (N + M)$. Let us assume that this function $\mathcal{M}^\mathcal{P}(\Psi)$ is provided, adding a memory clause to the CALL pragma defining the experiment. For the matrix example:

```
#pragma cll M M[0]+M[1]*N+M[2]*N^2+M[3]*N^3 \\
            memory (3*sizeof(double))*(N*N)
    for(i = 0; i < N; i++) {
        ...
    }
#pragma cll end M
```

We define the concept of *"memory interval"* as follows:

$$[a,b] = \{\Psi \in \mathbb{N}^d /\ a \leq \mathcal{M}^\mathcal{P}(\Psi) \leq b\}\ a,b \in \mathbb{N}$$

The general idea of piece-wise linear models is to extend linear models so that they have different "memory access parameters" corresponding to the different bandwidths of the memory hierarchy. The strategy is then to find a partition of the "memory space" of $\mathcal{P}$ in a number of intervals $\{[a_1, a_2), [a_2, a_3) \ldots [a_k, \infty)\}$ such that:

$$A_i(\Psi) = \sum_{s=1}^{k} A_i^s \times \chi_{[a_s, a_{s+1})}(\Psi)$$

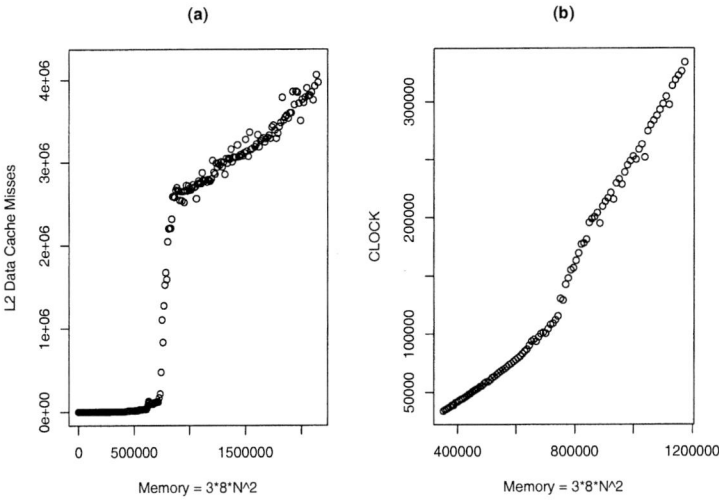

Fig. 3. Matrix Product. L2 = 256K. Finding a_2. a) Data Cache Misses. b) Time

where $\chi_{[a_s, a_{s+1})}$ is the characteristic function of the interval and A_i^s is a measure of the bandwidth ratio for the s-th interval.

To simplify, let us consider the case where we are only interested in two levels ($k = 2$) of the hierarchy: the L2 cache and main memory. Using *CALL* and PAPI we easily determine the values of a_2 in the available platforms. Figure 3 shows the variation of L2 data cache misses and time versus memory for a Intel Xeon CPUs at 1.40GHz with a L2 cache size of 256 KB. The clear change on the left curve is still appreciable as a fast increase in the time curve on the right. The change approximately occurs at $\mathcal{M}(N) = 3 \times sizeof(double) \times N^2 = 735000$, that is at $N = 175$.

The variation $\gamma_j^{\mathcal{P}}(\Psi)$ of a UIC j like, let us say, the number of memory accesses, is governed by the "time" complexity formula 2. Since Ψ is an input parameter and we know the memory use $\mathcal{M}^{\mathcal{P}}(\Psi)$ we can pick for the prediction the value of "memory access time" γ_j that specifically applies for such size.

6 Other Observables

Time is not the only performance observable designers are interested in. Is not rare the case that alternative measures provide useful information about the behaviour of the algorithm. The "performance analysis driven by the complexity" scheme outlined in the first section can be extended to consider these necessities. Figure 4 shows the way the *CALL* compiler facilitates the vigilance of the number of visited nodes (numvis) on a parallel branch and bound (B&B) solving the 0-1 Knapsack Problem. Figure 5 illustrates the predictions for the average and worst cases (left) and the load balance diagram (right). The last shows a strange property of parallel B&B: though the input instances for the 5 cases were the same, the number of visited nodes varies from one execution to the next.

```
1 #pragma cll code double numvis;
2   ...
3 #pragma cll kps kps[0]+kps[1]*numvis posteriori numvis
4   sol = knap(0, M, 0);
5 #pragma cll end kps
```

Fig. 4. B&B main code with *CALL* annotations

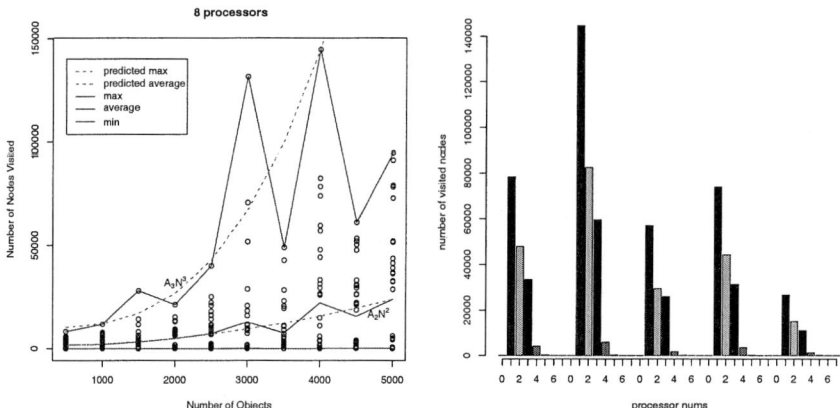

Fig. 5. Variation with the number of objects (left) and per processor (right)

Acknowledgements

Thanks to EPCC, CIEMAT, CEPBA, EC, FEDER, MCyT, TIC2002-04498-C05-05 and TIC2002-04400-C03-03.

References

1. Leslie G. Valiant. A bridging model for parallel computation. *Communications of the ACM*, 33(8):103–111, August 1990.
2. D. Culler, R. Karp, D. Patterson, A. Sahay, K. Schauser, E. Santos, R. Subramonian, and T. von Eicken. LogP: Towards a realistic model of parallel computation. In *4th ACM SIGPLAN Symposium on Principles and Practice of Parallel Programming*, May 1993.
3. J.L. Roda, F. Sande, C. León, J.A. González, and C. Rodríguez. The Collective Computing Model. In *Seventh Euromicro Workshop on Parallel and Distributed Processing*, pages 19–26, Funchal, Portugal, February 1999.
4. M. Goudreau, J. Hill, K. Lang, B. McColl, S. Rao, D. Stephanescu, T. Suel, and T. A. Tsantilas. Proposal for the BSP worldwide standard library. http://www.bsp-worldwide.org-/standard/stand2.htm, 1996.
5. X. Li, P. Lu, J. Schaefer, J. Shillington, P.S. Wong, and H. Shi. On the versatility of parallel sorting by regular sampling. In *Parallel Computing*, volume 19, pages 1079–1103, 1993.

Usefulness and Usage of SKaMPI-Bench

Werner Augustin and Thomas Worsch

Universität Karlsruhe, Karlsruhe, Germany
{augustin,worsch}@ira.uka.de
http://liinwww.ira.uka.de/~{augustin,worsch}/

Abstract. SKaMPI is a benchmark for measuring the performance of MPI implementations. Some examples of surprising behaviour of MPI libraries are presented. These result in certain new requirements for MPI benchmarks and will lead to major extensions in the new SKaMPI-Bench.

1 Introduction

The SKaMPI benchmark [6] already offers a broad spectrum of possibilities for investigating the performance of MPI platforms.

While recent development of SKaMPI focused on the improvement of the precision of the used measurement methods [8] it is time to pay attention to recent observations of unexpected behaviour of MPI implementations. In order to maintain SKaMPI's goal of providing the user with informations necessary to assess the performance of an MPI application and to give valuable hints for possible bottlenecks, extensions of SKaMPI are needed.

The rest of this paper is organised as follows. In Section 2 we demonstrate the necessity of very detailed benchmark data to get a clear picture of the quality of an MPI implementation. In Section 3 we argue that benchmarking an MPI implementation is not enough for this goal. Finally in Section 4 we give an outlook to the new SKaMPI-Bench which will provide the possibility to obtain these detailed informations about MPI implementations.

2 Benchmarking MPI Implementations

The goal of benchmarking MPI implementations is to provide most of the informations necessary to design efficient parallel programs.

This design already requires the consideration of two usually antagonistic properties: maintainability and performance. This situation becomes worse when several platforms are involved. Achievable performance improvements usually are machine specific. We do not think that in general there is something like performance portability; see Subsection 3.2 below for a counter example. Different parallel machines *are* different.

When a program has to run on a reasonably small number of different platforms, one can

- either clutter the code with hardware specific optimisations which are compiled into the program conditionally ("#ifdef deserts"). This makes the code difficult to maintain,
- or choose one implementation for a time critical part and accept a performance loss on some machines.

In both cases detailed data from MPI benchmark runs on the machines either help to find the fastest solutions or allow to assess the penalties for certain design decisions. See [5] for further discussions.

There is a number of pitfalls when benchmarking MPI implementations. Gropp and Lusk [1] give a list of them and describe the approach used by mpptest (part of the MPICH distribution) to avoid them. The results below show that there are even more aspects which require careful investigation.

2.1 Choosing the Right Parameters

It is obvious that the time required by a point-to-point communication operation depends on the message size and that the time required by collective operations in addition depends on the size of the communicator. But all of these functions have more parameters. Do they have an influence on the performance?

As a surprising example let us look at MPI_Reduce and the used reduction operation. It is clear that a no-op should result in a faster execution than say MPI_SUM. But what about different implementations of the latter? Figure 1 shows what happens on a Hitachi SR8000 using 32 processor on 4 SMP nodes and the pure MPI programming model without threads. The user supplied addition function was straightforwardly implemented as

```
void own_reduce_op(void *invec, void *inoutvec,
                   int *len, MPI_Datatype *type)
{
  int i;
  double *iv, *iov;

  iv = (double*) invec; iov = (double*) inoutvec;
  for(i=0 ; i<*len; i++) iov[i] = iov[i] + iv[i];
}
```

The result was a significantly faster execution compared to the usage of MPI_SUM. The speedup was about 3 for large message sizes.

2.2 Choosing the Right Parameter Values

Ranks of sender and/or receiver. One of the usual measurements is a pingpong pattern, i.e. sending data back and forth between two processes. But which processes? In general it is wrong to use the first two processes (which some benchmarks [3] are doing). On machines with SMP nodes only the communication bandwidth of the local shared memory is measured. Other benchmarks like MBL on the Earth Simulator [7] or b_{eff} [4] measure several performance numbers respectively a weighted sum of them.

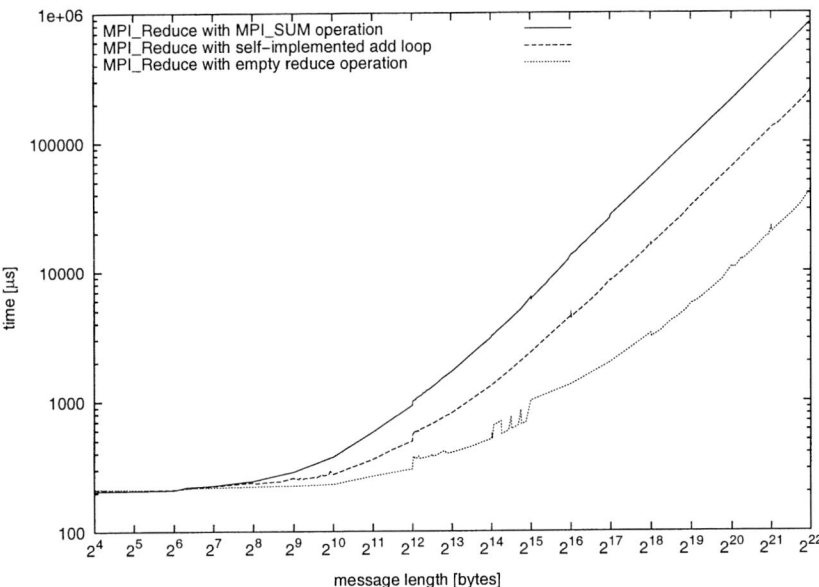

Fig. 1. Running times of `MPI_Reduce` for the built-in `MPI_SUM`, a self-implemented addition operation and the no-op.

Table 1. Distribution of running times of `MPI_Bcast` for different communicators of size 4 and 5.

machine	size	time	freq.	machine	size	time	freq.
SP2	4	210-240 ms	6	T3E	5	145-160 ms	44
SP2	4	310-350 ms	48	T3E	5	180-190 ms	12
SP2	4	380-410 ms	16	T3E	5	145-160 ms	40
T3E	4	95-105 ms	50	T3E	5	180-190 ms	16
T3E	4	130-135 ms	20				

Communicators. It turns out that a similar problem exists for collective operations. We claim that a number saying something like "`MPI_Bcast` for 1 MB in a communicator of size 8 takes 0.0436 s" is pretty useless. The reason is that on machines with SMP nodes the time significantly depends on how the processes participating in a collective operation are distributed across the nodes. But even on machines without SMP nodes the precise "shape" of a communicator has an influence on the communication time. Table 1 shows some experimental results for a Cray T3E and an IBM SP2. In all cases from an `MPI_COMM_WORLD` comprising 8 processes several communicators of size 4 and 5 were selected and used for broadcasts of a message of 2 MB. It turns out that not all times are (more or less) equal but clustered in a few groups, which differ from batch job to batch job.

Measurements for communicators of size 5 on the SP2 and for communicators of size 8 selected from 16 processes in `MPI_COMM_WORLD` do not show such a

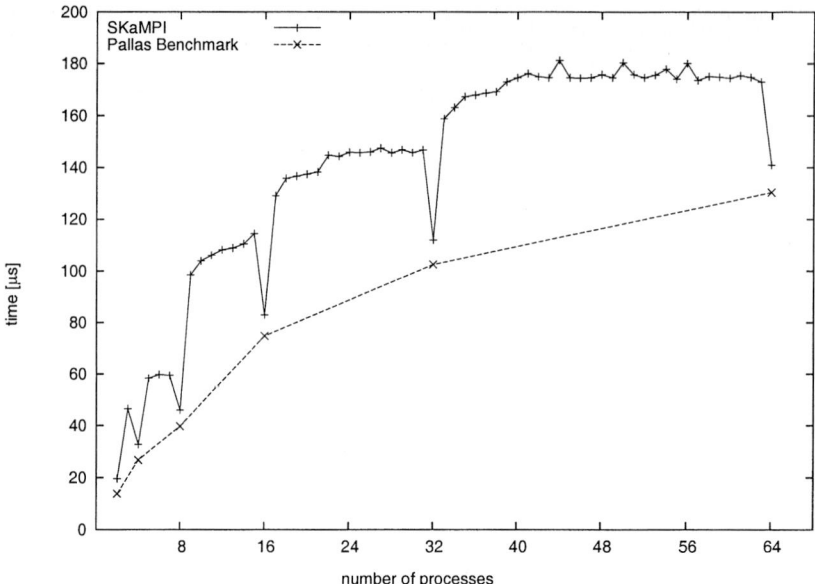

Fig. 2. MPI_Barrier on a Hitachi SR8000.

explicit clustering. But the times for a fast and a slow MPI_Bcast still differ by a factor of about 1.5.

Communicator sizes. For some reason some people like powers of two. As a results some benchmarks only use message lengths and communicator sizes which are a power of two. Unfortunately this does not always reveal the full truth about an MPI implementation. Figure 2 shows the behaviour of MPI_Barrier on an Hitachi SR8000. The lower line with measurements only for 2^k processes was made by the Pallas MPI benchmark using a loop repeatedly executing MPI_Barrier. The upper line was obtained by SKaMPI.

2.3 Choosing the Right Method

There is also something to say about the method used to obtain measurement data. In [8] a new approach has been described to benchmark collective operations. We see two advantages.

- It gives more reliable and understandable results than the method to synchronise the processes participating in a collective call using MPI_Barrier in advance (due to possible overlaps of the operations). Figure 2 also demonstrates this. For communicators of size 2^k SKaMPI gives larger numbers than the PMB.
- It allows to do more detailed benchmarks by varying the starting times according to some predefined known statistics and not relying on the time needed by the collective operation in the case of simultaneous start of all processes.

3 Benchmarking MPI Implementations Is Not Enough

We think that the proper thing to do for something like SKaMPI-Bench is to add the benchmarking of *"usage patterns"*. What we mean here is *not* what are called patterns in the current SKaMPI documentation. Nor do we mean what is called a pattern in software engineering.

3.1 Examples of Usage Patterns

When speaking of a usage pattern what we have in mind is some very basic, conceptually simple building block of a parallel algorithm which involves some communication and which can be implemented in several ways. Here are five examples of increasing complexity:

1. Pingpong: Sending a message back and forth between two processes is the well-known method to measure latency and bandwidth.
2. Broadcast: The transfer of a message to all processes in a communicator can be realized in different ways.
   - use one `MPI_Bcast`
   - use a couple of `MPI_Bcast` calls for partial chunks of data
   - use a combination of other collective operations (e.g. MPICH2 uses a combination of `MPI_Scatter` and `MPI_Allgather` under certain circumstances)
   - use several send operations
3. Non-contiguous sends: Assume that there are several chunks of data spread throughout the memory which have to be sent to another process. One might then for example
   - use several send operations, or
   - copy all data to a contiguous piece of memory and use one send operation, or
   - construct an MPI datatype comprising the chunks and use it for a send operation.
4. Simultaneous data exchange between neighbours in a lattice: Two or three dimensional decomposition is very often used for solving regular problems and the influence of specifying virtual topologies on these usage patterns should be measured.
5. Transposing a distributed matrix.

3.2 Benchmarking Different Implementations of Usage Patterns

PingPong. It can be implemented in different ways (blocking versus non-blocking communication, etc.) and may have different running times. The current SKaMPI already covers these possibilities.

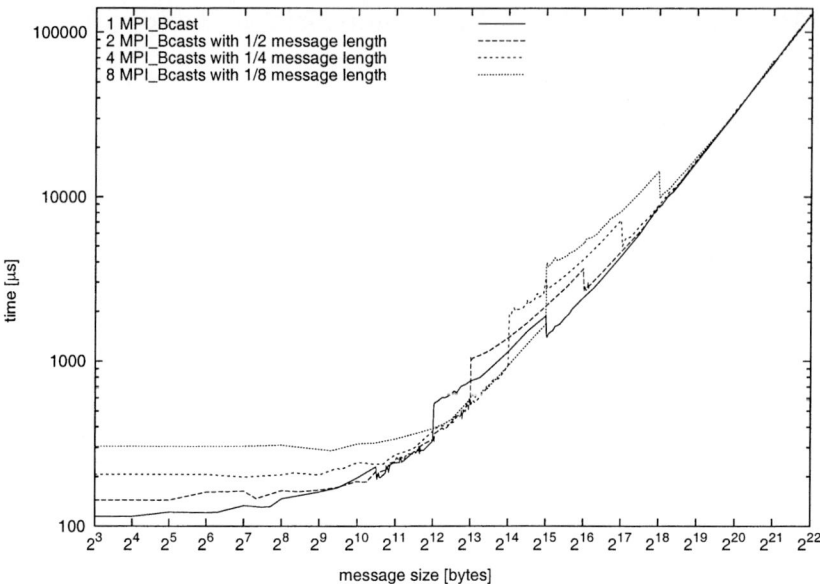

Fig. 3. Using several MPI_Bcast operations to realize the Broadcast usage pattern on an IBM SP2.

Broadcast on IBM SP2. Figure 3 shows the time needed to broadcast a message of size s using $k = 1, 2, 4, 8$ MPI_Bcast operations each of which transfers s/k bytes.

The implementation switches to a rendezvous protocol at a certain message size (default is 4 kB). After that point the communication becomes slower. Therefore it is in some situations advantageous to split one broadcast into several. For example for message sizes between 2^{14} and 2^{15} bytes the fastest method is using 8 broadcasts, the second fastest is using 1 broadcast, the third is using 2 and the slowest is using 4 broadcasts.

Changing the threshold for switching the protocol by setting the environment variable MP_EAGER_LIMIT to some larger value does shift the beginning of the step to the right until the effect disappears for values larger than 32768. Nevertheless MP_EAGER_LIMIT is a global and non-portable option for which the documentation only says that the programmer should try different values for tuning his program, so at least some precise measurement results would be useful.

Transposing a distributed matrix. Recently this problem has been investigated in [2]. One of the results was that compared to a naive implementation a speedup of approx. 20 % could be achieved on an IBM SP2 by making use of clever datatypes in an MPI_Alltoall which do the transposition of local parts of the matrix. On the other hand the same algorithm on an Hitachi SR8000 is significantly slower than the naive algorithm.

3.3 Pros and Cons of Looking at Usage Patterns

There is a famous quote by Donald Knuth (who attributes it to Hoare): "We should forget about small efficiencies, say about 97% of the time: premature optimization is the root of all evil."

Users of an MPI library should certainly think twice before replacing for example an easily understandable and maintainable call of MPI_Bcast with something more complicated.

On the other hand, for the *implementors* of an MPI library we consider it to be more enlightening to find out that 8 MPI_Bcasts of 1 kB are faster than 1 MPI_Bcast of 8 kB than to learn that one MPI_Bcast takes such and such time.

4 SKaMPI-Bench: How to Find Out Which Aspects Do Matter

It is impossible to anticipate (let alone implement in various ways) all possible usage patterns which might arise in parallel applications. Easy extendibility by users is therefore an important requirement for the new SKaMPI-Bench.

Until now SKaMPI is particularly difficult to extend for several reasons:

- Only in the course of time it became clear that benchmarking the obvious send/receive and collective operations in the obvious way is not enough.
- Thus extendibility (in the broad sense needed now) was not one of the design goals.
- One of the design goals was easy usability of SKaMPI. This lead to its distribution as one large source file, i.e. you do not even have to have the make utility to compile it. Since today's parallel machines have matured, we consider it no longer a necessity to require that.

Future development will remove these restrictions and in addition pursue the following aims:

- SKaMPI-Bench will allow to vary over not only one but an arbitrary set of parameters, possibly of different type. This will include not only parameters of MPI functions. One could for example also extend the benchmark by an experiment for measuring a sequence of function calls (as the MPI_Bcasts in Subsection 3.2 above) and vary the number of calls (and simultaneously the message size).
- Because the set of arbitrary parameters can lead to an explosion of the number of different measurements an adapted and improved algorithm for automatic choice of representative sampling points is required.
- The use of virtual topologies will be included into SKaMPI-Bench. Until now this part is missing from SKaMPI because it doesn't fit into the standard framework of usual benchmarking.
- The report generator which can be used to produce a readable document from the results produced by SKaMPI-Bench will be enhanced accordingly.

5 Conclusion

Several surprising results from experiments with MPI show that even benchmarks like the currently available SKaMPI leave room for several improvements:

- the possibility to vary more parameters;
- thus the requirement to vary over non-numeric parameters;
- the possibility to extend the benchmark by user defined experiments;

Currently the new SKaMPI-Bench is in its design phase while several ideas are being tested using simple test modules. Part of the above mentioned experimental results have been obtained that way, while the rest of the data has been determined using modified ad hoc versions of the current SKaMPI benchmark.

Acknowledgements

The authors would like to thank Michael Conrad and Michael Haller for pointing out some problems and surprises when benchmarking MPI implementations and anonymous referees for useful comments.

References

1. W. Gropp and E. Lusk. Reproducible measurements of MPI performance characteristics. In J. J. Dongarra, E. Luque, and T. Margalef, editors, *Proceedings 6th EuroPVM/MPI*, volume 1697 of *LNCS*, pages 11–18. Springer, 1999.
2. M. Haller. Parallele Transposition dreidimensionaler Felder im High Performance Computing. Diploma thesis, Fakultät für Informatik, Univ. Karlsruhe, 2003.
3. Pallas GmbH. Pallas MPI benchmark. http://www.pallas.de/e/products/pmb/.
4. R. Rabenseifner and G. Wellein. Communication and optimization aspects of parallel programming models on hybrid architectures. In *Proc. 4th EWOMP*, 2002.
5. R. Reussner. Using SKaMPI for developing high-performance MPI programs with performance portability. *Future Generation Computer Systems*, to appear.
6. SKaMPI Benchmark. http://liinwww.ira.uka.de/~skampi/.
7. H. Uehara, M. Tamura, and M. Yokokawa. An MPI benchmark program library and its application to the Earth simulator. *LNCS*, 2327:219–??, 2002.
8. Th. Worsch, R. Reussner, and W. Augustin. On benchmarking collective MPI operations. In D. Kranzlmüller et al., editor, *Proceedings 9th EuroPVM/MPI*, volume 2474 of *LNCS*, pages 271–279. Spinger, 2002.

The Performance of Parallel Disk Write Methods for Linux Multiprocessor Nodes

Gregory D. Benson, Kai Long, and Peter S. Pacheco

Keck Cluster Research Group
Department of Computer Science
University of San Francisco
2130 Fulton Street, San Francisco, CA 94117-1080
{benson,klong,peter}@cs.usfca.edu

Abstract. We experimentally evaluate several methods for implementing parallel computations that interleave a significant number of contiguous or strided writes to a local disk on Linux-based multiprocessor nodes. Using synthetic benchmark programs written with MPI and Pthreads, we have acquired detailed performance data for different application characteristics of programs running on dual processor nodes. In general, our results show that programs that perform a significant amount of I/O relative to pure computation benefit greatly from the use of threads, while programs that perform relatively little I/O obtain excellent results using only MPI. For a pure MPI approach, we have found that it is usually best to use two writing processes with mmap(). For Pthreads it is usually best to use two writing processes, write() for contiguous data, and writev() for strided data. Codes that use mmap() tend to benefit from periodic syncs of the data of the data to the disk, while codes that use write() or writev() tend to have better performance with few syncs. A straightforward use of ROMIO usually does not perform as well as these direct approaches for writing to the local disk.

1 Introduction

Many parallel simulation problems require a large number of writes to disk. Almost any time-dependent differential equation solver will interleave computation with disk writes [9]. Examples are climate modeling, simulation of groundwater flow, and circuit simulation. Such simulations require frequent writes to disk either because core memory must be used for support of the computation or simply too much data is generated to fit into an in-core buffer. The resulting data files can be used for simulation analysis and visualization. For example, we have developed a parallel program called NeuroSys [6] that will simulate the behavior of large networks of biologically accurate neurons. The output data consists of numerical values, such as membrane voltages, that represent the state of each neuron. A modest-sized simulation can result in several gigabytes of data.

Despite increasing attention paid to parallel I/O and the introduction of MPI-IO, there is limited, practical data to help guide a programmer in the choice of a good parallel write strategy in the absence of a parallel file system. This study investigates low-level, parallel disk write techniques for Linux clusters. In particular, we focus on methods that optimize the usage of dual-processor compute nodes with dedicated disks. We are interested in finding the most efficient methods for pushing large amounts of data onto the dedicated disks. Our goal is to establish the best write methods for a wide range of applications. Our results can be used to guide both application programmers and systems programmers, and the methods we study can be employed in parallel programs written using Pthreads, MPI, and OpenMP.

We have developed a synthetic benchmarking program that allows us to experimentally evaluate the performance of different methods given different application characteristics. The methods we evaluate consist of matching different Linux write mechanisms, such as `write()`, `writev()`, `mmap()`, and file syncing, with different strategies for parallelizing computation and I/O among multiple processes or threads on a multiprocessor node. For example, a straightforward, but sometimes inefficient strategy is to have two independent threads or MPI processes perform both computation and I/O on behalf of the simulation. It turns out that on a node with a single disk, uncoordinated file sync requests can compete for the disk and result in poor disk utilization. We also give preliminary results for the MPI-IO function, `MPI_File_write_all()` [3].

We also consider different simulation characteristics such as the ratio of I/O to computation on each simulation step. If a simulation produces very little output per simulation step, it is more important to ensure a balance in computation among the threads or processes, and most disk write strategies will not greatly affect application performance as long as the OS can buffer write requests and issue the disk writes asynchronously. However, as the output per simulation step increases it becomes less likely that the OS will be able to buffer all of the write requests, and it will be required to push the buffers to the disk. In this case, the write mechanism usage can determine how and when buffers are copied to disk.

Another application characteristic we consider is contiguous writes versus strided writes. Scientific simulations will often use strided writes to extract significant values from large vectors. The `write()` system call is well suited for contiguous writes, but not for strided writes unless memory copying is used within the application. Both `writev()` and `mmap()` files accommodate strided data. In MPI-IO, derived datatypes can be used to identify the strided data.

In our study we use a hardware and software configuration in which our systems represent nodes typical of a Linux cluster installation. The nodes are dual Pentium III 1GHz processors with a ServerWorks ServerSet III LE chipset and an 18GB SCSI disk. They run Linux kernel version 2.4.20, and we use the ext3 file system. For the benchmarks using MPI, we use MPICH-GM.1.2.5..8 and shared memory communication. For MPI-IO we use ROMIO 1.2.5.1. For parallel applications we assume that processes or threads running on a single node will write directly to the local disk. Such applications can benefit from the inherent I/O parallelism and achieve better communication bandwidth by eliminating I/O traffic on the network. We have not experimented with other

I/O configurations such as NFS mounted file systems or parallel file systems such as PVFS [2].

Our results show that when a program performs a large amount of I/O relative to computation, its performance can be substantially improved if it uses Pthreads. This result is in accordance with previous research in which threads are used to support asynchronous I/O [4]. However, programs with relatively little I/O obtain excellent performance using only MPI. Indeed, such programs may actually obtain better performance than a threaded program. For pure MPI programs, it is usually better to have both processes writing to the disk, and using the system call mmap() instead of write() or writev() usually results in better performance. Programs that use Pthreads also usually obtain the best results two writers. However, write() or writev() often performs better than mmap(). Programs that use mmap() instead of write() or writev() perform best if data is regularly synced to disk. Programs that use write() or writev() usually obtain little benefit from periodic syncing. If consistent performance is more important than raw speed, it is often better to use mmap() rather than write() or writev(). A straightforward use of the ROMIO [8] implementation of MPI_File_write_all() does not perform as well as the direct approaches for writing to the local disk.

This work was motivated by a practical need to implement efficient parallel disk writing in a locally developed scientific application, NeuroSys [6]. We found very little guidance in the research literature to help us optimize its I/O. Ideally, we would have liked to find experience summaries on a Linux cluster similar to ours (a cluster of 64 dual-processor nodes connected by Myrinet). A notable parallel I/O benchmark is b_eff_io [7], which is used to characterize the total parallel I/O performance of a parallel system. Unlike our benchmarks, which serve to identify an optimal disk write method for a specific system, b_eff_io is suited for comparing the I/O bandwidth of different systems. Furthermore, b_eff_io does not simulate computation, so while it can give an indication of the raw I/O throughput of a system, it does not reveal how well a system can overlap I/O with computation.

Our work is complementary to work in parallel file systems [2] and MPI-IO implementations [8]. The results of our parallel write experiments can be used to help guide in implementation of these I/O systems on Linux clusters. In addition, our benchmarks could be used as a framework for comparing the write performance of these I/O systems. Earlier results [5] indicate that performance gains from mixing MPI with explicit threading is not worth the added programming complexity when the application involves primarily in-core sparse-matrix computations. Our results show that for I/O intensive applications mixing threads with MPI is well worth the added complexity.

The rest of this paper is organized as follows. Section 2 describes the write methods we analyze in this paper. Section 3 describes our benchmarking approach. Section 4 evaluates our results and provides recommendations for application and system programmers who implement parallel I/O libraries. Finally, Section 5 makes some concluding remarks and discusses future work.

Acknowledgments. The first and third authors are grateful to the WM Keck Foundation for a grant to build a cluster for use in research and education and partial support of this research. The work of the third author was also partially supported by Lawrence Livermore National Laboratory. Work performed under the auspices of the U.S. Department of Energy by Lawrence Livermore National Laboratory under Contract W-7405-ENG-48.

2 Parallel Write Methods

We refer to a *parallel write method* as a write mechanism combined with a parallelization strategy.

Disk Write Mechanisms. Linux and most UNIX implementations support disk writing with the `write()` and `writev()` systems calls. Linux also supports memory mapped files with the `mmap()` system call. Both `write()` and `writev()` collect data from user space and transfer it to a kernel-space buffer. The buffer is usually written to the disk at a later time depending on system behavior and configuration. While `write()` supports the transfer of a single contiguous buffer, `writev()` allows a program to transfer a set of non-contiguous buffers. Using `mmap()` a program can establish a range of virtual memory in process address space to directly map to a named file. Thus writing to the file is as simple as writing directly to memory. The caching of memory mapped files is similar to ordinary file caching.

Programmers can affect when the kernel actually writes data to disk by "syncing" the data associated with a file. For writing with `write()` and `writev()` the `fsync()` system call can be used. On execution, `fsync()` blocks until all in-memory parts of a file are written to disk, including the file metadata. The `fdatasync()` system call is supposed to sync just the file data to disk, but as of Linux 2.4.20, `fdatasync()` is the same as `fsync()`, therefore introducing unnecessary disk writes. Note that although older versions of `fsync()` copied all of the in-core file buffers to disk, current versions only copy the buffers used by the file argument passed to `fsync()`. For `mmap()` regions, the `msync()` system call can be used. By syncing data to disk, it may be possible to achieve better disk write control and enable overlapping of computation with I/O. In a system with enough main memory, an application may write all its data to kernel buffers and only after the buffers have aged long enough or come under memory pressure, will the data be written to disk. Such behavior can result in large delays at the end of the program.

The `mmap()` system call can be used in two ways to write data to a file. The most straightforward technique is to use `mmap()` to map the entire length of the file into the user's virtual address space. In this mode, the user uses `mmap()` once and simply writes to contiguous memory locations. However, this approach limits the maximum file length to the amount of mappable virtual memory, which is just under 2 GB in Linux (for a default kernel configuration in Linux 2.4.20 and on a 32 bit x86 architecture). An alternate technique for writing files with `mmap()` is to map only a portion of the file into virtual memory. Once this *window* has

Table 1. Implementation Details for the Parallel Write Methods

MPI Implementations	
S1A	Two MPI processes compute and write to their own files. Each process performs periodic syncs to disk.
S1B	Similar to S1A except the periodic syncs are coordinated so that only one sync is issued at a time to the kernel: process 1 blocks in a receive while process 0 syncs first.
S2	Two MPI processes compute. One of the processes is a designated writer. The non-writing process sends its data to the writing process on each iteration. The writer issues periodic syncs.
S2DT	Similar to S2 except that derived datatypes are used to send strided data from the non-writer to the writer.
S3	Two MPI processes. One computes and one writes. The compute process sends data to the write process on each iteration.
S3DT	Similar to S3 except that derived datatypes are used to send strided data from the compute process to the write process.
MPI-IO	Two MPI processes compute and write using the `MPI_File_write_all()` function. Derived datatypes are used for strided data.
Pthread Implementations	
S1A	Two threads compute and write their own files. Each thread performs periodic syncs to disk.
S1B	Similar to S1A except the periodic syncs are coordinated so that only one sync is issued at a time to the kernel: thread 1 blocks in a barrier while thread 0 syncs first.
S2	Two threads compute. One of the threads is the designated writer. The non-writing thread passes a buffer to the writing thread on each iteration. The writer issues periodic syncs.
S3	Two threads. One computes and one writes. The compute thread passes a buffer to the write thread on each iteration.
S5	Similar to S2 except a separate sync thread is used. The writing thread notifies the sync thread when the sync size is reached. The sync thread allows disk flushing to occur asynchronously with the computation.

been written to, it is unmapped with `munmap()`, and the next window is mapped with `mmap()`. This approach does not place any limits on the maximum file size and it gives the programmer more control over the amount of memory used for file buffering.

The data to be written to a file may be *contiguous* or *strided*. Writing contiguous data is more straightforward than writing strided data. For example, using `write()` on a contiguous buffer simply requires the starting address and the length of the buffer to be written. Using `write()` on strided data requires several small writes or the non-contiguous data must be copied to an intermediate buffer. Alternatively, `writev()` can by used to directly write strided data. For `mmap()`, strided data must be copied into the mmapped memory region.

Parallelization Strategies. When assigning work to a dual processor node, the goal is to best utilize the processors for both the computation and I/O operations. Such utilization can be achieved with separate threads using Pthreads or separate MPI processes. For example, if very little data needs to be written to disk, then it makes sense to divide the computation between two threads or two processes. However, as an application writes more data to disk relative to the amount of computation it becomes less clear how the work should be divided. One consideration is whether to write two individual files, one for each thread, or have the threads combine the output data and write to a single file. The latter case may work better on nodes with a single disk. The parallelization strategies used for our study are listed in Table 1.

3 Experimental Methodology

We have developed a set of synthetic benchmarks that employ the disk write implementations given in Section 2. In this discussion the term "thread" is used to mean either Pthread or MPI process. The programs take several parameters: **iters, comptime, bufsize, syncsize,** and **winsize**. The **iters** parameter determines how many loop iterations to simulate. Each iteration represents a possible iteration in a real simulation. The **comptime** parameter determines how much total computation time should be simulated across all loop **iters**. The computation time per loop is **comptime / iters**. If there are two compute threads, the compute time per iteration is further divided between the two threads. If there are two write threads, the **bufsize** parameter is the amount of data to be written on each loop iteration by each thread. If there is only one write thread, then 2 × **bufsize** bytes are written by this thread on each iteration. Similarly, if there are two compute threads, each generates **bufsize** bytes of data for transferring to disk on each iteration, while if there is only one write thread, it will generate 2 × **bufsize** bytes. Thus, the total amount of data written to disk is 2 × **iters** × **bufsize**. Data is synced to disk every **syncsize** bytes. Finally, **winsize** is used with mmap() to determine the maximum size of an mmap region. Note that **syncsize** should be less than or equal to **winsize**. For the strided benchmarks two additional parameters are used: **len** and **stride**. The **len** is the number of bytes in a contiguous chunk of data. The **stride** is the number of bytes between the beginnings of successive chunks.

In the benchmarks, the compute time is generated by filling the compute buffer and having the thread spin on a timer. We found that there was virtually no difference between the results given by using Intel's cycle counter rdtsc() and the gettimeofday() system call. So for portability, we chose to use gettimeofday().

Each synthetic benchmark follows a common template: (1) Create threads or processes; (2) Warm up disk with writes; (3) Barrier; (4) Loop of (4a) Simulate computation and fill buffer, (4b) Barrier, (4c) Write buffer or transfer buffer, (4d) Possible sync; and (5) A final sync to ensure all data is flushed to disk. To record times, we start timing after (3) and end timing after (5).

4 Experimental Results

Using the benchmarks described in Section 3 we have obtained performance results for each parallel write method on the platform described in Section 1. All of the codes and libraries were compiled using the gcc 3.2 compiler with no optimization.

One of our main goals is to explore the impact of computation time relative to I/O time on each of the parallel write methods. We have chosen parameters that range from no compute time to a relatively large amount of compute time. The intuition is that some methods may do a better job at overlapping computation and I/O. Another goal is to determine the interaction between write mechanisms and parallelization strategies for our cluster configuration.

The specific parameters consist of 1024 iterations with 64 KB buffers. The total amount of data written for each simulation is 128 MB. Since all of the benchmarks include the time it takes to complete the actual disk transfer, the reported times are adequate for illustrating the behavior of the benchmark, provided the relative sizes of the files and compute times are preserved. For S1A and S1B, the output data will be split across two 64 MB files. For the other methods, the data will be stored in a single 128 MB file. We found that sync size and window sizes gave unpredictable results, so we experimented with a large range of values. We considered the following sync sizes (**syncsize**): 128 KB, 256 KB, 512 KB, 1 MB, 2 MB, 4 MB, 8 MB, 16 MB, 32 MB, 64 MB, and 128 MB. We also considered the following window sizes (**winsize**) for the `mmap()` write mechanism: 1 MB, 2 MB, 4 MB, 8 MB, 16 MB, 32 MB, 64 MB, and 128 MB. Note that we only run experiments with **syncsize** $\leq$ **winsize**. Each test is repeated 10 times and we report a 10% trimmed mean. For the strided data we used a **stride** of 32 bytes and a **len** of 8 bytes. For the MPI-IO results, we used a call to `MPI_File_write_all()` during each loop, a single call to `MPI_File_sync()` upon completion of the loop, and the the default ROMIO hints.

The results for our MPI and Pthread experiments are listed in Figure 1. The data in the table include the total execution time in seconds (we do not include program startup), the best **syncsize** found for the method (f), and the best **winsize** found for `mmap()` methods (w).

Pthreads and MPI. The results show that for our system configuration and the given parameters, if there is a large amount of I/O relative to computation, then using Pthreads provides much better performance than MPI. For contiguous data the best Pthread code for 0 seconds of compute provides a 66% improvement over the best MPI code for this time, and the best Pthread code for 2 seconds of compute provides a 35% improvement. For strided data the best Pthreads code for 0 and 2 seconds provide improvements of 33% and 13%, respectively. On the other hand, if the application is carrying out a relatively small amount of I/O (8 and 32 second compute), then the best MPI implementations do as well as, or somewhat better than, the best Pthread implementations. Our straightforward use of ROMIO is not competitive with the other methods unless the amount of computation is very large (32 seconds), and even in these cases it performs somewhat worse than MPI with `mmap()`.

Write method. For MPI codes, `mmap()` always outperforms `write()` and `writev()`. For example, for a compute time of 2 seconds, the best strided `mmap()` code provides an 18% improvement over the best `writev()` code. For Pthreads, the situation is almost reversed: in almost every case `write()` or `writev()` outperforms the corresponding `mmap()` code. The exceptions occur for contiguous buffers and relatively large amounts of compute time (8 and 32 seconds). In these situations, S5 with mmap performs best among the Pthreads codes. We expect that for these relatively large amounts of compute time, the extra sync thread is able to provide a significant amount of overlap with computation.

Distribution of work among threads. For the MPI codes, S1A or S1B usually performs best. In both methods, the processes perform equal amounts of

Table 1: MPI Contiguous Data

Comp time	write()				mmap()				MPI-IO
	S1A	S1B	S2	S3	S1A	S1B	S2	S3	
0	4.97 64Mf	**4.95** 64Mf	5.28 128Mf	5.00 128Mf	4.72 8Mf 64Mw	4.39 2Mf 2Mw	**4.37** 512Kf 1Mw	5.05 512Kf 1Mw	5.28
2	**6.63** 64Mf	6.77 64Mf	7.35 128Mf	8.29 128Mf	6.78 2Mf 64Mw	**6.37** 2Mf 4Mw	6.67 4Mf 8Mw	7.96 256Kf 32Mw	6.81
8	**10.1** 64Mf	10.40 64Mf	10.70 128Mf	17.5 128Mf	9.54 256Kf 1Mw	**9.05** 2Mf 4Mw	9.22 256Kf 1Mw	16.4 256Kf 128Mw	10.70
32	33.10 64Mf	**33.00** 64Mf	33.60 128Mf	64.50 128Mf	**33.00** 512Kf 2Mw	33.00 2Mf 2Mw	33.3 256Kf 2Mw	64.4 256Kf 1Mw	33.70

Table 2: MPI Strided Data

Comp time	writev()						mmap()						MPI-IO
	S1A	S1B	S2	S2DT	S3	S3DT	S1A	S1B	S2	S2DT	S3	S3DT	
0	8.35 64Mf	8.80 64Mf	10.60 128Mf	8.76 128Mf	12.30 128Mf	**7.60** 128Mf	9.54 512Kf 2Mw	**7.00** 1Mf 2Mw	8.59 256Kf 8Mw	7.62 512Kf 32Mw	9.14 128Kf 1Mw	7.30 512Kf 128Mw	9.71
2	9.82 64Mf	10.00 64Mf	11.00 128Mf	9.85 128Mf	11.50 128Mf	**9.75** 128Mf	9.20 128Kf 8Mw	8.64 512Kf 16Mw	9.67 256Kf 2Mw	8.54 512Kf 32Mw	9.51 512Kf 1Mw	**7.98** 512Kf 16Mw	10.00
8	**12.70** 64Mf	12.80 64Mf	15.90 128Mf	13.00 128Mf	19.90 128Mf	18.60 128Mf	**11.60** 1Mf 1Mw	11.90 4Mf 4Mw	14.70 128Kf 1Mw	12.20 512Kf 2Mw	18.70 128Kf 128Mw	17.70 128Kf 128Mw	15.00
32	**36.20** 64Mf	**36.20** 64Mf	40.10 128Mf	36.50 128Mf	67.30 128Mf	66.10 128Kf	35.50 256Kf 1Mw	**35.10** 4Mf 4Mw	38.70 512Kf 4Mw	35.50 256Kf 1Mw	66.70 256Kf 128Mw	65.70 128Kf 128Mw	38.70

Table 3: Pthreads Contiguous Data

Comp time	write()					mmap()				
	S1A	S1B	S2	S3	S5	S1A	S1B	S2	S3	S5
0	2.06 64Mf	**1.48** 64Mf	1.72 128Mf	1.76 128Mf	4.39 128Mf	5.08 32Mf 64Mw	5.03 16Mf 64Mw	5.47 4Mf 64Mw	5.50 4Mf 64Mw	**3.62** 16Mf 16Mw
2	4.73 64Mf	**4.13** 64Mf	4.52 128Mf	4.78 64Mf	4.92 128Mf	7.12 32Mf 64Mw	7.01 16Mf 64Mw	7.43 2Mf 4Mw	8.51 1Mf 1Mw	**5.01** 8Mf 8Mw
8	9.73 64Mf	10.96 32Mf	9.90 128Mf	16.43 64Mf	10.18 128Mf	13.15 32Mf 64Mw	12.73 256Kf 1Mw	13.20 512Kf 1Mw	16.75 256Kf 1Mw	**9.30** 512Kf 8Mw
32	33.37 64Mf	33.41 64Mf	33.32 128Mf	64.12 128Kf	**33.23** 256Kf	37.09 32Mf 64Mw	36.45 256Kf 1Mw	37.41 16Mf 64Mw	64.12 256Kf 2Mw	**33.20** 256Kf 2Mw

Table 4: Pthreads Strided Data

Comp time	writev()					mmap()				
	S1A	S1B	S2	S3	S5	S1A	S1B	S2	S3	S5
0	4.75 64Mf	**4.69** 64Mf	7.07 64Mf	7.46 64Mf	8.99 128Mf	7.36 16Mf 64Mw	7.11 16Mf 64Mw	9.26 16Mf 64Mw	9.25 64Mf 64Mw	**6.20** 8Mf 8Mw
2	**6.95** 64Mf	7.33 64Mf	9.84 128Mf	7.14 128Mf	9.88 128Mf	9.27 64Mf 64Mw	9.20 64Mf 64Mw	11.25 64Mf 64Mw	9.27 64Kf 64Mw	**7.75** 2Mf 8Mw
8	12.49 64Mf	**12.16** 64Mf	14.63 128Mf	16.24 64Mf	15.02 128Mf	15.42 64Mf 64Mw	15.00 256Kf 1Mw	17.31 16Mf 64Mw	17.43 128Kf 1Mw	**13.54** 1Mf 8Mw
32	36.25 64Mf	**36.06** 64Mf	38.33 64Mf	64.13 128Kf	38.26 512Kf	39.38 64Mf 64Mw	39.05 256Kf 1Mw	41.34 512Kf 1Mw	64.13 256Kf 1Mw	**37.46** 256Kf 2Mw

Fig. 1. Expermental Results for Parallel Write Methods (times in seconds, f is sync size, w is window size, K is kilobytes, M is megabytes)

computation and each writes to its own file. S1B differs from S1A in that it schedules the syncs, and, in most cases this seemed to either give some benefit or it didn't cause any significant degradation. The only clear exception to preferring S1A or S1B occurs in the strided benchmark with 2 seconds of compute time. In this situation, S3DT, is clearly superior.

For Pthreads making an optimal choice of the work distribution depends on whether `mmap()` or `write()`/`writev()` is being used. With `mmap()`, S5 is always preferred, while with `write()` or `writev()`, S1A or S1B is almost always the best choice.

Syncing and Window Size. Syncing allows the application to force the kernel to flush disk buffers to disk. However, we found that attempting to perform `fdatasync()` with `write()` or `writev()` with the benchmarks often resulted in worse performance than simply using one sync at the end of the benchmark. The degradation in performance may be due to the current implementation of `fdatasync()` in the Linux kernel, which is really an `fsync()` [1]. The main exceptions to this occur with Pthreads when there is a single writer (S2, S3, or S5). The most notable of these is S3, which usually benefits from at least one extra call to `fdatasync()`.

For `mmap()`, it is clear that periodic syncing provides significant benefits to performance. In the case of the contiguous MPI benchmarks, a 2 MB sync size provides the best performance with the preferred method, S1B. For the other benchmarks, though, a range of sync sizes resulted in optimal performance. For the strided MPI benchmarks, optimal sync sizes ranged from 512 Kbytes to 4 Mbytes. For Pthreads, the range was even greater: 256 Kbytes to 16 Mbytes. However, for S5, always the best performer with Pthreads and `mmap()`, as the compute times increased, the optimal sync sizes decreased.

The range of optimal window sizes is even larger than the range of optimal sync sizes. Each size we tested, from 1 MB to 128 MB, is optimal in some situation. Perhaps noteworthy in this context is the fact that for the optimal write method, the best window size is always less than the file size. So unmapping and remapping windows provides a clear benefit.

Variability. We do not have sufficient space to report the variability in the data we collected. We found a very wide range: the fastest and slowest times for a given benchmark could differ by as much as 300%. In general, however, it seems that for a given method, the use of `mmap()` results in somewhat less variation.

5 Conclusions and Future Work

Our study experimentally compares the performance of several parallel disk write methods using both MPI and Pthreads. We provide experimental results for one specific hardware configuration, a configuration that is typical of Linux clusters. Each benchmark was run on a constrained set of simulation parameters. The parameter set we studied was quite large, and we found that no one approach to I/O invariably results in the best performance. In particular, we have shown that using Pthreads gives the best performance when the ratio of I/O to computation is high, but that MPI provides excellent performance when the ratio of I/O to computation is low. We also found considerable differences in the performance of `write()`, `writev()`, and `mmap()`, and in the use of various other parameters. This suggests that any optimal implementation of I/O for dual processor nodes will need to use adaptive methods to identify the best combination of parameters.

Many directions for future work are available. Specifically, we want to explore the new asynchronous I/O API (aio) for Linux kernels. We also would like to implement benchmarks using the `O_DIRECT` option for writing files. This option allows applications to bypass the kernel disk caching mechanism. As of the writing of this paper, the `O_DIRECT` option is not supported in the Linux 2.4.20 kernel for the ext3 file system. We also want to increase our parameter space in a sensible way to make our results more general. Ideally, we would like to use our benchmarks to find the proper parallel write method for a specific application.

References

1. Daniel P. Bovet and Marco Cesati. *Understanding the Linux Kernel*. O'Reilly & Associates, Inc., 2nd edition, 2001.
2. Philip H. Carns, Walter B. Ligon III, Robert B. Ross, and Rajeev Thakur. PVFS: A parallel file system for linux clusters. In *Proceedings of the 4th Annual Linux Showcase and Conference*, pages 317–327, Atlanta, GA, 2000. USENIX Association.
3. William Gropp, Ewing Lusk, and Rajeev Thakur. *Using MPI-2: Advanced Features of the Message Passing Interface*. Scientific and Engineering Computation. MIT Press, Cambridge, MA, USA, November 1999.
4. S. More, A. Choudhary, I. Foster, and M. Xu. MTIO: A multi-threaded parallel I/O system. In *Proceedings of the 11th International Parallel Processing Symposium (IPPS-97)*, pages 368–373, Los Alamitos, April 1–5 1997. IEEE Computer Society Press.
5. Leonid Oliker, Xiaoye Li, Parry Husbands, and Rupak Biswas. Effects of ordering strategies and programming paradigms on sparse matrix computations. *SIAM Review*, 44(3):373–393, September 2002.
6. P. Pacheco, M. Camperi, and T Uchino. PARALLEL NEUROSYS: A system for the simulation of very large networks of biologically accurate neurons on parallel computers. *Neurocomputing*, 32–33(1–4):1095–1102, 2000.
7. Rolf Rabenseifner and Alice E. Koniges. Effective file-I/O bandwidth benchmark. *Lecture Notes in Computer Science*, 1900:1273–1283, 2001.
8. Rajeev Thakur, William Gropp, and Ewing Lusk. On implementing MPI-IO portably and with high performance. In *Proceedings of the Sixth Workshop on Input/Output in Parallel a nd Distributed Systems*, pages 23–32, 1999.
9. Rajeev Thakur, Ewing Lusk, and William Gropp. I/O in parallel applications: The weakest link. *The International Journal of High Performance Computing Applications*, 12(4):389–395, Winter 1998.

A Model for Performance Analysis of MPI Applications on Terascale Systems

Srigurunath Chakravarthi[1], C.R. Krishna Kumar[2], Anthony Skjellum[1],
H.A. Prahalad[2], and Bharath Seshadri[2]

[1] MPI Software Technology Inc., Suite #33
101 S Lafayette St., Starkville, MS 39759, USA
{ecap,tony}@mpi-softtech.com
[2] MPI Software Technology India Pvt. Ltd.
#351, 37th C Cross, 7th Main, Jayanagar 5th Block
Bangalore 560041, India
{crkkumar,sbharath,prahalad}@msti-india.com

Abstract. Profiling-based performance visualization and analysis of program execution is widely used for tuning and improving the performance of parallel applications. There are several profiler-based tools for effective application performance analysis and visualization. However, a majority of these tools are not equally effective for performance tuning of applications consisting of 100's to 10,000's of tasks or applications generating several gigabytes to terabytes of trace information. This paper identifies architectural and usability limitations applicable to majority of existing performance analysis tools and proposes an alternative design to improve analysis of large amounts of trace-data. The new design addresses architectural as well as user-interface issues for terascale systems by providing scalable, flexible and automated mechanisms to analyze trace data. Using the proposed design, the authors have implemented an MPI application performance analysis tool, *SeeWithin/Pro*, as a proof-of-concept that the design can support flexible query-based analysis mechanisms to reveal complex performance statistics

1 Background

Performance tuning of parallel applications executing on 100's to 10,000's of processors can be challenging for several reasons. Performance degradation may result from disparate causes such as poor mapping of tasks to processors, poor choice of parallel algorithm by the application, performance limitations of message passing software or device drivers, performance glitches in hardware, and others. At a large number of processors, it is difficult to isolate the cause of performance degradation from the relatively large amounts of trace data generated. Consequently, as the scale of computing grows, application programmers require more sophisticated support from performance visualization and analysis software. At the user-interface level the application programmer needs a degree of automated analysis, extreme flexibility to formulate and extract aggregate statistics as well as individual events of pertinence to the particular parallel application, and less reliance on "visually detecting" performance bottlenecks from a graphical view of the process timeline. At the level of the performance analysis software design, significantly better scalability is required to efficiently store and retrieve relevant information from several gigabytes to terabytes of trace data.

This paper examines the general design adopted by several existing performance analysis and visualization tools [3][5][7][12] and proposes a scalable and analyzable organization of, and access to, trace data using a relational database management system. It briefly discusses, *SeeWithin/Pro*, an implementation of our proposed design, as proof-of-concept that flexible analysis is possible using this design.

The rest of the paper is organized as follows: Section 2 examines suitability of currently adopted design of performance analysis software for terascale systems. Section 3 presents a new design for trace data organization and access suitable for terascale systems and reviews aspects of *SeeWithin/Pro* as an implementation of the design. Section 4 presents potential extensions to the proposed design for scalable on-the-fly analysis. Section 5 offers conclusions.

2 Design Adopted by Existing Tools

Several tools exist for performance debugging of parallel programs and many have been surveyed in [2]. A majority of these tools work well with parallel programs using popular standards such as MPI [11] and OpenMP [8] with several 10's up to a few 100's of tasks. VaMPIr [7] is a robust commercial tool for MPI applications. ParaVer [12] is a multi-purpose tool for performance visualization and analysis of parallel programs (OpenMP and MPI), standalone applications, system performance, thread-level performance etc.

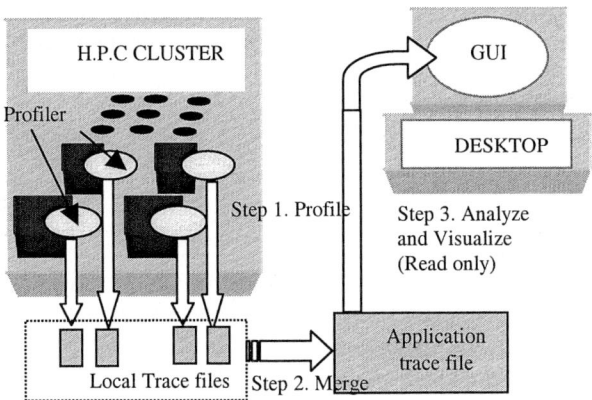

Fig. 1. Design adopted by conventional performance debugging software

Figure 1 shows the typical architecture of existing profiler-based performance debugging tools. In this paper, only post-mortem tools are considered; that is, tools that allow access to trace data after complete execution of the profiled application. A majority of existing tools support only post-mortem analysis with few exceptions such as SvPablo [6]. In Fig. 1. the two major modules of performance debugging tools are shown as ovals: the profiler and the Graphical User Interface (GUI). Typically the profiler library is linked with the HPC application and produces trace files for each task or thread in secondary storage local to each HPC node (Step 1). After execution of the application, the trace files are merged into one application trace file (Step 2). The application trace file could really be a collection of files for scalability or other reasons, but it is referred to here in the singular sense for convenience.

The following sections present some common aspects of existing tools unsuitable to the requirements specified for terascale systems in the previous section.

At an architectural level:

Stand-alone architecture: A majority of tools adopt standalone architecture as shown in Fig. 1. The GUI directly accesses data in the trace-file. The user interface module performs all tasks including reading trace-file into memory, execution of analysis logic on data loaded into memory, and display of timeline graphics. This design is known to scale relatively poorly compared to a 2-tier client-server model or N-tier models supported by more recent frameworks.

Trace-file format: Some tools use a proprietary trace-file format [7], some others use the somewhat open ALOG and CLOG formats [3][5], while some other tools use open ASCII [12] or XML-like self-defining formats [1]. Common to all these methods of storage is a problem that trace-files cannot be easily re-organized to optimize access times depending on the type of analysis the user wishes to perform. Tools for large scale systems should allow the user to "pre-process" raw data before an analysis session to optimize information retrieval times based on hints from the user.

Platform dependence: Many tools offer user interfaces (UIs) that are not portable across platforms. Platform dependence reduces easy deployment in Grid computing environments with heterogeneous resources. For some tools such as [7][8] this may be owed to the sophisticated visualization mechanisms they provide. A portable library such as Java Swing [4] provides less powerful graphics capability compared to a native graphics library.

At a user level:

Orientation towards visualization; Majority of tools offer sophisticated visualization of program execution but fall short of providing equally advanced mechanisms for analysis of trace data. Typically users have to load the process execution timeline (or a subset of timeline) into a GUI before they can begin analysis. This aspect gains significance for tera-scale systems because scalability of analysis of trace data is limited by memory available to load and display timeline graphics.

Difficult to extract user-specified information: Tools provide standard averages and aggregates for CPU and communication activity across the application, but fall short of providing statistics specific to communication patterns and parallel algorithms used by the application.

Required User Participation: Performance debugging is typically driven by the user. Most tools do not provide an easy interface for users to plug-in automatic performance analysis logic without great programming effort or intimate knowledge of trace-file format.

3 A New Model

3.1 Design Description

In this section a new model is presented that is designed to organize trace data efficiently and to provide scalable access to the user. represents a design based on this model.

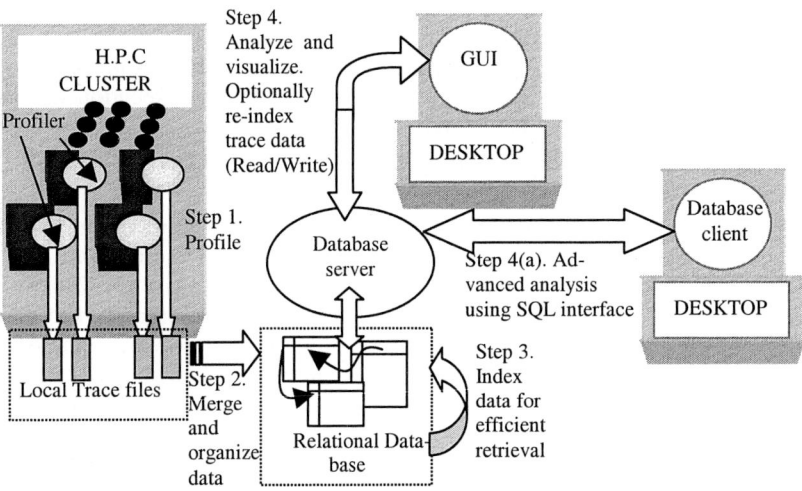

Fig. 2. Client-server design with scalable and optimized data access

In this design, the profiler module writes trace information to local storage as in the conventional design (Step 1). Trace files are then merged (in Step 2) into a set of relations in a relational database management system (RDBMS). The number and type of relations, primary keys, table fields, and other attributes of the database schema depend on the type of parallel systems or applications targeted by the tool. A schema suitable to message passing applications on distributed memory systems may be different from one that is suitable for parallel applications using a shared-memory paradigm. Step 3 sets up optimized trace-file access times for future analysis. Step 3 performs additional optimization by generating sequences (indices) on specific fields of specific relations and by allowing users to write stored-procedures [14], depending on what metrics users wish to analyze. Such optimization mechanisms are provided by every modern RDBMS [14]. For example, an index can be created on the *event timestamp* field to optimize access to analysis queries that seek information about time spent by communication functions or computational units.

Step 4 represents user access to trace data for performance analysis and visualization. This step is analogous to Step 3 in Fig. 1. except that the design permits analysis of data *without* loading all event records into memory of the User Interface process, through SQL queries [14]. This step also differs from the conventional case by allowing both read and write access to the user. Users can perform optional re-organization of trace data suitable to the type of analysis they intend to perform. Write access is possible in this design because additional information can be added as extra relations to the trace database, and unwanted trace information can be deleted by removing records from appropriate relations.

The design also allows direct access to trace data using the standard SQL interface (Step 4(a)), without need for a graphical user interface. This standard SQL interface facilitates easy plugging in of third party analysis software, without requiring programming constructs.

3.2 Advantages

The advantages of organizing trace data as relations using a database system are as follows:

1. *Efficient retrieval of performance data.* Currently available database systems are highly optimized and are generally more efficient than any proprietary file-access software.
2. *Flexible Analysis.* Any type of statistics or individual records can be retrieved from trace-data by constructing appropriate "queries". This will permit tools to provide a flexible interface to the user to unearth any performance metric desired by the user.
3. *Scalability.* Databases support organization of several terabytes of data. Trace data can be analyzed *without* requiring the loading of all event records into memory of the User Interface client.
4. *Standard Access through SQL.* A standard open interface makes easy to plug in third party software modules for automatic performance analysis of trace data. This interface is also useful for advanced users to directly access trace data for complex analysis.

3.3 Implementation

We have implemented a full-fledged performance analysis tool for MPI programs, *SeeWithin/Pro,* using the design shown in Detailed description of *SeeWithin/Pro* is beyond the scope of this paper. However, a brief summary of two unique analysis features of *SeeWithin/Pro* that are primarily possible because of the new design is presented below.

A *User Defined Query* UI allows users to graphically construct high-level "queries" that extract individual event records as well as aggregate statistics such as number of executions of, time spent in, or number of bytes transmitted by any specified set of MPI functions. Users can specify a set of conditions to limit the scope of their analysis query. For example, if value(s) for the communication tag [11], MPI communicator, or MPI Datatype are specified, then *SeeWithin/Pro* will search only records matching the specified values.

A *Comparison Query* UI allows users to compare performance statistics for two different trace-files. This UI can help users pinpoint exact sources of performance differences between two instances of an application. This is often useful to identify performance bottlenecks when an application does not perform as expected when ported to a new platform, or when run with an alternate MPI library, or when run on larger/smaller number of processors.

SeeWithin/Pro offers other such query-based analysis interfaces not discussed in this paper. It should be noted that the above-mentioned analysis interfaces demonstrate analysis of trace-data without requiring to load the trace-file into user memory. This contributes to the scalability of analysis with *SeeWithin/Pro*.

4 Future Extensions to Design

The design described in the previous section addresses many of the requirements for post-mortem performance debugging on terascale systems identified in section 2. In this section is presented extensions to the design that can provide further scalability and facilitate on-the-fly performance analysis and automatic performance analysis of trace data. These extensions pose several implementation challenges that limit their effective use and they are still being researched.

4.1 Distributed Trace data

The design shown in prominently suffers from the drawback of requiring a "merging" step (Step 2) as with conventional tools. This step involves transferring several Gigabytes of data to a central location and can consume several minutes even on a Gigabit network. Existing tools allow generation of trace data directly on a central storage (such as on an NFS mount), but this will interfere with the communication performance of the parallel application unless separate network backbones are used by the traced application and the distributed file system.

Using a distributed database mitigates the problem of merging intermediate trace data into a central location. Analysis queries are serviced by a distributed database that extracts appropriate data from local trace-files. This design however requires network bandwidth to access the distributed data for analysis and is consequently suitable for parallel systems with a separate dedicated network backbone for HPC applications. This design would also require HPC resources such as CPU and memory during analysis of the trace data and can potentially interfere with the performance of other applications using the HPC cluster at the time of performance analysis.

4.2 3-Tier Architecture

The models presented so far address scalability and performance analysis requirements for terascale systems. They do not specifically address portability and usability across the Internet in a Grid Computing environment. This framework is best suited for scalable on-the-fly performance analysis and tuning of applications deployed on the Grid. This design adds a new tier to the client-server design to enhance portability and transaction control of trace data access. The new tier consists of the "performance tool logic" residing on an *application server* [4]. This module contains all the logic for processing user inputs and generating output. The GUI is now relegated to a thin client such as a *Java applet* invoked from a browser. The user interface is now fully portable and can be launched on any web-capable device with *java* support. This model allows us to plug in additional automatic performance analysis modules at the application server that can directly access trace data to process it in real-time.

5 Conclusion

This paper puts forth requirements for effective performance debugging of parallel applications executing on terascale systems with 100's – 10,000's of nodes. Aspects of the stand-alone design adopted by majority of the tools that are unsuitable to scalable and efficient analysis on terascale systems are outlined. A new scalable client-server model is proposed. Future extensions are proposed to the model to support scalable on-the-fly performance analysis. *SeeWithin/Pro* is mentioned as a performance analysis tool that adopts the newly proposed design and provides flexible query-based analysis capability. Planned future work of the authors involves studying and quantifying scalability of this proposed design.

References

1. B. P. Miller, M. D. Callaghan, J. M. Cargille, J. K. Hollingsworth, R. B. Irvin, K. L. Karavanic, K. Kunchithapadam, and T. Newhall. *The Paradyn Parallel Performance Measurement Tools.* IEEE Computer 28, 11, November 1995.
2. Browne, Shirley, and Clay P. Breshears. *Usability Study of Portable Parallel Performance Tools.* http://www.hpcmo.hpc.mil/Htdocs/UGC/UGC98/papers/2c
3. C. Yan. *Performance Tuning with AIMS---An Automated Instrumentation and Monitoring System for Multicomputers.* Proceedings of the 27th Hawaii international Conference on Systems Sciences, ACM, Jan 1994.
4. Java 2 Platform, Enterprise Edition. J2EE. http://java.sun.com/j2ee/
5. Herrarte, V. and Lusk, E. (1991). *Studying parallel program behavior with Upshot.* Argonne National Laboratory - Technical Report ANL-91/15.
6. L. DeRose, Y. Zhang, and D. Reed. *SvPablo: A multi-language performance analysis system.* In Proceedings of 10th International Conference on Computer Performance Evaluation, September 1998.
7. Nagel W.E., Arnold A., Weber M., Hoppe H-C., and Solchenbach, K.:VAMPIR: *Visualization and Analysis of MPI Resources.* Supercomputer 63, Vol. 12, No. 1, 1996, pp. 69-80.
8. OpenMP. http://www.openmp.org
9. Parallel Virtual Machine (PVM). http://www.epm.ornl.gov/pvm
10. Riek, van Maurice, Bernard Tourancheau, Xavier-Francois Vigouroux. *Monitoring of Distributed Memory Multicomputer Programs.* Technical Report.
11. The Message Passing Interface (MPI) Forum. http://www.mpi-forum.org/
12. V. Pillet, J. Labuarta, J. Cortes, and S. Girona, *PARAVER: A Tool to visualize and Analyze Parallel Code,"* CEPBA#UPC Report RR-95#03, University of Politencia, Catalonia, 1995.
13. Automatic Performance Analysis: Real Tools (APART). http://www.fz-juelich.de/apart/
14. Hernandez, J. Michael, John L. Viescas. *SQL Queries for Mere Mortals: A Hands-On Guide to Data Manipulation in SQL.* Addison-Wesley Press, USA.

Evaluating the Performance of MPI-2 Dynamic Communicators and One-Sided Communication

Edgar Gabriel, Graham E. Fagg, and Jack J. Dongarra

Innovative Computing Laboratory, Computer Science Departement,
University of Tennessee, Suite 413, 1122 Volunteer Blvd.,
Knoxville, TN-37996, USA
{egabriel,fagg,dongarra}@cs.utk.edu

Abstract. This paper evaluates the performance of several MPI implementations regarding two chapters of the MPI-2 specification. First, we analyze, whether the performance using dynamically created communicators is comparable to the approach presented in MPI-1 using a static communicator for different MPI libraries. We than evaluate, whether the communication performance of one-sided communication on current machines, represents a benefit or a drawback to the end-user compared to the more conventional two-sided communication.

1 Introduction

The MPI-2 specification [3] extends the MPI-1 document [2] by three major chapters (dynamic process management, one-sided communication and parallel File-I/O), several minor ones and some corrections/clarifications for MPI-1 functions. Although it has been published since 1997, currently mainly the parallel File-I/O chapter has been accepted by the end-users. Clearly this is the reason, that despite of having many benchmarks for MPI-1 functionality [9–11], MPI-2 benchmarks have up to now just been developed for this area [4].

Assuming that the user really wants to use features of the MPI-2 specification, we would like to investigate in this paper, what the performance benefits and drawbacks of different features of MPI-2 are. Two questions are of specific interest in the context of this paper: first, do dynamically created communicators offer the same point-to-point performance on current implementations comparable to the static MPI_COMM_WORLD approach? And second, what is the achievable performance using one-sided operations compared to two-sided communication?

Since the number of available MPI implementations implementing some parts of the MPI-2 specification is meanwhile quite large, we would like to limit ourselves for the scope of this paper to analyze the performance and implementation of following libraries:

- **MPI/SX:** library version 6.7.2. Tests were executed on an NEC SX-5 consisting of 16 250 MHz processors with 32 GBytes of main memory.

- **Hitachi MPI:** library version 3.07. Tests were executed on a Hitachi SR8000 with 16 nodes, each having 8 250 MHz processors. Each node has 8 GBytes of main memory.
- **SUN MPI:** library version 6. Tests were executed on a SUN Fire 6800, with 24 750 MHz Sparc III processors, and 96 GBytes of main memory.
- **LAM MPI:** library version 6.5.9. Tests were executed on a cluster with 32 nodes, each having two 2.4 GHz Pentium 4 Xeon processors and 2 GBytes of memory. The nodes are connected by Gigabit Ethernet.

The library versions used in the tests are always the most recent versions available from the according vendors/implementors. We would like to emphasize at this point, that our intention is **not** to compare the numbers between the machines. Our goal is to compare the numbers achieved in the tests with the performance measured on the very same machine for the static MPI-1 scenario, and therefore comment on the quality of the implementation of the MPI-library.

2 Performance Results with Dynamic Communicators

The MPI-2 document gives the user three possibilities on how to create a new communicator that includes processes, which have not been part of the previous world-group:

1. Spawn additional processes using MPI_Comm_spawn/multiple
2. Connect two already running (parallel) applications using a socket-like interface, where one application connects using MPI_Comm_connect to another application, which calls MPI_Comm_accept.
3. Connect two already running application processes, which have already a socket connection established by using MPI_Comm_join.

The third method explicitly restricts itself to be used for socket communication. However, the goal of this paper is not to measure the socket performance on each machine, but we would like to measure the performance of methods, where the user might expect to get the same performance with a dynamically created communicator like with the static approach. Therefore, we are just considering the first two approaches in this paper.

The tests performed are a modification of a ping-pong benchmark, which has been adapted to work with variable communicator and partner arguments. The latter one is necessary, since in some of the cases we have to deal with intercommunicators, and therefore the rank of the communication partner might be different than in the static case using MPI_COMM_WORLD.

2.1 Results on the NEC SX-5

The first library which we would like to analyze regarding its performance and usability of this part of the MPI-2 specification, is the implementation of NEC. Starting an application which is using MPI_Comm_spawn, the user has to specify

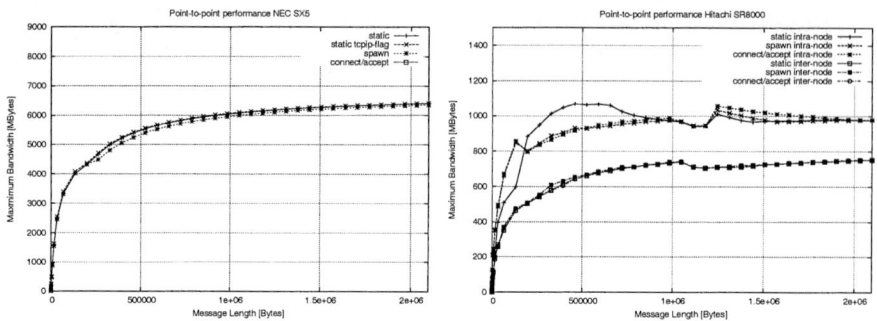

Fig. 1. Point to point performance on the SX-5 (left) and Hitachi SR8000 (right)

an additional parameter called `max_np`. For example, if the application is started originally with 4 processes and the user wants to spawn later on 4 more processes, the command line has to look like follows:

`mpirun -np 4 -max_np 8 ./<myapp>`

While this approach is explicitly allowed by the MPI-2 specification, it also clearly sets certain limits on the dynamic behavior of the application.

When using the connect/accept approach, the user has to set another flag for compiling and starting the application. The `tcpip` flag strongly indicates already, that the connect/accept model has been implemented in MPI/SX using TCP/IP. An interesting question regarding this flag is, whether communication in each of the independent, parallel applications is influenced by this flag, e.g. whether all communication is executed using TCP/IP, or whether just the communication between the two applications connected by the dynamically created inter-communicator is using TCP/IP.

Figure 1 shows on the left side the maximum bandwidth achieved with the different communicators. Obviously, the performance achieved with a communicator created by MPI_Comm_spawn is identical to the static approach. However, the line for the MPI_Comm_connect/accept approach is not visible, since the TCP/IP performance of the machine can not compete with the bandwidth achieved through the regular communication device.

At a first glance, the `tcpip` flag does not seem to have an affect on the maximum achievable bandwidth. However, our measurements showed, that the variance were somewhat higher than without the `tcpip` flag. The standard deviation from the average without the flag was usually below 1 %, while using the `tcpip` flag it was in the range of 5-10%. Therefore, the flag does have an influence on the performance of an application, even if it is not dramatic.

2.2 Results on the Hitachi SR8000

On the Hitachi SR8000 we conducted two sets for each experiment: all tests were executed using two processes on the same node, indicated in fig. 1 as intra-

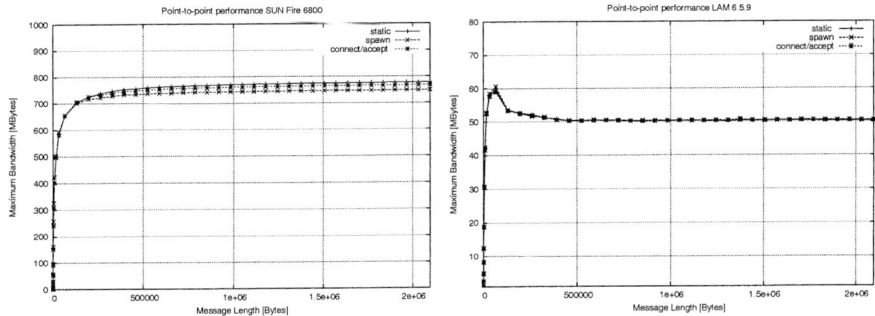

Fig. 2. Point to point performance on the SUN-Fire (left) and the with LAM (right)

node communication, and using two processes on different nodes, referred to as inter-node communication. As shown in the right section of fig. 1, for the intra-node tests as well as for the inter-node tests, the performance achieved with the MPI_Comm_spawn example and with the MPI_Comm_connect/accept example is comparable to the static approach.

2.3 Results on the SUN Fire 68000

The results achieved with SUN-MPI are presented in the left part of figure 2. To summarize these results and the experiences, no additional flags had to be used to make any of the examples work, and the performance achieved in all scenarios tested were always basically identical to the static MPI_COMM_WORLD scenario.

2.4 Results Using LAM 6.5.9

Using the most recent version of LAM, all three tests provided basically the same performance when connecting several processes on several nodes, (see right part of fig. 2).

We would like to comment on the behavior of LAM when using MPI_Comm_spawn. When booting the lam-hosts, the user has to specify in a hostfile the list of machines, which should be used for the parallel job. A LAM daemon is then started on each of these machines. The processes are started according to their order in the hostfile. When spawning new processes, it appears for the default configuration, the processes are started again using the first machine in the list. Optimally, the user would expect, that the first 'unused' machine (at least unused according to the job which spawns the processes) is chosen, to distribute the load appropriately. With the current scheme, it is probable that for compute intensive application by spawning additional processes on the machines which are running the MPI-job already, the overall job will be slowed down.

3 Performance of One-Sided Operations

The chapter about one-sided communication is supposed to be the most dramatic supplement to the MPI-1 specification, since it gives the user a completely new paradigm for exchanging data between processes. In contrary to the two-sided communication of MPI-1, a single processes can control the parameters for source and destination processes. However, since the goal was to design a portable interface for one-sided operations, the specification has become rather complex. It can be briefly summarized as follows:

- For moving data from the memory of one process to the memory of another processes, three operations are provided: MPI_Get, MPI_Put and MPI_Accumulate, the latter one combining the data of the processes in a similar fashion to MPI_Reduce.
- For the synchronization between the processes involved, three methods are provided: MPI_Win_fence, MPI_Win_start/post/wait/complete and MPI_Win_lock/unlock. The first two methods are called *active target synchronization*, since the destination processes is also involved in the operation. The last method is called *passive target synchronization*, since the destination process is not participating in any of the MPI-calls.

Another call from the MPI-2 document is of particular interest for the one-sided operation, namely the possibility to allocate some 'fast' memory using MPI_Alloc_mem [3]. On shared-memory architectures this might be for example a shared memory segment which can be directly accessed by a group of processes. Therefore, RMA operations and one-sided communication might be faster, if memory areas are involved, which have been allocated via this function.

3.1 Description of the Test Code

The ping-pong benchmark used in the last section has been further modified to work with one-sided operations. For this, we are creating first an access and exposure epoch on both processes and putting/getting data in/from the remote memory using a single MPI operation. After closing the access and exposure epoch on both processes and thus forcing all operations to finish, we create a second exposure and access epoch, transferring the data back. We are timing the overall execution time for both operations thus producing comparable results to the ping-pong benchmark.

For the passive target synchronization, we did not manage to create a reasonable version of this test. For measuring the achievable bandwidth using MPI_Win_lock/unlock, a streaming benchmark should be used instead. For producing comparable results (also with respect to the previous section), we omitted the passive target synchronization in the following tests and focused on communication methods using active target synchronization.

The MPI-2 specification gives the user many possibilities for optimizing the one-sided operations. For example, when creating a window object, the user has

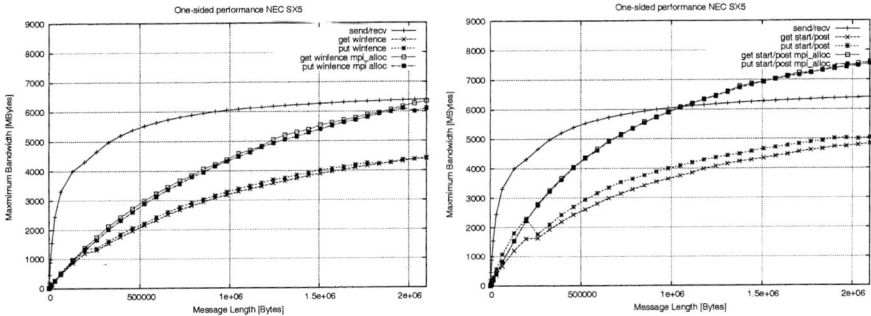

Fig. 3. Performance of one-sided operations using MPI_Win_fence (left) and MPI_Win_start/post for synchronization on the SX-5

to pass an MPI_Info object as an argument, where they can indicate, how the window is used in its application. Another optimization possibility is the assert argument in the synchronization routines. For our tests, we used the default values for both arguments, which are MPI_INFO_NULL and assert=0. An investigation of the effect of each of these parameters on different machines would be very interesting, but it would exceed the length-limit of this paper. Additionally, the usage of these arguments might optimize the communication performance on one platform, while being in the worst case a performance drawback on another one. Therefore, we expect most users to use just the default parameter settings.

3.2 Results on the NEC SX-5

The performance of one-sided operations with MPI/SX without using fast memory, is lower than regular point-to-point performance achieved by using MPI_Send and MPI_Recv. The user can still achieve the same maximum bandwidth with one-sided operations like in the MPI-1 scenario, however the message size has to reach up to 4 MBytes for achieving this bandwidth.

Using MPI_Alloc_mem to allocate the memory segments, which are then used in the one-sided operations, the user can improve the performance of one-sided operations for both, the winfence and the start/post test. While in the previous test without the usage of MPI_Alloc_mem, the start/post mechanism was achieving a slightly better performance than the winfence mechanism, with the 'fast' memory, the difference is increasing significantly. For messages larger than 1 MByte, it even outperforms the two-sided communication used as a reference.

3.3 Results on the Hitachi SR8000

The results for the Hitachi are shown in figure 4. Up to 1.5 MByte messages, the one-sided operations are partially more than 20 % slower than the two-sided communication. For messages exceeding this message size, the bandwidth achieved using one-sided operations is slowly converging towards the bandwidth

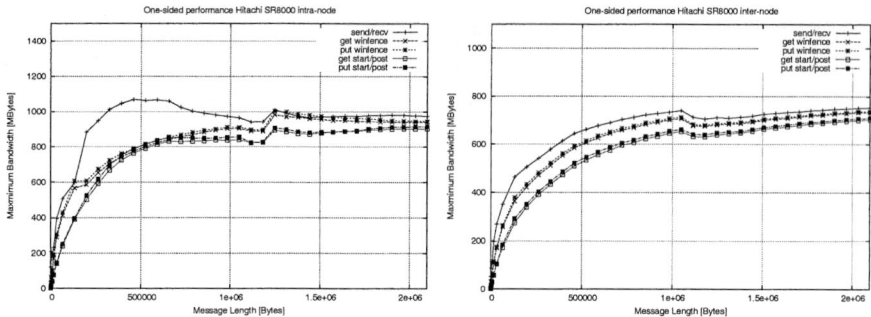

Fig. 4. Performance of one-sided operations for intra node (left) and inter-node communication on the Hitachi SR8000

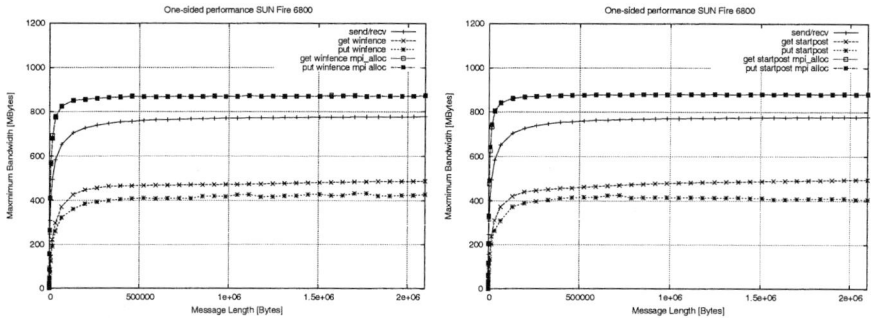

Fig. 5. Performance of one-sided operations using MPI_Win_fence (left) and MPI_Win_start/post for synchronization with SUN-MPI

of the send/recv test-case. There is also no real difference for the performance whether we are using MPI_Put or MPI_Get. However, the winfence test-case achieves usually a slightly better performance than the start/post mechanism.

The situation is similar for the inter-node case, the implementation of the test-suite using MPI_Win_fence for synchronization achieves a somewhat better performance than the test-case using MPI_Win_Start/ Post. For all tests, the usage of MPI_Alloc_mem did not show any effect on the performance.

3.4 Results on the SUN Fire 6800

The results achieved on with SUN-MPI are presented in figure 5. Two major effects can be observed: first, the usage of MPI_Alloc_mem has a huge influence on the performance achieved. In case where 'fast' memory is allocated using this function, the performance achieved with one-sided operations outperforms the point-to-point performance using send/recv operations. Without this routine however, the achievable bandwidth is roughly half of the bandwidth achieved for two-sided communication.

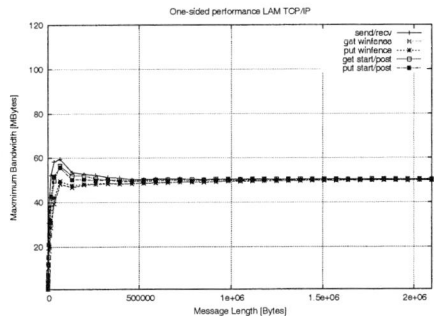

Fig. 6. Performance of one-sided operations for LAM 6.5.9

There is no real performance difference between the two synchronization mechanisms analyzed. However, if we are not allocating memory using the provided MPI-function, the performance using MPI_Get was always higher than the one achieved with MPI_Put.

3.5 Results Using LAM 6.5.9

The performance results achieved with LAM are presented in figure 6. For both communication drivers analyzed, the bandwidth achieved with one-sided communication is comparable to the send/recv tests. The only difference is, that the peak observed in both protocols between 32 and 64 Kilobyte messages, is somewhat lower.

3.6 Four-Byte Latency

While in the previous chapters we focused on the achievable bandwidth especially for large messages, we would like to summarize the results for small messages on all platforms by presenting the execution time for a data transfer of four bytes. Since we did not find any major differences in the performance between MPI_Put and MPI_Get, we present in this section just the results for MPI_Put. A minus in the table does not mean, that the function is not supported by the library, but it just indicates, that the usage of MPI_Alloc_mem did not have any influence on the performance. As shown in table 1, one-sided operations using active target synchronization have a much higher start-up overhead than two-sided communication. Only on SUN-MPI, when using memory allocated by MPI_Alloc_mem, the user can achieve a reasonable one-byte latency.

4 Summary

In this paper we presented our experiences and the performance of four MPI libraries, with respect to the handling of dynamically created communicators and

Table 1. Execution time for sending a 4-byte message using different communication methods

	Send/Recv	Win_fence	Win_fence + MPI_Alloc_mem	start/post	start/post + MPI_Alloc_mem
SX5	5.52	103.98	126.74	53.59	75.99
SR8K intra	11.21	64.95	-	182.93	-
SR8K inter	22.81	119.50	-	256.40	-
SUN	2.86	35.35	4.72	29.46	3.34
LAM	46.30	256.12	-	124.94	-

one-sided communication. The interpretation of the results presented are twofold: on one hand, we see a strong variance with respect to the performance of many MPI-2 functions, which can confuse the application developer and influence its decision whether to use MPI-2 functionality or not. On the other, the goal of MPI-libraries can not be to make everything 'equally slow', but to take advantage of as many optimization possibilities as possible. Additionally, one should not forget, that the library developers invested huge efforts for optimizing MPI-1 functionality, efforts, which might be invested in MPI-2 functions as soon as these sections are widely used.

While at the beginning of the 90s, a parallel application had to abstract the communication routines for supporting several communication libraries, it might now happen, that end-users have to do this again, if they want to make sure, that they are using the fastest possibility on each machine, even though all communication methods are provided by MPI.

Acknowledgements

The authors would like to thank the Innovative Computing Laboratory at the University of Tennessee, the High Performance Computing Center Stuttgart and the University of Ulm for providing their machines for the tests.

References

1. W. Gropp, E. Lusk, N. Doss, A. Skjellum: *A high-performance, portable implementation of the MPI message-passing interface standard*, Parallel Computing, 22 (1996).
2. Message Passing Interface Forum. *MPI: A Message-Passing Interface Standard (version 1.1)*. Technical report, June 1995. http://www.mpi-forum.org
3. Message Passing Interface Forum. *MPI-2: Extentions to the Message-Passing Interface* July 18, 1997.
4. Rolf Rabenseifner and Alice E. Koniges *Effective File-I/O Bandwidth Benchmark*, in A. Bode, T. Ludwig, R. Wissmueller (Eds.), 'Proceedings of the Euro-Par 2000', pp. 1273-1283, Springer, 2000.
5. Maciej Golebiewski and Jesper Larsson Traeff *MPI-2 One-Sided Communications in a Giganet SMP Cluster*, Yiannis Cotronis, Jack Dongarra (Eds.), 'Recent Advances in Parallel Virtual Machine and Message Passing Interface', pp. 16-23, Springer, 2001.

6. Glenn Luecke, Wei Hu *Evaluating the Performance of MPI-2 One-Sided Routines on a Cray SV-1*, technical report, December 21, 2002, http://www.public.iastete.edu/ grl/publications.html
7. S. Booth and E. Mourao *Single Sided MPI implementations for SUN MPI* in proceedings of Supercomputing 2000, Dallas, TX, USA.
8. Herrmann Mierendorff, Klaere Cassirer, and Helmut Schwamborn *Working with MPI Benchmark Suites on ccNUMA Architectures* in Jack Dongarra, Peter Kacsuk, Norbert Podhorszki (Eds.), 'Recent Advances in Parallel Virtual Machine and Message Passing Interface', pp. 18-26, Springer, 2000.
9. W. Gropp and E. Lusk *Reproducible measurements of MPI performance characteristics* in J.J. Dongarra, E.Luque and T. Margalef (Eds.), 'Recent advances in Parallel Virtual Vachine and Message Passing Interface', pp. 11-18, Springer, 1999.
10. R. H. Reussner, P. Sanders, L. Prechelt and M. Müller *SKaMPI: A Detailed Accurate MPI Benchmark*, in V. Alexandrov and J. J. Dongarra (Eds.), 'Recent advances in Parallel Virtual Vachine and Message Passing Interface', pp. 52-59, Springer, 1999.
11. R. Hempel *Basic message passing benchmarks, methodology and pitfalls* Presented at SPEC Workshop, Wuppertal, Germany, Sept. 1999.

Ring Algorithms on Heterogeneous Clusters with PVM: Performance Analysis and Modeling

Angelo Corana

IEIIT – National Research Council
Via De Marini 6, 16149 Genova, Italy
corana@ice.ge.cnr.it

Abstract. We analyze the performance obtainable on heterogeneous computing systems with data-parallel ring algorithms for the computation of long- and short-range interactions. The algorithms were originally developed for homogeneous parallel systems, where they yield a nearly linear speed-up. Two heterogeneous platforms are considered: a network of ALPHA Unix workstations and a network of Pentium PCs with Windows 2000. The parallel framework is PVM.
Our analysis shows that using a virtual ring of processes and assigning to each node a number of processes proportional to its relative speed, we greatly reduce load umbalancing and are able to achieve good performance even on highly heterogeneous systems. The analysis can be applied to similar problems.

1 Introduction

Heterogeneous parallel systems, like networks of workstations (NOW) and/or PCs, require, to fully exploit the available computational power, that the amount of computation varies among nodes according to node speed. Moreover, although interconnecting networks with a sufficiently large bandwidth are now commonly available, communication latency remains higher than the one of true parallel systems. So, the efficient porting to this kind of computing resources of parallel applications originally developed for homogeneous systems can be often not easy.

In this paper we deal with ring-based algorithms for the computation of long- and short-range interactions, which are perfectly balanced on homogeneous systems, thus providing nearly unitary efficiency. The straightforward porting of such algorithms on heterogeneous systems gives poor performance, since the slowest processor synchronizes the whole execution and the fastest ones have a high idle time. However, the use of a virtual ring of processes and the placement on each node of a number of processes proportional to its speed [3] is a simple and effective way to obtain good performance also on highly heterogeneous systems.

After the computational analysis of this approach, we present and compare some experimental results collected on two different heterogeneous platforms, namely a network of ALPHA workstations with Unix, and a cluster of PCs with Windows 2000. PVM is used as parallel framework.

The proposed problem is interesting both from an applicative and from a computational point of view. In particular, dealing with short-range interactions, we are able to change the computation to communication ratio of the algorithm simply by varying the neighbour size.

2 The Computational Problem

The basic algorithm (Alg. 1) solves the long-range interaction problem, in which a computation must be performed on all pairs of objects in a set; a modified version (Alg. 2), which uses a box-assisted approach with linked lists, computes short-range interactions, which involve only neighbouring pairs.

The general problem is exemplified considering the computation and histogramming of distances between points in a set. The algorithms have been originally developed for homogeneous systems, with one process per node, obtaining a nearly unitary efficiency in almost all situations [4].

2.1 Algorithm 1

Given a set X of N points in R^m, the basic algorithm processes all distinct pairs, with a cpu time per pair τ_o, measured on the reference node. The sequential execution time is therefore

$$T^{seq} = \frac{N \cdot (N-1)}{2} \cdot \tau_o \tag{1}$$

Let us consider now q processes arranged in a ring. Let us partition the set of points evenly into q subsets X_j, of size $N' = \frac{N}{q}$ and assign each subset to a process. The total number of distinct pairs is decomposed in the following way

$$\frac{N \cdot (N-1)}{2} = q \left(\frac{N' \cdot (N'-1)}{2} + \frac{q-1}{2} \cdot N'^2 \right) \tag{2}$$

The computation comprises two phases (Fig. 1). In phase one, which does not need communications, local pairs are processed. In the second phase, which consists of $L = \frac{q-1}{2}$ steps, local points of the generic process are moved forward along the ring in order to process pairs formed by local and visiting points.

We suppose that q is odd; otherwise a further phase is needed in which $q/2$ processes receive points from their opposite. In the end all the partial histograms are summed. It is easy to see that the fraction of total computation carried out in phases 1 and 2 is $1/q$ and $1 - 1/q$, respectively.

2.2 Algorithm 2

The same framework can be used for the computation of short-range interactions [6, 4], by adding auxiliary data structures for the fast search of neighbouring pairs, whose distance is less than a prefixed threshold ϵ, expressed a a fraction

$Proc_j$:
    compute distances in (X_j)
    for $l = 1, L$
        send data to next process
        receive data (X_r) from previous process
        compute distances in (X_r, X_j)
    endfor

Fig. 1. Process structure ($1 \leq j \leq q$).

of the diameter of the pointset. We use, in particular, the box-assisted approach described in [7, 4], in which an auxiliary m'-dimensional mesh of boxes, with $1/\epsilon$ boxes along each dimension, is used to build linked lists of points falling into the same m'-dim box. Usually $m' = 2$.

A detailed description of Alg. 2 can be found in [4]. Here, we only point out that: i) Alg. 2 needs more memory, owing to the additional data structures, but it has exactly the same communication pattern as Alg. 1; ii) the algorithm processes a fraction, which varies with ϵ, of total pairs with the same time per pair τ_o as the basic algorithm. Equivalently, to treat Alg. 1 and Alg. 2 in a uniform way, we can suppose that Alg. 2 processes all pairs with a time per pair $\tau_b(\epsilon) < \tau_o$. As ϵ decreases $\tau_b(\epsilon)$ decreases of several orders (see Table 2), and the computation to communication ratio worsens. It is equivalent to increase the CPU speed of all nodes by the same factor.

We assume that τ_b is the same for all subsets, i.e. the various subsets are statistically equivalent. In the following τ_x will denote generically τ_o or τ_b.

3 Implementation on Heterogeneous Systems

Let us consider a heterogeneous parallel system consisting of p nodes, connected by a switched communication network (e.g. Ethernet, Fast Ethernet, Gigabit Ethernet), with all links providing the same communication speed. Our analysis can be easily extended to mixed network.

Let be s_i the relative speed of node i with respect to a reference machine [2]. In this work we chose as reference node the lowest machine in each set. s_i depends both on the processor features and on the application under consideration, and can only be estimated in an approximate way.

Since we are mainly concerned on the impact of heterogeneity, we suppose that the system is dedicated. So, the total relative speed of the system

$$S = \sum_i s_i \qquad (3)$$

is the ideal speed-up.

The speed-up and the global efficiency are [2]:

$$SU = \frac{T^{seq}}{T^{par}} = \sum_i s_i \eta_i \qquad (4)$$

$$\eta = \frac{SU}{S} = \frac{\sum_i s_i \eta_i}{S} \tag{5}$$

where: T^{seq} and T^{par} are the execution time on the reference node and the parallel execution time on the heterogeneous system, respectively; η_i, $i = 1, \ldots, p$ are the node efficiencies.

3.1 Algorithm Analysis

Our application is split into a virtual ring of $q \geq p$ processes, with q_i (logically neighbouring) processes on the i-th node (Fig. 2).

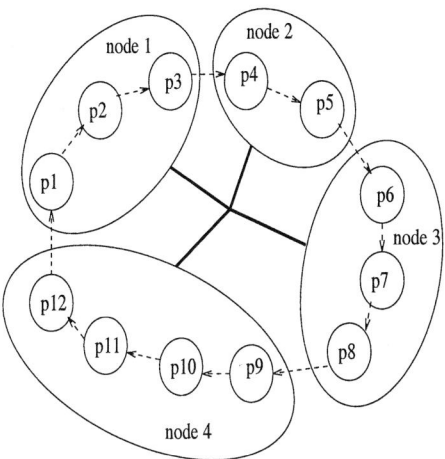

Fig. 2. Example with 12 processes and 4 nodes connected by a switched network.

The elapsed time on each node is the sum of computation time, context switching (cs) overhead, time needed for local activities involved with communications, and idle time (in general due to transmission time and umbalancing).

For each process, the cpu times spent in phase 1 and in each step of phase 2 are:

$$t_1^{cp} = \frac{N'(N'-1)}{2} \cdot \tau_x, \qquad t_2^{cp} = N'^2 \cdot \tau_x. \tag{6}$$

We assume that, for each step in phase 2, the transmission time over the network can be modeled as:

$$t_{tm} = \alpha + \beta \cdot M(N') \tag{7}$$

where α is the latency (average value over the NOW), β is the communication time per byte, and $M(N')$ is the number of bytes to be moved. Similarly, using suitable parameters $\alpha_0, \beta_0, \alpha_{pk}$ and β_{pk}, we can model the transmission time between two processes on the same node t_{tm}^0, and the time for packing/unpacking $t_{pk} = t_{upk}$ [9]. t_{tm}^0, t_{pk} and t_{upk} refer to the reference node.

Now we are able to express the elapsed time on the i-th node at the end of the local phase (t_i^1) and the elapsed time on the i-th node for the l-th step ($t_{i,l}$):

$$t_i^1 = q_i \frac{t_1^{cp}}{s_i} + t_i^{cs1} \qquad (8)$$

$$t_{i,l} = \frac{q_i}{s_i}(t_2^{cp} + t_{pk} + t_{upk}) + t_i^{cs2} + \frac{(q_i-1)}{s_i}t_{tm}^0 + t_{i,l}^{idle}$$

and the cumulative elapsed time $T_{i,l}$ on the i-th node at the end of the l-th step:

$$T_{i,0} = t_i^1 \qquad (9)$$
$$T_{i,l} = T_{i,l-1} + t_{i,l}, \quad l = 1, \ldots, L$$

t_i^{cs1} and t_i^{cs2} denote the time lost owing context switching on the i-th node in the local phase and in one step respectively.

$t_{i,l}^{idle}$ is related to umbalancing, and is computed at each step in the following way:

$$t_{i,l}^{idle} = \max(T_{i-1,l-1} + \frac{q_{i-1}}{s_{i-1}}(t_2^{cp} + t_{pk}) + \frac{(q_{i-1}-1)}{s_{i-1}}(t_{tm}^0 + t_{upk}) + t_{i-1}^{cs2} + t_{tm}$$
$$-T_{i,l-1} - \frac{q_i}{s_i}(t_2^{cp} + t_{pk}) - \frac{(q_i-1)}{s_i}(t_{tm}^0 + t_{upk}) - t_i^{cs2}, \ 0 \ ) \qquad (10)$$

The parallel execution time is therefore

$$T^{par} = \max_i T_{i,L} \qquad (11)$$

This formulation allows us to implement a computer simulator, whose accuracy depends on the number of overhead sources we consider. At a first approximation we can neglect the overheads due to the local communication activities (t_{pk}, t_{upk} and t_{tm}^0) and to context switching.

Considering the cpu times at the three levels (step l on node i, node i, whole system) and the corresponding elapsed times, we can obtain [2] the efficiencies $\eta_{i,l}, \eta_i$ and η. The system wide efficiency is related to the node-level quantities by eq. (5).

The system umbalancing at the step level can be defined as

$$U_s = \sum_i (t_2^{cp}(q_{i_o}/s_{i_o} - q_i/s_i)) \qquad (12)$$

where i_o denotes the node with the highest cpu time ($q_{i_o}/s_{i_o} = \max_i(q_i/s_i)$). For a given heterogeneous system and given the total number of processes q, the optimal allocation of processes is the one that minimizes U_s. This allocation can be found following the procedure described in [1], based on a dynamic programming approach, or, in a simpler but sub-optimal way, setting $q_i \simeq \frac{s_i}{S}q$, $i = 1, \ldots, p$, and approximating fractional results to the nearest integer. As q increases the umbalancing oscillates with a decreasing trend.

Table 1. Configurations C1 and C2, that include nodes up to the current row; s_i is the relative speed of component nodes, S the total computing power, H and h express the degree of heterogeneity.

Config. Id.	Node	Memory Size (MB)	s_i	S	H	h
-	ALPHA 200 4/233 (233 MHz)	192	1.00	-	-	-
-	ALPHA au 433 (433 MHz)	192	2.47	-	-	-
C1	ALPHA au 500 (500 MHz)	192	2.95	6.42	0.83	0.53
-	ALPHA 250 4/266 (266 MHz)	128	1.23	-	-	-
C2	ALPHA 667 (667 MHz)	256	6.40	14.05	1.94	0.64

Table 2. Values of τ_o and $\tau_b(\epsilon)$ (in μs) measured on the reference nodes for various ϵ values.

	ALPHA 233 MHz		PIII 600 MHz	
ϵ	τ_o	$\tau_b(\epsilon)$	τ_o	$\tau_b(\epsilon)$
1	6.20	6.99	2.05	2.34
0.1	-	0.308	-	0.1046
0.01	-	0.0187	-	0.00644
0.001	-	0.00154	-	0.00045

4 Experimental Results

The proposed approach is tested on two different heterogeneous clusters. We consider different problem sizes and, for Algorithm 2, various ϵ values. Points in R^m are obtained from the Henon attractor [4]; we choose $m = 20$ and $m' = 2$. The trials are executed on dedicated nodes and with a low traffic on the network. We start with one process per node and increase the total number of processes, allocated with the optimal strategy, until a suitable value q_{max}.

4.1 ALPHA NOW with Unix

The first platform is a Network of Workstations (NOW) composed of five Compaq ALPHA workstations connected by a switched Ethernet ($\alpha = 1\ ms$, $\beta \simeq 1\ \mu s/byte$), with PVM v. 3.4.3 and Fortran77 v.4.0. Table 1 describes the two configurations, with 3 and 5 nodes respectively, used for the trials.

The degree of heterogeneity is expressed by the standard deviation of speeds $H = (\sum_i (s_i - \bar{s})^2/p)^{1/2}$, and by $h = 1 - s_0/\bar{s}$, where $\bar{s}$ is the average relative speed and s_0 denotes the lowest relative speed in the NOW ($0 \leq h < 1$).

The measured values of the time per pair on the reference node (ALPHA 233 MHz) are reported in Table 2.

Table 3 reports, for each trial and for each configuration, the sequential execution time on the reference node, the performance obtained with the naive

Table 3. Execution time (in seconds) and measured (η) and simulated (η_s) efficiencies (naive porting and best performance) obtained with the two algorithms on C1 and C2; - in the ϵ field denotes Algorithm 1.

				C1				C2		
N	ϵ	T_{seq}	q	T	η	η_s	q	T	η	η_s
42 000	-	5448	3	2024	0.42	0.47	5	1114	0.35	0.36
”	-		75	884	0.96	0.96	75	407	0.95	0.96
”	0.1	272	3	94.2	0.45	0.47	5	57.7	0.34	0.36
”	”		75	40.1	1.06	0.95	21	20.5	0.94	0.90
”	0.01	16.5	3	6.13	0.42	0.46	5	4.29	0.27	0.35
”	”		15	2.56	1.00	0.90	15	1.67	0.70	0.82
210 000	0.1	7131	3	2667	0.42	0.46	5	1457	0.35	0.36
”	”		125	1015	1.09	0.97	125	496	1.02	0.97
”	0.01	424	3	164	0.40	0.47	5	101	0.30	0.35
”	”		75	65.0	1.02	0.93	21	33.3	0.91	0.89
”	0.001	35.3	3	12.6	0.43	0.45	5	7.70	0.32	0.34
”	”		7	5.57	0.99	0.83	15	3.80	0.66	0.78
420 000	0.1	29950	-	-	-	-	5	7854	0.27	0.35
”	”		-	-	-	-	125	1966	1.08	0.97
”	0.01	1699	3	686	0.39	0.47	5	420	0.29	0.36
”	”		75	269	0.98	0.95	75	129	0.94	0.94
”	0.001	141	3	48.8	0.45	0.46	5	29.3	0.34	0.35
”	”		15	20.6	1.07	0.90	15	10.6	0.94	0.82

porting, and the best performance. For comparison also the global simulated efficiency (η_s) is reported. In this case $q_{max} = 125$.

4.2 PC Cluster with Windows 2000

The second heterogeneous platform is a commodity cluster composed of seven Pentium PCs connected by a switched Fast-Ethernet with PVM v. 3.4.3 for Windows [5] and Compaq Visual Fortran v.6.6. The nodes are Pentium III and Pentium IV with clock from 600 MHz up to 2.8 GHz, with different memory sizes and speeds. Table 4 describes the two configurations, with 3 and 7 nodes respectively, used for the trials. Table 2 reports the values of the time per pair measured on the reference node (PIII 600 MHz).

The PC cluster is more powerful than the ALPHA NOW, but has a lower degree of heterogeneity (see H and h values in Tables 1 and 4). The communication bandwidth is higher (Fast-Ethernet vs. Ethernet), but the communication latency is also higher. From some communication trials that we performed on this platform, it results that communications are limited by the various software overheads at the OS and PVM levels ($\alpha \simeq 5\ ms$, $\beta \simeq 0.3\ \mu s/byte$). Moreover,

Table 4. Configurations C3 and C4, that include nodes up to the current row; s_i is the relative speed of component nodes, S the total computing power, H and h express the degree of heterogeneity.

Config. Id.	Node	Memory Size (MB)	s_i	S	H	h
-	PIII 600 MHz	128	1.00	-	-	-
-	PIV 1.8 GHz	256	1.79	-	-	-
C3	PIV 2.8 GHz	512	2.90	5.69	0.78	0.46
-	PIII 866 MHz	256	1.44	-	-	-
-	PIII 1.3 GHz	256	1.84	-	-	-
-	PIV 1.7 GHz	256	1.71	-	0.59	0.47
C4	PIV 2.4 GHz	256	2.48	13.16		

intra-processor communications are not significantly faster than inter-processor communications [8].

The results of the trials, carried out with $q_{max} = 35$ for configuration C3, and $q_{max} = 105$ for configuration C4, are reported in Table 5.

4.3 Analysis of Results

The trials confirm that the efficiency with the naive porting (a single process per node) is poor, especially for the most heterogeneous configurations. For both platforms, η increases steeply with q and remains nearly unitary for a large range of q values; over this range, performance starts to fall since a better balancing is paid with less efficient communications and more overhead in managing processes. Performance slightly worsens if the computation to communications ratio decreases (i.e. for a given N, ϵ decreases), and the best performance is obtained with a smaller mumber of processes. Fig. 3 shows a typical pattern of the measured global efficiency as a function of q for the four configurations.

Only when the total computational work is very small, η does not reach the unit value and decreases quite rapidly for $q > 30 - 40$, especially on the PC cluster, which pays in these cases for its higher communication latency.

The trials confirm that the context switching overhead is in most cases negligible, for both platforms.

Simulated efficiencies are in most cases in very good agreement with the experimental ones. On both platforms, the most relevant source of error is probably the variation of speeds with the amount of local data. On the PC cluster, performance modeling is a little more difficult, since timing measurements show a larger variance among trials.

Our simulations and trials show that the range of q values for which the optimal performance is nearly maximum is usually $2q_0 \leq q \leq 5q_0$ for the ALPHA NOW and $2q_0 \leq q \leq 3q_0$ for the PC cluster. The parameter q_0, defined as $q_0 = \sum_i \text{nint}(s_i/s_0)$ where nint is the nearest integer operator and $s_0 = \min_i s_i$, is related to the degree of heterogeneity of the cluster. For a more precise evaluation

Table 5. Execution time (in seconds) and measured (η) and simulated (η_s) efficiencies (naive porting and best performance) obtained with the two algorithms on C3 and C4; - in the ϵ field denotes Algorithm 1.

				C3				C4		
N	ϵ	T_{seq}	q	T	η	η_s	q	T	η	η_s
42 000	-	1800	3	603	0.52	0.53	7	257	0.53	0.53
"	-		35	344	0.92	0.99	105	152	0.90	0.95
"	0.1	92.3	3	31.3	0.52	0.53	7	13.4	0.52	0.53
"	"		25	16.1	1.01	0.95	21	7.48	0.94	0.89
"	0.01	5.68	3	1.90	0.53	0.52	7	0.83	0.52	0.52
"	"		7	1.23	0.81	0.85	7	0.83	0.52	0.52
210 000	0.1	2490	3	799	0.55	0.53	7	335	0.56	0.53
"	"		25	388	1.13	0.98	105	175	1.08	0.95
"	0.01	149	3	49.0	0.53	0.53	7	20.8	0.54	0.53
"	"		15	25.5	1.03	0.93	21	11.7	0.97	0.89
"	0.001	10.2	3	3.47	0.52	0.51	7	1.95	0.40	0.52
"	"		7	2.34	0.77	0.82	15	1.34	0.58	0.67
420 000	0.1	10146	3	3704	0.48	0.53	7	1387	0.56	0.53
"	"		25	1545	1.15	0.98	105	709	1.09	0.97
"	0.01	595	3	209	0.50	0.53	7	83.7	0.54	0.53
"	"		25	98	1.07	0.97	35	44.7	1.01	0.92
"	0.001	41.6	3	14.1	0.52	0.52	7	6.07	0.52	0.52
"	"		15	8.82	0.83	0.86	15	4.23	0.75	0.75

we can include the simulator in the parallel application, in order to automatically find at run-time a suitable q value.

5 Conclusions

We considered the problem of the efficient porting of ring algorithms, originally developed for homogeneous parallel systems, to heterogeneous platforms. The general problem is exemplified considering the computation of long- and short-range interactions. The use of a virtual ring of processes, with a number of processes much greater than the number of nodes, and with a number of processes in each node matching the node speed, allows the attainment of good performance, also on highly heterogeneous systems. The analysis is quite general and can be applied to other ring algorithms.

Two kinds of heterogeneous systems have been considered: a network of ALPHA workstations connected by switched Ethernet with Unix OS, and a cluster of PCs connected by switched Fast-Ethernet with Windows 2000 OS. Both platforms perform very well, fully exploiting the available computing power in almost all trials.

The PC cluster, more powerful and with a higher communication latency, is slightly less efficient when the granularity of the computation is very small.

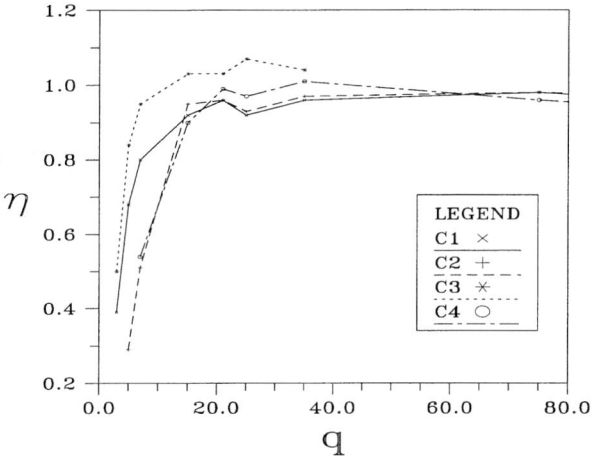

Fig. 3. Measured global efficiency vs. the total number of processes q, for the four configurations; $N = 420\,000$; $\epsilon = 0.01$.

Nevertheless, our trials show that a commodity PC cluster with Windows 2000 and PVM is a viable platform for the fast and cost-effective execution of large ring-based applications.

References

1. P. Boulet, J. Dongarra, Y. Robert, F. Vivien: Static tiling for heterogeneous computing platforms. Parallel Computing 25 (1999) 547-568.
2. A. Clematis, A. Corana: Porting regular applications on heterogeneous workstation networks: performance analysis and modeling. Parallel Algorithms and Applications 17 (2002) 205-226.
3. A. Clematis, G. Dodero, V. Gianuzzi: Efficient use of parallel libraries on heterogeneous networks of workstations. J. Systems Architecture 46 (2000) 641-653.
4. A. Corana: Parallel computation of the correlation dimension from a time series. Parallel Computing 25 (1999) 639-666.
5. M. Fischer, J. Dongarra: Experiences with Windows 95/NT as a cluster computing platform for parallel computing. J. Parallel and Distributed Computing Practices 2 2 (1999).
6. G.C. Fox, M.A. Johnson, G.A. Lyzenga, S.W. Otto, J.K. Salmon, D.W. Walker: Solving Problems on Concurrent Processors, Vol. 1. Prentice-Hall, Englewood Cliffs, NJ (1988).
7. P. Grassberger: An optimized box-assisted algorithm for fractal dimensions. Phys. Lett. A 148 (1990) 63-68.
8. J.K. Hollingsworth, E. Guven, C. Akinlar: Benchmarking a network of PCs running parallel applications, Proc. IEEE Int. Performance, Computing and Communications Conference, IEEE (1998) 1-7.
9. B.K. Schmidt, V.S. Sunderam: Empirical analysis of overheads in cluster environments. Concurrency: Practice and Experience 6 (1994) 1-32.

An MPI Tool to Measure Application Sensitivity to Variation in Communication Parameters

Edgar A. León[1], Arthur B. Maccabe[1], and Ron Brightwell[2]

[1] Computer Science Department, The University of New Mexico,
Albuquerque, NM 87131-1386
{leon,maccabe}@cs.unm.edu
[2] Scalable Computing Systems, Sandia National Laboratories,
Albuquerque, NM 87185-1110
bright@cs.sandia.gov

Abstract. This work describes an apparatus which can be used to vary communication performance parameters for MPI applications, and provides a tool to analyze the impact of communication performance on parallel applications. Our tool is based on Myrinet (along with GM). We use an extension of the LogP model to allow greater flexibility in determining the parameter(s) to which parallel applications may be sensitive. We show that individual communication parameters can be independently controlled within a small percentage error. We also present the results of using our tool on a suite of parallel benchmarks.

1 Introduction

Parallel architectures are driven by the needs of applications. Message-passing developers and parallel architecture designers often face optimization decisions that present trade-offs which affect the end performance of applications. A better understanding of the communication requirements of these applications is needed. To this end, we have created an apparatus which allows the alteration of communication parameters to measure their effects on application performance. This apparatus identifies the communication parameters to which an application is sensitive. Our apparatus is based on Myrinet along with the GM message-passing system. The communication parameters used are based on the LogP model [1] and have been instrumented into GM so we can vary communication performance. MPI applications can be analyzed through a port of MPICH on top of GM.

The remainder of this paper is organized as follows. Section 2 provides a brief overview of GM and the communication parameters used in this work. Section 3 describes the instrumentation and validation of our tool. Section 4 provides results of applying our tool to a collection of parallel benchmarks. Section 5 concludes with a discussion of related work and conclusions.

2 Background

GM is a low-level message-passing system created by Myricom as a communication layer for its Myrinet network. GM is comprised of a kernel driver, a user library, and a program that runs on the Myrinet network interface, called MCP (Myrinet Control Program). GM provides reliable, in order delivery of messages.

To characterize communication performance of a parallel system, we use an extension of the LogP model [1]. This model is characterized by four parameters: (L) latency, the time to transmit a small message from processor to processor; (o) overhead, the time the host processor is involved in message transmissions and receptions and cannot do any other work; (g) gap, the time between consecutive message transmissions and receptions (the reciprocal of g corresponds to the available per-node bandwidth); and (P) the number of nodes in the system. Considering that the send and receive operations are often not symmetric, the overhead and gap have been further separated into four parameters: o_s and o_r, the send and receive overhead; and g_s and g_r, the send and receive gap. This further separation provides a more detailed characterization of which communication parameters have a significant impact on applications. We also consider the gap per byte (Gap) to distinguish between short and long messages.

3 Instrumentation and Validation

To vary communication performance, we have modified GM to allow the alteration of communication parameters [2]. To empirically validate and calibrate our tool, we varied each communication parameter over a fixed-range of values while leaving the remaining parameters unmodified. Using a micro-benchmark [3], we measure the value of the parameters and verify that the average error difference (Err) between the desired value of the varied parameter and the measured value is small. We also verify that the remaining parameters remain fairly constant with low standard deviation (Std).

The results presented here were gathered using single-processor nodes on a Myrinet network. Each node has a 400 MHz Intel Pentium II processor with 512 MB of main memory and a Myrinet LANai 7.2 network interface card with 2 MB of memory. GM version 1.2.3 and a Linux 2.2.14 kernel were used.

Table 1 shows the results of varying o_s and g_s for 8 byte messages. The *Measured values* columns represent the values of the communication parameters measured using the micro-benchmark. As expected, the added overhead in Table 1.A is not independent of the gap (g). To keep the latency (L_1) constant when varying the gap (Table 1.B), we use only one ping-pong trial in the computation of the round-trip-time (RTT_1), as opposed to one-hundred as in Table 1.A (RTT). Since just one trial is considered, the value of the latency, L_1, is greater than L due to *warm-up issues*. The remaining communication parameters also show low error difference and low standard deviation on unmodified parameters [2].

4 Results

To test our tool on real applications, we measure the effects of varying the communication parameters on a collection of parallel benchmarks. This effect is quantified by measuring the running time slowdown of applications due to changing communication parameters. The variation in communication parameters is done by increasing each

Table 1. Varying o_s and g_s for 8 byte messages. All units are given in μs.

Table 1.A

%Err	Goal	o_s	o_r	g	RTT	L
	0.00	1.34	4.33	23.92	48.82	18.73
0.14	21.34	21.31	3.82	31.22	88.72	19.21
3.39	41.34	42.74	3.07	51.29	128.48	18.41
0.42	61.34	61.60	4.09	71.21	169.05	18.83
0.00	81.34	81.34	4.34	91.26	212.04	20.32
0.01	101.34	101.35	4.18	111.24	252.01	20.46
0.13	121.34	121.18	4.63	131.14	290.76	19.55
Avg 0.61			4.16			19.50
Std 1.05			0.39			0.82

Table 1.B

%Err	Goal	g	o_s	o_r	RTT_1	L_1
	0	23.91	1.36	4.33	125.07	56.84
	20	27.70	1.35	4.33	125.06	56.84
1.95	40	40.78	1.38	4.28	125.06	56.86
0.52	60	60.31	1.52	4.15	124.06	56.35
0.23	80	80.18	1.39	4.27	125.05	56.85
0.29	100	100.29	1.41	4.27	125.06	56.85
0.15	120	120.18	1.37	4.37	125.06	56.78
Avg 1.52			1.40	4.27	124.98	56.80
Std 3.31			0.05	0.06	0.63	0.31

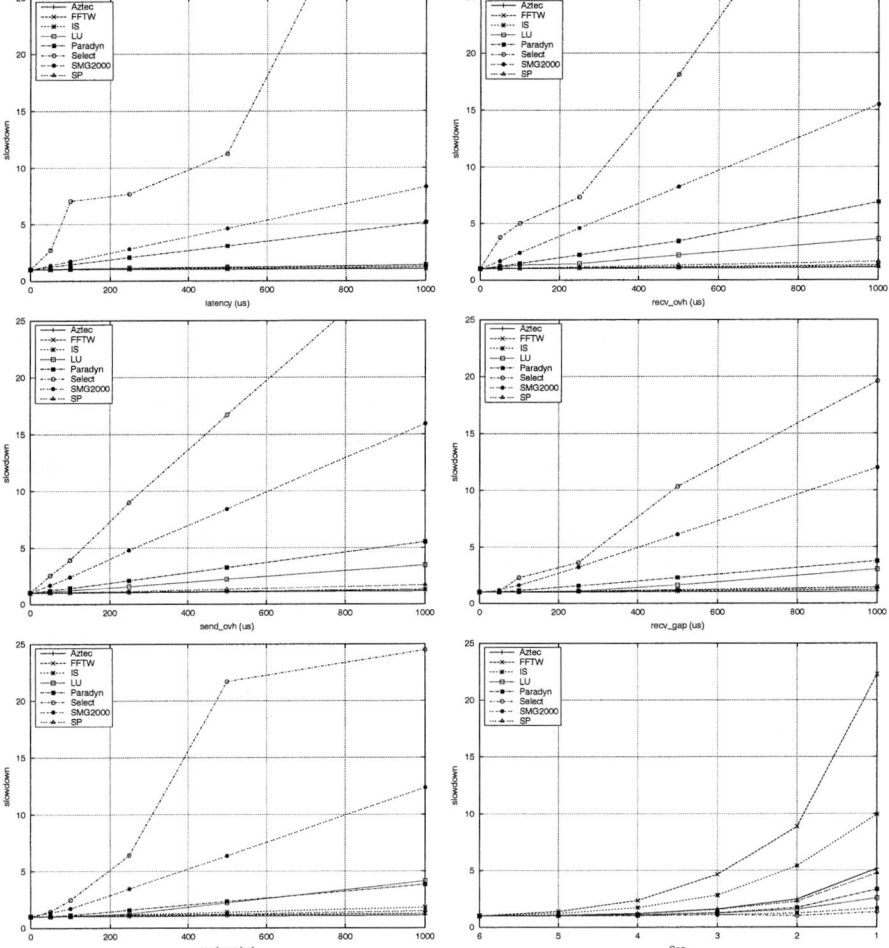

Fig. 1. Sensitivity to communication parameters. These set of figures plot the run time slowdown of applications vs. the communication parameters. The Gap is given by i, where 2^i represents the available bandwidth of the system.

parameter independently of the others. The results were gathered using 16 computational nodes with MPICH-GM version 1.2.1..7b. Our collection of benchmarks consists of eight applications: *FFTW* (Fast Fourier Transform) and *Select* (Selection problem); *Aztec*, *ParaDyn* and *SMG2000* from the ASCI Purple set of benchmarks; and *IS*, *LU* and *SP* from NPB2. These applications represent a variety of (a) degree of exploitable concurrency, (b) computation to communication ratio and (c) frequency and granularity of inter-processor communications.

Figure 1 shows the graphs of application sensitivity to variation in communication parameters. We found that the applications used in this work have no significant difference between sensitivity to send parameters (overhead and gap) and receive parameters due to the symmetry of their communication patterns. Also, overhead has a more significant impact on applications than the other communication parameters. With the exception of Select, applications are fairly insensitive to latency. Bandwidth or Gap per byte has been identified as a significant parameter to application performance due to the current trend of programmers to cluster small messages together into one message, reducing a significant amount of communication overhead and taking advantage of the increasing communication bandwidth.

5 Related Work and Conclusions

Martin and others studied the impact of LogGP communication parameters on parallel applications [4]. The applications used were written in Split-C on top of Generic Active Messages. They found the host overhead to be critical to application performance. Our work, in contrast, uses GM as the communication layer and focuses on applications written in MPI. Although the applications used in our work differ from those used by Martin, the results are similar. Applications were fairly insensitive to latency and sensitive to overhead.

We have created an apparatus to vary communication performance, based on the LogP model, on high-performance computational clusters. This tool is useful to designers of parallel architectures and message-passing developers to answer the question: What do applications really need? It can also be useful to parallel application developers and users to identify sources of performance degradation of an application on parallel architectures.

References

1. Culler, D., Karp, R., Patterson, D., Sahay, A., Schauser, K.E., Santos, E., Subramonian, R., von Eicken, T.: LogP: Towards a realistic model of parallel computation. In: Proceedings of the 4th ACM SIGPLAN PPoPP, San Diego, CA (1993) 262–273
2. León, E.A., Maccabe, A.B., Brightwell, R.: Instrumenting LogP parameters in GM: Implementation and validation. In: Workshop on HSLN, Tampa, FL (2002)
3. Culler, D.E., Liu, L.T., Martin, R.P., Yoshikawa, C.O.: Assessing fast network interfaces. IEEE Micro **16** (1996) 35–43
4. Martin, R.P., Vahdat, A.M., Culler, D.E., Anderson, T.E.: Effects of communication latency, overhead, and bandwidth in a cluster architecture. In: Proceedings of the 24th ISCA, Denver, CO (1997) 85–97

Measuring MPI Latency Variance

Rolf Riesen[1], Ron Brightwell[1], and Arthur B. Maccabe[2]

[1] Sandia National Laboratories*
Albuquerque, NM 87185-1110
{rolf,rbbrigh}@sandia.gov
[2] University of New Mexico
Albuquerque, NM 87131-1386
maccabe@cs.unm.edu

Abstract. Point to point latency and bandwidth measurements are often the first benchmarks run on a new machine or MPI implementation. In this paper we show that the common way of measuring latency hides valuable information about the transmission time characteristics. We introduce a simple benchmark to measure transmission time variance and report on the results from a variety of systems.

1 Introduction

Point to point latency and bandwidth measurements are often the first benchmarks run on a new machine or MPI implementation. Most people would agree that these two measurements give only a small indication of the scalability and overall performance of a complete parallel system. Martin et al. have shown in [4] that communication overhead, that is the time a CPU spends processing messages rather than running user code, is worse for an application than a higher latency. Nevertheless, latency measurements continue to be given a high importance.

Latency is defined as the time it takes for a zero-length MPI message to leave user space on one node, traverse the communication stack and the network link, and arrive in user space on the receiving node. Usually this is measured with a simple ping-pong program that sends n MPI messages back and forth and measures how long that takes. The total time is then divided by $2n$ to get the average time one message took to travel from one node to the other.

Figure 1 shows a graph where we have carried out this experiment on a variety of systems and operating modes. We have repeated the above ping-pong test 150 times and plotted the measured average latency for each run. The value of n was 200 for each of the 150 runs. We will give more details about the machines we ran on and the systems software we used in Section 2.

The ping-pong tests are usually run with a high number of iterations n for two reasons. On some systems the timing clock resolution is not fine grained enough. Repeatedly sending the zero-length message back and forth lets enough time pass for the timer function to return a meaningful result. The second reason is that the tests become more repeatable this way because a larger sample is used for the calculation of the average.

---

* Sandia is a multiprogram laboratory operated by Sandia Corporation, a Lockheed Martin Company, for the United States Department of Energy under contract DE-AC04-94AL85000.

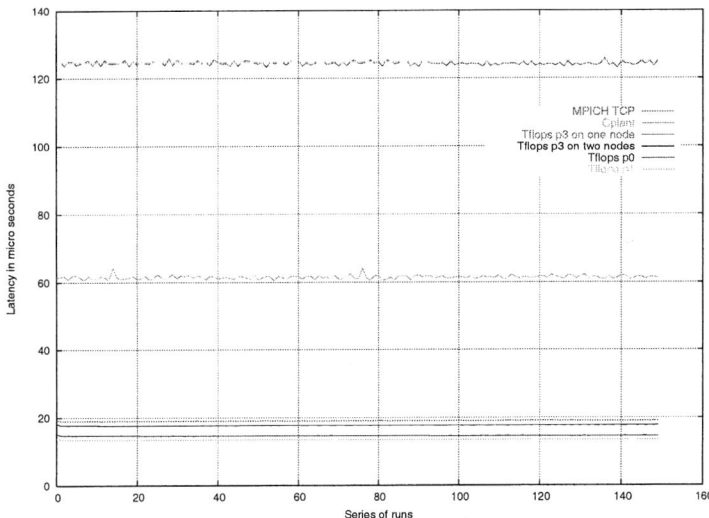

Fig. 1. Repeated Latency Measurements: A standard ping-pong test repeated 150 times.

From experience we suspected that that the practice of reporting average latency over many, many iterations is hiding information about the underlying MPI implementation and the system it is running on. In this paper we describe our attempt to peek below the standard ping-pong latency test and reveal what we have found.

2 Test Environment

We used two different parallel machines and several operating modes to carry out our experiments. The first system is a computational plant, or Cplant for short. The second system is Sandia's ASCI Red teraflop system.

2.1 Cplant

The Cplant [2] system at Sandia National Laboratories uses commercial off-the-shelf (COTS) components to build a massively parallel computer that can run scientific applications. We carried out our tests on the production system named Ross. Ross has about 1800 Compaq DS10 units which employ Alpha EV6 (21264) CPUs at 466 MHz. The nodes are connected by a Myrinet network with LANai 9 network interface cards (NICs). During the execution of these experiments, Ross was running the Cplant system software Release 2.0 using a version 2.2.21 Linux kernel.

For the data labeled *Cplant* we ran our test programs on two compute nodes that used the MPICH 1.2.0 library running over the Portals [1] message passing layer of Cplant. For the data labeled *MPICH/TCP* we ran between two service (login) nodes using MPICH 1.2.5 with the P4 device. Note that these use the slightly different XP1000 workstations and slower LANai 7 Myrinet NICs.

2.2 ASCI Red

ASCI Red [6] is a supercomputer comprised of more than 4500 dual-processor nodes connected by a high-performance custom network fabric. Each compute node has two 333 MHz Pentium II Xeon processors each with 256 MB of main memory, for a total of more than 9000 processors and more than a terabyte of distributed main memory.

Each compute node has a network interface that resides on the memory bus and allows for low-latency access to all of physical memory on a node. Each node is connected to a 3-d mesh network which provides a 400 MB/s uni-directional wormhole-routed connection between ASCI Red nodes. This interface appears essentially as two FIFOs on the system bus; one for transmitting and one for receiving.

The compute nodes of ASCI Red run Cougar, a variant of the Puma lightweight kernel that was designed and developed by Sandia and the University of New Mexico for maximizing both message passing throughput and application resource availability [5]. In Cougar, all of the resources on a compute node are managed by the *system processor*. This is the only processor that performs any significant processing in supervisor mode. The other processor runs application code and only rarely enters supervisor mode. This processor is called the *user processor*.

Cougar, just like Cplant, uses the Portals message passing interface. However, this is an older version of Portals which differs significantly from the version used in Cplant.

Cougar is not a traditional symmetric multi-processing operating system. Instead, Cougar supports four different modes [3] that allow different distributions of application processes on the two processors of each node. The following provides an overview of each of these processor modes.

The simplest processor usage mode, labeled *Tflops p0* in our data, is to run both the kernel and application process on the system processor. In this mode, the kernel runs only when responding to network events or in response to a system call from the application process.

In the second mode, message co-processor mode, the kernel runs on the system processor and the application process runs on the user processor. We label it *Tflops p1* in our graphs. When the processors are configured in this mode, the kernel runs continuously waiting to process events from external devices or service system call requests from the application process. Because the time to transition from user mode to supervisor mode and back can be significant, this mode offers the advantage of reduced network latency and faster system call response time.

In the third mode, known as virtual node mode and labeled as *Tflops p3*, the system processor runs both the kernel and an application process, while the second processor also runs the kernel and a full separate application process. This mode essentially allows a compute node to be split by the runtime system into two independent compute nodes. Since the two CPUs share the system bus and the NIC in this configuration, we also ran p3 mode tests on two nodes utilizing only one processor on each node. Since the second processor on each node is still active, it slows down our application and makes this different from p0 mode.

There is a fourth mode of operation (p2) which we are not using for this study, since it does not affect message passing performance.

3 Measuring Latency Variance

Ideally, we would like to measure the exact latency of a single zero-length message. This cannot usually be done because timer resolutions are not fine grained enough, and the clocks of the two nodes are not synchronized.

The results of the standard ping-pong test in Figure 1 tell us what the average latency is. In order to evaluate the variations in latency from one run to the next, we do not need to measure the actual latency, just the difference to the previous run. As long as the clocks on both nodes run at the same rate (within the short duration of the test), we will be able to measure differences in the time a message takes to be transmitted and received.

In order to measure the latency variation from one message to the next, we created a micro benchmark which works as follows. In a warm-up phase, the two nodes exchange w zero-length messages. This is necessary to get both nodes' caches warmed up and get the two programs ready.

Then, node 0 reads its timer and sends another zero-length message to node 1. We call this clock value t_s. When node 1 receives that message, it reads its own timer and sends that value (t_r) back to node 0. Node 0 now subtracts t_r from t_s. Since the clocks are not synchronized with each other, this simply gives us a value of the difference between the two clocks plus the time it took to transmit the message. We assume the difference between the two clocks does not vary during the short time the benchmark runs. Therefore, any variation we measure from one run to the next, is due to variations in the transmission time.

4 Results

We have run the micro benchmark described in the previous section on all six machine configurations available to us. We exchanged 10 warm-up messages and repeated the benchmark in a loop of 5000 iterations. We subtracted the minimum value measured for each configuration and counted the number of occurrences of each measurement. This gives us an indication of how far spread out the measured transmission times are.

For Cplant we found that the measurements are evenly spread out over a range of about 80 μs. Although this measurement does not tell us the actual latency, it does tell us that any given transmission time can be as far as 80 μs off from the minimum possible. For MPICH/TCP most of the message transmission times are within 10 μs of the minimum. However, there are a significant number of measurements are as far out as 417 μs for Cplant and 15669 μs for MPICH/TCP.

The spread of ASCI Red messages is within about 1 μs of the minimum measured. In other words, message transmission time is much more predictable in the ASCI Red system than the systems running Linux.

Another way to look at the data produced by our micro benchmark is to compare the relative latency measurement of one run with the one from the previous run. This shows us how erratic transmission time can be. We count how often transmission time has moved a given distance in μs. We found that Cplant's repeatability was within ± 10 μs; i.e. even though we measured latencies for Cplant as far apart as 80 μs from each other, it was most likely that two messages following each other were within 10 μs. For MPICH/TCP repeatability was within $\pm$ 20 μs for most messages, but a significant number were $\pm$ 40 μs and even further out. Tflops p0 and p3 (on one node) modes were within $\pm$ 0.5 μs, while p1 and p3 (on two nodes) modes were within $\pm$ 1 μs.

Comparing these results to the average ping-pong latency shown in Figure 1 reveals that a lot of information is hidden by averaging message latencies. The spread of message transmission times and the repeatability are a measure of quality of an MPI implementation and the underlying system. Having a high repeatability and a low message transmission time spread is important for optimizing collective operations and real-time systems. For example, Robert Van de Geijn [7] uses knowledge of transmission times to optimize global combine operations. If transmission times vary widely or are unknown, sophisticated optimizations cannot be done.

5 Summary

In this paper, we have shown that standard ping-pong latency measurements hide information about the true transmission times of short messages. The results of a simple micro benchmark we have written reveal that message transmission times on some systems vary widely. This can severely impact optimizations of global operations and other algorithms where knowledge of transmission times and repeatability are important.

References

1. Ron Brightwell, Tramm Hudson, Rolf Riesen, and Arthur B. Maccabe. The Portals 3.0 message passing interface. Technical report SAND99-2959, Sandia National Laboratories, 1999.
2. David S. Greenberg, Ron Brightwell, Lee Ann Fisk, Arthur B. Maccabe, and Rolf Riesen. A system software architecture for high-end computing. In *SC'97: High Performance Networking and Computing: Proceedings of the 1997 ACM/IEEE SC97 Conference: November 15–21, 1997, San Jose, California, USA.*, Raleigh, N.C., November 1997. ACM Press and IEEE Computer Society Press.
3. Arthur B. Maccabe, Rolf Riesen, and David W. van Dresser. Dynamic Processor Modes in Puma. *Bulletin of the Technical Committee on Operating Systems and Application Environments (TCOS)*, 8(2):4–12, 1996.
4. Richard P. Martin, Amin M. Vahdat, David E. Culler, and Thomas E. Anderson. Effects of communication latency, overhead, and bandwidth in a cluster architecture. In *Proceedings of the 24th Annual International Symposium on Computer Architecture (ISCA'97)*, volume 25,2 of *Computer Architecture News*, pages 85–97, New York, June 2–4 1997. ACM Press.
5. Lance Shuler, Chu Jong, Rolf Riesen, David van Dresser, Arthur B. Maccabe, Lee Ann Fisk, and T. Mack Stallcup. The Puma Operating System for Massively Parallel Computers. In *Proceeding of the 1995 Intel Supercomputer User's Group Conference*. Intel Supercomputer User's Group, 1995.
6. Stephen R. Wheat Timothy G. Mattson, David Scott. A TeraFLOPS Supercomputer in 1996: The ASCI TFLOP System. In *Proceedings of the 1996 International Parallel Processing Symposium*, 1996.
7. R. A. Van de Geijn. On global combine operations. *Journal of Parallel and Distributed Computing*, 22(2):324–328, August 1994.

CGM*graph*/CGM*lib*: Implementing and Testing CGM Graph Algorithms on PC Clusters

Albert Chan and Frank Dehne

School of Computer Science, Carleton University, Ottawa, Canada
http://www.scs.carleton.ca/~achan
http://www.dehne.net

Abstract. In this paper, we present CGM*graph*, the first integrated library of parallel graph methods for PC clusters based on CGM algorithms. CGM*graph* implements parallel methods for various graph problems. Our implementations of deterministic list ranking, Euler tour, connected components, spanning forest, and bipartite graph detection are, to our knowledge, the first efficient implementations for PC clusters. Our library also includes CGM*lib*, a library of basic CGM tools such as sorting, prefix sum, one to all broadcast, all to one gather, h-Relation, all to all broadcast, array balancing, and CGM partitioning. Both libraries are available for download at http://cgm.dehne.net.

1 Introduction

Parallel graph algorithms have been extensively studied in the literature (see e.g. [15] for a survey). However, most of the published parallel graph algorithms have traditionally been designed for the theoretical PRAM model. Following some previous experimental results for the MASPAR and Cray [14, 6, 18, 17, 11], parallel graph algorithms for more "PC cluster like" parallel models like the BSP [19] and CGM [7, 8] have been presented in [12, 1–4, 9, 10]. In this paper, we present CGM*graph*, the first integrated library of CGM methods for various graph problems including list ranking, Euler tour, connected components, spanning forest, and bipartite graph detection. Our library also includes a library CGM*lib* of basic CGM tools that are necessary for parallel graph methods as well as many other CGM algorithms: sorting, prefix sum, one to all broadcast, all to one gather, h-Relation, all to all broadcast, array balancing, and CGM partitioning. In comparison with [12], CGM*graph* implements both a randomized as well as a deterministic list ranking method. Our experimental results for randomized list ranking are similar to the ones reported in [12]. Our implementations of deterministic list ranking, Euler tour, connected components, spanning forest, and bipartite graph detection are, to our knowledge, the first efficient implementations for PC clusters. Both libraries are available for download at http://cgm.dehne.net. We demonstrate the performance of our methods on two different cluster architectures: a gigabit connected high performance PC cluster and a network of workstations. Our experiments show that our library

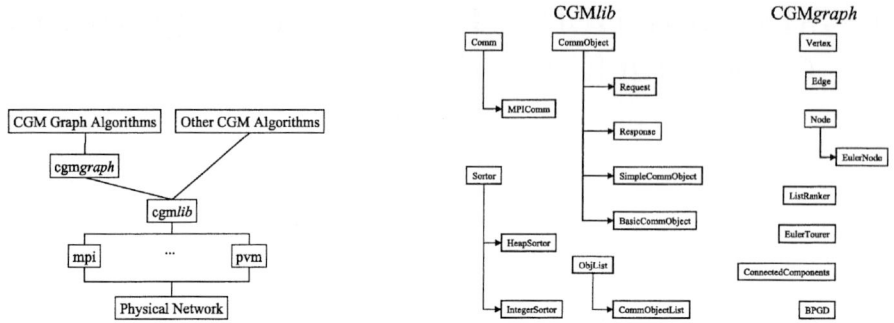

Fig. 1. Overview of CGM*lib* and CGM*graph*.

provides good parallel speedup and scalability on both platforms. The communication overhead is, in most cases, small and does not grow significantly with an increasing number of processors. This is a very important feature of CGM algorithms which makes them very efficient in practice.

2 Library Overview and Experimental Setup

Figure 1 illustrates the general use of CGM*lib* and CGM*graph* as well as the class hierarchy of the main classes. Note that all classes in CGM*graph*, except EulerNode, are independent. Both libraries require an underlying communication library such as MPI or PVM. CGM*lib* provides a class Comm which interfaces with the underlying communication library. It provides an interface for all communication operations used by CGM*lib* and CGM*graph* and thereby hides the details of the communication library from the user.

The performance of our library was evaluated on two parallel platforms: *THOG*, and *ULTRA*. The *THOG* cluster consists of $p = 64$ nodes, each with two Xeon processors. The nodes are of two different generations, with processors at 1.7 or 2.0GHz, 1.0 or 1.5GB RAM, and 60GB disk storage. The nodes are interconnected via a Cisco 6509 switch using Gigabit ethernet. The operating system is Linux Red Hat 7.1 together with LAM-MPI version 6.5.6. The *ULTRA* platform is a network of workstations consisting of $p = 10$ Sun Sparc Ultra 10. The processor speed is 440MHz. Each processor has 256MB RAM. The nodes are interconnected via 100Mb Switched Fast Ethernet. The operating system is Sun OS 5.7 and LAM-MPI version 6.3.2.

All times reported in the remainder of this paper are wall clock times in seconds. Each data point in the diagrams represents the average of three experiments (on different random test data of the same size) for CGM*graph* and ten experiments for CGM*lib*. The input data sets for our tests consisted of randomly created test data. For inputs consisting of lists or graphs, we generated random lists or graphs as follows. For random linked lists, we first created an arbitrary linked list and then permuted it over the processors via random permutations. For random graphs, we created a set of nodes and then added random edges. Unfortunately, different test data sizes had to be chosen for the different platforms because of the smaller memory capacity of *ULTRA*.

3 CGM*lib*: Basic Infrastructure and Utilities

3.1 CGM Communication Operations

The basic library, called CGM*lib*, provides basic functionality for CGM communication. An interface, Comm, defines the basic communication operations such as

- oneToAllBCast(int source, CommObjectList &data): Broadcast the list data from processor number source to all processors.
- allToOneGather(int target, CommObjectList &data): Gather the lists data from all processors to processor number target.
- hRelation(CommObjectList &data, int *ns): Perform an h-Relation on the lists data using the integer array ns to indicate for each processor which list objects are to be sent to which processor.
- allToAllBCast(CommObjectList &data): Every processor broadcasts its list data to all other processors.
- arrayBalancing(CommObjectList &data, int expectedN=-1): Shift the list elements between the lists data such that every processor contains the same number of elements.
- partitionCGM(int groupId): Partition the CGM into groups indicated by groupId. All subsequent communication operations, such as the ones listed above, operate within the respective processor's group only.
- unPartitionCGM(): Undo the previous partition operation.

All communication operations in CGM*lib* send and receive lists of type Comm ObjectList. A Comm ObjectList is a list of CommObject elements. The Comm Object interface defines the operations which every object that is to be sent or received has to support.

3.2 CGM Utilities

- Parallel Prefix Sum:
  calculatePrefixSum (CommObjectList &result, CommObjectList) &data).
- Parallel Sorting: sort(CommObjectList &data) using the deterministic parallel sample sort methods in [5] and [16].
- Request System for exchanging data requests between processors: The CGM*lib* provides methods sendRequests(...) and sendResponses(...) for routing the requests from their senders to their destinations and returning the responses to the senders, respectively.
- Other CGM Utilities: A class CGMTimers (with six timers measureing computation time, communication time, and total time, both in wall clock time and CPU ticks) and other utilities including a parallel random number generator.

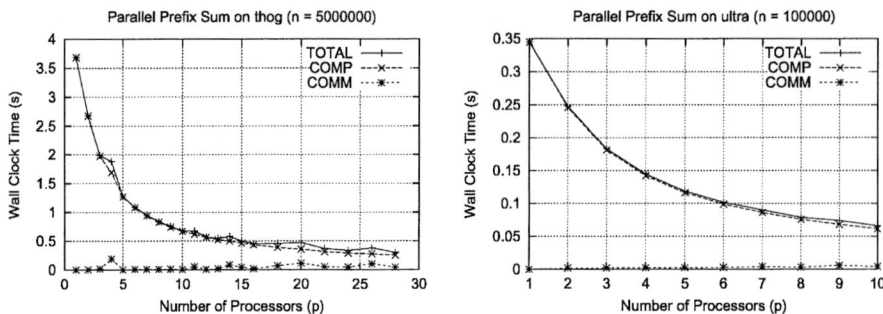

Fig. 2. Performance of our prefix sum implementation on *THOG* and *ULTRA*.

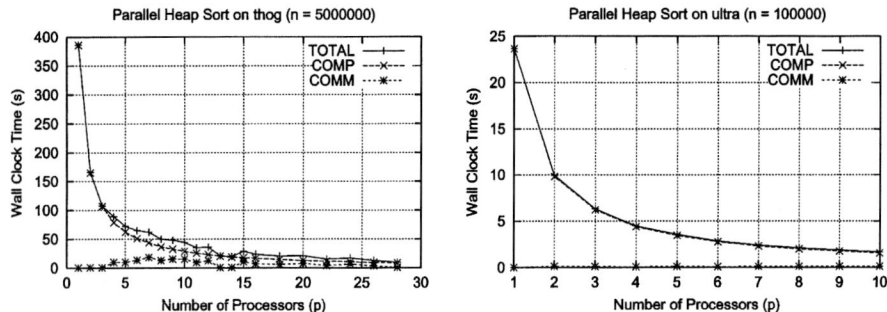

Fig. 3. Performance of our parallel sort implementation on *THOG* and *ULTRA*.

3.3 Performance Evaluation

Figure 2 shows the performance of our prefix sum implementation, and Figure 3 shows the performance of our parallel sort implementation. For our prefix sum implementation, we observe that all experiments show a close to zero communication time, except for some noise on *THOG*. The prefix sum method communicates only very few data items. The total wall clock time and computation time curves in all four diagrams are similar to $1/p$. For our parallel sort implementation, we observe a small fixed communication time, essentially independent of p. This is easily explained by the fact that the parallel sort uses of a fixed number of h-Relation operations, independent of p. Most of the total wall clock time is spent on local computation which consists mainly of local sorts of n/p data. Therefore, the curves for the local computation and the total parallel wall clock time are similar to $1/p$.

4 CGM*graph*: Parallel Graph Algorithms Utilizing the CGM Model

CGM*graph* provides a list ranking method `rankTheList(ObjList<Node> &nodes, ...)` which implements a randomized method as well as a deterministic method [15, 9]. The input to the list ranking method is a linear linked

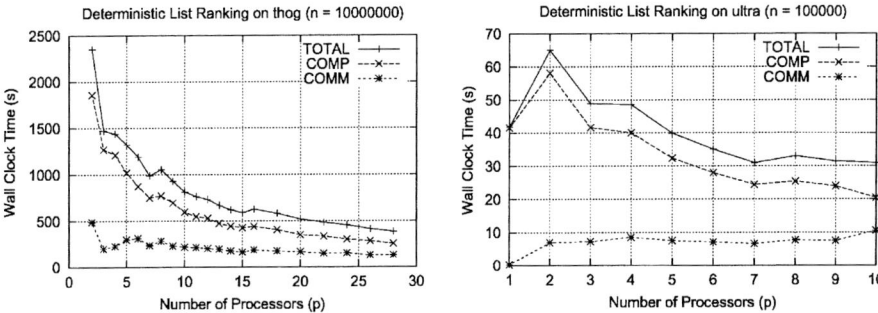

Fig. 4. Performance of the deterministic list ranking algorithm on *THOG* and *ULTRA*.

list where Tthe pointer is stored as the index of the next node. CGM*graph* also provides a method getEulerTour(ObjList <Vertex> &r, ...) for Euler tour traversal of a forest [9]. The forest is represented by a list of vertices, a list of edges and a list of roots. The input to the Euler tour method is a forest which is stored as follows: r is a set of vertices that represents the roots of the trees, v is the input set of vertices, e is the input set of edges, and eulerNodes is the output data of the method. We implemented the connected component method described in [9]. The method also provides immediately a spanning forest of the given graph. CGM*graph* provides a method findConnectedComponents(Graph &g, Comm *comm) for connected component computation and a method findSpanningForest(Graph &g, ...) for the calculation of the spanning forest of a graph. The input to the above two methods is a graph represented as a list of vertices and a list of edges. We also implemented the bipartite graph detection algorithm described in [3]. CGM*graph* provides a method isBipartiteGraph(Graph &g, Comm *comm) for detecting whether a graph is a bipartite graph. As in the case of connected component and spanning forest, the input is a graph represented as a list of vertices and a list of edges.

4.1 Performance Evaluation

In the following, we present the results of our experiment. For each operation, we measured the performance on *THOG* with $n = 10,000,000$ and on *ULTRA* with $n = 100,000$.

Figure 4 shows the performance of the deterministic list ranking algorithm. Again, we observe that for both machines, the communication time is a small, essentially fixed, portion of the total time. The deterministic list ranking requires between $c \log p$ and $2c \log p$ h-Relation operations. With $\log p$ in the range $[1,5]$, we expect between c and $10c$ h-Relation operations. Since the deterministic algorithm is more involved and incurs larger constants, c may be around 10 which would imply a range of $[10, 100]$ for the number of h-Relation operations. We measured usually around 20 h-Relation operations. The number is fairly stable, independent of p, which shows again that $\log p$ has little influence on the measured communication time. The small increases for $p = 4, 8, 16$ are due

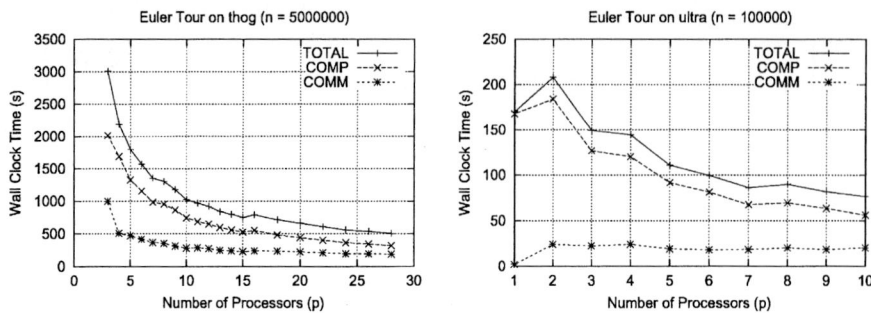

Fig. 5. Performance of the Euler tour algorithm on *THOG* and *ULTRA*.

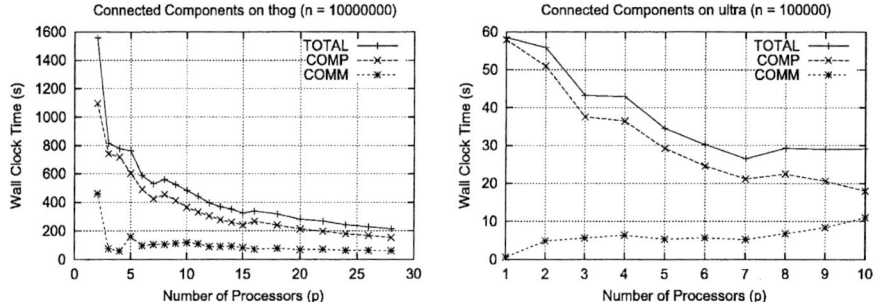

Fig. 6. Performance of the connected components algorithm on *THOG* and *ULTRA*.

to the fact that that the number of h-Relation operations grows with $\lfloor \log p \rfloor$, which gets incremented by 1 when p reaches a power of 2. In summary, since the communication time is only a small fixed value and the computation time is dominating and similar to $1/p$, the entire measured wall clock time is similar to $1/p$. Figure 5 shows the performance of the Euler tour algorithm on *THOG* and *ULTRA*. Our implementation uses the deterministic list ranking method for the Euler tour computation. Not surprisingly, the performance is essentially the same as for deterministic list ranking. Due to the fact that all tree edges need to be duplicated, the data size increases by a factor of three (original plus two copies). This is the reason why we could execute the Euler tour method on *THOG* for $n = 10,000,000$ only with $p \geq 10$.

Figure 6 shows the performance of the connected components algorithm on *THOG* and *ULTRA*. Figure 7 shows the performance of the spanning forest algorithm on *THOG*, and *ULTRA*. The only difference between the two methods is that the spanning forest algorithm has to create the spanning forests after the connected components have been identified. Therefore, the times shown in Figures 6 and 7 are very similar. Again, we observe that for both machines, the communication time is a small, essentially fixed, portion of the total time. The connected component method uses deterministic list ranking. It requires $c \log p$ h-Relation operations with $\log p$ in the range $[1,5]$. The communication time observed is fairly stable, independent of p, which shows that the $\log p$ factor has

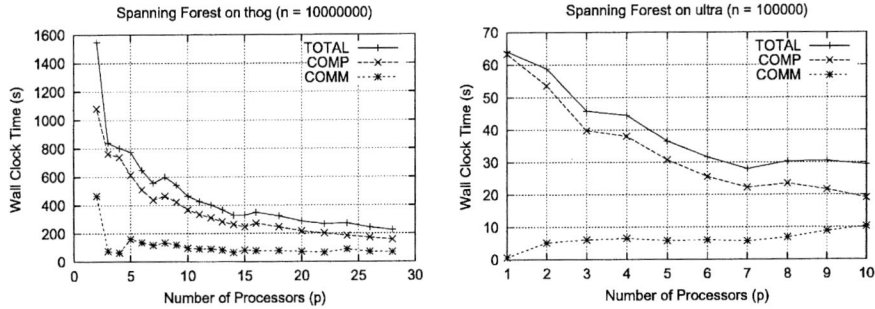

Fig. 7. Performance of the spanning forest algorithm on *THOG* and *ULTRA*.

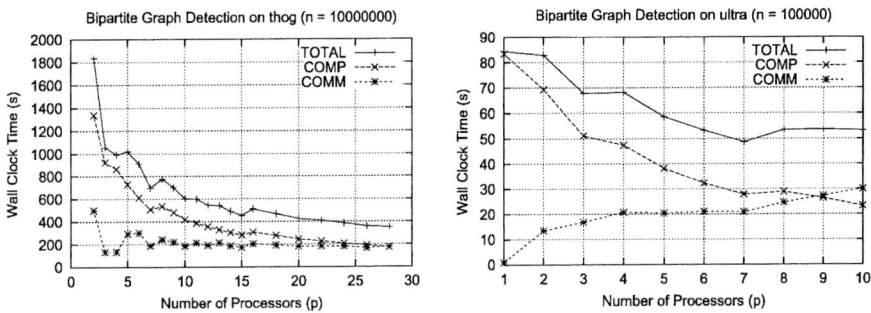

Fig. 8. Performance of the bipartite graph detection algorithm on *THOG* and *ULTRA*.

little influence on the measured communication time. The entire measured wall clock time is dominated by the computation time and similar to $1/p$.

Figure 8 shows the performance of the bipartite graph detection algorithm on *THOG*, and *ULTRA*. The results mirror the fact that the algorithm is essentially a combination of Euler tour traversal and spanning forest computation. The curves are similar to the former but the amount of communication time is now larger, representing the sum of the two. This effect is particularly strong on *ULTRA* which has the weakest network. Here, the $\log p$ in the number of communication rounds actually leads to a steadily increasing communication time which, for $p = 9$ starts to dominate the computation time. However, for *THOG* and *CGM1*, the effect is much smaller. For these machines, the communication time is still essentially fixed over the entire range of values of p. The computation time is similar to $1/p$ and determines the shape of the curves for the entire wall clock time. The computation and communication times become equal for larger p but only because of the decrease in computation time.

5 Future Work

Both, CGM*lib* and CGM*graph* are currently in beta state. Despite extensive work on performance tuning, there are still many possibilities for fine-tuning the code in order to obtain further improved performance. Of course, adding more parallel graph algorithm implementations to CGM*graph* is an important task for the near future. Other possible extensions include porting CGM*lib* and CGM*graph* to other communication libraries, e.g. PVM and OpenMP. We also plan to integrate CGM*lib* and CGM*graph* with other libraries, in particular the LEDA library [13].

References

1. P. Bose, A. Chan, F. Dehne, and M. Latzel. Coarse Grained Parallel Maximum Matching in Convex Bipartite Graphs. In *13th International Parallel Processing Symposium (IPPS'99)*, pages 125–129, 1999.
2. E. Cacere, A. Chan, F. Dehne, and G. Prencipe. Coarse Grained Parallel Algorithms for Detecting Convex Bipartite Graphs. In *26th Workshop on Graph-Theoretic Concepts in Computer Science (WG 2000)*, volume 1928 of *Lecture Notes in Computer Science*, pages 83–94. Springer, 2000.
3. E. Caceres, A. Chan, F. Dehne, and G. Prencipe. Coarse Grained Parallel Algorithms for Detecting Convex Bipartite Graphs. In *26th Workshop on Graph-Theoretic Concepts in Computer Science (WG 2000)*, volume 1928 of *Springer Lecture Notes in Computer Science*, pages 83–94, 2000.
4. E. Caceres, A. Chan, F. Dehne, and S. W. Song. Coarse Grained Parallel Graph Planarity Testing. In *International Conference on Parallel and Distributed Processing Techniques and Applications (PDPTA 2000)*. CSREA Press, 2000.
5. A. Chan and F. Dehne. A Note on Coarse Grained Parallel Integer Sorting. *Parallel Processing Letters*, 9(4):533–538., 1999.
6. S. Dascal and U. Vishkin. Experiments with List Ranking on Explicit Multi-Threaded (XMT) Instruction Parallelism. In *3rd Workshop on Algorithms Engineering (WAE-99)*, volume 1668 of *Lecture Notes in Computer Science*, page 43 ff, 1999.
7. F. Dehne. Guest Editor's Introduction, Special Issue on Coarse Grained Parallel Algorithms. *Algorithmica*, 24(3/4):173–176, 1999.
8. F. Dehne, A. Fabri, and A. Rau-Chaplin. Scalable Parallel Geometric Algorithms for Coarse Grained Multicomputers. In *ACM Symposium on Computational Geometry*, pages 298–307, 1993.
9. F. Dehne, A. Ferreira, E. Caceres, S. W. Song, and A. Roncato. Efficient Parallel Graph Algorithms for Coarse Grained Multicomputers and BSP. *Algorithmica*, 33(2):183–200, 2002.
10. F. Dehne and S. W. Song. Randomized Parallel List Ranking for Distributed Memory Multiprocessors. In *Asian Computer Science Conference (ASIAN '96)*, volume 1179 of *Lecture Notes in Computer Science*, pages 1–10. Springer, 1996.
11. T. Hsu, V. Ramachandran, and N. Dean. Parallel Implementation of Algorithms for Finding Connected Components in Graphs. In *AMS/DIMACS Parallel Implementation Challenge Workshop III*, 1997.
12. Isabelle Gurin Lassous, Jens Gustedt, and Michel Morvan. Feasability, Portability, Predictability and Efficiency : Four Ambitious Goals for the Design and Implementation of Parallel Coarse Grained Graph Algorithms. Technical Report RR-3885, INRIA, http://www.inria.fr/rrrt/rr-3885.html.
13. LEDA library. http://www.algorithmic-solutions.com/.
14. Margaret Reid-Miller. List Ranking and List Scan on the Cray C-90. In *ACM Symposium on Parallel Algorithms and Architectures*, pages 104–113, 1994.

15. J. Reif, editor. *Synthesis of Parallel Algorithms*. Morgan and Kaufmatin Publishers, 1993.
16. H. Shi and J. Schaeffer. Parallel Sorting by Regular Sampling. *Journal of Parallel and Distributed Computing*, 14:361–372, 1992.
17. Jop F. Sibeyn. List Ranking on Meshes. *Acta Informatica*, 35(7):543–566, 1998.
18. Jop F. Sibeyn, Frank Guillaume, and Tillmann Seidel. Practical Parallel List Ranking. *Journal of Parallel and Distributed Computing*, 56(2):156–180, 1999.
19. L. Valiant. A Bridging Model for Parallel Computation. *Communications of the ACM*, 33(8), 1990.

Efficient Parallel Implementation of Transitive Closure of Digraphs*

C.E.R. Alves[1], E.N. Cáceres[2], A.A. Castro Jr[3],
S.W. Song[4], and J.L. Szwarcfiter[5]

[1] Universidade São Judas Tadeu, São Paulo, Brazil
prof.carlos_r_alves@usjt.br
http://www.usjt.br/
[2] Universidade Federal de Mato Grosso do Sul, Campo Grande, Brazil
edson@dct.ufms.br
http://www.dct.ufms.br/~edson
[3] Universidade Católica Dom Bosco, Campo Grande, Brazil
amaury@ec.ucdb.br
http://www.ucdb.br/docentes/amaury
[4] Universidade de São Paulo, São Paulo, Brazil
song@ime.usp.br
http://www.ime.usp.br/~song
[5] Universidade Federal do Rio de Janeiro, Rio de Janeiro, Brazil
jayme@nce.ufrj.br
http://www.dcc.ufrj.br/docentes/szwarcfiter.html

Abstract. Based on a CGM/BSP parallel algorithm for computing the transitive closure of an acyclic directed graph (digraph), we present a modified version that works for any digraph and show very promising implementation results. The original CGM/BSP algorithm for acyclic digraphs uses a linear extension labeling of the vertices. With this labeling, the original algorithm can be shown to require $\log p + 1$ communication rounds, where p is the number of processors. The modified CGM/BSP algorithm works for any digraph and does not use the linear extension labeling. In theory the modified version no longer guarantees the $O(\log p)$ bound on the number of communication rounds, as shown by an artificially elaborated example that requires more than $\log p + 1$ communication rounds. In practice, however, all the graphs tested use at most $\log p + 1$ communication rounds. The implementation results are very promising and show the efficiency and scalability of the proposed modified algorithm, and compare favorably with other parallel implementations.

1 Introduction

The search for efficient algorithms to compute the *transitive closure* of a directed graph (*digraph*) has been around for many years. It was first considered in 1959

---

* Partially supported by FINEP-PRONEX-SAI Proc. No. 76.97.1022.00, FAPESP Proc. No. 1997/10982-0, CNPq Proc. No. 52.3778/96-1, 55.2028/02-9, and FAPERJ.

by B. Roy [13]. Since then a variety of sequential algorithms to solve this problem have been proposed [1, 14, 17]. Most of the sequential solutions are based on the adjacency Boolean matrix of the digraph or use the adjacency matrix in more directed terms as a problem representation.

Parallel algorithms for this problem have been proposed on the PRAM model [7, 9], on arrays and trees and meshes of trees [8], on highly scalable multiprocessors [15], on a cluster of workstations [10, 11], and on a coarse-grained multicomputer (CGM) [3].

The CGM/BSP algorithm for transitive closure [3] assumes an acyclic digraph and relies on the so-called linear extension labeling (also known as topological ordering) of the graph vertices. It requires $\log p + 1$ communication rounds, where p is the number of processors. In this paper we present a modified algorithm that is based on the ideas of [3] and works for general digraphs, without the acyclic restriction. Since the linear extension labeling can only be done on acyclic graphs, our algorithm does not use the linear extension labeling and is based on the simple, well-known and elegant Warshall's transitive closure algorithm. Without the linear extension labeling we can no longer guarantee the bound of $\log p + 1$ communication rounds. Nevertheless, all the graphs tested use at most $\log p + 1$ communication rounds. We show the efficiency and scalability of the modified algorithm and compare with other parallel implementations such as [10, 11].

2 Coarse-Grained Multicomputer (CGM) Model

The PRAM model [9] has been extensively utilized to produce important theoretical results on parallel algorithms. However, many of such algorithms could not be employed on real parallel machines. The limitations of the real machines, as compared to the requirements of the PRAM model, includes both the number of processors and the memory range accessed by each of the processors, in addition to synchronization and communication costs.

In this paper, we present a parallel algorithm for transitive closure that is based on a more practical parallel model. More precisely, we will use a version of the BSP model [16] referred to as the *Coarse Grained Multicomputer* (CGM) model [5, 6]. It uses only two parameters: the input size N and the number of processors p. The term *coarse grained* means the size of the local memory is much larger than $O(1)$. Dehne et al. [6] define "much larger" as $N/p \gg p$. In comparison to the BSP model, the CGM allows only bulk messages in order to minimize message overhead.

Let N denote the input size of the problem. A CGM consists of a set of p processors each with $O(N/p)$ local memory per processor and each processor is connected by a router that can send messages in a point-to-point fashion (or shared memory). A CGM algorithm consists of alternating local computation and global communication rounds separated by a barrier synchronization.

A computing round is equivalent to a superstep in the BSP model. In a computing round, we usually use the best sequential algorithm in each processor to process its data locally. In each communication round each processor sends $O(N/p)$ data and receives $O(N/p)$ data. Therefore, in terms of the BSP terminology, each communication round consists of routing a single h-relation with $h = O(N/p)$ per round. We require that all information sent from a given processor to another processor in one communication round be packed into one long message, thereby minimizing the message overhead. In the CGM model, the communication cost is modeled by the number of communication rounds.

A CGM computation/communication round corresponds to a BSP super-step with communication cost $g\frac{N}{p}$, where g is the cost, in steps per word, of delivering message data. Finding an optimal algorithm in the coarse grained multicomputer model is equivalent to minimizing the number of communication rounds as well as the total local computation time. The CGM model has the advantage of producing results which are closer to the actual performance on commercially available parallel machines. It is particularly suitable in current parallel machines in which the global computing speed is considerably larger than the global communication speed.

3 A CGM Transitive Closure Algorithm for Acyclic Digraphs

Algorithm 1 Parallel Transitive Closure for an Acyclic Digraph

---
Input: (i) An acyclic digraph D, with $|V(D)| = n$ vertices and $|E(D)| = m$ edges; (ii) p processors.
Output: D^t, the transitive closure of D.
1: Find a linear extension L of D
2: Let $S_1, \ldots, S_p$ be a partition of $V(D)$, whose parts have cardinalities as equal as possible, and where each S_j is formed by consecutive vertices in L.
   For $j = 1, \ldots, p$, assign the vertices of S_j to processor j;
3: In parallel, each processor j sequentially:
   . constructs the digraph $D(S_j)$ from D
   . computes the transitive closure $D^t(S_j)$ of $D(S_j)$
   . includes in D the edges of $D^t(S_j) \setminus D(S_j)$
4: After all processors have completed Step 3, verify if $D^t(S_j) = D(S_j)$, for all processors j. If true, the algorithm is terminated and D is the transitive closure of the input digraph. If false, go to Step 3.

We have presented a transitive closure algorithm for acyclic digraphs in [3]. We present without proof a summary of that result.

Let D be an acyclic digraph, with vertex set $V(D)$ and edge set $E(D)$, $|V(D)| = n$ and $|E(D)| = m$. Let $S \subseteq V(D)$. Denote by $D(S)$ the digraph formed exactly by the (directed) edges of D, having at least one of its extremes in S. If A is a path in D denote its length by $|A|$. A *linear extension* of D is a sequence $\{v_1, \ldots, v_n\}$ of its vertices, such that $(v_i, v_j) \in E(D) \Rightarrow i < j$.

The *transitive closure* of D is the digraph D^t, obtained from D by adding an edge (v_i, v_j), if there is a path from v_i to v_j in D, for all $v_i, v_j \in V(D)$.

Algorithm 1 computes the transitive closure of D, using p processors, where $1 \leq p \leq n$. It computes the transitive in at most $1 + \lceil \log p \rceil$ communication rounds. For details see [3].

4 A Modified CGM Algorithm for General Digraphs

The most well-known sequential algorithm for computing the transitive closure is due to Warshall [17]. Consider a digraph $G = (V, E)$ where $|V| = n$ and $|E| = m$. Let the vertices be $1, 2, \ldots, n$. The input to Warshall's algorithm is an $n \times n$ Boolean adjacency matrix M where the entry $M_{i,j}$ is 1 if there is a directed edge from vertex i to vertex j and 0 otherwise. Warshall's algorithm consists of a simple nested loop that transforms the input matrix M into the output matrix. The main idea is that if entries $M_{i,k}$ and $M_{k,j}$ are both 1, then we should set $M_{i,j}$ to 1. This is shown in Algorithm 2.

Algorithm 2 Warshall's Algorithm

Input: Adjacency matrix $M_{n \times n}$ of graph G
Output: Transitive closure of graph G

1: **for** $k \leftarrow 1$ **until** n **do**
2:    **for** $i \leftarrow 1$ **until** n **do**
3:       **for** $j \leftarrow 1$ **until** n **do**
4:          $M[i,j] \leftarrow M[i,j]$ **or** $(M[i,k]$ **and** $M[k,j])$
5:       **end for**
6:    **end for**
7: **end for**

The time complexity of this algorithm is $O(n^3)$. Its correctness is shown in the original paper [17], as well as in [2].

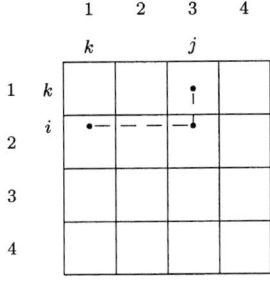

Fig. 1. Matrix M partitioned into 4 horizontal and 4 vertical stripes

We can modify Algorithm 1 and implement it by a parallelized version of Warshall's Algorithm. First partition and store the rows and columns of the adjacency matrix M in the p processors as follows. Divide the adjacency matrix M into p horizontal and p vertical stripes. Assume for simplicity that n/p is an integer, that is, n divides p exactly. Each horizontal stripe has thus n/p rows. Likewise each vertical stripe has n/p columns. This is shown in Fig. 1. Consider processors numbered as $1, 2, \ldots, p$. Then processor q stores the horizontal stripe q and the vertical stripe q. Notice that each adjacency matrix entry is thus stored in two processors.

Algorithm 3 Parallel Transitive Closure for a General Digraph
---
Input: Adjacency matrix M stored in the p processors: each processor q $(1 \leq q \leq p)$ stores submatrices $M[(q-1)\frac{n}{p}+1..q\frac{n}{p}][1..n]$ and $M[1..n][(q-1)\frac{n}{p}+1..q\frac{n}{p}]$.
Output: Transitive closure of graph G represented by the transformed matrix M.
Each processor q $(1 \leq q \leq p)$ does the following.

1: **repeat**
2:   **for** $k = (q-1)\frac{n}{p}+1$ **until** $q\frac{n}{p}$ **do**
3:     **for** $i = 0$ **until** $n-1$ **do**
4:       **for** $j = 0$ **until** $n-1$ **do**
5:         **if** $M[i][k] = 1$ **and** $M[k][j] = 1$ **then**
6:           $M[i][j] = 1$ (if $M[i][j]$ belongs to processor different from q then store it for subsequent transmission to the corresponding processor.)
7:         **end if**
8:       Send stored data to the corresponding processors.
9:       Receive data that belong to processor q from other processors.
10:     **end for**
11:     **end for**
12:   **end for**
13: **until** no new matrix entry updates are done

Notice a nice property of the way the matrix M is stored in the processors. Both $M[i][k]$ and $M[k][j]$ for any k are always stored in a same processor. See Fig. 1. This makes the test indicated at line 5 of the algorithm very easy to make. If both $M[i][k]$ and $M[k][j]$ are equal to 1 then $M[i][j]$ must also be made equal to 1. In this case, the update of $M[i][j]$ may be done immediately if it is also stored in processor q. Otherwise, the update will be done in the next communication round.

Algorithm 3 is derived from the original Algorithm 1 (without the linear extension labeling part) and implemented using the idea of Warshall's Algorithm. Its correctness derives from the original algorithm [3]. The bound of $\log p + 1$ communication rounds, however, is no longer valid. In fact, we can show that there exist cases where more than $\log p + 1$ communication rounds are required. For instance, consider $p = 4$ and a graph that is a linear list of $n = 16$ vertices (each labeled with two digits): $11 \rightarrow 31 \rightarrow 41 \rightarrow 21 \rightarrow 32 \rightarrow 12 \rightarrow 42 \rightarrow 33 \rightarrow 22 \rightarrow 43 \rightarrow 13 \rightarrow 23 \rightarrow 34 \rightarrow 14 \rightarrow 24 \rightarrow 44$. Assume that each vertex labeled with digits ij is stored in processor i. It can be shown that Algorithm 3 will need more than $\log 4 + 1 = 3$ communication rounds. It can be shown that at most p communication rounds suffices in the worst case.

In practice, however, this algorithm is very efficient and this special case has a very low probability to occur. Thus we obtain very good results as shown in the following.

5 Experimental Results

The problem of computing the transitive closure of a general digraph is an important problem that arises in many applications, when a graph is used to represent precedence relations between objects [8], such as in network planning, parallel and distributed systems, database management, and compiler designs, and thus may interest many users. It is our aim to present an efficient and portable implementation on low cost platforms.

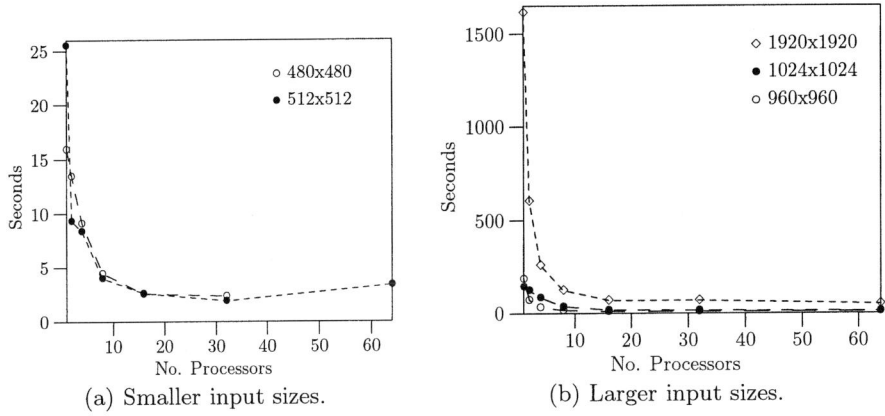

Fig. 2. Execution times for various input sizes

We implemented Algorithm 3 on a Beowulf cluster of 64 nodes consisting of low cost microcomputers with 256MB RAM, 256MB swap memory, CPU Intel Pentium III 448.956 MHz, 512KB cache, in addition to two access nodes consisting of two microcomputers each with 512MB RAM, 512MB swap memory, CPU Pentium 4 2.00 GHz, and 512KB cache. The cluster is divided into two blocks of 32 nodes each. The nodes of each block are connected through a 100 Mb fast-Ethernet switch. Each of the access nodes is connected to the switch that connects the block of nodes and the two switches are connected. Our code is written in standard ANSI C using the LAM-MPI library.

The test inputs consist of randomly generated digraphs where there is a 20 % probability of having an edge between two vertices. We tested graphs

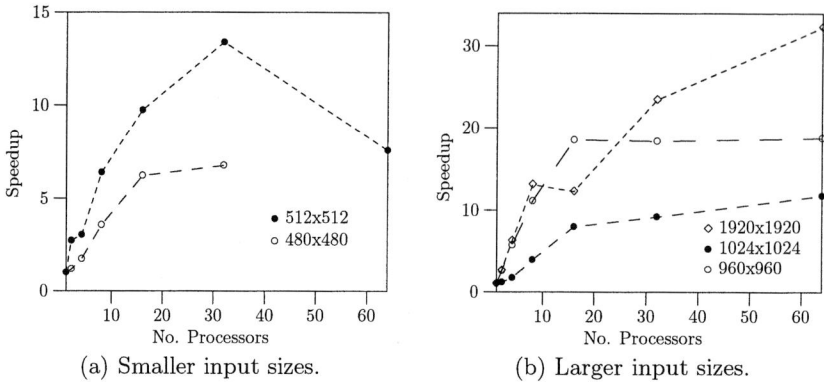

Fig. 3. Speedups for various input sizes

with $n=480, 512, 960, 1024,$ and 1920 vertices. In all the tests the number of communication rounds required are less than $\log p$.

The times curves for different problem sizes are shown in Fig. 2. The speedup curves are shown in Fig. 3. Notice the speedup curve for the input size of 1920×1920. It presents two ascending parts with different slopes. The first ascending part of the speedup can be seen to be superlinear. This is due to the memory swap overhead which is more severe for the sequential case ($p = 1$) which has to store the entire $n \times n$ input matrix whereas the parallel cases deal with input matrix of smaller size of $n/p \times n/p$.

For comparison purposes, our implementation considers inputs matrix sizes that include the same input sizes used in [10, 11], namely, $480 \times 480, 960 \times 960,$ and 1920×1920. As reported in [10], they use HP 720 workstations via a switched 10Mb Ethernet and PVM. Our implementation uses Pentium III processors on a switched 100Mb Ethernet and MPI. Our implementation results compare favorably. In particular observe the 1920×1920 case where our implementation obtains very substantial speedups.

6 Conclusion

Based on a CGM/BSP parallel algorithm for computing the transitive closure of an acyclic digraph, we have presented a modified version that works for any digraph. It can also be seen as a parallelized version of Warshall's algorithm. Although in theory the modified version no longer guarantees the $O(\log p)$ bound on the number of communication rounds, all the graphs we tested use at most $\log p + 1$ communication rounds. The implementation results are very promising and show the efficiency and scalability of the proposed modified algorithm, and compare favorably with other parallel implementations.

Acknowledgments

We would like to thank the anonymous referees for their review and helpful comments.

References

1. A. V. Aho, M. R. Garey and J. D. Ullman, The transitive reduction of a directed graph, *SIAM J. Comput.* **1** (1972) 131–137.
2. S. Baase. *Computer Algorithms - Introduction to Design and Analysis.* Addison-Wesley, 1993.
3. E. N. Cáceres, S. W. Song and J. L. Szwarcfiter. A Parallel Algorithm for Transitive Closure. *Proceedings the 14th IASTED International Conference on Parallel and Distributed Computing and Systems*, Cambridge, U.S.A., November 4-6, 2002, pp. 114-116.
4. H. Y. Chao and M. P. Harper, Minimizing redundant dependence and interprocessor synchronizations, *International Journal of Parallel Programming* **23** (1995) 245–262.
5. F. Dehne (Ed.), Coarse grained parallel algorithms, in: *Special Issue of Algorithmica* **24** (1999) 173–426.
6. F. Dehne, A. Fabri, and A. Rau-Chaplin, Scalable parallel computational geometry for coarse grained multicomputers, in: *Proc. ACM 9th Annual Computational Geometry* (1993) 298–307.
7. J. JáJá, *Introduction to Parallel Algorithms*, (Addison-Wesley Publishing Company, 1992).
8. F.T. Leighton, *Introduction to Parallel Algorithms and Architectures: Arrays - Trees - Hypercubes*, (Morgan Kaufmann Publishers, 1992).
9. R. M. Karp and V. Ramachandran, Parallel Algorithms for Shared-Memory Machines, in: J. van Leeuwen, ed., *Handbook of Theoretical Computer Science Vol. A*, (The MIT Press/Elsevier, 1990) Chapter 17, 869–941.
10. Aris Pagourtzis, Igor Potapov, and Wojciech Rytter. PVM Computation of the Transitive Closure: the Dependency Graph Approach, in: Y. Cotronis and J. Dongarra, eds., *Proceedings Euro PVM/MPI 2001*, Lecture Notes in Computer Science, V. 2131 (2001) 249–256.
11. Aris Pagourtzis, Igor Potapov, and Wojciech Rytter. Observations on Parallel Computation of Transitive and Max-Closure Problems, in: D. Kranzlmüller et al., eds., *Proceedings Euro PVM/MPI 2002*, Lecture Notes in Computer Science, V. 2474 (2002) 217–225.
12. P. Purdon Jr, A transitive closure algorithm, *BIT* **10** (1970) 76-94.
13. B. Roy, Transitivité et connexité, *C.R. Acad. Sci. Paris* **249** (1959) 216–218.
14. K. Simon, An improved algorithm for transitive closure on acyclic digraphs, *Theoretical Computer Science* **58** (1988) 325–346.
15. A.A. Toptsis, Parallel transitive closure for multiprocessor, in: *International Conference on Computing and Information*, Lecture Notes in Computer Science, V. 497 (1991) 197–206.
16. L. G. Valiant, A bridging model for parallel computation, *Communication of the ACM* **33** (1990) 103–111.
17. S. Warshall, A theorem on Boolean matrices, *J. Assoc. Comput. Mach.* **9** (1962) 11-12.

A Scalable Crystallographic FFT

Jaime Seguel and Daniel Burbano

University of Puerto Rico at Mayaguez, Mayaguez PR 00680, USA
{jaime.seguel,dburbano}@ece.uprm.edu

Abstract. Computational X-ray crystallography is the most accurate method for determining the atomic structure of crystals. Some large scale problems of current interest, such as the determination of macromolecular configurations at atomic level, demand a reiterated computation of large three-dimensional discrete Fourier transforms (DFT). Although fast Fourier transforms (FFT) are widely available, significant improvements in operation count and storage requirements can be obtained by using instead FFT variants tailored to crystal structure calculations. These are called crystallographic FFTs. A crystallographic FFT uses a-priori knowledge of the specimen's crystal symmetries to reduce the size of input and output data sets, and to eliminate redundant computations. Since in most cases of interest the modified FFT is still fairly large, parallel computation is regarded as an alternative to further speedup X-ray crystallography computations. Traditional divide-and-conquer multidimensional FFTs do not scale up well. In this paper we describe a parallel multidimensional crystallographic FFT for data arrays of prime edge-length that is endowed with good scalability properties. We perform a simple theoretical analysis and some computer experiments to validate our claim.

1 Introduction

Throughout this paper we assume that N is prime and denote by Z/N the set of integers modulo N. The *d-dimensional discrete Fourier transform* (DFT) of *edge length* N is the linear operator whose action on a real- or complex-valued mapping f defined in Z^d/N is described as

$$\hat{f}(\boldsymbol{k}) = \frac{1}{\sqrt{N}} \sum_{\boldsymbol{l} \in Z^d/N} f(\boldsymbol{l}) w_N^{\boldsymbol{k} \cdot \boldsymbol{l}}, \quad \boldsymbol{k} \in Z^d/N; \tag{1}$$

where $w_N = \exp(-2\pi i/N)$, $\cdot$ denotes the dot product modulo N, and $i = \sqrt{-1}$. By endowing Z^d/N with an order (1) is represented as the product of a $N^d \times N^d$ complex matrix by a N^d-point data vector. This matrix is denoted F_N for $d = 1$. It follows that, in general, the direct computation of (1) requires $O(N^{2d})$ time. However, for $d = 1$, a *fast Fourier transform* [3] (FFT) computes (1) in $O(N \log N)$ time. For $d \geq 2$, the usual FFT method consists of applying N^{d-1} one-dimensional FFTs along each of the d dimensions. Thus, (1) is computed in $O(N^d \log N)$ time. If N^{d-1} processors are available, a d-dimensional FFT can be computed in d parallel steps. Each step fixes all but one dimension and computes in parallel N^{d-1} one-dimensional FFTs of size N. The results are scattered across the processors in such a way that, in the next step, each processor computes the N-point one-dimensional FFT of a vector that corresponds to the next free dimension. This data exchange is, a gather/scatter operation in which each of the processors sends $N-1$ different data points to every other processor in a subset of $N-1$ processors. The amount of data exchanged between processors is $O(N^d)$, and data transmissions cannot be overlapped with computations. Variants of this method replace some one-dimensional by multidimensional FFTs lowering the number of parallel steps but keeping a similar order of complexity for the communication phase. Since gather/scatter operations are hard to parallelize, classical multidimensional FFTs scale poorly. This paper analyzes and tests the scalability of the prime edge-length crystallographic FFT proposed in [5].

2 Symmetries and Crystallographic FFTs

The atomic structure of a crystal is determined from X-ray diffraction intensity measurements through data intensive computer procedures. The complexity of the problem is largely due to the fact that measured intensities provide solely the magnitudes $|E|$ of the normalized structure factors $E = |E|\exp(i\phi)$ of the crystal. The elucidation of the crystal structure requires a knowledge of the *phase* ϕ, which is not obtainable from any physical experiment. The problem of reconstructing phases from magnitudes is solved by evaluating numerous trial structures. Each trial structure is refined through a sequence of steps which involve three-dimensional discrete Fourier transform (DFT) calculations. For instance, the *shake-and-bake* method [8], [9], alternates optimization in Fourier space with filtering in real space, performing thus, a forward and a backward three-dimensional DFT at each refinement step. Since crystal structures consist of repeating symmetric unit cells, their intensity data is highly redundant. In mathematical terms, intensities are represented by a real mapping f defined on Z^d/N, and redundancies described by the action of S, a $d \times d$ nonsingular matrix over Z/N. S and f are related by

$$f(l) = f(Sl) \quad \text{for all } l \in Z^d/N. \tag{2}$$

Matrix S is said to be a *symmetry* and f is said to be an S-symmetric mapping. For example, the mapping whose values on $Z^2/5$ are

$$[f(k,l)] = \begin{bmatrix} 8.0 & 2.2 & 5.9 & 5.9 & 2.2 \\ 2.2 & 4.0 & 1.2 & 6.0 & 4.0 \\ 5.9 & 6.0 & 7.7 & 7.7 & 1.2 \\ 5.9 & 1.2 & 7.7 & 7.7 & 6,0 \\ 2.2 & 4.0 & 6.0 & 1.2 & 4.0 \end{bmatrix}, \quad 0 \le k, l \le 4; \tag{3}$$

is S-symmetric with

$$S = \begin{bmatrix} 0 & 1 \\ -1 & 0 \end{bmatrix} = \begin{bmatrix} 0 & 1 \\ 4 & 0 \end{bmatrix} \quad \text{modulo 5}. \tag{4}$$

Indeed, an S-symmetric mapping satisfies $f(S^j a) = f(a)$ for all j. Therefore, f is constant over the subset of Z^d/N

$$O_S(a) = \{S^j a : j \text{ integer }\}; \qquad (5)$$

the so-called S-*orbit* of a. It follows that f is completely determined by its values on a set $\mathcal{F}_S$ formed by one and only one element from each S-orbit. This set is termed S-*fundamental set*. For example, the S-orbits and their images under f for symmetry (3) are

$$O_S(0,0) = \{(0,0)\}, f(O_S(0,0)) = \{8\} \qquad (6)$$
$$O_S(0,1) = \{(0,1),(1,0),(0,4),(4,0)\}, f(O_S(0,1)) = \{2.2\} \qquad (7)$$
$$O_S(0,2) = \{(0,2),(2,0),(0,3),(3,0)\}, f(O_S(0,2)) = \{5.9\} \qquad (8)$$
$$O_S(1,1) = \{(1,1),(1,4),(4,4),(4,1)\}, f(O_S(1,1)) = \{4\} \qquad (9)$$
$$O_S(1,2) = \{(1,2),(2,4),(4,3),(3,1)\}, f(O_S(1,2)) = \{1.2\} \qquad (10)$$
$$O_S(1,3) = \{(1,3),(3,4),(4,2),(2,1)\}, f(O_S(1,3)) = \{6\} \qquad (11)$$
$$O_S(2,2) = \{(2,2),(2,3),(3,3),(3,2)\}, f(O_S(2,2)) = \{7.7\}. \qquad (12)$$

A fundamental set for this symmetry is then,

$$\mathcal{F}_S = \{(0,0),(0,1),(0,2),(1,1),(1,2),(1,3),(2,2)\}. \qquad (13)$$

By a *fundamental data set* we understand the image of a fundamental set under f. It is easy to show that if f is S-symmetric, then $\hat{f}$ is S_*-symmetric, where S_* is the transpose of the inverse of S over Z/N. Therefore, $\hat{f}$ is determined by its values in a fundamental set $\mathcal{F}_{S_*}$, as well. Now, for each $a \in \mathcal{F}_S$, since $f(S^j a) = f(a)$ for all j, the input datum $f(a)$ is a common factor in all terms of $\hat{f}(k)$ that are indexed in $O_S(a)$ in (1). This is,

$$\sum_{l \in O_S(a)} f(l) w_N^{k \cdot l} = f(a) \left(\sum_{l \in O_S(a)} w_N^{k \cdot l} \right) = f(a) K_N(k, a). \qquad (14)$$

The expression $K_N(k, a) = \sum_{l \in O_S(a)} w_N^{k \cdot l}$ is called symmetrized DFT kernel, and the linear transformation

$$\hat{f}(k) = \sum_{a \in \mathcal{F}_S} K_N(k, a) f(a), \quad k \in \mathcal{F}_{S_*}, \qquad (15)$$

the symmetrized DFT. It turns out that a direct computation of the symmetrized DFT equations involves $O(M^2)$ operations, where M is the size of the fundamental set. Indeed, the efficient computation of 15 requires sophisticated methods, collectively known as *crystallographic FFTs*. A crystallographic FFT for composite edge-lengths was introduced by Ten Eyck in [7]. This method is not compatible with all crystal symmetries. A $O(M \log M)$ composite edge-length crystallographic FFT compatible with all crystal symmetries is proposed in [6].

The first prime edge-length crystallographic FFT method is described by Auslander et. al. in [1]. Although this method is compatible with all crystal symmetries, its time complexity is on average higher than that of the usual FFT [5]. A variant of Auslander's method whose serial time complexity bound varies with the crystal symmetry from an optimal $O(M \log M)$ to a worst case smaller but close to Auslander's bound, is proposed in [5]. The method computes 15 through as few as possible large-scale fast cyclic convolutions, whose results are combined to produce the symmetrized DFT output. In matrix format, a Q-point fast cyclic convolution can be viewed as the computation of $Y = HX$, where H is a $Q \times Q$ circulant matrix, and X a Q-point vector, through the equation

$$Y = F_Q^{-1} \Delta(H) F_Q^{-1} X. \tag{16}$$

This equation is based on a general result that states that if H is circulant, then

$$\Delta(H) = F_Q H F_Q \tag{17}$$

is a $Q \times Q$ diagonal matrix. Thus, a fast cyclic convolution computes $Y = HX$ in $O(Q \log Q)$ time. The decomposition of the symmetrized DFT matrix into circulant blocks [5] is a rather involved mathematical process which is out of the scope of this paper. However, in order to describe the parallel crystallographic FFT, we recall [5] that this decomposition results from the action of a matrix M that commutes with the symmetry S. M is chosen in a way such the lengths of the M-orbits are maximal. The action of M partitions both, input and output fundamental data sets, into Λ segments of approximately Q-points each. Since zero paddings are used to compensate irregularities, the actual size of the fundamental data set is, in general, less than or equal to ΛQ. These row and column decompositions, in turn, induce a block decomposition in the matrix representation the prime edge-length crystallographic FFT, of the form of

$$[U_a] = [H_{(a,b)}] [V_b]; \tag{18}$$

where $1 \leq a, b \leq \Lambda$, each $H_{(a,b)}$ is a $Q \times Q$ circulant block, and U_a and V_b are Q-point output and input vector segments, respectively. By applying (17) to each circulant block in (18) and factoring the Q-point DFT matrices we get a sparse matrix factorization of the form of

$$\begin{bmatrix} U_1 \\ U_2 \\ \vdots \\ U_\Lambda \end{bmatrix} = \begin{bmatrix} F_Q^{-1} & & & \\ & F_Q^{-1} & & \\ & & \ddots & \\ & & & F_Q^{-1} \end{bmatrix} \begin{bmatrix} \Delta(H_{(1,1)}) & \Delta(H_{(1,2)}) & \cdots & \Delta(H_{(1,\Lambda)}) \\ \Delta(H_{(2,1)}) & \Delta(H_{(2,2)}) & \cdots & \Delta(H_{(2,\Lambda)}) \\ \vdots & \ddots & \cdots & \vdots \\ \Delta(H_{(\Lambda,1)}) & \Delta(H_{(\Lambda,2)}) & \cdots & \Delta(H_{(\Lambda,\Lambda)}) \end{bmatrix}$$
$$\begin{bmatrix} F_Q^{-1} & & & \\ & F_Q^{-1} & & \\ & & \ddots & \\ & & & F_Q^{-1} \end{bmatrix} \begin{bmatrix} V_1 \\ V_2 \\ \vdots \\ V_\Lambda \end{bmatrix}.$$

This matrix factorization, which is the mathematical expression of the prime edge-length crystallographic FFT proposed in [5], shows that a large Λ, the matrix of diagonal blocks $[\Delta(H_{(a,b)})]$ becomes thicker, and therefore, dominant in the overall complexity of the method, which is $O(\Lambda Q \log Q + \Lambda^2 Q)$. It turns out that Λ is bounded below by a formula that depends on the symmetry S and the matrix M. In fact, only a few symmetries yield an optimal $\Lambda \equiv 1$. A way around to this limitation is parallelization. The method described above parallelizes very naturally. If $P \geq \Lambda$ processors are available, the Q-point FFTs can all be performed in parallel. Also, by assigning to each processor a different set of diagonal blocks of the form $D_b = \{\Delta(H_{(a,b)}) : 1 \leq a \leq \Lambda\}$, the multiplications of the outputs $Y_b = F_Q^{-1} V_b$ by the corresponding entries in $[\Delta(H_{(a,b)})]$ is performed in $O(\Lambda Q)$ time, reducing thus, the $O(\Lambda^2 Q)$ time of the serial counterpart. However, computing the additions in the matrix multiplication $[\Delta(H_{(a,b)})] [Y_b]$ require inter-processor communications. We use a hypercube nearest neighbor pattern for performing these interprocessor communications. However, since in general, Λ is not a power of two, we use a variant of the classical hypercube algorithm. Following is an illustration of this variant. Let $\Lambda = 3$ and $Q = 2$. Assume that $P = 4$ and that each processor has already computed and stored its results of the products of Y_b by each of the blocks $\Delta(H_{(a,b)})$. Let's represent these result in vector columns, each corresponding to the values stored in a different processor. Thus, before communications, the four processor have:

Proc. 0	Proc. 1	Proc. 2	Proc. 3
10	4	8	
15	10	12	
5	12	14	.
12	7	16	
3	11	20	
20	9	22	

(19)

We divide each data column in two segments, the upper of $\lceil \frac{\Lambda}{2} \rceil Q = 2\dot{2} = 4$ points, and the lower 2-point segment. The nearest neighbors that are loaded with data exchange their segments and add them together as illustrated in (20). If the nearest neighbor of a processor is unloaded, the loaded processor sends the lower segment to its unloaded neighbor, as illustrated in (20), as well. Thus, after the first communication step we get

Proc. 0	Proc. 1	Proc. 2	Proc. 3
14		8	
25		12	
17		14	.
19		16	
	14		20
	29		22

(20)

Each column that is still longer than Q is divided again in two segments. In this case, the columns in processors 0 and 2 are divided into data segments of two points each. Processor 2 sends its upper half to processor 0 and processor 0 sends its lower half to processor, just as in the previous step. Since no further divisions are possible in the data hold in processors 1 and 3, processor 3 simply sends its data to processor 1, which adds the columns together. The result is

$$\begin{array}{cccc} \text{Proc. 0} & \text{Proc. 1} & \text{Proc. 2} & \text{Proc. 3} \\ \hline 26 & & & \\ 37 & & & \\ & & 31 & \\ & & 35 & \\ & 34 & & \\ & 51 & & \end{array} \quad . \quad (21)$$

It is worth remarking that after this procedure, the indices of the the segments and those of the processors are related by a permutation. This is, processor 0 contains the segment V_0, processor 1 contains the segment V_2 and processor 2, the segment V_1. Fortunately, there is a very simple algorithm to compute this permutation. The algorithm consists of dividing the set $\{0, 1, ..., \Lambda - 1\}$ recursively in a upper and lower segment, an copying each subset below in a list of resulting subsets, as illustrated in the next example. Let $\Lambda = 5$.

$$\begin{aligned} \text{Initial Set} &: \begin{bmatrix} 0 \ 1 \ 2 \ 3 \ 4 \end{bmatrix} \\ \text{First Division (both segments)} &: \begin{bmatrix} 0 \ 1 \ 2 \end{bmatrix} \\ & \quad \begin{bmatrix} 3 \ 4 \end{bmatrix} \\ \text{Second Division (first segment only)} &: \begin{bmatrix} 0 \ 1 \end{bmatrix} \\ & \quad \begin{bmatrix} 3 \ 4 \end{bmatrix} \\ & \quad \begin{bmatrix} 2 \end{bmatrix} \\ \text{Final Division (first two segments)} &: \begin{bmatrix} 0 \end{bmatrix} \\ & \quad \begin{bmatrix} 3 \end{bmatrix} \\ & \quad \begin{bmatrix} 2 \end{bmatrix} \\ & \quad \begin{bmatrix} 1 \end{bmatrix} \\ & \quad \begin{bmatrix} 4 \end{bmatrix} \end{aligned}$$

If $\Lambda = 2^k$, this method produces the well-known bit-reversal permutation.

3 Analysis of the Parallel Crystallographic FFT (PCFFT) and Summary of Computer Experiments

The previously outlined method for parallel communications and additions compute the additions in $\left[\Delta(H_{(a,b)})\right][Y_b]$ in $O(kQ)$ time, for $2^{k-1} < \Lambda \leq 2^k$. Therefore, if $2^{k-1} < \Lambda \leq 2^k$, we have

Theorem 1. *Assuming that there are $P = 2^k$ processor and that $2^{k-1} < \Lambda \leq 2^k$; the parallel prime edge-length crystallographic FFT (PCFFT) computes (18) in $O(M \log M)$ time, where $M \equiv \Lambda Q$ is the size of the fundamental data set.*

Proof. As discussed above, the Q-points FFTs are performed in parallel in $O(Q \log Q)$ time. The multiplications and additions associated with the computation with the matrix of diagonal blocks are performed in $O(\Lambda Q)$ and $O(k\Lambda Q)$, respectively. Since

$$Q \log Q + \Lambda Q + k\Lambda Q \leq \Lambda Q \log Q + \Lambda Q + k\Lambda Q$$
$$\equiv M(\log Q + k + 1);$$

and $\log M \equiv \log Q + \log \Lambda \geq \log Q + k - 1$, we get the result.

We implemented a prototype of our algorithm in C/MPI and run it on a commodity cluster of eight 650 MHz Pentium III dual processors, interconnected by a 16-port switch. The cluster runs under Linux/OSCAR. The one-dimensional, Q-point FFTs were computed with the 1-D FFTW [4] package. We consider two symmetry. The first one,

$$S = \begin{bmatrix} 0 & 0 & 1 \\ 0 & 1 & 0 \\ -1 & 0 & 0 \end{bmatrix} \quad (22)$$

produces minimum values for Λ of the order of $N+1$. Since, in all our cases $P = 8$ is lower than Λ; this symmetry cannot be parallelized in our system without a significant agglomeration of parallel processes. However, the execution times in table 1 show a sustained relative speedup.

Table 1. Relative speedup with the first symmetry

Prime	P = 1	P = 2	P = 4	P = 8
199	176.767	92.487	52.456	32.488
223	506.488	137.350	76.397	47.292
239	603.016	204.512	130.962	85.196

We also considered the three dimensional even symmetry, which is described by

$$S = \begin{bmatrix} -1 & 0 & 0 \\ 0 & -1 & 0 \\ 0 & 0 & -1 \end{bmatrix}. \quad (23)$$

This symmetry yields values of Λ of the order of $(N-1)/2$, allowing thus a better parallelization of the crystallographic FFT in our system. Table 2 provides the performance measurements for this symmetry.

Table 3 is an attempt to validate our claim that the PCFFT is $O(M \log M)$, where M is the size of the fundamental set. The table shows the ratios between the execution time of the first symmetry and $M \log M$, in eight processors.

Table 2. Relative speedup with the three-dimensional even symmetry

Prime	P = 1	P = 2	P = 4	P = 8
199	65.146	43.041	27.420	19.474
223	134.413	72.227	45.193	30.467
239	176.377	97.680	60.436	40.733

Table 3. Ratio of time (T) over $M \log M$, where M is the problem size, and communications to computations ratio (R)

M	$\frac{T}{M \log M} * 10^8$	R
7880599	3.62	.42
11089576	2.93	.20
13651919	3.45	.19
18191447	4.81	.11
19902511	2.55	.19
30080231	24.3	.06

Acknowledgments

This work was partially supported by the NSF PRECISE project of the University of Puerto Rico at Mayagüez.

References

1. L. Auslander, and M. Shenefelt, *Fourier Transforms that Respect Crystallographic Symmetries*, IBM J. Res. and Dev., 31, pp. 213-223, 1987.
2. M. An, J. W. Cooley, and R. Tolimeri, *Factorization Methods for Crystallographic Fourier Transforms*, Advances in Appl. Math. 11, pp. 358-371, 1990.
3. J. Cooley, and J. Tukey, *An Algorithm for the Machine Calculation of Complex Fourier Series*, Math. Comp., 19, pp. 297-301, 1965.
4. M. Frigo, S. G. Johnson, *An adaptive software architecture for the FFT* ICASSP Conference Proceedings, 3 (1998), pp 1381-1384.
5. J. Seguel, D. Bollman, E. Orozco, *A New Prime Edge-length Crystallographic FFT*, ELSEVIER Lecture Notes in Computer Science, Vol. 2330, pp. 548-557,2002.
6. J. Seguel, *A Unified Treatment of Compact Symmetric FFT Code Generation*, IEEE Transactions on Signal Processing, Vol 50, No. 11, pp. 2789-2797, 2002.
7. L. F. Ten Eyck, *Crystallographic Fast Fourier Transforms*, ACTA Crystallogr. A, vol. 29, pp. 183-191, 1973.
8. C.M. Weeks, G.T. DeTitta, H.A. Hauptman, H.A Thuman, R. Miller, *Structure Solution by Minimal Function Phase Refinement and Fourier Filtering: II Implementation and Applications*, Acta Crystallogr. A50, pp. 210 - 220, 1994.
9. C.M. Weeks, R. Miller *Optimizing Shake-and-Bake for Proteins*, Acta Crystallogr. D55, pp 492-500, 1999.

Object-Oriented NeuroSys: Parallel Programs for Simulating Large Networks of Biologically Accurate Neurons

Peter S. Pacheco[1], Patrick Miller[2], Jin Kim[1],
Taylor Leese[1], and Yuliya Zabiyaka[1]

[1] Keck Cluster Research Group
Department of Computer Science
University of San Francisco
2130 Fulton Street, San Francisco, CA 94117
{peter,jhkim,tleese,yzabiyak}@cs.usfca.edu
[2] Lawrence Livermore National Laboratory
7000 East Avenue
Livermore, CA 94550
patmiller@llnl.gov

Abstract. Object-oriented NeuroSys is a collection of programs for simulating very large networks of biologically accurate neurons on distributed memory parallel computers. It includes two principle programs: ooNeuroSys, a parallel program for solving the systems of ordinary differential equations arising from the modelling of large networks of interconnected neurons, and Neurondiz, a parallel program for visualizing the results of ooNeuroSys. Both programs are designed to be run on clusters and use the MPI library to obtain parallelism. ooNeuroSys also includes an easy-to-use Python interface. This interface allows neuroscientists to quickly develop and test complex neuron models. Both ooNeuroSys and Neurondiz have a design that allows for both high performance and relative ease of maintenance.

1 Introduction

One of the most important problems in computational neuroscience is understanding how large populations of neurons represent, store and process information. Object-oriented NeuroSys is a collection of parallel programs that have been designed to provide computational neuroscientists with powerful, easy-to-use tools for the study of networks of millions of biologically accurate neurons. It consists of two principle programs: ooNeuroSys, a program for solving the systems of ordinary differential equations resulting from the modelling of large networks of interconnected neurons, and Neurondiz, a program for visualizing the results of ooNeuroSys. Both programs use an object-oriented design which makes it relatively easy to add features and change underlying data structures and algorithms. This design has also allowed us to achieve scalability comparable to earlier, structured versions of these programs [16].

In addition to improving maintainability, Object-oriented NeuroSys is much easier to use than the earlier versions. Inter alia, we have completely redesigned the GUI for Neurondiz and we have added a Python [17] interface to ooNeuroSys which allows users to code and test neuron models with relative ease.

The differential equation solver, ooNeuroSys, employs an adaptive communication scheme in which it determines at runtime how to structure interprocess communication. It also makes use of the parallel CVODE library [4] for the solution of the systems of ordinary differential equations.

In this paper we discuss the problems we encountered with an earlier version of NeuroSys and how we decided to address these in ooNeuroSys. We continue with a discussion of the communication schemes we used in ooNeuroSys, the new version of Neurondiz, the Python interface, the performance of Object-oriented NeuroSys, and directions for further development.

Acknowledgements. The first author thanks the W.M. Keck Foundation for a grant to build a cluster for use in research and education and partial support of this research. Work performed under the auspices of the U.S. Department of Energy by Lawrence Livermore National Laboratory under Contract W-7405-ENG-48.

2 ooNeuroSys Design

The original version of NeuroSys [14, 16] was written in the late 1990's by USF's Applied Mathematics Research Laboratory. It is a very powerful system: we were able to simulate sparsely interconnected systems consisting of 256,000 Hodgkin-Huxley type [7] neurons on a 32-processor cluster with parallel efficiencies of better than 90%. However, its design is essentially structured, and as it grew, it became very difficult to incorporate new, and to improve existing, features. So in the summer of 2001 we began a complete rebuilding of NeuroSys. One of the central features of the new system is an object-oriented design that makes maintenance relatively easy, but preserves scalability.

The original version of NeuroSys was written in C, and it used the MPI library to obtain parallelism. Because of the ease with which the performance and memory-usage of C code can be optimized, we decided to continue to use C for ooNeuroSys. Since our main target platform is clusters of relatively small SMPs, we also continued to use MPI. In our object-oriented design classes are defined in separate C source files. The data members are defined in a struct, and the methods are just C functions whose first argument is a pointer to the struct. Methods can be made private by declaring them to be static. During initial development, underlying data structures are hidden by using incomplete types in header files. That is, a data structure is declared in a dot-c file, and an incomplete type that is a pointer to the struct is declared in the corresponding header file. After initial development — when performance becomes a consideration — underlying data structures are selectively exposed in the header files, and some methods — especially accessor methods — are replaced by macros. A primitive, and for our purposes completely satisfactory, form of inheritance is obtained by declaring members of parent classes in macros in header files that are included in child classes.

Both the original version of NeuroSys and ooNeuroSys take as input two main data structures: a description of the neurons and their interconnections and a list of initial conditions for the variables associated with each neuron. For production simulations these data structures are stored in files and read in at the beginning of program execution. The output of the program is the raw data produced during the simulation, i.e., a collection of variable values as specified by the user.

The original version of NeuroSys used a very simple parallel implementation of a classical, fourth-order Runge-Kutta solver. Although we obtained excellent efficiencies with as many as 32 processors, because of the large amount of communication required, we did not expect this method to scale well for much larger numbers of processors. So in ooNeuroSys we wrote a solver class which interfaces with parallel CVODE [4], a general purpose ordinary differential equation solver for stiff and nonstiff ODE's. It obtains parallelism by partitioning the equations and variables of the system among the parallel processes. Since the equations we solve in ooNeuroSys are nonstiff, we use CVODE's variable-stepsize, variable-order Adams-Moulton solver. CVODE also uses an object-oriented design, and since it was written in C, and it uses the MPI library, writing the solver class interface was completely straightforward.

3   ooNeuroSys Communication

Since the equations and variables are partitioned among the processors, communication is required when an equation depends on a variable assigned to a different process. An interesting feature of neuronal interconnection networks is that the interdependence can have almost any form. At one extreme the problem can be almost perfectly parallel in that the equations assigned to each process have little or no dependence on variables assigned to other processes. At the other extreme, a problem may be almost "fully interconnected," i.e., every neuron depends on almost every neuron in the system. Thus the communication requirements of a problem are only known at runtime: after the neuronal interconnection structure has been read in. The original version of NeuroSys partially addressed this by providing compile-time options for choosing a communication scheme. This has the obvious weakness that the program needs to be recompiled for different interconnection networks. It has the added weakness that it requires the user to evaluate the interconnection network and then determine which communication program to use. Because of the nature of the problems (thousands or millions of neurons with possibly random interconnects), it may be impossible for a human to evaluate the interconnect, and expecting a neuroscientist to understand the intricacies of interprocess communication schemes may be unreasonable. Thus, ooNeuroSys determines automatically at runtime which communication scheme to use.

Although we have written a variety of communication classes, in the problems that we have studied thus far, we have found that only two of them are necessary for the best performance. The first, which corresponds to a fully interconnected system, is an implementation of `MPI_Allgather` that uses a rotating scheme of send/receive pairs in which, during the ith stage, $i = 0, 1, \ldots$, each process sends all its data to process

$$(\text{my\_rank} + 2^i) \bmod p,$$

where p is the number of processes. This is the "dissemination allgather algorithm" described in [1], which is based on the dissemination barrier algorithm described in [6]. The communication scheme requires $\lceil \log_2(p) \rceil$ stages. Its principle complication is that, in general, processes will not be communicating contiguous blocks of data. However, our benchmarks showed that for the data sets we expect to be of interest, both the MPICH [12] and LAM [10] implementations of `MPI_Type_indexed` allowed us to obtain excellent performance on fast-ethernet-connected clusters. We also found that using this implementation with the MPICH-GM [13] implementation resulted in excellent performance on Myrinet-connected clusters.

The second communication scheme is used for sparsely interconnected networks and is essentially that described in [20]. On the basis of the information describing its assigned subnetwork, each process can determine which variables it needs and to which process each variable is assigned. Thus, after a global communication phase, each process knows both which variables it should receive from which processes and which variables it should send to which processes. Once each process has built its communication structure, the interprocess communication is implemented by having each process post nonblocking receives for all of the messages it needs to receive and then making blocking sends of all the messages needed by the other processes. In experiments we found that this "lazy" approach outperformed any heuristic scheduling schemes we devised.

A key feature of the systems modelled by NeuroSys is that if the neuronal interconnection changes at all during a simulation, it usually doesn't change for hundreds or thousands of timesteps. We exploit this by building derived datatypes and persistent requests only at the beginning of a run and when the interconnect changes.

At the beginning of a run, after the neuronal interconnect has been read in, the communication class uses a simple heuristic in order to determine which of the two communication schemes is superior. If the number of processes is small (typically ≤ 4), we use the dense scheme. Otherwise we use a (heuristic) algorithm to construct a deterministic schedule for the sparse communications. If the maximum number of stages required by the schedule is less than $\lceil \log(p) \rceil$, then we expect the sparse scheme will outperform the dense scheme. On the other hand, empirical tests have shown that if the maximum number of stages is more than $\lceil 4 \log(p) \rceil$ in the sparse scheme, then the dense scheme is likely to be superior. For other interconnects, the program runs a short series of benchmarks of each scheme, and chooses the scheme with the smaller overall run time.

4 Neurondiz

Neurondiz takes the output data produced by ooNeuroSys and provides a graphic display of the simulation. For even modest-sized simulations, the datasets generated by ooNeuroSys can contain several gigabytes of data. Furthermore, some of the computations required for visualizing this data can involve all of the neurons. Thus, it is essential that Neurondiz include both high-performance I/O and high-performance computational capabilities. In order to handle the large amounts of data produced by ooNeuroSys, Neurondiz has been divided into two components: a backend that reads in and processes the ooNeuroSys data, and a frontend that manages the display. In order to provide maximum performance the backend is written in C, and it uses the MPI library. We are working on two versions of the frontend. For less demanding problems, we have a Java frontend. We chose Java to allow for future deployment of a Neurondiz applet, to provide an easy interface to other applications, and to allow for rapid development of new functionalities. For more demanding applications the second version of the frontend uses C++, the Qt application development framework [19] and the OpenGL graphics library [21].

Neurondiz was especially designed to support two hardware configurations. In one configuration, we assume the user is working with a parallel computer with no graphics capability. For example, a user with access to a powerful remote system at a supercomputer center could be considered to fall into this category. In the other, a single node of the parallel computer is directly connected to a display. For example, a user with a small local cluster might fall into this category. The frontend-backend division of Neurondiz makes it relatively easy to develop code for these two setups. In the first configuration, the frontend and backend run on separate computers and they communicate using sockets. In the second configuration, the frontend and backend reside on the same system and their communication depends on which frontend is being used. The C++ frontend can simply call functions defined in the C backend. On the other hand, the Java frontend can communicate with the C backend using sockets, but we expect that performance will be improved using Java's Native Interface, which allows a JVM to interoperate with programs written in other languages. At the time of this writing (July, 2003) we support direct communication with the C++ frontend and communication with sockets with the Java frontend.

When Neurondiz is started, the backend opens the data file(s) storing the results from ooNeuroSys, and some basic information on the neurons is sent to the frontend, which opens a display showing a rectangular grid of disks, one disk for each neuron. In the most basic execution of Neurondiz, the program provides an animated display of the firing of the individual neurons by changing the color of the disks. The user can either single-step through the simulation by using mouseclicks, or she can let the animation proceed without user interaction.

If, at any time, the user wants more detailed information, she can select a rectangular subset of neurons and the subset will be displayed in a new window, which supports all the functionality of the original window. For even more detail, the user can select a single neuron and display its membrane voltage as a function of time.

The computational neuroscientists that used the original version of Neurondiz requested that the display also provide information on the synaptic connections among the neurons. Of course, the interconnection network for only a few hundred neurons, can contain tens-of-thousands of synaptic interconnections, which would be impossible to display with any clarity. So after some discussion with the neuroscientists, we developed two additional functionalities for Neurondiz. For the first, we added an option that allows a user to select a subset of neurons and display the interconnections among these neurons by interfacing with the graph visualization software package, Graphviz [5]. The display showing the neurons and their synaptic interconnections will, in general, require changing the positions of the neurons relative to each other in order to achieve a reasonably clear image. Thus, the selected neurons in the original display are keyed to the neurons in the Graphviz display by assigning matching numbers to paired neurons. At the time of this writing (July, 2003), the Graphviz interface is available only with the Java frontend. It is supplied by a GraphViz program called *Grappa*. Grappa sends a graph description to another Graphviz program called *dot,* and dot generates the layout and sends the layout back to Grappa for display.

The second functionality allows neuroscientists to determine the density of synaptic connections between two neurons. After the user selects two neurons, a source and a destination, and enters a parameter specifying the maximum path length, the backend will identify the subgraph consisting of all directed paths of synaptic connections from the source to the destination that consist of a number of synaptic connections less than or equal to the bound. The algorithm for finding the subgraph uses two breadth-first searches. Both Neurondiz and ooNeuroSys store synaptic interconnection information by storing lists of neurons with synaptic connections *into* each neuron assigned to a process. Hence the first breadth-first search works backwards from the destination vertex. Essentially, the standard serial breadth-first algorithm is modified so that a globally replicated data structure records all visited vertices, and on each pass through the search loop, each process adds any vertices that can be reached from already visited vertices. At the end of the body of the search loop the structure recording visited vertices is updated. The loop terminates after it has searched the tree based at the destination with height equal to the user-specified bound.

At this point, we assume that the number of vertices visited by the breadth-first search is small enough so that the subgraph spanned by its neurons can be contained in the memory of a single process. So after the breadth-first search is completed, each process allocates enough storage for an adjacency matrix on the visited vertices. Each process initializes those columns of the matrix about which it has information, and a global reduction using logical-or creates a copy of the adjacency matrix on each process. The algorithm is completed by a breadth-

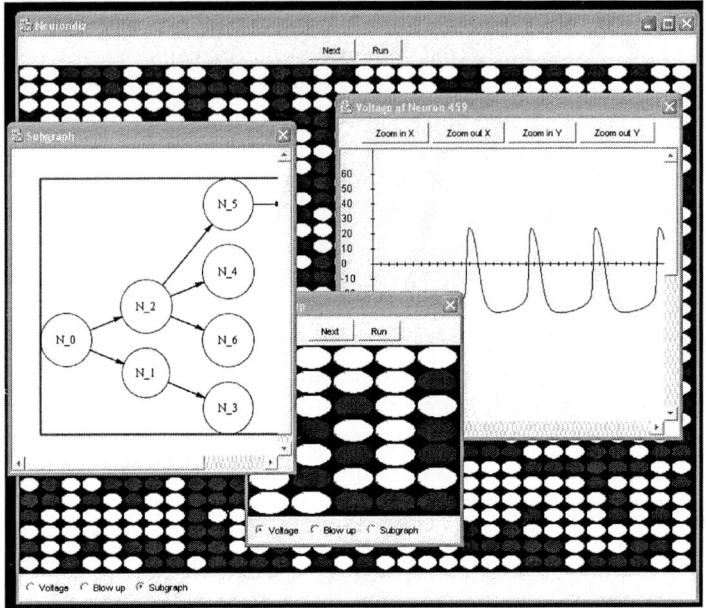

Fig. 1. Screenshot of Neurondiz

first-search from the source on the subgraph induced by the vertices visited in the first search. Any unvisited vertices and edges not lying on paths with length less than or equal to the the bound are deleted.

Figure 1 shows a screenshot of the Java frontend. It shows a blowup of a subset of neurons, a voltage vs. time plot, and a small subgraph with edges.

5 Python Interface

High speed and parallelism are certainly required for a high fidelity simulation. However, robust, accurate, and innovative models are also necessary to achieve understanding of neural processes. Herein lies one of the principle problems with the development of object-oriented NeuroSys. High speed and parallelism requirements decrease programmability, especially for non-computer scientists. This is discouraging, particularly for smaller runs in which a scientist is trying to develop new models. To require neuroscientists to write code in C and to compile and link a new equation model is too great a burden. In ooNeuroSys we provide an interface from the core simulation to the Python Interpreted language [17] so that users can develop and run new equation models and manipulate the neural simulation directly.

The most important considerations in the design of the Python interfaces are simplicity and flexibility. For instance, the equations that model a simulation variable should be simple to program and extend even for a non-programmer:

Table 1. Run Times of ooNeuroSys (in seconds).

Processes	\multicolumn{5}{c}{Neurons}				
	16,384	32,768	65,536	131,072	262,144
1	372	718	1453	—	—
2	239	463	981	1781	—
4	117	237	493	950	1930
8	51	119	239	483	978
16	22	52	123	248	495
32	11	24	57	125	258

```
def computeHPrime(self,h,V):
    def ah(v): return (0.128*exp(-(v+50.0)/18.0))
    def bh(v): return (4.0/(1.0+exp(-(v+27.0)/5.0)))

    h_prime = ah(V)*(1-h)-bh(V)*h

    return h_prime
```

The user should be able to examine and change state variables and connectivity:

```
for neuron in net:
    print 'my id is',neuron.id
    print 'my adjacency_list is',neuron.adjacency_list
    for neighbor in neuron.adjacency_list:
        print 'connect',neuron.id,'with',neighbor
    print 'voltage',neuron.V
```

Using these techniques, a user can setup and manipulate (steer) all relevant parts of a simulation. Interpreted languages may be slower than compiled languages like C, but Python of the sort used in the equations can be automatically compiled into high performance code [8, 11].

6 Performance

At the time of this writing (July, 2003), we have only been able to run a few small tests. However, these tests suggest that ooNeuroSys is as scalable as the original NeuroSys. Table 1 shows the run times in seconds of some simulations run on the Keck Cluster [9], a Myrinet connected cluster of 64 dual processor Pentium III's. The systems being simulated use two neuron models (excitatory and inhibitory neurons), and the synaptic interconnection network was randomly generated. Each neuron is modelled with 5 variables. The dashes in the table correspond to data which took too long to generate.

7 Conclusions and Directions for Future Work

Object-oriented NeuroSys provides many improvements over its predecessor. Its design provides both ease of maintenance and scalability. The Python interface to ooNeuroSys promises to make it much easier to use. The new version of Neurondiz has a much improved interface and considerably more functionality.

Among other improvements to ooNeuroSys, we plan to make use of graph partitioning software to further improve scalability. We have already begun work on improving the scalability of I/O by incorporating some of the recommendations in [2]. By using the results of this work we hope to be able to develop a scalable I/O scheme that is well-suited to clusters that don't have parallel file systems. Taken together, the Java and C++ versions of Neurondiz have all the desired functionality. However, both need to be completed.

There are several other programs for the parallel simulation of large networks of biologically accurate neurons. See, for example, [3, 15, 18]. While published parallel efficiencies of these programs are lower than those achieved by ooNeuroSys, it would be interesting to compare the programs when they are run on the same platforms with the same input data.

References

1. Gregory Benson, Cho-Wai Chu, Qing Huang, and Sadik G. Caglar. A comparison of MPICH allgather algorithms on switched networks. To appear.
2. Gregory Benson, Kai Long, and Peter Pacheco. The measured performance of parallel disk write methods on Linux multiprocessor nodes. To appear.
3. Mikael Djurfeldt, Anders Sandberg, Örjan Ekeberg, and Anders Lansner. See—a framework for simulation of biologically detailed and artificial neural networks and systems. *Neurocomputing,* 26–27: 997–1003, 1999.
4. George D. Byrne and Alan C. Hindmarsh. Correspondence: PVODE, an ODE solver for parallel computers. *The International Journal of High Performance Computing Applications,* 13(4): 354–365, 1999.
5. Emden R. Gansner and Stephen C. North. An open graph visualization system and its applications to software engineering. *Software—Practice and Experience,* 30(11): 1203–1233, 1999.
6. D. Hensgen, R. Finkel, and U. Manber. Two algorithms for barrier synchronization. *International Journal of Parallel Programming,* 17(1): 1–17, February 1988.
7. A.L. Hodgkin and A.F. Huxley. A quantitative description of membrane current and its application to conduction and excitation in nerve. *Journal of Physiology* (London), 117: 500–544, 1952.
8. Eric Jones and Patrick J. Miller. Weave — inlining C/C++ in Python. In *O'Reilly Open Source Convention,* July 2002. http://conferences.oreillynet.com/cs/os2002/view/e_sess/2919.
9. *The Keck Cluster.* http://keckclus.cs.usfca.edu/.
10. *LAM/MPI Parallel Computing.* http://www.lam-mpi.org/.
11. Patrick J. Miller. Parallel, Distributed Scripting with Python. In *Third International Conference on Linux Clusters: The HPC Revolution,* St. Petersburg, FL, Oct 23 - Oct 25, 2002. http://www.linuxclustersinstitute.org/Linux-HPC-Revolution/Archive/2002techpapers.html.

12. *MPICH-A Portable Implementation of MPI.* http://www-unix.mcs.anl.gov/mpi/mpich/index.html.
13. *Myrinet Software and Documentation,* http://www.myri.com/scs/.
14. Peter Pacheco, Marcelo Camperi, and Toshiyuki Uchino. Parallel NeuroSys: a system for the simulation of very large networks of biologically accurate neurons on parallel computers. *Neurocomputing,* 32–33: 1095-1102, 2000.
15. *Parallel Genesis.* http://www.psc.edu/Packages/PGENESIS/.
16. *Parallel NeuroSys.* http://www.cs.usfca.edu/neurosys.
17. *The Python Language.* http://www.python.org.
18. Evan Thomas. *Parallel Algorithms for Biologically Realistic, Large Scale Neural Modeling,* Master's Thesis, 1997. http://dirac.physiology.unimelb.edu.au/~evan/thesis/.
19. Trolltech. *Qt 3.1 Whitepaper.* www.trolltech.com.
20. Ray S. Tuminaro, John N. Shadid, and Scott A. Hutchinson. Parallel Sparse Matrix-Vector Multiply Software for Matrices with Data Locality. Sandia National Laboratories, SAND95-1540J, 1995.
21. Mason Woo, Jackie Neider, Tom Davis, and Dave Shreiner. *OpenGL(R) Programming Guide: The Official Guide to Learning OpenGL, Version 1.2,* 3rd ed., Addison-Wesley Publishing Co, 1999.

PageRank Computation Using PC Cluster

Arnon Rungsawang and Bundit Manaskasemsak

Massive **I**nformation & **K**nowledge **E**ngineering
Department of Computer Engineering
Kasetsart University, Bangkok 10900, Thailand
{arnon,un}@mikelab.net

Abstract. Link based analysis of web graphs has been extensively explored in many research projects. PageRank computation is one widely known approach which forms the basis of the Google search. PageRank assigns a global importance score to a web page based on the importance of other web pages pointing to it. PageRank is an iterative algorithm applying on a massively connected graph corresponding to several hundred millions of nodes and hyper-links. In this paper, we propose an efficient implementation of PageRank computation for a large sub-graph of the web on a PC cluster. A link structure file representing the web graph of several hundred million links, and an efficient PageRank algorithm capable of computing PageRank scores very fast, will be discussed. Experimental results on a small cluster of x86 based PC with artificial 776 million links of 87 million nodes derived from the TH domain report 30.77 seconds per iteration run.

1 Introduction

Web link analysis has been extensively explored in many research projects. Some recent examples are web mining [2], topic-specific web resource discovery [5, 11], quality measuring of web pages [16], URL ordering [8], web modelling [14], and especially in ranking the search results [3]. There exist many methods of web link analysis. Two well-known algorithms are the HITS [13] and the PageRank [3]. The PageRank algorithm for determining the web page importance has been introduced by Brin and Page [3] and used in the well known Google search engine. Since then, it can be seen as the most mentioned algorithm of link analysis in the web's literature.

The core of the PageRank algorithm involves iteratively computing the principal eigenvector of the Markov matrix representing the hyper-link structure of the web [7]. As the rapid growing of the web graph causes the web's hyper-link matrix computations very expensive, the development of techniques for computing PageRank efficiently of several hundred million nodes of web graphs is very important.

Former research exploiting sparse graph techniques to accelerate the PageRank computation has been reported in [4, 1]. There are also many fast numerical method based algorithms that can be applied to PageRank computational problem [15, 9], however most of them are very costly as they require matrix inversion. Recently, Kamvar et al. [12] exploit local block structure of the web and use successive intermediate results, as they become available, to estimate the PageRank scores rather than use only values from the previous iteration. Chen et al. [6] present a split-accumulate algorithm to speed up the iterative computation of PageRank. As well, Haveliwala [10] proposes an encoding scheme based on scalar quantization to efficiently compute the document rank vectors in main memory. There are many other research in this field, we rather mention a few.

As low-cost x86 based PC cluster can be affordable in many institutions this day, we thus believe that an implementation of a PageRank algorithm on a PC cluster platform is another promising way to serve the web link analysis research. Moreover, while the size of the web graph is exponentially expanded, the need for fast parallel PageRank computation becomes clear. In this paper, we present an efficient implementation of a PageRank algorithm on a PC cluster. We first introduce a simple link structure file to represent the connectivity of a large web graph, and propose a sequential algorithm to compute the PageRank scores. We then proceed to a parallel algorithm implementation on a cluster of x86 machines using a free message passing library MPICH. Both algorithms have been validated on a large web graph containing 776 million links, 87 million URLs. The wall-clock results for each PageRank iteration run is very promising.

2 Basic PageRank Description

Intuitive description of PageRank is based on an idea that if a page v of interest has many other pages u with high rank scores pointing to, then the authors of pages u are implicitly conferring some importance to page v. The importance that pages u confer to page v can be described as follows: Let N_u be the number of pages u point out (called later, "out-degree"), and let $Rank(p)$ represent the rank score of page p. Then a link $(u \to v)$ confers $Rank(u)/N_u$ units of rank to page v.

To compute the rank vector for all pages of a web graph, we then simply iteratively perform the following fixed point computation. If N is the number of pages in the underlying web graph, we assign all pages the initial score $1/N$. Let S_v represent the set of pages pointing to v. In each iteration, the successive rank scores of pages are recursively propagated from the previously computed rank scores of all other pages pointing to them:

$$\forall_v Rank_{i+1}(v) = \sum_{u \in S_v} \frac{Rank_i(u)}{N_u} \qquad (1)$$

The above PageRank computation equation ignores some important details. In general, the web graph is not strongly connected, and this may lead the PageRank computation of some pages to be trapped in a small isolated cluster of the graph. This problem is usually resolved by pruning nodes with zero out-degree, and by adding random jumps to the random surfer process underlying PageRank [6]. This leads to the following modification of Equation (1) to:

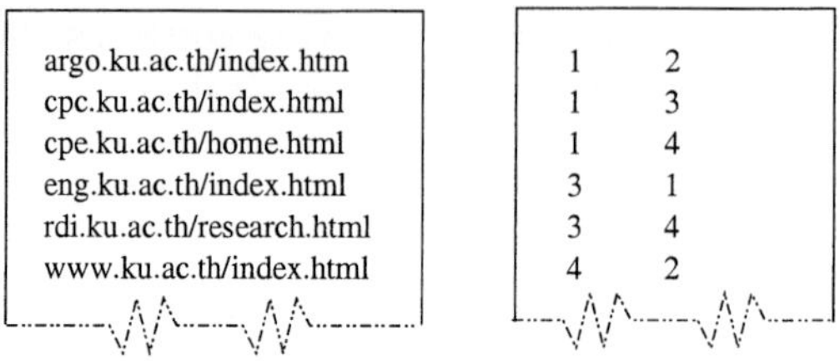

| argo.ku.ac.th/index.htm |
| cpc.ku.ac.th/index.html |
| cpe.ku.ac.th/home.html |
| eng.ku.ac.th/index.html |
| rdi.ku.ac.th/research.html |
| www.ku.ac.th/index.html |

1	2
1	3
1	4
3	1
3	4
4	2

Fig. 1. The input web graph files.

dest–id	in–degree (2 bytes)	source–id (4 bytes each)	
1	1	3	
2	2	1	4
3	1	1	
4	2	1	3

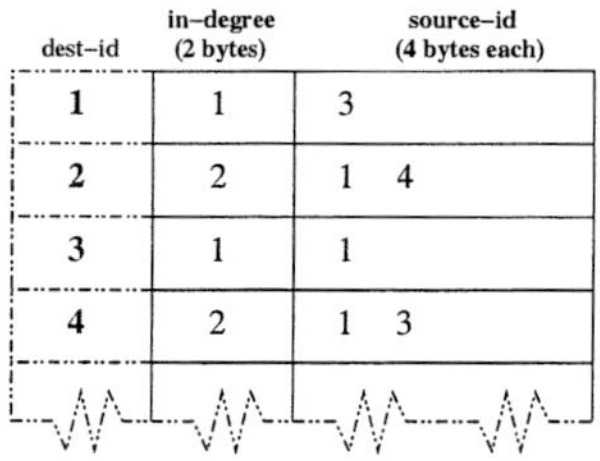

Fig. 2. The link structure file M.

$$\forall_v Rank_{i+1}(v) = (1-\alpha) + \alpha \sum_{u \in S_v} \frac{Rank_i(u)}{N_u} \quad (2)$$

where α, called "damping factor", is the value that we use to modify the distributional probability of the random surfer model. In the remainder of this paper, we will refer to the iterative processes stated in this Equation (2) to compute the PageRank scores.

3 Link Structure File and Algorithm Proposed

In general, the input web graph exists in form of a text file with two columns; a URL u in the first column which has an out-link to another URL v in the second column. To easily process, we then transform the input web graph into two files. The first one consists of all URLs sorted in alphabetical order. The second one is the "out-link file", which is equivalent to the underlying input web graph, but each line contains a pair of integers referring to line number (i.e. source and destination id) in the first file. The example of these two files is depicted on Figure 1.

The PageRank computational algorithm we propose in this paper does not directly take the input web graph files as depicted in Figure 1, we rather convert the out-link file into a binary "link structure file M" as illustrated in Figure 2. This link structure file contains one record for each URL (i.e., each line refers to a destination URL); the first column, storing in 2-byte integer, represents its in-degree (i.e. the number of URLs pointing to it), while the second column, storing a list of 4-byte integers, represents the ids referring to the source URLs. For example, reading from the Figure 1 and Figure 2, we obtain that the destination URL "cpc.ku.ac.th/index.html" has been pointed by source URLs "argo.ku.ac.th/index.htm" and "eng.ku.ac.th/index.html", respectively.

To iteratively compute the PageRank score for each URL in the web graph, we then create the two arrays of floating point representing the rank vectors, called hereby the "$rank_{src}$" and the "$rank_{dest}$". Each rank vector has T entries, where T is the total number of URLs in the web graph. We first initialize the $rank_{dest}$ to $\frac{1}{outarry[t]}$, where $outarry[t]$ is the number of out-degree of a URL t. For each iteration step, the $rank_{src}$ is referred to the rank score of iteration i and the $rank_{dest}$ is referred to the rank score of iteration $i+1$. The sequential version of the PageRank computation can be written in Algorithm 1 as follows:

Algorithm 1 : Sequential PageRank Algorithm.

1: $\forall_t rank_{dest}[t] = \frac{1}{outarry[t]}$, $\alpha = 0.85$
2: **for** $round = 1$ to 50 **do**
3: $\quad rank_{src} = rank_{dest}$
4: $\quad \forall_t rank_{dest}[t] = 0$, $sum = 0$
5: $\quad$ **for** $t = 1$ to T **do**
6: $\quad\quad$ **if** $M.read(indegree)! = 0$ **then**
7: $\quad\quad\quad$ **for** $j = 1$ to $indegree$ **do**
8: $\quad\quad\quad\quad M.read(src_j)$
9: $\quad\quad\quad\quad sum = sum + rank_{src}[src_j]$
10: $\quad\quad\quad$ **end for**
11: $\quad\quad\quad rank_{dest}[t] = \frac{(1-\alpha)+(\alpha \times sum)}{outarry[t]}$
12: $\quad\quad$ **end if**
13: $\quad$ **end for**
14: **end for**
15: $\forall_t rank_{dest}[t] = rank_{dest} \times outarry[t]$

---

4 Parallelization of PageRank Computation

To speed up computation of the PageRank scores for a large web graph using a cluster of β PC machines, we first partition the binary link structure file M into β chunks $M_0, M_1, ..., M_{\beta-1}$, such that each M_i contains only in-degree information of the URLs from the $(\frac{i \times T}{\beta} + 1)^{th}$ to the $(\frac{(i+1) \times T}{\beta})^{th}$. Figure 3 below gives the example of the modified link structure file M.

To iteratively compute the PageRank scores, we also create separate arrays of $rank_{dest,i}$, $outarry_i$, and $rank_{src,i}$ for each computing machine. The $rank_{dest,i}$ array and the $outarry_i$ array contain only the corresponding $\frac{T}{\beta}$ entries, while the $rank_{src,i}$ array contains the full set of rank scores that each machine needs to compute in each iteration step. The parallel version of the PageRank computation can be written in Algorithm 2.

Note that we first assign the MPI process identifier to each computing machine in line 1, then calculate the corresponding starting URL (B) and the ending

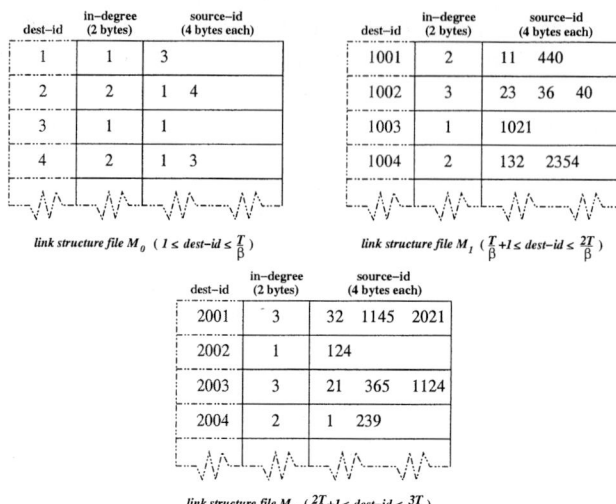

Fig. 3. The modified link structure file M used in parallel PageRank Algorithm.

URL (E), and initialize each destination rank score with its corresponding number of out-degree links. We refer to the machine with P_0 assigned as "master", and "slave" otherwise. Inspiring from the previous sequential algorithm, we use Algorithm 2 to iteratively compute the PageRank scores in each machine, and synchronize all final rank scores during each iteration step (see line 5-8 and 19-22) before recompute the PageRank scores in the consecutive iteration run.

As we can see that the computational cost of Algorithm 2 is still the same as that of Algorithm 1, plus the extra communication cost needed to send back and forth the subset of destination rank scores from slaves to master. To reduce this extra cost, we let the rank score synchronization occur once after 5 consecutive iteration steps (see line 5 and 19). From the experiments, the overall PageRank scores still converge.

5 Experimental Results and Discussion

5.1 Experimental Setup

Machine Setup: For all experiments, we use a PC cluster composing of four machines running Linux and SCE cluster management tool [17]. Each machine is equipped with an Athlon 1800XP CPU, 1 GB of main memory, and an ATA100 40GB, 7200 RPM hard disk. Both proposed algorithms were written in C language using the standard I/O library provided by the GCC compiler. The parallel version of Algorithm 2 is written using the message passing MPICH 1.2.5 library[1].

---

[1] http://www-unix.mcs.anl.gov/mpi/mpich/

Algorithm 2: Parallel PageRank Algorithm.
───
1: assign the rank of MPI calling process to P_{id}
2: $B = (\frac{T}{\beta} \times P_{id}) + 1$, $E = \frac{T}{\beta} \times (P_{id} + 1)$
3: $\forall_{t=B..E} rank_{dest,P_{id}}[t] = \frac{1}{outarry_{P_{id}}[t]}$, $\alpha = 0.85$
4: **for** $round = 1$ to 50 **do**
5:   **if** $round$ mod $5 == 0$ **then**
6:     **if** $P_{id} == 0$ **then** send merged $rank_{src,i}$ scores to all slaves
7:     **else** receive $rank_{src,i}$ scores **end if**
8:   **end if**
9:   $\forall_{t=B..E} rank_{dest,P_{id}}[t] = 0$, $sum = 0$
10:   **for** $t = B$ to E **do**
11:     **if** $M_{P_{id}}.read(indegree)! = 0$ **then**
12:       **for** $j = 1$ to $indegree$ **do**
13:         $M_{P_{id}}.read(src_j)$
14:         $sum = sum + rank_{src,P_{id}}[src_j]$
15:       **end for**
16:       $rank_{dest,P_{id}}[t] = \frac{(1-\alpha)+(\alpha \times sum)}{outarry_{P_{id}}[t]}$
17:     **end if**
18:   **end for**
19:   **if** $round$ mod $5 == 0$ **then**
20:     **if** $P_{id} == 0$ **then** receive slave's $rank_{dest,i}$ to be merged into $rank_{src,i}$
21:     **else** send own $rank_{dest,P_{id}}$ to master **end if**
22:   **end if**
23: **end for**
24: $\forall_{t=B..E} rank_{dest,P_{id}}[t] = rank_{dest,P_{id}} \times outarry_{P_{id}}[t]$

Input Data Set: We use a web graph derived from a crawl during January 2003 of roughly 10.9 million unique web pages, 97 million links, within the "TH" domain. This web graph was converted into the out-link file, as we depicted in previous Figure 1. We will hereafter name this file, the "1DB". We create additional artificial set of web graphs of larger size by concatenating several copies of the 1DB, and then connect those copies by rerouting some of the links. This creates larger out-link files representing large artificial web graphs of 2, 4, 8 times the size of the 1DB base graph, respectively. Before computing the PageRank scores, we preprocess and convert each DB data set into corresponding binary link structure file as mention in Section 4. Note that this preprocessing step takes several days of CPU time, which is much larger than the actual PageRank computational time reported in this paper.

5.2 Results and Discussion

In our experiments, we first run the sequential PageRank algorithm against all link structure files representing 1DB, 2DB, 4DB and 8DB. The average wall-clock times needed to complete an iteration run are 16.22, 28.54, 59.81, and 112.82 seconds, respectively. We then run the parallel PageRank algorithm against all link structure files again, using 2, and 4 machines. Using 4 machines, one Page-

Rank iteration run takes only 30.77 seconds on the 8DB data set (i.e., around 776 million links, 87 million URLs). Figure 4 concludes our experimental results by the four speedup curves. Remark that we also plot the ideal speedup curve for reference.

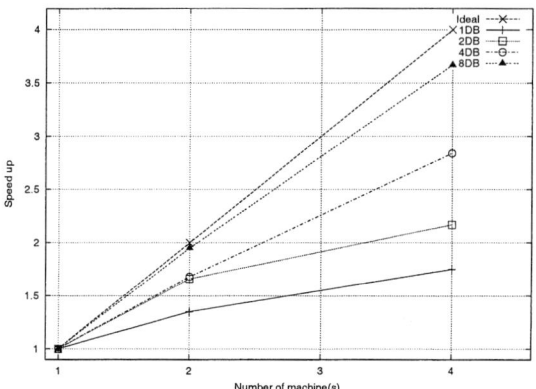

Fig. 4. The speedup results.

The experimental results make clear some characteristic of our proposed parallel PageRank algorithm. When we assign not enough data to each computing machine, most of the computational time would rather be spent on synchronization of the PageRank scores between machines (i.e., line 5-8 and 19-22 in Algorithm 2) than the PageRank score computation itself. The CPU utilization seems to be better when larger size of data has been assigned to each computing machine in the cluster.

6 Conclusion

The continuing growth of web graph containing several billion of URLs makes research that requires PageRank computation very expensive. Since low-cost x86 based PC machines running Linux can be affordable by many research institutions this day, using them to compute PageRank scores on large web graphs is another promising way. Here, we have proposed an efficient implementation of parallel PageRank algorithm on a PC cluster using a standard message passing library MPICH. A large web graph has been partitioned and distributed to several computing machines, and then we let the PageRank computation to be happened in parallel. Experimental results on an artificial web graph of 776 million links, 87 million URLs derived from a crawl within TH domain show that computing PageRank on a PC cluster give significant benefit if the sub-web graph assigned to each machine is large enough.

References

1. A. Arasu, J. Novak, A. Tomkins, and J. Tomlin. Pagerank computation and the structure of the web: Experiments and algorithms. *Proc. of the 11th WWW Conf.*, 2002. Poster Track.
2. K. Bharat, B.W. Chang, and M. Henzinger. Who links to whom: Mining linkage between web sites. *Proc. of the IEEE Conf. on Data Mining*, November 2001.
3. S. Brin and L. Page. The anatomy of a large-scale hypertextual web search engine. *Computer Networks*, 30 (1-7):107–117, 1998.
4. A. Broder, R. Kumar, F. Maghoul, P. Raghavan, S. Rajagopalan, and R. Stata. Graph structure in the web. *Proc. of the 9th WWW Conf.*, 2000.
5. S. Chakrabarti, M. van den Berg, and B. Dom. Focused crawling: A new approach to topic-specific web resource discovery. *Proc. of the 8th WWW Conf.*, 1999.
6. Y. Chen, Q. Gan, and T. Suel. I/O-efficient techniques for computing pagerank. *Proc. of the 11th ACM CIKM Conf.*, 2002.
7. S. Chien, C. Dwork anf R. Kumar, and D. Sivakumar. Towards exploting link evolution. *Workshop on Algorithms and Models for the Web Graph*, 2001.
8. J. Cho, H. Garcia-Molina, and L. Page. Efficient crawling through url ordering. *Proc. of the 7th WWW Conf.*, 1998.
9. G. Golub and C. Loan. *Matrix Computations*. Johns Hopkins U. Press, 1996.
10. T.H. Haveliwala. Efficient encodings for document ranking vectors. Technical report, Stanford University, November 2002.
11. T.H. Haveliwala. Topic-sensitive pagerank. *Proc. of the 11th WWW Conf.*, 2002.
12. S.D. Kamvar, T.H. Haveliwala, C.D. Manning, and G.H. Golub. Exploiting the block structure of the web for computing pagerank. Preprint, March 2003.
13. J.M. Kleinberg. Authoritative sources in a hyperlinked environment. *Proc. of the ACM-SIAM Symposium on Discrete Algorithms*, 1998.
14. J.M. Kleinberg, R. Kumar, P. Raghavan, S. Rajagopalan, and A.S. Tomkins. The web as a graph: Measurements, models and methods. *Proc. of the Inter. Conf. on Combinatorics and Computing*, 1999.
15. U. Krieger. Numerical solution of the large finite markov chains by algebraic multigrid techniques. *Proc. of the 2nd Workshop on the Numerical Solution of Markov Chains*, 1995.
16. M. Najork and J.L. Wiener. Breadth-first search crawling yields high-quality pages. *Proc. of the 10th WWW Conf.*, 2001.
17. P. Uthayopas, S. Phatanapherom, T. Angskun, and S. Sriprayoonsakul. SCE: A fully integrated software tool for beowulf cluster system. *Proc. of the Linux Cluster: the HPC Revol.*, 2001.

An Online Parallel Algorithm for Remote Visualization of Isosurfaces

Andrea Clematis[1], Daniele D'Agostino[1], and Vittoria Gianuzzi[2]

[1] IMATI-CNR, Via de Marini 6, 16149 Genova, Italy
{clematis,dago}@ge.imati.cnr.it
[2] DISI University of Genova, Via Dodecaneso 35, 16146 Genova, Italy
gianuzzi@disi.unige.it

Abstract. In this paper we present a parallel algorithm, implemented using MPICH, for isosurface extraction from volumetric data sets. The main contribution of this paper is in the analysis and performance improvements of the different phases of the isosurface production process including computation and output generation. The resulting algorithm is particularly well suited for online applications and for remote results visualization.

1 Introduction

Nowadays large collections of 3D and volumetric data are available, and many people with expertise in different disciplines access these data through the Web. Volumetric data are the product of different type of instruments such as medical equipments, or the result of time dependent simulations. Isosurface extraction [1] is a basic operation that permits to implement many types of queries on volumetric data. The product of an isosurface extraction is a Triangulated Irregular Network (TIN) containing a more or less large number of points and of topological elements (triangles, edges and vertices), depending on the amount of data in the original data set and on the specific isovalue.

Considering the huge size of volumetric data sets different algorithms have been developed in order to accelerate the isosurface extraction process [2–5]. These algorithms are based on parallel computing and on the use of out-of-core computations in order to reduce the computing time and to deal with main memory constraints. Parallel processing is exploited using data parallel approach and the main emphasis is on load balancing. In order to speed up out-of-core computation indices are created that permit a rapid access to relevant data for each specific interrogation. The creation of indices requires a preprocessing phase, normally executed out-of-line. Some parallel algorithms exploit the pre-computed indices in order to load balance the computation on the parallel system.

In many applications the result of isosurface extraction is immediately visualized and the interrogation and visualization system are tightly coupled.

In other applications, however data sets are created dynamically and users are interested to execute online query in a real time environment. This point makes it not convenient to prepare indices. Also the interrogation could start from a remote terminal and results should be visualized on it. This last point raises the problem of finding a suitable format for output considering both the necessity of reducing the file size to save time during data transmission, and to gain the benefits derived from the use of a standard format, like VRML [7], to easy accommodate heterogeneous client browsers.

In this paper we are interested in developing a practical parallel algorithm for online isosurface extraction without the support of precomputed indices. We are also interested in producing a suitable output for remote visualization on heterogeneous clients. Load balancing in our case cannot rely on the availability of a pre-computed index, and hence we adopt a low cost but enough efficient strategy at this aim. We are interested in improving performances of the whole isosurface extraction and output production process. In other papers we have found contribution that discuss how to optimize the computation (isosurface extraction) but not the output production phase.

At this aim we have to consider that the production of a consistent and space efficient output in a standard format need a sewing phase after parallel computation. This point is not addressed, at our knowledge, in previous works. Our solution tries to combine load balancing with the sewing and output production phase. In order to reduce the output size we adopt in the parallel algorithm an approach that avoids duplicating points during the isosurface extraction. This approach is derived from considerations that we originally applied to optimize existing sequential algorithms.

The remaining part of the paper is organized as follows. Section 2 describes some related works. Sect. 3 describes the sequential algorithm structure, its computational cost and our parallel algorithm. Sect. 4 shows the experimental results and Sect. 5 our conclusions and future works.

2 Related Work

Several isosurface extraction systems have the main purpose of locally visualize extracted meshes using cluster of workstation or PC. In [2] it is presented a scalable isosurface extraction and visualization algorithm that exploits parallel processing and parallel disks in conjunction with the use of specialized hardware for multiple displays handling. In [3] it is presented an unified infrastructure for parallel out-of-core isosurface extraction and volume rendering based on a pre-processing phase, the "meta-cells" technique. Other systems uses supercomputer to performs isosurface extraction. In [4] a parallel isosurface extraction module is presented in the context of IRIS explorer system. They adapt the VTK Marching Cubes class avoiding multiple computation of shared points, storing the resulting mesh in an own file formats. In [5] an approach to parallelization of isosurface extraction on a vector-parallel supercomputer is presented.

Our main contribution is the analysis of the cost and the performance improvement of the different phases of isosurface extraction including output production in a standard format. The aim is to develop, for a COTS cluster of PC, a load balanced parallel solution that limits inter process communications, data movement and data replication and provides a quite efficient output production.

3 The Algorithm

The Marching Cubes algorithm [1] is the classical approach to extract isosurfaces from volumetric data sets. Volumetric data set are normally structured as a set of slices where, for each slice, points have equal z, stored in an unique file ordered along z (often called "raw") or with a file for each slice. We will briefly describe the sequential algorithm structure, to analyze the computational cost in order to develop an efficient parallel version to improve it.

3.1 Sequential Algorithm Description

The algorithm traverses a volumetric data set processing a cube, called *cell*, at a time. Cells are obtained considering eight vertices, four belonging to the upper slice, four to the lower. There are 256 possible combinations of the vertices of a cell being above or below the threshold value. This means that there are 254 possible ways the cell can be intersected from the isosurface. In these cases linear interpolation is used to determine where the surface intersects cube edges. The original triangulation schema can (even if not so frequently) produces small "holes" as result of inconsistency in the connection of certain configuration of vertices on faces shared by two adjacent cells. We solved the problem using an alternative scheme proposed in [6] to obtain at least a *consistent* triangulation.

The Marching cubes algorithm is composed by three steps:

1. identification of *active cells*: every cell is analyzed to determine if it is intersected by the isosurface;
2. for each active cell the kind of intersection (and consequently triangulation) is determined;
3. the intersection points coordinates are computed using a linear interpolation of the vertices of intersected edges.

The first step is proportionally very expensive when the percentage of active cells is very small with respect to the total. To get round of this problem several proposals were made, that exploit a preprocessed search data structures. In this manner it is possible to skip step one and consider only active cells, but paying the time saving with the storage space for search data structure. We do not further consider the use of out-of-line preprocessing in this paper since we propose an online approach suitable for dynamic and one-shot data sets.

The second step consists in fast accesses to a lookup table containing information for each possible kind of intersection.

The third step produces the triangular mesh and it is the most expensive from the computational point of view.

Let us first of all shortly discuss the format of output produced by this step. To reduce communication between parallel processes meshes could be stored as a list of triangles, each of this represented by three records, with each record consisting of six single precision floating point numbers representing the triangle vertices coordinates plus, possibly, the vertices normal. However this representation is not space efficient because there are a lot of replicated data (in general a

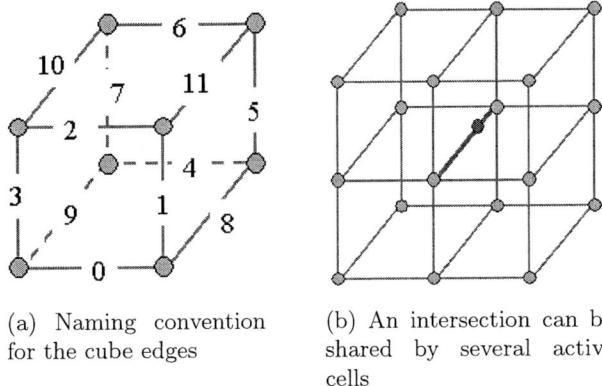

(a) Naming convention for the cube edges

(b) An intersection can be shared by several active cells

Fig. 1. The cubes considered for the isosurface extraction

point is shared by more than two triangles, both in the same cell and in adjacent ones, as the darker point in Fig. 1(b)). This problem has an heavy impact on the output dimension: to eliminate duplicates a postprocessing step can be performed, but is a very time expensive operation. On the contrary a smart format to store meshes uses two tables: the first, the **V table**, lists the Cartesian coordinates of each intersection point; the second, the **TV table**, lists each triangle providing the three indices to its vertices in the V table. In parallel processing the main problem is due to the intersections that lies on the border produced by data partitioning. Processes sharing points have to come to an agreement on who stores the points coordinates and what are the indices to use in the TV table to denote them.

To do it we use a technique proposed in [8] to avoid the multiple recomputation of a same point in the sequential algorithm. Typically the algorithm traverses the slices for the lower z value to the upper and for rows, so for a generic cell (see Fig. 1(a)) only intersections belonging to edges 1,2,11 are really new. In fact possible intersections in edges 0, 4, 8, 9, were computed in the lower cell, possible intersections in edges 7, 5, 6 were computed in the previous cell considering the column, and possible intersections in edges 10 and 3 were computed in the previous cell considering the row.

With this technique it is possible to maintain an unique copy of the coordinate of each intersection in the V table "remembering" some points from a cube to another and using coherently the same index to denote triangles vertices in the TV table avoiding a postprocessing step, reducing both the computation time and the output dimension. We point out that thanks to the independence of non-contiguous slices it is possible to load and process many slices at a time, storing in files points and triangles progressively collected, while solving in a smart way the problem of processing data shared by cells. This is very important for a parallel version of this algorithm, where data are partitioned among different processes.

3.2 Cost Analysis

The time necessary to perform the isosurface extraction, T, is given by $T_{Analysis} + T_{Computation}(isovalue)$.

- $T_{Analysis}$ corresponds to the first step of the Marching Cubes algorithm. It is independent from the isovalue because it represents the time spent in the analysis of each cell of the domain.
- $T_{Computation}(isovalue)$ corresponds to steps 2 and 3, and it is dependent from the numbers of active cells for a specific isovalue.

A preprocessing step can reduce $T_{Analysis}$, while the reuse of intersections can reduce the part related to step 3 of $T_{Computation}$. In the following, for a more compact notation, we consider $T_C = T_{Analysis} + T_{Computation}(isovalue)$. If we want a results in a unique file we must add the output production time T_{Output}. The more efficient way to obtain the output file is to append the TV file to the file containing points: in this case T_{Output} corresponds to the "appending" time.

An example of this subdivision of the total time to produce an isosurface we can consider Tab. 2 at page 167. Tests were performed on a 1.7 GHz Pentium Xeon equipped with 256 MB RAM using a 16 MB data set composed by 256*256*256 points.

3.3 Parallel Algorithm

The data parallel approach is the the natural way to parallelize the Marching Cubes algorithm since data can mostly be handled in an independent way. We developed a master-worker program using MPICH [9] for a cluster of almost dedicated machines. The domain is partitioned as a set of independent subdomains, but having the purpose to produce an output file in a compact and standard format the treatment of intersections belonging to the border must be carefully handled. Moreover we should pay attention to load balancing. To obtain of good performance figures heavily depends on these two aspects.

Our parallel algorithm is made by the following steps:

- *Initial Data Distribution*, done by the master.
- *Parallel Identification of active slices and cells for load balancing*. Information are collected for each pair of slices according to the specified isovalue, with the main purpose to balance the workload among the workers.
- *Data Redistribution for load balancing*, done by the master.
- *Parallel Isoextraction*. Every worker extracts the isosurface from its domain subset. The resulting mesh is stored into files.
- *Parallel Sewing*. The triangles are disguised as the three indices of the vertices composing it. Those having one or more vertices on the border with another worker can have negative indices denoting them. Processes then communicate each other these indices, in order to produce a coherent set of files that the master could concatenate together without further modifications.
- *Final Assembling*, done by the master.

The **Parallel Identification of active cells** step has the main purpose to collect, for each pair of slices, the number of intersections. Also the y coordinate of the first intersection are collected. We use in fact an ehuristic, useful when cell intersected are few and grouped, to reduce the following computation time: we start considering cells only from the row before the first intersection and we examine cells only until the number of intersections is met. In this phase the assignment for each worker consists of a set of contiguous slices, indicated by the start and stop indices of the set of slices. Data set is shared using NFS, without a considerable gain in time time and space with respect to send to each worker its slices, as showed in Tab. 1. Slices are partitioned in equal parts among workers because the identification of active cells is little dependent from the isovalue: the operation performed for each intersection founded is the increment of a counter. At the end workers return collected results (intersections number founded and y indices for each pair of slices) to the master.

In the **Data Redistribution** step the master subdivides the data set assigning a set of *active slices* to each worker so that each set has approximatively the same number of active cells. The workload balancing is a *static* solution based on the preprocessing step and the percentage of PC cpu idle collected at the beginning of each of the first two steps. In case of heterogeneous cluster it is possible to maintain the approach adding a weight to each PC. We chose to maintain the slice as data unit to reduce data collected in the second step and the borders between processes assignments. A further motivation is because data sets are stored for XY slices, hence the reading operations are faster using slice as processing unit.

Active slices are assigned in an ordered way, trying to keep contiguous slices assigned to the same worker. A worker reads as much as possible contiguous slices together in order to optimize disk accesses. The number of contiguous slices that can be read at once is determined considering the amount of free RAM.

Exploiting data locality we reduce the border between processes and, consequently, the exchange of information of the sewing.

In the **Parallel Isoextraction** step each worker extracts the isosurfaces considering its slices, and storing founded points and triangles into three files:

- *Points file*: it contains the coordinates of the computed intersection. The file created by worker W_i does not overlap with those created by workers W_{i-1} and W_{i+1}.
- *Triangles file*: it contains triangles represented by three positive indices
- *Border triangles file*: it contains triangles with one or two vertices on the boundary, represented by negative indices. The substitution of these negative value is made by the sewing step.

Index defines the position of each vertex in the Points file. Indices are coherent because, from the identification step, each process W_i knows how many points $(W_{i-1}, \ldots, W_0)$ have, so it starts its indices from that value. The aspect to take into account is related to the border points: consecutive processes W_{i-1} and W_i may share a slice and consequently the intersections belonging to it. We treat this border problem using the technique described for the sequential algorithm,

Table 1. Comparison between a parallel implementation that uses intermediate ASCII files ($MCPAR_A$) with that uses binary ones ($MCPAR_B$), with data set shared via NFS or (previously) replicated. Time are given in seconds

Version	Data set	No. Triangles	T_{Id}	T_{Comp}	T_{Out}	Total
$MCPAR_A$	NFS	286,954	1.34	2.45	1.4	4.88
$MCPAR_B$	NFS	286,954	1.9	2.25	1.36	5.54
$MCPAR_A$	LOCAL	286,954	1.36	2.53	1.17	4.91
$MCPAR_B$	LOCAL	286,954	1.9	2.25	1.29	5.46
$MCPAR_A$	NFS	3,896,986	2.29	18.39	19.97	40.6
$MCPAR_B$	NFS	3,896,986	1.51	7.07	17.75	26.33
$MCPAR_A$	LOCAL	3,896,986	1.36	16.1	21.7	39.32
$MCPAR_B$	LOCAL	3,896,986	1.33	6.47	18.56	26.36

so the ownership of shared points is given to W_{i-1}. In fact W_i, for its first slices, considers each square and precomputes first all intersections for edges 0, 4, and then for 8, 9, storing them in two matrices, respectively *xedge* and *yedge*. But W_i, instead of adding these points to its points file, stores in the matrices a progressive negative index, using it to denote one of this point in triangles representation.

It is to note that these intermediate file are binary. The I/O problem, in fact, is very relevant. A sequential version can store points and triangles using ASCII format, because it has only to concatenate the local triangles to the points file, having no problem on renaming triangles indices. A parallel version instead, to achieve a considerable speed-up, should limit communication cost and other possible overheads. Workers store their partial results in files, that should be accessed by the master in the final assembling step. We notice that to replicate data on local disks does not provide significative improvement with respect to the use of NFS. On the contrary the use of a binary format for intermediate files gives a consistent improvement with respect to the use of a ASCII format. A time comparison that put in evidence the efficiency of the different approaches is provided in Tab. 1. We use T_{Id} to denote steps 1 and 2, T_{Comp} for steps 3 and 4, T_{Out} for the remaining ones.

In the **Parallel Sewing** step at first processes send Points files to the master that provides to assemble them, adding the header. Then a process W_i extracts from the last xedge and yedge all the significant indices, sending it to the process W_{i+1} and receives the same information from process W_{i-1}. Using the absolute value of the negative index it is possible to replace the correct value.

Finally triangle files are given to the master that provides to **assemble** them, adding the other notation needed by the output format (e. g. VRML 2.0).

4 Experimental Results

We have experimented our algorithm using a data set representing a CT scan of a bonsai (available at URL http://www.volvis.org/). It is a 16 MB data set composed by 256 slices of 256*256 points with 8 bits values. In Tab. 2 are listed

Table 2. Characteristics of the meshes resulting from isovalues used for the tests and time (in seconds) subdivision between phases for a sequential out-of-core version of Marching Cubes algorithm. Output dimensions refers to a VRML 2.0 ASCII file

Isovalue	No. Points	No. Triangles	Output dimension	T_C	T_{Output}	T
254	3,245	6,348	871 KB	5.62	0.31	5.652
180	144,800	286,954	9.54 MB	6.86	0.84	7.70
2	1,962,635	3,896,986	170.8 MB	23.71	15.9	39.74

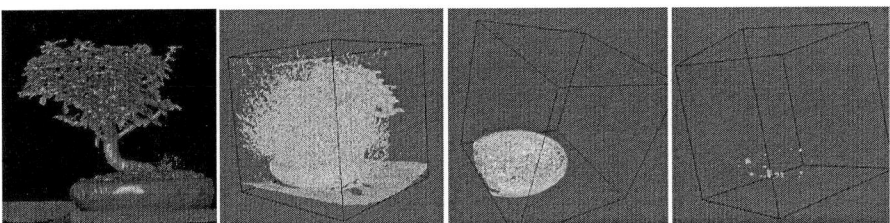

Fig. 2. Visualization of the meshes produced during the test. Starting from the original data set representation, meshes for isovalue 2, 180 and 254 are showed

the meshes characteristics for the isovalues considered in the experiments, and in Fig. 2 these meshes are showed.

For the tests we initially used a cluster of four PC, equipped with 1.7 GHz Pentium IV processor and 256 MB RAM, connected via Fast Ethernet and running Linux (RedHat 7.1) operative systems. NFS was used to share a disk partition. Our program uses a processors for the master and a processor for each worker. Tab. 3 shows tests results comparing the sequential results with the parallel executions. We used also a less powerful cluster of nine PC (266 MHz Pentium II with 128 MB RAM) to test the scalability of our algorithm. Results are showed in Fig. 3.

The performances of our algorithm are good both if we consider only the isosurface extraction or the whole process. In fact, over the four Pentium IV for isovalue 254 we have a speed-up value of, respectively, 1.53 and 1.51, for 180 we have 1.65 and 1.41, for 2 we have 3.04 and 1.51. The loss in speed-up and efficiency considering also the output step is due to the communication channel: for the isovalue 2 the sum of sizes of the files produced by the worker is about 67 MB, so the speed-up decrease from 3.04 to 1.51. The same situation happen for the execution on the cluster with 9 processors. The problem of performance reduction for the whole process could be partially solved using Parallel File Systems and/or faster connection as Gigabit Ethernet or Myrinet.

5 Conclusion and Future Works

The main contribution of this paper is a parallel algorithm for isosurface extraction that:

Table 3. A comparison between time (in sec.) spent in the various step of the Marching Cubes algorithm for a sequential and for our parallel version over 4 processors

Version	Isovalue	T_{Id}	T_{Comp}	T_{Out}	T
Sequential	254	0	5.62	0.31	5.65
Parallel	254	1.94	1.74	0.28	3.74
Sequential	180	0	6.86	0.84	7.7
Parallel	180	1.9	2.25	1.29	5.46
Sequential	2	0	23.71	15.9	39.74
Parallel	2	1.33	6.47	18.57	26.36

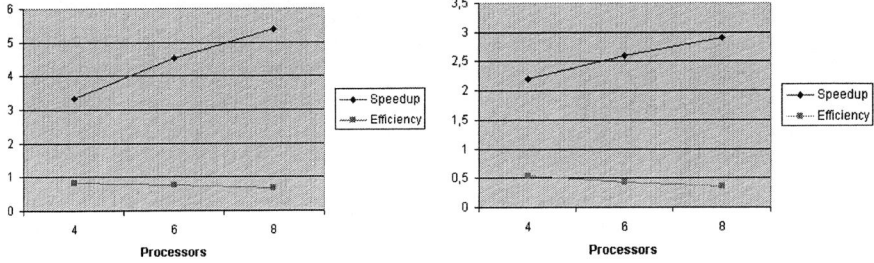

(a) Speed-up and Efficiency for the Isosurface extraction step.

(b) Speed-up and Efficiency for the whole process.

Fig. 3. Speed-up and Efficiency using 4, 6 and 8 workers for isovalue 180

- is able to treat huge data set exploiting out-of-core techniques;
- exploit spatial data coherence to speed-up the isosurface extraction step;
- produces an output using a standard format as VRML minimizing data postprocessing, communications between processes and sizes of data moved.

Future works will include a further and in-deep analysis of the load balancing step, in order to handle situations in which, for same isovalues, data are condensed in a very small number of slices.

Moreover we are interested in experimenting the use of advanced communication network and output devices to reduce the overhead during the sewing and assembling phases.

Finally we plan to develop a new version of this algorithm using an high level parallel programming environment [10].

Acknoledgements

This work has been supported by CNR Agenzia 2000 Programme "An Environment for the Development of Multiplatform and Multilanguage High Performance Applications based on the Object Model and Structured Parallel Programming" and by MIUR programme L. 449/97-99 SP3 "Grid Computing: enabling Technologies and Applications for eScience".

References

1. W. E. Lorensen and H. E. Cline: Marching Cubes: A High Resolution 3D Surface Construction Algorithm. In Computer Graphics (Proceedings of SIGGRAPH 87), 1987, vol. 21, no. 4, pp. 163-169.
2. X. Zhang, C. Bajaj, W. Blanke and D. Fussell: Scalable isosurface visualization of massive datasets on COTS clusters. In IEEE Symposium on Parallel and Large-Data Visualization and Graphics, 2001, pp. 51-58.
3. Y.-J. Chiang, R. Farias, C.T. Silva, and B. Wei: A Unified Infrastructure for Parallel Out-Of-Core Isosurface Extraction and Volume Rendering of Unstructured Grids.In IEEE Symposium on Parallel and Large-Data Visualization and Graphics 2001 proceedings, 2001, pp. 59-66.
4. S. Lombeyda, M. Aivazis and M. Rajan: Parallel Isosurface Calculation and Rendering of Large Datasets in IRIS Explorer. In Visualization Development Environments 2000 Proceedings, 2000.
5. T. S. Newman and N. Tang: Approaches that Exploit Vector-parallelism for three Rendering and Volume Visualization Techniques. In Computers & Graphics, 2000, vol. 24, no. 5, pp. 137-150.
6. C. Montani, R. Scateni, and R. Scopigno: A modified look-up table for implicit disambiguation of Marching Cubes. In The Visual Computer, 1994, vol. 10, no. 6, pp.353-355.
7. VRML: http://www.web3d.org/
8. Watt A. and Watt M: Advanced Animation and Rendering Techniques: Theory and Practice. ACM Press, 1996.
9. MPICH: http://www-unix.mcs.anl.gov/mpi/mpich/
10. M. Vanneschi: The programming model of ASSIST, an environment for parallel and distributed portable applications. In Parallel Computing, vol 28. no. 12, 2002, pp. 1709-1732.

Parallel Algorithms for Computing the Smith Normal Form of Large Matrices
(Extended Abstract)

Gerold Jäger

Mathematisches Seminar der Christian-Albrechts-Universität zu Kiel,
Christian-Albrechts-Platz 4, D-24118 Kiel, Germany
gej@numerik.uni-kiel.de

Abstract. Smith normal form computation has many applications in group theory, module theory and number theory. As the entries of the matrix and of its corresponding transformation matrices can explode during the computation, it is a very difficult problem to compute the Smith normal form of large dense matrices. The computation has two main problems: the high execution time and the memory requirements, which might exceed the memory of one processor. To avoid these problems, we develop two parallel Smith normal form algorithms using MPI. These are the first algorithms computing the Smith normal form with corresponding transformation matrices, both over the rings $\mathbb{Z}$ and $\mathbb{F}[x]$. We show that our parallel algorithms both have a good efficiency, i.e. by doubling the processes, the execution time is nearly halved, and succeed in computing the Smith normal form of dense example matrices over the rings $\mathbb{Z}$ and $\mathbb{F}_2[x]$ with more than thousand rows and columns.

1 Introduction

A matrix in $R^{m,n}$ over a Euclidean ring R with rank r is in *Smith normal form*, if it is a diagonal matrix with the first r diagonal elements being divisors of the next diagonal element and the last diagonal elements being zero. A theorem of Smith says that you can obtain from an arbitrary matrix in $R^{m,n}$ the uniquely determined Smith normal form by doing unimodular row and column operations.

The Smith normal form plays an important role in the theory of finite Abelian groups and in the theory of finitely generated modules over principal ideal rings. For many applications, for example the integer solutions of an integer system of linear equations, the transformation matrices describing the unimodular operations are important as well.

There are many algorithms for efficiently computing the Smith normal form, most of them only for one of the rings $\mathbb{Z}$ or $\mathbb{F}[x]$. Some of these algorithms are probabilistic ([2] for $R = \mathbb{Z}$, [16] for $R = \mathbb{Q}[x]$). Deterministic algorithms for $R = \mathbb{Z}$ often use modular techniques ([3], [5], [12, Chapter 8.4], [14], [15]). Unfortunately, these algorithms are unable to compute the corresponding transformation matrices.

We shortly introduce the two most important Smith normal form algorithms which work for both the ring $\mathbb{Z}$ and the ring $\mathbb{F}[x]$ and which are able to compute the corresponding transformation matrices. Both the algorithm of Kannan, Bachem [9] and the algorithm of Hartley, Hawkes [4] compute the diagonal form first and finally with an elementary algorithm the Smith normal form.

The disadvantage of these algorithms is that during the computation the entries of the matrix and the corresponding transformation matrices can be very large, even exponential [1]. For high-dimensional matrices with large entries this leads to high execution times and memory problems which can be solved by parallelization.

In [7], [8] and [17] parallel probabilistic algorithms are introduced for the ring $\mathbb{F}[x]$, but without experimental results, and in [11] a parallel algorithm is described, which only works for characteristic matrices.

In this paper we parallelize the general algorithms of Kannan, Bachem and Hartley, Hawkes for rectangular matrices. The main problem is how to uniformly distribute a large matrix to many processes. The key observation is that a row distribution is more efficient, if we use column operations, and column distribution is more efficient, if we use row operations. As we use both row and column operations, we develop an auxiliary algorithm which transforms a row distributed matrix into a column distributed one and vice versa. We estimate the parallel operations of our two algorithms and see that the complexity of the parallel Hartley-Hawkes-Algorithm is better than that of the parallel Kannan-Bachem-Algorithm.

We implement the algorithms and test it for large dense matrices over the rings $\mathbb{Z}$ and $\mathbb{F}_2[x]$. The experiments show that the parallel Kannan-Bachem-Algorithm leads to better results for the ring $\mathbb{Z}$ and the parallel Hartley-Hawkes-Algorithm to better results for the ring $\mathbb{F}_2[x]$. Considering medium-sized matrices, we see that the algorithms have a good efficiency, even for 64 processes. The algorithms are also able to compute the Smith normal form with its corresponding transformation matrices of very large matrices in reasonable time. Because of the memory requirements, the program package MAGMA is not able to do such computations.

2 Preliminaries

2.1 Notations and Definitions

Let R be a commutative, integral ring with 1. Let R be *Euclidean*, i.e. there is a mapping $\phi : R \setminus \{0\} \to \mathbb{N}_0$ such that for $a \in R, b \in R \setminus \{0\}$ exist $q, r \in R$ with $a = qb + r$ and $r = 0 \vee \phi(r) < \phi(b)$. We consider the following two examples:

a) The set $\mathbb{Z}$ of integers

We choose $\phi := |\cdot|$, $\mathcal{R} := \mathbb{N}_0$. For $a \in \mathbb{R}$ let $\lfloor a \rfloor$ be the largest integer $\leq a$. With the above notations we define $\psi(a,b) := r = a - \lfloor a/b \rfloor \cdot b$. For $A \in \mathbb{Z}^{m,n}$ let $\|A\|_\infty := \max_{1 \leq i,j \leq n}\{|A_{i,j}|\}$.

b) The polynomial ring $\mathbb{F}[x]$ with a field $\mathbb{F}$

We choose $\phi := \deg$, $\mathcal{R} := \{\text{Monic polynomials over } \mathbb{F}[x]\}$. With the above notations we define $\psi(a,b) := r$, where r is uniquely determined by polynomial division of a and b. For $A \in \mathbb{F}[x]^{m,n}$ let $\lceil A \rceil_{\deg} := \max_{1 \leq i,j \leq n} \{\deg(A_{i,j})\}$.

Definition 1. $GL_n(R)$ *is the group of matrices in* $R^{n,n}$ *whose determinant is a unit in the ring* R. *These matrices are called unimodular matrices.*

Definition 2. *A matrix* $A \in R^{m,n}$ *with rank* r *is in Hermite normal form (HNF), if the following conditions hold:*
a) $\exists i_1, \cdots, i_r$ *with* $1 \leq i_1 < \cdots < i_r \leq m$ *with* $A_{i_j,j} \in \mathcal{R} \setminus 0$ *for* $1 \leq j \leq r$.
b) $A_{i,j} = 0$ *for* $1 \leq i \leq i_j - 1$, $1 \leq j \leq r$.
c) *The columns* $r+1, \cdots, n$ *are zero.*
d) $A_{i_j,l} = \psi(A_{i_j,l}, A_{i_j,j})$ *for* $1 \leq l < j \leq r$.
The matrix A *is in left Hermite normal form (LHNF), if its transpose* A^T *is in HNF.*

Theorem 1. [6] *Let* $A \in R^{m,n}$. *There exists a matrix* $V \in GL_n(R)$ *such that* $H = AV$ *is in HNF. The matrix* H *is uniquely determined.*

Definition 3. *A matrix* $A \in R^{m,n}$ *with rank* r *is in Smith normal form (SNF), if the following conditions hold:*
a) A *is a diagonal matrix.*
b) $A_{i,i} \in \mathcal{R} \setminus \{0\}$ *for* $1 \leq i \leq r$.
c) $A_{i,i} \mid A_{i+1,i+1}$ *for* $1 \leq i \leq r-1$.
d) $A_{i,i} = 0$ *for* $r+1 \leq i \leq \min\{m,n\}$.

Theorem 2. [13] *Let* $A \in R^{m,n}$. *There exist matrices* $U \in GL_m(R)$ *and* $V \in GL_n(R)$ *such that* $C = UAV$ *is in SNF. The matrix* C *is uniquely determined. The matrices* U, V *are called the corresponding left hand and right hand transformation matrix for the Smith normal form.*

In the following Smith normal form algorithms we receive the corresponding transformation matrices, if we apply the row operations to E_m and the column operations to E_n.

2.2 Algorithm DIAGTOSMITH

In the SNF algorithms we use an elementary algorithm DIAGTOSMITH which computes the Smith normal form of a matrix in diagonal form [10, p. 318, Hilfssatz 11.5.14]. Two neighboring diagonal elements are substituted by its gcd and its lcm, until the matrix is in Smith normal form. The algorithm needs $\min\{m,n\}^2$ gcd computations.

2.3 Kannan-Bachem-Algorithm

The algorithm of Kannan and Bachem ([9]) alternately computes the Hermite normal form and the left Hermite normal form, until the matrix is in diagonal form. At the end the algorithm DIAGTOSMITH is applied.

Remark 1. Let $A \in R^{m,n}$ with $p = \max\{m,n\}$. Then the HNF and LHNF procedure of the Kannan-Bachem-Algorithm is executed $O(p^2 \log_2(p\|A\|_\infty))$ times for $R = \mathbb{Z}$ and $O(p^2 \lceil A \rceil_{\deg})$ times for $R = \mathbb{F}[x]$.

2.4 Hartley-Hawkes-Algorithm

For i, j with $1 \leq i \leq m$, $1 \leq j \leq n$ ROWGCD (A, i, j) transforms A so that $A_{i,j}^{\text{new}} = \gcd(A_{i,j}^{\text{old}}, A_{i,j+1}^{\text{old}}, \cdots, A_{i,n}^{\text{old}}) \in \mathcal{R}$, $A_{i,j+1}^{\text{new}} = \cdots = A_{i,n}^{\text{new}} = 0$. This is done by subtracting the multiple of a column from a different column very often. The procedure COLGCD is analogously defined with the role of rows and columns exchanged. The algorithm of Hartley and Hawkes [4, p. 112] alternately uses the procedures ROWGCD (l, l) and COLGCD (l, l), until the first $l - 1$ rows and columns have diagonal form. Finally the algorithm DIAGTOSMITH is used again.

Remark 2. Let $A \in R^{m,n}$ with $p = \max\{m,n\}$. Then the ROWGCD and COL-GCD procedure of the Hartley-Hawkes-Algorithm is executed at most $O(p^2 \log_2(p\|A\|_\infty))$ times for $R = \mathbb{Z}$ and at most $O(p^2 \lceil A \rceil_{\deg})$ times for $R = \mathbb{F}[x]$.

3 Parallelization of the Smith Normal Form Algorithms

3.1 Idea of Parallelization

A parallel program is a set of independent processes with data being interchanged between the processes. For interchanging the data we need the following procedures:

- With **BROADCAST x** a process sends a variable x to all other processes.
- With **BROADCAST-RECEIVE x FROM z** a process receives a variable x from the process with the number z which it has sent with BROADCAST.
- With **SEND x TO z** a process sends a variable x to the process with the number z.
- With **SEND-RECEIVE x FROM z** a process receives a variable x from the process with the number z which it has sent with SEND.

The matrix whose Smith normal form shall be computed has to be distributed to the different processes as uniformly as possible. It is straightforward to put different rows or different columns of a matrix to one process. For algorithms, in which mainly column operations are used, a column distribution is not sensible, as for column additions with multiplicity the columns involved in computations mostly belong to different processes, so that for each such computation a whole column has to be sent. So we decide to distribute rows, if column operations are used, and columns, if row operations are used. As for Smith normal form algorithms both operations are used, we have to switch between both distributions (see the procedures PAR-ROWTOCOL and PAR-COLTOROW).

We consider a row distribution. Let the matrix $\bar{A} \in R^{m,n}$ be distributed on q processes and let the z-th process consist of $k(z)$ rows. Every process z has as input a matrix $A \in R^{k(z),n}$ with $\sum_{z=1}^{q} k(z) = m$. For every process let the order of the rows be equal to the original order. At any time we can obtain the complete matrix by putting together these matrices. We choose the following uniform distribution:

The process with the number z receives the rows $z, z+q, \cdots, z+\lfloor (m-z)/q \rfloor \cdot q$. Further we need the following functions:

- For $1 \leq l \leq m$, ROW-TASK(l) returns the number of the process owning the l-th row.
- For $1 \leq l \leq m$, ROW-NUM(l) returns the row number of the original l-th row, if the row lies on its own process, and otherwise the row number, which it would get, if it would be inserted into its own process.

Analogously, we define the column distribution and the functions COL-TASK and COL-NUM. Since only column operations are performed on the right hand transformation matrix V, we choose for V a row distribution. Analogously, we choose a column distribution for the left hand transformation matrix U.

Theorem 3. [18] *Let $p = \max\{m, n\}$. There is a parallel HNF algorithm in which $O(p^2)$ BROADCAST operations are performed and $O(p^3)$ ring elements are sent with BROADCAST.*

3.2 Auxiliary Algorithm PAR-DIAGTOSMITH

As the original procedure DIAGTOSMITH is very fast in practice, it is sufficient to parallelize it trivially. Every diagonal element is broadcast from the process it lies on to all other processes so that the operations can be performed. In this algorithm $O(p^2)$ BROADCAST operations are performed and $O(p^2)$ ring elements are sent with BROADCAST. We use two versions of this algorithm, one for row distribution and one for column distribution.

3.3 Auxiliary Algorithms PAR-ROWTOCOL and PAR-COLTOROW

The algorithm PAR-ROWTOCOL changes a row distributed matrix into a column distributed matrix. Let $A \in R^{k(z),n}$ with $\sum_{z=1}^{q} k(z) = m$ be row distributed. A is transformed into a matrix $B \in R^{m,k'(z)}$ with $\sum_{z=1}^{q} k'(z) = n$. Every process communicates with every other process. For a process x the SEND operation has the following form:

SEND $\{A_{s,t} \mid 1 \leq s \leq k(x),\ 1 \leq t \leq n\}$ TO COL-TASK(t)

For a process x the SEND-RECEIVE operation has the following form:

SEND-RECEIVE $\{B_{s,t} \mid 1 \leq s \leq m,\ 1 \leq t \leq k'(x)\}$ FROM ROW-TASK(s)

This algorithm does not need to be applied to the corresponding transformation matrices, as we always transform the left hand transformation matrix U by row operations and the right hand transformation matrix V by column operations.

We obtain the algorithm PAR-COLTOROW from the algorithm PAR-ROWTOCOL by exchanging the role of rows and columns.

3.4 Parallel Kannan-Bachem-Algorithm

Algorithm 1
INPUT Number of processes q, number of its own process z,
$A \in R^{k(z),n}$, $\sum_{z=1}^{q} k(z) = m$ and whole matrix $\bar{A} \in R^{m,n}$
1 WHILE ($\bar{A}$ is not in diagonal form)
2         $A = PAR\text{-}HNF(A)$
3         $B = PAR\text{-}ROWTOCOL(A)$ $\left(B \in R^{m,k'(z)}, \sum_{z=1}^{q} k'(z) = n\right)$
4         $B = PAR\text{-}LHNF(B)$
5         $A = PAR\text{-}COLTOROW(B)$
6 $A = PAR\text{-}DIAGTOSMITH(A)$
OUTPUT $A = PAR\text{-}SNF(A) \in R^{k(z),n}$

Theorem 4. Let $\bar{A} \in R^{m,n}$ with $p = \max\{m,n\}$ and $R = \mathbb{Z}$ and $R = \mathbb{F}[x]$, respectively. In Algorithm 1 $O(p^4 \log_2(p\|\bar{A}\|_\infty))$ and $O(p^4 \lceil \bar{A} \rceil_{\deg})$ BROADCAST operations are performed, respectively, and $O(p^5 \log_2(p\|\bar{A}\|_\infty))$ and $O(p^5 \lceil \bar{A} \rceil_{\deg})$ ring elements are sent with BROADCAST, respectively. Further $O(q^2 p^2 \log_2(p \|\bar{A}\|_\infty))$ and $O(q^2 p^2 \lceil \bar{A} \rceil_{\deg})$ SEND operations are performed, respectively, and $O(p^4 \log_2(p\|\bar{A}\|_\infty))$ and $O(p^4 \lceil \bar{A} \rceil_{\deg})$ ring elements are sent with SEND, respectively.

Proof: Follows from Remark 1 and Theorem 3 and the definitions of PAR-ROWTOCOL and PAR-COLTOROW. □

3.5 Parallel Hartley-Hawkes-Algorithm

Algorithm 2
INPUT Number of processes q, number of its own process z,
$A = [a_1, \cdots, a_{k(z)}]^T \in R^{k(z),n}$ and $\sum_{z=1}^{q} k(z) = m$
1   $l = 1$
2   WHILE $l \leq \min\{m,n\}$
3         $y = ROW\text{-}TASK(l)$
4         $h = ROW\text{-}NUM(l)$
5   IF $y = z$
6   THEN BROADCAST a_h
7   ELSE BROADCAST-RECEIVE v FROM y
8   Insert v as h-th row vector of A
9   IF NOT $(A_{h,j})_{l+1 \leq j \leq n} = 0$
10   THEN $A = ROWGCD(A,h,l)$
11   IF NOT $y = z$
12   THEN Remove v as h-th row vector of A
13         $B = PAR\text{-}ROWTOCOL(A)$ $\left(B \in R^{m,k'(z)}, \sum_{z=1}^{q} k'(z) = n\right)$
14         $y = COL\text{-}TASK(l)$
15         $h = COL\text{-}NUM(l)$

```
16          IF y = z
17              THEN BROADCAST b_h (the h-th column of B)
18              ELSE BROADCAST-RECEIVE v FROM y
19                  Insert v as h-th column vector of B
20          IF (B_{i,h})_{l+1≤i≤m} = 0
21              THEN l = l + 1
22              ELSE B = COLGCD(B, l, h)
23          IF NOT y = z
24              THEN Remove v as h-th column vector of B
25      A = PAR-COLTOROW(B)
26  A = PAR-DIAGTOSMITH(A)
OUTPUT A = PAR-SNF(A) ∈ R^{k(z),n}
```

Correctness: The original algorithm consists of the steps 1, 2, 9, 10, 20, 21, 22 and 26 with l instead of h and A instead of B. We do the same steps as in the original algorithm, but on the processes owning the current elements.

At the beginning the matrix is row distributed. As in stage l of the WHILE-loop the original l-th row is decisive for the row operations which have to be done, in the steps 3 to 7 the l-th row is sent from the process it lies on to all other processes. In step 8 this row is inserted into the h-th place behind all rows, which are in the whole matrix above the l-th row. In step 9 and 10 the row at the h-th place and the rows behind it are transformed on all processes corresponding to the original algorithm. In the steps 11 and 12 the row is removed from all processes which have received it. In step 13 the matrix is transformed from row distribution to column distribution. In the steps 14 to 25 we do the analogous steps for the column distributed matrix. □

Theorem 5. Let $\bar{A} \in R^{m,n}$ with $p = \max\{m, n\}$ and $R = \mathbb{Z}$ and $R = \mathbb{F}[x]$, respectively. In Algorithm 2 $O(p^2 \log_2(p\|\bar{A}\|_\infty))$ and $O(p^2 \lceil \bar{A} \rceil_{\deg})$ BROADCAST operations are performed, respectively, and $O(p^3 \log_2(p\|\bar{A}\|_\infty))$ and $O(p^3 \lceil \bar{A} \rceil_{\deg})$ ring elements are sent with BROADCAST, respectively. Further $O(q^2 p^2 \log_2(p \|\bar{A}\|_\infty))$ and $O(q^2 p^2 \lceil \bar{A} \rceil_{\deg})$ SEND operations are performed, respectively, and $O(p^4 \log_2(p \|\bar{A}\|_\infty))$ and $O(p^4 \lceil \bar{A} \rceil_{\deg})$ ring elements are sent with SEND, respectively.

Proof: Follows from Remark 2 and the definitions of PAR-ROWTOCOL and PAR-COLTOROW. □

In comparison to Algorithm 1 the complexity of the BROADCAST operations improves by a factor of p^2, whereas the complexity of the SEND operations stays unchanged.

4 Experiments with the Parallel Versions of the Smith Normal Form Algorithms

The original algorithms of this paper were implemented in the language C++ with the compiler *ibmcxx*, version 3.6.4.0 and the parallel programs with *mpich*, version 1.1.1, an implementation of the message passing library MPI. The experiments were made under AIX 4.3.3 on a POWER3-II 375 MHz processor of a IBM RS/6000 SP-SMP computer at the SSC Karlsruhe. It is a distributed memory computer, which consists of altogether 128 POWER3-II multi processors with 1024 MB main memory for each processor. We use up to 64 processors, where 2 processors belong to a node. Every process of our parallel program runs on one of these processors. Additionally, we compare our results with the program package MAGMA V2.5-1, started under AIX 4.2 on a POWER2 66 MHz computer with main memory 1024 MB.

4.1 Efficiency

An important criterion for the quality of a parallel algorithm is the *efficiency* E, dependent on the number of processes q, which we define as $E(q) = \frac{T_s}{q \cdot T_q}$, where T_q is the execution time for the parallel algorithm with q processes and T_s the execution time for the corresponding original algorithm. The better is the parallel program the larger is the efficiency. The efficiency is at most 1.

We compute the Smith normal form with corresponding transformation matrices of a matrix of medium size on 1, 2, 4, 8, 16, 32 and 64 processes with the parallel Algorithms 1 and 2, and we also use the corresponding original algorithms. As parallel HNF algorithm we have implemented the algorithm of Theorem 3. For every parallel SNF computation we give the efficiency in %.

Matrices over the ring $\mathbb{Z}$: For the experiments we use the following class of matrices: $A_n = (a_{s,t} = (s-1)^{t-1} \mod n)$ for $1 \leq s, t \leq n$. These matrices have full rank, if n is a prime, and have rather large entries.

Table 1. Execution time and efficiency of the parallel Kannan-Bachem-Algorithm, applied to the matrix A_{389}

Pro.	1 (orig.)	1 (par.)	2	4	8	16	32	64	MAG.
Ti.	05:43:37	05:50:12	02:57:01	01:31:21	00:49:26	00:27:22	00:17:05	00:12:05	38:50:47
Eff.	-	98 %	97 %	94 %	87 %	78 %	63 %	44 %	-

The Hartley-Hawkes-Algorithm 2 produces a memory overflow even with 64 processes. The efficiency of the Kannan-Bachem-Algorithm 1 is rather high for up to 16 processes and lower for 32 and 64 processes.

Matrices over the ring $\mathbb{F}_2[x]$: We use the following class of matrices: $B_n^q = (b_{s,t} = p_{s-1}^{t-1} \mod q)$ for $1 \leq s, t \leq n$ with $(p_s(x))_{s \geq 0} = (0, 1, x, x+1, x^2, x^2+1, \cdots)$ and the irreducible polynom $q(x) = x^{10} + x^9 + x^8 + x^5 + 1$. These matrices also have full rank with large entries.

We see, that the Hartley-Hawkes-Algorithm 2 is the better SNF algorithm. The efficiency is from 16 processes on higher than for the ring $\mathbb{Z}$. MAGMA was not able to compute the Smith normal form of B_{400}^q with corresponding transformation matrices.

Table 2. Execution time and efficiency of the parallel Kannan-Bachem-Algorithm and Hartley-Hawkes-Algorithm, applied to the matrix B_{400}^q

Proc.	1 (orig.)	1 (par.)	2	4	8	16	32	64
Time (KB)	10:30:57	10:51:39	05:37:02	02:55:21	01:31:08	00:48:38	00:27:48	00:18:01
Eff. (KB)	-	97 %	94 %	90 %	87 %	81 %	71 %	55 %
Time (HH)	05:47:01	06:10:55	03:04:36	01:33:14	00:47:24	00:24:49	00:13:51	00:08:34
Eff. (HH)	-	94 %	94 %	93 %	92 %	87 %	78 %	63 %

4.2 Large Example Matrices

For the rings $\mathbb{Z}$ and $\mathbb{F}_2[x]$ we want to find out the maximum number of rows and columns of an input matrix we are able to compute the Smith normal form for. For some examples we additionally list the used memory in MB.

Matrices over the ring $\mathbb{Z}$: For the ring $\mathbb{Z}$ the Kannan-Bachem-Algorithm 1 is the best parallel algorithm (compare Table 1).

Table 3. Execution time and efficiency of the parallel Kannan-Bachem-Algorithm with 64 processes

Mat.	A_{967}	A_{983}	A_{997}	A_{1013}	A_{1117}	A_{1223}
Time	09:44:41	11:08:09	11:02:47	11:52:09	18:15:14	30:44:31 (129 MB)

We succeed in computing the Smith normal form of a (1223×1223) matrix with maximum absolute value 1222. The available memory of 1024 MB is not fully used, i.e. if we have more time, it is possible to compute the Smith normal form of larger matrices.

Matrices over the ring $\mathbb{F}_2[x]$: For the ring $\mathbb{F}_2[x]$ the Hartley-Hawkes-Algorithm 2 is the best parallel algorithm (compare Table 2). Additionally we use the test matrices $D_{1792}^{(1)}, D_{1792}^{(2)}, D_{1792}^{(3)}, D_{1792}^{(4)}$. These are characteristic matrices with full rank and elementary divisors which are mostly no unit ([11, example 7.3]).

Table 4. Execution time and efficiency of the parallel Hartley-Hawkes-Algorithm with 64 processes

Mat.	$D_{1792}^{(1)}$	$D_{1792}^{(2)}$	$D_{1792}^{(3)}$	$D_{1792}^{(4)}$	B_{1024}^q
Time	01:25:50	01:04:38	01:31:30	01:25:41 (82 MB)	07:04:31 (170 MB)

We succeed in computing the Smith normal form of a (1024×1024) matrix and of the four (1792×1792) matrices. The matrix B_{1024}^q is more difficult, as it contains polynomials up to degree 9, whereas the matrices $D_{1792}^{(i)}$ only contain polynomials of degree 0 and 1. The matrix B_{1024}^q needs more memory than all other large matrices considered. MAGMA was not able to compute the Smith normal form with corresponding transformation matrices of one of these large matrices.

References

1. X.G. Fang, G. Havas: On the worst-case complexity of integer gaussian elimination, Proc. of ISSAC (1997) 28-31.
2. M. Giesbrecht: Fast Computation of the Smith Normal Form of an Integer Matrix, Proc. of ISSAC (1995) 110-118.
3. J.L. Hafner, K.S. McCurley: Asymptotically Fast Triangularization of Matrices over Rings, SIAM J. Computing **20**(6) (1991) 1068-1083.
4. B. Hartley, T.O. Hawkes: Rings, Modules and Linear Algebra, Chapman and Hall, London (1976).
5. G. Havas, L.S. Sterling: Integer Matrices and Abelian Groups, Lecture Notes in Computer Science **72**, Springer-Verlag, New York (1979) 431-451.
6. C. Hermite: Sur l'introduction des variables continues dans la théorie des nombres, J. Reine Angew. Math. **41** (1851) 191-216.
7. E. Kaltofen, M.S. Krishnamoorthy, B.D. Saunders: Fast parallel computation of Hermite and Smith forms of polynomial matrices, SIAM J. Algebraic and Discrete Methods **8** (1987) 683-690.
8. E. Kaltofen, M.S. Krishnamoorthy, B.D. Saunders: Parallel Algorithms for Matrix Normal Forms, Linear Algebra and its Applications **136** (1990) 189-208.
9. R. Kannan, A. Bachem: Polynomial Algorithms for Computing the Smith and Hermite Normal Forms of an Integer Matrix, SIAM J. Computing **8**(4) (1979) 499-507.
10. H.-J. Kowalsky, G.O. Michler: Lineare Algebra, de Gruyter, Berlin (1998).
11. G.O. Michler, R. Staszewski: Diagonalizing Characteristic Matrices on Parallel Machines, Preprint 27, Institut für Experimentelle Mathematik, Universität/GH Essen (1995).
12. C.C. Sims: Computation with finitely presented groups, Cambridge University Press (1994).
13. H.J.S. Smith: On Systems of Linear Indeterminate Equations and Congruences, Philos. Trans. Royal Soc. London **151** (1861) 293-326.
14. A. Storjohann: Computing Hermite and Smith normal forms of triangular integer matrices, Linear Algebra and its Applications **282** (1998) 25-45.
15. A. Storjohann: Near Optimal Algorithms for Computing Smith Normal Forms of Integer Matrices, Proc. of ISSAC (1996) 267-274.
16. A. Storjohann, G. Labahn: A Fast Las Vegas Algorithm for Computing the Smith Normal Form of a Polynomial Matrix, Linear Algebra and its Applications **253** (1997) 155-173.
17. G. Villard: Fast parallel computation of the Smith normal form of poylynomial matrices, Proc. of ISSAC (1994) 312-317.
18. C. Wagner: Normalformenberechnung von Matrizen über euklidischen Ringen, Ph.D. Thesis, Institut für Experimentelle Mathematik, Universität/GH Essen (1997).

Hierarchical MPI+OpenMP Implementation of Parallel PIC Applications on Clusters of Symmetric MultiProcessors

Sergio Briguglio[1], Beniamino Di Martino[2],
Giuliana Fogaccia[1], and Gregorio Vlad[1]

[1] Associazione EURATOM-ENEA sulla Fusione, C.R. Frascati,
C.P. 65, 00044, Frascati, Rome, Italy
{briguglio,fogaccia,vlad}@frascati.enea.it
[2] Dip. Ingegneria dell'Informazione,
Second University of Naples, Italy
beniamino.dimartino@unina2.it*

Abstract. The hierarchical combination of decomposition strategies for the development of parallel Particle-in-cell simulation codes, targeted to hierarchical distributed-shared memory architectures, is discussed in this paper, along with its MPI+OpenMP implementation. Particular emphasis is given to the devised dynamic workload balancing technique.

1 Introduction

Particle-in-cell (PIC) simulation consists [1] in evolving the coordinates of a set of N_{part} particles in certain fluctuating fields computed (in terms of particle contributions) only at the points of a discrete spatial grid and then interpolated at each particle (continuous) position. Two main strategies have been developed for the workload decomposition related to porting PIC codes on parallel systems: the *particle decomposition* strategy [5] and the *domain decomposition* one [7, 6]. Domain decomposition consists in assigning different portions of the physical domain and the corresponding portions of the grid to different processes, along with the particles that reside on them. Particle decomposition, instead, statically distributes the particle population among the processes, while assigning the whole domain (and the grid) to each process. As a general fact, the particle decomposition is very efficient and yields a perfect load balancing, at the expenses of memory overheads. Conversely, the domain decomposition does not require a memory waste, while presenting particle migration between different portions of the domain, which causes communication overheads and the need for dynamic load balancing [3, 6].

Such workload decomposition strategies can be applied both for distributed-memory parallel systems [6, 5] and shared-memory ones [4]. They can also be

---

* This work has been partly supported by the CNR, Italy (Agenzia 2000 Project *ALCOR*) and by the Campania Reg. government (Projects "L41/96 Smart ISDN" and "Regional Competence Center on Information and Communication Technologies").

combined, when porting a PIC code on a hierarchical distributed-shared memory system (e.g., a cluster of SMPs), in two-level strategies: a distributed-memory level decomposition (among the n_{node} computational nodes), and a shared-memory one (among the n_{proc} processors of each node).

In previous papers we have investigated some of these two-level strategies applied to a specific application domain, namely the simulation of thermonuclear plasma confinement. In particular, we have designed and implemented the hierarchically combined particle-particle and particle-domain decomposition strategies, with the integrated use of HPF and OpenMP [2].

The task of a good scalability of the domain size with n_{node}, requires, however, to avoid the replication of the grid data proper of the particle decomposition at the distributed-memory level. The scenario of hierarchically-combined decomposition strategies has then to be completed by developing the domain-particle combination and, specially, the domain-domain one. A high-level data-parallel language like HPF is not suited, in these cases, to face problems like the inter-process particle migration and the related dynamic workload unbalance. We have then to resort to explicit message-passing libraries, such as MPI. Aim of this paper is discussing the MPI+OpenMP implementation of the integrated domain-particle and domain-domain decomposition strategies, with particular emphasis to the dynamic workload balancing technique we have devised and its MPI-based implementation.

In Sect. 2 we describe the inter-node, domain-decomposition strategy, adopted in the distributed-memory context, along with its MPI implementation, while the integration of such inter-node strategy with both intra-node particle and domain decomposition strategies is discussed in Sect. 3.

2 MPI Implementation of the Inter-node Domain Decomposition

The typical structure of a PIC code for plasma particle simulation can be represented as follows. At each time step, the code *i*) computes the electromagnetic fields only at the points of a discrete spatial grid (*field solver* phase); *ii*) interpolates the fields at the (continuous) particle positions in order to evolve particle phase-space coordinates (*particle pushing* phase); *iii*) collects particle contribution to the pressure field at the grid points to close the field equations (*pressure computation* phase). We can schematically represent the structure of this time-iteration by the following code excerpt:

```
call field_solver(pressure,field)
call pushing(field,x_part)
call compute_pressure(x_part,pressure)
```

Here, `pressure`, `field` and `x_part` represent pressure, electromagnetic-field and particle-position arrays, respectively. In order to simplify the notation, we will refer, in the pseudo-code excerpts, to a one-dimensional case, while the experimental results reported in the following refer to a three-dimensional (3-D) application.

In implementing a parallel version of the code, according to the distributed-memory domain-decomposition strategy, different portions of the physical domain and of the corresponding grid are assigned to the n_{node} different nodes, along with the particles that reside on them. This approach yields benefits and problems that are complementary to those yielded by the particle-decomposition one [5]: on the one hand, the memory resources required to each node are approximately reduced by the number of nodes; an almost linear scaling of the attainable physical-space resolution (i.e., the maximum size of the spatial grid) with the number of nodes is then obtained. On the other hand, inter-node communication is required to update the fields at the boundary between two different portions of the domain, as well as to transfer those particles that migrate from one domain portion to another. Such a particle migration possibly determines a severe load unbalancing of the different processes, then requiring a dynamic balancing, at the expenses of further computations and communications.

Three additional procedures then characterize the structure of the parallel code: at each time step

- the number of particles managed by a process has to be checked, in order to avoid excessive load unbalancing among the processes (if such an unbalancing is verified, the load-balancing procedure must be invoked);
- particles that moved from one subdomain to another because of particle pushing must be transferred from the original process to the new one;
- the values of the pressure array at the boundaries between two neighbor subdomains must be corrected, because their local computation takes into account only those particles which belong to the subdomain, neglecting the contribution of neighbor subdomain's particles.

Let us report here the schematic representation of the time iteration performed by each process, before giving some detail on the implementation of such procedures:

```
      call field_solver(pressure,field)
      call check_loads(i_check,n_part,n_part_left_v,
     &                 n_part_right_v)
      if(i_check.eq.1)then
        call load_balancing(n_part_left_v,
     &                      n_part_right_v,
     &                      n_cell_left,n_cell_right,
     &                      n_part_left,n_part_right)
        n_cell_new=n_cell+n_cell_left+n_cell_right
        if(n_cell_new.gt.n_cell)then
          allocate(field_aux(n_cell))
          field_aux=field
          deallocate(field)
          allocate(field(n_cell_new))
          field(1:n_cell)=field_aux(1:n_cell)
          deallocate(field_aux)
        endif
        n_cell=max(n_cell,n_cell_new)
```

```
      n_cell_old=n_cell
      call send_receive_cells(field,x_part,
     &                        n_cell_left,n_cell_right,
     &                        n_part_left,n_part_right)
      if(n_cell_new.lt.n_cell_old)then
        allocate(field_aux(n_cell_old))
        field_aux=field
        deallocate(field)
        allocate(field(n_cell_new))
        field(1:n_cell_new)=field_aux(1:n_cell_new)
        deallocate(field_aux)
      endif
      n_cell=n_cell_new
      n_part=n_part+n_part_left+n_part_right
     endif
     call pushing(field,x_part)
     call transfer_particles(x_part,n_part)
     allocate(pressure(n_cell))
     call compute_pressure(x_part,pressure)
     call correct_pressure(pressure)
```

In order to avoid continuous reallocation of particle arrays (here represented by x_part) because of the particle migration from one subdomain to another, we overdimension (e.g., +20%) such arrays with respect to the initial optimal-balance size, N_{part}/n_{node}. Fluctuations of n_part around this optimal size are allowed within a certain band of oscillation (e.g., ±10%). This band is defined in such a way to prevent, under normal conditions, index overflows and, at the same time, to avoid excessive load unbalancing. One of the processes (the MPI rank-0 process) collects, in subroutine check_loads, the values related to the occupation level of the other processes and checks whether the band boundaries are exceeded on any process. If this is the case, the "virtual" number of particles (n_part_left_v, n_part_right_v) each process should send to the neighbor processes to recover the optimal-balance level is calculated (negative values means that the process has to receive particles), and i_check is set equal to 1. Then, such informations are scattered to the other processes. These communications are easily performed with MPI by means of the collective communication primitives MPI_Gather, MPI_Scatter and MPI_Bcast. Load balancing is then performed as follows.

Particles are labelled (subroutine load_balancing) by each process according to their belonging to the units (e.g., the n_cell spatial-grid cells) of a finer subdivision of the corresponding subdomain. The portion of the subdomain (that is, the number of elementary units) the process has to release, along with the hosted particles, to neighbor subdomains in order to best approximate those virtual numbers (if positive) is then identified. Communication between neighbor processes allows each process to get the information related to the portion of subdomain it has to receive (in case of negative "virtual" numbers). Net transfer information is finally put into the variables n_cell_left, n_cell_right, n_part_left, n_part_right. Series of MPI_Sendrecv are suited to a deadlock-free implementation of the above described communication pattern.

As each process could be requested, in principle, to host (almost) the whole domain, overdimensioning the grid arrays (pressure and field) would cause losing of the desired memory scalability (there would be, indeed, no distribution of the memory-storage loads related to such arrays). We then have to resort to dynamical allocation of the grid arrays, possibly using auxiliary back-up arrays (field_aux), when their size is modified.

Portions of the array field have now to be exchanged between neighbor processes, along with the elements of the array x_part related to the particles residing in the corresponding cells. This is done in subroutine send_receive_cells by means of MPI_Send and MPI_Recv calls. The elements of the grid array to be sent are copied in suited buffers, and the remaining elements are shifted, if needed, in order to be able to receive the new elements or to fill possibly occurring holes. After sending and/or receiving the buffers to/from the neighbor processes, the array field comes out to be densely filled in the range 1:n_cell_new. Analogously, the elements of x_part corresponding to particles to be transferred are identified on the basis of the labelling procedure performed in subroutine load_balancing and copied into auxiliary buffers; the residual array is then compacted in order to avoid the presence of "holes" in the particle-index space. Buffers sent by the neighbor processes can then be stored in the higher-index part of the x_part (remember that such an array is overdimensioned).

After rearranging the subdomain, subroutine pushing is executed, producing the new particle coordinates, x_part. Particles whose new position falls outside the original subdomain have to be transferred to a different process. This is done by subroutine transfer_particles. First, particles to be transferred are identified, and the corresponding elements of x_part are copied into an auxiliary buffer, ordered by the destination process; the remaining elements of x_part are compacted in order to fill holes. Each process sends to the other processes the corresponding chunks of the auxiliary buffer, and receives the new-particle coordinates in the higher-index portion of the array x_part. This is a typical all-to-all communication; the fact that the chunk size is different for each destination process makes the MPI_Alltoallv call the tool of choice.

Finally, after reallocating the array pressure, subroutine compute_pressure is called. Pressure values at the boundary of the subdomain are then corrected by exchanging the locally-computed value with the neighbor process (subroutine correct_pressure), by means of MPI_Send and MPI_Recv calls. The true value is obtained by adding the two partial values. The array pressure can now be yielded to the subroutine field_solver for the next time iteration.

Note that, for the sake of simplicity, we referred, in the above description, to one-dimensional field arrays. In the real case we have to represent field informations by means of multi-dimensional arrays. This requires us to use MPI derived datatypes as arguments of MPI calls in order to communicate blocks of pages of such arrays.

3 Integration of the Inter-node Domain Decomposition with Intra-node Particle and Domain Decomposition Strategies

The implementation of particle and domain decomposition strategies for a PIC code at the shared-memory level in a high-level parallel programming environment like OpenMP has been discussed in Refs. [4, 2]. We refer the reader to those papers for the details of such implementation. Let us just recall the main differences between the two intra-node approaches, keeping in mind the inter-node domain-decomposition context. In order to avoid race conditions between different threads in updating the array pressure, the particle-decomposition strategy introduces a private auxiliary array with same rank and size of pressure, which can be privately updated by each thread; the updating of pressure is then obtained by a reduction of the different copies of the auxiliary array. The domain-decomposition strategy consists, instead, in further decomposing the node subdomain and assigning a pair of the resulting portions (we will refer to them as to "intervals", looking at the subdivision along one of the dimensions of the subdomain) along with the particles residing therein to each thread. This requires labelling particles according to the interval subdivision. The loop over particles in subroutine pressure can be restructured as follows. A pair of parallel loops are executed: one over to the odd intervals, the other over the even ones. A loop over the interval particles is nested inside each of the interval loops. Race conditions between threads are then removed from the pressure computation, because particles treated by different threads, will update different elements of pressure as they belong to different, not adjacent, intervals. Race conditions can still occur, however, in the labelling phase, in which each particle is assigned, within a parallel loop over particles, to its interval and labelled by the incremented value of a counter: different threads can try to update the counter of a certain interval at the same time. The negative impact of such race conditions on the parallelization efficiency can be contained by avoiding to execute a complete labelling procedure for all the particles at each time step, while updating such indexing "by intervals" only in correspondence to particles that have changed interval in the last time step [4].

The integration of the inter-node domain-decomposition strategy with the intra-node particle-decomposition one does not present any relevant problem. The only fact that should be noted is that, though the identification of particles to be transferred from one subdomain to the others can be performed, in subroutine transfer_particles, in a parallel fashion, race conditions can occur in updating the counters related to such migrating particles and their destination subdomains. The updating has then to be protected within critical sections.

The integration with the intra-node domain-decomposition strategy is more complicate. The need of containing the effect of the labelling-procedure race conditions requires indeed identifying particles whose interval indexing cannot be maintained. Two factors make such a task more delicate in comparison with the simple shared-memory case: the subdomain rearranging (due to load balancing) and the particle migration from one subdomain to another. The former

Table 1. Elapsed times (in seconds) for the different procedures of 3-D skeleton-code implementations of the domain-particle (d-p) and the domain-domain (d-d) decomposition strategies at different pairs n_{node}/n_{proc}.

		1/1	1/2	2/1	2/2	3/1	3/2	4/1	4/2
Load balancing	d-p	0.14	0.14	4.32	4.25	7.28	7.48	9.59	9.60
$\times 10^{-4}$	d-d	0.13	0.13	4.38	4.87	7.20	7.95	11.2	11.0
Pushing	d-p	8.58	4.39	4.28	2.14	2.78	1.40	2.11	1.06
	d-d	8.52	4.34	4.26	2.14	2.77	1.39	2.10	1.06
Particle transfer	d-p	0.85	0.43	0.42	0.21	0.29	0.15	0.22	0.11
	d-d	1.27	0.68	0.65	0.36	0.44	0.24	0.33	0.19
Pressure	d-p	9.82	4.89	4.82	2.42	3.16	1.58	2.40	1.20
	d-d	7.82	3.98	3.85	2.00	2.51	1.34	1.92	1.05

factor may even make the previous-step interval subdivision meaningless; we then choose to reset the interval assignment of particles after each invocation of the load-balancing procedure:

```
...
call send_receive_cells(...)
n_cell=n_cell_new
n_part=n_part+n_part_left+n_part_right
call assign_to_interval(x_part)
...
```

The latter factor enriches the family of particles that change interval: beside those leaving their interval for a different interval of the same subdomain, particles leaving the subdomain or coming from a different subdomain have to be taken into account. In the framework of such domain-domain decomposition strategy, subroutine transfer_particles will then include, in addition to the check on inter-subdomain particle migration, the check on inter-interval migration. Particles that left the subdomain will affect the internal ordering of the original interval only; particles who came into the subdomain will be assigned to the proper interval, then affecting only the internal ordering of the new interval; particles that changed interval without leaving the subdomain will continue to affect the ordering of both the original and the new interval.

The analysis aimed to identify, in subroutine transfer_particles, inter-subdomain or inter-interval migrating particles can still be performed by a parallel loop over intervals (with a nested loop over interval particles). Race conditions can occur when updating the counters related to particles leaving the subdomain (as in the above domain-particle case) and those related to particles reaching a new interval without changing subdomain. Race conditions can also be presented, of course, when parallelizing the interval assignment of the particles imported from the others subdomains.

Preliminary results obtained for a 3-D skeleton-code implementations of the domain-particle (d-p) and the domain-domain (d-d) hierarchical decomposition strategies are shown in Table 1. The elapsed time (in seconds) for the different

Table 2. Speed-up values for the 3-D skeleton-code implementations of the domain-particle and the domain-domain decomposition strategies at different pairs n_{node}/n_{proc}.

	1/1	1/2	2/1	2/2	3/1	3/2	4/1	4/2
d-p	0.92	1.82	1.83	3.39	2.78	4.98	3.71	7.32
d-d	1.00	1.88	1.99	3.54	3.01	5.84	4.04	7.56

procedures are reported for different pairs n_{node}/n_{proc}. Note that the "Pressure" procedure includes both compute_pressure and correct_pressure subroutines. A case with a spatial grid of $128 \times 32 \times 16$ cells and $N_{part} = 1048576$ particles has been considered. The overall speed-up values, defined as the ratio between the serial-execution elapsed times and the parallel execution ones, are reported in Table 2. These results have been obtained by running the code on an IBM SP parallel system, equipped with four 2-processors SMP Power3 nodes, with clock frequency of 200 MHz and 1 GB RAM.

We note that, for the considered case, the elapsed times decrease with the total number of processors for *pushing*, *particle transfer* and *pressure* procedures, while it increases for the *load balancing* procedure. This result can strongly depend, as far as the *particle transfer* procedure is concerned, on the rate of particle migration (which, in turn, depends on the specific dynamics considered).

Finally, we note that the domain-domain decomposition strategy comes out to be, for this case, more efficient than the domain-particle one. This is due to the need of reducing, in the framework of the latter decomposition strategy, the private copies of the array pressure.

References

1. Birdsall, C.K., Langdon, A.B.: Plasma Physics via Computer Simulation. (McGraw-Hill, New York, 1985).
2. Briguglio, S., Di Martino, B., Vlad, G.: Workload Decomposition Strategies for Hierarchical Distributed-Shared Memory Parallel Systems and their Implementation with Integration of High Level Parallel Languages. Concurrency and Computation: Practice and Experience, Wiley, Vol. **14**, n. 11, (2002) 933–956.
3. Cybenko, G.: Dynamic Load Balancing for Distributed Memory Multiprocessors. J. Parallel and Distributed Comput., **7**, (1989) 279–391.
4. Di Martino, B., Briguglio, S., Vlad, G., Fogaccia, G.: Workload Decomposition Strategies for Shared Memory Parallel Systems with OpenMP. Scientific Programming, IOS Press, **9**, n. 2-3, (2001) 109–122.
5. Di Martino, B., Briguglio, S., Vlad, G., Sguazzero, P.: Parallel PIC Plasma Simulation through Particle Decomposition Techniques. Parallel Computing **27**, n. 3, (2001) 295–314.
6. Ferraro, R.D., Liewer, P., Decyk, V.K.: Dynamic Load Balancing for a 2D Concurrent Plasma PIC Code, J. Comput. Phys. **109**, (1993) 329–341.
7. Fox, G.C., Johnson, M., Lyzenga, G., Otto, S., Salmon, J., Walker, D.: Solving Problems on Concurrent Processors (Prentice Hall, Englewood Cliffs, New Jersey, 1988).

Non-strict Evaluation of the FFT Algorithm in Distributed Memory Systems[*]

Alfredo Cristóbal-Salas[1], Andrei Tchernykh[2], and Jean-Luc Gaudiot[3]

[1] School of Chemistry Sciences and Engineering, University of Baja California,
Tijuana, B.C. Mexico 22390,
cristobal@uabc.mx
[2] Computer Science Department, CICESE Research Center
Ensenada, BC, Mexico 22830,
chernykh@cicese.mx
3 Electrical Engineering and Computer Science, University of California, Irvine, USA,
gaudiot@uci.edu

Abstract. This paper focuses on the partial evaluation of local and remote memory accesses of distributed applications, not only to remove much of the excess overhead of message passing implementations, but also to reduce the number of messages, when some information about the input data set is known. The use of split-phase memory operations, the exploitation of spatial data locality, and non-strict information processing are described. Through a detailed performance analysis, we establish conditions under which the technique is beneficial. We show that by incorporating non-strict information processing to FFT MPI, a significant reduction of the number of messages can be archived, and the overall system performance can be improved.

1 Introduction

Parallelization of scientific and engineering applications has become essential in modern computer systems. The variety of parallel paradigms, languages, runtime systems, and architectures makes optimization of parallel programs as equally demanding as the design of the parallel algorithm itself. High performance of the Fast Fourier Transform (FFT) is a key issue in many application [20]. There have been several attempts to parallelize FFT. For example, an algorithm suitable for 64-processor nCUBE 3200 hypercube multicomputer was presented in [17] where a speedup of up to 16 with 64 processors was demonstrated. In [10], the binary exchange algorithm for the parallel implementation of FFT was presented. Also, FFT for hypercube multicomputers and vector multiprocessors was discussed in [19]. The implementation of a parallel FFT algorithm on a 64-processor Intel iPSC was described in [3]. Finally, in [2], two FFT implementations (recursive and iterative), written in Id, were presented.

---

[*] This work is partly supported by CONACYT (Consejo Nacional de Ciencia y Tecnología de México) under grant #32989-Aand by the National Science Foundation under Grants No. CSA-0073527 and INT-9815742. Any opinions, findings, and conclusions or recommendations expressed in this material are those of the authors and do not necessarily reflect the views neither of the National Science Foundation nor of CONACYT.

Nevertheless, in spite of its reduction in complexity and time, FFT remains expensive mainly in distributed memory parallel computers where network latency significantly affects the performance of the algorithm. In most cases, the speedup which can be gained by parallelization is limited due to inter-process communication. Because of this, programming for distributed architectures has been somewhat restricted to regular, coarse-grained, and computation-intensive applications. FFT exploits fine grain parallelism, which means that an improvement at the communication level plays an extremely important role. Ideas for improvements include optimizating by pipelining of communications such as considered in [6] where a simple communication mechanism named Active Messages was proposed. Under Active Messages, the network is viewed as a pipeline operating at a rate determined by the communication overhead and with a latency which is directly related to the message length and the network depth.

Another approach to speeding up applications is based on Partial Evaluation (PE) [13]. PE [11] is an automatic program transformation technique which allows the partial execution of a program when only some of its input data are available, and it also "specializes" the program with respect to partial knowledge of the data. In [9], PE is incorporated in a library of general-purpose mathematical algorithms in order to allow the automatic generation of fast, special-purpose programs from generic algorithms. The results for the FFT show speedup factors between 1.83 and 5.05 if the size N of the input is available, where N ranges from 16 and 512. Good speedup for larger N is achieved despite the growth in code size which reaches $O(N \log_2 N)$.

In this paper, we present a 1D-FFT for distributed memory systems with an optimization at the communication level which reduces the number of messages by exploiting data locality and by applying a partial evaluation technique. We describe implementations based on multi-assignment and single-assignment data structures in distributed environments. Finally, we also discuss a caching mechanism for single-assignment data structures.

In the next section, we present several approaches to FFT parallelization. Description of our benchmark programs are made in section 3. In section 4, we discuss our experimental results. Lastly, conclusions are presented.

2 FFT Optimization

MPI provides many benefits for scalable parallel computations. However, one of its drawbacks is that it allows unrestricted access to data. The performance of MPI implementations is bounded by the performance of the underlying communication interface. However, an efficient interface does not necessarily guarantee a high performance implementation. One possible way to increase performance is to eliminate synchronization issues by non-strict data access and fully asynchronous operations, and to reduce the number of messages. We use single-assignment I-Structures [1] (ISs) to facilitate asynchronous access when structure production and consumption can be allowed to proceed with a looser synchronization than conventionally understood. In our implementation, ISs are managed by our Distributed I-Structure (DIS) memory system. We also use a mechanism to cache ISs memory requests; we call it Distributed I-Structures Software Cache (DISSC) to reduce number of messages by spatial and temporal locality exploitation, and by partial evaluation [4,21].

2.1 Non-strict Data Access and Software Caching

Our DIS [14] is a linked list of ISs where multiple updates of a data element are not permitted. In DIS, each element maintains a presence bit which has three possible states: full, empty, or deferred, indicating whether a valid data has been stored in the element. Split-phase operations are used to enable the tolerance of request latencies by decoupling initiators from receivers of communication/synchronization transactions. DISs facilitate the exploitation of parallelism while timing sequences and determinacy issues would otherwise complicate its detection, regain flexibility without losing determinacy, and avoid the cache coherence problem [16]. However, the overhead of DIS management becomes its major drawback [14]. In order to solve this problem, we use a caching mechanism, the Distributed I-Structure Software Cache (DISSC). Several efforts related to the optimization of IS memory systems using a caching mechanism have been presented in [5, 8, 12]. Our DISSC is a further development of the ISSC system designed for non-blocking multithreaded architectures and tested for the EARTH [14]. DISSC provides a software caching mechanism under a distributed address space. It takes advantage of spatial and temporal localities without hardware support. DISSC works as an interface between user applications and network and is implemented as an extension of the MPI library. It makes the cache system portable and provides non-blocking communication facilities. Accesses to DIS elements are naturally mapped to the split-phase transactions of MPI.

In DISSC, due to the long latency and unpredictable characteristics of a network, a second remote access to the data elements in the same data block (cache line) may be issued while the first request is still traveling. Hence, spatial data locality can be exploited. Temporal data exploitation refers to the reuse of data which is already in the cache. Because of the inherent cache coherence feature of DISs, no cache coherence problem exists. This significantly reduces the overhead of the cache system.

2.2 Partial Evaluation

In this section, an optimization technique based on partial evaluation is described. It enables the construction of general highly parameterized software systems without sacrificing efficiency. "Specialization" turns a general system into an efficient one, optimized for a specific parameter setting. It is similar in concept to, but in several ways stronger than, a highly optimizing compiler. Specialization can be done automatically or with human intervention. Partial evaluation may be considered a generalization of the conventional evaluation [7]. The use of partial evaluation for distributed applications has been considered in the recent past. For instance, in [18], a distributed partial evaluation model that considers distributing the work of creating the specializations to computational agents called specialization servers is presented. Also in [15], the OMPI (Optimizing MPI) system that removes much of the excess overhead by employing partial evaluation and exploiting static information of MPI calls is considered.

The question now becomes, would it be possible to use partial evaluation, not only to remove much of the excess overhead of a program, but also to reduce the number of messages? The answer is effectively yes. The problem is to assess how to partially evaluate of split-phase memory operations under a distributed address space.

In this paper, we focus on non-strict information processing of split-phase memory operations to demonstrate the possibility to optimize distributed applications at the communication level when some program inputs are known. The splitting of data requests on split-phase transactions such as *send-a-request, receive-a-request, send-a-value* and *receive-a-value*, together with the ability of ISs to defer reads, when the values are not available, allow evaluating MPI programs partially without losing determinacy. To completely evaluate a *send-a-request* transaction, the element being requested and the process that owns the element have to be specified. For the FFT, the size N of the input vector determines the control and data structures of the program. Hence, if N is available, an *MPI_Send* instruction can be executed. The *receive-a-request* transaction can also be completely evaluated. The owner of the element executes the *MPI_Receive* instruction, checks the status of the element, and, if it is available, sends a value back to the requester by the *MPI_Send* instruction. Otherwise, it stores the request as a deferred read to this element. Later, when the element is produced and written, the owner of the element finds the list of pending reads (continuation vectors) and sends a value to the requestors by executing *MPI_Send* instructions. A *receive-a-value* transaction executes an *MPI_Receive* instruction and writes the value to the local memory of a requester.

Distributed programs where parallel control structure is completely determined by the size of the problem (data-independent programs) can be partially evaluated even if the data bindings of the input vector are not performed. Residual programs only include *send-a-value* and *received-a-value* transactions. More details about non-strict evaluation and partial evaluation of DIS and DISSC can be found in [4].

3 Experimental Results

In this section, we discuss the performance evaluation of the 1-D FFT algorithm with 2048 double precision complex data on an SGI ORIGIN2000 with 8 MIPS R10000 processors running at 195MHz, with 1280MB of main memory, and a network bandwidth of 800MBs/sec. Six different MPI implementations have been compared:

1. *FFT* is the basic implementation with MPI.
2. *FFT-Residual*. This program differs from *FFT* in that all *send-a-request* and *receive-a-request* transactions are performed at the partial evaluation step. Hence, they are not included in the residual program. Each element of input vector has a vector of deferred reads. The residual program only binds elements, completes pending requests, and executes *send-a-value* and *receive-a-value* transactions.
3. *FFT-DIS*. Remote requests are managed by the DIS memory system.
4. *FFT-DIS-Residual*. A residual program differs from the original *FFT-DIS* program in that all requests for IS data items, local or remote, and *receive-a-request* operations are performed during the partial evaluation step.
5. *FFT-DISSC*. The DISSC system is used.
6. *FFT-DISSC-Residual*. Each element of the input vector has a vector of deferred reads. The residual program only binds elements, completes pending requests, and executes *send-a-value* and *receive-a-value* transactions. To support a cache line mechanism, the vector has one extra element which counts how many elements in a requested cache block have been produced.

3.1 Message Reduction by Caching Remote Memory Requests and Partial Evaluation

Table 1 shows the number of messages with a varying numbers of processors. DISSC does not reduce the number of messages when caching a single IS data item (CB=1). With caching 4 and 8 IS data items, the reduction of messages obtained by DISSC is respectively 4 and 8. This demonstrates that the FFT algorithm has no significant temporal data locality and re-use of data, and that only spatial locality is exploited. In the residual programs, the number of messages is reduced by a factor of two as compared to the original ones, irrespective of the number of PEs. Table 1 also shows how the DISSC contributes to the messages reduction. Increasing the size of the cache block proportionally decreases the number of messages, for example, the total reduction in the *FFT-DISSC*–Residual (CB=8) is 16 times comparing with the *FFT*.

It is important to note that a reduction in the number of messages not only diminishes the execution time of the program, but also improve the system behavior by reducing the saturation of the communication system.

Table 1. Number of messages varying the number of processors.

MPI programs		2 PEs	4 PEs	8 PEs
FFT		16,384	40,960	81,920
FFT-Residual		8,192	20,480	40,960
FFT-DIS		16,384	40,960	81,920
FFT-DIS Residual		8,192	20,480	40,960
FFT-DISSC	CB=1	16,384	40,960	81,920
FFT-DISSC-Residual		8,192	20,480	40,960
FFT-DISSC	CB=4	4,096	10,240	20,480
FFT-DISSC-Residual		2,048	5,120	10,240
FFT-DISSC	CB=8	2,048	5,120	10,240
FFT-DISSC-Residual		1,024	2,560	5,120

3.2 Time Reduction by Caching Remote Memory Requests

Figure 1 shows the speedup for varying numbers of PEs. *FFT-DIS* has a lower speedup than *FFT* because of the DISs management overhead. *FFT-DISSC* with CB=1 has a lower speedup than *FFT-DIS* because of the overhead and the lack of temporal data locality. Nevertheless, the spatial data locality exploited by the DISSC mechanism contributes to the acceleration of the *FFT* program. For instance, for eight PEs, the speedup varies from 1.19 to 4.39, varying CB from 1 to 8.

Figure 2 presents the relative time reduction of *FFT-DIS* and *FFT-DISSC*, with different cache block sizes over the original *FFT* program, varying the number of PEs. *FFT-DIS* and *FFT-DISSC* with CB=1 are not faster than *FFT*. The speedup is increased when CB=4, 8. For PEs=8, *FFT-DISSC* has a relative time reduction of 1.46 and 2.01, respectively. The time reduction is higher than the overhead of DISs and DISSC.

3.3 Time Optimization by Partial Evaluation

The degree of parallelizability of residual programs is presented in Figure 3. It shows speedups of residual programs with varying number of PEs. It shows that the speedup of *FFT-Residual*, *FFT-DIS-Residual* is relatively small, between 2 and 3 for 8 PEs. For the same number of PEs, the speedup of *FFT-DISSC-Residual* is increased from 2.1 to 5.35 varying CB from 1 to 8. To evaluate the impact of partial evaluation on the performance, a time optimization coefficient $S^o_p = T_o/T_r$ is calculated. S^o_p is the ratio of the execution time T_o taken by the original program over the time T_r taken by the residual one. Figure 4 shows the S^o_p for benchmark programs with and without cache system versus the number of processors.

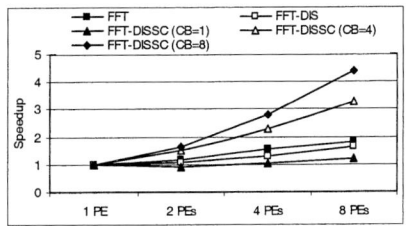

Fig. 1. Speedup of FFT, FFT-DIS and FFT-DISSC (with different cache block sizes 1, 4 and 8) varying number of Pes.

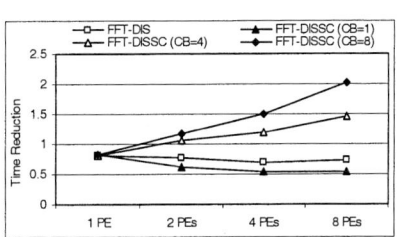

Fig. 2. Time reduction of *FFT-DIS* and *FFT-DISSC* (with different cache block sizes 1, 4 and 8) programs over *FFT*, when varying the number of PEs.

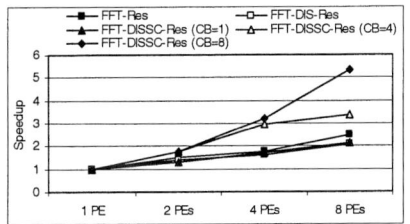

Fig. 3. Speedup of *FFT-Residual*, *FFT-DIS-Residual*, and *FFT-DISSC-Residual* (with cache block sizes equal 1, 4 and 8) programs with different number of PEs.

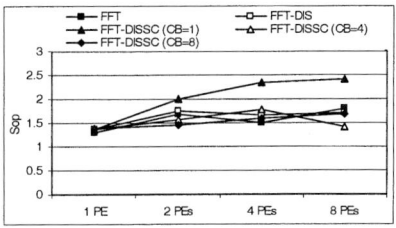

Fig. 4. S_{op} for benchmark programs with and without cache system versus the number of processors.

FFT-Residual is 20-50% faster (depending number of PEs) than *FFT*, *FFT-DIS-Residual* is about 70% faster than the original *FFT-DIS* program. The time reduction for *FFT-DISSC-Residual* program is slightly larger. It is about 90% when CB=1 and 46% for CB=8. Increasing the CB reduces the number of messages and, hence, fewer messages are removed by partial evaluation.

4 Conclusions

Many non-strict structures are known and have been experimentally evaluated for a variety of multithreaded shared memory systems. The problem is to assess how suited they are for the exploitation of parallelism in distributed memory systems which use the latency tolerance properties of MPI. In this paper, the design and experimental evaluation of parallel implementations of the FFT algorithm in MPI with DISs and

DISSC have been presented. We have shown that the split-phase memory access scheme of MPI and DISs allows not only an overlap of long communication latencies with useful computations, but also lifts the main restriction which conventional (and sequential) information processing usually implies: complete production of data before its consumption. It makes the concept of partial evaluation of distributed programs on the communication level feasible. Partial evaluation allows a reduction in the number of messages in data-independent applications. It can also be applied to program optimization by constant propagation, loop unrolling, and polyvariant specialization in order to get fully advantage of the static information available.

We have shown that MPI programs using DIS and DISSC can take advantage of data locality and can allow complete asynchronous memory accesses. Although the management of D-IS has a cost, the DISSC overcomes this cost and improves the program performance by eliminating messages. Although ISs help with the synchronization issues, there are some algorithms where re-assignment is a key issue. In this paper, we have also presented experimental results which show the gain of partial evaluation of MPI programs without ISs.

We have shown that DISSC and partial evaluation are a good programming mechanism which optimize both distributed programs and the use of the parallel systems by avoiding the saturation of the interconnection network, thereby leaving the resources free for other applications. Experiments have shown that if one were to take the total number of messages in the original MPI program as 100%, then introducing DISSC, it would reduce up to 88% of messages. The number of messages that are left (12%) can be reduced twice by partial evaluation, which means that only 6% of the original messages are left. Comparing the execution time of all benchmark programs versus the execution time of an FFT program running in a single process, the total execution time can then be reduced by a factor of 1.68, when CB=4, PEs=2; 2.38 when CB=8, PEs=4; and 3.37 when CB=8, PEs=8; with DISSC and partial evaluation together.

References

1. Arvind, Nikhil R.S., Pingali, K-K.: I-Structures: Data Structures for Parallel Computing. ACM Transaction on Programming Languages and Systems, Vol. 11 No. 4 (1989) 598-632
2. Böhm, A-P-W., Hiromoto, R-E.: The Data Flow Parallelism of FFT in Gao, G-R., Bic, L., Gaudiot, J-L.: Advanced topics in dataflow computing and multithreading ISBN: 0-8186-6542-4 (1995) 393-404
3. Chamberlain, R-M.: Gray codes, Fast Fourier Transforms and hypercubes. Parallel computing, vol. 6, (1988) 225-233
4. Cristobal A., Tchernykh A., Gaudiot J-L., Lin WY. Non-Strict Execution in Parallel and Distributed Computing, *International Journal of Parallel Programming*, Kluwer Academic Publishers, New York, U.S.A., vol. 31, 2, p. 77-105, 2003
5. Dennis, J-B., Gao, G-R.: On memory models and cache management for shared-memory multiprocessors. CSG MEMO 363, CSL, MIT. (1995)
6. Eicken, T., Culler, D-E., Goldstein, S-C., Schauser, K-E.: Active Messages: a Mechnisim for Integrated Communication and Computation. In Proceedings of the 19th International Symposium on Computer Architecture, 1992, 256-266
7. Ershov, A.P.: Mixed computation: potential applications and problems for study. Theoretical Computer Science, vol. 18 (1982)

8. Govindarajan R., Nemawarkar S, LeNir P: Design and performance evaluation of a multi-threaded architecture. In proceedings of the 1st international symposium on High-Performance Computer Architecture, Raliegh, 1995, 298-307
9. Gluck R., Nakashige R., Zochling R.: Binding-time analysis applied to mathematical algorithms. In Dolezal J., Fidler, J. (eds.) 17th IFIP Conference on System Modelling and Optimization; Prague, Czech Republic. (1995)
10. Gupta S-A,: A typed approach to layered programming language design. Thesis proposal, Laboratory of computer science, Department of EE&CS, MIT (1993)
11. Jones, N-D.: An introduction to Partial Evaluation. ACM computing surveys, Vol 28, No 3 (1996)
12. Kavi, K-M., Hurson, A-R., Patadia P., Abraham E., Shanmugam, P.: Design of cache memories for multithreaded dataflow architecture. In ISCA 1995, 253-264
13. Lawall, J-L.: Faster Fourier Transforms via automatic program specialization. IRISA research reports 1998; 28 pp.
14. Lin, W-Y., Gaudiot, J-L.: I-Structure Software Cache – A split-Phase Transaction runtime cache system. In: Proceedings of PACT '96 Boston, MA, 1996, 20-23
15. Ogawa, H., Matsuoka, S.: OMPI: Optimizing MPI programs using Partial Evaluation. In Proceedings IEEE/ACM Supercomputing Conference (1996)
16. Osamu, T., Yuetsu, K., Santoshi, S., Yoshinori, Y.: Highly efficient implementation of MPI point-to-point communication using remote memory operations. In: Proceedings of 12th ACM ICS98, Melbourne, Australia. (1998) 267-273
17. Quinn, M-J.: Parallel computing theory and practice. McGraw-Hill Inc. (1994)
18. Sperber, M., Klaeren, H., Thiemann P.: Distributed partial evaluation. In: Kaltofen, Erich (ed.): PASCO'97, Maui, Hawaii. (1997) 80-87
19. Swarztrauber, P-N.: Multiprocessor FFTs. Parallel computing, vol. 5. (1987) 197-210.
20. E. Oran Brigham. Fast Fourier Transform and Its Applications, Prentice-Hall, 1988
21. Amaral, J.N., W-Y. Lin, J-L. Gaudiot, and G.R. Gao, "Exploiting Locality in Single Assignment Data Structures Updated Through Split-Phase Transactions," International Journal of Cluster Computing, Special Issue on Internet Scalability: Advances in Parallel, Distributed, and Mobile Systems, Vol. 4, Issue 4, 2001.

A Parallel Approach for the Solution of Non-Markovian Petri Nets

M. Scarpa, S. Distefano, and A. Puliafito

Dipartimento di Matematica Università di Messina, 98166 Messina, Italy
{mscarpa,apulia,salvatdi}@ingegneria.unime.it

Abstract. This paper describes the new features implemented in the WebSPN modeling tool for the analysis of non-Markovian stochastic Petri nets *(NMSPN)*. In our approach, we envisage a discretization of time and an approximation of firing times for non-exponentially distributed transitions, by means of the Phase type distribution. In order to solve the problems related to the management of the state space (which can become very large) we managed to parallelize the solution algorithms by means of the MPI libraries [1].

Keywords: Non-Markovian *SPN,DPH*, parallel computation, message passing MPI.

1 Introduction

Sometimes ago, we developed a modeling tool for the analysis of non-Markovian stochastic Petri nets that relax some of the restrictions present in currently available modeling packages. This tool, called WebSPN [3], provided a discrete time approximation of the stochastic behavior of the marking process which results in the possibility to analyze a wider class of Petri net models. In [7], the technique implemented in WebSPN has been presented. It is based on a generation of *DTMCs* through a discretization of time and an approximation of firing times transitions, by means of the Phase type expansion. The state space created could be too large, thus limiting the area of application of the Petri net models proposed. One solution to this problem could be a formulation of the algorithm in parallel terms.

The idea we used to parallelize the expansion technique proposed is inspired to the work on parallel generation of reachability graph like [5, 4], but applied to a different context. In Section 2, we give a short introduction to *Non Markovian Stochastic Petri Nets (NMSPN)*. In Section 3, we briefly describe the algorithm used for generating the discrete process that approximates a *NMSPN*, starting from its reachability graph. After, in Section 4, we describe the parallel implementation of the algorithm. and, in Section 5 we give a short evaluation of algorithm performances.

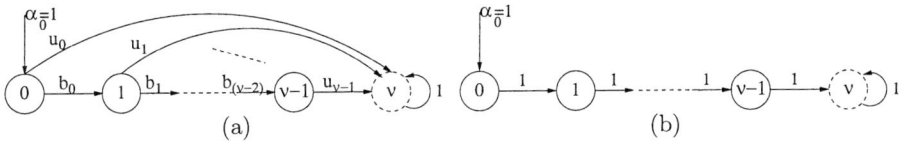

Fig. 1. Example of a generic *DPH* (a), and a *DPH* approximating a deterministic distribution (b).

2 Non-Markovian Stochastic Petri Nets

We define a non-Markovian *SPN* (*NMSPN*) as a stochastically timed *PN* in which the time evolution of the marking process cannot be mapped into a *Continuous Time Markov Chain (CTMC)*. In a *NMSPN* to each timed transition t_g is assigned a general random firing time γ_g with a cumulative distribution function $G_g(t)$. An *age variable* a_g associated to the timed transition t_g keeps track of the clock count. A timed transition fires as soon as the memory variable a_g reaches the value of the firing time γ_g. Three kinds of firing policies have been prosed (see [8] for more details): *preemptive repeat different (prd)*, *preemptive resume (prs)*, and *preemptive repeat identical (pri)*.

In the algorithm for solution of *NMSPN*s, we assume that the random variables of firing times for the transitions are *Discrete Phase Type (DPH)* [6], according to the definition provided by Neuts: *A DPH distribution is the cdf of the time to absorption in a discrete state discrete time Markov chain (DTMC) with ν transient states (numbered from 0 to $\nu - 1$) and one absorbing state (the ν-th), given an initial probability vector α.* (An example of *DPH* distribution is shown in Fig. 1 (a)). As it is shown in [7, 2], this class of Petri nets has several practical applications, and can also be used as an approximation of Petri nets whose firing times are continuous but are generally distributed.

3 How the Expansion Algorithm Works

The algorithm is based on the discretization of time into δ-wide time slots to discretize the distributions of the firing times for timed transitions, approximated with *DPH* distributions. With this representation, each activity is modeled by a graph whose states represent the *stage of firing* reached by the transition over the time. The stochastic process representing the net behavior in time is itself a homogeneous Discrete Time Markov process $\mathcal{D}$, whose states are identified by the net marking and the stage of firing of each transition. The Markov process can be constructed expanding the reachability graph $R(M_0)$ ([7]).

The expansion algorithm works with nodes defined as a $N = (M, V, S)$, where M is a marking of the Petri net, V is a vector that takes accounts of the actual phase of each *DPH* associated to a *prd* and *prs* transition, and S is a vector that takes into account of the actual level of memory of each *pri* transition. The expansion algorithm works as follows: the expanded graph is initially empty; at the beginning ($t = 0$) all system activities start anew, a set of initial nodes $\mathcal{N}_0$ is put in $\mathcal{N}$ and it is marked as non expanded.

An expansion step is then performed on each non expanded node. For each transition t_i enabled in M, its DPH model is searched for arcs outgoing from stage v_i. Then, for each k such that the arc from v_i to k exists in the model of t_i, a possible successor node $N' = (M, V', S)$ is generated, with $v'_i = k$, whereas the entries of V' corresponding to other enabled transitions shall be set according to the chosen memory policy. The so created successor node is entered in $\mathcal{N}$ (if not yet there), and an arc (N, N') is added to a set $\mathcal{A}$. When a new node N' is created, the probability of switching from N to N' is calculated according to the b_i and u_i probabilities of switching among the phases of DPHs. The details on how the new states and probabilities of $\mathcal{D}$ are computed can be found in [7].

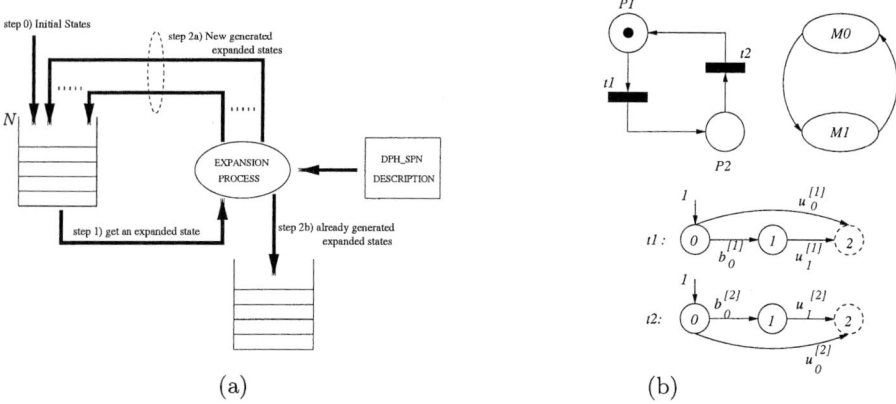

Fig. 2. Graphical representation of the expansion algorithm (a). Example of a simple Petri net (b).

This procedure is repeated until there are no more elements in $\mathcal{N}$. A graphical representation of the algorithm just described is provided in Fig. 2 (a). The result of the expansion algorithm is that each marking of the original PN is transformed into a macro-state in the new state space. In Fig. 3 (a), the steps for generating the expanded state space of the Petri Net depicted in Fig. 2 are shown.

4 Parallel Implementation of the Expansion Algorithm

The *step 1)* in Fig. 2 (a) can be assigned to several processors that expand different states of $\mathcal{N}$ at the same time, as it is shown in Fig. 3 (b). In order to parallelize the step 1) we chosen to use a *message passing* approach. Let us assume we have P processes available for the management of the expansion phase. The task of these processes is the *evaluation* of some states for the stochastic process $\mathcal{D} = (\mathcal{N}, \mathcal{A})$. This evaluation activity is organized in two different

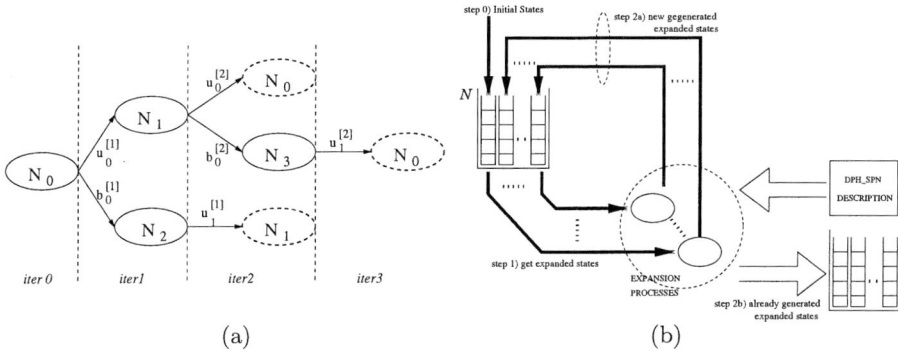

Fig. 3. Example of a simple expansion (a). Graphical representation of the parallel algorithm (b).

phases: the first one (called *expansion*) consists of expanding the states, generating new states; the second one (called *transmission*) consists of the distribution of a portion of the states generated to the other active processes. Both activities proceed concurrently. This means that, as long as new states are generated, they are transmitted and distributed in the input queues of the other processes. When a process has to evaluate a state that does not request to be expanded, the process stores this state in a local buffer. When a process no longer has states to be processed in its input queue, waits for any message coming from other processes, and containing further states to be evaluated.

When there are no processes left to be evaluated, the computation ends, and the information generated (that is, all the states expanded), are distributed in the local buffers of the single processes. Thus, at the end of the computation, each process will have saved a subset of the states of $\mathcal{D}$ locally. The computational scheme used is totally asynchronous. Each process maintains a vector of P lists, one for each active process, where the new states to be expanded are inserted. These states are distributed in the different lists, according to a *hash* function. The purpose of this function is that of trying to balance the work load among the active processes. The list associated to the same process is its work list (input queue). The states that do not belong to a process are inserted in the lists of the recipient processes, waiting to be sent. Such lists may grow until a fixed maximum value. Once this value is reached, the states are removed and sent to the processes they belong to.

Once the MASTER process has generated the initial states concerning the initial marking M_0 of the Petri net, a cycle starts, consisting of the following four phases. *Expansion*: during the phase of expansion, each process processes the state included in its work list. A verification is made for each new state generated, in order to make sure that it has not already been generated during a previous expansion. In this case, the state is discarded. The processing continues, until the work list is empty or the number of nodes present in one of the other lists reaches the highest value. *Sending*: during the phase of sending, a process sends the nodes included in the transmission lists to other processes. In this phase, data transmission is done by means of non-blocking calls. Thus the process immediately continues with the phase of receiving. *Receiving*: during the phase of receiving, a process checks whether other processes have sent messages to it. It also makes a distinction between termination messages (as we will clarify below) and messages containing states to be processed, thus inserting them in the input queue. *Termination*: the process enters this phase when its input queue remains empty for a time period longer than a fixed timeout. If all of the other processes are in the same condition, the expansion activity ends. Otherwise, any state received is processed. This phase synchronize all processes.

The *hash* function used, given the node $\mathcal{N}_a = (M_a, V_a, S_a)$, is: $n_p = (M_a + \sum_i [V_a]_i + \sum_i [S_a]_i) \bmod P$ where n_p is the number of the process which the node $\mathcal{N}_a$ has to be sent to, and $[V_a]_i$ ($[S_a]_i$) is the i-th component of the vector V_a (S_a). Since the markings and the phases of the *DPH*s are progressively numbered, the sum in the equation is an integer that identifies a new state. Moreover, the mod operation ensures that the state is sent to one of the P processes. We also experimented other kind of function (like that based on prime numbers), but without significant differences. Anyway, more research could be done on this point.

5 Performance Results

In this section, we discuss some performance indices of the parallel expansion algorithm. Due to the limited space it is not possible to report all the detailed performance measures computed, so here we only show the basic behavior of the algorithm in two extreme conditions. A deeper analisys will be given in a future work.

Our implementation has been tested with a Petri net that models a single-processor system where a multi-user and multi-threading operating system runs, shown in Fig. 4 (a). We are only going to point out that - in our graphical representation - an empty rectangle represents exponential transitions; a full rectangle represents transitions with non-exponential firing times. Finally, a segment represents immediate transitions.

We realized that the performances of the algorithm depend on the nature of the distributions for the firing times (*DPH*s) of transitions. For this reason here, we will show the behavior of the network in two extreme cases: the firing times for non-exponential transitions are uniformly distributed between 0 and τ (**case 1**); and the non-exponential transitions have a deterministic firing time equal to τ (**case 2**).

The parameter used for assessing the performances of the parallel algorithm is the gain obtained on the execution time, in comparison with a sequential execution calculated by using the formula $\sigma = \frac{T_s}{T_p}$, where T_s and T_p are the execution times of the sequential and parallel implementation of the expansion algorithm. We also notice that the execution time of the expansion program consists of two components: T_{exp}, which is the time spent for processing (expansion), and

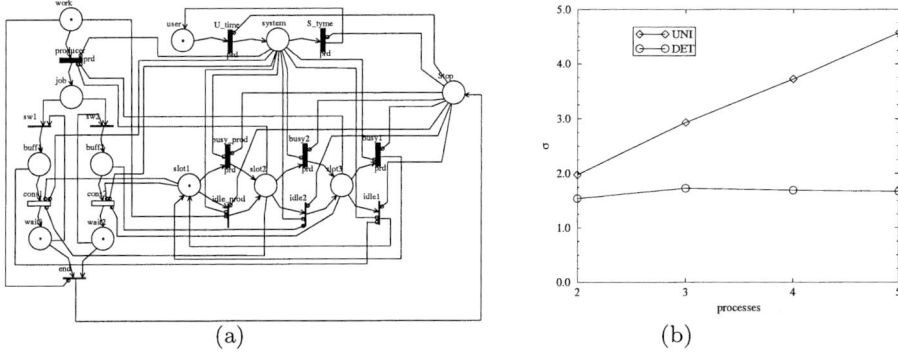

Fig. 4. Petri net used for the experiments (a). Speedup obtained by solving the reference Petri net model (b).

T_{com}, which is the time spent for communicating with other processes. T_{com} also includes the time that a process waits for receiving any state to be processed.

Our implementation has been done by using the C language on a Linux operating system. We have used a cluster of five PCs for tests. Each PC was equipped with an Intel Pentium II processor at 350MHz and 128 MB of RAM. These PCs were connected to a fast-Ethernet LAN at 100 Mbits.

The graph in Fig. 4 (b) shows the progress of the speedup in case the firing times of the general transitions are uniformly distributed (UNI curve), according to the variation of the number of nodes used for processing. This result shows a high level of parallelism in the execution of processes. This is pointed out by the linear increase of the speedup according to the number of processes. This therefore shows a good scalability.

In Fig. 4 (b), we also show the speedup that has been obtained through the parallel expansion of the network shown in Fig. 4 (a) with deterministic distributions (DET curve). Unlike the previous case, the use of deterministic transitions causes the speedup to decrease, when more than three processing nodes are used. The highest value of 1.7 is reached with three processing nodes.

This result is determined by the structure of the *DPH* that models a transition with a deterministic firing time. In fact, the *DPH* representing a deterministic firing time can be denoted as a chain of states, like in Fig. 1 (b). Since only one arc comes out from each phase of a *DPH*, only one state is generated (step **1** in section 4) for each expansion step if only deterministic transitions are present in the network. This means that only one processing node will be involved in the subsequent processing, with a very low level of parallelism.

Such behavior is confirmed also in Fig. 5 (a) and (b) where we show the percentage of the times T_{exp} and T_{com} spent by the parallel program in the **cases 1** and **2** (*np* indicates the number of processors used during the execution). In the deterministic case (Fig. 5 (b)), we can see how the most part of the time (more than 55%) is spent in communications with more than three processing nodes. Conversely, if transitions are uniform (Fig. 5 (a)) the most part of the

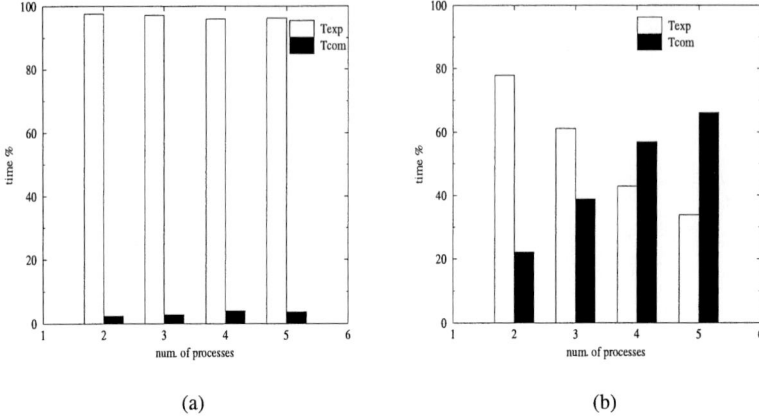

Fig. 5. Computing time with uniform (a) and deterministic (b) transitions.

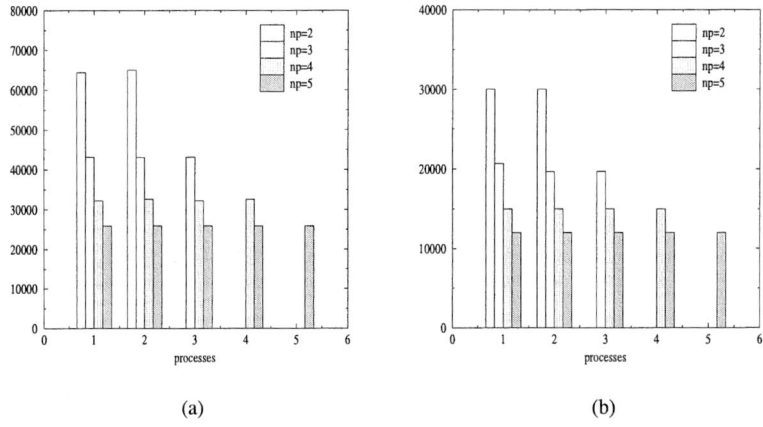

Fig. 6. Number of states distributed among the processes by solving the Petri net with uniform (a) and deterministic (b) transitions.

time is spent in the actual processing. Thus in **case 1** better performances can be obtained if processing is distributed among several nodes.

The results obtained by means of the hash function to compute n_p are shown in the graphs of Fig. 6 (a) and (b). As we can see, each process processes the same number of states in both cases. This means that, by working in parallel, a gain is always assured at least in terms of occupation of memory used on each machine.

6 Conclusions and Future Works

In this paper we have presented a new feature of WebSPN tool ([3]), constituted of a new parallel approach for the solution of non-Markovian Petri nets. This approach is based on the phase type expansion. The algorithms has been tested by using a cluster of workstations connected in fast Ethernet at 100 Mbit/s. The results obtained are encouraging, since they provide the evidence for a very high scalability of the algorithm. The algorithm provides performances that may change linearly, according to the variation of the number of processors available. Furthermore, we have proven a very good work load balancing among processors, thanks to the use of a mechanism based on an appropriately defined hash function. An optimization work over the parallel implementation is in progress to present a deeper analysis of the algorithm's performance throught several graphs and measures.

References

1. MPI: A Message Passing Interface Standard. Technical report, Message Passing Interface Forum, June 1995.
2. A. Bobbio, A. Horváth, M. Scarpa, and M. Telek. Acyclic Discrete Phase Type Distributions: Properties and a Parameter Extimation Algorithm. *To be appearing in Performance Evaluation*.
3. A. Bobbio, A. Puliafito, M. Scarpa, and M. Telek. Webspn: A WEB-accessible Petri Net Tool. In *Conf. on WEB-based Modeling & Simulation*, San Diego, California, January 1998.
4. G. Ciardo, J. Gluckman, and D. Nicol. Distributed state-space generation of discrete state stochastic models. *ORSA J. Comp. - To appear*, 1997.
5. P. Marenzoni, S. Caselli, and G. Conte. Analysis of large GSPN models: a distributed solution tool. In *7-th International Conference on Petri Nets and Performance Models - PNPM97*, pages 122–131. IEEE Computer Society, 1997.
6. M.F. Neuts and K.S. Meier. On the use of phase type distributions in reliability modelling of systems with two components. *OR Spektrum*, 2:227–234, 1981.
7. A. Puliafito, A. Horvath, M. Scarpa, and M. Telek. Analysis and Evaluation of non-Markovian Stochastic Petri Nets. In *Proceedings of 11th International Conference on Modelling Techniques and Tools for Performance Analysis*, Schaumburg, Illinois, March 2000. Springer Verlang.
8. M. Telek, A. Bobbio, and A. Puliafito. Steady state solution of MRSPN with mixed preemption policies. In *International Computer Performance and Dependability Symposium - IPDS96*, pages 106–115. IEEE Computer Society Press, 1996.

Advanced Hybrid MPI/OpenMP Parallelization Paradigms for Nested Loop Algorithms onto Clusters of SMPs

Nikolaos Drosinos and Nectarios Koziris

National Technical University of Athens
School of Electrical and Computer Engineering
Computing Systems Laboratory
Zografou Campus, Zografou 15773, Athens, Greece
{ndros,nkoziris}@cslab.ece.ntua.gr

Abstract. The parallelization process of nested-loop algorithms onto popular multi-level parallel architectures, such as clusters of SMPs, is not a trivial issue, since the existence of data dependencies in the algorithm impose severe restrictions on the task decomposition to be applied. In this paper we propose three techniques for the parallelization of such algorithms, namely pure MPI parallelization, fine-grain hybrid MPI/OpenMP parallelization and coarse-grain MPI/OpenMP parallelization. We further apply an advanced hyperplane scheduling scheme that enables pipelined execution and the overlapping of communication with useful computation, thus leading almost to full CPU utilization. We implement the three variations and perform a number of micro-kernel benchmarks to verify the intuition that the hybrid programming model could potentially exploit the characteristics of an SMP cluster more efficiently than the pure message-passing programming model. We conclude that the overall performance for each model is both application and hardware dependent, and propose some directions for the efficiency improvement of the hybrid model.

1 Introduction

Clusters of SMPs have emerged as the dominant high performance computing platform. For these platforms there is an active research concern that traditional parallelization programming paradigms may not deliver optimal performance, since pure message-passing parallel applications fail to take into consideration the 2-level SMP cluster architecture. Intuitively, a parallel paradigm that uses memory access for intra-node communication and message-passing for inter-node communication seems to match better the characteristics of an SMP cluster. Since MPI has become the de-facto message passing API, while OpenMP has grown into a popular multi-threading library, there is important scientific work that addresses the hybrid MPI/OpenMP programming model.

The hybrid model has already been applied to real scientific applications ([3], [6]). Nevertheless, a lot of important scientific work enlightens the complexity of the many aspects that affect the overall performance of hybrid programs ([2], [8], [10]). Also, the need for a multi-threading MPI implementation that will efficiently support the hybrid model has been spotted by the research community ([11], [9]).

However, most of the work on the hybrid OpenMP/MPI programming paradigm addresses fine-grain parallelization, e.g. usually incremental parallelization of computationally intensive code parts through OpenMP work sharing constructs. On the other hand, programming paradigms that allow parallelization and work distribution across the entire SMP cluster would be more beneficial in case of nested loop algorithms. The pure MPI code is generic enough to apply in this case too, but as aforementioned does not take into account the particular architectural features of an SMP cluster.

In this paper we propose two hybrid MPI/OpenMP programming paradigms for the efficient parallelization of perfectly nested loop algorithms, namely a fine-grain model, as well as a coarse-grain one. We further apply an advanced pipelined hyperplane scheduling that allows for minimal overall completion time. Finally, we conduct some experiments in order to verify the actual performance of each model.

The rest of the paper is organized as follows: Section 2 briefly presents our algorithmic model and our target architecture. Section 3 refers to the pure MPI parallelization paradigm, while Section 4 describes the variations of the hybrid parallelization paradigm, as well as the adopted pipelined hyperplane schedule. Section 5 analyzes the experimental results obtained for the ADI micro-kernel benchmark, while Section 6 summarizes our conclusions and proposes future work.

2 Algorithmic Model – Target Architecture

Our model concerns n-dimensional perfectly nested loops with uniform data dependencies of the following form:

```
FOR  j_0 = min_0 TO max_0 DO
   FOR  j_1 = min_1 TO max_1 DO
       ...
       FOR  j_{n-1} = min_{n-1} TO max_{n-1} DO
           Computation(j_0, j_1, ..., j_{n-1});
       ENDFOR
       ...
   ENDFOR
ENDFOR
```

The loop computation is a calculation involving an n-dimensional matrix A which is indexed by $j_0, j_1, \ldots, j_{n-1}$. For the ease of the analysis to follow, we assume that we deal with rectangular iteration spaces, e.g. loop bounds min_i, max_i are constant ($0 \leq i \leq n-1$). We also assume that the loop computation imposes arbitrary constant *flow* dependencies, that is the calculation at a given loop instance may require the values of certain elements of matrix A computed at previous iterations.

Our target architecture concerns an SMP cluster of PCs. We adopt a generic approach and assume num_nodes cluster nodes and $num\_threads$ threads of execution per node. Obviously, for a given SMP cluster architecture, one would probably select the number of execution threads to match the number of available CPUs in a node, but nevertheless our approach considers for the sake of generality both the number of nodes as well as the number of execution threads per node to be user-defined parameters.

3 Pure MPI Paradigm

Pure MPI parallelization is based on the tiling transformation. Tiling is a popular loop transformation used to achieve coarse-grain parallelism on multi-processors and enhance data locality on uni-processors. Tiling partitions the original iteration space into atomic units of execution, called tiles. Each MPI node assumes the execution of a sequence of tiles, successive along the longest dimension of the original iteration space. The complete methodology is described more extensively in [5]. It must be noted that since our prime objective was to experimentally verify the performance benefits of the different parallelization models, for the sake of simplicity we resorted to hand-made parallelization, as opposed to automatic parallelization. Nevertheless, all parallelization models can be automatically generated with minimal compilation time overhead according to the work presented in [4], which reflects the automatic parallelization method for the pure MPI model and can easily be applied in the hybrid model, as well.

Furthermore, an advanced pipelined scheduling scheme is adopted as follows: In each time step, an MPI node concurrently computes a tile, receives data required for the computation of the next tile and sends data computed at the previous tile. For the true overlapping of computation and communication, as theoretically implied by the above scheme, non-blocking MPI communication primitives are used and DMA support is assumed. Unfortunately, the MPICH implementation over FastEthernet (ch_p4 ADI-2 device) does not support such advanced DMA-driven non-blocking communication, but nevertheless the same limitations hold for our hybrid model and are thus not likely to affect the performance comparison.

Let $\textit{\textbf{tile}} = (tile_0, \ldots, tile_{n-1})$ identify a tile, $\textit{\textbf{nod}} = (nod_0, \ldots, nod_{n-2})$ identify an MPI node in Cartesian coordinates and $x = (x_0, \ldots, x_{n-1})$ denote the tile size. For the control index j_i of the original loop it holds $j_i = tile_i * x_i + min_i$, where $min_i \leq j_i \leq max_i$ and $0 \leq i \leq n-1$. The core of the pure MPI code resembles the following:

```
tile₀ = nod₀;
...
tileₙ₋₂ = nodₙ₋₂;
FOR tileₙ₋₁ = 0 TO ⌊(maxₙ₋₁-minₙ₋₁)/xₙ₋₁⌋ DO
   Pack(snd_buf, tileₙ₋₁ - 1, nod);
   MPI_Isend(snd_buf, dest(nod));
   MPI_Irecv(recv_buf, src(nod));
   compute(tile);
   MPI_Waitall;
   Unpack(recv_buf, tileₙ₋₁ + 1, nod);
END FOR
```

4 Hybrid MPI/OpenMP Paradigm

The hybrid MPI/OpenMP programming model intuitively matches the characteristics of an SMP cluster, since it allows for a two-level communication pattern that distinguishes between intra- and inter-node communication. More specifically, intra-node communication is implemented through common access to the node's memory, and appropriate synchronization must ensure that data are first calculated and then used, so that the execution order of the initial algorithm is preserved (thread-level synchronization). Inversely, inter-node communication is achieved through message passing, that implicitly enforces node-level synchronization to ensure valid execution order as far as the different nodes are concerned.

There are two main variations of the hybrid model, namely the *fine-grain* hybrid model and the *coarse-grain* one. According to the fine-grain model, the computationally intensive parts of the pure MPI code are usually incrementally parallelized with OpenMP work-sharing directives. According to the coarse-grain model, threads are spawned close to the creation of the MPI processes, and the thread ids are used to enforce an SPMD structure in the hybrid program, similar to the structure of the pure MPI code.

Both hybrid models implement the advanced hyperplane scheduling presented in [1] that allows for minimal overall completion time. The hyperplane scheduling, along with the variations of the hybrid model are the subject of the following Subsections.

4.1 Hyperplane Scheduling

The proposed hyperplane scheduling distributes the tiles assigned to all threads of a specific node into *groups* that can be concurrently executed. Each group contains all tiles that can be safely executed in parallel by an equal number of threads without violating the data dependencies of the initial algorithm. In a way, each group can be thought as of a distinct time step of a node's execution sequence, and determines which threads of that node will be executing a tile at that time step, and which ones will remain idle. This scheduling aims at minimizing the total number of execution steps required for the completion of the hybrid algorithms.

For our hybrid model, each group will be identified by an n-dimensional vector, where the first n-1 coordinates will identify the particular MPI node $\boldsymbol{nod}$ this group refers to, while the last coordinate can be thought of as the current time step and will implicitly determine whether a given thread $\boldsymbol{th} = (th_0, \ldots, th_{n-2})$ of $\boldsymbol{nod}$ will be computing at that time step, and if so which tile $\boldsymbol{tile}$. Formally, given a group denoted by the n-dimensional vector $\boldsymbol{group} = (group_0, \ldots, group_{n-1})$
the corresponding node $\boldsymbol{nod}$ can be determined by the first n-1 coordinates of $\boldsymbol{group}$, namely
$nod_i = group_i, 0 \leq i \leq n-2$
and the tile $\boldsymbol{tile}$ to be executed by thread $\boldsymbol{th}$ of $\boldsymbol{nod}$ can be obtained by
$tile_i = group_i \times m_i + th_i, 0 \leq i \leq n-2$
and
$tile_{n-1} = group_{n-1} - \sum_{i=0}^{n-2}(group_i \times m_i + th_i)$

where m_i the number of threads to the i-th dimension (it holds $0 \leq th_i \leq m_i - 1, 0 \leq i \leq n-2$).

The value of $tile_{n-1}$ will establish whether thread $\bm{th}$ will compute during group $\bm{group}$: If the calculated tile is valid, namely if it holds

$$0 \leq tile_{n-1} \leq \lfloor \frac{max_{n-1} - min_{n-1}}{t} \rfloor,$$

then $\bm{th}$ will execute tile $\bm{tile}$ at time step $\bm{group_{n-1}}$. In the opposite case, it will remain idle and wait for the next time step.

The hyperplane scheduling can be implemented in OpenMP according to the following pseudo-code scheme:

```
#pragma omp parallel num_threads(num_threads)
{
    group₀ = nod₀;
    ...
    groupₙ₋₂ = nodₙ₋₂;
    tile₀ = nod₀ * m₀ + th₀;
    ...
    tileₙ₋₂ = nodₙ₋₂ * mₙ₋₂ + thₙ₋₂;
    FOR(groupₙ₋₁){
        tileₙ₋₁ = groupₙ₋₁ - ∑ᵢ₌₀ⁿ⁻² tileᵢ;
        if(0 ≤ tileₙ₋₁ ≤ ⌊(maxₙ₋₁-minₙ₋₁)/t⌋)
            compute(tile);
#pragma omp barrier
    }
}
```

The hyperplane scheduling is more extensively analyzed in [1].

4.2 Fine-Grain Parallelization

The pseudo-code for the fine-grain hybrid parallelization is depicted in Table 1. The fine-grain hybrid implementation applies an OpenMP `parallel` work-sharing construct to the tile computation of the pure MPI code. According to the hyperplane scheduling described in Subsection 4.1, at each time step corresponding to a group instance the required threads that are needed for the tile computations are spawned. Inter-node communication occurs outside the OpenMP parallel region.

Note that the hyperplane scheduling ensures that all calculations concurrently executed by different threads do not violate the execution order of the original algorithm. The required barrier for the thread synchronization is implicitly enforced by exiting the OpenMP `parallel` construct. Note also that under the fine-grain approach there is an overhead of re-spawning threads for each time step of the pipelined schedule.

4.3 Coarse-Grain Parallelization

The pseudo-code for the coarse-grain hybrid parallelization is depicted in Table 2. Threads are only spawned once and their ids are used to determine their flow of ex-

Table 1. Fine-grain hybrid parallelization

```
group_0 = nod_0;
...
group_{n-2} = nod_{n-2};
/*for all time steps in current node*/
FOR(group_{n-1}){
    /*pack previously computed data*/
    Pack(snd_buf, tile_{n-1} − 1, nod);
    /*send communication data*/
    MPI_Isend(snd_buf, dest(nod));
    /*receive data for next tile*/
    MPI_Irecv(recv_buf, src(nod));
    #pragma omp parallel
    {
        tile_0 = nod_0 * m_0 + th_0;
        ...
        tile_{n-2} = nod_{n-2} * m_{n-2} + th_{n-2};
        /*calculate candidate tile for execution*/
        tile_{n-1} = group_{n-1} - \sum_{i=0}^{n-2} tile_i;
        /*if current thread is to execute a valid tile*/
        if(0 ≤ tile_{n-1} ≤ ⌊\frac{max_{n-1}-min_{n-1}}{t}⌋)
        /*compute current tile*/
        compute(tile);
    }
    /*wait for communication completion*/
    MPI_Waitall;
    /*unpack communication data*/
    Unpack(recv_buf, tile_{n-1} + 1, nod);
}
```

Table 2. Coarse-grain hybrid parallelization

```
#pragma omp parallel
{
    group_0 = nod_0;
    ...
    group_{n-2} = nod_{n-2};
    tile_0 = nod_0 * m_0 + th_0;
    ...
    tile_{n-2} = nod_{n-2} * m_{n-2} + th_{n-2};
    /*for all time steps in current node*/
    FOR(group_{n-1}){
        /*calculate candidate tile for execution*/
        tile_{n-1} = group_{n-1} - \sum_{i=0}^{n-2} tile_i;
        #pragma omp master
        {
            /*pack previously computed data*/
            Pack(snd_buf, tile_{n-1} − 1, nod);
            /*send communication data*/
            MPI_Isend(snd_buf, dest(nod));
            /*receive data for next tile*/
            MPI_Irecv(recv_buf, src(nod));
        }
        /*if current thread is to execute a valid tile*/
        if(0 ≤ tile_{n-1} ≤ ⌊\frac{max_{n-1}-min_{n-1}}{t}⌋)
        /*compute current tile*/
        compute(tile);
        #pragma omp master
        {
            /*wait for communication completion*/
            MPI_Waitall;
            /*unpack communication data*/
            Unpack(recv_buf, tile_{n-1} + 1, nod);
        }
        /*synchronize threads for next time step*/
        #pragma omp barrier
    }
}
```

ecution in the SPMD-like code. Inter-node communication occurs within the OpenMP `parallel` region, but is completely assumed by the master thread by means of the OpenMP `master` directive. The reason for this is that the MPICH implementation used provides at best an MPI_THREAD_FUNNELED level of thread safety, allowing only the master thread to call MPI routines. Intra-node synchronization between the threads is achieved with the aid of an OpenMP `barrier` directive.

It should be noted that the coarse-grain model, as compared to the fine-grain one, compensates the relatively higher programming complexity with the fact that threads are created only once, and thus the respective overhead of the fine-grain model is diminished. Furthermore, although communication is entirely assumed by the master thread, the other threads will be able to perform computation at the same time, since they have already been spawned (unlike the fine-grain model). Naturally, a thread-safe MPI im-

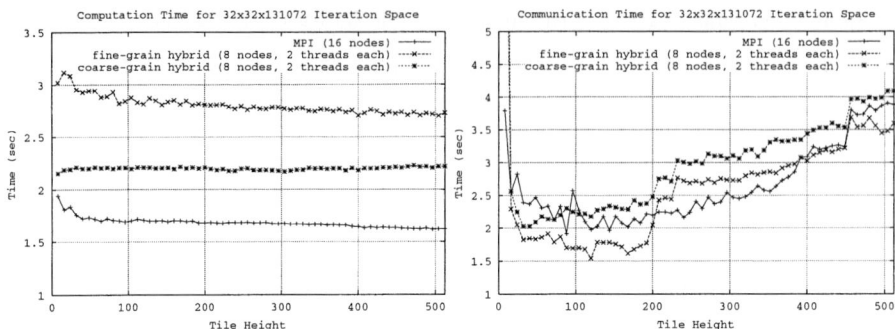

Fig. 1. Computation vs Communication Profiling for 32x32x131072 Iteration Space

plementation would allow for a much more efficient communication scheme, according to which all threads would be able to call MPI routines. Alternatively, under a non thread-safe environment, a more sophisticated load-balancing scheme that would compensate for the master-only communication with appropriately balanced computation distribution is being considered as future work.

5 Experimental Results

In order to evaluate the actual performance of the different programming paradigms, we have parallelized the Alternating Direction Implicit (ADI) Integration micro-kernel ([7]) and run several experiments for different iteration spaces and tile grains. Our platform is an 8-node dual-SMP cluster. Each node has 2 Pentium III CPUs at 800 MHz, 128 MB of RAM and 256 KB of cache, and runs Linux with 2.4.20 kernel. We used Intel icc compiler version 7.0 for Linux with following optimization flags: -O3 -mpcu=pentiumpro -static. Finally, we used MPI implementation MPICH v. 1.2.5, configured with the following options: --with-device=ch_p4 --with-comm=shared.

We performed two series on experiments in order to evaluate the relative performance of the three parallelization methods. More specifically, in the first case we used 8 MPI processes for the MPI model (1 process per SMP node), while we used 4 MPI processes × 2 OpenMP threads for the hybrid models. In the second case, we started the pure MPI program with 16 MPI processes (2 per SMP node), while we used 8 MPI processes × 2 OpenMP threads for the hybrid models. In both cases we run the ADI micro-kernel for various iteration spaces and variable tile heights in order to obtain the minimum overall completion time. Naturally, all experimental results depend largely on the micro-kernel benchmark used, its communication pattern, the shared-memory parallelism that can be achieved through OpenMP and the hardware characteristics of the platform (CPU, memory, network).

The experimental results are graphically displayed in Figure 2. Two conclusions that can easily be drawn are that the pure MPI model is almost in all cases the fastest, while on the other hand the coarse-grain hybrid model is always better than the fine-grain one. Nevertheless, in the 16 vs 8 × 2 series of experiments, the performance of the

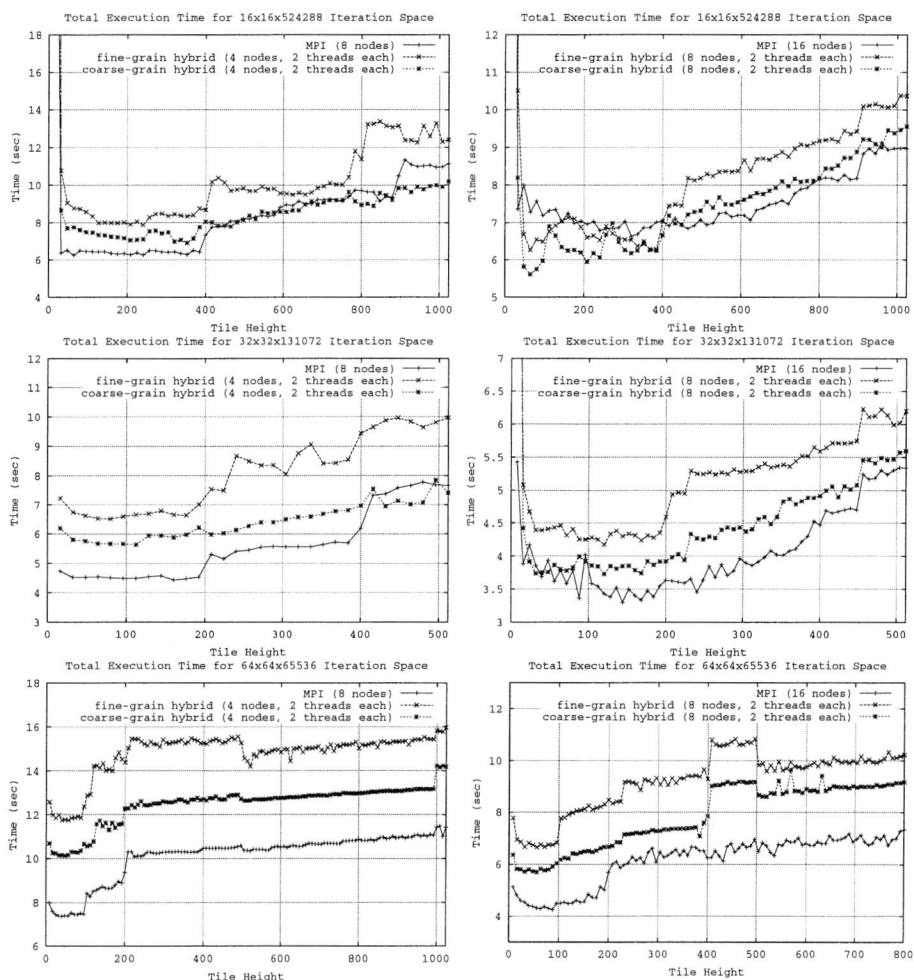

Fig. 2. Experimental Results for ADI Integration

coarse-grain hybrid model is comparable to that of the pure MPI, and in fact delivers the best results in 16 × 16 × 524288 iteration space.

In order to explain the differences in the overall performance of the 3 models, we conducted some more thorough profiling of the computation and communication times (Fig 1). The computation times clearly indicate that the pure MPI model achieves the most efficient parallelization of the computational part, while the fine-grain model is always worse than the coarse-grain one as regards the time spent on the computational part of the parallel code. The communication times follow a more irregular pattern, but on average they indicate a superior performance of the pure MPI model.

The advantage of the coarse-grain model compared to the fine-grain one lies in that, according to the first model threads are only spawned once, while according to the second threads need to be re-spawned in each time step. This additional overhead accounts for the higher computation times of the fine-grain model that were experimentally verified. However, the coarse-grain model suffers from the serious disadvantage of the inefficient communication pattern, since the master thread in each node assumes more communication than an MPI node in the pure MPI model. This disadvantage could be diminished by either a more efficient load-balancing computation distribution scheme, or by a thread-safe MPI implementation that would allow all threads to call MPI routines.

6 Conclusions-Future Work

In this paper we have presented three alternative parallel programming paradigms for nested loop algorithms and clusters of SMPs. We have implemented the three variations and tested their performance against the ADI Integration micro-kernel benchmark. It turns out that the performance of the hybrid coarse-grain OpenMP/MPI model looks quite promising for this class of algorithms, although the overall performance of each paradigm clearly depends on a number of factors, both application- and hardware-specific. We intend to investigate the behavior of the three paradigms more closely with a more extensive communication vs computation profiling, and apply a more efficient computation distribution, in order to mitigate the communication restrictions imposed by a non thread-safe MPI implementation.

References

1. M. Athanasaki, A. Sotiropoulos, G. Tsoukalas, and N. Koziris. Pipelined scheduling of tiled nested loops onto clusters of SMPs using memory mapped network interfaces. In *Proceedings of the 2002 ACM/IEEE conference on Supercomputing*, Baltimore, Maryland, USA, 2002. IEEE Computer Society Press.
2. F. Cappello and D. Etiemble. MPI versus MPI+OpenMP on IBM SP for the NAS benchmarks. In *Proceedings of the 2000 ACM/IEEE conference on Supercomputing*, Dallas, Texas, USA, 2000. IEEE Computer Society Press.
3. S. Dong and G. Em. Karniadakis. Dual-level parallelism for deterministic and stochastic CFD problems. In *Proceedings of the 2002 ACM/IEEE conference on Supercomputing*, Baltimore, Maryland, USA, 2002. IEEE Computer Society Press.
4. G. Goumas, M. Athanasaki, and N. Koziris. Automatic Code Generation for Executing Tiled Nested Loops Onto Parallel Architectures. In *Proceedings of the ACM Symposium on Applied Computing (SAC 2002)*, Madrid, Mar 2002.
5. G. Goumas, N. Drosinos, M. Athanasaki, and N. Koziris. Compiling Tiled Iteration Spaces for Clusters. In *Proceedings of the IEEE International Conference on Cluster Computing*, Chicago, Sep 2002.
6. Y. He and C. H. Q. Ding. MPI and OpenMP paradigms on cluster of SMP architectures: the vacancy tracking algorithm for multi-dimensional array transposition. In *Proceedings of the 2002 ACM/IEEE conference on Supercomputing*, Baltimore, Maryland, USA, 2002. IEEE Computer Society Press.
7. George Em. Karniadakis and Robert M. Kirby. *Parallel Scientific Computing in C++ and MPI : A Seamless Approach to Parallel Algorithms and their Implementation*. Cambridge University Press, 2002.

8. G. Krawezik and F. Cappello. Performance Comparison of MPI and three OpenMP Programming Styles on Shared Memory Multiprocessors. In *ACM SPAA 2003*, San Diego, USA, Jun 2003.
9. B. V. Protopopov and A. Skjellum. A multi-threaded Message Passing Interface (MPI) architecture: performance and program issues. *JPDC*, 2001.
10. R. Rabenseifner and G. Wellein. Communication and Optimization Aspects of Parallel Programming Models on Hybrid Architectures. *International Journal of High Performance Computing Applications*, 17(1):49–62, 2003.
11. H. Tang and T. Yang. Optimizing threaded MPI execution on SMP clusters. In *Proceedings of the 15th international conference on Supercomputing*, pages 381–392, Sorrento, Italy, 2001. ACM Press.

The AGEB Algorithm for Solving the Heat Equation in Two Space Dimensions and Its Parallelization on a Distributed Memory Machine

Norma Alias[1], Mohd Salleh Sahimi[2], and Abdul Rahman Abdullah[3]

[1] Department of Mathematics, Sciences Faculty
Universiti Teknologi Malaysia, 81310, Skudai, Johor, Malaysia
norm_ally@hotmail.com
[2] Department of Engineering Sciences and Mathematics,
Universiti Tenaga Nasional, Kajang, SEL
Sallehs@uniten.edu.my
[3] Department of Industrial Computing
FTSM, Universiti Kebangsaan Malaysia, 43600, Bangi, SEL, Malaysia
ara@ftsm.ukm.my

Abstract. In this paper, a computational analysis of parallelized a class of the AGE method based on the Brian variant (AGEB) is presented using (2 × 2) blocks. The resulting schemes are found to be effective in reducing data storage accesses and communication time on a distributed computer system. All the parallel strategies were developed on a cluster of workstations based on Parallel Virtual Machine environment [6]. The experiments were run on the homogeneous cluster of 20 Intel Pentium IV PCs, each with a storage of 20GB and speed of 1.6Mhz. Finally, the results of some computational experiments and performance measurements will be discussed. In conclusion, the communication cost and computational complexity have effected the efficiency of the parallel strategies.

1 Introduction

In this paper, we shall compare the numerical performance of the Alternating Group Explicit Method (AGE) with Douglas-Rachford variant (AGE_DR) of [3] with the Gauss Seidel Red Black (GSRB) iteration and newly-developed AGE algorithm based on the Brian variant. The domain decomposition parallelization strategy is employed to ascertain these performance indicators over the PVM environment using a cluster of workstations. We shall firstly present the formulation of AGEB method for the solution of the heat equation in two space dimensions and then describe its parallel implementation on the PVM on a model problem.

2 Formulation of the AGEB Method

The parallel strategies were tested on the two space dimensional parabolic partial differential equation as follows,

$$\frac{\partial U}{\partial t} = \frac{\partial^2 U}{\partial x^2} + \frac{\partial^2 U}{\partial y^2} + h(x,y,t), \quad (x,y,t) \in R \times (0,T] \tag{1}$$

subject to the initial condition $U(x,y,0) = f(x,y)$, $(x,y,t) \in R \times \{0\}$ and the boundary conditions $U(x,y,t) = G(x,y,t)$, $(x,y,t) \in \partial R \times (0,T]$. The region R is a rectangle defines by,

$$R = \{(x,y) : 0 \leq x \leq L, 0 \leq y \leq M\}$$

A generalized approximation to (1) at the point $(x_i, y_j, t_{k+1/2})$ is given by (with $0 \leq \theta \leq 1$),

$$\frac{\Delta_t u_{i,j,k}}{\Delta t} = \frac{1}{(\Delta x)^2} \theta(\delta_x^2 + \delta_y^2) u_{i,j,k+1} + (1-\theta)(\delta_x^2 + \delta_y^2) u_{i,j,k}$$
$$+ h_{i,j,k+\frac{1}{2}}, \quad i,j = 1,2,3,...,m \tag{2}$$

which leads to the *five-point* formula,

$$-\lambda\theta u_{i-1,j,k+1} + (1+4\lambda\theta)u_{i,j,k+1} - \lambda\theta u_{i+1,j,k+1} - \lambda\theta u_{i,j-1,k+1} - \lambda\theta u_{i,j+1,k+1}$$
$$= \lambda(1-\theta)u_{i-1,j,k} + [1-4\lambda(1-\theta)]u_{i,j,k} + \lambda(1-\theta)u_{i+1,j,k} + \lambda(1-\theta)u_{i,j-1,k}$$
$$+\lambda(1-\theta)u_{i,j+1,k} + \theta h_{i,j,k+\frac{1}{2}} \tag{3}$$

for $i = 1,2,3,...,m$ and $j = 1,2,3,...,n$. The weighed finite-difference equation (3) can be expressed in the more compact matrix form as,

$$\mathbf{A}\mathbf{u}_{(s)}^{(k+1)} = \mathbf{B}_{(s)}^{(k)} + \mathbf{b} + \mathbf{g} \tag{4}$$
$$= \mathbf{f}$$

Here $\mathbf{A}$ is split into the sum of its constituent symmetric and positive definite matrices $\mathbf{G}_1, \mathbf{G}_2, \mathbf{G}_3$ and $\mathbf{G}_4$, where

$$\mathbf{A} = \mathbf{G}_1 + \mathbf{G}_2 + \mathbf{G}_3 + \mathbf{G}_4 ,$$

with these matrices taking block banded structures where $\text{diag}(\mathbf{G}_1 + \mathbf{G}_2) = \text{diag}(\mathbf{A})/2$, $\text{diag}(\mathbf{G}_3 + \mathbf{G}_4) = \text{diag}(\mathbf{A})/2$. All are of order $(m^2 \times m^2)$. Using the well-known fact of the parabolic-elliptic correspondence and employing the fractional splitting of Brian [5], the AGEB method takes the form,

$$(\mathbf{G}_1 + r\mathbf{I})\mathbf{u}_{(r)}^{(k+\frac{1}{5})} = (r\mathbf{I} - \mathbf{G}_2 - \mathbf{G}_3 - \mathbf{G}_4)\mathbf{u}_{(r)}^{(k)} + \mathbf{f} \tag{5}$$

$$(\mathbf{G}_2 + r\mathbf{I})\mathbf{u}_{(r)}^{(k+\frac{2}{5})} = \mathbf{G}_2\mathbf{u}_{(r)}^{(k)} + r\mathbf{u}_{(r)}^{(k+\frac{1}{5})} \tag{6}$$

$$(\mathbf{G}_3 + r\mathbf{I})\mathbf{u}_{(r)}^{(k+\frac{3}{5})} = \mathbf{G}_3\mathbf{u}_{(r)}^{(k)} + r\mathbf{u}_{(r)}^{(k+\frac{2}{5})} \tag{7}$$

$$(\mathbf{G}_4 + r\mathbf{I})\mathbf{u}_{(r)}^{(k+\frac{4}{5})} = \mathbf{G}_4\mathbf{u}_{(r)}^{(k)} + r\mathbf{u}_{(r)}^{(k+\frac{3}{5})} \tag{8}$$

together with linear interpolation, we obtained,

$$u_{(r)}^{(k+1)} = 2u_{(r)}^{(k+\frac{4}{5})} - u_{(r)}^{(k)} \tag{9}$$

The approximations at the first and the second intermediate levels are computed directly by inverting $(rI+G_1)$ and $(rI+G_2)$. The computational formula for the third and fourth intermediate levels are derived by taking our approximations as sweeps parallel to the y-axis. The AGEB sweeps involved tridiagonal systems which in turn entails at each stage the solution of (2×2) block systems.

3 Parallel Implementation of the AGEB Algorithm

As the AGEB method is fully explicit, its feature can be fully utilized for parallelization. Firstly, the domain Ω is distributed to Ω^p subdomains by the master processor. The partitioning is based on the domain decomposition technique. Secondly, the subdomains Ω^p of AGEB method is assigned to p processors in block ordering. The domain decomposition for AGEB method is implemented for five time levels. The communication activities between the slave processors are needed for the computations in the next iterations. The parallelization of AGEB is achieved by assigning the explicit (2×2) blocks. Hence the computations involved are independent between processors. The parallelism strategy is straightforward with no overlapping subdomains. Based on the limited parallelism, this scheme can be effective in reducing computational complexity and data storage accesses in distributed parallel computer systems. The iterative procedure is continued until convergence is reached. The iterative procedure is continued until a specified convergence criterion is satisfied. That is when the requirement $|u_{i,j}^{(k+1)} - u_{i,j}^{(k)}| \leq \epsilon$ is met, where ϵ is the global convergence criterion.

4 Performance Measurements

The following definitions are used to measure the parallel performance of the three methods, speedup $S_p = \frac{T_1}{T_p}$, efficiency $C_p = \frac{S_p}{p}$ effectiveness $F_p = \frac{S_p}{C_p}$ and temporal performance $L_p = T_p^{-1}$. T_1 is the execution time on one processor, T_p is the execution time on p processors and the unit of L_p is work done per micro second. Now,

$$F_p = \frac{S_p}{pT_p} = \frac{C_p}{T_p} = \frac{C_p S_p}{T_1}$$

which shows that F_p measures both speedup and efficiency. Therefore, a parallel algorithm is said to be effective when it maximizes F_p hence, $F_p T_1 (= S_p C_p)$. The communication time will depend on many factors including network structure and network contention. Parallel execution time t_{para} is composed of two parts, computation time (t_{comp}) and communication time (t_{comm}). t_{comp} is the time to compute the arithmetic operations such as multiplication and addition operations of a sequential algorithm. If the number of iterations b and size of the messages for communication m, the formula for communication time is as follows,

$$t_{comm} = b(t_{startup} + mt_{data} + t_{idle})$$

where $t_{startup}$ is time to send a message with no data. The term t_{data} is the transmission time to send one data word. t_{idle} is the time for message latency and time to wait for all the processors to complete the process. Parallel and sequential algorithms of GSRB are chosen as the control schemes.

5 Numerical Results and Discussion

This paper presents the numerical properties of the parallel solver on the homogeneous architecture of 20 PCs with Linux operating, Intel Pentium IV processors, 20GB HDD, connected with internal network Intel 10/100 NIC and using message-passing libraries, PVM. The parallel implementation of the three methods were tested on two space dimensions parabolic partial differential equation as follows,

$$\frac{\partial U}{\partial t} = \frac{\partial^2 U}{\partial x^2} + \frac{\partial^2 U}{\partial y^2} + h(x, y, t),$$
$$(x, y, t) \in R \times (0, T] , \qquad (10)$$

subject to the initial condition $U(x, y, 0) = f(x, y)$, $(x, y, t) \in R \times 0$ and the boundary conditions $U(x, y, t) = G(x, y, t)$, $(x, y, t) \in \partial R \times (0, T]$ where $h(x, y, t) = sinx\ siny\ e^{-t} - 4$, $0 \le x \le 1$, $0 \le y \le 1$, $0 \le t$ and $U(x, y, 0) = sinx\ siny + x^2 + y^2$. The theoretical solution is given by,

$$U(x, y, t) = (sinx\ siny)\ e^{-t} + x^2 + y^2$$
$$0 \le x \le 1,\ 0 \le y \le 1,\ 0 \le t$$

The numerical results for sequential AGEB and AGE_DR are displayed in Table 1. This table provides the absolute errors of the numerical solutions based on matrices of size (600×600) and $(10^3 \times 10^3)$ respectively. The higher accuracy of the AGEB, AGE_DR and GSRB methods are observed from these errors. It is also reflected by the lower magnitude of the root mean square error (rmse). The rate of convergence of AGEB is faster than AGE_DR and GSRB methods. Table 2 and 3 show that the computational complexity and communication cost for parallel AGEB are lower than AGE_DR and GSRB methods. Plots of the graph of the execution time, speedup, efficiency and effectiveness versus number of the processors p used are shown in Fig. 1-4, where BRIAN for AGEB and DOUGLAS for AGE_DR. The parallel execution time and computation time are decreases with increasing p. The communication time expended indicates to some measure the size of messages send as well as the frequency of communication. Table 3 shows that the communication time of AGEB method is lower than AGE_DR and GSRB methods.

Table 1. Performance measurements of the sequential AGEB and AGE_DR methods

m	600 × 600			$10^3 \times 10^3$		
	AGEB	AGE_DR	GSRB	AGEB	AGE_DR	GSRB
$t_{para}(\mu s)$	33.885	35.689	40.159	138.981	143.2267	157.673
iter.	130	150	500	200	230	622
rmse	$3.0717E^{-12}$	$3.0739E^{-12}$	$3.0746E^{-12}$	$2.4396E^{-12}$	$2.4416E^{-12}$	$2.4482E^{-12}$
$|r|$	$6.6968E^{-13}$	$6.6302E^{-13}$	$6.6303E^{-13}$	$7.3807E^{-13}$	$7.3185E^{-13}$	$7.3988E^{-13}$
ave_rmse	$1.012E^{-11}$	$1.0116E^{-11}$	$1.0151E^{-11}$	$8.0722E^{-12}$	$8.0597E^{-12}$	$8.0979E^{-12}$
r.maxs	$1.5646E^{-23}$	$1.5668E^{-23}$	$1.5681E^{-23}$	$9.8766E^{-24}$	$9.8938E^{-24}$	$9.9535E^{-24}$
r	0.99	0.95	—	1.6	1.6	—
Δx	$1.67E^{-3}$	$1.67E^{-3}$	$1.67E^{-3}$	$1.00E^{-3}$	$1.00E^{-3}$	$1.00E^{-3}$
Δy	$1.67E^{-3}$	$1.67E^{-3}$	$1.67E^{-3}$	$1.00E^{-3}$	$1.00E^{-3}$	$1.00E^{-3}$
Δt	$1.00E^{-6}$	$1.00E^{-6}$	$1.00E^{-6}$	$1.00E^{-6}$	$1.00E^{-6}$	$1.00E^{-6}$
λ	$3.58E^{-1}$	$3.58E^{-1}$	$3.58E^{-1}$	1.00	1.00	1.00
θ	1.00	1.00	1.00	1.00	1.00	1.00
level	50	50	50	50	50	50
ϵ	$1.0E^{-12}$	$1.0E^{-12}$	$1.0E^{-16}$	$1.0E^{-12}$	$1.0E^{-12}$	$1.0E^{-17}$

rmse= root means square error, |r|= absolute error, r.maks = maximum error and ave_rmse = average of rmse

Table 2. Computational complexity for parallel AGEB and AGE_DR methods

m	600 × 600		$10^3 \times 10^3$	
	mult.	add.	mult.	add.
AGEB	$1832(m-1)^2$ $+\frac{1040m^2}{p}$	$3380(m-1)^2$ $+\frac{1690m^2}{p}$	$2800(m-1)^2$ $+\frac{1600m^2}{p}$	$5200(m-1)^2$ $+\frac{2600m^2}{p}$
AGE_DR	$3000(m-1)^2$ $+\frac{1500m^2}{p}$	$3900(m-1)^2$ $+\frac{1950m^2}{p}$	$4600(m-1)^2$ $+\frac{2300m^2}{p}$	$5980(m-1)^2$ $+\frac{2990m^2}{p}$
GSRB	$5000(m-1)^2$ $+\frac{7000m^2}{p}$	$5500(m-1)^2$ $+\frac{7500m^2}{p}$	$6220(m-1)^2$ $+\frac{8708m^2}{p}$	$6842(m-1)^2$ $+\frac{9330m^2}{p}$

Table 3. Communication cost for parallel AGEB and AGE_DR methods

m method	600 × 600 communication cost	$10^3 \times 10^3$ communication cost
AGEB	$1560mt_{data}$ $+780(t_{startup}+t_{idle})$	$2400mt_{data}$ $+1200(t_{startup}+t_{idle})$
AGE_DR	$1800mt_{data}$ $+900(t_{startup}+t_{idle})$	$2760mt_{data}$ $+1380(t_{startup}+t_{idle})$
GSRB	$6000mt_{data}$ $+3000(t_{startup}+t_{idle})$	$7464mt_{data}$ $+3732(t_{startup}+t_{idle})$

The reduction in execution time often becomes smaller when a large number of processors is used. Comparable speedups are obtained for all applications with 20 processors. The efficiency of the AGE_DR method decreases faster than the AGEB method. This could be explained by the fact that several factors lead

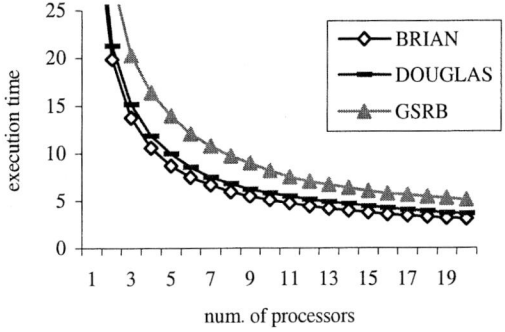

Fig. 1. The execution time vs. number of processors

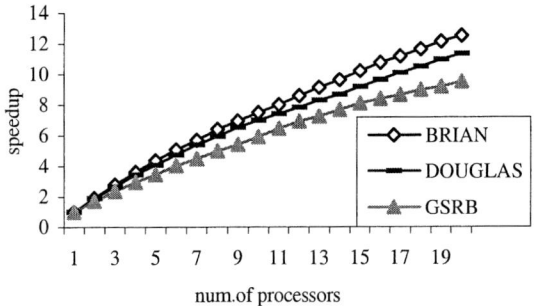

Fig. 2. The speedup vs. number of processors

to an increase in idle time such as network load, delay and load imbalance. The superiority of the AGEB method lies in its effectiveness and the temporal performance. The data decomposition runs asynchronously and concurrently at every time step with the limited communication cost. As a result, the AGEB method allows inconsistencies due to load balancing when the extra computation cost is needed for boundary condition.

6 Conclusions

The stable and highly accurate AGEB algorithm are found to be well suited for parallel implementation on the PVM platform where the data decomposition run asynchronously and concurrently at every time level. The AGEB sweeps involve tridiagonal systems which require the solution of (2×2) block systems. Existing parallel strategies could not be fully exploited to solve such systems. Since the AGEB method is inherently explicit, the domain decomposition strategy is efficiently utilized and straight forward to implement on a cluster of workstations. However, communication time is dependent on the size of messages and the frequency of communication. Therefore, it can be concluded that communication cost and computational complexity affect the speedup ratio, efficiency

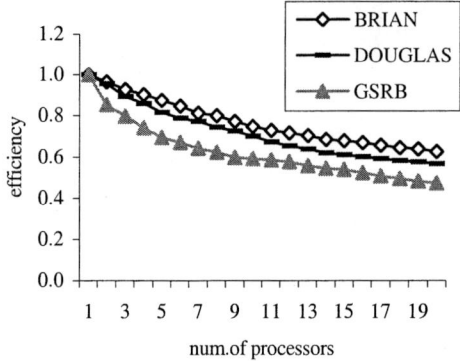

Fig. 3. The efficiency vs. number of processors

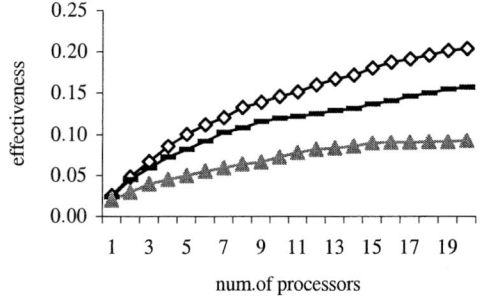

Fig. 4. The effectiveness vs. number of processors

and effectiveness of the parallel algorithm. Furthermore, we have already noted that higher speedups could be expected for a larger problems. Coupled with this is the advantage that the PVM has on its fault tolerant features. Hence, for a large real field problems which we hope to solve in the immediate future, these features become more important as the cluster gets larger.

Acknowledgment

We wish to express our gratitude and indebtedness to the Universiti Kebangsaan Malaysia, Universiti Tenaga Nasional and Malaysian Government for providing moral and financial support under IRPA grant for the successful completion of this project.

References

1. Alias, N., Sahimi, M.S., Abdullah, A.R.: Parallel Algorithms On Some Numerical Techniques Using PVM Platform On A Cluster Of Workstations. Proceedings of the 7th Asian Technology Conference in Mathematics. 7 (2002) 390–397

2. Alias, N., Sahimi, M.S., Abdullah, A.R.: Parallel Strategies For The Iterative lternating Decomposition Explicit Interpolation-Conjugate Gradient Method In solving Heat Conductor Equation On A Distributed Parallel Computer Systems. Proceedings of The 3rd International Conference On Numerical Analysis in Engineering. 3 (2003) 31–38
3. Evans, D.J., Sahimi, M.S.: The Alternating Group Explicit Iterative Method (AGE) to Solve Parabolic and Hyperbolic Partial Differential Equations. In: Tien, C.L., Chawla, T.C. (eds.): Annual Review of Numerical Fluid Mechanics and Heat Transfer, Vol. 2. Hemisphere Publication Corporation, New York Washington Philadelphia London (1989)
4. Evans, D.J., Sahimi, M.S.: The Alternating Group Explicit(AGE) Iterative Method for Solving Parabolic Equations I: 2-Dimensional Problems. Intern. J. Computer Math. 24 (1988) 311-341
5. Peaceman, D.W.: Fundamentals of Numerical Reservoir Simulation. Elsevier Scientific Publishing Company, Amsterdam Oxford New York (1977)
6. Geist, A., Beguelin, A., Dongarra, J., Jiang, W., Manchek, R., Sunderam, V., PVM: Parallel Virtual Machine & User's Guide and Tutorial for Networked Parallel Computing. MIT Press, Cambridge, Mass (1994)
7. Hwang, K. and Xu, Z., Scalable Parallel Computing: Technology, Architecture, Programming. McGraw Hill, (1998)
8. Lewis,T.G. and EL-Rewini,H., Distributed and Parallel Computing, Manning Publication, USA, (1998)
9. Wilkinson,.B. and Allen, M., Parallel Programming Techniques and Applications Using Networked Workstations and Parallel Computers, Prentice Hall,Upper Saddle River, New Jersey 07458 (1999)
10. Zamoya, A. Y. Parallel and Distribution Computing Handbook, McGraw Hill, (1996)

A Parallel Scheme for Solving a Tridiagonal Matrix with Pre-propagation

Akiyoshi Wakatani

Faculty of Science and Engineering, Konan University, Kobe, Japan
8-9-1, Okamoto, Higashinada,
Kobe, 658-0032, Japan
`wakatani@konan-u.ac.jp`

Abstract. A tridiagonal matrix for ADI method can be solved by Gaussian elimination with iterations of three substitutions, two of which need to be carefully parallelized in order to achieve high performance. We propose a parallel scheme for these substitutions (*first-order recurrence equations*) with scalability to the problem size and our experiment shows that it achieves $\frac{P}{2.1}$ speedup with P processors.

1 Introduction

1.1 ADI Method

Solving a linear system of equations is one of major applications for high performance computing, including the diffusion equation as shown in equation (1).

$$\frac{\partial u}{\partial t} = D(\frac{\partial^2 u}{\partial x^2} + \frac{\partial^2 u}{\partial y^2}) \tag{1}$$

ADI (Alternating Direction Iteration) method is an iterative algorithm by using finite difference method, which divides every iteration slot into the same number of micro iteration slots as the number of dimensions of the problem and updates the variable by solving a tridiagonal matrix every micro iteration slot[1]. The following equations are iterative scheme for two-dimensional problem.

$$u_{i,j}^{n+\frac{1}{2}} = u_{i,j}^n + \frac{1}{2}\alpha(\delta_x^2 u_{i,j}^{n+\frac{1}{2}} + \delta_y^2 u_{i,j}^n) \tag{2}$$

$$u_{i,j}^{n+1} = u_{i,j}^{n+\frac{1}{2}} + \frac{1}{2}\alpha(\delta_x^2 u_{i,j}^{n+\frac{1}{2}} + \delta_y^2 u_{i,j}^{n+1}) \tag{3}$$

$$\alpha \equiv \frac{D\Delta t}{\Delta^2}, \Delta \equiv \Delta x = \Delta y, \tag{4}$$

where Δ is a step size of difference and δ is difference operator.

Equation (2) solves $u_{i,j}^{n+\frac{1}{2}}$ by x-dimensional tridiagonal matrix and Equation (3) solves $u_{i,j}^{n+1}$ by y-dimensional tridiagonal matrix . This procedure should be iterated until the iterative solution is converged.

As a multidimensional ADI solver on parallel computers, several methods are known [3–5], which utilize the redistribution of arrays or the cell-partitioned method. However, both have drawbacks, that is, the redistribution of arrays is an expensive task and the cell-partitioned method requires the startup delay.

1.2 Purpose

Our purpose is to parallelize a solver for the following tridiagonal matrix of $A \times x = c$ where A is a tridiagonal matrix with $N \times N$ elements and x and c are vectors with N elements.

$$x_0 = c_0, \quad x_{N-1} = c_{N-1} \tag{5}$$

$$-b_i * x_{i-1} + a_i * x_i - b_i * x_{i+1} = c_i \quad (i = 1 \sim N-2) \tag{6}$$

where arrays a and b are elements of matrix A, arrays a, b and c are given in advance, array x is a unknown and N is the number of elements of the arrays.

It is known that this system can be deterministically solved by the following procedure, which utilizes two auxiliary arrays p and q.

$$p_0 = 0, q_0 = c_0 \tag{7}$$

$$p_i = \frac{b_i}{a_i - b_i \cdot p_{i-1}}, q_i = \frac{c_i + b_i \cdot q_{i-1}}{a_i - b_i \cdot p_{i-1}} \quad (i = 1 \sim N-2) \tag{8}$$

$$x_i = x_{i+1} \cdot p_i + q_i \quad (i = N-2 \sim 1) \tag{9}$$

The above procedure is called *Gaussian elimination*, which consists of a forward substitution (equation 8) and a backward substitution (equation 9). However, on parallel computers, the procedure cannot be straightforwardly parallelized due to the data dependency that resides on both forward and backward substitutions. For example, when it is assumed that the number of processor is P, $N = P * M + 2$ and arrays are block-distributed, processor k ($k = 0 \sim P-1$) is in charge of M elements of arrays from $k*M+1$ to $k*M+M$, thus p_{k*M+1} can be calculated on processor k only after $p_{(k-1)*M+M}$ is calculated on processor $k-1$. Meanwhile x_{k*M+M} can be calculated on processor k only after $x_{(k+1)*M+1}$ is calculated on processor $k+1$. These data-dependencies completely diminished the effectiveness of parallelism.

2 P-Scheme

Among these substitutions, the substitution for array p consists of only elements a and b, which are constant over iterations of ADI for the diffusion equation. Thus, since array p is fixed over rest of iterations if calculated once, we do not care about how to parallelize the substitution for array p [1].

However, on the context of ADI, array c is actually unknown variable that was calculated on other dimension, so array q is not fixed over iterations. Therefore we

---

[1] The substitution for array p can be also parallelized by using a similar method to ours. This issue will be discussed in a different paper.

```
local w', α, vv, tt;
parallel for k=0,P-1{ /* speculation */
    w'_0 = 0.0, α_0 = 0.0;
    for(i=1;i<=M;i++){
        w'_i = s_{k*M+i} × w'_{i-1} + t_{k*M+i};
        α_i = s_{k*M+i} × αi-1;
    }
}
/* propagation */
if(k==0){
    vv = C;
    tt = w'_M + α_M × vv;
    send(tt,k+1);
}
else if(k==P-1)
    receive(vv,k-1);
else{
    receive(vv,k-1);
    tt = w'_M + α_M × vv;
    send(tt,k+1);
}
parallel for k=0,P-1{ /* correction */
    for(i=1;i<=M;i++)
        w_{k*M+i} = w'_i + α_i × vv;
}
```

Fig. 1. P-scheme (Pre-Propagation scheme)

should focus on the substitutions for arrays q and x and consider the efficient parallel scheme for them.

These two substitutions can be expressed by the following first-order recurrence equation,

$$w_0 = C \tag{10}$$

$$w_i = s_i \times w_{i-1} + t_i, \quad (i = 0 \sim N-1) \tag{11}$$

where arrays s and t and C are known in advance and array w is unknown variable to be solved. For the system, we propose a scheme called *P-scheme(Pre-Propagation scheme)*, which consists of three phases. First of all, every processor starts its calculation by assuming that value of w_{k*M} is 0 and keeps the calculated value of w_i as w'_i. This is called *speculation* phase. Of course, since w_{k*M} is not necessarily 0, we have to correct the value of w_i. Let Δw_i to be $w_i - w'_i$.

$$\Delta w_i = w_i - w'_i = s_i \times (w_{i-1} - w'_{i-1}) = s_i \times \Delta w_{i-1} \tag{12}$$

$$= s_i \times s_{i-1} \times \ldots \times s_{k*M+1} \Delta w_{k*M} = \prod_{j=k*M+1}^{i} s_j \times \Delta w_{k*M} \tag{13}$$

Therefore, when w_{k*M} is determined on processor $k-1$, any value of array elements on processor k can be corrected to true value by using equation (13) as follows:

$$w_i = w'_i + \Delta w_i = w'_i + α_i \times w_{k*M}, \tag{14}$$

where α_i is $\prod_{j=k*M+1}^{i} s_j$. It should be noted that w_i can be corrected in any order (descendant, ascendant, random and so on) after w_{k*M} is determined. Thus, since the value of w_{k*M+M} is needed for processor $k+1$, w_{k*M+M} should be calculated first and sent to processor $k+1$. This is called *propagation* phase. Finally, all processors can correct w_{k*M+i} ($i = 1..M-1$) by using received data w_{k*M}. This is called *correction* phase. P-scheme is summarized in Fig.1.

As shown in the figure, the speculation and correction phases can be completely parallelized. Meanwhile the propagation phase is still sequential but the data to be exchanged is very slight, like just one data, so the communication cost is also expected to be very slight. The cost of the propagation phase is in proportion to the number of processors. Thus the total execution time is estimated by $O(\frac{N}{P}) + O(P) + O(\frac{N}{P})$.

Although the speculation and correction phases can be parallelized completely, the computational complexity is larger than the original substitution given by expression (11). Since the original substitution contains 1 multiplication, 1 addition, 3 loads and 1 store and P-scheme contains 3 multiplications, 2 additions, 7 loads and 3 store, P-scheme must carry out over twice computation than the original substitution. This ratio of computational complexity between the original substitution and P-scheme is called *complexity parameter* β. Therefore, by assuming that the communication cost for one element is Cm and the computation cost for one element by the original substitution is Cc, the estimation of speedup is expressed by,

$$speedup = \frac{Cc \times N}{\frac{Cc \times \beta \times P \times M}{P} + Cm \times (P-1)} \simeq \frac{1}{\frac{\beta}{P} + \frac{Cm}{M \times Cc}} \simeq \frac{P}{\beta}, \quad (15)$$

where $N = P*M+2$ and $Cm << M \times Cc$. When the size of array is sufficiently large and the cost of the communication of one data can be ignored, the maximal speedup, expressed by equation (15), can be achieved.

3 Experiment

In order to present the effectiveness of P-scheme, we implement the scheme on PC cluster system, which consists of 8 Celeron (1GHz) CPUs having 128MB memory with 100Mbps Ethernet under Linux 2.4.18 and MPICH 1.2.4. We measure the elapsed time for solving a tridiagonal matrix by using both the original substitution on one processor and P-scheme with varying the number of processors. The speedup of P-scheme is shown in Fig. 2 for the case where the speedup of the original substitution is assumed to be 1.

When the size of array is under 12800, the speedup is limited due to the communication cost for the propagation phase. For example, when the size of array is 6400, the speedup for 4 and 8 processors are 1.36 and 2.17 respectively, which are less than the estimated maximum speedup given by equation (15), 2.0 and 4.0. But, when the size of array is over 25600, the results are getting close to the estimation since the communication cost can be ignored. The speedup for 4 and 8 processors with the size of array of 4096000 is 1.86 and 3.68. Therefore it is proved that P-scheme works well for solving a tridiagonal matrix with enough large size of array and complexity parameter β is about 2.1.

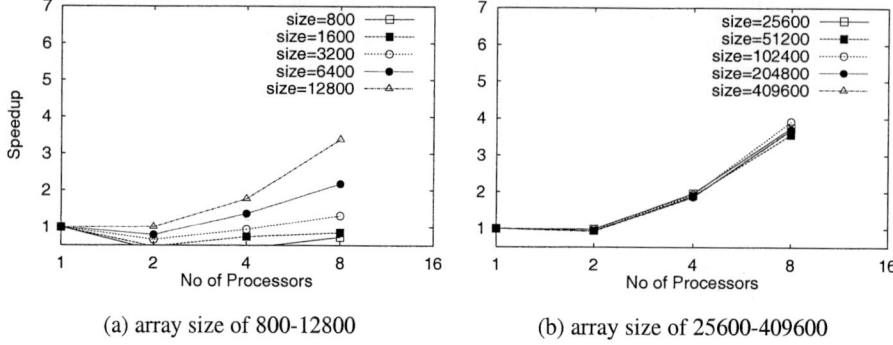

(a) array size of 800-12800   (b) array size of 25600-409600

Fig. 2. Speedup for 2, 4 and 8 processors with varying the size of array to be solved

4 Conclusion

We propose an alternative scheme, called P-scheme, for solving a tridiagonal matrix, which is suitable for parallel processing. Our experiment shows that the effective parallelism is about $\frac{P}{2.1}$ for the case of enough large size of arrays and even for the case of moderate size of multidimensional arrays, thus P-scheme is suitable for PC cluster system. We also shows that P-scheme can solve a tridiagonal matrix with enough accuracy.

References

1. Press, W.: Numerical Recipes in C. Cambridge, UK (1988)
2. Hockney, R.: Parallel Computer 2: Adam Hilger (1988)
3. Kadota, H. et al.: Parallel Computer ADENART -its Architecture and Application-. Proc. of Int'l Conf. on Supercomputing, (1991)
4. Kumar, B. et al.: A Parallel MIMD Cell Partitioned ADI Solver for Parabolic PDEs on VPP700. RIKEN Review **30** (2000)
5. Fox, G.: Spatial Differencing and ADI Solution of the NAS Benchmarks. http://www.npac.syr.edu/users/gcf/cps713nasii96 (1996)

Competitive Semantic Tree Theorem Prover with Resolutions

Choon Kyu Kim[1] and Monty Newborn[2]

[1] School of Computer Science, McGill University, Montreal, Canada
Current address: Korea Telecom Research Center, Seoul, Korea
cgkim@kt.co.kr
[2] School of Computer Science, McGill University, Montreal, Canada
newborn@cs.mcgill.ca

Abstract. Semantic trees have often been used as a theoretical tool for showing the unsatisfiability of clauses in first-order predicate logic. Their practicality has been overshadowed, however, by other strategies.

In this paper, we introduce unit clauses derived from resolutions when necessary to construct a semantic tree, leading to a strategy that combines the construction of semantic trees with resolution-refutation.

The parallel semantic tree theorem prover, called PrHERBY, combines semantic trees and resolution-refutation methods. The system presented is scalable by strategically selecting atoms with the help of dedicated resolutions. It performs significantly better and generally finds proof using fewer atoms than the semantic tree prover, HERBY.

1 Semantic Trees with Resolutions

The motivation for this research came from linear properties of semantic trees. The observation that many semantic trees found by HERBY are rather thin was clarified in an experiment, which showed that more than half of the proofs are almost linear [3]. It showed that 33 out of 78 proofs found by HERBY in the Stickel test set are completely linear; another 8 had all but one non-terminal node on a single path; and yet another 8 had all but two non-terminal nodes on a single path.

The linear semantic trees are semantic trees with all non-terminal nodes on one path. Unfortunately, a linear semantic tree exists for some but not all theorems. This tree reminds us of a *vine-form* proof in linear resolution proof or *input resolution*. This adds a further restriction in that each resolution in the proof has at least one base clause as an input. Not every theorem has a proof in vine-form.

To help to achieve linearity, we introduce resolution to the clauses when necessary. If a given set S of clauses is a theorem, one must obtain successively shorter clauses to deduce a contradiction. Providing unit clauses through resolution gives a way of progressing rapidly toward shorter clauses. If an atom is selected through a series of resolutions, the atom is more likely to trigger closure than the atom chosen arbitrarily from sets of clauses. Moreover, we can apply several strategies of resolution-refutation to generate these atoms.

2 Exploiting Parallelism: Highly Competitive Model

In this paper, we propose a competitive model that distributes the atoms collected by IDDFS(Iterative Deepening Depth-First Search) to processors so that each can construct a semantic tree. Each processor will construct a somewhat different semantic tree, depending on the atoms given by the master. The semantic tree will be different according to the behavior of the IDDFS execution and the number of unit clauses generated. Even the same atoms repeatedly collected by different iterations will be distributed in a different order in a very systematic way.

As an example, consider an atom distribution scenario. The atoms collected through IDDFS from Theorem A are shown in Figure 1. Atoms are numbered sequentially according to the order of generation by IDDFS.

Table 1. Theorem A and atoms collected at each iteration of IDDFS.

1.$P(x) \vee \neg Q(x)$	(a) 1st iteration	1 $\neg Q(x)$					
2.$Q(a) \vee Q(b)$	(b) 2nd iteration	2 $\neg Q(x)$	3 $Q(a)$	4 $\neg Q(x)$	5 $Q(b)$	6 $Q(a)$	7 $Q(b)$
3.$\neg P(x)$	(c) 3rd iteration	8 $\neg Q(x)$	9 $Q(a)$	10 $P(a)$			

Starting from the first atom in the Figure 1 (a), each is distributed to each slave. In this scheme, slave i receives (i **modulo** *number of slaves*)-th atom. The first slave receives the atom $\neg Q(x)$ and constructs a closed semantic tree. The second slave receives the same atom $\neg Q(x)$ as the first slave though it is grounded differently. We briefly show the tenth slave. With the tenth atom $P(a)$, the slave will construct a semantic tree with atoms:

1. $P(a)$ from the master. It closes a branch resolving with clause 3. The negated atom $\neg P(a)$ generates a resolvent (1a,1a) $\neg Q(a)$.
2. $\neg Q(a)$, $Q(b)$ and $P(b)$ from atom selection heuristics because the branch is closed by resolving (1a,1a) $\neg Q(a)$ with clause 2 and resolving the resolvent $Q(b)$ with clause 1, and resolving the resolvent $P(b)$ with clause 3.

Note that the atom $P(a)$ from the master is hidden inside the set of clauses and quite difficult to locate by means of atom selection heuristics without depending on luck. The scheme we propose provides the opportunity to generate these atoms.

We implemented a system named PrHERBY that embodies the ideas presented. This system is based on both HERBY and THEO. It uses the PVM (Parallel Virtual Machine environment) for message passing.

The master spawns several slaves and reads input clauses. After that, the master carries out an IDDFS in which it gathers atoms and simultaneously checks for messages from slaves. Atoms collected are sent to slaves according to the order of message arrival. Even the master can find a contradiction during IDDFS. After the master spawns several slaves, the slaves process input clauses.

Various atom selection heuristics are then tried to find an atom. Those that can close branches quickly are tried first. A semantic tree is constructed by resolving the atom with clauses on the path to the root.

3 The Experiments and Results

In this experiment, we used the selected subset of 420 theorems in the CADE '97 (Conference on Automated Deduction) competition. Using the same time parameter as in competition, 300 seconds, we carried out a series of experiments.

We chose *fifteen* 800MHz Pentium III machines with 256MB memories to obtain uniform test results. We varied the number of processors used by PrHERBY and presented the results of 5, 10, 15 machines. Results from 30 machines, however, used all kinds of available machines.

The results summarized in Table 2 show significantly improved performance of PrHERBY over HERBY in each category of the MIX division of the CADE-14 competition. Note that the number in parentheses beside each PrHERBY indicates the number of machines PrHERBY used.

Table 2. System performance by theorem category.

Category	Theorems	HERBY	PrHERBY(5)	PrHERBY(10)	PrHERBY(15)	PrHERBY(30)
HNE	128	20	49	50	50	50
HEQ	106	14	24	26	31	32
NNE	12	5	8	8	8	8
NEQ	174	58	76	77	80	92
Total	420	97	157	161	169	182

As the data show, the results of PrHERBY with 5, 10 and 15 machines, show improvement solving 60, 64 and 72 more theorems each than HERBY had been able to solve. PrHERBY with 10 and 15 machines on HNE and NNE category did not show any improvement after 5 machines. The NNE category has too small size. HNE category, however, mostly solved by master before slaves find a proof. Resolutions of the master are more appropriate than the semantic tree approach to attack the theorems in HNE group in this case. PrHERBY with 30 machines, outperformed HERBY by solving a total of 85 more theorems in the set of 420. The result shows an outstanding 87% (97 vs. 182) improvement over HERBY. For all configurations, PrHERBY solved significantly more theorems than HERBY.

In order to evaluate PrHERBY, besides the common criteria above, we compare the total work performed by the parallel algorithm to the original algorithm in terms of speed-up. We compare the run-times of PrHEBRY with HERBY for theorems to be proven. The run-time of PrHERBY is the time until one of the processors has found a proof.

The overall mean values for the speed-up are summarized in Table 3. In general, it is rather difficult to give a good estimation of a mean value for the speed-up over a set of examples, especially in cases where the speed-up shows a high variance. For our measurements, we give two common mean values: arithmetic and geometric mean.

For 77 theorems solved by all configurations, the arithmetic mean values are very high for all cases. It reflects the fact that a number of theorems with super-linear speed-up exist. In fact, a large number of theorems with super-linear speed- up exist for all cases. There are several cases in which PrHERBY is running slower than HERBY. The reason for this is that the unit clauses generated are not contributed to the proof of the theorem or misled the search of the proof. This negative effect can easily be overcome by using an additional machine that runs HERBY separately if the run-time is the only concern.

The geometric mean from $P = 15$ to $P = 30$ shows that the speed-up is decreased though the arithmetic mean shows some improvement. It seems that the high variance of the speed-up values that caused the increase of the arithmetic mean value was mitigated in the geometric mean. However, measuring the mean values for those theorems solved by all configurations is somewhat misleading because it does not take into account the prover's other strong point such as the number of solved theorems.

Table 3. Mean values of speed-up for different numbers of machines P.

Mean	PrHERBY(5)	PrHERBY(10)	PrHERBY(15)	PrHERBY(30)
For 77 theorems solved by all configurations				
Arithmetic mean	47.59	49.07	71.35	74.84
Geometric mean	2.05	2.15	2.83	2.71

4 Scalability

We measured system times for implementing the message passing mechanism between machines and the ratio of used atoms to generated atoms of master.

Given 300 seconds, each slave utilizes most of the time to construct semantic trees and the portion of receiving atoms from master is negligible according to experiments. On the other hand, the master divides the given time to perform IDDFS and to distribute atoms to each slave.

With the increasing number of machines, PrHERBY shows increasing system times but the increment is generally very small compared with the increment of the number of machines. Even if the number of machines is doubled, the system time is increased just by 2 to 3 seconds.

Figure 1 shows the system time for each category except NNE. HEQ and NEQ show smooth curves that do not present big differences of system times as the number of machines increases.

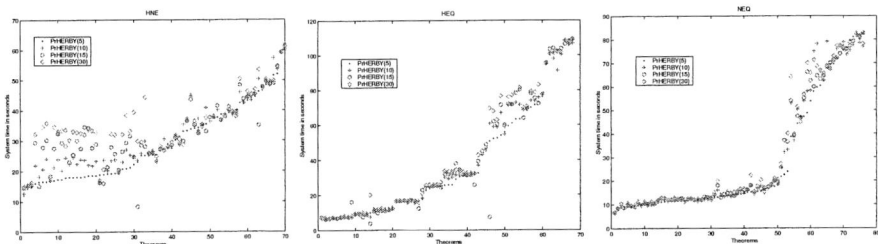

Fig. 1. Comparison of system times classified by system category.

For HNE category, the first half of the graph fluctuates according to the number of used machines. In fact, theorems of PLA (Planning) domain in the field of Computer Science show the behavior. The system time increases as the number of machines are added. The theorems in the domain are also hard to solve in PrHERBY experiments.

We compared the ratio of used atoms to generated atoms of PrHERBY. As the number of machines increases, the ratio is getting bigger meaning that PrHERBY with more machines consumes more atoms. The ratio, however, is below 10% in most cases. If the atom supply is sufficient, the system can use as many machines as the supply reaches its maximum if the overhead is negligible.

Performance generally improves for HEQ and NEQ categories as the number of slaves increases. From the discussions, we can infer the scalability of PrHERBY because the available numbers of atoms are large enough and the system overhead is not proportional to the number of machines.

Unlike SiCoTHEO [2], OCTOPUS [1] and PHERBY , which are limited by the number of available strategies, PrHERBY is scalable for theorems in many domains. As more slaves become involved, successful semantic trees can be built with resolutions for those theorems.

We strongly believe that the semantic tree generation can be as good as other methods for proving unsatisfiability, including the resolution-refutation method. Furthermore, it has unique possibilities of linearity, scalability as exploited in this paper.

References

1. M. Newborn, *Automated Theorem Proving: Theory and Practice*, Springer-Verlag, 2001.
2. Johann Schumann, *SiCoTHEO-simple competitive parallel theorem provers based on SETHEO*, Parallel Processing for Artificial Intelligence 3, 231-245, 1997.
3. Q. Yu, M. Almulla, and M. Newborn, *Heuristics used by HERBY for semantic tree theorem proving*, Annals of Math. and Artificial Intelligence, V.23, pp. 247-266, 1998.

Explicit Group Iterative Solver on a Message Passing Environment

Mohd Ali Norhashidah Hj.[1], Abdullah Rosni[2], and Jun Lee Kok[2]

[1] School of Mathematical Sciences, Universiti Sains Malaysia,
11800 Penang, Malaysia
shidah@cs.usm.my
[2] School of Computer Science, Universiti Sains Malaysia,
11800 Penang, Malaysia
rosni@cs.usm.my
kokjl@hotmail.com

Abstract. In Yousif and Evans [4], the explicit group iterative method for solving elliptic partial differential equations (p.d.e.'s) was introduced and investigated where the method was found to be more superior than the common block Successive Over Relaxation (S.O.R.) schemes. The method was also observed to possess inherent parallelism in its formulation. In this paper, we investigate the implementation of this group method on a message passing architecture, specifically on a cluster of workstations with PVM programming environment.

1 Introduction

During the mid 1980's, explicit p.d.e. solvers were extensively researched as they possess qualities which makes them amenable for use on parallel computers ([1, 2, 4]). Yousif and Evans(1986) in particular, uses small groups of equations in the iterative process to develop the explicit group methods for the solution of elliptic p.d.e.'s. This method has been shown to be suitable to be implemented on a shared memory parallel computer [3] using several variants of the multicoloring strategy. Due to this promising result, efforts are now being taken to test the versatility of this method on a message-passing paradigm. The explicit group method is presented in Section 2. In Section 3, we discuss the strategies used for parallelising the method and Section 4 presents the results of experiments performed.

2 The Explicit Group Iterative Method

Consider the two dimensional elliptic equation

$$u_{xx} + u_{yy} = f(x, y), \qquad (x, y) \in \Omega, . \qquad (1)$$

with Dirichlet boundary conditions $u(x, y) = g(x, y)$, $(x, y) \in \partial\Omega$. Here Ω is a continuous unit square solution domain. Let Ω be discretized uniformly in both x and y directions with a mesh size $h = 1/n$, where n is an integer. Assuming n to be odd, the mesh points are grouped in blocks of four points and the centred difference equation is applied to each of these points resulting in the following (4x4) system [4]: (here, $u_{ij} = u(x_i, y_j)$)

$$\begin{bmatrix} 4 & -1 & 0 & -1 \\ -1 & 4 & -1 & 0 \\ 0 & -1 & 4 & -1 \\ -1 & 0 & -1 & 4 \end{bmatrix} \begin{bmatrix} u_{ij} \\ u_{i+1,j} \\ u_{i+1,j+1} \\ u_{i,j+1} \end{bmatrix} = \begin{bmatrix} u_{i-1,j} + u_{i,j-1} - h^2 f_{ij} \\ u_{i+2,j} + u_{i+1,j-1} - h^2 f_{i+1,j} \\ u_{i+2,j+1} + u_{i+1,j+2} - h^2 f_{i+1,j+1} \\ u_{i-1,j+1} + u_{i,j+2} - h^2 f_{i,j+1} \end{bmatrix} \quad (2)$$

This 4x4 system can be easily inverted to produce a four-point explicit group equation

$$\begin{bmatrix} u_{ij} \\ u_{i+1,j} \\ u_{i+1,j+1} \\ u_{i,j+1} \end{bmatrix} = \frac{1}{24} \begin{bmatrix} 7 & 2 & 1 & 2 \\ 2 & 7 & 2 & 1 \\ 1 & 2 & 7 & 2 \\ 2 & 1 & 2 & 7 \end{bmatrix} \begin{bmatrix} u_{i-1,j} + u_{i,j-1} - h^2 f_{ij} \\ u_{i+2,j} + u_{i+1,j-1} - h^2 f_{i+1,j} \\ u_{i+2,j+1} + u_{i+1,j+2} - h^2 f_{i+1,j+1} \\ u_{i-1,j+1} + u_{i,j+2} - h^2 f_{i,j+1} \end{bmatrix} \quad (3)$$

whose individual explicit equations are given by

$$u_{ij} = \frac{1}{24}[7r1 + 2(r2 + r4) + r3], \qquad u_{i+1,j} = \frac{1}{24}[2(r1 + r3) + 7r2 + r4]$$

$$u_{i+1,j+1} = \frac{1}{24}[r1 + 2(r2 + r4) + 7r3], \qquad u_{i,j+1} = \frac{1}{24}[2(r1 + r3) + r2 + 7r4] \quad (4)$$

where

$r1 = u_{i-1,j} + u_{i,j-1} - h^2 f_{ij}, \qquad r2 = u_{i+2,j} + u_{i+1,j-1} - h^2 f_{i+1,j}$
$r3 = u_{i+2,j+1} + u_{i+1,j+2} - h^2 f_{i+1,j+1}, \qquad r4 = u_{i-1,j+1} + u_{i,j+2} - h^2 f_{i,j+1}.$ (5)

The EG method proceeds with iterative evaluation of solutions in blocks of four points using these formulae throughout the whole solution domain until convergence is achieved.

3 Parallelising Strategies on a Cluster of Workstations

Two strategies are proposed in parallelising the method. In the first strategy (Strategy 1), the solution domain is decomposed into a number of horizontal strips consisting of two rows of four point groups arranged in the order shown in Fig. 1(a) for the case n = 9. If we evaluate the solutions u using Equations (4)-(5) in this ordering, the coefficient matrix A in the linear system Au = B will have the following form

$$A = \begin{bmatrix} \underline{D} & C \\ F & \underline{D} \end{bmatrix} \begin{bmatrix} u_{Stage1} \\ u_{Stage2} \end{bmatrix}, \quad (6)$$

with $\underline{D}$, C and F being block diagonal, lower and upper triangular matrices respectively. The iterative evaluation of this system may then be written as

$$\underline{u}_{Stage1}^{(k+1)} = \underline{D}^{-1}[B_{Stage1} - C\underline{u}_{Stage2}^{(k)}]$$
$$\underline{u}_{Stage2}^{(k+1)} = \underline{D}^{-1}[B_{Stage2} - F\underline{u}_{Stage1}^{(k+1)}]. \qquad (7)$$

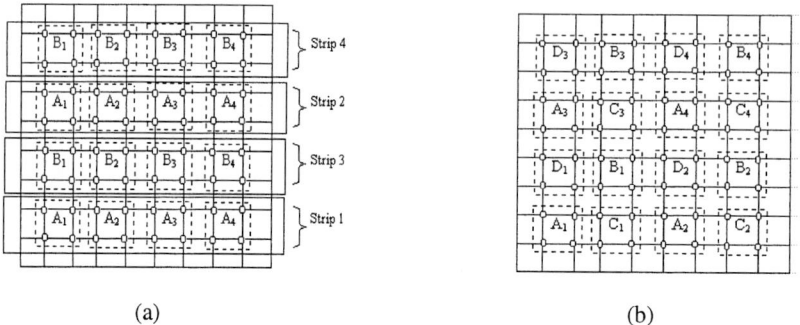

(a)   (b)

Fig. 1. Ordering of group of points in solution domain for (a) Strategy 1 and (b) Strategy 2

Thus, the computations in each stage are independent of each other and therefore parallelisable. In the second strategy (Strategy 2), the four-point groups are assigned to processors in block ordering as shown below for the case n = 9. As illustrated in Fig. 1(b), the iteration are firstly done on the blocks A_1, A_2, A_3, A_4 in parallel, followed by B_1, B_2, B_3, B_4, then C_1, C_2, C_3, C_4 and finally D_1, D_2, D_3, D_4, all in parallel. Thus, in this strategy, an iteration is split into four stages where the computations within each stage is independent of each other.

Figs. 2(i) illustrates the communication patterns which take place during the updates of points belonging to the A_i and B_i strips when the number of strips per processor is even (for example, here the number of processors is 3). One important observation about this case is that each processor assigned to the block of strips will require the same communication pattern when updating the points in the strips. For example, in Stage 1 of each iteration in this strategy, the values of points in the B_i blocks on the boundary of a subdomain held by a particular processor need to be sent to the processors holding adjacent subdomains in order to update the points in the A_i blocks on their boundaries. Then, in Stage 2, these updated values on the boundaries need to be sent to the appropriate processors to update the B_i points on the boundaries of adjacent subdomains. For the odd case, the communication patterns in updating the A and B strips is not the same for each processor specifically at the boundaries in each subdomain (see Fig. 2(ii)). Similar to Strategy 1, Strategy 2 imposes different communication patterns amongst the processors when updating the points if the number of strips per processor is odd.

4 Numerical Experimentation

To study the performance of the parallel algorithms, the Poisson equation on the unit square with Dirichlet boundary conditions was used as the model problem

$$\frac{\partial^2 U}{\partial x^2} + \frac{\partial^2 U}{\partial y^2} = (x^2 + y^2)e^{xy}, \qquad x, y \in \Omega = (0,1) \times (0,1) \tag{8}$$

with the boundary conditions satisfying its exact solution $u(x,y) = e^{xy}$. The experiments were ported to run on a cluster of Sun workstations at the School of Computer Science, USM with PVM programming environment. Table 1 depicts the CPU-times in seconds, error between the exact and computed solution, the speedup, and the efficiency values for the parallel EG (S.O.R.) method using Strategy 1 and 2 with the number of processors, p, ranging from 1 to 6. The grid size, n, is chosen such that each processor gets equal even number of strips in any one stage. Throughout the experiments a tolerance of $\varepsilon = 10^{-5}$ in the convergence test was used.

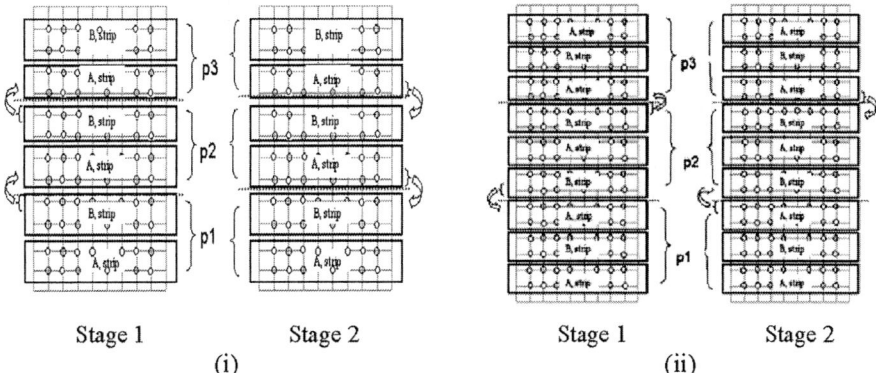

Fig. 2. The message passing communications involved in Strategy 1 in updating on the A_i and B_i strips when the number of strips per process is (i) even and (ii) odd

5 Results and Concluding Remarks

Between the two strategies, it is observed that the execution timings for Strategy 1 is less than Strategy 2 in almost all of the cases tested. This is due to the fact that the latter strategy impose more communication overheads in receiving and sending messages for the four stages involved in this strategy than the overheads incurred in the former strategy. It is also observed that the speedup and efficiency values for Strategy 1 are slightly better than Strategy 2 in almost all of the cases tested which indicates the amount of computations carried out over the total overheads in Strategy 1 is greater than the one in Strategy 2. In general, the two algorithms developed turned out to be relatively efficient and viable to be ported on a distributed system with Strategy 1 being the better one.

Acknowledgement
The authors acknowledge the Priority Research Grant funded by the Ministry of Science, Technology and Environment (305/PKOMP/6122012) that has resulted in this article.

Table 1. Performance of the parallel EG method using both strategies

Parallel Explicit Group (Strategy 1)						Parallel Explicit Group (Strategy 2)					
Grid size	p	Times(sec)	Error	iter	Speed up	Eff.	Grid size	Times(sec)	Error	iter	Speed up	Eff.
n=121 w: 1.9208	1	2.392611	0.000026	166	1.000	1.000	n=121 w: 1.9208	2.360774	0.000066	158	1.000	1.000
	2	1.835177	0.000026	166	1.304	0.652		1.982139	0.000066	158	1.191	0.595
	3	1.534026	0.000026	166	1.560	0.520		1.644802	0.000066	158	1.435	0.478
	4	1.544628	0.000026	166	1.549	0.387		1.909053	0.000066	158	1.236	0.309
	5	1.560656	0.000026	166	1.533	0.307		1.911274	0.000066	158	1.235	0.247
	6	1.978348	0.000026	166	1.209	0.202		2.410931	0.000066	158	0.979	0.163
n=241 w: 1.9628	1	18.975956	0.000128	323	1.000	1.000	n=241 w: 1.9631	18.440461	0.000069	308	1.000	1.000
	2	10.428801	0.000128	323	1.820	0.910		10.846364	0.000069	308	1.700	0.850
	3	7.740153	0.000128	323	2.452	0.817		8.160424	0.000069	308	2.257	0.752
	4	6.471082	0.000128	323	2.932	0.733		7.031195	0.000069	308	2.623	0.656
	5	5.928660	0.000128	323	3.202	0.640		6.726156	0.000069	308	2.742	0.548
	6	5.798748	0.000128	323	3.272	0.545		7.827797	0.000069	308	2.356	0.393
n=361 w: 1.9746	1	61.762393	0.000163	476	1.000	1.000	n=361 w: 1.9748	61.666080	0.000051	456	1.000	1.000
	2	33.300304	0.000163	476	1.854	0.927		33.917836	0.000051	456	1.818	0.909
	3	23.683028	0.000163	476	2.608	0.869		24.301238	0.000051	456	2.538	0.846
	4	19.843507	0.000163	476	3.112	0.778		22.261256	0.000051	456	2.770	0.693
	5	16.734022	0.000163	476	3.691	0.738		18.474603	0.000051	456	3.338	0.668
	6	15.675819	0.000163	476	3.940	0.657		17.836182	0.000051	456	3.457	0.576
n=481 w: 1.9805	1	145.408816	0.000199	628	1.000	1.000	n=481 w: 1.9805	147.621017	0.000077	609	1.000	1.000
	2	76.848287	0.000199	628	1.892	0.946		77.901479	0.000077	609	1.895	0.947
	3	53.811967	0.000199	628	2.702	0.901		54.801025	0.000077	609	2.693	0.898
	4	44.035463	0.000199	628	3.302	0.826		44.405671	0.000077	609	3.318	0.829
	5	37.175641	0.000199	628	3.911	0.782		39.191660	0.000077	609	3.767	0.753
	6	33.615684	0.000199	628	4.326	0.721		36.523845	0.000077	609	4.042	0.674
n=601 w: 1.9842	1	234.747902	0.000281	781	1.000	1.000	n=601 w: 1.9843	232.981012	0.000145	738	1.000	1.000
	2	147.675073	0.000281	781	1.923	0.964		144.860808	0.000145	738	1.954	0.977
	3	103.788805	0.000281	781	2.744	0.915		100.988379	0.000145	738	2.809	0.936
	4	82.405840	0.000281	781	3.455	0.864		84.830426	0.000145	738	3.331	0.833
	5	70.605206	0.000281	781	4.028	0.806		69.388261	0.000145	738	4.072	0.814
	6	61.262645	0.000281	781	4.648	0.775		62.970114	0.000145	738	4.488	0.748

References

1. D.J. Evans and A. R. Abdullah, A New Explicit Method for the Solution of $\frac{\partial u}{\partial t} = \frac{\partial^2 u}{\partial x^2} + \frac{\partial^2 u}{\partial y^2}$, *International Journal of Computer Mathematics*, **14**, (1983), 325-353.
2. D.J. Evans, and M. S. Sahimi, The Alternating Group Explicit(AGE) Iterative Method for Solving Parabolic Equations, 1-2 Dimensional Problems, *International Journal of Computer Mathematics*, **24**, (1988), 250-281.
3. D.J. Evans and W.S. Yousif, The Implementation of The Explicit Block Iterative Methods On the Balance 8000 Parallel Computer, *Parallel Computing*, **16**, (1990), 81-97.
4. W.S. Yousif, and D.J. Evans, Explicit group over-relaxation methods for solving elliptic partial differential equations, *Math. Computer Simulation*, **28**, (1986), 453-466.

Applying Load Balancing in Data Parallel Applications Using DASUD[*]

A. Cortés, M. Planas, J.L. Millán, A. Ripoll, M.A. Senar, and E. Luque

Universitat Autónoma de Barcelona, Dept. of Computer Science
08193 Bellaterra, Barcelona, Spain
{ana.cortes,ana.ripoll,miquelangel.senar,emilio.luque}@uab.es
{mercedes.planas,joseluis.millan}@campus.uab.es

Abstract. DASUD (Diffusion Algorithm Searching Unbalanced Domains) algorithm has been implemented in an SPMD parallel-image thinning application to balance the workload in the processors as computation proceeds and was found to be effective in reducing computation time. The average performance gain is about 40% for a test image of size 2688x1440 on a cluster of 12 PC's in a PVM environment.

1 Introduction

The problem of load balancing in parallel applications is concerned with how to distribute workload or the processes of a computation among the available processors so that each processor has the same or nearly the same amount of work to do. In most cases, load balancing is done prior to execution, and it is undertaken once only – this is called *static* mapping [1]. For computations whose runtime behavior is non-deterministic or else not so predictable, it might be better to perform the mapping more than once or periodically during runtime – this is called *dynamic load balancing*.

In SPMD (Single Program, Multiple Data) programming model a data parallel application decomposes its problem domain into a number of sub domains (data sets), and designates them to processes. These processes simultaneously perform the same functions across different data sets. Because the sub-domains are connected at their boundaries, processes in neighboring sub-domains have to periodically synchronize and exchange boundary information with each other. These synchronization points divide the computation into phases. During each phase, every process executes certain operations that might depend on the results from previous phases. Because of the need for synchronization between phases, a processor that has finished its work in the current phase has to wait for the more heavily loaded processors to finish their work before proceeding to the next. To lessen the penalty due to synchronization and load imbalances, we must dynamically balance the problem domain in the processors as the computation proceeds.

---

[*] This work has been financially supported by the *Comisión Interministerial de Ciencia y Tecnología* (CICYT) under contract TIC2001-2592

In this paper, we present the development of a parallel application frequently used in image processing and demonstrate the effectiveness of incorporating the dynamic load-balancing DASUD (Diffusion Algorithm Searching Unbalanced Domains) algorithm into the implementation [2].

2. The Parallel Thinning of Images with DASUD

DASUD is a dynamic load-balancing algorithms, which runs in each processor in a fully distributed way. Each processor plays an identical role in making load-balancing decisions, which is based on the knowledge of its nearest neighbor neighbors' states. DASUD is iterative, every processor successively balancing its workload with each one of the nearest neighbors in an iteration until a global balance state is reached. We analyzed the DASUD algorithm in our previous works [3] and showed that is effective for many network topologies.

Thinning is a fundamental pre-processing operation to be applied over a binary image so as to produce a version showing the significant features of the image (zoom out picture in figure 1(a)). In the process, redundant information is removed from the image. As input, it takes a binary picture consisting of objects and background which are represented by 1-valued pixels (dots) and 0-valued pixels (white spaces), respectively. It produces object skeletons, depicted with the asterisk symbol, which preserve the original shapes and connectivity. An iterative-thinning algorithm performs successive iterations on the picture by converting the 1-pixels that are judged not to belong to the skeletons into 0-pixels until no more conversions are necessary. In general, the conversion (or survival) condition of a pixel is dependent upon the values of its neighboring pixels.

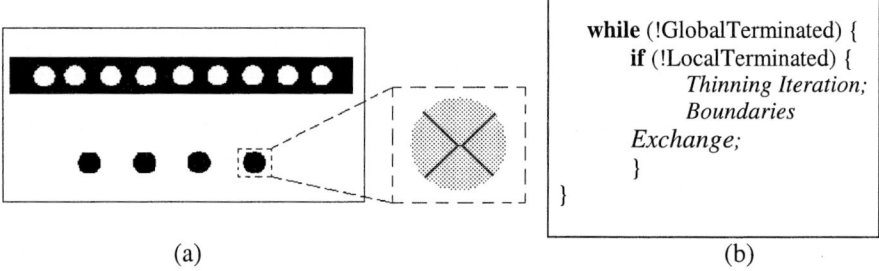

Fig. 1. The image pa77ttern and a partial thinning result (a) and a sketched of the algorithm (b)

A parallel thinning algorithm decomposes the image into a number of partitions, called strips (subset of rows of the image), and applies the thinning operator to all portions simultaneously. Since the study of the parallel thinning algorithm itself is beyond the scope of this study, we have selected an existing parallel thinning, the AFP3 algorithm [4], and implemented it on a chain-structured system using strip-wise decomposition (figure 1(b)).

At the end of each thinning iteration step, the boundary pixels of each strip are exchanged with those of the neighboring strips in the *Boundaries Exchange*. The core of the algorithm *Thinning Iteration* applies the thinning operator to each pixel, according to the survival conditions.

In the SPMD implementation of the Thinning Algorithm, all processes have the same code but there is a process that carries out data distribution and recollection (process 0). When a process finishes, it will send the result to this process. The processes should not finish until the whole image is computed. At the end of each iteration the processes can activate DASUD. In our current implementation, DASUD is activated every certain number x of iterations of Thinning. However, we are planning to include a mechanism, which activates the load balancing algorithm when the processor utilization decreases below a predefined threshold. Before each call to DASUD, the process calculates the resulting strip load and updates the data needed by DASUD. The strip load is calculated during a sequential reading of the strip as the sum of 1-pixels in every row.

Before starting a new iteration, each process checks if DASUD has been activated and whether any load balancing is required or not. As a result of executing the load-balancing process, some rows must necessarily be moved. These movements should be made according to certain rules to ensure data-coherence; they are only applicable to immediate neighboring processes and it is necessary to keep the redundancy within the boundary and, most importantly, the processes must synchronize the transfers undertaken between them.

3 Performance of Parallel Thinning

The experiment reported in this section was conducted on a 12 PC homogeneous cluster distributed architecture with Linux. This distributed architecture was interconnected by a 100 Mbs switched Fast Ethernet Network. The development of the parallel version of the Thinning algorithm was written in C++ using the PVM message passing library [5]. As a test pattern, we used 5 different images. Since the obtained results were very similar for all of them, we have chosen as a representative test, the image shown in figure 1. For the image of size 2688x1440, the number of total iterations required by the thinning algorithm is 246. The thinning time and other performance data of the algorithm for various numbers of the processors are given in table 1.

The 'efficiency' measure is used to reflect the effectiveness of using more processors to solve the same problem. Loss of efficiency as the number of processors increases is due to interprocessor-communication costs and load imbalances.

We see that in parallel thinning, the computational requirement of a node is mainly dependent on the 1-pixels. The amount of conversions of 1-pixels to 0-pixels in an iteration step is unpredictable, and hence the computational workload can be somewhat varied over time. We therefore resort to dynamic load-balancing so as to balance the workload over the course of thinning.

Table 1. Performance of parallel thinning

Number of Processors	1	2	4	6	8	10	12
Thinning time (seconds)	339	191	119	101	92	83	80
Speedup	1	1.775	2.849	3.356	3.685	4.084	4.238
Efficiency	1	0.887	0.712	0.559	0.460	0.408	0.353

As we have previously commented, an iterative application, as the parallel thinning, evolves in synchronized phases where the more heavily loaded processor during each phase, will denote the duration of each phase, let us now define some time values that will allow us to then define the concept of process utilization. Let T_k denote the duration of the k-th phase; the computation time of the processor i in this phase (t_{ik}) is given by the addition of the communication time and the calculation time spent by this processor during that phase. Therefore, the duration of the k-th phase will be given by:

$$T_k = \max(t_{1k}, t_{2k}, \ldots t_{Nk}) \quad (1)$$

where N is the total number of processors used. Thus, we can define processor utilization as:

$$U_k = \frac{\sum_{i=1}^{N} t_{ik}}{NT_k} \quad (2)$$

The objective of load balancing is to minimize the total elapsed time through maximizing the processor utilization U_k from phase to phase.

Since the execution of the load balancing procedure is expected to incur non-negligible delay, the decision of when to invoke a load balancing must be carefully made so that the load balancing cost would not outweigh the performance gain. The cost of load balancing includes the cost of interprocessor communication and the cost of subsequent workload transfers. Figure 2(a) plots the processor utilization across twelve processors at various iteration steps. Processor utilization has been measured for two different situations. On the one hand, we indicate the situation in which no load-balancing algorithm is applied. On the other hand, we depict the application execution when the load-balancing strategy has been considered. As we can observe, when no load balancing is applied, the processor's utilization quickly decreases since the idle times caused by the waiting time of the lightly loaded processors, are not overcome as the computation takes place. In contrast, when the load-balancing algorithm is included, we observe that the processors remain occupied most of the time. For the whole test pattern, we have experimentally obtained that DASUD must be iterated every 40 iterations of thinning to provide a good trade off between processor utilization and time spent carrying out balance operations. Figure 2(b) shows the improvement due to load-balancing in overall thinning time for different numbers of processors. This improvement is defined as follows,

$$\frac{t_{WithoutLB} - t_{WithLB}}{t_{WithoutLB}} \times 100\% \quad (3)$$

where $t_{WithoutLB}$ and t_{WithLB} are the execution times both without then with load-balancing, respectively. From figure 2(b), it is clear that the parallel thinning algorithm benefits from load balancing.

4 Conclusions

In this paper we have studied distributed load balancing with an emphasis on its applicability to real problems. We have used the DASUD (Diffusion Algorithm Searching Unbalanced Domains) algorithm, which has been developed for applications with a coarse and large granularity where workload must be treated as non-negative integer values. We have evaluated its performance with a parallel thinning application and we have shown the individual results obtained for a test image of 2688x1440 and improvements in total elapsed time in the order of 40 percent have been achieved. However, the improvements obtained for the whole test pattern, on average, were between 25% and 50% depending on the image. We consider that these gains in performance are due to maximizing processor utilization as the compute progresses towards becoming satisfactory for the test image analyzed.

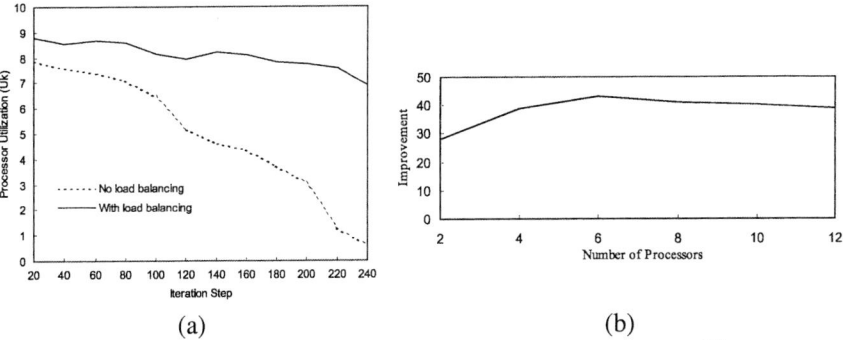

Fig. 2. Processor utilization at various iteration steps for 12 processors (a) and Improvement due to load balancing for various numbers of processors (b)

References

1. Parallel Program Development For Cluster Computing, methodology, Tools and Integrated Environemts, Editors: José Cunha, Peter Kacsuk ans Stephen C. Winter, Nova Science, 2001
2. A. Cortés, A. Ripoll, F. Cedó, M.A. Senar and E. Luque. An Asynchronous and Iterative Load-Balancing Algorithm for Discrete Load Model. Journal of Parallel and Distributed Computing. Vol 62/12, 1729-1746, January 2003.
3. A. Cortés, A. Ripoll, M. A. Senar, P. Pons and E. Luque. On the Performance of Nearest-Neighbors Load Balancing Algorithms in Parallel Systems. 7th Euromicro Workshop on Parallel and Distributed Processing (PDP-99). 170-177, 1999
4. Z. Guo and R.W. Hall, "Fast Fully Parallel Thinning Algorithms", CVGIP: Image Understanding, vol.55, no.3, pp. 317-328, May 1992.
5. A. Geist, A. Berguelín, J. Dongarra, W. Jiang, R. Mancheck and V. Sunderam, "PVM 3 User's guide and Reference Manual", Oak Ridge National Laboratory, September 1994.

Performance Analysis of Approximate String Searching Implementations for Heterogeneous Computing Platform

Panagiotis D. Michailidis and Konstantinos G. Margaritis

Parallel and Distributed Processing Laboratory
Department of Applied Informatics, University of Macedonia
156 Egnatia str., P.O. Box 1591, 54006 Thessaloniki, Greece
{panosm,kmarg}@uom.gr
http://macedonia.uom.gr/~{panosm,kmarg}

Abstract. This paper presents an analytical performance prediction model that can be used to predict the speedup and similar performance metrics of four approximate string searching implementations running on an MPI cluster of heterogeneous workstations. The four implementations are based on master-worker model using static and dynamic allocation of the text collection. The developed performance model has been validated on a 8-cluster of heterogeneous workstations and it has been shown that the model is able to predict the speedup of four parallel implementations accurately.

1 Introduction

Approximate string searching is one of the main problems in classical string algorithms, with applications to information retrieval, computational biology, artificial intelligence and text mining. It is defined as follows: given a large text collection $t = t_1 t_2 ... t_n$ of length n, a short pattern $p = p_1 p_2 ... p_m$ of length m and a maximal number of errors allowed k, we want to find all text positions where the pattern matches the text up to k errors. Errors can be substituting, deleting, or inserting a character. Distributed implementations of approximate string searching algorithm on a cluster of workstations can provide the computing power required for the speed up the process on large free text collections. Recently, in [1] four approximate string searching implementations were proposed and experimental results are reported on a cluster of heterogeneous workstations. The first implementation is the static master-worker with uniform distribution strategy, the second one is the dynamic master-worker with allocation of sub-texts and the third one is the dynamic master-worker with allocation of text pointers. Finally, the fourth hybrid implementation combines the advantages of static and dynamic parallel implementations in order to reduce the load imbalance and communication overhead. This hybrid implementation is based on the following optimal distribution strategy: the text collection is distributed proportional to workstation's speed. More detail for the experimental comparison of four parallel implementations are presented in [1].

2 Performance Model of Approximate String Searching Implementations

In this section, we develop a performance model of four approximate string searching implementations [1] on a cluster of heterogeneous workstations.

Static Master-Worker Implementation. The partitioning strategy of this approach is to partition the entire text collection into a number of subtext collections according to the number of workstations allocated. The size of each subtext collection contains $\lceil n/p \rceil + m - 1$ successive characters of the complete text collection (p is the number of workstations). There is an overlap of $m - 1$ pattern characters between successive subtexts. Also, we assume that the subtext collections stored in the local disk of the workstations. The execution time of the static master-worker implementation that is called P1, is composed of four terms: The first term, T_a, includes the communication time to broadcast the pattern string and the number of errors k to all workers. The second term, T_b, is the I/O time each worker to read its subtext collection with size $\lceil n/p \rceil + m - 1$ characters from the local disk in the main memory. The third term, T_c, is the string searching time across the heterogeneous cluster. Each worker performs the SEL dynamic programming algorithm [2] for an m pattern string in a subtext collection with size $\lceil n/p \rceil + m - 1$ characters. The fourth term, T_d, includes the communication time to gather the results from each worker.

Dynamic Master-Worker with Allocation of Subtexts. For the analysis, we assume that the entire text collection stored in the local disk of the master workstation. The execution time of the dynamic master-worker implementation that is called P2, composed of five terms: The first term, T_a, includes the communication time for broadcasting of the pattern string and the number of errors k to all workers. The second term, T_b, is the total I/O time to read the text collection into several chunks of size $sb + m - 1$ bytes from the local disk of the master. The sb is the optimal block size. The third term, T_c, is the total communication time to send all chunks of the text collection to all workers. The fourth term, T_d, is the average string searching time across the heterogeneous cluster. The fifth term, T_e, includes the communication time to receive $n/(sb + m - 1)$ results from all workers.

Dynamic Master-Worker with Allocation of Text Pointers. For the analysis, we assume that the complete text collection stored in the local disk of worker workstations. The execution time of the dynamic implementation with the text pointers that is called P3, is composed of same five terms as the P2 implementation. We note that the second term, T_b, of the P3 implementation is the average I/O time to read the text collection into several chunks of size $sb + m - 1$ bytes from the local disks of the workers. Further, the third term, T_c, includes the total communication time to send all text pointers instead of chunks of text to all workers.

Table 1. Performance analysis of the P1 and P4 implementations

Terms	P1	P4
T_a	$log_2 p(\alpha + (m+1)\beta)$	$log_2 p(\alpha + (m+1)\beta)$
T_b	$max_{j=1}^{p}\{\frac{\lceil n/p \rceil + m - 1}{(S_{i/o})_j}\}$	$max_{j=1}^{p}\{\frac{l_i*(n+m-1)}{(S_{i/o})_j}\}$
T_c	$max_{j=1}^{p}\{\frac{(\lceil n/p \rceil + m - 1)m}{(S_{search})_j}\}$	$max_{j=1}^{p}\{\frac{(l_i*(n+m-1))m}{(S_{search})_j}\}$
T_d	$log_2 p(\alpha + \beta)$	$log_2 p(\alpha + \beta)$
T_p	$T_a + T_b + T_c + T_d$	$T_a + T_b + T_c + T_d$

Table 2. Performance analysis of the P2 and P3 implementations

Terms	P2	P3
T_a	$log_2 p(\alpha + (m+1)\beta)$	$log_2 p(\alpha + (m+1)\beta)$
T_b	$\frac{n}{(S_{i/o})_{master}}$	$(\frac{n}{sb+m-1} - p)(sb+m-1) \over \sum_{j=1}^{p}(S_{i/o})_j$ $+ max_{j=1}^{p}\{\frac{sb+m-1}{(S_{i/o})_j}\}$
T_c	$\frac{n}{sb+m-1}(\alpha + (sb+m-1)\beta)$	$\frac{n}{sb+m-1}(\alpha + \beta)$
T_d	$(\frac{n}{sb+m-1} - p)[(sb+m-1)m] \over \sum_{j=1}^{p}(S_{search})_j$ $+ max_{j=1}^{p}\{\frac{(sb+m-1)m}{(S_{search})_j}\}$	$(\frac{n}{sb+m-1} - p)[(sb+m-1)m] \over \sum_{j=1}^{p}(S_{search})_j$ $+ max_{j=1}^{p}\{\frac{(sb+m-1)m}{(S_{search})_j}\}$
T_e	$\frac{n}{sb+m-1}(\alpha + \beta)$	$\frac{n}{sb+m-1}(\alpha + \beta)$
T_p	$T_a + T_b + max\{T_c + T_e, T_d\}$	$T_a + max\{T_c + T_e, T_b + T_d\}$

Hybrid Master-Worker Implementation. In order to achieve a good balanced distribution among heterogeneous workstations, the distribution strategy of this implementation is that the amount of text distributed to each workstation should be proportional to its processing capacity compared to the entire network:

$$l_i = \frac{S_i}{\sum_{j=1}^{p} S_j} \quad (1)$$

where S_j is the speed of the workstation j. Therefore, the amount of the text collection that is distributed to each workstation M_i ($1 \leq i \leq p$) is $l_i*(n+m-1)$ successive characters and stored in the local disk of workstation. There is an overlap of $m-1$ pattern characters between successive subtexts. The execution time of the hybrid master-worker implementation that is called P4, composed of same four terms as the P1 implementation. In this paper, the four implementations are based on parallelization of the SEL algorithm [2].

Tables 1 and 2 show the equations for each term of four master-worker implementations. We note that the parameter α is the latency time and β is the transmission time. Further, the parameters $(S_{i/o})_j$ and $(S_{search})_j$ are the I/O and string searching capacity of the heterogeneous network respectively when j workstation is used. Finally, we note that the P2 and P3 implementations in practice there is parallel communication and computation and this reason we take the maximum value between the communication time and the computation time as presented at the equations of the parallel execution time T_p in Table 2.

3 Validation of the Performance Model

The dedicated cluster of heterogeneous workstations connected with 100 Mb/s Fast Ethernet network is consisted of 4 Pentium MMX 166 MHz with 32 MB

Performance Analysis of Approximate String Searching Implementations 245

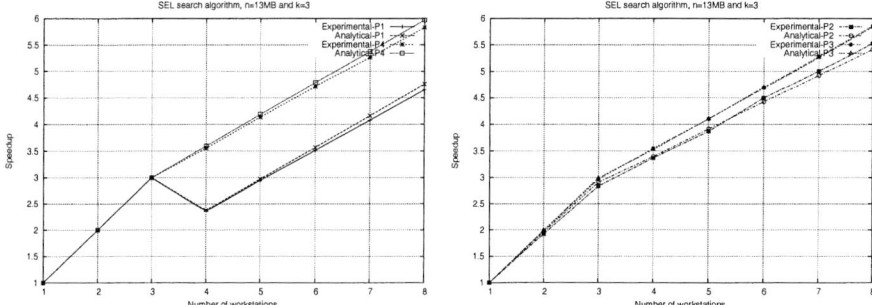

Fig. 1. The analytical and experimental speedups as a function of the number of workstations for text size of 13MB and $k=3$

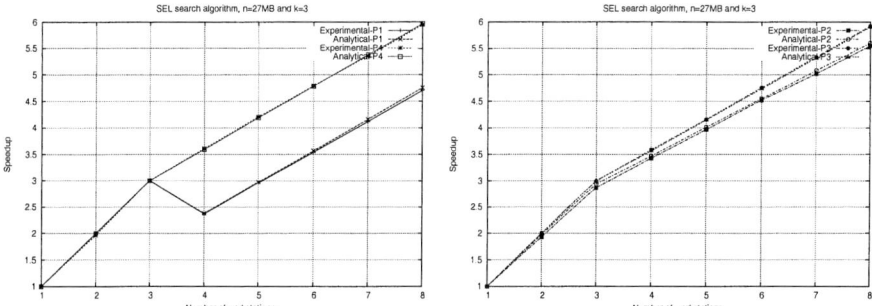

Fig. 2. The analytical and experimental speedups as a function of the number of workstations for text size of 27MB and $k=3$

RAM and 5 Pentium 100 MHz with 64 MB RAM. The parameters α and β which are used in our performance analysis are 4.11e-04 seconds and 9.27e-08 seconds, respectively. Finally, the average speeds $S_{i/o}$ and S_{search} of the fastest workstation were measured for different text sizes and are as follows, $S_{i/o} = 26225416$ chars/sec and $S_{search} = 3578514$ chars/sec for four implementations.

Figure 1 presents for text size of 13MB and $k=3$ the speedups obtained by experiments and those by the equations T_p for four implementations. Similarly, Figure 2 demonstrates for text size of 27MB and $k=3$ the speedups obtained by experiments and those by the equations T_p for four implementations. The experimental results of the four implementations are obtained from [1]. It is important to note that the speedups, which are plotted in Figures, are result of the average for five pattern lenghts $m = 5, 10, 20, 30$ and 60). Further, we used block size nearly $sb = 100,000$ characters for two dynamic implementations, P2 and P3, in the theoretical and experimental results according to the extensive study [1]. We observe that the estimated results for four implementations validate well the computational behaviour of the experimental results. Finally, we observe that the maximal difference between theoretical and experimental values are less than 9% and most of them are less than 3%. Consequently, the model for four distributed implementations is accuracy since the predictions need not be quantitatively exact, predition errors of 10-20% are acceptable.

4 Conclusions

In this paper has introduced an effective performance prediction model, which can help to users to predict the speedup of four master-worker implementations on larger clusters and problem sizes. The model requires only a small set of input parameters ($\alpha, \beta, S_{i/o}$ and S_{search}) that can be obtained from cluster specifications or from trial runs on a minimal system. It has been shown that the performance model is able to predict the speedup of parallel string searching implementations accurately.

References

1. P.D. Michailidis and K.G. Margaritis, A Performance study of load balancing strategies for approximate string matching on an MPI heterogeneous system environment, *in Proc. of the 9th Euro PVM/MPI 2002 Conference*, LNCS 2474, pp. 432-440, Springer-Verlag, 2002.
2. P.H. Sellers, The theory and computations of evolutionaly distances: pattern recognition, *Journal of Algorithms*, vol. 1, pp. 359-373, 1980.

Using a Self-connected Gigabit Ethernet Adapter as a `memcpy()` Low-Overhead Engine for MPI

Giuseppe Ciaccio

DISI, Università di Genova
via Dodecaneso, 35   16146 Genova, Italy
ciaccio@disi.unige.it

Abstract. Memory copies in messaging systems can be a major source of performance degradation in cluster computing. In this paper we discuss a system which can offload a host CPU from most of the overhead of copying data between distinct regions in the host physical memory. The sistem is implemented as a special-purpose Linux device driver operating a generic, non-programmable Gigabit Ethernet adapter connected to itself. Whenever the descriptor-based DMA engines of the adapter are instructed to start a data communication, the data are read from the host memory and written to the memory itself thanks to the loopback cable; this is semantically equivalent to a *non-blocking memory copy* operation performed by the two DMA engines. Suitable completion test/waiting routines are also implemented, in order to provide traditional, blocking semantics in a split-phase fashion. An implementation of MPI using this system in place of traditional `memcpy()` calls on receive shows a significantly lower receive overhead.

1 Introduction

Let us consider those parallel applications which tend to exchange messages of relatively large size, due to intrinsic algorithmic features or coarse run-time parallelism. Such applications incur a performance penalty when using traditional networking systems, in that they pay for the CPU-operated data movements between different regions of the host memory during data communications. This translates into inefficient use of the host CPU and cache hierarchy by all running programs, including user jobs and the Operating System (OS) itself. The ability of offloading the host CPU from the memory copy operations involved by communications has long been recognized as a key ingredient for such parallel application to scale up.

To offload the host CPU from some overhead we need additional hardware or additional features into existing hardware.

One possibility is to leverage an additional CPU for this. Assuming each PC in the cluster comes provided with two CPUs, one could think that dedicating one such CPU to computation and the other one to communication might be a good idea, as this would entirely offload the former CPU from all of the communication overhead. This however would not address the problem of a lower overall utilization of the computation resources available at the processing node.

Another possibility is to use so-called *zero-copy* communication systems, in which the CPU-consuming phases of the communication protocol like header processing, receive matching, device virtualization, and data movements, run on board of the Network Interface Card (NIC) [6, 5, 9, 11, 7, 10] This solution is thus restricted to programmable network devices (Myrinet and some Gigabit Ethernet adapters).

Zero-copy systems based on programmable NICs can also pose some issues. For instance, if the CPU located on the NIC is significantly slower compared to the host CPU, a wrong balance between NIC-operated and CPU-operated protocol phases may lead to an increased communication delay [6]. Message delivery must be restricted to prefetched memory pages marked as unswappable, so as to let the NIC know their physical address before communications take place (like in [9–11], for instance). But a perhaps more serious drawback concerns the efficient stacking of higher-level messaging primitives atop a zero-copy communication layer. For instance, stacking MPI atop the FM messaging system [4] required modifications and extensions of the set of FM routines: features like upcalls and streamed send and receive had to be added in order for MPI to take more advantage of the zero-copy features of FM. Basically, the problem lies in the fact that stacking higher-level communication primitives usually implies additional headers on messages and an extension of the matching algorithm on receive. If these extensions are not supported natively by the low-level, NIC-operated protocol, an intervention of the receiver CPU becomes necessary *before* the message payload could be delivered to any user-space destination; as a result, the computation-to-communication overlap, which is the main goal of zero-copy systems, becomes harder to obtain.

2 Demanding Memory Copies to a Dedicated Device

2.1 Performing Memory Copies through a Self-connected NIC

A modern NIC cooperates with the host computer using a data transfer mode called *Descriptor-based DMA* (DBDMA). With the DBDMA mode, the NIC is able to autonomously set up and start DMA data transfers. To do so, the NIC scans two pre-computed and static circular lists called *rings*, one for transmit and one for receive, both stored in host memory. Each entry of a ring is called a *DMA descriptor*.

A DMA descriptor in the transmit ring contains a pointer (a physical address) to a host memory region containing a *fragment* of an outgoing packet; therefore, an entire packet can be specified by chaining one or more send DMA descriptors, a feature called "gather".

Similar to a descriptor in the transmit ring, a DMA descriptor in the receive ring contains a pointer (a physical address, again) to a host memory region where an incoming packet could be stored. The analogous of the "gather" feature of the transmit ring is here called "scatter": more descriptors can be chained to specify a sequence of distinct memory areas, and an incoming packet could be scattered among them.

Now, let us consider a DBDMA-based full-duplex NIC networked to itself through a loopback wire (its output port connected to its input port).

Suppose the host CPU have to copy L bytes from source address S to destination address D; suppose S be in kernel address space and D be in a user space, as it occurs with a message receive in a communication system implemented in the OS kernel. Virtual addresses S and D can be translated to physical addresses, say P_S and P_D; a kernel-space address usually need not be translated at all, so the CPU overhead is just for one virtual to physical translation in this case (namely, D into P_D). At this point, the CPU can create two DMA descriptors for the NIC: one, in the transmit ring, points to address P_S, and the other, in the receive ring, points to address P_D. Both descriptors carry the same buffer size of L bytes. When the CPU commands to start a transmission, the NIC transmits L bytes of memory at address P_S to self, so receives them at address P_D. The data flow takes place at the network wire speed (supposedly lower than the DMA speed). At the end of the operation, the memory content has changed as if a memcpy(D,S,L) operation were issued, under the constraint that the two L byte sized memory regions P_S and P_D do not overlap.

The above procedure can be clearly extended to user-to-kernel as well as kernel-to-kernel or user-to-user cases, the latter requiring one more address translation.

Ethernet NICs usually exchange data using a MAC protocol which poses some requirements on data formatting, namely: data must be arranged into packets whose maximum size, called MTU, is fixed; and, each packet must be prepended by a header. These constraints make things a bit more complicated, but not too much. Indeed, copy operations whose size exceeds the maximum MTU size supported by the NIC can be easily broken into MTU-sized chunks. And, in order to eliminate the need for MAC packet headers, the NIC can be set up to operate in promiscuous mode so as the initial part of the packet will not be interpreted.

A number of Gigabit Ethernet adapters support non-standard MTU sizes of up to a few KBytes (to allow so called "jumbo frames") for efficiency reasons. Using one such NIC connected to itself, long memory copies can be operated on a page-by-page basis, with only a marginal intervention by the host CPU.

2.2 Split-Phase Memory Copies, and Notification of Completion

The sequence of events described in Section 2.1 gives rise to a copy of the content of a memory region to another, disjoint, memory region. In order for the events to take place, however, the host CPU must first set up two DMA descriptors, then command the NIC to start a transmission (to self). Actually, this latter operation only starts the memory copy. The operation will then proceed without any further involvement of the host CPU, but we need test/wait mechanisms to eventually synchronize the CPU to the end of a given copy operation, so as to prevent incorrect actions (e.g., reading the copied data before the copy itself has finished). This could be done by using *notification variables*, that is, memory locations whose stored value is to change as soon as the operation is complete.

Notifying completion of a copy operation by acting upon a notification variable can be done without the intervention of the host CPU. The gather/scatter features of the NIC can be exploited to this end. The idea is to extend the self-transmission trick by gathering together source data and notification *value*, then scattering them apart to destination buffer and notification *variable* on receive. To this end, we simply need to arrange a 2-way DMA descriptor in the transmit ring and a 2-way DMA descriptor in the receive ring, in place of traditional, single-entry descriptors.

At the end of the self-transmission, the presence of the notification value into the notification variable implies that the memory-to-memory copy is complete, because the notification value is delivered to memory *after* the actual data. No intervention by the host CPU is needed to accomplish such notification.

As a major advantage, such a split-phase memory copy would allow the host CPU to carry out useful work in between initiation and test/wait operations, this way overlapping the memory copy with other useful computation at the price of a initiation overhead.

3 A Working Prototype: DAMNICK

DAMNICK (DAta Moving through a NIC connected in loopbacK) is a working prototype of a system for demanding memory-to-memory copies to the DMA engines of an autonomous, self-connected Gigabit Ethernet adapter, located on the host I/O bus. It is implemented as a modified Linux device driver for the supported Gigabit Ethernet adapter. Currently, only the Alteon AceNIC and its lower-cost "clones" (the 3COM 3c985 and the Netgear GA620) are supported. The driver disables all sources of IRQ in the NIC, as they are unneeded.

The DAMNICK driver implements routines for initiating copy operations, according to the ideas sketched in Section 2.1. The driver also supports the NIC-operated notification of "end of copy" described in Section 2.2. There are routines for moving data from user space to user space of the same process, with or without notification of completion (resp. `icopy_notif()`, `icopy()`). Routines to move data from kernel space to user space are provided as well (`icopy_k2u_notif()`, `icopy_k2u()`). Testing/waiting for termination of initiated copy operations is done by the invoker by inspecting the current value of the given notification variable.

These routines can be invoked directly from OS kernel, in case of internal use; in addition, a trap address is set up to allow safe invocation of DAMNICK routines from application level, through a small library of stubs.

As pointed out in Section 2.1, the NIC must be set to promiscuous mode in order for DAMNICK to work. This is done at the time of opening the device before use (using the `ifconfig` UNIX utility).

3.1 Evaluation Framework, Performance Metrics, and Testbed

To evaluate the performance advantages of DAMNICK in a realistic scenario, we decided to integrate it into the receive part of a message-passing system running on a cluster of PCs. To this end, we decided to use the GAMMA messaging system [1], for which an implementation of MPI is available [2].

In the kernel-level receive thread of GAMMA, a traditional `memcpy()` operation delivers received message chunks from kernel buffers to application address space, followed by an "end of message" notification upon delivery of the last message chunk. The receiver CPU accomplishes the "end of message" notification by incrementing the value of a user-level variable.

The `memcpy()` has been replaced by an invocation of `icopy_k2u()` in the case of intermediate chunks of a message. For the last chunk, the `memcpy()` and the subsequent "end of message" notification have been replaced by a single invocation of `icopy_k2u_notif()`.

Our expectation was to observe a decisive decrease of the receive overhead when using DAMNICK in place of `memcpy()` on receive. Thus, next step has been to set up a proper benchmark written in MPI to evaluate the receive overhead at MPI level.

The testbed of our performance evaluation is a pair of PCs networked to each other by a dedicated, back-to-back Fast Ethernet connection. Both PCs have a single Athlon 800 MHz CPU, ASUS A7V motherboard (VIA KT133 chipset, 32 bit 33 MHz PCI bus, 133 MHz FSB), 256 MByte 133 MHz DRAM, and a 3COM 3c905C Fast Ethernet adapter. Each PC also mounts a Netgear GA620 Gigabit Ethernet adapter connected to itself through a fiber-optics loopback cable, along which the DAMNICK self-communications take place. The OS is GNU/Linux 2.4.16 including GAMMA and the DAMNICK device driver.

3.2 The Benchmark

A decisive decrease in MPI receive overhead at application level would only be helpful in case of overlap between useful computation and message arrivals at a given processing node.

A suitable benchmark could be one in which a process receives a stream of tasks, each represented by a message, and has to carry out some computation to consume each of them. Ideally the process of receiving tasks and consuming them should work like a pipeline, supposing that new tasks arrive at at least the same rate at which they are consumed. Clearly, overlapping computation to message receives can be of great help in a situation like this, as it would allow to increase the servicing throughput of the process. We then developed a proper MPI benchmark of this kind, for our performance evaluations.

A first, "naive" version of the program could be sketched as follows (receiver process only):

```
for (;;) {
  MPI_Recv(task);
  do_computation(task);
}
```

Here, the use of blocking receive allows limited overlap between computation and communication. A better solution could be obtained with non-blocking receives, by unrolling the loop twice then scheduling the activities in a proper way:

```
MPI_Irecv(task1,handle1);
for (;;) {
   MPI_Irecv(task2,handle2);
   MPI_Wait(handle1); do_computation(task1);
   MPI_Irecv(task1,handle1);
   MPI_Wait(handle2); do_computation(task2);
}
```

In this solution, activities on task1 are data-independent from activities on task2, so they can occur in between initiation and termination of communication activities concerning task2, and viceversa. The scheduling of activities shown in the program leads to a good *potential* overlap between task receive and task processing, and even between different phases of receive (of consecutive tasks).

However, the amount of *effective* overlap depends on the implementation of MPI in use. In the ideal case in which the whole implementation of MPI is operated by the NIC, the overlap takes place and the CPU never blocks on communication[1]. To the best of our knowledge, however, no fully NIC-operated implementation of MPI has been attempted so far. The best available MPI implementations are stacked atop lower-level, zero-copy, NIC-operated messaging systems, lacking significant parts of the MPI semantics, and especially the message matching (see [4, 8, 11, 2] for instance). In Section 1 we already pointed out that such architecture requires an intervention of the host CPU to match the MPI message envelope against MPI pending receives, and this must occur after the message arrival is detected but before the payload can be delivered to its destination address. As a result, it becomes difficult or impossible to achieve a good overlapping between communication and computation in spite of non-blocking receives and possibly zero-copy implementation of MPI.

With an MPI stacked atop a lower-level messaging system, the only way to get a significant computation-to-communication overlap is to extend MPI with an additional, blocking routine called poll() which waits for the low-level communication layer to notify a new message arrival, then performs the MPI message matching and computes destination address for the new message, and finally asks the low-level communication layer to deliver the payload to destination, without waiting for the delivery to complete. Usually, these steps are accomplished within the MPI_Wait() routine. Moving them away from the MPI_Wait() to the poll() routine allows to split the blocking receive semantics

---

[1] This is true under the aforementioned hypotesis that new tasks arrive at at least the same rate at which they are consumed. If this is not the case, the process will block on receive, waiting for incoming tasks.

into three phases rather than just two. That is, instead of accomplishing message receives by traditional split-phase pairs MPI_Irecv(); MPI_Wait(), we rather use triples of the kind MPI_Irecv(); poll(); MPI_Wait() and schedule the computation in the two slots between the three routines, which correspond to the two *separate* time slots in which the communication-to-computation overlap is allowed to take place.

The "three-phases" splitting requires unrolling the benchmark loop three times rather than just twice. Our MPI benchmark thus sketches as follows:

```
MPI_Irecv(task1,handle1);
MPI_Irecv(task2,handle2);
poll();   /* for task1  */
for (;;) {
   MPI_Irecv(task3,handle3);
   poll();   /* for task2  */
   MPI_Wait(handle1); do_computation(task1);
   MPI_Irecv(task1,handle1);
   poll();   /* for task3  */
   MPI_Wait(handle2); do_computation(task2);
   MPI_Irecv(task2,handle2);
   poll();   /* for task1  */
   MPI_Wait(handle3); do_computation(task3);
}
```

From the discussion above, it turns out that traditional, established MPI application benchmarks like the NAS NPB, which use standard split-phase send/receives to overlap computation to communication, could *never* detect the potential computation-to-communication overlap as provided by *any* MPI stacked atop a zero-copy messaging layer. This is the only reason why we could not provide any meaningful evaluation using established MPI application benchmarks.

3.3 Results

Figure 1 shows curves of MPI/GAMMA receive overhead as measured by the benchmark discussed before, as functions of the message size. Two distincs scenarios are reported about, namely, "hot cache" and "cold cache". In the "hot cache" case, all buffers touched during the receive operations are in cache; this is not the case with the "cold cache" scenario.

In all cases, the curves show the expected linear dependence of receive overhead on the message size. Non-data-touching receive overhead is reported as a lower bound, to highlight the portion of overhead where DAMNICK is expected to show its effects.

The memcpy() operation is clearly expected to be faster in the "hot cache" case compared to the "cold cache"; thus, it is no wonder that, when the messaging system uses a memcpy() to deliver data to final user-space destinations, the

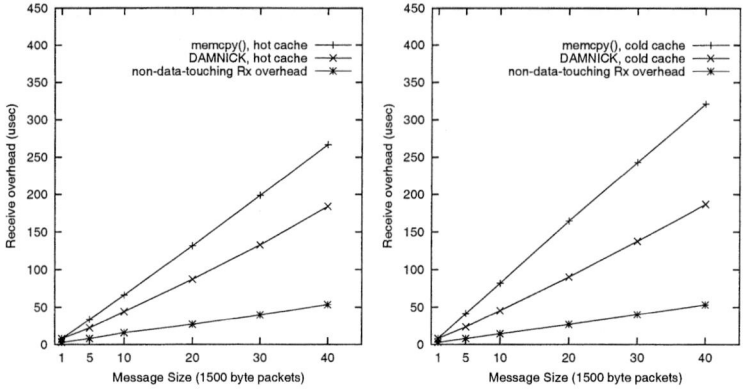

Fig. 1. Comparison of MPI/GAMMA receive overhead, using `memcpy()` vs. using `icopy_k2u_notif()` to deliver data to final destinations.

receive overhead is lower in the former case compared to the latter. It is no wonder as well, that the MPI/GAMMA receive overhead becomes insensitive to the caching state when `icopy_k2u_notif()` is used in place of `memcpy()` to deliver data to final destinations, as DAMNICK exploits DMA engines to move data, and DMA works in the host RAM, not cache.

The significant results come from comparing the MPI/GAMMA receive overhead, using `memcpy()` vs. using `icopy_k2u_notif()`. A clear advantage of the latter mechanism over the former one is shown in the two pictures. With "hot cache", the use of DAMNICK reduces the receive overhead by 31% with long messages. The difference is even more evident with "cold cache", with a decrease of 42%. If we are only concerned with the data-touching fraction of receive overhead, with DAMNICK this is reduced by 39% and 50%, respectively with "hot cache" and "cold cache".

4 Related Work

A problem which poses similar challenges to the ones addressed in this paper is that of intra-node communication, that is, message exchanges between processes running on the same processing node. In intra-node communication, two processes usually exploit a shared memory region to pass information to each other, at the cost of one memory copy performed by each. One of the two memory copies can be avoided in some cases, by running OS kernel privileged code which can directly access the virtual address spaces of both processes and thus can copy data from sender to receiver directly [3]. However, as an alternative, the two partner might pass messages to each other through the NIC, as they were remote to each other, provided that the interconnection switch be able to route data to the same NIC which originates them (loopback through first switch). Myrinet provides such a feature, which was exploited for intra-node communication by the Myricom GM communication library. Poor performance of such network-assisted intra-node communication is claimed in [3]. We could not carry out any experiments on Myrinet, but we suspect the poor performance claims of [3] actually refer to end-to-end communication delay, rather than CPU overhead.

5 Conclusions and Open Points

Our experiments demonstrate the practical feasibility of a system which is able to offload a substantial fraction (up to 42%) of the total receive overhead of MPI from the host CPU to a separate device. This is entirely based on cheap, *non-programmable* commodity components. By connecting a generic Gigabit Ethernet NIC back to itself with a loopback cable, and designing a suitable software to drive the NIC in a non-trivial way, it is possible to exploit the DMA capabilities of the NIC to perform memory-to-memory operations. This way, a larger fraction of host CPU time is delivered to user applications and OS tasks, without leveraging any custom hardware devices (expensive, due to their narrow marketplace segment) or programmable devices (expensive, due to their high complexity).

In order for such a system to work properly, the memory pages involved in the copy operation must be already loaded in RAM. Pages belonging to the OS kernel space are usually marked as non-swappable. For user space pages, it is the communication system that should check for page presence and possibly enforce page loading before use. This is already common practice with zero-copy messaging, and does not introduce any additional penalty compared to classical systems, based on memory copies with page fault management.

This system requires dedicating a Gigabit Ethernet NIC to memory copies; such a NIC could not be used for anything else. Needless to say, in a cluster of PCs we would rather prefer to find suitable DMA devices on each PC's motherboard, instead of adding a Gigabit Ethernet NIC to each node. Indeed, most motherboards come equipped with DMA devices for EIDE disk operation, but these have no descriptor queue; as a consequence, the CPU will block waiting for completion of the current DMA operation before submitting a new one, what makes this device unsuitable as an alternative to CPU-operated memory copies.

The addition of a Gigabit Ethernet adapter to each node in a cluster could be a questionable idea if the adapters were expensive. This is no longer the case, however, especially after the recent deployment of the Gigabit-over-copper low-cost technology. Indeed, modern high-end motherboards often come equipped with on-board Gigabit Ethernet controllers, whose price has become marginal compared to the cost of the entire motherboard.

Performance evaluation of DAMNICK as a support to MPI led us to a deeper understanding of the reason behind the relative insensitiveness of MPI parallel benchmarks to the receive overhead. From the arguments in Section 3.2, it follows that the classical split-phase approach to non-blocking send/receive routines is inappropriate whenever MPI is implemented in software; such an architecture cannot deliver a good computation-to-communication overlap to user applications on receive, regardless of it being zero-copy or not, because in this case the "overlapping window" offered by a MPI_Irecv(); MPI_Wait() pair is actually made up of two separate parts. Running the entire MPI in firmware on a programmable I/O device would be a satisfactory answer, but has not been attempted so far, probably due to excessive resource requirements.

Demanding memory copies to an I/O device forces data to travel across the PCI bus, which might show a higher bit error rate compared to the system bus. Extensive tests are to be carried out to investigate this aspect.

References

1. G. Chiola and G. Ciaccio. Efficient Parallel Processing on Low-cost Clusters with GAMMA Active Ports. *Parallel Computing*, (26):333–354, 2000.
2. G. Ciaccio. MPI/GAMMA home page, http://www.disi.unige.it/project/gamma/mpigamma/.
3. Patrick Geoffray, Loic Prylli, and Bernard Tourancheau. BIP-SMP: High performance message passing over a cluster of commodity SMPs. In *Proc. of 11th IEEE - ACM High Performance Networking and Computing Conference (SC99)*, 1999.
4. M. Lauria and A. Chien. MPI-FM: High Performance MPI on Workstation Clusters. *Journal of Parallel and Distributed Computing*, 40(1):4–18, January 1997.
5. Myricom. GM performance, http://www.myri.com/myrinet/performance/, 2000.
6. S. Pakin, M. Lauria, and A. Chien. High Performance Messaging on Workstations: Illinois Fast Messages (FM) for Myrinet. In *Proc. Supercomputing '95*, San Diego, California, 1995.
7. I. Pratt and K. Fraser. Arsenic: A User-Accessible Gigabit Ethernet Interface. In *Proc. Infocom 2001*, Anchorage, Alaska, April 2001. IEEE.
8. L. Prylli, B. Tourancheau, and R. Westrelin. The design for a high performance MPI implementation on the myrinet network. In *Proc. EuroPVM/MPI'99*, number 1697 in LNCS, pages 223–230, Barcelone, Spain, 1999.
9. L. Prylli and B. Tourancheau. BIP: a new protocol designed for high performance networking on Myrinet. In *Proc. Workshop PC-NOW, IPPS/SPDP'98*, number 1388 in Lecture Notes in Computer Science, pages 472–485, Orlando, Florida, April 1998. Springer.
10. P. Shivam, P. Wyckoff, and D. Panda. EMP: Zero-copy OS-bypass NIC-driven Gigabit Ethernet Message Passing. In *Proc. 2001 International Conference on Supercomputing (SC01)*, Denver, Colorado, November 2001.
11. T. Takahashi, S. Sumimoto, A. Hori, H. Harada, and Y. Ishikawa. PM2: High Performance Communication Middleware for Heterogeneous Network Environments. In *Proc. of High Performance Computing and Networking (HPCN'97)*, number 1225 in Lecture Notes in Computer Science, pages 708–717. Springer-Verlag, April 1997.

Improving the Performance of Collective Operations in MPICH

Rajeev Thakur and William D. Gropp

Mathematics and Computer Science Division
Argonne National Laboratory
9700 S. Cass Avenue
Argonne, IL 60439, USA
{thakur,gropp}@mcs.anl.gov

Abstract. We report on our work on improving the performance of collective operations in MPICH on clusters connected by switched networks. For each collective operation, we use multiple algorithms depending on the message size, with the goal of minimizing latency for short messages and minimizing bandwidth usage for long messages. Although we have implemented new algorithms for all MPI collective operations, because of limited space we describe only the algorithms for allgather, broadcast, reduce-scatter, and reduce. We present performance results using the SKaMPI benchmark on a Myrinet-connected Linux cluster and an IBM SP. In all cases, the new algorithms significantly outperform the old algorithms used in MPICH on the Myrinet cluster, and, in many cases, they outperform the algorithms used in IBM's MPI on the SP.

1 Introduction

Collective communication is an important and frequently used component of MPI and offers implementations considerable room for optimization. MPICH, although widely used as an MPI implementation, has until now had fairly rudimentary implementations of the collective operations. We have recently focused on improving the performance of all the collective operations in MPICH. Our initial target architecture is the one that is the most popular among our users, namely, clusters of machines connected by a switch, such as Myrinet or the IBM SP switch. For each collective operation, we use multiple algorithms based on message size: The short-message algorithms aim to minimize latency, and the long-message algorithms aim to minimize bandwidth usage. Our approach has been to identify the best algorithms known in the literature, improve on them where possible, and implement them efficiently. Our implementation of the algorithms handles derived datatypes as well as non-power-of-two number of processes.

We have implemented new algorithms in MPICH for all the collective operations, namely, scatter, gather, allgather, broadcast, reduce, allreduce, reduce-scatter, scan, and barrier. Because of limited space, however, we describe only the algorithms for allgather, broadcast, reduce-scatter, and reduce. We use the

SKaMPI benchmark [19] to measure the performance of the algorithms on two platforms: a Linux cluster at Argonne connected with Myrinet 2000 and the IBM SP at the San Diego Supercomputer Center. On the Myrinet cluster we use MPICH-GM and compare the performance of the new algorithms with the old algorithms in MPICH-GM. On the IBM SP, we use IBM's MPI and compare the performance of the new algorithms with the algorithms used in IBM's MPI. On both systems, we ran one MPI process per node. We implemented the new algorithms as functions on top of MPI point-to-point operations, so that we can compare performance simply by linking or not linking the new functions.

The rest of this paper is organized as follows. Section 2 describes related work in this area. Section 3 describes the cost model we use to guide the selection of the algorithms. The algorithms and their performance are described in Section 4. We conclude in Section 5 with a brief discussion of future work.

2 Related Work

Early work on collective communication focused on developing optimized algorithms for particular architectures, such as hypercube, mesh, or fat tree, with an emphasis on minimizing link contention, node contention, or the distance between communicating nodes [2–4, 13]. More recently, Dongarra et al. have developed automatically tuned collective communication algorithms [18]. Their approach consists of running tests to measure system parameters and then tuning their algorithms for those parameters. Researchers in Holland and at Argonne have optimized MPI collective communication for wide-area distributed environments [7, 8]. In such environments, the goal is to minimize communication over slow wide-area links at the expense of more communication over faster local-area connections. Research has also been done on developing collective communication algorithms for clusters of SMPs [12, 15–17], where communication within an SMP is done differently from communication across a cluster. Some efforts have focused on using different algorithms for different message sizes, such as the work by Van de Geijn et al. for the Intel Paragon [1, 9, 14], by Rabenseifner on reduce and allreduce [11], and by Kale et al. on all-to-all communication [6].

3 Cost Model

We use a simple model to estimate the cost of the collective communication algorithms in terms of latency and bandwidth usage and to guide the selection of algorithms for a particular collective communication operation. We assume that the time taken to send a message between any two nodes can be modeled as $\alpha + n\beta$, where α is the latency (or startup time) per message, independent of message size, β is the transfer time per byte, and n is the number of bytes transferred. We assume further that the time taken is independent of how many pairs of processes are communicating with each other, independent of the distance between the communicating nodes, and that the communication links are bidirectional (that is, a message can be transferred in both directions on the link in the same time as in one direction). The node's network interface is assumed to be single ported; that is, at most one message can be sent and one message can be received simultaneously. In the case of reduction operations, we assume that γ is the computation cost per byte for performing the reduction operation locally on any process.

4 Algorithms

In this section we describe the new algorithms and their performance.

4.1 Allgather

MPI_Allgather is a gather operation in which the data contributed by each process is gathered on all processes, instead of just the root process as in MPI_Gather.

The old algorithm for allgather in MPICH uses a ring method in which the data from each process is sent around a virtual ring of processes. In the first step, each process i sends its contribution to process $i+1$ and receives the contribution from process $i-1$ (with wrap-around). From the second step onwards each process i forwards to process $i+1$ the data it received from process $i-1$ in the previous step. If p is the number of processes, the entire algorithm takes $p-1$ steps. If n is the total amount of data to be gathered on each process, then at every step each process sends and receives $\frac{n}{p}$ amount of data. Therefore, the time taken by this algorithm is given by $T_{ring} = (p-1)\alpha + \frac{p-1}{p}n\beta$. Note that the bandwidth term cannot be reduced further because each process must receive $\frac{n}{p}$ data from $p-1$ other processes. The latency term, however, can be reduced if we use an algorithm that takes $\lg p$ steps. We use such an algorithm, called recursive doubling, for the new allgather in MPICH. Recursive doubling has been used in the past, particularly on hypercube systems; it is also used in the implementation of allreduce in [11].

Figure 1 illustrates how the recursive doubling algorithm works. In the first step, processes that are a distance 1 apart exchange their data. In the second step, processes that are a distance 2 apart exchange their own data as well as the data they received in the previous step. In the third step, processes that are a distance 4 apart exchange their own data as well the data they received in the previous two steps. In this way, for a power-of-two number of processes, all processes get all the data in $\lg p$ steps. The amount of data exchanged by each process is $\frac{n}{p}$ in the first step, $\frac{2n}{p}$ in the second step, and so forth, up to $\frac{2^{\lg p - 1}n}{p}$ in the last step. Therefore, the total time taken by this algorithm is $T_{rec\_dbl} = \lg p\, \alpha + \frac{p-1}{p}n\beta$.

The recursive-doubling algorithm is straightforward for a power-of-two number of processes but is a little tricky to get right for a non-power-of-two number of processes. We have implemented the non-power-of-two case as follows. At each step of recursive doubling, if the current subtree is not a power of two, we do additional communication to ensure that all processes get the data they would

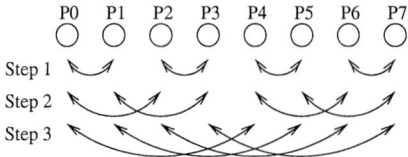

Fig. 1. Recursive doubling for allgather.

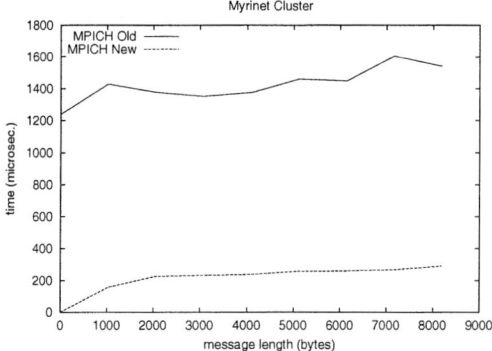

Fig. 2. Performance of allgather for short messages on the Myrinet cluster (64 nodes). The size on the x-axis is the total amount of data gathered on each process.

have gotten had the subtree been a power of two. This communication is done in a logarithmic fashion to minimize the additional latency. This approach is necessary for the subsequent steps of recursive doubling to work correctly. The total number of steps for the non-power-of-two case is bounded by $2\lfloor \lg p \rfloor$.

Note that the bandwidth term for recursive doubling is the same as for the ring algorithm, whereas the latency term is much better. Therefore, one would expect recursive doubling to perform better than the ring algorithm for short messages and the two algorithms to perform about the same for long messages. We find that this situation is true for short messages (see Figure 2). For long messages (> 512 KB), however, we find that recursive doubling runs much slower than the ring algorithm, as shown in Figure 3. We believe this difference is because of the difference in the communication pattern of the two algorithms: The ring algorithm has a nearest-neighbor communication pattern, whereas in recursive doubling, processes that are much farther apart communicate. To confirm this hypothesis, we used the b_eff MPI benchmark [10], which measures the performance of about 48 different communication patterns, and found that, for long messages on both the Myrinet cluster and the IBM SP, some communication patterns (particularly nearest neighbor) achieve more than twice the bandwidth of other communication patterns. In MPICH, therefore, we use the recursive-doubling algorithm for short- and medium-size messages (< 512 KB) and the ring algorithm for long messages (≥ 512 KB).

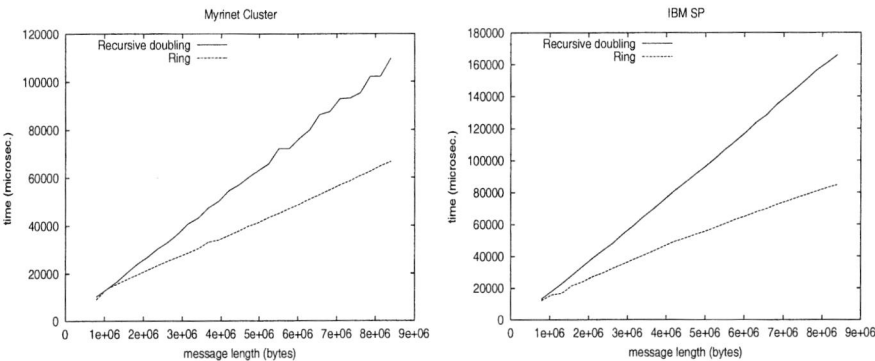

Fig. 3. Ring algorithm versus recursive doubling for long-message allgather (64 nodes). The size on the x-axis is the total amount of data gathered on each process.

We note that the dissemination algorithm [5] used to implement barrier operations is a better algorithm for non-power-of-two number of processes as it takes $\lceil \lg p \rceil$ steps. In each step k of this algorithm, process i sends a message to process $(i + 2^k)$ and receives a message from process $(i - 2^k)$ (with wrap-around). This algorithm works well for barrier operations, where no data needs to be communicated: Processes simply send 0-byte messages. We, however, find it not easy to use for collective operations that have to communicate data, because keeping track of which data must be routed to which process is nontrivial in this algorithm and requires extra bookkeeping and memory copies. With recursive doubling, on the other hand, keeping track of the data is trivial.

4.2 Broadcast

The old algorithm for broadcast in MPICH is the commonly used binary tree algorithm. In the first step, the root sends data to process (root + $\frac{p}{2}$). This process and the root then act as new roots within their own subtrees and recursively continue this algorithm. This communication takes a total of $\lceil \lg p \rceil$ steps. The amount of data communicated by a process at any step is n. Therefore, the time taken by this algorithm is $T_{tree} = \lceil \lg p \rceil (\alpha + n\beta)$.

This algorithm is good for short messages because it has a logarithmic latency term. For long messages, however, a better algorithm has been proposed by Van de Geijn et al. that has a lower bandwidth term [1, 14]. In this algorithm, the message to be broadcast is first divided up and scattered among the processes, similar to an MPI_Scatter; the scattered data is then collected back to all processes, similar to an MPI_Allgather. The time taken by this algorithm is the sum of the times taken by the scatter, which is $(\lg p\, \alpha + \frac{p-1}{p} n\beta)$ for a binary tree algorithm, and the allgather for which we use either recursive doubling or the ring algorithm depending on the message size. Therefore, for very long messages where we use the ring allgather, the time taken by the broadcast is $T_{vandegeijn} = (\lg p + p - 1)\alpha + 2\frac{p-1}{p} n\beta$.

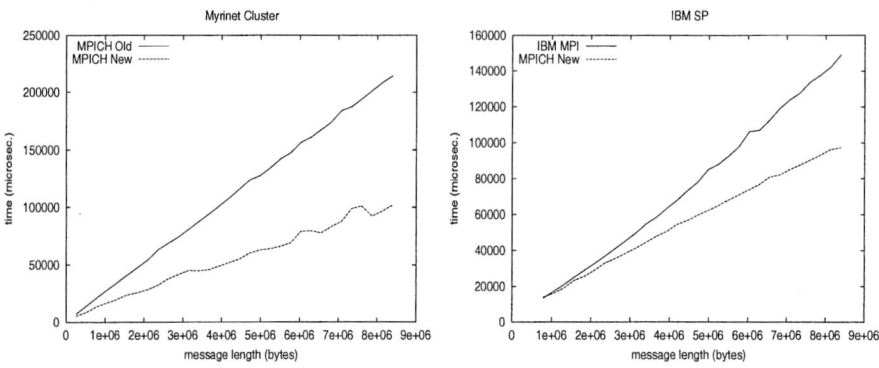

Fig. 4. Performance of long-message broadcast (64 nodes).

Comparing this time with that for the binary tree algorithm, we see that for long messages (where the latency term can be ignored) and when $\lg p > 2$ (or $p > 4$), the Van de Geijn algorithm is better than binary tree. The maximum improvement in performance that can be expected is $(\lg p)/2$. In other words, the larger the number of processes, the greater the expected improvement in performance. Figure 4 shows the performance for long messages of the new algorithm versus the old binary tree algorithm in MPICH as well as the algorithm used by IBM's MPI on the SP. In both cases, the new algorithm performs significantly better. Therefore, we use the binary tree algorithm for short messages (< 12 KB) and the Van de Geijn algorithm for long messages (≥ 12 KB).

4.3 Reduce-Scatter

Reduce-scatter is a variant of reduce in which the result, instead of being stored at the root, is scattered among all processes. The old algorithm in MPICH implements reduce-scatter by doing a binary tree reduce to rank 0 followed by a linear scatterv. This algorithm takes $\lg p + p - 1$ steps, and the bandwidth term is $(\lg p + \frac{p-1}{p})n\beta$. Therefore, the time taken by this algorithm is $T_{old} = (\lg p + p - 1)\alpha + (\lg p + \frac{p-1}{p})n\beta + n \lg p \, \gamma$.

In our new implementation of reduce-scatter, for short messages, we use different algorithms depending on whether the reduction operation is commutative or noncommutative. The commutative case occurs most commonly because all the predefined reduction operations in MPI (such as MPI_SUM, MPI_MAX) are commutative.

For commutative operations, we use a recursive-halving algorithm, which is analogous to the recursive-doubling algorithm used for allgather (see Figure 5). In the first step, each process exchanges data with a process that is a distance $\frac{p}{2}$ away: Each process sends the data needed by all processes in the other half, receives the data needed by all processes in its own half, and performs the reduction operation on the received data. The reduction can be done because the

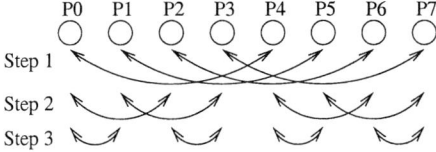

Fig. 5. Recursive halving for commutative reduce-scatter.

operation is commutative. In the second step, each process exchanges data with a process that is a distance $\frac{p}{4}$ away: Each process sends the data needed by all processes in the other half of the current subtree, receives the data needed by all processes in its own half of the current subtree, and performs the reduction on the received data. This procedure continues recursively, halving the data communicated at each step, for a total of $\lg p$ steps. Therefore, if p is a power of two, the time taken by this algorithm is $T_{rec\_half} = \lg p\, \alpha + \frac{p-1}{p} n\beta + \frac{p-1}{p} n\gamma$. We use this algorithm for messages up to 512 KB.

If p is not a power of two, we first reduce the number of processes to the nearest lower power of two by having the first few even-numbered processes send their data to the neighboring odd-numbered process (rank+1). These odd-numbered processes do a reduce on the received data, compute the result for themselves and their left neighbor during the recursive halving algorithm, and, at the end, send the result back to the left neighbor. Therefore, if p is not a power of two, the time taken by the algorithm is $T_{rec\_half} = (\lfloor \lg p \rfloor + 2)\alpha + 2n\beta + n(1 + \frac{p-1}{p})\gamma$. This cost is approximate because some imbalance exists in the amount of work each process does, since some processes do the work of their neighbors as well. A similar method for handling non-power-of-two cases is used in [11].

If the reduction operation is not commutative, recursive halving will not work. Instead, we use a recursive-doubling algorithm similar to the one in allgather. In the first step, pairs of neighboring processes exchange data; in the second step, pairs of processes at distance 2 apart exchange data; in the third step, processes at distance 4 apart exchange data; and so forth. However, more data is communicated than in allgather. In step 1, processes exchange all the data except the data needed for their own result $(n-\frac{n}{p})$; in step 2, processes exchange all data except the data needed by themselves and by the processes they communicated with in the previous step $(n-\frac{2n}{p})$; in step 3, it is $(n-\frac{4n}{p})$; and so forth. Therefore, the time taken by this algorithm is $T_{short} = \lg p\, \alpha + n(\lg p - \frac{p-1}{p})\beta + n(\lg p - \frac{p-1}{p})\gamma$. We use this algorithm for very short messages (< 512 bytes).

For long messages (≥ 512KB in the case of commutative operations and ≥ 512 bytes in the case of noncommutative operations), we use a pairwise exchange algorithm that takes $p-1$ steps. At step i, each process sends data to $rank+i$, receives data from $rank-i$, and performs the local reduction. The data exchanged is only the data needed for the scattered result on the process ($\approx \frac{n}{p}$). The time taken by this algorithm is $T_{long} = (p-1)\alpha + \frac{p-1}{p} n\beta + \frac{p-1}{p} n\gamma$. Note

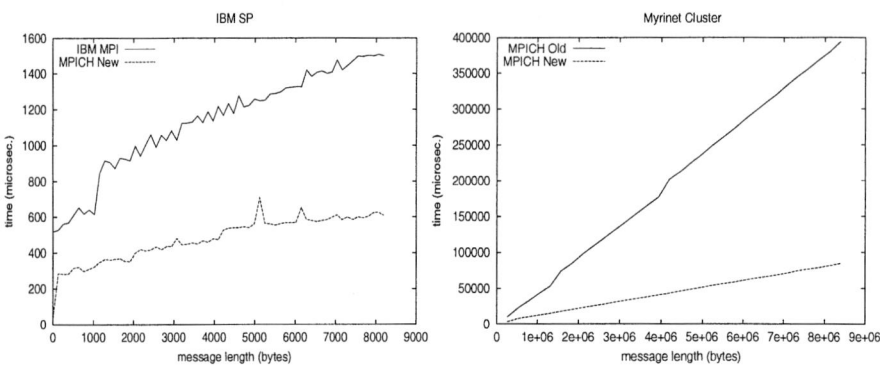

Fig. 6. Performance of reduce-scatter for short messages on the IBM SP (64 nodes) and for long messages on the Myrinet cluster (32 nodes).

that this algorithm has the same bandwidth requirement as the recursive halving algorithm. Nonetheless, we use this algorithm for long messages because it performs much better than recursive halving (similar to the results for recursive doubling versus ring algorithm for long-message allgather).

The SKaMPI benchmark, by default, uses a noncommutative user-defined reduction operation. Since commutative operations are more commonly used, we modified the benchmark to use a commutative operation, namely, MPI_SUM. Figure 6 shows the performance of the new algorithm for short messages on the IBM SP. The performance is significantly better than that of the algorithm used in IBM's MPI. For large messages, the new algorithm performs about the same as the one used in IBM's MPI. Because of a known problem in our Myrinet network, we were not able to test the old algorithm for short messages (the program hangs). We were able to test it for long messages on 32 nodes, and the results are shown in Figure 6. The new algorithm performs several times better than the old algorithm (reduce + scatterv) in MPICH.

4.4 Reduce

MPI_Reduce performs a global reduction operation and returns the result to the specified root. The old algorithm in MPICH uses a binary tree, which takes $\lg p$ steps, and the data communicated at each step is n. Therefore, the time taken by this algorithm is $T_{tree} = \lceil \lg p \rceil (\alpha + n\beta + n\gamma)$. This is a good algorithm for short messages because of the $\lg p$ steps, but a better algorithm, proposed by Rolf Rabenseifner [11], exists for long messages. The principle behind Rabenseifner's algorithm is similar to that behind Van de Geijn's algorithm for long-message broadcast. Van de Geijn implements the broadcast as a scatter followed by an allgather, which reduces the $n \lg p\, \beta$ bandwidth term in the binary tree algorithm to a $2n\beta$ term. Rabenseifner implements a long-message reduce effectively as a reduce-scatter followed by a gather to the root, which has the same effect of reducing the bandwidth term from $n \lg p\, \beta$ to $2n\beta$.

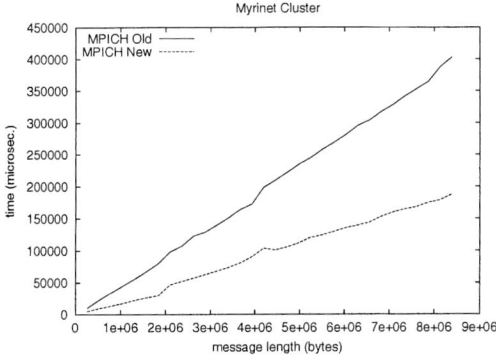

Fig. 7. Performance of reduce (64 nodes).

In the case of predefined reduction operations, we use Rabenseifner's algorithm for long messages (> 2 KB) and the binary tree algorithm for short messages (≤ 2 KB). In the case of user-defined reduction operations, we use the binary tree algorithm for all message sizes because in this case the user may pass derived datatypes, and breaking up derived datatypes to do the reduce-scatter is tricky. With predefined reduction operations, only basic datatypes are allowed.

The time taken by Rabenseifner's algorithm is the sum of the times taken by reduce-scatter (recursive halving) and gather (binary tree), which is $T_{rabenseifner} = 2\lg p\,\alpha + 2\frac{p-1}{p}n\beta + \frac{p-1}{p}n\gamma$.

Figure 7 shows the performance of reduce for long messages on the Myrinet cluster. The new algorithm is more than twice as fast as the old algorithm in some cases. On the IBM SP we found that the new algorithm performs about the same as the one in IBM's MPI.

5 Conclusions and Future Work

We have reported on our work on improving the performance of the collective communication algorithms in MPICH. All these algorithms will be available in the next release of MPICH (1.2.6). Since these algorithms distinguish between short and long messages, an important factor is the message size at which we switch between the short- and long-message algorithms. At present, we use experimentally determined cut-off points, which are different for different algorithms. We plan to develop a model to calculate the cutoff points automatically based on system parameters. We also plan to extend this work to incorporate topology awareness, particularly algorithms that are optimized for architectures comprising clusters of SMPs. Finally, we plan to explore the use of one-sided communication to improve performance of collective operations.

Acknowledgments

This work was supported by the Mathematical, Information, and Computational Sciences Division subprogram of the Office of Advanced Scientific Computing

Research, Office of Science, U.S. Department of Energy, under Contract W-31-109-ENG-38. We thank Rolf Rabenseifner for his careful reading and detailed comments on the paper.

References

1. M. Barnett, S. Gupta, D. Payne, L. Shuler, R. van de Geijn, and J. Watts. Interprocessor collective communication library (InterCom). In *Proceedings of Supercomputing '94*, November 1994.
2. M. Barnett, R. Littlefield, D. Payne, and R. van de Geijn. Global combine on mesh architectures with wormhole routing. In *Proceedings of the 7th International Parallel Processing Symposium*, April 1993.
3. S. Bokhari. Complete exchange on the iPSC/860. Technical Report 91-4, ICASE, NASA Langley Research Center, 1991.
4. S. Bokhari and H. Berryman. Complete exchange on a circuit switched mesh. In *Proceedings of the Scalable High Performance Computing Conference*, pages 300–306, 1992.
5. Debra Hensgen, Raphael Finkel, and Udi Manbet. Two algorithms for barrier synchronization. *International Journal of Parallel Programming*, 17(1):1–17, 1988.
6. L. V. Kale, Sameer Kumar, and Krishnan Vardarajan. A framework for collective personalized communication. In *Proceedings of the 17th International Parallel and Distributed Processing Symposium (IPDPS '03)*, 2003.
7. N. Karonis, B. de Supinski, I. Foster, W. Gropp, E. Lusk, and J. Bresnahan. Exploiting hierarchy in parallel computer networks to optimize collective operation performance. In *Proceedings of the Fourteenth International Parallel and Distributed Processing Symposium (IPDPS '00)*, pages 377–384, 2000.
8. T. Kielmann, R. F. H. Hofman, H. E. Bal, A. Plaat, and R. A. F. Bhoedjang. MagPIe: MPI's collective communication operations for clustered wide area systems. In *ACM SIGPLAN Symposium on Principles and Practice of Parallel Programming (PPoPP'99)*, pages 131–140. ACM, May 1999.
9. P. Mitra, D. Payne, L. Shuler, R. van de Geijn, and J. Watts. Fast collective communication libraries, please. In *Proceedings of the Intel Supercomputing Users' Group Meeting*, June 1995.
10. Rolf Rabenseifner. Effective bandwidth (b_eff) benchmark. http://www.hlrs.de/mpi/b_eff.
11. Rolf Rabenseifner. New optimized MPI reduce algorithm. http://www.hlrs.de/organization/par/services/models/mpi/myreduce.html.
12. Peter Sanders and Jesper Larsson Träff. The hierarchical factor algorithm for all-to-all communication. In B. Monien and R. Feldman, editors, *Euro-Par 2002 Parallel Processing*, pages 799–803. Lecture Notes in Computer Science 2400, Springer, August 2002.
13. D. Scott. Efficient all-to-all communication patterns in hypercube and mesh topologies. In *Proceedings of the 6th Distributed Memory Computing Conference*, pages 398–403, 1991.
14. Mohak Shroff and Robert A. van de Geijn. CollMark: MPI collective communication benchmark. Technical report, Dept. of Computer Sciences, University of Texas at Austin, December 1999.
15. Steve Sistare, Rolf vandeVaart, and Eugene Loh. Optimization of MPI collectives on clusters of large-scale SMPs. In *Proceedings of SC99: High Performance Networking and Computing*, November 1999.

16. V. Tipparaju, J. Nieplocha, and D.K. Panda. Fast collective operations using shared and remote memory access protocols on clusters. In *Proceedings of the 17th International Parallel and Distributed Processing Symposium (IPDPS '03)*, 2003.
17. Jesper Larsson Träff. Improved MPI all-to-all communication on a Giganet SMP cluster. In Dieter Kranzlmuller, Peter Kacsuk, Jack Dongarra, and Jens Volkert, editors, *Recent Advances in Parallel Virtual Machine and Message Passing Interface, 9th European PVM/MPI Users' Group Meeting*, pages 392–400. Lecture Notes in Computer Science 2474, Springer, September 2002.
18. Sathish S. Vadhiyar, Graham E. Fagg, and Jack Dongarra. Automatically tuned collective communications. In *Proceedings of SC99: High Performance Networking and Computing*, November 1999.
19. Thomas Worsch, Ralf Reussner, and Werner Augustin. On benchmarking collective MPI operations. In Dieter Kranzlmüller, Peter Kacsuk, Jack Dongarra, and Jens Volkert, editors, *Recent advances in Parallel Virtual Machine and Message Passing Interface, 9th European PVM/MPI Users' Group Meeting*, volume 2474 of *Lecture Notes in Computer Science*, pages 271–279. Springer, September 2002.

PVMWebCluster: Integration of PVM Clusters Using Web Services and CORBA

Pawel Czarnul

Faculty of Electronics, Telecommunications and Informatics
Gdansk University of Technology, Poland
pczarnul@eti.pg.gda.pl, http://www.ask.eti.pg.gda.pl/~pczarnul

Abstract. We propose a new architecture and its implementation called PVMWebCluster which enables easy parallelization of PVM task execution both onto geographically distributed PVM clusters and within them. Task submission is done by calling Web services that negotiate the best cluster(s) for the task and communicate with clusters via CORBA method invocation. PVMWebCluster supports tightly-coupled high performance demanding parallel applications by using PVM/DAMPVM, implements the idea of controlled cluster sharing among users as in grids and multi-tier applications and finally integrates the components using the latest Web services approach. This architecture gives flexibility, easy access for many users through simple code from many languages and operating systems and future development possibilities. We have implemented a testbed application and evaluated it on a testbed platform consisting of four clusters and eight nodes. Multiple copies have been run on the clusters and also parallelized within each of them using DAMPVM also implemented by the author.

1 Introduction

There are more and more technologies available for parallel and distributed programming. They range from message passing standards and environments like MPI, PVM ([1], [2]), client-server computing like CORBA ([3]), DCOM ([4]), through grids ([5], [6]) up to multi-tier Internet applications ([7]).

Grid architectures ([5], [6]) define Virtual Organizations (VOs). The grid architecture consists of the following layers: fabrics, connectivity, resource, collective and application that allow smart resource management and sharing for collaborative distributed computing. [8] explains the current trend of seeing the distributed computing world as a set of Web services offered by various parties and shows how the grid functionality can be incorporated into Web Service technologies by defining Open Grid Services Architecture (OGSA). [9] proposes Java Web Object Request Broker (JWORB) – a multiprotocol middleware implemented in Java that handles both HTTP and IIOP requests and passes them to the High Performance Commodity Computing backend like MPPs or NOWs. This model allows to add e.g. user collaboration to high performance computing. The recent research focuses on a new paradigm of distributed computing, namely Web services ([10], [11]). A distributed application is designed and executed by invoking available Web services to accomplish the given goal. [12] describes a WTABuilder architecture which allows users to build a complex task from multiple Web service components and then run the task by a Web Task Automation Server.

There have been attempts to integrate PVM/MPI clusters for high performance or collaborative computing ([13], [14]). [14] defines Web Remote Services Oriented Architecture that proposes three layers to provide the integration of Distributed Systems (DS) and the environment for coordinated resource sharing and task submission. The layers include the User Layer, Remote Service Interface Layer and Service Controller Layer and provide system access, request/data/user profile management and access to DSes respectively. The prototype implementation IONweb uses well-known technologies in multi-tier applications and also used in this work i.e. Web browsers/Tomcat/ CORBA/PVM. PVMWebCluster implements a highly distributed architecture where a distributed Web Service layer works as the client-system access protocol. On the other hand, [14] proposes the Service Controller Layer which consists of entry points to clusters implemented as CORBA servers. In this respect, PVMWebCluster has the important advantage of having the ability to access the distributed clusters and cluster services using one uniform API from code written in different languages like Java, C++, Perl that uses the HTTP protocol, not blocked by firewalls. Another important difference in the architectures of the two systems is that in IONweb CORBA servers communicate with PVM daemons while in this work CORBA managers interact with functionally enhanced DAMPVM schedulers, previously developed by the author ([15], [16], [17]).

2 System Architecture

The architecture of the proposed system is depicted in Figure 1. It is assumed that there are several, possibly geographically distributed, PVM clusters, possibly each running on a different user account. When a new cluster is to be added, only the entry address for the corresponding Web service must be registered in other clusters. It is also possible to create a simple servlet or a JSP page with a user-friendly interface to allow that. PVMWebCluster allows independent parallelization of:

1. incoming task submissions/Web service calls onto clusters,
2. applications within each cluster by either standard message passing programming in PVM or using automatic frameworks e.g. DAMPVM ([15], [16]).

Figure 1 shows a simplified sequence of running a task in the system:

1. Web service Run(program,criterion) is invoked on any of the available clusters. In the experiments this is done by a simple Java class Client (Figure 2). It can be done through a Web browser as well. Each cluster in the system has a Web service URL available. The criterion used in this case is to minimize the wall time across all the nodes in all clusters attached to the system.
2. The Web service calls Web services URL=FindBestCluster(sourceURL, criterion) on neighboring Web services which call this very Web service on their neighbors recursively in parallel. Given the criterion, the best cluster is chosen.

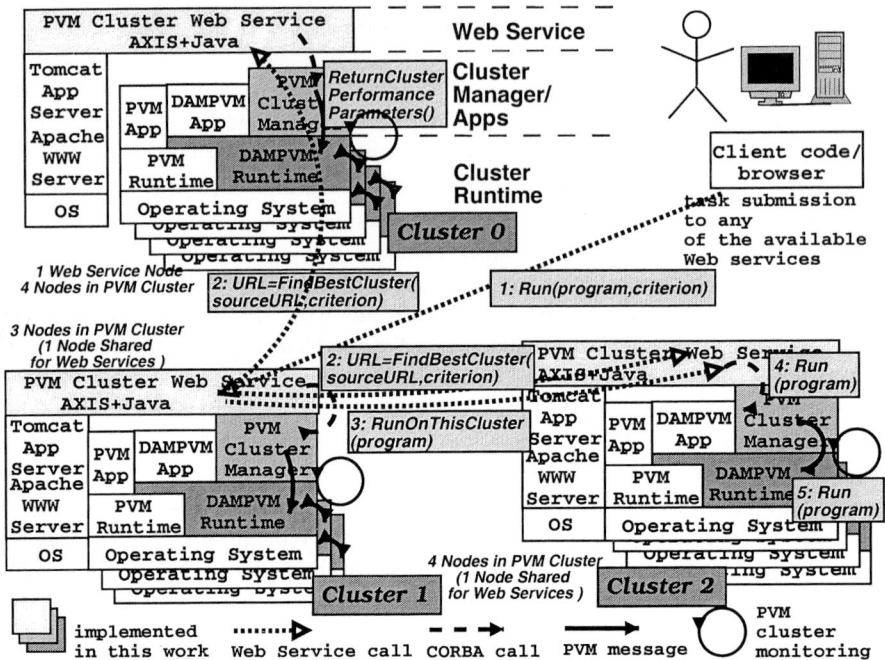

Fig. 1. PVMWebCluster Architecture

3. Web service `RunOnThisCluster(program)` is invoked on the selected cluster. The name of the program is given.
4. The Web service on the final cluster calls method `Run(program)` on the cluster manager being in charge of the cluster. The call is made via CORBA.
5. The cluster manager runs the specified program on the best node in the cluster given the criterion. In this case, this refers to the node with the lowest estimated execution time in the cluster as returned by DAMPVM ([15], [16], [17]) schedulers.

2.1 Cluster Layer

Each node in every cluster has PVM installed on it. The PVM runtime layer is used by system monitoring processes, namely DAMPVM ([15], [16], [17]) kernels. They monitor the states of the nodes including current loads, number of active processes, processor load captured by the processes of other users (time sharing the processors). DAMPVM exchanges such information between the nodes periodically which is then used for automatic load balancing techniques developed for DAMPVM applications. They include dynamic process allocation and migration ([18], [17]) which is additionally integrated with dynamic process partitioning techniques for irregular divide-and-conquer applications implemented in DAMPVM/DAC ([15], [16]). For regular PVM applications, DAMPVM is used only as the system monitoring layer that provides the aforementioned information to a PVM cluster manager.

2.2 Cluster Manager

The manager is implemented in C++ as a CORBA ([3], [4]) server that is multithreaded:

- one thread polls DAMPVM kernels for load information related to the PVM cluster the manager is responsible for,
- others wait for CORBA calls from the corresponding Web service that:
    - query the manager about the performance, current and past load information,
    - ask the manager to run a given application (parallel or sequential) on the cluster.

The CORBA manager is not an entry point to the cluster from the outside. This is because we want to be able to separate the entry point to the cluster and the PVM cluster physically i.e. so that they can run on physically different machines. This prevents incoming queries from being processed on a machine used by PVM.

2.3 Web Services as Entry Points to Clusters

The current system architecture proposes and implements cluster entry points using the latest Web technology, namely Web Services ([11], [10]). This solution enables:

- integration of distributed PVM clusters running on different user accounts,
- easy access which is not blocked by firewalls as it uses HTTP,
- easy task submission from various programming languages and Web browsers,
- modularization of the system which makes attaching or detaching various clusters possible by just adding or removing the URL of the corresponding Web service,
- easy, possibly remote system administration through Web services.

There is one entry point to every cluster. Such entry points have been implemented as Web services in Java (.jws files) with the AXIS server ([11], [10]) running in the Tomcat application server ([19]). AXIS is a SOAP engine that runs as a server within (this is how it is used in this work) or outside Tomcat, supports WSDL and a tool for monitoring TCP/IP packets. Tomcat runs on the popular Apache WWW server. It is possible to run separate PVMs in clusters, each running on a different user account.

Web service AddNeighboringServiceURL adds an URL to the vector of existing logical neighbors of a cluster (Figure 2). Web service Run executes the given command on the best cluster using the given criterion. The user receives the name of the Web service where the command has been run, the estimated execution time on this cluster (before submission) and waits for results (Figure 2).

3 Experimental Results

We achieved good parallel efficiency running several copies of a parallel application on a variety of Linux machines grouped into clusters and integrated using Web services. Each application was automatically parallelized inside the cluster thanks to the features incorporated into DAMPVM ([15], [16], [17]): automatic divide-and-conquer tree partitioning and dynamic process allocation. New processes are spawned on least loaded neighbors in the cluster. If a node is idle, it requests dynamic partitioning of divide-and-conquer trees assigned to other processes in the cluster. Subtrees are spawned as separate processes on the underloaded node ([15], [16]). This makes load balancing inside clusters possible but difficult because of different processor speeds (Table 1).

```
pvm & # start PVM
$HOME/pvm3/bin/LINUX/PCScheduler 'hostname' & # start DAMPVM
$HOME/pvm3/bin/LINUX/PCClusterManager & sleep 3 # start the PCClusterManager
java Client MonitorClusterPerformanceParametersLoop arg # start monitoring
[pczarnul@wolf]$ java Client AddNeighboringServiceURL fox.eti.pg.gda.pl
[pczarnul@wolf]$ java Client AddNeighboringServiceURL pluto.eti.pg.gda.pl
[pczarnul@wolf]$ java Client AddNeighboringServiceURL earth.eti.pg.gda.pl
[pczarnul@wolf]$ java Client Run /home/pczarnul/pvm3/bin/LINUX/dacintegrate 0
Got result : wolf.eti.pg.gda.pl>>0.0
...
[pczarnul@wolf]$ java Client Run /home/pczarnul/pvm3/bin/LINUX/dacintegrate 0
Got result : earth.eti.pg.gda.pl>>15.381059
[pczarnul@wolf]$ java Client Run /home/pczarnul/pvm3/bin/LINUX/dacintegrate 0
Got result : pluto.eti.pg.gda.pl>>10.819612
[pczarnul@wolf]$ java Client Run /home/pczarnul/pvm3/bin/LINUX/dacintegrate 0
Got result : fox.eti.pg.gda.pl>>0.0
```

Fig. 2. PVMWebCluster Configuration and Run of a Testbed Application

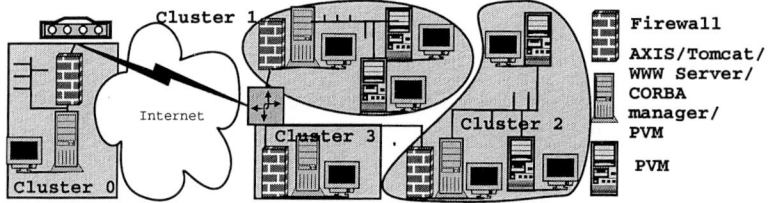

Fig. 3. Testbed Environment

3.1 Testbed Environment

We used the environment shown in Figure 3. It consists of four separate clusters, the total of eight nodes. The PVM clusters differ in the number of nodes and run separate PVMs. The computers run different Linux distributions and differ in speeds as shown in Table 1. The speed was measured by a run of a testbed adaptive integration application described below. Table 1 shows the host-to-host communication times as reported by the UNIX `ping` command. The clusters were secured by firewalls except ports open for incoming traffic: 8080 for the Tomcat and 80 for the Apache servers.

3.2 Testbed Application

In our experiments, we used a parallel implementation of the adaptive integration algorithm described in [16]. In this case, however, we submitted several runs of this application to the collection of clusters described above (Figure 2). Submission was done through a Java client invoking the Run() Web service. Each time the application was submitted, the Web service layer of the system chose the most suitable cluster to run the application. Since the criterion was to minimize the wall time across the clusters, PVM cluster managers computed maximum execution times across the clusters they were in charge of. Finally, the cluster with the lowest maximum execution time was chosen.

The applications run in every cluster have been parallelized automatically using the techniques available in DAMPVM ([15], [16], [17]). Thus, such a criterion would return the cluster with the lowest load, assuming the ideal load balance within clusters. The maximum execution time per cluster is computed as follows:

1. Compute the sum of the sizes S of all processes assigned to node N_i. DAMPVM applications provide this information to DAMPVM runtime by function PC_Instructions(). The adaptive integration example returned the value of $(b-a)$ where $[a, b]$ denotes the range to be integrated, assigned to the particular process.
2. Compute the execution time of node N_i as $estt_i(t) = \frac{S}{sp_i(1-\frac{othL_i(t)}{100})}$.
3. Compute the maximum execution time per cluster as $max_i \{estt_i(t)\}$.

3.3 Results

We performed experiments for three configurations as shown in Table 1:

A four clusters (one, three, three and one node respectively), eight nodes total,
B four clusters (one node in each cluster), four nodes total,
C one cluster, one node.

Table 1 shows that the computational speeds of the clusters differ significantly. The single node in the one cluster configuration is the slowest one. The obtained execution times for a series of 44 submissions of the aforementioned application are shown in Figure 4. This makes the parallelization/scheduling among clusters more difficult if the number of submitted applications is close to the number of clusters. Figure 4 shows the execution times as well the corresponding efficiency values.

The main reasons for the loss of efficiency in the experiments are as follows:

1. latency during submission – a task should run for at least several seconds so that the system can notice them running, latencies during performance monitoring – latencies propagate due to the flexible architecture of the system,
2. imprecise node speed measurement,
3. Web services/servers running on computers used by PVMs.

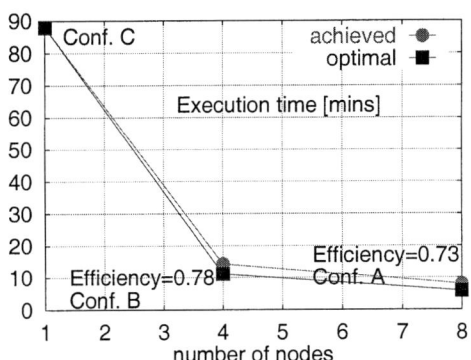

Fig. 4. Execution Time

4 Summary and Future Work

Considering that fact that the parallelization was done at the inter- and inner- cluster levels, the achieved preliminary values are good. This indicates that the integration of PVM clusters for demanding parallel scientific applications has been successful.

Table 1. Testbed Environment Configuration and Parameters

Node		Cluster Conf.			Ping Time to Cluster 64bytes (us)			
OS/kernel/Processor/Memory	Speed	A	B	C	0	1	2	3
RedHat/2.4.18/P4M 1.4GHz/768MB	1	0	0	0	40	1.1E5	1E5	1.3E5
Slackware/2.4.18/AthlonXP 1800+/256MB	2.3	1	1		x	20	100	281
Debian/2.4.18/Athlon XP 1800+/256MB	2.3							
Debian/2.4.18/Athlon 800MHz/512MB	1.2							
Slackware/2.4.18/AthlonXP 1800+/256MB	2.3	2	2		x	100	21	300
Mandrake 2.4.19/Athlon 850MHz/256MB	1.4							
Aurora/2.4.18/AthlonXP 1800+/256MB	2.3							
RedHat 2.4.18/AthlonXP 1800+/256MB	2.3	3	3		x	363	348	27

We plan to extend the implementation to support also MPI and other clusters as well as perform measurements on larger networks. Other planned additions include:

- queuing tasks within clusters based on their priorities - currently tasks are executed immediately after they were submitted,
- user and resource authentication and authorization (using MySQL databases),
- communication optimizations - automatic discovery of the best low latency graph for calling Web services between clusters,
- managing input and output data for tasks being submitted.

References

1. Geist, A., Beguelin, A., Dongarra, J., Jiang, W., Mancheck, R., Sunderam, V.: PVM Parallel Virtual Machine. A Users Guide and Tutorial for Networked Parallel Computing. MIT Press, Cambridge (1994) http://www.epm.ornl.gov/pvm/.
2. Wilkinson, B., Allen, M.: Parallel Programming: Techniques and Applications Using Networked Workstations and Parallel Computers. Prentice Hall (1999)
3. OMG (Object Management Group): Common Object Request Broker Architecture (CORBA/IIOP): Core Specification. v. 3.0.2 edn. (2002) http://www.omg.org/docs/formal/02-12-02.pdf.
4. Buyya, R., ed.: High Performance Cluster Computing, Programming and Applications. Prentice Hall (1999)
5. Foster, I., Kesselman, C., eds.: The Grid: Blueprint for a New Computing Infrastructure. Morgan Kaufmann (1998) ISBN 1558604758.
6. Foster, I., Kesselman, C., Tuecke, S.: The Anatomy of the Grid: Enabling Scalable Virtual Organizations. International Journal of High Performance Computing Applications **15** (2001) 200–222 http://www.globus.org/research/papers/anatomy.pdf.
7. Noack, J., Mehmaneche, H., Mehmaneche, H., Zendler, A.: Architectural Patterns for Web Applications. In Hamza, M., ed.: 18th IASTED International Conference on Applied Informatics (AI 2000), Proceedings, Innsbruck, Austria, ACTA Press (2000) citeseer.nj.nec.com/260788.html.

8. Foster, I., Kesselman, C., Nick, J., Tuecke, S.: The Physiology of the Grid: An Open Grid Services Architecture for Distributed Systems Integration. In: Open Grid Service Infrastructure WG. (2002) Global Grid Forum, http://www.globus.org/research/papers/ogsa.pdf.
9. Fox, G., Furmanski, W., Haupt, T., Akarsu, E., Ozdemir, H.: HPcc as High Performance Commodity Computing on Top of Integrated Java, CORBA, COM and Web Standards. In: 4th International Euro-Par Conference, Proceedings. Number 1470 in Lecture Notes in Computer Science, Southampton, UK, Springer-Verlag (1998) 55–74
10. Streicher, M.: Creating Web Services with AXIS: Apache's Latest SOAP Implementation Bootstraps Web Services. Linux Magazine (2002) http://www.linux-mag.com/2002-08/axis_01.html.
11. Butek, R., Chappell, D., Daniels, G., Davis, D., Haddad, C., Jordahl, T., Loughran, S., Nakamura, Y., Ruby, S., Rineholt, R., Sandholm, T., Scheuerle, R., Sedukhin, I., Seibert, M., Sitze, R., Srinivas, D.: Axis User's Guide. 1.1 edn. (2001) http://cvs.apache.org/viewcvs.cgi/~checkout~/xml-axis/java/docs/user-guide.html.
12. Lu, J., Chen, L.: An Architecture for Building User-Driven Web Tasks via Web Services. In: Third International Conference, E-Commerce and Web Technologies EC-Web 2002, Proceedings. Number 2455 in Lecture Notes in Computer Science, Aix-en-Provence, France, Springer-Verlag (2002) 77–86
13. Furtado, A., Reboucas, A., de Souza, J., Rexachs, D., Luque, E.: Architectures for an Efficient Application Execution in a Collection of HNOWS. In: Recent Advances in Parallel Virtual Machine and Message Passing Interface. Number 2474 in LNCS, Springer-Verlag (2002) 450–460 9th European PVM/MPI Users' Group Meeting, Linz, Austria, September/October 2002, Proceedings.
14. Jorba, J., Bustos, R., Casquero, A., Margalef, T., Luque, E.: Web Remote Services Oriented Architecture for Cluster Management. In: Recent Advances in Parallel Virtual Machine and Message Passing Interface. Number 2474 in LNCS, Springer-Verlag (2002) 368–375 9th European PVM/MPI Users' Group Meeting, Linz, Austria, Sept/Oct 2002, Proceedings.
15. Czarnul, P.: Programming, Tuning and Automatic Parallelization of Irregular Divide-and-Conquer Applications in DAMPVM/DAC. International Journal of High Performance Computing Applications 17 (2003) 77–93
16. Czarnul, P., Tomko, K., Krawczyk, H.: Dynamic Partitioning of the Divide-and-Conquer Scheme with Migration in PVM Environment. In: Recent Advances in Parallel Virtual Machine and Message Passing Interface. Number 2131 in Lecture Notes in Computer Science, Springer-Verlag (2001) 174–182 8th European PVM/MPI Users' Group Meeting, Santorini/Thera, Greece, September 23-26, 2001, Proceedings.
17. Czarnul, P., Krawczyk, H.: Dynamic Assignment with Process Migration in Distributed Environments. In: Recent Advances in Parallel Virtual Machine and Message Passing Interface. Number 1697 in Lecture Notes in Computer Science (1999) 509–516
18. Czarnul, P.: Dynamic Process Partitioning and Migration for Irregular Applications. In: International Conference on Parallel Computing in Electrical Engineering PARELEC'2002, Proceedings, Warsaw, Poland (2002) http://www.parelec.org.
19. McClanahan, C.R.: Tomcat: Application Developer's Guide. (2002) Apache Jakarta Project, http://jakarta.apache.org/tomcat/tomcat-4.1-doc/appdev/index.html.

Lock-Free Collective Operations

Alexander Supalov

Pallas GmbH, a member of ExperTeam Group,
Hermülheimer Str. 10, D-50321 Brühl, Germany
supalov@pallas.com

Abstract. This paper describes an extension of the lock-free message passing idea to the native implementation of the MPI-2 collective operations for the shared memory based platforms. A handy notation is introduced for the description of the collective algorithms. The results of benchmarking demonstrate viability and competitiveness of this approach by comparing the performance of Sun HPC and Fujitsu MPI-2 with and without proposed native collective optimizations.

1 Introduction

Collective operations had been an area of intensive research well before the the MPI standards were introduced. In those days the efforts were focused on identifying the set of the most useful and universal collective operations, improving the underlying communication patterns, and optimizing their mapping onto the more or less bizarre interconnects [1].

Introduction of a rich set of predefined collectives by the MPI standards [2, 3] allowed the implementors to concentrate on optimizing performance instead of wondering about what operations had to be supported and why. However, the earlier involvement with the interconnects persisted in the sense that the natural ways of collective communication were not actively pursued even in those situations when they hold an inherent advantage over the indirect point-to-point message passing approach routinely used for implementing the MPI-2 collectives.

This is particularly striking in the area of the shared memory based MPI implementations. A lot of solid work has been done on implementing fast point-to-point communication within the MPI context [4] and ever faster interprocess synchronization primitives elsewhere, but no visible effort has been undertaken to exploit the shared memory to the full advantage of the MPI collective operations.

This paper attempts to correct this situation somewhat. It presents an extension of the lock-free message passing idea to the native implementation of the optimized MPI-2 collective operations for the Solaris/Sparc SMP platform, one of the architectures supported by Fujitsu MPI-2 [5].

The discussion is organized as follows. Section 2 analyzes the requirements imposed on the low level collective operations by the extended semantics of the MPI-2 collectives. Section 3 introduces a handy notation used for formulating selected lock-free collective algorithms in Section 4. Section 5 presents the results of comparative benchmarking that demonstrate viability and competitiveness of the described approach. Finally, Section 6 concludes the discussion and dwells upon the further research directions.

2 Requirements

There are several factors to keep in mind while designing the basic lock-free collective operations.

First of all, these operations should be able to work on any subset of processes, not only all of the MPI_COMM_WORLD or a particular number of processes (like some power of two, for example).

Next, the operations should not be limited to particular buffer sizes. This is especially true of the indexed operations that should be able to exchange variable amounts of data without the processes deciding first between themselves which algorithm - optimized or non-optimized - is to be used.

In addition to this, the operations have to support the MPI_IN_PLACE argument when necessary. It turns out that this requirement can easily be met by avoiding copying of a respective data buffer portion (that can adequately represent the MPI_IN_PLACE) upon itself.

Although processing of the noncontiguous data types can be handled by the upper MPI layer, optimal handling of the noncontiguous data types should be delegated to the lowest level possible, where unnecessary extra memory copying can be avoided in the most natural way.

Finally, by disregarding the split collective communication outlined in the MPI-2 Journal of Development [6], it appears possible to formulate the native collectives as blocking operations, provided that the MPI progress requirement is taken care of.

3 Notation

Compared to the more conventional lock-based shared memory implementations, the lock-free approach avoids the overheads associated with the use of the interprocess synchronization primitives (such as SVR3 semaphores, POSIX mutexes, etc.) by separating the interprocess communication paths with the help of a two-dimensional buffer table held in the shared memory segment. This allows the processes to independently poll the respective parts of this table without fear of unexpected interprocess interference, provided that the sequential consistency requirements are properly enforced either in hardware or by software [7].

Extension of this idea to the native collective operations requires careful analysis of the possible deadlock and runaway conditions. This is made very difficult by the naturally obfuscated program code. Hence, there arises a need for some clear way of expressing in sufficient detail the individual actions of each of the processes, as well as interaction between them.

This need is adequately met by the following notation that is used throughout this paper to describe the lock-free collective algorithms.

```
Operation(argument,list)
----------------------------------------------------------------
0 or root actions            other processes' actions
----------------------------------------------------------------
```

This header describes the operation together with its essential arguments, and provides the place for specifying actions performed by the root process (if it exists) and other processes during the operation.

Some actions may be performed by some process(es) only after another action has been finished by other process(es). In this case, the dependent action is placed on the string following the one it depends upon. Actions that may be performed simultaneously by the root and nonroot processes are put onto the same line. Empty lines are used sparingly as comments to separate stages of the operation.

The argument list always starts with a description of the process group spanned by the operation. This description should include at least the list of process ranks in the group, their number, and the MPI communication context. The value of the latter is guaranteed to be unique on a per process basis, which is necessary for ensuring that simultaneous or closely timed operations across different communicators don't interfere with each other.

Any other argument that starts with letter d refers to the destination process; any other argument starting with letter s refers to the source process.

Rank 0 or root is used to designate the root process if it exists. An expression like [1..(n-1)], or [!0], or [!root] specifies all other processes. Index i is conventionally used for signifying the current nonroot process out of n processes of the group. A star (*) denotes all processes of the group.

All operations are performed in a shared memory segment allocated once at the start of the MPI job. In this segment, each MPI process has dedicated parts that are used for performing the point-to-point, collective, and one-sided operations.

The variables data[i], valid[i], sync[i], and lock[i] are used to designate portions of the shared memory segment allocated for performing collective operations by process of rank i within the group spanned by the operation involved. The valid[i] cells are used to indicate that the data in the respective data[i] cell is valid. The sync[i] and lock[i] cells are used for two-way synchronization between the processes.

The sync[i], lock[i], and valid[i] cells are always found and left in empty (zero) state. They must be able to contain all legal values of the MPI context identifier mentioned above. The data[i] cells should be big enough to contain the most typical data buffers. When user data buffers become larger than the preallocated space, double buffering techniques can be used to sequence the processing. The details of this are left outside the scope of this paper.

Assignments are designated by the sign <- (left arrow) and may also be performed over the index ranges described above. It is required that the assignments to the aforementioned synchronization variables be atomic with respect to read access by other processes. It is also assumed for simplicity that the sequential consistency is provided by the underlying hardware, but the corresponding changes for the opposite case are rather trivial [4].

A waiting primitive (condition[range])? can be thought of as a loop over all the specified process ranks performed until the condition becomes true everywhere. The conventional C like notation is used for specifying the conditions. Note that while waiting, the collective primitives must ensure that the point-to-point message passing does not stall.

The rather rare loop constructs take the following form:

{ body }[range]

that may be considered equivalent to the C for loop with the index variable k going over the indicated index range.

A condition preceding a block

(condition[range])? { body }

means that the action within the curled braces is performed for every process within the given range once the condition involved becomes true there. The work is terminated once the action has been performed for all the indicated processes.

Finally, some functions call the earlier defined primitives using the usual C convention, namely, function(argument,list). On one count (see Reduce), the usual C notation for a conditional operation is also used.

4 Algorithms

The MPI-2 standard specifies no less than 15 collective operations. Of them, the most application relevant appear to be [8]: Allreduce (the most frequently used), Broadcast, Alltoall, Scatter, Barrier, Reduce, and Allgather. Due to the size constraints, only some of these operations will be considered in detail below, while others will only be touched upon.

It is assumed that a reasonable memory model (like SPARC TSO [7]) is exploited by the system involved. An extension of these algorithms to the case of the more complicated memory models is possible but lies beyond the scope of this paper.

4.1 Barrier

```
Barrier(pproc,nproc,id)
------------------------------------------------------------
0                              [!0]
------------------------------------------------------------
                               sync[i] <- id
(sync[!0] == id)?
lock[0] <- id
                               (lock[0] == id)?
```

```
                              sync[i] <- 0
(sync[!0] == 0)?
lock[0] <- 0
                              (lock[0] == 0)?
```

The first part of the Barrier operation makes sure that the processes enter the operation within the same group, and barriers performed within overlapping groups of processes in close succession do not spoil each other's act. The second part ensures that the synchronization cells are left in a properly zeroed state and no race or runaway condition occurs when the processes are preempted at an awkward moment. Below, these parts are referred to as `BarrierEnter(root)` and `BarrierLeave(root)`, respectively, where the `root` argument is meant to take the place of the index 0 in the aforementioned diagram.

Of course, this is a very naive implementation, the scalability of which can be improved by applying a communication pattern that would relieve the read contention over the `lock[0]` variable. Note also that the double synchronization inherent in this scheme is largely superfluous for the Barrier itself and can be substantially improved upon, which exercise is left to the inquisitive reader.

At the same time, the partial Barrier stages described above appear indispensable in preventing the runaway conditions in the following operations that may be started in close succession by different root processes in the same MPI communicator.

4.2 Broadcast

```
Bcast(pproc,nproc,id,root,buf,len)
---------------------------------------------------------------
root                         [!root]
---------------------------------------------------------------
data[root] <- buf
valid[root] <- id
                             (valid[root] == id)?
                             buf <- data[root]

BarrierEnter(root)           BarrierEnter(root)
valid[root] <- 0
BarrierLeave(root)           BarrierLeave(root)
---------------------------------------------------------------
```

The root process copies buffer contents into its own `data` cell, then sets its `valid` cell to `id`. Of course, at some point it may be beneficial to introduce a spanning tree or another structure, and resort to the linear copying only at some depth from the root process.

4.3 Allgather

```
Allgather(pproc,nproc,id,dbuf,sbuf,len)
---------------------------------------------------------------
*
---------------------------------------------------------------
data[i] <- sbuf
valid[i] <- id

(valid[*] = id)?
{
  dbuf[k] <- data[k]
}

BarrierEnter(0)
valid[i] <- 0
BarrierLeave(0)
---------------------------------------------------------------
```

In this case, it's unnecessary to differentiate between the local and remote contributions unless access to the shared memory segment is considered to be more costly than local memory references. The indexed version is formulated analogously to the strided version presented above.

4.4 Reduce

```
Reduce(pproc,nproc,id,root,op,dbuf,sbuf,len,...)
---------------------------------------------------------------
root                    [!root]
---------------------------------------------------------------
dbuf <- sbuf            data[i] <- sbuf
                        {
                          if (subroot(k,i,root,nproc)) {
                            j <- (i + 1<<(k-1))%nproc
                            data[i] <- op(data[j],data[i],...)
                          }
                          else {
                            valid[i] <- id
                            break
                          }
                        }[1..int(log2(n))]
{
  (valid[(root + 1<<(k-1))%nproc] == i)?
  dbuf <- op(data[k],dbuf,...)
```

```
   valid[(root + 1<<(k-1))%nproc] <- 0
}[1..int(log2(nproc))]

Barrier(root)                   Barrier(root)
```

Upon copying of the source buffers into the respective places, a tree-like computation is performed, with the root using the `dbuf` as the result storage, and the appropriate tree subroots computing intermediate results and using their respective `data[i]` cells to store them. Note that the reduction function `op` has to be passed extra arguments - the MPI item count and data type description - to perform its work.

The `valid[i]` cells are used to indicate the stage of the tree reduction, with the initial stage being indicated by 1, and the stage preceding the last computation at root being indicated by `int(log2(nproc))`.

It is quite possible that under certain conditions (small data buffers, not so many processes, fast computational units) it may be advantageous to let the root node compute the result at once, and thus save on the synchronization overhead.

4.5 Other Operations

The Gather operation can be formulated very similarly to the Allgather operations presented above. The Scatter operation can be thought of as a generalization of the Bcast. This is true of both the strided and indexed versions of these operations.

Due to the possible rounding errors, as well as under- and overflow conditions, it is generally safer if suboptimal to represent the Allreduce operation as a Reduce to process 0 followed by a Broadcast. This can lead worse performance compared to a direct Allreduce implementation, so that a direct implementation should be considered for the truly associative operations (like MIN and MAX). In some cases, simultaneous calculation by all processes, with due attention paid to the cache contention problems, can be beneficial as well.

The Reduce_scatter operations can be adequately implemented as Reduce followed by Scatter (indexed) operation.

Finally, although the Alltoall can be thought of as a series of Gather or Scatter operations, this simple approach proves to be vastly inferior even to the layered point-to-point implementation, and a proper direct algorithm is to be devised.

5 Results

The following results were obtained by comparing the highly tuned high level MPI-2 collectives of the Fujitsu MPI-2 that use the MPI point-to-point message passing, on the one hand, and the lock-free variants of the same operations on the other hand. Note that the results span the whole range of the MPI-2 collectives, for Fujitsu MPI-2 provides native lock-free support for all of them.

The methodology and assumptions are similar to those adopted in our earlier paper [5]. The vendor independent and well proven Pallas MPI Benchmark (PMB) version 2.2 is used for measuring performance of a wide range of the application repevant MPI-1 point-to-point and collective operations at 4 byte and 4 Megabyte message lengths. The former guarantees bypassing of the zero size message shortcuts allowed for some MPI collectives, and also makes reductions work on the sensibly sized data buffers. All results are presented as timings, thus providing for a direct universal measure for all operations at all buffer sizes, and avoiding the tricky bandwidth definition in the case of collectives.

This time the measurements were again performed on the Sun Starfire 9500 cluster at the RWTH Aachen, Germany. Sun HPC 5.0 installed at the machine was used as a reference to assess the relative and absolute quality of the Fujitsu MPI-2 with and without the lock-free collectives enabled. Note that in these uniform timing diagrams, *smaller* means *better* (see Figures 1-4).

It can be seen that the Fujitsu MPI-2 point-to-point operations are sometimes superior to the Sun HPC ones. Even though, the nonoptimized Fujitsu MPI-2 collectives appear to be quite slower on some counts. The use of the optimized collectives described above helps to achieve a remarkable relative speed-up in a number of cases (cf., for example, Allreduce, Reduce, ReduceScatter, Allgather, Allgatherv, and Barrier).

There are however some tougher operations (like Allreduce, Alltoall, and Barrier) that still work better in Sun HPC on some processor numbers and buffer sizes. These constitute the focus of our ongoing development efforts.

6 Conclusions

This paper presents a handy notation used for description of the lock-free collective operations. Being more abstract than the C language, this notation simplifies detection of contention, deadlocks, race and runaway conditions, and other synchronization issues much more readily than the naturally obfuscated program source code.

The results produced by applying the lock-free technique directly at the collective operation level indicate a good potential for improving their performance basing on the direct shared memory approach alone. At the same time it must be noted that the somewhat naive linear access patterns described above have to be replaced by the more scalable ones for the growing number of processors.

In addition to this, since the Barrier operation constitutes an integral part of all operations, any improvement in the latency of the Barrier suboperations will be translated directly into the corresponding improvement of all other latencies. This makes hardware-assisted Barrier implementation an attractive option for further performance improvement.

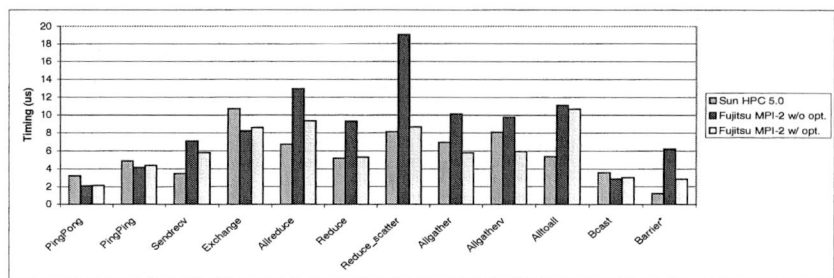

Fig. 1. PMB-MPI1 version 2.2 timings at 4 byte message size on 2 processors.

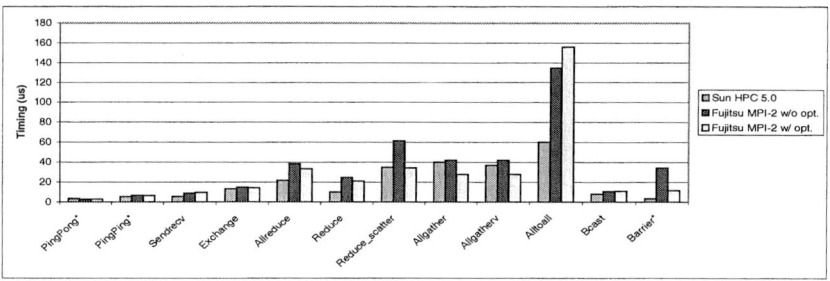

Fig. 2. PMB-MPI1 version 2.2 timings at 4 byte message size on 16 processors.

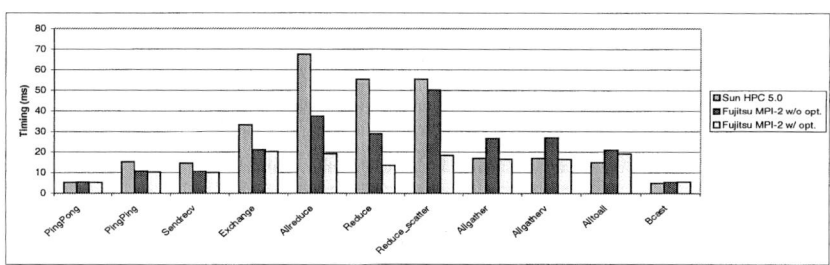

Fig. 3. PMB-MPI1 version 2.2 timings at 4 Megabyte message size on 2 processors.

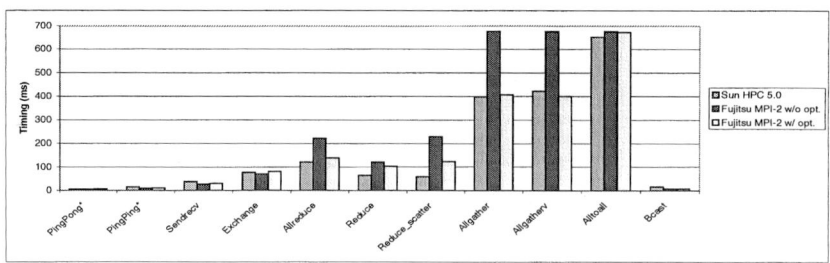

Fig. 4. PMB-MPI1 version 2.2 timings at 4 Megabyte message size on 16 processors.

References

1. Mitra, P., Payne, D., Shuler, L., Geijn, R. van de, Watts, J.: Fast Collective Communication Libraries, Please. Tech. Rep. TR-95-22, Department of Computer Sciences, The University of Texas, (1995)
2. Message Passing Interface Forum: MPI: A Message-Passing Interface Standard. June 12, 1995
3. Message Passing Interface Forum: MPI-2: Extensions to the Message-Passing Interface. July 18, 1997
4. Gropp, W., Lusk,E.: A High-Performance MPI Implementation on a Shared-Memory Vector Supercomputer. Parallel Computing **22(11)** (1997) 1513-1526
5. Bißeling, G., Hoppe, H.-C., Supalov, A., Lagier, P., Latour, J.: Fujitsu MPI-2: Fast Locally, Reaching Globally. Rec. Adv. in PVM and MPI (2002) 401–409
6. Message Passing Interface Forum: MPI-2 Journal of Development. July 18, 1997
7. Adve, S. V., and Gharachorloo, K.: Shared Memory Consistency Models: A Tutorial. Computer **29(12)** (1996) 66–76.
8. Rabenseifner, R.: Automatic MPI Counter Profiling of All Users: First Results on a CRAY T3E 900-512. In proc. of the Message Passing Interface Developer's and User's Conference 1999 (MPIDC'99), Atlanta, USA, March 10-12 (1999) 77–85

Efficient Message-Passing within SMP Systems

Xuehua Chen and Dave Turner

Ames Laboratory – Iowa State University
327 Wilhelm Hall, Ames, Iowa, 50011
turner@ameslab.gov

Abstract. Message-passing libraries have made great strides in delivering a high percentage of the performance that the network hardware offers. There has been much less effort focused on improving the communications between processes within an SMP system. SMP nodes are becoming an integral part of many clusters and MPP systems. These SMP nodes are also growing in size, requiring attention to scalable solutions to passing messages through shared-memory segments. The research presented in this paper will focus on an analysis of the performance of existing message-passing libraries, as well as new methods being evaluated using the MP_Lite message-passing library. The NetPIPE utility is used to provide point-to-point measurements that are backed up by tests with a real application.

1 Introduction

Symmetric Multi-Processor (SMP) systems are increasingly becoming an integral part of clusters and Massively Parallel Processing (MPP) systems. In the most basic x86 clusters, adding a 2nd processor to each node typically adds only 20% to the cost while doubling the potential computational power. Not all this power will be realized due to memory bandwidth limitations, but the economics will almost always favor choosing the additional processor. Exceptions include applications that push the memory limitations of a system, where adding a 2nd processor would cut the memory/processor in half, and communication-bound applications where having 2 processes/node would cut the effective bandwidth out of each process in half.

There are many examples of larger SMP nodes in use today. Quad-processor Alpha systems and IBM PowerX nodes using 2-16 processors use larger secondary and tertiary caches combined with greater bandwidth on the shared memory bus to efficiently apply the greater processing power.

Parallel applications use either the MPI standard [1-3] or the PVM library [4-5] to communicate between nodes. Message-passing libraries such as MPICH [6-7], LAM/MPI [8-9], MPI/Pro [10], MP_Lite [11-12], and PVM now pass along a majority of the performance that the underlying network hardware offers in most cases [13].

An application can divide work between processors in an SMP node by adding a second level of parallelism using a thread-based approach such as with the OpenMP standard [14]. The drawback to this approach is that it requires extra programming knowledge and effort.

One alternative, typically chosen since it requires no additional effort, is to treat each processor as a node and handle the communication between processors the same as between nodes, with MPI or PVM message-passing calls. The graphs presented later will show that there is a very broad range in message-passing performance between the various implementations, showing that more focus is needed in this area.

There are many case studies available comparing the efficiency of the message-passing paradigm with OpenMP [15-16]. The goal of this research is to optimize the message-passing performance between processes within SMP nodes. Only when this is completed is it time to weigh in on the debate of performance and ease of use for each approach.

2 The MP_Lite Message-Passing Library

MP_Lite is a lightweight message-passing library designed to provide optimal performance for the environments it supports. It is a small, streamlined package that is ideal for research into new message-passing techniques. It supports a core set of the MPI commands including basic and asynchronous 2-sided functions, 1-sided *get* and *put* operations, and the most common global operations. Enough of the MPI functionality is provided to ensure that any techniques being investigated within MP_Lite will be applicable to full MPI implementations. MP_Lite was implemented as an MPICH channel device [17] to show that the performance benefits of MP_Lite could be passed on to the full MPICH library.

MP_Lite has a SIGIO-based TCP module, an M-VIA module, a Cray/SGI SHMEM module, a new InfiniBand module based on the Mellanox VAPI, and an SMP module that is the focus of this paper. There are actually many variations of the MP_Lite SMP module that have been analyzed. All pass messages through a shared-memory segment that is attached to each process on an SMP node. They vary in the method used to manage the shared segment, the locking mechanism (or lack of one) used to prevent processes from trampling on one another, the method a destination process uses to block for a receive, and how the source process notifies the destination process that a new message is ready.

Most SMP message-passing libraries use a shared-memory segment as a shared resource for transferring messages between all processes. These messages may be linked together for fast search using linked lists, or the headers may be put in circular queues for each destination process. Since all processes must add new messages to and retrieve messages from this shared area, a locking mechanism is needed to ensure that operations from different processes do not interfere with each other. Semaphores are designed for this, but each use of a semaphore can cost 3 μs or more. Implementations commonly require multiple locks, so this can quickly add to the latency for passing small messages.

One alternative is to use a locking mechanism that is more efficient than a semaphore operation. Atomic functions such as the x86 assembly operation *btsl* can be used to test and set a memory lock in the same operation. The atomic lock function repeatedly tests and sets a given memory location to 1 until the test returns a 0, indicating that any previous lock had been removed. If the locking variable is set up to be the only thing in an entire cache line, then repeated testing is done from cache placing no burden on the shared memory bus. Processes are usually running on separate processors, so having a CPU spin is usually not detrimental. However, since multiple processes can share the same processor, a schedule yield function taking around 1 µs must also be called after a given period to avoid possible lockups.

Care must be taken to make lock-based approaches scalable to large SMP systems. Processes only need to lock the shared-memory segment when they are adding or deleting headers, not when they are copying data in or out. MP_Lite goes even further by implementing a shared-memory FIFO pipe between each pair of processes. These pipes contain only the pointers to messages in the shared pool for a given source/destination pair. The shared pool then only needs to be locked during memory allocation and de-allocation, and not when processes need to traverse the linked list or header queue in the shared-memory segment. De-allocation is done on messages marked as received by the destination node during subsequent allocation phases by that source node, further reducing the number of locks. A spinlock function is used to efficiently block for the next pointer to be put into the FIFO pipe. The MP_Lite graphs presented in this paper use these shared-memory FIFO pipes to transfer pointers to the messages in the shared pool that is managed using atomic locks.

Another approach is to avoid locking mechanisms altogether. The shared-memory segment can be divided into sections, one for each source process, with the source process being responsible for all management of its section. The outgoing messages from each process are written to its section and added to the end of the linked list. The destination process traverses this linked list, copies the message, and marks a 'garbage' flag indicating to the source process that the message has been received and can be removed from the linked list. This is an efficient method for managing the shared-memory segment without requiring any locking mechanism. The only drawback is that the shared-memory segment has been subdivided, so unbalanced message traffic may fill up the resources more quickly.

There are several approaches that can be used to allow the destination process to block for an incoming message when needed, and for the source process to signal the destination when a new message is ready in the segment. The most efficient approach is simply to have the destination process do a spinlock waiting for the 'next' pointer in the linked list to change from NULL. The destination process could also wait in a sig_suspend function, to be woken up by a SIGUSR1 signal sent by the source process, but this was found to take around 10 µs to propagate the signal.

3 Message-Passing Implementations

The various MPI implementations and the PVM library use a variety of techniques for passing messages between processes on SMP nodes. MPICH (1.2.5) uses a small number of fixed size shared packets to transfer small messages between processes. Larger messages are sent through the shared-memory segment that is managed using semaphore locks. Very long messages also use a rendezvous mechanism.

MPICH2 (0.93 beta) is a rewrite of the MPICH library that is due for official release in the fall of 2003. This beta version shows much improvement in latency and bandwidth over previous versions of MPICH.

LAM/MPI (6.5.9 usys) uses several mechanisms to provide optimal performance. Messages smaller than 16 kB are sent through an 8 kB postbox set up between each pair of processes. A spinlock function is used to prevent subsequent messages from trampling on each other, so the source process will block on a subsequent message until the previous one has been received and the lock cleared. The LAM implementation packs the header with the data so it can be streamed between processes very efficiently, producing extremely low small message latencies. Larger messages are transferred through a shared-memory segment managed using semaphore locks.

MPI/Pro (1.6.4-1) is the first SMP implementation from MPI Software Technology. This is a commercial product distributed as an RPM without source code, so little is known at this point about its implementation details.

PVM (3.4.4-2) is the Parallel Virtual Machine library. It is a message-passing library, not a standard like MPI, and has a different syntax but some similarities in functionality to MPI. This message-passing library appears to have an extra memcpy embedded in its code that slows communications between processes.

4 Performance Comparisons

The NetPIPE utility [18-19] was used to measure the point-to-point message-passing performance of each library. NetPIPE performs a series of ping-pong measurements for increasingly large message sizes, including perturbations from regular points to ensure a complete analysis of each message-passing system. The latencies reported are the round trip time for small messages (8 Bytes) divided by 2. Tests were done on a wide variety of systems, including dual Xeon, Athlon, Alpha, IBM, and Pentium 3 systems. The graphs presented here are from a 1.7 GHz dual-Xeon system running RedHat 8.0 with the 2.4.18-14smp kernel. These results are representative of the other systems, and any deviations will be discussed.

Fig. 1 shows the performance of all message-passing libraries running in their optimal configurations. These results include cache effects, which are achieved by using the same memory buffer to send and receive the messages. This is therefore representative of the results that would be expected if the data in an application started in cache.

Fig. 2 shows the performance without cache effects. This is achieved by sending a message from a different window in main memory each time, and is representative of the performance an application would see if the data was not cached before being sent. Both of these graphs are needed to understand what performance an application might get out of each message-passing system.

LAM/MPI clearly provides the best performance for small messages with a 1 μs latency. In some practical cases, the synchronization that could be imposed by the postbox approach could hurt performance. MP_Lite and MPICH2 also have low latencies of 2 μs and 3 μs respectively. The semaphore locks in MPICH produce a longer latency of 8 μs, while PVM at 31 μs and MPI/Pro 48 μs are much slower. The performance for small messages varies by almost a factor of 50 from best to worst.

The performance in the cache region also varies greatly between the message-passing libraries. The minimal use of locks in MP_Lite, and the efficiency of the atomic locks used, proves best in this regime. LAM/MPI and MPICH2 benefit in the primary cache regime from their low latencies, while LAM/MPI and MPICH show good performance in secondary cache. The overall performance can vary by as much as a factor of 5. Fig. 2 shows that the performance varies by as much as a factor of 2-3 in this intermediate regime even when data starts in main memory.

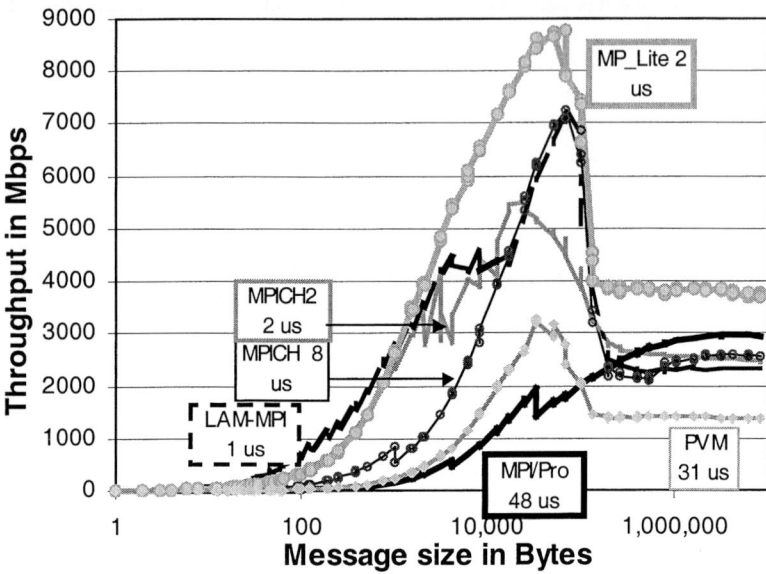

Fig. 1. The SMP message-passing performance with cache effects for MPI implementations and PVM on a 1.7 GHz dual-Xeon system running RedHat 8.0 (2.4.18-14smp kernel). The small message latencies are given in microseconds for each library.

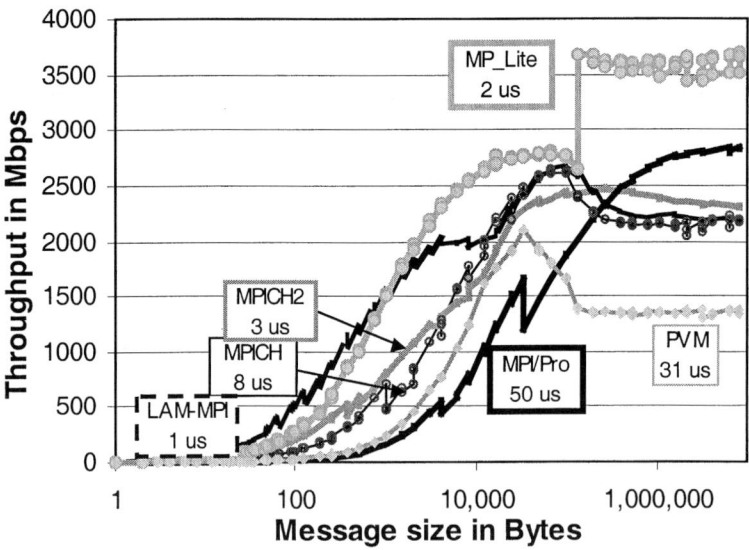

Fig. 2. The SMP message-passing performance without cache effects for MPI implementations and PVM on a 1.7 GHz dual-Xeon system running RedHat 8.0 (2.4.18-14smp kernel). The small message latencies are given in microseconds for each library.

MP_Lite tests with a lock-free approach show equally good performance on most multi-processor Unix systems, but have poorer cache performance in x86 systems. PAPI and VTune show more cache misses during the send operation due to each process using a separate part of the shared-memory segment for outgoing messages.

Performance on large messages depends solely on the memory copy rate. Most libraries use the standard memcpy function, which provides adequate performance. However, MP_Lite uses an optimized memory copy routine that uses a non-temporal memory copy available for this processor. This increases the communication rate by 50%, which would obviously benefit the other message-passing libraries as well. The jump in the MP_Lite performance in fig. 2 is due to this non-temporal copy. The cutoff is optimized for the cache case, though applications might benefit more from optimizing it for the non-cache case by lowering the cutoff.

Table 1. The communication time in one section of the ALCMD code run with 2 MPI processes on a 1.7 GHz dual-Xeon system for each MPI implementation.

	1 kB messages	32 kB messages	163 kB messages
MPICH	101 ms	609 ms	245 ms
LAM/MPI	54 ms	669 ms	419 ms
MPI/Pro	445 ms	1550 ms	693 ms
MP_Lite	44 ms	538 ms	257 ms

While the raw performance graphs from NetPIPE provide an important part of the story, they should be viewed as an upper limit to the performance that each message-passing library might deliver. Testing with real applications is a necessary, but often neglected, component of a full analysis. At this point, one application has been used to try to validate these NetPIPE results.

The Ames Laboratory Classical Molecular Dynamics (ALCMD) code [20-21] is ideal for this purpose. The system size can be adjusted to alter the range of message sizes so that the tests can be aimed at the small message, cache, and RAM regimes in the performance curves. The code requires enough communication to show off any benefits from better message-passing techniques, even when run on as few as 2 processes.

Table 1 shows results from 3 runs designed for the different regimes, for several of the message-passing libraries (MPICH2 is still in the pre-release stage, and a bug prevented its inclusion in these tests). In general, these measurements validate the NetPIPE results. MP_Lite and LAM/MPI are best for small messages, with MPICH not too far behind and MPI/Pro lagging significantly. Runs using 32 kB and 163 kB message sizes bracket the cache-based performance. The ALCMD code is doing bi-directional transfers while NetPIPE is only measuring communications in one direction. More research is needed to understand the role that the cache effects are playing in practical situations. It may also be possible to tune the SMP message-passing system to take better advantage of the cache effects demonstrated using Net-PIPE. Additional measurements are also needed for even larger systems, though these should clearly show the benefits from the non-temporal memory copy that MP_Lite uses.

5 Conclusions

There are very large variations in performance between the message-passing libraries. Performance varies by a factor of 50 for small messages, up to a factor of 5 in the cache region, and by as much as a factor of 2 for messages larger than the cache size. Choosing an appropriate message-passing library is therefore extremely important in an SMP environment. LAM/MPI performs best for small messages below 1 kB, with MP_Lite and MPICH2 not far behind. The lock-based version of MP_Lite using the non-temporal copy performs best for message sizes above 1 kB. The exception is for systems where hyper-threading is turned on, which makes the non-temporal memory copy perform poorly.

Recent advances are being made to bring latencies down to the 1 µs range by using fewer and faster locking mechanisms that should also provide reasonable scaling characteristics. More work is needed to fully understand the cache effects and to determine how they can be passed on to applications. Optimized memory copy routines can make a large difference for all implementations by removing performance problems stemming from alignment and odd message sizes, and by adding functionality such as with the non-temporal memory copy for x86 systems.

More testing with the ALCMD code is needed to help pass on the cache benefits to real applications. Testing with more codes, and on larger SMP systems, is needed to provide a better basis for judging each message-passing library and the techniques that they rely upon.

Acknowledgements

This project is funded by the DOE MICS department through the Applied Mathematical Sciences Program at Ames Laboratory. Ames Laboratory is operated for the U.S. Department of Energy by Iowa State University under Contract No. W-7405-Eng-82. The authors would like to thank MPI Software Technology for providing an evaluation copy of the MPI/Pro software.

References

1. The MPI Standard: http://www.mcs.anl.gov/mpi/
2. MPI Forum. MPI: A Message-Passing Interface Standard. International Journal of Supercomputer Applications 8 (3/4). (1994) 165-416
3. Snir, M., Otto, S., Huss-Lederman, S., Walker, D., and Dongarra, J.: MPI – The Complete Reference. Second edn. The MIT Press. Cambridge Massachusetts. (2000)
4. PVM webpage: http://www.epm.ornl.gov/pvm/
5. Geist, A., Beguelin, A., Dongarra, J., Jiang, W., Manchek, R., and Sunderam, V.: PVM: Parallel Virtual Machine. The MIT Press (1994)
6. MPICH webpage: http://www.mcs.anl.gov/mpi/mpich/

7. Gropp, W., Lusk, E., Doss, N., and Skjellum, A.: High-Performance, Portable Implementation of the MPI Message Passing Interface Standard. Parallel Computing 22(6). (September 1996) 789-828
8. LAM/MPI webpage: http://www.osc.edu/Lam/lam.html
9. Burns, G., and Daoud, R.: Robust Message Delivery with Guaranteed Resources. MPI Developers Conference. University of Notre Dame. (June 22-23, 1995)
10. MPI/Pro webpage: http://www.mpi-softtech.com/
11. MP_Lite webpage: http://www.scl.ameslab.gov/Projects/MP_Lite/
12. Turner, D., Chen, W., and Kendall, R.: Performance of the MP_Lite Message-Passing Library on Linux Clusters. Linux Clusters: The HPC Revolution. University of Illinois, Urbana-Champaign (June 25-27, 2001)
13. Turner, D., and Chen, X.: Protocol-Dependent Message-Passing Performance on Linux Clusters. Proceedings of the IEEE International Conference on Cluster Computing. (September of 2002) 187-194
14. OpenMP webpage: http://www.openmp.org/
15. Krawezik, G., and Cappello, F.: Performance Comparison of MPI and Three OpenMP Programming Styles on Shared Memory Multiprocessors. SPAA'03. San Diego. (June 7-9, 2003)
16. Cappello, F., Richard, O., and Etiemble, D.: Understanding Performance of SMP Clusters Running MPI Programs: Future Generation Computer Systems 17(6). (April 2001) 711-720
17. Turner, D., Selvarajan, S., Chen, X., and Chen, W.: The MP_Lite Message-Passing Library. Fourteenth IASTED International Conference on Parallel and Distributed Computing and Systems. Cambridge Massachusetts. (November 4-6, 2002) 434-439
18. NetPIPE webpage: http://www.scl.ameslab.gov/Projects/NetPIPE/
19. Snell, Q., Mikler, A., and Gustafson, J.: NetPIPE: A Network Protocol Independent Performance Evaluator. IASTED International Conference on Intelligent Management and Systems. (June 1996)
20. ALCMD: http://www.cmp.ameslab.gov/cmp/CMP_Theory/cmd/cmd.html
21. Zhang, B., Wang, C., Ho, K., Turner, D., and Ye, Y.: Anomalous Phonon Behavior and Phase Fluctuations in BCC Zr: Physical Review Letters 74. (1995) 1375

The Network Agnostic MPI – Scali MPI Connect

Lars Paul Huse and Ole W. Saastad

Scali AS, Olaf Helsets vei 6, PObox 150, Oppsal, N-0619 Oslo, Norway
ole@scali.com, http://www.scali.com

Abstract. This paper presents features and performance of Scali MPI Connect (SMC). Key features in SMC are presented, such as dynamic selection of interconnect at runtime, automatic fail-over and runtime selection of optimized collective operations. Performance is measured both for basic communication functions such as bandwidth and latency and for real applications. Comparisons are made with MPICH and LAM.

1 Introduction

Scali MPI Connect (SMC) is a native implementation of the MPI-1.2 standard [12]. SMC has builtin a large number of features like trace, timing, profiling in addition to a large number of runtime selectable collective algorithms. SMC is thread-safe and thread-hot and includes a number of features that can be activated at user-level during runtime through environment variables. The features include tracing, timing and profiling and the ability to select different algorithms for the collective operations. SMC also supports concurrent use of multiple interconnects with selection done at runtime. This means that the user only needs one executable of a given application independent of interconnect. This is in contrast to most other MPI implementations where combinations of interconnects and MPI versions must be determined at compile time to generate different executables for each combination. An example is MPICH [13] that exists in several flavors optimized for specific networks; a standard version for TCP/IP sockets or shared memory, MPICH-GM for Myrinet [2], MPICH-SCI for SCI [7], MPICH-G2 for Grids etc. MPICH-G2 for Grids etc. SMC supports a MIMD execution model, establishing a fundament for seamless communication between machines with processors having different architecture or word lengths. SMC allows an application to execute in a heterogeneous cluster environment with a combination of Ia64 (e.g. Intel Itanium) and Ia32 based machines (e.g. Intel Xeon and AMD Athlon).

Section 2 discusses related work and Section 3 presents the design details of SMC. Section 4 compares performance with other MPI implementations.

2 Related Work

The most common open source MPI implementations for clustering are MPICH [13] and LAM [10]. Many projects have adapted and optimized MPICH to their own communication API, e.g. MPICH-VMI use VMI [14] to address heterogeneous networks and failover. Another commercial MPI implementation is

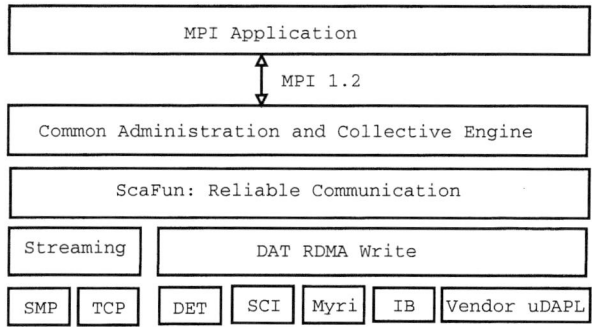

Fig. 1. SMC layering

MPI/Pro [21] from MPI Software Technology Inc. Due to difficulties in acquiring the appropriate licenses for testing, this software has not been included in this evaluation. Most of the optimization of collective operations in MPI implementations is done with specific hardware in mind. In [20] however, a framework for automatic collective algorithm selection is described in detail.

3 Design

Most of the software framework (daemon, debugger, and application launch environment) and some of the basic design ideas in SMC are inherited from ScaMPI [4]. Several new features have been added and are described in this article. SMC supports a wide selection of interconnects: local shared memory, any Ethernet (Standard-, Fast- and Gigabit-Ethernet) [6], SCI [7], Myrinet [2], InfiniBand [8], and any network with a MAC address or a 3rd party uDAPL (User Direct Access Programming Library) [3] (see section 3.1).

Figure 1 shows the SMC layering. The top layer performs parameter checking and conversion. Other complementary services in the top layer include trapping of application errors, extended data sanity-checking and extraction of CPU usage, communication statistics and timing & tracing details. The network devices are divided in two classes: streaming and remote memory write. These require different administrative semantics that are detailed later in this section. The network selection is done independently for each point-to-point Connection based on availability and priority. If several data paths are available between two processes, one is selected according to the network priority list (while the others are kept for a possible failover) - given from:

1. A command line option to SMC's application launcher *mpimon*.
2. An environment variable.
3. A configuration file in the current directory (./ScaMPI.conf).
4. A configuration file in the users home directory ($\sim$/ScaMPI.conf).
5. The system wide configuration file (/opt/scali/etc/ScaMPI.conf).

All SMC parameters (e.g. network buffer adaptation, statistics, tracing and timing) can be specified in any of these levels. For details refer to [17].

3.1 Data Transport Using Remote Memory Write

In a remote memory write protocol the sender deposits data and control information using RDMA (Remote Direct Memory Access), over a network or local shared memory, directly into the receivers memory. In a zero-copy protocol the data is deposited directly to user memory, otherwise the receiver has to to complete the transfer by copying the data from the receive buffer(s) to user memory. This model is best suited for a polling receiver, but can also be made blocking.

SMC's high-level transport using remote memory writes are based on a "classical" MPI division of messages based on size. Short messages are transferred as self-synchronizing messages. For medium sized messages there are a fixed number of *eager* buffers for asynchronous transfers. If there are no available eager-buffers or if the message is too large, the *transporter* protocol is applied requiring a rendezvous between sender and receiver. All data is deposited in dedicated receiver buffers i.e. a one-copy model. For details refer to [5].

One of the design objectives for SMC was to allow an open modular selection of network with a standardized ABI (Application Binary Interface) and dynamic linking. A DAT (Direct Access Transport) [3] was chosen as the preferred low-level ABI. The DAT Consortium standardized DAT in 2002 with several major computer vendors as members. In SMC several independent uDAPL's can be used concurrently, enabling full freedom of network selection. Currently the Scali DAT portfolio contains *DET* (Direct Ethernet Transport) and *SHM0* (over local shared memory). *MY* (over GM for Myrinet) and *IB* (for InfiniBand) are under development. DET is Scali's channel bonding/aggregation DAT device for all networks with a MAC address, e.g. all Ethernet adapters. DET's main features are low overhead and better out-of-order packet handling than TCP which is required to deliver acceptable performance when bonding two or more network adapters. An open source uDAPL implementation is available on Source Forge.

For networks with peak bandwidth (below a few percentage of memory Bandwidth) the "extra" copy from communication buffers to user memory on the receiver side introduces little performance degradation. On the machines in section 4 an internal memory copy bandwidth of 2.26 Gbyte/s (using a hand-optimized STREAM benchmark [11]) was measured, while GbE has a theoretical peek inbound bandwidth of 125 Mbyte/s. In this case the internal copy has minor impact on performance. To minimize performance loss for high bandwidth networks and SMP internal transfers, a zero-copy transfer mode was introduced in SMC. The receiver and sender register the user buffers to the uDAPL, and the transfer can be performed by a single RDMA directly from user to user buffer. Compared to the SMC transporter mode [17], only one extra control message, containing remote memory region details, is required to administrate the zero-copy. The long messages bandwidth for the SHM0 device was increased from 230 Mbyte/s in transporter mode to 1040 Mbyte/s (close to peak) using zero-copy transfers.

Direct communication using RDMA usually requires the communication buffers to be pinned down in memory. Since pinning and unpinning memory is a costly operation [18], memory administration can become a bottleneck. Reusing memory regions is therefore essential to achieve good performance. Reusing the fixed communication buffers on the receiver side is trivial, while for user sendbuffers and buffers for zero-copy, the situation is more complex. Between transfers the application memory can be released back to the OS and a new memory allocation can acquire the same virtual address space, but with different physical pages. SMC handles this by applying communication buffer caching. Upon releasing memory, the affected entries in the cache have to be invalidated. MPICH-GM traces dynamic memory by replacing the *libc* memory administration (e.g. *malloc()*) with library local functions. This approach locks the library to a given *libc* version. MVICH [15] disables releasing of allocated memory by setting *malloc* tuning parameters using *mallopt()*. This approach limits the application-usable memory to ≈ 1 GByte on 32 bit machines and forces compilers to use *malloc* and *free*. SMC processes subscribe to changes in physical memory allocation by using a device driver that snoops the process' calls to *sbrk()* and *munmap()*. This approach does not have the disadvantages that the two others may suffer.

To ensure failover on network errors, all remote memory writes are made idempotent i.e., multiple writes of the same data have the same effect as writing them once [7]. To overtake a failing RDMA transaction, the transaction has to be inhibited from further retransmission and then retransmitted over another communication network. For example, if parts of a cluster's high-speed network is temporarily unavailable, the affected nodes can switch to the infrastructure Ethernet while it is down. Since any transaction is idempotent is the order between the two actions indifferent. This implies that all valid networks for a pt2pt connection use the same physical buffers and unify their buffering parameters. This is done automatically in SMC.

3.2 Data Transport Using Streaming Devices

The streaming devices have a "socket like" behavior. Data is written as a byte stream on the sender-side, and is read in-order on the receiver-side. Each pt2pt connection has a fixed buffer capacity. An SMC message is coded as a small header (envelope) directly followed by the user data. A basic assumption of the socket is that it delivers reliable communication, hence no data check or synchronization is applied. To keep the protocol as simple as possible, all sends over streaming devices are initiated instantly in the same order they are issued by the application. To support out-of-order MPI communication a dynamic unexpected message queue has been implemented on the receiver side. To ensure forward progress, all writes and reads are performed non-blocking, keeping an updated transfer-state between each socket read & write. Currently the Scali streaming portfolio contains *TCP* (socket over TCP) and *SMP* (over local shared memory).

TCP offers reliable connections, where transfer acknowledges are given when data has entered the internal buffer memory. In standard mode the unsent buffered data is unavailable when a socket is broken or transfers otherwise fail. Failover from streaming devices is therefore currently not implemented.

3.3 Collective Algorithm Selection and Bundling

Optimal collective algorithms are very dependent on network properties [1, 9, 5, 19]. SMC therefore has a flexible design, where users can select algorithms though environment variables. The operations with a common data volume have the possibility to select two algorithms and a threshold, while for simplicity the vectorized operations only can select one algorithm.

To further ease specifying collective operations the user can choose between a set of predefined profiles adapted to low/high latency networks or application dominant communication sensitivity e.g. asynchronicity, latency or bandwidth. For production code or running on clusters with heterogeneous network, the user may perform an educated guess or try all algorithms of the dominant collective operation(s) - that can be identified using SMC's built-in timing facility [17].

4 Performance

This section will present performance of SMC and compare it to other MPI implementations. The performance experiments were run on a cluster of eight Dell 2650 nodes with dual Pentium Xeon's running at 2.4 GHz under RH 8.0 Linux. Each node had 1 GB of memory and embedded Broadcom Gigabit Ethernet adapters using the tg3 driver. A Netgear GS524 switch was used to interconnect the cluster. The software tested was SMC 4.0.0, LAM 6.5.6 and MPICH 1.2.5.

Communication performance is highly dependent on the switch fabric, Ethernet driver and kernel version, and results may defer on other configurations.

4.1 Point-to-Point Performance

Figure 2 and 3 present Gigabit Ethernet performance for SMC using the TCP device (*smc-tcp*), LAM (*lam*), MPICH (*mpich*), direct socket communication using TCP/IP (*socket*) and operating directly on the adapter HW (*eth-raw*). In contrast to *socket* in figure 2, any MPI implementation includes a message envelope i.e. increased data volume and multiple data vectors. Hence, SMC only adds a few μs to direct socket communication, giving latency slightly better than LAM and MPICH. Figure 3 shows that SMC bandwidth generally outperforms LAM and MPICH.

4.2 Application Benchmark Performance

NPB (NAS Parallel Benchmarks) 2.3 [16] constitutes eight CFD (Computational Fluid Dynamics) problems, coded in MPI and standard C and Fortran 77/90. Each benchmark is also associated with an operation count, *op*, which scales with the problem size. Table 1 shows performance of size A of the NPB 2.3 for

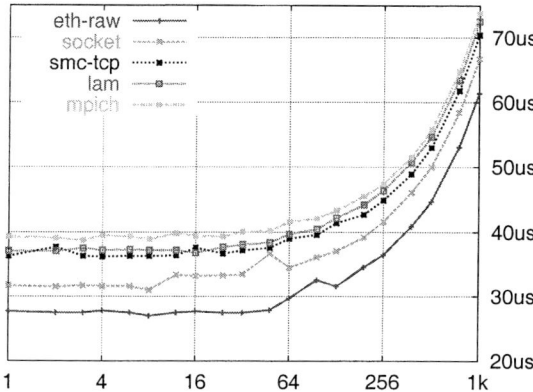

Fig. 2. Ping-pong communication latency in μs

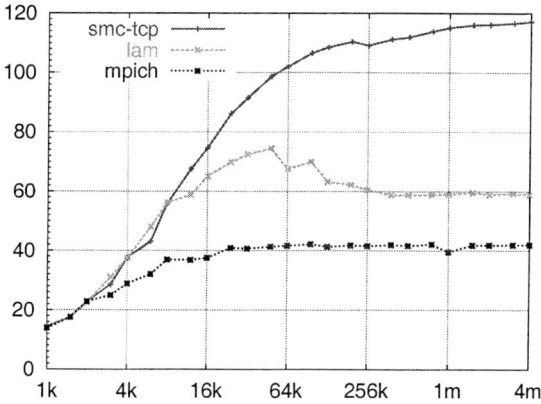

Fig. 3. Ping-pong communication bandwidth in MByte/s

SMC, LAM and MPICH - with 16 processes on 8 nodes. As can be observed, SMC outperforms the others on all tests but IS. IS is, however, very sensitive to *MPI_alltoallv()* implementation, and by altering this (see section 3.3) the SMC performance reached an impressive 111.73 Mop/s for IS.

4.3 Real World Applications

Since users run real applications, should MPI implementations also be compared and judged by real application performance?

Fluent performs flow and heat transfer modeling using CFD. The Fluent benchmark comprises nine different benchmarks carefully selected to explore a large set of possible application space. It is divided into classes of different sizes; each class with a different solver and application. The benchmarks run 25

Table 1. NAS parallel benchmark performance in Mop/s (higher is better)

MPI	BT	CG	EP	FT	IS	LU	MG	SP
SMC	2591.26	1023.46	194.07	2205.36	34.46	5700.27	2214.29	1739.07
MPICH	2123.89	676.37	184.01	1607.88	45.75	-	1487.59	1510.01
LAM	2506.77	758.57	143.62	1793.82	33.60	5255.07	1702.94	1610.00

Table 2. Fluent performance in jobs/day (higher is better)

MPI	S1	S2	S3	M1	M2	M3	L1	L2	L3
SMC	3632	6279	5067	1087	4397	501	731	577	107
MPICH	1513	2637	2831	577	3111	330	601	458	107

iterations, and are denoted by size; Small, Medium, Large and application areas; 1, 2 and 3. Version 6.0.21 of Fluent was used.

The Fluent metric is jobs/day (i.e. the number of successive runs with can be performed in 24 hours). Table 2 shows the results from running the Fluent benchmarks with all 16 CPUs in the cluster. For most tests SMC outperforms MPICH.

MM5) is an open source meteorological application (PSU/NCAR mesoscale model). Since SMC and MPICH are header compatible, only the linking differs between the two application binaries. Running MM5, SMC performance is slightly better than MPICH. Performance for MM5 is reported in Gflop/s for the *T3A* dataset running one time step within the application.

Magma is an application to simulate casting and molding. The application highlights the outstanding performance of the SMC. Magma performance is reported for the *pumpengine* dataset in jobs/day.

LS-DYNA is an application that simulates mechanical structure deformation (simulation of crashing cars or other objects). This application is not very dependent of interconnect performance for small clusters, but very dependent for larger clusters with 32 nodes or more. It responds to the MPI implementation as it runs faster with both LAM and SMC than with MPICH. LS-DYNA performance is reported for the *neoncar* dataset in jobs/day.

StarCD is a CFD application. The communication sensitivity is relatively large, and the speedup when changing from MPICH to SMC is significant. StarCD performance is reported for the *engine* dataset in jobs/day.

5 Conclusions

In the paper SMC design and performance have been detailed. Relying on a standard network connection ABI, SMC has with its flexible and open design enabled easy adaptation to new networks. Compared to other MPI implementations for clusters, SMC have demonstrated superior application performance.

Table 3. Application performance (higher is better)

MPI	MM5	Magma	LS-DYNA	StarCD
SMC	4.2	48.3	25.48	701
MPICH	3.9	28.0	21.90	585
LAM	-	-	25.26	-

References

1. M.Barnett, L.Shuler, R.van de Geijn, S.Gupta, D.G.Payne, J.Watts: Interprocessor collective communication library. Proceedings of Scalable High Performance Computing Conference (1994).
2. N.J.Boden, D.Cohen, R.E.Felderman, A.E.Kulawik, C.E.Seitz. J.N.Seizovic, W-K.Su: Myrinet: A Gigabit-per-Second Local Area Network. IEEE Micro (1996).
3. Direct Access Transport (DAT) Collaborative: uDAPL: User Direct Access Programming Library - version 1.0 (2002).
4. L.P.Huse, K.Omang, H.Bugge, H.W.Ry, A.T.Haugsdal, E.Rustad: ScaMPI - Design and Implementation. LNCS 11734; SCI: Scalable Coherent Interface. Architecture & Software for High-Performance Compute Clusters (1999)
5. L.P.Huse: Collective Communication on Dedicated Clusters of Workstations. Proceedings of 6th PVM/MPI European Users Meeting - EuroPVM/MPI (1999)
6. IEEE Standard for Gigabit Ethernet, ANSI/IEEE Std 802.3z-1998 (1999)
7. IEEE Standard for Scalable Coherent Interface (SCI), IEEE Std 1596-1992 (1993).
8. InfiniBand Trade Association: IB Architecture Specification Release 1.1 (2002)
9. Thilo Kielmann et.al.: MagPIe: MPI's Collective Communication Operations for Clustered Wide Area Systems. Proceedings of ACM SIGPLAN Symposium on Principles and Practice of Parallel Programming (1999).
10. LAM/MPI (Local Area Multicomputer) Parallel Computing Environment - Version 6.5.9 (2003) Available from http://www.lam-mpi.org.
11. John McCalpin: STREAM: Sustainable Memory Bandwidth in High Performance Computers. Online at http://www.cs.virginia.edu/stream.
12. MPI Forum: MPI: A Message-Passing Interface Standard. Version 1.1 (1995)
13. MPICH: Portable MPI Model Implementation. Version 1.2.5 (2003). Available from http://www-unix.mcs.anl.gov/mpi/mpich.
14. The National Center for Supercomputing Applications (NCSA): VMI (Virtual Machine Interface) homepage at http://vmi.ncsa.uiuc.edu.
15. National Energy Research Supercomputer Center (NERSC): MVICH (MPI for Virtual Interface Architecture) homepage at http://www.nersc.go/research/FTG/mvich
16. The Numerical Aerospace Simulation Facility at NASA Ames Research Centre: NAS Parallel Benchmarks. Online at http://www.nas.nasa.gov/NAS/NPB.
17. Scali AS: Scali MPI Connect Users Guide Version 1.0 (2003).
18. F.Seifert, J.Worringen, W.Rehm: Using Arbitrary Memory Regions for SCI Communication. Proceedings of the 4th SCI-Europe (2001).
19. S.Sistare, E.Dorenkamp, N.Nevin, E.Loh: Optimization of MPI Collectives on Clusters of Large-Scale SMP's. Proceedings of Supercomputing 1999.
20. S.S.Vadhiyar, G.E.Fagg, J.Dongarra: Automatically Tuned Collective Communications. Proceedings of Supercomputing 2000.
21. V.Velusamy, C.Rao, J.Neelamegam, W.Chen, S.Verma, A.Skjellum: Programming the InfiniBand Network Architecture. MPI Software Technology WP (2003).

PC/MPI: Design and Implementation of a Portable MPI Checkpointer

Sunil Ahn[1], Junghwan Kim[2], and Sangyong Han[1]

[1] School of Computer Science and Engineering Seoul National University 56-1 Sinlim, Kwanak Seoul, Korea
{siahn,syhan}@pplab.snu.ac.kr
[2] School of Computer Science Kunguk University 322 Danwol-Dong, Chungju-Si ChungCheongBuk-Do, Korea
jhkim@kku.ac.kr

Abstract. Most MPI checkpointers are substantially or even totally dependent on a specific MPI implementation or platform, so they may not be portable. In this paper we present design and implementation issues as well as solutions to enhance portability of an MPI checkpointer. We actually developed PC/MPI (Portable Checkpointer for MPI) to which the presented solutions are applied, and verified that it is applicable to various MPI implementations and platforms.

1 Introduction

Large-scale parallel processing computers might have short MTTF (mean time to failure) because they are usually composed of many autonomous hardware components. Most parallel applications, which are executed in these parallel computers, require many computational resources and are long-running. Hence, fault-tolerance has significant importance in not only distributed computing but also parallel computing.

MPI (message passing interface) states that if any error occurs, the MPI application should abort immediately by default [1]. Therefore, if one process fails, all of the remaining processes participated in that computation would be aborted in many implementations of MPI [2,3].

Checkpointing and rollback is a useful technique to provide fault-tolerance. Fault-tolerance is achieved by periodically using stable storage to save the processes' states during failure-free execution. Upon a failure, failed processes are restarted from one of their saved states, thereby reducing the amount of lost computation. Many previous researches [4–8] have been undertaken to provide checkpointing capability for MPI applications. But they are substantially or even totally dependent on a specific MPI implementation or platform, so they may not be portable. Portability of the MPI checkpointer is important because it can give users more freedom to select platforms or MPI implementations. And it becomes more important where heterogeneous platforms are assumed as in GRID [9].

In this paper we present design and implementation issues on an MPI checkpointer which should be addressed to make it portable for various underlying platforms and MPI implementations. And we present PC/MPI, a portable MPI checkpointer, to which the presented solutions are applied, and introduce our experiences with it.

The rest of the paper is organized as follows: The overview on related researches is given in Section 2. The design issues and implementation issues for portability are presented in Section 3. The architecture, programming model, and implementation of PC/MPI are discussed in Section 4. And finally we conclude with the future work in Section 5.

2 Related Researches

Cocheck [4] is one of the earliest researches towards incorporating a fault tolerance capability in MPI. It extends an SPC (single process checkpointer) called Condor [10] to checkpoint MPI processes' images and all the messages in transit. Cocheck aimed to be layered on top of MPI to achieve portability, but actually it is integrated into an MPI implementation called tuMPI because calling MPI_Init subroutine several times can not be handled properly over MPI.

CLIP [5] is a checkpointing tool for the Intel Paragon. It uses user-defined checkpointing rather than system-level checkpointing, because the latter may not guarantee correct global consistency [11] and may degrade the performance of the Paragon. MPICH-V [6], Egida [7], and MPI/FT [8] provide a checkpointing capability for MPI and in addition they log every message. By utilizing the message logs, a failed MPI process can restart without interrupting other correctly working processes. But they have high overhead in managing the logs. All of these MPI checkpointers [4–8] are substantially or even totally dependent on a specific MPI implementation or platform, so they may not be portable.

3 Design and Implementation Issues for Portability

To enhance portability of MPI checkpointer, we considered following issues. First, checkpointing a running process is platform dependent. Second, checkpointing in-transit messages is MPI implementation dependent. Third, reinitializing the network connections is MPI implementation dependent too. And finally, checkpointing MPI internal states also depends on an MPI implementation. We will describe these issues in detail in each sub-section.

3.1 Process Checkpointing

Because checkpointing a running process is inherently machine dependent and difficult to implement, it may be more desirable to utilize existing SPCs such as [10, 12, 13]. Since there is no standard interface to the existing SPCs, an MPI checkpointer should be integrated with a specific SPC partially or entirely.

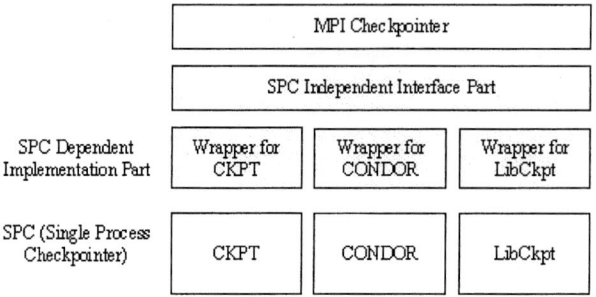

Fig. 1. Conceptual structure of the SPC abstraction layer.

We considered two methods to enhance portability. First, it is considered to use a portable SPC such as LibCkpt [12], which is applicable in most Unix platforms. Second, we designed an abstraction layer over the existing SPCs. Figure 1 depicts the conceptual structure of the SPC abstraction layer. The SPC abstraction layer is divided into the SPC dependent implementation part and the SPC independent interface part. If an MPI checkpointer needs other SPC, only SPC dependent implementation part needs to be modified, so this can minimize dependency on a specific SPC or platform.

We actually implemented the SPC dependent implementation part for CKPT [13], and this required to insert only less than 20 source lines and a little effort to understand how to use CKPT. So we expect that adopting other SPCs may not require too much efforts.

3.2 Message Checkpointing

To checkpoint an MPI application, it is necessary to save messages, which have been sent in one MPI process but not received in other MPI process. Because MPI implementations may use diverse underlying mechanism to send a message and have different message formats, message checkpointing depends on a specific MPI implementation.

To remove such dependency, we avoid message checkpointing under the assumption that there are no in-transit messages when checkpointing occurs. If system-level checkpointing is used, message checkpointing is not avoidable because it is possible that there are messages in transit. But if user-defined checkpointing is used, a programmer can select proper points where no in-transit messages are. Figure 2 shows some examples of user-defined checkpointing. The example (1) and (2) in Figure 2 place the matching MPI_Send and MPI_Recv subroutine calls in the group before the checkpoint or after the checkpoint. In this case, it is guaranteed that there are no in-transit messages when the MPI_Ckpt subroutine is called. Conversely, there may be in-transit messages in case of (3), because the MPI_Send is placed before the checkpoint and the match MPI_Recv is placed after the checkpoint. The example (4) causes inconsistency problem of checkpointing or deadlock problem.

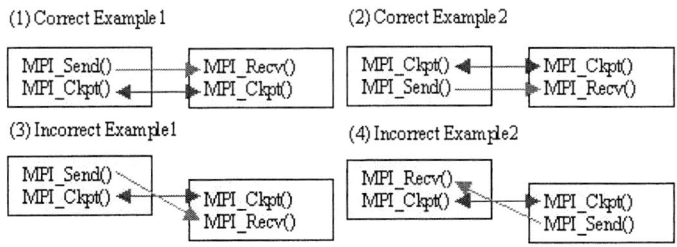

Fig. 2. User-defined checkpointing examples.

Such user-defined checkpointing mechanism may place a little burden on programmers compared to system-level checkpointing where source codes need not be modified. But the burden was very little according to our experience. After implementing out prototype system, we tested it with the NAS parallel benchmark suites [14], which have been known as very close to real applications. Even though we did not understand the benchmark codes, we could find proper checkpoint locations easily at the end of coarse-grained iterations, or just before of after a natural communication phase of the programs.

3.3 Network Connection Re-initialization

If an MPI application should be restarted in voluntary nodes, it is useless to checkpoint network connections. That is because IP addresses and port numbers may change after restarting. Hence, it is necessary to reinitialize the network connections instead of checkpointing. But reinitializing the network connections is not defined in the MPI standard, and most MPI implementations [2,3] do not support this functionality. So, MPI checkpointers such as [4-8] are integrated into a specific MPI implementation, so that they support this functionality.

To solve such a dependency problem, we let the restarted process call the MPI_Init subroutine to reinitialize the network connections before it calls an SPC subroutine to restart the failed process from the checkpoint. Because this method only depends on the MPI_Init subroutine, it improves portability. But if network connections are created dynamically or the order that network connections to the other MPI processes are created is not fixed, this method may not guarantee correct network connections. So, for portability we place a slight limitation to MPI implementations. That is the order, which network connections are created to the other MPI processes, should be always uniform.

According to MPI implementations, the source code needs to be modified to satisfy such a limitation. But the amount of modification needed is very slight compared to inserting functionality of reinitializing network connections. We tested this method with LAM [2] and MPICH/P4 [3], which are the most popular MPI implementations currently, and actually they did not require any modification on their implementations. LAM keeps our limitation so that it requires no modification. But MPICH/P4 does not keep the limitation because it creates connections dynamically. Nevertheless, we could easily let MPICH/P4 satisfy our limitation by adding a wrapper function of the MPI_Init subroutine. This wrapper function sends messages properly to other MPI processes in order to create the network connections in a fixed order.

The limitation, which we pose, may degrade the performance a little when all network connections are not necessary (e.g. master/slave model), but it is very trivial if it comes to an MPI application, which is long-running so that it requires checkpointing functionality.

3.4 MPI Internal State Checkpointing

MPI internal state is usually maintained inside the MPI process image, so that it can be checkpointed by an SPC. In a few MPI implementations, they include a process number as an MPI internal state. Because a process number may differ after the restart, this may cause incorrect checkpointing and recovery.

Such case does not come under MPICH/P4 and the c2c mode of LAM, which is the default mode of network connection. But in lamd mode of LAM, which is not the default, process number inconsistency after the restart causes incorrect network connection. Nevertheless, this problem could be handled easily by just calling a "kattach" subroutine after restarting, which is an internal subroutine in the LAM implementation. A "kattach" subroutine plays a part in informing a process number to the lamd daemon process.

In short, the major MPI implementations do not need to be modified to checkpoint the MPI internal state. So, just providing the abstraction layer that is similar to the one used in the process checkpointing may be sufficient to checkpoint the MPI internal states for a portable MPI checkpointer. In most cases the implementation part of the abstraction layer may be empty unless there are unusual MPI internal states such as a process number.

4 Architecture, Programming Model, and Implementation of PC/MPI

PC/MPI is an MPI checkpointer that the presented solutions in Section 3 are applied. The overall structure of PC/MPI is depicted in Figure 3. PC/MPI is constructed on top of the MPI standard to avoid dependency on a specific MPI implementation. However PC/MPI depends on an SPC. To minimize platform dependency, we use an SPC abstraction layer that is described in Section 3.1. When we need to change an SPC, it is necessary to modify only the implementation part of the SPC abstraction layer instead of the whole PC/MPI.

PC/MPI uses a user-defined checkpointing technique, which is similar to the one used in CLIP [5]. A user may place one or more MPI_Ckpt subroutine calls in the code specifying when checkpoints can occur. Calls to the MPI_Ckpt subroutine should be made in places where synchronization for all MPI processes is possible, and no in-transit messages remain. The MPI_Ckpt subroutine is

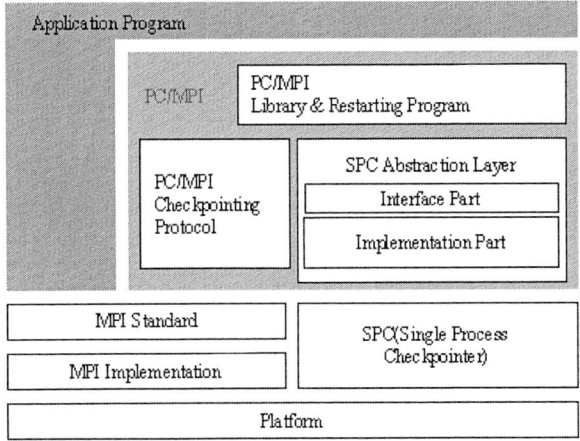

Fig. 3. Overall structure of PC/MPI.

provided as a PC/MPI library. So, a user should link the PC/MPI library with his or her MPI program to use PC/MPI.

When the MPI_Ckpt subroutine is called, each MPI process checkpoints its process image to a checkpoint file. At some later stage if an error occurs, the MPI program can be restarted from the checkpoint files just after the place where the MPI_Ckpt subroutine is called. PC/MPI does not always checkpoint whenever the MPI_Ckpt subroutine is called. The minimum time-interval between the MPI_Ckpt subroutine calls can be set to avoid too frequent checkpointing.

A globally consistent checkpoint means a state, in which a message sent after the checkpoint is not received before the checkpoint [11]. Because PC/MPI assumes no in-transit messages when it calls the MPI_Ckpt subroutine, a message sent after the checkpoint can not be received before the checkpoint. Thus a globally consistent checkpoint can be guaranteed in PC/MPI.

The current PC/MPI implementation is based on the Linux operating system, and uses CKPT [13], an SPC. Linux was chosen because it is the most prevalent operating system for high performance computing, and CKPT was selected because it is freely available to the public and worked stable on the Linux operating system. Currently PC/MPI works stable on MPICH/P4 and LAM, which are the most popular MPI implementations. We expect that PC/MPI can be used for various underlying platforms, because it does not have direct dependency on the Linux platform.

5 Conclusion and Future Work

In this paper we presented design and implementation issues as well as solutions to enhance portability of an MPI checkpointer. Portability is achieved from user-defined checkpointing, wrapping an SPC, and placing a slight limitation on an MPI implementation. We actually developed PC/MPI to which the presented solutions are applied, and verified that it is applicable to various MPI implementations and platforms.

Because PC/MPI supports the synchronous checkpointing mechanism, it may be awkward to the Master/Slave programming model. But PC/MPI supports the Master/Slave model with other checkpointing protocol, which is not explained in this paper on account of space considerations. Future research will be going in several directions. Integrating with existing batch job schedulers, and an automatic error detection and recovery technique should be researched further. And reducing checkpointing time and file size by adapting other optimized SPCs is one of the remains.

References

1. MPI Forum. Mpi: A message-passing interface standard. *International Journal of Supercomputer Applications*, 8(3):165–414, 1994.
2. G. Burns, R. Daoud, and J. Vaigl. Lam: An open cluster environment for mpi. In *Proceedings of Supercomp. Symp.*, 1994.
3. W. Gropp, E. Lusk, N. Doss, and A. Skjellum. Mpich: A high-performance, portable implementation of the mpi message passing interface standard. *Parallel computing*, 22(6):789–828, 1996.
4. G. Stellner. Cocheck: Checkpointing and process migration for mpi. In *Proceedings of the International Parallel Processing Symposium*, 1996.
5. Y. Chen, J.S. Plank, and K. Li. Clip: A checkpointing tool for message-passing parallel programs. In *Proceedings of the ACM/IEEE conference on Supercomputing*, 1997.
6. G. Bosilca, A. Bouteiller, F. Cappelllo, S. Djilali, G. Fedak, C. Germain, T. Herault, P. Lemarinier, O. Lodygensky, F. Magniette, and V. Neri. Mpich-v: Toward a scalable fault tolerant mpi for volatile nodes. In *Proceedings of SC2002*, 2002.
7. S.L. Alvisi and M. Harrick. Egida: An extensible toolkit for low-overhead fault-tolerance. In *Symposium on Fault-Tolerant Computing*, 1999.
8. R. Batchu, Y.S. Dandass, A. Skjellum, and M. Beddhu. Mpi/ft: Architecture and taxonomies for fault-tolerant message-passing middleware for performance-portable parallel computing. In *1st International Symposium on Cluster Computing and the Grid*, 2001.
9. I. Foster and C. Kesselman. *The Grid: Blueprint for a New Computing Infrastructure*. Morgan Kaufmann, 1999.
10. T. Tannenbaum and M. Litzkow. Checkpointing and migration of unix processes in the condor distributed system. *D. Dobbs Journal*, pages 40–48, 1995.
11. K.M. Chandy and L. Lamport. Distributed snapshots: Determining global states of distributed system. *ACM Trans. On Computer Systems*, 3(1):63–75, 1985.
12. RJ.S. Plank, M. Beck, G. Kingsley, and K. Li. Libckpt: Transparent checkpointing under unix. In *Usenix Winter 1995 Technical Conference*, 1995.
13. V.C. Zandy, B.P. Miller, and M. Livny. Process hijacking. In *Eighth IEEE International Symposium on High Performance Distributed Computing*, 1999.
14. D. Baile, T. Harris, W. Saphir, R. Wijngaart, and A. Wooand M. Yarrow. The nas parallel benchmarks 2.0. Technical report, NSA-95-020 Ames Research Center, 1995.

Improving Generic Non-contiguous File Access for MPI-IO

Joachim Worringen, Jesper Larsson Träff, and Hubert Ritzdorf

C&C Research Laboratories, NEC Europe Ltd.
Rathausallee 10, D-53757 Sankt Augustin, Germany
{worringen,traff,ritzdorf}@ccrl-nece.de
http://www.ccrl-nece.de

Abstract. We present a fundamental improvement of the generic techniques for non-contiguous file access in MPI-IO. The improvement consists in the replacement of the conventional data management algorithms based on a representation of the non-contiguous fileview as a list of ⟨offset, length⟩ tuples. The improvement is termed *listless i/o* as it instead makes use of space- and time-efficient datatype handling functionality that is completely free of lists for processing non-contiguous data in the file or in memory. *Listless i/o* has been implemented for both independent and collective file accesses and improves access performance by increasing the data throughput between user buffers and file buffers. Additionally, it reduces the memory footprint of the process performing non-contiguous I/O. In this paper we give results for a synthetic benchmark on a PC cluster using different file systems. We demonstrate improvements in I/O bandwidth that exceed a factor of 10.

1 Introduction

For high-performance parallel file access, MPI-IO is the preferred interface for MPI applications or libraries as it provides a portable syntax and efficient semantics for I/O purposes [4]. An important part of the semantics is the concept of a *fileview* which makes it possible for different application processes to access different parts of a file even though they all call the same MPI-IO functions with the same parameters. The access granularity can be set to any MPI datatype. This is useful for partitioning data from a file into the memory of a process (and vice versa). It is achieved by employing a filter between the process and the file which makes only specified parts of the file visible to the process. The filter is also described by an MPI datatype. The default fileview of a file gives a contiguous view of the complete file with single-byte access granularity. However, using a fileview based on a non-contiguous datatype is very common, and results in non-contiguous file accesses which require different handling than accesses to a single contiguous block of data in a file.

MPI-IO is usually implemented as a run-time library on top of an actual file system. Many file systems, however, only support contiguous file access as defined by the POSIX interface [6]. Only a few file systems provide for non-contiguous access. Even in such cases, they use a different description for the access than MPI datatypes. Usually, lists (or arrays) of ⟨offset, length⟩ tuples are used. In both cases, the MPI-IO runtime library needs to transform the file access of the application, filtered through the fileview, into calls to the file system. The independent access of a file with a non-contiguous fileview is performed via datasieving, while collective accesses of such files use two-phase I/O. Both techniques are also used in ROMIO [8, 9, 11], a freely available open-source MPI-IO runtime library [10].

ROMIO can be used with many MPI implementations and is the starting point for the MPI-IO sections of NEC's MPI implementations MPI/SX (for the SX-series of parallel vector computers) and MPI/PC-32 (for Myrinet-coupled PC clusters) [3]. In Section 2 we briefly describe how ROMIO performs the aforementioned transformation in a generic way for file systems which support only contiguous file access. Our work on *listless i/o*, a new technique that avoids any use of lists of ⟨offset, length⟩ tuples, is described in Section 3. Section 4 compares the performance of the conventional solution (as employed in ROMIO) and *listless i/o* on a PC cluster platform. Related work is discussed in Section 5. A more detailed description of our work, together with performance results on SX-series vector computers can be found in [13].

The following definitions will be helpful for the remainder of the paper: A *filetype* is an MPI datatype used to set up the fileview of a file. A *memtype* is an MPI datatype used to describe the source or destination buffer of an MPI-IO operation. A *non-contiguous file* is a file that is accessed through a non-contiguous filetype. Finally, an *ol-list* is a list (possibly in an array) of ⟨offset, length⟩ tuples.

2 Conventional Techniques for Non-contiguous File Access

MPI-IO defines *independent* and *collective* file access routines. Independent routines can be executed by each process without coordination with other processes. Collective file access requires that all processes which have opened the file perform the same call before it can complete at any process. This allows for optimizations inside of MPI-IO to create more efficient types of file accesses.

2.1 Flat Representation of MPI Datatypes

The straightforward representation of an MPI datatype is an *ol-list*, with each tuple describing a contiguous block of data. This is used by ROMIO and will be referred to as *list-based i/o*. This approach has *significant inherent drawbacks*: high memory consumption, long traversal time and reduced bandwidth for copy operations. Each time a new non-contiguous fileview is set up for a file, ROMIO creates the *ol-list* for the associated datatype. If a non-contiguous memtype is used, another *ol-list* is created for this datatype.

2.2 Independent List-Based File Access

A process accessing a non-contiguous file independently uses the *ol-lists* to find the offset in the file of the first byte. Although the fileview is a single MPI datatype, the file can be accessed with the granularity of the *elementary type (etype)*. An etype is another MPI datatype on which the fileview is built. Thus the file can be accessed at offsets located inside a fileview[1].

Once the offsets are determined, the specified part of the file is read block-wise into a file buffer. For each block, data between file buffer and user buffer are exchanged, using the *ol-lists* for filetype and, possibly, memtype. For write accesses, the file buffer is written back for each block.

2.3 Collective List-Based File Access

Collective access of P processes is performed via a generalized version of the extended two-phase method described in [10]. The part of the file accessed by any of the P processes is partitioned among a number of $P_{io} \le P$ io-processes. Each io-process p_{io}, $0 \le p_{io} < P_{io}$ performs I/O operations for itself and all other $P_{acc}(p_{io})$ access-processes that need to access data from its part of the file.

For this, p_{io} needs to know the access pattern of every $P_{acc}(p_{io})$ as determined by its fileview. However, each process can have (and usually has) its own fileview different from the fileviews of all other processes. In ROMIO, this information is also exchanged as an *ol-list*. Based on its fileview, each access-process creates a specific *ol-list* for each of the io-processes. All these *ol-lists* need to be exchanged between the access- and io-process. Obviously, these lists can become very large. The size of each list scales linearly with N_{blocks} (the number of contiguous blocks that makes up the non-contiguous datatype) and the extent of the access that the remote process performs on behalf of the local process. In the worst case it can actually exceed the size of the data accessed. The io-processes read their part of the file block-wise into a file buffer. For each block, an indexed MPI datatype is created for each process based on the list of tuples received. This datatype describes the distribution of the data in the buffer that this access-process wants to access. For a read access, the io-process then sends a message to the access-process using this datatype. For a write access, the io-process receives the data to be written from the access-process into the file buffer using this datatype. At the end of each iteration, all datatypes are freed again. In case of a write access, the file buffer is written back to the file.

2.4 Summary of Overheads

The overheads for list-based, non-contiguous file access can be summarized as:

- Creation and exchange of *ol-lists* for file and user buffer datatypes takes $O(N_{blocks})$ time.

---
[1] This is different from packing or unpacking with MPI_Pack and MPI_Unpack which only handle entire datatypes.

- Memory requirements are significant, amounting to $N_{\text{blocks}} \cdot (\text{sizeof}(\texttt{MPI\_Offset}) + \text{sizeof}(\texttt{MPI\_Aint}))$ bytes.
- Navigating within the file (like positioning the file pointer) requires list traversal of on average $N_{\text{blocks}}/2$ list elements per access.
- Copying a contiguous block of data of a non-contiguous datatype in addition requires to read the corresponding ⟨offset, length⟩ tuple before the copy operation.

3 Improving Non-contiguous File Access

To avoid the time- and memory-consuming usage of *ol-lists*, a different way to handle non-contiguous MPI datatypes is required. In the following we describe our new approach called *listless i/o* which does not use any *ol-lists*, and how it was integrated into the existing ROMIO-based MPI-IO section of NEC's MPI library.

3.1 Flattening on the Fly

Träff et. al. [12] describe a new technique named *flattening-on-the-fly* to pack and unpack non-contiguous data described by an MPI datatype in a more efficient way than the generic, recursive algorithm used in e.g. MPICH. The technique radically reduces the number of recursive function calls, and provides for more structured memory accesses. The method was originally developed for vector architectures with gather-scatter hardware support, but has been extended to be efficient on scalar architectures, too. For the purposes of MPI-IO (as well as all other MPI functions requiring datatype support), the ADI provides functions for packing and unpacking data arbitrarily from/to non-contiguous buffers.

3.2 Integration into ROMIO

The first step is to replace the list-based packing and unpacking functionality in ROMIO with the efficient pack and unpack functions mentioned above. However, there are certain differences to the packing and unpacking performed by MPI when sending messages of non-contiguous data.

Access granularity: When sending messages of non-contiguous data, the access granularity is the datatype. For accessing a file, the access granularity is the *etype*. Thus, file accesses may start or end *within* a datatype. This requires additional means to navigate within a datatype.

Buffer limits: When packing or unpacking non-contiguous data for sending and receiving messages, it is always the "transport buffer" holding the packed data which is limited in size. The buffer which holds the non-contiguous data is provided by the application, and is therefore sufficient for the complete non-contiguous user data. This is not true when accessing a file with a non-contiguous fileview using the two-phase method: the temporary buffer which is read from the file can hold only a fraction of the data to be accessed, but has to do so using the non-contiguous representation of the data as it was read from the file.

Datatype Navigation. The possible positioning of the file pointer inside the filetype requires that we can determine the extent of a data buffer of which a given number of bytes of typed data has been written or read. Conversely, we need to be able to determine how many bytes of data are contained in an arbitrary typed buffer. This functionality is provided by two new internal ADI functions:

The function `MPIR_Get_type_dataextent(dtype, skip, length)` returns the extent for the case that `length` bytes of data are "unpacked" according to the datatype `dtype` skipping over the first `skip` bytes.

The function `MPIR_Get_size_for_extent(dtype, skip, extent)` returns the amount of data that can be "contained" in a buffer of size `extent` bytes with datatype `dtype` after skipping the first `skip` in the datatype.

Using these functions, we can easily perform the needed calculations to toggle between absolute and filetype-relative positioning in the file, and determine the amount or extent of data that a buffer currently contains or is able to hold.

Buffer Limit Handling. An example for the aforementioned problem of lack of control of buffer limits with two-phased I/O techniques is the case when writing contiguous data into a file with a non-contiguous fileview: a fraction of the file is read into a temporary buffer, and data from memory is *unpacked* into it. Normally, the amount of data to unpack is determined by the size of the source buffer to unpack *from*. Here, it is the other way round: the size of the destination buffer to unpack *into* is the limiting factor. To be able to use the unpack function here, we first need to determine the amount of (unpacked) data in the contiguous source buffer that the destination buffer can hold. This is done by `MPIR_Get_size_for_extent`.

Independent and Collective Access. We continue using the basic techniques of *data sieving* and *two-phased i/o* for non-contiguous file access in our implementation [9]. However, most of the related code was replaced with the *listless i/o* algorithms, eliminating all use of *ol-lists* in the generic I/O functions. Accordingly, *ol-lists* are no longer created[2].

A notable improvement of the two-phase i/o technique is the handling of the fileviews of remote processes. In the list-based approach of ROMIO, *ol-lists* have to be exchanged for each collective access. In our approach (which we named *fileview caching*), a very compact representation of each process' filetype and its displacement are exchanged *once* when the fileview is set up. For all collective accesses, each io-process can perform the necessary file accesses with an access-process fileview using this cached information without the need to exchange any information besides the actual file data.

Similarly, all other overheads listed in Section 2.4 have been eliminated by *listless i/o*: no *ol-lists* have to be created, stored, traversed or exchanged, and

---

[2] Some file systems like NFS and PVFS use their own file access functions for independent accesses and thus still require the list-based representation. In these cases, the *ol-lists* are still created, but not used in the generic collective access functions which are based on *listless i/o*.

the actual data copy operations are performed efficiently using flattening-on-the-fly. Thus, by sticking to the same basic file-access strategies *data-sieving* and *two-phase i/o*, any performance differences that may be observed between the original ROMIO code and our approach are solely due to the improved handling of datatypes.

4 Performance Evaluation

In this section we present a first evaluation of *listless i/o* by comparing it to the current ROMIO implementation. We designed a customizable, synthetic benchmark, called *noncontig*, which employs a non-contiguous fileview based on a vector datatype. It writes and subsequently reads back data using contiguous or non-contiguous memtype and filetype, and measures the resulting I/O bandwidth. The most important test parameters are the number of elements in the vector datatype and the size of the file to be created. The file access can be performed using independent or collective operations.

The system used for the evaluation is a 6-node IA-32 PC-Cluster with a Myrinet 2000 interconnect. The nodes are 4-CPU Pentium-III Xeon systems with 1GB of RAM, running Linux 2.4. Although this system is not the latest technology, it is well suited to compare the two different approaches. It allows 4 processes to access a local file system concurrently.

Each node has a local disk, and has a disk from the head node mounted via NFS. Additionally, the parallel file system PVFS [1] (version 1.5.6) was set up for this cluster with each node being an I/O server from its local disk[3]. The parallel environment is SCore [5] together with NEC's MPI/PC-32, a full implementation of MPI-2 for this platform. MPI/PC-32 can be configured to use either ROMIO or *listless i/o* for MPI-IO.

For a first evaluation of our approach, we have performed tests using *noncontig* with the three available file systems, namely any local *unix file system* (UFS) for the local disk, NFS for the mounted server disk and PVFS for the parallel file system across all nodes. The number of processes was chosen from $P = \{1, 4, 16\}$ as applicable. With UFS, up to $P = 4$ processes on a single node could be used. The tests for NFS and PVFS where run across multiple nodes with the processes evenly distributed across four nodes.

On UFS, we ran with two fixed filesizes $S_{\text{small}} = 20MB$ and $S_{\text{big}} = 2GB$. The repetition count for the vector is set to maintain the chosen filesize. Tests for S_{small} will be influenced by the cache of the file system (leading to a potentially higher bandwidth), while tests for S_{big} will mostly nullify any cache effects on this test platform. It makes sense to also perform tests including file system caching effects as we strive to *compare* the two different techniques. For the file systems NFS and PVFS, which access remote storage, there were no significant differences for the test with S_{small} or S_{big}. Therefore, we only show the results for S_{small}. The datatype used as memtype and as filetype is a vector of MPI_INT with a block length of 1, a block count of $1024/P$ and a stride of P.

---

[3] PVFS uses fast ethernet for data transfers between nodes.

Table 1. Bandwidth per process (MB/s) for UFS file system. Filesize are 20MB (upper half) and 2GB (lower half).

	list-based i/o						listless i/o						contig	
	nc-nc		nc-c		c-nc		nc-nc		nc-c		c-nc		c-c	
P r/w	ind	coll	ind	coll	ind	coll	ind	coll	ind	coll	ind	coll	ind	coll
1 r	4.74	3.20	11.93	11.94	5.76	3.77	8.82	9.59	25.87	25.79	12.4	15.29	84.1	81.5
w	3.75	2.74	9.22	10.25	5.58	3.08	6.06	6.05	15.27	16.66	9.62	8.73	85.0	55.7
4 r	3.12	0.63	7.33	7.38	3.97	0.77	3.15	3.48	7.09	6.79	4.4	6.60	13.5	25.1
w	0.64	0.56	6.44	6.04	1.02	0.65	1.09	2.78	5.89	4.68	1.37	3.02	22.2	20.1
1 r	0.86	**0.45**	8.00	7.87	1.47	0.79	5.04	**4.98**	10.13	10.07	5.8	5.85	14.1	16.3
w	0.87	0.45	7.81	7.78	1.45	0.79	4.45	4.49	9.32	9.36	5.26	5.25	12.2	10.9
4 r	0.74	0.33	1.87	1.89	1.59	0.49	2.22	1.59	2.54	2.10	2.90	2.06	2.9	2.8
w	0.48	0.36	2.54	2.52	0.66	0.39	0.77	2.09	2.77	2.82	0.95	2.28	2.8	2.7

The results of our tests are shown in Tables 1, 2 and 3. The values are the average bandwidth per process in MB/s. The abbreviations characterize the type of file access: independent *(ind)* or collective access *(coll)*; accesses with non-contiguous memtype and non-contiguous filetype *(nc-nc)*, non-contiguous memtype and contiguous filetype *(nc-c)*, or contiguous memtype and a non-contiguous filetype *(c-nc)*. Read and write accesses are indicated by the letters r and w, respectively. For comparison, the bandwidth for fully contiguous accesses (which is the same for both *list-based i/o* and *listless i/o*) is also given *(c-c)*.

The performance gain of *listless i/o* for the UFS file system over *list-based i/o* can exceed a factor of 10 (indicated in bold). Typically, the factor is between 2 and 5. As expected, the bandwidth increase is especially significant for non-contiguous files. It is also notable that for *list-based i/o* the performance for collective accesses is *lower* than for independent accesses. This is due to the exchange of the *ol-lists*. Interestingly, this also happens with just one process. In contrast, with *listless i/o* collective accesses are faster than independent accesses, and about the same for the single-process case. Generally, the performance advantage of *listless i/o* will increase for filetypes and memtypes with a larger value of N_{blocks} for independent accesses. For collective accesses, it is the number of blocks per file block (the density) which increases the overhead for *list-based i/o*.

For NFS, Table 2 shows results for collective file accesses only, as the differences in performance for independent file access is not significant. The reason for this is that the bottleneck for independent accesses is the low I/O bandwidth. For collective accesses, we see that for non-contiguous files, the required exchange of *ol-lists* for *list-based i/o* leads to a drop in bandwidth when going from 1 to 4 processes, although the per-process bandwidth for contiguous access remains nearly constant. Using *listless i/o*, the bandwidth even increases for this transition. However, when going from 4 to 16 processes, the available per-process bandwidth is divided by 4 which shows in all bandwidth values for non-contiguous file access, too.

Table 2. Bandwidth per process (MB/s) of non-contiguous file access for NFS file system. Filesize is 20MB.

		list-based i/o			listless i/o			contig
		nc-nc	nc-c	c-nc	nc-nc	nc-c	c-nc	c-c
P	r/w	coll	coll	coll	coll	coll	coll	coll
1	r	1.90	5.53	2.36	2.50	5.78	3.01	6.6
	w	1.09	3.64	1.28	1.17	3.16	1.24	4.6
4	r	0.80	4.87	0.98	4.68	5.71	3.72	8.1
	w	0.65	2.57	0.78	2.25	2.75	2.51	4.2
16	r	0.45	1.20	0.52	1.18	1.28	1.12	1.5
	w	0.30	0.80	0.40	0.46	0.79	0.47	0.9

Table 3. Bandwidth per process (MB/s) of non-contiguous file access for PVFS file system. Filesize is 20MB.

		list-based i/o						listless i/o						contig	
		nc-nc		nc-c		c-nc		nc-nc		nc-c		c-nc		c-c	
P	r/w	ind	coll	ind	coll	ind	coll	ind	coll	ind	coll	ind	coll	ind	coll
1	r	2.80	2.14	6.51	6.51	3.32	2.52	4.23	4.27	8.47	8.58	5.14	5.19	9.3	13.5
	w	>0	>0	>0	>0	>0	>0	0.01	0.01	0.01	0.01	0.01	0.01	9.9	8.6
4	r	1.86	0.76	6.23	6.16	2.03	1.01	2.14	5.08	6.02	5.71	2.29	6.24	12.1	10.9
	w	>0	0.71	>0	0.05	>0	0.81	0.01	3.35	0.11	0.01	0.01	4.45	9.2	9.2
16	r	0.19	0.48	1.92	1.77	0.19	0.58	0.19	0.77	0.70	0.47	0.19	0.74	3.0	2.8
	w	>0	0.35	>0	0.05	>0	0.35	0.01	0.53	0.01	>0	0.01	1.03	2.5	2.3

The results for PVFS in Table 3 show that this file system has problems with non-contiguous file access which can only to a limited degree be compensated by *list-based i/o*. PVFS does not support file-locking which hinders efficient write operations for non-contiguous files. Additionally, the `pvfs_writev()` function used for the *nc-c*-case seems to have a performance problem. Extremely low write bandwidth results from this. An exception are collective write operations with non-contiguous files for $P > 1$ which do not require file locking and thus can be performed via *listless i/o*.

For that reason, it makes sense to look more at the results for read-accesses. For $P = 1$, we see that *listless i/o* is between 50 to 100% faster than *list-based i/o* due to its more efficient handling of non-contiguous datatypes. For collective accesses of non-contiguous files, this advantage steps up with increasing values of P. For independent accesses *list-based i/o* is sometimes faster – this effect requires further investigation as we currently see no reason why *listless i/o* should by slower than *list-based i/o*.

5 Related Work

Most work that deals with non-contiguous file access in MPI-IO covers collective buffering or the two-phase method [8, 10, 11]. Our work is complementary: it

Table 4. Accumulated bandwidth (MB/s) of non-contiguous independent file access for the PVFS file system. Filesize is 2MB.

	list-based i/o			listless i/o			listio			
P r/w	nc-nc	nc-c	c-nc	nc-nc	nc-c	c-nc	nc-nc	nc-c	c-nc	c-c
16 r	2.89	8.45	2.99	2.74	8.22	3.14	0.05	0.93	0.05	53.9
w	0.03	0.03	0.03	0.07	0.08	0.07	0.14	0.77	0.51	63.1

deals with determining the relations of and performing the transfers between data placed in memory and in the file. We could not find any previous work on this specific, but obviously important part of the implementation of MPI-IO. It has to be assumed that all existing approaches use a list-based technique.

Only [2] describes the benefits of using a file system which provides an interface for non-contiguous I/O named *listio*. The authors achieve impressive performance improvements compared with *list-based i/o* for the evaluated workloads. Their work is still based on *ol-lists* and is limited to independent accesses. For write accesses, a comparison with the data sieving approach was not possible because the file system used (PVFS [1]) does not support file locking. We performed another experiment as in Section 4 to compare *listio* with plain *list-based i/o* and with *listless i/o*.

The results in Table 4 show that for the simple test case, *listio* has a significantly higher write-bandwidth than *list-based i/o* and *listless i/o*. However, it is still on a very low absolute level of about 1% of the bandwidth for contiguous write accesses. For read accesses, both *list-based i/o* and *listless i/o* operate on the same level of performance as for independent accesses with 16 processes. The performance bottleneck in this case is the raw I/O bandwidth. The read-bandwidth of *listio* remains on an extremely low level.

6 Summary and Outlook

We have presented a new technique for accessing non-contiguous data on generic, POSIX-compliant file systems through MPI-IO. It avoids the large overheads associated with the traditional technique based on a list-style representation of the disjoint blocks to be accessed and thus achieves significant performance improvements for all typical file systems used in component-of-the-shelf clusters.

It will be interesting to see how *listless i/o* performs on more recent (cluster) systems. As *listless i/o* reduces the load on the CPU, the memory and the interconnect, faster implementations of those system components may reduce the advantage of *listless i/o* relative to *list-based i/o*. On the other hand, faster system components for I/O reduce the amount of time needed for read-/write-operations, which again favors *listless i/o* as these operations are the same for *listless i/o* and *listbased i/o*.

References

1. P. H. Carns, W. B. L. III, R. B. Ross, and R. Thakur. PVFS: A parallel file system for Linux clusters. In *Proceedings of the 4th Annual Linux Showcase and Conference*, pages 317–327, 2000.
2. A. Ching, A. Choudhary, W.-K. Liao, R. Ross, and W. Gropp. Noncontiguous I/O through PVFS. In *International Conference on Cluster Computing*, pages 405–414, 2002.
3. M. Gołebiewski, H. Ritzdorf, J. L. Träff, and F. Zimmermann. The MPI/SX implementation of MPI for NEC's SX-6 and other NEC platforms. *NEC Research & Development*, 44(1):69–74, 2003.
4. W. Gropp, S. Huss-Lederman, A. Lumsdaine, E. Lusk, B. Nitzberg, W. Saphir, and M. Snir. *MPI - The Complete Reference*, volume 2, The MPI Extensions. MIT Press, 1998.
5. Y. Ishikawa, H. Tezuka, A. Hori, S. Sumimoto, T. Takahashi, F. O'Carroll, and H. Harada. RWC PC cluster II and SCore cluster system software – high performance Linux cluster. In *Proceedings of the 5th Annual Linux Expo*, pages 55–62, 1999.
6. D. Lewine. *POSIX Programmer's Guide*. O'Reilly and Associates, Inc., 1991.
7. M. Snir, S. Otto, S. Huss-Lederman, D. Walker, and J. Dongarra. *MPI - The Complete Reference*, volume 1, The MPI Core. MIT Press, second edition, 1998.
8. R. Thakur, W. Gropp, and E. Lusk. A case for using MPI's derived datatypes to improve I/O performance. In *Proceedings of SC98: High Performance Networking and Computing*. ACM/IEEE Press, 1998.
9. R. Thakur, W. Gropp, and E. Lusk. Data sieving and collective I/O in ROMIO. In *Proceedings of the 7th Symposium on the Frontiers of Massively Parallel Computation*, pages 182–189, 1999.
10. R. Thakur, W. Gropp, and E. Lusk. On implementaing MPI-IO portably and with high performance. In *Proceedings of the 6th Workshop on I/O in Parallel and Distributed Systems (IOPADS)*, pages 23–32, 1999.
11. R. Thakur, W. Gropp, and E. Lusk. Optimizing noncontiguous accesses in MPI-IO. *Parallel Computing*, 28:83–105, 2002.
12. J. L. Träff, R. Hempel, H. Ritzdorf, and F. Zimmermann. Flattening on the fly: efficient handling of MPI derived datatypes. In *Recent Advances in Parallel Virtual Machine and Message Passing Interface. 6th European PVM/MPI Users' Group Meeting*, volume 1697 of *Lecture Notes in Computer Science*, pages 109–116, 1999.
13. J. Worringen, J. L. Träff, and H. Ritzdorf. Fast Parallel Non-contiguous IO. Accepted for *Supercomputing*, 2003. http://www.sc-conference.org/sc2003/.

Remote Exception Handling for PVM Processes

Paweł L. Kaczmarek and Henryk Krawczyk

Faculty of Electronics, Telecommunications and Informatics
Gdańsk University of Technology, Poland
{pkacz,hkrawk}@eti.pg.gda.pl

Abstract. The paper presents a model for local and remote exception handling in the PVM library. A running process is augmented with the ability to throw remote exceptions to its master process and to receive exception handling actions. Main exception handling patterns for distributed applications were presented and Remote Exception Handler (REH) is introduced. REH is a dedicated server process that receives all remote exception events and maintains coherent information about the system. It has the ability to control each process in the virtual machine. Its impact on PVM environment is discussed.

1 Introduction

The size of parallel applications grows very fast and inevitably a number of errors occur both in them and in their executing environment. Different techniques were developed to support reliability of applications [Jal94], but achieving high fault tolerance in distributed systems is not an easy task.

Exception handling (eh) is one of fault tolerance techniques that separates normal and exceptional control flow. This causes the program to be more readable and the structure to be clearer. The programmer specifies *guarded regions* together with *handling functions*[PB00]. If an error occurs in a guarded region, the normal execution is terminated and the exceptional code is called. In sequential programming the application of guarded regions and call to handling functions require specific stack operations that are managed by compiler.

The PVM standard library does not support explicit exception handling, however a number of error handling mechanisms were offered. The JPVM [Fer97] and CPPVM [Gor00] projects are related to object oriented programming and support exception handling by using standard functionalities of C++ and Java. Asynchronous communication can be achieved in PVM by pvm_sendsig [Kow94] routine that sends a Unix signal to the specified process. Message handler was included in the PVM3.4 standard [Gei97] as another way of asynchronous communication. The receipt of the specified message causes an asynchronous invocation of a receiving function. The notification mechanism allows informing about specific problems in PVM processes, but explicit receipt of the notification message is required, what could be inconvenient to implement. Error handlers provide a mechanism for local error handling in MPI [Sni96]. The user of MPI specifies functions that are called each time an error occurs.

The Signal mechanism allows achieving asynchronous communication in the Unix system. If a signal is sent to a process, the process performs one of the actions: terminates, ignores the signal or calls a specified handling function.

Most of current research related to exception handling and distributed systems is focused on object oriented environments. The concept of *remote exception* is used in such systems like CORBA [Obj02], RMI or J2EE [Sha02]. A remote exception is thrown when an abnormal situation occurs during communication with remote server or during a call to a remote function. A problem of coordinating exception occurrences arises in transactions and atomic actions, i.e. if an exception occurs in one process it must be known to other processes. The work of Xu, Romanovsky [JX00] presents algorithms for solving this problem and the work of Issarny [Iss01] presents solutions for multiple exception occurrences. The concept of event notification servers was presented by Souza et al. [dSea02]. The idea links the awareness functionality with a monitoring tool.

We choose the PVM library as a representative environment for research in the field of exception handling techniques for parallel applications. PVM offers a number of fault-tolerance mechanisms, but there is no profound distributed exception handling available. We offer a new mechanism that is able to handle remote programming exceptions. The paper is organized as follows: in the next section we present the design of exception throwing and handling for master-slave model. In section 3 we introduce the Remote Exception Handler (REH) concept to handle exceptions in distributed processing. In section 4 we present some experimental results evaluating the suitability of the designed strategies. The last section presents conclusions and remarks about future work.

2 Local and Remote Exception Handling

Below we present a model for local and remote exception handling that is based on the standard PVM library for the C language. Notice that the C language does not support explicit exception handling. In this context an error means any discrepancy between the expected result of an operation and the actual result. We define an exception as a special event in an erroneous situation that causes the change in the control flow of a program. In the proposed solution, errors occurring in PVM programs cause exceptions to be thrown that are handled in two different ways:

- local exception handling - where an exception is handled by the process where it occurs,
- remote exception handling - where an exception is handled by a process different than the process where the exception occurred.

The model allows a user to define specific actions in the case of exception occurrence or to use one of the predefined repair strategies. The model is thought as resumption [PB00] one for both local and remote exception handling. However, termination actions could be done as it is discussed further.

Local exception handling is implemented in the following way. We have implemented an extension of the library allowing to call a specified exception handling

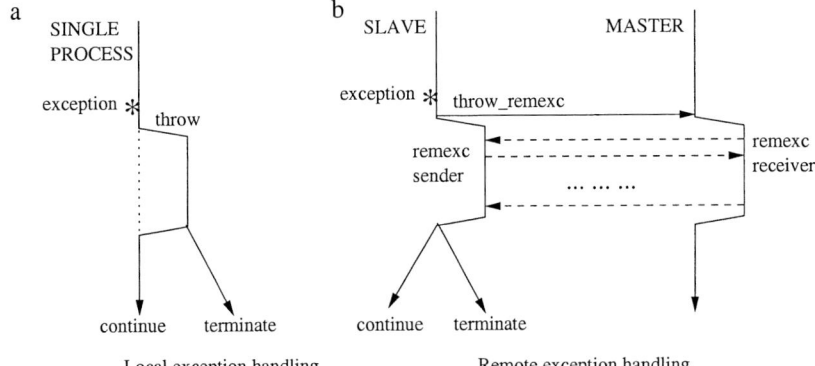

Fig. 1. Local (a) and remote (b) exception throwing in master-slave model

function in the case of errors, called *local_exception_handler* (see Figure 1a). The function call is local and is only linked with local execution. It is possible to establish application specific communication within user-defined functions.

When the handling function is defined, it is called each time a PVM exception occurs. The handling functions could be set, unset or changed, but only one function is active at a time. The call to local exception handler is synchronous and after it the control flow returns to the instruction following the erroneous one. In consequence, if a C++ compiler is used, PVM functions can throw local exceptions with PVM error numbers using the try-catch-throw mechanism. Such solution is dedicated for local exception handling only.

Remote exception throwing and handling is organized in the following way. If an error occurs in one of PVM processes, an exception may be sent to a remote process that is a process collaborating with the previous one. Let us concentrate on the master-slave model, where slaves throw remote exceptions to the master. We assume, that a user defines application specific functions for handling exceptions in throwing and receiving processes. If no functions are defined, processes take a default action (usually termination or restart of the erroneous process).

For instance we propose the pvm_throw_remexc function for throwing remote exceptions and the set_remexc_receiver (set_remexc_sender) function to define which function is called in the master (slave) process if a remote exception arrives as shown in Figure 1b.

If an error occurs in a slave process, the master-slave model works as follows:

- The slave process throws a *remote exception* to the master process using the *pvm_throw_remexc* routine. The exception contains an integer that indicates what kind of error occurred in the sending process.
- The master process receives asynchronously the exception and suspends current execution. Then it calls a user defined *remexc_receiver* function.
- The functions remexc_sender(_receiver) are used to exchange application specific data between the master and the slave to take appropriate repair actions.

- The master returns to the slave further actions that is either continuation or termination of execution.

The pvm_throw_remexc function communicates with the master in two phases. First it sends a signal to notify about its request and to force the master to suspend and then it sends any required data by normal PVM communication.

The master process may take some error correction actions concerning either the whole application or a specified process. Using the presented model the following repair actions could be taken for one process:

- restart the corrupted process,
- restart the corrupted process and send data for second calculations,
- start a new, alternative process or algorithm to perform the task.

Further repair actions could be taken concerning the whole application. However, they might give partial results or cause the final result to differ from the origin. The actions are:

- take results from correct slaves only,
- take initial or default value as the result value,
- perform the work of a collapsed slave in the master process,
- restart the corrupted process, perform a random, negligible modifications to input data and send for second calculation,
- take results from correct slaves and estimate the result from the erroneous slave,
- notify the user of the application.

Let note that some of the methods require programmer attention, though most of them are done automatically. The programmer needs only to define once the correction strategy and it will be applied each time an error occurs. Certainly some actions taken by the master process introduce errors in the final result, which is most visible in calculation-oriented applications. However in this model we are able to hold calculations even in case of exceptions. If the result may slightly differ from the original one (e.g. weather prediction), the partial repair actions may be taken even in case of severe errors. To support the restart and resend facility the library implements a logging mechanism for sent messages.

Let suppose we want to simulate movements of molecules in a limited area. The program consists of (n+1) processes: 1 master that takes the results and n slaves that take each $1/n$ of the whole area. The simulation is done in turns lasting a quantum of time. Suppose further that an error exists either in the source code or in the environment. The application of the strategies pointed out above allows to achieve results even in case of errors as presented in section 4.

In normal PVM programs we could use many different fault tolerance mechanisms: pvm_notify, message handlers or pvm_sendsig. In the proposed model the programmer work is reduced because of the ability to assign one strategy for exception handling and one local exception handling function.

3 Remote Exception Handler Concept

In master-slave applications some exceptions that occurre in slaves are handled by the master. It means that the functionality of the master could be extended with handling functions. In peer-to-peer applications all processes (objects) should have such an extra functionality, what is an impractical solution. Therefore we proposed extra process as *Remote Exception Handler* (REH). The number of REHs is at least one and it can be chosen in accordance to complexity of the control structure of an application. The functionality of REH is either defined by a user or it is taken from the available set of different REH handling patterns.

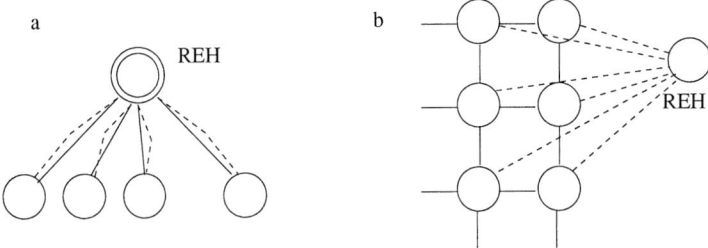

Fig. 2. Remote Exception Handler: double role of master (a), extra REH process (b)

REH needs to be started before any other PVM process is started. It is registered in MessageBox [Gei97] and every process checks for its existence on startup. REH supplies a library of functions for initiating fault-tolerance mechanisms, manipulating data related to exceptions and throwing remote exceptions. A user needs to define functions that perform application specific operations. All exceptions are managed though *Exception Box* mechanism that is maintained by REH and offered as a part of its functionality. The implementation of Exception Box contains information about:

- current state of processes - number, status, restart status, parent process,
- information about exceptions signaled by each processes - the type of an operation, parameters, error number, other involved processes,
- information about exceptions signaled about each process - the type of an operation, parameters, error number, sending process number.

Exception Box is used in master-slave and cooperation exception handling by REH. An example of Exception Box usage is storing information about restarted processes. If a collapsed process is restarted the new process number is stored as a link. Other processes are informed about the restart and they are able to identify the new process number. The implementation of Exception Box is realized by storing information as internal data of REH. REH supports a set of functions (put, get, change, etc.) to access data and to put new information.

REHs implement a handling pattern that allows to develop an application with exception handling mechanisms independently from application logic design. In consequence, functions implemented by REH could be divided into:

- actions - actions force other processes to change their states and processes treat them as asynchronous events,
- answers - answers are given by REH in response to questions send by other processes, this could either be a data or a recommended behavior

The proposed implementation supports actions of sending restarted process number, forcing process termination and forcing data resend to a specified process. The mechanism allows to implement user defined actions and to perform communication between the REH and other processes.

4 Experimental Results

Below we present results from experiments with various local and remote exception handling strategies. We tested two application models: the master-slave model and the peer-to-peer model. Tests were executed in a network of four stations each having a 1,5GHz processor and a 10 Mb network connection and running the Linux operating system. The tests were executed on dedicated machines and were not interfered by other users. In the first set of tests, the master sends in turns data to slaves for calculations, after the calculations the slaves return results to the master. The test simulates a molecule modeling program with 8 slave processes each calculating 100 molecules in a turn. Figures show experimental results for various repair actions discussed in section 2.

The difference between remote exception handling by the master process and by REH is shown in Figure 3. In this test, if an exception occurs, data is send either to the master or to REH and the remote process repeats the whole calculation work. As we can see the REH handling is faster because the REH process is loaded with exceptional work only. In contrast, if the master process handles remote exceptions, it is loaded with regular and exceptional work.

In Figure 4 we present the execution time for remote exception handling done by the master process. If an exception occurs, the master executes a repair operation that lasts a time unit relative to actual calculations - 50% or 100% respectively. The 100% case represents a complete recalculation done by the master.

Figure 5 shows the execution time for three exception handling strategies. If an exception occurs in a slave, the calculations are repeated in one of the ways: (i) locally by the slave, (ii) remotely by the master, (iii) by a restarted slave. The total execution time is comparable for local and remote handling. The slave restart handling is the most expensive way as it involves both the master machine for identification of an exception and the slave machine for process restart.

The second application executes parallel matrix multiplication as presented in [Akl89]. In this model slaves communicate with each other, so the master process has a limited knowledge about the system. The matrix size is set to

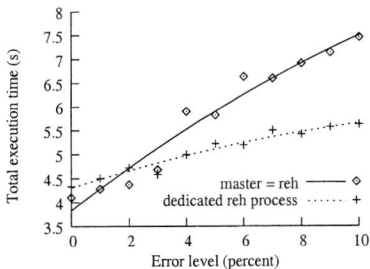
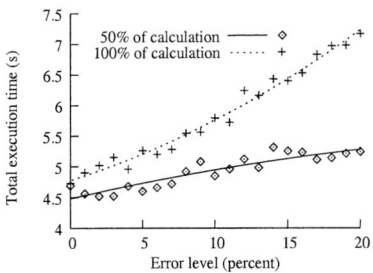

Fig. 3. Remote exception handling by the master and by a dedicated REH

Fig. 4. Remote exception handling with different handling time

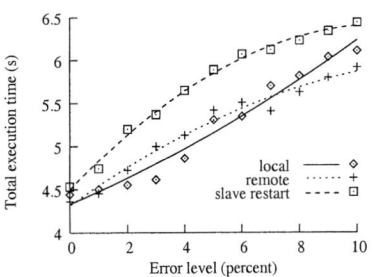
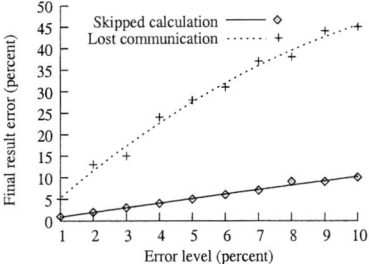

Fig. 5. Local, remote and slave restart handling strategies

Fig. 6. Comparison between different errors for matrix multiplication

8×8 and the input values range from 0 to 1. In this test we assume that the exception handling mechanism allows to retrieve from errors, but the result of the erroneous operation is lost, i.e. if an exception occurs, the value is set to zero. This corresponds to the repair action of taking default value as discussed in section 2. We have analyzed two types of anomalies: exceptions cause calculation to be skipped and exceptions cause communication to be lost. Figure 6 shows error level of the final result if the exception handling model can not restore the complete functionality. The error of losing communication affects the result in a much higher level than losing calculations, because calculation losing concerns one process only in contrast to communication losing.

5 Final Remarks

In the paper we have presented an exception handling model for parallel applications. The model allows to separate the normal and exceptional control flow for the body of an application. Main advantages of the presented solution are:

- it increases reliability of applications,
- it extends standard programming models with mechanisms for remote handling of abnormal situations,
- it separates the normal and exceptional code in the global scope of distributed applications,

- a simple distributed exception handling mechanism can be implemented with negligible programmer attention.

The future work can be concentrated on the two main aspects:

- further research in local and remote exception handling for different communication models,
- the suitable number of REH to cover representative exceptions.

Further we notice the problem of extending PVM library with other fault tolerance mechanisms, in particular *replication* and *transactions* (multitasking, rollback and commit). The PVM REH library could easily be extended by replication as this requires actually of one function prototype and an extended concept of identifier. The function *pvm_replicative_ spawn* spawns a new task with replication mechanism. The newly spawned task is assigned a *multiidentifier* to emphasize its replicative nature. Another very popular mechanism for achieving reliability is transaction, but achieving standard and efficient solutions faces some difficulties. The transactional service can be provided by the set of functions *pvm_begin_trans*, *pvm_ end_trans*, *pvm_rollback_trans*. A complete implementation needs to define *shared data* - the data that is accessed by each process within the transaction. The transaction mechanism requires complete and effective solutions of remote exception problems.

References

[Akl89]   S. G. Akl. *The Design and Analysis of Parallel Algorithms*. Prentice-Hall Int., 1989.
[dSea02] C. R. B. de Souza et al. Using event notification servers to support application awareness. In *6th Int. Conf. Software Eng. and Applications, USA*, 2002.
[Fer97]   A. J. Ferrari. Jpvm: Network parallel computing in java. Technical report, Univ. of Virginia, Charlottesville, 1997.
[Gei97]   A. Geist. *Advanced Tutorial on PVM3.4 New Features and Capabilities*. EuroPVM-MPI, 1997.
[Gor00]   S. Gorzig. Cppvm - parallel programming in c++. Technical report, University of Stuttgart, 2000.
[Iss01]   V. Issarny. Concurrent exception handling. *LNCS - Advances in Exception Handling Technique*, 2001.
[Jal94]   P. Jalote. *Fault Tolerance in Distributed Systems*. Prentice Hall PTR, 1994.
[JX00]   B. Tandell J. Xu, A. Romanovsky. Concurrent exception handling and resolution in distributed object systems. *IEEE Trans. on PDS*, Oct 2000.
[Kow94]   J. Kowalik, editor. *PVM: Parallel Virtual Machine*. MIT Press, 1994.
[Obj02]   Object Management Group. *CORBA: core specification*, 2002.
[PB00]   W.Y.R. Mok P.A. Buhr. Advanced exception handling mechanisms. *IEEE Trans. Software Eng*, Sept. 2000.
[Sha02]   B. Shannon. *J2EE Platform Specification*. Sun Microsystems Inc., 2002.
[Sni96]   M. Snir. *MPI: The Complete Reference*. The MIT Press, 1996.

Evaluation of an Eager Protocol Optimization for MPI

Ron Brightwell and Keith Underwood

Center for Computation, Computers, Information, and Mathematics
Sandia National Laboratories*
PO Box 5800
Albuquerque, NM 87185-1110
{rbbrigh,kdunder}@sandia.gov

Abstract. Nearly all implementations of the Message Passing Interface (MPI) employ a two-level protocol for point-to-point messages. Short messages are sent eagerly to optimize for latency, and long messages are typically implemented using a rendezvous mechanism. In a rendezvous implementation, the sender must first send a request and receive an acknowledgment before the data can be transferred. While there are several possible reasons for using this strategy for long messages, most implementations are forced to use a rendezvous strategy due to operating system and/or network limitations. In this paper, we compare an implementation that uses a rendezvous protocol for long messages with an implementation that adds an eager optimization for long messages. We discuss implementation issues and provide a performance comparison for several micro-benchmarks. We also present a new micro-benchmark that may provide better insight into how these different protocols effect application performance. Results for this new benchmark indicate that, for larger messages, a significant number of receives must be pre-posted in order for an eager protocol optimization to outperform a rendezvous protocol.

1 Introduction

Nearly all implementations of the Message Passing Interface (MPI) employ a two-level protocol for implementing the peer communication functions. This strategy is an attempt to optimize short messages for latency and long messages for bandwidth. For short messages, data is eagerly sent along with the MPI envelope information (context, tag, etc.). This allows the send operation to complete without any interaction with the receiver. The long message protocol is typically implemented using a rendezvous mechanism where the sender must first send a request and receive an acknowledgment before the data can be transferred. Since the message to be sent is large, the overhead of the protocol exchange with the receiver is amortized by the transfer of the data.

While there are several possible reasons for using a rendezvous protocol for long messages, most implementations are forced to use it due to operating system and/or network limitations. In the case of a network that uses remote DMA to transfer a long message, the receiver may have to perform resource management activities, such as

---

* Sandia is a multiprogram laboratory operated by Sandia Corporation, a Lockheed Martin Company, for the United States Department of Energy under contract DE-AC04-94AL85000.

pinning down memory pages, and provide the sender with information necessary to start the data transfer. One machine where there are no such restrictions is the ASCI Red machine at Sandia National Laboratories. The production implementation of MPI for this machine uses eager sends for all message sizes. We believe that this approach has some benefits, and previous research has demonstrated a significant performance gain for using an eager protocol for larger messages for certain benchmarks [7]. In order to analyze the effect of using eager sends for all messages, we have modified the implementation to use a standard rendezvous protocol for large messages.

In this paper, we compare the strategy of using a rendezvous protocol with an eager optimization with a standard non-eager rendezvous protocol. We discuss implementation issues and provide a performance comparison for several micro-benchmarks. In addition, we present a new micro-benchmark that we have developed that may provide better insight into the effect of these different protocols on application performance. This new micro-benchmark varies the number of pre-posted receives to show the impact of unexpected messages on bandwidth.

The rest of this paper is organized as follows. The following section describes the hardware and software environment of ASCI Red, including the original MPI implementation. Section 3 describes the new rendezvous implementation. In Section 4, we discuss the micro-benchmarks that were run and present performance results and analysis. We discuss the limitation of these benchmarks and present a new micro-benchmark together with performance results in Section 5. Section 6 summarizes the important results, and we conclude in Section 7 with a discussion of future work.

2 ASCI Red

The Sandia/Intel ASCI/Red machine [6] is the United States Department of Energy's Accelerated Strategic Computing Initiative (ASCI) Option Red machine. It was installed at Sandia National Laboratories in 1997 and was the first computing system to demonstrate a sustained teraFLOPS level of performance. The following briefly describes the hardware and system software environment of the machine and discusses some unique features that are relevant to this particular study.

2.1 Hardware

ASCI/Red is composed of over nine thousand 333 MHz Pentium II Xeon processors. Each compute node has two processors and 256 MB of memory. Each node is connected to a wormhole-routed network capable of delivering 800 MB/s of bi-directional communication bandwidth. The network is arranged in a 38x32x2 mesh topology, providing 51.2 GB/s of bisection bandwidth. The network interface on each node resides on the memory bus, allowing for low-latency access between host memory and the network.

Despite its age, we feel that the ratio of peak network bandwidth to peak compute node floating-point performance makes ASCI Red a viable platform for this study. We believe this balance to be an important characteristic of a highly scalable machine, and few machines exist today that exhibit this level of balance. Clusters composed of commodity hardware, for example, have floating-point performance that greatly exceeds their network capability.

2.2 Software

The compute nodes of ASCI/Red run a variant of a lightweight kernel, called Puma [4], that was designed and developed by Sandia and the University of New Mexico. A key component of the design of Puma is a high-performance data movement layer called Portals. Portals are data structures in an application's address space that determine how the kernel should respond to message passing events. Portals allow the kernel to deliver messages directly from the network to application memory. Once a Portal has been set up, the kernel has sufficient information to deliver a message directly to the application. Messages for which there is no corresponding Portal description are simply discarded. Portals also allows for only the header of a message to be saved. This keeps a record of the message, but the message data is discarded.

The network hardware, the lightweight kernel, and Portals combine to offer some very unique and interesting properties. For example, messages between compute nodes are not packetized. An outgoing message to another compute node is simply streamed from memory onto the network. The receiving node determines the destination in memory of the message and streams it in off of the network. Also, reliability is handled at the flit level at each hop in the network, but there is no end-to-end reliability protocol. The observed bit error rate of the network is at least 10^{-20} eliminating the need for higher-level reliability protocols.

2.3 MPI Implementation

The MPI library for Portals on ASCI Red is a port of the MPICH [2] implementation version 1.0.12. This implementation was validated as a product by Intel for ASCI/Red in 1997, and has been in production use with few changes since. Because this paper focuses on long messages, we only describe the long message protocol in this paper. See [1] for a more complete description of the entire implementation. In the rest of this paper, we will refer to this protocol as the eager-rendezvous protocol.

When the MPI library is initialized, it sets up a Portal for receiving MPI messages. Attached to this Portal is the posted receive queue, which is traversed when an incoming message arrives. At the end of this queue are two entries that accept messages for which there is no matching posted receive. The first entry handles short messages, while the second entry handles long messages. The entry for long messages is configured such that it matches any incoming long protocol message and deposits only the message header into a list. The corresponding message data is discarded. An acknowledgment is generated back to the sender that indicates that none of the data was received.

For long protocol sends, the sender first sets up a Portal that will allow the receiver to perform a remote read operation on the message. The sender then sends the message header and data eagerly. If a matching receive has been pre-posted, the message is deposited directly into the appropriately user-designated memory, and an acknowledgment indicating that the entire message was accepted is delivered to the sender. The sender receives the acknowledgment and recognizes that the entire message was accepted. At this point the send operation is complete.

If the message was unexpected, then the incoming message will fall into the long unexpected message entry described above. In this case, the sender receives the acknowledgment and recognizes that the entire message was discarded. The sender must then wait for the receiver to perform a remote read operation on the data. Once the receiver has read the data, the send operation completes.

There are several reasons why we chose to implement an eager-rendezvous protocol for long messages. Portals are based on the concept of expected messages, so we wanted to be able to take advantage of that feature as much as possible. We wanted to reward applications that pre-post receives, rather than penalizing them. We believed that we were optimizing the implementation for the common case, although we had no real data to indicate that long messages were usually pre-posted. Because the network performance of ASCI Red is so high, the penalty for not pre-posting receives is not that large. The compute node allocator is topology-aware, so jobs are placed on compute nodes in such a way as to reduce network contention as much as possible. The impact of extra contention on the network resulting from sending a large unexpected message twice (once when the message is first sent and once again when the receiver reads it) is minimal. As mentioned above, previous research results had indicated that an eager protocol could provide significant performance benefits. Finally, using an eager protocol insures that progress for non-blocking messages is made regardless of whether the application makes MPI calls. The implementation need not use a separate progress engine, such as a thread or timer interrupt or require the application to make MPI library calls frequently, to insure that asynchronous message requests make progress. This greatly simplifies the MPI implementation.

3 Standard-Rendezvous Implementation

In this section, we describe the standard-rendezvous implementation. We have added this capability to the existing eager-rendezvous implementation. The standard-rendezvous protocol can be selected at run time by setting an environment variable, so there is no need to re-link codes.

On the send side, the rendezvous implementation essentially skips the step of sending data when a long send is initiated. It also does not wait for an acknowledgment from the receiver. It sets up a Portal that will allow the receiver to perform a remote read operation, sends a zero-length message, and waits for an indication that the buffer has been read by the receiver. While this change may appear to be minor and straightforward, it has a large impact on how completion of message operations is handled.

Assuming an MPI application with two processes, we examine the two rendezvous protocols for the following legal sequence of calls on both processes:

```
MPI_Irecv( buf, count, datatype, destination, tag, communicator, request );
MPI_Send( buf1, count, datatype, destination, tag, communicator );
MPI_Wait( request, status );
```

For the eager-rendezvous protocol, the MPI_Irecv() call sets up the necessary match entry on the receive Portal (assuming the message has not arrived) and returns. The MPI_Send() call sends the message eagerly and waits for an acknowledgment. Because the receive was pre-posted, the entire message is deposited into the receive buffer, an acknowledgment indicating this is generated, and the send completes when this acknowledgment is received. The MPI_Wait() call waits for the incoming message to arrive. Once the entire message is received, the wait call completes. Alternatively, if the send is unexpected (on either process), the receive call will find the unexpected message and read it from the sender. The send call will wait for the receiver to pull the message before completing. The wait call will block until the entire message is pulled. In all of these scenatrios, the MPI implementation is only concerned with initiating or completing the specific request made by the function call. That is, completing a send or receive operation only involves that specific send or receive operation.

In contrast, the standard-rendezvous implementation is more complex. If the receive call is pre-posted, the send call only sends a message indicating that it has data to send. In order to complete the send call, the receiver must receive this request and pull the data from the sender. This means that a send call cannot simply block waiting for the receiver to pull the message. It may itself have to respond to an incoming send request. In the above code example, if both processes block in the send call waiting for a response from the receiver, both will deadlock. Instead, the implementation must maintain a queue of posted receives. The send call must continuously traverse this queue to see if any posted receives can be progressed. In general, the implementation cannot just try to complete the incoming request from the function call. It must be concerned with *all* outstanding send and receive requests. This can be less efficient, since Asynchronous messaging requests only make progress when the application calls any of the test or wait family of functions.

4 Micro-benchmark Performance

This section presents the micro-benchmarks used and compares the performance of the two MPI implementations. All of the tests were run in the interactive partition of ASCI Red. This partition is set aside for short runs associated with development. There is some impact of running these benchmarks on a shared machine, but repeated runs showed this impact to be minimal.

The first micro-benchmark is a ping-pong bandwidth test. The sender and receiver both pre-post receives and then exchange a message. The bandwidth is based on the time to send the message and receive the reply. Bandwidth is calculated by averaging the results of repeated transfers. Figure 1(a) shows the ping-pong bandwidth performance. The eager-rendezvous protocol outperforms the standard-rendezvous protocol by nearly 50 MB/s for 5 KB messages and 15 MB/s for 100 KB messages.

The second micro-benchmark is the Post-Work-Wait (PWW) method of the COMB [3] benchmark suite. This benchmark calculates effective bandwidth for a given simulated work interval, which measures bandwidth relative to the host processor overhead. Since PWW is aimed at measuring the achievable overlap of computation and communication, it uses pre-posted receives to allow the MPI implementation to make progress on outstanding operations. Figure 1(b) shows the PWW performance of the two protocols for 50 KB, 100 KB, and 500 KB messages. Again, the eager-rendezvous outperforms the standard-rendezvous for all message sizes. For 500 KB messages, the difference is slight. PWW shows less of a difference than the ping-pong benchmark.

The third micro-benchmark, NetPIPE [5], measures aggregate throughput for different block sizes. It also uses a ping-pong strategy, but it determines bandwidth by exchanging messages for a fixed period of time rather than a fixed number of ex-

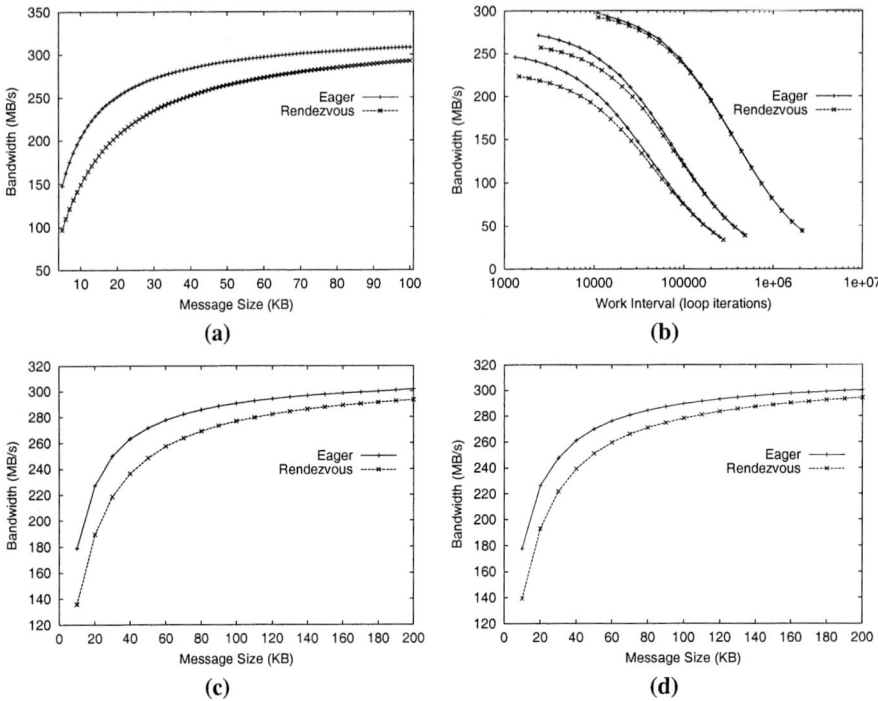

Fig. 1. Bandwidth comparisons of rendezvous and eager for: **(a)** Ping-pong, **(b)** COMB PWW, **(c)** NetPIPE ping-pong, and **(d)** NetPIPE pipeline

changes. By default, NetPIPE does not insure that receives are pre-posted, but it does have an option to enable this feature. We used the default settings and did not enable pre-posted receives for our tests. In addition to the ping-pong strategy, NetPIPE also has a pipelined test that sends several messages in a burst. Figure 1(c) shows the performance of the ping-pong version, while Figure 1(d) shows the pipelined version. As with the previous benchmarks, the eager-rendezvous protocol significantly outperforms the standard-rendezvous protocol for all message sizes.

5 New Micro-benchmark

Benchmark results in Section 4 indicate that the eager-rendezvous protocol could provide significantly more performance to applications. However, only the NetPIPE benchmark considers the possibility of unexpected messages. Real applications are likely to have a mixture of pre-posted and unexpected messages. It follows that the eager-rendezvous protocol would be beneficial to applications that pre-post a majority of their receives, while the standard-rendezvous protocol would be more appropriate for applications that do not.

In order to test this hypothesis, we designed and implemented a micro-benchmark that measures bandwidth performance with a parameterized percentage of pre-posted receives. This micro-benchmark allows us to analyze bandwidth performance for both

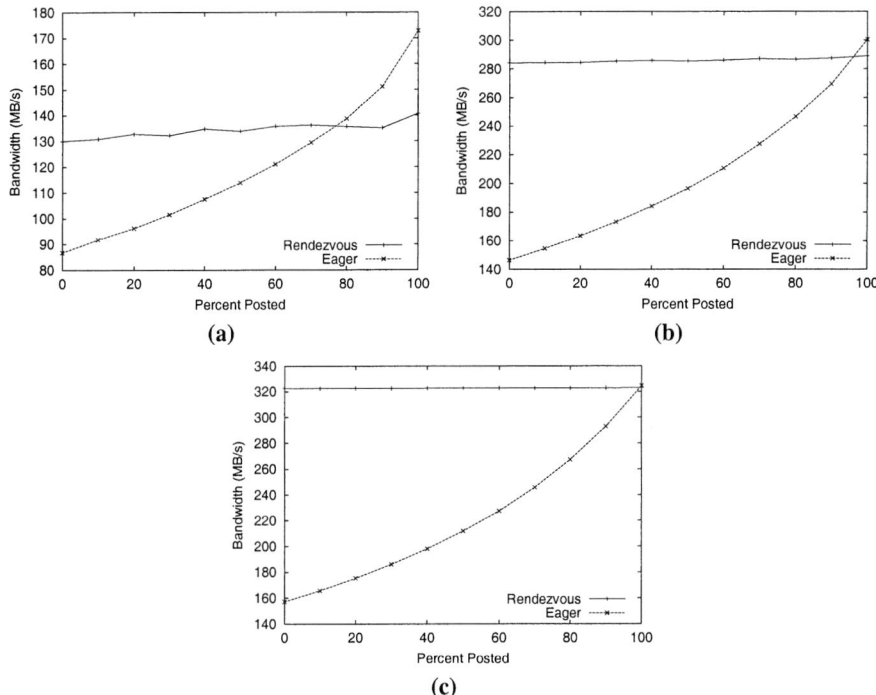

Fig. 2. Unexpected message bandwidth for **(a)** 10 KB, **(b)** 100 KB, and **(c)** 1 MB messages

protocols while varying the number of unexpected messages. The results of this new micro-benchmark are displayed in Figure 2. The results are somewhat surprising. For 10 KB messages shown in Figure 2(a), the standard-rendezvous protocol outperforms the eager-rendezvous protocol until nearly 80% of the receives are pre-posted. As the message size is increased, the standard-rendezvous protocol continues to significantly outperform the eager-rendezvous version. The eager-rendezvous protocol is only more effective when more than 90% of 100 KB message are pre-posted, and when nearly all of the 1 MB messages are pre-posted.

6 Summary

In this paper, we have described an implementation of a standard-rendezvous protocol for long messages and compared its performance against a rendezvous protocol with an eager optimization. Our initial premise was that the eager optimization could provide a possible performance advantage for applications that pre-post receives.

We described the extra complexity of the standard-rendezvous protocol. It must maintain a list of posted receives and must continually try to process receives, even while waiting to complete send operations. This can potentially be less efficient, since progress can only be made on outstanding requests when the application makes an MPI library call.

We compared the performance of these two different long message protocols using three different micro-benchmarks. We then designed and implemented a fourth micro-benchmark that attempts to provide more insight into how these protocols would perform in the context of real applications. Surprisingly, the results of this more realistic benchmark indicate that the eager optimization only outperforms the standard-rendezvous protocol if a large percentage of receive operations are pre-posted.

7 Future Work

We are continuing to evaluate the two different protocols presented in this paper for real applicaions. We have instrumented our MPI implementation to keep track of expected and unexpected messages, and we hope to be able to correlate the performance of the different protocols with the percentage of pre-posted receives. We are also trying to understand trends as applications are run on increasing numbers of nodes. We also hope to quantify other factors, such as the dependence on progress independent of making MPI calls, and their impact on the performance of these two protocols.

We believe that this work will help us to better understand the message passing characteristics of our important applications. We hope to use information about application behavior, MPI protocols, and resource usage in our design of the network hardware and software for the follow-on to the ASCI Red machine, called Red Storm. This machine is a joint project between Cray, Inc. and Sandia. The hardware and software architecture of this new machine is very similar to ASCI Red, so this data should be of great benefit.

References

1. Ron Brightwell and Lance Shuler. Design and Implementation of MPI on Puma Portals. In *Proceedings of the Second MPI Developer's Conference*, pages 18–25, July 1996.
2. William Gropp, Ewing Lusk, Nathan Doss, and Anthony Skjellum. A High-Performance, Portable Implementation of the MPI Message Passing Interface Standard. *Parallel Computing*, 22(6):789–828, September 1996.
3. William Lawry, Christopher Wilson, Arthur B. Maccabe, and Ron Brightwell. Comb: A portable benchmark suite for assessing mpi overlap. Technical Report TR-CS-2002-13, Computer Science Department, The University of New Mexico, April 2002.
4. Lance Shuler, Chu Jong, Rolf Riesen, David van Dresser, Arthur B. Maccabe, Lee Ann Fisk, and T. Mack Stallcup. The Puma Operating System for Massively Parallel Computers. In *Proceeding of the 1995 Intel Supercomputer User's Group Conference*. Intel Supercomputer User's Group, 1995.
5. Q.O. Snell, A. Mikler, and J.L. Gustafson. NetPIPE: A Network Protocol Independent Performance Evaluator . In *Proceedings of the IASTED International Conference on Intelligent Information Management and Systems*, June 1996.
6. Stephen R. Wheat Timothy G. Mattson, David Scott. A TeraFLOPS Supercomputer in 1996: The ASCI TFLOP System. In *Proceedings of the 1996 International Parallel Processing Symposium*, 1996.
7. F. C. Wong, R. P. Martin, R. H. Arpaci-Dusseau, and D. E. Culler. Architectural Requirements and Scalability of the NAS Parallel Benchmarks. In *Proceedings of SC'99*, November 1999.

A Comparison of MPICH Allgather Algorithms on Switched Networks*

Gregory D. Benson, Cho-Wai Chu, Qing Huang, and Sadik G. Caglar

Keck Cluster Research Group
Department of Computer Science
University of San Francisco
2130 Fulton Street, San Francisco, CA 94117-1080
{benson,cchu,qhuang,gcaglar}@cs.usfca.edu

Abstract. This study evaluates the performance of MPI_Allgather() in MPICH 1.2.5 on a Linux cluster. This implementation of MPICH improves on the performance of allgather compared to previous versions by using a *recursive doubling* algorithm. We have developed a *dissemination allgather* based on the dissemination barrier algorithm. This algorithm takes $\log_2 p$ stages for any values of p. We experimentally evaluate MPICH allgather and our implementations on a Linux cluster of dual-processor nodes using both TCP over FastEthernet and GM over Myrinet. We show that on Myrinet, variations of the dissemination algorithm perform best for both large and small messages. However, when using TCP, the dissemination allgather algorithm performs poorly because data is not exchanged in a pair-wise fashion. Therefore, we recommend the dissemination allgather for low-latency switched networks.

1 Introduction

The MPI_Allgather() function is a useful, high-level collective communication function. Each process that participates in an allgather contributes a portion of data. At the end of the allgather, each participating process ends up with the contributions from all the other processes. Allgather is often used in simulation and modeling applications where each process is responsible for the calculation of a subregion that depends on the results of all the other subregions. A poor implementation of allgather can have a significant, negative impact on the performance of applications.

The MPICH [1] and LAM [3] implementations of MPI are widely used on clusters with switched networks, such as FastEthernet or Myrinet. However, the collective communication functions in MPICH and LAM have long suffered from poor performance due to unoptimized implementations. Due to the poor performance of collective communication in MPICH and LAM, programmers often resort to writing their own collective functions on top of the point to point functions.

---
*This work was supported by the the W. M. Keck Foundation.

For our own local applications we have experimented with improved implementations of allgather. We have developed several implementations of *dissemination allgather* based on the dissemination barrier algorithm [2]. This approach is attractive because, for p processes, it requires at most $\lceil \log_2 p \rceil$ stages for any value of p. However, some processes may have to send non-contiguous data in some stages. For non-contiguous data, either copying must be used or two sends to transfer the two regions of data. We have experimented with both approaches.

Recently, many of the collective routines in MPICH have been greatly improved. In particular, allgather is now implemented with a *recursive doubling* algorithm. This algorithm avoids the need to send noncontiguous data, but can require up to $2\lfloor \log_2 p \rfloor$ stages.

In this paper we report on an experimental evaluation of our dissemination allgather algorithms and the new recursive doubling algorithm in MPICH 1.2.5 on a Linux cluster connected by switched FastEthernet and Myrinet. We show that on Myrinet, variations of the dissemination algorithm generally performs best for both large and small messages. For TCP over Fast Ethernet, the recursive doubling algorithm performs best when using small messages and for large messages all of the algorithms perform similarly, with MPICH doing slightly better. Our results suggest that for a low-latency network, like Myrinet, the dissemination allgather that supports both copying for short messages and two sends for large messages should be used. For TCP, an algorithm that incorporates pair-wise exchange, such as recursive doubling or the butterfly algorithm, is best in order to minimize TCP traffic.

The rest of this paper is organized as follows. Section 2 describes the allgather algorithms used in this study. Section 3 presents our experimental data and analyzes the results. Finally, Section 4 makes some concluding remarks.

2 Allgather Algorithms

Early implementations of allgather used simple approaches. One such approach is to gather all the contributed data regions on to process 0 then have process 0 broadcast all of the collected data regions to all the other participating processes. This approach is used in LAM version 6.5.9. It is dependent, in part, on the implementation of the gather and broadcast functions. However, in LAM, gather and broadcast also have simple and inefficient implementations. Another approach is the ring algorithm used in previous versions of MPICH. The ring algorithm requires $p - 1$ stages. This section describes two, more sophisticated, algorithms: recursive doubling and dissemination allgather.

2.1 Recusive Doubling

In the latest version of MPICH, 1.2.5, a new algorithm based on *recursive doubling* is used to implement allgather. First consider the power-of-2 case. In the first stage, all neighboring pairs of processes exchange their contributions. Thus, in the first stage, each process exchanges data with a process that is distance 1 away. In stage one, process 0 exchanges data with process 1, 2 exchanges with 3,

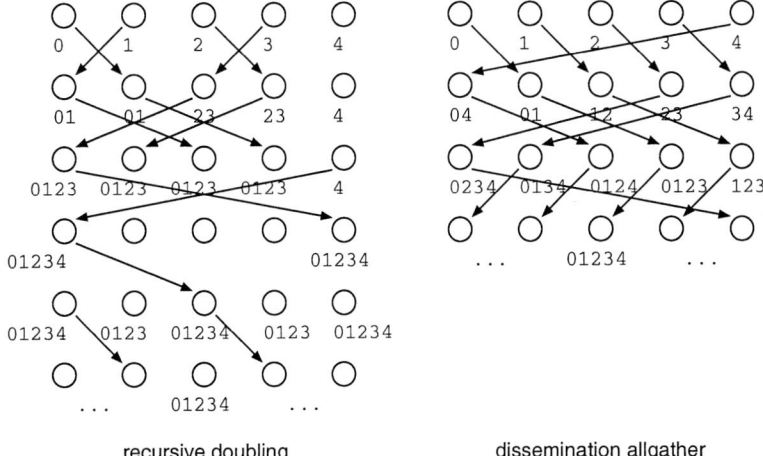

Fig. 1. An example of recusive doubling and dissemination allgather for 5 processes

and so on. In the next stage, groups of 4 are formed. In this stage, each process exchanges all of its data with a process that is distance 2 away within its group. For example, 0 exchanges with 2 and 1 exchanges with 3. In the next stage, the group size is doubled again to a group of 8 and each process exchanges data with a process that is distance 4 apart. After $\log_2 p$ stages all processes will have all the contributions.

For the non-power-of-2 case, correction steps are introduced to ensure that all processes receive the data they would have received in the power-of-two case. The left column of Figure 1 shows how recursive doubling works for 5 processes. The first two stages are just like the first two stages of the power-of-2 case. The third stage marks the beginning of the correction step; it can be thought of as a backward butterfly. In the third stage, 4 exchanges with 0. In the fourth and fifth stages, the contribution of process 4 is propagated to the first four processes.

To accommodate the non-power-of-2 cases, recursive doubling with correction can take $2\lfloor \log_2 p \rfloor$ stages. From Figure 1 it can be seen that data is always exchanged in contiguous chunks. Therefore, the exchange steps are simple. Furthermore, processes always exchange data in a pairwise manner. As we will see in the experimental results, this property benefits a TCP implementation of MPI.

2.2 Dissemination Allgather

We have developed an allgather algorithm based on the dissemination barrier algorithm [2]. Every process is involved in each stage. In the first stage, each process i sends to process $(i + 1) \bmod p$. Note that this is not an exchange, it is just a send. On the second stage each process i sends to process $(i + 2) \bmod p$ and on the third stage process i sends to process $(i + 4) \bmod p$. This pattern continues until $\lceil \log_2 p \rceil$ stages have completed. See the right column of Figure 1 for an example of dissemination allgather for 5 processes. Note that the number of stages is bounded by $\lceil \log_2 p \rceil$ for all values of p, which is much better than the bound for recursive doubling.

An important aspect of the dissemination algorithm is determining which data needs to be sent on each stage. The data to be sent can be determined using the process rank (i) and the stage number (s), starting at 0. First we consider all stages other than the final stage. Each process will send 2^s chunks. The starting chunk that process i will send is $((i+1) - (2^s + p)) \bmod p$. The starting chunk that process i will receive is $((i+1) + (2^s \times (p-2))) \bmod p$. For the final stage, each process will send $p - 2^s$ chunks. The starting chunk that process i will send is $((i+1) + 2^s) \bmod p$ and the starting chunk that process i will receive is $(i+1) \bmod p$.

It is possible that a sequence of chunks is non-contiguous because the chunk wraps around to the beginning of the chunk array. This can also be seen in Figure 1. This means that either copying is needed or at most two sends, one for each chunk of data. If copying is used, the non-contiguous chunks must be copied into a contiguous buffer before a transfer. After the buffer is received the chunks must be copied into their proper locations. We have implemented three versions of the dissemination allgather algorithm; each deals with the non-contiguous data in a different way:

- **One send** copy non-contiguous regions into a buffer and issue one send.
- **Two sends** send each non-contiguous region one at a time.
- **Indexed type** Use MPI_Type_Indexed to send the non-contiguous regions.

All of our implementations are built using MPI point to point functions. We use non-blocking sends and receives. During experimentation we found that we could achieve better performance if we varied the order of which processes send first and which processes receive first. For example, in the first stage, every other process, starting at process 0, sends first. Every other process starting at process 1 receives first. In the second stage the first two processes send first, the second two receive first, and so on. We tried having all processes issue an MPI_Irecv() first, but this did not achieve the same performance as the alternating send/receive approach. Finally, we also tried using MPI_sendrecv(), but the resulted in slightly lower performance than using individual non-blocking sends and receives.

3 Experimental Results

We ran several experiments to compare the performance of the new MPICH recursive doubling algorithm to our implementations of dissemination allgather. Our test environment is a cluster of dual Pentium III 1GHz nodes connected by Myrinet and FastEthernet. Our test program simply measures the time to complete an allgather operation for a given number of processes and a given data size. We measure 500 to 2000 iterations and divide by the iteration count to determine the cost of a single allgather operation. We take the mean of three runs for each data point. The variance in the data was quite small; the normalized standard deviation for each data point was never larger than 0.02. Our

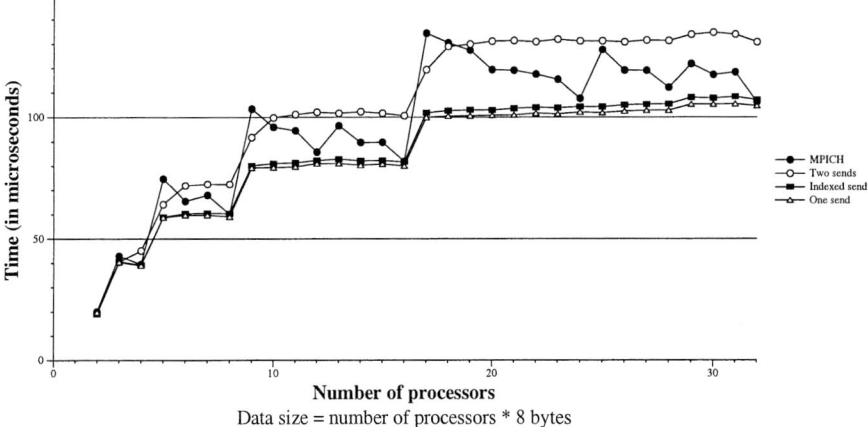

Fig. 2. Allgather performance for small messages on MPICH-GM-Myrinet (1 process per node)

benchmarking methodology is simple and suffers from some of the problems noted in [5]. However, the experiments are reproducible and all the algorithms are compared using the same technique. More work is needed to better measure the cost of a single allgather invocation and to predict allgather performance in real applications.

We present the results in terms of the data size; it is the amount of data contributed by each process in a run. Thus if the data size is 64K and we use 4 processes, the total data accumulated at each process is 256K. In the graphs, MPICH denotes the recursive doubling algorithm.

3.1 MPICH-GM on Myrinet

Figures 2, 3, 4, and 5 show the performance of the different allgather algorithms using MPICH-GM over Myrinet. The first two figures, 2 and 3, give results in which we assign a single process to each node. The second two figures, 4 and 5, give results in which we assign two processes per node.

The small message (8 bytes) results in Figure 2 shows that one send and indexed dissemination allgather perform the best for almost all process counts. For the powers-of-two, the recursive doubling algorithm does just as well because only $\log_2 p$ stages are used. In this case, recursive doubling reduces to the butterfly algorithm. The graph also reveals the varying number of stages required for recursive doubling in the non-power-of-2 cases. Note that the two sends approach generally performs the worst due to the small message size. The two sends incur two start up latencies. The one send approach performs slightly better than the indexed send approach. This is due to the overhead of setting up the index type.

Figure 3 shows the results for large messages (64K bytes). In this case, the two send dissemination approach consistently performs better, up to 40% faster, than the recursive doubling approach for the non-power-of-2 cases. The one send

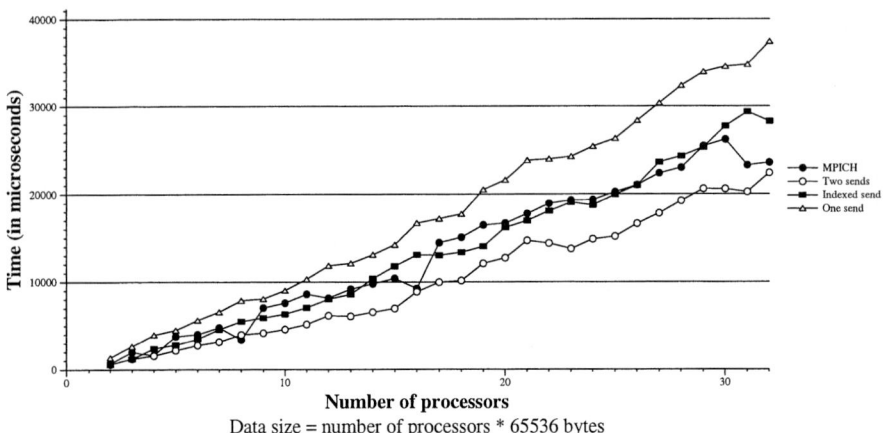

Fig. 3. Allgather performance for large messages on MPICH-GM-Myrinet (1 process per node)

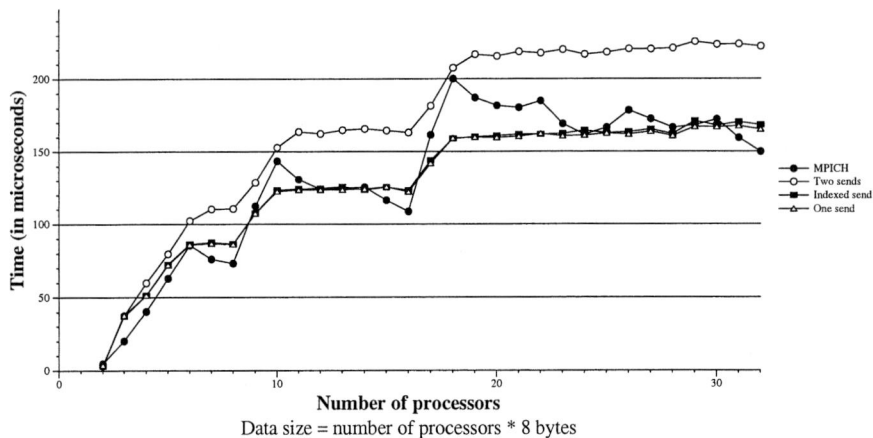

Fig. 4. Allgather performance for small messages on MPICH-GM-Myrinet (2 processes per node)

approach performs the worst because it incurs a large amount of copying. The indexed send appear to minimize some of the copying. In additional experiments not shown here, we found the break even point for one send versus two sends to be 1024 bytes.

The 2 processes per node results in Figures 4 and 5 are similar to the one process per node results. A notable exception is for short messages in Figure 4 in which recursive doubling performs much better than the dissemination allgather in the power-of-two cases. This is because recursive doubling uses pairwise exchange and in the first stage, all the pairs of processes reside on the same node.

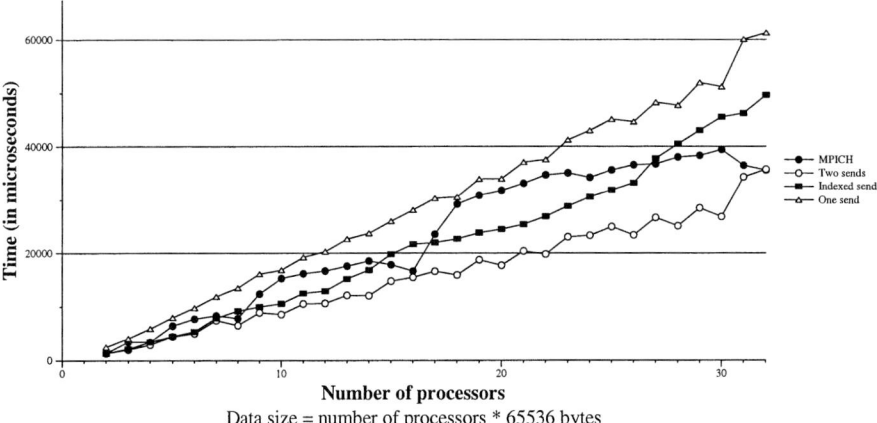

Fig. 5. Allgather performance for large messages on MPICH-GM-Myrinet (2 processes per node)

This suggests that for 2 processor per node assignments a hybrid of dissemination allgather and recursive doubling is desired.

3.2 TCP on FastEthernet

Figures 6 and 7 show the performance of the different allgather algorithms using TCP over FastEthernet. Due to limited space we only show the results for 1 process per node. For small messages in Figure 6 the results are highly erratic. We found large variances in our collected data for TCP an small messages. This is likely due to buffering in TCP. However, the recursive doubling approach is clearly the best in all cases. As expected, two sends performs the worst. However, one send and indexed send seem to do much more poorly than expected, especially considering the good small message results for Myrinet.

The source of the difference between recursive doubling and dissemination allgather comes from the use of pairwise exchange. Because recursive doubling uses pairwise exchange, TCP can optimize the exchange by piggybacking data on ACK packets. The dissemination allgather never does a pairwise exchange; in each stage a process sends to a different process than from which it receives. To test our hypothesis we ran tcpdump [4] to observe the TCP traffic during an allgather operation. We monitored the rank 0 process. With a data size of 8 bytes and using 7 processes we found for recursive doubling 3654 packets were transmitted and only 114 (3.1%) ACKs were pure ACKs. A pure ACK is an ACK without piggybacked data. For the same parameters we found that dissemination allgather resulted in 6746 total packets transmitted and 2161 (32%) ACKs were pure ACKs. Dissemination allgather generates much more TCP traffic.

Figure 7 shows the results for TCP and large messages. As the data size increases, the advantage of pairwise exchange begins to diminish. However, in the

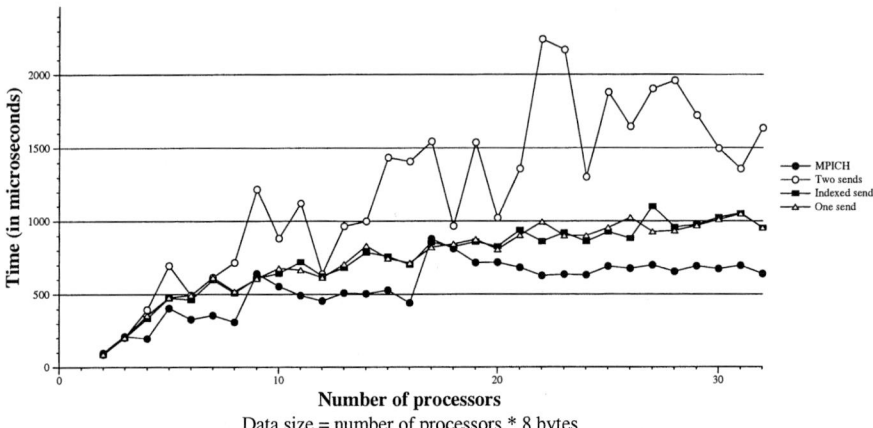

Fig. 6. Allgather performance for small messages on MPICH-TCP-Ethernet (1 process per node)

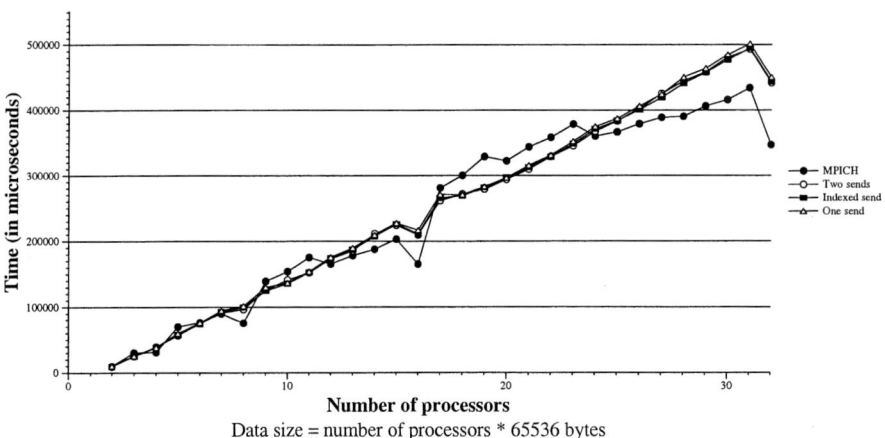

Fig. 7. Allgather performance for large messages on MPICH-TCP-Ethernet (1 process per node)

power-of-2 cases, the recursive doubling algorithm still shows better performance than dissemination allgather.

4 Conclusions

We have presented the dissemination allgather algorithm and compared its performance to the recursive doubling approach used in MPICH 1.2.5. We showed that for GM over Myrinet, dissemination allgather consistently performs better than recursive doubling except in the power of two cases with 1 process per node assignment. For 2 process per node assignment a hybrid of dissemination allgather and recursive doubling should be used. A general purpose implementation will have to utilize both one send and two sends in order to achieve good performance for both small and large messages. For TCP over FastEthernet the best choice is recursive doubling due to its use of pairwise exchange. Our results suggest that a version of the dissemination algorithm should be used to implement allgather for MPICH-GM.

For future work we plan to improve our benchmarking methodology. We also plan to apply our results by developing an allgather implementation that can choose the most efficient algorithm based on input parameters and the underlying network. Finally we plan to analyze the other collective operations to see where the dissemination approach can be applied.

Acknowledgements

We thank Peter Pacheco and Yuliya Zabiyaka for insightful discussions on different allgather algorithms. Peter Pacheco also provided feedback on an earlier version of this paper. Amol Dharmadhikari helped us verify the correctness of our dissemination algorithm. Alex Fedosov provided system support for the Keck Cluster and responded to last minute requests during data collection. Finally, we thank the anonymous reviewers for their useful feedback and pointers to related work.

References

1. Argonne National Laboratory. *MPICH - A Portable Implementation of MPI*, 2003. http://www-unix.mcs.anl.gov/mpi/mpich/.
2. D. Hensgen, R. Finkel, and U. Manber. Two algorithms for barrier synchronization. *International Journal of Parallel Programming*, 17(1):1–17, February 1988.
3. Indiana University. *LAM / MPI Parallel Computing*, 2003. http://www.lam-mpi.org/.
4. Lawrence Berkeley National Laboratory. *tcpdump*, 2003. http://www.tcpdump.org/.
5. Thomas Worsch, Ralf H. Reussner, and Werner Augustin. On benchmarking collective MPI operations. In J. Volkert, D. Kranzlmüller, and J. J. Dongarra, editors, *Recent advances in parallel virtual machine and message passing interface: 9th European PVM/MPI Users' Group Meeting, Linz, Austria, September 29 – October 02, 2002*, Lecture Notes in Computer Science, 2002.

Network Fault Tolerance in LA-MPI

Rob T. Aulwes, David J. Daniel, Nehal N. Desai,
Richard L. Graham, L. Dean Risinger,
Mitchel W. Sukalski, and Mark A. Taylor*

Los Alamos National Laboratory, Advanced Computing Laboratory,
MS-B287, P. O. Box 1663, Los Alamos NM 87545, USA
lampi-support@lanl.gov
http://www.acl.lanl.gov/la-mpi/

Abstract. LA-MPI is a high-performance, network-fault-tolerant implementation of MPI designed for terascale clusters that are inherently unreliable due to their very large number of system components and to trade-offs between cost and performance. This paper reviews the architectural design of LA-MPI, focusing on our approach to guaranteeing data integrity. We discuss our network data path abstraction that makes LA-MPI highly portable, gives high-performance through message striping, and most importantly provides the basis for network fault tolerance. Finally we include some performance numbers for Quadrics Elan, Myrinet GM and UDP network data paths.

1 Introduction

LA-MPI [1, 2] is an implementation of the Message Passing Interface (MPI) [3, 4] motivated by a growing need for fault tolerance at the software level in large high-performance computing (HPC) systems.

This need is caused by the sheer number of components present in modern HPC systems, particularly clusters. The individual components – processors, memory modules, network interface cards (NICs), etc. – are typically manufactured to tolerances adequate for small or desktop systems. When aggregated into a large HPC system, however, system-wide error rates may be too great to successfully complete a long application run [5]. For example, a network device may have an error rate which is perfectly acceptable for a desktop system, but not in a cluster of thousands of nodes, which must run error free for many hours or even days to complete a scientific calculation.

LA-MPI has two primary goals: *network fault tolerance* and *high performance*. Fortunately these goals are partially complimentary, since the flexible approach we take to the use of redundant network data paths to support fault tolerance also allows LA-MPI to exploit all the available network bandwidth

---

* Los Alamos report LA-UR-03-2939. Los Alamos National Laboratory is operated by the University of California for the National Nuclear Security Administration of the United States Department of Energy under contract W-7405-ENG-36. Project support was provided through ASCI/PSE and the Los Alamos Computer Science Institute.

in a network-device-rich system by sending different messages and/or messagefragments over multiple network paths.

A well-known solution to the network fault tolerance problem is to use the TCP/IP protocol. We believe, however, that this protocol – developed to handle unreliable, inhomogeneous and oversubscribed networks – performs poorly and is overly complex for HPC system messaging. Instead LA-MPI implements a more limited but highly efficient checksum/retransmission protocol, which we discuss in detail in section 3.

There are several other approaches to fault-tolerant message passing systems [6–9], but these have tended to focus on the issues of *process* fault tolerance and assume the existence of a perfectly reliable network (typically TCP/IP). We do intend to explore process fault tolerance in future, but believe that a high performance, network-fault-tolerant messaging system is a necessary first step.

Other important features of LA-MPI include an open source license, standards compliance (MPI version 1.2 integrated with ROMIO [10] for MPI-IO v2 support), thread safety, and portability to many operating systems, processor architectures and network devices.

In the following sections we will first review the architecture of LA-MPI emphasizing the important role of our network data path abstraction. A detailed discussion of LA-MPI's data integrity protocol is given in section 3, while a selection of performance results are presented in section 4.

2 Architecture

At a high level, LA-MPI's architecture falls into two layers: an upper MPI layer, implementing the full richness of the MPI standard, and a lower User Level Messaging (ULM) layer that provides a simpler reliable message passing API. Looking deeper, ULM is itself composed of two layers: a Memory and Message Layer (MML), and a Send and Receive Layer (SRL). The MML consists of code common to all systems and data paths, while the SRL is highly device-specific.

Before discussing these layers and their interaction in more detail, it is helpful to discuss what types of network fault tolerance are provided by LA-MPI. We distinguish two separate functionalities: (a) guaranteed data integrity of delivered messages; and (b) the ability to fail-over from one network device to another if the first is generating too many errors. Both of these require that we are able to treat each available network device on an equal footing, and this has led us to develop an abstraction called a *network data path object* or, more succinctly, a *path*.

A path is an abstraction of lower-level network transports and devices that are available to LA-MPI. Each path can represent a single network adapter, or a set of common adapters, or even a common protocol over many different network adapters. Currently, paths are implemented for shared memory, UDP (over all IP-enabled devices), Quadrics Elan3 [11, 12] remote direct memory access (RDMA) and Myrinet GM [13], and is currently being developed for Infiniband and TCP. In all of our current paths except UDP/IP, which treats multiple net-

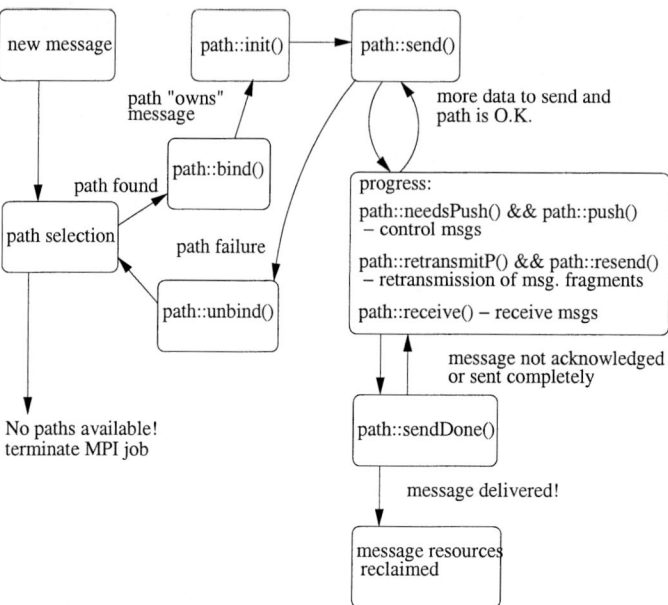

Fig. 1. Message-Path Interactions.

work adapters as a single Internet Protocol "device", multiple network adapters are used by a single path instantiation, if they exist on the machine.

The path object provides the interface between the portable common code of the MML and device-specific SRL. The interaction of the MML with the various paths is described schematically in figure 1.

As noted in the introduction, the path model enables us to implement message striping, where different messages may be sent along different data paths. For paths that comprise several NICs, we also stripe fragments of a single message across the NICs, and so achieve excellent network bandwidth.

An additional benefit of the path abstraction is that it enforces a high degree of portability in LA-MPI. For example, since differenct messages may be sent along different paths, all tag matching must be done in the MML in a path-independent way in order to respect MPI ordering semantics. We have found that there is no performance penalty for this approach (see section 4), while we gain in terms of an increasingly clean and maintainable code base.

In the next section we give an in-depth discussion of one aspect of network fault tolerance in LA-MPI, namely support for reliable message delivery, that is, the guaranteed integrity of delivered data. The other aspects of LA-MPI's architecture are described in more detail elsewhere [2].

3 Reliability

Unlike many MPI libraries that consider all underlying communication perfectly reliable, LA-MPI optionally supports sender-side retransmission of messages by

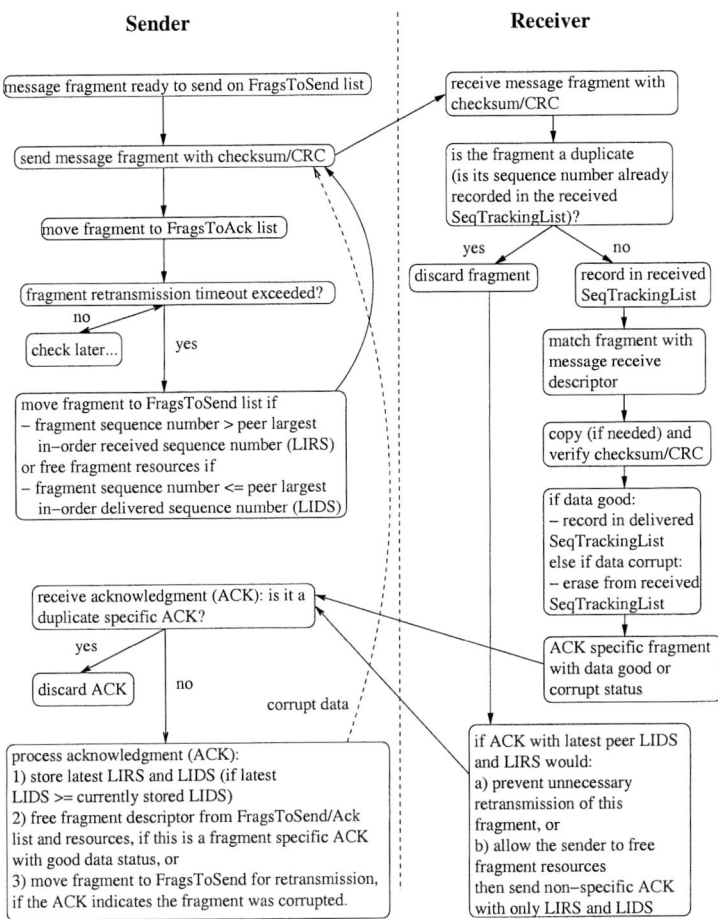

Fig. 2. Retransmission and Checksumming.

checking an "unacknowledged" list periodically for message send descriptors that have exceeded their timeout periods. This retransmission scheme is appropriate for low error rate environments, typical of most clusters. Each network transport is responsible for arranging to retransmit the necessary fragments. Each fragment's retransmission time is calculated using a truncated exponential back-off scheme; this avoids resource exhaustion at a receiving process that is busy doing non-MPI computation. Fragments that must be retransmitted are moved from the `FragsToAck` list to the `FragsToSend` list, and the associated message send descriptor is placed on the incomplete list.

Each network transport is also responsible for providing a main memory-to-main memory 32-bit additive checksum or 32-bit cyclic redundancy code (CRC), if it is needed. This checksum/CRC protects against network and I/O bus corruption, and is generated at the same time data is copied, if at all possible. By

Table 1. Zero-byte latency and peak point-to-point bandwidth for various LA-MPI paths. For the Quadrics path, we also give (in parentheses) the performance numbers with reliability (guaranteed data integrity) turned off (a run-time option).

System	Path	Latency (μs)	Bandwidth (MB/s)
alpha	Shared Memory	2.93	935
alpha	Quadrics/Elan (1 NIC)	11.23 (8.39)	257 (273)
alpha	Quadrics/Elan (2 NICs)	11.37 (8.43)	438 (468)
alpha	Quadrics/Elan (UDP/IP)	156	67
i686	UDP/IP gigE	125.1	91
i686	Shared Memory	3.09	455
i686	Myrinet/GM (1 NIC)	11.91	241
i686	Myrinet/GM (2 NICs)	12.26	403
i686	Myrinet/GM (UDP/IP)	125.2	94
i686	UDP/IP gigE	125.1	91

delaying checksumming to avoid wasting memory bandwidth, a received fragment is not necessarily a deliverable, or uncorrupted, fragment. The checksum can be disabled at run-time for additional performance at the cost of guaranteed data integrity.

Several MML generic features aid in the implementation of this retransmission and checksumming scheme. Every byte of data sent between a given pair of processes is associated with a monotonically increasing 64-bit sequence number. A fragment is therefore labeled by a range of sequence numbers (as a special case, zero-byte messages are assigned a single sequence number). The receiving process records the sequence numbers of arriving fragments in a special object, SeqTrackingList, as an ordered set of possibly non-contiguous ranges of sequence numbers. These lists use internal hint pointers to exploit any temporal locality in accessing these lists to minimize access overhead. The receiver maintains two SeqTrackingList lists for each peer with which it communicates to distinguish between fragments that have been received, and those that have been received and delivered successfully (i.e., no data corruption). Duplicate fragments are easily detected by checking the received fragment's sequence number range against the received SeqTrackingList.

We use per-byte rather than per-fragment sequence numbers to support network fault tolerance: by keeping track of the delivery of individual bytes we can more easily rebind failed fragment transmissions to alternate network paths with different fragment sizes. This is outlined in figure 1 and discussed more fully elsewhere [2].

Upon processing fragment acknowledgments from a receiver, a sender will store two special values that are carried in every acknowledgment: the largest in-order peer received sequence number (LIRS), and the largest in-order peer delivered sequence number (LIDS). The LIRS is used to prevent the retransmission of fragments that have been received, but whose data integrity has not been checked yet; it may increase or decrease over time, depending upon transmission and I/O bus errors. The LIDS is used to free any fragments whose acknowl-

Table 2. Zero-byte latency and peak point-to-point bandwidth for several MPI implementations (LA-MPI, MPICH and HP/Compaq MPI ("alaska"), on the alpha system described in table 1. The LA-MPI numbers in parentheses are those with reliability turned off (a run-time option).

Implementation	Path	Latency (μs)	Bandwidth (MB/s)
LA-MPI	Shared Memory	2.93	935
LA-MPI	Quadrics/Elan (1 NIC)	11.23 (8.39)	257 (273)
LA-MPI	Quadrics/Elan (2 NICs)	11.37 (8.43)	438 (468)
MPICH	Quadrics/Elan (1 NIC)	4.65	228
MPICH	Quadrics/Elan (2 NICs)	4.57	257
HP/Compaq	Quadrics/Elan (1 NIC)	4.89	292
HP/Compaq	Quadrics/Elan (2 NICs)	4.99	258

edgment was lost. The LIDS is always less than or equal to the LIRS. Figure 2 shows the interaction of these sequence numbers, the retransmission scheme, and checksumming.

4 Performance

In this section we present benchmark results that characterize the performance of LA-MPI on a variety of computer architectures, and allow a comparison with other implementations of MPI.

In table 1 we give "ping-pong" performance results from two systems currently of interest to us: (a) an alpha/Tru64 system consisting of HP/Compaq ES45 4-way nodes with 1.25 GHz alpha ev68 processors, and a "dual rail" Quadrics Elan/Elite interconnect; and (b) an i686/Linux system composed of 2 GHz dual Xeon nodes with 2 Myrinet 2000 cards.

Also included in table 1 are results for LA-MPI's UDP/IP path run over Elan/IP, and Myrinet GM/IP. These numbers give an indication of the very large cost associated with a complete IP implementation, and why LA-MPI uses the light-weight checksum/retransmission protocol described in section 3.

For the Quadrics path on alpha we quote the results with and without data integrity guaranteed. As can be seen the impact of reliability on performance is relatively small, increasing latency by about a third and reducing bandwidth by less than 10 %.

Table 2 gives a comparison of LA-MPI with two vendor supplied MPI implementations: MPICH as optimized by Quadrics for the Elan/Elite network, and HP/Compaq MPI version r11 (also known as "alaska"). Both of these implementations are based on the native Quadrics `libelan` tagged-messaging primitive `elan_tport`, whereas LA-MPI uses the common code in the MML for tag matching and accesses the Elan using `libelan3` chained DMAs [11].

In fairness we should point out that the Quadrics native Elan library achieves a ping-pong latency of about 4.5 μs. There are several structural reasons for our higher latency (8.39), mainly related to the way that tag matching is implemented – in order to support all paths LA-MPI can make fewer assumptions about message-fragment arrival. We believe, however, that further refinements to LA-MPI's MML and SRL will reduce this gap.

For "on-host" messages, on the other hand, LA-MPI can use its shared memory path which easily out-performs the Elan network; this option is not available to the `elan_tport`-based approaches.

LA-MPI truly excels in the bandwidth benchmarks, for two reasons. Firstly, on-host traffic is handled by the shared memory path which has a much higher bandwidth than the Elan devices. Secondly, on systems with two "rails" of Elan/Elite network (i.e. two Elan devices per node), LA-MPI highly efficiently sends message fragments along both rails. In this simple ping-pong benchmark the `elan_tport`-based libraries show little or negative improvement with two rails, because they use the rails by assigning messages between a process pair to a fixed rail. For some communication patterns this approach may be reasonably efficient, but we emphasize that LA-MPI's fragment-based scheduling across the rails is efficient for all communication patterns.

5 Conclusions

With the rise of terascale distributed computing environments consisting of thousands of processors and network adapters, the need for fault tolerant software has become critical to their successful use. Negligible component error and failure rates in small to medium size clusters are no longer negligible in these large clusters, due to their complexity, sheer number of components, and amount of data transferred.

LA-MPI addresses the network-related challenges of this environment by providing a production-quality, reliable, high-performance MPI library for applications capable of (a) surviving network and I/O bus data corruption and loss, and (b) surviving network hardware and software failure if other connectivity is available.

Future development efforts will address (a) the implementation of a fault-tolerant, scalable, administrative network for job control, standard I/O redirection, and MPI wire-up; (b) the implementation of process fault-tolerance in the face of multiple process failures; and (c) the implementation of dynamic topology reconfiguration and addition of MPI processes to support dynamic process migration and MPI-2 dynamic processes.

LA-MPI is currently available as open source software under an LGPL license. It currently runs on Linux (i686 and Alpha processors), HP's Tru64 (Alpha only), SGI's IRIX 6.5 (MIPS), and Apple's Mac OS X (PowerPC). It supports an increasing variety of paths (network devices) as discussed in section 2. LA-MPI supports job spawning and control with Platform LSF, Quadrics RMS (Tru64 only), Bproc [14], and standard BSD `rsh`. Please send email to `lampi-support@lanl.gov`, and for more information visit our web site [15]. All fault tolerance features described in this paper have been fully implemented, except for on-going work on automatic network fail-over support.

References

1. Richard L. Graham, Sung-Eun Choi, David J. Daniel, Nehal N. Desai, Ronald G. Minnich, Craig E. Rasmussen, L. Dean Risinger, and Mitchel W. Sukalski. A network-failure-tolerant message-passing system for terascale clusters. In *Proceedings of the 16th international conference on Supercomputing*, pages 77–83. ACM Press, 2002.
2. Rob T. Aulwes, David J. Daniel, Nehal N. Desai, Richard L. Graham, L. Dean Risinger, and Mitchel W. Sukalski. LA-MPI: The design and implementation of a network-fault-tolerant MPI for terascale clusters. Technical Report LA-UR-03-0939, Los Alamos National Laboratory, 2003.
3. Message Passing Interface Forum. MPI: A Message Passing Interface Standard. Technical report, 1994.
4. Message Passing Interface Forum. MPI-2.0: Extensions to the Message-Passing Interface. Technical report, 1997.
5. C. Partridge, J. Hughes, and J. Stone. Performance of checksums and CRCs over real data. *Computer Communication Review*, v. 25 n. 4:68–76, 1995.
6. Georg Stellner. CoCheck: Checkpointing and Process Migration for MPI. In *Proceedings of the 10th International Parallel Processing Symposium (IPPS '96)*, Honolulu, Hawaii, 1996.
7. M. Litzkow, M. Livny, and M. Mutka. Condor - a hunter of idle workstations. In *8th International Conference on Distributed Computing System*, pages 108–111. IEEE Computer Society Press, 1988.
8. A. Agbaria and R. Friedman. Starfish: Fault-tolerant dynamic MPI programs on clusters of workstations. In *8th IEEE International Symposium on High Performance Distributed Computing*, 1999.
9. G. Fagg and a Dongarra. FT-MPI: Fault Tolerant MPI, Supporting Dynamic Applications in a Dynamic World. In *EuroPVM/ MPI User's Group Meeting 2000, Springer-Verlag, Berlin, Germany, 2000*, 2000.
10. Rajeev Thakur, William Gropp, and Ewing Lusk. *Users Guide for ROMIO: A High-Performance, Portable MPI-IO Implementation.* Mathematics and Computer Science Division, Argonne National Laboratory, October 1997. ANL/MCS-TM-234.
11. Quadrics Ltd. http://www.quadrics.com/.
12. Fabrizio Petrini, Wu-Chun Feng, Adolfy Hoisie, Salvador Coll, and Eitan Frachtenberg. The Quadrics network: High-performance clustering technology. *IEEE Micro*, v. 22 n. 1:46–57, 2002.
13. Myricom, Inc. http://www.myri.com/.
14. Advanced Computing Laboratory, Los Alamos National Laboratory. http://public.lanl.gov/cluster/index.html.
15. Advanced Computing Laboratory, Los Alamos National Laboratory. http://www.acl.lanl.gov/la-mpi.

MPI on BlueGene/L: Designing an Efficient General Purpose Messaging Solution for a Large Cellular System

George Almási[1], Charles Archer[2], José G. Castaños[1], Manish Gupta[1], Xavier Martorell[1], José E. Moreira[1], William D. Gropp[3], Silvius Rus[4], and Brian Toonen[3]

[1] IBM T. J. Watson Research Center, Yorktown Heights NY 10598-0218
{gheorghe,castanos,jmoreira,mgupta,xavim}@us.ibm.com
[2] IBM Systems Group, Rochester MN 55901
archerc@us.ibm.com
[3] Argonne National Laboratory, Argonne IL 60439
{gropp,toonen}@mcs.anl.gov
[4] Texas A&M University, College Station TX 77840
rus@tamu.edu

Abstract. The BlueGene/L computer uses system-on-a-chip integration and a highly scalable 65,536-node cellular architecture to deliver 360 Tflops of peak computing power. Efficient operation of the machine requires a fast, scalable, and standards compliant MPI library. In this paper, we discuss our efforts to port the MPICH2 library to BlueGene/L.

1 Introduction

BlueGene/L [1] is a 65,536-compute node massively parallel system being developed by IBM in partnership with Lawrence Livermore National Laboratory. Through the use of system-on-a-chip integration [2], coupled with a highly scalable cellular architecture, BlueGene/L will deliver 360 Tflops of peak computing power.

In this paper we present and analyze the software design for a fast, scalable, and standards compliant MPI communication library, based on MPICH2 [15], for the BlueGene/L machine. MPICH2 is an all-new implementation of MPI that is intended to support both MPI-1 and MPI-2. The MPICH2 design features optimized MPI datatypes, optimized remote memory access (RMA), high scalability, usability, and robustness.

The rest of this paper is organized as follows. Section 2 presents a brief description of the BlueGene/L computer. Section 3 discusses its system software. Section 4 gives a high level architectural overview of the communication library, and Section 5 discusses the design choices we are facing during implementation. Section 6 describes the methodology we employed to measure performance and presents preliminary results. We conclude with Section 7.

2 BlueGene/L Hardware Overview

The basic building block of BlueGene/L is a custom chip that integrates processors, memory, and communications logic. A chip contains two 32-bit embedded PowerPC

440 cores with custom *dual* floating-point units that operate on two-element vectors. The theoretical peak performance of the chip is 5.6 Gflops at the target clock speed of 700 MHz. An external double data rate (DDR) memory system completes a BlueGene/L node. The complete BlueGene/L machine consists of 65,536 compute nodes and 1,024 I/O nodes. I/O nodes are connected to a Gigabit Ethernet network and serve as control and file concentrators for the compute nodes.

The compute nodes of BlueGene/L are organized into a partitionable $64 \times 32 \times 32$ three-dimensional torus network. Each compute node contains six bi-directional torus links for direct connection with nearest neighbors. The network hardware guarantees reliable and deadlock-free, but unordered, delivery of variable length (up to 256 bytes) packets, using a minimal adaptive routing algorithm. It also provides simple broadcast functionality by depositing packets along a route. At 1.4 Gb/s per direction, the bisection bandwidth of the system is 360 GB/s per direction. The I/O nodes are not connected to the torus network.

All compute and I/O nodes of BlueGene/L are interconnect by a tree network. The tree network supports fast point-to-point, broadcast, and reduction operations on packets, with a hardware latency of approximately 2 microseconds for a 64k-node system. An ALU in the network can combine incoming packets using bitwise and integer operations, forwarding a resulting packet along the tree. Floating-point reductions can be performed in two phases (one for the exponent and another one for the mantissa) or in one phase by converting the floating-point number to an extended 2048-bit representation.

3 BlueGene/L System Software Overview

The smallest unit independently controlled by software is called a processing set (or pset) and consists of 64 compute nodes and an associated I/O node. Components of a pset communicate through the tree network. File I/O and control operations are performed by the I/O node of the pset through the Ethernet network.

The I/O nodes run a Linux kernel with custom drivers for the Ethernet and tree devices. The main function of I/O nodes is to run a program called **ciod** (control and I/O daemon) that implements system management services and supports file I/O operations by the compute nodes.

The control software running on compute nodes is a minimalist POSIX compliant *compute node kernel* (CNK) that provides a simple, flat, fixed-size address space for a single user process. The CNK plays a role similar to PUMA [12] in the ASCI Red machine. The torus network is mapped directly into user space and the tree network is partitioned between the kernel and the user.

The system management software provides a range of services for the machine, including machine initialization and booting, system monitoring, job launch and termination, and job scheduling. System management is provided by external service nodes that act upon the I/O and compute nodes, both directly and through the **ciod** daemons. The partitioning of the system into compute, I/O, and service nodes leads to a hierarchical system management software.

4 Communication Software Architecture

The BlueGene/L communication software architecture is divided into three layers. At the bottom is the *packet layer*, a thin software library that allows access to network hardware. At the top is the MPI library. The *message layer* glues the packet layer and MPI together.

Packet layer. The torus/tree packet layer is a thin layer of software designed to abstract and simplify access to hardware. It abstracts hardware FIFOs into torus and tree *devices* and presents an API consisting of essentially three functions: initialization, packet send and packet receive. The packet layer provides a *mechanism* to use the network hardware but does not impose any *policies* on how to use it.

Some restrictions imposed by hardware are not abstracted at packet level for performance reasons. For example, the length of a torus packet must be a multiple of 32 bytes, and can be no more than 256 bytes. Tree packets have exactly 256 bytes. Packets sent and received by the packet layer have to be aligned to a 16-byte address boundary, to enable the efficient use of 128-bit loads and stores to the network hardware through the dual floating-point units.

All packet layer send and receive operations are non-blocking, leaving it up to the higher layers to implement synchronous, blocking and/or interrupt driven communication models. In its current implementation the packet layer is stateless.

Message layer. The message layer is an active message system [6, 11, 13, 14], built on top of the packet layer, that allows the transmission of arbitrary buffers among compute nodes. Its architecture is shown by Figure 1.

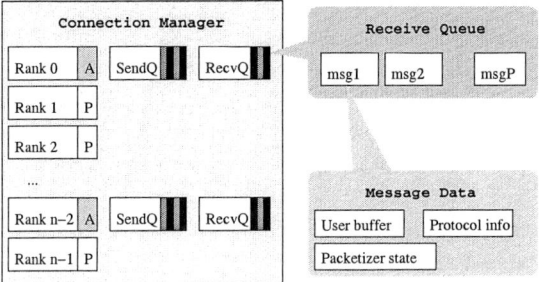

Fig. 1. The message layer architecture.

The connection manager controls the overall progress of the system and contains a list of virtual connections to other nodes. Each virtual connection is responsible for communicating with one peer. The connection has a send queue and a receive queue. Outgoing messages are always sent in order. Incoming packets, however, can arrive out of order. The message layer has to determine which message a packet belongs to. Thus, each packet has to carry a message identifier.

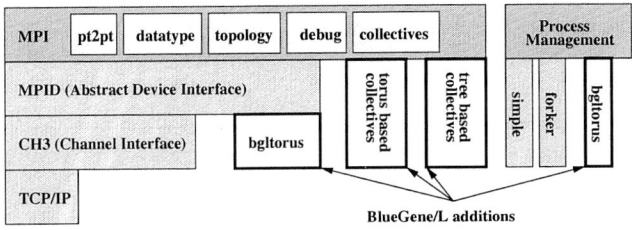

Fig. 2. The BlueGene/L MPI roadmap.

Message buffers are used for sending and receiving packets belonging to the same message. A message buffer contains the state of the message (in progress, complete, etc). It also has an associated region of user memory, and a *packetizer/unpacketizer* that is able to generate packets or to place incoming packets into memory. Message buffers also handle the message protocol (*i.e.*, what packets to send when).

Packetizers and unpacketizers drive the packet layer. Packetizers build and send packets out of message buffers. Unpacketizers rebuild messages from the component packets. Packetizers also handle the alignment and packet size limitations imposed by the network hardware.

The three main functions implemented by the message layer API are Init, advance and postsend: Init initializes the message layer; advance is called to ensure that the message layer makes progress (*i.e.*, sends the packets it has to send, checks the torus hardware for incoming packets and processes them accordingly); postsend allows a message to be submitted into the send queue.

Just like packet layer functions, message layer functions are non-blocking and designed to be used in either polling mode, or driven by hardware interrupts. Completion of a send, and the beginning and end of a receive are all signaled through *callbacks*. Thus, when a message is sent and is ready to be taken off the send queue the senddone function is invoked. When a new message starts arriving, the recvnew callback is invoked. At the end of reception recvdone is invoked.

MPICH2. MPICH2, currently under development at Argonne National Laboratory, is an MPI implementation designed from the ground up for scalability to hundreds of thousands of processors. Figure 2 shows the roadmap of developing an MPI library for BlueGene/L. MPICH2 has a modular structure, and therefore the BlueGene/L port consists of a number of plug-in modules, leaving the code structure of MPICH2 intact.

The most important addition of the BlueGene/L port is an implementation of ADI3, the MPICH2 Abstract Device Interface [8]. A thin layer of code transforms (for example) MPI Request objects and MPI_Send function calls into sequences of message layer postsend function calls and various message layer callbacks.

Another part of the BlueGene/L port is related to the process management primitives. In MPICH2, process management is split into two parts: a process management interface (PMI), called from within the MPI library, and a set of process managers (PM) which are responsible for starting up and terminating down MPI jobs and implementing the PMI functions. The BlueGene/L process manager makes full use of its hierarchical system management software to start up and shut down MPI jobs, dealing with the scalability problem inherent in starting up, synchronizing, and killing 65,536 MPI processes.

MPICH2 has default implementations for all MPI collectives and becomes functional the moment point-to-point primitives are implemented. The default implementations are oblivious of the underlying physical topology of the torus and tree networks. Optimized collective operations can be implemented for communicators whose physical layouts conform to certain properties. Building optimized collectives for MPICH2 involves several steps. First, the process manager interface needs to be expanded to allow the calculation of the torus and tree layouts of particular communicators. Next, a list of optimized collectives, for particular combinations of communicator layouts and message types, needs to be implemented. The best implementation of a particular MPI collective will be selected at run-time, based on the type of communicator involved (as calculated using the process manager interface).

- The torus hardware can be used to efficiently implement broadcasts on contiguous 1-, 2-, and 3-dimensional meshes, using the feature of the torus that allows depositing a packet on every node it traverses. Collectives best suited for this implementation include Bcast, Allgather, Alltoall, and Barrier.
- The tree hardware can be used for almost every collective that is executed on the MPI_COMM_WORLD communicator, including reduction operations.
- Non-MPI_COMM_WORLD collectives can also be implemented using the tree, but care must be taken to ensure deadlock free operation. The tree network guarantees deadlock-free simultaneous delivery of two virtual channels. One of these channels is used for control and file I/O purposes; the other is available for use by collectives.

5 Design Decisions in the Message Layer

The design of the message layer was influenced by specific BlueGene/L hardware features, such as network reliability, packetization and alignment restrictions, out-of-order arrival of torus packets, and the existence of non-coherent processors in a chip. These hardware features, together with the requirements for a low overhead scalable solution, led us to design decisions that deserve closer examination.

The impact of hardware reliability. The BlueGene/L network hardware is completely reliable. Once a packet is injected into the network, hardware guarantees its arrival at the destination. The BlueGene/L message layer does not implement a packet recovery protocol, allowing for better scaling and a large reduction of software overhead.

Packetizing and alignment. The packet layer requires data to be sent in (up to) 256-byte chunks aligned at 16-byte boundaries. This forces the message layer to either optimize the alignment of arbitrary buffers or to copy memory to/from aligned data buffers.

Figure 3 illustrates the principle of optimizing the alignment of long buffers. The buffer is carved up into aligned chunks where possible. The two non-aligned chunks at the beginning and at the end of the buffer are copied and sent together. This strategy is not always applicable, because the alignment *phase* (*i.e.*, the offset from the

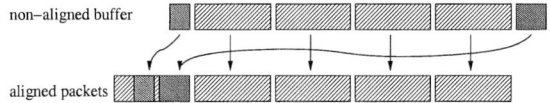

Fig. 3. Packetizing non-aligned data.

closest aligned address) of the sending and receiving buffers may differ. MPI has no control over the allocation of user buffers. In such cases at least one of the participating peers, preferably the sender, has to adjust alignment by performing memory to memory copies. For rendezvous messages the receiver can send back the *desired alignment phase* with the first acknowledgment packet. We note that the alignment problem only affects zero copy message sending strategies, since a memory copy can absorb the cost of re-alignment.

Out-of-order packets. The routing algorithm of the torus network allows packets from the same sender to arrive at the receiver out of order. The task of re-ordering packets falls to the message layer.

Packet order anomalies affect the message layer in one of two ways. The simpler case occurs when packets belonging to the same message are received out of order. This affects the way in which packets are re-assembled into messages, and the way in which MPI matching is done at the receiver (since typically MPI matching information is in the *first* packet of a message).

Packet order reversal can also occur to packets belonging to different messages. To prevent the mixing of packets belonging to different messages, each packet has to carry a message identifier. To comply with MPI semantics, the receiver is responsible to present incoming messages to MPI in strictly increasing order of the message identifier.

Cache coherence and processor use policy. Each BlueGene/L compute node incorporates two non-cache-coherent PowerPC 440 cores sharing the main memory and devices. Several modes of operation for these two cores have been proposed.

- *Heater mode* puts the second core into an idle loop. It is easy to implement because it sidesteps all issues of cache coherency and resource sharing.
- *Virtual node mode* executes a different application process in each core. Virtual node mode doubles the processing power available to the user at the cost of halving all other resources per process. It is well suited for computation-intensive jobs that require little in the way of memory or communication. We are still in the beginning of our research on virtual node mode and do not discuss it further in this paper.
- *Communication coprocessor mode* is considered the default mode of operation. It assigns one processor to computation and another to communication, effectively overlapping them by freeing the compute processor from communication tasks.

The main obstacle to implementing communication coprocessor mode efficiently is the lack of cache coherence between processors. A naive solution is to set up a non-cached shared memory area and implement a virtual torus device in that area. The computation processor communicates only with the virtual torus device. The communication processor simply moves data between the real device and the virtual device.

The naive implementation of coprocessor mode still requires the compute processor to packetize and copy data into the shared memory area. However, reads and writes to/from the shared memory area can be done about four times faster than to/from the network devices, reducing the load on the compute processor by the same amount.

For better performance, we want to develop a mechanism in which the communication processor moves data to and from the application memory directly. Before sending an MPI message, the compute processor has to insure that the application buffer has been flushed to main memory. The communication processor can then move that data directly to the hardware torus. When receiving a message, the compute processor has to invalidate the cache lines associated with its receive buffer before allowing the communication processor to fill it in with incoming data.

Scaling issues and virtual connections. In MPICH2, point to point communication is executed over virtual connections between pairs of nodes. Because the network hardware guarantees packet delivery, virtual connections in BlueGene/L do not have to execute a per-connection wake-up protocol when the job starts. Thus startup time on the BlueGene/L machine will be constant for any number of participating nodes.

Another factor limiting scalability is the amount of memory needed by an MPI process to maintain state for each virtual connection. The current design of the message layer uses only about 50 bytes of data for every virtual connection for the torus coordinates of the peer, pointer sets for the send and receive queues, and state information. Even so, 65,536 virtual connections add up to 3 MBytes of main memory per node, or more than 1% of the available total (256 MBytes), just to maintain the connection table.

Transmitting non-contiguous data. The MPICH2 abstract device interface allows non-contiguous data buffers to percolate down to message layer level, affording us the opportunity to optimize the marshalling and unmarshalling of these data types at the lowest (packet) level. Our current strategy centers on `iovec` data structures generated by utility functions in the ADI [8] layer.

Communication protocol in the message layer. Early in the design we made the decision to implement the communication protocol in the message layer for performance reasons. Integration with MPICH2 is somewhat harder, forcing us to implement an abstract device interface (ADI3) port instead of using the easier, but less flexible, channel interface [8]. In our view, the additional flexibility gained by this decision is well worth the effort. The protocol design is crucial because it is influenced by virtually every aspect of the BlueGene/L system: the reliability and out of order nature of the network, scalability issues, and latency and bandwidth requirements.

- Because of the reliable nature of the network no acknowledgments are needed. A simple "fire and forget" eager protocol is a viable proposition. Any packet out the send FIFO can be considered safely received by the other end.
- A special case of the eager protocol is represented by single-packet messages, which should be handled with a minimum of overhead to achieve good latency.

- The main limitation of the eager protocol is the inability of the receiver to control incoming traffic. For high volume messages, the rendezvous protocol is called for, possibly the optimistic form implemented in Portals [4].
- The message protocol is also influenced by out-of-order arrival of packets. The first packet of any message contains information not repeated in other packets, such as the message length and MPI matching information. If this packet is delayed on the network, the receiver is unable to handle the subsequent packets, and has to allocate temporary buffers or discard the packets, with obvious undesirable consequences. This problem does not affect the rendezvous protocol because the first packet is always explicitly acknowledged and thus cannot arrive out of order.
- A solution to the out-of-order problem for mid-size messages involves a variation on the rendezvous protocol that replicates the MPI matching information in the first few packets belonging to a message, and requires the receiver to acknowledge the first packet it receives. The number of packets that have to carry extra information is determined by the average roundtrip latency of the torus network. The sender will not have to stop and wait for an acknowledgment if it is received before the allotment of special packets carrying extra information has been exhausted.

6 Simulation Framework and Measurements

This section illustrates the measurement methodology we are using to drive our design decisions, and how we are planning to optimize the implementation of the MPI port. The numbers presented here are current as of April 2003, and were measured with the first version of the BlueGene/L port of MPICH2 that was able to run in the BGLsim multichip simulation environment [5]. BGLsim is equipped with an implementation of HPM [7, 9] which allows us to measure the number of instructions executed by regions of instrumented code. We measure the software overhead in the MPICH2 port and in the message layer. The workloads for our experiments consisted of the NAS Parallel Benchmarks [3, 10], running on 8 or 9 processors, depending on the benchmark.

Figure 4 shows a simplified call graph for sending a blocking MPI message, with the functions of interest to us highlighted. We instrumented these functions, and their counterparts on the receive end, with HPM library calls. HPM counted the average number of instructions per invocation.

Table 1 summarizes the measurements. The left panel in the table contains measurements for the high level functions of the MPICH2 port. As the table shows, blocking operations (MPI_Send and MPI_Recv) are not very good indicators of software overhead, because the instruction counts include those spent waiting for the simulated network to deliver packages. The numbers associated with non-blocking calls like MPI_Isend and MPI_Irecv are a much better measure of software overhead.

The right panel in the table contains data for message layer functions. The function postsend is called to post a message for sending. It includes the overhead for sending the first packet. The senddonecb function is called at the end of every message send. It shows the same number of instructions in every benchmark. The recvnewcb function has a slightly higher overhead because this is the function that performs the matching of an incoming message to the requests posted in the MPI request queue.

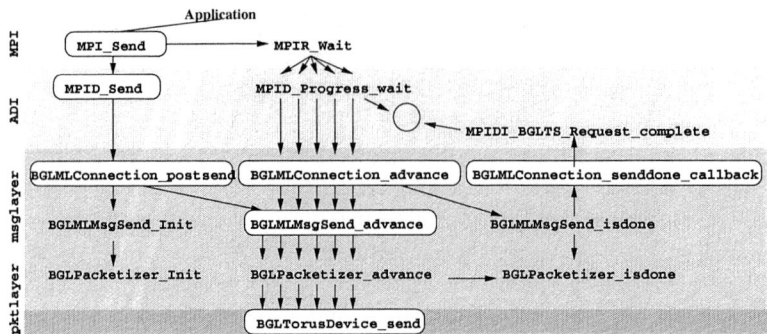

Fig. 4. The callgraph of an MPI_Send() call.

Table 1. Software overhead measurements for MPICH2 and message layer functions.

	FT	BT	SP	CG	MG	IS	LU
MPI_Send				11652	10479	3746	7129
MPID_Send				1759	1613	1536	1744
MPI_Isend		2043	2162				
MPID_Isend	1833	1782	1901				
MPI_Irecv		541	542	549	564	536	557
MPID_Irecv	280	279	280	293	308	280	301
MPI_Recv							13811
MPID_Recv							406

	FT	BT	SP	CG	MG	IS	LU
postsend	1107	1271	1401	1230	1114	1220	1265
senddonecb	115	115	115	115	115	115	115
recvnewcb	445	344	353	349	335	341	328
recvdonecb	16179	418	333	267	150	204	127
advance	2181	1643	1781	1429	1669	2865	955
msgsend_adv	671	653	648	620	556	642	594
dispatch	520	518	516	598	661	533	620

The recvdonecb numbers show a high variance, because in certain conditions this callback copies the message buffer from the unexpected queue to the posted queue. In our measurements this happened in the FT benchmark. The table also shows the amount of instructions spent by the message layer to get a packet into the torus hardware (msgsend_adv) or out of the torus hardware (dispatch).

An MPI_Isend call in the BT benchmark takes about 2000 instructions. Out of these, the call to postsend in the message layer accounts for 1300 instructions. The postsend function calls msgsend_adv to send the first packet of the message. The msgsend_adv function spends an average of 650 instructions sending the packet. Thus the software overhead of MPID_Send can be broken down as $2000 - 1300 = 700$ instructions spent in the MPICH2 software layers, $1300 - 650 = 650$ instructions spent in administering the message layer itself, and 650 instructions spent to send each packet from the message layer.

The above reasoning points at least one place to where the message layer can be improved. The minimum number of instructions necessary to send/receive an aligned packet is 50. However, the message layer spends approximately 650 instructions for the same purpose, partially because of suboptimal implementation, alignment adjustment through memory copies and packet layer overhead. We are confident that a better implementation of the message sender/receiver can reduce the packet sending overhead by 25-50%.

7 Conclusions

In this paper we have presented a software design for a communications library for the BlueGene/L supercomputer based on the MPICH2 software package. The design concentrates on achieving very low software overheads. Concentrating on point-to-point communication, the paper presents the design decisions we have already made and the measurement methodology we are planning to use to drive our optimization work.

References

1. N. R. Adiga et al. An overview of the BlueGene/L supercomputer. In *SC2002 – High Performance Networking and Computing*, Baltimore, MD, November 2002.
2. G. Almasi et al. Cellular supercomputing with system-on-a-chip. In *IEEE International Solid-state Circuits Conference ISSCC*, 2001.
3. D. H. Bailey, E. Barszcz, J. T. Barton, D. S. Browning, R. L. Carter, D. Dagum, R. A. Fatoohi, P. O. Frederickson, T. A. Lasinski, R. S. Schreiber, H. D. Simon, V. Venkatakrishnan, and S. K. Weeratunga. The NAS Parallel Benchmarks. *The International Journal of Supercomputer Applications*, 5(3):63–73, Fall 1991.
4. R. Brightwell and L. Shuler. Design and Implementation of MPI on Puma portals. In *In Proceedings of the Second MPI Developer's Conference*, pages 18–25, July 1996.
5. L. Ceze, K. Strauss, G. Almási, P. J. Bohrer, J. R. Brunheroto, C. Caşcaval, J. G. Castanos, D. Lieber, X. Martorell, J. E. Moreira, A. Sanomiya, and E. Schenfeld. Full circle: Simulating Linux clusters on Linux clusters. In *Proceedings of the Fourth LCI International Conference on Linux Clusters: The HPC Revolution 2003*, San Jose, CA, June 2003.
6. G. Chiola and G. Ciaccio. Gamma: a low cost network of workstations based on active messages. In *Proc. Euromicro PDP'97, London, UK, January 1997, IEEE Computer Society.*, 1997.
7. L. DeRose. The Hardware Performance Monitor Toolkit. In *Proceedings of Euro-Par*, pages 122–131, August 2001.
8. W. Gropp, E. Lusk, D. Ashton, R. Ross, R. Thakur, and B. Toonen. MPICH Abstract Device Interface Version 3.4 Reference Manual: Draft of May 20, 2003.
http://www-unix.mcs.anl.gov/mpi/mpich/adi3/adi3man.pdf.
9. P. Mindlin, J. R. Brunheroto, L. DeRose, and J. E. Moreira. Obtaining hardware performance metrics for the BlueGene/L supercomputer. In *Proceedings of Euro-Par 2003 Conference*, Lecture Notes in Computer Science, Klagenfurt, Austria, August 2003. Springer-Verlag.
10. NAS Parallel Benchmarks. http://www.nas.nasa.gov/Software/NPB.
11. S. Pakin, M. Lauria, and A. Chien. High performance messaging on workstations: Illinois Fast Messages (FM) for Myrinet. In *Supercomputing '95, San Diego, CA, December 1999*, 1995.
12. L. Shuler, R. Riesen, C. Jong, D. van Dresser, A. B. Maccabe, L. A. Fisk, and T. M. Stallcup. The PUMA operating system for massively parallel computers. In *In Proceedings of the Intel Supercomputer Users' Group. 1995 Annual North America Users' Conference*, June 1995.
13. T. von Eicken, A. Basu, V. Buch, and W. Vogels. U-net: A user-level network interface for parallel and distributed computing. In *Proceedings of the 15th ACM Symposium on Operating Systems Principles, Copper Mountain, Colorado*, December 1995.
14. T. von Eicken, D. E. Culler, S. C. Goldstein, and K. E. Schauser. Active Messages: a mechanism for integrated communication and computation. In *Proceedings of the 19th International Symposium on Computer Architecture*, May 1992.
15. The MPICH and MPICH2 homepage.
http://www-unix.mcs.anl.gov/mpi/mpich.

Porting P4 to Digital Signal Processing Platforms

Juan A. Rico[1], Juan C. Díaz Martín[1], José M. Rodríguez García[1],
Jesús M. Álvarez Llorente[1], and Juan L. García Zapata[2]

[1]Department of Computer Science, University of Extremadura. Spain
{jarico,juancarl,jmrodri,llorente}@unex.es
[2]Department of Mathematics,University of Extremadura. Spain
{jgzapata}@unex.es

Abstract. This paper presents preliminary work on bringing the Message Passing Interface standard to the DSP distributed real time applications world. MPICH is a thin implementation of MPI built upon the P4 parallel programming library. Originally built upon UNIX, our work deals with the issues of porting P4 to commercial multi-computers based on the Texas Instruments TMS320C6000 digital signal processor. We show that this implementation is possible and give performance figures.

1 Introduction and Goals

DSP processors show specialized architectures to run real time signal processing. They are currently used in a broad range of fields, including communications, like voice and data compression or mobile telephony, multimedia, like speech and image processing, medicine, like diagnostic imaging, etc. These applications have a high computational complexity, usually overcoming the personal computer power. Fortunately, most of applications and algorithms can be decoupled and distributed among two or more processors ([5], [6]). DSP multi-computers are nowadays available in the market at affordable prices. For instance, Sundance ([7]) manufactures this kind of machines; based on Texas Instruments TMS320C6000 DSPs. System software support for these parallel computers consists mainly on low-level communication libraries that the manufacturer of the platform provides. In the better case, it tends to be hardware specific and, therefore, a poor tool to build scalable and portable distributed DSP applications and systems. In our view, a distributed programming standard will ease the exploitation of DSP parallelism. Thus, our ultimate goal is to attack distributed signal processing via the parallel and distributed programming standard MPI. This work describes some efforts made on this sense. MPICH ([1]) is a well-known implementation of MPI, based in the P4 parallel programming library ([2]). We got MPICH and tried to make it run on an industrial DSP development environment. At this moment, we are able of running the P4 interface on the Texas Instruments DSK (DSP Starter Kit) development environment.

The rest of paper is structured as follows. Section 2 presents IDSP; a distributed real time framework targeted to Texas Instruments TMS320C6000 based multi-computers. Section 3 discusses some issues on porting P4 upon the IDSP interface. Section 4 deals with the problem of the overhead that P4 imposes to real time DSP applications. Section 5 presents some conclusions and ongoing and future work.

2 IDSP: A Distributed Real Time Framework for DSPs

DSP/BIOS ([4]) is the real time kernel that Texas Instruments provides for its DSP processors. It provides timing services and basic support for management and synchronization of threads, as well as a rich set of tools for tracing and analysis. IDSP ([3]) is a distributed framework that extends DSP/BIOS with inter-processor control and communication facilities (Fig. 1). IDSP is manly intended to provide transparency to location of threads. We have used it as the software layer that supports P4. We have devised and developed IDSP in the TMS320C6711 Texas Instruments DSK platform and we are now in the process of running it on a Sundance SMT310Q multi-computer board with four Sundance SMT335 modules. Each SMT335 holds a Texas Instruments TMS320C6201 processor.

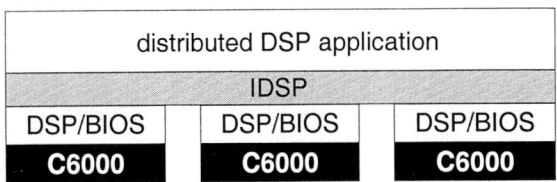

Fig. 1. The IDSP framework

The IDSP cornerstone is the concept of group (Fig. 2). The distributed application that Fig. 2 shows is a directed graph of related algorithms that cooperate in solving a DSP task. The Levinson-Durving algorithm, for instance, collaborates in a speech recognition engine application. An arrow in the graph represents a data stream between two algorithms. A *group* is an application in execution, and it is known by a single identifier in a global scope. A group is therefore a graph of *operators* running on one or more processors. An operator is a single independent thread of execution dedicated to run an algorithm. Operators communicate by using the *communicator* object. A communicator is something similar to a UNIX Berkeley socket and it has nothing to do with the MPI communicator concept.

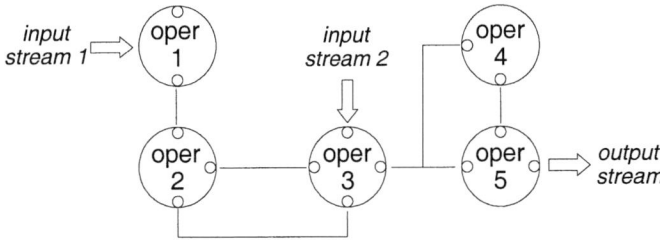

Fig. 2. A group of operators: The IDSP model of a distributed application

IDSP is able of dynamically creating one or more instances of a given application, assigning operators to processors following a load-balancing approach. Communicator objects can be also dynamically created. There are two kinds of operators: *user* operators, that run DSP algorithms, and *server* operators, that provide IDSP system services, such as the creation of new operators and groups. A server operator runs a service loop, working as a RPC skeleton. The group service implements the GROUP interface, the operator service implements the OPER interface, etc. Fig. 3 illustrates the microkernel architecture of the IDSP framework. The so named *kernel* module is dedicated to implement the COMM message passing API.

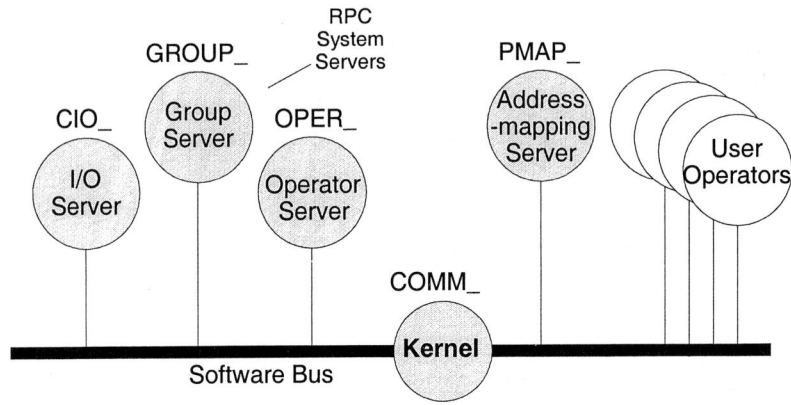

Fig. 3. The IDSP Architecture

An important aspect of IDSP is its addressing scheme. Each communicator has assigned an address known as a *port*. The port is composed by three integer numbers *(gix, oix, cix)* –the group index, the operator index and the communicator index. The group index is allocated by the system at group creation time. The operator index identifies an operator inside a group. The communicator index identifies a communicator inside an operator. This definition makes ports to be transparent to the specific machine location of its operator. Operators use the communicators via the COMM interface in order to interchange messages. Fig. 4 shows the message format. Note that the same format is used to send and receive either DSP data or RPC parameters and results.

SRC address	DST address	SIZE	DATA/METHOD

Fig. 4. The IDSP message format

Algorithm operators communicate data streams through *channels*, library objects built upon the communicator object. The channel API eases the writing and porting of algorithms to the IDSP environment even more by hiding the communicator concept. There are two kinds of channels, input and output ones. Every input communicator has a *timeout* attribute for real time purposes.

Fig. 5 shows that IDSP is internally structured as four sub-layers. The *library level* provides the operator, group, and channel APIs. The *kernel level* supports the communication API. The *network level*, has been written in a hardware independent way, leaving to the *link level* the true relation with each particular configuration of communication hardware. Up to time of writing, the actual devices used by the link level are, on one hand, the serial port McBSP in loop-back mode, assisted by the EDMA for improved performance, and, on other hand, shared memory. A TCP/IP device is under construction. Adding other communicating devices just conveys replacing the module that implements the Link level and the way of using it.

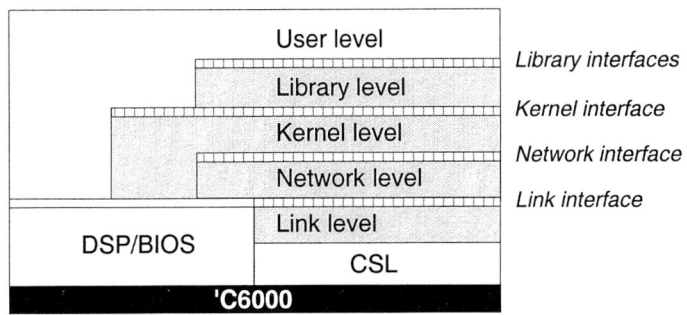

Fig. 5. The layered design of IDSP

3 Implementing the P4 Functionality upon IDSP

The purpose of DSP/BIOS is helping to build applications of digital signal processing. It is not POSIX compliant. It is not even an UNIX-like system. The same considerations apply, therefore, to IDSP. P4, in contrast, relies on the classic UNIX primitives for concurrency and on Berkeley sockets or internal shared memory mechanisms for communication. Table 1, however, demonstrate that there exists a certain correspondence between both interfaces.

Table 1. Correspondence of P4 basic primitives with UNIX and IDSP

P4	IDSP	UNIX
`P4_initenv(argc, argv)`	`OPER_create(&oper,`	`fork, rsh, exec`
`P4_create_procgroup()`	`fxn, app, addr,`	
	`param)`	
	`GROUP_create(&gix,`	
	`app, param)`	
	`COMM_create`	`socket, bind, listen,`
		`connect, accept`
`P4_send(type, buff,`	`COMM_send(comm,`	`send(sock, buff,`
`    dst, bytes)`	`    dst, buff, bytes)`	`    bytes, flags)`
`P4_recv(type, buff,`	`COMM_receive(comm,`	`recv(sock, buff,`
`    src, bytes)`	`    src, buff, bytes)`	`    bytes, flags)`
`P4_wait_for_end()`	`OPER_destroy(oper,`	`exit, close`
	`    addr)`	
	`GROUP_destroy(gix)`	

Once we know the IDSP interface and internal design, the following questions arise: Is it possible to implement the P4 functionality upon IDSP? What will be its resultant performance? We have explored the problem by building the P4/IDSP stack shown in Fig. 6. This section discusses this issue.

We deal in first place with concurrency aspects. P4 is based on UNIX processes, creating them in local and remote machines. P4, on other hand, is not a thread-safe library because assumes the classic process of a single thread. IDSP, however, is a thread-based system, being a thread a DSP/BIOS task. As Fig. 6 shows, IDSP threads re-enter P4. Thus, migrating P4 to IDSP bring us the problem of dealing with global variables shared by threads. Some variables have to be put in threads private memory to save their values while the remaining ones have to be protected with mutual exclusion mechanisms. An example is the *proc_info* structure. There is a data structure of this kind in every process to store information of the other processes in the application. This data structure is shared under IDSP, so we had to put it in the private zone of every thread.

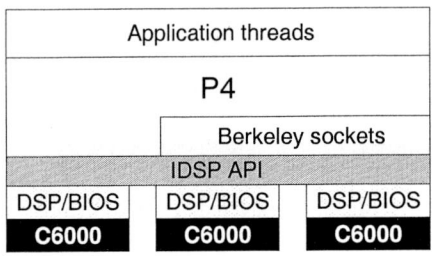

Fig. 6. The P4/IDSP stack

A second problem is the communication pattern and the addressing scheme. Targeted to DSP multi-computer environments, the IDSP communicator object supports a connectionless service, mainly due to there are not communication errors in this kind of hardware. P4, however, is based upon Berkeley Sockets on TCP, a connection-oriented protocol useful in wide area networks, but not in a reliable channel, where it just adds overhead. To fill this gap we have ported the Berkeley socket API upon the COMM API of IDSP. This implementation has resulted quite thin and efficient, as we will see in Fig. 9. The key design issue here is to consider the group as the frame or container for an IDSP/P4 application. All MPI groups and processes of the application run into the environment of the IDSP group as Fig. 7 shows.

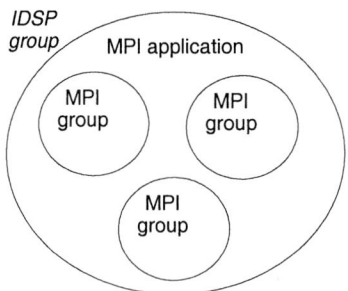

Fig. 7. An IDSP group contains an MPICH or P4 application

This strategy leaves unmodified the P4 communication code when running on IDSP, but poses the problem of mapping the Internet address (machine, port) to the IDSP address. An IDSP server operator solves it (Fig. 3) by managing a table that stores the mapping. It listens in a well-known IDSP port. Client operators communicate with it to register their Internet addresses and to get the IDSP addresses of message destinations. Operators have a cache to store these addresses that minimize the communication overhead with this server.

P4 uses UNIX signals for timeouts and for process termination among other purposes. As DSP/BIOS does not provide signals, we have constructed timeouts upon DSP/BIOS clock services and termination through IDSP messages.

UNIX P4 start-up procedure begins by reading the `procgroup` file and executable files. IDSP P4, in contrast, reads the application register, which plays the role of a file system in a conventional UNIX computer.

Finally, the P4 listener is a daemon process charged to do some background work for every P4 process, such as accepting new connections. The overhead of this process is high in a real time application. Fortunately, every IDSP operator has a well-known port in an operator to receive asynchronous data. Because an IDSP operator runs their main function without parameters, we need this port to send initial information to any new process.

4 Measuring the P4 Overhead

IDSP has been tested primarily in speech processing applications, paying a good performance as Fig. 8 shows. We have evaluated the overhead introduced by P4 on the IDSP communication primitives. Fig. 8 shows the time it takes doing a rendezvous for different sized messages under P4/IDSP and IDSP. In our view, the overhead is remarkable, but not quite bad. Moreover P4/IDSP is been further improved.

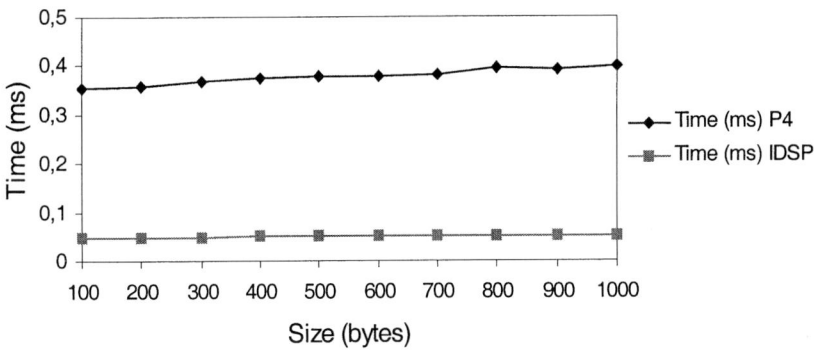

Fig. 8. The P4 performance

Fig. 9 shows the same tests comparing IDSP against our before mentioned thin binding of the Berkeley sockets interface upon IDSP. The performance degradation is here quite low, what validates our approach.

5 Conclusions and Current Work

To our knowledge, we have made the first reported migration of P4 to a stand-alone DSP environment. In our view, the use of the IDSP framework has been a key aspect in the success of this work. IDSP interface has resulted flexible enough to support the P4 functionality with a reasonable and expected overhead.

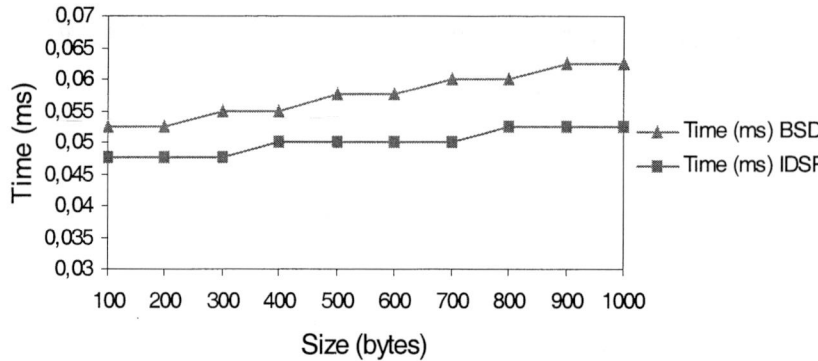

Fig. 9. The overhead introduced by the socket/IDSP binding results minimum

We are currently working on the optimisation of P4/IDSP and using it to support a distributed speech recognition engine, as well as building the MPI API upon MPICH/P4. We are also extending IDSP link layer to take P4 to a Sundance SMT310Q multi-computer board with four DSP processors.

We plan future work on implementing and testing the MPI/RT specifications on the DSP world.

Acknowledgements

The Junta de Extremadura founded this work under IPR00C032 project.

References

1. William Gropp, Ewing Lusk, Nathan Doss, Anthony Skjellum, "A High Performance, Portable Implementation of the MPI Message Passing Interface Standard". Parallel Computing, 22, pp. 789-828 (1996).
2. Ralph Butler, Ewng Lusk: User´s Guide to the P4 Parallel Programming System. Technical Report ANL-92/17, Argonne National Laboratory (1992).
3. Díaz Martín, J.C., Rodríguez García, José M., Álvarez Llorente, Jesús M, Juan I. García, Rico Gallego, Juan A.: "On Group Communication for Speech Processing", Submitted to the 8th European Conference on Speech Communication and Technology, September, 1-4, 2003. Geneva, Switzerland.
4. Texas Instruments: TMS320C6000 DSP/BIOS User´s Guide. Literature Number SPRU303B, Texas Instruments (2002).
5. Díaz Martín, J.C., Rodríguez García, J.M., García Zapata J.L., Gómez Vilda, P., "Robust Voice Recognition as a Distributed Service", Proc. of 8th IEEE Int. Conf. on Emerging Technologies and Factory Automation, EFTA 2001, Antibes, France, V2, pp. 571-575.
6. Díaz Martin, JC. Garcia Zapata, JL. Rodriguez Garcia, J.M., Alvarez Salgado, J.F., Espada Bueno, P. Gómez Vilda, P.," DIARCA: A Component Approach to Voice Recognition", Proc. of 7th European Conference on Speech Communication and Technology, Eurospeech 2001, Aalborg, Denmark, 2001, V4, pp. 2393-2396
7. http://www.sundance.com

Fast and Scalable Barrier Using RDMA and Multicast Mechanisms for InfiniBand-Based Clusters*

Sushmitha P. Kini[1], Jiuxing Liu[1], Jiesheng Wu[1],
Pete Wyckoff[2], and Dhabaleswar K. Panda[1]

[1] Dept. of CIS, The Ohio State University, Columbus, OH - 43210
{kinis,liuj,wuj,panda}@cis.ohio-state.edu
[2] Ohio Supercomputer Center, 1224 Kinnear Road,
Columbus, OH - 43212
pw@osc.edu

Abstract. This paper describes a methodology for efficiently implementing the barrier operation, on clusters with the emerging InfiniBand Architecture (IBA). IBA provides hardware level support for the Remote Direct Memory Access (RDMA) message passing model as well as the multicast operation. This paper describes the design, implementation and evaluation of three barrier algorithms that leverage these mechanisms. Performance evaluation studies indicate that considerable benefits can be achieved using these mechanisms compared to the traditional implementation based on the point-to-point message passing model. Our experimental results show a performance benefit of up to 1.29 times for a 16-node barrier and up to 1.71 times for non-powers-of-2 group size barriers. Each proposed algorithm performs the best for certain ranges of group sizes and the optimal algorithm can be chosen based on this range. To the best of our knowledge, this is the first attempt to characterize the multicast performance in IBA and to demonstrate the benefits achieved by combining it with RDMA operations for efficient implementations of barrier. This framework has significant potential for developing scalable collective communication libraries for IBA-based clusters.

1 Introduction

Barriers are used for synchronizing the parallel processes in applications based on the Message Passing Interface (MPI) [11] programming model. The MPI_Barrier function call is invoked by all the processes in a group. This call blocks a process until all the other members in the group have invoked it. An efficient implementation of the barrier is essential because it is a blocking call and no computation can be performed in parallel with this call. Faster barriers improve the parallel speedup of applications and helps in scalability.

---
* This research is supported in part by Sandia National Laboratory's contract #30505, Department of Energy's Grant #DE-FC02-01ER25506, and National Science Foundation's grants #EIA-9986052 and #CCR-0204429.

Recent communication technologies like VIA and InfiniBand Architecture [3] offer a model of data transport based on memory semantics. They allow transfer of data directly between user level buffers on remote nodes without the active participation of either the sender or the receiver. This is a one-sided operation that does not incur a software overhead at the remote side. This method of operation is called Remote Direct Memory Access (RDMA).

In current generation clusters the MPI collective operations are implemented using algorithms that use the MPI point-to-point communication calls. When an operation like barrier is executed the nodes make explicit send and receive calls. The receive operation is generally an expensive operation since it involves posting a descriptor for the message. This overhead can be effectively eliminated using RDMA operations.

Another attractive feature in the IBA network is the support for hardware-based multicast. Multicast is the ability to send a single message to a specific address and have it delivered to multiple processes which may be on different end nodes. This primitive is provided under the Unreliable Datagram (UD) transport mode, which is connectionless and unacknowledged. IBA allows processes to attach to a multicast group and then the message sent to the group will be delivered to all the processes in the group. Performance evaluations of this multicast primitive with the InfiniHost HCAs [8], InfiniScale switch and VAPI interface [9] show that it takes about $9.6 \mu s$ to send a 1-byte message to 1 node and $9.8 \mu s$ to send the message to 7 nodes. This shows that the operation is quite scalable and can be used effectively to design scalable collective operations.

In this paper, we aim to provide answers to the following two questions:

1. Can we optimize the MPI collective operations by using algorithms that leverage the RDMA primitives in IBA instead of algorithms that use the existing MPI point-to-point operations?

2. Can the multicast primitives in IBA be used to implement scalable collective communication operations?

The paper shows that replacing the point-to-point communication calls in the collective operations with faster lower-level operations can provide significant performance gains. Performance improvement is possible due to various reasons. Primarily, the number of data copies is reduced by avoiding point-to-point messaging protocols. Also, software overheads like tag matching and unexpected message handling are eliminated. The hardware multicast feature fits in well with the semantics of collective operations and hence can be utilized to our advantage. We propose three algorithms that utilize these features of IBA.

MVAPICH [12] is the implementation of Abstract Device Interface (ADI) [15] for the VAPI interface of the InfiniHost HCAs and is derived from MVICH [6] from Lawrence Berkeley National Laboratory. The algorithms for the barrier were implemented and integrated into the MVAPICH implementation of MPI over IBA, and we discuss the design and implementation issues here. We also present the results of our performance evaluations and show that considerable benefits are achieved using the proposed techniques.

2 Overview of RDMA and Multicast in InfiniBand

The InfiniBand Architecture (IBA) [3] defines a System Area Network (SAN) for interconnecting processing nodes and I/O nodes. It supports both channel and memory semantics. In channel semantics, send/receive operations are used for communication. In memory semantics, RDMA write and RDMA read operations are used instead of send and receive operations. These operations can directly access the memory address space of a remote process. They are one-sided and do not incur software overhead at the remote side.

InfiniBand provides hardware support for multicast. In some cases, this mechanism can greatly reduce communication traffic as well as latency and host overhead. InfiniBand also provides flexible mechanisms to manage multicast groups. However, multicast is only available for the Unreliable Datagram (UD) service. Therefore, tasks such as fragmentation, acknowledgment and retransmission, may be needed on top of UD to make multicast work reliably.

3 Barrier Algorithms

In this section we describe the three algorithms that we have designed and implemented for the barrier operation. In the following subsections we denote processes using symbols i, j, k and the total number of processes involved in the barrier is denoted by N. We refer to the process that has a distinguished role to play in some algorithms as the *root*. We indicate the number of the current barrier by the symbol *barrier_id*.

3.1 RDMA-Based Pairwise Exchange (RPE)

The algorithm for the barrier operation in the MPICH distribution is called the Pairwise Exchange (PE) recursive doubling algorithm. MPICH makes use of the MPI_Send and MPI_Recv calls for the implementation of this algorithm. If the number of nodes performing the barrier is a power of two, then the number of steps in the algorithm is $\log_2 N$ and it is $\lfloor \log_2 N \rfloor + 2$ otherwise.

Now we describe how this algorithm can be performed using the RDMA Write primitive. The barrier is a collective call, and so each process keeps a running count of the current barrier number, *barrier_id*. Each process has an array of bytes of length N. In each step of the PE, process i writes the *barrier_id* in the ith position of the array of the partner process j. It then waits for the *barrier_id* to appear in the jth position of its own array. Since each process is directly polling on memory for the reception of data, it avoids the overhead of posting descriptors and copying of data from temporary buffers, as is the case when the MPI_Recv call is used.

Figure 1 gives a pictorial representation of this algorithm. Here N is 4, and the processes are called P0, P1, P2, and P3. In the first step P0 does an RDMA write of *barrier_id*, in this case 1, to index 0 of P1's array and waits for P1 to write in index 1 of its own array. In the second step it performs the same operations with P2.

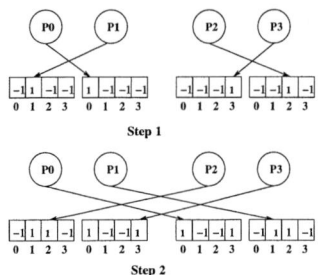

Fig. 1. Steps performed in RPE for a 4-node barrier

3.2 RDMA-Based Dissemination (RDS)

In the Dissemination Barrier algorithm as described in [10], the synchronization is not done pairwise as in the previous algorithm. In round m, process i sends a message to process $j = (i + 2^m) \mod N$. It then waits for a message from the process $k = (i + N - 2^m) \mod N$. This algorithm takes $\lceil \log_2 N \rceil$ steps at each process, irrespective of whether there are power of two or non-power of two number of nodes and thus is a more efficient pattern of synchronizations. More details on this algorithm are discussed in [4, 5].

The barrier signaling operations using RDMA write are done exactly as in the RPE algorithm, and this algorithm only varies in way in which the processes are grouped for communication in each step.

3.3 RDMA-Based Gather and Multicast (RGM)

In this scheme, the barrier operation is divided into two phases. In the first phase called the gather, every node indicates its arrival at the barrier by sending a message to a special process, *root*. This process of gather can be done in a hierarchical fashion by imposing a logical tree structure on the processes. Once *root* has received the messages from all its children, it enters the multicast phase. In this phase *root* broadcasts a message to all the nodes to signal that they can now exit the barrier.

In this two-step technique we use RDMA writes in the gather phase. The processes are arranged in a tree structure. Each process has an array of bytes on which it polls for messages from its children. Once it receives messages from all its children, the process forwards the message to its parent.

When *root* receives all the RDMA messages, it does a hardware multicast to all the processes. The multicast message contains the *barrier_id*. This phase is a one step process, since the multicast primitive is such that the single message gets sent to all the members of the multicast group.

Let us assume that the gather phase is done with a maximum fan-in of l. The value of l is chosen to be a $(power of 2 - 1)$ value, and $l < N$. So the number of levels in the tree created in this phase will be $\lceil \log_{l+1} N \rceil$, and this is the number of hops done by the barrier signal to reach *root*. In the multicast phase just one step is taken by the *root* to signal completion of the barrier to all nodes.

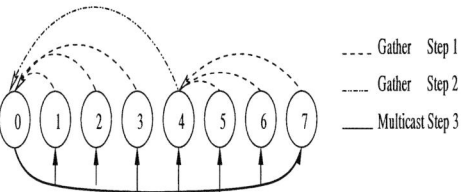

Fig. 2. Gather and Multicast Algorithm

Figure 2 shows how this algorithm works for a barrier on 8 processes. Here the gather is done using a 2 stage tree with the value of l as 3. Process 0 is *root*. The value for l can be chosen based on the number of nodes and the performance of the RDMA write operation.

4 Design Issues

We now discuss the intrinsic issues associated with the design and implementation of the proposed algorithms.

4.1 Buffer Management

IBA specification requires that all the data transfer be done only between buffers that are registered. Implementing collective operations on top of point-to-point message passing calls leads us to rely on the internal buffer management and data transfer schemes which might not always be optimal in the collective operations context. In order to use the RDMA method of data transfer, each node is required to pin some buffers and send/receive data using them. Also, the remote nodes should be aware of the local buffer address and memory handle, which means that a handshake for the address exchange should be done. The allocation and registration can be done at various stages during the life of the MPI application.

In our implementation, the buffers are allocated and registered during the first barrier call made by a process. This ensures that the memory is registered only if the application is involved in collective operations. Since the barrier is a collective call, during the first MPI_Barrier call, all the processes allocate memory for the barrier and perform the exchange of the virtual addresses. The size of the memory allocated is the same as the size of the communicator. Each element in this allocated array will be written by the corresponding process using an RDMA write call. Since every process in the communicator is identified by a *rank* the array elements can be indexed using this *rank* value. Other options of registering buffers, including a dynamic scheme, are discussed in [4, 5].

4.2 Data Reception

The RDMA write operation is transparent at the receiving end and hence the receiver is not aware of the arrival of data. We need a mechanism to notify the receiver of the completion of the RDMA write.

We make use of a scheme where the receiver polls on the buffers for arrival of data. This means that when the buffers are allocated, they will need to be initialized with some special data so that the data arrival can be recognized. There is a static count called the *barrier_id* that is maintained by each process. This value is always positive. So during the initialization we assign a negative value to all the array elements. When a process needs a message from a remote process, it polls the corresponding array element. It waits for the value to be greater than or equal to the current *barrier_id*. This is needed to handle cases with consecutive barriers. If one process is faster than the other, it will enter the second barrier before the other can exit the first one. Thus it will write the larger barrier number in the array.

4.3 Reliability for Unreliable Multicast Operations

The MPI specification assumes that the underlying communication interface is reliable and that the user need not cope with communication failures. Since the multicast operation in IBA is unreliable, reliability has to be handled in our design. One alternative is to provide an acknowledgment (ACK) message from the processes after every multicast message is received. The sending process waits for the ACKs from all the nodes and retransmits otherwise. This technique is very expensive.

In our implementation each receiving process maintains a timer and sends a negative acknowledgment (NAK) when it has not received a message. When the root process receives this message, it retransmits the multicast message. Processes that have already received the message discard this retransmitted message.

The IB specification allows for event handlers to be executed when a completion queue entry is generated. There is the option of triggering these event handlers on the receive side only if the "solicit" flag is set in the message by the sender. This facility can be used in the NAK message. By setting the solicit flag, this message triggers the event handler at the *root*, which then does a retransmission of the multicast message.

We have seen in our clusters that the rate of dropping UD packets is very low, and hence this reliability feature is not called upon often. Also, since IBA allows us to specify service levels to QPs, we could assign high priority service levels to the UD QPs. Thus the chances of these messages getting dropped is reduced even further. We also see that in the normal scenarios where there are no packets dropped, there is no overhead imposed by the reliability component.

5 Performance Evaluation

We conducted our performance evaluations on the following two clusters.

Cluster 1: A cluster of 8 SuperMicro SUPER P4DL6 nodes, each with dual Intel Xeon 2.4GHz processors, 512MB memory, PCI-X 64-bit 133MHz bus, and connected to a Mellanox InfiniHost MT23108 DualPort 4x HCA. The nodes are connected using the Mellanox InfiniScale MT43132 eight 4x port switch. The Linux kernel version is 2.4.7-10smp. The InfiniHost SDK version is 0.1.2 and the HCA firmware version is 1.17.

Cluster 2: A cluster of 16 Microway nodes, each with dual Intel Xeon 2.4GHz processors, 2GB memory, PCI-X 64-bit 133MHz bus, and connected to a Topspin InfiniBand 4x HCA [16]. The HCAs are connected to the Topspin 360 Switched Computing System, which is a 24 port 4x InfiniBand switch with the ability to include up to 12 gateway cards in the chassis. The Linux kernel version is 2.4.18-10smp. The HCA SDK version is 0.1.2 and firmware version is 1.17.

The barrier latency was obtained by executing MPI_Barrier 1000 times and the average of the latencies across all the nodes was calculated.

Figure 3 shows the performance comparisons of the three proposed barrier algorithms with MPI-PE, the standard pairwise exchange MPICH implementation of the barrier. We see that RPE and RDS perform better than MPI-PE for all cases. The pairwise exchange algorithms, MPI-PE and RPE, always penalize the non-power-of-2 cases, and this is not seen in RDS and RGM. Hence on Cluster 1, RDS and RGM gain a performance improvement of up to 1.64 and 1.71 respectively. On Cluster 2, we see that RGM performs best in most cases and the maximum factor of improvement seen is 1.59. For group sizes of 2 and 4, RGM does worse because the base latency of the UD multicast operation is greater than that of a single RDMA write. The performance of RPE and RDS for powers-of-2 group sizes is very similar. We see that for 8 nodes in Cluster 1, we gain as much as 1.25 factor of improvement with RPE and 1.27 with RDS. On Cluster 2 RGM does the best for 16 nodes with an improvement of 1.29. This is because for larger group sizes, RGM has the benefit of the constant time multicast phase.

The factor of improvement for RPE is almost a constant in all cases because the benefit is obtained by the constant difference in the latency between a point-to-point send/receive operation and an RDMA-Write/poll operation.

The performance of the RGM algorithm varies with the values for maximum fan-in in the gather phase. As this value decreases, the height of the tree increases and this will increase the number of RDMA writes being done. But if this value is large, the parent node becomes a hot-spot, that could possibly cause degradation in performance. Based on our experiments, we observed that a fan-in of 7 gives the best performance, and hence have chosen this value in our implementations.

As mentioned earlier, the pairwise exchange algorithm does badly for non-power-of-2 group sizes because of 2 extra operations. Hence in order to do a fair comparison, we implemented the Dissemination algorithm with the point-to-point MPI functions. We refer to this as MPI-DS. The barrier latencies of the proposed algorithms are better than that of MPI-DS too. Figure 4 shows the comparison of the RDS and RGM implementations with MPI-DS. It is to be noted that inspite of providing benefits to the current MPI implementation, RDS achieves up to 1.36 factor of improvement, and RGM achieves 1.46 on Cluster 1. We see an improvement of 1.32 with RDS and 1.48 with RGM on cluster 2.

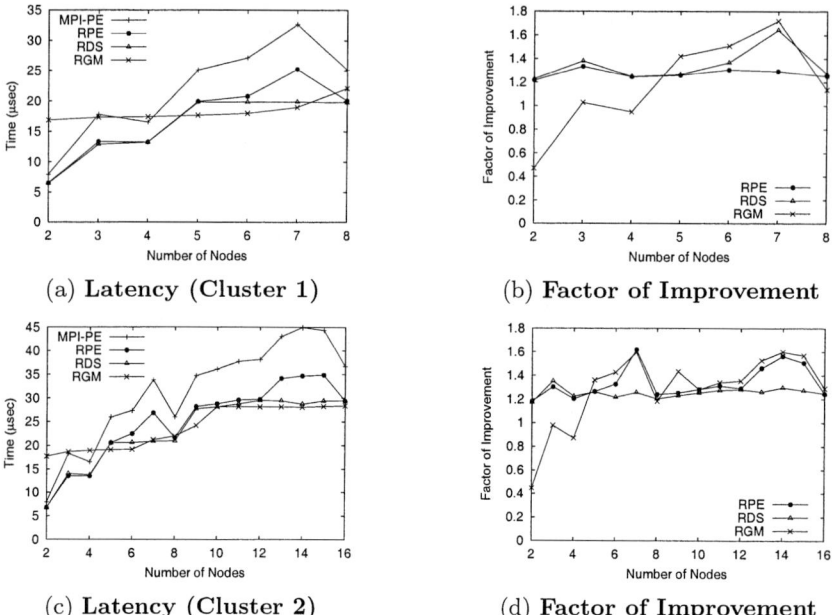

Fig. 3. Comparison of MPI-PE with the proposed algorithms for all group sizes on Clusters 1 and 2

6 Related Work

The benefits of using RDMA for point-to-point message passing operations for IBA clusters has been described in [7]. The methods and issues involved in implementing point-to-point operations over one-sided communication protocols in LAPI are presented in [1]. However using these optimized point-to-point operations does not eliminate the data copy, buffering and tag matching overheads. A lot of research has taken place in the past to design and develop optimal algorithms for collective operations on various networks using point-to-point primitives, but not much work has been done on selection of the communication primitives themselves.

RDMA based design of collective operations for VIA based clusters [13, 14] has been studied earlier. Combining remote memory and intra-node shared memory for efficient collective operations on IBM SP has been presented in [17]. The implementations and performance evaluations of the barrier operation using remote mapped memory on the SCI interconnect was presented in [2]. However these papers do not focus on taking advantage of novel mechanisms in IBA to develop efficient collective operations.

7 Conclusions and Future Work

In this paper, we have presented three new approaches (RPE, RDS, and RGM) to efficiently implement the barrier operation on IBA-based clusters while taking

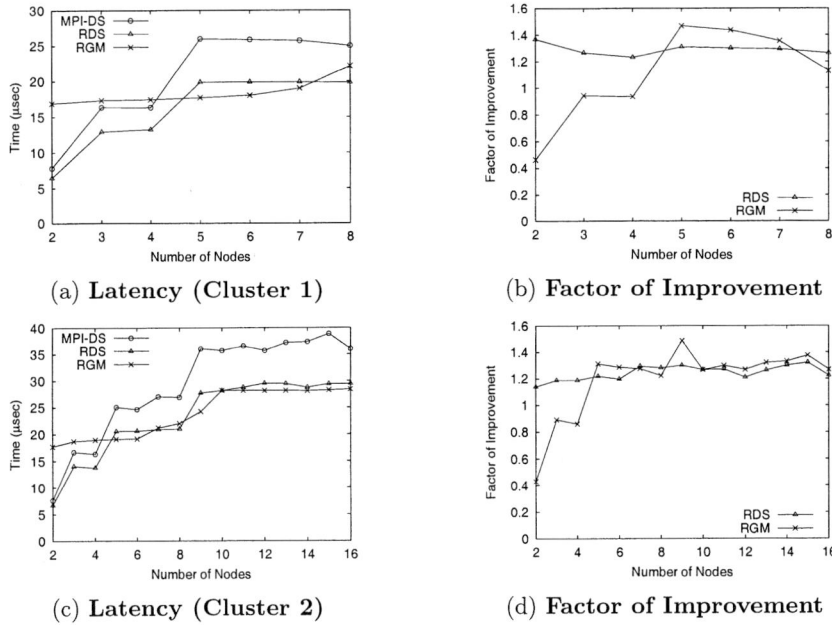

Fig. 4. Comparison of MPI-DS with the proposed algorithms on Clusters 1 and 2

advantage of the RDMA and multicast functionalities of IBA. The experimental results we achieved show that the proposed approaches significantly outperform the current barrier implementations in MPI that use point-to-point messaging. The RGM scheme tends to perform well for larger group sizes, while RPE and RDS perform better for smaller groups. The results also show that the schemes are scalable with system size and will provide better benefits for larger clusters. Therefore we arrive at the conclusion that the efficiency of the barrier operations can be considerably improved compared to the traditional point-to-point messaging calls based implementations by using the novel mechanisms of IBA.

We are working on extending these ideas to implement other collective operations like broadcast and allreduce. We expect the challenges and scope for improvement to be greater in these cases because of the data transfer involved in these operations. We are also planning to use the other features of IBA, like support for atomic and RDMA read operations to implement the collective operations efficiently.

Acknowledgments

We would like to thank Kevin Deierling and Jeff Kirk from Mellanox Technologies for their support with the InfiniBand hardware and software. We would also like to thank Ben Eiref, Robert Starmer, and Lorne Boden from Topspin Communications for all their efforts in providing us access to their 16 node InfiniBand cluster. We would like to thank Rinku Gupta, Amith Rajith Mamidala, Pavan

Balaji and Balasubramaniam Chandrasekaran from our research group for their help and valuable suggestions.

References

1. Mohammad Banikazemi, Rama K. Govindaraju, Robert Blackmore, and Dhabaleswar K. Panda. MPI-LAPI: An Efficeint Implementation of MPI for IBM RS/6000 SP Systems. *IEEE TPDS*, pages 1081–1093, October 2001.
2. Lars Paul Huse. Collective communication on dedicated clusters of workstations. In *PVM/MPI*, pages 469–476, 1999.
3. InfiniBand Trade Association. InfiniBand Architecture Specification, Release 1.0, October 24 2000.
4. Sushmitha P. Kini. Efficient Collective Communication using RDMA and Multicast Operations for InfiniBand-Based Clusters. Master Thesis, The Ohio State University, June 2003.
5. Sushmitha P. Kini, Jiuxing Liu, Jiesheng Wu, Pete Wyckoff, and Dhabaleswar K. Panda. Fast and Scalable Barrier using RDMA and Multicast Mechanisms for InfiniBand-Based Clusters. Technical Report, OSU-CISRC-05/03-TR24, May 2003.
6. Lawrence Livermore National Laboratory. MVICH: MPI for Virtual Interface Architecture, August 2001.
7. Jiuxing Liu, Jiesheng Wu, Sushmitha P. Kini, Pete Wyckoff, and Dhabaleswar K. Panda. High Performance RDMA-Based MPI Implementation over InfiniBand. In *ICS '03*, June 2003.
8. Mellanox Technologies. Mellanox InfiniBand InfiniHost Adapters, July 2002.
9. Mellanox Technologies. Mellanox IB-Verbs API (VAPI), Rev. 0.97, May 2003.
10. John M. Mellor-Crummey and Michael L. Scott. Algorithms for scalable synchronization on shared-memory multiprocessors. *ACM ToCS*, 9(1):21–65, 1991.
11. Message Passing Interface Forum. MPI: A Message Passing Interface. In *Supercomputing '93*, pages 878–883. IEEE Computer Society Press, 1993.
12. Network-Based Computing Laboratory. MVAPICH: MPI for InfiniBand on VAPI Layer. http://nowlab.cis.ohio-state.edu/projects/mpi-iba/index.html, January 2003.
13. R. Gupta, P. Balaji, D. K. Panda, and J. Nieplocha. Efficient Collective Operations using Remote Memory Operations on VIA-Based Clusters. In *IPDPS '03*, April 2003.
14. R. Gupta, V. Tipparaju, J. Nieplocha and D. K. Panda. Efficient Barrier using Remote Memory Operations on VIA-Based Clusters. In *Cluster 02*, September 2002.
15. Rajeev Thakur, William Gropp, and Ewing Lusk. An Abstract-Device Interface for Implementing Portable Parallel-I/O Interfaces. In *Frontiers '96*. IEEE Computer Society, Oct 1996.
16. Topspin Communications, Inc. Topspin InfiniBand Host Channel Adapter, http://www.topspin.com/solutions/hca.html.
17. V. Tipparaju, J. Nieplocha, D. K. Panda. Fast Collective Operations Using Shared and Remote Memory Access Protocols on Clusters. In *IPDPS '03*, April 2003.

A Component Architecture for LAM/MPI*

Jeffrey M. Squyres and Andrew Lumsdaine

Open Systems Lab, Indiana University
{jsquyres,lums}@lam-mpi.org

Abstract. To better manage the ever increasing complexity of LAM/MPI, we have created a lightweight component architecture for it that is specifically designed for high-performance message passing. This paper describes the basic design of the component architecture, as well as some of the particular component instances that constitute the latest release of LAM/MPI. Performance comparisons against the previous, monolithic, version of LAM/MPI show no performance impact due to the new architecture—in fact, the newest version is slightly faster. The modular and extensible nature of this implementation is intended to make it significantly easier to add new functionality and to conduct new research using LAM/MPI as a development platform.

1 Introduction

The Message Passing Interface (MPI) is the *de facto* standard for message passing parallel programming on large-scale distributed systems [1–3]. Implementations of MPI comprise the middleware layer for many large-scale, high-performance applications [4, 5]. LAM/MPI is an open source, freely available implementation of the MPI standard. Since its inception in 1989, the LAM project has grown into a mature code base that is both rich with features and efficient in its implementation, delivering both high performance and convenience to MPI users and developers.

LAM/MPI is a large software package, consisting of over 150 directories and nearly 1,400 files of source code. Research, development, and maintenance of this code base—even for the LAM/MPI developers—is a complex task. Even though the LAM/MPI source code is fairly well structured (in terms of file and directory organization), contains many well-abstracted and logically separated functional code designs, and includes several highly flexible internal APIs, new LAM/MPI developers are inevitably overwhelmed when learning to work in the code base. Third party developers and researchers attempting to extend the LAM/MPI code base—or even to *understand* the code base—are frequently stymied because of the intrinsic complexities of such a large software system. Hence, not only does it take a long time to train new LAM developers, external contributions to LAM/MPI are fairly rare and typically only small, specific patches.

---

* Supported by a grant from the Lilly Endowment and by National Science Foundation grant 0116050.

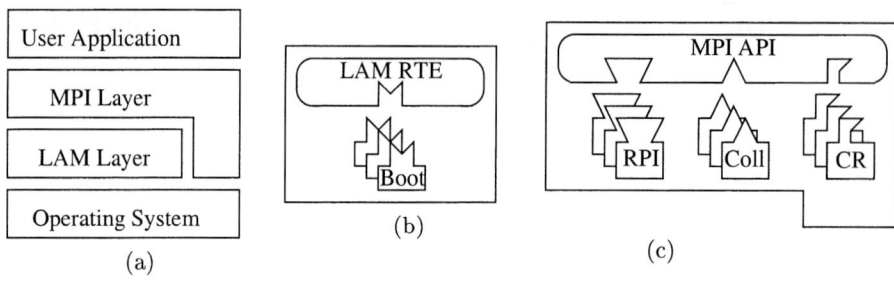

Fig. 1. (a) High-level architecture showing the user's MPI application, the MPI layer, the LAM layer, and the underlying operating system. The LAM layer (b) and MPI layer (c) each have public interfaces that are implemented with back-end components

For these reasons, a natural evolutionary step for LAM is a modular, component-based architecture. In this paper, we present the component architecture of LAM/MPI: the *System Services Interface* (SSI), first available in LAM version 7.0. To create this architecture, existing abstractions within the LAM/MPI code base have been identified and re-factored, and their concepts and interfaces formalized. Components for new functionality were also added. Hence, it is now possible to write (and maintain) small, independent, component modules that "plug in" to LAM's overall framework. It was a specific design goal to allow multiple modules of the same component type to co-exist in a process, one (or more) of which and be selected for use at run-time. Hence, different implementations of the same component can be created to experiment with new research directions, provide new functionality, etc. The architecture was designed to be lightweight, high-performance, and domain-specific (in contrast to general purpose component architectures such as CORBA [6] or CCA [7]).

The result is not simply an MPI implementation, but rather a framework that effects an MPI implementation from specified components. The rest of this paper is organized as follows. Section 2 provides a brief overview of LAM/MPI. LAM's component architecture and component implementations are described in Section 3. Future work and conclusions are given in Sections 5 and 6.

2 Overview of LAM/MPI

LAM/MPI is an open source implementation of the MPI standard developed and maintained at Indiana University. It implements the complete MPI-1 standard and much of the MPI-2 standard. LAM/MPI is made up of the LAM run-time environment (RTE) and the MPI communications layer (see Fig. 1). For performance reasons, both layers interact directly with the operating system; requiring the MPI layer to utilize the LAM layer for all MPI communications would impose a significant overhead.

Table 1. Modules that are available for each component type

Component type	Modules available
RPI	gm, lamd, tcp, sysv, usysv
Coll	lam_basic, smp
CR	blcr
Boot	bproc, globus, rsh, tm

2.1 LAM Layer

The LAM layer includes both the LAM RTE and a companion library providing C API functions to interact with the RTE. The RTE is based on user-level daemons (the "lamds"), and provides services such as message passing, process control, remote file access, and I/O forwarding. A user starts the LAM RTE with the lamboot command which, in turn, launches a lamd on each node (from a user-specified list) using a back-end component to start processes on a remote node (see Fig. 1). After the RTE is up, MPI programs can be run. When the user is finished with the RTE, the lamhalt command is used to terminate the RTE by killing the lamd on every node.

2.2 MPI Communications Layer

The MPI layer itself consists of multiple layers. The upper layer includes the standardized MPI API function calls and associated bookkeeping logic. The lower layer has recently been re-architected into a component framework. As such, the upper layer acts as the public interface to multiple types of back-end components that implement MPI functionality (see Fig. 1).

3 Component Architecture

The LAM/MPI component architecture supports four major types of components [8]. "RPI" (Request Progression Interface) components provide the back-end implementation of MPI point-to-point communication [9]. "Coll" components provide the back-end implementations of MPI collective algorithms [10]. "CR" components provide interfaces to checkpoint-restart systems to allow parallel MPI jobs to be checkpointed [11]. Finally, "Boot" components provide the capability for launching the LAM RTE in different execution environments [12]. Table 1 lists the modules that are available in LAM for each component type. RPI, Coll, and Boot were selected to be converted to components because they already had well-defined abstractions within the LAM/MPI code base. The CR type represented new functionality to LAM/MPI; it only made sense to design it as a component from its initial implementation.

3.1 Supporting Framework

Before transforming LAM's code base to utilize components, it was necessary to create a supporting framework within LAM/MPI that could handle component configuration, compilation, installation, and arbitrary parameters, both at compile-time and run-time. The following were design goals of the supporting framework:

- Design the component types to be implemented as plug-in modules, allowing both static and dynamic linkage.
- Simplify the configuration and building of plug-in modules; explicitly do not require the module to be aware of the larger LAM/MPI configuration and build system.
- Enable multiple modules of the same component type to exist in the same MPI process, and allow the selection of which module(s) to use to be a run-time decision.
- Allow a flexible system of passing arbitrary compile-time defaults and user-specified run-time parameters to each module.

This supporting infrastructure is responsible for the configuration and compilation of modules, and initializes relevant modules at run-time. It is used to provide a small number of run-time utility services to modules for cross-component functionality. Each of the component types has its own "base" that offers common utility functionality to all of its modules. This allows modules to share some functionality for tasks that are likely to be common across modules of the same component type.

3.2 MPI Point-to-Point Communication Components

The Request Progression Interface (RPI) is responsible for the movement of messages from one process to another. The RPI revolved around the concept of an MPI request; its API functions essentially follow the life of the request (creating, starting, advancing, finishing). The actual message passing is almost a side-effect of the life cycle of the request; implementation of how the bytes actually move from one process to another is not directly addressed in the API.

LAM/MPI has long supported a formal API and set of abstractions for the RPI. However, prior to converting the RPI to be component-based, selection of which RPI to use was a compile-time decision; only one RPI could be compiled into a LAM installation; LAM had to be installed multiple times to support different underlying communication mechanisms. As such, the RPI was a natural choice to be LAM's first component design. Converting the existing RPI code to be component-based provided not only a sound basis for testing the base SSI framework, but also added the capability to support different underlying message passing transports in a single installation of LAM (by allowing multiple RPI modules to co-exist in the same MPI process).

In addition to the previously existing RPIs for TCP and shared memory, two new RPI modules have been added: native support for Myrinet networks using the gm message passing library [13], and a modified version of the TCP RPI that supports checkpointing (named "CRTCP").

3.3 MPI Collective Communication Components

The design and implementation of the majority of the collective communication component was straightforward: the main public functions are identical to the MPI collective functions themselves. Hence, LAM's top-level MPI API functions check arguments for errors and perform minimal bookkeeping, and then simply invoke the corresponding underlying component function with the same arguments that it received.

The collective components provide two versions of each collective operation—one for intracommunicators and one for intercommunicators. If a module does not support intercommunicator algorithms, for example, it can provide NULL for its function pointer. This design provides a clear method for modules to indicate whether they support intercommunicator collectives. Hence, LAM/MPI fully supports the capability to have intercommunicator collectives (although no collective modules implement them yet).

The collective component was designed such that each communicator may use a different module. For example, collectives invoked on MPI_COMM_WORLD may use one set of algorithms, while collectives invoked on my_comm may use an entirely different set of algorithms (i.e., a different module). As such, significant effort was put into the design of the query and initialization of the collective component functions. Modules can be manually selected by the user, or automatically nominate which module is "best" for a given communicator.

Although all current collective modules are implemented as "layered" implementations of the MPI collective algorithms (i.e., they use MPI point-to-point functions for message passing), this is not required. For example, it is possible that future collective modules may provide their own communication channels.

In addition, to support complex communication patterns, collective modules can utilize other collective modules in a hierarchical pattern. That is, a collective module can create sub-communicators to simplify the execution of its algorithms. A new module was written that utilized this concept: collective algorithms tuned for SMPs on a LAN [14]. For example, the SMP-based algorithm for an MPI barrier is to perform a fan-in to a local manager, followed by a barrier among the set of managers, and then a local fan-out from the managers. The SMP module implements this algorithm by creating two sub-communicators: one that group processes on the local node, and another for the set of managers. For example, the local fan-in and fan-out is implemented as a zero-byte MPI gather and MPI broadcast (respectively) on the local communicator. Invoking collective operations on the sub-communicators simply invokes LAM's basic collective algorithms.

3.4 Checkpoint/Restart Components

The checkpoint/restart (CR) component represents new functionality in LAM/MPI. Parallel MPI jobs can be involuntarily checkpointed and restarted essentially any time between MPI_INIT and MPI_FINALIZE using a coordinated approach. The role of the CR component is twofold: interface with a back-end checkpointing system and coordinate other MPI SSI modules to checkpoint and restart themselves.

Three abstract actions are defined for CR components: **checkpoint**, **continue**, and **restart**. The **checkpoint** action is invoked when a checkpoint is initiated. It is intended to be a bounded-time action that allows an MPI process to prepare itself to be checkpointed. The **continue** action is activated after a successful checkpoint. This can be an empty action, but if migration is supported, communication channels may need to be re-established if processes have moved. The **restart** action is invoked after an MPI process has been restored from a prior checkpoint. This action will almost always need to re-discover its MPI process peers and re-establish communication channels to them.

The CR functionality requires that all MPI SSI modules that are selected at run-time support the ability to checkpoint and restart themselves. Specifically, API functions are included in both the MPI collective and point-to-point components that are invoked at checkpoint, continue, and restart time. Each SSI module can do whatever it needs for these three actions. For example, RPI modules may need to consume all "in-flight" messages and ensure that the communications network is fully quiesced before allowing the checkpoint to continue (this is exactly what the CRTCP RPI does to support checkpointing).

Since the checkpoint/restart capability is new to LAM/MPI, there is only one module available: an interface to the BLCR single-node checkpointer [15]. The CR functionality in LAM/MPI is discussed in further detail in [11].

3.5 Boot Components

Boot components are used as the back-end implementations for starting and expanding the LAM RTE. Previously, LAM only had the capability to launch `lamds` on remote nodes via `rsh` or `ssh`. The creation of the boot component formalized the abstractions required to identify remote hosts, start a process on a remote node, and communicate initialization protocol information with the newly-started process(es). Inspiration for the design of this interface was strongly influenced by the existing `rsh`/`ssh` boot code, as well as expectations of what would be necessary to utilize the native remote execution facilities under the PBS batch queue system [16].

Once these actions were identified and prototyped into functions, the `rsh`/`ssh` code was converted into a module. A second boot module was also written to verify the design that uses the Task Management (TM) interface to PBS to launch arbitrary processes on allocated nodes. After these two modules were completed, support was also added for BProc systems [17] and Globus-enabled systems [18]. With each of these boot modules in place, LAM can now be "natively" booted in a wide variety of execution environments.

4 Performance

To ensure that the new architecture of LAM/MPI does not negatively impact performance, the new component architecture (version 7.0) was compared

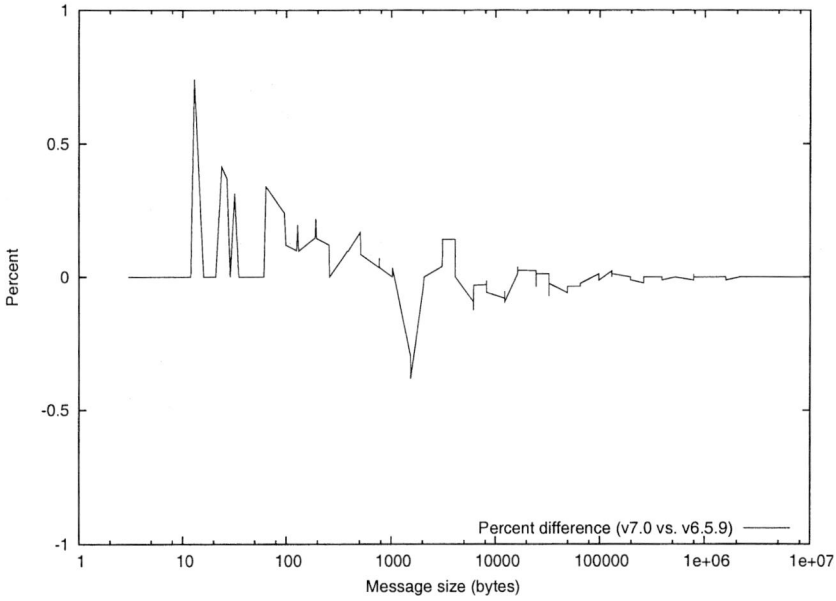

Fig. 2. TCP bandwidth percentage difference between LAM/MPI versions 7.0 (component architecture) and 6.5.9 (monolithic architecture)

against the last stable monolithic version of LAM (version 6.5.9) using the NetPIPE MPI benchmarks [19]. NetPIPE measures both the latency and the bandwidth for MPI message passing over a range of message sizes. Fig. 2 shows the percentage difference of TCP bandwidth between versions 7.0 and 6.5.9 using NetPIPE 2.4 under Linux 2.4.18-smp (RedHat 7.3) on a pair of 1.5GHz Pentium IV nodes, each with 768MB of RAM, connected via fast Ethernet (on the same switch). The figure shows that the performance difference between the two architectures is literally in the noise (less than $+/-1\%$).

5 Future Work

Our main focus for future work will be equally divided among three directions:

1. Continued refinement and evolution of component interfaces. Expansion to allow concurrent multithreaded message passing progress, for example, will necessitate some changes in the current component designs.
2. Creating more component types for both the MPI and LAM layers. Possible candidates for new component types include: MPI topology functions, MPI one-sided functions, MPI I/O functions, operating system thread support, and out-of-band messaging.
3. Creating more modules for the component types that already exist. Possible candidates include: native MPI point-to-point modules for other high-speed networks, and further refinement of SMP and wide-area MPI collectives.

6 Conclusions

The component architecture of LAM/MPI allows for much more fine-grained research and development than has previously been possible with MPI implementations. The current set of components not only allows independent research in MPI functional areas, it also fosters the spirit of open source development and collaboration. For example, researchers studying new MPI collective implementations can simply write a small run-time module and focus on their algorithms without having to deal with the intrinsic complexities of LAM/MPI itself. This freedom has been previously unavailable in widely-used MPI implementations and is a significant reason why researchers have been forced to either create small research-quality MPI subsets that focus on their specific work, or create entire derivative MPI implementations to show their methodologies.

The overall size of the LAM/MPI code base grew with the new component architecture; new code had to be written to selectively configure, compile, and select modules at run-time. However, this new code was essentially a one-time cost since it will change much less frequently than the code of the modules themselves. Additionally, with the segregation of code into orthogonal, functionally distinct modules, the impact on maintenance and new functionality has been dramatic. In short: the use of a component architecture has resulted in a significantly simpler code base to develop and maintain.

LAM/MPI, including the source code, technical specifications, and documentation of all the component architectures described in this paper [8–12], is freely available from http://www.lam-mpi.org/.

Acknowledgments

This work was performed using computational facilities at Indiana University and the College of William and Mary. These resources were enabled by grants from Sun Microsystems, the National Science Foundation, and Virginia's Commonwealth Technology Research Fund.

References

1. Gropp, W., Huss-Lederman, S., Lumsdaine, A., Lusk, E., Nitzberg, B., Saphir, W., Snir, M.: MPI — The Complete Reference: Volume 2, the MPI-2 Extensions. MIT Press (1998)
2. Message Passing Interface Forum: MPI: A Message Passing Interface. In: Proc. of Supercomputing '93, IEEE Computer Society Press (1993) 878–883
3. Snir, M., Otto, S.W., Huss-Lederman, S., Walker, D.W., Dongarra, J.: MPI: The Complete Reference. MIT Press, Cambridge, MA (1996)
4. Burns, G., Daoud, R., Vaigl, J.: LAM: An Open Cluster Environment for MPI. In Ross, J.W., ed.: Proceedings of Supercomputing Symposium '94, University of Toronto (1994) 379–386
5. Gropp, W., Lusk, E., Doss, N., Skjellum, A.: A high-performance, portable implementation of the MPI message passing interface standard. Parallel Computing **22** (1996) 789–828

6. Object Management Group: The common object request broker: Architecture and specification (1999) Revision2.3.1.
7. Armstrong, R., Gannon, D., Geist, A., Keahey, K., Kohn, S.R., McInnes, L., Parker, S.R., Smolinski, B.A.: Toward a common component architecture for high-performance scientific computing. In: HPDC. (1999)
8. Squyres, J.M., Barrett, B., Lumsdaine, A.: The system services interface (SSI) to LAM/MPI. Technical Report TR575, Indiana University, Computer Science Department (2003)
9. Squyres, J.M., Barrett, B., Lumsdaine, A.: Request progression interface (RPI) system services interface (SSI) modules for LAM/MPI. Technical Report TR579, Indiana University, Computer Science Department (2003)
10. Squyres, J.M., Barrett, B., Lumsdaine, A.: MPI collective operations system services interface (SSI) modules for LAM/MPI. Technical Report TR577, Indiana University, Computer Science Department (2003)
11. Sankaran, S., Squyres, J.M., Barrett, B., Lumsdaine, A.: Checkpoint-restart support system services interface (SSI) modules for LAM/MPI. Technical Report TR578, Indiana University, Computer Science Department (2003)
12. Squyres, J.M., Barrett, B., Lumsdaine, A.: Boot system services interface (SSI) modules for LAM/MPI. Technical Report TR576, Indiana University, Computer Science Department (2003)
13. Myricom http://www.myri.com/scs/GM/doc/html/: GM: A message passing system for Myrinet networks. (2003)
14. Kielmann, T., Bal, H.E., Gorlatch, S.: Bandwidth-efficient Collective Communication for Clustered Wide Area Systems. In: International Parallel and Distributed Processing Symposium (IPDPS 2000), Cancun, Mexico, IEEE (2000) 492–499
15. Duell, J., Hargrove, P., Roman, E.: The design and implementation of Berkeley Lab's linux checkpoint/restart (2002) http://www.nersc.gov/research/FTG/checkpoint/reports.html.
16. Veridian Systems: Portable Batch System / OpenPBS Release 2.3, Administrator Guide. (2000)
17. Hendriks, E.: BProc Manual, http://bproc.sourceforge.net/. (2001)
18. Foster, I.: The anatomy of the Grid: Enabling scalable virtual organizations. International Journal of Supercomputer Applications **15** (2001)
19. Snell, Q., Mikler, A., Gustafson, J.: Netpipe: A network protocol independent performace evaluator. In: IASTED Internation Conference on Intelligent Information Management and Systems. (1996)

ORNL-RSH Package and Windows '03 PVM 3.4

Phil Pfeiffer[1], Stephen L. Scott[2], and Hardik Shukla[2]

[1] East Tennessee State University, Dept. of Computer and Information Sciences,
Box 70391, Johnson City, TN 37614-1266
phil@etsu.edu

[2] Oak Ridge National Laboratory, Computer Science & Mathematics Division,
Bethel Valley Road, Oak Ridge, TN 37831-3637
{scottsl,hs2}@ornl.gov

1 Introduction

The first public release of PVM was version 2.0 in February 1991; the first PVM release from Oak Ridge National Laboratory that supported the Windows operating system was version 3.4 (beta 5) at the end of 1997 and then with the formal release of PVM version 3.4.0 in January 1999. While this initial release provided the PVM framework and functionality to the Windows world, there were a number of shortcomings that created undue difficulties for users. Some of the problems encountered included the difficulty of the installation process itself, the necessity for a 3rd party and costly rsh package, and the lack of Windows user level documentation of the entire process (from install to use). Thus, the general goal of this work and its resulting release is to simplify the use of Windows PVM by its user community. To achieve this goal, the new package will have to include: a simplified installation process on individual and networked machines (clusters), a simplified and free (open source preferred) rsh package for PVM, and of course the associated documentation so that others may more easily use all the new software. This paper contains a brief introduction of new features included in the latest Windows PVM release and spends the remainder of the paper discussing the details of the new ORNL-RSH package that greatly simplifies the use PVM on Windows based machines.

2 Windows PVM v3.4

Windows '03 PVM v3.4 differs from earlier versions of Windows PVM in three key ways:

- '03 supports Windows 2000 and Windows XP (new), as well as Windows 98 and Windows NT.
- '03 includes ORNL-rsh, an open-source rsh daemon for Windows platforms (new). ORNL-RSH, which was created expressly for Windows PVM v3.4, is described in more detail in Section 3.
- '03 supports a simplified installation procedure, as follows:
  - Support for client-mode installation, a subset of the standard PVM package designed for hosts that only issue commands, was dropped, to make the PVM installation dialogue less confusing to novice PVM users.

- Support for remote installation was enhanced, with the aid of a new PVM installer that fully supports remote PVM installation. Prior to v3.4, anyone who installed Windows PVM on a host H had to make hands-on contact with H to complete the installation. Even when a network share was used to distribute PVM to host H, the administrator was required to physically visit H, and run a script locally on H that downloaded PVM to H, then configured PVM for local use.

To use the PVM installer, a user must have an administrator-level account on every host involved in the PVM installation procedure—local and remote hosts alike. Any remote account that the administrator intends to use must also be network accessible. Under Windows XP, network access for administrator accounts must be explicitly enabled using XP's security settings.

The new PVM installer's look and feel resembles that of the earlier, InstallShield™ based installer. A new screen for configuring remote installation supports the use of wildcards to target sets of hosts and IP addresses for PVM installation. Other new screens confirm a configuration's parameters before starting an install, and confirm daemon installation.

3 ORNL-RSH

Windows PVM uses the *rsh* protocol to execute commands on remote machines: e.g., to start a PVM daemon on a remote host. In rsh, a string like

```
rsh -l remote-user remote-host hostname
```

represents a request to run a command *hostname* on a host *remote-host* as user *remote-user*. A request is typically accepted by a program known as an *rsh client*, which relays it to the specified host for further processing. This processing is done by programs known as *rsh servers,* or *rsh daemons*. Both clients and servers are needed for full rsh operation: a host that lacks rsh client code cannot initiate remote commands, and a host that lacks an rsh daemon cannot respond to requests from remote hosts.

Heretofore, the use of PVM under Windows has been impeded by a lack of public domain rsh servers for the Windows environment. rsh servers, which were originally developed under BSD Unix, do not port readily to the Windows environment, thanks to important differences between the Unix and Windows models for user logins, tasking, and security. Commercially available implementations of rsh servers for Windows PVM currently cost as much as $120 (USD) per machine to license.

The ORNL-RSH software package, which is installed as part of Windows PVM v3.4, is a freeware product, distributed under an open source license similar to PVM's [1]. This package, which can be obtained from [1], includes an rsh daemon for Microsoft's Win32 subsystem, and supporting utilities that install this daemon on local and remote hosts; manage its operation on remote hosts; and uninstall the package's utilities and files.

The ORNL-rsh daemon is installed as a Win32 service that runs under a Windows administrator account. A supporting database holds Windows-specific process execution parameters—information that cannot be obtained via the basic rsh protocol. This database also allows administrators to restrict every remote user's access to a prespecified set of local accounts.

The balance of this section discusses ORNL-RSH's features, supporting tools, and security limitations in more detail. The section, which assumes a prior familiarity with rsh, focuses primarily on extensions and accommodations for the Windows environment.

3.1 ORNL-RSH Features

The ORNL and BSD rsh daemons implement similar protocols for processing user requests. For example, executing a command like

```
rsh   -l   someuser   someWindowsHost   hostname
```

on an ORNL-rsh daemon returns the name of the remote host. Executing a command like

```
rsh   -l   someuser   someWindowsHost   cmd.exe
```

has the effect of opening an interactive session on the remote host.

The two daemons also differ in four important regards. ORNL-rsh eliminates interactive challenges for user passwords; limits remote access to prespecified users; supports Windows-specific options for managing command execution; and supports syntax extensions for the Windows environment.

No password challenge. The BSD daemon, by default, uses an interactive password challenge to authenticate requests for service. Depending on how an rsh client is implemented, this challenge is made visible to the remote user—

```
user@host> rsh -l targetacct targethost hostname
password:           # challenge returned by targethost
login
```

—or managed transparently, with an additional command-line parameter—

```
user@host> rsh -l targetacct -p passwd targethost hostname
```

Neither style of challenge is secure: rsh fails to encrypt passwords in transit, thereby rendering them vulnerable to scanning [2]. ORNL-RSH currently omits this interactive password challenge, along with two BSD rsh mechanisms for challenge bypass: *.rhosts* and *hosts.allow* files.

Explicit limits on remote access. BSD rsh uses "implicit allow/explicit deny" to manage access to a server host. BSD's rsh daemon vets any request from any host not named in *hosts.deny*, an auxiliary file of untrusted hosts, regardless of the account from which the request came, or the account that it targets.

ORNL-rsh uses an "explicit allow/implicit deny" policy to manage access. The daemon *accepts* a request of the form

```
user@host> rsh -l targetacct targethost hostname
```

if and only if *targetacct* is registered in an ORNL auxiliary database of *rsh* accounts; *someuser@somehost* matches an entry in the list of *targetacct's* users; and the request originates from *somehost*—as determined by a check of the logical connection between *somehost* and *targethost*.

Support for Win32-style command execution. The ORNL and BSD rsh daemons respond to a request to run a command as *targetacct* by creating a new process that runs as *targetacct*, and then using this process to run that command. The ORNL mechanism for command execution, however, is more complex than the corresponding Unix mechanism, thanks to three key differences between the Unix and Win32 environments.

Difference 1: domains. The standard UNIX login mechanism presents a one-level view of the network environment, associating every computer with a unique set of accounts. The Win32 subsystem presents users with a *two*-level view of the networked environment. Every computer in a Win32 environment is associated with one *or more* uniquely named views of the network, known as *domains or workgroups*, that capture distinct views of a network's directories, devices, and servers. Every workgroup or domain, in turn, is associated with its own set of accounts.

Under the Windows model of system access, a user, at time of login, can access one of several accounts that bear his name: *e.g.*, an account named *phil* in a domain specific to the local host, or an account named *phil* in a domain specific to the larger network. Accordingly, Win32 logins require three, rather than two, parameters: an account, a password, *and* a domain. This third, domain parameter is sometimes hidden from the Windows user with a special login screen that automatically supplies a default domain—but such screens simply mask the need for the domain parameter, and do not eliminate it.

Difference 2: stricter security. UNIX allows root users to configure daemons can "impersonate" any user U at any time. The Win32 model of process security allows impersonation only when the daemon has explicit permission to become user U (cf. [3]). This permission can be obtained in one of two ways:

- Using named pipe *authentication*. A daemon can use *named pipe authentication* to get permission to impersonate user U. Permission must be obtained from a task that is already running as U; that has *explicit* permission to grant other tasks the right to impersonate U; and that is running in a domain that the daemon's host domain trusts.
- *Using passwords.* A daemon may also obtain permission to impersonate U by supplying the operating system with U's password.

Difference 3: No home directories. Every Unix account is associated with a home directory, which the BSD rsh daemon uses as an initial directory for running commands. Windows accounts have no default home directories, which makes the BSD strategy for determining an initial directory unworkable.

These three differences create a need for three new task-creation parameters in ORNL-rsh: the name of a default domain to access when logging into an account; the local account's password, which is needed to support the impersonation of local users in a non-interactive way; and the name of a directory to be used as a local working directory. The ORNL-rsh daemon obtains these three parameters from its auxiliary database, which must be preconfigured before using ORNL-rsh.

Extended command line syntax. ORNL-rsh supports the use of Unix-style and Windows-style command-line syntax.

- ORNL-RSH recognizes Unix- and Windows-style environment variables—i.e., $THIS and %THIS%—and expands variables in the context of the current user's environment.
- ORNL-rsh recognizes Unix- and Windows-style pathname separators—e.g., treating, "C:/WinNT" and "C:\WinNT" as synonyms for the standard Win32 master directory.
- ORNL-RSH recognizes UNC-style syntax for account names—e.g., treating a reference to user \\DOMAIN\USER as a reference to an account named USER in a domain named DOMAIN. Any account name that is not prefixed with \\DOMAIN\ is treated as a request that specifies the default local domain, \\.

3.2 ORNL-RSH Tools

The ORNL-rsh daemon is distributed with four supporting utilities: an installer utility that installs the daemon on local and remote hosts; a configuration tool that configures the rsh daemon for use on a local host; a manager tool that exports a local rsh configuration to a set of remote hosts; and an uninstaller.

ORNL-RSH Installer. The ORNL-RSH distribution consists of a single, self-installing executable. This program installs the ORNL-RSH package in four phases:

1. The administrator first configures ORNL-RSH for the target environment. The administrator selects the directory in which to install the RSH package; specifies the account under which the rsh daemon will run; and specifies what files, if any, will be installed remotely.
2. The administrator specifies what remote hosts, if any, to target for package installation.
3. The installer utility installs the specified pieces of the ORNL-RSH package on the specified hosts, displaying a running update of the package's installation status.
4. The installer gives the administrator the option of restarting the targeted hosts, for the purpose of activating the ORNL-RSH service.

ORNL-RSH Configuration Tool. After ORNL-RSH has been installed, the rsh daemon must be configured for every host on which it resides. The ORNL-RSH configuration tool allows an administrator to configure a daemon for use on the *local* host—the host on which the configuration tool is running. The tool's options allow the administrator to

- configure an account for use as an *rsh account*—i.e., a local account that remote rsh users can use to run commands. This task requires the administrator to specify the account's domain and password, as well as an initial directory for running commands.
- associate an rsh account with remote users—i.e., users authorized to use that account to run their commands.
- list all remote users that are associated with a particular rsh account.
- end an association between an rsh account A and a remote user.
- remove an account from the list of rsh accounts.

ORNL-RSH Manager. The ORNL-RSH manager utility allows the administrator to manage *remotely* installed copies of ORNL-RSH. The utility supports options that install ORNL-RSH on an administrator-specified set of hosts; export a locally configured rsh database to these hosts; start and stop remote ORNL-RSH services; and uninstall ORNL-RSH remotely.

ORNL-RSH Uninstaller. The uninstaller removes ORNL-RSH and its supporting databases from the specified hosts, deactivating rsh daemons in the process.

3.3 ORNL-RSH Security Limitations

Authentication based on point of origin. Shortly after it was developed, the rsh password challenge protocol, which transmits passwords in clear text, was rendered insecure by devices like protocol analyzers. The strategy for remote user authentication described here "solves" the clear text password transmission problem by authenticating requests based on their points of origin. Unfortunately, accepting requests based on point of origin allows anyone who can compromise a remote account, or spoof their point of origin with techniques like DNS poisoning [2], to run commands on a rsh server.

A better strategy for secure authentication uses encrypted channels to protect user passwords. The main problem with such protocols, from the standpoint of PVM, is a lack of backward compatibility with existing implementations of rsh.

Stored passwords. Section 3.1 noted that Win32's non-support for unrestricted impersonation forces any third-party service that acts on behalf of a user U, in the worst case, to supply the Win32 subsystem with U's password. Moreover, if this service is to run without direct user interaction, passwords must be stored on electronic media—thereby rendering passwords vulnerable to compromise.

ORNL-RSH stores the password for every local rsh account in its host system's registry. All of these passwords are encrypted using Blowfish [4], with a single master key. This key is stored in a second registry key, *HKEY_LOCAL_MACHINE\ Software\Rshd*, in a field named *Rshd_Key*. Access to this registry key is limited to users with administrator privileges. The master key is generated once, at random, when the password database is generated, and used for all subsequent password encryptions.

One serious problem with storing any password on any system is that the systems themselves are vulnerable to hacking. For example, Scambray et. al. describe a variety of strategies for obtaining unauthorized access to protected data in the Windows registry [5]. A typical hack involves first dumping the registry, using security holes like improperly secured network connections, improperly secured bootstrap procedures, and registry backup utilities, and then analyzing the dump on a second, hacker-friendly system. The registry can be made more secure, using strategies like disallowing remote registry access (which would render ORNL-RSH inoperable); password-protecting BIOSes; and registry encryption (cf. [6]): even so, the password remains on the system.

An alternative approach to protecting the master key would be to store this key outside the registry—for example, in a main memory location whose contents are generated at runtime, using a "secret" key generation algorithm. The authors' desire to make ORNL-RSH an open source utility precludes the use of secret algorithms to protect keys. In any case, a blind reliance on obfuscation to secure data is a practice that is held in low esteem by most of the security community, particularly in light of unsuccessful attempts to use "secret" approaches to protect data (e.g., DIVX, DeCSS).

4 Conclusion

As stated at the beginning of this paper, the general goal of this work and its resulting release is to simplify the use of Windows PVM for the user community. Due to the page limitation we were only able to provide significant details regarding the ORNL-rsh package and much of that is at the design and administrator level. Comprehensive user level documentation is undergoing an external beta test and review process as of this writing and will be released on the ORNL PVM web site [1] prior to the EuroPVM/MPI 2003 meeting in September.

Regarding our future plans for Windows development, one significant goal for the development team is to leverage the experience gained in this effort to enable us to expand the current state of Windows based high-performance computing and cluster computing to a more Windows centric manner while: still supporting native HPC codes written in their original UNIX/Linux format, transitioning new codes to be written for Windows HPC in a Windows centric manner, and enabling both the aforementioned items to coexist. While some have proclaimed Windows HPC as dead, we have seen a recent resurgence of interest in cluster computing using the Windows computing environment. In some cases, a business is looking to leverage Windows desktops during non-peak utilization. In other instances it is a new type of user that has never even considered traditional HPC but is instead looking for a way to leverage cluster and HPC characteristics in manners not traditionally considered in either of these two camps.

Regardless of your use, we hope that this will serve as an impetus for you to further investigate the new Windows PVM release, ORNL-rsh, and associated packages.

References

1. Oak Ridge National Laboratories, "PVM: Parallel Virtual Machine", www.csm.ornl.gov/pvm/, (last accessed April 5, 2003).
2. W. Cheswick and S. Bellovin, Firewalls and Internet Security: Repelling the Wily Hacker, © 1994, Addison-Wesley.
3. D. Solomon and M. Russinovich, Inside Microsoft Windows 2000 (Microsoft Programming Series), © 2000, Microsoft Press.
4. B. Schneier, Applied Cryptography, 2nd Edition, c. 1996, John Wiley and Sons
5. S. McClure, J. Scambray; and G. Kurtz, Hacking Exposed: Network Security Secrets & Solutions, Third Edition, © 2001, McGraw-Hill Osborne.
6. M. Edwards and D. LeBlanc, "Where NT Stores Passwords", *Windows & .NET Magazine*, Aug. 1999 [www.winnetmag.com/Articles/Index.cfm?ArticleID=5705], (last accessed January 29, 2003).

MPI for the Clint Gb/s Interconnect

Nicolas Fugier[1], Marc Herbert[1,2], Eric Lemoine[1,2], and Bernard Tourancheau[1]

[1] SUN labs Europe, 38334 Saint Ismier, France
{Nicolas.Fugier,Bernard.Tourancheau}@sun.com
[2] RESO-INRIA at LIP, ENS-Lyon, France

Abstract. The Clint network provides an FPGA-based segregated architecture with a bulk channel controlled by a quick channel. We report in this paper how, in order to implement efficiently the MPI APIs on top of this network, we "codesigned" the interface between the Sun™ MPI communication stack and the network FPGAs.
The Sun™ MPI "Protocol Module" we developed implements functions to enable a full support of Sun MPI and gave us an insightful view of the design problems and performance bottlenecks. Hence, we were able to provide pertinent feedback to the hardware designers who then, thanks to the use of rapid FPGA-prototyping, implemented the corresponding hardware enhancements. As a result, our software architecture fits as much as possible with the hardware capabilities and the resulting prototype exploits the best of the overall architecture.

1 Introduction

Thanks to publicly available software libraries such as implementations of MPI [8], developing parallel applications for clustered systems has become increasingly popular. Typically, these applications require tight coupling of the processing nodes and, thus, an interconnect that provides high bandwidth as well as low latency.

Unfortunately, interconnects typically provide low latency only as long as they are lightly loaded. Thus there is a tradeoff between high throughput and low latency. Clint[1] aims to provide high throughput and low latency by providing a segregated architecture. Moreover, in order to propose these performances at the application level, a very good coupling between the hardware and software has to be designed and this is the object of that paper.

We have structured the paper as follows. Section 2 gives an overview of the Clint architecture. Section 3 describes the Sun™ MPI[2] environment. Section 4 describes our software architecture and prototype for the port of Sun MPI on Clint. Section 5 explains our "codesign" approach and results. Section 6 contrasts our experience with related work. Finally, section 7 gives the conclusions.

---

[1] Clint is the code name of a Sun Microsystems Laboratories internal project.
[2] Sun, Sun Microsystems, the Sun Logo, Sun MPI, Sun HPC ClusterTools, Sun Parallel File System, Sun Prism, Sun Scalable Scientific Subroutine Library (Sun S3L), and Sun Cluster Runtime Environment are trademarks or registered trademarks of Sun Microsystems, Inc. in the U.S. and other countries.

2 Overview of the Clint Network

The segregated architecture motivation for Clint comes from the observation that network traffic is usually a bimodal distribution as reported in [13]. Two types of packets are wanted: large packets for which high throughput is needed and small packets for which low latency is preferable. Clint segregates the interconnect into two physically separate channels: a bulk channel optimized for the transmission of large packets and a quick channel optimized for short packets .

The Clint interconnect[6] uses physically separated networks to implement a bulk and a quick channels with different scheduling strategies. The quick channel is also responsible of the control messages for the scheduling of the bulk channel. While the quick channel has to be implemented as a new device, the bulk channel can be any off-the-shelf switched network, as long as an analog interface is available.

Figure 1 shows the organization of the bulk and the quick switches. In this example, a 2x2 switch connects two nodes. Most notably, the switches do not contain any buffer memory, it is located in the nodes.

The hardware prototype uses an off-the-shelf 16x16 crosspoint switch as the bulk switch and Field-Programmable Gate Arrays (FPGA) to implement the "quick switch" ports and the NICs. The prototype raw latencies are 1.5 ns for the analog switch of the bulk channel and 90 ns for the pipelined switch of the quick channel. Of more interest are the round-trip times: 20 μs for the bulk channel with 2KB packets and 1 μs for the quick channel with 32B packets. Links are serial copper cables with a length of up to 5 m. The full-duplex bandwidth[3] is 2+2 Gbit/s for the bulk channel and 0.53+0.53 Gbit/s for the quick channel.

2.1 Quick Channel and Switch Scheduling and Arbitration

The quick channel takes a best-effort approach and packets are sent whenever they are available. Quick packets are 32 bytes long and can contain 28 bytes of payload. All the received packets are acknowledged. Because the quick channel physical layer is not reliable, the link layer implements retransmission in case of errors. These retransmissions are done when errors are detected after the transmission (CRC checksums) or after a timeout thanks to the acknowledgment strategy.

Collisions happen infrequently because the quick channel is only lightly loaded due to the provision of excess bandwidth. However in case of collision, the packet that arrives first wins and is forwarded. Packets that arrive later will lose and be dropped. If colliding packets arrive simultaneously, a round-robin scheme is used to pick the winner and avoid starvation. This arbiter makes its routing decisions very quickly to keep forwarding latencies low.

2.2 Bulk Channel and Switch Scheduling and Arbitration

Bulk packets are 2086-byte long and contain 2048 bytes of payload. The bulk channel uses a scheduler that globally allocates time slots on the transmission

---

[3] The physical layer uses 8B/10B encoding; thus, the link rates is 25% more.

paths before packets are sent off. This way collisions that lead to locks are avoided and, thus, performance loss too. In contrast with the quick channel, the bulk channel is reliably scheduled and controlled by a hardware scheduler and control messages on the quick channel. Thus, no packet is dropped during transmission. However, transmission errors could happen, and acknowledgment packets through the quick channel are used to check the integrity of the transmission.

The bulk channel scheduler applies a relatively compute-intensive algorithm described in [12] that avoids end-of-line-blocking and conflicts, and optimizes the aggregate throughput of the switch. For a pair of source and destination, packets are transferred in order, while the ordering between pairs is not specified. The arbiter uses a proprietary algorithm called *Least Choice First Arbiter*[9] where the arbiter allocates connections between sources and destinations based on the number of requests. For the Clint prototype, the transmission of the acknowledgment and scheduling packets consumes 5% of the quick channel bandwidth.

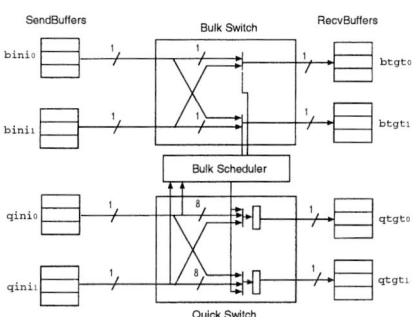

Fig. 1. Organization of the switches.

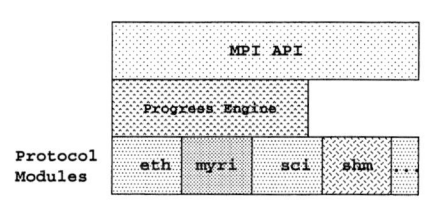

Fig. 2. Sun MPI layered structure.

3 Sun HPC ClusterTools™

Sun HPC ClusterTools™ [10] Software includes Sun MPI [11], Sun MPI I/O, Sun™ Parallel File System, Sun Prism™ debugger, Sun™ Scalable Scientific Subroutine Library (Sun S3L), Sun™ Cluster Runtime Environment, Cluster Console Manager environments. These components provide the features needed to effectively develop, execute, and monitor parallel applications.

The Sun MPI implementation is an optimized, thread-safe version of Message Passing Interface 2 (MPI-2) portable message-passing standard [15].

Sun MPI is made out from 3 layers as shown in Figure 2: the Sun MPI API is the layer dealing with the calls to the MPI library; the Progress Engine is the layer in charge of doing the progress calls to the networks. It manages calls to each Protocol Module (PM) functions used to perform the communications in order to be fair with each current communication; and finally the PM layer is a collection of modules in charge of their own specific network.

4 Clint Driver Architecture

We had to choose between two very different implementation alternatives for the NIC driver. The first possibility was a standard kernel space network driver. This approach was not chosen because:

- It is now well-known that a heavy layered protocol model in general, and TCP/IP in particular, is not well suited for performance [19, 7].
- Controlling the network interface from user mode is easier,
- We were not interested in the benefits brought by a *standard* network driver because only high performance is targeted.

The alternative was a simple kernel driver which would be in charge of initializing the NIC and setting up user memory mappings. Then all the critical, communication part of the driver would run in user space. This solution avoids system calls and thus context-switches in the critical path. Because all the code is in user space, debugging is much easier. Figure 3 gives a picture of the memory mappings done between the NIC and the kernel module, and between the kernel module and the user-space.

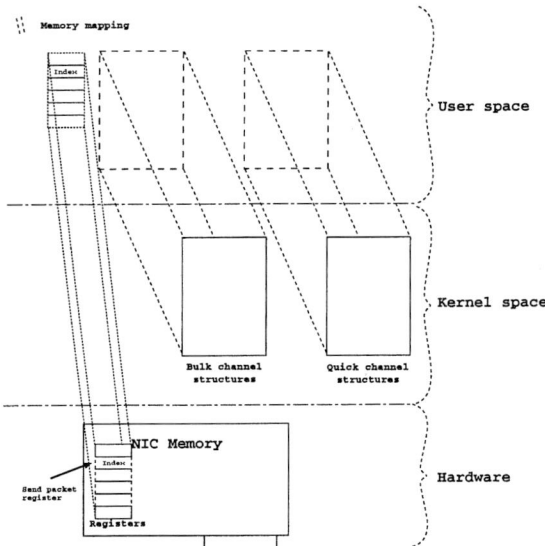

Fig. 3. Memory mappings between NIC and user-level driver through kernel space.

The drawbacks of this approach are that we do not provide a generic network functionality and we do not handle interrupts but this does not matter in our experimental context.

5 FPGA & Software "Codesign"

Thanks to the FPGA hardware programmability, we were able to influence and feedback the hardware design in order to facilitate our development and then to optimize our software on a short time-frame. Moreover, the prototype provides reasonable performances (Gb/s order) with off-the-shelf technologies.

The FPGA programmability is very comparable to software, with the VHDL language, compiler and loader. FPGAs makes the hardware development similar to the software development. What we called "codesign" describes our "development loop" where the software designers are interacting regularly with the hardware designers to modify the prototype.

In the following sections, we'll describe examples in which some implementation or performance issues occurred and where we solved them by a "codesign" effort between the software and the hardware.

5.1 Blocking and Non-blocking Semantics, Pipelined Data-Paths

Our protocol implementation took advantage of the reliable FIFO semantics insured by the hardware. This, for instance, simplifies the implementation of the MPI blocking semantics at the user level and of the pipelined data transfers between the receiving buffer-rings and the user buffers.

5.2 Message Size Match

The targeted MPI is usually implemented with separated mechanisms to transport short and long messages. We mapped these characteristics to the hardware features. Thus, the MPI small messages, up to 112 Bytes travel on the quick channel while the larger than 112 Bytes ones use the bulk channel. Notice that the packet data unit payload on the quick channel is 28 bytes and some segmentation/re-assembly must be done. This has a cost that leads to the 112 bytes threshold to determine which channel to use.

5.3 Flow Control Exposure

The flow control mechanism in Gb/s architecture can cost a lot if all implemented in software because it requires computation as well as some control information on the link. In Clint, some flow control mechanism is done by the hardware because the physical layer was designed to be reliable. However, the software layer needs to be informed about the state of the communication between two nodes to be able to actively manage it. For instance, in the case of receiving node overflow, the sending side NIC driver needs to know about it to be able to stop sending packets. In the initial version of the FPGA hardware configuration, the flow control information sent back to the driver was difficult to deal with because it was mixed with other information. Dealing with that issue in software is complex, error prone and slow.

A codesigned solution was directly implemented into the FPGA and the hardware then exposed the needed flow control information at almost no cost. This allowed us to easily implement the flow control mechanisms in the software layers. The gain was not only on performance but also on software implementation easiness and this diminishes errors and bugs, shortening the development cycle.

5.4 PCI Transfer Performance Issue

The Sun Psycho+ PCI chipsets we were using in our platform are targeting short transactions and multi-threading with a strong requirement on fairness as well as compliance with the Unix stream mode. The corresponding chipset can be programmed in 2 modes:

Consistent mode is the default mode of operation. All DMAs are reliable in the sense that there is no cache coherency issues like the ones we can have in the streaming mode. Unfortunately, performances are then limited: the DMA Read maximum throughput was 125.5MB/s.

Streaming mode is a little trickier to use because of some cache coherency issues. The chipset implements a STreaming Cache (STC). This STC has 16x64-bytes cache lines, each one is associated with a different memory page on the host memory. When doing a DMA, data go through the corresponding cache line from/to the device to/from the memory. Thus, data is flushed only on 64-bytes boundaries. Performances reach 222.1MB/s for the best case DMA Read.

We initially used the consistent mode. We faced some difficulties while designing for the streaming mode because the structures used by the Clint hardware network are less than 64-byte long and in particular the message descriptors which are 32-byte long.

The software workaround was to force the PCI cache line flushing by an `ioctl()` before reading structures that are less than 64 byte long. The hardware solution was to modify all structures at the FPGA level to be 64-byte long to be sure that each minimal data transfer is always automatically flushed. We implemented the software solution and we were able to have a 30% throughput gain against the consistent mode. Much additional gain was expected with the hardware specification passed back to the FPGA designers. Unfortunately, while these changes seems easy for software designers they were in fact very complex because buffers are costly in FPGA, either in terms of space, wire and also the associated logic for clock propagation. Thus this modification exceeded our FPGA platform capacity.

5.5 Preliminary Performance Results

The Clint hardware and its MPI Protocol Module resulting from our "codesign" is giving its first set of results. For small packets, the latencies stays small with 64 micro-seconds round trip time for a 28 bytes payload, see Figure 4.

For large packets, while the maximum throughput is limited by the PCI platform performances in consistent mode, but the half maximum throughput is obtained for 2K Bytes packets, see Figure 5, i.e. for the first full size bulk transfer. This shows the interest of such a segregated approach where the bulk channel is always at high speed as soon as enough data fills the fixed size packet data unit.

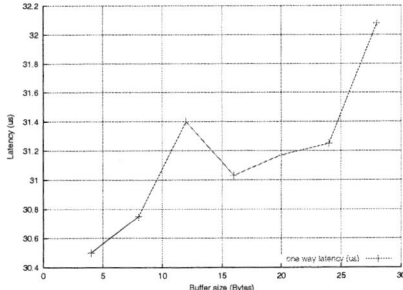
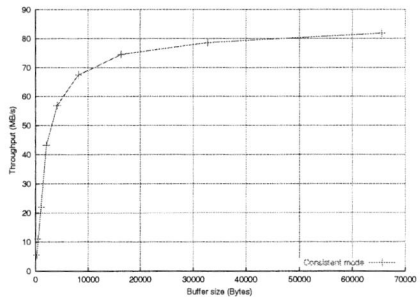

Fig. 4. One-way latencies for small messages on the quick channel.

Fig. 5. Throughput for messages up to 64K bytes on the bulk channel.

6 Related Work

The use of multiple channels has been examined in the network community for performance improvement [13][14], for path reservation [23][17], for hybrid wormhole/circuit-switched networks [5]. Compared with these architectures Clint is unique because both Clint's channels are available to user programs and because it applies a global schedule to the switches as well as the NICs.

The use of separate mechanisms to transport short and long messages has been proposed, for instance, in the Illinois Fast Messages (FM) protocol [16] and the Scheduled Transfer protocol [20] for HIPPI-6400. The decoupling between small and large messages in order to optimize latency and throughput was extensively studied in clusters[16, 18, 19, 7, 2] and is part of the MPI standard [15] implementations. The design of user-level communication stacks targeting MPI for cluster has been well studied with programmable interfaces [18, 19, 7, 21, 1] or with regular NICs [4, 3].

The usage of codesign surfaced in the 90s for application specific systems and embedded systems designed with ASICs[22]. Codesign exploits largely the FPGA technology for real time systems, signal processing etc. and also is now targeting CMP. On the contrary, in the MPI for cluster context, the "codesign" approach using FPGA is, to our knowledge, a novelty.

7 Conclusion

We described an efficient MPI-2 port on a the Clint networking prototype architecture which provides two physically separated channels for large packets at high bandwidth and for small packets with low forwarding latency.

The targeted architecture is based on reconfigurable FPGA hardware and flow through switch chip. In order to fit best our software stack, we "codesigned" several enhancement of the FPGA hardware by providing new specifications.

This solved some of the performances issues by adding the necessary semantic to the hardware physical layer and by exposing some available pertinent control information into the hardware API for the software stack. Another advantage of such an approach was the improvement in the code design easiness which allowed for a nice efficient overall design in a short time frame.

The results shows up to date performances with an off-the-shelf cheap switch and basic FPGA development boards. However, the continuation of such an approach would be the production of ASIC chips corresponding to the FPGAs boards in order to get higher performances and cheap NICs. The approach seems to be scalable because the bulk switch chips can be cascaded and they now exist with a bigger number of ports and higher bandwidth. Also the quick switch design can be extended easily on an ASIC.

If codesign is always at the beginning of any hardware specification, eventually it usually stays at this very low level initial interaction. We pushed such an idea, outside of the classical RT-embedded system arena, and a little bit closer to the application, with the design of a Gb-range MPI-2 network for cluster.

Acknowledgments

We thank Hans Eberle and Nils Gura who were in charge of the hardware part of the "codesign" and Roland Westrelin and Loic Prylli who helped with some driver and MPI issues.

References

1. G Bibeling, HC Hoppe, A Supalov, P Lagier, and J Latour. Fujitsu mpi-2: fast locally, reaching globally. In *Recent Advances in Parallel virtual Machine and Message Passing Interface*, number 2474 in LNCS, pages 401–409. springer, 2002.
2. R Brightwell, A Maccabe, and R Riesen. Design and implementation of mpi on portals 3.0. In *Recent Advances in Parallel virtual Machine and Message Passing Interface*, number 2474 in LNCS, pages 331–340. springer, 2002.
3. G. Chiola and G. Ciaccio. Gamma: a low-cost network of workstations based on active messages. In *PDP'97 (5th EUROMICRO workshop on Parallel and Distributed Processing)*, London, UK, January 1997.
4. G. Chiola and G. Ciaccio. Porting MPICH ADI on GAMMA with flow control. In *MWPP'99 (1999 Midwest Workshop on Parallel Processing)*, Kent, Ohio, August 1999.
5. J. Duato, P. López, and F. Silla. A High Performance Router Architecture for Interconnection Networks. In *Proc. Int. Conf. On Parallel Processing*, 1996.
6. Hans Eberle and Nils Gura. Separated high-bandwidth and low-latency communication in the cluster interconnect clint. IEEE, 2002.
7. Patrick Geoffray, Loïc Prylli, and Bernard Tourancheau. BIP-SMP: High performance message passing over a cluster of commodity SMPs. In *Supercomputing (SC '99)*, Portland, OR, November 1999.
8. W. Gropp, E. Lusk, N. Doss, and A. Skjellum. A high-performance, portable implementation of the MPI message passing interface standard. *Parallel Computing*, 22(6):789–828, September 1996.
9. Nils Gura and Hans Eberle. The least choice first scheduling method for high-speed network switches. In *Proceedings of the International Parallel and Distributed Processing Symposium*. IEEE, April 2002.

10. Sun Microsystems Inc. Sun hpc clustertools. Technical report, 2003. http://www.sun.com/servers/hpc/software/.
11. Sun Microsystems Inc. Sun mpi. Technical report, 2003. http://www.sun.com/servers/hpc/software/specifications.html#sunmpi.
12. M. Karol, M. Hluchyi, and S. Morgan. Input versus Output Queuing on a Space-Division Packet Switch. *IEEE Transactions on Communications*, C-35(12):1347–1356, December 1987.
13. J. Kim and D. Lilja. Utilizing Heterogeneous Networks in Distributed Parallel Computing Systems. In *Proc. of the 6th Int. Symposium on High Performance Computing*, 1997.
14. J. Kim and D. Lilja. Performance-Based Path Determination for Interprocessor Communication in Distributed Computing Systems. *IEEE Trans. on Parallel and Distributed Systems*, 10(3):316–327, 1999.
15. MPI-comittee. Message passing interface forum. Technical report. http://www-unix.mcs.anl.gov/mpi/.
16. S. Pakin, V. Karamcheti, and A. Chien. Fast Messages (FM): Efficient, Portable Communication for Workstation Clusters and Massively-Parallel Processor. *IEEE Concurrency*, 5(2):60–73, 1997.
17. L. Peh and W. Dally. Flit-Reservation Flow Control. In *Proc. 6th Int. Symposium on High-Performance Computer Architecture*, pages 73–84, Toulouse, France, January 2000.
18. Loïc Prylli, Bernard Tourancheau, and Roland Westrelin. The design for a high performance MPI implementation on the Myrinet network. In *Recent Advances in Parallel Virtual Machine and Message Passing Interface. Proc. 6th European PVM/MPI Users' Group (EuroPVM/MPI '99)*, volume 1697 of *Lect. Notes in Comp. Science*, pages 223–230, Barcelona, Spain, 1999. Springer Verlag.
19. Loïc Prylli and Bernard Tourancheau. BIP: a new protocol designed for high performance networking on Myrinet. In *1st Workshop on Personal Computer based Networks Of Workstations (PC-NOW '98)*, volume 1388 of *Lect. Notes in Comp. Science*, pages 472–485. Held in conjunction with IPPS/SPDP 1998. IEEE, Springer-Verlag, April 1998.
20. Task-Group-btgt11.1. Scheduled Transfer Protocol (ST). Technical Report 3.6, National Committee for Information Technology Standardization, January 2000. www.hippi.org.
21. Bernard Tourancheau and Roland Westrelin. Support for MPI at the network interface level. In *8th European PVM/MPI Users Group Meeting: Euro PVM/MPI 2001*, Santorini (Thera) Island, Greece, April 2002. Springer - Verlag.
22. W Wolf. A decade of hardware/software codesign. *IEEE Computer*, 36(4):38–44, apr 2003.
23. X. Yuan, R. Melhelm, and R. Gupta. Distributed Path Reservation Algorithms for Multiplexed All-optical Interconnection Networks. In *3rd IEEE Symposium on High-Performance Computer Architecture*, San Antonio, Texas, February 1997.

Implementing Fast and Reusable Datatype Processing

Robert Ross, Neill Miller, and William D. Gropp

Mathematics and Computer Science Division
Argonne National Laboratory, Argonne IL 60439, USA
{rross,neillm,gropp}@mcs.anl.gov

Abstract. Methods for describing structured data are a key aid in application development. The MPI standard defines a system for creating "MPI types" at run time and using these types when passing messages, performing RMA operations, and accessing data in files. Similar capabilities are available in other middleware. Unfortunately many implementations perform poorly when processing these structured data types. This situation leads application developers to avoid these components entirely, instead performing any necessary data processing by hand.

In this paper we describe an internal representation of types and a system for processing this representation that helps maintain the highest possible performance during processing. The performance of this system, used in the MPICH2 implementation, is compared to well-written manual processing routines and other available MPI implementations. We show that performance for most tested types is comparable to manual processing. We identify additional opportunities for optimization and other software where this implementation can be leveraged.

1 Introduction

Many middleware packages now provide mechanisms for building *datatypes*, descriptions of structured data, and using these types in other operations, such as message passing, remote memory access, and I/O. These mechanisms typically allow regularity of structured data to be described, leading to concise descriptions of sometimes complicated layouts.

The problem with many implementations of these systems is that they perform poorly [9]. Hence, application programmers often avoid the systems altogether and instead perform this processing manually in the application code. A common instance of this is manually *packing* structured data (placing noncontiguous data into a contiguous region for efficiently sending in a message) and then manually copying the data back into structured form on the other side.

Obviously, no implementors providing mechanisms for structured data description and manipulation intend these systems to be unusably slow. Further, the MPI datatype specification does not preclude high-performance implementations. Several groups have investigated possibilities for improving MPI datatype processing performance [10, 5] with some success, but the techniques described in these works have not yet made it into widely-used MPI implementations.

This work describes the implementation of a generic datatype processing system and its use in the context of a portable, high-performance MPI implementation, MPICH2. The goal of this work is to provide a high-performance implementation of datatype processing that will allow application programmers to leverage the power of datatypes without sacrificing performance. While we will show the use of this system in the context of MPI datatypes, the implementation is built in such a way that it can be leveraged in other environments as well by providing a simple but complete representation for structured types, a mechanism for efficiently performing arbitrary operations on data types (not just packing and unpacking), and support for partial processing of types.

2 Design

Previous work presented a taxonomy of MPI types and a methodology for representing these in a concise way [5]. It further discussed the use of an explicit stack-based approach for processing that avoids recursive calls seen in simple implementations. At the time, however, only preliminary work was done in this direction, and no implementation was made available. This effort builds on that preliminary work, implementing many of the ideas, extending and generalizing the approach for use in additional roles, and providing this implementation as part of a portable MPI implementation. There are three characteristics of this implementation that we will consider in more detail:

- Simplified type representation (over MPI types)
- Support for partial processing of types
- Separation of type parsing from action to perform on data

2.1 Representing Types: Dataloops

We describe types by combining a concise set of descriptors that we call *dataloops*. Dataloops can be of five types: contig, vector, blockindexed, indexed, and struct [5]. These five types allow us to capture the maximum amount of regularity possible, keeping our representation concise. At the same time, these are sufficient to describe the entire range of MPI types. Simplifying the set of descriptors aids greatly in implementing support for fast datatype processing because it reduces the number of cases that our processing code must handle. Further, we maintain the type's extent in this representation (a general concept) while eliminating any future need for the MPI-specific LB and UB values. This simplification has the added benefit of allowing us to process resized types with no additional overhead in our representation.

For MPI we create the dataloop representation of the type within the MPI type creation calls (e.g., MPI_Type_vector), building on the dataloop representation of the input type. We also take this opportunity to perform optimizations based on the input type and new constructor, such as coalescing of adjacent regions in indexed types.

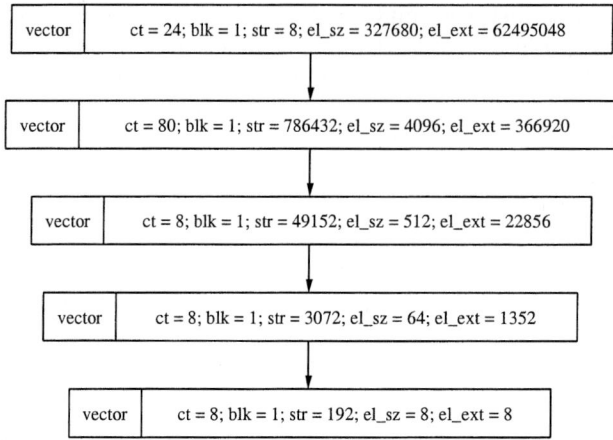

Fig. 1. Dataloop representation of Flash test type.

Figure 1 shows the dataloop representation of the type used in the Flash I/O datatype test described in Section 3. Converting from the nested MPI vectors in the Flash type results in a similarly nested set of vector dataloops. At the bottom of the diagram is the *leaf* dataloop; in this case it is a vector with a count of 8, a stride of 192 bytes, and an element size and extent of 8 bytes (a double). Dataloops above the leaf describe where data resides in the buffer, but do not require processing of the buffer. Thus processing consists of two steps, recalculating the relative location of data based on upper (non-leaf) dataloops, and processing data at the leaf. In a heterogeneous system there would be two slight differences: type information would be stored in the dataloops rather than simple byte sizes, and struct dataloops might allow for "forks" in the tree that result in multiple leaf dataloops. The overall process would remain the same.

2.2 Partial Processing: Segments

In many cases processing of a type must be broken into a number of steps. For example, when sending a message we may need to copy data into a contiguous buffer for sending. If the message is large, we may have to break the data into chunks in order to limit our use of available memory. We call this action of operating on data in chunks *partial processing*. This action is often necessary in other areas as well, such as I/O, where buffer sizes or underlying interfaces may be limiting factors.

For the purpose of partial processing, we need some structure to maintain state between calls to datatype processing routines. We call this structure a **segment**. Segments are allocated before processing and freed afterwards. Segments contain the stack used to process the type and state describing the last position processed. With this information, processing can be broken into multiple steps or performed out of order.

2.3 Actions on Data

So far we haven't discussed actions that might be performed as we are processing a type, other than alluding to copying data to and from contiguous buffers. However, there are actually a variety of actions that one might perform.

For MPICH2 the use of type processing occurs in three locations. The first and most obvious is the `MPI_Pack` and `MPI_Unpack` routines that allow users to pack a type into a contiguous buffer. The second use is in the point-to-point messaging code itself. In this code we must in some cases pack or unpack from contiguous buffers of limited size in order to bound the memory requirements of the implementation, so partial processing is needed. In other cases we can leverage the `readv` and `writev` calls to avoid the need for data copy. In these cases we instead convert the type to a list of $(offset, length)$ pairs to be passed to these calls. Here, too, we must partial process, as these calls will accept only a limited number of these pairs. The third use of type processing is in parallel I/O. The MPI-IO component of MPICH2 requires similar $(offset, length)$ pairs for use with noncontiguous file views. The sizes of these types do not match the sizes of the types for `readv` and `writev` calls on all platforms, so separate routines are required.

Clearly, in the context of MPI alone a number of operations might be performed. We thus separate the code that understands how to process the type from the *action* that will be performed on pieces of the type. For a given action to perform on types, we need functions (or possibly macros for performance reasons) that understand each of the leaf dataloop types. By providing code that can process entire leaf dataloops, we avoid processing the type as a collection of contiguous pieces, thereby maintaining performance. Returning to the example dataloops in Figure 1, a function for processing vector leaf dataloops will be used to copy data during the `MPI_Pack` operation. This function will then perform an optimized strided copy, rather than copying an element at a time.

2.4 Implementation Details

Currently we implement our system using a core "loop manipulation" function that processes non-leaf dataloops and calls action-specific functions to handle leaf dataloops. For each action a set of functions are implemented that understand contiguous, vector, indexed, block indexed, and struct loops. The ability to process entire leaf dataloops in this manner leads directly to the performance seen in the following section. We have investigated conversion of these routines into macros in order to eliminate function call overhead, but at this time the overhead does not appear significant. The current implementation supports only homogeneous systems.

Optimizations of the loop representation are currently applied at two points. First, when types are built, we perform optimizations such as conversion of struct types into indexed types (for homogeneous systems) and coalescing of contiguous indexed regions. Second, at the time the segment is created (the first step in a `MPI_Pack`), we examine the type and the count used in the segment. We use this opportunity to optimize for cases such as a count of a contiguous type, converting this into a larger contiguous type or a vector (depending on the extent of the base type). We will see the results of this optimization in the Struct Array and Struct Vector tests in the following section.

In addition to loop optimization we are able to preload the entire stack at segment creation time. This preloading is possible because of conversion of structs into indexed loops; our homogeneous type representation never has more than one leaf dataloop. The preloading optimization may also be used in heterogeneous systems when struct types are not present in the datatype and may be used to a limited extent even when struct types are present.

3 Benchmarking

When choosing benchmarks for this work, we first examined the SKaMPI benchmark and datatype testing performed with this tool [7, 8]. While this tool did seem appropriate for testing of type processing within a single MPI implementation, it does so in the context of point to point message passing or collectives. Because we wanted to look at a number of different implementations and were concerned solely with type processing, we desired tests that isolated datatype processing. We implemented a collection of synthetic tests for this purpose. These tests compare the MPI_Pack and MPI_Unpack routines with hand-coded routines that manually pack and unpack data, effectively isolating type processing from other aspects of the MPI implementation. Each test begins by allocating memory, initializing the data region, and creating a MPI type describing the region. Next, a set of iterations are performed using MPI_Pack and MPI_Unpack in order to get a rough estimate of the time of runs. Using this data, we then calculate a number of iterations to time and execute those iterations. The process is repeated for our manual packing and unpacking routines. Only pack results are presented here.

The *Contig* and *Struct Array* set of tests both test performance operating on contiguous data. The Contig tests are simple contiguous cases using MPI_INT, MPI_FLOAT, and MPI_DOUBLE types. A contiguous type of 1048576 elements is created, and a count of 1 is passed to the MPI_Pack and MPI_Unpack routines. We expect in these tests that most MPI implementations will perform competitively with the manual routines. The Struct Array test creates a single struct type, and an array of 64K of these are manipulated. The structure consists of two integers, followed by a 64-byte char array, two doubles, and a float. The structure is defined to be packed, so there are no gaps between elements or between structures in the array. This provides an opportunity for implementations to automatically optimize their internal representation of the type, and we would expect performance to be virtually identical to the Contig test.

The *Vector* and *Struct Vector* tests both examine performance when operating on a vector of 1,048,576 basic types with a stride of 2 types (i.e. accessing every other type). In the Vector tests, we build a vector type and pack and unpack using a count of 1. In the Struct Vector tests we first build a struct type using MPI_LB and MPI_UB to increase the extent, and then we pack and unpack with a count of 1048576. This is a useful method of operating on strided data when the number of elements might change from call to call. Examining the relative performance of these two tests allows us to see the importance of optimizations that are applied after the type is created based on the count passed to MPI calls.

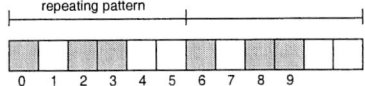

Fig. 2. Pattern of elements in Indexed tests.

The *Indexed* set of tests use an indexed type with a fixed, regular pattern. Every block in the indexed type consists of a single element (of type MPI_INT, MPI_FLOAT, or MPI_DOUBLE, depending on the particular test run). There are 1,048,576 such blocks in the type. As shown in Figure 2, some pieces in the pattern are adjacent, allowing for underlying optimization of the region representation. A particularly clever implementation could refactor this as a vector of an indexed base type, but we do not expect any current implementations to do this, and ours does not. These tests showcase the importance of handling indexed leaf dataloops efficiently.

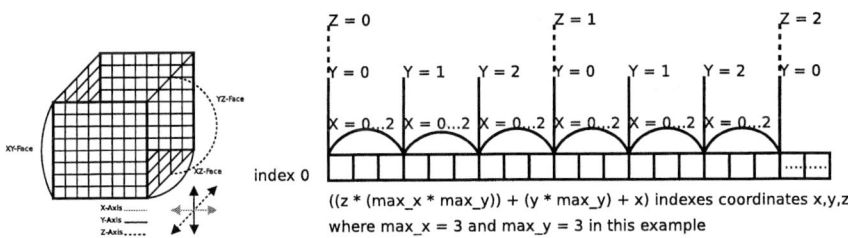

Fig. 3. Data layout in 3D Face tests.

The *3D Face* tests pull entire faces off a 3D cube of elements (Figure 3, described in Appendix E of [4]). Element types are varied between MPI_INT, MPI_FLOAT, and MPI_DOUBLE types. The 3D cube is 256 elements on a side. We separate the manipulation of sides of the cube in order to observe the performance impact of locality and contiguity. The XY side of the cube has the the greatest locality, while the YZ side of the cube has the least locality.

The *Flash I/O* test examines performance when operating on the data kept in core by the Flash astrophysics application. The Flash code is an adaptive mesh refinement application that solves fully compressible, reactive hydrodynamic equations, developed mainly for the study of nuclear flashes on neutron stars and white dwarfs [3].

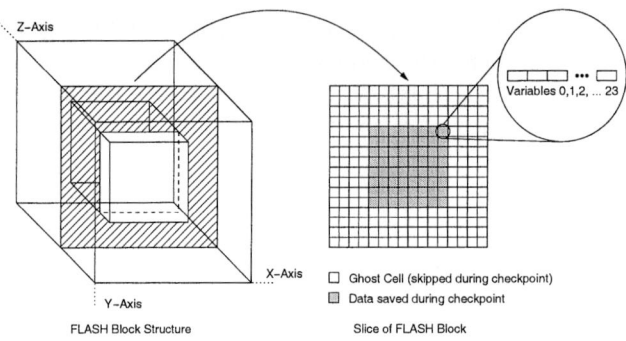

Fig. 4. Data layout in Flash test.

Figure 4 depicts the in-memory representation of data used by Flash. The data consists of 80 3D blocks of data. Each block consists of a $8 \times 8 \times 8$ block of elements surrounded by a guard cell region four elements deep on each side. Each element consists of 24 variables, each an `MPI_DOUBLE`. For postprocessing reasons the Flash code writes data out by variable, while variables are interleaved in memory during computation. In the Flash I/O test we describe the data in terms of this by-variable organization used in writing checkpoints. This leads to a very noncontiguous access pattern across memory. Further, this is the most deeply nested type tested in this suite, showcasing the need for nonrecursive approaches to processing.

3.1 Performance Results

Measurements on the IA32 platform were performed on a dual-processor 2.0 GHz Xeon system with 1 GByte of main memory. The machine has 512 Kbytes of L2 cache. Results for the Stream benchmark [6] show a copy rate of 1230.77 Mbytes/sec on this machine. This gives us an upper bound for main memory manipulation, although in specific cases we will see cache effects.

Table 1 shows the performance of our synthetic benchmarks for manual packing, MPICH2, MPICH1, and the LAM MPI implementations. Also listed are the size and extent of the data region manipulated (in MBytes). Results with `MPI_INT` types were removed; they were virtually identical to `MPI_FLOAT` results. LAM 6.5.9, MPICH 1.2.5-1a, and a CVS version of MPICH2 (as of May 7, 2003) were used in the testing. The `CFLAGS` used to compile test programs and MPI implementations were "-O6 -DNDEBUG -fomit-frame-pointer -ffast-math -fexpensive-optimizations".

The data extent in the Contig test is large enough that caching isn't a factor, and in all cases performance is very close to the peak identified by the Stream benchmark. The Struct Array test shows similar results for all but LAM. LAM does not detect that this is really a large contiguous region, resulting in significant performance degradation.

Table 1. Comparison of processing performance.

Test	Manual	MPICH2	MPICH1	LAM	Size	Extent
	\multicolumn{4}{c}{(Mbytes/sec)}		(MB)	(MB)
Contig (FLOAT)	1156.37	1124.04	1136.48	1002.38	4.00	4.00
Contig (DOUBLE)	1132.26	1126.22	1125.05	1010.81	8.00	8.00
Struct Array	1055.02	1131.39	1131.28	512.72	5.75	5.75
Vector (FLOAT)	754.37	753.81	744.42	491.31	4.00	8.00
Vector (DOUBLE)	747.98	743.88	744.81	632.77	8.00	16.00
Struct Vector (FLOAT)	746.04	750.76	36.57	141.60	4.00	8.00
Struct Vector (DOUBLE)	747.31	743.70	72.81	252.34	8.00	16.00
Indexed (FLOAT)	654.35	401.26	82.79	122.85	2.00	4.00
Indexed (DOUBLE)	696.59	530.29	161.52	204.43	4.00	8.00
3D, XY Face (FLOAT)	1807.91	1798.52	1754.45	1139.04	0.25	0.25
3D, XZ Face (FLOAT)	1244.52	1237.68	1210.53	992.80	0.25	63.75
3D, YZ Face (FLOAT)	111.85	112.06	112.15	64.22	0.25	63.99
3D, XY Face (DOUBLE)	1149.84	1133.86	1132.43	1011.11	0.50	0.50
3D, XZ Face (DOUBLE)	1213.10	1201.54	1157.93	969.46	0.50	127.50
3D, YZ Face (DOUBLE)	206.41	206.39	201.82	103.24	0.50	127.99
Flash I/O (DOUBLE)	245.60	212.55	215.80	159.63	7.50	59.60

The Vector and Struct Vector tests show that the same pattern can be processed very differently depending on how it is described. Our implementation detects the vector pattern in the Struct Vector tests at segment creation time, converting the loop into a vector and processing in the same way. This optimization is not applied in the other two implementations, leading to poor performance.

The Indexed tests showcase the importance of handling indexed leaf dataloops well. With the inclusion of action-specific functions that handle indexed dataloops we attain 60% of the manual processing rate at the smaller data type sizes and 76% for MPI_DOUBLE, while the other implementations lag behind significantly. We intend to spend additional time examining the code path for this case, as we would expect to more closely match manual packing performance.

The 3D Face test using MPI_FLOAT types shows two interesting effects. First, because in the XY case the extent of the data is such that it all fits in cache, performance actually exceeds the Stream benchmark performance for this case. In the YZ case data elements are strided but laid out in groups of 256; this is more than adequate to maintain high performance. In the last (YZ) case we see the effect of very strided data; we are accessing only one type for every 256 in a row, and performance is less than 10% of peak for manual routines and all the tested MPI implementations.

The Flash I/O type processing test shows that while we are able to maintain the performance of a manual packing implementation, performance overall is quite bad. Just as with the YZ 3D Face test, this type, with its many nested loops, provides opportunities for optimization that we do not currently exploit. This type will serve as a test case for application of additional optimizations.

4 Related Work

The work by Träff et al. on datatypes is in many ways similar to this approach [10]. They also consider derived types as a tree. However, their leaf nodes are always basic (primitive) types, and they allow branches to occur at indexed types, while we maintain a single child in these cases. Further they have rules for each type of MPI constructor, rather than converting to a more general, yet simpler, set of component types. At the same time, they leverage some loop reordering optimizations that are not used in this work.

5 Conclusions and Future Work

This work presents a concise abstraction for representing types coupled with a well-engineered algorithm for processing this representation. With this system we are able to maintain a high percentage of manual processing performance under a wide variety of situations. This system is integrated into MPICH2, ensuring that many scientists will have the opportunity to leverage this work.

The study presented here was performed on commodity components and a homogeneous system. It would be interesting to examine the performance on vector-type machines. Other fast datatype approaches have been applied on these machines [10], we should compare this work and look for ways in which multiple techniques might be used to move beyond matching manual processing performance. Techniques such as loop reordering and optimizing based on memory access characteristics [1] offer opportunities for improved performance and should match well to the dataloop representation used in our system. However, loop reordering has implications on partial processing that must be taken into account. If we think of dataloops as a representation of a program for processing types, runtime code generation is another avenue for performance gains. Support for heterogeneous platforms is also important. While many of the optimizations shown here are equally applicable in heterogeneous systems, further study is warranted, including examining previous work in the area.

We are also looking at other applications of this component in scientific computing software. For example, we are incorporating this work into PVFS [2] as a type processing component. By passing serialized dataloops as I/O descriptions, we obtain a concise I/O request and can leverage this high-performance type processing code for processing at the server. Similarly, this component could be used to replace the datatype processing system in MPICH1, or the system in HDF5 that was the source of performance problems in a previous study [9].

Acknowledgment

This work was supported by the Mathematical, Information, and Computational Sciences Division subprogram of the Office of Advanced Scientific Computing Research, Office of Science, U.S. Department of Energy, under Contract W-31-109-ENG-38.

References

1. S. Byna, W. Gropp, X. Sun, and R. Thakur. Improving the performance of mpi derived datatypes by optimizing memory-access cost. Technical Report Preprint ANL/MCS-P1045-0403, Mathematics and Computer Science Division, Argonne National Laboratory, April 2003.
2. P. Carns, W. Ligon, R. Ross, and R. Thakur. PVFS: A parallel file system for Linux clusters. In *Proceedings of the 4th Annual Linux Showcase and Conference*, pages 317–327, Atlanta, GA, October 2000. USENIX Association.
3. B. Fryxell, K. Olson, P. Ricker, F. X. Timmes, M. Zingale, D. Q. Lamb, P. MacNeice, R. Rosner, and H. Tufo. FLASH: An adaptive mesh hydrodynamics code for modelling astrophysical thermonuclear flashes. *Astrophysical Journal Suppliment*, 131:273, 2000.
4. W. Gropp, E. Lusk, and A. Skjellum. *Using MPI: Portable Parallel Programming with the Message-Passing Interface*. MIT Press, Cambridge, MA, 1994.
5. W. Gropp, E. Lusk, and D. Swider. Improving the performance of MPI derived datatypes. In Anthony Skjellum, Purushotham V. Bangalore, and Yoginder S. Dandass, editors, *Proceedings of the Third MPI Developer's and User's Conference*, pages 25–30. MPI Software Technology Press, 1999.
6. J. McCalpin. Sustainable memory bandwidth in current high performance computers. Technical report, Advanced Systems Division, Silicon Graphics, Inc., Revised to October 12, 1995.
7. R. Reussner, P. Sanders, L. Prechelt, and M Müller. SKaMPI: A detailed, accurate MPI benchmark. In Vassuk Alexandrov and Jack Dongarra, editors, *Recent advances in Parallel Virtual Machine and Message Passing Interface*, volume 1497 of *Lecture Notes in Computer Science*, pages 52–59. Springer, 1998.
8. R. Reussner, J. Träff, and G. Hunzelmann. A benchmark for MPI derived datatypes. In Jack Dongarra, Peter Kacsuk, and Norbert Podhorszki, editors, *Recent Advances in Parallel Virutal Machine and Message Passing Interface*, number 1908 in Springer Lecture Notes in Computer Science, pages 10–17, September 2000.
9. R. Ross, D. Nurmi, A. Cheng, and M. Zingale. A case study in application I/O on linux clusters. In *Proceedings of SC2001*, November 2001.
10. J. Träff, R. Hempel, H. Ritzdoff, and F. Zimmermann. Flattening on the fly: Efficient handling of MPI derived datatypes. In J. J. Dongarra, E. Luque, and Tomas Margalef, editors, *Recent Advances in Parallel Virtual Machine and Message Passing Interface*, number 1697 in Lecture Notes in Computer Science, pages 109–116, Berlin, 1999. Springer-Verlag.

An MPI Implementation Supported by Process Migration and Load Balancing

A. Maloney, A. Goscinski, and M. Hobbs

School of Information Technology
Deakin University
Geelong, Vic 3216, Australia
{asmalone,ang,mick}@deakin.edu.au

Abstract. This report describes an implementation of MPI-1 on the GENESIS cluster operating system and compares this implementation to a UNIX based MPI implementation. The changes that were made to the implementation are compared between the two, and the advantages of porting to GENESIS are detailed. This report demonstrates how GENESIS' load balancing supported by process migration improves the execution performance of an MPI application. The significance of this report is in demonstrating how these services can enhance parallel programming tools to improve performance and how future parallel programming tool design could take advantage of these services.

1 Introduction

The execution of parallel applications on non-dedicated clusters is both different from execution on not only MPPs and SMPs but also dedicated clusters, and challenging. Non-dedicated clusters are characterized by communication latency and multiprocessing supported by individual cluster computers. Computers could be removed from the cluster or fail and new computers can be added, they can become idle, lightly loaded or heavy loaded. This naturally generates a need for not only static allocation of application processes but also load balancing supported by migration. Due to communication latency, sequential creation of many identical parallel processes on many computers could take unacceptable long time.

The known implementations of MPI on clusters require the programmer to be involved in activities, which are of the operating system nature [1] [2]. In particular, the programmer must define the number of computers and select those that can satisfy their requirements. Parallel processes are instantiated on remote computers sequentially and cannot change their location during the application execution.

Currently, operating systems do not provide services to deal with the existing problems and to relieve the programmer from the burden of executing MPI applications on non-dedicated clusters. The only trials to improve the situation are demonstrated by Mosix that offers load balancing supported by process migration, however it suffers from the problems of initial allocation of parallel processes [3]; and also adaptive MPI [4], which uses process migration, however requires some modification of existing MPI code to satisfy load balancing requirements.

GENESIS is a cluster operating system currently being developed at Deakin University, as a proof of concept system [5]. It is because of the services that GENESIS provides that GENESIS makes an ideal candidate to port MPI onto, to investigate how the services can benefit the implementation of MPI. PVM has previously been ported to GENESIS, and hence would also allow for the outcomes of the MPI port to be analyzed further by comparing performance data of the two parallel programming tools [6].

The first goal of this paper is to present an implementation of MPI-1 on GENESIS, in particular the differences in the architecture of both UNIX MPI and GENESIS MPI, discuss the advanced services that GENESIS provides, which can improve the performance of MPI application, and to measure the performance of the GENESIS MPI library by comparing the test results gathered with those from previous tests conducted using GENESIS PVM and basic GENESIS message passing. The second goal is to demonstrate how load balancing supported by process migration improves the execution performance of an MPI application.

2 UNIX MPI

Many implementations of MPI exist, each with their own slightly varying architectures that meet the goals of MPI and adhere to the MPI specification. As this is the case, an implementation needed to be chosen that was designed for the UNIX system and would be ideal for porting to GENESIS. Two main implementations were considered for porting: MPICH [1] and LAM-MPI [7]. The MPICH implementation was selected.

The Architecture of MPICH. The design of MPICH is that of many layers, each being stacked on top of each other to form the overall MPI implementation. The top layer is probably the most simple of the four layers. This layer represents the API, which means that the programmer using MPI only has to deal with the MPI calls and their semantics. The second is the 'MPI Point-to-point' layer. It contains the actual code that defines how each MPI library call operates, and the algorithms that allow MPI to actually work the way that it is defined in the MPI specification. From this layer down, the programmer does not need to know what is going on within the layer hierarchy. The next layer is the 'Abstract Data Interface' (ADI) layer. The job of the ADI layer is to provide a way for the higher layer to achieve its goal independent of the system that MPI is running on. The layer must hide the differences and limitations of the underlying system from the 'MPI Point-to-Point' layer so that it can still achieve what is needed. The lowest, the 'Channel Interface' layer is the most system specific, and hence has to deal with the actual interactions with the system that MPI is executing on.

The use of these layers is how MPICH achieves its high portability, by allowing the MPICH implementation to be dissected at a certain layer, and then having the lower layers replaced with a new layer(s) designed for the target system.

Process Management. The runtime environment of MPICH is relatively simple, as it does not rely on any coordinating servers to provide a way for each of the processes to communicate to each other. The processes use a peer-to-peer model, whereby each process knows of each other process that is part of the MPI applications execution.

With this knowledge, each process can communicate directly with another process. Each process learns of the other processes during the process instantiation stage. Once a process has been created on a computer, then that process must continue to execute on that same computer until it has finished. MPICH does not provide process migration.

Process Instantiation. Process instantiation is not defined within the MPI specification. It is up to the individual implementation to decide how processes are to be instantiated and where. MPICH achieves process instantiation through the use of an executable application called 'mpirun' that allows a user to execute their desired MPI applications and at the same time to pass any command line arguments that may be necessary to the applications. The basic 'mpirun' syntax is as follows:

mpirun <number of processes> <executable> <arguments for the MPI application>

Once 'mpirun' has managed to start the execution of the processes, it then terminates and leaves the processes to continue on their own. The computer(s) for which to start these processes on also needs to be specified by the user before the execution of the application. This is done by listing these computers in a specific file.

Process Communication. The method of process communication is not strictly defined in the MPI specification. Within the MPICH implementation, the TCP protocol is used in order to facilitate the exchange of data between processes. This requires that each process establish a connection with each of the other processes within the executing group of processes for this communication to take place.

3 GENESIS MPI

Many of the services provided by GENESIS can be incorporated into the design to simplify the MPI library. These services are interprocess communication, group process creation and duplication, global scheduling and process migration.

3.1 GENESIS

The design of GENESIS is based on the microkernel approach executing on a homogenous cluster of computers [5]. A separate server has been defined for managing each basic resource, such as processor, main memory, network, interprocess communication, and file I/O. These servers, together with the microkernel cooperate to provide a cluster operating system for user applications. The servers and application parallel processes communicate using messages based on a peer-to-peer model.

GENESIS provides many services to the applications that are executed on the system. These services include, among other services, interprocess communication, process creation and duplication, global scheduling and process migration. Process creation and duplication allow an application process to be created or duplicated onto multiple computers simultaneously. These services are supported by group communications. These mechanisms improve performance dramatically as processes do not need to be created sequentially. Global scheduling allows for the many computers within the cluster to be equally loaded in terms of the amount of processing. The global scheduler determines the initial placement of processes on the cluster, and if need be, can offer dynamic load balancing during execution. This dynamic load balancing is achieved by the use of process migration.

The cornerstone of the GENESIS architecture is its communication services [5]. Their placement in the GENESIS architecture has been designed to produce high performances for application execution as well as offering transparency.

3.2 The Architecture of GENESIS MPI

To port MPICH to GENESIS, the two lowest layers of MPICH (the 'Channel Interface' and the 'Abstract Device Interface' layers) were removed from the implementation and replaced with a new 'Services of GENESIS' layer, which provided the functionality for the MPI implementation to use.

The underlying functionality of MPICH has just been enhanced through the use of services that are provided by GENESIS. These services allow GENESIS MPI to provide better process management, both during instantiation and execution. GENESIS also allowed the ported implementation to use an improved communications service that is already incorporated into the GENESIS system.

Dynamic Process Management. Process management is handled very differently under GENESIS MPI compared to MPICH. This is because of the services that GENESIS provides at the lower level to processes.

Remote Process Creation. GENESIS provides the services of local and remote group process creation to improve the performance of the creation of many processes on many computers, which is more efficient than the traditional sequential process creation. Group process creation works by using group communication to simultaneously create a group of processes on many computers using an identical process image [5]. The destination computers are selected by the global scheduler, and then the execution managers cooperate to create the processes on the appropriate computers. This is implemented in GENESIS MPI during the initial process creation of the MPI processes when the application is first instantiated.

Global Scheduling. The global scheduler is involved with the initial placement of processes that are first instantiated. The placement of the processes is not permanent. The global scheduler also aids during mid-execution of MPI applications. This is the case when choosing if and when a process should be migrated to another computer if the workload on a computer becomes heavily loaded or a computer becomes idle.

Process Migration. The migration services of GENESIS can be used effectively when a computer in the cluster becomes heavily loaded or a computer becomes idle, a MPI process that is currently executing on one computer can be migrated to another computer within the cluster. This improves the overall performance of the MPI application. To provide migration within GENESIS, a migration manager is used. The migration manager acts as a coordinator for the migration of the various resources that combine to form a process. The global schedular triggers the migration by informing the migration manager on the source computer that a migration needs to take place. The global schedular provides the appropriate details of which process needs to be migrated and to which computer the process needs to be migrated. To perform the migration, the migration manager contacts the process manager, space manager and IPC manager to migrate the associated process entries, memory, and communication resources, respectively.

Process Instantiation. The instantiation of processes in GENESIS MPI is handled by the 'mpirun' application. This application is needed to create the processes specified by the user and to prepare them for execution. The use of 'mpirun' provides a familiar interface to users as 'mpirun' is used as the method for executing MPI applications in the MPICH implementation. 'mpirun' operates by creating the processes to be executed for the MPI application, and then waits until all of the executing processes have finalized and terminated, before terminating itself.

To select the executables that the user wishes to execute, and the number of processes of each, 'mpirun' prompts the user for this information. 'mpirun' first prompts the user for the name of the executable to be executed on the GENESIS system and then for the number of processes of this executable to create. This is recursive, and continues to prompt the user for another executable name and number of processes until the user leaves the executable name blank. At this point 'mpirun' begins to create the specified executables and initialize the processes. From this point forward, GENESIS services are used to create and initialize user processes (Figure 1). This provides instantiation transparency as the user need not provide any more information for the instantiation of the user processes. In the MPICH implementation of MPI, the user had to provide additional information, such as the computers for executing the MPI processes.

Interprocess Communication. Using the service of interprocess communication that GENESIS provides can aid MPI's communications services. GENESIS provides send and receive primitives for use in user applications. This simplifies the communication process of MPI, as many of the communication calls provided by MPI have been directly mapped on top of these two GENESIS primitives. This simplification occurs because the MPI library no longer needs to distinguish between local and remote processes when attempting to communicate with them. The delivery of the messages is instead handled by the GENESIS system. The lower level workings of the MPI library therefore do not need to specify which computer the destination process is on.

Network communication in GENESIS MPI is different to that of UNIX MPI. UNIX MPI uses the TCP protocol to support process to communication, GENESIS does not use TCP. It provides its own high performance reliable datagram protocol known as RHODOS Reliable Datagram Protocol (RRDP).

4 Performance Study

This section presents the results of some tests to determine how the port of MPI to the GENESIS system compares to the current message passing facilities that are already existent on GENESIS. It also demonstrates how load balancing supported by process migration improves the execution performance of an MPI application.

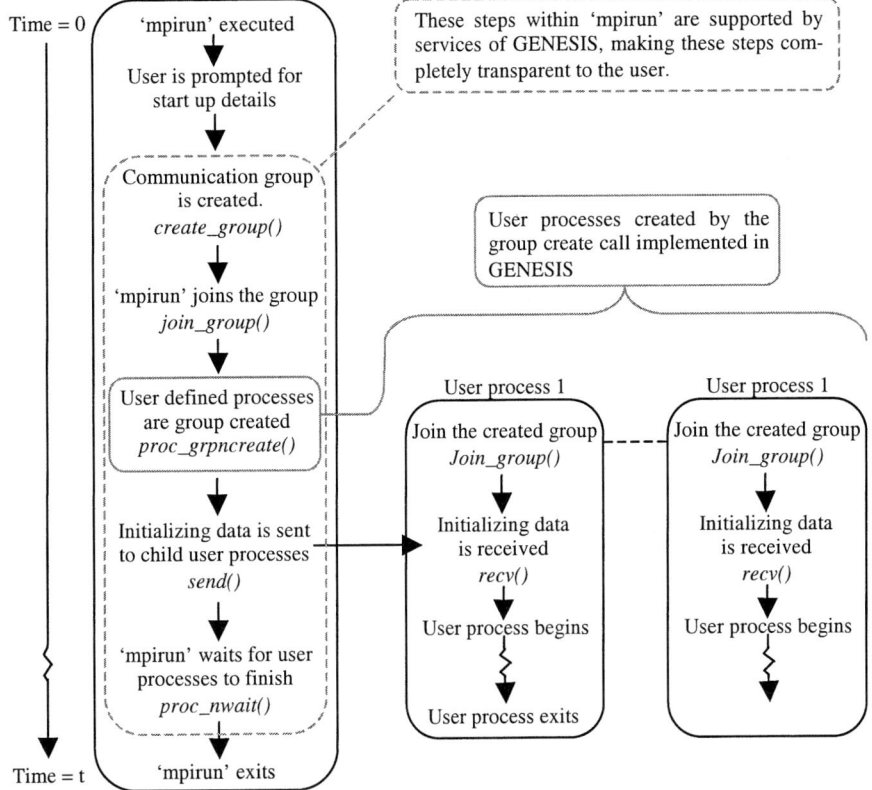

Fig. 1. Execution of 'mpirun' and instantiation of user processes

The facilities are GENESIS PVM and GENESIS' standard message passing (It was demonstrated in [6] that the GENESIS PVM offers better execution performance than UNIX PVM. This was the reason for using GENESIS PVM as a basis for performance comparison). To compare these three systems, two simple, commonly used applications (SOR-NZ and TSP) were executed and the overall time of the applications to execute was measured and graphed. These tests were conducted on the Sun Microsystems 3/50 cluster. A total of four Sun 3/50 computers connected by a switched Ethernet were used for the testing of MPI.

4.1 GENESIS MPI vs. GENESIS PVM vs. GENESIS Message Passing

The following results were obtained from the execution of the test applications. The results for the PVM and message passing based applications were taken from [5]. Figure 2 shows that both the GENESIS Message Passing (MP) and PVM version of SOR-NZ provides slightly better completion times than the MPI version. Although it is also noticed that the speedup of both MPI and PVM being quite close, and it is not until more computers are added that a noticeable difference can be observed (Figure 3). The slower completion times of MPI are due to extra overheads that have been implemented in the MPI library used. The reason for these extra overheads, compared to the PVM library and MP, is the extensive range of functionality that MPI provides.

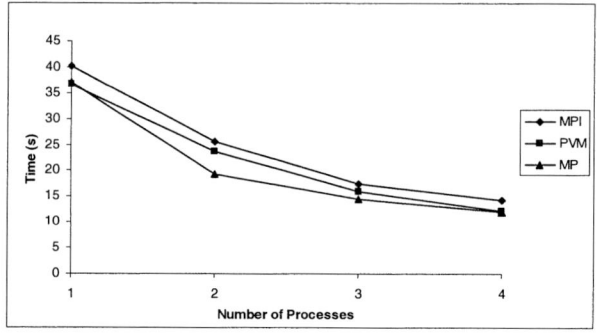

Fig. 2. Performance results achieved using SOR-NZ

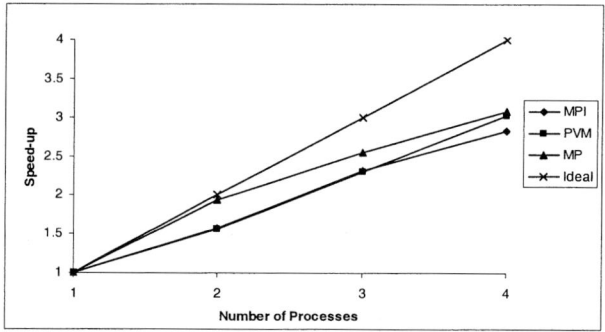

Fig. 3. Speedup achieved using SOR-NZ

The results for the TSP performance tests are much the same as the results for the SOR-NZ tests. The MPI version of the applications was slower in overall execution time than the PVM and MP version (Figure 4). The speedups achieved were slightly in favor of the PVM version of the application (Figure 5), with MPI coming second, in between PVM and MP. Again the reasoning behind these outcomes is much the same as for the SOR-NZ results.

4.2 Execution Supported by Global Scheduling and Process Migration

Experiment Environment. To successfully show how the use of the global scheduular, aided by process migration, can help to allow applications to complete in their shortest time possible, an experiment was conducted using two tests on the GENESIS cluster, as shown in Figure 6. The first test did not used process migration during its execution, whilst the second test was executed with support of process migration. The applications that were used in these tests were TSP, Interactive 1, and Interactive 2.

The last two simulate the behavior of interactive applications executed on a non-dedicated cluster.

Interactive 1 is a simple application that sits idle for 60 seconds and then it infinitely loops. Interactive 2 sits in a loop for the first 20 seconds and then exits, this application is used to represent a computer that is heavily loaded and then exiting, leaving the computer idle.

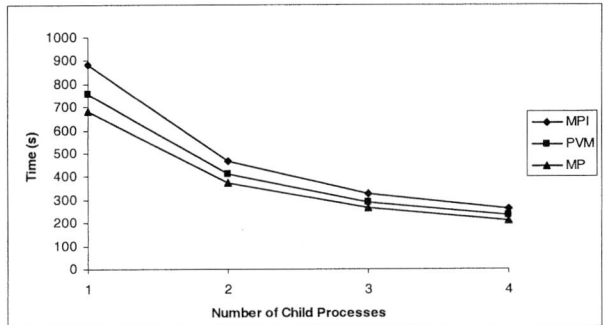

Fig. 4. Performance results achieved for TSP

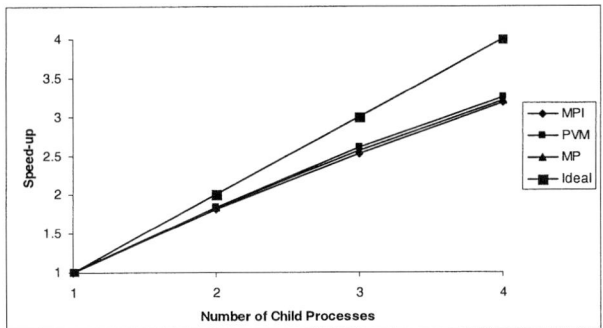

Fig. 5. Speedup achieved using TSP

Experiment Execution and Results. The first test that was conducted did not incorporate process migration into the execution. The TSP application was executed using three processes. The execution of all processes is shown in Figure 7. At the beginning, all three TSP processes started executing, along with Interactive 2, whilst Interactive 1 sits idle at this point in time. After the first 20 seconds, Interactive 2 completes its execution and the process is terminated; this means that computer 4 becomes idle. At the 60 second mark, Interactive 1 starts its computing, this means that both the TSP process and Interactive 1 have to share the computer, making it heavily loaded. The execution of the TSP process then completes and the execution time is recorded.

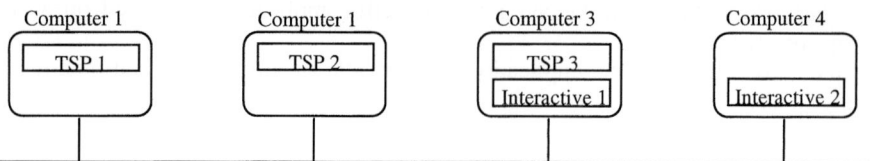

Fig. 6. Execution environment

The second test takes advantage of global scheduling and process migration. The initial execution of this test is the same as in test 1. However, at the 60 second mark, Interactive 1 starts its computation, making computer 3 heavily loaded. At this point in time, the global scheduler is informed of the load change, and attempts to balance the load over the cluster. The global scheduler identifies that the TSP process on computer 3 can be migrated to the currently idle computer 4 and informs the migration manager to do so, effectively balancing the load of the cluster (Figure 8).

The results of the experiment (Table 1) showed that the use of global scheduling and process migration provides excellent improvement in overall execution times on a heavily loaded cluster when compared to static allocation of processes on the cluster.

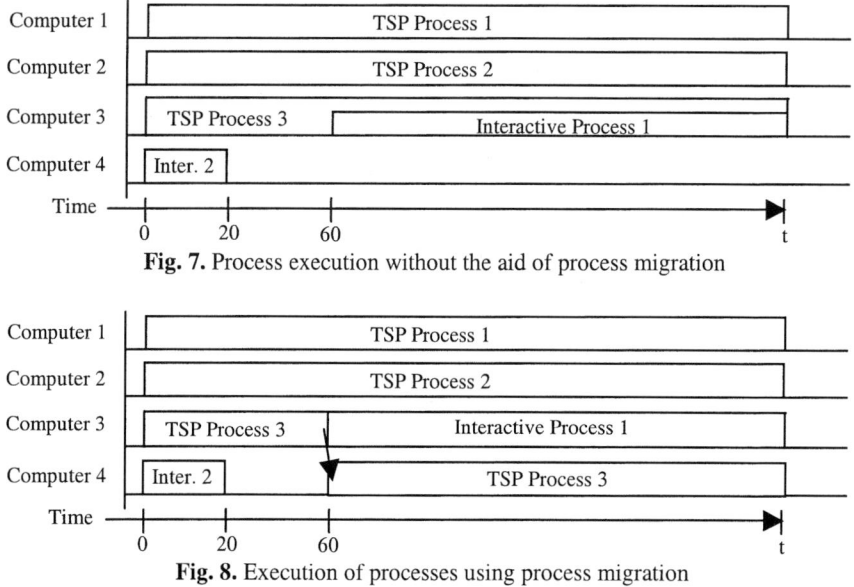

Fig. 7. Process execution without the aid of process migration

Fig. 8. Execution of processes using process migration

Table 1. Resulting times of process migration tests

System Configuration	Execution time of TSP
Dynamic load balancing with additional load	470.70000 seconds
Static allocation of processes with additional load	617.81000 seconds
Execution with no additional load on the cluster	469.17000 seconds

5 Conclusions

The porting of MPI from the UNIX environment to GENESIS has shown that there have been several large changes to the underlying structure of MPI to improve the ported implementation of MPI. The move to GENESIS has been achieved by replacing the two lower layers of MPICH with the services that GENESIS provides. These services were group communications, group process creation, process migration, and global scheduling, including static allocation and dynamic load balancing. Incorporating these services to MPI has shown promising results and provided a better solution for implementing parallel programming tools. It is hoped that future parallel programming tools can take advantage of what was learnt whilst porting MPI to a cluster operating system.

Currently, 'mpirun' is used in order to instantiate MPI applications. This will be improved further in the future by automating the instantiation process through exploiting automatic and dynamic establishment of a parallel virtual cluster.

References

1. Gropp W., Lusk E., Doss N., Skjellum A.: A High-Performance, Portable Implementation of the MPI Message Passing Interface Standard. Mathematics and Computer Science Division, Argonne National Laboratory (1996)
2. Brightwell R., Maccabe A.B., Riesen R.: Design and Implementation of MPI on Portals 3.0. In: proceedings of Ninth Euro PVM/MPI Conf, Linz, (2002)
3. Shaaban D., Jenne J.E.N.: Distributed Computing: PVM, MPI, and MOSIX Multiple Processor Systems (1999)
4. Bhandarkar M., Kale L.V., de Sturler E., Hoeinger J.: Object-Based Adaptive Load Balancing for MPI Programs. Center for Simulationof Advanced Rockets, University of Illinois at Urbana-Champaign (2000)
5. Goscinski A., Hobbs M., Silcock J.: GENESIS: An Efficient, Transparent and Easy to Use Cluster Operating System. In: Parallel Computing Vol 28, Elsevier Science (2002)
6. Rough J., Goscinski A., DePaoli D.: PVM on the RHODOS Distributed Operating System. In: Recent Advances in Parallel Virtual Computer and Message Passing Interface, 4th European PVM/MPI Users' Group Meeting, Cracow, Poland (1997)
7. Burns G., Daoud R., Vaigl J.: LAM: An open cluster environment for MPI. In: Ross J.W. (ed.): Proceedings of Supercomputing Symposium '94, University of Toronto (1994)

PVM over the CLAN Network

Ripduman Sohan[1] and Steve Pope[2]

[1] Laboratory for Communications Engineering
Department of Engineering
University of Cambridge, England
rss39@eng.cam.ac.uk

[2] Level 5 Networks, 25 Metcalfe Road
Cambridge, CB4 2DB, England
spope@level5networks.com

Abstract. In this paper we present an integration of PVM with a user-level network called CLAN (Collapsed LAN). CLAN is a high-performance network targeted at the server room. It presents a non-coherent shared memory approach to data transfer, coupled with a unique synchronisation mechanism called Tripwire. The essential details of the CLAN interface are outlined, along with a version of PVM modified to take advantage of the underlying hardware. The paper also provides a quantitative comparison between CLAN and ordinary Gigabit Ethernet, concluding that the CLAN interface allows PVM to achieve a significant performance increase in inter-host communication latency.

1 Introduction

Recent years have seen substantial improvement in the capabilities of the underlying hardware in terms of bandwidth and latency, nevertheless, few applications have been able to harness these improvements due to the temporal software overheads incurred in data transfer [1]. One solution to this problem has been the use of *user-level* network stacks, whereby all network operations are performed in user space, bypassing the kernel entirely [2, 3]. A variety of research projects [1, 5] have used this approach to significantly reduce communication latency.

This direct access approach does not usually perform well with regards to parallel computing due to the following limitations:

- User-level network interfaces are designed to support a particular communications paradigm. Foreign paradigms are poorly emulated.
- User-level network interfaces rarely provide adequate synchronisation primitives.

This paper presents the integration and performance of PVM over CLAN [6], a unique distributed shared-memory network.

2 The CLAN Network

The Collapsed LAN (CLAN) project is a high-performance user-level network designed at AT&T Laboratories-Cambridge [7]. Communication is provided by non-coherent distributed shared memory (DSM). Data transfer is achieved by reading or writing to the shared memory, and abstractions are created on top of this interface. The network is described in detail elsewhere [6], but a brief overview of the key features follow:

2.1 Endpoints

An endpoint identifies a host address and port number pair. An API is provided to create and destroy endpoints and manage connections. Endpoint creation and destruction are relatively expensive operations and thus they are usually cached.

Multiple endpoints are managed in the form of a circular *asynchronous event queue*. All messages are delivered into this queue. Applications register interest in or poll for wanted events. The cost of event delivery is $O(1)$ regardless of the number of active endpoints, providing a scalable delivery interface. The queue itself is integrated with the system's `select()` variant allowing easy integration with applications.

2.2 Synchronisation

On the receiver side, data is placed into application buffers asynchronously making synchronisation complex. CLAN provides a novel solution to synchronisation: the *tripwire*. A tripwire is a programmable entry in a content addressable memory (CAM) on the NIC, matching a particular address in an application address space. When a memory access to a location matching the tripwire is detected, the application receives a notification. This makes synchronisation orthogonal to data transfer and allows association with control, data or both.

3 Integration

3.1 Endpoint Management

Every node creates an initial listening CLAN endpoint on startup. Transfer endpoints between hosts are dynamically instantiated and kept open for the entire lifetime of the daemon process. The data channels of different child tasks are multiplexed over open endpoints. This allows for efficient endpoint use.

Direct route communication between tasks follows a similar procedure. However, unlike in the daemon, endpoints may be closed if left unused. This ensures conservation of available endpoint resources. Attempts to transfer data over a closed endpoint will incur the overhead of re-establishing the connection, providing a good balance between endpoint efficiency, conservation and fast communication.

3.2 Data Transfer

For the transmission and storage of message packets, PVM uses dynamically allocated memory. Maximum message size is limited by available memory. The CLAN network depends on mapping virtual address space over the network into physical address space of a remote host and dynamic alteration of these mappings is an expensive process involving breaking an existing mapping to create a new one.

This problem was overcome by the use of a *Distributed Message Queue*. Illustrated in Fig. 1, it shows that messages are copied across the network into the free buffers on the receiver queue, indicated by the write pointer (write_i). The write pointer is then incremented modulo the size of the buffer, and new value copied to the receiver (lazy_write_i).

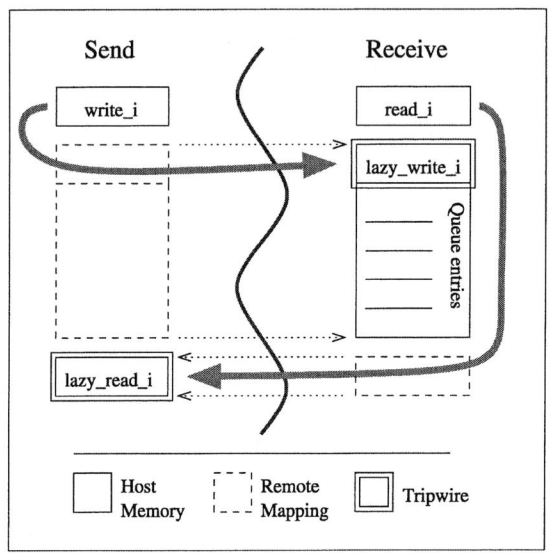

Fig. 1. Distributed Message Queue.

The receiver compares the lazy copy of the write pointer with the read pointer (read_i) to determine data availability. Messages are dequeued by reading from the buffer, incrementing the read pointer and copying its value to the sender (lazy_read_i). Tripwires notify of pointer updates.

Every endpoint contains a separate queue, enabling endpoints to function independently. Currently, each endpoint consists of 32,768 [1] buffers, each of UDPMAXLEN size. This design allows unlimited data transfer with receiver based flow control.

4 Performance

4.1 Setup

The test nodes comprised a pair of 650 MHz Pentium III systems, containing 256 MB RAM and running Linux 2.4. Both machines were equipped with a CLAN NIC and a 3Com 3c985 series Gigabit Ethernet adaptor. The benchmark consists of two micro-benchmarks designed to measure latency and throughput respectively. All tests relied on the PVM daemon for routing.

---

[1] This number was chosen in an attempt to try and maximise both queue size and the number of possible open endpoints.

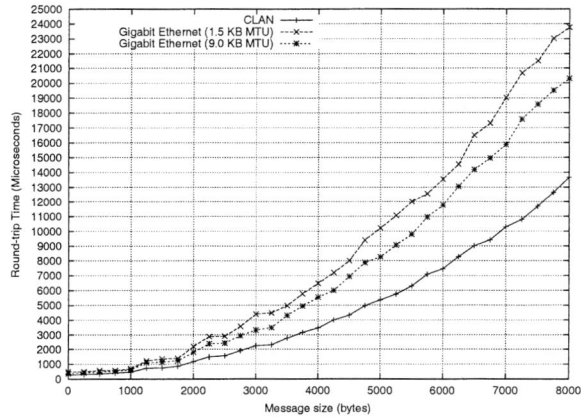

Fig. 2. Latency vs. Message Size.

4.2 Latency

Latency was measured by taking the mean round-trip time of a large number (10,000) of ping-pongs, with small-medium packet sizes (0-8KB).

As the results in Fig. 2 show, CLAN has the lowest message latency. The difference becomes appreciable as message size grows reflecting the low software overhead of CLAN. By comparison, the closest result we could find was Direct Network Access PVM [8] which reports a round-trip time double ours for equivalent message size.

4.3 Throughput

Throughput was measured in a similar fashion to Latency. 10,000 messages per packet size were sent without waiting on acknowledgement. Testing was concentrated on medium-large packet size (8-16KB).

Fig. 3 shows CLAN achieves a higher throughput for medium size packets (8-10KB). However, as packet sizes increase, available throughput drops drastically, until eventually the performance for CLAN and Gigabit Ethernet become identical.

4.4 Analysis

CLAN performance demonstrates the benefit of lightweight interfaces. Lack-lustre performance of Gigabit Ethernet may be attributed to overhead in multiple data-copy operations while traversing the TCP/IP stack and data fragmentation for Ethernet transmission. Data copy is the most significant contributor to poor performance; however larger packets have poorer performance with a small MTU. Larger MTUs outperforming smaller ones hint at significant overhead either in PVM or the network layer when fragmenting/re-assembling PVM data.

Throughput results denote that as message size increases, throughput performance decreases for both systems. Efforts to analyse this counter-intuitive result has shown that this may be attributed to overhead in the PVM daemon associated with message copying and fragmentation. From message packing to delivery by the network, multiple copy's

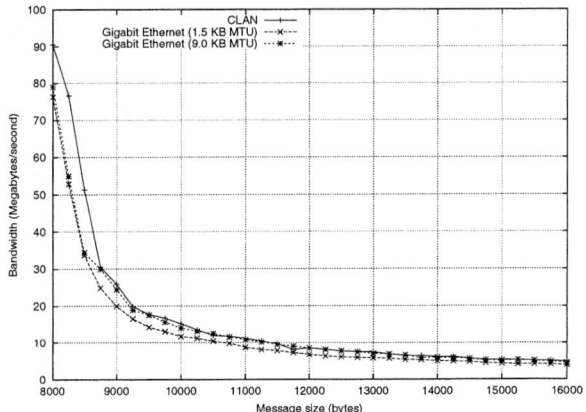

Fig. 3. Available Throughput vs. Message Size.

are made of data. Even with `PvmDataInPlace` encoding, the figures improve but the general trend is unchanged, indicating an upper bound on performance achievable before the design of PVM itself becomes an issue.

5 Future Work and Conclusion

PVM design is a bottleneck with large packets. This is being further studied to pinpoint design deficiency, along with porting of real-world applications. Finally, RDMA is being investigated as an alternative transfer mechanism for large packet sizes.

References

1. T.Von Eicken, et. Al. U-Net: A user-level network interface for parallel and distributed computing. In *Proceedings of the 15th ACM Symposium on Operating Systems Principles*, Dec. 1995, pp. 40-53
2. E. V. Carrera, et Al. User-Level Communication in Cluster-Based Servers. *Proceedings of the 8th IEEE International Symposium on High-Performance Computer Architecture (HPCA 8)*, February 2002
3. T. Warschko, et. Al. On the Design and Semantics of UserSpace Communication Subsystems. In *Proceedings of the International Conference on Parallel and Distributed Processing, Techniques and Applications (PDPTA'99)*, volume V, pages 2344-2350, Las Vegas, Nevada, USA, June 28 - July 1, 1999
4. M. Fischer and J. Simon. Embedding SCI into PVM. In *EuroPVM97*, Krakow,Poland, 1997.
5. I. Pratt and K. Fraser. Arsenic: a user-accessible Gigabit Ethernet interface. In *Proceedings of Infocom*, April 2001
6. D. Riddoch, S. Pope, et. Al. Tripwire: A Synchronisation Primitive for Virtual Memory Mapped Communication. *Journal of Interconnection Networks*, 2(3):345-364, Sep. 2001
7. AT&T Laboratories-Cambridge, England: `http://www.uk.research.att.com`
8. R. Lavi and A. Barak: Improving the PVM Daemon Network Performance by Direct Network Access. In *Proceedings of the 5th EuroPVM/MPI'98*, LNCS 1497, pp. 44-51, Springer-Verlag, 1998

Distributed Configurable Application Monitoring on SMP Clusters[*]

Karl Fürlinger and Michael Gerndt

Institut für Informatik
Lehrstuhl für Rechnertechnik und Rechnerorganisation
Technische Universität München
{fuerling,gerndt}@in.tum.de

Abstract. Performance analysis of applications on large clusters of SMPs requires a monitoring approach that supports tools realizing concepts like automation, distribution and on-line operations. Key goals are a minimization of the perturbation of the target application and flexibility and efficiency with respect to data pre-processing and filtering. To achieve these goals, our approach separates the monitor into a passive monitoring library linked to the application and an active 'runtime information producer' (RIP) which handles monitoring requests and performs pre-processing (e.g., aggregation) of performance data for individual cluster nodes. A directory service can be queried to discover which RIPs handle which nodes.

1 Introduction

Performance analysis of applications in terascale computing requires a combination of new concepts to cope with the problems arising with thousands of processors and gigabytes of performance data. The classic approach of collecting the performance data in a central file and running a post-mortem analysis tool (e.g., Vampir [15]) is hardly feasible in this context.

The new concepts include the *distribution* of the performance analysis system and *on-line processing*, together enabling the analysis of performance data close to its origin in the target application. In addition, *automation* seeks to alleviate the user from the burden of manually locating performance problems in the interaction of thousands of processors hidden behind massive amounts of data.

Monitoring in the context of these new concepts must support on-line operation, i.e., tools requests performance data at run-time which are delivered by the monitor as soon as they become available. Tools access the required data by submitting monitoring requests and receiving the desired data through a monitoring request interface (MRI).

On-line operation implies an active monitor waiting to serve monitoring requests. Since we want to avoid the possible perturbation of the target application

---

[*] Part of this work is funded by the Competence Network for High-Performance Computing in Bavaria KONWIHR (http://konwihr.in.tum.de) and by the European Commission via the APART working group (http://www.fz-juelich.de/apart).

by spawning additional processes or threads, our approach is to split the monitor in a lightweight, passive monitoring library linked to the application and an active component called runtime information producer (RIP) that executes on a processor set-aside to host the performance tool.

Our monitoring library is based on static instrumentation, but the kind of data gathered (if any) can be configured at run-time. This is important, since a performance tool might require different data in different phases of the analysis process.

Before we present our monitoring approach in detail in Section 4, we first give a short overview of existing monitoring solutions in Section 2. Then we briefly describe our design of a performance tool for applications in terascale computing in Section 3.

2 Related Work

As an overview of the available monitoring techniques we present three classes of approaches and describe one representative for each.

The *classic* approach to performance analysis relies on a monitoring library that is linked to the application writing event records to a tracefile that is analyzed after the application has terminated. A good representative here is Vampirtrace, the monitoring library that comes with Vampir [15], a powerful visualization tool that is available for many platforms. For performance reasons, the trace data is held in local memory and dumped to a file at the end of the target application or when the buffer is full. The library supports flexible filtering based on the event type through a configuration file, but this cannot be changed at runtime.

An innovative approach to minimize the monitoring overhead and to limit the amount of data that is generated is the *dynamic instrumentation* of DPCL [11] which is based on Dyninst [12]. Executable instrumentation code patches ('probes') can be inserted to and removed from a target application at runtime by calling functions of the API of the DPCL C++ class library. DPCL translates these calls to requests that are sent to DPCL daemons that attach themselves to the target application processes and install or remove the probes. The probes within the target application send data to the DPCL daemon which forwards the data to the analysis tool, triggering the appropriate callback routine.

In the context of *Grid* computing the existing monitoring approaches have been found to be unsuitable and several projects for grid monitoring were initiated. As an example, OCM-G [1], the grid-enabled OMIS compliant monitor, is an autonomous and distributed grid application monitoring system currently being developed in the CrossGrid [9] project. The OCM-G features transient as well as permanent components. The transient component is called the local monitor and is embedded in the address space of the application. The persistent component consists of one service manager per grid site. OCM-G supports selective (activated or deactivated) monitoring to minimize overhead and perturbation and to limit the amount of monitored data to the really relevant parts. It also supports higher-level performance properties and application defined metrics and it allows the manipulation of the executable (e.g., stopping a thread) besides pure monitoring.

3 The Peridot Project

Each of the monitoring solutions presented in Section 2 was considered unsuitable for the Peridot project, where we plan to implement a distributed automated on-line performance analysis system, primarily for the Hitachi SR8000 system installed at the Leibnitz-Rechenzentrum in Munich and similar clustered SMP architectures. Here we provide an overview of the target architecture and then briefly introduce the design of our performance analysis system.

3.1 The Hitachi SR8000

The Hitachi SR8000 features a clustered SMP design, each node consists of eight application processors plus one system processor sharing a common memory through a crossbar switch. A storage controller supports efficient access to memory on remote nodes (remote direct memory access, RDMA) and takes care of cache coherency. Using RDMA it is possible for a processor to read and write memory on a remote node without intervention of the remote node's processors.

The SR8000 can be used for pure message passing (inter- and intra-node) as well as for hybrid shared memory/message passing programming. OpenMP and COMPAS (COoperative MicroProcessors in single Address Space) are supported for shared memory programming within a single node. The machines' processors have support for eight fixed performance counters: instruction and data TLB miss count, instruction and data cache miss count, number of memory access and floating point instructions, total number of executed instructions and number of cycles.

3.2 Automated Distributed On-Line Analysis

This section outlines the general architecture of the analysis system currently under development within the Peridot project, for details please consult [4].

Our distributed performance analysis system is composed of a set of analysis agents that cooperate in the detection of performance properties and problems. The agents are logically arranged into a hierarchy and each agent is responsible for the detection of performance problems related to its level in the hierarchy. Specifically, the leaf agents (the lowest level of the hierarchy) are responsible for the collection and analysis of performance data from one or more nodes, which they request form monitors.

The detection of performance problems is based on an automatic evaluation of performance *properties* specified in the APART specification language [7, 8]. Higher level agents combine properties detected by lower level agents and they assign subtasks for the evaluation for a global property to the appropriate lower level agents.

The interaction among the agents and between leaf agent and monitor can be regarded as a producer–consumer relation. On the lowest level, the monitors generate the performance data and leaf agents request and receive this data. On higher levels, agents act as consumers as well as producers of refined (higher-grade) performance data in the form of (partially evaluated) performance properties. The monitors and the agents register their producer and consumer parts in a central directory service together with the type of performance data they are able to produce or consume.

4 Distributed Monitoring

As mentioned in Section 3.2 in our approach, the monitor acts as a producer of performance data. This implies an *active* implementation where the monitor is waiting to serve requests from agents. Since we want to avoid the overhead and perturbation of the target application resulting form a monitoring library spawning its own thread or process, we split the monitor in two components connected by a ring (circular) buffer.

The first (passive) component is the *monitoring library* linked to the application and the second (active) component is the *runtime information producer (RIP)*. This separation keeps the monitoring overhead and the perturbation of the target application small while flexibility with respect to filtering and pre-processing of performance data can be retained.

4.1 Monitoring Library

The monitoring library is completely passive, i.e., it executes only through calls of the instrumented application.

Instrumentation. We use static instrumentation for OpenMP and MPI related application events. OpenMP regions are instrumented by OPARI [2] (a source-to-source instrumenter), while MPI calls are captured using the usual MPI wrapper technique.

For each *event* (i.e., call to one of the procedures of the monitoring library) an event packet is assembled and stored in a ring buffer. The event packet consists of a header that specifies the size of the packet, the type of the event and a sequence number. The body of the packet contains a wall-clock time stamp and the current values of selected performance counters. Additionally, event-type specific data is stored in the body. For OpenMP regions this includes the name of the OpenMP construct affected and its location in the source code (file name and line numbers denoting beginning and end of the construct).

On the Hitachi, the eight fixed performance counters are accessible through a library provided by the Leibnitz-Rechenzentrum. On other architectures we use PAPI [6] to configure (see Section 4.3) and read the hardware counters.

Ring Buffer. The ring buffer connects the two components of our monitoring approach. Data written by the monitoring library is read by runtime information producers (RIPs). A separate ring buffer is allocated by the monitoring library

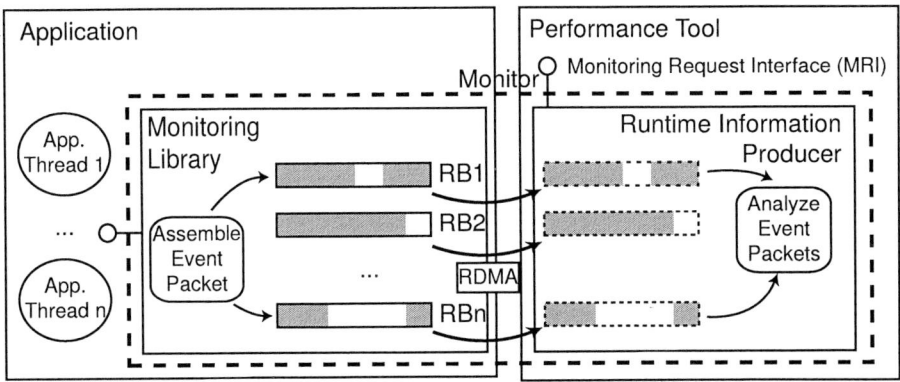

Fig. 1. The monitoring library writes event packets to ring buffers (one per application thread). In the RDMA setting on the Hitachi SR8000, the runtime information producer works on a copy transferred into its own address space.

for each OpenMP thread, avoiding the overhead associated with locking a single buffer per process for several threads.

In order to process the event packets, a RIP must acquire access to ring buffers embedded in the monitoring library. This can be organized in two ways. The first approach is to assign one RIP per application node which is responsible for all ring buffers of that node. A RIP can then simply map these buffers into its own virtual address spaces, provided they are allocated in shared memory segments (for example using System V shmget() and shmat()). Although this approach is feasible for any SMP machine, it can lead to artificial load imbalance since one processor per node must execute the RIP in addition to its application load.

To circumvent this problem, it would be convenient to take advantage of the system processor on the Hitachi. However, this special processor is used internally by the operating system and special (root) privileges are required to execute programs there. Currently we are working together with the Leibnitz-Rechenzentrum to investigate the requirements concerning the utilization of the system processor for our analysis system, in order not to disturb normal operation of the operating system.

The second approach is to use the remote direct memory access (RDMA) facility of the Hitachi, allowing the RIP to execute on any processor of the machine. The RIP transfers a *copy* of the ring buffers of a node into its own address space and works on this copy when analyzing events (Fig. 1). As this does not require intervention of the processors of the remote node (holding the ring buffer and executing the target application), this approach is very efficient and does not lead to artificial load imbalance. However, it requires one or more nodes being set aside for the performance analysis system.

In both approaches, the buffers must be locked by the monitoring library as well as the RIPs for write or read access, fortunately the Hitachi supports efficient locks across nodes. Note that the original ring buffer is never emptied in RDMA case, since the RIP always works on a copy of the original buffer.

4.2 Runtime Information Producer

The runtime information producer (RIP) forms the active part of our monitoring approach. Its task is to provide the consumers (the analysis agents of our system) with the required performance data. The functionality and the data are accessed through a monitoring request interface (MRI) implemented by the RIP. A request submitted to the RIP specifies what to measure, where to measure and possible aggregation. Current efforts in the APART working group to standardize the MRI will enable other tools to use the functionality of our monitors as well.

Node-Level Monitoring. A runtime information producer (RIP) is responsible for reading and processing event packets from ring buffers of its assigned application nodes. On startup, it queries the directory service that is part of our performance analysis system for the information required to access the memory holding the buffer. In the shared memory case, this is the key and the size of the shared memory segment, in the RDMA case, the coordinates of the affected node are required additionally. Subsequently, in regular intervals (one second, say) the RIP acquires access to the buffers and processes them.

High-Level Monitoring. Analyzing certain application behavior, notably for MPI applications, requires the collection of data from several nodes. For example, to analyze message transit time we need to monitor matching `MPI_Sends` and `MPI_Recvs`. Hence, we need to integrate data from several nodes, generally not covered by the same RIP.

In our approach we deliberately do not provide this cross-node data at the monitoring level. Instead we focus on efficient monitoring of single nodes at minimal cost and RIPs can be queried not only for metrics or other aggregated data, but also for single events. Hence, a tool which requires cross-node event data registers with the RIPs responsible for the respective nodes and is then able to access the desired information. We feel that this 'flat' monitoring it is advantageous to a hierarchical approach (e.g., OCM-G) since the latter requires considerable complexity in the monitor to distribute the performance requests and to integrate the results.

4.3 Configuration of the Monitor

For performance reasons it is desirable to limit the data that is passed from the monitoring library to the RIP to those actually needed by the RIP to satisfy monitoring requests. Additionally, on some Architectures (Power4, for example) a large number of countable hardware events are accessed through a smaller number of counters that need to be programmed according to current needs.

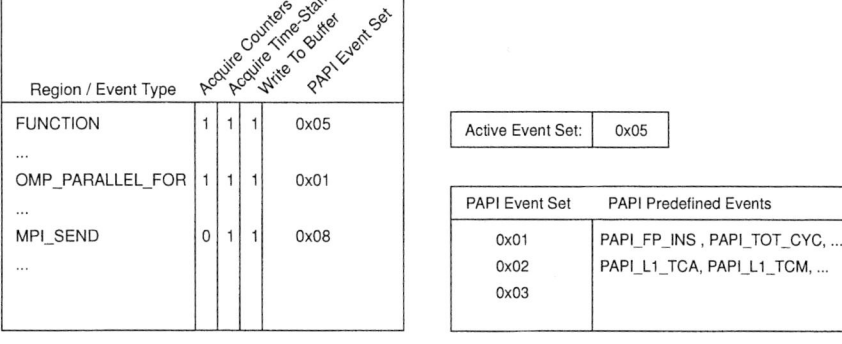

Fig. 2. The configuration tables for event/region type specific monitoring.

Figure 2 shows our approach to configuring the monitoring library on a per event/region *type* basis. The library allocates space for the configuration table similarly to the event ring buffer. The table holds the configuration data for the individual event or region types (left part of Fig. 2). This includes flags indicating (a) whether to acquire the current values of the performance counters (b) acquire a time-stamp (c) write an event packet to the ring buffer. Additionally, this table indicates the PAPI event set to use when requesting performance counters. This is an index into a second table (right part of Fig. 2) that lists the PAPI events in the events set.

In PAPI it is possible to have multiple active event sets. However, this complicates the monitoring library since it would be necessary to keep information on which event sets can be active simultaneously. Hence we restrict the library to one active event set at a time.

When the instrumented application makes a call of one of the libraries' functions we can retrieve the configuration for the affected region/event type easily since it is located at a fixed, known location. Then the currently active event set is checked against the configured event set and if necessary the current set is PAPI_stop()ed and the new one is PAPI_start()ed.

It is the RIP's responsibility to make entries in the configuration tables such that the monitoring library generates the information the RIP needs to satisfy its monitoring requests. The monitoring library only reads the tables entries, it does not modify them.

Note that our current approach limits configurability to event/region types (i.e., all functions) instead of individual regions (i.e., function foo()). This is necessary because we want to keep the monitoring function calls as lightweight as possible and a time-consuming search in dynamic data structures has to be avoided. To circumvent this problem it would be necessary to have a list of all instrumented regions in target application at program start. Then, similar to the event/region type based table described above, a fixed size table can be allocated for all regions in the program and the configuration information can be looked up at a known fixed location. Work is currently in progress in the

APART working group to define a standard for this static program information down to individual data structures.

5 Conclusion

We have presented our approach for monitoring clustered SMP architectures with the goal of minimizing overhead while enabling flexible on-line analysis. This is achieved by separating the required active component from the monitoring library into a distinct component, called runtime information producer (RIP). A ring buffer allocated in a shared memory segment couples the monitoring library and the RIP. To efficiently access the ring buffer we can take advantage of service processor and the RDMA facility of the Hitachi SR8000, our primary target machine.

The third component of our monitoring approach is the directory service used by the RIP to retrieve the required information to access he ring buffers. Additionally, RIPs publish the type of performance data they provide in the directory service. Consumers, such as the agents of our distributed analysis system can then locate and query the RIPs to access the desired performance data.

References

1. Bartosz Balis, Marian Bubak, Wlodzimierz Funika, Tomasz Szepieniec, and Roland Wismller. Monitoring of Interactive Grid Applications. To appear in Proceedings of Dagstuhl Seminar 02341 on Performance Analysis and Distributed Computing. Kluiver Academi Publishers. 2003.
2. Bernd Mohr, Allen D. Malony, Sameer Shende, and Felix Wolf. Towards a Performance Tool Interface for OpenMP: An Approach Based on Directive Rewriting. In EWOMP'01 Third European Workshop on OpenMP, Sept. 2001.
3. The Top 500 Supercomputer Sites. http://www.top500.org
4. Michael Gerndt and Karl Frlinger. Towards Automatic Performance Analysis for Large Scale Systems. At the 10th International Workshop on Compilers for Parallel Computers (CPC 2003). Amsterdam, The Netherlands. January 2003.
5. The Hitachi Performance Monitor Function (Hitachi Confidential).
6. S. Browne and J. Dongarra and N. Garner and K. London and P. Mucci. A Scalable Cross-Platform Infrastructure for Application Performance Tuning Using Hardware Counters. Proc. SC'2000, November 2000.
7. T. Fahringer, M. Gerndt, G. Riley, and J.L. Trff. Formalizing OpenMP Performance Properties with the APART Specification Language (ASL), International Workshop on OpenMP: Experiences and Implementation, Lecture Notes in Computer Science, Springer Verlag, Tokyo, Japan, pp. 428–439, October 2000.
8. T. Fahringer, M. Gerndt, G. Riley, and J.L. Trff. Knowledge Specification for Automatic Performance Analysis. APART Technical Report. http://www.fz-juelich.de/apart. 2001.
9. CrossGrid Project: http://www.eu-crossgrid.org
10. T. Ludwig, R. Wismller, V. Sunderam, and A. Bode. OMIS – On-line Monitoring Interface Specification (Version 2.0). Shaker Verlag, Aachen Vol 9, LRR-TUM Research Report Series, (1997). http://wwwbode.in.tum.de/ omis/OMIS/Version-2.0/version-2.0.ps.gz

11. Dynamic Probe Class Library. http://oss.software.ibm.com/dpcl/
12. Dyninst. An Application Program Interface (API) for Runtime Code Generation. http://www.dyninst.org
13. Ch. Thiffault, M. Voss, S. T. Healey and S. W. Kim. Dynamic Instrumentation of Large-Scale MPI/OpenMP Applications. To appear in Proc. of IPDPS'2003: International Parallel and Distrubuted Processing Symposium, Nice, France, April 2003.
14. B. Tierney, R. Aydt, D. Gunter, W. Smith, M. Swany, V. Taylor, and R. Wolski. A Grid Monitoring Architecture. http://www-didc.lbl.gov/GGF-PERF/GMA-WG/papers/GWD-GP-16-2.pdf
15. W. E. Nagel, A. Arnold, M. Weber, H. C. Hoppe, and K. Solchenbach. VAMPIR: Visualization and analysis of MPI resources. Supercomputer, 12(1):69–80, January 1996. http://www.pallas.com/e/products/vampir/index.htm

Integrating Multiple Implementations and Structure Exploitation in the Component-Based Design of Parallel ODE Solvers

J.M. Mantas[1], J. Ortega Lopera[2], and J.A. Carrillo[3]

[1] Software Engineering Department, University of Granada
C/ P. Daniel de Saucedo s/n. 18071 Granada, Spain
jmmantas@ugr.es
[2] Computer Architecture and Technology Department
University of Granada
C/ P. Daniel de Saucedo s/n. 18071 Granada, Spain
jortega@atc.ugr.es
[3] Departament de Matematiques - ICREA
Universitat Autonoma de Barcelona Bellaterra E-08193
carrillo@mat.uab.es

Abstract. A COmponent-based Methodology to derive Parallel programs to solve Ordinary Differential Equation (ODE) Solvers, termed COMPODES, is presented. The approach is useful to obtain distributed implementations of numerical algorithms which can be specified by combining linear algebra operations. The main contribution of the approach is the possibility of managing several implementations of the operations and exploiting the problem structure in an elegant and systematic way. As a result, software reusability is enhanced and a clear structuring of the derivation process is achieved. The approach includes a technique to take the lowest level decisions systematically and is illustrated by deriving several implementations of a numerical scheme to solve stiff ODEs.

1 Introduction

One important formulation for the ODEs arising from the modelling process is that of the *Initial Value Problem* (IVP) for ODE [3]. The goal in the IVP is to find a function $y : \mathbb{R} \to \mathbb{R}^d$ at an interval $[t_0, t_f]$ given its value at t_0, $y(t_0) = y_0$, and a system function $f : \mathbb{R} \times \mathbb{R}^d \to \mathbb{R}^d$ fulfilling that $y'(t) = f(t,y)$.

The computational demands of the numerical methods to solve IVPs, and the complexity of the IVPs which arise in practical applications, suggests the use of efficient algorithms for Distributed-Memory Parallel Machines (DMPMs).

In order to achieve an acceptable performance on a DMPM, the parallel design of this kind of numerical software must take into account 1) the task and data parallelism exhibited by the method (usually, several subcomputations in a time step can be executed simultaneously and each one is composed of linear algebra operations) 2) the characteristics of the particular DMPM and 3) the particular structure of the IVP whose exploitation is fundamental.

Currently, the development of parallel software for these applications benefits from two contributions:
- The development of reusable software components of parallel linear algebra libraries [2] for DMPMs, which encapsulate the details about the efficient SPMD implementation of many standard solution methods.
- The hierarchical execution systems to exploit the mixed parallelism [7, 8] facilitate the generation of group SPMD programs in which several SPMD subprograms are executed by disjoint processor groups in parallel. This execution model is specially suitable to exploit the potential task and data parallelism of these applications and the MPI standard makes it possible its implementation on DMPMs. The *TwoL* framework [8] for the derivation of parallel programs and the PARADIGM compiler system [7] are relevant contributions in this area. However, these approaches may benefit from explicit constructs to: a) maintain and select among multiple implementations of an operation in an elegant and systematic way (called *performance polymorphism* in [5, 4]), and b) exploit the particular structure of the IVPs.

We propose a methodological approach based on linear algebra components for deriving group SPMD programs to solve ODEs. This approach, termed COMPODES, includes explicit constructs for performance polymorphism, takes into account the exploitation of the problem structure and enables the structuring of the derivation process by including three clearly defined phases in which optimizations of different types can be carried out. The proposal is illustrated by deriving parallel implementations, adapted to two different IVPs, of an advanced numerical scheme [9, 4] to solve stiff ODEs.

A brief introduction to COMPODES is presented in section 2. The three following sections illustrate the COMPODES phases and introduce a technique to complete the last phase. Some conclusions are drawn in section 6.

2 COMPODES Overview

In COMPODES, the description of the functional behaviour of a linear algebra operation is decoupled from the multiple implementations which provide the same functionality. This is achieved by encapsulating each entity as separate software components [5, 4]: *concepts* (formal definitions of operations) and *realizations* (particular implementations). Each concept can have several associated realizations. This explicit distinction allows us to select the implementation that offers the best performance in a particular context (target machine, IVP, etc.).

A concept (`MJacobian`) that denotes the computation of an approximation to the Jacobian of a function f at a point $(t, y) \in \mathbb{R}^{d+1}$ is presented in Figure 1. Two different realizations for `MJacobian` are shown: $Seq\_MJacobian$ encapsulates a sequential implementation of the operation and the parallel realization $Block\_MJacobian$ obtains a block column distribution of the Jacobian matrix.

A realization has a client-visible part, called the *header*, which describes the aspects that must be known to use the code (called the *body*) including: a) the distribution of the array arguments among the processors [4], b) a formula which

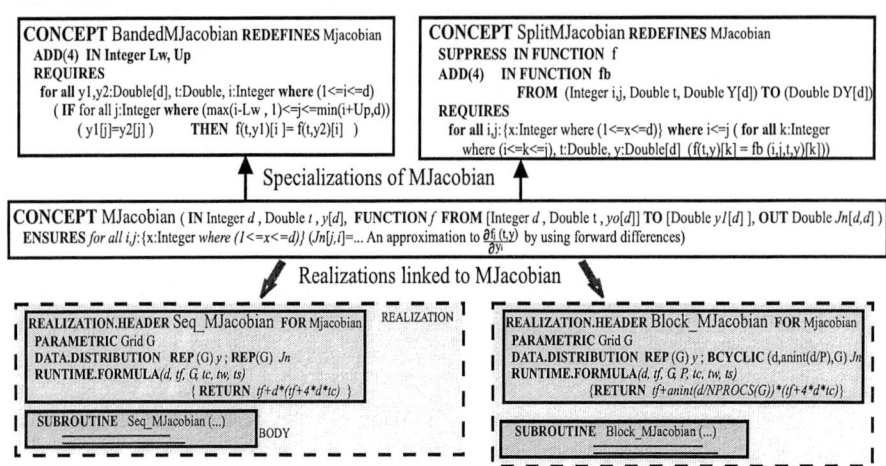

Fig. 1. The MJacobian concept with several realizations and specializations.

estimates its runtime from parameters describing the data distributions, the target machine (number of processors P, per word communication cost t_w, startup time t_s, etc.), and problem size, and c) the storage scheme of the arguments.

We have defined a specialization mechanism to adapt a concept to deal with the particular structure of its arguments. When a concept has not been obtained by the specialization of a previously existing one, we say that it is a *general concept*. A specialized concept might admit more efficient implementations than a general one because the implementation can take advantage of the special structure of its arguments. We can consider two types of specialization:

• Specializations based on the array structure [5]. For instance, we can specialize a concept which denotes the usual matrix-vector product operation (MVproduct) to deal with banded matrices (BandedMVproduct).

• Specializations based on the function structure. In Figure 1, several specializations of the MJacobian concept based on the function structure are shown. BandedMJacobian specializes MJacobian to deal with a banded system function with bandwith $Lw + Up + 1$. A system function f is banded when a component of the output vector $f(t, y)$ only depends on a consecutive band of the input vector y. This kind of function enables the minimization of the remote communication when the function is evaluated on several processors. The Jacobian matrix generated with Banded_MJacobian must also be banded. The concept SplitMJacobian indicates that the argument f is cost-separable. A system function is *cost-separable* when it is possible to define a *partitioning function fb* which allows the evaluation of f homogeneously by pieces without introducing redundant computation. This property is important to enable the easy exploitation of the data parallelism in the block parallel evaluation of f.

The derivation process in COMPODES starts from a mathematical description of the numerical method to solve ODEs and proceeds through several phases. During the first phase, called **functional composition**, several general concepts

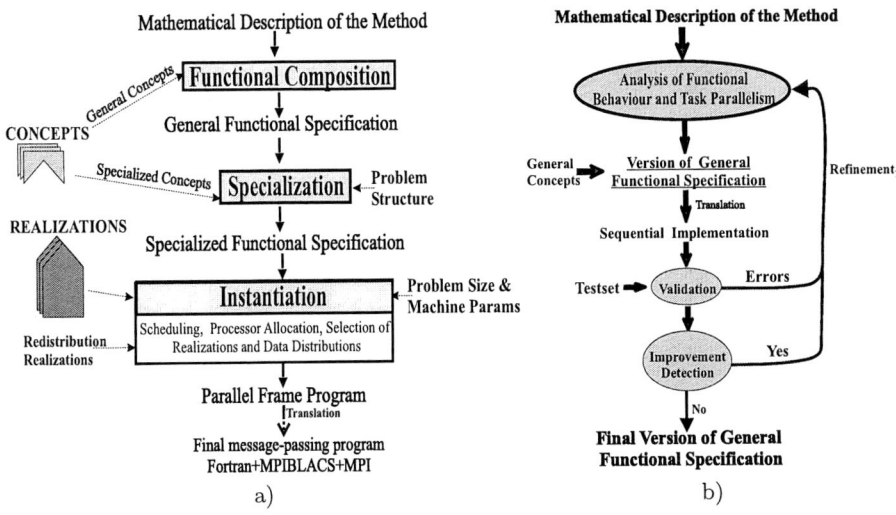

Fig. 2. a) Overview of COMPODES, b) Funtional Composition.

are selected and combined by using constructors of sequential and concurrent composition to describe the functionality of the method and the maximum degree of task parallelism. As a result, a version of *general functional specification* is obtained (see Figure 2b). From this representation, one can obtain a sequential program automatically (by using the sequential realizations linked to the general concepts which appear in the specification), which makes it possible to validate the numerical properties of the method. If the validation detects neither anomalies nor improvement possibilities, we obtain a definitive version of the general specification which can be used in the solution in different contexts of different IVPs on different architectures.

During the **specialization** phase, the general specification is modified according to the structural characteristics of the particular IVP to be solved. These modifications consist fundamentally of replacing general concepts by specializations. The user must provide a sequential routine to evaluate the system function and a sequential prototype can also be generated to validate the specification. As a result, a *specialized specification* is obtained which allows the exploitation of the special structure of the problem because realizations adapted to the structure of the arrays and functions can be selected in the next phase.

Finally, the **instantiation** phase [4] takes into account both the parameters of the IVP and of the target machine in order to: 1) schedule the tasks and allocate processors to each task, 2) select the best realization for each concept reference of the specification and the most suitable data distribution parameters for each realization chosen and 3) insert the required data redistribution routines. The goal is to obtain a good global runtime solution. This last phase can be performed systematically to obtain a description called *parallel frame program* which can be translated into a Fortran program augmented with MPI routines.

442   J.M. Mantas, J. Ortega Lopera, and J.A. Carrillo

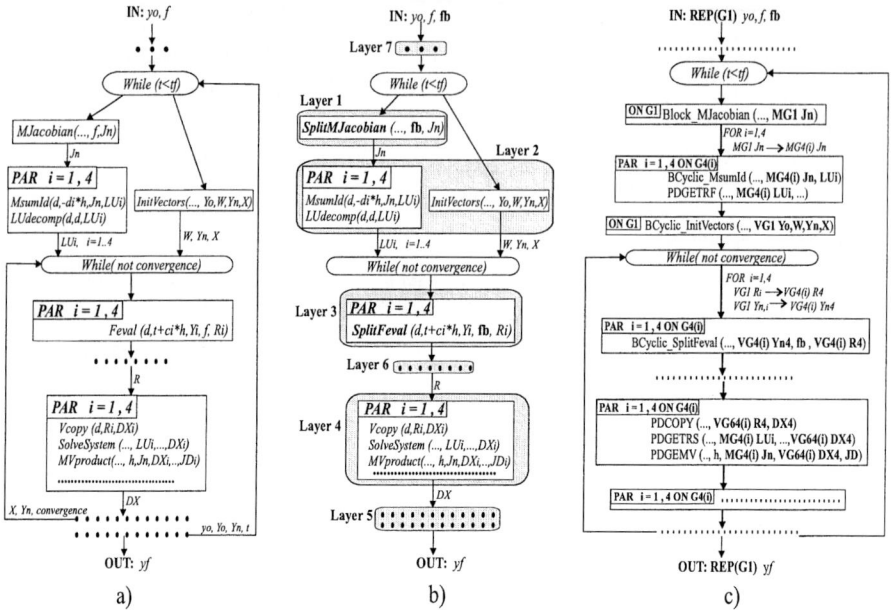

Fig. 3. a) General specification of the ONPILSRK method, b) Layered specialized specification ONPILSRK-VORTEX, c) Parallel frame program.

3 Functional Composition

To illustrate this phase, we employ an advanced numerical method to solve stiff ODEs [9], which is a parallelization across the Radau IIA method with 4 stages [3]. The analysis of this numerical scheme [4], makes it possible to derive an improvement of this scheme (called ONPILSRK) which presents a lower computational cost and exhibits greater task parallelism. We have selected several general concepts to specify this method. For instance, LUdecomp(.., A, ..) denotes the LU Factorization of A, SolveSystem(.., A, ..., X) denotes the computation of $X \longleftarrow A^{-1}X$ (assuming LUdecomp(.., A, ..)) and the Feval(.., t, f, y, dy) concept denotes the evaluation of the function f. These operations are the main sources of data parallelism exhibited by the method. To combine these concepts, we can use a graphical notation which expresses the concurrent and sequential composition as a task directed graph. A summarized description of the definitive general specification of the scheme is presented in Figure 3a, where the edges denote data dependencies between operations and in which the main sources of task parallelism in the method are represented with concurrent loops ($PAR\ i = 1, 4$).

4 Specialization

To illustrate this phase, we adapt the ONPILSRK method to two stiff IVPs:
• An IVP, noted as VORTEX, which models the evolution of two singular vortex patches governed by a two-dimensional incompressible fluid flow [1]. Assuming

each vortex patch boundary has been parameterized by using $N/2$ points, we obtain a system with 2N ODEs where the evaluation of the equations of a point depends on all the other points (it involves a dense Jacobian) and the system function is cost-separable. The specialization of the functional specification for this problem consists of incorporating the cost-separable property of the system function f. This includes 1) defining a partitioning function **fb** as a sequential routine, and 2) substituting the general Feval and MJacobian concepts by specialized concepts which manage cost-separable functions as shown in Figure 3b. This enables the exploitation of the data parallelism existing in the evaluation of f by selecting specialized parallel implementations in the instantiation phase.

• An ODE system, noted as BRELAX, which describes a 1D rarefied gas shock [6]. The resulting system has 5N ODEs when the 1D space is discretized by using N grid points. The system function is also cost-separable and has a narrow banded structure with lower bandwith $Lw = 9$ and upper bandwidth $Up = 7$. To obtain the specialized specification for this IVP, several general concepts, which deal with matrices maintaining the banded structure of the Jacobian (for instance, LUdecomp) must be replaced by specializations which assume a banded structure for these matrices. The concepts MJacobian and Feval must be replaced by specializations which assume a cost-separable banded system function.

5 An Approximation Method to Perform the Instantiation

We propose an approximation method to perform the last phase, which assumes that these algorithms exhibit a task parallelism with a layered structure [8]. The method selects the most suitable realizations and data distributions in an ordered way, by giving priority to the most costly layers in the layered specification.

Following this method, we have obtained parallel implementations of the ONPILSRK scheme adapted to the VORTEX and BRELAX IVPs for the $P = 4$ and $P = 8$ nodes of a PC cluster with a switched fast Ethernet network. To illustrate the method, the instantiation of the ONPILSRK-VORTEX specification for $P = 8$ will be considered. Figure 3c presents a graphical description of the parallel frame program obtained. The nodes can represent a realization call or parallel loops applied on a sequence of calls. Every call is assigned to a processor group and some edges are labelled with redistribution operations [4].

The method uses the task layer definition which is introduced in [8] to identify layers in the graph. The layers are ordered taking into account the estimated execution time of the sequential realizations linked to the nodes of each layer, and then the layers are instantiated in an ordered way starting with the most costly ones. Figure 3b shows how the layers have been ordered in our example.

The instantiation of a layer depends on its internal structure and is based on the constrained instantiation of a concept reference. Given a layered functional graph, where several nodes may have been instantiated, and a reference to a concept C which belongs to a layer, the *constrained instantiation* of C on P_m processors, consists of selecting (R, P_R, D), where R represents a realization linked to C, $P_R \leq P_m$ denotes a number of processors and D is a set of parameters describing the distribution of the array arguments of R on P_R processors. This selection is performed such that the estimated execution time for the operation C is minimized taking into account the cost associated with the redistribution operations needed to adapt the data distributions of R (given by D) with the distributions followed in previously instantiated nodes. The constrained instantiation also involves inserting redistribution operations to adapt the data distributions.

When a layer encapsulates a chain of concept references, it is a **linear layer**. To instantiate a linear layer, its nodes are sorted according to the estimated sequential time and the constrained instantiation of each reference concept on the total number of processors is carried out starting with the most costly nodes in the chain. In our example, the instantiation starts with the linear layer 1 (see Figure 3b) (the most costly one) which only contains one operation. Since there is no fixed data distribution which affects this layer, the optimal realization for the group with the 8 processors ($G1$) is chosen. This realization generates a block column distribution of the Jn matrix (distribution type MG1).

When a layer includes several concurrent chains, it is a **concurrent layer**. To instantiate a concurrent layer, all the possibilities of scheduling the chains are evaluated. To evaluate a scheduling choice where there are concurrent chains, the total number of processors is divided among the resultant concurrent chains, in proportion to the estimated sequential time of each chain. Next, every chain is instantiated as in a linear layer but on the previously assigned number of processors. The result of instantiating each chain is evaluated by combining the runtime formulas of the realizations selected and the redistribution costs. Finally, the choice which minimizes the estimated runtime for the layer is chosen.

In our example, layer 2 is a concurrent layer with 5 chains. The scheduling choice which gives the lowest cost consists of assigning each chain of the concurrent loop to disjointed groups with 2 processors ($G4(i)$, $i = 1, ..., 4$) and then executing the other one on the $G1$ group. This involves the use of a ScaLAPACK realization (LU factorization) [2], which assumes a 64×64 block-cyclic distribution of the matrix ($MG4(i)$, $i = 1, ..., 4$). Therefore the selection of this choice must take into consideration the redistribution of the matrix Jn. To instantiate layer 3, a realization to perform a parallel block evaluation of the function system which uses the partitioning function is chosen. The remaining layers are instantiated in an ordered way but taking into account the fixed distributions.

We have compared the runtime of the parallel programs obtained with two sequential solvers: $RADAU5$ [3], an efficient stiff ODE solver, and the sequential implementation of the ONPILSRK scheme, called here SNPILSRK (see Figure 4). The implementations for the VORTEX IVP achieve a speedup of 3 to 3.7 on 4 processors and a speedup of 6.5 to 7.5 on 8 processors with regard to SNPILSRK. The implementations for BRELAX achieve a speedup of 3.65 to 4 on 4 processors and a speedup of 7.15 to 7.85 on 8 processors with regard to SNPILSRK. The results obtained with regard to RADAU5 are slightly better.

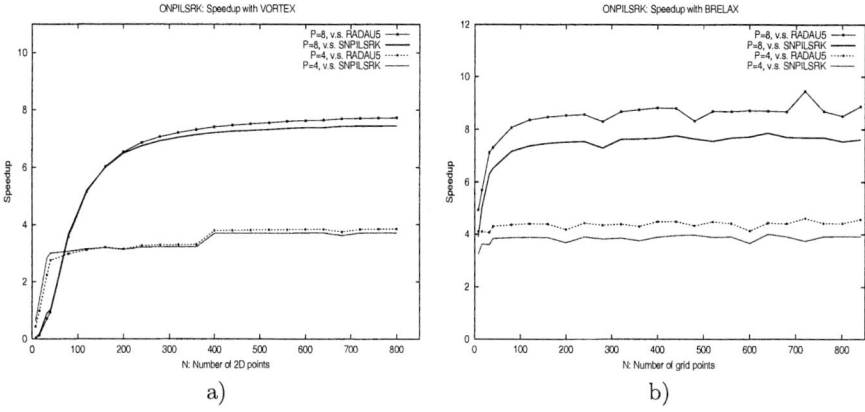

Fig. 4. Speedup Results for a) VORTEX IVP and b) BRELAX IVP.

6 Conclusions

The COMPODES approach to deriving parallel ODE solvers is proposed. The approach makes it possible to manage several implementations of the operations and enables the separate treatment of different aspects during the derivation:

a) *Functional aspects*: A generic description of the functionality and the task parallelism of the method is obtained in the initial phase by focusing on optimizations independent of the machine and the problem.

b) *Problem structure*: In the *specialization* phase, all the structural characteristics of the problem are integrated into the method description in order to enable its exploitation in the next phase.

c) *Performance aspects dependent on both the architecture and the problem*: A simple approximation method has been proposed to take systematically all the parallel design decisions which affect the performance of the final program by considering both the parameters of the problem and the machine.

The approach is illustrated by deriving several efficient implementations of a stiff ODE solver for a PC cluster. Following this approach, satisfactory results have been obtained in the solution of two different problems.

Acknowledgements

This work was supported by the projects TIC2000-1348 and BFM2002-01710 of the Ministerio de Ciencia y Tecnología.

References

1. Carrillo, J. A., and Soler, J.: On the Evolution of an angle in a Vortex Patch. The Journal of Nonlinear Science, 10:23–47, 2000.
2. Dongarra, J., Walker D.: Software libraries for linear Algebra Computations on High Performance Computers. SIAM Review, 37(2):151–180, Jun. 1995.

3. Hairer, E., Wanner., G.: Solving Ordinary Differential Equations II: Stiff and Differential Algebraic Problems. Springer-Verlag, 1996.
4. Mantas, J. M., Ortega, J., Carrillo J. A.: Component-Based Derivation of a Stiff ODE Solver implemented on a PC Cluster. International Journal of Parallel Programming, 30(2), Apr. (2002).
5. Mantas, J. M., Ortega, J., Carrillo J. A.: Exploiting the Multilevel Parallelism and the Problem Structure in the Numerical Solution of Stiff ODEs. 10th Euromicro Workshop on Parallel, Distributed and Network-based Processing, (2002).
6. Mantas, J. M., Ortega, J., Pareschi, L., Carrillo J. A.: Parallel Integration of Hydrodynamical Approximations of the Boltzmann Equation for rarefied gases on a Cluster of Computers. Journal of Computational Methods in Science and Engineering, JCMSE, 3(3):337–346, 2003.
7. Ramaswamy, S., Sapatnekar, S., Banerjee, P.: A Framework for Exploiting Data and Functional Parallelism on Distributed Memory Multicomputers. IEEE Trans. Parallel and Distributed Systems, 8:1098–1116, Nov. 1997.
8. Rauber, T., Rünger, G.: Compiler support for task scheduling in hierarchical execution models. Journal of Systems Architecture, 45:483–503, 1998.
9. Van der Houwen, P. J., de Swart, J. J. B.: Parallel linear system solvers for Runge-Kutta methods. Advances in Computational Mathematics, 7:157–181, Jan. 1997.

Architecture of Monitoring System for Distributed Java Applications

Marian Bubak[1,2], Włodzimierz Funika[1], Marcin Smętek[1], Zbigniew Kiliański[1], and Roland Wismüller[3]

[1] Institute of Computer Science
AGH, al. Mickiewicza 30, 30-059 Kraków, Poland
[2] Academic Computer Centre – CYFRONET
Nawojki 11, 30-950 Kraków, Poland
[3] LRR-TUM – Technische Universität München
D-80290 München, Germany
{bubak,funika}@uci.agh.edu.pl
{smentos,zkilian}@icslab.agh.edu.pl
wismuell@in.tum.de
phone: (+48 12) 6173964, fax: (+48 12) 6338054
phone: (+49 89) 289 28243

Abstract. Recently, the demand in tool support (performance analyzers, debuggers etc.) for efficient Java programming increases considerably. A universal, open interface between tools and a monitoring system, On-line Monitoring Interface Specification (OMIS), and the OMIS compliant monitoring system (OCM) enable to specify such a Java oriented monitoring infrastructure which allows for an extensible range of functionality intended for supporting various kinds of tools. The paper presents an approach to building a monitoring system which underlies this infrastructure.

Keywords: Java, monitoring system, monitoring interface, distributed object system, tools, OMIS

1 Introduction

Java technology has grown in popularity and usage because of its portability. This simple, object oriented, secure language supports multithreading and distributed programming including remote method invocation, garbage collection and dynamic class file loading. There are many performance problems for Java programmers. *The Garbage Collection mechanism* may influence the performance of application due to a possibly large heap and the asynchronous mode of operation. *The Object Oriented* nature of Java programming causes the use of a very large number of classes and therefore a lot of jumps in control flow between pieces of software, which may need to be optimized. *The Dynamic Class Loading* can have a significant impact on the amount of memory used, moreover the JVM sometimes loads classes before they are needed. *Memory leaks* occur when an instance of a longer life cycle has a reference to an instance of a shorter life cycler, which prevents the instance with a shorter life cycle from being garbage collected. Remote Method Invocation (RMI) combines the problems of pure Java with those stemming from the distributed Java programming: *downloading of stubs* needed by a client may cause downloading of indispensable classes through a web server, thus generating large network traffic; the use of *Distributed Garbage Collection* protocol and *Object Serialization* introduce a substantial overhead on the performance of RMI calls.

Our goal is to build a comprehensive tool support for building distributed Java applications by providing uniformed, extendible monitoring facilities for communication between components, for analyzing application's execution to understand system behaviour, and for detecting bugs. The paper is organised as follows. A short overview of related work in Section 2, followed by a general consideration of Java tools functionality and implications for monitoring (Section 3). Then follows an overview of OMIS and OMIS-compliant Monitoring System, OCM. Section 4 gives a characteristics of Java-oriented extension to OMIS. Next, an overview of the Java-oriented monitoring system architecture is presented (Section 5). Conclusions and future work are summarised in Section 6.

2 Overview of Java Support Tools

To assist the user in dealing with problems mentioned in Section 1, many tools have been developed. Most of them are based on Java Virtual Machine profiling interface (JVMPI) [16]. From JDK 1.2 SDK it also includes an example profiler agent for examining efficiency called hprof [8] which can be used to build professional profilers. Heap Analysis Tool (Hat) [9] enables to read and analyze profile reports of the heap generated by hprof tool and may be used e.g. for debugging "memory leaks". JTracer [10] is a debugger which provides traditional features, e.g. a variable watcher, breakpoints and line by line execution. J-Sprint [11] provides information about what parts of a program consume most of execution time and memory. JProfiler [12], targeted at J2EE and J2SE applications, provides information on CPU and memory usage, thread profiling, and VM. It's visualization tool shows the object references chain, execution control flow, threads hierarchy and general information about JVM using special displays. There is also a group of powerful commercial tools, with friendly graphical interfaces: OptimizeIt [13], Jtest [14] and JProbe [15] which allow to identify performance bottleneck.

All these tools have the similar features: memory, performance, code coverage analysis, program debugging, thread deadlock detection, class instrumentation, but many of them are designed to observe a single process Java application and do not support directly monitoring a distributed environment based on RMI middleware. A notable exception is JaViz [7] which is intended to supplement existing performance analysis tools with tracing client/server activities to extend Java's profiling support for a distributed environment. JaViz focuses on a method-level trace with sufficient details to resolve RMI calls. It caches profiling data in files in each involved node, which are merged after an execution and presented. The profiling is presented with one graph for each client call. The main disadvantage of JaViz is that trace recording is performed by modified JVMs what disagrees with the JVM standard.

All above described tools for distributed Java application provide a wide range of advanced functionality but practically each of them only provides a subset of desired functions. Distributed systems are very complex and the best monitoring of a such system could be achieved by using diverse observation techniques and mechanisms, therefore it is often desirable to have a suite of specialized tools such as debuggers, performance analyzers each of them addressing a different task and allowing developers to explore the program's behaviour from various viewpoints. The existing tools are as a rule incompatible to each other, inflexible with respect to their extensibility and cannot be used at the same time. Most tool concentrate on simple scenarios where only certain aspects of a distributed application can be observed. In result, there is a need to establish a more general approach to build flexible, portable, and efficient monitoring-based tools.

3 Building of a Monitoring System

In order to provide comprehensive support for distributed programming, the tools need to be able to *manipulate* and *observe* the whole application distributed over different machines at runtime. The tools with this ability are called *on-line* tools, in contrast to *off-line* tools that only collect information at runtime for later analysis (e.g. JaViz). To provide a flexible functionality of tools monitoring activities underlying the access to and manipulation of the observed application should be concentrated in a separate module which usually is called *monitoring system*. The monitoring system should ideally provide a uniform on-line interface for different kinds of tools, which allows to easily build tools without a need to understand the implementation of monitoring. This monitoring interface has to permit scalability and cover a wide range of analysis methods.

Nowadays, there are no suitable generic monitoring systems supporting Java distributed applications. Most tool environments usually consolidate tools with a monitoring facility into one monolithic system. However, there are some approaches which can underly the construction of particular types of tools. Java Platform Debugger Architecture (JPDA) [17] provides an infrastructure to build a debugger tool by allowing access to the internals of a program running on one JVM from within another one. The debugger and the debuggee are running in completely separate memory spaces, which minimizes the impact what they will have on each other. JPDA can be a good platform for remote debugging, but it does not offer support for distributed debugging and monitoring, moreover, it only allows for a single connection to a target JVM at the same time, what means that different tools cannot be used to monitor the same JVM simultaneously. Java-based Monitoring Application Programming Interface (JMAPI) [4] is a monitoring component integrated into the Secure Open Mobile Agent (SOMA)[5] platform and developed for Java-based Mobile Agents environments. A monitoring tool (agent), based on this interface can *instrument* JVM to handle several types of events produced by Java programs, via JVMPI [16] and JNI

[18] interfaces, and *inspect* the state of machine specific information (e.g., CPU, memory usage) typically hidden by JVM, and available via platform-dependent modules. JMAPI is used by SOMA to get information about Mobile Agents resource usage and is intended to perform the on-line resource management and profiling of SOMA-based services. JMAPI and JPDA provide a useful functionality to obtain information about monitored Java programs and VM internal state. The advantages of the above architectures are very desirable but there are still other requirements which are not met by them, e.g. concerning possibility of simultaneous use by different tools and support for their different types.

4 From OMIS to J-OMIS

The constraints mentioned above made us to choose another approach. To build a versatile monitoring system we used a monitor/tool interface specification, OMIS [2], and a monitoring system, the OCM [3], which implements this specification. OMIS follows the idea of separation of a tool from a monitoring system through a standardized interface. The cooperation between the tool and monitoring system bases on the service request/reply mechanism. A tool sends a service request to the monitoring system e.g. as a coded string which describes a condition (event) (if any) and activities (action list) which have to be invoked (when the condition gets true). In this way the tool programs the monitoring system to listen for event occurrences, perform needed actions, and transfer results to the tool. OMIS relies on a hierarchy of the abstract objects: *nodes, processes, threads, messages queue and messages*. Every object is represented by an abstract identifier (*token*) which can be converted into other token types by conversion functions *localization* and *expansion* which are automatically applied to every service definition that has tokens as parameter that refer to an object type different from that for which service is defined. Each tool at each moment has a well define scope, i.e. it can observe and manipulate a specific set of objects *attached* on a request from a tool. The OCM is the first OMIS compliant monitoring system which was built to support parallel programming environments. Due to the distributed nature of parallel application, the monitoring system must itself be distributed and needs one monitoring component per node, which in case of OCM is called local monitor (LM). The OCM also comprises a component, called the Node Distribution Unit (NDU) that has to analyze each request issued by a tool and split it into separate requests that can be processed locally by LMs on proper nodes. OMIS allows the monitoring system to be expanded with a tool extension or monitor extension, via adding new services and new types of objects to the basic monitoring system. This allows to provide the monitoring support for specific programming environments.

Java-bound On-line Monitoring Interface Specification (J-OMIS) is a monitor extension to OMIS for Java applications that is intended to support the development of Java distributed applications with on-line tools. J-OMIS introduces a range of new types of objects, new services and conversion functions. The extension divides a new Java-bound object hierarchy into two kinds of system objects: execution objects, i.e. *nodes, JVMs, threads* and application ones, i.e. *interfaces, classes, objects, methods*. J-OMIS defines a set of services operating on each object. As in the original OMIS, J-OMIS specifies tree types of services: *information services* that provide information about an object, *manipulation services* which allow to change the state of an object, and *events services* to trigger some arbitrary actions whenever a matching event takes place. J-OMIS defines relations between the objects of a running application, which are expressed by conversion functions, e.g. *"implements"* or *"downcast/upcast"*. The idea of conversion comes from OMIS 2.0 where the *localization/expansion* conversion has been defined. J-OMIS enlarges this ability by a few additional operations that result from the object-oriented nature of Java. E.g., a request :method_get_info([class_id], 1) relates to a *method* information service to obtain information on all methods implemented in the specified class. The *class_id* token is expanded by the conversion mechanism into a set of *method* objects [1].

5 Architecture of Java-Oriented Monitoring System

Based on J-OMIS, we have designed a Java-oriented extension to the OCM, J-OCM, by extending the functionality of OCM, adding new software components and adapting existing ones. This approach allows to combine the existing functionality of the OCM with Java platform to support Java homogeneous and heterogeneous in the future computing. Fig. 1 shows which components have been added and which modified. The *Node Distribution Unit* (NDU) is a unchanged part of the whole monitoring infrastructure, which is still responsible for distributing requests and assembling replies. E.g. a tool may issue a request in order to run Garbage Collector on specified JVMs, therefore the NDU must determine the nodes executing the JVMs and, if needed, to split the request into separate subrequests to be sent to the proper nodes. The NDU must also assemble the partial replies from local monitors into a global reply. The NDU is aimed to make the whole system manageable, thus it has to program the local monitors of all the currently observed nodes. As the set of monitored nodes may changed over time, the NDU must properly react to these changes: to create local monitors on newly added nodes or to re-arrange its list of the objects being involved in the execution of requests that have been issued by tools, when some nodes are deleted. The *Local Monitor* is a monitor process, independent from the whole global monitoring infrastructure. Each monitor process provides an interface similar to that of the NDU, with the exception that it only accepts requests to operate on local objects. To support the monitoring of Java applications, the LM's extension, JVMEXT, provides new services defined by J-OMIS, which control JVM via agents. JVMEXT is linked to LMs as a dynamically linked library at runtime using the *dlopen* interface, whenever the tool issues a service request to JVMEXT. LM stores information about the target Java application's objects such as *JVMs, threads, classes, interfaces, objects, methods etc.* referred by tokens. The *Java Virtual Machine Local Monitor* is an agent embedded into a JVM process, which is responsible for execution of the requests received from the LM. It uses Virtual Machine native interfaces such as JVMPI, JVMDI, JNI that provide low level mechanisms for interactive monitoring, independent of

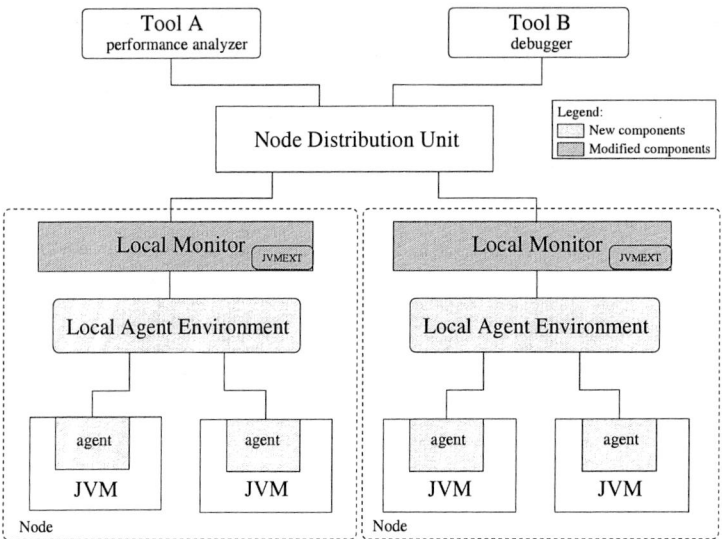

Fig. 1. J-OCM architecture.

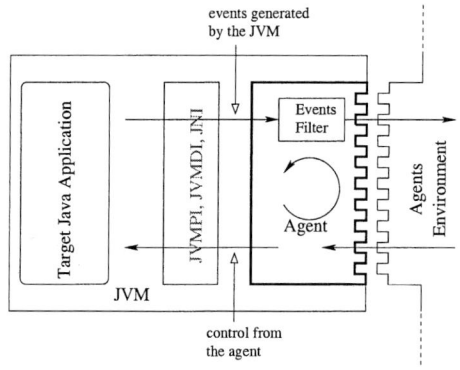

Fig. 2. JVM agent.

a JVM implementation. The *Shared Memory based Local Agents Environment* (SHMLAE) is a communication layer to support cooperation between agents and the LM. It provides an application programming interface (API) for the parallel programming model based on signals and shared memory regions. It offers *non-blocking send* and *interrupt/poll driven receive* operations to support monitoring techniques used in the OCM, based on the event-action paradigm. The asynchronous communication is needed to avoid blocking of the monitoring processes and Java agents in order to provide fast reactions on occurring events. To provide a better performance of Java agents, we use a mechanism we call *interrupt/poll driven receive*, which in fact is a combination of two different communication techniques. In order to receive messages the agent needs to specify a *callback function*, which is activated by the environment whenever a message comes. Signals are used for asynchronous notification and in order to keep the agent system properly working, each signal used to notify of incoming message has to be handled by the communication environment. There may arise a situation, when a signal is being received within its own signal handler. It means that the signal handler can only perform atomic operations such as changing state of the file descriptor that is being polled by the agent at a specified period of time. The agent may also disable this method of notification of the event occurrence and specify its own one.

The asynchronous communication provided by the SHMLAE supports the manipulation and event services specified by OMIS. Manipulation services usually comprise just one request which is sent to change the state of JVM via the profiling agent. In case of the event service, information about events which occur in JVM are sent by the agent also in a single request. The information services often need to perform one or more transactions with the Java agent inside its body. Information service requests cause sending requests and waiting for a reply. This model of data exchange is performed synchronously. To support this model, the SHMLAE introduces an additional communication channel based on Unix Domain Sockets. The *proxy* module shown in Fig. 3 is a transparent software layer responsible for packing outgoing and unpacking incoming messages. It is implemented as a separate library linked with the whole environment.

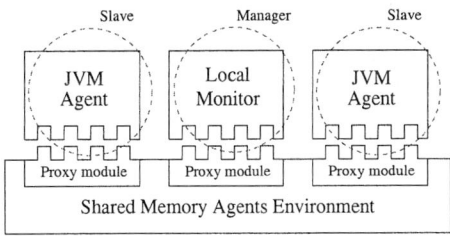

Fig. 3. Shared Memory based Local Agents Environment.

6 Conclusions

The work on building a Java-oriented tools followed the idea of separating the layer of tools from a monitoring system's functionality. We extended the On-line Monitoring Interface Specification by a Java specific hierarchy of objects and a set of relevant services. The corresponding work on a Java-oriented monitoring system, the J-OCM, concentrated on extending the functionality of Local Monitors which are the distributed part of the system and introducing new software levels interfacing the J-OCM to JVM and providing a communication mechanism for the low-level layers. Our on-going work focuses on completing the implementation of the J-OCM and designing a suite of Java-oriented performance analysis tools.

Acknowledgement

This research was carried out within the Polish-German collaboration and it was partially supported by the KBN grant 4 T11C 032 23.

References

1. M. Bubak, W. Funika, P. Mętel, R. Orłowski, and R. Wismüller: Towards a Monitoring Interface Specification for Distributed Java Applications. In Proc. 4th Int. Conf. PPAM 2001, Nałęczów, Poland, September 2001, LNCS 2328, pp. 315-322, Springer, 2002.
2. T. Ludwig, R. Wismüller, V. Sunderam, and A. Bode: OMIS – On-line Monitoring Interface Specification (Version 2.0). Shaker Verlag, Aachen, vol. 9, LRR-TUM Research Report Series, (1997)
http://wwwbode.in.tum.de/~omis/OMIS/Version-2.0/version-2.0.ps.gz
3. R. Wismüller, J. Trinitis and T. Ludwig: A Universal Infrastructure for the Runtime Monitoring of Parallel and Distributed Applications. In Euro-Par'98, Parallel Processing, volume 1470 of Lecture Notes in Computer Science, pages 173-180, Southampton, UK, September 1998. Springer-Verlag.
4. P. Bellavista, A. Corradi and C. Stefanelli: Java-based On-line Monitoring of Heterogeneous Resources and Systems. In 7th Workshop HP OpenView University Association, Santorini, Greece, June 2000.
http://lia.deis.unibo.it/Staff/PaoloBellavista/papers/hpovua00.pdf
http://lia.deis.unibo.it/Research/ubiQoS/monitoring.shtml
5. P. Bellavista, A. Corradi, C. Stefanelli A Secure and Open Mobile Agent Programming Environment. WET ICE '98, Stanford University, California, USA, June 1998, http://lia.deis.unibo.it/Research/SOMA/
6. G. Pennington and R. Watson: JProf – a JVMPI Based Profiler
http://starship.python.net/crew/garyp/jProf.html
7. I.H. Kazi, D.P. Jose, B. Ben-Hamida, C.J. Hescott, C. Kwok, J. Konstan, D.J. Lilja, and P.-C. Yew: JaViz: A Client/Server Java Profiling Tool, *IBM Systems Journal*, **39**(1), (2000) 96-117.
http://www.research.ibm.com/journal/sj/391/kazi.html
8. The SDK profiler.
http://www.javaworld.com/javaworld/jw-12-2001/jw-1207-hprof.html
9. Sun's Heap Analysis Tool (HAT) for analysing output from hprof.
http://java.sun.com/people/billf/heap/index.html
10. JTracer tool. http://www.amslib.com/jtracer/
11. Cheap fully featured Java profiler http://www.j-sprint.com/
12. JProfiler. http://www.ej-technologies.com/jprofiler/overview.html
13. The OptimizeIt! performance profiler. http://www.optimizeit.com/
14. JTest. http://www.parasoft.com/jsp/products/home.jsp?product=Jtest
15. JProbe. http://java.quest.com/jprobe/jprobe.shtml
16. Sun Microsystems: Java Virtual Machine Profiler Interface (JVMPI)
http://java.sun.com/products/jdk/1.2/docs/guide/jvmpi/jvmpi.html
17. Sun Microsystems: Java Platform Debug Architecture (JPDA)
http://java.sun.com/j2se/1.4.1/docs/guide/jpda/index.html
18. Sun Microsystems: Java Native Interface (JNI)
http://java.sun.com/products/jdk/1.2/docs/guide/jni/

A Communication API for Implementing Irregular Algorithms on SMP Clusters

Judith Hippold* and Gudula Rünger

Chemnitz University of Technology
Department of Computer Science
09107 Chemnitz, Germany
{juh,ruenger}@informatik.tu-chemnitz.de

Abstract. Clusters of SMPs (symmetric multiprocessors) gain more and more importance in high performance computing and are often used with a hybrid programming model based on message passing and multithreading. For irregular application programs with dynamically changing computation and data access behavior a flexible programming model is needed to achieve load balance and efficiency. We have proposed *task pool teams* as a new hybrid concept to realize irregular algorithms on clusters of SMPs efficiently. Task pool teams offer implicit load balance on single cluster nodes together with multithreaded, MPI-based communication for the exchange of remote data. This paper introduces the programming model and library support with an easy to use application programmer interface for task pool teams.

1 Introduction

Irregular algorithms are characterized by an unknown access behavior to data structures, varying computational effort, or irregular dependencies between computations resulting in an input dependent program behavior. The characteristics of irregular algorithms make an efficient parallel implementation difficult. Especially when an irregular algorithm has unpredictably evolving computational work, dynamic load balance is required to employ all processors evenly.

For shared memory platforms the concept of task pools can be used to realize dynamic load balance. A task pool is a global data structure to store and manage the tasks created for one specific program combined with a fixed number of threads processing these tasks. Each thread can extract tasks for execution and can insert dynamically created tasks. Task pools are classified according to the internal organization or access strategies. Central task pools offer good load balance because each thread can get a new task from the central queue when ready with previous work. Decentralized pools usually have as many queues as threads. The advantage is that there are no access conflicts between several threads, however, dynamic load balance can only be achieved with task stealing. That means, if the private task queue of a thread is empty, it tries to steal

---

* Supported by DFG, SFB393 *Numerical Simulation on Massively Parallel Computers*

tasks from other queues which requires a lock mechanism. Detailed investigations of different task pool versions are given in [1]. Task pool implementations for dynamic load balance have been presented in e.g. [2][3].

In [4] we have introduced task pool teams, a generalization of the task pool concept, for realizing irregular algorithms on SMP clusters. Task pool teams combine task pools on single nodes implemented with Pthreads for load balance with explicit message passing using MPI for irregularly occurring, remote data accesses. The resulting implementation of an irregular algorithm with task pool teams is entirely realized on the application programmers level so that the characteristics of the specific algorithm can be exploited.

This paper presents the hybrid programming model and the application programmer interface. The API clarifies the concept and improves the structure of the resulting program while no additional overhead compared to the hand-coded version is introduced. Moreover, we present several communication protocols and corresponding functions which can be used to realize different communication characteristics. This allows an easy adaptation to the communication requirements of different irregular algorithms.

The paper is structured as follows: Section 2 introduces the hybrid programming model and the communication scheme for task pool teams. Sections 3 and 4 describe the API for task pools and communication. Experimental results are presented in Section 5. Section 6 discusses related work and Section 7 concludes.

2 Hybrid Programming Model

We assume the following basic programming model: Programs are written in an SPMD style, and each cluster node runs the same program containing MPI and Pthread operations as well as calls to the task pool team interface. Within the program there are code sections with task-oriented structure processed in parallel by a task pool. There exists one pool for each cluster node. Mutual communication between nodes is realized with message passing. The task pools of all cluster nodes form a task pool team.

At the beginning and at the end of a program run only the main thread is active. It can use MPI operations arbitrarily, for example to distribute data or to collect data from other processors. The program switches to multithreaded mode when the main thread starts the processing of tasks and switches back to single-threaded when it leaves the task pool. Task pools are realized with a fixed number of *worker threads* (WT) and are re-usable in different multithreaded sections.

Irregular application programs may have irregular communication requirements with communication partners working asynchronously on different parts of the code. Thus the counterpart of the communication operation to be issued by the remote communication partner might be missing when using MPI communication operations. To ensure correct communication, we introduce a communication scheme with a separate *communication thread* (CT) for each task pool and distinguish between two cases of communication (see Figure 1).

a)
1. send_data
2. receive_data

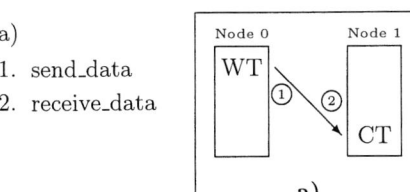
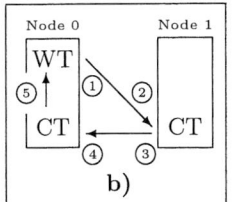

b)
1. initial_send
2. initial_receive
3. final_send
4. final_receive
5. awake WT

Fig. 1. Simplified illustration of a) simple and b) complex communication between two task pools only showing one worker thread and the communication threads.

Simple communication can be used e.g. in parallel backtracking algorithms using treelike solution spaces where locally calculated, intermediate results are exchanged to restrict the search space. Figure 1 a) illustrates this communication process consisting of the following steps: *(1) A worker thread of Node 0 sends calculated data to Node 1. (2) The remote communication thread receives and processes the data.*

Complex communication occurs if intermediate results or data structures of one process are needed by another process to continue the calculations, as in the hierarchical radiosity algorithm. The following steps have to be performed as illustrated in Figure 1 b): *(1) A worker thread of Node 0 needs data situated in the address space of Node 1. Thus it sends a request and waits passively. (2) The communication thread of Node 1 receives the request, reacts according to the message tag, and (3) sends the data back. (4) The CT of Node 0 receives the message and (5) signals the waiting worker thread that non-local data are available.*

Within every communication situation there are actually two distinct kinds of thread interactions to manage: the local cooperation of worker thread and communication thread and the handling of remote communication needs. We have decoupled the local cooperation and the remote communication in order to avoid conflicting requirements for the CT which might occur when initializing data requests interferes with the receipt of asynchronously arriving messages. The decoupling realized in the complex communication scheme makes this scheme suitable for the unknown data requests within irregular algorithms.

3 User Interface for Task Pools

The interface for task pools was modified compared to the former version (see [4]) concerning an implicit re-initialization of the task pools and an explicit selection of the task pool run mode to provide a more general and optimized implementation. If there is no exchange of messages between different MPI processes, the pools should run in the WITHOUT_CT mode (see function (4)) because this results in a smaller execution time.

(1) **void** tp_init (**unsigned** number_of_threads, **void** (* ct_routine)()) ;
   allocates and initializes the task pool. number_of_threads denotes the total number of threads including the main thread and the communication thread. ct_routine points to the function performed by the communication thread (see Section 4.3).

(2) **void** tp_destroy ( ) ;
deallocates the task pool structure and destroys all threads except the main thread.
(3) **void** tp_initial_put (**void** (* task_routine)(), arg_type *arguments) ;
inserts an initial task into the task pool. task_routine is a pointer to the function representing the task. The arguments for that function are given by **arguments**.
(4) **void** tp_run (**unsigned** type) ;
starts the processing of tasks. Depending on the **type** (WITH_CT or WITHOUT_CT) the task pool runs with or without a communication thread.
(5) **void** tp_put (**void** (* task_routine)(), arg_type *arguments, **unsigned** thread_id) ;
inserts dynamically created tasks into the pool. The parameter **thread_id** is the identifier of the thread inserting the task.

Functions (1)-(4) are performed by the main thread. Function (5) can be used by each thread working on the pool. The main thread becomes a worker thread after calling tp_run. When the task pool is empty, the main thread prepares the pool for re-use and returns. There is no need to destroy the pool and to create a new one when it might be used again which saves thread creation time. Each worker thread is identified by its **thread_id**. This identifier is assigned after thread creation and different from the identifier provided for Pthreads.

4 User Interface for Communication in Task Pool Teams

Task pool teams are created by combining task pools (see Section 3) with the communication schemes from Section 2. We present an interface for simple and complex communication and further distinguish between the cases of a) the size of incoming messages is not known and b) the size of incoming messages is known in advance. The provided functions in Subsections 4.1 and 4.2 encapsulate MPI and Pthread operations. The use of those functions is illustrated in 4.3.

4.1 Complex Communication

(1) **void** *initial_send(**void** *buffer, **int** count, **MPI_Datatype** type, **int** dest, **int** tag, **unsigned** thread_id);
sends a data request to processor **dest**. The pointer **buffer** denotes the data of length **count** and data type **type** necessary to identify the requested data. **tag** denotes the message in order to initiate a specific action on the destination process. The function returns a pointer to the requested data.
(2) **int** get_size(**unsigned** thread_id) ;
determines the size of the data requested by initial_send. The parameter **thread_id** identifies the requesting thread. (only necessary for case a))
(3) a) **void** *initial_receive(**int** *count, **MPI_Datatype** type) ;
receives the data request and returns a pointer to the received data. After finishing initial_receive, **count** contains the length of the received data of type **type**.
b) **void** initial_receive_buf(**void** *buffer, **int** count, **MPI_Datatype** type) ;
receives the data request. The user provides the buffer **buffer** of length **count**.
(4) **void** final_send(**void** *buffer, **int** count, **MPI_Datatype** type) ;
sends the requested data in **buffer** of length **count** and data type **type** back to the requesting process.

(5) a) **void** final_receive(**MPI_Datatype** type) ;
receives the requested data of data type type and awakes the waiting worker thread.
b) **void** final_receive_buf(**void** *buffer, **int** count, **MPI_Datatype** type) ;
receives the requested data of data type type and length count in the user provided buffer buffer and awakes the waiting worker thread.

Function (1) initiates a data request by a worker thread. The calling WT is blocked until the data are available. (2) provides the size of the received data to this worker thread. Functions (3)-(5) are performed by the communication threads of the communication partners. The finally received data are available in the shared memory of the node.

4.2 Simple Communication

(1) **void** send_data(**void** *buffer, **int** count, **MPI_Datatype** type, **int** dest, **int** tag) ;
sends the data in buffer of length count and data type type to process dest. tag identifies the message.
(2) a) **void** *receive_data(**int** *source, **int** *count, **MPI_Datatype** type) ;
receives the data of data type type. After finishing this function, the sender and the size are stored in source and count, and a pointer to the received data is returned.
b) **void** receive_data_buf(**void** *buffer, **int** *source, **int** count, **MPI_Datatype** type) ;
receives the data of data type type and length count in the user provided buffer buffer. After finishing this function, the sender is stored in source.

The worker thread performs function (1) and the communication thread performs function (2). There is no need to block the worker thread because the communication process is finished. The CT performs algorithm specific computations on the received data.

4.3 Communication Thread

The application programmer has to code the function performed by the communication thread according to algorithmic needs and gives a pointer to it as a parameter of tp_init. The following pseudo-code illustrates the core structure of this function with examples for complex and simple communication. /*... ...*/ labels the location for algorithm specific code.

```
while(1) {
   if(message_check(&tag)) {
      /* COMPLEX COMMUNICATION */        /* SIMPLE COMMUNICATION */
      if(tag == 1) {                     else if(tag == 3) {
         initial_receive();                 receive_data();
         /*... get data ...*/               /*... process data ...*/
         final_send();                   }
      }                                  else if ...
      else if(tag == 2) {             } /* end if(message_check()) */
         final_receive();           } /* end while(1) */
      }
```

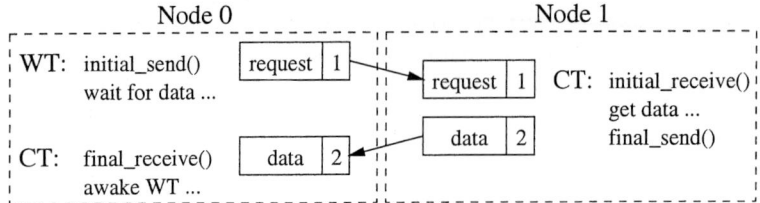

Fig. 2. Communication protocol for complex communication using the tags 1 and 2.

We provide the function int message_check(int *tag) to check for incoming messages. If there is a message available, it returns TRUE and tag contains the tag of the message. According to this message tag the communication thread selects the specific action to perform. The application programmer chooses an arbitrary, odd, and unique integer as tag for a specific type of request. If a message with an odd tag arrives, the communication thread automatically increments the tag and uses it for the response message. Thus the pair $(2i+1, 2i+2), i \in I\!N$, labels a complex communication process of a specific type. The simple communication process needs only one tag because there are no final_send and final_receive operations necessary. The pseudo-code shows a complex communication process with the tags 1 and 2. Figure 2 illustrates the corresponding communication protocol.

4.4 Synchronization Hierarchy

Although programs with task pool teams have SPMD style, the task-oriented structure and the irregularity of the algorithm lead to different, asynchronous program runs on different cluster nodes. Implicit synchronization is only necessary for switching from multi- to single-threaded mode to guarantee that the remote communication partners are active and can handle data requests. Task pool teams ensure this by a synchronization hierarchy (see Figure 3) completely hidden to the user.

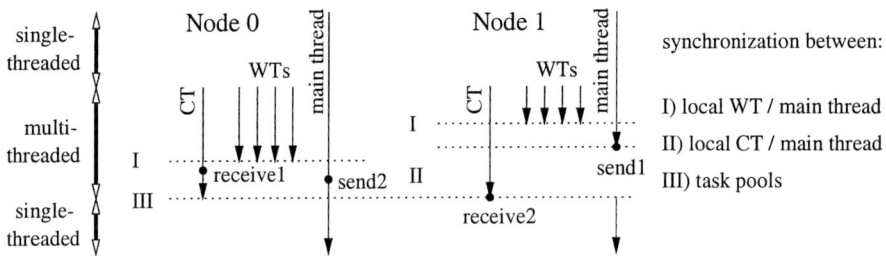

Fig. 3. Synchronization hierarchy illustrated with two cluster nodes. The main thread of Node 1 has to wait till the local CT receives a synchronization message of Node 0. The main thread of Node 0 continues with computation after sending the synchronization message because the message of Node 1 was already received.

The synchronization of task pools (Figure 3, III) and local main thread and communication thread (Figure 3, II) is closely connected. Task pools are synchronized by sending synchronization messages after all local tasks are processed. This is done by the main thread. Each communication thread gathers these messages and awakes the waiting main thread when an acknowledge of every task pool has arrived. The following pseudo-code illustrates that mechanism:

```
/* MAIN THREAD LOOP */              /* COMMUNICATION THREAD LOOP */
CT_run = TRUE;                      while(!CT_run) wait();
signal_communication_thread();      /* handle communication till synchro-
/* ... process tasks ... */            nization message of all pools */
send_synchronization_message();     CT_run = FALSE;
while(CT_run) wait();               signal_main_thread();
```

To ensure correct program behavior, the main thread is not allowed to leave the task pool till every other local worker thread is ready and waits passively for re-activation (Figure 3, I). Otherwise, it would be possible that the communication thread is stopped by the main thread while there are worker threads still waiting for non-local data. The pseudo-code realizes such a barrier:

```
waiting_threads += 1;                        Threads entering the barrier
if(waiting_threads < number_of_WT) wait();   wait passively except the last
else { if(main_thread) return;               thread which awakes the main
       else {   signal_main_thread();        thread and blocks, unless it is
                wait();                      the main thread itself. Then it
}     }                                      returns.
```

5 Experimental Results

We have implemented the hierarchical radiosity algorithm using our application programmer interface for task pool teams and compare this realization with a former hand-coded version of [4], where more detailed investigations and evaluations about the basic task pools can be found. We use three example scenes: "largeroom" (532 initial polygons) of the SPLASH2 benchmark suite [5], "hall" (1157 initial polygons) and "xlroom" (2979 initial polygons) from [2]. We have investigated our API on a small SMP cluster of 4 SunBlade 1000 with two 750 MHz UltraSPARC3 processors and SCI network.

On the left of Figure 4 the speedups depending on the number of threads and processors are shown for the scene "xlroom" with the best-suited task pool. Each cluster node runs one MPI process. Although there are only two processors per cluster node, an increased number of threads leads to better speedups caused by the reduction of the allocated CPU time for the communication thread and by the overlapping of computation and communication. That means, while a worker thread waits for data, another worker thread might perform calculations. Due to the overhead for threads and the sm aller workload per thread with growing numbers of processes the speedups reach a saturation point.

On the right of Figure 4 a comparison between the former hand-coded version and the radiosity version using the API is shown. The runtimes of the best-suited task pools with 20 threads per pool are presented for varying example scenes and

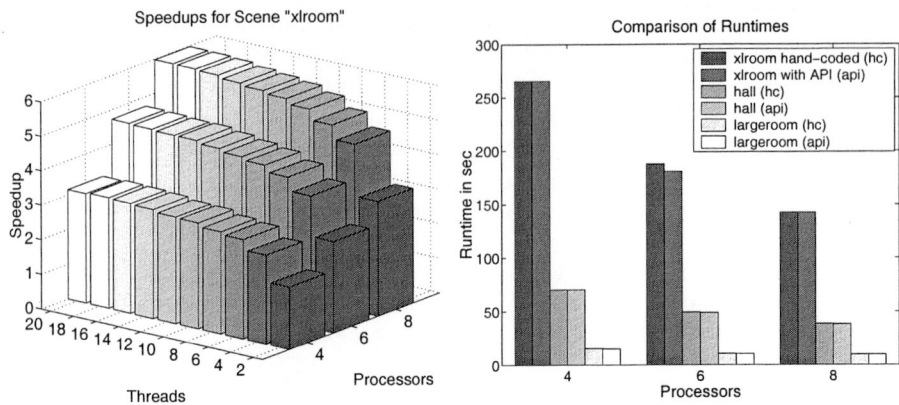

Fig. 4. Left: Speedups for model "xlroom". Right: Speedups of the hand-coded version (*hc*) compared with the radiosity version using the API (*api*).

numbers of processors. It is shown that there are only slight changes in execution times between both radiosity versions. Thus our interface for communication induces only a marginal overhead.

6 Related Work

There are several approaches for hybrid programming of SMP clusters: SIMPLE [6] can be used for applications which allow a strict separation of computation and communication phases. NICAM [7] supports overlapping of communication and computation for data parallel applications. Some packages provide threads on distributed memory. Nexus [8] is a runtime environment for irregular, heterogeneous, and task-parallel applications. Chant [9] presents threads capable of direct communication on distributed memory. In contrast, our approach is entirely situated within the application programmers level in order to provide a systematic programming approach without hiding important details and implicit load balance.

7 Conclusion

We have presented an easy to use interface for task pool teams suitable for the parallelization of irregular algorithms on clusters of SMPs. Our model offers dynamic load balance on individual cluster nodes and multithreaded communication for the task-oriented sections. The efficiency results are good and depend on the specific input data. Task pool teams are also advantageous for PC clusters since communication and computation overlap in task-oriented sections.

References

1. Korch, M., Rauber, T.: Evaluation of Task Pools for the Implementation of Parallel Irregular Algorithms. Proc. of ICPP'02 Workshops, CRTPC 2002, Vancouver, Canada (2002) 597–604
2. Podehl, A., Rauber, T., Rünger, G.: A Shared-Memory Implementation of the Hierarchical Radiosity Method. Theoretical Computer Science **196** (1998) 215–240
3. Singh, J.P., Holt, C., Totsuka, T., Gupta, A., Hennessy, J.: Load Balancing and Data Locality in Adaptive Hierarchical N-body Methods: Barnes-Hut, Fast Multipole, and Radiosity. Journal of Parallel and Distributed Computing **27** (1995) 118–141
4. Hippold, J., Rünger, G.: Task Pool Teams for Implementing Irregular Algorithms on Clusters of SMPs. In Proc. of the 17th IPDPS, Nice, France. (2003)
5. Woo, S.C., Ohara, M., Torrie, E., Singh, J.P., Gupta, A.: The SPLASH-2 Programs: Characterization and Methodological Considerations. In: Proc. of the 22nd Annual Int. Symposium on Computer Architecture. (1995) 24–36
6. Bader, D.A., JáJá, J.: SIMPLE: A Methodology for Programming High Performance Algorithms on Clusters of Symmetric Multiprocessors (SMPs). Journal of Parallel and Distributed Computing **58** (1999) 92–108
7. Tanaka, Y.: Performance Improvement by Overlapping Computation and Communication on SMP Clusters. In Proc. of the 1998 Int. Conf. on Parallel and Distributed Processing Techniques and Applications **1** (1998) 275–282
8. Foster, I., Kesselman, C., Tuecke, S.: The Nexus Approach to Integrating Multithreading and Communication. Journal of Parallel and Distributed Computing **37** (1996) 70–82
9. Haines, M., Mehrotra, P., Cronk, D.: Chant: Lightweight Threads in a Distributed Memory Environment. Technical report, ICASE. (1995)

TOM – Efficient Monitoring Infrastructure for Multithreaded Programs*

Bartosz Baliś[1], Marian Bubak[1,2], Włodzimierz Funika[1],
Roland Wismüller[3,4], and Grzegorz Kaplita[1]

[1] Institute of Computer Science
AGH, al. Mickiewicza 30, 30-059 Kraków, Poland
[2] Academic Computer Centre – CYFRONET
Nawojki 11, 30-950 Kraków, Poland
[3] LRR-TUM – Technische Universität München
D-80290 München, Germany
[4] Institute for Software Sciences
University of Vienna, A-1090, Wien Austria
{balis,bubak,funika}@agh.edu.pl, wismuell@in.tum.de,
orkid@student.uci.agh.edu.pl
phone: (+48 12) 6173964, fax: (+48 12) 6338054
phone: (+49 89) 289-28243

Abstract. Multithreading is an efficient and powerful solution for parallel programming. However, multithreaded programming is difficult and there are few tools that support the development of multithreaded applications. Even fewer or no tools introduce portable concepts to deal with threads on many platforms. In this paper, we describe the TOM monitoring infrastructure for multithreaded applications. The key concept of TOM are Application Monitors which are additional monitoring threads in the monitored application. The concept of Application Monitors allows efficient and portable solutions to the most important problems in thread monitoring. We describe the current implementation of TOM with a focus on Application Monitors. In addition, we provide a case study implementation of fast breakpoints based on these Application Monitors.

Keywords: multithreading, monitoring, debugging, performance analysis, parallel tools

1 Introduction

The most popular thread standard today is POSIX threads, called pthreads [9]. Pthreads define a standardized interface and behaviour for thread creation and management subroutines, as well as related data types. Almost every operating system (OS) provides a pthreads library, although the underlying implementation is strongly system-dependent. This makes it hard to develop tools that

---

* This work has been carried out within the Polish-German collaboration and is supported, in part, by KBN under grant 4 T11C 026 22, and, in part concerning SGI, under grant 6 T11 0052.

support the debugging of pthreads applications – there is no standard interface for accessing pthreads internals, and standard system mechanisms such as ptrace or procfs [11] are often not pthreads-enabled. Besides debugging, application developers are also interested in the monitoring of running applications in order to analyse the application performance, to find how large are the delays due to synchronization, etc. These features are offered by tools such as performance analyzers or visualizers. Instrumentation of an application is necessary to collect information for performance measurements. Efficient instrumentation is not trivial and multithreading introduces even more problems such as transparency due to the single code image [5].

In this paper, we describe the TOM monitoring infrastructure for multithreaded applications, which supports the development of portable tools, such as debuggers or performance analyzers. The key concept in TOM are Application Monitors which are additional monitoring threads in the monitored application. The Application Monitors concept allows for efficient and portable solutions to the most important problems of thread monitoring. We describe the current implementation of TOM with special focus on Application Monitors and provide a case study of fast breakpoints based on this concept.

2 Troubles with Thread Monitoring

Below we shortly summarize the most important problems related to the monitoring of multithreaded programs.

Asynchronous Control. We wish to deal with threads asynchronously like with processes, for example, execute step-by-step only one thread of a process while others are still running. Unfortunately, OS interfaces used for this purpose, such as ptrace or procfs, usually do not support threads. This means that manipulating one of the threads with ptrace would require stopping the whole process.

Single Code Image. Threads share not only data but also code address space. This introduces *transparency* problems when the monitoring system instruments a thread's code. A breakpoint set in one thread is immediately visible in all other ones while we are going to apply the breakpoint to one thread only.

Portability. Though the common pthreads interface is widely agreed, the underlying implementations of libraries are very different from system to system or even between two versions of the same system (such as in IRIX 6.4 and IRIX 6.5). In addition, there is no standard debug-interface for pthreads. Some vendors do provide a pthreads debug library, but it is not portable and sometimes not even available to the public. As a result, in some cases only the vendor tools are thread-aware, as it is the case for IRIX.

3 TOM – Thread-Enabled OMIS Monitor

The architecture of TOM is shown in Fig. 1. TOM is an autonomous infrastructure composed of three types of components: Service Managers (SM), Local

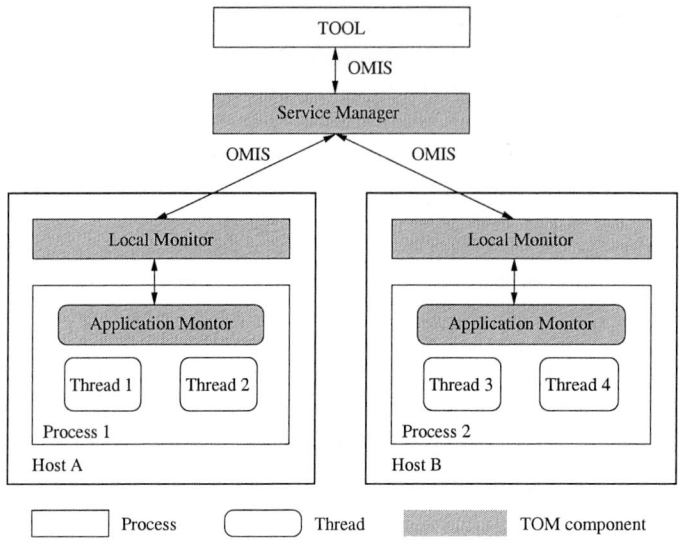

Fig. 1. Thread enabled OMIS Monitor.

Monitors (LM), and Application Monitors (AM). Tools connect to TOM via SMs, send monitoring requests and receive replies. The communication interface is based on the OMIS specification (On-line Monitoring Interface Specification) [10, 2]. On each local unit of the system, which tightly shares a common memory, one LM is supposed to reside. For example, on a cluster there is a single SM and one LM per host, while on a multiprocessor shared-memory machine, such as SGI Origin, there may be one SM, and one LM per each SMP node. Finally, there is one AM thread per each process of the application. The monitoring requests are executed by either LMs or AMs, while the SM's task is to distribute the requests to appropriate LMs and collect the corresponding replies.

In the rest of the paper, we focus on the Application Monitors, which are the key concept in TOM enabling efficient and portable monitoring of threads.

4 Application Monitors

4.1 General Concept

The Application Monitors (AMs) are designed for two main objectives: portability and efficiency of monitoring. An AM is an additional thread in each process of the application. The main benefit is that, as an AM shares address space with the application, it can perform some actions directly, without OS mechanisms involved.

An LM sends asynchronous requests to an AM and waits for responses. In this way, we can read the address space (e.g., variable values), set breakpoints or even insert a general instrumentation code dynamically. The asynchronous control of threads is addressed owing to the communication pattern: asynchronous queries/replies as opposed to synchronous mechanisms such as ptrace. At the same time we also benefit from a higher portability. With AMs we can also easily solve the single code image problem. This can be done in such a way that when an instrumentation point is hit, the AM checks if it was hit in the appropriate thread, and only in this case the instrumentation code will be executed.

4.2 Avoiding of AM Corruption and Transparency

Since AMs share the address space with the other application threads, they may be subject to corruption by the code of the user's application as a result of bugs. This may render debugging impossible while this is exactly the situation when we especially wish to do that. A solution could be to mprotect the appropriate pages. In this case, write attempts would simply cause page faults which should be enough to fix the problem. However, the disadvantage of this solution is a loss of efficiency. For a full protection, we would need to protect both text and data pages of the AM. This would mean that whenever we need to write the AM's memory, we would have to temporarily unprotect the appropriate pages. This is a high-cost operation since it involves a switch to kernel mode. An alternative solution, efficient though not perfect, is to ensure that the AM's data is allocated in memory segments located far away from the pages of other threads. This considerably reduces the probability that a thread accidentally writes the AM's data space. We can achieve that by providing our own memory allocation subroutines or by using a shared memory segment to store the AM data. In our case, the latter option is natural, since in the current implementation the AMs and the Local Monitor already use a shared memory segment for communication.

A second problem is transparency. The additional thread must not be seen by other threads and must not affect the execution of the application. In general, this can be achieved by proper instrumentation of all thread library functions which are affected by this problem. These are usually the operations that involve 'all' threads (e.g., return number of all threads) or 'any' thread. However, in case of pthreads there are no such operations, thus the problem of transparency is not a serious one.

5 Case Study: Breakpoints

In this section, we present a detailed design and implementation of fast breakpoints based on the concept of Application Monitors. Though the concept of fast breakpoints itself is not new, and similar approaches have been proposed [8, 4], we believe that it can illustrate the advantage of the AMs concept. Furthermore, multithreading poses new problems related to fast breakpoints which will be described below.

5.1 Description of the Fast Breakpoints Concept

The general idea is as follows. As a prerequisite, we need a way to stop an arbitrary thread. The AM achieves this by sending the thread a signal. The signal handler for this signal will then wait for a condition variable, which effectively stops the thread. When the thread should be continued again, the AM signals this condition variable to wake-up the thread.

At start-up, the AM creates a configurable number of condition variables and handler functions. This number determines the maximum number of breakpoints allowed. Each handler function contains two parts: a call to the pthreads routine that waits for a condition variable, and 'empty space' (i.e. a couple of NOP-instructions) to save the original instruction when the breakpoint is set (see below). Thus, the process of setting a breakpoint is done in the following stages:

1. The debugger sends the AM a request 'set breakpoint at address AAA'.
2. The AM thread receives the request and saves the original instruction at address AAA in the space reserved in the handler function.
3. The AM replaces the instruction at address AAA with a jump to the handler function.

This solution seems quite obvious and relatively easy to implement, however, there are serious problems related to the third operation. The following subsection discusses them.

5.2 Troubles with Instrumentation of Fast Breakpoints

The question is: how can we safely replace the original instruction with another one, e.g., a jump to the breakpoint handler? In general, we must distinguish two cases:

– the jump instruction is not longer than the shortest possible instruction for the architecture (usually one word),
– the jump is longer than the shortest possible instruction.

In the first case, the original instruction can be replaced using an atomic memory-write operation. This means that we can safely do the replacement on-the-fly, since any thread either will see the original state or the new state; there are no intermediate, inconsistent states possible.

In the second case, we may run into serious problems, since we cannot do the replacement atomically. Even if we stop all threads before the replacement, and continue them again afterwards, some of the threads might accidentally have been stopped in the middle of the code region we wish to change. After the replacement they may be executing an incorrect instruction (e.g., the 'second half' of our jump). It is still possible to handle this case by careful examination of the threads' stacks. If any thread happens to execute the 'forbidden' code, we may continue it for a while and stop it again until we get the desired result. However, if the thread happens to be waiting in this region of code, the retry strategy will not work. The most serious problem though, is when the application's code contains a jump into the code region to be replaced. After changing the code region, this jump will branch into 'the middle' of an instruction, which usually will crash the application. Since at the level of the machine code there is no easy way to check whether a given address is a branch target, it is extremely difficult to properly handle this case.

The only reliable solution is to always try to use a short jump instruction. However, while on most architectures such jump instructions are available, they are usually 'short' jumps, i.e., the range of the jump is limited to a nearby memory region. Since it is not easy to guarantee that the handler function is always within a nearby memory region, using short jumps is not always possible.

5.3 Optimal Fast Breakpoints Instrumentation

Fortunately, on each processor, there is an instruction which is not longer than the shortest possible instruction for the architecture, and which can be used instead of a jump. This is the trap instruction which is used by 'normal' debuggers to set breakpoints. Although this solution is guaranteed to work, its disadvantage is that it is not as efficient as a normal jump instruction, since the trap instruction involves a switch into kernel mode and a signal delivery. Still, in our approach there is an advantage over traditional debuggers – the signal is caught by the same process, which avoids an additional process switch and is therefore considerably faster.

The optimal solution is a mixture of the options described above. If the address of the handler function is within the short-jump range, we use a jump instruction. Otherwise, we use the trap instruction.

5.4 Evaluation

We have performed a test to compare the efficiency of breakpoints implemented in three different ways: 1) trap instruction with signal handled by an external process, 2) trap instruction with signal handled inside the AM, 3) with a jump instruction. The test procedure was very simple – a thread was hitting a breakpoint, and the handler immediately continued execution; this was done a number of times in a loop. The total time to execute the loop was measured. The test was performed on an 128-processor SGI Origin machine with R14k processors installed, and IRIX 6.5 OS. Table 1 shows the results. The leftmost column indicates the number of iterations, the following columns provide the real time in system tics.

Table 1. Evaluation of different implementations of breakpoints.

No. iterations	TRAP / signal ext.	TRAP / signal AM	JUMP
10,000	3213 ± 74	15.7 ± 0.48	0 ± 0
100,000	32112 ± 544	159 ± 2.1	0.8 ± 0.42
1,000,000	323870 ± 3532	1585 ± 14.5	6.8 ± 0.42

The table shows clearly that with application monitors and trap instruction we obtain a result two orders of magnitude better than with the traditional method. Additionally using the jump instruction improves the result by still another two orders of magnitude!

6 Related Work

Until now, thread-enabled tools for parallel programming are still not as well supported as those for multiprocess applications. Most of existing tools are debuggers, for example, Wildebeest, TotalView, kdb, NodePrism and LPdbx. Wildebeest [1] is an example of a debugger based on gdb, which supports both kernel and user threads. However, it is strictly limited to HP-UX platforms and implements only a synchronous thread control. TotalView [6] is a commercial debugger which supports a variety of platforms and offers a rich set of debugging capabilities. It is well suited for multithreaded applications and even provides support for applications developed in OpenMP. However, it does not allow for asynchronous thread control unless this feature is supported by the operating system. Kdb [4] was designed to overcome the limitations of other debuggers, specifically for handling user-level threads and for controlling each target thread independently. It does not support pthreads, though.

There are some efforts to address performance analysis of multithreaded applications. One example is the Tmon tool [7], which is a monitoring system combined with a visualization module used to present *waiting graphs* for multithreaded applications. An interesting approach is the thread-enabled Paradyn tool [12]. Paradyn is able to associate performance data with individual threads and relies on dynamic instrumentation to lower the instrumentation cost and overall monitoring intrusiveness.

7 Comparison of AMs with Other Concepts

Our approach is different from those described above not only because it unites the main benefits of the mentioned projects, but – what is more important – it introduces the concept of Application Monitors, which are *active* monitoring components and thus more powerful. The benefits of using AMs are manifold: **AMs encapsulate their functionality in a standardized protocol**. External users (a debugger, a monitoring system, etc.) just send standardized request and receive replies. This increases portability, since all platform-specific details are hidden in the implementation, and interoperability, since multiple users can potentially concurrently use the AM's services. **AMs can access the application's address space directly**, without the need to deal with interfaces such as ptrace or procfs. This greatly eases and speeds up many operations, for example reading memory, which is the basis for sophisticated data visualization capabilities of debuggers. **AMs enable dynamic insertion of arbitrary instrumentation** into the application's code. The only project which so far offers such a possibility, is DynInst [3]. DynInst is a very powerful approach, which allows to insert (nearly) arbitrarily complex code at run-time. AMs are more restricted, since only the jump to the handler function is inserted dynamically; all the other required code is included into the application by linking it with the AM library. This restriction, however, makes our approach much more lightweight and portable; for example, we do not need a complex code generator like DynInst. The simpler structure also makes the AM approach easier to maintain and less error-prone. **AMs enable asynchronous control of threads.** For example, the concept of fast breakpoints described in this paper allows independent debugging of a single thread while keeping others running, even if the particular implementation is based entirely on user-level threads, which are not supported by the OS. Finally, **AMs enable the portable monitoring of threads**, independent of the concrete pthreads implementation (e.g. user level vs. kernel threads) and independent of OS support.

8 Conclusion and Future Work

We have described our experience in design and implementation of a portable and efficient monitoring system which supports multithreaded applications. The key concept of our solution are Application Monitors which are additional threads for each process of the application. The presented concept is generic – it is designed to support a variety of tools, for example, debuggers and performance analyzers. We have shown a case study of fast breakpoints based on the concept of Application Monitors.

Currently, we have implemented the first prototype of TOM which contains the infrastructure for Application Monitors with basic monitoring services, and a simple external monitoring infrastructure. The tasks for the future are as follows. First, an existing OMIS-compliant monitoring system for clusters – the OCM [2] will be extended with threads support so that we can benefit from the full monitoring functionality offered by OMIS. Second, the Application Monitors will be extended by additional monitoring functionality. Finally, the thread-enabled OCM will be integrated with Application Monitors to obtain a fully functional OMIS-based thread-enabled monitoring system – TOM.

References

1. S. S. Adayapalam. In Search of Yeti: Footprint Analysis with Wildebeest. In Mireille Ducassé, editor, *Proceedings of AADEBUG 2000, Fourth International Workshop on Automated Debugging*, Munich, Germany, August 2000.
2. M. Bubak, W. Funika, B. Baliś, R. Wismüller. On-line OCM-based Tool Support for Parallel Applications. In *Annual Review of Scalable Computing*, vol. 3, pp. 32–62. World Scientific Publishing and Singapore University Press, Singapore, 2001.
3. B. Buck and J. Hollingsworth. An API for Runtime Code Patching. *The International Journal of High Performance Computing Applications*, 14(4):317–329, Winter 2000.
4. P. A. Buhr, M. Karsten, and J. Shih. KDB: A Multi-threaded Debugger for Multi-threaded Applications. In *Proc. SPDT'96: SIGMETRICS Symposium on Par. and Distrib. Tools*, pp. 80–89, Philadelphia, Pennsylvania, USA, May 1996. ACM Press.

5. J. Cargille and B. P. Miller. Binary Wrapping: A Technique for Instrumenting Object Code. *ACM SIGPLAN Notices*, 27(6):17–18, June 1992.
6. TotalView Multiprocess Debugger. WWW-Site of Etnus Inc., Framingham, MA, USA, 1999. http://www.etnus.com/products/totalview/index.html.
7. M. Ji, E. W. Felten, and K. Li. Performance Measurements for Multithreaded Programs. In *Measurement and Modeling of Computer Systems*, pp. 161–170, 1998.
8. P. B. Kessler. Fast Breakpoints. Design and Implementation. *ACM SIGPLAN Notices*, 25(6):78–84, June 1990.
9. Portable Operating System Interface: The Pthreads standard (POSIX 1003.1c).
10. Ludwig, T., Wismüller, R., Sunderam, V., and Bode, A. OMIS – On-line Monitoring Interface Specification (Version 2.0). Shaker Verlag, Aachen, vol. 9, LRR-TUM Research Report Series, 1997. http://wwwbode.in.tum.de/~omis
11. J. B. Rosenberg. *How Debuggers Work: Algorithms, Data Structures, and Architecture*. John Wiley & Sons, 1996.
12. Z. Xu, B. Miller, O. Naim. Dynamic Instrumentation of Threaded Applications. In: Proc. *7th ACM SIGPLAN Symposium on Principles and Practice of Parallel Programming*. Atlanta, Georgia, May 4-6, 1999.

MPI Farm Programs on Non-dedicated Clusters

Nuno Fonseca[1] and João Gabriel Silva[2]

[1] CISUC - Polytechnic Institute of Leiria, Portugal
nfonseca@estg.ipleiria.pt
[2] CISUC - University of Coimbra, Portugal
jgabriel@dei.uc.pt

Abstract. MPI has been extremely successful. In areas like e.g. particle physics most of the available parallel programs are based on MPI. Unfortunately, they must be run in dedicated clusters or parallel machines, being unable to use for long running applications the growing pool of idle time of general-purpose desktop computers. Additionally, MPI offers a quite low level interface, which is hard to use for most scientist programmers. In the research described in this paper, we tried to see how far we could go to solve those two problems, keeping the portability of MPI programs, but drawing upon one restriction - only programs following the FARM paradigm were to be supported. The developed library - MpiFL - did provide us significant insight. It is now being successfully used at the physics department of the University of Coimbra, despite some shortcomings.

1 Introduction[1]

MPI has made possible a very important development among scientists: parallel program portability. Up to not many years ago, parallel number crunching programs in areas like e.g. particle physics were made for particular combinations of operating systems and communication libraries, severely hindering their widespread use. With MPI, things changed. An MPI program made for a very expensive massively parallel machine also runs on a cheap cluster made of PCs. Other middleware communication packages had the same potential, but none managed to become a de facto standard like MPI did.

Unfortunately, MPI does not tolerate node failures. If a single machine in a cluster fails, the whole computation is lost. Non-dedicated clusters, built by bringing together the idle time of workstations with other uses, are out-of-reach of MPI programs, since in those ad-hoc clusters nodes become unavailable quite often. The reason can be a network cable that is plugged out, or a computer

---

[1] The authors would like to thank Hernani Pedroso and João Brito (Critical Software); Paulo Marques and Fernando Nogueira (University of Coimbra); Nelson Marques and Patrício Domingues (Polytechnic Institute of Leiria) for their help. This work was partially supported by the Portuguese Ministry of Science and Technology and by the European Union, under R&D Unit 326/94 (CISUC), projects POSI/EEI/1625/95 (PARQUANTUM) and POSI/CHS/34832/99 (FT-MPI).

switched off, or simply because the owner of a node launches a task that uses up all available CPU time. Even in dedicated clusters failures do happen, although much less frequently, forcing many programmers to resort to "hand-made" checkpointing, regularly saving intermediate data, and manually restarting application from that data when the computation crashes. There are essentially two approaches to deal with this problem.

One is to use a different middleware altogether, capable of tolerating failures and cycle stealing. The best example is probably the Condor system [16], which can handle non-dedicated clusters in a very efficient way. Still, Condor has a different API, and quite different execution model, from MPI. Switching to Condor means losing the main advantage of MPI: program portability. While Condor is becoming popular in clusters, it has little expression in dedicated parallel machines. If Condor usage becomes more widespread, it may be able to offer similar portability to MPI, but it is hard to say whether that will happen. It is true that Condor is capable of running MPI programs, but to do so fault-tolerance is lost. MPI and non-dedicated clusters are thus not brought together by Condor.

The other solution is to change MPI to make it fault tolerant. There have been several attempts for doing that, like Co-check [15], Startfish [1], MPI-FT [8], FT-MPI [5] and MPI/FT [2]. Some of these systems provide transparent fault-tolerance and run unmodified programs, others require changes to user programs, with some (like e.g. Startfish) supporting both mechanisms. The underlying tradeoff is that there is a bigger performance penalty for transparent checkpointing, and implementation is significantly more complex. Still, none of these systems are readily available, and most did not go beyond the state of limited prototypes. This is anyhow a promising approach, but a complex one, that will still take some time before becoming mainstream.

Without denying the merits of any of these approaches, we decided to explore a different route. In order to keep full portability, we tried to build a layer above MPI that could run over any unmodified MPI implementation, but would support non-dedicated clusters by offering fault-tolerance.

As a secondary goal, we wanted to offer a higher-level API, better adapted to the type of problems scientists were facing, e.g. at the Physics department of the University of Coimbra. After analyzing their programs were concluded that all of them were already implemented in the farm paradigm (also known as master/worker), or could be easily changed to fit that paradigm. In the farm paradigm there is one master node that distributes subtasks to the other nodes (known as workers or slaves). The slaves do not communicate among themselves, only with the master, which collects the slave outputs and from them computes the collective result of the computation (for a discussion of the main paradigms of parallel programs see [14]).

The farm paradigm is very interesting for fault-tolerance purposes because, since everything goes through the master, that node becomes an obvious place to do checkpointing. Since non-dedicated clusters are generally heterogeneous, load balancing is also required; otherwise the slowest node would limit the whole computation. Fortunately, in the farm paradigm this balancing is obtained almost for free: faster nodes will finish their jobs first, and request more jobs from the master, thus getting a bigger share of the job pool than slower nodes, which will get less jobs to perform. This works well as long as the number of jobs to distribute is significantly above the number of available nodes.

The library we built was thus called MpiFL (MPI-Farm Library).

Any library so devised necessarily has a drawback, similar to what was pointed before to Condor - it has a different API than MPI. This is the price to pay to provide the user a higher level API. But, contrary to Condor, we have the potential not to lose the main advantage of MPI - portability. If, of course, we are able to build such a library to run over any MPI implementation, from big machines to small clusters.

The idea to build such libraries is not new. Among them is MW, built over Condor [6]; we have developed in the past something similar for the Helios OS [11]; and in the Edinburgh Parallel Computing Centre a number of such libraries was also developed some years ago over MPI, but with no fault tolerance [3]. The *algorithmic skeleton* community has also started to work on libraries for MPI, which promise some level of standardization of the particular skeletons used, and allow the programmer to go on using their familiar environments, like C++ and MPI [7], but do not address the complex issues of faults, errors and failures.

In spite of several other variations reported in the literature, we could not find any other farm library over MPI that had been built with our set of requirements in mind: high portability over MPI implementations, support for non-dedicated clusters (i.e. fault-tolerance) and an high-level, easy to use API. These are the goals of MpiFL.

The paper is structured as follows. After this introduction, section 2 discusses how far fault-tolerance can be obtained under the chosen constraints. Section 3 then discusses the interface the library offers to programmers. Section 4 describes the internals of the library and some results of its usage. Section 5 closes the paper, presenting some conclusions and future research directions.

2 Fault-Tolerance over MPI

Loss of Nodes. In both version 1 and 2 of the MPI standard [9][10], fault tolerance is specified only for the communication channels, which are guaranteed to be reliable, but not for process faults. If a process or machine fails the default behavior is for all other nodes participating in the computation to abort. The user may change this by providing error handlers, but the system may not even be able to call them, and even if it does they are useful only for diagnostic purposes, as only sometimes (implementation dependant) will it be possible to continue the computation after the execution of the error handler, as the standard does not specify the state of a computation after an error occurs.

In a master worker configuration we would like to be able to continue using the remaining workers if one of them fails. Although the standard does not guarantee that, a particular implementation may sometimes make it possible to just ignore the failed processor and go on using the others, depending on the type of fault. We can benefit from that possibility whenever it is available, through what we call "lazy fault-recovery": the default behavior of aborting everything when a single process is lost is switched off by defining new error handlers and, as long as most of the worker nodes still make progress, the computation is kept alive. When it is judged that the price of a global restart of the application is outweighed by the benefit of adding to the virtual machine the nodes that in the meantime became available (possibly including some or all of the failed workers, if the problem that led them to stop was transient) the computation should be stopped and relaunched with the full set of available machines. With this approach we manage to use up as much capacity to work in a degraded mode as each MPI implementation provides.

"Lazy fault-recovery" is made possible because of another feature of MpiFL, which is also useful for load balancing. Even in the absence of faults, since in non-dedicated clusters nodes can have quite different processing capabilities, when the list of tasks to be distributed to the workers is exhausted, MpiFL distributes to the idle workers the jobs that have already been distributed to some worker but whose result is not yet available. In this way, a fast node may finish a job faster than the slow node it was originally distributed to. This also works when a task is assigned to a node that fails - since that node will not return a result, the task will eventually be sent to a different worker, and the application reaches completion.

Please note that the notion of "failed node" includes the case when the rightful owner of a machine starts using it heavily and stalls the process running on behalf of MPI, which runs with low priority. A slow node is thus equivalent to a failed node. If later the slow node still produces the result of its assigned job, it will simply be ignored. There is one drawback to this scheme - we are not able to stop a worker that is processing a job whose result we already know is not needed. The only way to do that is abort the whole computation and restart it. MpiFL gives the user the possibility of specifying this behavior.

System Monitoring. As should result clear from the previous section, MPI has no mechanism no determine when a node fails, or when a new one becomes available. An external monitoring service is needed. This service is operating system (OS) specific, and so is not portable across different MPI implementations running on different OSs, constituting the biggest limitation to a full MpiFL portability. Even if such a monitor could be based only on MPI calls, we would need to have it separate from the main computation, so that the monitor could survive when the MPI computation aborts, not only to be able to signal that a particular MPI process died, but also to be able to relaunch an MPI application that aborted because a remote machine died.

The type of diagnostic made by this monitor must be more fine-grained than just the usual detection of machine crashes - even if a machine is up, it has to detect whether all the requirements for an MPI process to run are satisfied, and also whether the machine has sufficient idle time to be able to constructively participate in a computation.

In the current version of MpiFL, the loss of the monitor in the master machine is the sole case that requires manual intervention to restart the MPI computation. A mechanism to do this automatically is not difficult to build, and may be included in a future version.

Recovery and Restart. To recover a computation after a crash we use periodic checkpoints, which are written to disk by the master (optionally to several disks in different machines, to make the system tolerant to crashes of the master machine). The content of the checkpoints is basically the results of the already executed tasks, which makes it easy to migrate the checkpoints, even across different architectures and OSs.

Since there are still very few implementation of the MPI-2 standard, we decided to base MpiFL on MPI version 1.1 [9]. On MPI-2 we could add dynamically new processes, but on MPI 1.1 a restart is needed to add new machines, which results in some wasted processing. When a restart is needed because of a computation crash, we obviously seize the opportunity to include all available nodes. Otherwise the monitor has to force an abort to include new machines, a decision that is only taken when the estimate of the time to complete the application with the new machines is clearly lower than without them, even taking into account the cost of the abort and the restart.

3 High-Level Interface for Farm Programs

The programmer only has to provide the master, that produces the jobs for the workers and collects the results, the workers that process the jobs (see Fig. 1), and the configuration file, that indicates where the master, workers and checkpoints should be. The library does everything else.

When the MPI computation crashes, the monitor restarts it. The master executes from the beginning, and at the call to *MpiFL_MasterInit* the library reads the checkpoint contents. The master then proceeds to generate the jobs again, but the library will recognize those that have already been processed before and replays their results to the master without calling any worker. Only those that had not been processed before will be forwarded to the workers. The master redoes all its processing after each restart, which can be inconvenient; but to do otherwise, we would have to ask the user to do additional calls to the library to set checkpoints, or do transparent checkpoints and lose portability [12][13]. We chose portability and the simpler interface.

With this model, the programmer must assure that in the case of a restart, the master deterministically recreates identical jobs. If it has non-deterministic code, it will have to execute that code only once, using the *MpiFL_FirstStart* function (see Fig. 1). Since the *MpiFL_FirstStart* function only returns *true* in the first execution of the program, the code inside the *if* will only be executed once. The variables that store the outcome of that non-deterministic code (a and b in the example of Fig. 1), are saved by the call to *MpiFL_Restart* in the first execution, and restored in executions that result from a restart caused by a failure.

Master	Slave
| ```
#include <mpifl.h>
main() {
int a,b;
MpiFL_MasterInit();

// Handle Non-deterministic
//   code here (optional)
if (MpiFL_FirstStart()) {
    scanf("%d",&a);
    b=rand(); }
MpiFL_Restart (&a, sizeof(a));
MpiFL_Restart (&b, sizeof(b));

//deterministic code
// Produce jobs
for ()
    MpiFL_SendJob(..);
// Consume
for ()
    MpiFL_GetResults(..);
...
MpiFL_MasterClose();
}
``` | ```
#include <mpifl.h>
main() {

MpiFL_SlaveInit();


while
 (MpiFL_GetJob()>0){
    //Process
    ...
    MpiFL_SendResults()
}
MpiFL_SlaveClose();
}
``` |

Fig. 1. Templates for master and slave. Other more complex variations are also possible, like generating new jobs based on the results of the previous ones.

4 MpiFL Library

The internal structure of MpiFL is presented in Fig. 2. All communication is done through MPI, except between the master and the monitor, that use pipes, although they could use TCP sockets. The checkpoints can be replicated in several machines to ensure their survivability.

We have made two implementations of MpiFL, one for Windows (using WMPI from Critical Software - http://www.criticalsoftware.com/HPC/), and one for Linux (using MPICH - http://www-unix.mcs.anl.gov/mpi/mpich/). Both versions of the library support C, C++ and Fortran90.

We have subject both versions of MpiFL to many faults, like the abrupt killing of MpiFL process, many kinds of communication problems (removal of network cables, disabling of NIC's, stopping networking services, etc.), machine problems (reboots, stopping MPI services, etc), checkpoint problems (inconsistent checkpoint files, removal of checkpoint files, etc), and the library recovered always, except when the monitor in the master machine was affected.

The library was also tested for two weeks in a non-dedicated cluster composed of 30 machines in computer rooms used by computer engineering students, a particularly hostile environment (only the master machine was in a restricted access lab), and it was never down, in spite of the frequent node losses and additions.

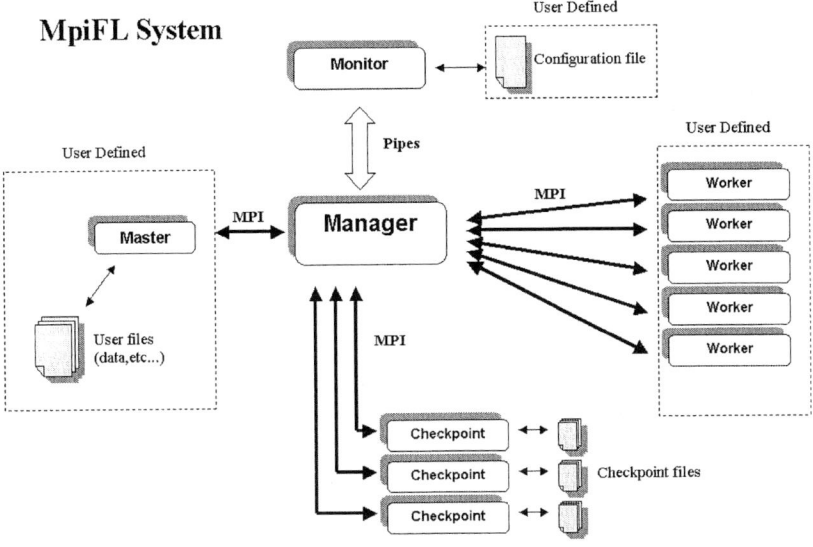

Fig. 2. MpiFL.

To judge the performance penalty the library might represent, many test were made with a travelling salesman optimization problem, with different mixes of machines and granularity of tasks, and the overhead introduced by the library was always negligible (below 1%). The experience of usage in real problems in the Physics department points in the same direction, although measurements were not done systematically there. Generically, with different programs the performance overhead can become relevant, being determined essentially by the amount of data that has to be saved to disk, as is well known for a long time [4].

5 Conclusions and Future Work

The main conclusion of this research is indeed the strong need for a clean failure semantics in MPI. The parallel machines that were dominant when MPI was first devised have now been largely replaced by clusters that have high failure rates that must be dealt with. In the case of non-dedicated clusters because these are inherently unstable environments; in the case of dedicated clusters because of the rapidly growing number of machines. If MPI is not able to solve this problem, it will probably soon lose the dominant position it now has as the preferred execution environment for parallel programs.

In spite of this shortcoming of MPI, we have shown that very useful levels of fault-tolerance can be achieved without significantly compromising portability, while at the same time offering the average scientist programmer a much easier programming model for the farm paradigm.

For the MpiFL library we are considering three enhancements: a fully automatic restart also for the case of loss of the monitor in the master machine; using the dynamic process creation capability of MPI 2.0 to add new nodes without having to restart the whole computation; and perfecting the "lazy fault recovery" mechanism to better use all capability that each particular MPI implementation may have to go on working with lost nodes.

References

1. Agbaria, A., Friedman, R.: Starfish: Fault-Tolerant Dynamic MPI Programs on Clusters of Workstations. 8th IEEE International Symposium on High Performance Distributed Computing (Aug 1999) 167–176
2. Batchu, R., Neelamegam, J.P., Cui, Z., Beddhu, M., Skjellum, A., Dandass, Y., Apte, M.: MPI/FT(tm): Architecture and Taxonomies for Fault-Tolerant, Message-Passing Middleware for Performance-Portable Parallel Computing. 3th International Workshop on Software Distributed Shared Memory (WSDSM'01), May 16 18, Brisbane, Australia (2001)
3. Chapple, S., Clarke, L.: PUL: The Parallel Utilities Library. Procedings of the IEEE Second Scalabe Parallel Libraries Conference, Mississipi, USA, 12-14 Oct (1994), IEEE Computer Society Press, ISBN 0-8186-6895-4
4. Elnozahy, E.N., Johnson, D.B., Zwaenepoel, W.: The Performance of Consistent Checkpointing. Proc. 11th Symposium on Reliable Distributed Systems, IEEE Computer Society Press (1992) 39–47
5. Fag, E.G., Dongarra, J.J.: FT-MPI: Fault Tolerant MPI, supporting dynamic applications in a dynamic world. EuroPVM/MPI, User's Group Meeting 2000, Springer-Verlag, Hungary (Sep. 2000) 346–353
6. Goux, J.-P., Kulkarni, S., Linderoth, J.T., Yoder, M.E.: Master-Worker: An Enabling Framework for Applications on the Computational Grid. Cluster Computing 4 (2001) 63–70
7. Kuchen, H.: A Skeleton Library. Procedings of Euro-Par 2002, LNCS, Springer-Verlag (2002)
8. Louca S., Neophytou N., Lachanas, A., Evripidou, P.: MPI-FT: Portable Fault Tolerance Scheme for Mpi. Parallel Processing Letters, Vol. 10, No. 4 (2000) 371–382
9. MPI: A Message Passing Interface Standard. Version 1.1, Message Passing Interface Forum (June 12 1995). http:\\www.mpi-forum.com
10. MPI-2: Extensions to the Message-Passing Interface Standard. Message Passing Interface Forum (July 18 1997). http:\\www.mpi-forum.com
11. Silva, L.M., Veer B., Silva, J.G.: How to Get a Fault Tolerant Farm. Transputer Applications and Systems' 93, R. Grebe, J. Hektor, S.C. Hilton, M.R. Jane, P.H. Welch (eds.), Vol. 36 in the series Transputer and Occam Engineering, IOS Press, Amsterdam, Vol. 2, ISBN 90-5199-140-1 (1993) 923–938
12. Silva, L.M., Silva, J.G., Chapple, S., Clarke, L.:Portable Checkpointing and Recovery. 4th IEEE International Symposium on High Performance Distributed Computing (HPDC-4), Pentagon City, Virginia, USA, August 2-4, IEEE Computer Society Press, ISBN 0-8186-7088-6 (1995) 188–195

13. Silva, L.M., Silva, J.G.: System-Level versus User-Defined Checkpointing. 17th IEEE Symposium on Reliable Distributed Systems, October 20-23, West Lafayette, USA, IEEE Computer Society, ISBN 0-8186-9218-9 (1998) 68–74
14. Silva, L.M., Buyya, R.: Parallel Programming Models and Paradigms. High Performance Cluster Computing: Archtectures and Systems: Vol. 2, R. Buyya (ed.), Prentice Hall PTR, NJ, USA (1999)
15. Stellner, G.: CoCheck: Checkpointing and Process Migration for MPI. Procedings of the International Parallel Processing Symposium, Honolulu, HI, IEEE Computer Society Press (April 1996) 526–531
16. Tannenbaum, T., Wright, D., Miller, K., Livny, M.: Condor: A Distributed Jub Scheduler. Beowulf Cluster Computing with Linux, Thomas Sterling editor, The MIT Press, ISBN 0-262-69274-0 (2002)

Application Composition in Ensemble Using Intercommunicators and Process Topologies

Yiannis Cotronis

Dept. of Informatics and Telecommunications, Univ. of Athens, 15784 Athens, Greece
cotronis@di.uoa.gr

Abstract. Ensemble has been proposed as an enabling technology, for composing different MPI application configurations maintaining a single code for each of the components involved, possibly maintained by different teams. Ensemble enables a) the design and implementation of MPI components, b) the specification of symbolic application composition directives and c) the composition of MPI applications. Composed MP applications are pure MPI programs and do not use any external environment for process communication. In this paper we describe application composition using intercommunicators and process topologies. We demonstrate on a climate model configuration.

1 Introduction

Significant progress has been made in developing models, which solve computationally complex problems. Typical examples are environment related models: for weather prediction (e.g. atmosphere, ocean, land), for pollution (e.g. air, sea) and natural disasters or crises (e.g. forest fire propagation, flooding). As these models require critical time responses their code has been parallelised to run on parallel machines, clusters and lately grids [3]. The most successful parallel model is Message Passing (MP) and MPI [6] has become its de-facto implementation standard; it seems that it will also be the standard for grid enabled parallel applications.

Each model requires an initial set of data, which are of two types: internal or boundary. Internal data is manipulated by the model itself, simulating some natural quantity, whereas Boundary data is not modified by the model. Usually, the Internal data of one model is the Boundary of another. The models and their codes are being improved and maintained by different research teams. Due to their complexity and their multi-disciplinary nature of the models their implementation codes are designed to run stand alone, using boundary data, which remains the same throughout the run. Nevertheless, models require the synergy with other models by updating their initial boundary data with the latest values computed internally by another model. This synergy does not only improve the accuracy of the results of the models involved, but also extends their modelling possibilities. For example, the atmospheric, hydrological and hydraulic models may run in synergy to forecast floods and give early warnings. Application synergy is presently achieved by code coupling, which has a number of drawbacks:

- Code coupling produces rigid coupled codes.
- Code modifications and maintenance require significant effort.

- Code coupling requires cooperation of teams, sometimes reluctant to share codes.
- The almost continuous evolution of models and codes makes coupling a moving target and single code maintenance of individual applications a difficult task.

We have proposed the Ensemble methodology [1,2] in which MPI components are developed separately and applications are composed into different configurations, maintaining a single code for each component. Ensemble enables the composition of genuine MPMD applications, where P indicates *"Source Programs"* and not *"Program Execution Behaviors"*. Ensemble is particularly appropriate for composing MPI applications on grids, where individual components are developed and maintained by different teams. Applications may be composed in various configurations (SPMD, MPMD, regular, irregular) specified symbolically in a high-level composition language. Composed programs though, are pure MPI programs running directly on MPICH [4] or MPICH-G2 [5]. In the past we have presented Ensemble supporting process groups in intracommunicators and their (point-to-point [2] and collective [1]) communication. In this paper we present process groups in intercommunicators and topologies.

The structure of the paper is as follows: In section 2, we present the composition principles. In section 3, we outline the structure of three MPI components (atmospheric, ocean and land models), which we use in section 4 to compose a climate model configuration. In section 5 we present our conclusions.

2 The Composition Principles

If processes are to be coupled together in various configurations they should not have any specific envelope data (which implicitly determine topologies) built into their code, but rather be provided individually to each process dynamically. In Ensemble components all envelope data of MPI calls (i.e., communicators, ranks, message tags and roots) are specified as "formal communication parameters" and "actual communication parameters" are passed dynamically to each process in its command line arguments (CLA).

Let us first show the feasibility of the approach. Envelope data in MPI calls are bound to three types: communicators, ranks (roots are ranks) and message tags. The first two cannot be passed directly in CLA: the communicator, because it is not a basic type and the rank, although an integer, because it is not known before process spawning. We overcome the problems by constructing communicators and indirectly determining ranks. We associate with each process a unique integer, namely the Unique Ensemble Rank (UER). We use UERs in CLA to specify "actual communication parameters" for point-to-point and reduction (roots) operations. Processes determine ranks from UERs (e.g. in a communication call a UER has to be interpreted as the rank of the process associated with it). To this end, a communicator `Ensemble_Comm_World` is constructed by "splitting" all processes in `MPI_COMM_WORLD` with a common color using as key their unique UERs. The new communicator reorders processes, with MPI ranks equal to UERs. For constructing other communicators we pass an integer indicating a color and construct the required communicator by splitting `Ensemble_Comm_World`. To find the rank of a process associated with a UER in a constructed communicator we use `MPI_Group_translate_ranks` and its rank (=UER) in `Ensemble_Comm_World`.

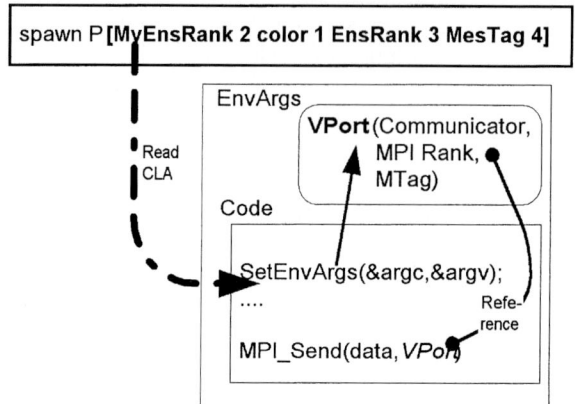

Fig. 1. The low level composition principles

For developing components and composing programs we need to specify four inter-depended entities, as depicted in figure 1. The structure of CLAs, which specify the actual communication and effectively the composition directives for each process. A routine, say `SetEnvArgs`, which parses and interprets CLAs, and produces MPI envelope data. A data structure, say `EnvArgs`, for storing the produced MPI envelope data. Finally, the usage of elements of `EnvArgs` in MPI calls.

2.1 The Structure EnvArgs and MPI Envelope Bindings

Envelope data in `EnvArgs` is organized in MPI contexts. For point-to-point communication ports are introduced, which are abstractions of the envelope pair (rank, message tag). Ports with similar usage form arrays of ports (MultiPorts).

```
Context EnvArgs[NrContexts];/*Context Arguments */
typedef struct    /* Envelope in a context*/
{ MPI_Comm IntraComm; /* the intracommunicator */
  MultiPortType MultiPorts[NrMultiPorts];
}Context;
```

Communicating processes are in the same communicator, whether intra or inter. Each multiport may specify a separate inter or topology communicator. As point-to-point communication is performed by the same send/receive routines irrespective of the type of communicator, envelope data in all point-to-point calls refers to ports. The type of the actual communicator (intra, inter or topology) would be specified in the CLA and set by `SetEnvArgs` together with all other data port consistent with their semantics (e.g. if inter then rank will indicate the rank of a process in the remote intracommunicator).

```
typedef struct    /* A MultiPort*/
{ MPI_Comm Comm; /* intra, inter or topology */
  PortType Ports[NrPorts];
}MultiPortType;
```

```
typedef struct      /* A single Port */
{ int Rank;         /* Rank of Communicating Process */
  int MessageTag;   /* Message Tag */
}PortType;
```

As the focus of this paper is intercommunicators and process topologies, we do not present other aspects of `EnvArgs` such as collective communications (for this refer to [1,2]). We may use elements of `EnvArgs` in MPI calls directly, as for example in

```
MPI_Send(Data, count, type,
         EnvArgs[2].Multiports[3].Ports[1].Rank
         EnvArgs[2].Multiports[3].Ports[1].MessageTag,
         EnvArgs[2].Multiports[3].Comm);
```

However, for convenience we have defined virtual envelope names for communicators and multiports and instead of using envelope data directly, we use macros, which refer to virtual envelope names. We present virtual envelopes and the use of macros in section 3.

2.2 The CLA Structure and SetEnvArgs

The CLAs for each process are used to construct envelope data, being effectively the composition directives, relevant to each process. The structure of CLA is:

- UER
- Number of splits of `MPI_COMM_WOLRD`. For each split:
  - Its color. If color >= 0 (process belongs in the intracommunicator):
    - Ctxindex (an index of array `EnvArgs`)
    - The number of multiports in intra; for each multiport:
      - Its MPindex and number of ports; for each port: UER and Msg Tag
    - The number of Topologies constructed from intra; for each topology
      - Orderkey; Cartesian or graph
      - If Cartesian: ndims, dims array, period array
      - If Graph: nnodes, index array, edges array
      - The number of multiports in topology; for each multiport:
        - Its MPindex and Number of ports; for each port: UER and Msg Tag
    - The number of InterCommunicators using intra as local; for each intercomm
      - UER of local and remote leaders; MsgTag
      - The number of multiports in intercommunicator; for each multiport:
        - Its MPindex and Number of ports; for each port: UER and Msg Tag

The call of `SetEnvArgs` follows `MPI_Init` and its actions are directed by CLAs. It first reads UER and the number of splits of `MPI_COMM_WORLD` and enters a split loop. For each split it reads its color and constructs a new communicator (if negative no communicator is constructed). It reads its index in `EnvArgs` (Ctxindex). The first split (usually Ctxindex=0) must be for `Ensemble_Comm_World` reordering ranks (all processes use a common color). The new communicator is stored in `EnvArgs[Ctxindex].IntraComm`.

It then reads the number of multiports in the constructed intracommunicator and enters a multiport loop. For each multiport it reads its index in the context (MPindex), sets `MultiPorts[MPindex].Comm` to `IntraComm` and reads the number of ports; enters a port loop. For each port it reads UER and MsgTag; translates UER to MPI rank and stores rank and MsgTag.

It then reads the number of topologies to be constructed from `IntraComm` (superposition of topologies is supported) and enters a topology loop. For each topology a temporary communicator is constructed, reordering processes in `IntraComm` according to the orderkey given in the CLAs (the orderkey should be consistent with row major numbering in cartesian topologies and the index and edges arrays for graph topologies). From this temporary communicator cartesian or graph topology communicators are constructed by passing appropriate arguments. For Cartesian: ndims, dims array and period array; reorder=false as we would like to maintain orderkey ordering. For graph: nnodes, index array, edges array; again reorder=false. It then reads the number of multiports using the topology; it then enters a multiport loop, as in the case of the intracommunicator.

It reads the number of intercommunicators, which use `IntraComm` as the local communicator. It reads and interprets the UERs of the local and remote leaders, reads MsgTag and constructs the intercommunicator, using `Ensemble_Comm_World` as the bridge communicator. It then reads the number of multiports using this intercommunicator and enters a multiport loop, as in the case of intracommunicators.

The CLAs are tedious to construct and error prone and they cannot be parameterized. For this purpose, we are developing a symbolic and parametric high-level composition language, from which low-level CLA composition directives are generated; the language is outlined by example in section 4.

3 The Component Structure

In the previous section we presented the low level composition principles related to point-to-point communication in intra, inter and topology communicators. We will demonstrate these principles on an example application inspired from the climate model involving Atmospheric, Ocean and Land models. In this section, we outline the three components and in the next section we compose the climate model.

Atm processes communicate within the model with atm neighbors in a two-dimensional mesh, exchanging halo rows and columns of data internal to the atmospheric model. In the virtual envelope of the Atm component (table 1) we specify context `Internal`, having multiports N, S, E, W, within which all such communication is performed. Atm processes may also communicate with other processes (e.g. ocean or land) in the vertical boundary. For this, we specify context `VerticalBoundary` having only multiport `Down`. For simplicity, we have specified at most one port, indicating a one-to-one correspondence of atm and surface processes. The code structure of Atm component is just sketched; the two MPI_Send calls show the use of macros (boxed italics) in the envelope data (cf. section 2.1).

Ocean component requires three contexts. One for communicating halo data internal to the model (`Internal`), a second for communicating surface boundary data to land processes (`SurfaceBoundary`) and a third for communicating vertical boundary data to atm processes (VerticalBoundary). The first two have N, S, E, W and respectively BN, BS, BE, BW multiports. The third has just one multiport Up.

Table 1. The Virtual Envelope and PseudoCode of Atm

```
Context Internal;
    Ports N[0..1], S[0..1], E[0..1], W[0..1];
Context VerticalBoundary;
    Ports Down[0..1];
repeat
  Model Computations
  Communication in context Internal
      MPI_Send(HaloDA,HN,HTA,ENVport(N,1,Internal));
  Communication in context VerticalBoundary
      MPI_Send(VD,VN,VT,ENVport(Down,1,VerticalBoundary));
until termination;
```

Table 2. The Virtual Envelope and PseudoCode of Ocean

```
Context Internal;
    Ports N[0..1], S[0..1], E[0..1], W[0..1];
Context SurfaceBoundary;
    Ports BN[0..1], BS[0..1], BE[0..1], BW[0..1];
Context VerticalBoundary;
    Ports Up[0..1];
repeat
  Model Computations
  Communication in context Internal
      MPI_Send(HD,HN,HTO,ENVport(N,1,Internal));
  Communication in context SurfaceBoundary
      MPI_Send(SBD,SBN,SBT,ENVport(BN,1,SurfaceBoundary));
  Communication in context VerticalBoundary
      MPI_Send(VD,V,VT,ENVport(Up,1,VerticalBoundary));
until termination
```

The virtual envelope and code structure of Land component is similar to Ocean.

Table 3. The Virtual Envelope of Land

```
Context Internal;
    Ports N[0..1], S[0..1], E[0..1], W[0..1];
Context SurfaceBoundary;
    Ports N[0..1], S[0..1], E[0..1], W[0..1];
Context VerticalBoundary;
    Ports Up[0..1];
```

4 The High Level Composition

The composition of applications is specified in three levels each representing an abstraction of application composition. The top level is the Reconfigurable High Level Composition (RHLC) in which symbolic names for processes are used as component instances. The number of processes is parametrically specified and they are grouped into symbolic communicators (intra, inter and topology). In each communicator point-to-point communication channels between process ports are defined. RHLC specifies reconfigurable applications, in two aspects: a) different configurations may be obtained, depending on the values and the generality of parameters, and b) they are independent of any execution environment resources (machines, files, etc). By setting values to parameters and specifying execution resources of RHLC we obtain the Configured High Level Composition (CHLC). The actual configuration decisions are outside the scope of Ensemble. From CHLC the Low Level Composition (LLC) directives (cf. section 2.2) are generated.

We demonstrate the RHLC of a climate application, composing the three models (fig. 2). Atm processes form a cartesian topology (AtmPlane) exchanging data internal to the model. Ocean and Land (depicted as grey) processes together also form a Cartesian topology (SurfacePlane). Here however, there are two kinds of communications: internal to each model (ocean to ocean and land to land) or boundary (ocean to land). Finally, there is a vertical exchange of data, between the two planes, for which we will use an intercommunicator. Node that in the components' code there is no indication of the communicator type used in the point-to-point communication. This is considered a design decision for the RHLC.

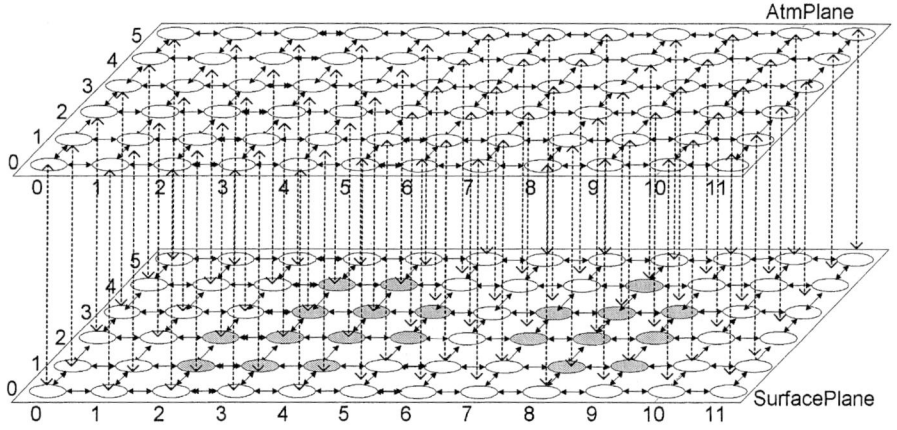

Fig. 2. A Composition of Three Simulation Models

In the Parameter section of RHLC (table 4), integer identifiers are declared, which parameterize the design: AtmRows, AtmCols and SurfRows, SurfCols respectively, determine the sizes of the two process meshes; elements of array OLmask determine the covering of SurfacePlane by Ocean (=0) or Land (=1).

Next all processes in Ensemble_Comm_World are specified as instances of components. All AtmP processes are instances of Atm; however SurfP processes are either instances of Ocean or Land determined by OLmask. Processes are then grouped into communicators (intra, inter, topology) and within each communicator its point-to-point communications are specified.

The first group is AtmPlane, in which AtmPs participate in their Internal context. They form a Cartesian geometry and the communication channels are explicitly specified by channel-patterns. A basic channel-pattern is a guarded point-to-point pattern: Guard:Proc.Context.Port<->Proc.Context.Port. Only point-to-point patterns with guards=true are valid. Proc indicates the symbolic name of a process, Context is the virtual context within which communication takes place and Port is a communication port. The symbol ^ indicates the default context in the group. A channel-pattern may also be a for-structure controlling channel-patterns #index:from(step)to[{channel-pattern[expr]}+]. **Cartesian on** N, S, E, W indicates a Cartesian topology and the multiports using it.

Table 4. A Reconfigurable High Level Composition of a Climate model

```
Parameter
  AtmRows, AtmCols, SurfRows, SurfCols;
  OLmask[SurfRows,SurfCols];
IntraComm Ensemble_Comm_World;
  processes AtmP(AtmRows,AtmCols) from component Atm;
  processes SurfP(SurfRows,SurfCols)from component
  {#i:0(1)SurfRows [#j:0(1)SurfCols
    [(OLmask[i,j]=0):Ocean; (OLmask[i,j]=1):Land]]};
IntraComm AtmPlane;
  processes AtmP(*,*)in Internal;
  cartesian on N, S, E, W;
  channels
  #i:0(1)AtmRows [#j:0(1)AtmCols [
    (i<AtmRows): AtmP(i,j).^S[1] <-> AtmP(i+1,j).^N[1];
    (j<AtmCols): AtmP(i,j).^E[1] <-> AtmP(i,j+1).^W[1]]]
IntraComm SurfaceInternal;
  processes SurfP(*,*) in Internal;
  cartesian on N ,S ,E , W;
  channels
  #i:0(1)SurfRows [#j:0(1)SurfCols [
    (i<SurfRows)&(OLmask[i,j]=OLmask[i+1,j]):
         SurfP(i,j).^S[1] <-> SurfP(i+1,j).^N[1];
    (j<SurfCols)&(OLmask[i,j]=OLmask[i,j+1]):
         SurfP(i,j).^E[1] <-> SurfP(i,j+1).^W[1];]]
IntraComm SurfaceOther;
  processes SurfP(*,*) in SurfaceBoundary;
  cartesian on BN, BS, BE, BW;
  channels
  #i:0(1)SurfRows [#j:0(1)SurfCols [
    (i<SurfRows)&(OLmask[i,j]!=OLmask[i+1,j]):
         SurfP(i,j).^BS[1] <-> SurfP(i+1,j).^BN[1];
    (j<SurfCols)&(OLmask[i,j]!=OLmask[i,j+1]):
         SurfP(i,j).^BE[1] <-> SurfP(i,j+1).^BW[1]]]
IntraComm SurfaceGroup;
  processes SurfP(*,*) in VerticalBoundary;
InterComm Coupling;
  Intra1 AtmPlane;        leader AtmP(0,0);
  Intra2 SurfaceGroup;    leader SurfP(0,0);
  channels
  #i:0(1)AtmRows [#j:0(1)AtmCols[
    AtmP(i,j).VerticalBoundary.Down[1] <->
    SurfP(i,j).VerticalBoundary.Up[1]]]
```

For SurfacePlane we specify two groups in Cartesian geometry: SurfaceInternal in the context of Internal and a SurfaceOther in SurfaceBoundary. The former connects ports within each model and the latter between models. We then construct `SurfaceGroup` of all surface processes and use it together with `AtmPlane` to construct the intercommunicator `Coupling` and specify the communication channels between `AtmP` and `SurfP` processes.

5 Conclusions

We presented application composition in Ensemble using intercommunicators and topologies, thus supporting all aspects of MPI application composition. The low-level composition aspects (CLA structure, SetEnvArgs, EnvArgs and macros) have been completed and the High Level Composition is under development.

Ensemble alleviates the drawbacks of code coupling. Ensemble also reduces effort for developing single components (code only involves data movement, reduction and synchronization). As components are neutral to the communicator type (intra, inter, topology) for point-to-point communication, a process spawned from a component may be in a topology or in an intercommunicator, as specified by the composition directives. Consequently, Ensemble may even offer some advantages in configuring dynamically SPMD applications.

Acknowledgment

Supported by Special Account for Research of Univ. of Athens.

References

1. Cotronis, J.Y, (2002) Modular MPI Components and the Composition of Grid Applications, Proc. PDP 2002, IEEE Press pp 154-161.
2. Cotronis, J.Y., Tsiatsoulis Z., Modular MPI and PVM components, PVM/MPI'02, LNCS 2474, pp. 252-259, Springer.
3. Foster, I. and Kesselman, C (eds.) The Grid, Blueprint for the New Computing Infrastructure, Morgan Kaufmann, 1999.
4. Gropp, W. and Lusk, E. Installation and user's guide for mpich, a portable implementation of MPI, ANL-01/x, Argone National Laboratory, 2001.
5. Karonis, N., Toonen B., Foster, I.: MPICH-G2: A Grid-Enabled Implementation of the Message Passing Interface, preprint ANL/MCS-P942-0402, April 2002 (to appear in JPDC).
6. Message Passing Interface Forum MPI: A Message Passing Interface Standard. International Journal of Supercomputer Applications, 8(3/4): 165-414, 1994.

Improving Properties of a Parallel Program in ParJava Environment*

Victor Ivannikov, Serguei Gaissaryan,
Arutyun Avetisyan, and Vartan Padaryan

Institute for System Programming Russian Academy of Sciences
25 B. Kommunisticheskaya st., Moscow, 109004, Russia
{ivan,ssg,arut,vartan}@ispras.ru

Abstract. ParJava integrated environment supporting development and maintenance of data parallel Java-programs is discussed. When a parallel program is developed it is necessary to assure not only its correctness, but also its efficiency and scalability. For this purpose it is useful to know some dynamic properties of the program. This information may help to modify the program in order to improve its parallel features. ParJava provides a collection of such tools. Symbolic execution allows to estimate expected execution time and limits of scalability of Java SPMD-program.

1 Introduction

In the present work the ParJava [1] integrated environment supporting the development and maintenance of data parallel Java-programs is discussed. There is a great deal of interest in using Java for parallel computations. The most part of SPMD-programs are implemented using MPI (C+MPI, Fortran+MPI). There are several implementations of MPI for Java.

When a parallel program is developed it is necessary to assure not only its correctness, but also its efficiency and scalability. Profiles and traces of the program indicate the order and the interference of its interprocess communications. A programming system supporting the development of parallel programs should provide several tools allowing to discover semantic properties of a program being developed. ParJava is such an integrated environment.

Section 2 is devoted to a brief description of ParJava. Section 3 presents ParJava tools that help to estimate scalability of a program and expected execution time as well as tools that visualize its stored history traces. In Section 4 we compare ParJava with the related systems. In Section 5 some conclusions are made.

2 Brief Description of ParJava Environment

ParJava supports development and improvement of the behavior of Java SPMD-programs. The parallel computing is mainly concerned with symmetric commu-

---
* This work is supported by RFBR, grants 02-01-00961, 02-07-90302

nications implemented in the MPI standard. In ParJava MPI is implemented using native MPI bindings similar to Java wrappers [2]. The main menu of ParJava GUI includes the following items: File, Edit, View, Search, Execute, Debug, Analyze, Transform, Visualize, Help. Menus File, Edit, View, Search support common facilities. Other menus provide access to specific ParJava tools.

The result of analyzes and symbolic execution allows to investigate parallel properties of SPMD-program during the stage of its development and estimate limits of its scalability. The details see in Section 3. Fig. 1 demonstrates the portability of ParJava program.

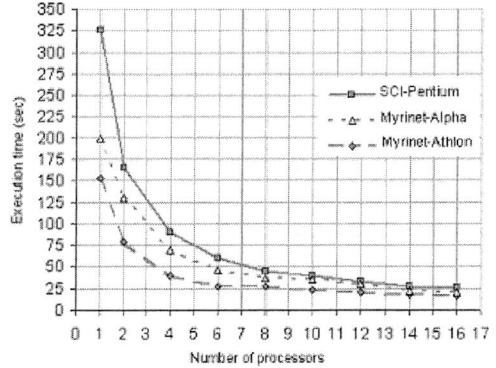

Fig. 1. The linear algebraic equation solution by Jacobi iteration process using all listed clusters.

The same sample program was executed using various clusters having different performances: SCI cluster (18 dual PIII) and two Myrinet clusters (16 dual Alpha and 16 dual Athlon XP).

3 ParJava Tools Supporting the Development of SPMD-Programs

To define frequency (or time) profile we use the notion of a step (execution of a basic block). The following types of blocks are considered: sequence of assignments, condition, function call, and communication function call. Frequency profile of a sequential program is defined as mapping associating each step of the program with the frequency of its execution. Each profile may be represented as a vector with dimension equal to number of program steps. The profile of the SPMD program is represented by matrix whose lines are profiles of the program's parts executed in parallel. To obtain frequency profiles of a program it should be insrumentated, i.e. calls of instrumental functions should be included in its basic blocks. Instrumental functions should not distort dependences between program's parts executed in parallel. Therefore compensation statements

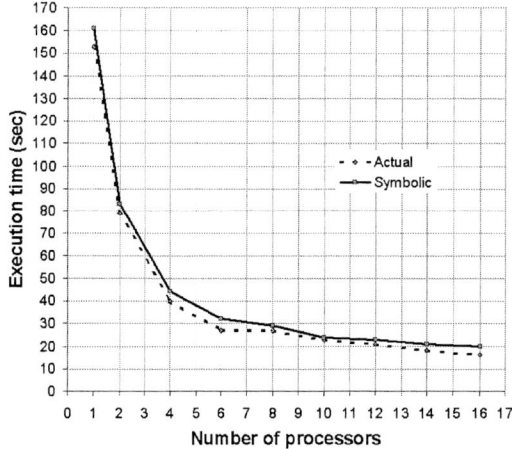

Fig. 2. Actual and symbolic execution of the sample program.

are added. Symbolic execution allows to estimate limits of scalability and hence expected execution time for the program during the stage of its development. The advantage of symbolic execution against actual execution is that the first one can be performed much faster.

There are defined several execution models of various precision. During the symbolic execution basic blocks that lie on the path defined by the specified input data, are interpreted: assignment statements are evaluated, transfer conditions are calculated to select the next basic block. The execution starts from the entry block and ends with the exit block. When the basic blocks containing calls to communication functions are executed the a priori information about the communication subsystem is used. This information allows us to determine the duration of transfer of n bytes from one node to another. Symbolic execution allows to estimate program execution time, as well as maximal number of nodes for which scalability is hold. Fig. 2 shows that such estimations may be precise enough.

A parallel program may be executed in the "Test mode", when instead of MPI library its instrumented copy is used. It allows to fix all communication function calls, as well as the execution time of each communication function. Parallel execution trace is represented as partially ordered set of events. User can visualize the stored history traces by means of the "Trace Visualization" item of the menu.

4 Related Works

Unlike Java extensions in the HPF style [3] that extend Java language with additional statements we avoid any additions to Java language to remain in the pure Java environment. All our extensions to Java are implemented as the Java class libraries.

All integrated environments (research and commercial) are connected with Fortran and C languages. We may mention such freeware environments as AIMS [4], commercial systems as Vampir [5] and others. All these systems employ post-mortem analysis of the program. They provide wide opportunities for trace viewing, gathering of parallel applications profiles and statistics. The analogic tools are realized in ParJava.

AIMS is most similar to ParJava. It provides the symbolic execution, but during the instrumenting in AIMS, unlike ParJava, the quantity and position optimization of instrumental function calls is not used. The interpreted program in AIMS contains three kinds of blocks: "cycle", "communication" and "sequence". In ParJava the program is presented by its control flow graph that supplies more adequate interpretation. Moreover, in ParJava some facilities of control of the symbolic execution are realized. It is also possible to gather the trace of the symbolically executed program, to monitor the states of the program parts executed in parallel and to determine the deadlock automatically.

5 Conclusion

ParJava allows to develop portable scalable SPMD Java-programs, providing the application programmer with tools that help him to improve his parallel Java-program. ParJava is on the stage of evolution. The new tools are being developed (the automatic program parallelizer, the relative debugger of SPMD-programs and others), the problem of performance growth of parallel Java programs is under investigation, the possibilities to apply Java during the preparation of programs for GRID are also studied.

References

1. A. Avetisyan, S. Gaissaryan, O. Samovarov. *Extension of Java Environment by Facilities Supporting Development of SPMD Java-programs.* //V. Malyshkin (Ed.): PaCT 2001, LNCS 2127, pp. 175 - 180.
2. S. Mintchev. *Writing Programs in JavaMPI.* //TR MAN-CSPE-02, Univ. of Westminster, UK, 1997.
3. H.K. Lee, B. Carpenter, G. Fox, and S. Boem Lim. *Benchmarking HPJava: Prospects for Performance.* // In 6th Workshop on Languages, Compilers and Run-time Systems for Scalable Computers, March 2002.
4. J. C. Yan and S. R. Sarukkai. *Analyzing Parallel Program Performance Using Normalized Performance Indices and Trace Transformation Techniques.* //Parallel Computing. V. 22, No. 9, November 1996. pp. 1215-1237
5. W. E. Nagel, A. Arnold, M. Weber, H.-C. Hoppe, and K. Solchenbach. *VAMPIR: Visualization and analysis of MPI resources.* //Supercomputer, 12(1): 69–80, January 1996.

Flow Pattern and Heat Transfer Rate in Three-Dimensional Rayleigh-Benard Convection

Tadashi Watanabe

Center for Promotion of Computational Science and Engineering,
Japan Atomic Energy Research Institute, Tokai-mura, Ibaraki-ken, 319-1195, Japan
watanabe@sugar.tokai.jaeri.go.jp

Abstract. The three-dimensional Rayleigh-Benard convection is simulated numerically using the lattice Boltzmann method. Parallel calculations are performed on a distributed shared-memory system. Flow patterns are observed in a rectangular box with an aspect ratio ranging from 2:2:1 to 6:6:1, and the heat transfer rate is estimated in terms of the Nusselt number. The dependency of the Nusselt number on the Rayleigh number is shown to agree well with that obtained by the two-dimensional calculations of the Navier-Stokes equations. It is found that several roll patterns are possible under the same condition and the heat transfer rate changes according to the flow pattern.

1 Introduction

The Rayleigh-Benard (RB) system, in which a fluid is contained between two horizontal parallel walls and the bottom wall is kept at a higher temperature than the top wall, is one of the most representative nonequilibrium hydrodynamic systems. In the RB system, a heat conduction state is established when the temperature difference between the top and bottom walls is smaller than a critical value, while convection rolls appear when the temperature difference exceeds the critical value. Convection in the RB system has been extensively studied experimentally and numerically, and reviewed by Ahlers [1], and Cross and Hohenberg [2]. Efforts to describe complex spatio-temporal convection patterns in the RB system were reviewed by Pesch [3].

The RB convection has been studied using particle simulation methods such as the molecular dynamics (MD) method in order to study the microscopic behavior of the macroscopic flow. The convection rolls were simulated using the MD method by Mareschal and Kestemont [4,5] and Rapaport [6]. Mareschal et al. [7], Puhl et al. [8], and Given and Clementi [9] compared the field variables in the convection rolls obtained by the MD method with the results by the hydrodynamic calculations. The chaotic motion of atoms in the transition between heat conduction and convection was studied using the MD method by Watanabe and Kaburaki [10]. Posch et al. studied the RB system using the smooth-particle applied mechanics (SPAM), which is a grid-free particle method for solving the partial differential equations of fluid or solid mechanics [11,12]. The good agreement between the smooth-particle and the Navier-Stokes results was obtained, and SPAM was shown to be an interesting bridge between continuum mechanics and molecular dynamics [13]. The convection rolls were also simulated using the direct simulation Monte Carlo (DSMC) method, where the Boltzmann equation is solved using particles, by Garcia [14], and Stefanov and Cercignani [15]. Garcia and Penland [16] compared velocity distributions in the convection rolls with the numerical solution of the Navier-Stokes equations. The transition between conduction and convection was shown by Watanabe et al. using the DSMC method [17,18], and the spatial correlations of temperature fluctuations were shown to grow in the transition [19]. The transition and the hysteresis of three-dimensional convection patterns were also simulated [20]. Recently, the transition and the chaotic behavior of convection rolls were studied by Stefanov et al. [21,22]. The RB system was also studied using the lattice Boltzmann (LB) method, where motions of particles with distribution functions are calculated on a lattice based on the Boltzmann equation. The convection rolls were simulated by Shan [23] and He et al. [24] up to high Rayleigh numbers, and the dependency of the Nusselt number on the Rayleigh number was shown to be the same as that obtained by the Navier-Stokes equations. The effect of the Van der Waals fluid on the onset of convection was studied by Palmer and Rector [25]. Through these studies, the macroscopic flow phenomena in the RB system were shown to be simulated qualitatively and quantitatively using the particle simulation methods. These microscopic simulations were, in many cases, performed in a two-dimensional region with a small aspect ratio, since a large number of particles are necessary to simulate a three-dimensional flow or even the two-dimensional flow with a large aspect ratio.

In this study, the LB method proposed by He et al. [24] is applied to simulate the RB system in a three-dimensional rectangular box with an aspect ratio ranging from 2:2:1 to 6:6:1. The dependency of the Nusselt number on the Rayleigh number and the relation between the heat transfer rate and the flow pattern are discussed.

2 Lattice Boltzmann Thermal Model

The LB thermal model proposed by He et al. [24] is used in this study. In this model, the evolution equation of distribution function is solved for the internal-energy density as well as for the particle density. The Boltzmann equation with the BGK approximation [26] for the particle density is given by

$$\partial_t f + (\xi \cdot \nabla) f = -\frac{f - f^{eq}}{\tau_v}, \tag{1}$$

where f is the single-particle density distribution function, ξ is the microscopic velocity, f^{eq} is the Maxwell-Boltzmann equilibrium distribution, and τ_v is the relaxation time. The equilibrium distribution is

$$f^{eq} = \frac{\rho}{(2\pi RT)^{D/2}} \exp[-\frac{(\xi - u)^2}{2RT}], \tag{2}$$

where ρ, T, and u are the macroscopic density, temperature, and velocity, respectively, and R is the gas constant and D is the dimension. The evolution equation for the internal-energy density is

$$\partial_t g + (\xi \cdot \nabla) g = -\frac{g - g^{eq}}{\tau_c} - f(\xi - u) \cdot [\partial_t u + (\xi \cdot \nabla) u], \qquad (3)$$

where τ_c is the relaxation time and g is the internal-energy density distribution function defined by

$$g = \frac{(\xi - u)^2}{2} f. \qquad (4)$$

The equilibrium distribution is

$$g^{eq} = \frac{\rho(\xi - u)^2}{2(2\pi RT)^{D/2}} \exp[-\frac{(\xi - u)^2}{2RT}]. \qquad (5)$$

The macroscopic variables are calculated using

$$\rho = \int f d\xi, \qquad (6)$$

$$\rho u = \int \xi f d\xi, \text{ and} \qquad (7)$$

$$\frac{\rho DRT}{2} = \int g d\xi. \qquad (8)$$

Using the Chapman-Enskog expansion, the Boltzmann-BGK equations recover the continuity, momentum, and energy equations:

$$\partial_t \rho + \nabla \cdot (\rho u) = 0, \qquad (9)$$

$$\rho[\partial_t u + (u \cdot \nabla) u] = -\nabla p + \nabla \cdot \Pi, \text{ and} \qquad (10)$$

$$\partial_t (\rho \varepsilon) + \partial (\rho u \varepsilon) = \nabla \cdot (\rho \chi \nabla \varepsilon) + \Pi : \nabla u - p \nabla \cdot u. \qquad (11)$$

In the above equations, ε is the internal energy,

$$\varepsilon = \frac{DRT}{2}, \qquad (12)$$

χ is the thermal conductivity,

$$\chi = \frac{(D+2)\tau_c RT}{D}, \qquad (13)$$

and Π is the stress tensor,

$$\Pi = \rho \upsilon (\nabla u + u \nabla), \qquad (14)$$

where υ is the kinetic viscosity,

$$\upsilon = \tau_v RT. \qquad (15)$$

An external force term, which results in ρG in the macroscopic momentum equation,

$$\frac{G \cdot (\xi - u)}{RT} f^{eq}, \qquad (16)$$

is included in the right-hand side of Eq. (1), where G is the external force acting per unit mass.

3 Numerical Simulation

The three-dimensional RB convection is simulated numerically using the LB thermal model. The 3-D 27-direction lattice is used in this study. The simulation region is a rectangular box with an aspect ratio ranging from 2:2:1 to 6:6:1. The height of the simulation region is determined by the sensitivity calculations for the grid size, and is set equal to 60. The Prandtl number, $Pr=\nu/\chi$, is fixed at 0.71, and the Rayleigh number, $Ra=(\beta\Delta TgH^3)/(\nu\chi)$, is varied, where β is the thermal expansion coefficient, ΔT is the temperature difference between the top and bottom walls, g is the acceleration due to gravity, and H is the height of the simulation region. The parameter in the Rayleigh number, $\beta\Delta TgH$, is fixed at 0.1. The no-slip boundary condition is applied at the top and bottom walls using the bounce-back rule of the nonequilibrium density distribution [27]. The periodic boundary condition is used for the side boundaries. The linear temperature field is applied from the bottom to the top walls as the initial condition.

3.1 Efficiency of Parallel Calculations

The LB method consists of streaming and collision processes of the distribution function. The collision process is calculated locally, and high efficiency of parallel calculation is expected. The parallel computer system, HITACHI SR8000, is used, where one node consists of a 12 GB shared memory and 8 processors. The on-node-parallel function is used in a node: calculation procedures are divided into 8 parts using the shared memory, and the data transfer is not necessary in the node. The message passing interface (MPI) is used between two nodes. Purely MPI calculations are also possible in a node without using the on-node-parallel function.

An example of speedup for parallel LB simulations is shown in Fig. 1, where the on-node-parallel calculations are compared with purely MPI calculations. It is shown that the speedup of the purely MPI calculations is better than that of the on-node-parallel calculations when the number of nodes is one or two. The rate of the data transfer time to the elapsed time is shown in Fig. 2. The data transfer time is smaller for the on-node-parallel calculations, but the speedup is not much different between the purely MPI and the (On-Node-Parallel)+MPI calculations as shown in Fig. 1. This is because additional calculations are necessary for the on-node-parallel calculations. The effect of on-node-parallel functions appears as the number of nodes increases.

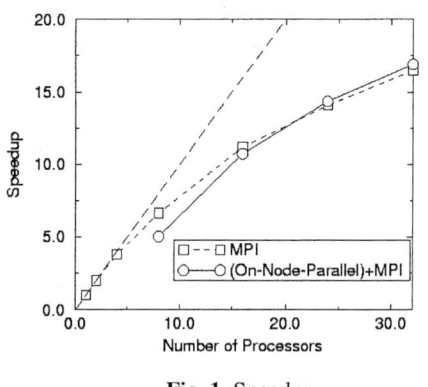

Fig. 1. Speedup

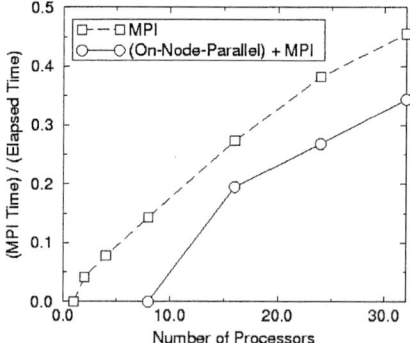

Fig.2. Data transfer time

The memory size of the simulation program is increased as the number of processors increases in both cases as shown in Fig. 3. Large memory is, however, shown to be necessary for the MPI calculations. The difference of the memory size is due to the additional buffer memory needed for MPI. Variables are divided into 8 parts in one node for the purely MPI calculations, while they are not divided for the on-node-parallel calculations. The amount of buffer memory is thus about 8 times larger for the purely MPI calculations. It is found that the shared memory system is effective from the viewpoint of the memory size.

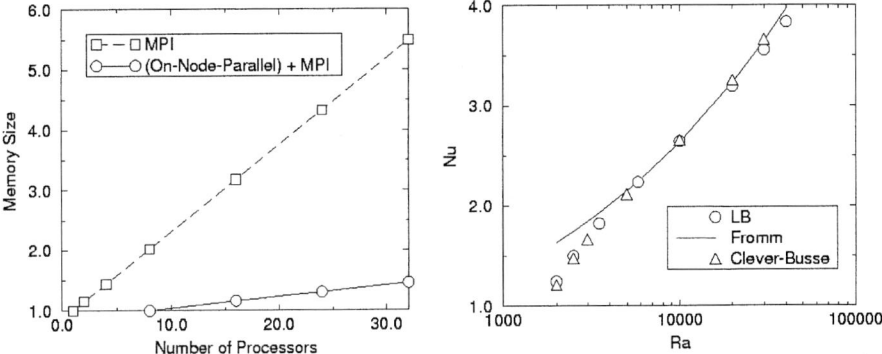

Fig. 3. Memory size

Fig. 4. Dependence of the Nusselt number on the Rayleigh number

3.2 Dependence of the Heat Transfer Rate on the Rayleigh Number

The heat transfer rate is estimated in terms of the Nusselt number defined by

$$Nu = 1 + \frac{<u_y T>}{\chi \Delta T / H}, \quad (17)$$

where u_y is the vertical velocity and $<>$ denotes the average over the whole simulation region. The dependence of the Nusselt number on the Rayleigh number is shown in Fig. 4. The aspect ratio of the simulation region is 2:2:1 (120x120x60) in this case. The solid line denotes the correlation obtained by Fromm [28] for relatively high Rayleigh numbers using the finite difference method, and thus the difference from the LB results in this study is notable at low Rayleigh numbers. The numerical results by Clever and Busse [29] using the Fourier expansion method are also shown in Fig. 4. Although these two numerical results are obtained in two dimensions, the agreement with the three-dimensional results in this study is satisfactory. An example of the three-dimensional temperature field in a steady state is shown in Fig. 5, where the surface of the average temperature between the top and bottom walls is depicted. The two-dimensional roll parallel to one of the side boundaries is established with the wave number of 3.142. The results by Fromm and by Clever and Busse are obtained for the wave number of 3.117, which corresponds to the lowest mode of instability at the onset of convection [30]. The three-dimensional heat transfer rate is thus in good agreement with the two-dimensional results.

3.3 Flow Pattern

The flow pattern in the steady state is shown as the temperature field. The Rayleigh number is fixed at 5805 in the following simulations. The temperature field in the simulation region with the aspect ratio of 2:2:1 is shown in Fig. 5. The left half in the region is the downward flow region, and the right half is the upward flow region.

The temperature fields in the simulation region with the aspect ratio of 4:4:1 (240x240x60) and 6:6:1 (360x360x60) are shown in Figs. 6 and 7, respectively. The stable convection rolls are established in both cases. The wave number is 2.221 for Fig. 6 and 2.342 for Fig. 7, and corresponds to the stable region in the macroscopic stability map [29]. The ratio of the horizontal size to the vertical size of the simulation region is a multiple of 2:1 in Figs. 6 and 7, and the wave number may be 3.142 when the convection roll is parallel to one of the side boundaries as shown in Fig. 5. The convection roll is, however, inclined in Figs. 6 and 7. It is thus found that several flow patterns are possible though the ratio of the horizontal size to the vertical size is a multiple of 2:1.

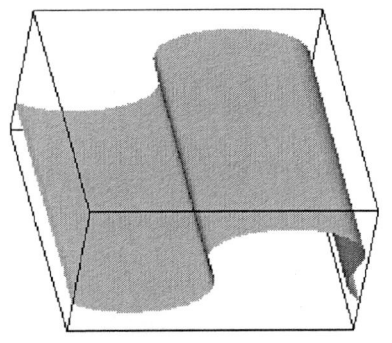

Fig.5. Temperature field in the region of 2:2:1

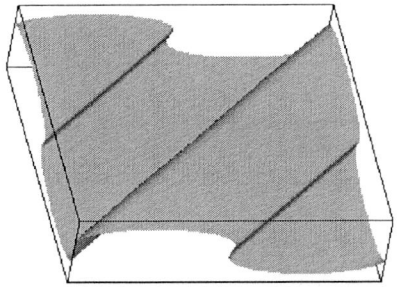

Fig.6. Temperature field in the region with 4:4:1

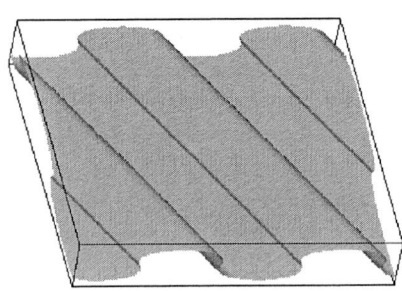

Fig.7. Temperature field in the region of 6:6:1

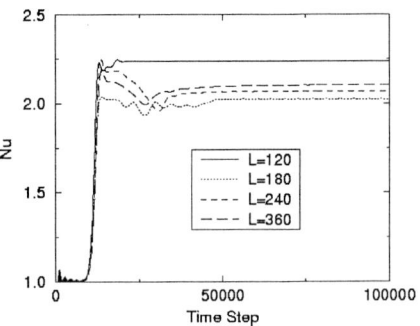

Fig.8. Effect of the region size on the Nusselt number

3.4 Heat Transfer Rate

The effect of the region size on the heat transfer rate is shown in Fig. 8, where the Nusselt numbers obtained in the simulation region with the aspect ratio of 2:2:1(L=120), 3:3:1(L=180), 4:4:1(L=240) and 6:6:1(L=360) are shown. The Nusselt number is almost constant in the convection state after 50000 time steps. The Nusselt numbers in the steady state are 2.238, 2.022, 2.069 and 2.105 for the aspect ratio of 2:2:1, 3:3:1, 4:4:1 and 6:6:1, respectively. The wave numbers are 3.142, 2.094, 2.221 and 2.342, respectively. It is thus found that the heat transfer rate decreases as the wave number decreases and the wavelength increases.

4 Summary

The three-dimensional RB convection has been numerically simulated using the LB method. It was shown in the parallel calculations that the on-node-parallel calculations using shared memory were effective from the viewpoint of the memory usage in comparison with the purely MPI calculations.

Flow patterns were observed in a rectangular box with an aspect ratio ranging from 2:2:1 to 6:6:1, and the heat transfer rate was estimated in terms of the Nusselt number. The dependency of the Nusselt number on the Rayleigh number was shown to agree well with that obtained by the two-dimensional calculations of the Navier-Stokes equations. It was found that several roll patterns were possible under the same conditions and the heat transfer rate decreased as the wave number decreased.

References

1. Ahlers, G.: Experiments with Pattern-Forming Systems. Physica D, 51(1991)421.
2. Cross, M. C., Hohenberg, P. C.: Pattern Formation Outside of Equilibrium. Rev. Mod. Phys., 65(1993)851.
3. Pesch, W.: Complex Spatiotemporal Convection Patterns. CHAOS, 6(1996)348.
4. Mareschal, M., Kestemont, E.: Order and Fluctuations in Nonequilibrium Molecular Dynamics Simuations of Two-Dimensional Fluids. J. Stat. Phys., 48(1987)1187.
5. Mareschal, M., Kestemont, E.: Experimental Evidence for Convective Rolls in Finite Two-Dimensional Moecular Models. Nature, 239(1987)427.
6. Rapaport, D. C.: Molecular-Dynamics Study of Rayleigh-Benard Convection. Phys. Rev. Lett., 60(1988)2480.
7. Mareschal, M., Mansour, M. M., Puhl, A., Kestemont, E.: Molecular Dynamics versus Hydrodynamics in a Two-Dimensiona Rayleigh-Benrad System. Phys. Rev. Lett., 61(1988)2550.
8. Puhl, A., Mansour, M. M., Mareschal, M.: Quantitative Comparison of Molecular Dynamics with Hydrodynamics in Rayleigh-Benard Convection. Phys. Rev. A, 40(1989)1999.
9. Given, J. A., Clementi, E.: Molecular Dynamics and Rayleigh-Benard Convection. J. Chem. Phys., 90(1989)7376.

10. Watanabe, T., Kaburaki, H.: Increase in Chaotic Motions of Atoms in a Large-Scale Self-Organized Motion. Phys. Rev. E, 54(1996)1504.
11. Posch, H. A., Hoover, W. G., Kum, O.: Steady-State Shear Flows via Nonequilibrium Molecular Dynamics and Smooth-Particle Applied Mechanics. Phys. Rev. E, 52(1995)1711.
12. Kum, O., Hoover, W. G., Posch, H. A.: Viscous Conducting Flows with Smooth-Particle Applied Mechanics. Phys. Rev. E, 52(1995)4899.
13. Hoover, W. G., Kum, O.: Non-Equilibrium Simulations. Molec. Phys., 86(1995)685.
14. Garcia, A. L.: Hydrodynamic Fluctuations and the Direct Simulation Monte Carlo Method. In: Mareschal, M. (ed.): Microscopic Simulations of Complex Flows, Plenum Press, New York(1990)177.
15. Stefanov, S., Cercignani, C.: Monte Carlo Simulation of Benard's Instability in a Rarefied Gas. Eur. J. Mech. B, 11(1992)543.
16. Garcia, A., Penland, C.: Fluctuating Hydrodynamics and Principal Oscillation Patter Analysis. J. Stat. Phys., 64(1991)1121.
17. Watanabe, T., Kaburaki, H., Yokokawa, M.: Simulation of a Two-Dimensional Rayleigh-Benard System using the Direct Simulation Monte Carlo Method. Phys. Rev. E, 49(1994)4060.
18. Watanabe, T., Kaburaki, H., Yokokawa, M.: Reply to "Comment on 'Simulation of a Two-Dimensional Rayleigh-Benard System using the Direct Simulation Monte Carlo Method'". Phys. Rev. E, 51(1995)3786.
19. Watanabe, T., Kaburaki, H., Machida, M., Yokokawa, M.: Growth of Long-Range Correlations in a Transition Between Heat Conduction and Convection. Phys. Rev. E, 52(1995)1601.
20. Watanabe, T., Kaburaki, H.: Particle Simulation of Three-Dimensional Convection Patterns in a Rayleigh-Benard System. Phys. Rev. E, 56(1997)1218.
21. Stefanov, S., Roussinov, V., Cercignani, C.: Rayleigh-Benard Flow of a Rarefied Gas and its Attractors. I. Convection Regime. Phys.Fluids, 14(2002)2255.
22. Stefanov, S., Roussinov, V., Cercignani, C.: Rayleigh-Benard Flow of a Rarefied Gas and its Attractors. II. Chaotic and Periodic Convective Regimes. Phys. Fluids, 14(2002)2270.
23. Shan, X.: Simulation of Rayleigh-Benard Convection using a Lattice Boltzmann Method. Phys. Rev. E, 55(1997)2780.
24. He, X., Chen, S., Doolen, G. D.: A Novel Thermal Model for the Lattice Boltzmann Method in Incompressible Limit. J. Comp. Phys., 146(1998)282.
25. Palmer, B. J., Rector, D. R.: Lattice Boltzmann Algorithm for Simulating Thermal Flow in Compressible Fluids. J. Comp. Phys., 161(2000)1.
26. Bhatnagar, P. L., Gross, E. P., Krook, M: A Model for Collision Processes in Gases, I: Small Amplitude Processes in Charged and Neutral One-Component System. Phys. Rev., 94(1954)511.
27. Zou, Q., He, X.: On Pressure and Velocity Boundary Conditions for the Lattice Boltzmann BGK Model. Phys. Fluids, 9(1997)1591.
28. Fromm, J. E.: Numerical Solutions of the Nonlinear Equations for a Heated Fluid Layer. Phys. Fluids, 8(1965)1757.
29. Clever, R. M., Busse, F. H.: Transition to Time-Dependent Convection. J. Fluid Mech., 65(1974)625.
30. Chandrasekhar, S.: Hydrodynamic and Hydromagnetic Stability. Oxford University Press(1961).

A Parallel Split Operator Method for the Time Dependent Schrödinger Equation

Jan P. Hansen[1], Thierry Matthey[2], and Tor Sørevik[3]

[1] Dept. of Physics, University of Bergen, Norway
   http://www.fi.uib.no/~janp
[2] Parallab, UNIFOB, Bergen, Norway
   http://www.parallab.no/~matthey
[3] Dept. of Informatics, University of Bergen, Norway
   http://www.ii.uib.no/~tors

Abstract. We describe the parallelization of a spectral method for solving the time dependent Schrödinger equation in spherical coordinates. Two different implementation of the necessary communication have been implemented and experiments on a real application are presented. The excellent runtime and accuracy figures demonstrate that our approach is very efficient. With the very encouraging speed-up, we claim that the numerical scheme is parallelizable and our MPI-implementation efficient.

1 Introduction

The time dependent Schrödinger equation is of fundamental importance in a wide range of scientific disciplines, such as femto- and attosecond laser physics [DR96], quantum optics [SZ97], atomic collisions [BM92] and in cold matter physics [KDSK99]. In the non-perturbative regime, the equation can in general only be solved numerically, even for single-particle systems. A large number of methods have been developed and applied. Most methods are based on finite difference or spectral discretization, and in particular the latter approach dominates since the basis functions often can be connected to physical properties of a part of the system. Numerical schemes based on Cartesian [RR99], cylindrical [Dun02] and spherical geometry [HJ88] have for example been used. The description based on spherical geometry seems to be less popular in recent works. This is at first surprising, since spherical outgoing waves are often dominating final states, thus making physical interpretation (post processing) straightforward. However, up to now, there has been no known implementation of efficient direct spectral schemes in three dimensions.

Hermann and Fleck[HJ88] describe a split-operator technique for advancing the system in time based on spherical coordinates with a limitation to spectral propagation of the system in the radial and polar coordinates. The clue in this approach is to notice that the Hamiltonian operator is composed of simpler operators with well known eigenfunctions. Selecting these eigenfunctions as basis for the spectral approximations allows us to do an extremely simple and accurate time stepping.

In this paper we present an efficient parallelization of the above mentioned algorithm and provide experimental evidence of its speed-up and efficiency on real physical problems. The basic algorithm is presented in section 2, the parallelization in section 3 and the numerical experiments in section 4. In section 5 we conclude with some remarks and point to future works.

2 The Algorithm

Here we briefly outline the split-operator technique applied to the time dependent Schrödinger equation (1), and detail the algorithms for the time propagation of the separate operators.

$$i\frac{\partial}{\partial t}\Psi(\mathbf{x},t) = H\Psi(\mathbf{x},t). \qquad (1)$$

The Hamiltonian operator, H, consists of the Laplacian plus a potential $V(\mathbf{x},t)$

$$H\Psi(\mathbf{x},t) = \Delta\Psi(\mathbf{x},t) + V(\mathbf{x},t)\Psi(\mathbf{x},t). \qquad (2)$$

Transforming to spherical coordinates and introducing the reduced wave function $\Phi = r\Psi$ gives the following form of the Hamiltonian

$$H = -\frac{\partial^2}{2\partial r^2} + \frac{L^2}{2r^2} - \frac{1}{r} + V(r,\theta), \qquad (3)$$

where L^2 is the angular momentum operator. To highlight the basic idea we make the simplifying assumption that V is time-independent as well as independent of ϕ. The same basic algorithm and the same parallelization strategy holds without these assumption, but the details become more involved.

As shown by equation (3) the Hamiltonian is nothing, but a sum of linear operators, each relatively simple to deal with. As the separate operators of the Hamiltonian are linear and time independent, the solution to the initial value problem is formally

$$\Phi(t_{n+1}) = e^{\Delta t(A+B)}\Phi(t_n), \qquad (4)$$

which could be approximated by

$$\Phi(t_{n+1}) = e^{\Delta t A}e^{\Delta t B}\Phi(t_n), \qquad (5)$$

allowing us to apply the operators separately[1]. If A and B commute these two expressions provides identical results, if not we have a splitting error, which is the case here. The straightforward splitting leads to a local error of $O(\Delta t^2)$. This can be reduced to $O(\Delta t^3)$ locally if a Strang [Str68] splitting is applied. The Strang splitting does $e^{\Delta t/2 A}e^{\Delta t B}e^{\Delta t/2 A}\Phi(t_n)$. This introduction of "symmetry" eliminates a term in the error expansion and increasing the order of

---
[1] For simplicity we here split the Hamiltonian in only two operators. For more operators we can apply the formalism recursively, which is done in our implementation.

the method. When the Strang splitting is done repeatedly in a time loop, we get $e^{\Delta t/2A}e^{\Delta tB}e^{\Delta t/2A}e^{\Delta t/2A}e^{\Delta tB}e^{\Delta t/2A}\cdots e^{\Delta t/2A}e^{\Delta tB}e^{\Delta t/2A}\Phi(t_n)$ which reduces to $e^{\Delta t/2A}e^{\Delta tB}e^{\Delta tA}e^{\Delta tB}\cdots e^{\Delta tA}e^{\Delta tB}e^{\Delta t/2A}\Phi(t_n)$. Hence provided some care is taken with startup and clean up the Strang splitting can be implemented without extra cost.

The clue to efficient and accurate application of the spatial differential operators is to expand Φ in terms of spherical harmonics $\Psi_{lm}(\theta,\phi)$ and Fourier functions, e^{ikr}, since these are the eigenfunctions of the angular momentum operator and $\frac{\partial^2}{\partial r^2}$, respectively. Application of these operators to the associated eigenfunctions independently then becomes not only efficient and simple, but exact as well.

The Split-step algorithm is outlined in Algorithm 1.

Algorithm 1 (The split-step algorithm)

$\Phi^*(t_{1/2}) = rprop(\Phi(t_0), dt/2)$
for n = 1,nsteps-1
    $\Phi^{**}(t_{n-1/2}) = vprop(\Phi^*(t_{n-1/2}), dt)$
    $\Phi^*(t_{n+1/2}) = rprop(\Phi^{**}(t_{n-1/2}), dt)$
end for
$\Phi^{**}(t_{nsteps-1/2}) = vprop(\Phi^*(t_{nsteps-1/2}), dt)$
$\Phi(t_{nsteps}) = rprop(\Phi^{**}(t_{nsteps-1/2}), dt/2)$

The computational work is carried out in *vprop* and *rprop*. They operate on a computational grid, $F(k,j)$; $k = 1,...,n_r$; $j = 1,...,n_z$, which approximate the function at a tensor product of the collocation points in the radial coordinate (row-index) and the angular coordinates (column-index). In Algorithm 2 we display how *rprop* works. Here F contains the spatial values of the function at a fixed point in time, while $\tilde{F}$ represents the coefficients for its Fourier expansion.

Algorithm 2 (Propagation in r-direction)

/* Transform to Fourier space */
for $j = 1, n_z$
    $\tilde{F}(:,j) \leftarrow FFT(F(:,j));$
end
/* Propagate in time by scaling with appropriate eigenvalues */
for $k = 1, n_r$
    $\tilde{F}(k,:) = \tilde{F}(k,:)e^{-i\Delta t\pi^2 k^2/(2R_{max}^2)}$
end
/* Inverse Transform back from Fourier space */
for $j = 1, n_z$
    $F(:,j) \leftarrow IFFT(\tilde{F}(:,j));$
end

The propagation in the angular direction, *vprop*, is similar to *rprop*, with the obvious difference that we need an other transform as the basis functions for the expansion are different. If, as in (3), V is independent of ϕ, the problem reduces to 2-dim and the appropriate basis functions are the Legendre polynomials. The discrete Legendre transform correspond to a matrix-vector multiply[2]. $\hat{F}(i,:) = F(i,:)L$. L being the Legendre transformation matrix with entries $L_{kj} = P_j(x_k)w_k$ where $P_j(x)$ is the j-th Legendre polynomial, x_k; $k = 1, ..., n_z$ are the zeroes of the Legendre polynomial of degree n_z and w_k; $k = 1, ..., n_z$ are the weights of the corresponding Gauss-Legendre quadrature rule. When applied to multiple vectors the Legendre transform can be formulated as a matrix-matrix multiply. The transformation matrix is of size $n_z \times n_z$ and should be applied to n_r vectors of size n_z, lined up in an $n_z \times n_r$ matrix. This matrix is F^T. In other words, the Legendre transform works on rows of F, while the Fourier transform works on columns.

Spectral methods are famous for their impressive accuracy provided the approximated function is smooth enough and care is taken at the boundaries. The smoothness of Φ is not a problem and the spherical harmonics are of course periodic, making the treatment of boundaries easy. In the radial direction, however, the computational domain is in principle $[0, \infty)$. For the problem we are studying, we truncate the infinite interval to $[0, R_{max}]$, and as long as $\Phi(t, r, \theta, \phi) = 0$; for all $t \leq T_{max}$, and $r \geq R_{max}$ the smoothness at R_{max} is assured. To make sure this is true we need to chose R_{max} sufficiently large. To avoid aliasing errors a sufficiently fine resolution of r is needed. Combined with a large and safe $R_{\max}$ this makes the number of grid points (n_r) in the r-direction pretty high. The number of grid points (n_z) in the angular direction is substantial smaller.

3 Parallel Implementation

The work in the above algorithm is done within *rprop* and *vprop*. Here the Fourier transforms in *rprop* and the Legendre transform in *vprop* are the dominating computational costs. The propagation itself is only a scaling of each element in the coefficient matrix which is cheap as well as embarrassingly parallel. Each transform is a global operation on the vector in question. But with multiple vectors in each directions, we can simply parallelize the transforms by assigning n_z/N_p transforms to each processor in the radial direction, or n_r/N_p in the angular direction. N_p being the number of processors. Thus the coefficient matrix has to be distributed column-wise for the Fourier transform and row-wise for the Legendre transform. Given these distributions the computation itself takes place without any need of communication. However, in between a Fourier transform and a Legendre transform, we need to redistribute the data from "row-splitting" to "column-splitting" or visa versa.

---

[2] There exists a "Fast Legendre Transform" with asymptotic complexity $O(n(\log n)^2)$. However, for the relative small n_z we are targeting, the matrix-vector product is faster.

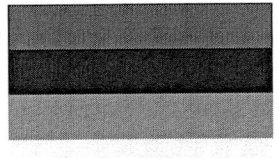  

Fig. 1. Color coding shows the distribution of data to processors in the left and right part of the figure. The middle part indicates which blocks might be sent simultaneously (those with the same color).

Our code is parallelized for distributed memory system, using MPI. The communication described above correspond to the collective communication routine MPI_ALLTOALL provided each matrix block could be treated as an element. This is accomplished using the MPI-derived datatype [GLS94].

An alternative implementation is obtained using point-to-point send and receive with a packing/unpacking of the blocks of the column- (row-) distributed data. In this case each block is sent as one item. We have implementation both alternatives. The point-to-point version is implemented by a separate subroutine where the non-blocking MPI-routines are used to minimize synchronization overhead. All that is needed to move from the sequential version of the code to the parallel, is inserting the redistribution routines between the alternating calls to *rprop* and *vprop* and adjusting the index space accordingly.

As seen in Figure 1 the redistribution requires that all processors gather $N_p - 1$ blocks of data of size $n_r n_z / N_p^2$ from the other $N_p - 1$ processors. Thus $N_p - 1$ communication steps are needed for each of the N_p processors. These can however be executed in $N_p - 1$ parallel steps where all the processors at each step send to and receive from different processors. This can easily be achieved by letting each processor sending block $(i + p) \pmod{N_p}$ to the appropriate processor at step i. Where $p = 0, 1, \cdots, N_p - 1$ is the processor number and $i = 1, \cdots, N_p - 1$.

This corresponds exactly to the algorithm we have implemented in our point-to-point MPI-implementation (and presumably it is also the underlying algorithm for MPI_ALLTOALL). The algorithm is optimal in the sense that it uses the minimum number of steps, sends the minimum amount of data and keeps all the processors busy all the time. What is beyond our control, is the optimal use of the underlying network. A well tuned vendor implementation of MPI_ALLTOALL might outpace our handcoded point-to-point by taking this into account.

In the parallel version the $n_z \times n_z$ coefficient matrix for the Legendre transform is replicated across all the participating processors.

IO is handled by one processor only, and the appropriate broadcast and gather operations are used to distribute and gather data to all processors when needed. All remaining computational work, not covered here, is point-wise and can be carried out locally regardless of whether the data are row- or column-splitted. For n_r and n_z being a multiplum of N_p the load is evenly distributed and any sublinear parallel speed-up can be contributed to communication overhead. The above communication algorithm minimizes the number of communication steps and keeps all processors busy provided the interconnecting network has sufficient bisectional bandwidth.

4 Numerical Experiments

Our test case is related to strong field laser-atom physics: A strong femtosecond laser pulse with linear polarized light in the $z-$direction and with peak intensity $E_0 = 0.2$ (around 10^{15} W/cm^2) is modeled as a time dependent potential $V(z,t) = E_0 sin^2 \left(\frac{\pi}{T}t\right) cos(w_L t)$, with $t \in (0,T)$, and $w_L = 0.25$ the laser frequency (Atomic units are used). For this case we get an acceptable accuracy by setting, $n_r \times n_z = 2048 \times 32$. We run the simulation up to $T_N = 50$ using $dt = 0.001$ as step size, implying a total of $N = 50000$ time steps. These discretization parameters are required for accurate simulation of the physical problem.

To see how our technique works on a computational more demanding problem, we run the same problem on the grid, $n_r \times n_z = 8192 \times 64$, and a reduced number of time steps. We have ran the tests on an IBM Regatta with 32 1.3 GHz Power4 processors. For FFT and BLAS we have used the vendor supplied essl-library on the regatta system. When IO and initialization are excluded from the timing, all computation should scale perfectly provided the number of processors divide the size parameters n_r and n_z. Thus any sublinear speed-up should be contributed to communication cost, synchronization and overhead associated with the subroutine calls to the communication layer, including associated index juggling.

Table 1. Timing in seconds for the 8192 × 64 problem on the IBM Regatta.

	MPI_ALLTOALL				point-to-point			
p	total	vprops	rprop	Comm	total	vprops	rprop	Comm
1	26128	16863	7455	1811	25630	17087	7573	970
2	12772	8320	3687	764	12399	8077	3588	734
4	6452	4152	1880	418	6434	4088	1868	478
8	3386	2049	1003	334	3370	2031	996	343
16	1900	1001	578	320	1847	997	573	276
32	1166	531	353	282	1148	528	355	266

Timings are wall clock time on a system in production mode, and as such only crude estimates[3]. The table shows how the pure number-crunching parts (*vprop* and *rprop*) scales almost perfectly with the number of processors. There

---
[3] The copying of the diagonal block is a part of the communication routine and this is the time consuming part for 1 processor.

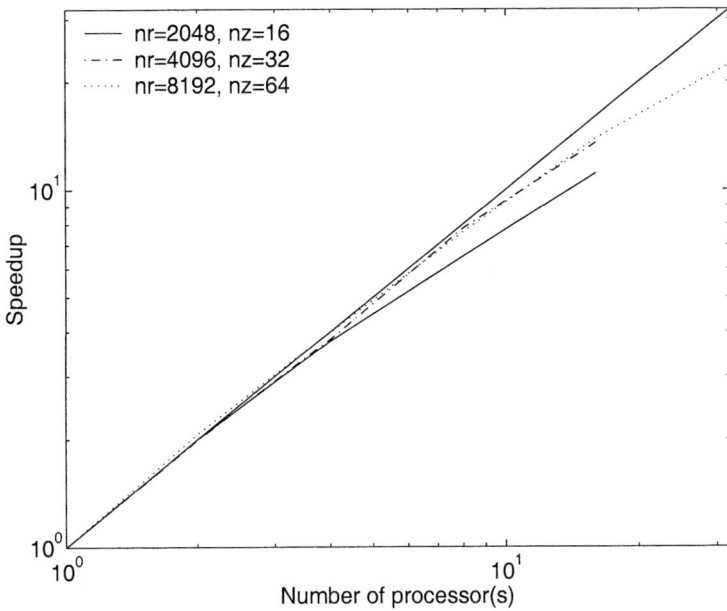

Fig. 2. Speed-up curves for different problem-sizes. Here the point-to-point communication has been used.

is little if any difference in the runtime for the two different implementation of the communication operations. Except for the curious behavior of all-to-all on one processor. In this case the real work is only a memory copy of the entire matrix.

The amount of data to be sent is proportional to $(N_p - 1)/N_p^2$ and thus decreases nicely, the numbers of startups is $N_p - 1$ and contributes to a linearly increasing term. As always the synchronization overhead increases with the number of processors and may eventually dominate the communication time. Thus as expected the communication does not scale well. However, as the arithmetic work dominates the total time the overall scaling is quite acceptable, as displayed by the speed-up curves in Figure 2. As always we see that larger problems scale better than small ones.

5 Conclusions and Future Work

We are currently working on a port of this code to Linux based Itanium systems, which we recently have been give access to. For this version we will use the public domain library FFTW [Fri98], [Fri99] and ATLAS [WD99] for FFT-routines and BLAS respectively.

Where we meet the real demanding computational problems are for the 3-D cases. These can not be carried out with sufficient accuracy and in reasonable time without parallelism. We already have a prototype ready for the 3-D case where the parallelization applies as for the 2-D case, without any modification. The only difference we expect is that as the arithmetic work explode, the parallel scaling becomes even better.

References

[BM92]   B.H. Bransden and M.R.C. McDowell. *Charge Exchange and the Theory of Ion-Atom Collisions.* Clarendon, 1992.

[DR96]   Jean-Claude Diels and Wolfgang Rudolph. *Ultrashort laser pulse phenomena.* Academic Press, 1996.

[Dun02] Daniel Dundas. Efficient grid treatment of the ionization dynamics of laser-driven h_2^+. *Phys. Rev. A*, 65, 2002.

[Fri98] M. Frigo. Fftw: An adaptive software architecture for the fft. In *Proceedings of the ICASSP Conference*, volume 3, page 1381, 1998.

[Fri99] M. Frigo. A fast fourier transform compiler. In *Proceedings of the ACM SIGPLAN Conference on Programming Language Design and Implementation (PLDI'99)*, 1999.

[GLS94] William Gropp, Ewing Lusk, and Antony Skjellum. *USING MPI, Portable Parallel Programming with the Message-Passing Interface.* MIT Press, 1994.

[HJ88]   Mark R. Hermann and J. A. Fleck Jr. Split-operator spectral method for solving the time-dependent schrödinger equation in spherical coordinates. *Physical Review A*, 38(12):6000–6012, 1988.

[KDSK99] W. Ketterle, D. S. Durfee, and D. M. Stamper-Kurn. Making, probing and understanding bose-einstein condensates. In M. Inguscio, S. Stringari, and C. E. Wieman, editors, *Bose-Einstein Condensation of Atomic Gasesi, Proceedings of the International School of Physics, "Enrico Fermi", Cource CXL.* IOS Press, 1999.

[RR99]   M. E. Riley and B. Ritchie. Numerical time-dependent schrödinger description of charge-exchange. *Phys. Rev. A*, 59:3544–3547, 1999.

[Str68] Gilbert Strang. On the construction and comparison of difference scheme. *SIAM Journal of Numerical Analysis*, 5:506–517, 1968.

[SZ97]   Marlan O. Scully and M. Suhail Zubairy. *Quantum Optics.* Cambridge University Press, 1997.

[WD99]   R. Clint Whaley and Jack Dongarra. Automatically tuned linear algebra software. In *Ninth SIAM Conference on Parallel processing for Scientific Computing*, 1999.

A Parallel Software for the Reconstruction of Dynamic MRI Sequences*

G. Landi, E. Loli Piccolomini, and F. Zama

Department of Mathematics,
Piazza Porta S. Donato 5, Bologna, Italy
piccolom@dm.unibo.it
http://www.dm.unibo.it/~piccolom

Abstract. In this paper we present a parallel version of an existing Matlab software for dynamic Magnetic Resonance Imaging which implements a reconstruction technique based on B-spline Reduced-encoding Imaging by Generalized series Reconstruction. The parallel primitives used are provided by MatlabMPI. The parallel Matlab application is tested on a network of Linux workstations.

1 Introduction

In many type of Magnetic Resonance Imaging (MRI) experiments such as contrast-enhanced imaging and MRI during the course of a medical intervention, it is necessary to quickly acquire the dynamic image series with high time resolution. The increase of the temporal resolution is obtained at the expense of the spatial resolution.

For example, in a typical functional MRI experiment, series of low resolution images are acquired over time and only one or two high resolution images are acquired and used later, to point out the brain area activated by the external stimuli.

In general, the data acquired in a MRI experiment are frequency-encoded in the so-called k-space and the image is reconstructed by means of inverse Fourier transforms. The time sequence of the dynamic MR Images is obtained by recovering each image independently. Since during a dynamic experiment only a small part of the structure of the image changes, it is possible to accelerate the data acquisition process by collecting truncated samplings of the data. In particular in the k-space, only the low frequency signal changes dynamically, while the high frequency signal remains essentially unchanged. Consequently, only a small (usually central and symmetric with respect to the origin) subset of the k-space data in the phase encoding direction is acquired with maximum time resolution.

Unfortunately, when the data are reduced-encoded, the Fourier traditional methods have many limitations and the reconstructed images present ringing

---

* This work was completed with the support FIRB Project "Parallel algorithms and Nonlinear Numerical Optimization" RBAU01JYPN

effects from the edge of the objects. For this reason, some methods have been developed for the estimation of the images of the sequence from a limited amount of the sampled data [3], [8]. These methods, using prior information of the first and last images in the sequence, called *references images*, allow good quality reconstruction at a high computational cost. In the method proposed in [9], the reconstructed images are modelled with B-Spline functions and are obtained by solving ill-conditioned linear systems with Tikhonov regularization method.

A Matlab software with graphical interface, called MRITool[1], has been developed: it implements the reconstruction technique based on B-spline Reduced-encoding Imaging by Generalized series Reconstruction (BRIGR) [9]. For clinical needs, the execution time for the reconstruction of a whole sequence of images is too high. For this reason, in this paper we present a parallel version of the reconstruction method in substitution of the sequential MRItool computational kernel. Several parallel Matlab toolboxes have been built, differing each other in the underlying communication method. In [2], it can be found an overview of the current available software for parallel Matlab. In the development of our Matlab application on parallel distributed memory systems we choose a standard message passing library such as Message Passing Interface (MPI) [4]. As a preliminary step we use MatlabMPI which is a set of full Matlab routines that implement a subset of MPI functions on top of the Matlab I/O system. It is a very small "pure" Matlab implementation and does not require the installation of MPI. The simplicity and performance of MatlabMPI provides a reasonable choice for speeding up an existing Matlab code on distributed memory parallel architectures. In section 2 the mathematical problem is presented with the sequential algorithm. In section 3 we describe the parallel algorithm. The numerical results are reported in section 4.

2 Numerical Method and Sequential Algorithm

Numerically, the problem described in the introduction can be formulated as follows. At successive times t_j, $j = 0, \ldots, Q$, the j-th image of the sequence is represented by a function $I_j(x, y)$ which solves:

$$D_j(h, k) = \iint_{-\infty}^{+\infty} I_j(x, y) e^{-2\pi i(hx + ky)} dx dy.$$

where $D_j(h, k)$, $j = 0, \ldots, Q$, are the data sets acquired independently in the Fourier space.

We suppose that, at times t_0 and t_Q, two complete discrete high resolution reference sets are available:

$$D_0(\ell \Delta h, m \Delta k) \text{ and } D_Q(\ell \Delta h, m \Delta k) \quad \begin{array}{l} \ell = -N/2, \ldots, N/2 - 1 \\ m = -M/2, \ldots, M/2 - 1 \end{array}$$

---

[1] MRITool 2.0 can be downloaded at
http://www.dm.unibo.it/~piccolom/WebTool/ToolFrame.htm

where N is the number of *frequency encodings* measured at intervals Δh and M is the number of *phase encodings* measured at intervals Δk. At times t_j, $j = 1, \ldots, Q-1$ we have reduced spatial resolution; the sets $D_j(\ell\Delta h, m\Delta k)$, $\ell = -N/2, \ldots, N/2 - 1$, $m = -N_m/2, \ldots, N_m/2 - 1$, $N_m \ll M$, are called *dynamic sets*.

For $j = 0$ and $j = Q$ we can apply a 2D discrete inverse Fourier transform to the reference sets $D_0(\ell\Delta h, m\Delta k)$ and $D_Q(\ell\Delta h, m\Delta k)$ and compute the discrete image functions $I_0(\ell\Delta x, m\Delta y)$ and $I_Q(\ell\Delta x, m\Delta y)$.

Since the dynamic data $D_j(\ell\Delta h, m\Delta k)$ are undersampled only along the k direction, by applying a discrete Fourier inverse transform along the h direction, we obtain the discrete functions:

$$\hat{D}_j(\ell\Delta x, m\Delta k) = \int_{-\infty}^{+\infty} I_j(\ell\Delta x, y) e^{-2\pi i (m\Delta k) y} dy, \quad j = 1, \ldots, Q-1 \quad (1)$$

We represent the dynamic changes by means of the difference function:

$$\hat{\mathcal{D}}_j^{(\ell)}(m\Delta k) \equiv \hat{D}_j^{(\ell)}(m\Delta k) - \hat{D}_0^{(\ell)}(m\Delta k)$$

where $\hat{D}_j^{(\ell)}(m\Delta k) \equiv \hat{D}_j(\ell\Delta x, m\Delta k)$. Using the relation (1) we obtain:

$$\hat{\mathcal{D}}_j^{(\ell)}(m\Delta k) = \int_{-\infty}^{\infty} (I_j^{(\ell)}(y) - I_0^{(\ell)}(y)) e^{-2\pi i (m\Delta k) y} dy \quad \begin{array}{l} j = 1, \ldots, Q-1 \\ \ell = -N/2, \ldots, N/2 - 1 \end{array} \quad (2)$$

where $I_j^{(\ell)}(y) \equiv I_j(\ell\Delta x, y)$. In order to reconstruct the whole images sequence we have to solve $N \cdot (Q-1)$ integral equations (2).

In our method, proposed in [9], we represent the unknown function (in this case the difference between the image I_j and the reference image I_0), using cubic B-Spline functions:

$$I_j^{(\ell)}(y) - I_0^{(\ell)}(y) = G^{(\ell)}(y) \sum_{p=0}^{N_m-1} \alpha_p^{(j,\ell)} \mathcal{B}_p(y) \quad (3)$$

where $G^{(\ell)}(y) = |I_Q^{(\ell)}(y) - I_0^{(\ell)}(y)|$ accounts for given *a priori* information and the set $\{\mathcal{B}_0(y), \ldots, \mathcal{B}_{N_m-1}(y)\}$ is the basis of cubic B-Spline functions (see [9] for the details). Hence, the problem (2) leads to the solution of the following linear equation:

$$\hat{\mathcal{D}}_j^{(\ell)}(m\Delta k) = \sum_{p=0}^{N_m-1} \alpha_p^{(j,\ell)} \sum_{q=0}^{N_m-1} \mathcal{F}(G^{(\ell)})((m-q)\Delta k) \mathcal{F}(\mathcal{B}_p)(q\Delta k) \quad (4)$$

where $\mathcal{F}(f)$ represents the Fourier transform of f. Introducing the square matrices:

$$\left(H^{(\ell)}\right)_{s,t} = \mathcal{F}(G^{(\ell)})\left((s-t)\Delta k\right), \quad s, t = 0, \ldots, N_m - 1, \quad (5)$$

$$(B)_{u,v} = \mathcal{F}(\mathcal{B}_v)(u\Delta k), \quad u, v = 0, \ldots, N_m - 1,$$

```
INPUT: First reference set: D_0(ℓΔh, mΔk) of N · M values;
       Q − 1 intermediate dynamic sets D_j(ℓΔh, mΔk) each of N · N_m values;
       Last Reference set: D_Q(ℓΔh, mΔk) with N · M values.
(1) Compute the N_m × N_m matrix B through N_m FFTs of vectors of length N_m.
(2) for j = 1, ..., Q − 1
    (2.1) for m = −N_m/2, ..., N_m/2 − 1
       (2.1.1) D̂_j(·, mΔk) = IFFT(D_j(·, mΔk))
(3) Compute I_0(ℓΔx, mΔy) = IFFT2(D_0(ℓΔh, mΔk))
(4) Compute I_Q(ℓΔx, mΔy) = IFFT2(D_Q(ℓΔh, mΔk))
(5) for ℓ = −N/2, ..., N/2 − 1
    (5.1) Compute G^(ℓ)(y)
    (5.2) Compute the matrices H^(ℓ) and A^(ℓ) (eqs. (5) and (6))
    (5.3) Compute the Singular Value Decomposition of A^(ℓ)
    (5.4) for j = 1, ..., Q − 1
       (5.4.1) Solve the system A^(ℓ) α_j^(ℓ) = d_j^(ℓ)
       (5.4.2) Represent the function:
          I_j^(ℓ)(mΔy) − I_0^(ℓ)(mΔy) = G^(ℓ)(mΔy) Σ_{p=0}^{N_m−1} α_p^(j,ℓ) B_p(mΔy)
OUTPUT: High resolution sequence: I_j(ℓΔx, mΔy) − I_0(ℓΔx, mΔy), j = 1, ..., Q − 1
```

Fig. 1. BRIGR Algorithm

we can write (4) as a linear system of N_m equations:

$$A^{(\ell)} \alpha_j^{(\ell)} = d_j^{(\ell)}$$

with right hand side: $d_j^{(\ell)} = \left(\hat{D}_j^{(\ell)}(0), \ldots, \hat{D}_j^{(\ell)}((N_m - 1)\Delta k) \right)^T$, coefficient matrix:

$$A^{(\ell)} = H^{(\ell)} B \qquad (6)$$

and unknowns: $\alpha_j^{(\ell)} = \left(\alpha_0^{(j,\ell)}, \ldots, \alpha_{N_m-1}^{(j,\ell)} \right)^T$.

The algorithm for reconstructing the whole sequence is described in figure 1; its total computational cost is:

$$FLOPS_{seq} = FLOPS_{FT} + FLOPS_{Reg} \qquad (7)$$

where $FLOPS_{FT}$ contains the flops of the fast Fourier transforms (FFT) or inverse fast Fourier transforms (IFFT), required in steps (1),(2), (3), (4) and (5.2) in figure 1. Using the Matlab FFT function we have that:

$$FLOPS_{FT} \propto N_m^2 \log_2(N_m) + (Q-1)N_m N \log_2(N) + $$
$$+ 2NM \log_2(NM) + NM \log_2(M) \qquad (8)$$

The parameter $FLOPS_{Reg}$ is relative to the computational cost of the regularization algorithm required in steps (5.3) and (5.4.1) in figure 1. In our program, the value of $FLOPS_{Reg}$ is relative to the Tikhonov Regularization method which requires the computation of the Singular Value Decomposition (SVD) of the matrix $A^{(\ell)}$ and the choice of the optimal regularization parameter λ by means of the Generalized Cross Validation method. Then $FLOPS_{Reg} = N\ FLOPS_{SVD} + N(Q-1)FLOPS_\lambda$ where [1]:

$$FLOPS_{SVD} \propto \left(5 + \frac{11}{3}\right) N_m^3 \sim 9N_m^3$$

Using the primitives of the Regularization Tools Matlab package [5, 6], we found that, in our application:

$$FLOPS_\lambda \propto 25 FLOPS_{SVD}$$

and then

$$FLOPS_{Reg} \propto 9N \cdot N_m^3 \left(1 + 25(Q-1)\right) \qquad (9)$$

In figure 2 we report the total computational time with respect to the components $FLOPS_{FT}$ and $FLOPS_{Reg}$. The greatest computational work load is given by the contribution of $FLOPS_{Reg}$: the parallel splitting of this part of the algorithm can improve significantly the efficiency of the whole application.

3 Parallel Algorithm

The parallel version of the algorithm reported in figure 1 is obtained observing that the computations in ℓ cycle in step (5) are completely independent each other and can be distributed among different processors. The parallel algorithm is implemented on a master-slave basis, using message passing primitives for the data communications. The master and slave algorithms are reported in figures 4 and 5, respectively.

Given P the number of homogeneous slave processors, we can describe the computational cost of the parallel algorithm as:

$$FLOPS_{par} = FLOPS_{master} + FLOPS_{slave} + FLOPS_{comm} \qquad (10)$$

where $FLOPS_{comm}$ is the number of floating point operations performed during the time spent in communication. Observing the structure of the algorithm and recalling (9), (8) we have that:

$$FLOPS_{master} \propto 2NM \log_2(NM) + (Q-1)N_m N \log_2(N)$$

$$FLOPS_{slave} \propto \frac{N}{P} \left(M \log_2(M) + 9N_m^3 \left(1 + 25(Q-1)\right)\right)$$

In this last case, the $FLOPS$ required in the computation of matrix B (step (1) in figure 5) are not taken into account since they are completely overlapped by the value of $FLOPS_{master}$.

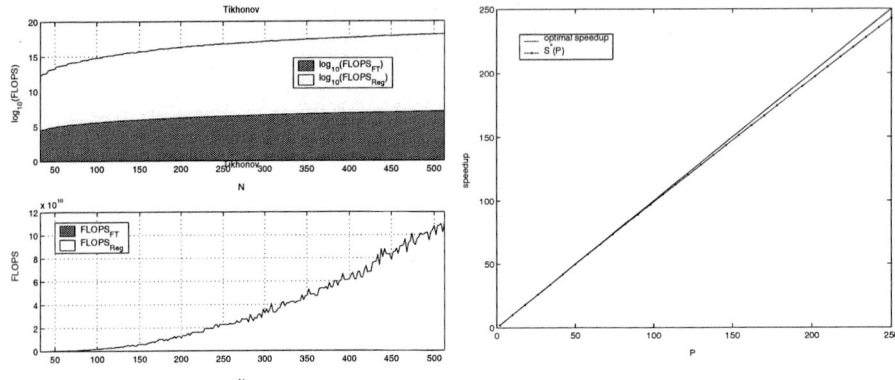

Fig. 2. Values of $FLOPS_{seq}$ in the case: $Q = 58$, $M \simeq 0.3N$, $N_m \sim 0.3M$

Fig. 3. Values of Asymptotic Speed up in the case: $Q = 58$, $N = 256$, $M = 70$, $N_m = 19$

The parallel performance is measured by means of the speedup parameter as a function of the number of processors used:

$$Su(P) = \frac{timesequential}{timeparallel}$$

Using relations (7) and (10) we define the asymptotic speedup parameter by ignoring the communication time:

$$S^*(P) = \frac{FLOPS_{seq}}{FLOPS_{master} + FLOPS_{slave}}$$

Analyzing the plot of $S^*(P)$ (figure 3) we notice that for values of P less then 100 optimal speedups are still obtained.

4 Numerical Results

The experiments have been performed on a cluster of 17 PC Pentium III 600 Mhz with 256 Mb RAM connected through a 10 Mbit/sec network. The PCs are equipped with Matlab 6.5 and MatlabMPI version 0.95 [7] that provides Message Passing primitives. The parallel algorithm has been tested on real dynamic MRI data. The data sequence is constituted of two reference data sets of 256×70 samples and of 57 dynamic data sets of 256×19 samples. In the notation used in the previous sections:

$$N = 256, \ M = 70, \ Q = 58, \ N_m = 19.$$

The total time for the parallel algorithm is given as the sum of the times necessary for the following algorithm chunks:

MASTER

INPUT: First reference set: $D_0(\ell\Delta h, m\Delta k)$ of $N \cdot M$ values;
$Q - 1$ intermediate dynamic sets $D_j(\ell\Delta h, m\Delta k)$,
each of $N \cdot N_m$ values;
Last Reference set: $D_Q(\ell\Delta h, m\Delta k)$ with $N \cdot M$ values.

(1) for $j = 1, \ldots, Q - 1$
   (2.1) for $m = -N_m/2, \ldots, N_m/2 - 1$
      (2.1.1) $\hat{D}_j(\cdot, m\Delta k) = IFFT(D_j(\cdot, m\Delta k))$
(2) Compute $I_0(\ell\Delta x, m\Delta y) = IFFT2(D_0(\ell\Delta h, m\Delta k))$
(3) Compute $I_Q(\ell\Delta x, m\Delta y) = IFFT2(D_Q(\ell\Delta h, m\Delta k))$
(4) for $\ell = -N/2, \ldots, N/2 - 1$
   (4.1) Compute $G^{(\ell)}(m\Delta y)$ and $\hat{D}_j^{(\ell)}(\eta\Delta k)$
(5) $\mathcal{N} = N/\text{Num}_{\text{Slaves}}$
(6) for $Np = 1 : \text{Num}_{\text{Slaves}}$
   (6.1) Send to Slave Np:
$$\begin{array}{ll} & m = -M/2, \ldots, M/2 - 1 \\ G^{(\ell)}(m\Delta y) & \eta = -N_m/2, \ldots, N_m/2 - 1 \\ \hat{D}_j^{(\ell)}(\eta\Delta k) & \ell = (Np - 1) \cdot \mathcal{N} + 1 : Np \cdot \mathcal{N} \\ & j = 1, \ldots, Q - 1 \end{array}$$
   (6.2) Receive from Slave Np:
$$\begin{array}{ll} & m = -M/2, \ldots, M/2 - 1 \\ (I_j^{(\ell)} - I_0^{(\ell)})(m\Delta y) & \ell = (Np - 1) \cdot \mathcal{N} + 1 : Np \cdot \mathcal{N} \\ & j = 1, \ldots, Q - 1 \end{array}$$

OUTPUT: High resolution sequence:
$I_j(\ell\Delta x, m\Delta y) - I_0(\ell\Delta x, m\Delta y), \quad j = 1, \ldots, Q - 1$

Fig. 4. Parallel Algorithm: Master Processor

1. the sequential operations in the master program ((1)-(4) in figure 4);
2. the broadcasting of input data from the master to the slaves ((6.1) in figure 4);
3. the computation in the slave programs ((3) in figure 5);
4. the sending of computed results from each slave to the master ((4) in figure 5).

We present here the results obtained for the available data in our cluster; we have tested the application on 4, 8 and 16 slaves and the computational times in seconds are reported in table 1. The reconstructed images are not shown here, but they can be reproduced using MRITool 2.0 or they can be found in [9].

The time for chunk 1 is constant and it is about 0.65 seconds. The time for the broadcast in chunk 2 (t.b.) is reported in the first row. The message length decreases but the overhead increases from 4 to 16 nodes, hence the time is oscillating. The time for chunk 3 (t.s.) is dominant over the others. It depends on the processor power and it has inverse ratio with respect to the number of processors, as it is evident from figure 5. Indeed, the aim of this parallel

```
┌─────────────────────────────────────────────────────┐
│                    SLAVE Np                         │
│                                                     │
│ (1) Compute the Nm × Nm matrix B.                   │
│ (2) Receive from Master:                            │
│                    m = −M/2,..., M/2 − 1            │
│        G^(ℓ)(mΔy)  η = −Nm/2,..., Nm/2 − 1          │
│        D̂_j^(ℓ)(ηΔk) ℓ = (Np − 1)·N + 1 : Np·N      │
│                    j = 1,..., Q − 1                 │
│                                                     │
│ (3) for ℓ = (Np − 1)·N + 1 : Np·N                   │
│     (3.3) Compute the matrix A^(ℓ) = H^(ℓ)·B        │
│     (3.4) Compute the SVD of A^(ℓ)                  │
│     (3.5) for j = 1,..., Q − 1                      │
│         (3.6.1) Solve A^(ℓ) α_j^(ℓ) = d_j^(ℓ)       │
│         (3.6.2) Compute I_j^(ℓ)(mΔy) − I_0^(ℓ)(mΔy) =│
│             G^(ℓ)(mΔy) Σ_{p=0}^{Nm−1} α_p^(j,ℓ) B_p(mΔy) │
│                                                     │
│ (4) Send to Master:                                 │
│                    m = −M/2,..., M/2 − 1            │
│     (I_j^(ℓ) − I_0^(ℓ))(mΔy)  ℓ = (Np − 1)·N + 1 : Np·N │
│                    j = 1,..., Q − 1                 │
└─────────────────────────────────────────────────────┘
```

Fig. 5. Parallel Algorithm: Slave Processor

application is to decrease the execution time by splitting the computational workload of chunk 3 among an increasing number of processors. If Tikhonov regularization method is used together with the GCV method for the choice of the regularization parameter (from the Regularization Tools Matlab package [5,6]), then the reconstruction time of a single image row ((3.6.1) and (3.6.2) in figure 5) is of about 0.4 seconds on Pentium III 600 Mhz. The time for the execution of the whole chunk 3 is reported in row 2 of table 1. The time for executing chunk 4 (t.f.) is the time for a communication of a message between two nodes, since we can presume that the slave do not send concurrently to the master. Finally, the last row of the table shows the total time for the described application; figure 6 plots the obtained speedup that is almost equal to the ideal speedup. If the application is executed on Pentium IV 1.5Ghz processors, the application scales again very well up to 16 processors, even if the time for the execution of chunk 3 is reduced of about 90%. This agrees with the theoretical results predicted in figure 3.

5 Conclusions

In this paper we presented a parallel software for dynamic MRI reconstructions. The computational cost of the parallel application has been analyzed in term of

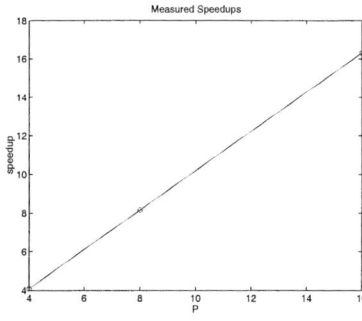

P	4	8	16
broadcasting time (t.b.)	0.85	0.65	0.8
slave computational time (t.s.)	1429	715	357
sending time (t.f.)	0.9	0.6	0.3
total time	1431	716	358

Table 1. Execution times in seconds on P processors

Fig. 6. Values of measured speedup in the case: $Q = 58$, $N = 256$, $M = 70$, $N_m = 19$

number of floating point operations by varying the number of processors. The parallel application is tested on real MR data on a network of Linux workstations using MatlabMPI primitives. The results obtained completely agree with the predictions giving optimal speedups with up to 20 processors. In our future work we are planning to test our application on larger and more powerful parallel computing environments, investigating among different parallel matlab implementations based on MPI.

References

1. A. Bjorck, *Numerical methods for least squares problems*, SIAM, 1996.
2. J. Fenandez-Baldomero, *Message Passing under Matlab*, Proceedings of the HPC 2001 (Seattle, Ws) (Adrian Tentner, ed.), 2001, pp. 73–82.
3. E. Loli Piccolomini F. Zama G. Zanghirati A.R. Formiconi, *Regularization methods in dynamic MRI*, Applied Mathematics and Computation **132, n. 2** (2002), 325–339.
4. MPI Forum, *MPI: a message passing interface standard*, International Journal of Supercomputer Applications **8** (1994), 3–4.
5. P.C. Hansen, *Regularization Tools: : A Matlab package for analysis and solution of discrete ill-posed problems*, Numerical Algorithms **6** (1994), 1–35.
6. P.C. Hansen, *Regularization Tool 3.1*, http://www.imm.dtu.dk/ pch/Regutools/index.html, 2002.
7. Jeremy Kepner, *Parallel programming with MatlabMPI*, http://www.astro.princeton.edu/ jvkepner/, 2001.
8. A.R. Formiconi E. Loli Piccolomini S. Martini F. Zama and G. Zanghirati, *Numerical methods and software for functional Magnetic Resonance Images reconstruction*, Annali dell'Universita' di Ferrara, sez. VII Scienze Matematiche, suppl. vol. XLVI, Ferrara, 2000.
9. E. Loli Piccolomini G. Landi F. Zama, *A B-spline parametric model for high resolution dynamic Magnetic Resonance Imaging*, Tech. report, Department of Mathematics, University of Bologna, Piazza Porta S.Donato 5, Bologna, Italy, March 2003.

Improving Wildland Fire Prediction on MPI Clusters*

B. Abdalhaq, G. Bianchini, A. Cortés, T. Margalef, and E. Luque

Departament d'Informàtica, E.T.S.E, Universitat Autònoma de Barcelona,
08193-Bellaterra (Barcelona) Spain
{baker,german}@aows10.uab.es
{ana.cortes,tomas.margalef,emilio.luque}@uab.es

Abstract. One of the challenges still open to wildland fire simulators is the capacity of working under real-time constrains with the aim of providing fire spread predictions that could be useful in fire mitigation interventions. In this paper, a parallel optimization framework for improving wildland fire prediction is applied to a real laboratory fire. The proposed prediction methodology has been tested on a Linux cluster using MPI.

1 Introduction

One of the goals of fire model developers is that of providing physical or heuristic rules that can explain and emulate fire behavior and, consequently, might be applied to creating robust prediction and prevention tools. However, as knowledge of several factors affecting fire spread is limited, most of the existing wildland fire models are not able to exactly predict real-fire spread behavior. Fire simulators [1],[2],[3],[4], which only are a translation of the fire models' equations into code, cannot therefore provide good fire spread predictions. The disagreement between real and simulated propagation basically arises because of uncertainties stemming not only from the respective mathematical models (coded on the simulators) and their numerical solutions, but also from the difficulty of providing the model with accurate input values. A way to overcome the latest problem consists of applying optimization techniques to the input parameters of the simulator/model, with the aim of finding an input setting so that the predicted fire propagation matches the real fire propagation. Although similar ways of approaching that problem can be found in the literature [5],[6], no analysis of its applicability under real time constraints has been carried out.

Optimization is an iterative process that starts from an initial set of guesses for the input parameters and, at each iteration, generates an enhanced set of input parameter guesses. The optimization process will stop when a feasible solution is reached. In other words, for the fire case, the aim of the optimization process is to find a set of input parameters that, if fed to the simulator, best describe fire behavior in the past. Therefore, we expect that the same set of parameters could be used to improve the prediction of fire behavior in the near future. Obviously, this prediction scheme will

---

* This work has been financially supported by the *Comisión Interministerial de Ciencia y Tecnología* (CICYT) under contract TIC2001-2592 and by the European Commission under contract EVG1-CT-2001-00043 SPREAD.

be useful if it can provide a prediction (a new fire-line situation) within a time frame that is substantially before that of the real time being predicted. Otherwise, this prediction scheme will be of no value. Consequently, we are interested in accelerating the optimization process as much as possible.

Typically, any optimization technique involves a large number of simulation executions, all of which usually require considerable time. In particular, we have used a Genetic Algorithm (GA) as optimization strategy, which has been parallelized under a master-worker programming paradigm to speed up its convergence. This enhanced prediction method was implemented using MPI as a message-passing interface and was executed on a Linux PC cluster. In this paper, we analyze the improvements provided by the proposed prediction scheme in terms of prediction quality and speed-up gains for a real laboratory fire.

The organization of this paper is as follows. The enhanced prediction method is presented in section 2. Its parallel version is described in section 3. Section 4 includes the experimental results obtained when the proposed prediction method is applied to a laboratory fire. Finally, the main conclusions are reported in section 5.

2 The Wildland Fire Prediction Method

As we have mentioned, the classical prediction scheme consists of using any existing fire simulator to evaluate the fire position after a certain time. This classical approach is depicted in figure 1 in which FS corresponds to the Fire Simulator, which is seen as a black-box. RFL0 is the real fire line at time t_0 (initial fire line), whereas RFL1 corresponds to the real fire line at time t_1. If the prediction process works, after executing FS (which should be fed with its input parameters and RFL0) the predicted/simulated fire line at time t_1 (PFL) should concord with the real fire line (RFL1).

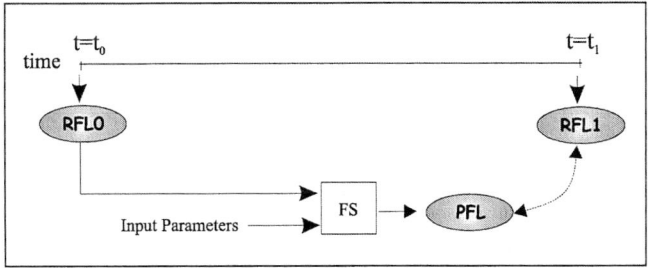

Fig. 1. Classical prediction of wildland fire propagation.

Our prediction method is a step forward with respect to this classical methodology. The proposed approach focuses its efforts on overcoming the input-parameter uncertainty problem. It introduces the idea of applying an optimisation scheme to calibrate the set of input parameter with the aim of finding an "optimal" set of inputs, which improves the results provided by the fire-spread simulator. The resulting scheme is shown in figure 2. As we can see, in order to evaluate the goodness of the results provided by the simulator, a fitness function should be included (FF box). This function will determine the degree of matching between the predicted fire line and the real fire line. We can also observe from figure 2 the way in which the optimisation strategy is included into the framework to close a feedback loop. This loop will be repeated until a "good" solution is found or until a predetermined number of iterations has been reached. At that point, an "optimal" set of inputs should be found, which will be used as the input set for the fire simulator, in order to obtain the position of the fire front in the very near future (t_2 in figure 2). Obviously, this process will not be useful if the time incurred in optimizing is superior to the time interval between two consecutive updates of the real-fire spread information (for the example of figure 2, the interval time between t_1 and t_2). For this reason, it is necessary to accelerate the optimization process as much as possible. In the following section, we describe how we have parallelized the optimization method and executed it on an MPI cluster in order to accelerate the entire prediction process.

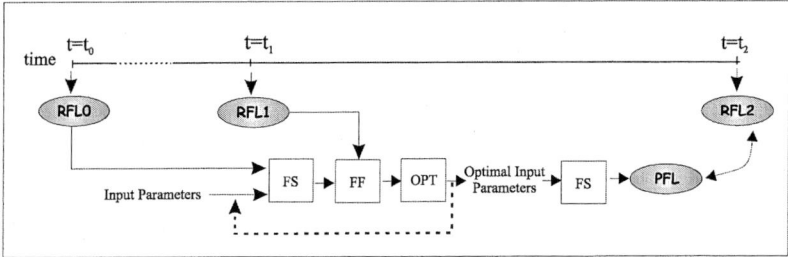

Fig. 2. Enhanced wildland fire prediction method

3 A Parallel Implementation of the Enhanced Prediction Method

For optimization purposes, we used the optimization framework called BBOF (Black-Box Optimization Framework) [7], which consists of a set of C++ abstract-based classes that must be re-implemented in order to fit both the particular function being optimized and the specific optimization technique. BBOF works in an iterative fashion, in which it moves step-by-step from an initial set of guesses for the set of parameters to be optimized to a final value that is expected to be closer to the optimal set of parameters than the initial guesses. This goal is achieved because, at each iteration of this process, a preset optimization technique is applied to generate a new set of guesses that should be better than the previous set. This optimization scheme fits well into the master-worker programming paradigm working in an iterative scheme. In particular, since the evaluation of the function to be optimized for each guess is independent, the guesses can be identified as the work (tasks) done by the workers. The responsibility for collecting all the results from the different workers and for generating the next set of guesses by applying a given optimization technique will be taken on by the master process. For the purposes of master-worker communication, BBOF uses the MPICH (Message Passing Interface) library [8],[9]. In our case, the master will execute a GA as optimisation strategy and will also be in charge of distributing the guesses of the candidate solutions to the workers. The workers themselves will execute, the underlying fire-spread simulator and will also provide the prediction error (evaluation of the fitness function). Figure 3 shows how this master-worker scheme provided by BBOF is matched in our fire prediction environment. For this particular case, the OPT box is directly identified to the master process, whereas the FS and FF box pair define the code at each worker.

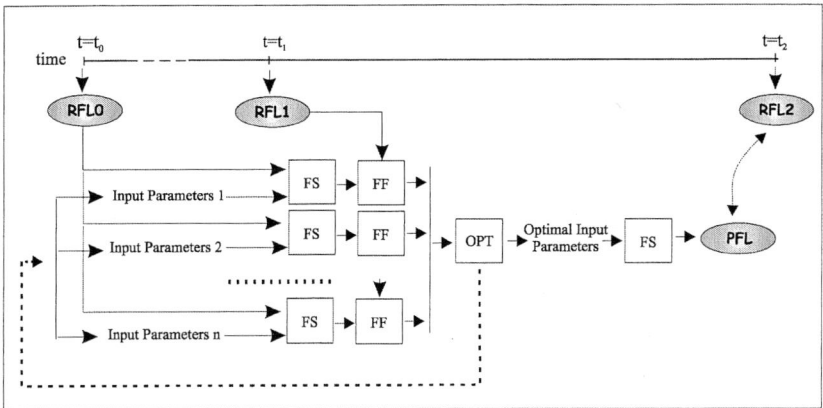

Fig. 3. Enhanced wildland fire prediction method on a master-worker scheme

4 Experimental Results

The proposed fire-prediction model has been studied using a purposely-built experimental device. This set is composed by a burn table of 3x3 m^2 that can be inclined at any desired angle (slope) and by a group of fans that can produce a horizontal flow above the table with an arbitrary velocity. In our experimental study, the laboratory environment was set up as follows: the table inclination was set to 35 grades; there was no wind and the fuel bed consisted of maritime pine ("pinus pinaster"). In order to gather as much information as possible about the fire-spread behavior, an infrared camera recorded the complete evolution of the fire. Subsequently, the obtained video was analyzed and several images were extracted, from which the corresponding fire contours were obtained. Figure 4.a and 4.b show the recorded images for the ignition fire and fire spread after 1 minute, respectively. It should be taken into account that the slope increases from the bottom of the images towards the top. Fire time was about 1m 30" from the moment of ignition. Despite the duration of this laboratory experiment, its *post-mortem* analysis allows us to validate the behavior of our prediction method, as will be shown in the following sections.

Subsequently, we will briefly describe the FS and FF component of the enhanced-prediction method depicted in figure 2 for our particular case. The Optimization strategy used in this framework is a Genetic Algorithm (GA) [10]. Since GAs are well known optimization strategies, in this paper we will make no further comment on its method of working.

4.1 The Simulator

For wildland fire simulation purpose, we have used the wildland simulator proposed by Collin D. Bevins, which is based on the FireLib library [11]. FireLib is a library that encapsulates the BEHAVE fire behavior algorithm [12]. In particular, this simulator uses a cell automata approach to evaluate fire spread. The terrain is divided into square cells and a neighborhood relationship is used to evaluate whether a cell is to be burnt and at what time the fire will reach the burnt cells. As inputs, this simulator accepts the maps of the terrain, the vegetation characteristics, the wind and the initial ignition map. The output generated by the simulator consists of the map of the terrain where each cell is tagged with its ignition time. In our experiment, we divided the terrain (burn table) into 40x40 cells.

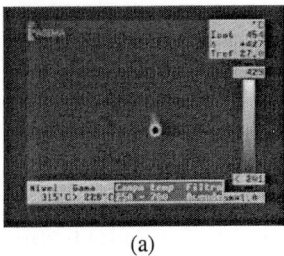 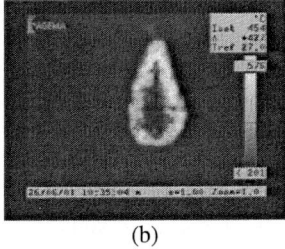

(a) (b)

Fig. 4. Image recorded as an ignition fire (a), and fire spread after 1 minute (b).

4.2 The Fitness Function

As we describe in section 2, in order to measure the goodness of the predicted fire line, we need to define a fitness function. Taking into account the particular implementation of the simulator used in this experiment, where the terrain is treated as a square matrix of terrain cells, in order to ascertain whether or not the simulated fire spread exactly matches real fire propagation, we define the fitness function as the minimization of the number of cells that are burned in the simulation but are not burned in the real fire map, and vice versa. This expression is known as the XOR function. Figure 5 shows an example of how this fitness function is evaluated for a 5x5 cell terrain. The obtained value will be referred to as the prediction error that, for this example, is 3.

4.3 Classical Wildland Fire Prediction

We used the laboratory fire described above to compare the prediction results provided by classical prediction with respect to the proposed enhanced prediction method. As previously commented, any fire-spread simulator needs to be fed with certain input parameters. Since our experimental fire was carried out under determined conditions (laboratory conditions), we have fairly good estimations values for the input parameters. Table 1 shows the values of these parameters, which have been grouped into three different categories: wind, moisture and fuel description. Since in this paper we are not interested in the model description, we will not describe in detail each individual input parameter.

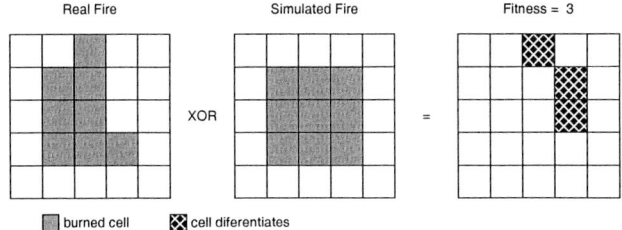

Fig. 5. Evaluation of the XOR function as a fitness function for a 5x5 cell terrain.

Table 1. Input parameter values measured at the laboratory fire

Wind		Moisture				Fuel			
Speed	Dir.	1 hour	10 hours	100 hours	Herb	Depth	Load	M. ext	ar/vol
0,0	0,0	0,1536	0,1536	0,1536	0,1536	0,25	0,134	1	2500

We used the prediction scheme described in figure 1 for two different situations. In the first case, the initial time t_0 was chosen as 30", consequently, the fire line at that time was RFL1. For this initial situation, we predicted the new situation of the fire front at time 1 minute by executing the fire simulator in an isolated way. The second prediction was performed by considering 1 minute as the initial time and the predicted fire line was obtained for time instant 1min 30". Table 2 summarizes the obtained results. If we consider the prediction errors in terms of percentage according to the total number of cells burnt, we have 52% and 25% for the first and second prediction, respectively. Bearing in mind the dimension of the fire (3x3 m^2), this percentage of error is considerable high.

Table 2. Prediction error for the classical prediciton method applied to the laboratory fire

Initial time	Prediction time	Total burn cells	Prediction error
30"	1 min	180	95
1 min	1min 30"	401	101

4.4 Prediction Quality Improvement

The above numbers show that the classical prediction method does not provide accurate predictions, despite the study case being well known due to its laboratory nature. Therefore, what would happen in a real fire situation where there are several types of uncertainty? We therefore applied the enhanced prediction method to the same lab fire analysed in the previous section in order to compare the obtained prediction with that from the earlier experiment. As commented, we used the Genetic Algorithm as an optimisation strategy, which will be iterated 1000 times. The input parameters to be tuned are the same as those shown in table 1, and the optimisation process will work under the assumption that there is no previous knowledge of the input parameters. The complete enhanced prediction method, depicted in figure 3, was applied twice, once at 30" and again at 60". The first optimisation process provided an "optimal" set of input parameters, which were used to predict the new fire line situation at 60". This prediction was obtained by executing the fire spread simulator once, feeding it with the real fire line at 30" and with the "optimal" set of parameters obtained for that time. Subsequently, we continue the process of optimisation to predict the fire line at 1m 30". We used the optimised parameters at 30" as the initial generation, repeating the same process using the real-fire line at 1 minute as reference. Optimised parameters were used to predict the fire line at 1min30". The result obtained in terms of improvement in prediction quality are shown in figure 6. This figure plots both, the enhanced and classical predicted fire line versus the real fire line. As we can observe from both, the plotted fire lines and the obtained prediction errors, the proposed prediction scheme outperforms the results obtained applying the classical scheme. In particular, the prediction errors obtained, in percentage, are 40% and 11% for both predictions, respectively. That means a reduction of 20% in the first case with respect to the classical approach and a reduction of more than 50% for the prediction at 90".

We can therefore conclude that the enhanced prediction method provides better results than the classical prediction scheme. In particular, we observe that the accumulation effect of the optimisation method (1000 iterations at 30" plus an additional 1000 iterations at 60") provides better prediction quality. We should thus be able to iterate the process as much as possible under real-time constraints in order to guarantee good prediction quality. For this reason, we apply parallel processing to accelerate the optimisation process. In the following section, we analyse the speed-up improvement of the prediction process, as the number of processors involved in the prediction process increases.

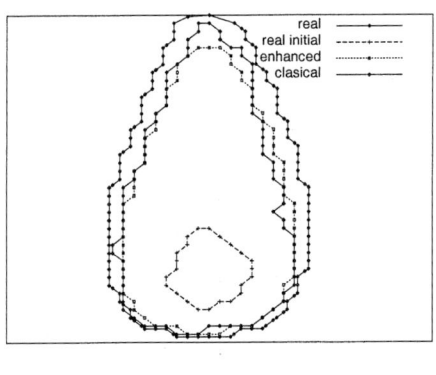

Initial time	Prediction time	Prediction error	
		Classical Prediction	Enhanced Prediction
30"	60"	95	72
60"	90"	101	45

(a) (b)

Fig 6. Predicted fire lines (a) for the laboratory fire at 90" applying the classical and the enhanced prediction methods and their corresponding prediction errors (b)

4.5 Speed up Improvement

As it has been shown, in order to provide useful fire spread prediction, it is necessary to work under real-time constrains, which must be accomplished for the proposed enhanced prediction method. For this reason, we have analysed the speed up improvement for the prediction process as the number of processors increases.

The proposed method has been executed on a Linux cluster under an MPI environment. The number of processors used were 1, 2, 4, 8, 11 and 13. Figure 7 shows the evolution of the speed up for this particular example. Let's notice that the speed up for 2 processors is less than the sequential execution of the method in 1 processor. Although this result seems to be anomalous, this situation can easily be explained. We should bear in mind the master-worker approach described in section 3. When the prediction process is executed on a single processor, the master and worker processes are in the same machine and there is no network delays involved. However, when the prediction process is executed in 2 processors, we still have one master and one worker but, in this case, both processes must communicate each other through the network and, consequently, there is a time increase due to this fact. From 4 processors (1 master and 3 workers) we clearly observe a speed up improvement, which continues as the number of processors increases. For the maximum number of processors available, we can observe a considerable time reduction despite of not accomplishing the real-time constraints required by our experiment. The prediction time for the laboratory experiment should be less than 30", however, with the available computational resource, we have not been able to accomplish such time requirement. Figure 7 illustrates that by using more machines we can carry out more iterations in a predetermined limitation of time and a better quality of prediction could be obtain. Therefore, if we want to predict fire evolution faster than real fire spread, the use of parallel processing becomes crucial.

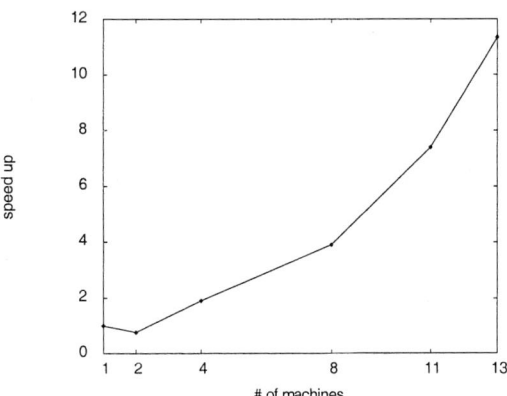

Fig. 7 Speed up for the enhanced prediction method for different number of processors

5 Conclusions

In this paper, we have described an enhanced fire spread prediction methodology, whose goal is to work under real time constraints. The proposed prediction scheme uses real fire information from the recent past of an ongoing fire to tune the input parameters of the underlying fire simulator. The obtained parameters will be used to predict the fire spread in a near future. Since this process should work under real time constraints, we have parallelized the technique using MPI to improve the prediction speed up. The methodology has been tested using a laboratory fire. Although the results obtained are only for one isolate experiment, they are illustrative enough to conclude that the enhanced prediction scheme could accomplish the real-time constraints when enough computing power (in terms of processors) is available.

References

1. Finney, M.A. "FARSITE: Fire Area Simulator-- Model Development and Evaluation." USDA For. Serv. Res. Pap. RMRS-RP-4. (1998).
2. Lopes,A.M.G., Viegas, D.X. & Cruz, M.G. "FireStation - An Integrated System for the Simulation of Fire Spread and Wind Flow Over Complex Topography Spreading", III International Conference on Forest Fire Research, Vol. B.40, pp. 741-754. (1998). [6] Martine-Millán and Saura, 1998
3. Martinez-Millán, J. and Saura, S. "CARDIN 3.2: Forest Fires Spread and Fighting Simulation System", III International Conference on Forest Fire Research. (1998).
4. Jorba J., Margalef T., Luque E., J. Campos da Silva Andre, D. X Viegas "Parallel Approah to the Simulation Of Forest Fire Propagation". Proc. 13 Internationales Symposium "Informatik fur den Umweltshutz" der Gesellshaft Fur Informatik (GI). Magdeburg (1999) pp. 69-81
5. Keith Beven and Andrew Binley. The Future of Distributed Models: Models Calibration and Uncertainty Prediction. Hydrological Process, Vol. 6, pp. 279-298 (1992).
6. K.Chetehouna, A. DeGiovanni., J. Margerit., O. Séro-Guillaume. Technical Report, INFLAME Project, October 1999.
7. Baker Abdalhaq, Ana Cortés, Tomàs Margalef, Emilio Luque: "Evolutionary Optimization Techniques on Computational Grids. International Conference on Computational Science" (1) 2002, pp. 513-522.
8. W. Gropp and E. Lusk and N. Doss and A. Skjellum,"A high-performance, portable implementation of the MPI message passing interface standard", "Parallel Computing", volume22-6, pp.789-828, sep,1996.
9. William D. Gropp and Ewing Lusk, User's Guide for mpich, a Portable Implementation of MPI Mathematics and Computer Science Division, Argonne National Laboratory, 1996.
10. Coley David A.: An Introduction to Genetic Algorithms for Scientists and Engineers, World Scientific, (1999)
11. Collin D. Bevins , FireLib User Manual & Technical Reference, 1996, www.fire.org
12. Andrews P.L. BEHAVE: fire behavior prediction and modeling systems- Burn subsytem, part1. General Technical Report INT-194. Ogden, UT, US Department of Agriculture, Forest Service, Intermountain Research Station; 1986, 130 pp.

Building 3D State Spaces of Virtual Environments with a TDS-Based Algorithm

Aleš Křenek, Igor Peterlík, and Luděk Matyska

Faculty of Informatics, Masaryk University
Brno, Czech Republic
{ljocha,xpeterl,ludek}@fi.muni.cz

Abstract. We present an extension of the TDS parallel state space search, building the state space of a certain class of haptic virtual environments. We evaluate its properties on a concrete example from computational chemistry. The scalability of the algorithm is distorted by several abnormalities whose causes are discussed.

1 The Application Area

1.1 Haptic Rendering

During the last decade, haptic human-computer interfaces grew into an important phenomenon of interaction with virtual environments while still presenting a challenge for development of computational methods to create realistic virtual environments.

The time interval of at most 1 ms is available to compute a force reaction, as at least 1 kHz refresh rate is required to create tactile illusion of surface ([5, 7]), and up to 5 kHz are needed for smooth perception [2]. Only simple models, like spring model of surface penetration, are usable under such strong restrictions.

A straightforward solution lies in pre-computing the involved force field on a sufficiently fine 3D grid. The actual device position would be mapped to the grid and the resulting force computed by interpolation with only few floating-point operations. However, this approach is too restrictive to cover many interesting applications as it does not take into account any internal state of the environment. We proposed an enriched 3D grid structure that keeps track of the environment internal state. This grid can be computed in advance and is described in Sect. 2 (for detailed description, see [3]), with major focus on parallel implementation of the generating algorithm.

1.2 Conformational Behaviour

Many complex organic molecules are *flexible*, capable to change shape without changing the chemical structure. We call *conformations* the relatively stable shapes, and by *conformational behaviour* we mean the process of changing conformations. Conformational behaviour is studied mainly due to its critical role in understanding biochemical processes in living organisms.

We build interactive models of flexible molecules based on results of computational analysis of conformational behaviour [4]. The user is presented, both in visual and haptic rendering, a van der Waals surface of the examined molecule. The haptic device is attached to another virtual object in the model, a spherical *probe*. With the probe the user can apply force on the molecular surface and make it undergo a conformational change. The energy required for the particular change is delivered to the user via the force feedback of the haptic device.

2 3D Grid with Level Conversions

To overcome the limitations of in-haptic-loop computation we proposed two stage process [3]: Exhaustively search through the state space, performing all the computationally extensive evaluations and store the results in a 3D grid data structure enriched with level conversions (abstraction of directionality in the state space). This stage is a focus of this paper.

The second stage, described in [3], runs the actual haptic interaction, using the pre-computed 3D data and interpolating between them when necessary.

2.1 The Data

The data structure used is based on a 3D rectangular grid of evenly distributed samples of the haptic device position. In addition, there may be more than one *level* in each grid point. A level represents a distinct state of the modelled system possible for a given device position (i.e. the grid point). Each record, i.e. a grid point and a level, stores exactly a state vector s_l, and $3 \times 3 \times 3$ cube D_l of *destination levels*. The state vector describes completely the state of the modelled system. The cube of the destination levels encodes *conversions* among the grid points and levels. We ignore the centre of the cube and interpret its remaining 26 elements as vectors $\bm{d} \in \mathcal{D}$,

$$\mathcal{D} = \left\{ (d_1, d_2, d_3) : d_1, d_2, d_3 \in \{-\bar{d}, 0, \bar{d}\} \text{ and } |(d_1, d_2, d_3)| \neq 0 \right\}$$

where $\bar{d}$ is the axial distance between two adjacent grid points. For each such $\bm{d}$, the corresponding value in the D array indicates that if the haptic device moves from the current position (grid point) $\bm{x}$ to $\bm{x} + \bm{d}$ the system reaches the state stored there at the level $D_l[\bm{d}]$.

We require *completeness* of the data, i.e. for each grid point $\bm{x}$, level l at this point and a shift vector $\bm{d}$ such that $\bm{x} + \bm{d}$ is still within the computation bounding box, the destination level $D_l[\bm{d}]$ must exist at $\bm{x} + \bm{d}$.

2.2 The Algorithm

The parallel version shown in Alg. 1 follows the *Transposition-Table-Driven Work Scheduling* (TDS for short) scheme [1]. By *transposition table* we mean a storage of discovered states. The TDS approach unifies partitioning the transposition table with scheduling work among the computing nodes. Whenever

Algorithm 1 Compute the 3D grid with level conversions, parallel version

1: initialize Q with all local seed points
2: **while** not terminating **do**
3:   **while** there is incoming message **do**
4:     **if** the message is STEP(s, x, d, l') **then**
5:       $Q \leftarrow (s, x, d, l')$
6:     **else if** the message is RESULT(x, l', d, l) **then**
7:       $X[x, l'].D[d] := l$
8:     **end if**
9:   **end while**
10:   $(s, x, d, l') \leftarrow Q$
11:   find level l where s is stored in x
12:   send RESULT$(x - d, l', d, l)$ to node_of$(x - d)$
13:   **if** $X[x, l]$ does not exist **then**
14:     $X[x, l].s := s$
15:     expand_state(x, s, l)
16:   **end if**
17: **end while**

procedure expand_state(x, s, l)
  for $d \in \mathcal{D}$ **do**
    if $x + d \in A$ **then**
      $s' = conv(s, x, d)$
      send STEP$(s', x + d, d, l)$ to node_of$(x + d)$
    end if
  end for

a new state is discovered during the search it is pushed towards its *home node*, i.e. the node which may keep the state in its partition of the transposition table. If the new state is not already in the table, it triggers further computation carried by the home node.

Besides that our extension also sends back messages to update the destination level cubes. Due to the required search through levels (line 11) the states are distributed according to x exclusively. The algorithm works with a distributed queue Q of quadruplets (s, x, d, l) — requests to store a data record consisting of a state s at the device position x, having been found as an appropriate conversion from position $x - d$ and level l. The queue is initialised with *seed points* whose states are known — usually the corners of the bounding box. The output of the algorithm is the array X, split among the nodes.

The parallel processes interchange two types of messages: STEP(s, x, d, l) — a forward request to store a data record (it implements a distributed insert into the queue, acually done at line 5 at the destination node of the message), and RESULT(x, l', d, l) — a reverse flow of information on the level l where a forward STEP$(s, x+d, d, l')$ request was actually stored (or the matching state s found).

The function node_of(x) finds the home node of the grid point x. The procedure expand_state performs computation of conversions and sends the generated requests to appropriate computing nodes.

We implemented the parallel version using MPI point-to-point communication. One of the TDS advantages we benefit from is an independence on any synchronisation (see also [6]), allowing to use CPU for computation as much as possible. Therefore a non-blocking communication is required as well. We use the `MPI_IBSEND` call that matches the semantics exactly.

The detection of global termination, deliberately omitted from Alg. 1, is based on sending another type of messages around a virtual circle among the nodes when they are idle. However, due to the asynchronous mode of communication, the process is rather complicated.

3 Performance Analysis

3.1 Experiments Overview

All the experiments we discuss in this section were run on the same input data— a conformation and two adjacent transition states of the alanine amino acid, using 3D grid resolution of 20. This represents a simple but real problem solved in an appropriate resolution.

All the experiments were performed in the following environments:

- SGI Origin 2000, 40 × MIPS 10k 195 MHz, IRIX 6.5, SGI MPI native implementation bundled with the operating system.
- Cluster of 16 PC's, each node 2 × Intel Xeon 2.4 GHz, Linux Debian 3.0, kernel 2.4.20, MPICH 1.2.5 using Myrinet network via native GM drivers (bypassing TCP/IP).
- The same cluster but using ch_p4 communication over gigabit Ethernet.
- Two clusters of 16 PC's, 2×Intel Pentium III 1 GHz, the same Linux environment, MPICH 1.2.5 using ch_p4. The clusters are located at two sites approx. 350 km far from each other, connected with gigabit WAN (RTT=5.5 ms).

The numerical part of the problem is represented by 187,112 invocations of the *conv* function and 374,224 data messages sent (total size approx. 20 MB) and is the same for all the experiments.

3.2 Evaluation Criteria

For the purpose of performance and scalability analysis we instrumented the program to produce a detailed trace output. The processing was classified into four distinct phases:

Work. Time corresponding to the *conv* function calls. Should be same for all the experiments on the same platform.
I/O. Writing the output files with states. Proved to have negligible effect and therefore neglected.
Receive-Idle. Waiting for an incoming message while the local queue is empty.
Send-Idle. Time spent in MPI send calls. Despite the implementation use of non-blocking send calls only, they turned up to consume considerable amount of time in certain situations (see details bellow).

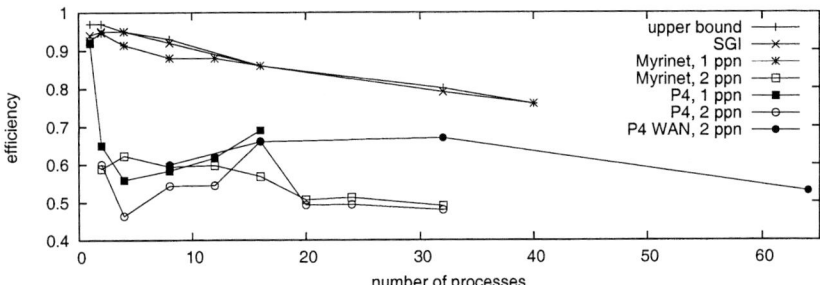

Fig. 1. Efficiency curves of all the experiments. "ppn" stands for "processes per node"

Whenever any of the parallel processes switches from one of the phases to another, it records the fact to the trace file together with an accurate timestamp.

We compare results of the experiments mainly in terms of *efficiency* that is calculated as the ratio:

$$efficiency = \frac{sequential\ time}{N \times wall\ clock\ time}$$

where the *sequential time* refers to a sequential version of the algorithm, i.e. it is the net CPU time necessary to solve the problem, N is the number of CPUs, and *wall clock time* is the duration of the parallel computation.

The efficiency should be close to 1 in an ideal case. However, despite the uniform distribution of grid points among computing nodes, there is a non-uniformity in the number of *conv* invocations given by the different number of discovered levels in each point. Moreover, there is huge difference in the time required for a single *conv* calculation depending on the actual originating position and state. Consequently, the *Work* times per node differ by as much as 30 % in our concrete computation[1]. Therefore there is a principal upper bound of the efficiency that cannot be surpassed (a consequence of the Amdahl's law).

$$efficiency\ upper\ bound = \frac{sequential\ time}{N \times \max_{i=1...N} work\ time\ of\ process\ i}$$

3.3 Observed Behaviour

Figure 1 presents the efficiency curves of all the performed experiments. In an optimal environment—the SGI Origin or the PC cluster using Myrinet and running one process per node in our experiments—the efficiency closely follows the theoretical upper limit given by the work distribution non-uniformity.

The *Work* time (see Tab. 1) in these two experiments is almost constant indicating an optimal CPU usage. In case of SGI Origin, the observed increase

---

[1] The situation rapidly improves with higher grid resolutions. Therefore we achieve better efficiency with more complicated problems which is promising in general.

Table 1. *Work* times (minutes), i.e. the sum of time spent exclusively in numeric calculations by all processes. It is expected to be constant on a given platform.

			Processes	1	2	4	8	12	16	20	24	32	40
Platform	Communication	ppn											
SGI	SGI	–		1012	974	976	981	–	974	–	–	1009	996
Linux	Myrinet	1		128	124	126	126	125	126	–	–	–	–
Linux	ch_p4	1		129	124	127	126	125	126	–	–	–	–
Linux	Myrinet	2		–	199	171	174	151	158	173	171	161	–
Linux	ch_p4	2		–	134	142	133	133	127	147	148	155	–

for 1, 32, and 40 processes is due to the lack of free CPU (serving system calls for I/O and network) in the partition of the machine allocated for the experiment.

The detailed traces show virtually all the *Receive-Idle* time is cumulated at the end of the computation of each process, forming a "drain-out" phase when no work for the process is available.

Blocking Send Calls. Switching to the ch_p4 device in place of Myrinet the `MPI_IBSEND` calls (counted as *Send-Idle* times, see Tab. 2) start taking considerable time (up to 30 seconds per call) after several hundreds messages were sent. Consequently, the efficiency drops down by about 30 %. Moreover, the behaviour is non-deterministic and random — the measured times vary with standard deviation 10 %. We do not know reason for this behaviour yet, but we assume a saturation of the MPI layer.

When the computation is split among more processes, the number of messages per process is lower. The lower rate of saturation explains the decreased overall *Send-Idle* time. However, currently we cannot explain the clear maximum at 4 processes.

The decreasing overall *Send-Idle* time is also responsible for the visible increase in efficiency. Because the local queues grow to several hundreds requests at the beginning (before the blocking sends actually occur) the *Receive-Idle* phase would cumulate at the end of computation again. However, due to the "wasted" CPU time in the *Send-Idle* phases the *Receive-Idle* phase is partially or completely reduced.

Interference on Dual-CPU Nodes. When two MPI processes are run on a dual-CPU node, they start to mutually interfere preventing an optimal CPU usage. The effect is observed as an increased *Work* time (see Tab. 1). Again, the behaviour is rather random, measured times vary with standard deviation about 10 %.

In the Myrinet experiments, the consequence is the visible drop of the efficiency. With ch_p4 this is still apparent but not so deep — the discussed *Send-Idle* phases do not contribute to CPU load, hence the interference does not occur when one of the processes is blocked, and consequently the *Work* times are shorter.

Table 2. *Receive-Idle* time (minutes) — the sum of time spent by all processes waiting for an incoming message while being idle — and *Send-Idle* time (minutes) — being blocked while sending a message. The *Send-Idle* times are shown in parentheses and omitted where negligible. In the ideal case the *Receive-Idle* time grows according to non-uniformity of work distribution and the *Send-Idle* time is always negligible.

Platf.	Comm.	ppn	Processes 1	2	4	8	12	16	20	24	32	40
SGI	SGI	–	0	32	42	68	–	156	–	–	214	259
Linux	Myrinet	1	0	4	8	13	15	16	–	–	–	–
Linux	ch_p4	1	0(5)	0(63)	0(90)	1(78)	6(68)	7(45)	–	–	–	–
Linux	Myrinet	2	–	7	14	11	48	44	53	59	68	–
Linux	ch_p4	2	–	0(71)	4(97)	5(88)	16(71)	11(48)	41(50)	46(45)	52(33)	–

Table 3. Compared results of "2n" (local) and "n + n" (distributed) experiments.

Processes	8	4 + 4	16	8 + 8	16 + 16	32 + 32
Efficiency	0.60	0.60	0.66	0.66	0.67	0.53
Work	283	283	283	282	278	279
Receive-Idle	8	1	27	21	63	143
Send-Idle	175	178	103	102	52	17

3.4 Geographically Distributed Runs

The motivation to run the program in a geographically distributed environment was twofold: confirm the hypothesis that the computation is independent on communication latency, and observe the behaviour on higher number of CPU's. Unfortunately, there is not a distant counterpart to the cluster where we performed the previous experiments, and vice versa, we could not run all the experiments on this pair of clusters. This makes interpretation of the results harder.

The first important outcome is that the results of "2n" and "n + n" experiments, i. e. the same number of processes running on the same cluster and split to both clusters respectively, are very close to each other (see Tab. 3). This is a strong evidence of the independence on the network latency.

Confusingly, the measured efficiency is higher in all comparable experiments. The reason of this phenomenon has to be traced to the CPU technology. The more advanced CPU's used in the previous experiments are more sensitive to the 2-ppn interference effect therefore it shows up more apparently[2].

The initial increase of efficiency corresponds to the decreasing *Send-Idle* time and has been already discussed in Sect. 3.3. From 32 processes the curve follows the slope of the theoretical upper bound witnessing a persisting scalability of the algorithm itself.

---

[2] While preparing the experiments we ran a set of calculations on an even older CPU's. Their results confirm this reasoning.

4 Conclusions

We presented a parallel algorithm to build a specialized 3D state space applicable to a class of problems coming mainly from human-computer interaction applications. The algorithm is based on transposition table driven work scheduling approach (originally designed for state-space searching), preserving its principal property — no need for explicit synchronisation.

The experimental results confirm this claim — the algorithm is virtually independent on network latency and can be efficiently used even in grid environments with high latencies. The achieved scalability is very close to theoretical limits given by non-ideal, slightly non-uniform distribution of actual work.

As a side effect we discovered certain limits of the current MPICH implementation on the Linux platform, with severe negative impact on performance. Despite these limitations the efficiency remains above 0.5 in all cases.

The implementation of the algorithm had been already used to solve large real problems, that are untractable without the parallel implementation [3].

In the following research we will concentrate on more even work distribution and we will consider using a simpler communication layer (instead of MPI) primary to avoid the "send" blocking.

Acknowledgement

The work presented in this paper was supported by the Grant Agency of the Czech Republic, grant no. 201/98/K041, and the Czech Ministry of Education, research programme CEZ:J07/98:143300003. Special thanks to the Supercomputer Centre Brno and the MetaCentre project for providing the computing resources.

References

1. J. W. Romein A. Plaat, H. E. Bal, and J. Schaeffer. Transposition table driven work scheduling in distributed search. In *Proc. 16th National Conference on Artificial Intelligence (AAAI)*, pages 725–731. 1999.
2. Z. Kabeláč. Rendering stiff walls with phantom. In *Proc. 2nd PHANToM User's Research Symposium*, 2000.
3. A. Křenek. Haptic rendering of complex force fields. In *Proc. 9th Eurographics Workshop on Virtual Environments*, pages 231–240. 2003. ISBN 3-905673-00-2.
4. J. Koča. Traveling through conformational space: an approach for analyzing the conformational behaviour of flexible molecules. *Progress in Biophys. and Mol. Biol.*, 70:137–173, 1998.
5. W. R. Mark, S. C. Randolph, M. Finch, J. M. Van Verth, and R. M. Taylor. Adding force feedback to graphics systems: Issues and solutions. In *Proc. SIGGRAPH*, 1996.
6. J. W. Romein, H. E. Bal, J. Schaeffer, and A. Plaat. A performance analysis of transposition-table-driven work scheduling in distributed search. *IEEE Trans. on Parallel and Distributed Systems*, 13(5):447–459, May 2002.
7. D. C. Ruspini, K. Kolarov, and O. Khatib. The haptic display of complex graphical environments. In *Proc. SIGGRAPH*, pages 345–352, 1997.

Parallel Pencil-Beam Redefinition Algorithm

Paul Alderson[1], Mark Wright[1], Amit Jain[1], and Robert Boyd[2]

[1] Department of Computer Science
Boise State University, Boise, Idaho 83725, USA
{mwright,aalderso}@onyx.boisestate.edu, amit@cs.boisestate.edu
[2] MD Anderson Cancer Center
University of Texas, 1515 Holcombe Blvd, Houston, TX 77030, USA
rboyd@mdanderson.org

Abstract. The growing sophistication in radiation treatment strategies requires the utilization of increasingly accurate, but computationally intense, dose algorithms, such as the electron pencil-beam redefinition algorithm (PBRA). The sequential implementation of the PBRA is in production use at the MD Anderson Cancer center. The PBRA is difficult to parallelize because of the large amounts of data involved that is accessed in an irregular pattern taking varying amounts of time in each iteration. A case study of the parallelization of the PBRA code on a Beowulf cluster using PVM and PThreads is presented. The solution uses a non-trivial way of exchanging minimal amount of data between processes to allow a natural partitioning to work. Multi-threading is used to cut down on the communication times between CPUs in the same box. Finally, an adaptive load-balancing technique is used to further improve the speedup.

1 Introduction

Radiation therapy was one of the first medical disciplines where computers were used to aid the process of planning treatments; the first paper on the use of computers to calculate radiation dose distributions appeared almost 50 years ago [1]. Today, computers are involved in practically all areas of radiation therapy. Treatment planning functions include image-based tumor localization, image segmentation, virtual therapy simulation, dose calculation, and optimization. Treatment delivery functions include controlling delivery systems and treatment verification. The growing sophistication in radiation treatment strategies requires the utilization of increasingly accurate, but computationally intense, dose algorithms, such as the electron pencil-beam redefinition algorithm (PBRA) [2]. The demanding pace of the radiation therapy clinic requires the employment of these advanced dose algorithms under the most optimum conditions available in terms of computation speed. Parallel processing using multi-computer clusters or multi-processor platforms are now being introduced to the clinic for this purpose, and the PBRA, with its extensive use of multi-dimensional arrays, is a good candidate for parallel processing.

In Section 2, we present an analysis of the PBRA sequential code. In Section 3, we describe the parallelization of the PBRA code as a series of refinements that were implemented along with the results obtained after each refinement. Section 4 further discusses some properties of the current parallel implementation. Finally, in Section 5, some conclusions are presented.

2 Sequential Code

The PBRA algorithm was implemented in FORTRAN by Robert Boyd in 1999. It is in production use at the University of Texas MD Andersen Cancer Center. We will highlight some features of the PBRA code that are relevant to the parallel implementation.

The PBRA code uses 16 three-dimensional arrays and several other lower dimensional arrays. The size of the arrays is about 45MB. The inner core of the code is the function pencil_beam_redefinition(), which has a triply-nested loop that is iterated several times. Profiling shows that this function takes up about 99.8% of the total execution time. The following code sketch shows the structure of the pencil_beam_redefinition() function.

```
kz = 0;
while (!stop_pbra && kz <= beam.nz)
{
  kz++;
  /* some initialization code here */

  /* the beam grid loop */
  for (int ix=1; ix <=beam.nx; ix++) {
    for (int jy=1; jy <= beam.ny; jy++) {
      for (int ne=1; ne <= beam.nebin; ne++) {
        ...
        /* calculate angular distribution in x direction */
        pbr_kernel(...);
        /* calculate angular distribution in y direction */
        pbr_kernel(...);
        /* bin electrons to temp parameter arrays */
        pbr_bin(...);
        ...
      }
    }
  } /* end of the beam grid loop */
  /* redefine pencil beam parameters and calculate dose */
  pbr_redefine(...);
}
```

The main loop of pencil_beam_redefinition() also contains some additional straight-line code that takes constant time and some function calls that perform binary search. However, these take an insignificant amount of time and are hence omitted from the sketch shown above. Currently the code uses beam.nx = 91, beam.ny = 91, beam.nz = 25, and nebin = 25. Profiling on sample data shows that the functions pbr_kernel() and pbr_bin() take up about 97.6% of the total execution time.

The function pbr_kernel() takes linear time ($O($beam.nx$)$ or $O($beam.ny$)$). The pbr_kernel() function computes new ranges in x and y direction that are used in the pbr_bin() function to update the main three-dimensional arrays. The execution time for pbr_bin() is dominated by a doubly-nested loop that is $O(($xmax $-$ xmin $+ 1) \times ($ymax $-$ ymin $+ 1))$, where the parameters xmin, xmax, ymin, ymax are computed in the two invocations of the pbr_kernel() function. The function pbr_bin() function updates the main three-dimensional arrays in an irregular manner, which makes it difficult to come up with a simple partitioning scheme for a parallel implementation.

3 Parallelization of PBRA

Initially, the PBRA code was rewritten in C/C++. The C/C++ version is used as the basis for comparing performance. During this section, we will discuss timing results that are all generated using the same data set. For this data set, the **sequential PBRA code ran in 2050 seconds**. In production use, the PBRA code may be used to run on several data sets in a sequence. In the next section, we will present results for different data sets.

The sequential timing skips the initialization of data structures and the final writing of the dosage data to disk. These two take insignificant amount of time relative to the total running time. Before we describe the parallel implementation, we need to describe the experimental setup.

3.1 Experimental Setup

A Beowulf-cluster was used for demonstrating the viability of parallel PBRA code. The cluster has 6 dual-processor 166MHz Pentium PCs, each with 64 MB of memory, connected via a 100 MBits/s Ethernet hub.

The PCs are running RedHat Linux 7.1 with 2.4.2-2 SMP kernel. The compiler is GNU C/C++ version 2.96, with the optimizer enabled. PVM version 3.4.3 and XPVM version 1.2.5 [3] are being used. For threads, the native POSIX threads library in Linux is being used.

3.2 Initial PVM Implementation

The parallel implementation uses the PVM Master/Slave model. The master process initializes some data structures, spawns off the PVM daemon, adds machines to PVM, spawns off slave processes, multicasts some data structures to the slave processes and then waits to get the dosage arrays back from the slave processes. Embedding PVM makes it transparent to the users.

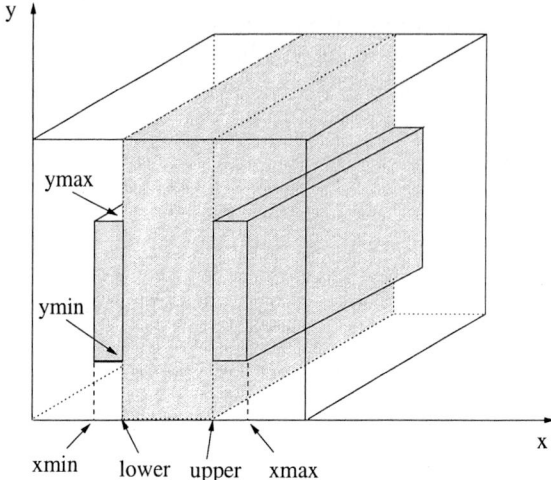

Fig. 1. Spreading of a beam being processed in one slice by one process

The main loop in pencil_beam_redefinition is being run by each slave process. However, each process works on one slice of the main three-dimensional arrays. The slicing was chosen to be done in the X-axis. If we have p processes and n is the size in the X dimension, then each process is responsible for a three-dimensional slice of about n/p width in the X axis. However, as each process simulates the beam through its slice, the beam may scatter to other slices. See Figure 1 for an illustration. Most of the time the scattering is to adjoining slices but the scattering could be throughout. One effect of this observation is that each slave process has to fully allocate some of the three-dimensional arrays even though they only work on one slice.

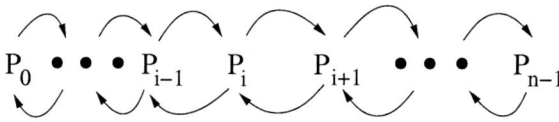

Fig. 2. Compensation for beam scattering at the end of each outer iteration

To solve the problem of beam-scattering, the processes exchange partial amounts of data at the end of each iteration (which also synchronizes the processes). The communication pattern is shown in Figure 2. Each process P_i receives appropriate parts of the three-dimensional arrays from P_{i-1} as well as P_{i+1}. Each process P_i combines the received data with its computed data. Then P_i sends the appropriate parts of the data off to its two neighbors. The processes P_0 and P_{n-1} bootstrap the process, one in each direction. The amount of data exchanged is dependent upon how much the beam scatters.

After some more fine-tuning, the best timing with the initial implementation was 657 seconds with 12 slave processes, for a speedup of 3.12. The reason for the low speedup is due to large amount of communication as well as load-imbalance.

3.3 Using PThreads on Each Machine

Using XPVM the communication patterns of the PBRA parallel code was observed. It was realized that the communication time can be reduced by letting only one process run per machine but use two threads (since each machine was a SMP machine with 2 CPUs). The main advantage was that threads would share the memory, so no communication would be required.

Each thread is now running the entire triply-nested for loop. To obtain a better load balance, the threads are assigned iterations in a round-robin fashion. Another problem is the need to synchronize threads in between calls to pbr_kernel and for the call to pbr_bin, since during the call to pbr_bin the partial results from the threads were being combined. The net effect of multi-threading is that the calls to pbr_kernel were now happening concurrently while communication is reduced significantly. The sketch of the thread main function (pbra_grid) is shown below.

```
/* inside pbra_grid: main function for each thread */
for (int ix=lower; ix <=upper; ix=ix+procPerMachine)
    for (int jy=1; jy <= beam.ny; jy++)
        for (int ne=1; ne <= beam.nebin; ne++)
        {
            ...
            /* calculate angular distribution in x direction */
            pbr_kernel(...);
            <use semaphore to update parameters in critical section>
            /* calculate angular distribution in y direction */
            pbr_kernel(...);
            <use semaphore to update parameters in critical section>
            /* bin electrons to temp parameter arrays */
            <semaphore_down to protect access to pbr_bin */
            pbr_bin(...);
            <semaphore_up to release access to pbr_bin */
            ...
        }
```

Compared to the sequential program, the multi-threaded version running on one machine with 2 CPUs took 1434 seconds, for a speedup of 1.43. When we ran the PVM program with multi-threading on 12 CPUs, we got a time of 550 seconds for a speedup of 3.73, about a 20% improvement.

3.4 Adaptive Load Balancing

Using XPVM and with the help of code instrumentation, it was discovered that although each process had an equal amount of data, the amount of time required is not distributed equally. Also, the uneven distribution had an irregular pattern that varies with each outer iteration. A general load balancing scheme is described below to deal with the unbalanced workloads.

Each slave process sends the time taken for the last outer iteration to the master. Suppose that these times are $t_0, t_1, t_2, \ldots, t_{n-1}$ for n processes. The master computes the average time, say t_{avg}. Based on that, process P_i needs to retain a fraction t_{avg}/t_i for the next round. We are using the past iteration to predict the times for the next iteration. We also made the frequency of load balancing be a parameter; that is, whether to load-balance every iteration or every second iteration and so on. The following code shows a sketch of the main function for the slave processes after incorporating the load-balancing.

```
kz = 0;
while (!stop_pbra && kz <= beam.nz)
{
   kz++;
   /* the pbra_grid does most of the work now */
   for (int i=0; i<procPerMachine; i++)
     pthread_create(...,pbra_grid,...);
   for (int i=0; i<procPerMachine; i++)
     pthread_join(...);
   <send compute times for main loop to master>
   <exchange appropriate data with P(i-1) and P(i+1)>
   /* redefine pencil beam parameters and calculate dose */
   pbr_redefine(...);
   <send or receive data to rebalance based on
     feedback from master and slackness factor>
}
```

Table 1 shows the effect of load balancing frequency on the parallel runtime.

Table 1. Effect of load balancing frequency on runtime for parallel PBRA code running on 6 machines with 2 CPUs each

Load Balancing Frequency	Runtime (seconds)
none	550
1	475
2	380
3	391
4	379
5	415

The next improvement comes from the observation that if a process finishes very fast, it might receive too much data for the next round. The slackness factor allows us to specify a percentage to curtail this effect. If it is set to 80%,

Table 2. Parallel runtime versus number of CPUs on a sample data set

CPUs	Runtime (secs)	Speedup
1	2050	1.00
2	1434	1.42
4	1144	1.79
6	713	2.87
8	500	4.00
10	405	5.06
12	369	5.56

Table 3. Comparison of various refinements to the parallel PBRA program. All times are for 12 CPUs

Technique	Time (seconds)	Speedup
Sequential	2050	1.00
Partitioning with PVM	657	3.12
Multithreading + PVM	550	3.73
Load balancing + Multithreading + PVM	369	5.56

then the process receives only 80% of the data specified by the load-balancing scheme. This allows the data received to be limited but still enables receiving a fair amount to be load-balanced. We experimented with various slackness factors: 90%, 80%, 70%, 60%, 50%. A slack factor of 80% gave an additional 5% improvement in runtime.

Finally, Table 2 shows the runtime and speedup for the sample data set with all the above refinements in place. The load balancing frequency was set to 4 and the slackness factor was 80%.

4 Further Results and Discussion

Table 3 summarizes the improvements obtained with the various refinements on one sample data set.

Table 4 shows the runtime and speedup for six additional data sets. The first column shows the density of the matter through which the beam is traveling. Note that when the density of the matter is high, the electron pencil-beam stops early and thus the computation time is smaller. When the density is low, then the beam goes farther but does not scatter as much, which would also tend to reduce the time. In both cases the beam scatter less, which leads to less communication among the processes resulting in higher speedups. Human tissue has density values close to 1.0, which is the most important case. That is why the density was 1.0 in the sample data set used in the previous section. The average speedup for all the data sets tested was around 8. The load balancing frequency was set to 4 and the slackness factor was 80%.

Table 4. Parallel runtime and speedups for different data sets. The density column shows the density of the matter through which the beam is traveling. All times are for 12 CPUs

Density (gm/cm^3)	Sequential (seconds)	Parallel (seconds)	Speedup
0.5	1246	131	9.51
0.7	2908	352	8.26
0.9	3214	364	8.83
1.1	2958	370	7.99
1.3	2641	321	8.22
1.5	2334	300	7.78

Although the speedups obtained are encouraging, further work remains to be done. We would like to test the parallel PBRA program on a larger cluster. Further tuning of the parallel code could lead to more speedups. Testing on a wider variety of data sets should allow us to further customize the load balancing frequency and the slackness factor.

5 Conclusions

We have presented a parallelization of electron Pencil Beam Redefinition Algorithm program originally written by Robert Boyd. The program was difficult to parallelize because of the large amounts of data that is accessed in an irregular pattern, requiring varying amounts of time in each iteration. We were able to obtain speedups in the range of 5.56 to 9.5 using 12 CPUs. The speedups obtained were based on three techniques: (1) using a simple partitioning scheme but compensating for the irregularity of data with an interesting data exchange technique that attempts to minimize the amount of data traffic on the network; (2) using threads in conjunction with PVM to reduce communication time for SMP machines; (3) using an adaptive load-balancing technique.

References

1. K. C. Tsien, "The application of automatic computing machines to radiation treatment," Brit. J. Radiology 28:432-439, 1955.
2. A. S. Shiu and K. R. Hogstrom, "Pencil-beam redefinition algorithm for electron dose distributions," Med. Phys. 18: 7-18, 1991.
3. PVM Home Page: http://www.csm.ornl.gov/pvm/pvm_home.html

Dynamic Load Balancing for the Parallel Simulation of Cavitating Flows

Frank Wrona[2], Panagiotis A. Adamidis[1], Uwe Iben[2],
Rolf Rabenseifner[1], and Claus-Dieter Munz[3]

[1] High-Performance Computing-Center Stuttgart (HLRS),
Allmandring 30, D-70550 Stuttgart, Germany
{adamidis,rabenseifner}@hlrs.de
[2] Robert Bosch GmbH, Dept. FV/FLM, P.O. Box 106050, D-70059 Stuttgart
{frank.wrona,uwe.iben}@de.bosch.com
[3] Institute for Aero- and Gasdynamics (IAG),
Pfaffenwaldring 21, D-70550 Stuttgart, Germany
munz@iag.uni-stuttgart.de

Abstract. This paper deals with the parallel numerical simulation of cavitating flows. The governing equations are the compressible, time dependent Euler equations for a homogeneous two-phase mixture. These equations are solved by an explicit finite volume approach. In opposite to the ideal gas, after each time step fluid properties, namely pressure and temperature, must be obtained iteratively for each cell. This is the most time consuming part, particularly if cavitation occurs. For this reason the algorithms has been parallelized by domain decomposition. In case where different sizes of cavitated regions occur on the different processes a huge load imbalance problem arises. In this paper a new dynamic load balancing algorithm is presented, which solves this problem efficiently.

1 Introduction

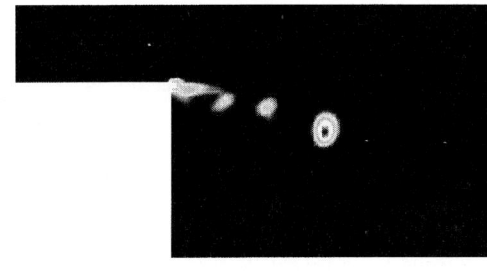

Fig. 1. Cavity formation behind a backward-facing step

Cavitation is the physical phenomenon of phase transition from liquid to vapor. The reason for fluid evaporation is that the pressure drops beneath a certain threshold, the so called steam pressure. Once generated the vapor fragments can be transported through the whole fluid domain, as been depicted in Fig.1. Finally, they are often destroyed at rigid walls which leads to damages. The work in this paper is extended for high pressure injection systems. In such systems cavitation occurs as small vapor pockets and clouds. Due to the structure of cavities, the assumption that the flow field is homogenous, i.e. pressure, temperature and velocity of both phases are the same, is justified. The more complicated challenge is to model the cavitation process, in a fashion that is valid for all pressure levels, which can occur in such injection systems. Therefore the fluid properties are described by ordinary equations of state [1].

Further, the complete flow field is treated as compressible, even if the fluid does not evaporate. Additionally, enormous changes in the magnitude of all flow properties occur, if the fluid is cavitating. Therefore such simulations are very CPU time consuming and parallelization is unavoidable if one wants to calculate large problems.

2 Governing Equations

The governing equations are the two dimensional Euler equations, symbolically written as

$$\mathbf{u}_t + \mathbf{f}(\mathbf{u})_x + \mathbf{g}(\mathbf{u})_y = 0, \tag{1}$$

with $\mathbf{u} = (\rho, \rho v, \rho w, E)^T$, $\mathbf{f}(\mathbf{u}) = (\rho v, \rho v^2 + p, \rho v w, v(E+p))^T$ and $\mathbf{g}(\mathbf{u}) = (\rho w, \rho v w, \rho w^2 + p, w(E+p))^T$. Here, derivatives are denoted by an index. Further, ρ is the density, v and w the velocity in x-, respectively in y-direction. The property E is also introduced, which describes the total energy $\rho(e + 1/2(v^2 + w^2))$ per unit volume.

The density and the internal energy e are functions of the pressure p and the temperature T and are expressed as mixture properties

$$1/\rho = \mu/\rho_G + (1-\mu)/\rho_L \quad \text{and} \quad e = \mu e_G + (1-\mu)e_L. \tag{2}$$

The regarded fluid is water, where the gaseous phase (subscript G) is treated as ideal gas and the functions of the liquid phase (subscript L) are obtained from the IAPWS97 [2]. The mass fraction μ, the void fraction ε and their relation are defined by

$$\mu = m_G/(m_G + m_L), \quad \varepsilon = V_G/(V_G + V_L) \quad \text{and} \quad \varepsilon = \mu\rho/\rho_G \tag{3}$$

For solving the governing equations numerically, eq.(1) is discretized as

$$\mathbf{u}_i^{n+1} = \mathbf{u}_i^n + (\Delta t/\Omega_i) \sum_{j \in \mathcal{N}(i)} \mathcal{L}(\mathbf{u}_i^n, \mathbf{u}_j^n) \tilde{f}(\mathbf{u}_i^n, \mathbf{u}_j^n) l_{ij}, \tag{4}$$

where $\mathcal{N}(i)$ are the set of the neighbor cells of the ith cell and Ω_i its volume. $\mathcal{L}(\mathbf{u}_i^n, \mathbf{u}_j^n)$ denotes an operator for different time integration methods. The underlying mesh is unstructured and consists of triangles and rectangles. The fluxes $\tilde{f}$ are calculated by approximate Riemann solvers, namely the HLLC-Solver [3]. Finally, the mass fraction – which describes the fractional mass portion of the gaseous phase to the total mass in each cell – must also be expressed as a function of pressure and temperature. After the flux calculation and the update of the conservative variables from $\mathbf{u}_i^n$ to $\mathbf{u}_i^{n+1}$, the primitive variables ρ, v, w, e can be computed analytically for each cell from the conserved quantities. However the pressure and the temperature for every cell cannot be calculated directly. Their values can be obtained iteratively from equations (2), because the internal energy and the density are already known

$$h_1(p,T) = 1/\rho - \mu/\rho_\mathrm{G} - (1-\mu)/\rho_\mathrm{L} = 0 \quad \text{and} \quad h_2(p,T) = e - \mu e_\mathrm{G} - (1-\mu)e_\mathrm{L} = 0. \tag{5}$$

These two equations are iterated by a two dimensional bisection method for p and T, until this two values converge. This step is the most time consuming part in the whole solution algorithm and even takes much more time if in a cell cavitation arises. Therefore simulations of realistic problems take several days. A more detailed description of the equations is presented in [1].

3 Parallel Algorithm

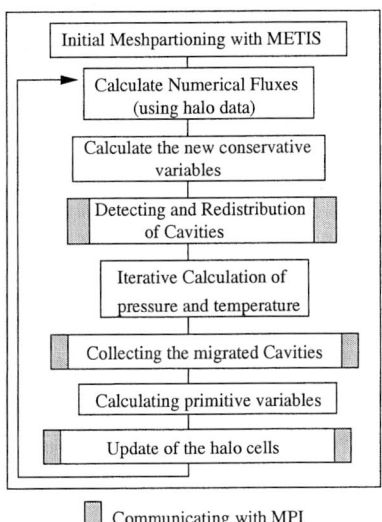

Fig. 2. Flow chart of parallel algorithm with dynamic load balance

In this work, we parallelize the algorithm by domain decomposition using the MPI paradigm. The target computing platform is a PC cluster. The phenomenon of cavitation affects the parallel algorithm in two ways. On one hand, the cavitating cells are not distributed homogeneously over the subdomains. This causes a very heavy load imbalance. On the other hand, the locations of the cavities move across subdomains. For this reason, using state of the art strategies [4] results in repartitioning at every time step. In our algorithm, only the work done on cavitating cells, during the iterative calculation of pressure and temperature (see Fig. 2), is redistributed at each time step. The parallel algorithm starts with an initial mesh partitioning, using the tool METIS [5] (see Fig. 2). After calculating the fluxes and conservative variables on the subdomains, cavities are detected by checking the void fraction ϵ. After this, every process knows how many cavitating cells reside in its subdomain. Denoting with cav_i this number for process i, the optimal number of cavities in each subdomain cav_opt is determined by

$$cav_\mathrm{opt} = 1/nprocs \sum_{i=1}^{nprocs} cav_i, \tag{6}$$

where $nprocs$ is the number of processes. Now the processes are classified into senders and receivers of cavities in the following manner: Depending on whether $cav_i - cav_\mathrm{opt}$ is greater than, less than or equal zero, the ith process is going to migrate part of its cavitating cells, or will be a receiver of such cells, or will not redistribute any cell. With this migration, only a small part of the cell-information must be sent. All other cell-information remains at the original owner of the cell. Halo data is not needed, because the time-consuming iterative calculation of pressure and temperature is done locally on each cell.

The implementation is based on an all-gather communication which sends the cav_i values to all processes. The computation time needed for a cavitating cell is about 1 ms and only about the sixth part is needed for a non cavitating cell, on a PentiumIII 800 MHz processor. Furthermore, the senders take for each cavitating cell, which they move to a receiver, a corresponding non cavitating cell from the specific receiver. With this approach the number of cavitating and non cavitating cells is the same on each process, which leads to a well balanced system. Due to the small number of bytes for each cell, the approach of transferring non cavitating cells as compensation implies only a very small communication overhead. After this, the calculation of pressure and temperatures is carried out, and afterwards, the results are sent back to the owners of the cells, and the remaining of the calculations is executed on the initial partitioning of the mesh. For this redistribution, 128 Bytes for each cell must be communicated, which means on a 100 Mbit/s Ethernet a communication time of nearly 10 μs. In this way we avoid expanding the halos, because we outsource only the time-consuming part of the computation done on the cavitating cells, and recollect the results.

4 Results

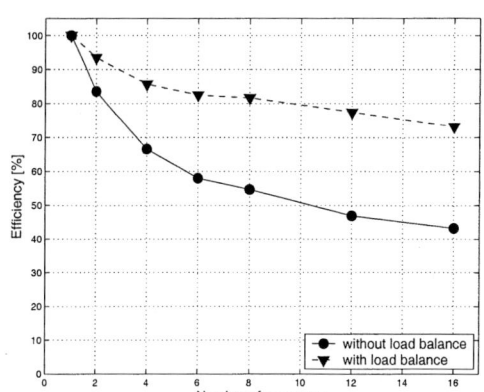

Fig. 3. Efficiency

As benchmark, a shock tube problem is defined. The tube has a length of one meter. The mesh is a Cartesian grid with ten cells in y-direction and 1000 in x-direction. At the initial step the computational domain consists of a cavity, which is embedded in pure liquid, and the initial velocity is directed in positive x-direction. Therefore it is an excellent benchmark for checking the load balance algorithm, because the position of the cavity moves from subdomain to subdomain. The computing platform was a cluster consisting of dual-CPU PCs, with Pentium III 1GHz processors. The results are summarized in Tab. 1 and Fig. 3 for several parallel runs. From these results it is obvious that a tremendous gain in efficiency has been achieved by the implemented load balancing strategy. In the runs without dynamic load balancing the efficiency drops down to 66.6% even when using only 4 processors and getting worse in the case

Table 1. CPU Time in seconds and Speedup

	# Processes	1	2	4	6	8	12	16
not load balanced	CPU Time	12401.4	7412.12	4649.84	3558.7	2830.16	2201.29	1791.68
not load balanced	Speedup	1	1.67	2.66	3.48	4.38	5.63	6.92
load balanced	CPU Time	-	6626.94	3616.51	2503.19	1897.14	1333.28	1058.19
load balanced	Speedup	1	1.87	3.42	4.95	6.53	9.30	11.72

of 16 processors (43.2%). In contrast the efficiency, with dynamic load balancing is over 80%, up to 8 processors, and in case of 16 processors still at 73.2%, which is a profit of 30% compared to the case without load balancing.

5 Conclusion

The simulation of cavitating flows is a CPU time demanding process. To obtain results in an adequate time it is necessary to use parallel computing architectures. In order to achieve high performance, the parallel algorithm has to deal with the problem of load imbalance, introduced by the cavities. In this work a new dynamic load balancing algorithm was developed, which treats this problem very efficiently. Future work will be concentrated on new criteria to detect the cavitating regions, and simulating 3D problems.

References

1. U. Iben, F. Wrona, C.-D. Munz, and M. Beck. Cavitation in Hydraulic Tools Based on Thermodynamic Properties of Liquid and Gas. *Journal of Fluids Engineering*, 124(4):1011–1017, 2002.
2. W. Wagner et al. The IAPWS Industrial Formulation 1997 for the Thermodynamic Properties of Water and Steam. *J. Eng. Gas Turbines and Power*, 12, January 2000. ASME.
3. P. Batten, N. Clarke, C. Lambert, and D.M. Causon. On the choice of wavespeeds for the HLLC Riemann solver. *SIAM J. Sci. Comp.*, 18(6):1553–1570, November 1997.
4. C. Walshaw, M. Cross, and M. G. Everett. Parallel Dynamic Graph Partitioning for Adaptive Unstructured Meshes. *J. Parallel Distrib. Comput.*, 47(2):102–108, 1997. (originally published as Univ. Greenwich Tech. Rep. 97/IM/20).
5. G. Karypis and V. Kumar. METIS:A Software Package for Partitioning Unstructured Graphs, Partitioning Meshes, and Computing Fill-Reducing Orderings of Sparse Matrices. Technical report, University of Minnesota,Department of Computer Science / Army HPC Research Center, 1998.

Message Passing Fluids: Molecules as Processes in Parallel Computational Fluids

Gianluca Argentini

New Technologies & Models
Information & Communication Technology Department
Riello Group, 37045 Legnago (Verona), Italy
gianluca.argentini@riellogroup.com

Abstract. In this paper we present the concept of MPF, Message Passing Fluid, an abstract fluid where the molecules move by mean of the informations that they exchange each other, on the basis of rules and methods of a generalized Cellular Automaton. The model is intended for its simulation by mean of message passing libraries on the field of parallel computing, which seems to offer a natural environment for this model. The first results show that by mean of simple mathematical models it's possible to obtain realistic simulations of fluid motion, even for general geometries. Also a possible implementation for the MPI library is developed.

1 Background of the Work

The work discussed in this paper is a first part of a company internal project on computational fluid dynamics about the flow of fluids into the combustion chamber of some models of industrial burners. The necessity of obtaining good realistic simulations implies the use of great numbers of physical and technical entities, as fluid molecules and graphic resolution. The methods usually adopted in our company for fluids motion simulations, are based on software with a poor degree of parallelism or with a too difficult approach for specific implementations. For this reason we use for our experiments some parallel computing hardware systems and message passing libraries for the parallelization of the software.

For the description of the fluid motion I have developed a mathematical and computational model by mean of techniques of *generalized Cellular Automata* (e.g., [1]). In this manner I have obtained a simple tool with a good level of parallelism and a good adaptability for generic geometries. The tool is based on the concept of Message Passing Fluid.

2 Concept of MPF and the Abstract Model

A *MPF*, Message Passing Fluid, is an abstract computational model of fluid into which the molecules move on the basis of some predefined rules which prescribe a mutual exchange of informations among the particles. A single molecule, once it has obtained these informations from the other neighbouring molecules, computes the value of the physical quantities prescribed by the rules of the MPF, and moves into the fluid on the basis of an appropriate combination of such values.

In a real fluid there are many physical quantities which determine the motion of the molecules. For the description of the intermolecular relations are yet determinant some short-range forces, as Van der Waals interactions, that the molecules exercise in a reciprocal manner by mean of an *exchange of informations*, (e.g., [2], where is offered a description for computational purposes).

MPF can be simulated by mean of a 2D or 3D computational grid, and the exchange of informations can be implemented by mean of opportune libraries as *MPI*, Message Passing Interface (e.g., [3]). In this manner the simulation can profit by the benefits of a parallel computing environment: as shown forward, the molecules are comparable to independent processes which in the same computational step exchange informations each other. Hence a MPF can be considered as a computational parallel environment (for these aspects, see e.g. [4]).

In the MPF model the fluid is described by a $n \times m$ grid of quadratic equal cells in the 2D case, and from a $n \times m \times h$ grid of cubic cells in the 3D case. The cells where the molecules can move are inside a space delimited by walls, which are represented by geometric cells of the same kind too and that constitute the physical boundary into which the fluid is contained. The molecules can receive and send messages, which in the physical reality correspond to intermolecular forces fields. Even the single walls cells can send to molecules some messages, corresponding to forces fields especially of electromagnetic nature. or the messages exchange is useful to define a neighbourhood relative to a specific fluid molecule, constituted by the set of those molecules of the fluid itself and, if necessary, of those of the extra-fluid objects which can exchange messages with the involved molecule.

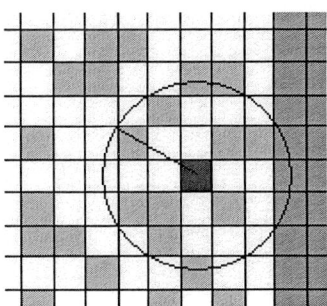

Fig. 1. A possible circular neighbourhood of a molecule for determining the objects to which send messages at every computational step. With gray shade are represented the molecules of a wall or of an obstacle.

Moreover one should define the rules by which one molecule moves, on the basis of the received messages. These rules are used for determining the cell of the grid where the molecule will move, after the receiving of the relative necessary informations by mean of the messages of the objects contained in its neighbourhood. For example, a possible rule in the 2D case could require the motion, among the eight cells adjacent to that where the molecule lies, to the cell where the sum of the potential values received via message is minimum. As supplementary rule one might require that, in the case that cell is already occupied, the molecule moves towards a cell immediately close to that determined before, on the basis of a random choice between right and left, or up and down.

3 The Computational Model

One MPF has a native computational implementation by mean of techniques of messages passing among independent processes in a multithreading program. A first possible ideal computational accomplishment might be so modelled:
- every molecule corresponds to a process of the simulative program;
- the messages passing among the molecules is obtained by mean of interprocess calls to suitable functions; therefore the fluid is represented by a set of parallel processes;
- for every computational step, a molecule, hence a process, sends its data to the other molecules of the fluid, receives the data from the other objects contained in its neighbourhood, and then calcules and determines its shifting on the grid on the basis of the predefined rules;
- the grid is completly computed with the new positions of the molecules, and the program move to the next computational step.

Therefore a computational realization of a MPF fluid requires the use of a message passing library in a parallel program. The concrete cases that we have studied have been implemented by mean of the MPI library, interfaced to a C language program.

A complexity analysis (e.g., [5]) shows that the described algorithm, native and not optimized, presents a polynomial complexity of the second order respect to the ratio of the total number N of molecules with the number P of parallel processes used for the simulation.

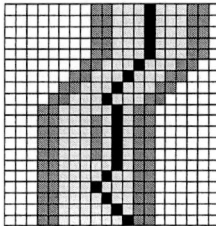

Fig. 2. Trajectory of a single molecule between walls and obstacle. The figure is the result of a computation with P = 4 on the Beowulf-like Linux cluster at CINECA, Bologna, Italy.

A first example with newtonian potentials and a single molecule has been implemented by mean of a C program interfaced to MPI calls. The program starts P independent processes; one of the processes traces in memory the position of the molecule on the grid and sends it to the other P-1 processes by mean of the function MPI_Bcast; these processes are associated to the static objects (walls and obstacle) and at every computational step transmit via MPI_Send to the process-molecule the positions of the objects contained into the neighbourhood centred on the particle; then the molecule-process computes the relative potentials.

Message Passing Fluids: Molecules as Processes in Parallel Computational Fluids 553

4 A Code for MPI

In this section we present some fragments of a possible code for MPI using the C language.
For the representation of the cells of the grid where the molecules can move, it is convenient numbering the cells in a progressive way, p.e. assigning a number to a cell of every row. In this way, if the grid is a cube $d \times d \times d$, the cell number n has three cartesian coordinates so computed:

```
if ( temp = n%d² )
{ row = temp/d; column = temp%d; }
else
{ row = n/d; column = n%d; };
height = n/d² + 1;
```

If the total number of molecules at every computational step is N and the number of used processes is P, divisor of N, then each process can manage M=N/P molecules and one can use a two-dimensional array as global variable for representing the positions of the molecules in the grid:

```
int global_positions[P][M];
.........
MPI_Comm_rank( MPI_COMM_WORLD, &myrank );
mol_number = global_positions[myrank][i];   /* this is the
number associated to the (i+1)-th molecule of the process myrank */
```

At the beginning, a manager process, p.e. that of rank 0, can divide the initial set of molecules among all the other worker processes. Every single process can use a one-dimensional array as local variable to store the positions of its molecules:

```
int local_positions[M];
.........
MPI_Scatter( &global_positions[0][0], M, MPI_INT, lo-
cal_positions, M, MPI_INT, 0, MPI_COMM_WORLD );
```

If necessary the array `global_positions` should be initialized in an appropriate manner, for example when the flow is entering into the grid from one side and exiting from another side. At every computational step a process can broadcast its own array to the others and receive the informations about the positions of all the other molecules by a collective MPI routine, in the communicator group representing the fluid:

```
MPI_Allgather( local_positions, M, MPI_INT,
global_positions, M, MPI_INT, MPI_COMM_WORLD );
```

In this manner the processes receive these informations by an optimized MPI technique. Once all the processes have received the data, they can operate on the basis of the predefined rules for the fluid, and then they update the array `local_positions` with the new values of the cells occupied by their own molecules.

5 Possible Further Works

We are studying some implementations of the MPF model with a realistic number of molecules on an arbitrary geometry. The computation is made on the Linux cluster of Cineca, using the MPICH implementation of the parallel library (e.g., [5]). The figure below shows a picture of the simulation of a 3D air flow in a chamber with a turbine. The experiment has been conducted with 32 processors and 320 molecules, and the action of the turbine on the molecules has been treated as an external sinusoidal force.

Fig. 3. 3D air flow in a turbine. The rule of the associated MPF requires that the molecules move to the cells where a repulsive newtonian potential is minimum. The picture shows the trajectories of four molecules with initial positions 90 ° out of phase with each other.

References

1. Wolfram, S.: Cellular Automata and complexity, collected papers, Perseus Publishing, (2002)
2. Rapaport, D.C.: An introduction to interactive molecular dynamics simulations, Computers in Physics, **11**, 4, (1997)
3. Pacheco, P.: *Parallel programming with MPI*, Morgan Kaufmann, San Francisco, (1997)
4. Wolfram, S.: *Cellular automaton supercomputing*, in: High-Speed Computing: Scientific Applications and Algorithm Design, ed. Robert B. Wilhelmson (University of Illinois Press, 1988)
5. Gropp, W.: *Parallel programming with MPI*, in: Sterling, T.: Beowulf cluster computing with Linux, MIT, (2002)

Parallel Implementation of Interval Analysis for Equations Solving

Yves Papegay, David Daney, and Jean-Pierre Merlet

INRIA Sophia Antipolis – COPRIN Team,
2004 route des Lucioles, F-06902 Sophia Antipolis, France,
Yves.Papegay@sophia.inria.fr

Abstract. ALIAS is a C++ library implementing interval analysis and constraint programming methods for studying and solving set of equation over the reals. In this paper, we describes a distributed implementation of the library.

1 Introduction

ALIAS[1] is a C++ library of algorithms for solving set of equations and related problems, e.g finding an approximation of the real roots of a 0-dimensional system, giving bounds of the roots of an univariate polynomial, or performing global optimization of a function with interval coefficients. Most of this algorithms are based on interval analysis and constraint programming methods and their scope is not restricted to algebraic expressions.

Although if most of the algorithms of the library have a structure that allows a parallel implementation, we will focus in this paper on the systems solving algorithms.

2 Interval Analysis and Systems Solving

Interval Analysis is based on *interval arithmetics* which is a well-known extension of classical arithmetics. Even if there are numerous ways to calculate the mapping Y of an interval X by a function f (see [1,2]), interval arithmetics guarantee that $\forall x \in X, f(x) \in Y$ and allows to take into account round-off errors[3].

The basic solving algorithm of interval analysis is based on interval evaluation and bissection:

Let $B = \{X_1, \ldots, X_n\}$ be a box and $\{F_i(X_1, \ldots, X_n) = 0\}$ a set of equations to be solved within B. Let L be a list of boxes initially restricted to $\{B\}$. Let ϵ be a threshold for width of intervals. The algorithm proceed as follows:

boxes loop: while L is not empty, let select a box b from L and
– if $\forall i, 0 \in F_i(b)$ and size of b is less than *epsilon*,

---

[1] http://www.inria-sop.fr/coprin/logiciel/ALIAS/ALIAS.html

- then store b in the solution list and remove b from L
- else, if it exists at least one $F_j(b)$ not containing 0, then remove b from L
- else, select one of the direction i and bisect B among this direction, creating 2 new boxes. Store them in L.

This basic method may be drastically improved by *filtering* i.e. decreasing the width of the current box "in place". ALIAS implements namely the 2B method [4] which is a *local method* as it proceeds equation by equation without looking at the whole system but *global methods* also exist, such as the classical Newton interval method [5]. A second type of improvement relies on the use of *unicity operators* whose purpose is to determine eventually a box, called a *unicity box*, that contains a unique solution of the system, that furthermore can be numerically computed in a certified manner. The most classical unicity operator is based on Kantorovitch theorem [6].

3 Parallel Implementation of ALIAS

A simple distributed implementation scheme based on a master computer and a set of slave computers may be used:

- The master will maintains a list of unprocessed boxes. These boxes will be dispatched to the slave computers.
- The slave computers run the solving algorithm with as initial search space the box received from the master. This slave program performs iterations within the boxes loop until either some stop criteria is fulfilled or if the boxes list has been exhausted. The list of unprocessed boxes (that may be empty) and, eventually, the solutions that have been found is sent back to the master.
- The master will periodically check if any slave computer has terminated its job and may eventually process a box in the meantime.

We use different stop criterion to stop an ongoing slave process:

1. The number of boxes still to be processed is greater than a given threshold N: this allows to limit the size of the message that is sent back to the master. However it may be acceptable to have more than N boxes in the boxes list of the slave process if we may assume that the slave will be able to process all the boxes in a reasonable amount of time. Indeed not stopping the slave will avoid a large number of message exchanges between the master and slave processes. For that purpose if the width of the box received by the slave is lower than a given threshold the slave process is allowed to perform at most M iterations of the solving algorithm. If the process is not completed after this number of iteration a FAIL message is sent to the master process.
2. the computation time has exceeded a fixed amount of time, in which case a FAIL message is sent to the master process: this indicates that it is necessary to distribute the treatment of the processed box among different slaves.

3.1 Efficiency

To obtain an efficient parallelization of the procedure it is necessary to choose carefully the threshold values for the stopping criteria and the values of the solving parameters for the slave process.

Indeed if the time necessary for the slave process to produce the N returned boxes is very small, then most of the computation time will be devoted to message passing, thus leading to a poor efficiency. On the other hand if this time is too large for a given box it may happen that the computer receiving this box will do most of the job, while the other slaves are free.

There is no general rule of a thumb for finding the right compromise but in our experience a first run with standard value for the parameters and then eventually a few additional run for fine tuning the parameters allows to determine near optimal values for the parameters, that are valid not only for the current problem but for a class of problems.

3.2 Implementation

A particularity of the ALIAS library is that it is mostly interfaced with Maple. Without going into the details the system of equations may be written in Maple and can be solved directly within Maple. The procedures invoqued create the necessary C++ code specific of the equations for solving the system, compile it and then execute it, returning the results to the Maple session (furthermore the symbolic treatment of the equations allows also for a better efficiency of the solving algorithm). The purpose of our implementation is to allow the use of a distributed implementation within Maple with a minimal modification of the Maple code.

For a parallel implementation it is hence necessary to have a message passing mechanism that enable to send a box to a slave program on another computer and to receive data from the slave computers. For the parallel implementation we use the message passing mechanism PVM10.1.

Simple master programs using PVM may be found in the ALIAS distribution along with its corresponding slave programs: these programs are used by Maple for creating the distributed implementation of the general solving procedures.

Basically a message sent through PVM is composed of a few control characters and a set of floating point numbers. Each box sent to a slave machine is saved in a backup box. The slave process uses the same coding for returning the boxes to process (if any): if there is no return box the slave process will return the keyword N, while solutions are returned with a message starting with the keyword S.

Within the master program an array of integers is used to determine the state of the slave machines: 0 if the machine is free, 1 if the machine is processing a box and has not returned, 2 if the machine is out of order. If a machine has status 1 the master process checks periodically if the machine has returned a message (using pvm_nrecv) or is not responding (using pvm_mstat): if this the case the master process will use the backup box of the machine, performs a bisection of this box and add the result in its list.

Both master and slave process use the same C++ solving code but a flag allows to determine if the algorithm is run by a slave or by the master. In the first case at each iteration of the algorithm the slave process will check if a stop criteria is verified while in the second case the master process checks at some key points if a slave has returned a message, in which case the master program stop the processing of the current box. The master process stops and the result is returned in a file as soon as all the boxes have been processed and all the machines are free.

4 Experiments

Our first experiment with the distributed implementation was to solve a very difficult problem in mechanism theory: the synthesis of a spatial RRR manipulator [7]. A RRR manipulator has three links connected by revolute joints and the geometry of the mechanism is defined by 15 parameters. The problem is to determine the possible values of these parameters under the constraints that the robot should be able to reach a set of 5 defined positions. For each such position we have new unknowns, namely the three angles of the revolute joints and the full problem is to solve a set of 30 non-linear equations in 30 unknowns. A first approach to solve this problem was to use a continuation method on a parallel computer with 64 processors, but after one month of calculation the problem was not solved. We then use the distributed implementation of ALIAS on a cluster of 20 PC's and get the solutions in about 5 days.

4.1 Chebyquad Function

For this experiments we compare the performances of the non-parallel version running on an EVO 410 C (1.2 Ghz) and a cluster of 11 medium-level PC's (850 MHz) with the master process running on a Sun Blade.

This system [8] is a system of n equations $f_i = 0$ with

$$f_i = \frac{1}{n} \sum_{j=1}^{j=n} T_i(x_j) + a_i$$

where T_i is the ith Chebyshev polynomial and $a_i = 0$ if i is odd and $a_i = -1/(i^2-1)$ if i is even. This system has 24 solutions for $n = 4$ and 0 for $n = 5, 6$. The computation times for a search space of [-100,100] are respectively 25s, 279s and 11286s with the sequential implementation and 27s, 84s and 1523s with the parallel one.

This example allows to establish a rough model for the gain of a distributed implementation. For a sequential implementation the computation time t_s is roughly proportional to the number of boxes processed during the algorithm which is $2^{n \log(w/\epsilon)}$ where w is the initial width of the range in the search space and ϵ the mean value of the width of a box that is either deleted or in which a solution is found.

$$t_s = a 2^{n \log(w/\epsilon)} + b \qquad (1)$$

Using the first line of the table we find $a = 0.17e^{-5}, b = 19, \epsilon = 0.87$. For the distributed implementation the computation time t_d should be t_s divided by the number m of slaves, to which should be added a communication time which is proportional to n:

$$t_d = t_s/m + a_1 n + b_1 \qquad (2)$$

Using the 2 first values of the second line of the table we get $a_1 = 24.418, b_1 = -73.88$. Using these values for $n = 6$ we get $t_d = 1520.44$ which is coherent with the experimental data. The theoretical maximal ratio t_s/t_d in that case is about 7.8.

5 Conclusion

Interval analysis algorithms have a structure that is highly appropriate for a distributed implementation. We have shown the use of PVM in the distributed implementation of the ALIAS C++ library and presented some examples.

Prospectives for this work are:

- an adaptive control of the solving parameters to improve the load distribution among the slaves.
- a possible modification of the parallel scheme in which expensive global filtering methods will benefit of a distributed implementation while the core of the solving algorithm will be run on a master computer (or a mix between the current scheme and the proposed one).

References

1. Hansen E., *Global Optimization using Interval Analysis*. Marcel Dekker, 1992.
2. Moore R.E., *Methods and Apllications of Interval Analysis*. SIAM Studies in Applied Mathematics, 1979.
3. Revol N. and Rouillier F., *Motivations for an Arbitrary Precision Interval Arithmetics and the MPFI Library*. In Validated Computing Conference, Toronto, 2002.
4. Collavizza, H. Deloble, F. and Rueher M., *Comparing Partial Consistencies*. Reliable Computing, 5:1–16, 1999.
5. Ratscheck H. and Rockne J., *Interval Methods*. In Horst R. and Pardalos P.M. editors, Handbook of Global Optimization, pages 751–819. Kluwer, 1995
6. Tapia R.A., *The Kantorovitch Theorem for Newton's Method*. american Mathematic Monthly, 78(1.ea):389–392, 1971.
7. Lee E., Mavroidis C. and Merlet J-P., *Five Precision Points Synthesis of Spatial RRR Manipulators using Interval Analysis*. In ASME 27th Biennal Mechanisms and Robotics Conf. Montreal, 2002.
8. Moré J.J., Garbow B.S. and Hillstrom K.E., *Testing Unconstrained Optimization Software*. ACM Trans. Math. Software, 7(1):136–140, March 1981.

A Parallel System for Performing Colonic Tissue Classification by Means of a Genetic Algorithm

S.A. Amin[1], J. Filippas[1], R.N.G. Naguib[1], and M.K. Bennett[2]

[1] BIOCORE, School of Mathematical and Information Sciences
Biomedical Computing Research Group, Coventry University, Coventry, UK
[2] Department of Histopathology, Royal Victoria Infirmary, Newcastle Upon Tyne, UK

Abstract. Tissue analysis is essential for dealing with a number of problems in cancer research. This research tries to address the problem of identifying normal, dysplastic and cancerous colonic mucosa by means of Texture analysis techniques. A genetic algorithm is used to interpret the results of those operations. Image-processing operations and genetic algorithms are both tasks requiring vast processing power. PVM (Parallel Virtual Machine), a message-passing library for distributed programming has been selected for implementing a parallel classification system. To further enhance PVM functionality a C++ object-oriented "PVM wrapper" was constructed.

1 Introduction

Analysis of tissue is a task typically undertaken by specialized pathologists. However there is an increasing interest in developing computerized systems capable of performing the task. In this paper a number of texture analysis algorithms have been employed as the means of classifying colonic tissue images. A number of studies in that area have attained impressive accuracy of success, reaching 90%, using a variety of methods [1], [2], [3]. It is our belief there can be further improvement.

A genetic algorithm (GA) uses the feature extraction algorithms (FEAs) results for classification purposes. The FEA and the GA are tasks suited for parallelizing [4], [5]. PVM (Parallel Virtual Machine), a message-passing library for distributed programming has been selected for implementing a classification tool [6]. A C++ object-oriented PVM wrapper was implemented in order to simplify the implementation of the tool.

2 Image-Processing Operations

Normal, dysplastic and cancerous tissue structures vary. Typically normal images contain easy to identify, well-defined shapes, in contrast with the cancerous ones. The image-processing operations chosen are concentrated on texture analysis thus all color information was discarded from the images prior to processing. Three different feature extraction algorithm (FEA) families were employed for this paper [7].

Histogram FEAs operate on the histogram (grey-level frequency table) of an image. Histogram FEAs are simple with limited processing power requirements. Mean value, Variance, Skewness, and Kurtosis histogram FEAs were used.

Grey-level difference statistics FEAs are used to extract information from a histogram of grey-level differences. Each pixel I, J is paired with a pixel I+DX, J+DY (where DX and DY are two displacement values). Their absolute difference is the index to the histogram array position to be increased during the histogram calculation. Mean value, Variance, and Contrast FEAs were used.

The third FEA family employed is based on Co-occurrence Matrix information. A co-occurrence matrix for a grey-level image of size X*Y, is a two dimensional array of size G*G, where G is the number of grey-levels. Each position (K, L) of the matrix holds the number of image pixels with intensity K, related to image pixels with intensity L. The pixel pairs are related in terms of two displacement values DX and DY. A single parameter distance (D) is used to define four basic directions (0°, 45°, 90°, 135°) for both grey-level different statistics and co-occurrence FEAs [8]. Maximum probability, Dissimilarity, Difference Moment, Homogeneity, and Inverse Difference Moment co-occurrence matrix FEAs were used. Entropy and Angular Second Moment operations have been implemented for all three families.

Table 1. The training and testing tissue image sets composition

Magnification	SET	Normal	Displastic	Cancerous
x100	Training 1A	10 Images	10 Images	10 Images
x100	Testing 1A	5 Images	5 Images	6 Images
x40	Training 2A	10 Images	10 Images	10 Images
x40	Testing 2A	5 Images	5 Images	6 Images

3 Classification

Two sets of images corresponding to different magnification levels are considered. Both sets consist of 15 normal, 15 dysplastic and 16 cancerous tissue images each. Each set is divided into two subsets (see table 1), a training set and a testing set.

A genetic algorithm (GA) has been chosen as a classification method [9], [10]. Adopting such a method requires choosing an appropriate way of modeling the problem. Our model has each position (gene) of the solution string (chromosome) corresponding to one term of an expression. After some experimentation it was decided to use formula 1 in order to generate that expression.

$$(F1+F2+..+Fn)^1 + (F1+F2+..+Fn)^2 + .. + (F1+F2+..+Fn)^m \tag{1}$$

Where F stands for FEA, n is the number of FEAs considered, and m is an integer number in the range 1 to n. Expanding this formula generates a number of terms, each corresponding to a gene. For instance an m value of 2 results in a quadratic expression. Formula 1 can be used to produce a vast amount of terms. Each chromosome constitutes a solution to the problem. During training, solution evaluation is achieved using the diagnosis for images of the training set.

Several parameters, such as the number of iterations, the size of the solution population, the chance of a gene getting a zero value, and the mutation rate, are needed to control the behavior of the GA. During the initialization state a random population of solutions is generated. In each GA iteration the fitness of each solution is calculated and a new solution population is created. The fittest members of the population survive and mate producing even stronger members, while the less fit members gradually die down. It was decided to use short integers to store the gene values. The range of co-efficient values is -127 to 128. Having negative values makes sense since some features measure opposing characteristics of the image.

4 Parallel Computing

Parallel computing techniques are used to enhance the performance of both the FEA calculation and the GA PVM, a message-passing library, has been employed for that purpose. PVM provides a number of programming functions for sending and receiving messages (packets) amongst processes. It is up to the programmer to use those functions in order to define and debug a processor intercommunication model (and in essence define a virtual machine).

When using PVM building different VMs require the construction of new programs or the modifying of old ones. Experimenting with various VMs is important since certain configurations are more appropriate for certain tasks; it was thus considered necessary building a tool with higher flexibility [11]. This lead to the decision of constructing an object oriented PVM wrapper that would allow the definition of VMs by more sophisticated and application specific mechanisms. Some compromises were made to make this feasible. The PVM wrapper for instance supports only the master-slave programming paradigm. The wrapper hides the existence of PVM from the application. Instead of using PVM functions, calls to wrapper methods are made. A configuration file format was devised for defining different VMs. It contains a number of commands, which describe the configuration in terms of slave numbers, topology, node transmit modes and operations (see Table 2).

Table 2. Configuration file command summary

Command	Description
TITLE <string>	Set script title
SLAVES <int>	Set number of slaves
MODE <int> <bool>	Set node transmit mode to broadcast or distribute
CONNECT <int> <int>	Connects two nodes
COMMAND <int> <int>	Assign a command to a slave
PARAM <float>	Set a parameter value for the last command defined
END	End of script file; anything beyond this point is ignored

The wrapper handles node communications through transmit and receive methods, which replace the "send/receive" PVM functions. The data is either distributed to, or broadcasted to. Multiple commands and parameter for each command can be used. A simple program written using PVM calls and a PVM wrapper one, share a similar structure. However complexity increases dramatically when using PVM to implement complex topologies. In contrast the PVM wrapper version looks almost the same.

FEA calculations were performed using task parallelism. The master process loads the images, and broadcast them to the slaves; each slave (worker) performs a different FEA. The images were segmented in order to achieve better processor utilization.

Several GA processes were started on different slaves. They communicated occasionally through the master. In such an event the master process gathers the best solutions and distributes them to the GA processes where they are added to the mating pool. Having several GA processes running simultaneously means a larger number of solutions are evaluated. Due to the random factor each GA process starts with a different initial population and follows a different path to a solution. This tackles one of the fundamental problems of GAs, that of converging to a local solution.

Table 3. Execution time in seconds for 7 FEAs (various segment sizes)

Processors	50x50	100x100	150x150	200x200	250x250
1	602.18	201.63	136.04	113.24	98.98
2	300.91	103.17	72.03	56.95	49.79
3	227.74	77.95	53.03	42.67	37.17

5 Results

A three-computer cluster was used for testing. Table 3 shows the time in seconds taken for processing a set of images using 7 co-occurrence matrix FEAs. Since there were more processes than processors some had to be executed on the same computers. The execution time decreases when larger image segments are used. The program seems to scale well. However those results are somehow inconclusive since an equivalent serial program was not constructed.

Table 4. Accuracy for different FEA groups and complexities (m)

FEA	m	Train 1A	Test 1A	Train 2A	Test 2A
Grey difference statistics – Best distance parameter estimates	2	83.33%	50.00%	90.00%	37.50%
	3	83.33%	50.00%	90.00%	50.00%
Co-occurrence matrix features – Best distance parameter estimates	2	86.67%	31.25%	93.33%	68.75%
	3	86.67%	31.25%	96.66%	68.75%
Selection of 10 best features – Best distance parameter estimates	2	96.67%	62.50%	93.33%	68.75%
	3	93.33%	62.50%	96.66%	68.75%
All 18 FEAs	2	93.33%	56.25%	100%	81.25%
	3	93.33%	56.25%	100%	68.75%

The accuracy results appear to be better for the images of the second set (lower magnification) (see Table 4). In general the results seem to be quite low compared to those of other researches. This is mainly due to the fact that we are considering three different classes rather than two, as other researchers have done.

6 Conclusions

More work is needed to verify the validity of the results. Experimenting with more images is necessary to verify if the accuracies results are realistic or not. Enlarging the workstation cluster size and constructing a serial program are required to proper assess the benefits of parallel computing techniques. The current implementation seems promising at this stage both in terms of accuracy and performance. Large improvements in performance seem to be achieved by the addition of more processors, while the accuracy is decent when the fact that three classes are considered is taken into account.

References

1. Hamilton P.W., Bartels P.H., Thompson D., Anderson N.H., Montironi R.: Automated location of dysplastic fields in colorectal histology using image texture analysis, Journal of pathology, vol. 182, (1997) 68-75
2. Esgiar A.N., Naguib R.N.G., Sharif B.S., Bennett M.K., Murray A.: Microscopic image analysis for quantitative measurement and identification of normal and cancerous colonic mucosa, IEEE Transactions on information technology in biomedicine, vol. 2, no. 3, (1998) 197-203
3. Esgiar A.N., Naguib R.N.G.,. Bannett M.K,. Murray A,: Automated extraction and identification of colon carcinoma, Analytical and quantitative cytology and histology, vol. 20, no. 4, (1998) 297-301
4. Lee C.K., Hamdi M.:Parallel Image-Processing Applications on a Network of Workstations, Parallel Computing 21, (1994) 137-160,.
5. Lee C.,. Wang Y.F, Yang T.: Global Optimisation for Mapping Parallel Image processing Tasks on Distributed Memory Machines, Journal of Parallel and Distributed Computing 45, (1997) 29-45
6. Geist A., Beguelin A., Dongarra J., Jiang W., Manchek R., Sunderam V.: PVM: Parallel Virtual Machine, A Users' Guide and Tutorial for Networked Parallel Computing, The MIT Press, (1994)
7. Pitas I.: Digital Image Processing Algorithms and Applications, Wiley-Interscience Publications, ISBN 0-471-37739-2, (2000)
8. Bovis K., Singh S.: Detection of Masses in Mammograms Using Texture Features, Proc. 15th International Conference on Pattern Recognition, IEEE Press, vol 2, (2000).267-270
9. Goldberd D.E.: Genetic Algorithms in Search Optimization & Machine Learning, Addison-Wesley Publishing Company Inc., ISBN 0-201-15767-5, (1989).
10. Bevilacqua A., Campanini R., Lanconelli N.: A Distributed Genetic Algorithm for Parameters Optimization to Detect Microcalcifications in Digital Mamograms, EvoWorkshop 2001, LNCS 2037, (2001) 278-287
11. Downton A., Crookes D.: Parallel Architectures for Image Processing, Electronics & Communication Engineering Journal 10(3) (1998), 139-151

Eigenanalysis of Finite Element 3D Flow Models by Parallel Jacobi–Davidson

Luca Bergamaschi[1], Angeles Martinez[1], Giorgio Pini[1], and Flavio Sartoretto[2]

[1] Dipartimento di Metodi e Modelli Matematici per le Scienze Applicate
Via Belzoni 7, 35173 Padova, Italy
{berga,pini}@dmsa.unipd.it
http://www.dmsa.unipd.it/

[2] Università di Venezia, Dipartimento di Informatica
Via Torino 155, 30173 Venezia, Italy
sartoret@dsi.unive.it
http://www.dsi.unive.it/~sartoret/

Abstract. Computing some eigenpairs of a Finite Element (FE) flow model is an important task. Parallel computations are unavoidable, in order to accurately analyze in an acceptable time large structures, e.g. regional groundwater systems, by fully 3D FE models.
The eigenpairs can be efficiently computed by Jacobi–Davidson (JD) algorithm, provided it is efficiently preconditioned.
Parallelization of JD exploiting FSAI preconditioning technique was completed under a distributed memory paradigm, by a Fortan 90 code performing MPI calls. In this paper we show that our code allows for the fast eigensolution of huge real–life flow problems on a parallel IBM SP4 machine.

1 Introduction

Assume we need to compute the transient 3D porous media flow inside a multi–aquifer system. A linear system of partial differential equations is to be integrated in space over a 3D FE N–node grid, yielding the so–called stiffness, H, and capacity, P, $N \times N$ matrices. H and P are symmetric, positive definite (SPD) matrices. Further integration in time by finite difference methods, leads to a linear algebraic system.

Computing a number, r, of the leftmost eigenpairs (i.e. the smallest eigenvalues, $0 < \lambda_1 \leq \ldots \leq \lambda_r$, and corresponding eigenvectors $\mathbf{u}_1, \ldots, \mathbf{u}_r$) of the generalized eigenproblem $H\mathbf{u}_i = \lambda_i P \mathbf{u}_i$, is an important task for determining the eigenmodes of the aquifer under analysis [1]. Using a technique called *mass lumping*, the matrix P is reduced to diagonal form, hence P^{-1} is straightforward to evaluate and the problem is computationally equivalent to the SPD classical eigenvalue problem

$$A\mathbf{u}_i = \lambda_i \mathbf{u}_i, \quad A = P^{-1}H. \tag{1}$$

When real–life models are considered, N can be so large that the wall–clock time needed to compute a suitable number of eigenpairs on sequential computers becomes unacceptably large. Thus, one *must* switch to parallel computing systems. Many algorithms were proposed for solving problem (1). We elected the iterative Jacobi–Davidson (JD) algorithm [2], which displays fast convergence [3], and includes many parallelizable cores.

JD algorithm computes the eigenpairs by projecting problem (1) onto a set of *search spaces*, S_k, $k = 1, 2, \ldots$, $\dim(S_k) = k$.

2 Parallelization

We developed a parallel code which assembles the FE matrices, then solves the partial eigenproblem (1) by JD technique. Our code avoids the *global* assemblage of H and P matrices, which are splitted among the processors. Moreover, we implemented a parallel version of FSAI [4] preconditioner. Appropriate preconditioning techniques are mandatory in order to guarantee the convergence of JD on large problems [3]. FSAI preconditioning allows for the efficient parallel solution of our very large problems. FSAI technique requires the computation of a triangular matrix, called the *approximate inverse factor*, before JD iterations start. Afterwards, *preconditioning* amounts to performing suitable matrix–vector (MV) products.

JD algorithm can be decomposed into a number of scalar products, daxpy-like linear combinations of vectors, $\alpha \mathbf{v} + \beta \mathbf{w}$, and MV operations. We focussed on parallelizing these tasks, assuming that the code is to be run on a fully distributed *uniform memory access (UMA) machine with p identical, powerful processors*. This assumption is nowadays not usually true for parallel systems, but we defer a discussion of this point to the next Section.

A data–splitting approach was applied to store the H and P matrices. Our flow problems are efficiently solved by linear FE 3D meshes with well-known tetrahedral elements. The portion of each matrix which pertain to each processor is identified by assigning to the processor a subset of the nodes in the global mesh, which leads to store merely the rows of H and P corresponding to that nodes. Note that our test matrices have nearly uniform distributed entries, thus evenly distributed row partitioning yields quite a uniform distribution of nonzero elements among the processors. Hence we expect that a reasonable load balance is attained.

We tailored the implementation of parallel MV products for application to sparse matrices, using a technique for minimizing data communication between processors [5]. In the greedy matrix-vector algorithm, each processor communicates with each other. Using our approach, which takes into account the structure of our sparse FE matrices, usually each processor sends/receives data to/from at most 2 other ones, and the amount of data exchanged is far smaller than $[N/p]$, when running on p processors. Communication tasks were accomplished by suitable calls to MPI_SEND and MPI_RECV routines.

Scalar products, $\mathbf{v} \cdot \mathbf{w}$, were distributed among the p processors by uniform block mapping, and MPI_ALLREDUCE were performed to collect the results.

The FSAI technique [4] computes a factorized approximate inverse of A, let it be $M = G_L^T G_L$, where G_L is a sparse nonsingular *lower triangular* matrix, with the same pattern as the lower part of A. Any row of the matrix G_L is computed in parallel, by solving a small SPD dense linear $m \times m$ system, where $m \ll N$ is the number of nonzero entries in that row. Communication tasks were performed by suitable MPI_SEND and MPI_RECV calls. One preconditioner application (PA) amounts to performing a $\mathbf{w} = G_L \mathbf{v}$ operation, followed by a $\mathbf{z} = G_L^T \mathbf{w}$ one.

Our parallel JD algorithm was implemented into a Fortran 90 code. Parallel tasks were accomplished under a distributed memory paradigm, using IBM MPI Ver. 3, Rel. 1, routines.

3 Performance Results

Our numerical tests were performed on an IBM SP4 Supercomputer, located at the CINECA Supercomputing Center in Bologna, Italy[1]. The machine is equipped with 512 POWER 4, 1.3 GHz CPUs. The current configuration counts 16 nodes encompassing 32 processors each. All nodes but one have a 64 GByte RAM, the remaining one being equipped with a 128 GByte RAM, totalizing 1088 GB RAM. Inside each node the RAM can be shared among all the processors. The physical nodes are *virtually partitioned*, in order to improve parallel performance. Each partition is connected with 2 interfaces to a dual plane switch. This machine is not an UMA system. A discussion of this point is carried on in the sequel.

The wall clock time of one parallel run does not accurately measure the parallel efficiency of a code. Each SP4 processor consumes highly oscillating wall-clock solution times, when the size of data changes. Moreover, conflicts on shared memory slots can be an important source of idle time. In order to obtain meaningful wall-clock times, by suitably setting the parameters of the scheduler [6], at each run we reserved to our own use one of the 16–processor, 64 GB *virtual* nodes. Such requirement raises very much the time each job waits on batch queues, but allows for at most an acceptable 10% fluctuation in wall–clock time. Since time fluctuations are still present, we performed four or more runs for solving each eigenproblem, on each given number of processors, giving in the sequel *the average elapsed time*.

Table 1 shows the average wall–clock time seconds, T_p, spent to compute $r = 10$ smallest eigenpairs of our FE matrices. The size of each matrix, N, is given. Each larger FE problem is obtained by refining the mesh of the first one, i.e. by subdividing in a suitable manner each element of the coarsest FE mesh. The number of entries per row in the H (and hence A) matrices is quite the same for all problems, since the geometry of the meshes does not essentially change. On average, there are 14.7 entries per row in each matrix.

Recall that we reserved to our own use a 16–processor 64 GB node, hence each processor can address *at most* 4 GB of memory. This limitation prevented us from solving both Problem 4 by a 1-processor run, and Problem 5 using 1, 2, and 4 processors.

Inspecting Table 1 one can see that the reduction of the wall–clock time when p increases is worth *per se*, allowing the validation of real–life FE models in acceptable times.

---

[1] http://www.cineca.it

Table 1. Computation of $r = 10$ eigenpairs by p-processor runs. The dash symbol means that the computation cannot be performed under the memory limitations required. Average elapsed seconds spent, T_p, and number of computational kernels performed, K_p.

#	N	T_p 1	2	4	8	16	K_p 1	2	4	8	16
1	268,515	349	204	121	66	44	4554	4678	4773	4676	4779
2	531,765	1589	894	493	275	171	7841	8062	8396	7629	8062
3	1,059,219	2378	1125	642	379	271	5443	5433	5209	5429	5434
4	2,097,669	—	3933	2441	1360	844	—	8261	9869	8480	8600
5	4,027,347	—	—	—	2631	1761	—	—	—	7628	7616

Table 2. Problem and symbols as in Table 1. Elapsed seconds per computational kernel, $T_p^{(K)}$, and relative speedup values, $S_p^{(r)}$.

#	$T_p^{(K)}$ 1	2	4	8	16	$S_p^{(r)}$ 2	4	8	16
1	0.077	0.044	0.025	0.014	0.009	1.8	1.7	1.8	1.5
2	0.203	0.111	0.059	0.036	0.021	1.8	1.9	1.6	1.7
3	0.437	0.207	0.123	0.070	0.050	2.1	1.7	1.8	1.4
4	—	0.476	0.247	0.160	0.098	—	1.9	1.5	1.6
5	—	—	—	0.345	0.231	—	—	—	1.5

The number of JD and Bi–CGSTAB iterations change both with N and p. This is a well-known numerical effect, due in the former case to change in the eigenproblem conditioning with N, in the latter to the change in the sequence of floating point operations. Hence, the computational cost of JD depends upon N *and* the conditioning of the problem. Inside JD algorithm, the matrix vector (MV) products and the applications of the preconditioner (PA) are the most expensive tasks, accounting for the main cost of the algorithm. MV and PA operations spend quite the same computational cost; we call them *computational kernels*. Table 1 shows the total number of computational kernels, K_p, performed. In order to estimate the computational cost of JD vs N, dropping the dependence upon numerical convergence speed, we use the time per computational kernel, $T_p^{(K)} = T_p/K_p$.

Table 2 shows that $T_p^{(K)}$ decreases when p raises, confirming that useful parallelism is performed. Since $T_1^{(K)}$ is not available in a number of tests, classical $T_1^{(K)}/T_p^{(K)}$ speed up can be evaluated in a small number of cases. Thus, we report the relative speedup values

$$S_p^{(r)} = T_{p/2}^{(K)}/T_p^{(K)}, \quad p = 2, 4, 8, 16, \qquad (2)$$

which are shown in Table 2. Ideal linear parallel performance could be attained when $S_p^{(r)} = 2$ for each p. Note that solving Problem 3 with $p = 2$, we report $S_2^{(r)} > 2$, which in principle cannot appear. This result is likely to be ascribed to cache–effects. Roughly, best speedup is obtained for small p values, suggesting that communications spoil the parallel performance, as usual. Notwithstanding, let us consider Problem 3 in Table 2, as an example. One can compute the classical 16–processor speedup, $S_{16} = T_1^{(K)}/T_{16}^{(K)} \simeq 8.7$. which can be scored appreciable, taking into account that we consider a complex eigenvalue procedure, which is applied to large, real–life problems. As a support to this statement, see the results in [7], where poor speedups on an IBM SP2, for matrix–vector products, are documented. We argue that the SP4 has improved network and processor speed, but the ratio between tham is already low. Concerning the difference in performance that could be found when running on different virtual nodes, rahter than on a single node, we fulfilled test runs dividing the tasks between different *nodes*, obtaining performance results which are comparable with those reported when running on a *single node*.

4 Conclusions

The results show that our code has an appreciable parallel performance, which allows for solving *huge* 3D FE eigenproblems by a very reasonable amount of elapsed time, on a parallel SP4 machine.

Future work relies upon (a) developing parallel preconditioners which allows for faster numerical convergence, and (b) the solution of flow problems by using the computed eigenvalues, i.e. by exploiting the so–called *superposition modes* approach.

References

1. Gambolati, G.: On time integration of groundwater flow equations by spectral methods. Water Resour. Res. **29** (1993) 1257–1267
2. Sleijpen, G.L.G., van der Vorst, H.A.: A Jacobi-Davidson method for linear eigenvalue problems. SIAM J. Matrix Anal. Appl. **17** (1996) 401–425
3. Bergamaschi, L., Pini, G., Sartoretto, F.: Computational experience with sequential and parallel preconditioned Jacobi Davidson for large sparse symmetric matrices. J. Comput. Phys. **188** (2003) 318–331
4. Kolotilina, L.Y., Yeremin, A.Y.: Factorized sparse approximate inverse preconditioning I. Theory. SIAM J. Matrix Anal. Appl. **14** (1993) 45–58
5. Bergamaschi, L., Putti, M.: Efficient parallelization of preconditioned conjugate gradient schemes for matrices arising from discretizations of diffusion equations. In: Proceedings of the Ninth SIAM Conference on Parallel Processing for Scientific Computing. (March, 1999) (CD–ROM).
6. IBM Poughkeepsie, NY: IBM Load Leveler for AIX 5L. Using and Administering. First edn. (2001) Available at the URL http://www-1.ibm.com/servers/eserver-/pseries/library/sp_books/loadleveler.html. Last accessed April 30, 2003.
7. Röllin, S., Geus, R.: Towards a fast parallel sparse matrix-vector multiplication. In D'Hollander, E.H., Joubert, J.R., Peters, F.J., Sips, H., eds.: Parallel Computing: Fundamentals & Applications, Proceedings of the International Conference ParCo'99, 17-20 August 1999, Delft, The Netherlands, Imperial College Press (2000) 308–315

Executing and Monitoring PVM Programs in Computational Grids with Jini *

Gergely Sipos and Péter Kacsuk

MTA SZTAKI Computer and Automation Research Institute, Hungarian Academy of Sciences
1518 Budapest, P.O. Box 63., Hungary
{sipos,kacsuk}@sztaki.hu

Abstract. This paper presents a way to build a computational Grid for PVM programs. The Grid applies Jini to handle the dynamically changing set of participants, and to make the communication between Grid-clients and Grid-machines possible. In case of a PVM-Grid the grid-resources are Parallel Virtual Machines. Our system provides a high-level interface for them, which through the users can submit their locally compiled PVM-programs. Our Grid-implementation gives support for run-time monitoring of the submitted PVM-programs as well. To achieve this functionality, clients have to use in their PVM source codes the Instrumentation API developed by SZTAKI.

1 Introduction

One solution for the problem of executing a large-scale application is to divide the program into parallel processes and execute them on different processors. Each process solves just a small part of the original problem, so the total execution time of the application is shorter than in case of the original approach. The PVM offers a framework for this process communication: processes in the same Parallel Virtual Machine can send and receive messages to and from each other using the PVM API [4].

However, to execute a PVM-application efficiently, one needs a cluster or a supercomputer. Grid computing tries to make this dream attainable for everybody with the notion of remote program execution using other sites of the same network [3]. For any computational PVM-Grid, in which users can execute their programs on any virtual machine of the network, an infrastructure has to be used. This infrastructure joins the PVMs and the clients into one logical entity. Minimally it has to provide the opportunity of join to the offered resources, and the support of finding an appropriate PVM. After a client chose the most suitable provider, there should be no more tasks for it, the rest of the work must be performed by the service just had been chosen. The transport of the program-code together with its input files, the execution process itself, and finally the returning of the results are the tasks of the high level Grid application service that runs on the top of the basic infrastructure.

In this paper we present a service-implementation that applies Jini as the infrastructure of the Grid, and offers the above mentioned high level execution facility. Our system builds only on the lookup services, the most basic service in every Jini network.

---
* The work presented in this paper was supported by the Ministry of Education under No. IKTA5-089/2002 and the Hungarian Scientific Research Fund No. T042459.

This work is strongly connected to the Hungarian Cluster Grid project, where 99 PC clusters each with 20 PCs and a server machine are connected into a country-wide Grid system via the 2.5 Gbit/s academic network of Hungary. Each PC-cluster realizes a PVM and the goal is to develop a computational PVM-Grid on top of this infrastructure containing more than 2000 PCs. Our task in the project is to create the highest-layer that will be used directly by the users, while the developers from the University of Veszprém work on the enhancement of Jini towards a scalable Grid infrastructure by extending Jini with an intelligent broker architecture [5].

In the next section we discuss how a PVM-Grid can be created with Jini. Afterwards we present the way we developed the execution and monitor architecture of our PVM-Grid.

2 Overview of the Jini Based PVM-Grid

The purpose what Jini tries to achieve is to transform TCP/IP based networks into self-managing, scalable entities, in which participants can offer fault tolerant services to each other [9]. This objective is similar to the one of the first generation computational Grids. In those Grids the customers of the services are solely computer programs and the only things they need are processing power, special hardware resources and other software components. In djinns any physical device, which accomplishes the protocol requirements can act as a service provider [8], and this universal notion is the most important reason why Jini is suitable to attend the job of the infrastructure in PVM-Grids.

Handling the registrations of computational resources, and keeping this list up-to-date is the most difficult thing one has to face during the development of a computational Grid. We assigned this task to the machines acting as the providers of the most obvious service in djinns, to the lookup services. Because there must be at least one lookup service in every djinn, our computational Grid can be established in every network that uses Jini.

We entrusted the following tasks to the lookup services:

1. Keep the list of the offered PVMs up-to-date.
2. Give the opportunity for every PVM of the network to join the Grid as a provider.
3. Provide the necessary information for clients to find a PVM.

The first task is the most difficult to fulfill in every computational Grid. The creation of a new entry in the information database when a new resource appears is self-evident. The real problem is to appoint the necessity of an erasure when a virtual machine disappears. Jini lookup services try to correspond to the challenge of this dynamic behavior with the adaptation of leasing based registration. In our Grid they store information about PVMs just for a limited amount of time - called the duration of the lease - which period is estimated during the registration process of a physical resource, and can be renewed any time before its expiration. If service providers desire short expiration periods for their registrations, the databases inside the lookup services will represent the perfect copy of the Grid's present state.

The computational resources and the Grid-clients can find these Grid information services with the discovery protocols of Jini. With these protocols lookup service hosts

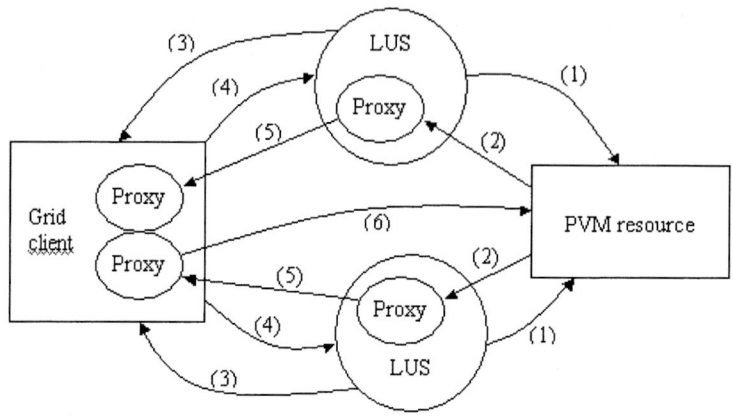

Fig. 1. The PVM registration and PVM discovery procedures in the Jini based Grid.

located anywhere on the Internet can be found. The usage of our Jini based PVM-Grid can be seen in Fig. 1.

One machine of every PVM has to host a Java program, which accomplishes the registration process of that parallel virtual machine. This program finds the lookup services (LUS) of the network using Jini discovery (1), and places a proxy at each LUS (2). The renewing of the lookup registrations' leases is this program's task as well. A client machine from the same physical network can find any PVM by sending its attributes to the lookup service hosts (4) discovered with the same discovery procedure that the provider used earlier (3). These attributes describe the the needed PVM (number of nodes, amount of memory per node, architecture of the machines, ...), and this is the way how clients can specify their requirements. Every lookup service answers to these requests with a set of proxies that match the requirements (5). A client can choose any proxy from the returned set - because they all provide the same functionality - and can ask its service side appropriate to execute the compiled PVM application (6).

The Jini API gives support for both the join and the lookup procedures. Our task was to develop the service program and its suitable proxy that can perform the program execution procedure and registers this availability at the lookup services. Moreover we had to write a client program that knows how to find and use a registered instance of this Grid-service. This client has to know nothing about the service except the interface of the proxy, which interface has to be given to the lookup services as a criterion for the needed service.

3 The Development of the Grid Service

During the development process of the PVM-Grid, our first task was to create the server side Java program and its downloadable proxy. These two programs together represent the PVM service provider for the clients. The client programs of the Grid have to download an instance of the proxy and send request to it through its well-known interface.

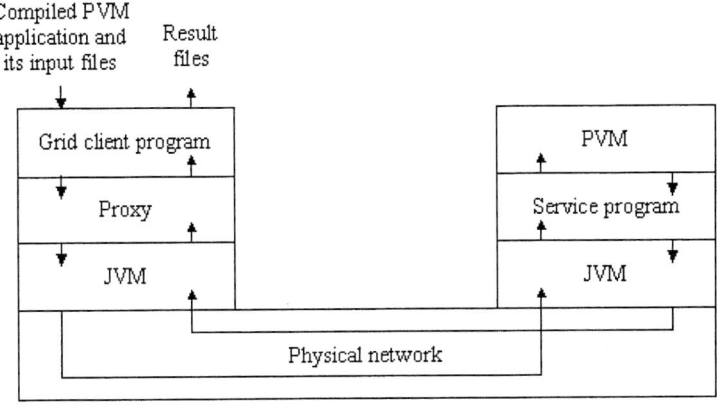

Fig. 2. The communicating layers of the provider and client sites in the PVM-Grid.

Fig. 2. shows how an application is forwarded to the remote PVM, and how the results returned back to the user.

Every user who knows the interface of the proxy can write its own client program. Our implementation offers a graphical interface to chose a PVM application from the local disc, and than submits the selected program to the proxy. The proxy can perform some kind of preprocessing on the received data and then it forwards the program to the server side Java program listening on one machine of the remote PVM. During this communication the proxy can use any protocol that the service program knows, because these messages are hidden from the client. The server side program has to be able to communicate with the local PVM to execute the received application. After the execution finished, the results can be sent back to the client.

We wanted to provide an easy to use execution facility for clients, and that is why we kept the interface of the proxy as simple as it was possible. The execution process can be initiated by calling one method on the proxy. This method call returns a unique id to the client. This id is generated by the server side Java program. After the id is returned, the client can disconnect from the network. The possibility of disconnection during execution time can be very useful in case of long running, large-scale parallel applications, especially if the submission was performed by a mobile device. After the execution finished on the PVM side, the user can ask the proxy to bring back the results by calling another method on it. The user in this method call can refer to the PVM program with the id that was returned from the service program during the submission.

Our proxy communicates with the server side program via RMI method calls, because our service implementation is a Java RMI server. During the lookup registration process the wrapper class starts this server and creates the proxy with a reference to it. This reference assures that the remote proxy - downloaded to client hosts - will be able to send request to the server side. Because with RMI only Java objects can be transported, we had to find another way to export the PVM application and its input files from the client to the resource, and the results files from the resource to the client. To make this non-Java code transportation possible we use file-server programs (HTTP or FTP servers) on both sites. On the service side, this server must be started before the

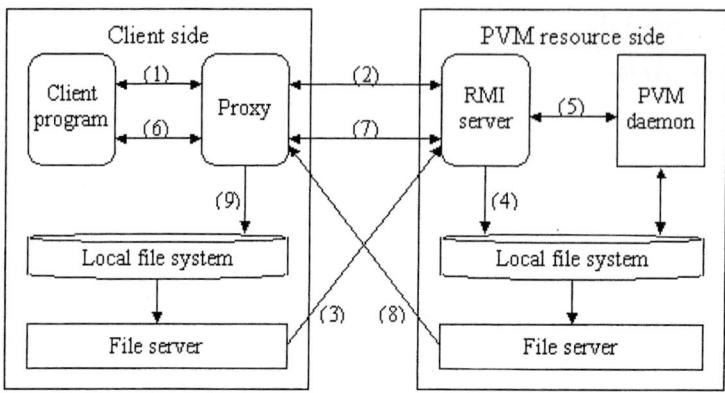

Fig. 3. The components of the system and the ways of communication among them.

registration of the proxy, and it has to be able to access the directory that contains the results of every terminated PVM program. On the client side the file server has to be started by the user before the PVM program submission. The proxy can not provide this functionality for clients, because it does not know the file systems of the client machines. Every component that takes part in the usage of the service can be seen in Fig. 3, and this figure also shows how the service is provided.

The client program gives a file path and an URL to the proxy (1). The path refers to a directory in the local file system that contains the compiled PVM application together with its input files and a job description file. The URL is the address through which this directory can be accessed from a remote machine. The proxy archives the content of the directory into a JAR file and sends the URL of this file to the service program via an RMI call. The service program replies with an id, which is than forwarded to the client (2). The service program downloads the application JAR file (3) to the local file system, extracts it (4), and than executes the content using the local PVM daemon (5). The previously mentioned description file assures that the service program will know how to start the application. After the termination of the PVM program the RMI server archives the result files into another JAR file that can be accessed through the service side file server. Later, when the client asks the proxy to download the results (6), first it gets the URL of this JAR file with another RMI call (7), and than downloads (8) and extracts it to the client's file system (9).

The usage of archive files during the data transmission is hidden from the user, and in a later version digitally signed JAR files could be used to authenticate the client and the service provider.

4 Monitoring PVM Programs in the Jini-Grid

The monitoring of a PVM application means that the state of its PVM processes can be observed at any time during the execution. Such a support is indispensable in case of big applications, especially if the processing power of the machines being used in the PVM is different, or their current load balance is not satisfactory. This demand claims the

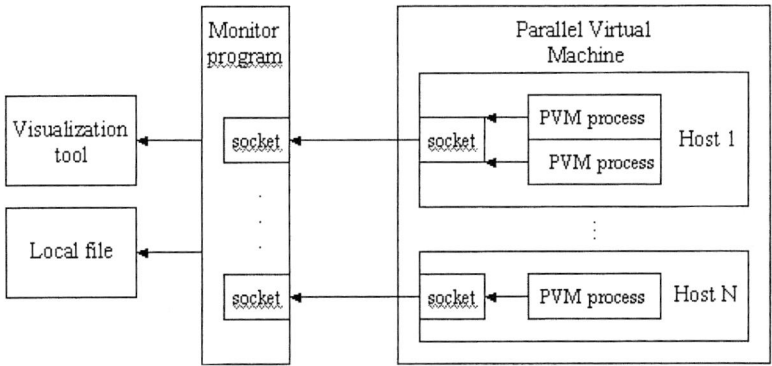

Fig. 4. Dataflow during application monitoring with the GRM/PROVE tools of SZTAKI.

necessity of a continuous data flow between the PVM-processes and a monitor program, which accepts and understands the data, and provides some visualization. Unfortunately the PVM API gives no support at all for such a framework, so PVM-developers have to find a tool that meets these requirements.

Instrumentation of the source code with function calls that write data to a file is suitable if the PVM processes have common file system with the monitor [2]. In our Grid environment an internal file buffer cannot be applied, because the monitor program on the client side, and the PVM application on the executor side use different file systems.

The developers in SZTAKI wrote an API and an appropriate monitor and visualization tool for it, to support the task of application monitoring in Grid environments [7]. Using this API during the development process of a PVM application results that the PVM processes will be able to provide data for the monitor program situated anywhere in the network.

The way this tool provides the solution is based on sockets [1]. The architecture of a monitored application can be seen on Fig. 4. The incremented PVM processes open one socket from every host of the PVM to sockets previously opened by the client side monitor program. The PVM processes can send trace data through these sockets to the monitor, which can save it to a local file or forward it to the visualization tool.

To make this way of monitoring possible in any distributed system, a particular environment variable has to be set for the PVM program. This variable contains the IP address of the machine where the client's monitor program is running, and the port number it is listening on.

Our service implementation gives support for this type of monitoring, because it can set environment variables for the submitted PVM programs. To resort the monitoring functionality, clients have to do two things. First: increment the source code of the PVM application with function calls from the above-mentioned API, second: write the name and the value of the appropriate environment variable into the description file of the job. The service side Java program will set this environment variable for the application, so the PVM processes will be able to connect to the client side monitor.

5 Summary and Related Works

In this paper we described a way in which computational Grid environment for PVM-programs can be created. Compare to the approach of Harness [6], our system can overgrow the border of a LAN or an organization, and it could act as the middleware in a country-, or continent-wide grid. This is because we use the PVM infrastructure at the cluster level, but we built a layer above it that connects these PVMs to the clients. Another benefit of our PVM-Grid is that it uses standard and publicly known discovery, lookup and registration procedures. These procedures are based on the platform independent Java language, which means that it causes no restriction for the platforms of the Grid's machines.

We have an operational prototype from the service and the client, and we successfully tested them on a network of PVM-clusters. Now we are working on the integration of our client program into P-GRADE, the PVM-developer environment of SZTAKI. After this integration, P-GRADE will cover the whole life cycle of PVM application development and execution, and will be able to act as the front end for users in the Hungarian PVM-Grid discussed in the introduction.

Another goal we would like to achieve is to give support for local jobmanagers on the service side. A local jobmanager could start a new PVM for every client program, which guarantees that processes belonging to different applications will not interfere with each other.

References

1. Z. Balaton, P. Kacsuk, N. Podhorszki: Application Monitoring in the Grid with GRM and PROVE. Proceedings of the International Conference on Computational Science - ICCS 2001, San Francisco, CA., USA, (2001) 253-262.
2. Z. Balaton, P. Kacsuk, N. Podhorszki, F. Vajda: From Cluster Monitoring to Grid Monitoring Based on GRM. Conference paper, 7th EuroPar'2001 Parallel Processings, Manchester, UK, (2001) 874-881.
3. I. Foster, C. Kesselman, The Grid (ed): Blueprint for a New Computing Infrastructure. Morgan Kaufmann, USA (1999)
4. A. Giest, A. Beguelin, J. Dongarra, W. Jiang, R. Mancheck, V. Sonderam: PVM: Parallel Virtual Machine-A Users' Guide and Tutorial for Networked Parallel Computing. MIT Press, London (1994)
5. Z. Juhász, Á. Andics, Sz. Póta: Towards a Robust and Fault-Tolerant Multicast Discovery Architecture for Global Computing Grids, Proceedings of the 4th DAPSYS workshop, Linz, (2002) 74-81
6. D. Kurzyniec, V. Sunderam, M. Migliardi: PVM emulation in the Harness metacomputing framework - design and performance evaluation. In Second IEEE International Symposium on Cluster Computing and the Grid (CCGrid), Berlin, Germany, (2002)
7. N. Podhordszki: Semi-on-line Monitoring of P-Grade Applications. PDPC Journal, to appear in (2003)
8. Sun Microsystems, Jini Device Architecture Specification v1.2. http://java.sun.com/products/jini, (2001)
9. Sun Microsystems, Jini Technology Core Platform Specification v1.2. http://java.sun.com/products/jini, (2001)

Multiprogramming Level of PVM Jobs in a Non-dedicated Linux NOW*

Francesc Giné[1], Francesc Solsona[1], Jesus Barrientos[1], Porfidio Hernández[2], Mauricio Hanzich[2], and Emilio Luque[2]

[1] Departamento de Informática e Ingeniería Industrial, Universitat de Lleida, Spain
{sisco,francesc,jesusb}@eup.udl.es
[2] Departamento de Informática, Universitat Autònoma de Barcelona, Spain
{porfidio.hernandez,emilio.luque}@uab.es, mauricio@aows10.uab.es

Abstract. Our research is focussed on keeping both local and PVM jobs together in a time-sharing Network Of Workstations (NOW) and efficiently scheduling them by means of dynamic coscheduling mechanisms. In this framework, we study the sensitivity of PVM jobs to multiprogramming. According to the results obtained, we propose a new extension of the dynamic coscheduling technique, named Cooperating Coscheduling. Its feasibility is shown experimentally in a PVM-Linux cluster.

1 Introduction

The challenge of exploiting underloaded workstations in a NOW to host parallel computation has led researchers to develop new techniques in an attempt to adapt the traditional time-shared scheduler to the new situation of mixing local and distributed workloads. These techniques [6, 7] deal in improving parallel job performance without disturbing the response time of local processes excessively. In this framework, the coscheduling of parallel jobs becomes a critical issue.

One such form of coscheduling is explicit coscheduling [1]. This technique schedules and de-schedules all tasks of a job together using global context switches. The centralized nature of explicit coscheduling limits its efficient development in a non-dedicated NOW. The alternative is to identify the need for coscheduling during execution. This way, only a sub-set of processes of the same job are scheduled together, leading to *dynamic coscheduling* [8]. Dynamic coscheduling [2, 5, 9] uses an incoming message to schedule the process for which it is intended, even causing CPU preemption of the task being executed inside. The underlying rationale is that the receipt of a message denotes the higher likelihood of the sender process of that job being scheduled at the remote workstation at that time.

Some studies on non-dedicated NOWs [2, 9] have shown the good performance of dynamic coscheduling when many local users compete with a single

---

* This work was supported by the MCyT under contract TIC 2001-2592 and partially supported by the Generalitat de Catalunya -Grup de Recerca Consolidat 2001SGR-00218.

parallel job. Unfortunately, our work shows that dynamic coscheduling performance falls when the number of parallel jobs competing against each other (MultiProgramming Level (MPL)) is increased. Basically, this is due to two reasons: a) one node can give priority to one parallel task while the priorities of the remaining tasks forming the same job may be decreased in the rest of the nodes (also named *cooperating nodes*) due to the presence of local users; and b) when the competing parallel jobs have similar communication behavior, the single analisys of communication events is not enough to distinguish which tasks of the same parallel job should be cosheduled. These non-coordinated local decisions could drastically slow down the performance of the NOW.

A new technique, called Cooperating CoScheduling (CCS), is presented in this paper. CCS improves dynamic coscheduling by solving both the problems explained above. Each CCS node manages its resources efficiently by combining local and foreign runtime information provided by its cooperating nodes. CCS is implemented in a PVM-Linux NOW.

The rest of the paper is organized as follows. In Section 2, we describe the initial implementation of dynamic coscheduling and our experimental environment. In section 3, we examine the response of local and parallel jobs to different values of multiprogramming. In Section 4, we describe and evaluate the performance of the CCS technique. Finally, the conclusions and future work are detailed.

2 Background

This section describes the main assumptions, our experimental environment and the initial implementation of dynamic coscheduling that serves as the basis for our study of sensitivity to multiprogramming.

2.1 Assumptions

Some of the following assumptions are made taking Linux o.s. properties into account to make the subsequent implementation easier.

Our framework is a non-dedicated NOW, where all nodes are under the control of our scheduling scheme. In each node, a time-sharing scheduler is assumed with task preemption based on the ranking of tasks according to their priority. The scheduler works by dividing the CPU time into *epochs*. In every epoch, each task is assigned a specific time slice. When the running process has expired its time slice or is blocked waiting for an event (for example a communication event), the process with highest priority from the Ready Queue (RQ) is selected to run and the original process is made to wait. The epoch ends when all the processes in the RQ have exhausted their time slice.

With regard to parallel jobs, a SPMD model is assumed. Each parallel job consists of several tasks of similar size each allocated to a different workstation. Every task alternates computation with communication phases.

2.2 Job Interaction

We propose to limit the computational resources assigned to parallel tasks with the aim of preserving the performance of local tasks. When the $node_i$ scheduler detects[1] the presence of a local user, it will assign a time slice to parallel and local tasks equal to $DEF\_QUANTUM_i * L$ and $DEF\_QUANTUM_i$, respectively. $DEF\_QUANTUM_i$ is the base time slice (200ms in Linux) of $node_i$ and L is the percentage of resources assigned to parallel jobs. It is assumed that L has the same value across the cluster.

2.3 Implementation of Dynamic Coscheduling in a Linux NOW

In order to minimize the communication waiting time, we want to coschedule tasks of the same parallel job according to their own communication needs. With this aim, we implemented a dynamic coscheduling technique in the Linux 2.2.15 [9]. Every local scheduler increases the receiving task priority according to the number of packets in the receive socket queue. So, the task with most pending receiving messages will have the highest priority. Thus, the scheduler, which is invoked every time that a process is woken up, will schedule this task if it has a higher priority than the current scheduled task. Coscheduling is thus achieved.

2.4 Experimental Environment

The experimental environment was composed of eight Pentium III with 256 MB of memory. All of them were connected through a Fast Ethernet network.

The performance of the PVM jobs was evaluated by running four class A benchmarks from the NAS suite: IS ($ET^2=192s$; communication bound), SP and LU ($ET^2 = 250s$ and $ET^2 = 142s$, respectively; computation and communication are balanced) and BT ($ET^2 = 279s$; computation bound). They were run in route_direct PVM mode with a size of 8 tasks. Three parallel workloads (Wrk1, Wrk2 and Wrk3) were defined. Wrk1 is made up of the four benchmarks (SP, LU, IS and BT), Wrk2 is made up of two copies of the IS and LU benchmarks; while Wrk3 is made up of four copies of the IS benchmark. For one hour, every workload was continuously executing MPL benchmarks concurrently, which were chosen randomly according to a discrete uniform distribution. The multiprogramming level (MPL) was varied in the range from 1 to 4. The highest value of MPL was set at four because over this value the main memory was overloaded. Thus, our study was isolated from the pernicious effect of paging [3, 4].

The local workload was carried out by running one synthetic benchmark, called local. This allowed the CPU load, memory requirements and network traffic used by the local user to be fixed. In order to assign these values in a realistic way, we monitored the average resources used by 10 different local users

---
[1] Every epoch, the scheduler checks the keyboard and mouse activity.
[2] ET: Execution time on a dedicated environment.

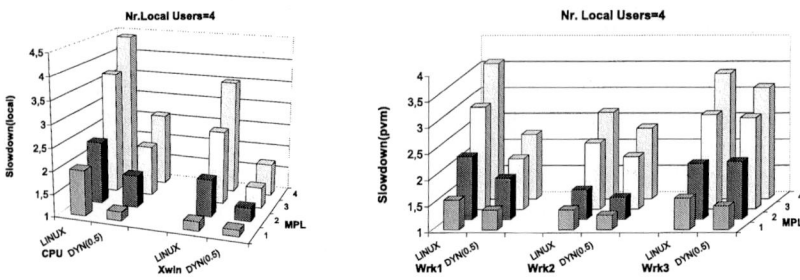

Fig. 1. (left) Slowdown of local and (right) PVM jobs with four local users.

for one week. According to this monitoring, we defined two different local user profiles: a user with high CPU requirements, denoted as *CPU*, and a user with high requirements of interactivity, denoted as *Xwin*. These parameters (cpu, memory[3] and network) were set at (0.65, 35MB and 0KB/s) and (0.15, 85MB and 3Kb/s) for *CPU* and *Xwin* users, respectively.

Two environments were evaluated: the plain LINUX scheduler and the DYNAMIC scheduler (denoted as DYN). Note that DYNAMIC scheduler applies the job interaction mechanism (see section 2.2) and the dynamic coscheduling technique (see section 2.3). The performance of the parallel and local jobs for these environments was validated by means of the *Slowdown* metric. Slowdown is the response-time ratio of a job in a non-dedicated system in relation to the time taken in a system dedicated solely to this job. It was averaged over all the jobs in the cluster.

3 Sensitivity of Local and PVM Jobs to Multiprogramming

This section evaluates the slowdown on the performance of local and PVM jobs for different numbers of MPL $(1, ..., 4)$ and local users $(0, ..., 8)$.

Fig. 1(left) shows the average slowdown of the local workload, when two *CPU* and two *Xwin local* benchmarks[4] were executed together with the *Wrk1* PVM workload (the most demanding computation one). Every trial was repeated twice: once with the plain *LINUX* and the other incorporating the Dynamic coscheduling and Job Interaction mechanism (see section 2.2) with $L = 0.5$ (denoted as DYN). This value of L was chosen because L under 0.5 could excessively disturb the performance of PVM jobs due mainly to the degradation of cache performance with applications with a large working set [5]. Focusing on the obtained results, we can see the high slowdown introduced by the plain LINUX when MPL is increased. This reflects the necessity of preserving CPU resources for local tasks. On the other hand, DYN impact rises gradually when the MPL

---

[3] Memory requirements do not include kernel memory.
[4] One instance of the *local* benchmark was ran in each node.

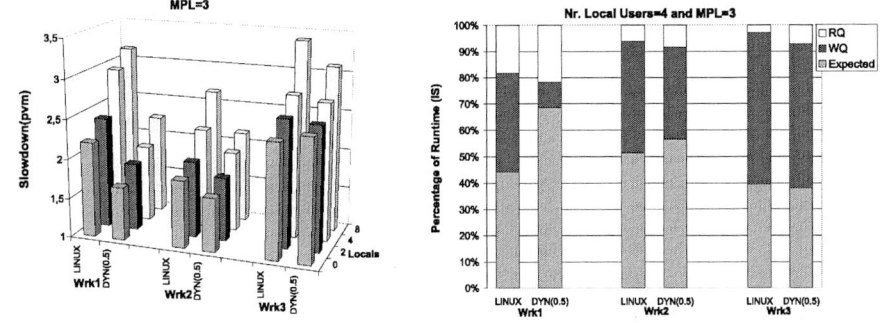

Fig. 2. (left) Slowdown of PVM jobs varying the number of local users. (right) Execution time breakdown of the IS benchmark.

is increased, although this is always much smaller than in the LINUX case (even in the worst case, $MPL = 4$, the slowdown is under 2.5 and 1.7 for a *CPU and Xwin* user, respectively). For the rest of the trials, the local workload is exclusively made up of CPU local users (the most unfavorable case for parallel tasks performance).

Fig. 1(right) shows the slowdown in the performance of PVM jobs when every PVM workload was executed with the plain LINUX and the DYN modes. The number of CPU local users was set at four. First of all, it is worth pointing out that the slowdown is always below the *MPL* value. This proves the feasibility of increasing the parallel multiprogramming in non-dedicated NOWs. Focusing on DYN behavior, we can see that DYN drastically improves the performance of PVM jobs for *Wrk1*. In fact, this improvement increases according to the value of MPL. However, this gain in DYN with regard to Linux is reduced for *Wrk2* workload and practically disappears when all the competing PVM jobs are equal *(Wrk3)*. This means that DYN performance behaves worse when the competing parallel tasks tend to be equal.

We repeated the above trial setting $MPL = 3$ and varying the number of local users. Fig. 2(left) shows the PVM job slowdown. In general, we can see that the improvement of DYN in comparison with LINUX increased with the number of local users. It means that DYN performance is much less sensitive to the variation in the number of users. It proves that dynamic coscheduling is able to coschedule well when PVM jobs are competing against local tasks.

To further understand the behavior of dynamic coscheduling, we profiled the execution time[5] of the IS benchmark in the case of four local users and an $MPL = 3$ (see fig. 2(right)). With this aim, we introduced two counters in the Linux kernel to measure the extra time spent by IS processes in the Waiting Queue *(WQ)* and in the Ready Queue *(RQ)*. The *Expected time* is the execution time of the IS benchmark in a dedicated environment. The high WQ time obtained with DYN mode for *Wrk2* and *Wrk3* workloads reflects the

---

[5] These values are averaged over all the nodes.

poor performance of dynamic coscheduling in these cases. This is due to two different reasons. The first one, which will be named *similitude problem*, arises when some competing PVM processes have the same communication rate. In these cases, a situation where a set of different PVM processes have the same number of receiving packets in their reception queues can happen frequently. In such cases, and taking into account the implementation of dynamic coscheduling, the scheduler assigns the same priority to all these processes so the next PVM process to run is selected randomly by the scheduler. In this way, there is a high likelihood that coscheduling was not achieved. The second problem, which will be named *resource balancing* problem, is due to the fact that processes belonging to the same PVM job can have different amounts of CPU resources assigned in each node depending on the local user activity. This means that PVM processes belonging to the same job will progress in a non-synchronized manner. As a consequence, the waiting time of PVM processes run in nodes without local activity will be unnecessarily increased.

4 CCS: Cooperating CoScheduling

In order to solve both problems related to dynamic coscheduling performance, some improvements were introduced in the original dynamic technique. According to the nature of our proposal, this new extension of dynamic coscheduling is named Cooperating CoScheduling (CCS).

Previous results show that when the competing PVM jobs have similar communication behavior (*similitude problem*), coscheduling is not achieved. This problem shows the need, apart from the receiving packets, to take a second parameter into account, one which provides the local scheduler with the ability to distinguish between processes belonging to different jobs. Thus, every scheduler will be able to select PVM jobs according to a global order across the NOW. Taking the nature of the SPMD programs into account, whenever there are several PVM processes with the same priority in the Ready Queue, the CCS scheduler will select the PVM process with the lowest execution time. Note that this value is provided by the Linux Kernel. Given that the same criterion will be applied throughout the NOW, the likelihood of achieving coscheduling will be increased.

Regarding the *resource balancing* problem, we propose to assign the same amount of local computational resources to each process belonging to the same job. Thus, all the processes of the same job will progress uniformly across the cluster. With this aim, nodes running the same job (cooperating nodes) should interchange status information. The key question is which information should be interchanged. An excess of information could slow down the performance of the system, increasing its complexity and limiting its scalability. For this reason, only the following two events are notified:

1. *LOCAL:* when there is local user activity in a *node*, it sends the identifier of the running PVM jobs in this node to all its cooperating nodes.
2. *NO_LOCAL:* if the local activity finishes, the node sends a notification message to its cooperating nodes.

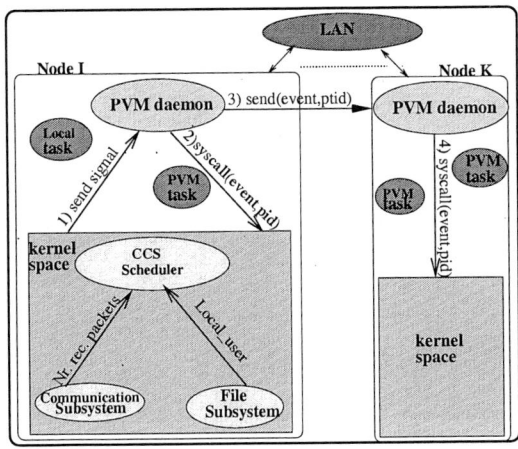

Fig. 3. Cooperating Coscheduling Architecture.

When a cooperating node receives one of the above events, it will reassign the resources according to the following rules: (1) The CCS scheduler with more than one PVM task under its management will assign a quantum equal to $(DEFAULT\_QUANTUM_i * L)$ to those PVM tasks notified by $LOCAL$ events. (2) The CCS scheduler will reassign the default quantum to a PVM task notified by a NO_LOCAL event, only when the number of $LOCAL$ received events coincides with the NO_LOCAL received events. This way, we assure that a PVM job is not slowed down by any local users across the cluster,

4.1 Implementation of CCS in a *PVM-Linux* Cluster

CCS was implemented in a PVM (v.3.4) - Linux (v.2.2.15) cluster. PVM provides useful information to implement the cooperating scheme. Every node of a PVM system has a daemon, which maintains information of the PVM jobs under its management. It contains the identifier of each job $(ptid)$ and a host table with the addresses of its cooperating nodes. A patch, with the following modifications must be introduced into the Linux Kernel:

File Subsystem: CCS sends the LOCAL (NO_LOCAL) events when there is (no) user interactivity for more than 1 minute. This value ensures that the machine is likely to remain available and does not lead the system to squander a large amount of idle resources. At the beginning of every epoch, the access time to the keyboard and mouse files is checked, setting a new kernel variable *(LOCAL_USER)* to True (False).

Communication Subsystem: We have implemented a new function to collect the receiving packets from the socket queues in the Linux kernel.

Scheduler: CCS implementation involved the modification of the Linux scheduler according to the algorithm explained in section 2.2 and 4.

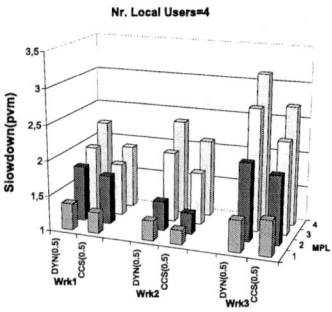 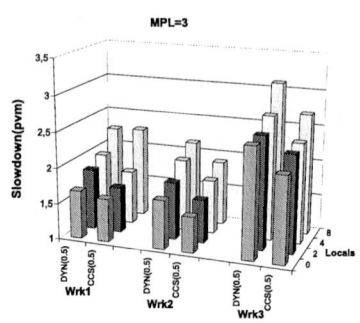

Fig. 4. Slowdown of PVM jobs varying the MPL (left) and the number of local users (right).

Fig. 3 shows the steps involved in the process of sending the notification of an event from $node_i$ to $node_k$. When the kernel of $node_i$ detects a new event, it sends a signal to the local *PVM daemon* (1). After that, the PVM daemon (by means of a system call) obtains the process identifiers *(pids)* of the delayed/resumed PVM tasks together with the event's tag (LOCAL/NO_LOCAL) from the kernel (2). Once the PVM daemon has changed the process identifier (*pid*) into the PVM job identifier (*ptid*), it sends the event's tag and the *ptids* of the associated jobs to its cooperating nodes(3). Finally, when $node_k$ receives the message, it communicates this event to its kernel by means of a new system call(4).

4.2 CCS Performance

This section discusses the performance characteristics of both coscheduling strategies (CCS and DYN). Fig. 4 shows the slowdown on *Wrk1*, *Wrk2* and *Wrk3* when the MPL was varied from 1 to 4 (left) and the number of local users was varied between 0 and 8 (right). From fig. 4(left), we can see how CCS improves the DYN behavior when the value of MPL is increased. This is due to the fact that the resources are better balanced under CCS and thus, all PVM jobs can progress across the NOW in a coordinated way. For the same reason, CCS improves DYN performance when the number of local users varies from 2 to 4 (see fig. 4(right)). From this fig. 4(right)), it is worth pointing out the improvement obtained by CCS for *Wrk2* and *Wrk3* workloads with 0 local users. This proves that CCS is able to coordinate the coscheduling of PVM jobs better when there is a high similitude between competing processes.

5 Conclusions and Future Work

This paper studies the feasibility of executing multiple PVM jobs simultaneously in a non-dedicated Linux NOW without disturbing local jobs excessively. Our results reveal that this can be achieved by means of combining techniques that limit the computational resources assigned to parallel workloads together with dynamic coscheduling techniques that maximize the use of these resources. A detailed analisys of these results shows that the performance of PVM jobs falls when the competing tasks have similar communication behavior and when parallel tasks from the same job have been assigned different resources. In order to solve both problems, a new extension of dynamic coscheduling, named Cooperating CoScheduling (CCS), is presented. The results obtained by CCS prove its good behavior. CCS reduces substantially the slowdown of parallel tasks with respect to dynamic policy. In addition, the CCS performance shows a high stability in contrast to the high variability of a non-dedicated NOW.

Future work is directed towards researching the optimal MPL value according to the characteristics the parallel workload (computation, communication and memory requirements) and the local one. In addition, we are interested in testing CCS in a real environment composed of computational laboratories with different degrees of heterogeneity, local users profiles and a larger number of nodes.

References

1. D.G. Feitelson and L. Rudolph. Gang scheduling performance benefits for fine-grain synchronization. *J. Parallel and Distributed Computing*, 164(4):306–318, 1992.
2. A. Gaito, M. Rak, and U. Villano. Adding dynamic coscheduling support to pvm. *LNCS*, 2131:106–113, 2001.
3. F. Giné, F. Solsona, P. Hernández, and E. Luque. Coscheduling under memory constraints in a now environment. *LNCS*, 2221:41–65, 2001.
4. F. Giné, F. Solsona, P. Hernández, and E. Luque. Adjusting the lengths of time slices when scheduling pvm jobs with high memory requirements. *LNCS*, 2474:156–164, 2002.
5. F. Giné, F. Solsona, P. Hernández, and E. Luque. Adjusting time slices to apply coscheduling techniques in a non-dedicated now. *LNCS*, 2400:234–239, 2002.
6. P. Krueger and D. Babbar. Stealth: a liberal approach to distributed scheduling for network of workstations. Technical report, OSU-CISRCI/93-TR6, Ohio State University, 1993.
7. K.D. Ryu and J.K. Hollingsworth. Linger longer: Fine-grain cycle stealing for networks of workstations. In *Proceedings Supercomputing'99 Conference*, 1999.
8. P.G. Sobalvarro, S. Pakin, W.E. Weihl, and A.A. Chien. Dynamic coscheduling on workstation clusters. *LNCS*, 1459:231–256, 1998.
9. F. Solsona, F. Giné, P. Hernández, and E. Luque. Predictive coscheduling implementation in a non-dedicated linux cluster. *LNCS*, 2150:732–741, 2001.

Mapping and Load-Balancing Iterative Computations on Heterogeneous Clusters

Arnaud Legrand, Hélène Renard, Yves Robert, and Frédéric Vivien

LIP, UMR CNRS-INRIA-UCBL 5668, École Normale Supérieure de Lyon, France

Abstract. This paper is devoted to mapping iterative algorithms onto heterogeneous clusters. The application data is partitioned over the processors, which are arranged along a virtual ring. At each iteration, independent calculations are carried out in parallel, and some communications take place between consecutive processors in the ring. The question is to determine how to slice the application data into chunks, and to assign these chunks to the processors, so that the total execution time is minimized. One major difficulty is to embed a processor ring into a network that typically is not fully connected, so that some communication links have to be shared by several processor pairs. We establish a complexity result that assesses the difficulty of this problem, and we design a practical heuristic that provides efficient mapping, routing, and data distribution schemes.

1 Introduction

We investigate the mapping of iterative algorithms onto heterogeneous clusters. Such algorithms typically operate on a large collection of application data, which is partitioned over the processors. At each iteration, some independent calculations are carried out in parallel, and then some communications take place. This scheme encompasses a broad spectrum of scientific computations, from mesh based solvers to signal processing, and image processing algorithms. An abstract view of the problem is the following: the iterative algorithm repeatedly operates on a rectangular matrix of data samples. This matrix is split into vertical slices that are allocated to the computing resources. At each step of the algorithm, the slices are updated locally, and then boundary information is exchanged between consecutive slices. This geometrical constraint advocates that processors be organized as a virtual ring. Then each processor only communicates twice, once with its predecessor in the ring, and once with its successor. There is no reason to restrict to a uni-dimensional partitioning of the data, and to map it onto a uni-dimensional ring of processors. But uni-dimensional partitionings are very natural for most applications, and we show that finding the optimal one is already very difficult.

The target architecture is a fully heterogeneous cluster, composed of different-speed processors that communicate through links of different bandwidths. On the architecture side, the problem is twofold: (i) select the processors that participate in the solution and decide for their ordering (which defines the ring); (ii) assign communication routes between each pair of consecutive processors in the ring. One major difficulty of this ring embedding process is that some of the communication routes will (most probably) have to share some physical communication links: indeed, the communication networks of heterogeneous clusters typically are far from being fully connected. If two or more routes share the same physical link, we have to decide which fraction of the link bandwidth is assigned to each route. Once the ring and the routing have been decided, there remains to determine the best partitioning of the application data. Clearly, the quality of the final solution depends on many application and architecture parameters.

To assess the impact of sharing the link bandwidths, we deal with the simplified version of the problem where we view the target interconnection network as fully connected: between any node pair, the routing is fixed (shortest paths in terms of bandwidth), and the bandwidth is assumed to be that of the slowest link in the routing path. This model is not very realistic, as no link contention is taken into account, but it will lead to a solution ring that can be compared to that obtained with link sharing, providing a way to evaluate the significance of the different hypotheses on the communications.

The rest of the paper is organized as follows. Section 2 is devoted to the precise and formal specification of the previous optimization problem, denoted as SHAREDRING. We also specify the simplified version of the problem denoted as SLICERING. We show that the decision problem associated to SHAREDRING is NP-complete. Section 3 deals with the design of polynomial-time heuristics to solve the SHAREDRING optimization problem. Section 4 is the counterpart for the SLICERING problem. We report some experimental data in Section 5. We state some concluding remarks in Section 6. Due to the lack of space, we refer the reader to [4, 3] for a survey of related papers.

2 Framework

2.1 Modeling the Platform Graph

Computing Costs. The target computing platform is modeled as a directed graph $G = (P, E)$. Each node P_i in the graph, $1 \leq i \leq |P| = p$, models a computing resource, and is weighted by its relative cycle-time w_i: P_i requires w_i time-steps to process a unit-size task. Of course the absolute value of the time-unit is application-dependent, what matters is the relative speed of one processor versus the other.

Communication Costs. Graph edges represent communication links and are labeled with available bandwidths. If there is an oriented link $e \in E$ from P_i to P_j, b_e denotes the link bandwidth. It takes L/b_e time-units to transfer one message of size L from P_i to P_j using link e. When several messages share the link, each of them receives a fraction of the available bandwidth. The fractions of the bandwidth allocated to the messages can be freely determined by the user, except that the sum of all these fractions cannot exceed the total link bandwidth. The eXplicit Control Protocol XCP [2] does enable to implement a bandwidth allocation strategy that complies with our hypotheses.

Routing. We assume we can freely decide how to route messages between processors. Assume we route a message of size L from P_i to P_j, along a path composed of k edges $e_1, e_2, \ldots, e_k$. Along each edge e_m, the message is allocated a fraction f_m of the bandwidth b_{e_m}. The communication speed along the path is bounded by the link allocating the smallest bandwidth fraction: we need L/b time-units to route the message, where $b = \min_{1 \leq m \leq k} f_m$. If several messages simultaneously circulate on the network and happen to share links, the total bandwidth capacity of each link cannot be exceeded.

Application Parameters: Computations. W is the total size of the work to be performed at each step of the algorithm. Processor P_i performs a share $\alpha_i.W$, where $\alpha_i \geq 0$ for $1 \leq i \leq p$ and $\sum_{i=1}^{p} \alpha_i = 1$. We allow $\alpha_j = 0$, meaning that processor P_j do not participate: all resources are not involved if extra communications incurred by adding more processors slow down the whole process, despite the increased cumulated speed.

Application Parameters: Communications in the Ring. We arrange the participating processors along a ring. After updating its data slice, each active processor sends a message of fixed length H to its successor. To illustrate the relationship between W and H, we can view the original data matrix as a rectangle composed of W columns of height H, so that one single column is exchanged between consecutive processors in the ring.

Let $\text{succ}(i)$ and $\text{pred}(i)$ denote the successor and the predecessor of P_i in the virtual ring. There is a communication path $\mathcal{S}_i$ from P_i to $P_{\text{succ}(i)}$ in the network: let $s_{i,m}$ be the fraction of the bandwidth b_{e_m} of the physical link e_m that is allocated to the path $\mathcal{S}_i$. If a link e_r is not used in the path, then $s_{i,r} = 0$. Let $c_{i,\text{succ}(i)} = \frac{1}{\min_{e_m \in \mathcal{S}_i} s_{i,m}}$: P_i requires $H.c_{i,\text{succ}(i)}$ time-units to send its message of size H to its successor $P_{\text{succ}(i)}$. Similarly, we define the path $\mathcal{P}_i$ from P_i to $P_{\text{pred}(i)}$, the bandwidth fraction $p_{i,m}$ of e_m allocated to $\mathcal{P}_i$, and $c_{i,\text{pred}(i)} = \frac{1}{\min_{e_m \in \mathcal{P}_i} p_{i,m}}$.

Objective Function. The total cost of one step in the iterative algorithm is the maximum, over all participating processors, of the time spent computing and communicating:

$$T_{\text{step}} = \max_{1 \leq i \leq p} \mathbb{I}\{i\}[\alpha_i.W.w_i + H.(c_{i,\text{pred}(i)} + c_{i,\text{succ}(i)})]$$

where $\mathbb{I}\{i\}[x] = x$ if P_i is involved in the computation, and 0 otherwise. In summary, the goal is to determine the best way to select q processors out of the p available, to assign them computational workloads, to arrange them along a ring and to share the network bandwidth so that the total execution time per step is minimized.

2.2 The SHAREDRING Optimization Problem

Definition 1 (SHAREDRING(p,w_i,E,b_{e_m},W,H)). *Given p processors P_i of cycle-times w_i and $|E|$ communication links e_m of bandwidth b_{e_m}, given the total workload W and the communication volume H at each step, minimize*

$$T_{step} = \min_{1 \leq q \leq p} \min_{\substack{\sigma \in \Theta_{q,p} \\ \sum_{i=1}^{q} \alpha_{\sigma(i)} = 1}} \max_{1 \leq i \leq q} \left(\alpha_{\sigma(i)}.W.w_{\sigma(i)} + H.(c_{\sigma(i),\sigma(i-1 \bmod q)} + c_{\sigma(i),\sigma(i+1 \bmod q)}) \right) \quad (1)$$

In Equation 1, $\Theta_{q,p}$ denotes the set of one-to-one functions $\sigma : [1..q] \rightarrow [1..p]$ which index the q selected processors that form the ring, for all candidate values of q between 1 and p. For each candidate ring represented by such a σ function, there are constraints hidden by the introduction of the quantities $c_{\sigma(i),\sigma(i-1 \bmod q)}$ and $c_{\sigma(i),\sigma(i+1 \bmod q)}$, which we gather now. There are $2q$ communicating paths, the path $\mathcal{S}_i$ from $P_{\sigma(i)}$ to its successor $P_{\text{succ}(\sigma(i))} = P_{\sigma(i+1 \bmod q)}$ and the path $\mathcal{P}_i$ from $P_{\sigma(i)}$ to its predecessor $P_{\text{pred}(\sigma(i))} = P_{\sigma(i-1 \bmod q)}$, for $1 \leq i \leq q$. For each link e_m in the interconnection network, let $s_{\sigma(i),m}$ (resp. $p_{\sigma(i),m}$) be the fraction of the bandwidth b_{e_m} that is allocated to the path $\mathcal{S}_{\sigma(i)}$ (resp. $\mathcal{P}_{\sigma(i)}$). We have the equations:

$$\begin{cases} 1 \leq i \leq q, \ 1 \leq m \leq E, \ s_{\sigma(i),m} \geq 0, \ p_{\sigma(i),m} \geq 0, \ \sum_{i=1}^{q}(s_{\sigma(i),m} + p_{\sigma(i),m}) \leq b_{e_m} \\ 1 \leq i \leq q, \ c_{\sigma(i),\mathrm{succ}(\sigma(i))} = \frac{1}{\min_{e_m \in \mathcal{S}_{\sigma(i)}} s_{\sigma(i),m}}, \ c_{\sigma(i),\mathrm{pred}(\sigma(i))} = \frac{1}{\min_{e_m \in \mathcal{P}_{\sigma(i)}} p_{\sigma(i),m}} \end{cases}$$

Since each communicating path $\mathcal{S}_{\sigma(i)}$ or $\mathcal{P}_{\sigma(i)}$ will typically involve a few edges, most of the quantities $s_{\sigma(i),m}$ and $p_{\sigma(i),m}$ will be zero. In fact, we have written $e_m \in \mathcal{S}_{\sigma(i)}$ if the edge e_m is actually used in the path $\mathcal{S}_{\sigma(i)}$, i.e. if $s_{i,m}$ is not zero.

From Equation 1, we see that the optimal solution involves all processors as soon as the ratio $\frac{W}{H}$ is large enough: then the impact of the communications becomes small in front of the cost of the computations, and the computations should be distributed to all resources. Even in that case, we have to decide how to arrange the processors along a ring, to construct the communicating paths, to assign bandwidths ratios and to allocate data chunks. Extracting the "best" ring seems to be a difficult combinatorial problem.

2.3 The SLICERING Optimization Problem

We denote by SLICERING the simplified version of the problem without link sharing. The SLICERING problem is exactly given by Equation 1 with an important simplification concerning routing paths and communication costs: the routing path between any node pair is fixed, as well as its bandwidth. This amounts to assuming a fully connected interconnection network where the bandwidth between P_i and P_j has a constant value. Given a "real" network, we define $c_{i,j}$ as the inverse of the smallest link bandwidth of a path of maximal bandwidth that goes from P_i to P_j. This construction does not take contentions into account: if the same link is shared by several paths, the available bandwidth for each path is over-estimated.

We summarize the construction of the simplified problem as follows: take the actual network as input, and compute shortest paths (in terms of bandwidths) between all processor pairs. This leads to a (fake) fully connected network. Now in Equation 1, the cost of all communication paths is given. But there remains to determine the optimal ring, and to assign computing workloads to the processors that belong to the ring.

2.4 Complexity

The following result states the intrinsic difficulty of the SHAREDRING problem (the same result holds for the simplified SLICERING problem; see [3,4] for the proofs):

Theorem 1. *The decision problem associated to the* SHAREDRING *optimization problem is NP-complete.*

3 Heuristic for the SHAREDRING Problem

We describe, in three steps, a polynomial-time heuristic to solve SHAREDRING: (i) the greedy algorithm used to construct a solution ring; (ii) the strategy used to assign bandwidth fractions during the construction; and (iii) a final refinement.

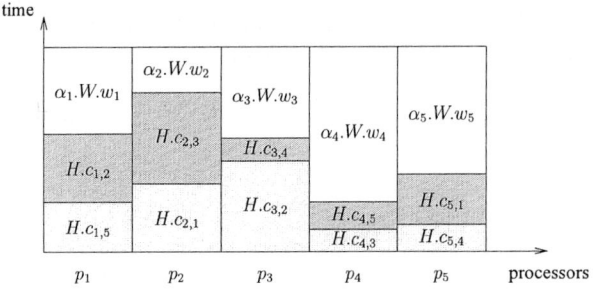

Fig. 1. Summary of computation and communication times with $q = 5$ processors.

3.1 Ring Construction

We consider a solution ring involving q processors, numbered from P_1 to P_q. Ideally, all these processors should require the same amount of time to compute and communicate: otherwise, we would slightly decrease the computing load of the last processor and assign extra work to another one (we are implicitly using the "divisible load" framework [3]). Hence (see Figure 1) we have for all i (indices being taken modulo q):

$$T_{\text{step}} = \alpha_i.W.w_i + H.(c_{i,i-1} + c_{i,i+1}). \tag{2}$$

Since $\sum_{i=1}^{q} \alpha_i = 1$, $\sum_{i=1}^{q} \frac{T_{\text{step}} - H.(c_{i,i-1}+c_{i,i+1})}{W.w_i} = 1$. With $w_{\text{cumul}} = \frac{1}{\sum_{i=1}^{q} \frac{1}{w_i}}$:

$$T_{\text{step}} = W.w_{\text{cumul}} \left(1 + \frac{H}{W} \sum_{i=1}^{q} \frac{c_{i,i-1} + c_{i,i+1}}{w_i} \right) \tag{3}$$

We use Equation 3 as a basis for a greedy algorithm which grows a solution ring iteratively, starting with the best pair of processors. Then, it iteratively includes a new node in the current solution ring. Assume we already have a ring of r processors. We search where to insert each remaining processor P_i in the current ring: for each pair of successive processors (P_j, P_k) in the ring, we compute the cost of inserting P_i between P_j and P_k. We retain the processor and pair that minimize the insertion cost. To compute the cost of inserting P_i between P_j and P_k, we resort to another heuristic to construct communicating paths and allocate bandwidth fractions (see Section 3.2) in order to compute the new costs $c_{k,j}$ (path from P_k to its successor P_j), $c_{j,k}$, $c_{k,i}$, and $c_{i,k}$. Once we have these costs, we compute the new value of T_{step} as follows:

- We update w_{cumul} by adding the new processor P_k into the formula.
- In $\sum_{s=1}^{r} \frac{c_{\sigma(s),\sigma(s-1)} + c_{\sigma(s),\sigma(s+1)}}{w_{\sigma(s)}}$, we suppress the two terms corresponding to the two paths between P_i to P_j and we insert the new terms $\frac{c_{k,j}+c_{k,i}}{w_k}$, $\frac{c_{j,k}}{w_j}$ and $\frac{c_{i,k}}{w_i}$.

This step of the heuristic has a complexity proportional to $(p - r).r$ times the cost to compute four communicating paths. Finally, we grow the ring until we have p processors. We return the minimal value obtained for T_{step}. The total complexity is

$\sum_{r=1}^{p}(p-r)rC = O(p^3)C$, where C is the cost of computing four paths in the network. Note that it is important to try all values of r, because T_{step} may not vary monotonically with r.

3.2 Bandwidth Allocation

We now assume we have a r-processor ring, a pair (P_i, P_j) of successive processors in the ring, and a processor P_k to be inserted between P_i and P_j. Together with the ring, we have built $2r$ communicating paths to which a fraction of the initial bandwidth has been allocated. To build the four paths involving P_k, we use the graph $G = (V, E, b)$ where $b(e_m)$ is what has been left by the $2r$ paths of the bandwidth of edge e_m. First we re-inject the bandwidths fractions used by the communication paths between P_i and P_j. Then to determine the four paths, from P_k to P_i and P_j and vice-versa:

- We independently compute four paths of maximal bandwidth, using a standard shortest path algorithm in G.
- If some paths happen to share some links, we use a brute force analytical method to compute the bandwidth fractions minimizing Equation 3 to be allocated.

Then we can compute the new value of T_{step} as explained above, and derive the values of the workloads α_i. The cost C of computing four paths in the network is $O(p + E)$.

3.3 Refinements

Schematically, the heuristic greedily grows a ring by peeling off the bandwidths to insert new processors. To diminish the cost of the heuristic, we never re-calculate the bandwidth fractions that have been previously assigned. When the heuristic ends, we have a q-processor ring, q workloads, $2q$ communicating paths, bandwidth fractions and communication costs for these paths, and a feasible value of T_{step}. As the heuristic could appear over-simplistic, we have implemented two variants aimed at refining its solution. The idea is to keep everything but the bandwidth fractions and workloads. Once we have selected the processor and the pair minimizing the insertion cost in the current ring, we perform the insertion and recompute all bandwidth fractions and workloads. We can re-evaluate bandwidth fractions using a global approach (see [3] for details):

Method 1: Max-min fairness. We compute the bandwidths fractions using the traditional bandwidth-sharing algorithm [1] which maximizes the minimum bandwidth allocated to a path. Then we compute the α_i so as to equate all execution times (computations followed by communications), thereby minimizing T_{step}.

Method 2: quadratic resolution using the KINSOL software. Once we have a ring and all the communicating paths, the program to minimize T_{step} is quadratic in the unknowns α_i, $s_{i,j}$ and $p_{i,j}$. We use the KINSOL library [5] to solve it.

4 Heuristic for the SLICERING Problem

The greedy heuristic for the SLICERING problem is similar to the previous one. It starts by selecting the fastest processor and iteratively includes a new node in the current

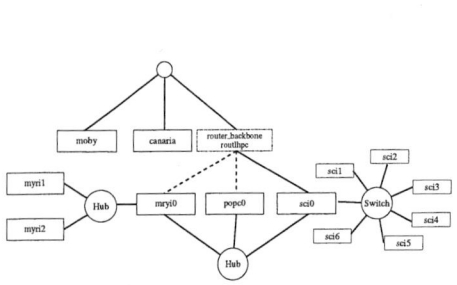
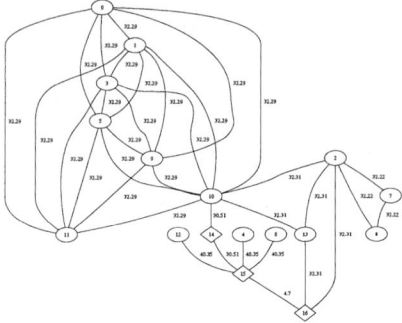

Fig. 2. Topology of the Lyon platform. **Fig. 3.** Abstraction of the Lyon platform.

Table 1. Processor cycle-times (in seconds per megaflop) for the Lyon and Strasbourg platforms.

P_0	P_1	P_2	P_3	P_4	P_5	P_6	P_7	P_8	P_9	P_{10}	P_{11}	P_{12}	P_{13}	P_{14}	P_{15}	P_{16}
0.0206	0.0206	0.0206	0.0206	0.0291	0.0206	0.0087	0.0206	0.0206	0.0206	0.0206	0.0206	0.0291	0.0451	0	0	0

P_0	P_1	P_2	P_3	P_4	P_5	P_6	P_7	P_8	P_9	P_{10}	P_{11}	P_{12}	P_{13}	P_{14}	P_{15}	P_{16}	P_{17}	P_{18}
0.0087	0.0072	0.0087	0.0131	0.016	0.0058	0.0087	0.0262	0.0102	0.0131	0.0072	0.0058	0.0072	0	0	0	0	0	0

solution ring. Assume we have a ring of r processors. For each remaining processor P_i, for each pair of successive processors (P_j, P_k) in the ring, we compute the cost of inserting P_i between P_j and P_k. We retain the processor and the pair minimizing the insertion cost. This step of the heuristic has a complexity proportional to $(p - r).r$. We grow the ring until we have p processors, and we return the minimal value obtained for T_{step}. The total complexity is $\sum_{r=1}^{p}(p-r)r = O(p^3)$. It is important to try all values of r as T_{step} may not vary monotically with r. See [4] for further details.

5 Experimental Results

5.1 Platform Description

We experimented with two platforms, one located in ENS Lyon and the other one in the University of Strasbourg. Figures 2 and 3 show the Lyon platform which is composed of 14 computing resources and 3 routers. In Figure 3, circled nodes 0 to 13 are the processors, and diamond nodes 14 to 16 are the routers. Edges are labeled with link bandwidths. Similarly, the Strasbourg platform is composed of 13 computing resources and 6 routers. Processor cycle-times for both platforms are gathered in Table 1.

5.2 Results

For both topologies, we evaluate the impact of link sharing as follows. In the first heuristic, we build the solution ring without taking link sharing into account. Using the abstract graph in Figure 3, we run an all-pair shortest distance algorithm to determine the bandwidth between any pair of nodes, thereby simulating a fully connected interconnection network. Then we return the solution ring computed by the greedy heuristic

Table 2. T_{step}/W for each heuristic for the Lyon and Strasbourg platforms respectively.

Ratio H/W	H1 : slice-ring	H2 : shared-ring	Improvement	Ratio H/W	H1 : slice-ring	H2 : shared-ring	Improvement
0.1	3.17	3.15	0.63%	0.1	7.32	7.26	0.82%
1	3.46	3.22	6.94%	1	9.65	7.53	21.97%
10	10.39	3.9	62.46%	10	19.24	10.26	46.67%

for the SLICERING problem, as described in Section 4. The value of T_{step} achieved by the heuristic may well not be feasible, as the actual network is not fully connected. Therefore, we keep the ring and the communicating paths between adjacent processors in the ring, and we compute feasible bandwidth fractions using the quadratic programming software. The second heuristic is the greedy heuristic designed in Section 3 for the SHAREDRING problem, using the quadratic programming refinement. The major difference between the two heuristics is that the latter takes link contention into account when building up the solution ring. To compare the value of $\frac{T_{step}}{W}$ returned by both algorithms, we use various communication-to-computation ratios. Table 2 shows these values for each platform. From these experiments we conclude that:

– When the impact of communication costs is low, the main goal is to balance computations, and both heuristics are equivalent.
– When the communication-to-computation ratio becomes more important, the effect of link contention becomes clear, and the second heuristic's solution is much better.

As a conclusion, we point out that an accurate modeling of the communications has a dramatic impact on the performance of the load-balancing strategies.

6 Conclusion

The major limitation to programming heterogeneous platforms arises from the additional difficulty of balancing the load. Data and computations are not evenly distributed to processors. Minimizing communication overhead becomes a challenging task. In this paper, the major emphasis was towards a realistic modeling of concurrent communications in cluster networks. One major result is the NP-completeness of the SHAREDRING problem. Rather than the proof, the result itself is interesting, because it provides yet another evidence of the intrinsic difficulty of designing heterogeneous algorithms. But this negative result should not be over-emphasized. Indeed, another important contribution of this paper is the design of an efficient heuristic, that provides a pragmatic guidance to the designer of iterative scientific computations. The importance of an accurate modeling of the communications, that takes contentions into full account, has been made clear by the experimental results. Our heuristic makes it possible to efficiently implement iterative computations on commodity clusters made up of several heterogeneous resources, which is a promising alternative to using costly supercomputers.

References

1. D. Bertsekas and R. Gallager. *Data Networks*. Prentice Hall, 1987.
2. D. Katabi, M. Handley, and C. Rohrs. Congestion control for high bandwidth-delay product networks. In *Proceedings of ACM SIGCOMM 2002*, pages 89–102. ACM Press, 2002.
3. A. Legrand, H. Renard, Y. Robert, and F. Vivien. Load-balancing iterative computations in heterogeneous clusters with shared communication links. Research Report RR-2003-23, LIP, ENS Lyon, France, Apr. 2003.
4. H. Renard, Y. Robert, and F. Vivien. Static load-balancing techniques for iterative computations on heterogeneous clusters. Research Report RR-2003-12, LIP, ENS Lyon, 2003.
5. A. Taylor and A. Hindmarsh. User documentation for KINSOL. Tech. Rep. UCRL-ID-131185, Lawrence Livermore Nat. Lab., July 1998.

Dynamic Topology Selection for High Performance MPI in the Grid Environments

Kyung-Lang Park[1], Hwang-Jik Lee[1], Kwang-Won Koh[1], Oh-Young Kwon[2], Sung-Yong Park[3], Hyoung-Woo Park[4], and Shin-Dug Kim[1]

[1] Dept. of Computer Science, Yonsei University 134 Shinchon-Dong, Seodaemun-Gu
Seoul 120-749, Korea
{lanx,bear22,sugare,sdkim}@parallel.yonsei.ac.kr
[2] Dept. of Computer Engineering, Korea University of Technology and Education
P.O. BOX 55, Chonan, 330-600, Korea
oykwon@kut.ac.kr
[3] Dept. of Computer Science, Sogang University
1 Shinsoo-Dong, Mapo-Gu, Seoul 121-742, Korea
parksy@ccs.sogang.ac.kr
[4] Korea Institute of Science and Technology Information
P.O. BOX 122, Yusong, Taejun, 305-806, Korea
hwpark@hpcnet.ne.kr

Abstract. MPI (Message Passing Interface) is getting more popular and important even in the Grid, but its performance still remains a problem, which is caused by the communication bottleneck on wide area links. To overcome such performance wall problem, we propose a dynamic topology selection which provides an effective resource selection service based on the principles of wide area message passing. It attempts to match the communication pattern of application with the topology of resources. Consequently, the proposed method provides an optimized set of resources and improves overall application performance by reducing the communication delay. To demonstrate the proposed method, we executed parallel benchmark programs and measured each execution time in five geometrically distributed clusters by changing resource selection method. When using topology selection method, experimental results show that performance gain can be achieved by up to 200%.

1 Introduction

The Grid [1] is an emerging technology considered as a next generation computing infrastructure. In the Grid environment, users can use practically unlimited resources as a single entity. However, there is a significant gap between the ideal Grid and current implementations. Especially, it is difficult to find useful Grid applications. In this situation, MPI (Message Passing Interface) [2] is the most significant technology to make Grid applications. It is a parallel programming library which was widely used for supercomputers and massive parallel processors. As the computational Grid emerges, MPI starts to be used for the Grid environments.

The Grid-enabled MPI library represented as MPICH-G2 [3] has a lot of new features derived from characteristics of the Grid. For example, it supports the multi-requests on distributed machine environments and provides security. But, the main purpose of the MPI is high-performance computing, so that the most important requirement must be performance rather than other functionalities. Nevertheless, conventional Grid-enabled MPI implementations do not show any reasonable performance advantage for existing commercial network environments. Therefore, many researchers have attempted to improve performance of MPI applications.

Performance gain can be achieved by enhancing the physical network features or by applying an efficient communication algorithm. However, these approaches need large amount of costs to change current communication infrastructure. Therefore, resource selection methods are considered as an alternative way to gain the performance without changing infrastructure. In Grid environment, resource selection can affect performance more significantly because the Grid implicitly includes heterogeneous resources for both computation and communication.

Different from previous resource selection methods, the proposed topology selection considers not only the capacity of individual resources, but also network status and communication pattern of applications. It attempts to match communication pattern of applications with the topology of resources. Thus it provides a group of efficient nodes for a given MPI application and improves overall performance by reducing communication delay. To demonstrate the proposed method, we implement topology selection framework. When measuring application execution time in five distributed clusters, topology selection method provides 200% performance gain compared with general sequential resource selection method.

In Section 2, the basic concept of resource selection on Grid environments is introduced. In Section 3, the topology selection mechanisms are described in detail. Section 4 shows several results of the proposed implementation to demonstrate its effectiveness. Finally, we present the conclusions of the research in Section 5.

2 Background

Resource selection method has aroused many researchers' interest after Grid and distributed computing technologies were appeared. Especially in the field of parallel computing with MPI programming environment, it must be a crucial issue in the aspect of high performance. But, previous resource selection methods neither support distributed resources nor consider the characteristics of parallel programs. PBS [4] and LSF [5] are system schedulers, which include simple resource selection methods. But these are designed only for a single supercomputer or cluster and concentrate on computation capacity, so that these are too simple to work on Grid environments. Advanced are the AppLes [6] and Condor [7]. AppLes support for writing specific resource selection method to be embedded into AppLes system. Condor also provides ClassAds and Matchmaker for the user to inform his request. However, those are focused on selecting individual resource, so that those were are not suitable for the

Dynamic Topology Selection for High Performance MPI in the Grid Environments 597

MPI on Grid environments that need a set of resources which include communication delay.

As shown in Figure 1, MPI execution environments are being changed into multi-site (multi-cluster) environments that include heterogeneous networks. In this situation, the communication latency between clusters can be a new parameter, so that performance of MPI applications can be affected by not also the computing power of individual nodes but also the relationship between any two processes. Namely, overall application performance can be dominated by the entire resource topology rather than by the status of each process. Therefore the algorithm reflecting the topology will be needed.

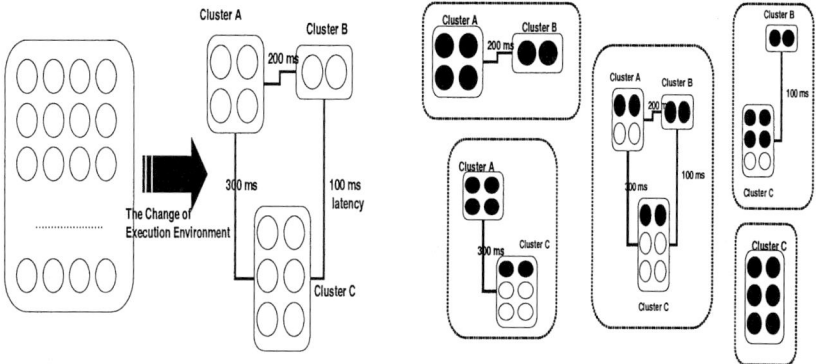

Fig. 1. Change of MPI execution environment (left). Assume that a user wants 6 resources to run MPI application, there are various cases of resource topology and performance must be different in each case (right). Circles mean resources and a black circle means that a process is allocated to the resource.

3 Dynamic Topology Selection

3.1 Design Methodology

To design proposed topology selection method, we apply two basic principles specified from wide area message passing environments and consider two additional principles that are related to application characteristics. The basic concept reflected from the characteristics of the wide area message passing environment is that communication should be performed via wide area links as few as possible [8]. As mentioned before, the Grid environment is constructed as many wide area networks, so that communications through geometrically distributed sites can be significant performance bottleneck. This basic concept teaches us that it can reduce the amount of communication bottleneck to decrease the number of communications through wide area networks. To apply this concept more easily, we expanded it into two phases, the *use of minimum number of clusters* (A) and *giving priority to the cluster which has the lowest value of latencies over other clusters* (B). Principle A can decrease the frequency in use of wide area links. Also, it is more favorable to use a collection of clusters having better network performance according to Principle B.

Two additional principles are specified as HBPTS (High Burden Process based Topology Selection) and HBCTS (High Burden Channel based Topology Selection), which are both based on application characteristics. HBPTS is to *give higher priority to the high burden processes, which have more responsibility about the communication* (C). If previous two principles are used to determine which clusters should be used, Principle C is used to determine the order of processes in assigning resources with high performance. At last, HBCTS is *to allocate high burden channels into intra-cluster* (D) to minimize the communication latencies. It can improve performance for the applications that have heavy communications among specific processes. By applying Principle D, heavy communication channels are not used for wide area links.

Finally, our topology selection policy is constructed by combining above four principles. By using topology selection policy, the topology selection framework is implemented and explained next section.

3.2 Topology Selection Framework

In this section, we will explain the topology selection method and its detailed operational flow with a practical example. The architecture of our topology selection framework is shown in Figure 2.

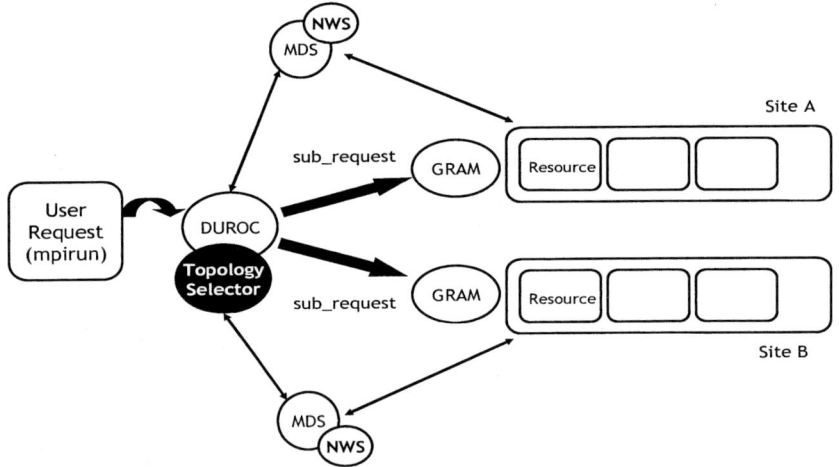

Fig. 2. Architecture of topology selection framework.

To make the topology selection framework simple, we leverage conventional Grid components in Globus Toolkit [9] and just add a topology selector drawn as black circle as in Figure 2. MDS (Monitoring and Discovery Service) [10] provides necessary information to the topology selector, constructed as local queue information and dynamic network status. NWS (Network Weather Service) [11] is coupled with MDS

Dynamic Topology Selection for High Performance MPI in the Grid Environments

to provide accurate network information. The topology selector makes a process list and a resource list by using given information from MDS and/or NWS, and decides a collection of resource, where MPI processes will be executed. After that, DUROC and GRAM perform co-allocation procedure on selected resources [12].

The flow of the topology selection comprises of 6 steps. The first step is to make a resource list by using the information from MDS. Secondary, the topology selector sorts the resource list by the order of communication performance. Those two steps are derived from Principle A and B. In the third step, the topology selector makes a process list by using user's requests. In step 4, the topology selector tries to find high burden channels. If a high burden channel is discovered, it groups a pair of processes which are connected to the high burden channel. In step 5, topology selector sorts the process and group list by order of communication rate. Finally, in step 6, the selector simply allocates sorted processes into the sorted resources one by one.

A following example shows clear sequence of the topology selection steps. Assume that the workload is the LU solver included in NAS Parallel Benchmark [13] and the execution environment consists of five distributed clusters which have four nodes in each cluster. When using 16 processes, the LU solver has the communication pattern as shown in Figure 3. Process 5, 6, 9, and 10 are high burden processes and the channels between process 4 to 8 and process 7 to 11 are high burden channels. No high burden channels exist in original LU solver, but we insert redundant communication code for easy-of-understanding. When we execute such a workload, topology selection step will be performed as in Figure 4. As shown in the figure, high burden processes (5, 6, 9, and 10) are allocated in cluster C which has the best network performance. Also, high burden channels (4 to 8 and 7 to 11) are allocated in the same clusters. The example introduced in this section was experimented in the real testbed, and the result will be shown in Section 4.

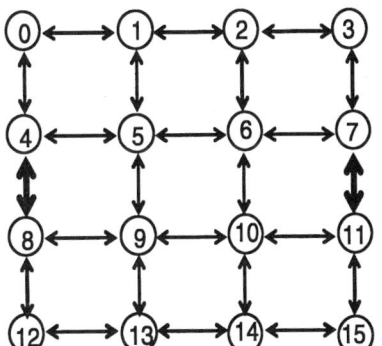 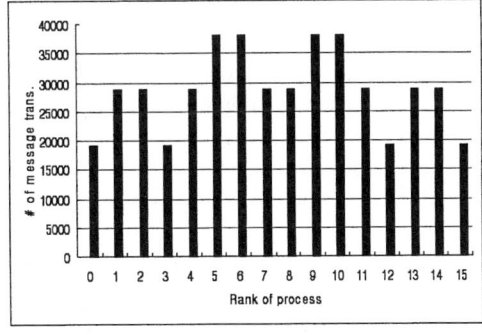

Fig. 3. Communication patterns in LU solver is shown in left side and the number of message transmission are depicted in the right graph. Process 5,6,9, and 10 have more responsibility for communication (high burden processes), and two channels between process 4-8 and 7-11 have more communication (high burden channel).

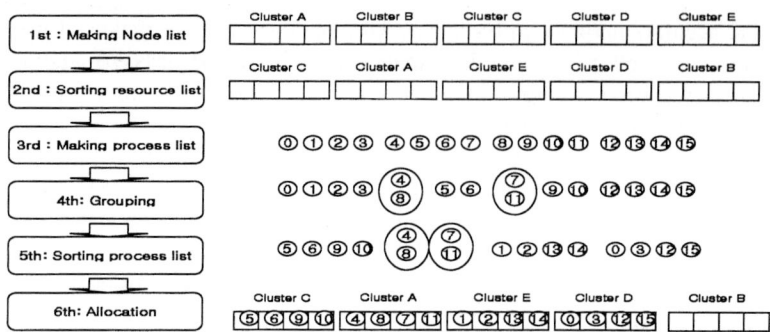

Fig. 4. Operation steps for dynamic topology selection (Assume that communication performance of clusters: C > A > E > D > B).

4 Experimental Result

To evaluate the impact of our topology selection, we will show the experimental results in a practical Grid environment. Table 1 shows our MPI testbed which consists of four clusters of Pentium machines connected by general purpose Internet in five universities located at different cities in Korea [14].

Table 1. MPI Testbed Status.

Name	Type	# of resource	resource on test	Job-Manager	Globus	CPU	Location
Yonsei	Cluster	24	4	PBS	2.0	P4/1G	Seoul
Ajou	Cluster	8	4	PBS	2.0	P4/1.6G	Soowon
KISTI	Cluster	80	4	PBS	2.0	P4/2G	Daejun
KUT	Cluster	4	4	PBS	2.0	P3/850	Chonan
Postech	Cluster	8	4	PBS	2.0	P4/1.7G	Pohang

In this environment, we executed four benchmark programs and compared execution time by changing scheduling policy and problem size. To experiment more precisely, we collect sufficient samples in 95% confidence interval.

Figure 5 shows the results of four benchmark programs. Each program has its own unique communication pattern [15]. In this figure, the sorted node list means that only two steps are performed in resource selection. Surely, the full topology selection means that all six steps are performed and no policy means that there is no resource selection service. In the case of LU benchmark as explained in the previous section, the topology selection method improves the performance by up to 200% compared with no policy. IS (Integer Sort) comprises of a number of broadcast and reduce functions. Thus the root process can be a high burden process. In this case, there is a little difference between the full topology selection and the sorted list because root process can be considered as a high burden process automatically. MG (Multi Grid) has similar communication pattern with LU. It shows the 4D hypercube topology in 16 processes and process 4, 5, 6, 7, 12, 13, 14, and 15 has more communication rate than others. In MG benchmark, performance improvement can be achieved by 180%. Differently, the processes merely communicate each other in EP benchmark. Topology selection cannot help such application because topology selection is based on communication pattern and network status.

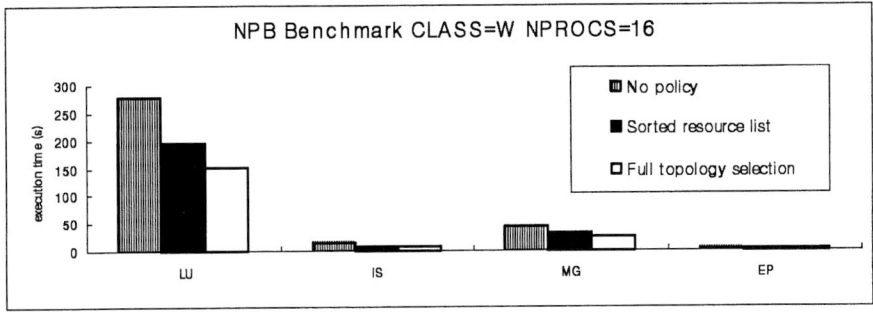

Fig. 5. Execution time of four type parallel benchmark programs with 16 processes and W class.

Also we experimented by changing problem size. NPB benchmark suite provides 5 classes of problem size, which are S, W, A, B and C, where S is the smallest and C is the largest. As shown in the figure, for the class C which is the largest, performance gain can be achieved by 200% compare with no policy and by 140% compared with sorted node list. We also can see that the performance gain become bigger if the problem size is larger because larger problem size causes more communication overhead.

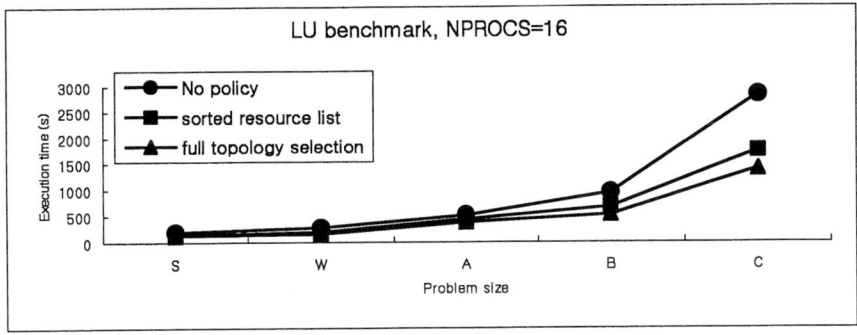

Fig. 6. Execution time according to the change of problem size.

5 Conclusion

Since the emergency of the Grid, many previous experiments show us that applications cannot be executed in Grid environments without tuning performance and functionalities of software or hardware components which comprise of the Grid. Proposed dynamic topology selection is one of the tuning methods for MPI applications. It provides an efficient resource selection service based on four principles which are derived from wide area message passing paradigm. Those principles are the use of minimum number of clusters, giving priority to the cluster which has the lowest value of latencies over other clusters, giving priority to the high burden processes, and allocating high burden channels into the intra-cluster. Consequently, the topology selection can improve the overall application performance by reducing the communication load. To demonstrate the proposed method, we measured application's execution time in four geometrically distributed clusters by changing resource selection method. When using topology selection method, performance gain can be achieved by 200% compared with no policy and by 140% compared with sorted list only policy in given execution environments.

References

1. I. Foster and C. Kesselman, eds. The GRID: Blueprint for a New Computing Infrastructure, Morgan Kaufmann, (1998).
2. Message Passing Interface Forum, MPI: A Message-Passing Interface standard, International Journal of Supercomputer Applications, 8(3/4), (1994), 165-414.
3. I. Foster and N. Karonis, A grid-enabled MPI: Message passing in heterogeneous distributed computing systems, In Proc. Supercomputing '98, 11 (1998).
4. R. Henderson, and D. Tweten, Portable Batch System: External reference specification, Ames Research Center, (1996).
5. S. Zhou, LSF: Load Sharing in Large-scale Heterogeneous Distributed System, In Proc. Workshop on Cluster Computing, (1992).
6. H. Casanova, G. Obertelli, F. Berman, and R. Wolski. The AppLeS Parameter Sweep Template: User-Level Middleware for the Grid, In Proc. Super Computing 00, Dallas, Texas, 11 (2000).
7. J. Frey, T. Tannenbaum, I. Foster, M. Livny, and S. Tuecke, Condor-G: A computation Management Agent for Multi-Institutional Grids, Cluster Computing, 5(3), (2002).
8. T. Kielmann, R. F. H. Hofman, H. E. Bal, A. Plaat, and R. A. F. Bhoedjang, MagPIe: MPI's Collective Communication Operations for Clustered Wide Area Systems, In Proc. Symposium on Principles and Practice of Parallel Programming, Atlanta, GA, 5 (1999).
9. I. Foster and C. Kesselman, Globus: A metacomputing infrastructure toolkit, International Journal of Supercomputer Applications, 11(2), (1997), 115-128.
10. K. Czajkowski, S. Fitzgerald, I. Foster, C. Kesselman, Grid Information Service for Wide Area Distributed Computations, In Proc. International Symposium on High Performance Distributed Computing, 8 (2001)
11. R. Wolski, N. Spring, and J. Hayes, The Network Weather Service: A Distributed Resource Performance Forecasting Service for Metacomputing, Journal of Future Generation Computing Systems, 15(5-6), (1999), 757-768
12. I. Foster, and C. Kesselman, Resource Co-Allocation in Computational Grids, In Proc. International Symposium on High Performance Distributed Computing, (1999), 217-228
13. D. Bailey, T. Harris, W. Saphir, R. Wijngaart, A. Woo, and M. Yarrow, NAS Parallel benchmark 2.0, Technical Report 95-020, NASA Ames Research Center, 12 (1995).
14. Antz Grid testbed, online at http://www.antz.or.kr
15. J. Subhlok, S. Venkataramaiah, and A. Singh, Characterizing NAS Benchmark Performance on Shared Heterogeneous Networks, In Proc. International Parallel and Distributed Processing Symposium, (2002)

Monitoring Message Passing Applications in the Grid with GRM and R-GMA

Norbert Podhorszki and Peter Kacsuk

MTA SZTAKI, Budapest, H-1528 P.O.Box 63, Hungary
{pnorbert,kacsuk}@sztaki.hu

Abstract. Although there are several tools for monitoring parallel applications running on clusters and supercomputers they cannot be used in the grid without modifications. GRM, a message-passing parallel application monitoring tool for clusters, is connected to the infrastructure of R-GMA, the information and monitoring system of the EU-DataGrid project in order to collect trace information about message-passing parallel applications executed in the grid. In this paper, their connection is described.

1 Introduction

The monitoring of grid applications is a new area for research. Existing tools developed for clusters and supercomputers are not usable without redesign. One of the main reasons is that they cannot be set-up on the grid for monitoring at all. The direct access rights to the resources and the a priori knowledge of the machines where the target application is executed are required for the tools to be set-up on a cluster or supercomputer. Without this knowledge on the grid the tools cannot be started and used for collecting information about the application.

This is also the case for GRM [1], a semi-on-line monitor for message-passing parallel applications. To adapt it to the grid, the start-up mechanism as well as the data transfer had to be modified. Within the EU-DataGrid project [2], GRM is connected to R-GMA, the grid information and monitoring system. GRM uses R-GMA as a service to publish trace information about the monitored application and to transfer the trace to the user's site.

In this paper, the connection of the two tools is described. First, GRM and R-GMA are shortly introduced. Then their connection is presented. Finally, about a small MPI example show visualised trace information as a result.

2 GRM Application Monitor

GRM [3] is an on-line monitoring tool for performance monitoring of message passing parallel applications running in the grid. PROVE is a performance visualisation tool for GRM traces. When requested, GRM collects trace data from all machines where the application is running and transfers it to the machine where the trace is visualised by PROVE.

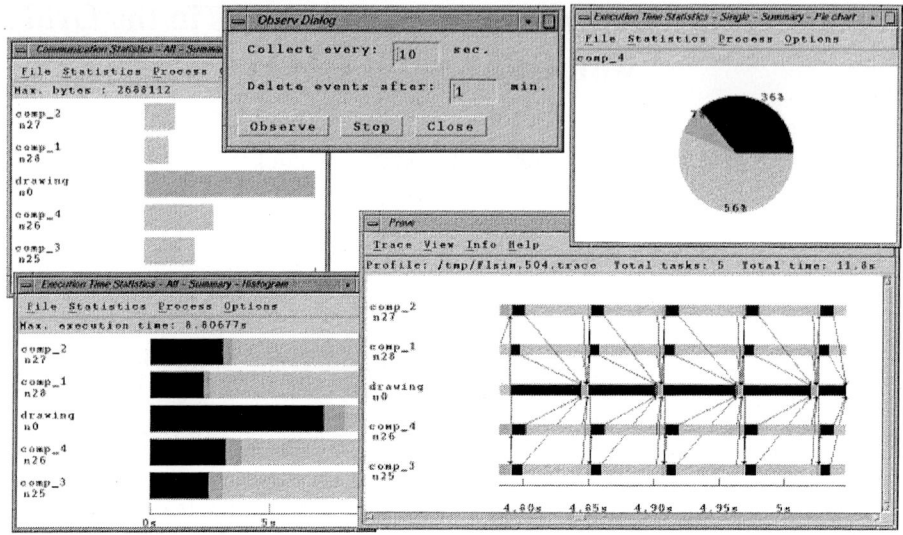

Fig. 1. Visualisation of trace and statistics in PROVE

To enable monitoring of an application, the user should first instrument the application with trace generation functions. GRM provides an instrumentation API and library for tracing. The instrumentation API is available for C/C++ and Fortran. The basic instrumentation functions are for the start and exit, send and receive, multicast, block begin and end events. However, more general tracing is possible by *user defined events*. For this purpose, first the format string of a new user event should be defined, similarly to C printf format strings. Then the predefined event format can be used for trace event generation, always passing the arguments only. The instrumentation is explained in detail in [4].

The trace is event record oriented. One record (line) in the trace file represents one trace event of the application. Each record starts with a header containing information about the type of the event, generation time and id of the generating process. The remainder of the record contains the values for that given type of event.

PROVE is a trace visualisation tool to present traces of parallel programs (see Fig. 1) collected by GRM. Its main purpose is to show a time-space diagram from the trace but it also generates several statistics from the trace that help to discover the performance problems, e.g. Gannt chart, communication statistics among the processes/hosts and detailed run-time statistics for the different blocks in the application process.

These tools have been the basis in the development of a grid application monitor that supports on-line monitoring and visualisation of parallel/distributed applications in the grid. GRM can be used as a stand-alone tool for grid application monitoring, as its architecture is described in [3]. However, the problem of firewalls cannot be overcome by GRM itself. If a firewall disables a connection between the components of GRM, the tool is not able to collect trace from the application processes. To solve this problem, a proxy-like solution is needed which enables the connection of two components by making a chain of connections from one of the components towards the other through some hops in the network. Such solution should be a service which is always available in the grid. Instead of creating a new GRM-service, we turned to R-GMA that is a continuously running grid monitoring service and that also can be used to transfer trace data through the network.

3 R-GMA, a Relational Grid Monitoring Architecture

R-GMA (Relational Grid Monitoring Architecture, [5]) is being developed as a Grid Information and Monitoring System for both the grid itself and for use by applications. It is based on the GMA concept [6] from Global Grid Forum, which is a simple Consumer-Producer model. The special strength of this implementation comes from the power of the relational model. It offers a global view of the information as if each Virtual Organisation had one large relational database.

It provides a number of different Producer types with different characteristics; for example some of them support streaming of information. It also provides combined Consumer/Producers, which are able to combine information and republish it. At the heart of the system is the mediator, which for any query is able to find and connect to the best Producers to do the job.

R-GMA is not a general distributed RDBMS but it provides a way of using the relational data model in a Grid environment [7]. All the producers of information are quite independent. It is relational in the sense that Producers announce what they have to publish via an SQL CREATE TABLE statement and publish with an SQL INSERT and that Consumers use an SQL SELECT to collect the information they need. R-GMA is built using servlet technology and is being migrated rapidly to web services and specifically to fit into an OGSA (Open Grid Services Architecture, [8]) framework.

It is important to emphasize here that R-GMA is a grid service providing an infrastructure to enable developers to create special producers and consumers for specific tasks and not a tool usable for any purpose (like application monitoring) in itself.

4 Connection of GRM and R-GMA

GRM uses R-GMA to deliver trace data from the application process to the machine where the user is running the visualisation tool. The basic structure of the connection can be seen in Fig. 2. The application processes contain the instrumentation library that produces events. The main monitor of GRM is running at the user's host (where PROVE is running as well) and reads trace data from R-GMA. The instrumentation library is a Producer while GRM's main monitor is a Consumer of R-GMA. R-GMA is distributed among several hosts. It consists of servlets: Registry servlets are placed somewhere in the grid providing a fault-tolerant service for publishing information about available producers. Other servlets connect to the registry to find a way to communicate with each other. ProducerServlets are placed on several machines. Any producer of data should connect to one of the ProducerServlets (whose address is set on the host where the producer is running). Similarly, every consumer connects to a ConsumerServlet. The

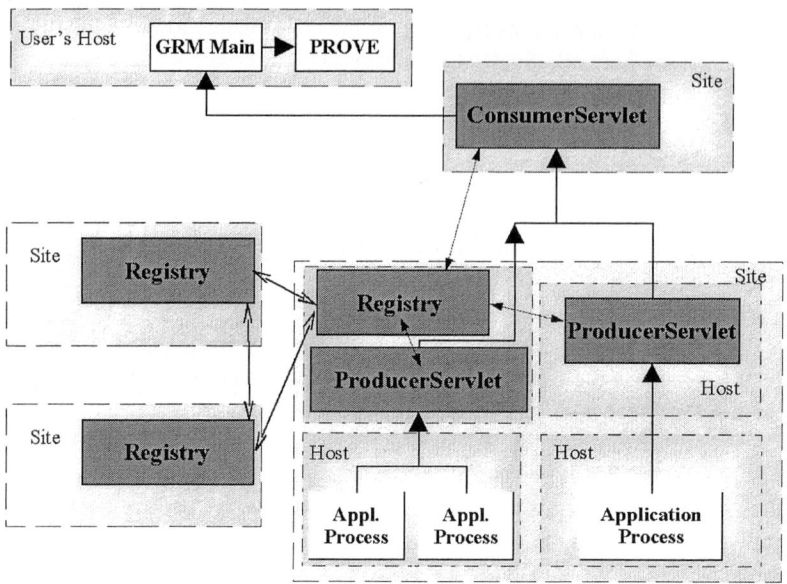

Fig. 2. Structure of GRM in R-GMA

configuration of R-GMA is very flexible to fit to the current grid infrastructure. For more detailed information see the architecture documentation of R-GMA [9].

R-GMA is always running in the grid as a service while GRM's main monitor is started by the user when the job is submitted. The application processes start to behave as producers of R-GMA when they are launched. This way, the structure of the monitoring chain is built-up with the application start.

The instrumentation functions automatically connect to R-GMA at the start of the processes and trace events are published to R-GMA. GRM's main monitor acts as a Consumer of R-GMA, looking for trace data and receiving it from R-GMA. The delivery of data from the machines of the running processes to the collection host is the task of R-GMA now. As it can be seen in Fig. 3, R-GMA is using several servlets and buffers to deliver the trace data to the consumers. There is a local buffer in the application process itself that can be used to temporarily store data if a large amount of trace is generated fast. The processes are connected to ProducerServlets that are further connected to ConsumerServlets. Both kind of servlets create distinguished buffers for each Producer/Consumer that connect to them.

The mediator functionality of R-GMA ensures that all matching information for a specific query are merged from several data sources and the consumer receives all information in one data stream. Thus, GRM's main monitor receives the whole application trace data in one single stream.

The distinction between the traces of different applications is made by a unique id for each application. This id works as a key in the relational database schema and one instance of GRM is looking for one application with a given id/key. A proper id can be the global job id of the application which is defined by the grid brokering system. Cur-

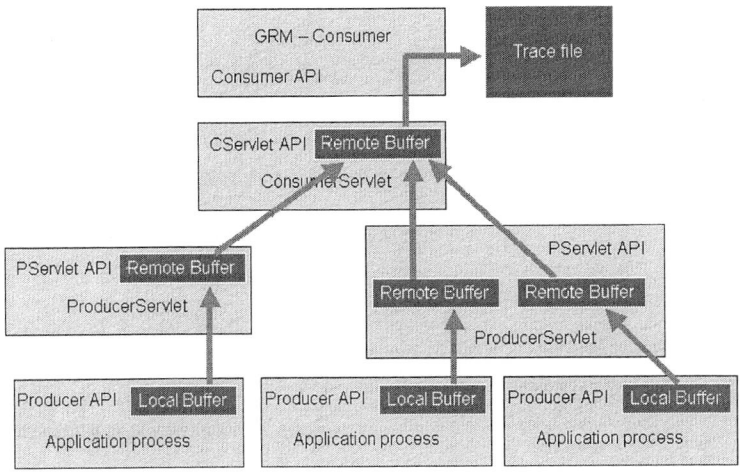

Fig. 3. Buffering and delivery of trace data within R-GMA

rently, there is no defined way how the instrumentation functions within the application processes can get this id. So, the user should define a unique id for its application in the current version of GRM.

After the application is submitted and GRM's main monitor is started, the main monitor connects R-GMA immediately and subscribes for traces with the id of the application. When R-GMA gives a positive response GRM starts continuously reading trace from R-GMA.

4.1 Monitoring of MPI Applications

As an example, the code of the systest demo application of the MPICH package is instrumented and the generated trace in PROVE is shown. The systest program performs two different tests. In the "Hello" test each process sends a short message to all the others. In the "Ring" test, the processes form a ring based on their ranks, the process 0 is connected to process 1 and N-1, where N is the number of processes. Starting from process 0, a messages with ever increasing size are sent around the ring, finally arriving at process 0 again.

In the top window of the screenshots in Fig. 4. PROVE presents the full execution. The arrows on the left side of the picture represent the messages of the "Hello" test while the many arrows in the right side of the picture represent the "Ring" test. In between, the large section with light color represent an artifically inserted sleep statement in the program to make the different phases clearly distinguishable.

The bottom left screenshot is the zoom to the left part. In this test each process sent a message to all the others, one by one. The first blocks with light color represent the barrier in the program. Also the triangle symbol representing the start of process P0 can be seen on the left. The blocks with light color on the right are the sleeping section in the processes.

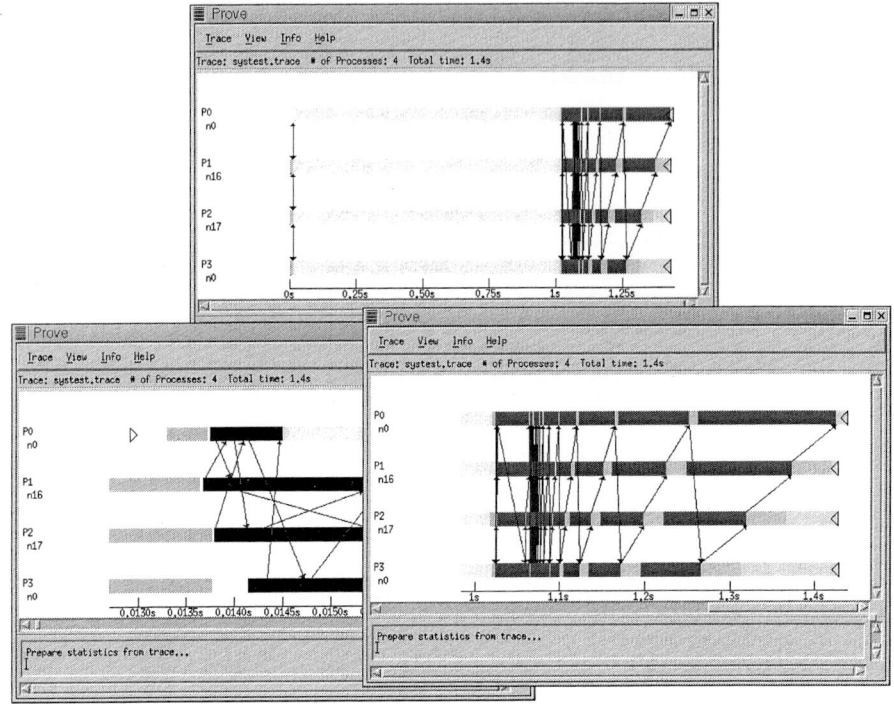

Fig. 4. Trace of MPI *systest* example application

The bottom right screenshot shows the right side of the full trace. In this test messages with sizes 1, 2, 4, ..., 524288 bytes are sent around the processes. The time of the communication is growing with the size of the message. The sending and receiving phases in the processes are distinguished by the alternating lighter and darker blocks. The triangles representing the exit statement in the instrumentation can also be seen on the right side of the picture.

5 Related Work

R-GMA is deployed within the EU-DataGrid project [2]. Other grid projects are mostly based on MDS [10], the LDAP based information system of Globus but, e.g., the GridLab [11] project is extending the MDS to provide an information system and it is developing a new monitoring system [12]. OGSA [8] specifications and developments also address the issue of information systems and all projects above (including R-GMA) will have to redesign their information systems according to OGSA specifications in the future.

In the area of application monitoring, the OMIS [13] on-line monitoring interface, developed for clusters and supercomuters (similarly to the case of GRM) is the basis for a grid application monitoring system within the CrossGrid [14] project.

Netlogger is used for monitoring distributed applications in the grid rather then for parallel programs. Its time-space visualisation display concept is orthogonal to PROVE. In the vertical axis different types of events are defined while in PROVE the processes of the parallel programs are presented. Netlogger can be used for finding performance/behaviour problems in a communicating group of distributed applications/services while PROVE for a parallel program that is heavily communicating within itself. Netlogger, PROVE and other tools like Network Weather Service and Autopilot has been compared in the beginning of the DataGrid project in detail, see [15].

GRM and R-GMA are the first tools that can be used for on-line monitoring of parallel applications running in the grid.

6 Conclusion

R-GMA is a relational Grid Monitoring Architecture delivering the information generated by the resources, services and application processes in the grid. GRM/PROVE is a parallel application monitoring toolset that is now connected to R-GMA. The two systems together can be used for on-line monitoring and performance analysis of message-passing parallel applications running in the grid environment.

Acknowledgement

We would like to thank for the efforts of the developers of R-GMA in the EU-DataGrid project helping us to use their system together with GRM to monitor applications. The development of the tools described in this paper has been supported by the following grants: EU DataGrid IST-2000-25182, Hungarian DemoGrid OMFB-01549/2001 and OTKA T042459.

References

1. N. Podhorszki. Semi-on-line Monitoring of P-GRADE Applications. PDPC Journal, to appear in 2003
2. EU DataGrid Project Home Page: *http://www.eu-datagrid.org*
3. Z. Balaton, P. Kacsuk, N. Podhorszki, F. Vajda. From Cluster Monitoring to Grid Monitoring based on GRM. Proc. of EuroPar'2001, Manchester, pp. 874–881
4. GRM User's Manual. Available at *http://hepunx.rl.ac.uk/edg/wp3/documentation/*
5. S. Fisher et al. R-GMA: A Relational Grid Information and Monitoring System. 2nd Cracow Grid Workshop, Cracow, Poland, 2002
6. B. Tierney, R. Aydt, D. Gunter, W. Smith, V. Taylor, R. Wolski and M. Swany. A grid monitoring architecture. GGF Informational Document, GFD-I.7, GGF, 2001, URL: *http://www.gridforum.org/Documents/GFD/GFD-I.7.pdf*
7. Steve Fisher. Relational Model for Information and Monitoring. GGF Technical Report GWDPerf-7-1, 2001. URL: *http://www-didc.lbl.gov/GGF-PERF/GMA-WG/papers/GWD-GP-7-1.pdf*
8. S. Tuecke, K. Czajkowski, I. Foster, J. Frey, S. Graham, C. Kesselman, and P. Vanderbilt. Grid service specification. GGF Draft Document, 2002, URL: *http://www.gridforum.org/meetings/ggf6/ggf6_wg_papers/draft-ggf-ogsi-gridservice-04_2002-10-04.pdf*

9. The R-GMA Relational Monitoring Architecture. DataGrid WP3 Report, DataGrid-01-D1.2-0112-0-3, 2001, Available at *http://hepunx.rl.ac.uk/edg/wp3/documentation/*
10. K. Czajkowski, S. Fitzgerald, I. Foster, C. Kesselman. Grid Information Services for Distributed Resource Sharing. Proc. of the Tenth IEEE International Symposium on High-Performance Distributed Computing (HPDC-10), IEEE Press, August 2001.
11. GridLab project. URL *http://www.gridlab.org*
12. G. Gombás and Z. Balaton. A Flexible Multi-level Grid Monitoring Architecture. 1st European Across Grids Conference, Universidad de Santiago de Compostela, Spain, Feb. 2003
13. T. Ludwig and R. Wismüller. OMIS 2.0 – A Universal Interface for Monitoring Systems. In M. Bubak, J. Dongarra, and J. Wasniewski, eds., Recent Advances in Parallel Virtual Machine and Messag Passing Interface, Proc. 4th European PVM/MPI Users' Group Meeting, LNCS vol. 1332, pp. 267–276, Cracow, Poland, 1997. Springer Verlag.
14. B. Balis, M. Bubak, W. Funika, T. Szepienic, and R. Wismller. An Infrastructure for Grid Application Monitoring. In D. Kranzlmller, P. Kacsuk, J. Dongarra, and J. Volk ert, editors, Recent Advances in Parallel Virtual Machine and Message Passing Interface, 9th European-PVM/MPI Users' Group Meeting, volume 2474 of Lecture Notes in Computer Science, pp. 41–49, Linz, Austria, September 2002. Springer-Verlag.
15. Information and Monitoring: Current Technology. DataGrid Deliverable DataGrid-03-D3.1. URL: *https://edms.cern.ch/document/332476/2-0*

Component-Based System for Grid Application Workflow Composition

Marian Bubak[1,2], Kamil Górka[1], Tomasz Gubała[1],
Maciej Malawski[1], and Katarzyna Zając[1]

[1] Institute of Computer Science, AGH, al. Mickiewicza 30, 30-059 Kraków, Poland
[2] Academic Computer Centre – CYFRONET, Nawojki 11, 30-950 Kraków, Poland
{bubak,malawski,kzajac}@uci.agh.edu.pl
{kgorka,gubala}@student.uci.agh.edu.pl
phone: (+48 12) 617 39 64, fax: (+48 12) 633 80 54

Abstract. An application working within a Grid environment can be very complex, with distributed modules and decentralized computation. It is not a simple task to dispatch that kind of application, especially when the environment is changing. This paper presents the design and the implementation of the Application Flow Composer system which supports building the description of the Grid application flow by combining its elements from a loose set of components distributed in the Grid. The system is based on the Common Component Architecture (CCA) and uses the CCA distributed component description model. OGSA Registry Grid Service is applied for storing component description documents. The performance tests confirm the feasibility of this approach.

Keywords: Grid computations, workflow composition, CCA, OGSA

1 Introduction

Grid computations may be performed in different locations, remote both logically and geographically. In the consequence there is a need for effective and standardized ways of communication between Grid modules: software systems, computers, tertiary storage. One can view an application of the Grid technology as an assembly combined of multiple heterogeneous systems interacting together in order to obtain the application goal. It is distributed, decentralized and even may dynamically change its topology [1–3].

Designing and developing systems capable of working in the Grid environment is a difficult task. The methodology is often determined by designers of the framework within which the application is being constructed, and this means that various techniques of development may result in an incompatibility of the resultant software systems. To overcome this, standards of Grid application architectures are under development so systems constructed in the future should achieve sufficient level of compatibility in a communication layer as well as in an internal design. Two examples are Common Component Architecture (CCA) [4] and Open Grid Service Architecture (OGSA) [5]. In both CCA and OGSA environments, the Grid applications are composed of modules connected by defined links (CCA components, Grid Services).

2   Workflow Composition

The Grid application is a set of cooperating heterogeneous components with different roles in the assembly: human-friendly visualization components, data delivering components, computational scientific components and many others. The components perform different tasks, expose different functionalities to the external peers, and require different input data. Both CCA and OGSA introduce the idea of *ports*. Every Grid Service can expose some ports, each of them including one or more methods ready to be invoked. Similarly, CCA Components can incorporate a set of CCA Ports, divided into Provides Ports and CCA Uses Ports. CCA Provides Port, similarly to OGSA Ports, publish a handful of methods. CCA Uses Port tells what kind of Port the component needs to function properly, i.e. what kind of CCA Provides Port should be connected to this component. While the connection is established, the CCA component can perform its internal computations and produce output. So, the Grid application is defined by a set of components and a set of connections between them.

Let's assume there are systems capable of dispatching such application by building all needed components and establishing all required connections required. Some solutions have been proposed like the *Application Factory* concept [8] for CCA environment or GSFL [9] flow-building engines for Grid Services. Such facility requires input information describing the main internals of a newly created application, the compounds building it and the workflow of method invocation within. On the output, the system should produce complete description of the Grid application. Such a system must have at its disposal information about components available on the Grid, and not every system may discover such information. The application may be very complicated so no one can easily specify directly components and connections.

As a solution to this *Workflow Composition Problem*, we present a system capable of reading incomplete input information and, using proper knowledge about the environment, composing a complete description of a Grid application workflow as an output. It is called *Application Flow Composer System* (AFC System). The AFC system may be useful in situations described below.

Grid Prototyping. This consists of building an application which has not been run in the Grid environment yet, and trying to combine available software components in a way that the whole will deliver desired functionality. It would be dull and time consuming to scribe manually every workflow combination into a new document and send it to application dispatching facility.

Changed Component/Port. The application is well known and fully described but some component or port names have been changed. This may be typical for the Grid environment where the set of components are changing all the time. For example, the component provider may introduce some innovations to the component and, to distinguish it from the previous version, name it in another way what will render the application workflow document useless.

Automatic Construction. For more sophisticated examples of Grid computations there is a need to automatically construct internal Grid application which structure is not clear until the very moment of composition. It is helpful then to contact some entity capable of composing the ready new Grid application on demand.

3 Application Flow Composer System

3.1 The AFC System Concept

The system we propose must implement the functionality of constructing application workflows. This requirement imposes the need of some source of information about the current state of the environment, i.e. what components are available now, what ports do they provide and where to find them on the Grid. There should be continuous communication between the composer part of the AFC system and the informational part, providing the former with necessary data as frequently as it asks for it. In consequence, there are two main modules (see Fig. 1), the one responsible for workflow document composition (we call it *Flow Composer Component* or FCC) and the other, which should obtain every piece of information which can be used by the system (*Flow Composer Registry*, FCR). This module is called 'Registry' because its main function is to receive, contain and publish on demand the information about the application components available on the Grid.

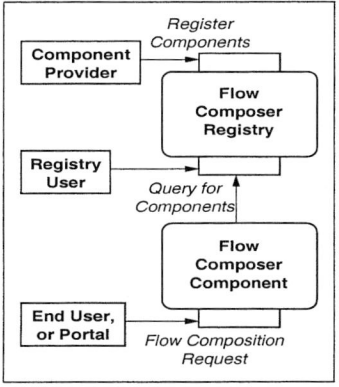

Fig. 1. AFC System overview

3.2 Use Cases of the AFC System

In the early design phase it is helpful to establish future system use cases. They are presented below.

Workflow Composition. The user describes requirements constraining the Grid application, and submits this description (as an XML *Initial Workflow Description* (IWD) document) to FCC composition facility. This document should specify components important for composed application and the links which are known to the user. Then, the AFC system tries to construct every component-based workflow fulfilling those requirements using the information contained in FCR Registry. It is very likely that the system presents more then one resultant workflows. They will be concatenated into one XML document which has very similar format to the initial IWD document it is called *Final Workflow Description* (FWD) document.

Component Registration. Every external institution may register its own component within FCR provided it is authorized to. This registration equals to submission of the document describing the component which we will call *Component Information Document* (CID). Depending on component's implementation technology, different information will be within this document. For example, if it is a CCA Component, the CID document will contain its name, identification and a list of CCA Uses Ports and CCA Provides Ports.

Component Lookup. The external system which requires some information about components, performs a query to the registry which specifies what type of component it is looking for. This query is another document in XML format, called *Component Query Document* (CQD), and it can ask either for a component of a given name or for a component providing specified functionality (in CCA technology it means a component containing specified CCA Provides Port). The Component Lookup interface is used by FCC Composer to obtain the information needed for successful workflow composition.

It is clear that the first use case is the most important one and so we will concentrate on it.

3.3 Description of Implementation

We have decided that the CCA technology will be the most suitable for application composition. The reason is simple - it is just the purpose for which this technology has been defined (actually, it is still in definition phase since the final version of specification [4] has not been published yet). Whole CCA environment is tailored with the scientific Grid application construction in mind, the main idea of this technology is to build applications from smaller modules, called CCA components, and connections established between them. There are few implementations of the CCA technology (i.e. CCA frameworks) in the scientific community being developed (CCAFFEINE [11], SciRun2 [12], XCAT [7]) and we have chosen to use the XCAT Framework 1.0. It has been the most mature project in the moment we had to choose, and, what is important, it is the only truly dedicated to totally distributed, Grid-based applications. Also, to make our future system CCA-compliant too, we have assumed that both modules of the system, the FCC Composer and the FCR Registry, will be CCA components. The other issue has been to choose the registry capable of containing the CID documents within and being able to be an implementation of FCR Registry concept. Here, our choice has been the Open Grid Services Infrastructure (OGSI) technology with its widely known implementation, Globus Toolkit 3.0 [6]. Although it would be better to have the registry issue solution within CCA technology, there is no such implementation already available (actually, there is only sketch description of such entity, called *Component Browser*, capable of registering and publishing CCA components information). To overcome this we have decided to use Virtual Organization GS Registry available in Globus Toolkit 3.0, and we applied it as a Component Browser (or, at least, something similar). In result, we have implemented the FCR Registry as a CCA component using Grid Service with Registry Port Type.

Figure 2 shows main components of the AFC system. The FCR Registry cooperates with the Registry Grid Service from Globus Toolkit package. It exposes

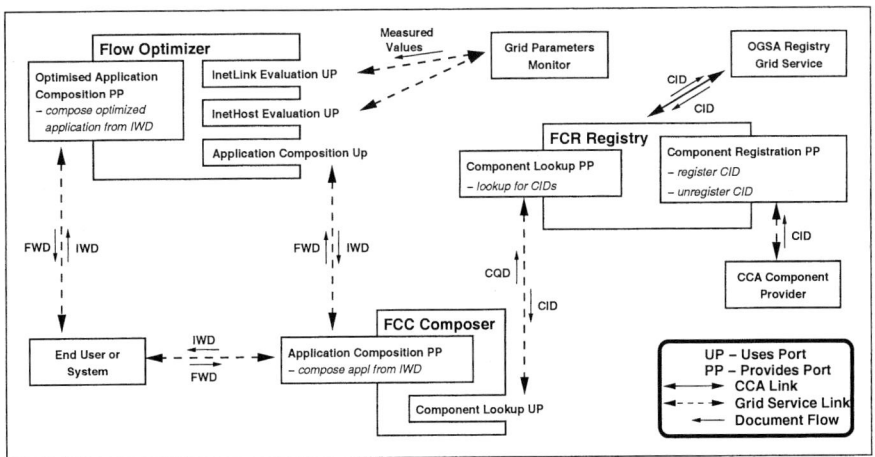

Fig. 2. Main components building AFC System

two CCA Provides Ports, *Component Lookup* Provides Port and *Component Registration* Provides Port which resemble two main use cases of the FCR Registry, component querying and component registration, respectively. The FCC Composer has two ports, one of Provides Port type (*Application Composition Provides Port*) and the other of Uses Port type what indicates that it uses the functionality of the FCR Registry to obtain needed information. To make the AFC system working, the user has to dispatch one instance of these two components and connect them with one link.

The third component, *Flow Optimizer* (FO), is not obligatory (the user can easily do without it by contacting FCC directly). The need for optimization component arisen when it has become clear that the amount of flows produced by the FCC Composer can be enormous. We have included such an optimizer which tries to choose better solutions and discard worse, so the volume of output is reduced. The FO component decisions depend on the information it can achieve from some kind of Grid monitoring facility, measuring values important for Grid application performance; it could be Internet hosts speed or Internet links throughput (see Fig. 2). With this information at its disposal, the FO can pick the flows which hopefully reveal better performance then others.

3.4 Composition Algorithm

This Subsection describes briefly the flow of internal information in the AFC system. The user submits IWD document and starts the computation (Fig. 2). For every component mentioned in that document, the FCC does one query to FCR in order to acquire its CID document. Within contents of this document there is a list of every CCA Uses Port the found component requires, so the FCC tries to find (again within FCR Registry) any component providing such port. This new component may have its own Uses Ports, so the algorithm goes into the next iteration. This procedure lasts until every component marked by

- **Monitoring.** The source of the Grid environmental data for FO should be discussed and some real solutions proposed (a candidate is the Grid Index Information Service (GIIS) [10] infrastructure).
- **Version Upgrade.** It will be very profitable if the system could be compatible with Application Factories [8], so if announced XCAT Framework 2.0 is published, the AFC system should be upgraded to work within this new environment.

Acknowledgements

We are very grateful to Mr Michał Kapałka for his contribution. This work was partly funded by the EU Project CrossGrid IST-2001-32243 and KBN Grant 4 T11C 032 23.

References

1. Foster I, Kesselman C., Nick J., Tuecke S.: The Physiology of the Grid: An Open Grid Services Architecture for Distributed Systems Integration. Open Grid Service Infrastructure WG, Global Grid Forum, June 22, 2002.
2. Foster I., Gannon D.: Open Grid Services Architecture Platform, February 16, 2003 http://www.ggf.org/ogsa-wg
3. Fox G., Balsoy O., Pallickara S., Uyar A., Gannon D., Slominski A: Community Grids in: Proceedings of the International Conference on Computational Science (ICCS 2002). Amsterdam, Netherlands April 2002, LNCS 2329, pp 22-38, Springer 2002
4. The Common Component Architecture Technical Specification, http://www.cca-forum.org/documents
5. Tuecke S., Czajkowski K., Foster I., Frey J., Graham S., Kesselman C., Vanderbilt P.: Grid Service Specification, version 4. Draft 4 October 2002
6. Argonne National Lab.: Globus Toolkit 3.0 Alpha Version 3, March 2003, http://www.globus.org
7. Indiana Univ.: XCAT Framework 1.0.1, http://www.extreme.indiana.edu/xcat
8. Gannon D., Ananthakrishnan K., Krishnan S., Govindaraju M., Ramakrishnan L., Slominski A.: Grid Web Services and Application Factories. Indiana University, http://www.extreme.indiana.edu/xgws/af/
9. Krishnan S., Wagstrom P., von Laszewski G.: GSFL: A Workflow Framework for Grid Services, draft 19 July 2002
10. Grid Information Index Service, http://www-fp.globus.org/toolkit/information-infrastructure.html
11. Allan B., Armstrong C., Wolfe A., Ray J., Bernholdt D., Kohl J.: The CCA Core Specification in a Distributed Memory SPMD Framework, Sandia National Lab.
12. Johnson C., Parker S., Weinstein D., Heffernan S.: Component-Based Problem Solving for Large-Scale Scientific Computing, in *Journal on Concurrency and Computation: Practice and Experience on Concurrency and Computation: Practice and Experience*, 2002 No. 14 pp. 1337-1349

Evaluating and Enhancing the Use of the GridFTP Protocol for Efficient Data Transfer on the Grid

Mario Cannataro[1], Carlo Mastroianni[2], Domenico Talia[3], and Paolo Trunfio[3]

[1] University "Magna Græcia" of Catanzaro, Via T. Campanella 115, 88100 Catanzaro, Italy
cannataro@unicz.it
[2] ICAR-CNR, Via P. Bucci 41/c, 87036 Rende, Italy
mastroianni@icar.cnr.it
[3] University of Calabria, Via P. Bucci 41/c, 87036 Rende, Italy
{talia,trunfio}@deis.unical.it

Abstract. Grid applications often require large data transfers along heterogeneous networks having different latencies and bandwidths, therefore efficient support for data transfer is a key issue in Grid computing. The paper presents a performance evaluation of the GridFTP protocol along some typical network scenarios, giving indications and rules of thumb useful to select the "best" GridFTP parameters. Following some recent approaches that make use of experimental results to optimize data transfers, the paper presents a simple algorithm that suggests the "best" GridFTP parameters for a required transfer session on the basis of historical file transfer data.

1 Introduction

The *Grid* is an integrated infrastructure for coordinated resource sharing and problem solving in distributed computing environments. Grid applications often involve large amounts of data and/or computing, therefore efficient support for data transfer on networks with different latencies and bandwidths is a key issue.

GridFTP [1] is a protocol, developed within the context of the Globus Toolkit, that supports the efficient transfer of large amounts of data on Grids, facing high latency and low bandwidth problems often encountered in geographical networks.

GridFTP is based on the FTP protocol but, opposite to many implementations of that protocol, it supports and extends a large subset of the features defined in the RFC 969 standard [2]. The major contribution of the GridFTP protocol is the use of the security services of Globus to assure the authentication of Grid applications. Other peculiar features of GridFTP are: the manual setting of the TCP buffer size, the use of multiple parallel streams, the third-party transfer option, and the partial file transfer option.

Some recent works report performance evaluations of the GridFTP protocol or propose techniques that make use of experiment results to optimize data transfers. In [3], GridFTP is compared with the Remote File I/O protocol developed at CERN, and it is shown that GridFTP is generally more efficient if TCP buffer size and the number of sockets are properly tuned. In [4], a client library that provides a set of high level functionalities based on GridFTP and other basic Globus services, is proposed. Some performance evaluations are also reported for file transfers between Italy, UK and USA. In [5], the problem of efficient data transfer is tackled within the context of the Data Grid project. The goal was to predict future data transfer performances by using statistical functions calculated over past experiments. All file transfers use 8 parallel streams and a TCP buffer size equal to the theoretical optimum value (Bandwidth times Round Trip Time). In [6], a method is proposed to combine active tests (i.e., when test data are sent through the network) and passive tests (i.e., when useful data are transferred and results are used as test results). That work proposes to publish summarized test results on the Grid information services, in particular on the Monitoring and Discovery Service of Globus, to make them accessible by Grid hosts. Hosts are therefore aware of end-to-end connection properties before starting a file transfer.

This paper discusses a work that follows the approach suggested by [5] and [6]. After a performance evaluation of the GridFTP protocol along some typical network scenarios, the paper describes a tool for the collection and summarization of GridFTP usage data (collected for each transfer session activated on a node), that implements a simple procedure whose purpose is to suggest the "best" GridFTP parameters for a required transfer session.

The rest of the paper is organized as follows. Section 2 presents the performance evaluation of GridFTP through different data transfer scenarios and summarizes the main results obtained and some possible indications on how to choose the GridFTP parameters. Section 3 presents a tool that automatically configures the GridFTP parameters to minimize file transfer times between Globus hosts. Finally, Section 4 concludes the paper.

2 GridFTP Performance Evaluation

In order to evaluate the performance of the GridFTP protocol in different network scenarios, we tested GridFTP along three different kinds of connections with the following tests:

1. Tests on adjacent Local Area Networks (LAN). Files were transferred between two hosts belonging to different LANs connected through a router.
2. Tests on two different long distance Internet connections; we chose connections with similar bandwidth characteristics but different latency values.

The `pipechar` tool [7] was used to evaluate the main characteristics of the connections, that is the RTT (Round Trip Time) delay and the bottleneck bandwidth (i.e., the minimum bandwidth measured on the path followed by IP packets).

Transfers were executed during the night to avoid network congestion, and, more important for the objective of this work, to minimize the effect of the network load variability during the experiments. The low variance of the measurements we obtained shows that this goal has been achieved.

We used the `globus-url-copy` command of the Globus Toolkit version 2.2, with the following syntax:

```
globus-url-copy -vb -notpt -tcp-bs <buffer> \
-p <parallel> gsiftp://<source-file> gsiftp://<dest-file>.
```

Where `<buffer>` is the TCP buffer size (in Kbytes) and `<parallel>` is the number of parallel streams (i.e., the number of sockets used in parallel for the transfers).

The following parameters have been varied in the tests:

- the TCP buffers on sender and receiver, with values from 1 Kbyte to 64 Kbytes, that is the maximum allowed size on many operating systems;
- the number of parallel streams: tests were made using 1, 2, 4, 8, 16, 32, and 64 sockets;
- the file size, with values from 32 Kbytes to 64 Mbytes.

For each combination of these parameters, we performed 20 file transfers and calculated the average data transfer value after discarding values that differ more than 20% with respect to the overall average.

2.1 Tests between Adjacent LANs

These tests have been performed between a host (`telesio.cs.icar.cnr.it`) at ICAR-CNR (Institute for High Performance Networks and Applications) and a host (`griso.deis.unical.it`) at University of Calabria. These hosts belong to 100 Mbps LANs connected through 10 Mbps links to a router.

Preliminary tests run with `pipechar` showed that for this connection the mean RTT delay is 31.5 msec, while the bottleneck bandwidth is 4.7 Mbps, with a theoretical optimum TCP buffer size equal to 18.5 Kbytes (TCP buffer size = RTT × bandwidth).

File transfer experiments confirmed the presence of an optimum TCP buffer, even if its size is lower than the theoretical one. Figure 1a reports the data transfer rates obtained with the transfers of a 16 Mbytes file, w.r.t. the TCP buffer size, for different value of the number of sockets. Figure 1b shows the same performances w.r.t. the number of sockets, to highlight the effect of using several sockets. From those figures two considerations arise:

(i) a high number of sockets is not advantageous for a high bandwidth connection like this, because the amount of time needed to set up and release the connections outweighs the possible advantage of having many parallel streams; the use of a small number of sockets (from 4 to 8) seems to be a good choice for all the values of the TCP buffer size;

(ii) the buffer size that gives the best performance decreases as the number of sockets increases: while with 1 or 2 sockets a 8 Kbyte buffer is the best choice, with 4, 8 or 16 it is better to use a 4 Kbyte buffer, and an even smaller buffer (2 Kbytes) is preferable if 32 sockets are used. A motivation can be that, with a high number of sockets, the operating system is requested to manage a large amount of TCP buffer memory: e.g., with 32 sockets and a 64 Kbyte buffer, the overall buffer memory is equal to 2 Mbytes.

Similar qualitative results were obtained for transfers of larger files. Figure 2 reports a summary of data transfer rates for different file sizes, and confirms that the use of several sockets is not effective for this kind of connection. We also can note that, as expected, the transfer data rate increases when the file size increases, due to the lower relative impact of connection set up and release phases. Figure 2 also shows that it is not necessary to test transfers of very large files, since curves tend to get to a saturation.

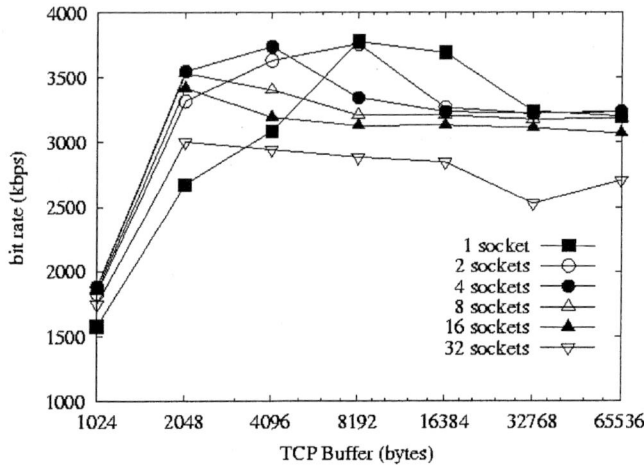

Fig. 1a. Data transfer rates for a 16 Mbyte file, versus the TCP buffer, for different values of the number of parallel streams.

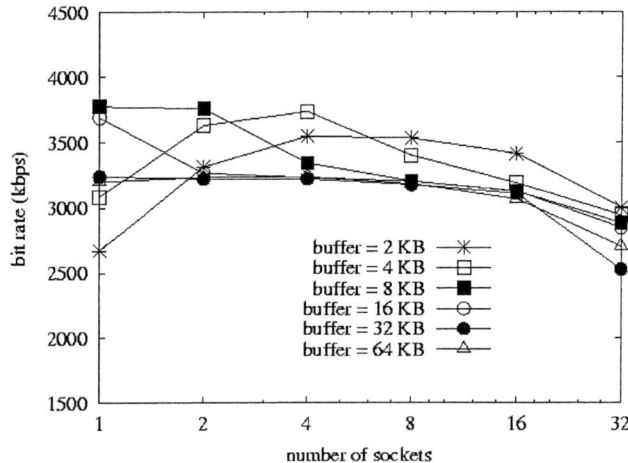

Fig. 1b. Data transfer rates for a 16 Mbyte file, versus the number of sockets, for different values of the TCP buffer size.

2.2 Tests on Internet Connections – Case A

GridFTP tests were also made from an ICAR-CNR host (`icarus.cs.icar.cnr.it`) to a host at the University of Calabria (`griso.deis.unical.it`). Differently from the case analyzed in Section 2.1, routers were configured so that the LANs were not directly linked, but IP packets followed a path along the Italian high-bandwidth GARR network (with a number of hops equal to 8). The resulting bottleneck bandwidth is about 1.6 Mbps, while the mean RTT delay is 80 milliseconds, with a theoretical optimum TCP buffer size equal to about 16 Kbytes.

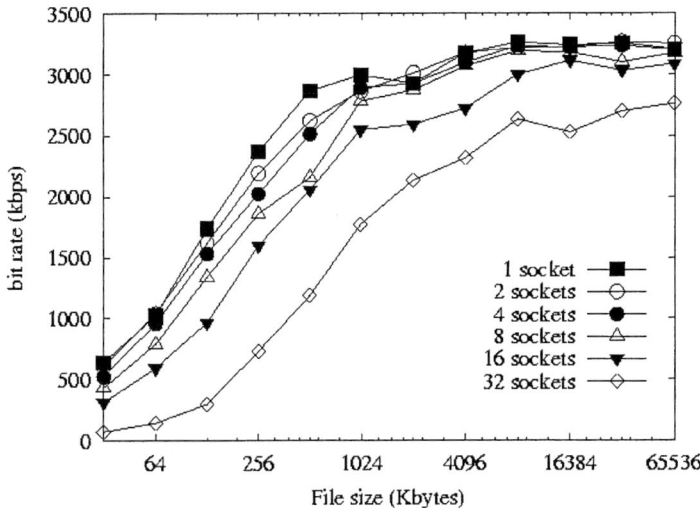

Fig. 2. Data transfer rates versus the file size, for different values of the number of sockets. The TCP buffer size is set to 32 Kbytes.

Figure 3a depicts data transfer rates obtained with a 16 Mbyte file. It appears that when the number of sockets increases, the larger potential transfer rate is balanced by the longer connection procedures: a good trade-off seems to be reached when the number of streams is between 16 and 32.

For what concerns the TCP buffer size, the most convenient size strongly depends on the number of sockets: with only 1 socket, a 64 Kbyte buffer is to be chosen, while with 32 or 64 sockets a 8 Kbyte buffer gives the best performance. With 8 or 16 sockets the performance obtained with different buffer sizes is similar. As a consequence, we may note that a non optimal choice of the buffer size would not cause a notable performance degradation.

Figure 3b shows the performance obtained transferring a 64 Mbyte file. The larger file size causes two remarkable phenomena: (i) performance does not worsen when the number of sockets increases, and (ii) the buffer size influence is very small with a large number of sockets. Therefore, it results that transfers of 64 Mbytes or larger files should be made with 32 or 64 sockets, while the choice of the buffer size is almost ineffective.

Figure 4 shows that a number of sockets ranging from 4 to 8 gives the best performance, w.r.t. to lower or larger numbers of sockets, with almost the considered file sizes. When using a higher number of sockets (e.g., 32), we also may obtain good performance if the file size exceeds 32 Mbytes, but experiment poorer performance when transferring smaller files.

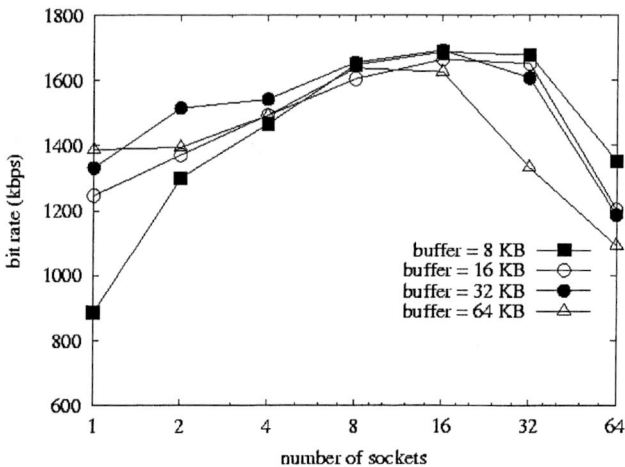

Fig. 3a. Data transfer rates for a 16 Mbyte file, versus the number of sockets, for different values of the TCP buffer size.

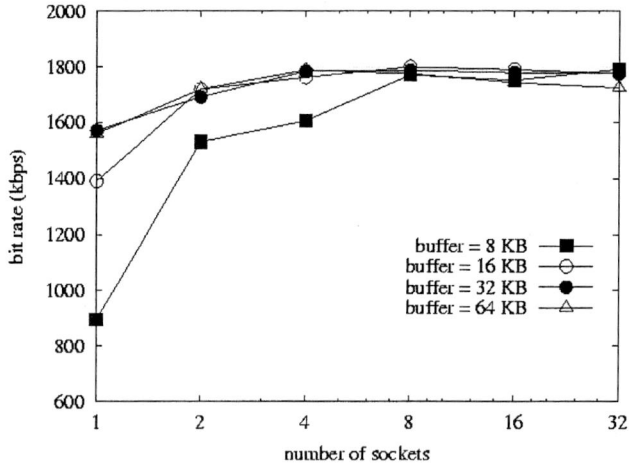

Fig. 3b. Data transfer rates for a 64 Mbyte file, versus the number of sockets, for different values of the TCP buffer size.

2.3 Tests on Internet Connections – Case B

These tests were performed between an ICAR-CNR host (icarus.cs.icar.cnr.it) and a host at the CNUCE-CNR institute in Pisa (novello.cnuce.cnr.it). The path between these two nodes includes both inter-LAN connections and Internet links. With respect to the connection discussed in Section 2.2, this connection has a similar bottleneck bandwidth (about 1.7 Mbps), but a higher RTT delay (125 msec). These parameters lead to a theoretical optimum TCP buffer equal to about 26.5 Kbytes.

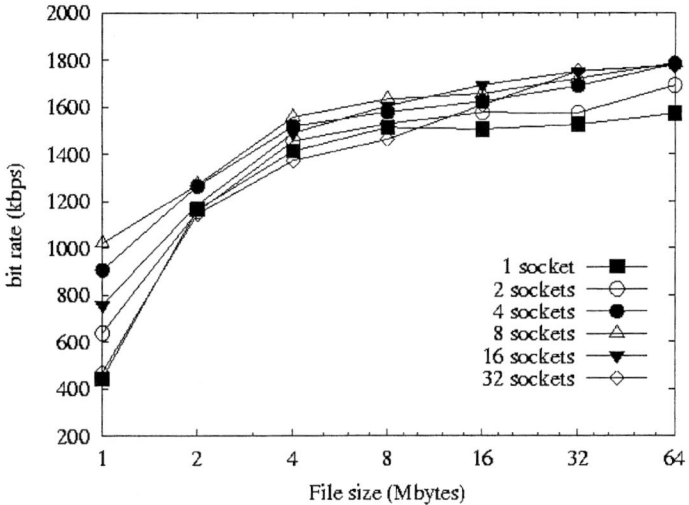

Fig. 4. Data transfer rates versus the file size, for different values of the number of sockets. The TCP buffer size is set to 32 Kbytes.

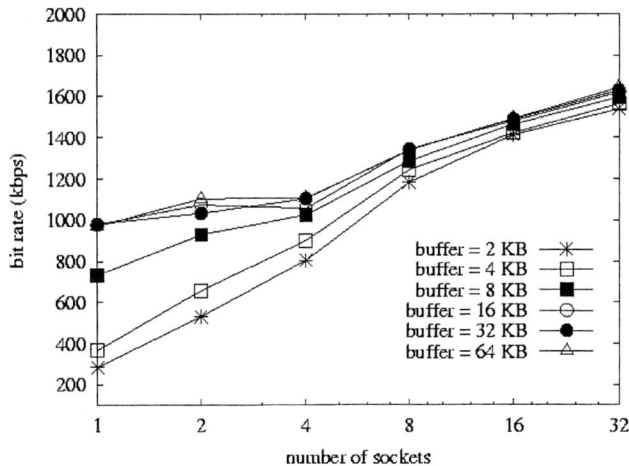

Fig. 5. Data transfer rates for a 16 Mbyte file, versus the number of sockets, for different values of the TCP buffer size.

We experimented that, due to the higher latency, performance figures show some remarkable differences when they are compared to the figures reported in Section 2.2, though the maximum data rates that are achievable with both connections are similar.

In Figure 5 we see that, when transferring a 16 Mbyte file, performance increases with the number of sockets for all values of the TCP buffer. Furthermore, a high TCP buffer is advantageous with any number of sockets, though the advantage decreases as that number increases. Therefore, with this file size, the best choice is to have a number of sockets and a TCP buffer size as large as possible.

This is not true for all file sizes. Figure 6 shows performances w.r.t. the file size, with a 32 Kbyte TCP buffer: we see that a high number of sockets is beneficial only for big-sized files, while for small files 1 or 2 sockets are preferable. Note that curves related to different numbers of sockets get crossed in the range between 512 Kbytes and 2 Mbytes.

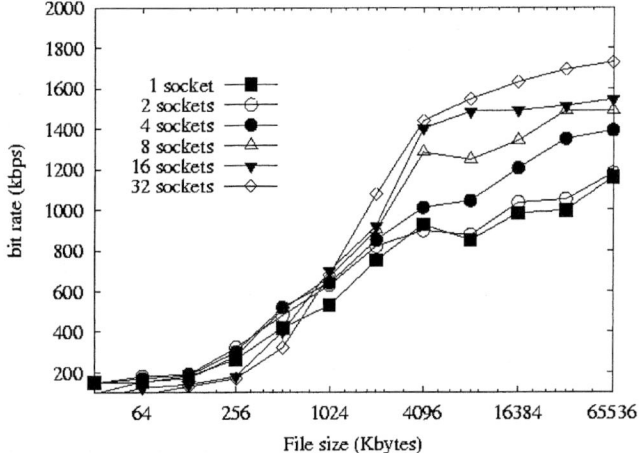

Fig. 6. Data transfer rates versus the file size, for different values of the number of sockets. The TCP buffer size is set to 32 Kbytes.

2.4 Summary Results

On the basis of the experiments presented along the paper, we can draw some conclusions on performance trends obtained by varying the file size, the TCP buffer and the number of sockets:

1. The optimal number of sockets strongly depends on the type of connection, particularly on the latency value: for low-latency connections, a small number of sockets is sufficient, while as the latency increases the use of more sockets can lead to a significant advantage;
2. The file size has also an impact on the choice of the number of sockets: a high number of sockets becomes convenient only for files whose sizes exceed a certain value. This cross value depends on the Grid connection and decreases as the latency increases: for example for the Internet connection reported in Section 2.2 (lower latency), the cross value is about 32 Mbytes, while for the connection reported in Section 2.3 (higher latency), the cross value is about 2 Mbytes.

3. The optimal TCP buffer size depends on the network connection (latency and bandwidth), the file size, and the number of sockets. Dependencies are complex but a rule of thumb can be the following: large TCP buffers are advantageous with high RTT × BW products and for transfers of large files; but the use of a high number of sockets often requires small TCP buffers.

In summary, supposing to know the network characteristics (latency and bandwidth) and given the file size, a possible approach to choose the GridFTP parameters could start finding the number of sockets, on the basis of latency and file size, and then finding the TCP buffer size.

3 A Tool for Enhanced GridFTP File Transfers

In Section 2 we reported some of the performance results we obtained with GridFTP tests on three different types of network connections.

At completion of this work, we built a tool, written in Java and executable on machines running the Globus Toolkit, that uses the GridFTP protocol to perform efficient file transfer on a Globus-based Grid.

Such tool has two main goals:

- *to build a file transfer log*, by collecting the performance data about the executed file transfers;
- *to enhance the file transfer*, by automatically setting the GridFTP parameters (TCP buffer and number of sockets) to those values that are supposed to minimize the transfer time for a given file on a given Grid connection.

The automatic setup of the GridFTP parameters is made on the basis of the experience, i.e., of the transfer times obtained in previous file transfers and stored in the file transfer log.

In particular, when a file transfer between hosts A and B is requested, the following steps are executed:

(i) the tool tries to determine the type of Grid connection, in order to select the historical data that can be useful. For example, if nodes A and B belong to Internet domains for which historical data are already available, the tool will refer to those data. The connection type can also be derived by measurements on network parameters (RTT, BW) made with the `pipechar` tool. If data are available for another connection with similar parameter values, those data can be referred. If none of those cases applies, the tool generates a new connection type and suggests the user to perform a set of tests that can be used in the future.

(ii) once the reference historical data have been chosen, the tool determines the GridFTP parameter values that are the most convenient on the basis of the experience.

(iii) the file transfer is executed with the chosen parameters, and the transfer times are used to update the historical data for the connection type under consideration.

To transfer a very large file, it can be convenient to split the file in several parts and separately transfer those parts. In this way, GridFTP parameters could be adapted on the fly to network conditions that may vary between transfers of file parts.

The tool provides a graphical interface allowing a user to navigate in the file systems of the Grid hosts and to execute transfers of one or more files with intuitive drag and drop operations. Before starting the transfer, the tool proposes to the user the convenient parameters (that she/he can modify) and shows the estimated transfer time. Moreover, the tool automatically manages the Globus authentication procedures needed prior to start the GridFTP transfers.

4 Conclusions and Future Work

In this paper we discussed a performance evaluation of the Globus GridFTP protocol along some typical network scenarios. We obtained some indications and rules of thumb useful to choice the GridFTP parameters if main network characteristics are known. The high variability of network conditions makes it hard to find analytical, close formulas to find such parameters.

Following some recent approaches that make use of experimental results to optimize data transfers, we built a Java tool executable on Globus-based machines, whose objective is to allow the user to perform efficient data transfers on the Grid by means of a user-friendly graphical interface. Such tool suggests the "best" GridFTP parameters for a required transfer session on the basis of historical data. Currently, the finding of stored historical data exploitable for the requested file transfer to be optimized is obtained through a simple similarity function. However, we are designing a tool extension that will make use of data mining techniques, such as clustering and classification techniques, that will produce a categorization of Grid connections and will allow a more effective selection of historical data exploitable for the current file transfer. In the next future we will offer the file transfer tool to interested users through the Web.

Acknowledgments
We acknowledge the CNUCE-CNR Institute (now ISTI-CNR), for kindly providing the access to their Grid hosts and allowing the execution of our GridFTP tests.

This work has been partially funded by the project "MIUR Fondo Speciale SP3: GRID COMPUTING: Tecnologie abilitanti e applicazioni per eScience".

References

1. The Globus Project: the GridFTP protocol, http://www.globus.org/datagrid/gridftp.html
2. RFC 969: NETBLT: A Bulk Data Transfer Protocol, http://www.faqs.org/rfcs/rfc969.html
3. Kalmady, R., Tierney, B.: A Comparison of GSIFTP and RFIO on a WAN. Technical Report for the Work Package 2 of the European DataGrid project, http://edg-wp2.web.cern.ch/edg-wp2/publications.html (2001)
4. Aloisio, G., Cafaro, M., Epicoco, I.: Early experiences with the GridFTP protocol using the GRB-GSIFTP library. Future Generation Computer Systems 18 (2002)
5. Vazhkudai, S., Schopf, J. M., Foster, I.: Predicting the Performance of Wide Area Data Transfers. Proc. International Parallel and Distributed Processing Symposium (2002)
6. The European Datagrid Project: DataGrid Network Monitoring Scheme Proposal, document DataGrid-07-TED-nnnn-0_1 (2001)
7. The Pipechar Tool: http://www-didc.lbl.gov/pipechar

Resource Monitoring and Management in Metacomputing Environments[*]

Tomasz Wrzosek, Dawid Kurzyniec, Dominik Drzewiecki, and Vaidy Sunderam

Dept. of Math and Computer Science, Emory University
Atlanta, GA 30322, USA
{yrd,dawidk,drzewo,vss}@mathcs.emory.edu

Abstract. Sharing of computational resources across multiple administrative domains (sometimes called grid computing) is rapidly gaining in popularity and adoption. Resource sharing middleware must deal with ownership issues, heterogeneity, and multiple types of resources that include compute cycles, data, and services. Design principles and software approaches for monitoring and management tools in such environments are the focus of this paper. A basic set of requirements for resource administration tools is first proposed. A specific tool, the GUI for the H2O metacomputing substrate is then described. Initial experiences are reported, and ongoing as well as future enhancements to the tool are discussed.

1 Introduction

A growing number of high-performance computational environments consist of, and use, resources that are not only distributed over the network but also owned and administered by different entities. This form of resource sharing is very attractive for a number of reasons [2]. However, the very aspects of heterogeneity, distribution, and multiple ownership, make such systems much more complex to monitor, manage, and administer than local clusters or massively parallel processor machines. Therefore, there is a need for sophisticated, reliable, and user-friendly management tools fulfilling several essential requirements:

- Authorized individuals should be allowed to check the status, availability and load of shared resources.
- Owners should be able to (remotely) control access to their resources.
- Resource usage information should be dynamically updated at appropriate intervals, and presented in a clear and comprehensible form.
- As with all types of monitoring tools, perturbation to the underlying system should be minimized to the extent possible.
- Especially in shared computing environments where multiple administrators control different resources, abrupt unavailability of resources is more likely. Monitoring tools should be responsive to such events and provide informational and correctional options.

---

[*] Research supported in part by U.S. DoE grant DE-FG02-02ER25537 and NSF grant ACI-0220183

– In addition, the usual graphical user interface guidelines should be followed to make tools convenient and easy to use and to allow users to focus on their own domains and applications.

A graphical monitoring and management tool that follows these guidelines has been developed for use with the H2O metacomputing environment [10]. Some background information about this underlying distributed computing substrate, the salient features of the GUI tool, and its projected use in shared-resource settings, are described in Section 2. The following section discusses related tools for other distributed computing environments, while Section 4 describes the detailed design and implementation of the GUI. The paper concludes with a discussion of our early experiences with the tool, and plans for further development.

2 The H2O Framework and Its Graphical User Interface

The H2O metacomputing system is an evolving framework for loosely coupled resource sharing in environments consisting of multiple administrative domains. Its architectural model is provider-centric and based on the premise that resource providers act locally and independently of each other and of clients, and that by minimizing or even eliminating coordination middleware and global state at the low level, self-organizing distributed computing systems can be enabled. In H2O, a software backplane within each resource supports component-based services that are completely under owner control; yet, authorized clients may configure and securely use each resource through components that deliver compute, data, and application services. A detailed description of the core H2O framework is outside the scope of this paper [10, 5]; however, selected aspects will be explained further in this paper as appropriate.

In H2O, various types of entities (providers, clients, developers, third-party resellers) interact with distributed computing resources and software units (pluglets and kernels), as shown in Figure 1. "Providers" are resource owners, e.g. users that control and/or have login id's on computer systems. They instantiate the H2O kernel on machines they wish to share and specify their sharing policies. Clients avail of resources to suit their own needs via "pluglets", which are componentized modules providing remote services. These services may range from end-user-applications (e.g. a computational fluid dynamics pluglet) to generic programming environments (e.g. a collection of pluglets implementing an MPI environment). Service deployment may be performed by end-clients, by providers, as well as by third-party resellers that may offer to clients a value-added over a raw resource served by the provider.

It is evident that without appropriate tools, management of such multi-actor, dynamic environment can be unwieldy. Therefore, the graphical tool termed the H2O GUI has been developed that assists users in managing H2O kernels, pluglets, policies and other associated aspects through a convenient and friendly interface. Providers may use the GUI to start, stop, and dynamically attach to and detach from specific kernels, as well as to control sharing policies and user access privileges. Pluglet deployers (i.e. third-party resellers or end-clients) may use the GUI to load pluglets into specific kernels, search for previously loaded

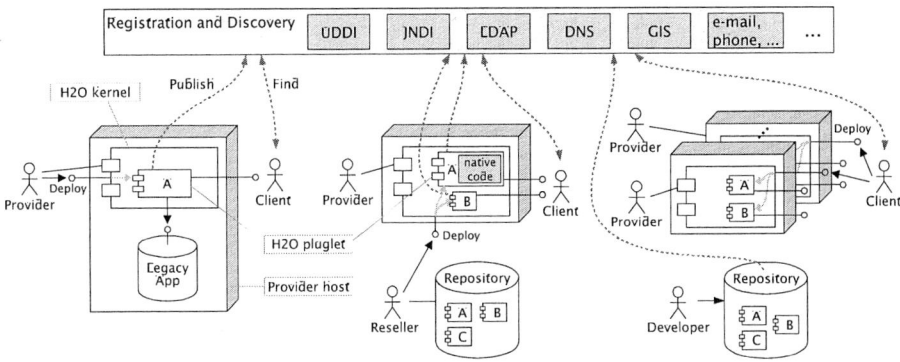

Fig. 1. Various example usage scenarios of H2O

pluglets, and aggregate pluglet management tasks. The GUI enables rapid determination of resource usage types and levels, pluglet configurations on various resources, and execution control of distributed tasks.

3 Related Work

In large, loosely coupled, heterogeneous, and somewhat fragile environments of today, tremendous potential and need exists for the evolution of effective tools for resource environment monitoring. Our GUI project is one effort that attempts to address this issue; other similar research efforts are mentioned below.

A few tools oriented towards distributed resource administration have been available for some time; an example is XPVM [6], a graphical console and monitor for PVM. XPVM enables the assembly of a parallel virtual machine, and provides interfaces to run tasks on PVM nodes. In addition, XPVM can also gather task output, provide consoles for distributed debugging, and display task interaction diagrams. Adopting a different premise, MATtool [1] was written to aid system administrators; it permits uploading and execution of a task (process) simultaneously on many machines, and provides monitoring services running on hosts to inspect current machine status.

Sun Grid Engine, Enterprise Edition is a software infrastructure that enables "Campus Grids" [8]. It orchestrates the delivery of computational power based upon distributed resource policies set by a grid administrator. The SGEEE package includes a graphic user interface tool (qmod) that is used to define Sun's grid resource access policies (e.g. memory, CPU time, and I/O activity). Not a tool in the traditional sense but rather a library providing specific API is the Globus' GRAM package [4]. It is used by the Globus framework [3] to process requests for, and to allocate resources, and provides an API to submit, cancel, and manage active jobs.

Another category of systems created to help users with distributed computing and resource management are Grid Portals [13]. Such interfaces enable job submission, job monitoring, component discovery, data sharing, and persistent object storage. Examples of such portals include Astrophysics Simulation Collaboratory Grid Portal [7], the NPACI HotPage framework [12], and JiPANG [11]. These portals present resources in a coherent form through simple, secure and transparent interfaces, abstracting away the details of the resources.

The H2O GUI builds on the experience of the tools mentioned above. It supports controlled resource sharing by permitting the definition and application of sharing policies, aids in the deployment and monitoring of new services, as well as in their discovery and usage, and, finally, presents collected resources and services in the form of kernels and pluglets abstracting away their origin and nature. However, the target user constituency of the H2O GUI is different from the tools above, which were created either for resource administration or for resource usage. The H2O GUI combines these two target groups and may be used by resource providers (administrators) as well as service deployers and/or third-party resellers. The main distinguishing feature of the H2O GUI concerns the resource aggregates that it monitors. In other metacomputing environments, there is usually the notion of the distributed system (with a certain amount of global state) that is being monitored. In contrast, resource aggregation in H2O does not involve distributed state and is only an abstraction at the client side – H2O kernels maintain no information about other kernels. Hence, the H2O GUI provides the *convenience* of managing a scalable set of resources from a single portal even though the resources themselves are independent and disjoint.

4 The H2O GUI - How It Works

From an operational viewpoint, the first action in the use of H2O generally involves the instantiation of kernels by providers. Active kernels are represented by kernel "references"; as indicated in Figure 1, clients lookup and discover kernel references via situation-specific mechanisms that can range from UDDI repositories to LDAP servers to informal means such as phone calls or email. Clients login to kernels, instantiate (or upload) pluglets and deploy their applications. The H2O GUI can help with all aspects of these phases.

4.1 Profiles

To facilitate operational convenience, stable data concerning resources from a given provider (or a set of providers) may be maintained on persistent storage in the form of a "profile" file. The profile contains key data concerning provider's kernels and is retained in XML-format to enhance interoperability. It is a collection of entries, each holding both static, and, after instantiation, dynamic information about an H2O kernel. The latter has a form of a kernel reference, that is of paramount importance as it is the only way to contact the kernel.

An example of a kernel entry is shown in Figure 2. The "RemoteRef" field contains the aforementioned kernel reference; it encapsulates the information about the kernel identity, kernel endpoint, and the protocol that client must use when connecting to the kernel via this endpoint. The "startup" element is specified and used only by resource owners, as it allows for starting the kernel directly from the GUI. The (open) set of supported kernel instantiation methods is configured globally via the GUI configuration dialog and it may include any method invokable from command line interface.

```
<kernelEntry>
  <name>my_red_kernel</name>
  <RemoteRef provider='edu.emory.mathcs.rmix.spi.xsoap.XSoapProvider'
    binding='' interfaces='edu.emory.mathcs.h2o.server.GateKeeperSrv'
    location='http://170.140.150.185:34787/11d1def534ea1be0:1b26af32aa43251b:2'
    guid='11d1def534ea1be0:1b26af32aa43251b:0'/>
  <startup method='ssh' autostart='true'>
    <parameter name="user" value="neo"/>
    <parameter name="command" value="/home/neo/h2o/bin/h2o-kernel"/>
    <parameter name="host" value="matrix.mathcs.emory.edu"/>
  </startup>
</kernelEntry>
```

Fig. 2. Example profile entry

4.2 The GUI Functionality

The GUI has two main operating windows. The first one, displayed after GUI startup, is a small panel designed to provide a user with all general information about the kernels in the profile at glance. It also facilitates controls allowing shutdown and/or restart of all kernels (i.e. the entire profile). A user may also access information about kernels in a more detailed manner. Second GUI window, shown in Figure 3, is more comprehensive and provides the user with a number of new options that include detailed on-line monitoring and management of the distributed resources (kernels) – the focus is on separate access to individual kernels. The left panel in the main GUI window displays a list of kernel entries that are contained in the currently loaded profile. A user may edit this list – changing the aforementioned static kernel data, adding new, or removing unused kernel entries. The first two operations are conducted within a dialog divided into two sections corresponding to the structure of a profile entry. As in the case of a profile entry the usage of this dialog varies between different classes of users. *Resource providers* may use it to specify how their kernels are to be started. On the other hand, *service deployers* (entities loading pluglets into H2O kernels) may use it to manually enter remote references to kernels of their interest that are controlled by somebody else.

From the perspective of resource providers, H2O kernel may be viewed as a mechanism of controlled resource sharing. Thus for them, the GUI serves as a tool for collective management of resources that are shared via H2O kernels and utilized by H2O pluglets. To support such management tasks, the GUI provides ways of controlling kernels as well as separate pluglets, thus enabling provider to independently handle raw resources and services running on them. This separate access to resources (kernels) is realized through the kernel list which allows providers to start or shutdown a selected kernel as appropriate. Pluglets loaded into a kernel are shown in the second (right) panel and may be suspended, reactivated, or terminated via the GUI. These options might be used to manage already running jobs or to enqueue new ones on a kernel, change their priorities, grant or refuse resources etc.

The GUI is also designed for use as an accounting tool for H2O kernels. Since H2O requires a security policy to be defined and users' accounts to be created, the GUI goal is to provide convenient interfaces to facilitate these tasks. A kernel provider may define entities that are allowed to use the provider's kernel and/or

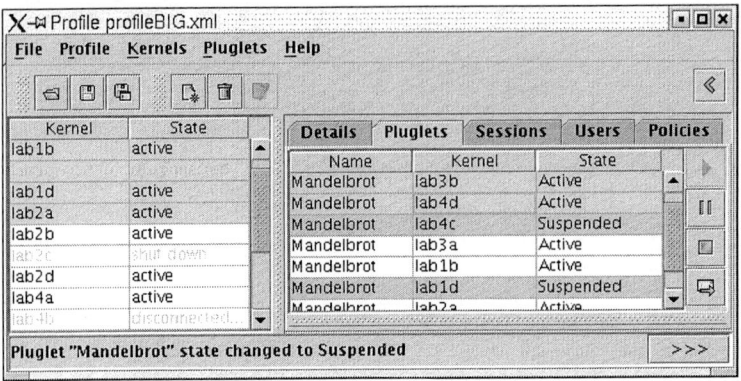

Fig. 3. Main GUI window

may define a set of permissions that will be used as the kernel security policy. The interface utilizes the fact that H2O security policies are based on the set of standard Java policies [5, 9]. The policy may be uploaded into, and used in, multiple kernels in the current profile, or may be exported to a file. These options will simplify housekeeping and security management.

The GUI also provides a form of a remote console onto which kernel messages are printed. Examples of useful display messages include: a kernel reference that may later be used to advertise this kernel to potential users, pluglet loading messages, or pluglet and kernel exception stack traces. All events that take place within the GUI as well as within monitored kernels and pluglets (e.g. kernel/pluglet state changes, pluglet loading events, and policy changes) are logged, thus enabling a GUI user to keep track of happenings in the system and to inspect causes of possible errors and exceptions in the system.

Apart from resource providers, the GUI may also be used by service deployers in order to upload new services into already running kernels and control them. The mandatory information needed to load a pluglet include its class path and a main class name. Some additional data may also be specified, thus allowing deployer to personalize the service instance. This information may later be used for discovery or advertisement purposes. The necessary data may either be typed by hand or loaded from an XML-based descriptor file that would typically be provided by the supplier of pluglet binaries.

5 Discussion and Future Work

This paper has presented the preliminary facilities provided by the H2O GUI, a graphical interface for the management and monitoring of shared resources in the H2O metacomputing framework. Based on the belief that ease of management of shared resources in grids and metacomputing environments is critical to their success, the H2O GUI attempts to combine simplicity and industry standards (XML, JAAS, Swing) with utility and convenience for the different entities that interact with H2O, namely resource providers, clients, pluglet developers and third-party resellers. In this initial version of the GUI, the focus is on resource provider and service deployer facilities. The prototype implementation enables user-friendly operation for both types of entities. In follow-on versions of the GUI, we intend to offer new features that assist in policy control and lookup and discovery interfaces for pluglets. We also are exploring more complex monitoring features e.g. network connection displays, bandwidth and memory usage indicators, and service usage statistics. We believe that these features and facilities will lead to substantial increases in adoption of computational resource sharing across multiple administrative domains as a mainstream paradigm.

References

1. S. M. Black. MATtool. Monitoring and administration tool. Available at http://www.ee.ryerson.ca:8080/ sblack/mat/.
2. I. Foster, C. Kesselman, and S. Tuecke. The anatomy of the grid: Enabling scalable virtual organizations. *The International Journal of Supercomputer Applications*, 15(3), 2001.
3. Globus. Available at: http://www.globus.org.
4. GRAM: Globus Resource Allocation Manager. Available at: http://www-unix.globus.org/api/c-globus-2.2/globus_gram_documentation/html/index.html.
5. D. Kurzyniec, T. Wrzosek, D. Drzewiecki, and V. Sunderam. Towards self-organizing distributed computing frameworks: The H2O approach. *preprint*, 2003.
6. Maui High Performance Supercomputing Center. XPVM. Available at http://www.uni-karlsruhe.de/Uni/RZ/Hardware/SP2/Workshop.mhtml.
7. M. Russell et. al. The astrophysics simulation collaboratory: A science portal enabling community software development. In *Proceedings of the 10th IEEE International Symposium on High Performance Distributed Computing*, pages 207–215, San Francisco, CA, 7-9 Aug. 2001.
8. SGEEE: Sun Grid Engine, Enterprise Edition. Papers available at: http://wwws.sun.com/software/gridware/sge.html.
9. Sun Microsystems. Default policy implementation and policy file syntax. http://java.sun.com/j2se/1.4.1/docs/guide/security/PolicyFiles.html.
10. V. Sunderam and D. Kurzyniec. Lightweight self-organizing frameworks for metacomputing. In *The 11th International Symposium on High Performance Distributed Computing*, Edinburgh, Scotland, July 2002.
11. T. Suzumura, S. Matsuoka, and H. Nakada. A Jini-based computing portal system. In *Super Computing 2001*, Denver, CO, USA, November 10-16 2001.
12. M. Thomas, S. Mock, and J. Boisseau. NPACI HotPage: A framework for scientific computing portals. In *3rd International Computing Portals Workshop*, San Francisco, CA, December 7 1999.
13. G. von Laszewski and I. Foster. Grid Infrastructure to Support Science Portals for Large Scale Instruments. In *Proceedings of the Workshop Distributed Computing on the Web (DCW)*, pages 1–16. University of Rostock, Germany, 21-23 June 1999.

Generating an Efficient Dynamics Multicast Tree under Grid Environment*

Theewara Vorakosit and Putchong Uthayopas

High Performance Computing and Networking Center Faculty of Engineering
Kasetsart University, 50 Phaholyotin Rd, Chatuchak Bangkok, 10900, Thailand
thvo@hpcnc.cpe.ku.ac.th, pu@ku.ac.th

Abstract. The use of an efficient multicast tree can substantially speed up many communication-intensive MPI applications. This is even more crucial for Grid environment since MPI runtime has to work on wide area network with very different and unbalanced network bandwidth. This paper proposes a new and efficient algorithm called, GADT (Genetics Algorithm based Dynamics Tree) that can be used to generate an efficient multicast tree under Grid environment. The algorithm takes into consideration the unbalanced network speed of Grid system in order to generate a multicast tree. The experiments are conducted to compare GADT with binomial tree and optimal algorithm. The results show that GADT can produce a multicast tree that has communication performance close to the optimal multicast tree deriving from exhaustive search. Moreover, the multicast tree generated results in a substantially faster communication than a traditional binomial tree algorithm. Therefore, GADT can be used to speed up the collective operation for MPI runtime system under Grid environment.

1 Introduction

The performance of MPI libraries depends on many factors such as the data buffering, communication protocol and algorithm used. Many of the communication-intensive algorithms in MPI runtime system (such as gather, scatter, and reduce) rely heavily on the collective communication. In the emerging Grid system [4], the MPI tasks are distributed over a wide area network. Therefore, there are two important issues need to be addressed. First, the bandwidth that links multiple clusters over a wide area network may be very different. Thus, the traditional binomial tree algorithm is no longer optimal anymore. The multicast tree for WAN environment can be any tree, including flat tree or sequential tree. Although the true optimal multicast tree for WAN (and Grid) can be found using an exhaustive search algorithm, the complexity of this brute force algorithm can be as high as $O((n-1)!^2)$. Second, since the links among multiple clusters are shared by nodes in the cluster, the multicast algorithm is more complex because the task allocation and sharing have to be taken into consideration. Therefore, finding a good multicast tree for MPI runtime system under this environment is not a trivial task.

---

* This research is supported in part by Kasetsart University Research and Development Institute /SRU Grant and AMD Far East Inc.

Recently, many works address the problem of finding a good multicast tree in cluster and Grid environment. Karp [5] proposed the optimal multicast and summation algorithms based on LogP model [3]. Karp discussed about the six fundamental communication problems, namely, single-item multicast, k-item multicast, continuous multicast, all-to-all multicast, combining-multicast, and summing. For the single-item multicast, which is the focus in this paper, binomial algorithm is used. LogP model is used by Karp to prove that the model is optimal. However, optimality of algorithm used is only valid inside cluster system where the inter-node bandwidth can be assumed to be equal. Kielmann [6] proposed a model named *parameterized LogP* model and a multicast algorithm for message size M that is divided into k segments of size m. So, the goal is to find a tree shape and a segment size m that minimize the completion time. For the two layer multicast, the coordinator of each cluster is voted. The coordinator nodes first participate in the wide-area multicast. Then, they forward the message inside their clusters.

For the Grid system, the algorithm for finding the optimal multicast tree is NP-hard problem. Therefore, many heuristics algorithm has been applied. For example, Bernaschi [1] proposed a multicast algorithm based on α-tree. The value α must be given by users before the α tree is generated. MAGPIE [7] uses this model to implement the library as an add-on to MPICH implementation. Bhat [2] proposed a heuristic algorithm called *Fastest Edge First* or *FEF* for creating a communication schedule. In FEF, sender is a set of nodes that already has data and receiver is a set of nodes that need the data. For each communication step, the fastest edge from sender to receiver is selected. The process continues until receiver is empty. However, this paper did not mention how to overlap communication because sender can be more than one node except the first time.

This paper proposes a genetic-based algorithm GADT (*Genetic-Based Dynamic Tree*). This algorithm generates an efficient multicast tree for Grid system. The experimental results show that GADT produce a multicast tree which has the communication performance close to the optimal tree. Moreover, the result is much faster than the traditional binomial tree. This GADT algorithm can be used in MPI communication library to substantially improve the overall performance.

This paper is organized as followed: Section 2 presents a system model being used throughout this paper. Section 3 presents the proposed GADT algorithm. The experimental results are shown in Section 4. Finally, the conclusion and future works are given in Section 5.

2 The System Model

In order to solve the problem, a Grid system is represented as a weighted graph G(V, E), where vertices V is a cluster, and directed edges E is an interconnection link between each cluster. Each edge has a weight B_i which is the bandwidth available for the Grid application. Fig. 2 shows an example of a Grid system graph. This graph can also represented by a *bandwidth matrix*. A *bandwidth matrix* (B) is defined as an $n \times n$ matrix, where n is a number of clusters in the Grid. Each element b_{ij} is a link bandwidth from cluster i to cluster j. The diagonal value of the bandwidth matrix is an internal bandwidth of each cluster. Here, the assumption is that the cluster internal network is a non-blocking, fully connected network. Fig. 1(b) shows the bandwidth matrix obtained from the Grid graph in Fig. 1(a).

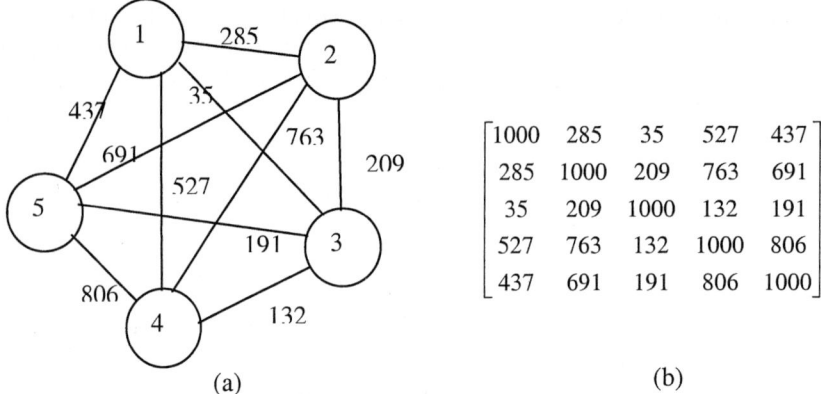

Fig. 1. (a) The Grid system graph and (b) bandwidth matrix derived from the graph

Multicast operation is the communication among a set of processes. In order to send the multicast message, a multicast tree must be built. Multicast tree is a tree that the originator of the data is root node and all nodes involved in the multicast is a member of this tree. The performance of the multicast tree can be defined as the total time used to propagate the data to all member of the tree. So, the problem addressed here is how to find the best performance tree multicast tree after the location of process is known.

In this paper, each instance of the multicast operation is called *multicast schedule*. There are many feasible multicast schedule which can results in a different finish time for the over all multicast operation. Multicast schedule has two parts: *multicast topology* and *multicast order*. Multicast topology is the organizations of the send receive operations among nodes. Since the bandwidth of each link is not equal, the different order of transmission can results in a substantially different overall transmission time. This leads to the second part of the multicast schedule, *the multicast order* which defines the dependency or order of the transmission. In each multicast schedule, a node can execute the ith step operation if and only if it has already finished the $(i-1)$th step. In each step, sender selects receiver based on their priorities. The multicast tree and order are as shown in Fig. 2.

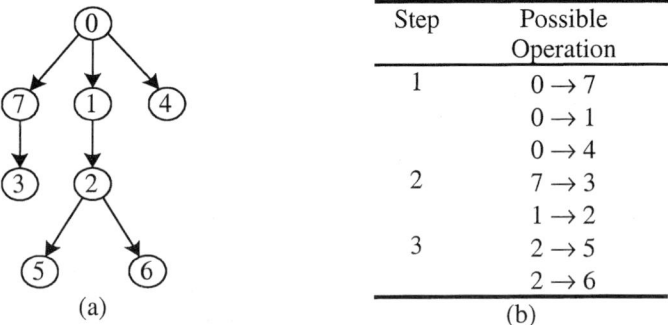

Fig. 2. (a) A multicast tree and (b) multicast order

The performance of multicast operation depends on three factors. First factor is the structure of the multicast tree. The second factor is how the tree is being mapped into the Grid topology. The third factor is the schedule of the data transmission used. These factors must be considered simultaneously in order to obtain the best solution.

From the model mentioned earlier, finding the optimal cost multicast schedule can be done by constructing all variations of the schedule, calculating the cost, and finding the optimal one. However, performing this operation is too expensive to be practical except for the use as a theoretical cost lower bound. For this problem, one of the conventional heuristics being used in this situation is to use genetics algorithm to evolve the schedule. The detail of the proposed heuristics is as discussed in the following section.

3 Proposed Genetic Algorithms-Based Dynamic Tree (GADT)

A proposed *GADT (Genetic Algorithms-based Dynamic Tree)* algorithm is a multicast tree generating algorithm based on genetic algorithm. GADT uses a total transmission time as a fitness function. The total transmission time is defined as an elapse time required finishing the multicast operation. To solve this problem using genetic algorithm, the problem is encoded as follows.

The DNA string is a concatenation of two arrays. The index of these arrays starting from 1. The first array is called *parent array*. The value in index *i* of the parent array, denoted by *p[i]*, is the value of parent node of node number *i*. Note that node 0 does not have any parent, so only $n - 1$ entry is require for n nodes. The other array is called *priority array*. The priority value is used by parent node to choose which nodes to send the data first. The priority value begins at 0 to 1,000,000. The lower value means greater priority. If two nodes have the same parent and priority, the lower node number will be chosen first. Fig. 3 shows an example DNA string for eight nodes and the tree represented.

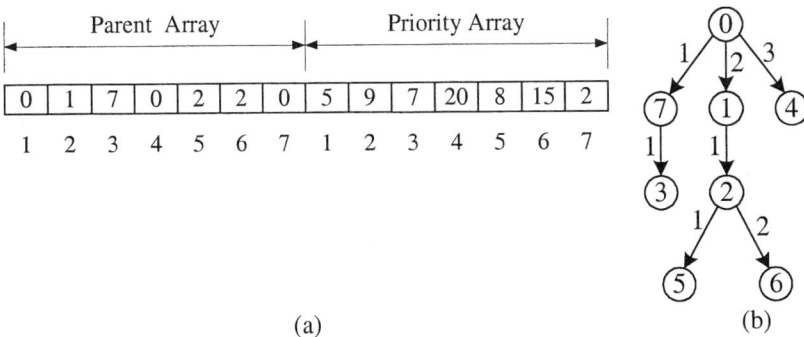

Fig. 3. (a) GADT Encoding and (b) multicast tree

GADT algorithm starts by setting a pre-defined fitness value to the DNA string. If loop or unconnected node is detected, the predefined fitness value is set to 1000 time of maximum transmission time. (The maximum transmission time is computed from *(datasize/minimal bandwidth)×(number of node - 1)*. This is a bias such that the bad multicast pattern will have a much higher chance to be dropped out. The genetic operations are then applied.

In order to find the fitness value of a given multicast schedule, the total transmission time must be calculated. These steps must take into consideration the grid system model mentioned earlier. Therefore, a small simulator named *Treesim* is developed. Treesim is a library module that is called by the main genetic algorithm. The main program passes the value of bandwidth matrix, Grid table, multicast schedule, and process assignment information to Treesim. Treesim then computes the transmission time of a given schedule and return the value to the caller. This simulator also supports the bandwidth sharing computation. If two processes use the same link at the same time, the finish time of their running tasks will be recomputed reflect to the lower bandwidth. Finally, the value of the transmission time obtained is returned to the main genetic algorithm as a fitness value of the multicast schedule passed to the simulator. This process continues until the near optimal answer is obtained or the predefined number of iterations is reached.

4 Experimental Results

In order to evaluate the performance of GADT algorithm, it is compared with two other algorithms. The first one is the optimal algorithm (OPT) based on brute force search to see how close GADT perform compared to the best possible algorithm. The second algorithm being compared is the binomial tree (BT) which is very efficient in cluster environment. These algorithms are tested under the simulation. The simulation is tested on HP Net Server, dual Pentium III 933 MHz with 2048 MB SDRAM.

PGAPack 1.0 library [8] is used to implement the genetic algorithm. The parameters used for the genetic algorithm evaluation are as follows. Population size is 100. The iteration is 1000. Crossover type is two points crossover with crossover probability of 0.85. The mutation probability is 1/L where L is a string length.

First, a Grid of 10 clusters is used. The reason only 10 clusters are used because the computation time of the optimal algorithm is very long. The bandwidth matrix and number of node in each cluster are randomly generated. Table 1 shows number of node in each cluster used while Table 2 shows the bandwidth between clusters (in Mbps).

From this Grid Graph, 10 test cases has been generated by randomly selected a set of 8 nodes from the graph. The multicast message size is set to 1 Mbits. The performance of a multicast tree has been calculated as shown in Table 3.
From these results, a few facts can be observed such as:

1. The GADT can generate a multicast tree which has a performance very close to the optimal multicast algorithm from all test cases. The average ratio of GADT/OPT is 1.09 which means that GADT can generate a tree that is within 9% of the best performance attainable for all test case.
2. The tree generated from GADT is about 1.59-6.43 times faster than traditional binomial tree algorithm. The reason is that binomial tree does not take into account the unbalance bandwidth in Grid environment.

The standard derivation of ratio of transmission time shows that GADT has less derivation than binomial algorithm. This means that the algorithm will generate a tree which is usually provides a good performance all the time.

Table 1. Number of nodes in each cluster

Cluster Id	0	1	2	3	4	5	6	7	8	9
No. of Nodes	155	254	987	356	679	457	255	300	122	98

Table 2. Bandwidth matrix in the test grid environment (unit in Mbps)

	0	1	2	3	4	5	6	7	8	9
0	1000	345	489	423	744	769	509	471	19	599
1	345	1000	543	482	934	152	915	295	668	972
2	489	543	1000	183	640	418	108	571	316	302
3	423	482	183	1000	687	673	981	163	706	475
4	744	934	640	687	1000	373	51	964	149	147
5	769	152	418	673	373	1000	734	658	618	105
6	509	915	108	981	51	734	1000	609	161	588
7	471	295	571	163	964	658	609	1000	543	665
8	19	668	316	706	149	618	161	543	1000	503
	599	972	302	475	147	105	588	665	503	1000

Table 3. Comparison of multicast algorithms

Test case No.	OPT (μsec)	GADT (μsec)	BT (μsec)	GADT/OPT	BT/GADT
0	5680.97	5680.97	9042.90	1.00	1.59
1	3949.63	4599.84	14989.28	1.16	3.80
2	4954.84	5088.77	9775.74	1.03	1.97
3	4392.34	5292.42	13425.24	1.20	3.06
4	4055.45	4833.57	26091.69	1.19	6.43
5	4199.14	5271.07	12636.79	1.26	3.01
6	4599.84	4599.84	13055.05	1.00	2.84
7	5364.11	5878.23	20188.22	1.10	3.76
8	4790.83	4878.23	8654.73	1.02	1.81
9	5018.10	5311.29	9365.22	1.06	1.75
Average		5143.42	13722.49	1.09	3.00
Standard Derivation		428.93	5580.36	0.10	1.46

For the next experiment, the running time of GADT and binomial algorithm is considered. For the optimal algorithm, the computing time is usually very high. Thus, OPT is not evaluated here. Both BT and GADT have been tested by increasing the number of nodes involved from 8 to 2048. The results are shown in Table 4.

From the result shown in Fig. 5, it can be seen that BT is much faster than GADT in term of the computation time since the evaluation of BT is much less complex. But for less than 256 nodes, the computation time of GADT is less than 100 seconds. Hence, it is still practical to add the support of GADT in MPI run time. Also, the computation time of GADT and binomial tree seems to be a linear function of number of nodes. So, both algorithms seem to scale well although GADT is much slower than BT. Anyway, Fig. 8 shows that GADT can generate much better tree for a very large number of nodes (2048).

Table 4. Running time of GADT and binomial algorithm

Number of Node	Multicast time(μsec)		Running time (sec)	
	GADT	BT	GADT	BT
8	5143.42	13722.49	0.87	0.01
16	6502.27	26194.34	2.01	0.01
32	10012.30	32978.33	5.05	0.02
64	20126.81	50988.54	12.87	0.01
128	32985.22	62545.36	32.10	0.03
256	67866.07	177943.33	97.18	0.04
512	142775.44	163871.07	336.61	0.13
1024	224383.74	241309.33	1039.68	0.18
2048	384247.71	646205.70	3561.85	0.45

5 Conclusion and Future Works

This paper proposed a multicast tree generation algorithm for Grid system called, GADT (Genetic Algorithm based Dynamic Tree). The experiment shows that GADT can generate a multicast tree and schedule which is very close to the one obtained from pure Optimal algorithm (OPT). GADT can be used to establish a baseline performance for multicast algorithm. This uses will allow the researchers to evaluate the performance of various heuristics using GADT as a near optimal solution. This eliminates the need for running the time consuming brute force algorithm. The evaluation system being build and used in this paper can be well extended to support a new kind of grid model, parameters, and new algorithm to be evaluated.

In practice, this algorithm can be added in MPI runtime system as well. GADT can be implemented into MPI runtime library at the MPI_Init function. After MPI runtime finish the process assignment, GADT can be used to determine the best multicast tree. Then, this information can be propagated to all of the participant process and used to optimize MPI collective operations such as MPI_Bcast, MPI_Scatter, and MPI_Gather. The GADT algorithm proposed is this paper can be easily extended to support other operations. In the future, this algorithm will be added into a runtime of experimental MPITH runtime system.

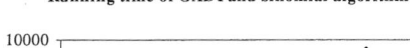

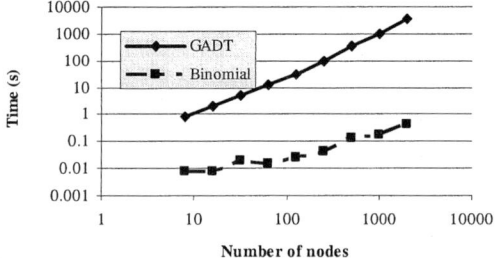

Fig. 4. Running time of GADT and BT

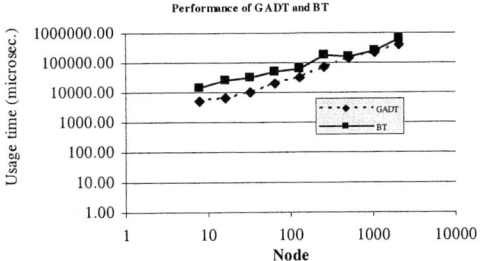

Fig. 5. Performance of GADT and BT

References

M. Bernaschi, and G. Iannello. 1998. Collective Communication Operations: Experimental Results vs. Theory. **Concurrency: Practice and Experience** 10(5):359-386

P.B. Bhat, C.S. Raghavendra, and V.K. Prasanna. 1999. Efficient Collective Communication in Distributed Heterogeneous Systems, pp 15 – 24. In **The International Conference on Distributed Computing Systems (ICDCS)**. Austin, Texas.

Culler, E. E., R. Karp, D. Patterson, A. Sahay, K.E. Schauser, E. Santos, R. Subramonian, and T. von Eicke. 1993. LogP: Towards a realistic model of parallel computation, pp 1 – 12. In **The 4th ACM SIGPLAN Symposium on Principles and Practice of Parallel Programming**. San Dieego, CA.

Foster, I. and C. Kesselman. 1997. Globus: A Metacomputing ifrastructure Toolkit. International Journal of Supercomputer Applications 11(2):115 – 128.

Karp, R. M., A. Sahay, E.E. Santos, and K.E. Schauser. 1993. Optimal Multicast and Summation in the LogP model, pp. 142 – 153. In **Symposium on Parallel Algorithms and Architectures (SPAA)**. Velen, Germany

Kielmann, T., H.E. Bal, and S. Gorlatch. 1999. Bandwidth-efficient Collective Communication for Clustered Wide Area Systems. Submitted for publication.

_____, R.F.H. Hofman, H.E. Bal, A. Plaat, and R.A.F. Bhoedjang. 1999. MAGPIE: MPI's Collective Communication Operations for Clustered Wide Area Systems, pp. 131 – 140. In **The Seventh ACM SIGPLAN Symposium on Principles and Practice of Parallel Programming (PPoPP)**, Atlanta, GA.

Levine, D. 1996. PGAPack Parallel Genetic Algorithm Library, Argonne National Laboratory, ANL95 /18, Argonne, Il.

Topology-Aware Communication in Wide-Area Message-Passing

Craig A. Lee

Computer Systems Research Department
The Aerospace Corporation, P.O. Box 92957
El Segundo, CA 90009
lee@aero.org

Abstract. This position paper examines the use of topology-aware communication services to support message-passing in wide-area, distributed environments, i.e., grids. Grid computing promises great benefits in the flexible sharing of resources but poses equally great challenges for high-performance computing, that is to say, how to execute large-scale computations on a grid with reasonable utilization of the machines involved. For wide-area computations using a message-passing paradigm, these issues can be addressed by using topology-aware communication, i.e., communication services that are aware of and can exploit the topology of the network connecting all relevant machines. Such services can include augmented communication semantics (e.g., filtering), collective operations, content-based and policy-based routing, and managing communication scope to manage feasibility. While such services can be implemented and deployed in a variety of ways, we propose the use of a peer-to-peer, middleware forwarding and routing layer. In a related application domain (time management in distributed simulations) we provide emulation results showing that such topology-awareness can play a major role in performance and scalability. Besides these benefits, such communication services raise a host of implementation and integration issues for their operational deployment and use in grid environments. Hence, we discuss the need for proper APIs and high-level models.

1 Introduction

Communication performance is a common motivating factor in many application domains. In grid computations, understanding and utilizing the network topology will be increasingly important since overall grid performance will be increasingly dominated by bandwidth and propagation delays. That is to say, in the next five to ten years and beyond, network "pipes" will be getting fatter (as bandwidths increase) but not commensurately shorter (due to latency limitations) [1]. To maintain performance, programming tools such as MPI will have to become *topology-aware*. An example of this is MagPIe [2]. MagPie transparently accommodates wide-area clusters by minimizing the data traffic for collective operations over the slow links using a two-level approach. Other work reported in [3] uses a multi-level approach to manage wide-area, local-area, cluster and machine communication. PACX-MPI [4] and MetaMPI [5] are other examples of work in this area.

While the level of topology-awareness in these systems is necessary, they do not necessarily exploit the topology of the network itself. To this end, we consider the use of a *middleware layer* that can provide application-specific routing and forwarding. The fact that such middleware can be implemented as a peer-to-peer framework reinforces the notion of a possible convergence between peer-to-peer and grid computing [6].

Topology-aware communication services could also be provided that have fundamentally different communication properties. Such advanced communication services can be classified into several broad categories.

- **Augmented simple communication semantics.** Common examples include caching (web caching), filtering, compression, encryption, quality of service, data-transcoding, or other user-defined functions.
- **Collective operations.** Rather than implementing operations, such as barriers, scans and reductions, using end-to-end communication, they could be implemented using a topology that matches the physical network.
- **Content-based and policy-based routing.** Content- and policy-based routing would facilitate publish/subscribe services, event services, tuple spaces, and quality of service.
- **Communication scope.** Applications could define multiple *named topologies* that each have their own communication *scope* to limit the problem size and improve performance.

How are such services to be designed, built, and deployed? The issue is clearly to find the right set of abstractions that allows functionality to be encapsulated and hidden at the right level. Hence, we could speak of communicators (perhaps in the MPI sense of the word) for grid applications or services that "live" in the network.

We begin by discussing some fundamental abstractions. We then investigate how topology-awareness could be exploited in a message-passing paradigm, specifically MPI. To illustrate the potential of this approach, we present emulation results for a related application domain, time management in distributed simulations. This is followed by a discussion of the organization and management of communication services. We conclude with a review of outstanding issues.

2 Topology-Aware Communication

Advanced communication services can be viewed as a *programmable communication service object* that is comprised of *service routers* or *hosts* in a grid, as illustrated in Figure 1. Such services could be statically or dynamically defined over a set of service hosts where end-hosts dynamically join and leave. An abstract communication services could have separate *control* and *data planes* where the application end-hosts can explicitly control the behavior of the communication service in terms that are meaningful to the abstraction being provided. A

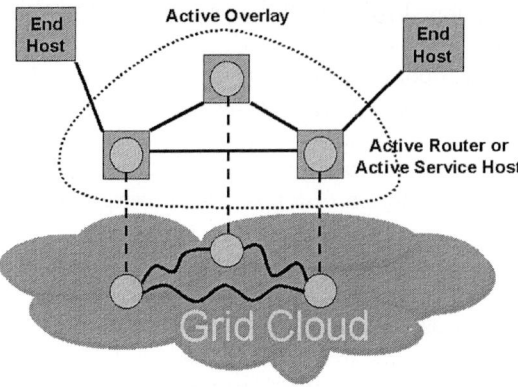

Fig. 1. A Communication Service composed of specific, service-capable routers or hosts.

crucial property is that any such communication service can exploit the topology of the physical connectivity among the service hosts. For operations other than simple point-to-point data transfer, operation costs can be greatly reduced by using structures such as trees.

Equally important is that the API presented by the abstract service object should represent the highest-level model and API meaningful to the application. This model and API must hide all possible details of operating a communication service in a distributed, heterogeneous environment while providing significant benefits.

3 Application to Distributed Message-Passing

Any such API could, of course, be hidden under a message-passing API presented to the end-user. Message-passing APIs, such as MPI, have been developed to facilitate a number of common operations useful in the message-passing paradigm besides that of simple, point-to-point data transfer. Some of these operations that could exploit topology-aware communication include:

- **Broadcast.** Clearly broadcast could benefit. Broadcast can be easily supported using multicast groups but this is generally not supported across wide areas. A middleware service would provide very similar advantages.
- **Scatter/Gather.** Scatter is actually similar to broadcast in that one-to-all communication takes place but not the same data item. Rather than n smaller, point-to-point transfers of individual items, aggregate transfers of multiple items could be used that ultimately split apart as different routes to destination hosts must be taken.
- **Barriers and Reductions.** Barrier and reductions could also clearly benefit. Generally speaking, $O(log n)$ behavior could be realized rather than $O(n log n)$. An example demonstrating this is presented in the next section. We note that *split-phase* or em fuzzy barriers/reductions could also be used in a topology-aware context.

- **Scans.** Scans can be thought of as a progressive reduction. For simple, well-behaved topologies (such as complete, binary trees), it is easy to show that $O(n)$ behavior can be reduced to $O(logn)$ behavior while using an equivalent number of messages. In practice, of course, the real benefit would lie somewhere inbetween depending on the actual topology involved.
- **Communicators.** The *communicator* concept is central to MPI for providing disjoint scopes for many operations, including the ones above. Creating, splitting and deleting communicators would correspond to managing different named scopes across the service hosts.

Current distributed message-passing tools, such as MPICH-G2 [7], generally open a point-to-point connection for each host-pair in a computation. These point-to-point connections are used for simple, point-to-point data transfer as well as the operations above. For simple transfers, a distributed middleware layer may introduce a performance penalty but there are situations where it may provide other advantages. In the extreme case, it would be possible to push all routing into the middleware layer where each communication server forwards each message based on the communicator, operation, and rank involved. This would allow end-hosts to greatly limit file descriptor consumption and avoid depletion, but this is generally not a problem. The middleware layer could, however, also manage routing over high-speed pipes without having to manage the routing tables in hardware routers. As some point in the future, it might be possible to manage such things using *flow IDs* in IPv6 but the adoption of that standard over IPv4 has been slow.

4 A Related Application Domain

We now present a concrete example of a topology-aware communication service in a grid environment. We will use a communication service to support *time management* in a distributed simulation. The High Level Architecture (HLA) [8] is a framework defined by the Defense Modeling and Simulation Office to support distributed simulations through the use of several well-defined services. HLA services include, for example, Data Distribution Management, Ownership Management, and *Time Management*.

4.1 Time Management and the DRN Algorithm

Time Management is essentially the mechanism whereby simulations can enforce causality in a variety of situations. Time Management is commonly supported by a *Time Stamp Order delivery service* whereby events and messages are time stamped and delivered in nondecreasing time stamp order. Rather than enforce a strict synchronization across all hosts in a simulation, however, just the t_{min} of some *lower bound time stamp* is sufficient to know when delivery can be done.

Parallel and distributed simulations, however, have an additional complication. Messages sent between hosts have a time stamp and take some non-negligible time to be delivered. In a heterogeneous, networked environment, it

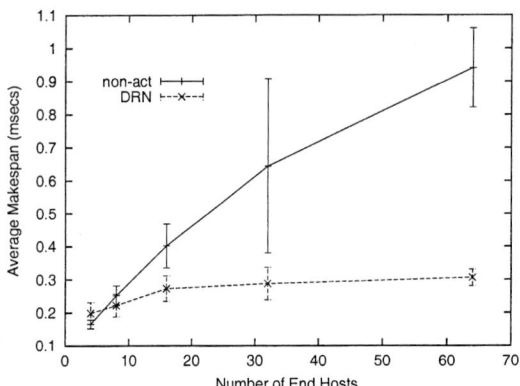

Fig. 2. Average Makespans on Emulab Testbed. Vertical bars give standard deviation.

is possible that t_{min} could be computed and then a message with $t_{msg} < t_{min}$ arrives. To prevent this problem, the *Lower Bound Time Stamp (LBTS)* computation is defined over all hosts *and in-transit messages*:

$$LBTS = min(\ t_1,\ \ldots,\ t_n,\ in-transit\ messages\ ).$$

While the LBTS computation is essentially a *min* reduction on the time stamps, the inclusion of in-transit messages means that the reduction is over a variable number of time stamps. Hence, LBTS is essentially an instance of the Distributed Termination Problem. That is to say, doing the reduction is the easy part; knowing when it's done is the hard part.

To compute LBTS by exploiting the topology of the network, we developed the *Distinguished Root Node* (DRN) algorithm [9]. DRN computes LBTS "on-the-fly in the network" and was derived from a class of Distributed Termination algorithms. As the name implies, the DRN algorithm relies on a distinguished root node in a tree of time management daemons that are on the "interior" of the network. Complete details are presented in [9] and [10].

To evaluate the DRN algorithm, we integrated it with the Georgia Tech HLA/RTI [11] and drove it with *Airport Sim*, a simple HLA-compliant code that simulates m airplanes flying among n airports. This entire system was run in a metropolitan environment using the Globus toolkit to deploy a time management overlay and the Georgia Tech HLA/RTI that subsequently discovered the overlay through the Globus MDS. While it was very important to demonstrate the entire system integration, no real performance benefit was realized since the metropolitan environment only consisted of four nodes. Given the difficulty of large-scale deployment for experimental evaluation purposes, we instead decided to use emulation to show the expected performance gains.

4.2 Emulation Results

Hence, both the DRN and traditional (non-active) time management algorithms were hosted on *Emulab* at the University of Utah [12]. Emulab is essentially a cluster of 168 PCs, where each PC has five 100Mbit ethernet interfaces connected to programmable switches. Experiments have exclusive access to a subset of nodes. Besides loading user code, an experiment can load customized operating systems, and specify NS scripts that program the switches and *the physical connectivity among the nodes*. This means that each experiment can be run on an exclusive set of nodes connected by a customized hardware topology.

A set of quasi-random, tree topologies were generated that had 4, 8, 16, 32, and 64 end-hosts. These topologies had 9, 15, 22, 29, and 34 interior service hosts, respectively, that were constrained to have an average 2.5 degree of connectedness. For each algorithm and each topology, 550 LBTS computations were done. The average LBTS makespan for all experiments is shown in Figure 2. Above 8 end-hosts, the DRN algorithm clearly out-performs the non-topology-aware algorithm. There is considerable variability in these measurements since relatively small time intervals are being measured. Also, unrelated OS operations have contributed to this variability. Nonetheless, the expected $O(logn)$ and $O(nlogn)$ behaviors of these two algorithms come to dominate their performance. Hence, the superior performance of the DRN algorithm under suitable conditions is demonstrated, along with that of other tree-structured communication services.

5 Service Organization

Besides using an explicit network of servers, advanced communication services could also be encapsulated in a layer of middleware. A prime example here is *FLAPPS (Forwarding Layer for Application-level Peer-to-Peer Services)* [13], a general-purpose peer-to-peer distributed computing and service infrastructure.

5.1 A Forwarding and Routing Middleware Layer

In *FLAPPS*, communication is managed by interposing a routing and forwarding middleware layer between the application and the operating system, in userspace. This service is comprised of three interdependent elements: peer network topology construction protocols, application-layer routing protocols and explicit request forwarding. *FLAPPS* is based on the store-and-forward networking model, where messages and requests are relayed hop-by-hop from a source peer through one or more transit peers en route to a remote peer. Hop-by-hop relaying relies on an interconnected application-layer network, in which some peers act as intelligent routers between connected peer groups and potentially between different peer networks as inter-service gateways. Routing protocols propagate reachability of remote peer resource and object names across different paths defined by the constructed peer network. Resources and objects offered by a peer in a *FLAPPS*-based service are chosen from the service's namespace which an application can define to uniquely identify a resource or object within the service. The service's namespace is also hierarchically decomposable so that collections of resources and objects can be expressed compactly in routing updates.

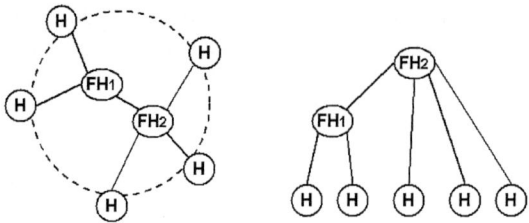

Fig. 3. A Simple Example.

5.2 Namespace Organization

Consider Figure 3 which illustrates a simple set of end-hosts (H) connected to FLAPPS hosts (FH). This is shown as an arbitrary set of hosts in a wide-area, distributed environment, and also as a tree structure with some FLAPPS host chosen as the root. Each end-host in the MPI computation has one socket connection to its local FLAPPS host. All routing and collective operations are managed by FLAPPS using the namespace defined by the application.

One possible way to construct a FLAPPS namespace is to associate a dotted name string with each communicator where the last name field is always the processor rank. Within a communicator, the rank determines the routing at any given FLAPPS host. When a communicator is created or duplicated, a new namespace can be created by "incrementing" the last non-rank name element of the dotted name. Note that if a newly created communicator is smaller, then it may have a different root FLAPPS host. Similarly when a communicator is split where several new, smaller communicators are defined, each may have a different root. Since all communicator constructors are collective operations, these operations will start at the end-hosts, propagate up to the root host, and back down to the end-hosts.

Dotted names can also be used to keep track of the relationship between "parent" and "child" communicators by appending a new, non-rank name element, instead of incrementing the last one. FLAPPS could also be used to manage inter-communicator traffic, as well as facilitate the discovery and management of suitable FLAPPS hosts.

5.3 Service Management

Clearly the creation, management, discovery, and termination of such a middleware layer is an important issue. These are precisely the issues being addressed in grid computing. Grid computing tools and services include information services (that can support resource discovery and allocation), process management, performance monitoring, and security. Under Globus [14], the de facto standard for grid computing, resource discovery is provided by the MDS-2, the second version of the Metacomputing Directory Service [15]. Clearly a grid information service could be used for the discovery or allocation of an advanced communication service. Existing services could be registered with enough metadata to enable an end-host to find a service with the desired capabilities and to join.

The functions that a router or service host is capable of could also be registered, thereby enabling a new service to be instantiated among a selected set of routers.

6 Summary and Discussion

We have discussed the concept of topology-aware communication services in grid environments. Such services can exploit the physical network topology connecting a set of service hosts to reduce operation costs where possible. In the message-passing paradigm, and specifically MPI, there are a number of communication-related functions that could take advantage of such a service. To support these claims, we presented emulation results for a related application domain, time management in distributed simulations, that does a reduction "in the network" over a variable number of elements. We argue that a middleware routing and forwarding layer managed using the emerging grid computing tools is probably the most practical avenue of implementation and deployment at this time. The fact that such middleware can easily be implemented as a peer-to-peer framework is advantageous given the emerging practices of grid computing.

While it is clear that many communication-related functions can benefit significantly from topology-awareness, there are still many hurdles to their practical, wide-scale deployment. These hurdles are, in fact, inherent to the grid environment. Security is certainly a concern. It is common to use X.509 certificates for authentication among parts of a grid computation. Should the same approach be used for joining and managing a communication service over a set of FLAPPS hosts? Reliability is also important. The networking community has gone through great lengths to make basic network functions very robust with a very loosely coupled, distributed control structure based on soft state. The middleware layer approach promoted here can require reliable statefulness across groups of service hosts. This will certainly make reliability more difficult for very large, distributed computations, but this issue can actually be raised for the message-passing paradigm, in general. As these computations grow in size concomitantly with the growth in the number of easily available grid resources, reliability will have to be addressed as a whole for the entire computation.

The final issue is how much overall performance improvement a typical message-passing application will realize in a wide-area environment from essentially improving its collective operations. Tightly coupled models of computations are, in fact, inappropriate for very heterogeneous environments with possibly very low and variable performance. Many applications, however, will be run in more suitable environments, such as the TeraGrid where network bandwidth is high with less competition. Hence, the open issue for further work is to quantify exactly where the performance boundaries are that will govern the effective use of message-passing with topology-aware communication.

Acknowledgement

I wish to thank B. Scott "Scooter" Michel for many fruitful conversations about FLAPPS.

References

1. C. Lee and J. Stepanek. On future global grid communication performance. *10th IEEE Heterogeneous Computing Workshop*, May 2001.
2. T. Kielmann et al. MagPIe: MPI's collective communication operations for clustered wide area systems. In *Symposium on Principles and Practice of Parallel Programming*, pages 131–140, May 1999. Atlanta, GA.
3. N. Karonis, B. de Supinski, I. Foster, W. Gropp, E. Lusk, and J. Bresnahan. Exploiting hierarchy in parallel computer networks to optimize collective operation performance. In *IPDPS*, pages 377–384, 2000.
4. Edgar Gabriel, Michael Resch, Thomas Beisel, and Rainer Keller. Distributed computing in a heterogenous computing environment. In *Recent Advances in Parallel Virtual Machine and Message Passing Interface*, Lecture Notes in Computer Science. Springer, 1998.
5. T. Eickermann, H. Grund, and J. Henrichs. Performance issues of distributed mpi applications in a german gigabit testbed. In *Proc. of the 6th European PVM/MPI Users' Group Meeting*, 1999.
6. I. Foster and A. Iamnitchi. On death, taxes, and the convergence of peer-to-peer and grid computing. In *2nd International Workshop on Peer-to-Peer Systems (IPTPS'03)*, February 2003.
7. N. Karonis, B. Toonen, and I. Foster. MPICH-G2: A Grid-Enabled Implementation of the Message Passing Interface. *Journal of Parallel and Distributed Computing (JPDC)*, 2003. To appear.
8. The Defense Modeling and Simulation Office. The High Level Architecture. *http://hla.dmso.mil*, 2000.
9. C. Lee, E. Coe, C. Raghavendra, et al. Scalable time management algorithms using active networks for distributed simulation. *DARPA Active Network Conference and Exposition*, pages 366–378, May 29-30 2002.
10. C. Lee, E. Coe, B.S. Michel, I. Solis, J. Stepanek, J.M. Clark, and B. Davis. Using topology-aware communication services in grid environments. In *Workshop on Grids and Advanced Networks, International Symposium on Cluster Computing and the Grid*, May 2003.
11. R. Fujimoto and P. Hoare. HLA RTI performance in high speed LAN environments. In *Fall Simulation Interoperability Workshop*, 1998.
12. B. White et al. An integrated experimental environment for distributed systems and networks. In *Proc. of the Fifth Symposium on Operating Systems Design and Implementation*, pages 255–270, Boston, MA, December 2002.
13. B.S. Michel and P. Reiher. Peer-to-Peer Internetworking. In *OPENSIG*, September 2001.
14. The Globus Team. The Globus Metacomputing Project. *www.globus.org*, 1998.
15. K. Czajkowski, S. Fitzgerald, I. Foster, and C. Kesselman. Grid information services for distributed resource sharing. In *HPDC-10*, pages 181–194, 2001.

Design and Implementation of Dynamic Process Management for Grid-Enabled MPICH

Sangbum Kim[1], Namyoon Woo[1], Heon Y. Yeom[1],
Taesoon Park[2], and Hyoung-Woo Park[3]

[1] School of Computer Science and Engineering
Seoul National University, Seoul, 151-742, Korea
{ksb,nywoo,yeom}@dcslab.snu.ac.kr
[2] Department of Computer Engineering
Sejong University, Seoul, 143-747, Korea
tspark@kunja.sejong.ac.kr
[3] Supercomputing Center, KISTI, Taejon, Korea
hwpark@hpcnet.ne.kr

Abstract. This paper presents the design and impementation of MPI_Rejoin() for MPICH-GF, a grid-enabled fault tolerant MPICH implementation. To provide fault tolerance to the MPI applications, it is mandatory for a failed process to recover and continue execution. However, current MPI implementations do not support dynamic process management and it is not possible to restore the information regarding communication channels. The *'rejoin'* operation allows the restored process to rejoin the existing group by updating the corresponding entries of the channel table with the new physical address. We have verified that our implementation can correctly reconstruct the MPI communication structure by running NPB applications. We also report on the cost of *'rejoin'* operation.

1 Introduction

The grid has attracted much attention for its ability to utilize ubiquitous computational resources with a single system view. However, most grid-related studies have concentrated on the static resource management. The dynamic resource management, especially useful for the fault tolerance, has not been discussed enough in the grid research area. Several fault tolerant implementations of the message passing systems have been reported, which exploits the dynamic process management of PVM[5] or LAM-MPI[3, 1, 4]. These implementations, however, are based on the indirect communication mechanism where the messages are transferred via intermediates like daemons. Channel reconstruction is simply accomplished by connecting the local daemon and the increase of message delay is inevitable. MPICH-G2 proposed by Argonne National Laboratory[2] is a grid-enabled MPICH that runs on Globus middleware. Each MPI process is aware of the physical channel information of the other processes and it can send messages to the target processes directly. Once the process group set is initialized, no addition or deletion is possible. Assuming that the failed process has been restored, there is no way for the restored process to take the place of the old process as part of the group.

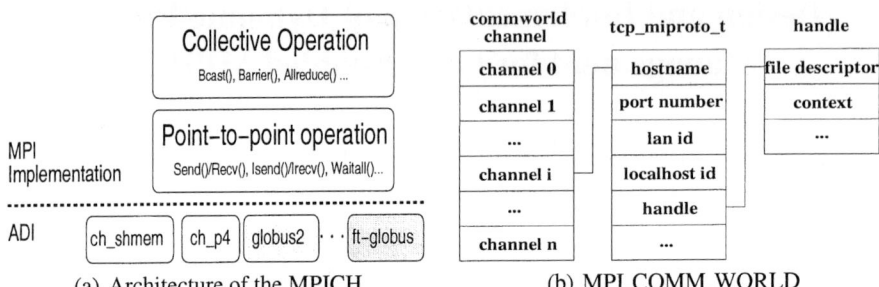

(a) Architecture of the MPICH (b) MPI_COMM_WORLD

Fig. 1. Architecture of the MPICH and Description of MPI_COMM_WORLD

We propose to remedy the situation using the new operation, MPI_Rejoin(). The proposed operation allows the restored process to rejoin the existing group by updating the corresponding entry of the channel table with the new physical address.

2 Communication Mechanism of MPICH-G2

The communication of MPICH-G2 is based on non-blocking TCP sockets and active polling. In order to accept a request for channel construction, each MPI process opens a *listener port* and registers it on the file descriptor set with callback function to poll it. On the receipt of a request, the receiver opens another socket and accepts the connection. Then both processes enter the *await_instruction* state where they exchange the metadata of the connection point. During this channel construction, the process with the larger rank ID plays a master role whether it is a sender or a receiver. Every process is aware of the listener ports for all processes after the initialization. The initialization in MPICH-G2 consists of two main procedures: the rank resolution and the exchange of listener information. Rank is the logical process ID in the group that is determined through the check-in procedure. After check-in procedure, the master process with rank 0 becomes aware of other processes' ranks and broadcasts it. Then, each process creates the listener socket and exchanges its address with the siblings processes to construct the MPI_COMM_WORLD. Figure 1 presents MPI_COMM_WORLD, the data structure containing the listener and channel information for all processes.

3 MPICH-GF

MPICH-GF[6] is our own fault tolerant MPICH implementation on grids that is originated from MPICH-G2. It supports the coordination checkpointing, the sender-based message logging and the receiver-based optimistic message logging. We have implemented these recovery algorithms using the user-level checkpoint library and the process rejoining module described in Section 4. Our MPICH-GF implementation is accomplished at the virtual device level only and it does not require any modification of application source code or the MPICH sublayer upon ADI. MPICH-GF is aided by the hierarchical management system which is responsible for the failure detection and the process recovery.

Table 1. Rejoin message format

global rank (4 Bytes)	hostname (256 Bytes)	port number (10 Bytes)	lan id (4 Bytes)	localhost id (40 Bytes)	fd (4 Bytes)

4 Design of MPI_Rejoin

We have devised MPI_Rejoin() function in order to allow the recovered process to be recognized as the previous process instance. MPICH-G2 has many reference variables related to the system level information. These variables are used by select() system call for non-blocking TCP communication. The read / write callback functions also are stored in these variables. Since these sytem level information are not valid any more in a new process instance, they should be re-initialized in order to prevent a recovered process from accessing the invalid file descriptors. Then, the new physical address of the restored process should be notified to the other processes. Figure 2(a) shows the rejoin protocol incurred by MPI_Rejoin(). When a process failure is detected, the failed process is restored using the latest checkpoint image by local manager and the MPI_Rejoin() function is called. MPI_Rejoin() function executes the following operations.

 – clearing the reference variables related to the system level information.
 – reopening its listener port.
 – sending its new channel information (Table 1) to the local manager.

Then the local manager forwards this report to the central manager. The central manager broadcasts this update report to all local managers. On the receipt of the update report, each local manager sends its process the channel information by using message queue and SIGUSR1 signal. All survived processes modify the corresponding entries of their MPI_COMM_WORLD and set the value of *handle* as NULL. This enables the survived processes to access the failed process's new listener port in order to reconstruct the channel. All this can be done without changing the application source code. The only limitation is that MPI-2 is not yet supported.

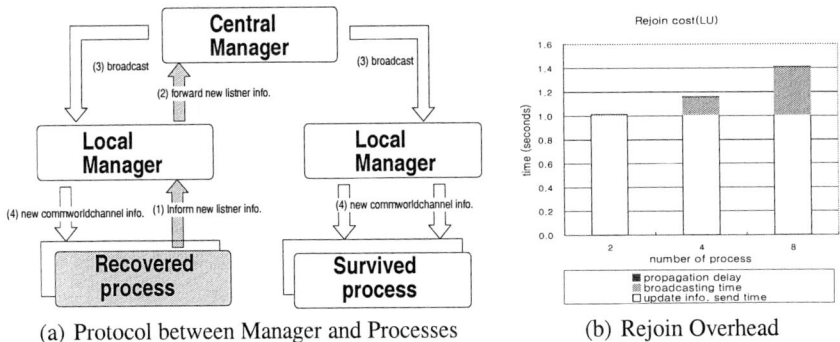

(a) Protocol between Manager and Processes   (b) Rejoin Overhead

Fig. 2. Protocol and Performance result

5 Experimental Results

The *'rejoin'* cost per single failure is presented in Figure 2. We have tested NAS Parallel Benchmark applications(LU). *'update info. send time'* is the time at a failed process from re-lauching and reading the checkpoint file from hard disk to sending the update channel information to local manager . Since this cost is not influenced by the number of processes which participate in the current working group, it shows nearly constant time. We have measured *'broadcasting time'* at central manager from receiving the a failed process's update channel informatioin to receiving the acknowledgement from all proces in current working group. Figure 2 shows that *'broadcasting time'* increase over the number of processes. *'propagation delay'* is pretty small and almost constant.

6 Conclusion

We have presented the design and implementation of process rejoining for MPICH on grids. The proposed operation is an essential primitive of the message passing system for fault tolerance or task migration.

References

1. G. E. Fagg and J. Dongarra : FP-MPI : Fault tolerant MPI, supporting dynamic applications in a dynamic world. In PVM/MPI 2000, pages 346-353, 2000.
2. I. Foster and N. T. Karonis : A grid-enabled MPI : Message passing in heterogeneous distributed computing systems. In Proceedings of SC 98. ACM press, 1998.
3. W. J. Li and J. J. Tsay : Checkpointing message-passing interface(MPI) parallel programs. In Pacific Rim International Symposium on Fault-Tolerant Systems(PRFTS), 1997.
4. S. Louca, N. Neophytou, A. Lachanas, and P. Evripidou : Portable fault tolerance scheme for MPI. Parallel Processing Letters, 10(4):371-382, 2000.
5. J. Menden and G. Stellner : Proving properties of pvm applications - a case study with cocheck. In PVM/MPI 1996, pages 134-141, 1996.
6. N. Woo, S. Choi, H. Jung, J. Moon, H. Y. Yeom, T. Park, and H. Park : MPICH-GF : providing fault tolerance on grid environments. In the 3rd IEEE/ACM International Symposium on Cluster Computing and the Grid(CCGrid2003), the poster and research demo session, MAY, 2003.

Scheduling Tasks Sharing Files on Heterogeneous Clusters

Arnaud Giersch[1], Yves Robert[2], and Frédéric Vivien[2]

[1] ICPS/LSIIT, UMR CNRS-ULP 7005, Strasbourg, France
[2] LIP, UMR CNRS-INRIA 5668, École Normale Supérieure de Lyon, France

Abstract. This paper is devoted to scheduling a large collection of independent tasks onto heterogeneous clusters. The tasks depend upon (input) files which initially reside on a master processor. A given file may well be shared by several tasks. The role of the master is to distribute the files to the processors, so that they can execute the tasks. The objective for the master is to select which file to send to which slave, and in which order, so as to minimize the total execution time. The contribution of this paper is twofold. On the theoretical side, we establish complexity results that assess the difficulty of the problem. On the practical side, we design several new heuristics, which are shown to perform as efficiently as the best heuristics in [3,2]although their cost is an order of magnitude lower.

1 Introduction

In this paper, we are interested in scheduling independent tasks onto heterogeneous clusters. These independent tasks depend upon files (corresponding to input data, for example), and difficulty arises from the fact that some files may well be shared by several tasks. This paper is motivated by the work of Casanova et al. [3,2], who target the scheduling of tasks in APST, the AppLeS Parameter Sweep Template [1]. Typically, an APST application consists of a *large* number of independent tasks, with possible input data sharing. When deploying an APST application, the intuitive idea is to map tasks that depend upon the same files onto the same computational resource, so as to minimize communication requirements. Casanova et al. [3,2] have considered three heuristics designed for completely independent tasks (no input file sharing) that were proposed in [5]. They have modified these three heuristics (originally called Min-min, Max-min, and Sufferage in [5]) to adapt them to the additional constraint that input files are shared between tasks. As was already pointed out, the number of tasks to schedule is expected to be very large, and special attention should be devoted to keeping the cost of the scheduling heuristics reasonably low.

We restrict to the same special case of the scheduling problem as Casanova et al. [3, 2]: we assume the existence of a master processor, which serves as the repository for all files. The role of the master is to distribute the files to the processors, so that they can execute the tasks. The objective for the master is to select which file to send to which slave, and in which order, so as to minimize the total execution time. The contribution of this paper is twofold. On the theoretical side, we establish complexity results that assess the difficulty of the problem. On the practical side, we design several new heuristics, which are shown to perform as efficiently as the best heuristics in [3, 2] although their cost is an order of magnitude lower.

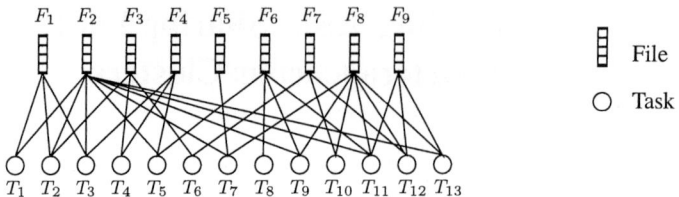

Fig. 1. Bipartite graph gathering the relations between the files and the tasks.

2 Framework

The problem is to schedule a set of n tasks $\mathcal{T} = \{T_1, T_2, \ldots, T_n\}$. Theses tasks have different sizes: the weight of task T_j is t_j, $1 \leq j \leq n$. There are no dependence constraints between the tasks, so they can be viewed as independent. However, the execution of each task depends upon one or several files, and a given file may be shared by several tasks. Altogether, there are m files in the set $\mathcal{F} = \{F_1, F_2, \ldots, F_m\}$. The size of file F_i is f_i, $1 \leq i \leq m$. We use a bipartite graph (see Figure 1 for an example) to represent the relations between files and tasks. Intuitively, a file F_i linked by an edge to a task T_j corresponds to some data that is needed for the execution of T_j to begin.

The tasks are scheduled and executed on a master-slave heterogeneous platform, with a master-processor P_0 and p slaves P_i, $1 \leq i \leq p$. Each slave P_q has a (relative) computing power w_q: it takes $t_j.w_q$ time-units to execute task T_j on processor P_q. The master processor P_0 initially holds all the m files in $\mathcal{F}$. The slaves are responsible for executing the n tasks in $\mathcal{T}$. Before it can execute a task T_j, a slave must have received from the master all the files that T_j depends upon. For communications, we use the one-port model: the master can only communicate with a single slave at a given time-step. We let c_q denote the inverse of the bandwidth of the link between P_0 and P_q, so that $f_i.c_q$ time-units are required to send file F_i from the master to slave P_q. We assume that communications can overlap computations on the slaves: a slave can process one task while receiving the files necessary for the execution of another task.

The objective is to minimize the total execution time. The schedule must decide which tasks will be executed by each slave, and it must determine the ordering in which the master sends the files to the slaves. Some files may well be sent several times, so that several slaves can independently process tasks that depend upon these files. Also, a file sent to some processor remains available for the rest of the schedule: if two tasks depending on the same file are scheduled on the same processor, the file must only be sent once.

3 Complexity

See the extended version [4] for a survey of existing results, and for the proof that the restricted instance of the problem with two slaves, and where all files and tasks have unit size ($t_j = f_i = 1$ for all j, i), remains NP-complete. Note that in that case, the heterogeneity only comes from the computing platform.

4 Heuristics

We compare our new heuristics to the three *reference heuristics* Min-min, Max-Min and Sufferage presented by Casanova et al. [3,2]. All the reference heuristics are built on the following model: for each remaining task T_j, loop over all processors P_i and evaluate OBJECTIVE(T_j, P_i); pick the "best" task-processor pair (T_j, P_i) and schedule T_j on P_i as soon as possible. Here, OBJECTIVE(T_j, P_i) is the minimum completion time of task T_j if mapped on processor P_i, given the scheduling decisions that have already been made. The heuristics only differ by the definition of the "best" couple (T_j, P_i). For instance in Min-min, the "best" task T_j is the one minimizing the objective function when mapped on its most favorable processor: The computational complexity is at least $O(p.n^2 + p.n.|\mathcal{E}|)$, where $\mathcal{E}$ is the set of the edges in the bipartite graph.

When designing new heuristics, we took special care to decreasing the computational complexity. In order to avoid the loop on all the pairs of processors and tasks in the reference heuristics, we need to be able to pick (more or less) in constant time the next task to be scheduled. Thus we decided to sort the tasks *a priori* according to an objective function. However, since our platform is heterogeneous, the task characteristics may vary from one processor to the other. Therefore, we compute one sorted list of tasks for each processor. This sorted list is computed *a priori* and is not modified during the execution of the heuristic. Once the sorted lists are computed, we still have to map the tasks to the processors and to schedule them. The tasks are scheduled one-at-a-time. When we want to schedule a new task, on each processor P_i we evaluate the completion time of the first task (according to the sorted list) which has not yet been scheduled. Then we pick the pair task/processor with the lowest completion time. This way, we obtain an overall execution time reduced to $O(p.n.(\log n + |\mathcal{E}|))$.

Six different objective functions, and three refinement policies are described in [4], for a total of 48 variants. Here is a brief description of those that appear in Table 1 below:

- *Computation:* execution time of the task as if it was not depending on any file
- *Duration:* execution time of the task as if it was the only task to be scheduled on the platform
- *Payoff:* ratio of task duration over the sum of the sizes of its input files (when mapping a task, the time spent by the master to send the required files is payed by all the waiting processors, but the whole system gains the completion of the task)

The *readiness* refinement policy states to give priority to tasks whose input files are all already available at a given processor location, even though they are not ranked high in the priority list of that processor.

5 Experimental Results

Table 1 summarizes all the experiments. In this table, we report the best ten heuristics, together with their cost. This is a summary of $12,000$ random tests ($1,000$ tests over four graph types and three communication-to-computation cost ratios for the platforms, each with 20 heterogeneous processors and communication links). Each test involves 53 heuristics (5 reference heuristics and 48 combinations for our new heuristics). For each

Table 1. Relative performance and cost of the best ten heuristics.

Heuristic	Relative performance	Standard deviation	Relative cost	Standard deviation
Sufferage	1.110	0.1641	376.7	153.4
Min-min	1.130	0.1981	419.2	191.7
Computation+readiness	1.133	0.1097	1.569	0.4249
Computation+shared+readiness	1.133	0.1097	1.569	0.4249
Duration+locality+readiness	1.133	0.1295	1.499	0.4543
Duration+readiness	1.133	0.1299	1.446	0.3672
Payoff+shared+readiness	1.138	0.126	1.496	0.6052
Payoff+readiness	1.139	0.1266	1.246	0.2494
Payoff+shared+locality+readiness	1.145	0.1265	1.567	0.5765
Payoff+locality+readiness	1.145	0.1270	1.318	0.2329

test, we compute the ratio of the performance of all heuristics over the best heuristic. The best heuristic differs from test to test, which explains why no heuristic in Table 1 can achieve an average relative performance exactly equal to 1. In other words, the best heuristic is not always the best of each test, but it is closest to the best of each test in the average. The optimal relative performance of 1 would be achieved by picking, for any of the 12, 000 tests, the best heuristic for this particular case.

We see that *Sufferage* gives the best results: in average, it is within 11% of the optimal. The next nine heuristics closely follow: they are within 13% to 14.5% of the optimal. Out of these nine heuristics, only *Min-min* is a reference heuristic. In Table 1, we also report computational costs (CPU time needed by each heuristic). The theoretical analysis is confirmed: our new heuristics are an order of magnitude faster than the reference heuristics. We report more detailed performance data in [4]. As a conclusion, given their good performance compared to *Sufferage*, we believe that the eight new variants listed in Table 1 provide a very good alternative to the costly reference heuristics.

References

1. F. Berman. High-performance schedulers. In I. Foster and C. Kesselman, editors, *The Grid: Blueprint for a New Computing Infrastructure*, pages 279–309. Morgan-Kaufmann, 1999.
2. H. Casanova, A. Legrand, D. Zagorodnov, and F. Berman. Using Simulation to Evaluate Scheduling Heuristics for a Class of Applications in Grid Environments. Research Report 99-46, Laboratoire de l'Informatique du Paralllisme, ENS Lyon, Sept. 1999.
3. H. Casanova, A. Legrand, D. Zagorodnov, and F. Berman. Heuristics for Scheduling Parameter Sweep Applications in Grid Environments. In *Ninth Heterogeneous Computing Workshop*, pages 349–363. IEEE Computer Society Press, 2000.
4. A. Giersch, Y. Robert, and F. Vivien. Scheduling tasks sharing files on heterogeneous clusters. Research Report RR-2003-28, LIP, ENS Lyon, France, May 2003. Available at www.ens-lyon.fr/~yrobert.
5. M. Maheswaran, S. Ali, H. Siegel, D. Hensgen, and R. Freund. Dynamic matching and scheduling of a class of independent tasks onto heterogeneous computing systems. In *Eight Heterogeneous Computing Workshop*, pages 30–44. IEEE Computer Society Press, 1999.

Special Session of EuroPVM/MPI 2003:

Current Trends in Numerical Simulation for Parallel Engineering Environments

ParSim 2003

Carsten Trinitis[1] and Martin Schulz[2]

[1] Lehrstuhl für Rechnertechnik und Rechnerorganisation (LRR)
Institut für Informatik
Technische Universität München, Germany
Carsten.Trinitis@in.tum.de
[2] Computer Systems Laboratory (CSL)
School of Electrical and Computer Engineering
Cornell University, USA
schulz@csl.cornell.edu

Simulating practical problems in engineering disciplines has become a key field for the use of parallel programming environments. Remarkable progress in both CPU power and network technology has been paralleled by developments in numerical simulation and software integration resulting in the support for a large variety of engineering applications. Besides these traditional approaches for parallel simulation and their constant improvement, the appearance of new paradigms like Computational Grids or E-Services has introduced new opportunities and challenges for parallel computation in the field of engineering.

Following the successful introduction of ParSim as a special session at EuroPVM/MPI in 2002, ParSim continues to bring together scientists from both the engineering disciplines and computer science. It provides a forum to discuss current trends in parallel simulation from both perspectives and offers the opportunity to foster cooperations across disciplines. The EuroPVM/MPI conference series, as one of Europe's prime events in parallel computation, serves as an ideal surrounding for this special session. This combination enables the participants to present and discuss their work within the scope of both the session and the host conference.

This year, 15 papers were submitted to ParSim and we selected six of them to be included in the proceedings and to be presented at the special session. These papers come from different backgrounds and cover both specific simulation applications and general frameworks for the efficient execution of parallel simulations. This selection thereby represents the intended mix between specific problems and requirements given with particular applications or environments and general solutions to cope with them. We are confident that this resulted in an attractive program and we hope that this session will be an informal setting for lively discussions.

Several people contributed to this event. Thanks go to Jack Dongarra, the EuroPVM/MPI general chair, and to Domenico Laforenza and Salvatore Orlando, the PC chairs, for giving us the opportunity to continue the ParSim series at EuroPVM/MPI 2003. We would also like to thank the numerous reviewers, who provided us with their reviews in less than a week and thereby helped us to maintain the tight schedule. Last, but certainly not least, we would like to thank all those who took the time to submit papers and hence made this event possible in the first place.

We hope this session will fulfill its purpose to encourage interdisciplinary cooperation between computer scientists and engineers in the various application disciplines, and we hope ParSim will continue to develop into a long and successful tradition in the context of EuroPVM/MPI.

Efficient and Easy Parallel Implementation of Large Numerical Simulations

Rémi Revire, Florence Zara, and Thierry Gautier

Projet APACHE* ID-IMAG, Antenne ENSIMAG, ZIRST
51, av. J. Kuntzmann, F38330 Montbonnot Saint Martin, France.
{remi.revire,florence.zara,thierry.gautier}@imag.fr

Abstract. This paper presents an efficient implementation of two large numerical simulations using a parallel programming environment called Athapascan. This library eases parallel implementations by managing communications and synchronisations. It provides facilities to adapt the schedule to efficiently map the application on the target architecture.

Keywords: Parallel Molecular Dynamics, Parallel Cloth Simulation, Parallel Programming Environment, Scheduling.

1 Introduction

In the past decade, computer science applications in simulation have become a key point for parallel programming environments. Many of these applications have been developed using MPI (Message Passing Interface) or PVM (Parallel Virtual Machine). Even if these low level libraries are efficient for fine grained applications, writing and debugging them remain difficult. Other works such as NAMD [3], a molecular dynamic simulation, implemented with an higher level programming library (Charm) have shown good speed-up. The Charm library integrates load balancing strategies within the runtime system. Despite the higher level of the programming interface, it does not provide an uniform portability across different parallel architectures.

In this paper, we present the implementation of a cloth simulation and a molecular dynamic simulation using Athapascan. This library is well suited for this kind of application for two main reasons. It eases applications implementation. For instance, an MPI version of our molecular dynamic application is about 100,000 lines of code while the Athapascan [7, 4] version is about 10,000 lines of code. Next, performances portability is made possible by adapting the scheduling algorithm to the specificities of the application and the target architecture.

The next section presents the two numerical simulations. Section 3 describes an overview of Athapascan and section 4 gives some implantation details and experimental results.

---
* Project funded by CNRS, INPG, INRIA, UJF. SAPPE was partly financed by the Rhône-Alpes region. This work is made in collaboration with François Faure (GRAVIR-IMAG), Jean-Louis Roch and Jean-Marc Vincent (ID-IMAG APACHE project).

2 Parallel Algorithms of Two Numerical Simulations

The first numerical simulation, TUKTUT [2] is a molecular dynamics simulation. It aims at emulating the dynamic behaviour of multiple-particle systems to study mechanical and structural properties of proteins and other biological molecules. The second one, called Sappe [9] is a cloth simulation [1]. It provides a 3D and realistic modelling of dressed humans in real time. SAPPE is based on a physical model: a cloth is represented as a triangular mesh of particles linked up by springs emulate the material properties. The mesh topology describes how particles interact and exert forces on each other.

The loop iteration of each simulation is composed of two main parts: (1) Computation of forces that act on each particle or atom; (2) Computation of each particle or atom states (acceleration, velocity, position) by integrating the dynamic equations of the system. The two simulations differ only by the nature of the forces.

To design parallel algorithms for these two simulations, computations are partitioned in a set of tasks. Two techniques are used to obtain these partitions: a particle decomposition for SAPPE [9] and a domain decomposition for TUKTUT [2]. A particle decomposition consists in splitting the set of particles in several subsets, while a domain decomposition consists in splitting the simulation space. With both applications, the numerous interactions between particles leads to many data dependencies between computation tasks. Consequently, the distribution of tasks among distant processors induces non-trivial communication patterns. Tasks scheduling is thus a key point for performance.

3 Advantages of Athapascan for a Parallel Programming

This section is dedicated to the description of the Athapascan library. The programming interface is first briefly described before to present functionalities to handle the scheduling algorithm.

3.1 Overview of the Programming Interface

Parallelism is expressed using remote asynchronous procedure calls that create objects named *tasks*. Tasks communicate with each others using a virtual shared memory and synchronisations are deduced from the type of access made by the tasks on shared objects (read access, write access). The simplicity of Athapascan is mainly due to its sequential semantics: each read operation on a shared object returns the last value written as defined by the sequential order of the execution [4].

Athapascan programs are described independently of the target architecture and the chosen scheduling algorithm. Thus, the programmer can focus on algorithms letting the Athapascan runtime managing synchronisations and communications between tasks. Moreover the programming interface, described in [7], relies on two keywords only.

3.2 Scheduling Facilities for Efficient Executions

In order to get efficient executions, the scheduling should be adapted to the target application and architecture. The programmer can use general algorithms already implemented or design its own specific scheduling strategy. These algorithms can take advantage of some specific scheduling attributes associated to tasks and shared data.

In the context of our numerical simulations, several scheduling algorithms have been implemented. In these algorithms, shared data are first distributed among execution nodes. Tasks are scheduled according to the mapping of their parameters using the Owner Compute Rule as for HPF Compiler [5]. We distinguish three strategies to distribute data. In the first one, data are Cyclically distributed (Cyclic). In the second one, the set of shared objects is recursively partitioned according to 3D position and estimated costs (attributes of shared objects). This strategy is called Orthogonal Recursive Bisection (ORB). In the third one, a data dependency graph is built and the Scotch partition library [6] is used to compute the mapping. These strategies only give the shared and data mapping. The execution according to this mapping is fully handled by Athapascan runtime.

4 Implementation of Applications and Results

The implementation of both applications in Athapascan is intuitive. We first declare a set of Athapascan shared objects representing either a geometric region of space and the associated atoms (TUKTUT), or a set of particles (SAPPE). Then, Athapascan tasks are iteratively created to compute forces between atoms or particles of each shared object. Finally the program creates tasks to integrate positions and velocities. This kind of shared decomposition makes the granularity of tasks easily adaptable by increasing or decreasing the number of atoms or particles encapsulated in shared objects. At runtime, Athapascan manages synchronisations and communications between tasks according to the schedule strategy.

SAPPE has been implemented and tested on a cluster of PCs composed of 120 mono-processor Pentium III running at 733MHz, with 256MBytes of main memory and interconnected through a switched 100Mbit/s network. The left part of figure 1 presents execution time for one iteration of the cloth simulation. Performances are obtained with a cyclic data mapping. We simulate system of one million of particles with a good speedup. Notice that Romero and Zapata have presented results of a parallel cloth simulation with collision detection for 3,520 particles on 8 processors [8] in 2000. This is three orders-of-magnitude less than our simulation size. Although they perform collision detection, we guess that with a similar detection we still be able to compute large simulation.

TUKTUT has been tested on a cluster of 10 SMPs dual Pentium III processors running at 866MHz with 512MBytes of main memory and interconnected through a switched Ethernet 100Mbit/s network. We report experiments using two molecular structures on figure 1. The first one has 11,615 atoms (called GPIK). The second one (an hydrated β-galactosidase, called BGLA) has 413,039 atoms. In these experiences, we compare two scheduling strategies, ORB and Scotch, on an average of ten iterations. We obtain a significant speed-up for each strategy. Also notice that the chosen scheduling has an important impact on the results that shows the importance of scheduling facilities of Athapascan.

# particles	#nodes	speedup
490,000	2	1.81
490,000	4	3.17
490,000	6	4.19
490,000	8	5.35
1,000,000	2	1.75
1,000,000	4	2.65
1,000,000	6	3.29

BGLA (413,039 atoms)			GPIK (11,615 atoms)		
#nodes	ORB	Scotch	#nodes	ORB	Scotch
2	3.09	2.91	2	3.83	2.7
4	6.35	6.12	4	3.83	3.53
8	8.1	8.92	8	4.18	5.11

Fig. 1. SAPPE speed-up (left) on a cluster of PCs and TUKTUT speed-up (right) on a cluster of SMPs.

5 Conclusion

We have presented an efficient fine grain implementation of two numerical simulations (SAPPE and TUKTUT) with Athapascan. Experimental results confirm that the choice of a scheduling strategy is a key point for high performance. Athapascan is a parallel programming environment suited to this kind of applications. It offer facilities to adapt the scheduling strategy to the specificities of the applications and the target architecture. Furthermore the high level programming interface helps to implement applications in an easier way than with MPI or PVM.

References

1. D. Baraff and A. Witkin, *Large steps in cloth simulation*, Computer Graphics Proceedings, Annual Conference Series, SIGGRAPH, 1998, pp. 43–54.
2. P.-E. Bernard, T. Gautier, and D. Trystram, *Large scale simulation of parallel molecular dynamics*, Proceedings of Second Merged Symposium IPPS/SPDP (San Juan, Puerto Rico), April 1999.
3. R.K. Brunner, J.C. Phillips, and Kale L.V., *Scalable Molecular Dynamics for Large Biomolecular Systems*, Proceedings of Supercomputing (SC) 2000, Dallas, TX, November 2000.
4. F. Galilée, J.-L. Roch, G. Cavalheiro, and M. Doreille, *Athapascan-1: On-line building data flow graph in a parallel language*, Pact'98 (Paris, France) (IEEE, ed.), October 1998, pp. 88–95.
5. High Performance Fortran Forum, *High Performance Fortran language specification, version 1.0*, Tech. Report CRPC-TR92225, Houston, Tex., 1993.
6. F. Pellegrini and J. Roman, *Experimental analysis of the dual recursive bipartitioning algorithm for static mapping*, Tech. Report 1038-96, 1996.
7. J.-L. Roch and et al., *Athapascan: Api for asynchronous parallel programming*, Tech. Report RR-0276, INRIA Rhône-Alpes, projet APACHE, February 2003.
8. S. Romero, L.F. Romero, and E.L. Zapata, *Fast cloth simulation with parallel computers*, Euro-Par 2000 (Munich), August 2000, pp. 491–499.
9. F. Zara, F. Faure, and J-M. Vincent, *Physical cloth simulation on a pc cluster*, Fourth Eurographics Workshop on Parallel Graphics and Visualization 2002 (Blaubeuren, Germany) (X. Pueyo D. Bartz and E. Reinhard, eds.), September 2002.

Toward a Scalable Algorithm for Distributed Computing of Air-Quality Problems*

Marc Garbey[1], Rainer Keller[2], and Michael Resch[2]

[1] Dept. of Computer Science – University of Houston, USA
[2] HLRS – University of Stuttgart, Germany

1 Introduction and Numerical Method

In this paper, we present a fast parallel solver designed for system of reaction diffusion convection equations **RDCE**. A typical application is the large scale computing of air quality model for which the main solver corresponds to

$$\frac{\partial C}{\partial t} = \nabla.(K\nabla C) + (\boldsymbol{a}.\nabla)C + F(t,x,C), \quad (1)$$

with $C \equiv C(x,t) \in R^m$, $x \in \Omega \subset \mathbf{R}^3, t > 0$. In air pollution model $\boldsymbol{a}$ is the given wind field, and F is the reaction term combined with source/sink terms. For such a model m is usually very large, and the corresponding ODE system is stiff [2, 3, 8].

Using the total derivative notation $\frac{D}{Dt}$, the equation (1) can be rewritten as

$$\frac{DC}{Dt} = \nabla.(K\nabla C) + F(t,x,C). \quad (2)$$

For the time integration of RDCE, one can distinguish three different time scales. Let us denote dt the time step and h the minimum size of the mesh in all space directions. Let us assume $||\boldsymbol{a}|| = O(1)$ and $||K|| = O(1)$, which correspond usually to the scaling with fine grid approximation. First the Courant-Friedrichs-Lewy (**CFL**) condition imposes $dt = O(h)$ with the explicit treatment of the convective term. Second the stability condition for the explicit treatment of the diffusion term gives $dt = O(h^2)$. It is standard for reaction-diffusion-convection solver used in air-quality to have a second order scheme in space and time. We have then to look for an implicit scheme such that $dt = O(h)$. It is therefore critical to implicit the treatment of the diffusion term, while it is not so critical for the convective term. The discretisation of the convective term might be done with second order one side finite differences approximation of first order derivatives [8] or the method of characteristics that provides a good combination of space-time accuracy, while it is fairly simple to code and straightforward to parallelize with no global data dependency in space. The third time scale in the RDCE comes

---

* This work was supported in part by NSF Grant ACI-0305405.

from the reactive source term that is usually stiff in air quality application. One typically applies non-linear ODE implicit schemes [8].

The main problem we address is the design of a fast solver for reaction-diffusion that has good stability properties with respect to the time step but avoids the computation of the full Jacobian matrix. Usually one introduces an operator splitting combining a fast non linear ODE solver with an efficient linear solver for the diffusion(-convection) operator. However the stiffness of the reaction terms induces some unusual miss-performance problems for high order operator splitting. In fact, the classical splitting of Strang might perform less well than a first order source splitting [7]. We use here some alternative methodology in this paper that consists of stabilizing with a posteriori filtering, the explicit treatment of the diffusion term. The diffusion term is then an additional term in the fast ODE solver and the problem is parametrized by space dependency, introduced in [6]. This stabilizing technique based on filtering is limited to grid that can be mapped to regular space discretization or grids that can be decompose into sub-domains with regular space discretization. It follows the fundamental observation that only the high frequencies are responsible for the time step constraint $dt = O(h^2)$, and they are poorly handled by second order finite differences or finite volume methods. Therefore the main mathematical idea is to construct a filtering technique that can remove the high frequencies in order to relax the constraint on the time step while keeping second order accuracy in space.

We have demonstrated the potential of our numerical scheme with two examples in air quality models that usually require the implicit treatment of diffusion terms, that is local refinement in space via domain decomposition to improve accuracy around source points of pollution or stretched vertical space coordinate to capture better ground effect [4]. For general reaction-diffusion problems on tensorial product grids with regular space step, the filtering process can be applied as a black box post-processing procedure. We will present here new results using overlapping domain decomposition and the parallel filtering procedure for each sub-domain.

2 On the Structure and Performance of the Parallel Algorithm

For simplicity we restrict the presentation to two space dimensions while the performances are given for the 3 dimensional case.

The code has to process a 3 dimensional array $U(1 : N_c, 1 : Nx, 1 : Ny)$ where the first index corresponds to the chemical species, the second and third corresponds to space dependency. This set of data is decomposed in space into a set of nd overlapping sub-domains exactly as one will do with the Schwarz algorithm. The data are therefore distributed on a grid of processors of dimension $nd \times px_{local}$ in horizontal direction x, and py in horizontal direction y. In the three space dimension case, each processor own a vertical column of atmosphere for all chemical components. The total number of processors is then $nd \times px_{local} \times py$. For each sub-domain, the computation is decomposed into two phases:

- Step 1: Solution of the formula

$$U(:,i,j) := G(U(:,i,j), U(:,i+1,j), U(:,i-1,j), U(:,i,j+1), U(:,i,j-1)),$$

at each grid point with appropriate boundary conditions with a Newton loop.
- Step 2: Evaluation of the filtered solution $U(i,j)$ using the stabilization technique of [6].

Step 1 relates to the semi-explicit time marching and is basically parametrized by space variables. In addition the data dependencies with respect to i and j correspond to the classical five points graph common in second order central finite differences. The parallel implementation of Step 1 is straightforward: one decomposes the array $U(:,1:Nx,1:Ny)$ into sub-blocks distributed on a two dimensional cartesian grid of $px \times py$ processors with an overlap of one (or two) row(s) and column(s) in each directions (depending on the stencil used for convection). Parallel performance of this algorithm is well known. If the load per processor is high enough, (which is likely the case with the pointwise integration of the chemistry,) this algorithm scales very well – i.e. see the parallel CFD test case in http://www.parcfd.org.

The data structure is imposed by Step 1. Step 2 introduces a global data dependency across i and j. It is therefore more difficult to parallelize the filtering algorithm. The kernel of this algorithm is to construct the two dimensional sine expansion of $U(:,i,j)$ modulo a shift, and its inverse. One may use an off the shelf parallel FFT library that supports two dimension distribution of matrices – see e.g. http://www.fftw.org. In principle the arithmetic complexity of this algorithm is of order $N_c N^2 \log(N)$ if $Nx \sim N, Ny \sim N$. It is well known that the inefficiency of the parallel implementation of the FFTs comes from the global transpose of $U(:,i,j)$ across the two dimensional network of processors. Although thanks to domain decomposition, we can keep the dimension per sub-domain of order 100 or less. In this case an alternative approach to FFTs that can use fully the vector data structure of $U(:,i,j,)$ is to write Step 2 in matrix multiply form:

$$\forall k = 1..N_c, \; U(k,:,:) := A_{x,sin}^{-1} \times (F_x \cdot A_{x,sin}) U(k,:,:) (A_{y,sin}^t \cdot F_y) \times A_{y,sin}^{-t}, \quad (3)$$

where $A_{x,sin}$ (resp. $A_{y,sin}$) is the matrix corresponding to the sine expansion transform in x direction and F_x (resp. F_y) is the matrix corresponding to the filtering process. In (3), $\cdot$ denotes the multiplication of matrices component by component. Let us define $A_{left} = A_{x,sin}^{-1} \times (F_x \cdot A_{x,sin})$ and $A_{right} = (A_{y,sin}^t \cdot F_y) \times A_{y,sin}^{-t}$. These two matrices A_{left} and A_{right} can be computed once for all and stored in the local memory of each processors. Since $U(:,i,j)$ is distributed on a two dimensional network of processors, one can use an approach very similar to the systolic algorithm to realize in parallel the matrix multiply $A_{left} U(k,:,:) A_{right}$ for all $k = 1..N_c$. Let $px_{local} \times py$ be the size of the two dimensional grid of processors. First one does $py - 1$ shifts of every sub-blocks of $U(k,:,:)$ in y direction assuming periodicity in order to construct $\forall k$, $V(k,:,:) = A_{left} U(k,:,:)$. Second one does $px_{local} - 1$ shifts of every sub-blocks of $V(k,:,:)$ in x direction assuming periodicity in order to construct $\forall k$, $U(k,:,:) = V(k,:,:) A_{right}$. Non-blocking communication is used in order to overlap the communication by the computation. The time necessary to move the data in x and then y direction is negligible in comparison with the time spent in the matrix multiply.

Further the matrices involved in filtering can be approximated by sparses matrices, neglecting matrix coefficients smaller than some tolerance number tol. This method is competitive to a filtering process using FFT for large N_c and not so large N_x and N_y. But the parallel efficiency of the algorithm as opposed to FFT on such small data sets is very high [5].

We present here new performance analysis results for the 3 dimensional problem,

$$\frac{\partial C}{\partial t} = \Delta C + F(C, x, y, z, t), \ (x,y) \in (-L, L)^2, (z) \in (0, h), \ \text{with} \quad (4)$$

$$\Delta C = \partial_x^2 C + \partial_y^2 C + \frac{\partial}{\partial z}(\mathbf{K} \frac{\partial C}{\partial z}), \quad (5)$$

with the four equations simplified ozone model in [8].

In order to analyze the performance of the most critical step of our algorithm, that is excluding the point wise integration of the chemistry that has embarrassing parallelism, we look for the performance of the code with four linear heat equations. For each number of sub-domains we test the scalability, i.e. we increase linearly the size of the global domain in x direction as a function of the number of processors px_{local} while py stays fixed. In the mean time we manage the global size of the problem for the same number of px_{local} to be the same for all nd within one percent while the overlap stays 3 meshes. We can therefore get the scalability for a fixed number of sub-domains. The tests were all done on a Cray T3e/512, an MPP installed at the High-performance Computing Center at Stuttgart, HLRS. The architecture of this machine is well-known and offers a balanced communication- and computation performance. Fig. 1 shows the efficiency of the parallelization according to the domain decomposition with growing size i.e. $124 \times 258 \times 32$ for curve 'o', $244 \times 258 \times 32$ for curve '+', $484 \times 258 \times 32$ for curve '*' and $960 \times 128 \times 32$ for curve 'v'. Fig. 2 shows the elapsed time in seconds for 5 configurations with increasing number of sub-domains nd: curve 'o' respectively '+', '*', 'd' 'v' for growing sizes from $nd = 1$, to $nd = 5$. We can observe that (1) the larger is the number of sub-domains, the better is the scalability and (2) that the domain decomposition has a super-linear speed-up.

This is already a good result, but the salient feature of this method is that the computation per sub-domains is fairly intense, while there are only two local communication between neighbor sub-domains in order to exchange boundaries at every time steps. Therefore this algorithm should give excellent performance with meta-computing architectures for the same reason as explained in [1], while it has a satisfactory numerical efficiency and parallel efficiency on a single parallel computer.

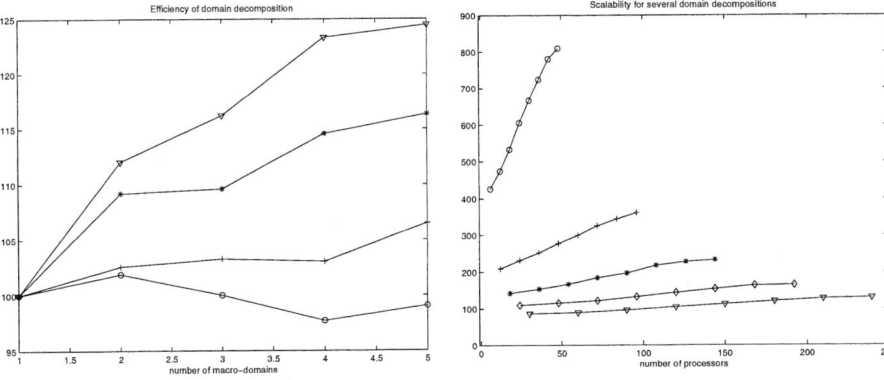

Fig. 1. Parallel efficiency with respect to the number of subdomains.

Fig. 2. Scalability for several domain decomposition configurations.

References

1. N. Barberou, M. Garbey, M. Hess, M. Resch, T. Rossi, J. Toivanen and D. Tromeur Dervout, *On the Efficient Meta-computing of linear and nonlinear elliptic problems*, to appear in Journal of Parallel and Distributed Computing - special issue on grid computing.
2. P. J. F. Berkvens, M. A. Botchev, J. G. Verwer, M. C. Krol and W. Peters, *Solving vertical transport and chemistry in air pollution models*, MAS-R0023 August 31, 2000.
3. D. Dabdub and J. H. Steinfeld, *Parallel Computation in Atmospheric Chemical Modeling*, Parallel Computing Vol22, pp. 111–130, 1996.
4. F. Dupros, M. Garbey and W. E. Fitzgibbon, *A Filtering technique for System of Reaction Diffusion equations*, submitted to JCP.
5. W. E. Fitzgibbon, M. Garbey and F. Dupros, *On a Fast Parallel Solver for Reaction-Diffusion Problems: Application to Air Quality-Simulation*, Parallel Computational Fluid Dynamics – Practice and Theory, North Holland Publisher, P. Wilders et al (edt.), pp. 111–118, 2002.
6. M. Garbey, H. G. Kaper and N. Romanyukha, *A Some Fast Solver for System of Reaction-Diffusion Equations*, 13th Int. Conf. on Domain Decomposition DD13, Domain Decomposition Methods in Science and Engineering, CIMNE, Bracelona, N. Debit et al (edt.), pp. 387–394, 2002.
7. J. G. Verwer and B. Sportisse, *A Note on Operator Splitting in a Stiff Linear Case*, MAS-R9830, http://www.cwi.nl, Dec 1998.
8. J. G. Verwer, W. H. Hundsdorfer and J. G. Blom, *Numerical Time Integration for Air Pollution Models*, MAS-R9825, http://www.cwi.nl, Int. Conf. on Air Pollution Modelling and Simulation APMS'98.

A Piloting SIMulator for Maritime and Fluvial Navigation: SimNav

Michel Vayssade[1] and Alain Pourplanche[2]

[1] Université de Technologie de Compiègne
B.P.20.529 60205 Compiègne, Cedex, France
Michel.Vayssade@UTC.fr
[2] CETMEF - Centre d'Études Techniques Maritimes et Fluviales
2, boulevard Gambetta 60321 Compiègne, Cedex, France
alain.pourplanche@equipement.gouv.fr

Abstract. SimNav is a simulator of ship piloting for port and river navigation. It puts together in an integrated system a set of programs running models of the physical phenomena involved in a ship movement.
These physical models compute at any time the ship position according to the environmental conditions (wind, currents, bank effects) and to the orders given by the student pilot. A virtual model (in the 3D graphic meaning) of the simulated ship is embedded in a 3D virtual model of the geographic site studied. The student pilot give steering and engine orders in order to have the ship following a "good" trajectory.
SimNav uses a cluster of "PC" like machines, in which each machine is dedicated to a particular task. SimNav includes also cooperative input from the professional end-users: Pilots and Authority from Le Havre and Paris.

1 Introduction and Background

1.1 Maritime and Fluvial Context

Entering a ship inside a maritime harbour is always a difficult and dangerous task: there are always a lot of local traps just as high bottoms, local currents which depend on the tide, winds, etc ... If ignored or underestimated, theses traps can lead even a big ship to be runned aground or to collide another one.

So, in quite all maritime harbors, a local pilot, attached to the harbor, is taken to the ship, and is responsible to get the ship safely into the harbour. These local pilots are chosen for their high degree of knowledge of the local navigating conditions and traps.

But, like any professionals, the pilots have to be trained to keep their skills at the best, to learn new regulation rules, to learn how to manage new ships or how to drive through new harbour equipments (channel, sea-marks, sea-walls,...). This learning process can be somewhat abreviated and greatly enhanced by the use of simulators.

A Piloting SIMulator for Maritime and Fluvial Navigation: SimNav   673

Maritime simulators do exists for a while, but they are big and expensive installations. They are built for one harbour, embedding inside them the geography and local conditions of this harbour. So, in most cases, an installed simulator is not very useful for the pilots of another harbour.

In the context of fluvial navigation things are worse. As far as we know, nobody has tried to build a simulator for canal-boats. People learn to drive them by looking at their parents doing it, and so on...

Furthermore, predicting with a model the behaviour of a ship in a river, is much difficult than in the open field: there is some additional fluid mechanics effect such as bank effect or shallow bottom.

And, by the way, the habits of the fluvial navigation sphere, doesn't lean to a demand for that sort of tools. Even, the idea of a school to learn fluvial navigation is quite recent.

1.2 The SimNav Project

SimNav is a cooperating work between a National Technical Service for River and Maritime Studies and a University, but it includes also cooperative input from the professional end-users: Navigation Service of Paris, Port of le Havre Authority and Pilotes Company of le Havre. SimNav is a research project of the "RNTL", french national action on software technology.

The goal of the project is to build a light simulator prototype of a piloting post for a reasonable cost so that it can be widely dispatched and intensively used for training professionals.

For the 3D visual part of the simulator we include a private company, SIRIATech, which has developped a 3D OpenGL visualization library. Having access to the source code, allowed us to put hooks in the library to make it controlled from the outside by the controller of the simulator.

The SimNav project had to be innovative. This is achieved by addressing some weaknesses of existing simulators, in particular, we focus on two points: the cost, by building a simulator an order of magnitude cheaper, the realistic behaviour of the ship with respect to currents, winds, and steering and engine orders from the pilot.

1.3 Constraints and Requirements Meets Technology

At a first glance these specifications seem unrealistic. But the development and spreading of cluster technology with off the shelf components make an opportunity to achieve them.

The SimNav prototype is entirely built upon off the shelf components, all linked in a cluster where message passing is the glue between processes, each process doing a little part of the job.

This allows us to meet the initial specs and will enable a continuous improvment process over time, as users ask for more sophisticated simulated situations, without leading to a "change all or die" alternative.

2 The Prototype SimNav Simulator

The SimNav prototype can be thought of four main parts: the immersive visualization subsystem, the ship behaviour computational model, the instructor and simulation control subsystem, the dashboard and control panel.

All four subsystems run on standard off the shelf Intel-PC machines, linked together by a 100Mbits ethernet network. Most of them are running Linux while some are running Win2K (the 3D library is not yet fully operational on Linux).

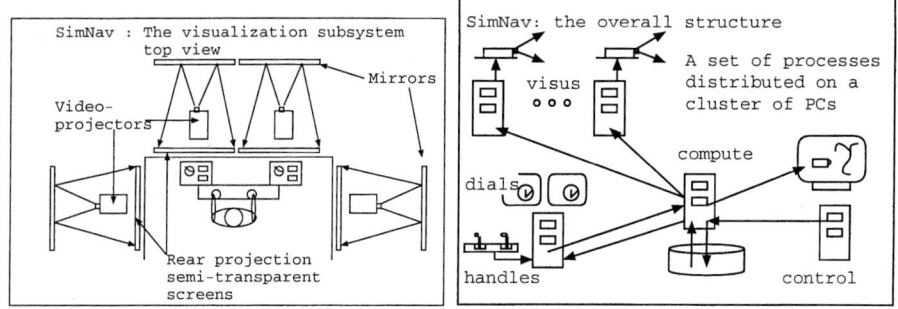

Fig. 1. The visualization subsystem and the overall structure

At startup, each visualization program loads the same 3D world inside its memory. So all display show a view of the same virtual world. Some of the virtual objects can be moved inside the virtual world. In order to keep in sync all visus, they all use the same data, they all receive the same updating commands from the controler.

Currents in the field are computed by a finite element model. This process has been described in previous papers [3], [4].

The simulator is not a computer game. Its main purpose is a professional learning process. The learning pilot is tutored by an instructor. The instructor plays the part of the harbour authority (equivalent of air-control), chooses the case (which ship, which tide, winds ...), etc ...

So, the instructor uses a set of software tools to prepare the case: set-up trajectories of other ships in the field, set-up the initials conditions, use a tugboat management module, etc...

The pilot has some instruments to help him in the navigation process and some handles to control the ship: at least a helm and an engine command. Most of the instruments give information: the radar screen, the GPS info system, steering-compass, ... All these dials are simulated on computer screens positionned in front of the trainee. The displayed values are extracted from the results of the behaviour computation and sent via a message to the process in charge of the display.

A Piloting SIMulator for Maritime and Fluvial Navigation: SimNav   675

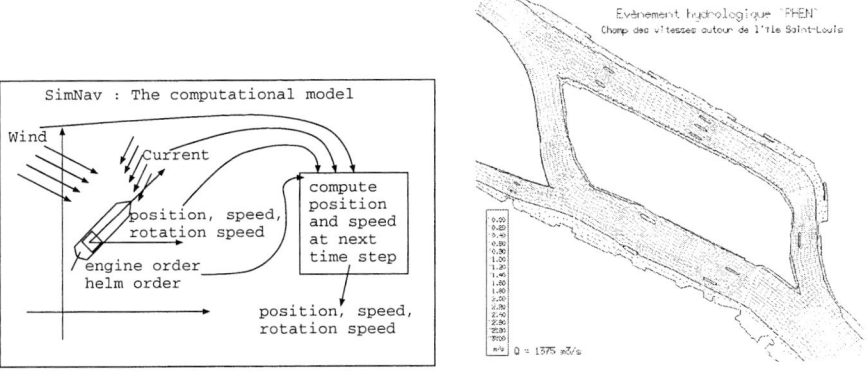

Fig. 2. the computational model and an example of computed currents

Fig. 3. A view of Antifer and a view of Paris

3 Domains of Applications

This project is a response to the queries of several actors of the shipping world: pilots, harbour controls, navigation services which are very concerned with passengers safety and with environmental risks due to ships accidents. The SimNav simulator is expected to have several domains of application, such as pilots's training, impact of harbours or rivers developments and accidents or incidents analysis.

To demonstrate that the initial goals of the project could be achieved we choose two sites, and for each site, we involved in the project the professional concerned on the site.

For the maritime case, we choose the site of petroleum harbour of Le Havre-Antifer; we work with the Pilot Society of Le-Havre and with the harbour authority responsible of Le-Havre and Antifer.

For the fluvial case, we choose the site of Paris, with the river Seine from Austerlitz bridge to Mirabeau bridge; we work with the Navigation service of the Seine and with a society of passenger ships for the pilots.

Each of these sites has specific advantages from the point of view of showing the usefullness of a simulator.

For Antifer, a good training of pilots is very important in terms of security (dangerous product) and in terms of economy (very high costs of ships and infrastructures). The site of Antifer can be difficult to navigate when winds and currents are coming from South-West. Furthermore pilots rarely go on this site (two ships a month) and it is very necessary for them to have a possibility of training.

The site of Paris is very interesting by its complexity and its security requirements: very high traffic, traffic is very mixed, a lot of constructions, and this site is very sensitive in terms of risks and navigation security.

The set of boats chosen to validate the simulator prototype was suggested by professional partners of this project. For maritime domain it will be tankers of 180 000 and 300 000 tons in loading configuration or not. The set of boats for river domain is composed with river boats and "boat-buses".

4 Results and Perspectives

The prototype is nearly operationnal (june 2003). We start an evaluation process with professional pilots in order to modify, if any, some features to make the simulator more usable.

In the futur, we plan to extend the prototype on three directions: add more types of simulated boats, add new sites and extend the functionalities, for example a multi-simulator interacting capability.

From the developers point of view, one very interesting aspect of this work has been the close relationship between applied fluid mechanics scientists, software specialists and operational professionals. This complex cooperation between a lot of different peoples would not have been possible without the support of the RNTL action which plays a key role in the setup of such a project.

References

1. Hollocou Y., Thuillier H. and Kanshine A.: "Mathematical model of the behaviour of a 278000 Ton Oil Tanker", p1-25, XIème Conference of the International Association of Lighthouse Authorities, Brighton, 1985.
2. Hollocou Y. et Lam Son Ha: "Simulation de la manœuvrabilité des navires. Présentation du modèle NAVMER", p1-22,Colloque de l'Institut Français de Navigation (simulation aérienne et maritime), Décembre 1991.
3. P.Sergent, F.Ropert, O.Orcel, M.Houari, D.Duhamel, G.Dhatt - Water waves in harbour areas: appreciation of open boundary conditions, Journal of waterway, port, coastal and ocean engineering - volume 128 N 5, 2002, pp 184 -189.
4. P. Sergent, B. Zhang, J.L Souldadié, P.A Rielland, J.M Tanguy - (1999) - Utilisations du modèle hydrodynamique REFLUX sur l'estuaire de la Seine - Colloque l'Estuaire de la Seine, fonctionnements, perspectives, Rouen

Methods and Experiences of Parallelizing Flood Models*

L. Hluchy[1], V.D. Tran[1], D. Froehlich[2], and W. Castaings[3]

[1] Institute of Informatics, Slovak Academy of Sciences
Dubravska cesta 9, 842 37 Bratislava, Slovakia
viet.ui@savba.sk
[2] Parsons Brinckerhoff Quade and Douglas, Inc
909 Aviation Parkway, Suite 1500
Morrisville, North Carolina 27560 USA
Froehlich@pbworld.com
[3] LMC-IMAG
Domaine Universitaire BP 53
38041 Grenoble Cedex 9
william.castaings@inrialpes.fr

Abstract. This paper focuses on parallelization process of DaveF, a new two-dimensional depth-averaged flow and sediment transport model that allows breach development and the resulting flood wave to be simulated simultaneously. Problems encountered during parallelization and techniques used to solve them are described. The experimental results with different input data on different machines are also included.

1 Introduction

Over the past few years, floods have caused widespread damages throughout the world. Most of the continents were heavily threatened. Therefore, modeling and simulation of floods in order to forecast and to make necessary prevention is very important. The kernel of flood simulation is a numerical model, which requires an appropriate physical model and robust numerical schemes for a good representation of reality.

Simulating river floods is an extremely computation-intensive undertaking specially for situations where the flow is significantly 2D in nature. Several days of CPU-time may be needed to simulate floods along large river reaches using shallow water models. For critical situations, e.g. when an advancing flood is simulated in order to predict which areas will be threatened so that necessary prevention measures can be implemented in time, long computation times are unacceptable. Therefore, using high-performance platforms to reduce the computational time of flood simulation is a critical issue. The high-performance versions of hydraulic models not only reduce computational time but also allow simulation of large scale problems, allow extensive calibration and validation, and consequently provide more reliable results.

At the beginning of ANFAS project [4], many surface-water flow models are studied in order to find suitable high-performance models for pilot sites at Vah river in

---

* This work is supported by EU 5FP ANFAS IST-1999-11676 RTD and the Slovak Scientific Grant Agency within Research Project No. 2/7186/20

Slovakia and Loire river in France. The result of the study showed that many models exist only in sequential forms. Two models were chosen for the pilot site; one is FESWMS which is based on finite element approach and is distributed with commercial package SMS [9] by EMS-I. The second model is DaveF, a new model based on time-explicit, cell-centered, Godunov-type, finite volume scheme finite-volume approach. Both models were developed by Dr. Dave Froehlich. Both models are parallelized with MPI duding ANFAS project. In this paper, the methods of parallelization of the models and the learned experiences are presented, which may help readers to parallelize other sequential models.

2 Computational Approaches of Flood Models

Although both models are used for modeling river flows, they are based on completely different numerical approaches. Detailed descriptions of the numerical approaches of the models can be found in [5] or [10]. This paper focuses on problem encountered during its parallelization and solutions to those problems. Therefore, the following descriptions of computational approaches are purely from the view of parallel programming.

In FESWMS, Newton iteration scheme is used to solve the system of non-linear equation generated by Galerkin finite element method of solving the governing system of differential equations. In each iteration step, a large sparse matrix is generated and solved using frontal scheme. Solving the large sparse matrices is the most computation-intensive part of the model, which require over 90% of total CPU time and a lot of additional memory for storing triangular matrices.

In DaveF, time steps are explicitly calculated using a threshold on Courant numbers. In each time step, DaveF computes the solutions (water levels and velocities) of each cell from its current values and the values of its neighbors. At first sight, it seems to be easily parallelized, however, more careful study shows a big parallelization problem of the computation: the fine granularity. DaveF generally uses very small time steps for numerical stability of the solution; and a small amount computation is needed in each time step (to compensate for the large number of steps).

Source codes of the model have about 66000 lines for FESWMS and 24000 lines for DaveF. The topography data (elements, nodes) are declared as global arrays that are used in nearly all computational routine. The solutions (water levels and velocities) are stored in the cell and node arrays. There are cross-references between the arrays (e.g. elements contains indexes of its nodes in the node arrays) which make big problems for data distribution in the parallel versions using MPI.

3 Parallelization Methods

One of the biggest problems of parallelization of the model is data distribution. Unlike finite-difference method, the finite element and finite volume networks used here are usually irregular and contain a mix of triangular and quadrilateral elements. As the arrays are global variables and are accessed in nearly all routines in the program, modification of the arrays may cause modification of whole program.

Our approach is to use data duplication/replication instead of data distribution that is usually used in MPI programs. The same arrays exist on every MPI process although the process may use only a part of the arrays. The amount of memory needed for the arrays is negligible in comparison with the memory needed for storing matrices in FESWMS. Using data duplication slightly increases the memory requirement of parallel versions (in any case each MPI process still needs less memory than the sequential versions), but it significantly reduce then amount of modified code. In fact, the parallel versions of the models have only about 200-300 lines of code that are modified from total 66000 lines of FESWMS code or 24000 lines of DaveF code. Smaller amount of modified codes means also less time needed for development and testing of parallel versions and easier to maintain and upgrade the parallel version to newer versions of the sequential codes.

Other significant method of parallelizing FESWMS is to replace the frontal method of solving sparse matrix by iterative methods (variations of conjugate gradient method, most significantly the bi-conjugate gradient stabilized (BiCGStab) algorithm). Iterative methods are easier to parallelized (in fact, we used Petsc library [11] which has the parallel iterative methods implemented) and have less memory requirement than the frontal method. Our experiments show that the iterative method BiCGStab is about 10 times faster than the frontal method. As solving the sparse matrices is the most computation-intensive part of FESWMS, the performance of the solver is extremely important. The only drawback of the iterative methods is their instability, which can be reduced using preconditioners.

4 Experimental Results

Experiments have been carried out using Linux clusters on two sites: a Linux cluster at II-SAS of 16 Pentium IV 1800 MHz nodes connected by an Ethernet 100Mb/s switch and the INRIA icluster [6] of 216 Pentium III 733 MHz nodes connected by 100Mb/s Ethernet. Input data for the experiments are taken from Vah river in Slovakia and Loire river in France.

The speedup of FESWMS is difficult to describe in a table or graph. There to several iterative solvers and preconditioners, each of them has also several additional parameters. The combination BiCGStab method and ILU preconditioner is the fasted (about 10x faster than the original frontal method) according to our experiments but GMRES/ILU is the most stable in sequential version. ILU preconditioner is not suitable for running in parallel due to its recurrent nature, so it is applied only for local sub-matrix in the CPU (sub-preconditioner) while additive Schwarz (ASM) preconditioner is used for the global matrix. For larger number of processors, the combination BiCGStab/ASM/ILU suffers problem of stability (it need larger number of iterations to converge). Finding the best combination for certain size of matrix and number of processors is our future work with parallel version of FESWMS.

Fig.1 shows the speedup of DaveF with two different input data from Loire river, one is four time larger than the second one. It is easy to see that the speedup is increased with the size of input data, especially for larger number of processors. The reason is the fine granularity of DaveF, the more processors are used the larger is effect of the granularity performance. The speedup on INRIA icluster is smaller than on II-SAS cluster because the network interference with other applications running on the system, especially when the nodes are not on the same segment (nodes are assigned to applications by PBS batch scheduling system). The speedup reaches maximum for 32 processors, for more processors, the speedup begins decrease because communication delays become to large for computations.

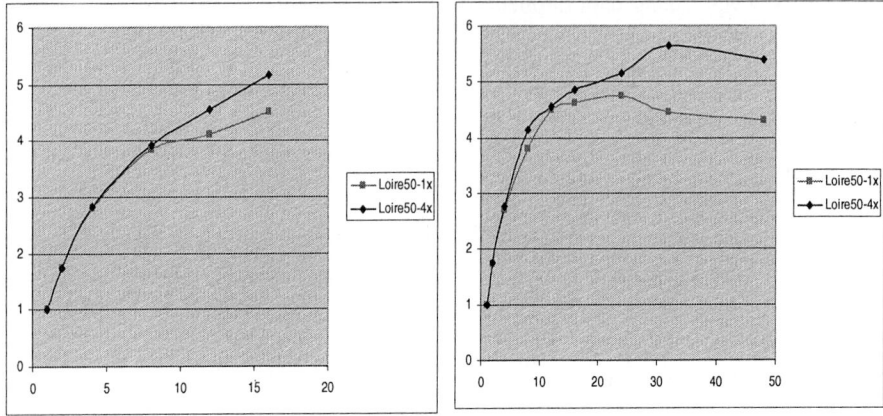

Fig. 1. Speedup of DaveF on II SAS cluster (left) and on INRIA icluster (right)

5 Conclusion and Future Work

In this paper, parallelization process of two flood models has been shown. The problems encountered and their solutions during parallelization process can be applied for parallelizing other applications, too. At the moment, both models have been ported to Grid environment in CrossGrid project [7] and are running in CrossGrid testbed [8]. The details of Grid-aware Flood Virtual Orgranization, where the models are used, are described in a separate paper [2].

References

1. L. Hluchy, V. D. Tran, J. Astalos, M. Dobrucky, G. T. Nguyen, D. Froehlich: Parallel Flood Modeling Systems. International Conference on Computational Science ICCS'2002, pp. 543-551.
2. L. Hluchy, V. D. Tran, O. Habala, J. Astalos, B. Simo, D. Froehlich: Problem Solving Environment for Flood Forecasting. Recent Advances in Parallel Virtual Machine and Message Passing Interface, 9th European PVM/MPI Users' Group Meeting 2002, pp. 105-113.
3. FESWMS- Finite Element Surface Water Modeling.
http://www.bossintl.com/html/feswms.html
4. ANFAS Data Fusion for Flood Analysis and Decision Support.
http://www.ercim.org/anfas/
5. D. Froehlich: IMPACT Project Field Tests 1 and 2: "Blind" Simulation by DaveF. 2002.
6. icluster project. http://www-id.imag.fr/Grappes/icluster/materiel.html
7. EU 5FP project CROSSGRID. http://www.crossgrid.org/
8. Marco, R.: Detailed Planning for Testbed Setup. The CrossGrid Project, 2002. http://grid.ifca.unican.es/crossgrid/wp4/deliverables/CG-4-D4.1-001-PLAN.pdf
9. Surface-water Modeling System. http://www.ems-i.com/SMS/sms.html.
10. D. Froehlich: User's Manual for FESWMS Flo2DH
11. PETSC: Portable, Extensible Toolkit for Scientific Computation.
http://www-unix.mcs.anl.gov/petsc/petsc-2/

padfem2 – An Efficient, Comfortable Framework for Massively Parallel FEM-Applications[*]

Stephan Blazy, Odej Kao, and Oliver Marquardt

Paderborn Center for Parallel Computing
Paderborn University, Fuerstenallee 11, 33102 Paderborn, Germany
{blazy,okao,marquardt}@uni-paderborn.de
http://www.upb.de/pc2/

Abstract. In this paper a new MPI-based framework *padfem2* for finite elements methods (FEM) is presented allowing an efficient execution of FEM applications on clusters with SMP nodes. This paper focuses on the global architecture and on an unique parallel data structure for high-performance object management on structured and unstructured grids. The efficiency and scalability of the parallel FEM processing is evaluated using Poisson and Navier-Stokes numerical solvers as an example.

1 Introduction

In this paper we present an MPI-based framework for massively parallel simulations of finite elements named *padfem2* which is based on the completely re-designed FEM-Tool PadFEM [1]. A re-design was necessary to integrate a highly modular architecture and to support modern software engineering methods. The main *padfem2* targets are the efficient implementation of FEM codes for massively parallel architectures (currently clusters and SMPs) combined with plug-in based environments for creation, specification, and development of modern numerical FEM algorithms, e.g. for computational fluid dynamics or crack simulation [2]. The abstraction of the complex architecture details, the support for the parallelization of novel algorithms and the transparent access to high-performance resources allow researchers – currently from chemistry, physics, mathematics, engineers, etc. – to focus on research-specific details.

This paper gives an overview about the global architecture of *padfem2* and demonstrates the performance characteristics by considering the Poisson and Navier-Stokes solvers as an example. The performance measurements are executed on a cluster with 32 SMP nodes. Due to the limited space details on the modules for numerical algorithms, adaptation, load balancing, mesh generation, pre- and post-processing, and visualization are omitted.

---

[*] This work is partly supported by the German Science Foundation (DFG) project SFB-376.

2 The *padfem2* Architecture

The *padfem2* architecture is based on a modular concept with two application levels – *padfem2* kernel and user level – which are depicted in Fig. 1. The kernel level provides core functionality to all FEM applications and consists of the following modules: a runtime environment, communication management in SMPs (threads) and tightly-coupled architectures (MPI, hive), a parallel and distributed data structure, and a module for basic and complex numerical algorithms/techniques. Additional modules support the management of massively parallel architectures dealing with grid partitioning or load-balancing, etc.

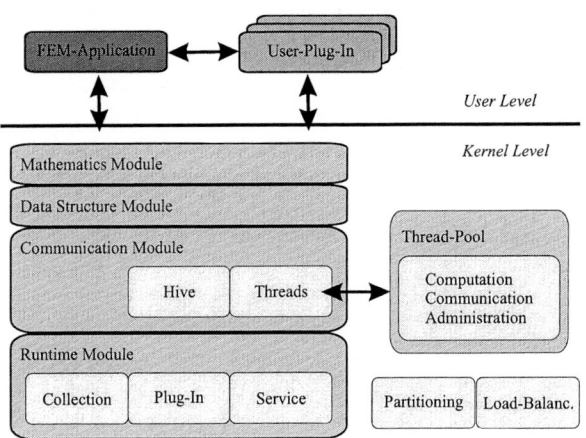

Fig. 1. Schematic overview of the *padfem2* architecture components

The *padfem2* user level allows the specification of FEM applications by using a combination of a-priori given and user-defined numerical algorithms/ techniques. Development of the latter is supported by the data structure kernel module, which contains C++ classes for efficient memory management and an iterator concept for traversing objects such as vertices, volumes, etc. The user level modules are developed as plug-ins and loaded from the kernel during runtime. Thus, a flexible *padfem2* extension with an additional functionality such as a special grid management or the support for parallel tasks is provided.

A unique property and functionality of *padfem2* is provided by a sophisticated, machine-close data structure, which forms the building block for a highly efficient, parallel and distributed object management. The corresponding module determines and manages information about the partitioning of grids and its partition halo with different depths for parallel computation. Moreover, computations on structured and unstructured grids with basic (vertex, edge, face, volume) and complex (region, halo) objects are supported. This data structure also provides an automatically determinable but user configurable neighborhood relationship detection. The user can select if he/she needs a partial or full knowledge of the neighborhood relation for each object type. Using this application-dependent knowledge the specification as well as the performance of numerical algorithms can be improved significantly. Furthermore, special requirements on physical or chemical data can be modeled by the user through a container concept, so called attachment. Attachments are defined in plug-ins, bundled with *padfem2* object types, and can be accessed in the numerical algorithms for further usage. The supporting functions for partitioning and load balancing are currently based on well-known methods such as PARTY [6]. The adaptation is executed by tetrahedron refinement based on problem-dependent error estimators.

Building a complete FEM application out of the framework is done with less effort. Firstly, one has to define the set of numerical data to compute on (e.g. temperature or velocity values). This data is enclosed in an attachment class and appended to each mesh object. The framework provides easy-to-use functions for that purpose. Secondly, own numerical algorithms may be added in a user-defined plug-in working on the attachments. These algorithms are supported by basic or complex help functions from the *padfem2* kernel. Finally, the user has to specify the FEM domain for the problem (i.e. mesh including boundary condition specifications). The user-defined plug-in and the FEM domain are the inputs for the *padfem2* main program.

3 Parallelism with MPI and Threads

The *padfem2* system combines two parallelism paradigms in one application framework and thus supports the current trends in parallel processing, where powerful SMP compute nodes are combined into a cluster with high-speed interconnects and message passing.

The SMP parallelism for the compute nodes is realized using the POSIX thread model, as this standard allows a manual optimization of the program code. A grid partition is mapped exclusively onto a single SMP compute node and the data structure takes care of the partition and global grid consistency. The provided C++ algorithm classes and functions hide the complex thread management from the user and ease the development of numerical algorithms significantly.

The message passing interface (MPI) is used to run *padfem2* on massively parallel systems. Analogously to the SMP thread model the MPI mechanism is also hidden in C++ classes. Hence, the underlying communication software can be replaced by alternative low-level communication packages (GM, GM-2, VMI, etc.) in order to exploit the characteristics of the application and HPC-architecture in the most suitable and efficient way. The inter node communication is optimized by minimizing the submitted information for communication steps, as the transmission of redundant data is avoided. The communication latency is hidden by thread-based communication architecture, where the computation and communication tasks are run in parallel. The provided numerical algorithms and management modules assist this concept in a consistent way.

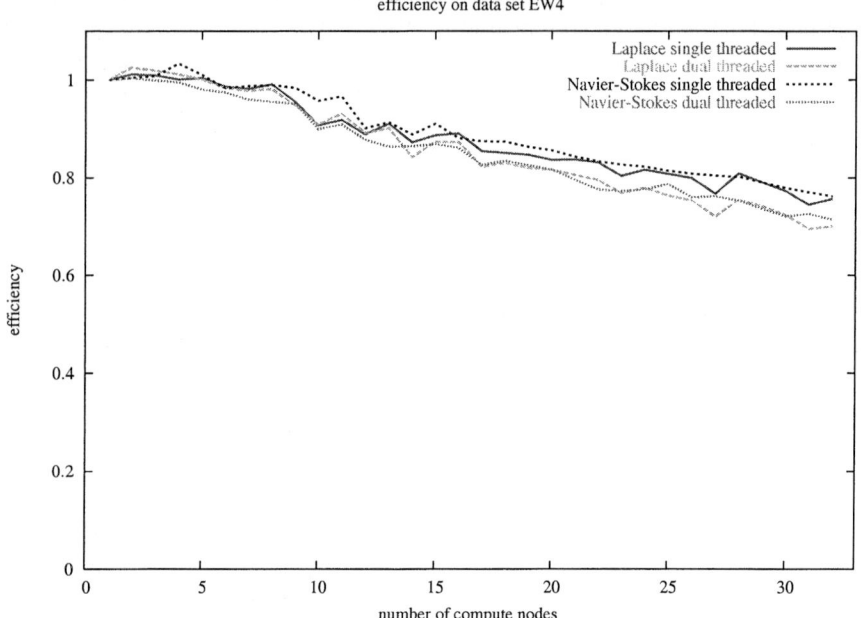

Fig. 2. Efficiency on FEM data set

A thread pool is allocated in the *padfem2* kernel level managing several tasks during runtime (see Fig. 1). The pool determines autonomously how many threads will be created and maps the tasks of computation, communication and miscellaneous services to them. This, together with the latency hiding approach, leads to a balanced load on each SMP compute node in a tightly-coupled environment with up to 256 nodes.

4 Numerical Applications

In *padfem2* we provide finite element methods using linear ansatz-functions on three dimensional tetrahedral grids. The generated linear systems of equations are solved by using a conjugate gradient method. *padfem2* also supports other iterative solvers (e.g. algebraic multi-grid methods). Furthermore, it is possible to implement own method as external modules.

We consider two numerical examples to measure the performance of the conjugate gradient method and the efficiency of the data structure. For the first, we solve the standard 3D Poisson problem in a cube with zero Dirichlet boundary conditions: $-\Delta u(x) = f(x)$ $x \in \Omega$, $u_{|\partial \Omega} = 0$. In the second test case we consider the 3D Navier-Stokes equation:

$$\left. \begin{array}{r} \frac{\partial}{\partial t}v + (v \cdot \nabla)v - \nu \Delta v + \nabla p = 0 \\ div\ v = 0 \end{array} \right\} \text{ in } \Omega.$$

For solving this equation, we use a characteristic pressure correction scheme, which leads to a three step algorithm [3–5].

For the performance measurements of these examples we used a FEM data set consisting of a 3D cube with 48423 vertices forming 236762 tetrahedrons. During the simulation the FEM data set was handled as a static grid with no 3D adaptation. The simulation is executed on a Siemens hpc$L$ine cluster system with 32 SMP compute nodes, each of them with two Pentium3-850 MHz, 512 MByte RAM. The measurement results in Fig. 2 show that the efficiency of the parallel FEM applications ranges from 70% to 75% using all 32 compute nodes. Please note, that we worked with a static grid, thus the efficiency results will be improved significantly, as soon as dynamic grid adaptation is integrated. The efficiency values greater than 100% can be explained by operating system activities (e.g. swapping of concurrent processes) during the performance measurement on a single compute node.

5 Conclusion and Future Work

This paper presented the efficient and comfortable framework *padfem2* for specification and execution of FEM applications on massively parallel architectures. This work-in-progress is supported by a number of users in science and industry, thus the individual specification and computational needs of the users are considered during the design and implementation.

Future work is related to the development of further massively parallel algorithms for the three dimensional Navier Stokes equation on unstructured, adaptive grids using a self-organizing 3D grid adaptation technique with motion support. The technical effort is currently directed to optimization of *padfem2* for 64bit architectures in tightly-coupled clusters with modern high speed interconnects.

References

1. Diekmann, R., Dralle, U., Neugebauer, F.: PadFEM: A Portable Parallel FEM-Tool, Proc. Int. Conf. High-Performance Computing and Networking, Apr. 1996.
2. *padfem2* A Parallel adaptive Finite Element Method tool box, http://www.padfem.de.
3. S. Blazy, O. Marquardt: A characteristic algorithm for the 3D Navier-Stokes equation using *padfem2*, TR-RSFB-03-74, 2003.
4. Blazy, S., Borchers, W., Dralle, U.: Parallelization methods for a characteristic's pressure correction scheme. In: E.H. Hirschel (ed), Flow Simulation with High-Performance Computers II, Notes on Numerical Fluid Mechanics, 1995.
5. Gilles, F.: Une méthode des caractéristiques d'ordre deux sur maillages mobiles pour la résolution des équations de Navier-Stokes incompressible par élements finis, INRIA, Report RR 4448, 2002.
6. Preis,R., Diekmann, R.: PARTY - A Software Library for Graph Partitioning, Advances in Computational Mechanics with Parallel and Distributed Processing, Civil-Comp Press, 1997, pp. 63-71

AUTOBENCH/AUTO-OPT:
Towards an Integrated Construction Environment for Virtual Prototyping in the Automotive Industry

A. Kuhlmann, C.-A. Thole, and U. Trottenberg

Fraunhofer Institute for Algorithms and Scientific Computing
Schloss Birlinghoven, 53754 Sankt Augustin, Germany
{kuhlmann,thole,trottenberg}@scai.fhg.de

Abstract. The present paper describes two cooperative projects (AUTO-BENCH and AUTO-OPT) carried out with partners in the automotive industries (AUDI, BMW, DaimlerChrysler, Karmann and Porsche), software vendors of simulation software (ESI, INTES, INPRO, SFE) and technology providers (Uni Stuttgart, FhG-SCAI and DLR-SISTEC). Both projects aim at the development of integrated working environments for virtual automotive prototypes. Special focus is on simulation of functional behaviour of the car body, production of its parts and their improvement. New technologies have been developed for the handling of numerical grids, integration of CAE tools, numerical algorithms and visualisation. Parallel computing is supported throughout the projects on a simulation level as well as for optimisation purposes. Ongoing work concentrates on the interactive simulation and optimisation as well as the reuse of the vast amount of resulting data.

1 Introduction

Simulation in the automotive industries has become well established as an application for parallel computing, where crash simulation is the most demanding area in terms of computing requirements, but computational fluid dynamics, noise and vibration analysis and virtual reality are further important applications. Most commercial simulation codes are now available in parallel versions [5].

The goal of AUTOBENCH[1] was to improve the workflow of construction loops for car development by introducing high performance parallel computing, communication on distributed networks and virtual reality. An integrated working environment was developed that allows the administration and execution of the software tools involved to carry out a simulation from beginning to end. Some of the tools are now in industrial use [1].

AUTO-OPT[1] emphasises the need for integrated engineering environments by focusing on optimisation and the reuse of simulation results and design decisions. Another objective is to carry simulations into an earlier stage of the design process.

---

[1] The AUTOBENCH and AUTO-OPT projects were funded by the German Ministry for Education and Research. The duration of AUTOBENCH was 1998 till 2001. The follow-on project AUTO-OPT is running till 2005.

2 Finite Element Models for Crash Simulation

In order to carry out a crash simulation a model of the vehicle is passed from the CAD development division to the crash division of the automotive company. The CAD design is based on the single components of the car, i.e. each component is described by its own model. For crash testing the whole car has to be covered with a finite element model (a crash test of only a fender makes no sense). A diagram with the steps involved in crash testing is shown in Figure 1.

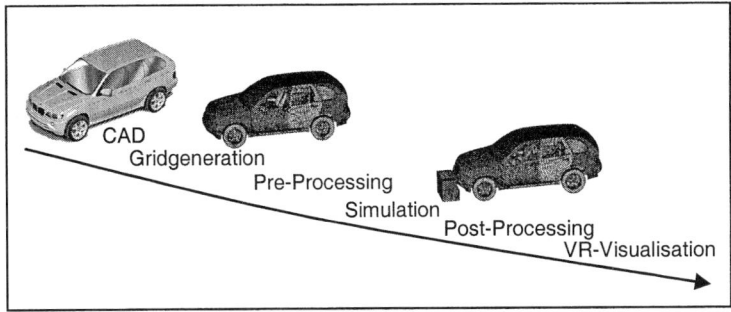

Fig. 1. Process chain for crash simulation

2.1 Incompatible Grids

Traditionally the finite element model was generated homogenously for the whole car, i.e. the entire vehicle was covered with one closed net of finite elements. This process had two major drawbacks:

- Meshing the whole car with an automated tool could not be attempted since the resulting grid quality with today's tool would be poor.
- Component redesigns may change the grid for the complete car, i.e. the grid generation process had to be repeated when one component was modified.

In AUTOBENCH PAM-Crash (crash simulation) and PERMAS (FE-Solver) have been extended in order to be able to deal with incompatible grids. In this way the components can now be covered with independent numerical grids. These grids can be connected to a model for crash simulation – with connections representing the characteristics of the components of the car rather than being restricted to the elements and nodes of the grid. A solution has also been found to model spot welds and welding lines in order to give a more realistic description of the entire car.

2.2 Simulation in the Conceptional Phase

In order to evaluate and select a certain design from a variety of design concepts the behaviour of a car structure has to be assessed. In a design software (SFEConcept) the design is performed in a purely declarative manner using abstract high order elements to describe a structure. Today structural behaviour can be assessed in this manner. AUTO-OPT aims at carrying this early analysis into crash simulation.

3 Integration of the CAE Work Flow

CAE simulation involves many processes and different tools that have to work together. First the model has to be pre-processed for the set-up of a simulation. Then simulation has to be run in different constellations and the results have to be post-processed for analysis and visualisation. This work flow requires a considerable amount of management. Different software tools are applied, each requiring a different file format, simulations are run on parallel computers, i.e. computer clusters have to be supported, etc. Thus AUTOBENCH aimed at the creation of simulation environments in order to support workflows of this type.

CAE-BENCH [2] as specified by and implemented for BMW has the following specific characteristics:
1. The user interface to CAE-BENCH is web-based in order to be accessible from all computers inside an automotive company.
2. All intermediate results can be retrieved by searching its data base.
3. Activities of the user are logged.
4. As a next step AUTO-OPT aims at the integration of stability analysis [3] and data mining tools such that these can be handled from CAE Bench.

4 Optimisation

Optimisation means searching – and finding - the best possible solution for a stated problem, for example changing geometries, materials and other parameters of a vehicle until the simulation result is as good as it can get. In automotive design simulations tend to have long running times of several hours or even days. This makes optimisation a slow process. Here the application of optimisation routines specifically adapted to suit these problems may be beneficial. Also parallel computing can accelerate the solution by

- Employing an optimisation strategy that calls for several simulation runs in parallel
- Utilise parallel computing within the simulation code [4].

In AUTOBENCH/AUTO-OPT both possibilities are accounted for (see also [5]).

4.1 Topology Optimisation

Within AUTOBENCH an integrated topology optimisation module for the structural analysis code PERMAS was developed: A design space can be defined for the respective component of the car together with the boundary conditions and the load. The design objective is the compliance and eigenfrequency. At the beginning of the optimisation the component fills the whole space area. The optimisation module then gradually removes material and finds the structure that can fulfil the design objective intended for the component while minimising its material.

The resulting structures may be somewhat rough, but serve as a good initial guess for the design of this component.

4.2 Multidisciplinary Optimisation

In cases where different disciplines affect the quality of a design multidisciplinary optimisation may shorten the optimisation phase. An example are the conflicting disciplines "crash" and "nvh" (noise vibration, harshness) simulated with separate software applications. Within AUTO-OPT a tool for multidisciplinary optimisation is developed [6]. The objective function is a weighted sum of several objectives from different disciplines and the engineer can adopt the weights according to the needs.

5 Data Analysis

5.1 Stability of Crash Simulation

Small changes in parameters, load cases or model specifications for crash simulation may result in large changes in the result, characterising the crash behaviour of an automotive design.

As part of AUTO-OPT/AUTOBENCH the reasons for the scatter of the results were investigated in detail. It turned out that in some cases numerical effects may bring about this scatter. In most cases, however, the instable behaviour stems from the actual algorithm applied in the simulation or even turned out to be a feature of the car design.

The tool DIFFCRASH [7] supports the analysis of an ensemble of crash simulation results with respect to stability and traces instable behaviour back to its origin. For a BMW analysed in the project the scatter could be traced back to a certain point at which the motor carrier starts its deformation. By changing the design in the area of this motor carrier the instability could be eliminated.

5.2 Data Mining

The development of an integrated engineering environment in the AUTOBENCH project allows storing and reusing results from previous analysis or different disciplines in a unified and reliable fashion. AUTO-OPT exploits these results via the application of data mining methods in order to improve the design process. An example is to use the data about all components present in any of the crash tests performed during the development process to evaluate which components actually do play a role for certain vital quality criteria.

6 Conclusions

AUTOBENCH/AUTO-OPT were set up to enhance the integration of software tools for simulation in the automotive industries as well as improving various software tools involved in the workflow of vehicle design. This paper has shown some of the results achieved throughout the projects.

A number of those results are now in use by the industrial partners or marketed by the software vendors involved in the project. Overall a further step towards an integrated environment for virtual prototyping was achieved.

References

1. Thole, C., Kolibal, S., Wolf, K., AUTOBENCH- Virtual prototypes for Automotive Industry, In M., Owen, R., (eds): 16th EMACS World Congress 2000, Proc. EMACS, Rutgers University, New Brunswick (2000)
2. CAEBENCH is marketed as MSC.VirtualInsight by MSC.Software,
3. Mei, L., Thole, C., Cluster Algorithms for Crash Simulation Analysis, Proc. 5th Workshop on Datamining Scientific and Engineering Datasets MSD'02-V, pp.51-56
4. Galbas, H.G., Kolb, O.: Multiphase Overpartitioning in Crashworthiness Simulation, COMPLAS 2003,
5. Thole, C., Stüben, K., Industrial Simulation on parallel Computers, Parallel Computing, v25, pp 2015-2037, 1999
6. Jakumeit, J., Herdy, M., Nietsche, M., Parameter Optimisation of the Sheet Metal Forming Process using an Iterative Parameter Kriging Algorithm, submitted to Design Optimisation,. 2003,
7. Thole, C., Mei, L., Reasons for Scatter in Crash Simulation Results, 4th European LS-DYNA User Conference,
http://www.dynamore.de/event/eu03/con_event_eu03_agenda.html.

Author Index

Abdalhaq, B. 520
Abdullah, A.R. 214
Adamidis, P.A. 545
Ahn, S. 302
Alderson, P. 537
Alias, N. 214
Almási, G. 352
Álvarez Llorente, J.M. 362
Alves, C.E.R. 126
Amin, S.A. 560
Archer, C. 352
Argentini, G. 550
Augustin, W. 63
Aulwes, R.T. 344
Avetisyan, A. 491

Balis, B. 464
Barrientos, J. 577
Benjegerdes, T. 37
Bennett, M.K. 560
Benson, G.D. 71, 335
Bergamaschi, L. 565
Bianchini, G. 520
Blazy, S. 681
Boyd, R. 537
Brightwell, R. 108, 112, 327
Briguglio, S. 180
Bubak, M. 447, 464, 611
Burbano, D. 134

Cáceres, E.N. 126
Caglar, S.G. 335
Cannataro, M. 619
Carrillo, J.A. 438
Castaings, W. 677
Castaños, J.G. 352
Castro Jr, A.A. 126
Chakravarthi, S. 81
Chan, A. 117
Chen, X. 37, 286
Chu, C.-W. 335
Ciaccio, G. 247
Clematis, A. 160
Corana, A. 98
Cortés, A. 237, 520

Cotronis, Y. 482
Cristóbal-Salas, A. 188
Czarnul, P. 268

D'Agostino, D. 160
Daney, D. 555
Daniel, D.J. 344
Dehne, F. 117
Desai, N.N. 344
Díaz Martín J.C. 362
Distefano, S. 196
Doallo, R. 29
Dongarra, J.J. 88
Drosinos, N. 204
Drzewiecki, D. 629

Fagg, G.E. 88
Filippas, J. 560
Fogaccia, G. 180
Fonseca, N. 473
Fox, G. 1
Froehlich, D. 677
Fugier, N. 395
Funika, W. 447, 464
Fürlinger, K. 429

Gabriel, E. 88
Gaissaryan, S. 491
Garbey, M. 667
García, L. 55
García Zapata, J.L. 362
Gaudiot, J.-L. 188
Gautier, T. 663
Geist, A. 10
Gerndt, M. 429
Gianuzzi, V. 160
Giersch, A. 657
Giné, F. 577
González, J.A. 55
González, J.C. 55
Górka, K. 611
Goscinski, A. 414
Graham, R.L. 344
Gropp, W.D. 15, 27, 257, 352, 404

Gubała, T. 611
Gupta, M. 352

Han, S. 302
Hansen, J.P. 503
Hanzich, M. 577
Herbert, M. 395
Hernández, P. 577
Hippold, J. 455
Hluchy, L. 677
Hobbs, M. 414
Huang, Q. 335
Huse, L.P. 294

Iben, U. 545
Ivannikov, V. 491

Jäger, G. 170
Jain, A. 537

Kacsuk, P. 570, 603
Kaczmarek, P.L. 319
Kao, O. 681
Kaplita, G. 464
Keller, R. 667
Kiliański, Z. 447
Kim, C.K. 227
Kim, J. 142, 302
Kim, S.-D. 595
Kim, S. 653
Kini, S.P. 369
Koh, K.-W. 595
Kok, J.L. 232
Koziris, N. 204
Krawczyk, H. 319
Krishna Kumar, C.R. 81
Kuhlmann, A. 686
Kurzyniec, D. 629
Křenek, A. 529
Kwon, O.-Y. 595

Landi, G. 511
Larsson Träff, J. 309
Lee, C.A. 644
Lee, H.-J. 595
Leese, T. 142
Legrand, A. 586
Lemoine, E. 395

León, C. 55
León, E.A. 108
Liu, J. 369
Loli Piccolomini, E. 511
Long, K. 71
Lumsdaine, A. 379
Luque, E. 237, 520, 577
Lusk, E. 16, 27

Maccabe, A.B. 108, 112
Malawski, M. 611
Maloney, A. 414
Manaskasemsak, B. 152
Mancini, E. 45
Mantas, J.M. 438
Margalef, T. 520
Margaritis, K.G. 242
Marquardt, O. 681
Martinez, A. 565
Martino, B. Di 180
Martorell, X. 352
Mastroianni, C. 619
Matthey, T. 503
Matyska, L. 529
Merlet, J.-P. 555
Michailidis, P.D. 242
Millán, J.L. 237
Miller, N. 404
Miller, P. 142
Moreira, J.E. 352
Munz, C.-D. 545

Naguib, R.N.G. 560
Newborn, M. 227
Norhashidah Hj., M.A. 232

Oline, A. 37
Ortega Lopera, J. 438

Pacheco, P.S. 71, 142
Padaryan, V. 491
Panda, D.K. 369
Papegay, Y. 555
Park, H.-W. 595, 653
Park, K.-L. 595
Park, S.-Y. 595
Park, T. 653
Peterlík, I. 529
Pfeiffer, P. 388

Author Index 693

Pini, G. 565
Planas, M. 237
Podhorszki, N. 603
Pope, S. 424
Pourplanche, A. 672
Prahalad, H.A. 81
Priol, T. 23
Puliafito, A. 196

Rabenseifner, R. 545
Rak, M. 45
Renard, H. 586
Resch, M. 667
Revire, R. 663
Rico, J.A. 362
Riesen, R. 112
Ripoll, A. 237
Risinger, L.D. 344
Ritzdorf, H. 309
Robert, Y. 586, 657
Rodríguez, C. 55
Rodríguez, G. 55
Rodríguez García, J.M. 362
Rosni, A. 232
Ross, R. 404
Rünger, G. 455
Rungsawang, A. 152
Rus, S. 352

Saastad, O.W. 294
Sahimi, M.S. 214
Sartoretto, F. 565
Scarpa, M. 196
Schulz, M. 661
Scott, S.L. 388
Seguel, J. 134
Senar, M.A. 237
Seshadri, B. 81
Shukla, H. 388
Silva, J.G. 473
Sipos, G. 570
Skjellum, A. 81
Smętek, M. 447
Sohan, R. 424
Solsona, F. 577
Song, S.W. 126
Sørevik, T. 503
Squyres, J.M. 379
Sukalski, M.W. 344

Sunderam, V. 28, 629
Supalov, A. 276
Szwarcfiter, J.L. 126

Taboada, G.L. 29
Talia, D. 619
Taylor, M.A. 344
Tchernykh, A. 188
Thakur, R. 257
Thole, C.-A. 686
Toonen, B. 352
Torella, R. 45
Tourancheau, B. 395
Touriño, J. 29
Tran, V.D. 677
Trinitis, C. 661
Trottenberg, U. 686
Trunfio, P. 619
Turner, D. 37, 286

Underwood, K. 327
Uthayopas, P. 636

Vanneschi, M. 24
Vayssade, M. 672
Villano, U. 45
Vivien, F. 586, 657
Vlad, G. 180
Vorakosit, T. 636

Wakatani, A. 222
Watanabe, T. 495
Wismüller, R. 447, 464
Woo, N. 653
Worringen, J. 309
Worsch, T. 63
Wright, M. 537
Wrona, F. 545
Wrzosek, T. 629
Wu, J. 369
Wyckoff, P. 369

Yeom, H.Y. 653

Zabiyaka, Y. 142
Zając, K. 611
Zama, F. 511
Zara, F. 663

Lecture Notes in Computer Science

For information about Vols. 1–2735
please contact your bookseller or Springer-Verlag

Vol. 2736: V. Mařík, W. Retschitzegger, O.Štěpánková (Eds.), Database and Expert Systems Applications. Proceedings, 2003. XX, 945 pages. 2003.

Vol. 2737: Y. Kambayashi, M. Mohania, W. Wöß (Eds.), Data Warehousing and Knowledge Discovery. Proceedings, 2003. XIV, 432 pages. 2003.

Vol. 2738: K. Bauknecht, A M. Tjoa, G. Quirchmayr (Eds.), E-Commerce and Web Technologies. Proceedings, 2003. XII, 452 pages. 2003.

Vol. 2739: R. Traunmüller (Ed.), Electronic Government. Proceedings, 2003. XVIII, 511 pages. 2003.

Vol. 2740: E. Burke, P. De Causmaecker (Eds.), Practice and Theory of Automated Timetabling IV. Proceedings, 2002. XII, 361 pages. 2003.

Vol. 2741: F. Baader (Ed.), Automated Deduction – CADE-19. Proceedings, 2003. XII, 503 pages. 2003. (Subseries LNAI).

Vol. 2742: R. N. Wright (Ed.), Financial Cryptography. Proceedings, 2003. VIII, 321 pages. 2003.

Vol. 2743: L. Cardelli (Ed.), ECOOP 2003 – Object-Oriented Programming. Proceedings, 2003. X, 501 pages. 2003.

Vol. 2744: V. Mařík, D. McFarlane, P. Valckenaers (Eds.), Holonic and Multi-Agent Systems for Manufacturing. Proceedings, 2003. XI, 322 pages. 2003. (Subseries LNAI).

Vol. 2745: M. Guo, L.T. Yang (Eds.), Parallel and Distributed Processing and Applications. Proceedings, 2003. XII, 450 pages. 2003.

Vol. 2746: A. de Moor, W. Lex, B. Ganter (Eds.), Conceptual Structures for Knowledge Creation and Communication. Proceedings, 2003. XI, 405 pages. 2003. (Subseries LNAI).

Vol. 2747: B. Rovan, P. Vojtáš (Eds.), Mathematical Foundations of Computer Science 2003. Proceedings, 2003. XIII, 692 pages. 2003.

Vol. 2748: F. Dehne, J.-R. Sack, M. Smid (Eds.), Algorithms and Data Structures. Proceedings, 2003. XII, 522 pages. 2003.

Vol. 2749: J. Bigun, T. Gustavsson (Eds.), Image Analysis. Proceedings, 2003. XXII, 1174 pages. 2003.

Vol. 2750: T. Hadzilacos, Y. Manolopoulos, J.F. Roddick, Y. Theodoridis (Eds.), Advances in Spatial and Temporal Databases. Proceedings, 2003. XIII, 525 pages. 2003.

Vol. 2751: A. Lingas, B.J. Nilsson (Eds.), Fundamentals of Computation Theory. Proceedings, 2003. XII, 433 pages. 2003.

Vol. 2752: G.A. Kaminka, P.U. Lima, R. Rojas (Eds.), RoboCup 2002: Robot Soccer World Cup VI. XVI, 498 pages. 2003. (Subseries LNAI).

Vol. 2753: F. Maurer, D. Wells (Eds.), Extreme Programming and Agile Methods – XP/Agile Universe 2003. Proceedings, 2003. XI, 215 pages. 2003.

Vol. 2754: M. Schumacher, Security Engineering with Patterns. XIV, 208 pages. 2003.

Vol. 2756: N. Petkov, M.A. Westenberg (Eds.), Computer Analysis of Images and Patterns. Proceedings, 2003. XVIII, 781 pages. 2003.

Vol. 2758: D. Basin, B. Wolff (Eds.), Theorem Proving in Higher Order Logics. Proceedings, 2003. X, 367 pages. 2003.

Vol. 2759: O.H. Ibarra, Z. Dang (Eds.), Implementation and Application of Automata. Proceedings, 2003. XI, 312 pages. 2003.

Vol. 2761: R. Amadio, D. Lugiez (Eds.), CONCUR 2003 - Concurrency Theory. Proceedings, 2003. XI, 524 pages. 2003.

Vol. 2762: G. Dong, C. Tang, W. Wang (Eds.), Advances in Web-Age Information Management. Proceedings, 2003. XIII, 512 pages. 2003.

Vol. 2763: V. Malyshkin (Ed.), Parallel Computing Technologies. Proceedings, 2003. XIII, 570 pages. 2003.

Vol. 2764: S. Arora, K. Jansen, J.D.P. Rolim, A. Sahai (Eds.), Approximation, Randomization, and Combinatorial Optimization. Proceedings, 2003. IX, 409 pages. 2003.

Vol. 2765: R. Conradi, A.I. Wang (Eds.), Empirical Methods and Studies in Software Engineering. VIII, 279 pages. 2003.

Vol. 2766: S. Behnke, Hierarchical Neural Networks for Image Interpretation. XII, 224 pages. 2003.

Vol. 2768: M.J. Wilson, R.R. Martin (Eds.), Mathematics of Surfaces. Proceedings, 2003. VIII, 393 pages. 2003.

Vol. 2769: T. Koch, I. T. Sølvberg (Eds.), Research and Advanced Technology for Digital Libraries. Proceedings, 2003. XV, 536 pages. 2003.

Vol. 2773: V. Palade, R.J. Howlett, L. Jain (Eds.), Knowledge-Based Intelligent Information and Engineering Systems. Proceedings, Part I, 2003. LI, 1473 pages. 2003. (Subseries LNAI).

Vol. 2774: V. Palade, R.J. Howlett, L. Jain (Eds.), Knowledge-Based Intelligent Information and Engineering Systems. Proceedings, Part II, 2003. LI, 1443 pages. 2003. (Subseries LNAI).

Vol. 2776: V. Gorodetsky, L. Popyack, V. Skormin (Eds.), Computer Network Security. Proceedings, 2003. XIV, 470 pages. 2003.

Vol. 2777: B. Schölkopf, M.K. Warmuth (Eds.), Learning Theory and Kernel Machines. Proceedings, 2003. XIV, 746 pages. 2003. (Subseries LNAI).

Vol. 2778: P.Y.K. Cheung, G.A. Constantinides, J.T. de Sousa (Eds.), Field-Programmable Logic and Applications. Proceedings, 2003. XXVI, 1179 pages. 2003.

Vol. 2779: C.D. Walter, Ç.K. Koç, C. Paar (Eds.), Cryptographic Hardware and Embedded Systems – CHES 2003. Proceedings, 2003. XIII, 441 pages. 2003.

Vol. 2781: B. Michaelis, G. Krell (Eds.), Pattern Recognition. Proceedings, 2003. XVII, 621 pages. 2003.

Vol. 2782: M. Klusch, A. Omicini, S. Ossowski, H. Laamanen (Eds.), Cooperative Information Agents VII. Proceedings, 2003. XI, 345 pages. 2003. (Subseries LNAI).

Vol. 2783: W. Zhou, P. Nicholson, B. Corbitt, J. Fong (Eds.), Advances in Web-Based Learning – ICWL 2003. Proceedings, 2003. XV, 552 pages. 2003.

Vol. 2786: F. Oquendo (Ed.), Software Process Technology. Proceedings, 2003. X, 173 pages. 2003.

Vol. 2787: J. Timmis, P. Bentley, E. Hart (Eds.), Artificial Immune Systems. Proceedings, 2003. XI, 299 pages. 2003.

Vol. 2789: L. Böszörményi, P. Schojer (Eds.), Modular Programming Languages. Proceedings, 2003. XIII, 271 pages. 2003.

Vol. 2790: H. Kosch, L. Böszörményi, H. Hellwagner (Eds.), Euro-Par 2003 Parallel Processing. Proceedings, 2003. XXXV, 1320 pages. 2003.

Vol. 2792: T. Rist, R. Aylett, D. Ballin, J. Rickel (Eds.), Intelligent Virtual Agents. Proceedings, 2003. XV, 364 pages. 2003. (Subseries LNAI).

Vol. 2794: P. Kemper, W. H. Sanders (Eds.), Computer Performance Evaluation. Proceedings, 2003. X, 309 pages. 2003.

Vol. 2795: L. Chittaro (Ed.), Human-Computer Interaction with Mobile Devices and Services. Proceedings, 2003. XV, 494 pages. 2003.

Vol. 2796: M. Cialdea Mayer, F. Pirri (Eds.), Automated Reasoning with Analytic Tableaux and Related Methods. Proceedings, 2003. X, 271 pages. 2003. (Subseries LNAI).

Vol. 2798: L. Kalinichenko, R. Manthey, B. Thalheim, U. Wloka (Eds.), Advances in Databases and Information Systems. Proceedings, 2003. XIII, 431 pages. 2003.

Vol. 2799: J.J. Chico, E. Macii (Eds.), Integrated Circuit and System Design. Proceedings, 2003. XVII, 631 pages. 2003.

Vol. 2801: W. Banzhaf, T. Christaller, P. Dittrich, J.T. Kim, J. Ziegler (Eds.), Advances in Artificial Life. Proceedings, 2003. XVI, 905 pages. 2003. (Subseries LNAI).

Vol. 2803: M. Baaz, J.A. Makowsky (Eds.), Computer Science Logic. Proceedings, 2003. XII, 589 pages. 2003.

Vol. 2804: M. Bernardo, P. Inverardi (Eds.), Formal Methods for Software Architectures. Proceedings, 2003. VII, 287 pages. 2003.

Vol. 2805: K. Araki, S. Gnesi, D. Mandrioli (Eds.), FME 2003: Formal Methods. Proceedings, 2003. XVII, 942 pages. 2003.

Vol. 2806: J. Favela, D. Decouchant (Eds.), Groupware: Design, Implementation, and Use. Proceedings, 2003. XII, 382 pages. 2003.

Vol. 2807: V. Matoušek, P. Mautner (Eds.), Text, Speech and Dialogue. Proceedings, 2003. XIII, 426 pages. 2003. (Subseries LNAI).

Vol. 2810: M.R. Berthold, H.-J. Lenz, E. Bradley, R. Kruse, C. Borgelt (Eds.), Advances in Intelligent Data Analysis V. Proceedings, 2003. XV, 624 pages. 2003.

Vol. 2812: G. Benson, R. Page (Eds.), Algorithms in Bioinformatics. Proceedings, 2003. X, 528 pages. 2003. (Subseries LNBI).

Vol. 2815: Y. Lindell, Composition of Secure Multi-Party Protocols. XVI, 192 pages. 2003.

Vol. 2816: B. Stiller, G. Carle, M. Karsten, P. Reichl (Eds.), Group Communications and Charges. Proceedings, 2003. XIII, 354 pages. 2003.

Vol. 2817: D. Konstantas, M. Leonard, Y. Pigneur, S. Patel (Eds.), Object-Oriented Information Systems. Proceedings, 2003. XII, 426 pages. 2003.

Vol. 2818: H. Blanken, T. Grabs, H.-J. Schek, R. Schenkel, G. Weikum (Eds.), Intelligent Search on XML Data. XVII, 319 pages. 2003.

Vol. 2819: B. Benatallah, M.-C. Shan (Eds.), Technologies for E-Services. Proceedings, 2003. X, 203 pages. 2003.

Vol. 2820: G. Vigna, E. Jonsson, C. Kruegel (Eds.), Recent Advances in Intrusion Detection. Proceedings, 2003. X, 239 pages. 2003.

Vol. 2821: A. Günter, R. Kruse, B. Neumann (Eds.), KI 2003: Advances in Artificial Intelligence. Proceedings, 2003. XII, 662 pages. 2003. (Subseries LNAI).

Vol. 2822: N. Bianchi-Berthouze (Ed.), Databases in Networked Information Systems. Proceedings, 2003. X, 271 pages. 2003.

Vol. 2823: A. Omondi, S. Sedukhin (Eds.), Advances in Computer Systems Architecture. Proceedings, 2003. XIII, 409 pages. 2003.

Vol. 2824: Z. Bellahsène, A.B. Chaudhri, E. Rahm, M. Rys, R. Unland (Eds.), Database and XML Technologies. Proceedings, 2003. X, 283 pages. 2003.

Vol. 2825: W. Kuhn, M. Worboys, S. Timpf (Eds.), Spatial Information Theory. Proceedings, 2003. XI, 399 pages. 2003.

Vol. 2827: A. Albrecht, K. Steinhöfel (Eds.), Stochastic Algorithms: Foundations and Applications. Proceedings, 2003. VIII, 167 pages. 2003.

Vol. 2830: F. Pfenning, Y. Smaragdakis (Eds.), Generative Programming and Component Engineering. Proceedings, 2003. IX, 397 pages. 2003.

Vol. 2831: M. Schillo, M. Klusch, J. Müller, H. Tianfield (Eds.), Multiagent System Technologies. Proceedings, 2003. X, 229 pages. 2003. (Subseries LNAI).

Vol. 2832: G. Di Battista, U. Zwick (Eds.), Algorithms – ESA 2003. Proceedings, 2003. XIV, 790 pages. 2003.

Vol. 2834: X. Zhou, S. Jähnichen, M. Xu, J. Cao (Eds.), Advanced Parallel Processing Technologies. Proceedings, 2003. XIV, 679 pages. 2003.

Vol. 2836: S. Qing, D. Gollmann, J. Zhou (Eds.), Information and Communications Security. Proceedings, 2003. XI, 416 pages. 2003.

Vol. 2837: N. Lavrač, D. Gamberger, H. Blockeel, L. Todorovski (Eds.), Machine Learning: ECML 2003. Proceedings, 2003. XVI, 504 pages. 2003. (Subseries LNAI).

Vol. 2838: N. Lavrač, D. Gamberger, L. Todorovski, H. Blockeel (Eds.), Knowledge Discovery in Databases: PKDD 2003. Proceedings, 2003. XVI, 508 pages. 2003. (Subseries LNAI).

Vol. 2839: A. Marshall, N. Agoulmine (Eds.), Management of Multimedia Networks and Services. Proceedings 2003. XIV, 532 pages. 2003.

Vol. 2840: J. Dongarra, D. Laforenza, S. Orlando (Eds.), Recent Advances in Parallel Virtual Machine and Message Passing Interface. Proceedings, 2003. XVIII, 693 pages. 2003.

Vol. 2849: N. García, J.M. Martínez, L. Salgado (Eds.), Visual Content Processing and Representation. Proceedings, 2003. XII, 352 pages. 2003.